AMERICA

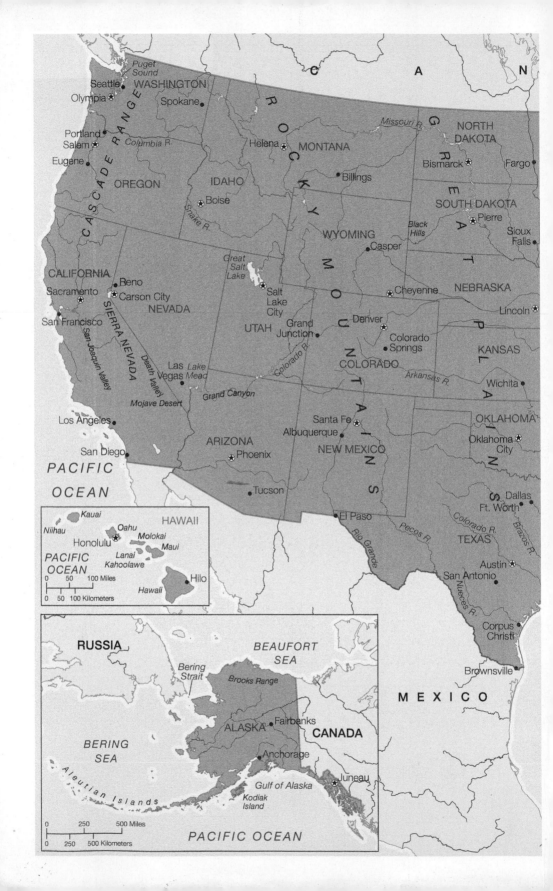

C A N A D A

Puget
Sound

Seattle WASHINGTON

Olympia

Spokane

R
O
C
K
Y

Missouri R.

NORTH
DAKOTA

G
R
E
A
T

Bismarck

Fargo

Portland
Salem

Columbia R.

Helena

MONTANA

Billings

Eugene

OREGON

IDAHO

Boise

Snake R.

SOUTH DAKOTA

Pierre

Black
Hills

Sioux
Falls

CASCADE RANGE

CALIFORNIA

Reno

WYOMING

Casper

Great
Salt
Lake

Sacramento

Carson City

NEVADA

Salt
Lake
City

Cheyenne

NEBRASKA

Lincoln

M
O
U
N
T
A
I
N
S

San Francisco

SIERRA NEVADA

UTAH

Grand
Junction

Denver

San Joaquin Valley

Colorado
Springs

KANSAS

Death Valley

Colorado R.

COLORADO

Las
Vegas

Lake
Mead

Arkansas R.

Wichita

G
R
E
A
T

P
L
A
I
N
S

Mojave Desert

Grand Canyon

Los Angeles

Santa Fe

San Diego

ARIZONA

Albuquerque

Phoenix

NEW MEXICO

OKLAHOMA

Oklahoma
City

PACIFIC

Tucson

OCEAN

El Paso

Dallas

Ft. Worth

Colorado R.

HAWAII

Kauai

Niihau

Oahu

Honolulu

Molokai

Maui

PACIFIC
OCEAN

Lanai

Kahoolawe

Hawaii

Hilo

0   50   100 Miles

0   50 100 Kilometers

Rio Grande

Pecos R.

Brazos R.

TEXAS

Austin

San Antonio

Nueces R.

Corpus
Christi

M E X I C O

Brownsville

RUSSIA

BEAUFORT
SEA

Bering
Strait

Brooks Range

BERING
SEA

ALASKA

Fairbanks

CANADA

Anchorage

Juneau

Aleutian Islands

Gulf of Alaska

Kodiak
Island

0   250   500 Miles

0   250   500 Kilometers

PACIFIC OCEAN

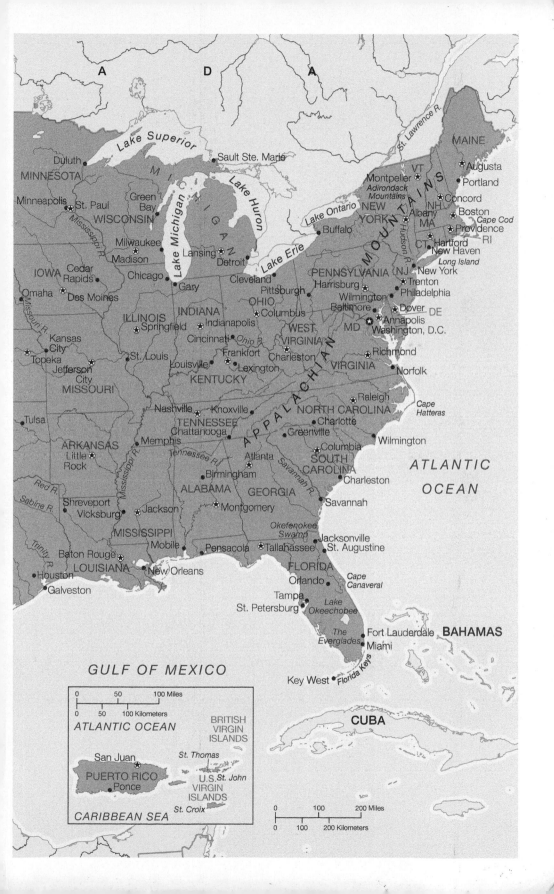

twelfth edition
VOLUME 2

AMERICA

A Narrative History

David Emory Shi

W. W. NORTON & COMPANY, INC.
New York · London

Copyright © 2022, 2019, 2016, 2013, 2010, 2007, 2004, 1999, 1996, 1992, 1988, 1984 by W. W. Norton & Company, Inc.

Editor: Jon Durbin
Senior Project Editor: David Bradley
Assistant Editor: Lily Gellman
Editorial Assistant: Allen Chen
Managing Editor, College: Marian Johnson
Associate Director of Production: Benjamin Reynolds
Media Editor: Carson Russell
Associate Media Editor: Hillary Roegelein
Media Project Editor: Rachel Mayer
Media Editorial Assistant: Jennifer Jussel
Managing Editor, College Digital Media: Kim Yi
Ebook Production Manager: Megan Crayne
Marketing Manager, History: Sarah England Bartley
Design Director: Jillian Burr
Director of College Permissions: Megan Schindel
College Permissions Manager: Bethany Salminen
Text Permissions Specialist: Elizabeth Trammell
Photo Department Manager: Stacey Stambaugh
Photo Editor: Amla Sanghvi
Photo Researcher: Julie Tesser
Composition: Graphic World/Project Manager: Gary Clark
Cartography by Mapping Specialists
Manufacturing: King Printing Co., Inc.

Permission to use copyrighted material is included on page C-1.

ISBN: 978-0-393-54365-0

W. W. Norton & Company, Inc., 500 Fifth Avenue, New York, NY 10110-0017
wwnorton.com

W. W. Norton & Company Ltd., 15 Carlisle Street, London W1D 3BS
2 3 4 5 6 7 8 9 0

FOR

W. W. NORTON & COMPANY

A GROUP OF EXCEPTIONAL PROFESSIONALS WHO SHAPE

THE FUTURE BY REMEMBERING THE PAST

ABOUT THE AUTHOR

DAVID EMORY SHI is president emeritus at Furman University in Greenville, South Carolina. He is the author of several books focusing on American cultural history, including the award-winning *The Simple Life: Plain Living and High Thinking in American Culture* and *Facing Facts: Realism in American Thought and Culture, 1850–1920*. He remains highly engaged with students and instructors around the country with his many annual "author-in-residence" visits to campuses. Learn more about David Shi at usahistorian.com.

BRIEF CONTENTS

CONTENTS

MAPS

PREFACE

With this Twelfth Edition of *America: A Narrative History*, I have sought to improve on a textbook celebrated for its compelling narrative history of the American experience. In the late eighteenth century, the new republic of the United States of America emerged from a revolutionary war with Great Britain that was fought over hotly debated principles, especially the ideals of freedom and equality. To be sure, the integrity of those ideals was corrupted by the deeply rooted institution of slavery and equally entrenched notions of female inequality and racial and ethnic prejudice. Yet the founding principles, however unrealized in practice, remain the distinguishing element of American development. The United States has always been a work in progress, an experiment in building a republic based on the ideals of liberty and justice for all. Conflicts over how best to define and embody those ideals continue to be the shaping dynamic of the American experience. The nation is not perfect, but it remains committed to becoming less imperfect.

That commitment has generated much of the ambition, fortitude, and creativity that have distinguished the American experiment in representative democracy from the rest of the world. The ongoing struggle to create a beacon of freedom and equality to the world is what animates this textbook. I have sought to write an engaging account of the American experiment centered on political and economic developments animated by colorful characters, informed by balanced analysis and social texture, and guided by the unfolding of transformational events. Those classic principles, combined with its affordable, trade-style format, have helped make *America: A Narrative History* one of the most popular, enduring, and well-respected textbooks in the field.

The overarching theme of this Twelfth Edition of *America* is the importance of the Latino and Latina experience in American history (a phrase I use to encompass the experiences of those variously called Hispanics, Chicano/Chicana, Latinx, and more specific national identities, for example, Cuban American, Mexican American, and Puerto Rican American).

The story starts with the Spanish, who were the first Europeans to settle vast regions of what became the United States. Their efforts to create a "New Spain" empire began a violent and often deadly process of colonial settlement. The frequent mixing of Spanish and indigenous peoples and the resulting fusion of their cultures formed the social fabric of the southern borderlands and far western regions across several hundred years.

These regions would be acquired by the United States during the nineteenth century. After Mexico gained its independence from Spain in 1821 and Americans of European descent accelerated their expansion westward, more and more Spanish-speaking peoples would come to America to work and settle, joining those Spanish-speaking peoples already there. Many would face the ongoing challenges of poor working and living conditions and racial injustice.

Through all the challenges they faced, Mexican Americans and those from other Latin American nations who have come to this country have persevered to exercise a profound influence on the development of American society and history. And they still do so today. American politics, prosperity, clothing, music, architecture, literature, language, food, and history have all been influenced by the growing presence of Latino and Latina people living throughout the entire country.

In 2003, Latinos (the term that displaced *Hispanics*, an earlier label used by the U.S. Census over several decades) surpassed African Americans as the nation's largest ethnic minority group. Today, immigrants from Spanish-speaking countries and their descendants occupy a more significant place in American cultural life than ever before. The Latino population in 2020 was more than 61 million, or nearly 20 percent of the total U.S. population.

While an introductory textbook must necessarily focus on major political, constitutional, diplomatic, economic, and social changes, it is also essential to highlight the diverse range of people who have contributed to the dynamic nature of the American experience. In addition to the focus on the Latino/Latina experience I just discussed, the Twelfth Edition includes ongoing enhanced coverage of diverse voices from women, African Americans, Native Americans, Asian Americans, immigrants, and LGBTQ Americans.

I also have enriched the political history that is the backbone of *America*'s narrative with an ongoing assessment of both the achievements and contradictions of well-known historical figures and fresh treatment of major historical events. This textbook also incorporates more social and cultural history by revealing how ordinary people managed everyday concerns—housing, jobs, food, recreation, religion, and entertainment. In doing so, they often overcame exceptional challenges to enhance the quality of American life in the face of depressions, wars, epidemics, and racial injustice.

Whether your interests are political, social, cultural, or economic, you'll find new material to consider in what remains the most well-balanced narrative history of America.

To better align the textbook with semester schedules, I have reduced the number of chapters from thirty-two to thirty in the Full and Brief Editions. Accordingly, I have combined in Volume 1 the materials that were in Chapter 13, Western Expansion, 1830–1848 with Chapter 14, The Gathering Storm, 1848–1860 in previous editions. In Volume 2, I have combined the materials that were in Chapter 23, A Clash of Cultures, 1920–1929 with Chapter 24, The Reactionary Twenties in previous editions.

Among the new coverage in this Twelfth Edition are the following:

Chapter 1: The Collision of Cultures in the Sixteenth Century

- New coverage on how gender status and the caste system based on ethnic hierarchy in Spanish America (Mestizos and Criollos) grew out of the impact of the ravages of smallpox.
- New discussions on how the crops native to the Americas crossed the Atlantic and improved the health of Europeans while spurring a dramatic population increase.

Chapter 2: England and Its American Colonies, 1607–1732

- New insights into how the population explosion in Europe in the seventeenth century led to the beginnings of mass migration to the New World.
- New coverage on the arrival of the first enslaved Africans brought to Jamestown in 1619 and how the growing European desire for new beverages—tea and coffee—dramatically increased the number and size of British sugar plantations in the Caribbean and the need for more enslaved Africans to work there.
- Discussion of how South Carolina became the wealthiest colony through its purposeful focus on developing coastal rice plantations using the forced labor of enslaved Africans and Native Americans.
- An expanded portrait of William Penn and how he developed strong relationships with Native Americans through the purchase of land titles from them.

Chapter 3: Colonial Ways of Life, 1607–1750

- New summaries comparing different types of slavery in different regions in colonial America.
- New segments explaining why the British first embraced enslaving Native Americans but then came to prefer enslaved Africans and what the slave system was like in New York City.

- A new vignette on a freedom seeker named Antonio, an enslaved West African man shipped to New Amsterdam and then to Maryland, who after his last escape attempt, in 1656, was tortured and killed by his owner, who was acquitted of murder by an all-White jury.

Chapter 4: From Colonies to States, 1607–1776

- New discussions on how French Jesuit missionaries integrated themselves into the Huron and Algonquin societies in French Canada.
- Updated discussions on how the American Revolution was often a civil war between colonists—Loyalists and Patriots—as demonstrated at the Battle of Moore's Creek Bridge, where the combatants were virtually all Americans.
- An updated and expanded biographical portrait of Thomas Paine and his writing of *Common Sense*.

Chapter 5: The American Revolution, 1775–1783

- New explanations of the British treatment of American prisoners of war during the Revolution and how the British policy to recruit enslaved men in the southern colonies to join the British army pushed many slave owners into the Patriots camp and motivated George Washington to allow free Blacks to fight with the Patriots.
- Expanded discussions of the American army's brutal winter encampment at Valley Forge, Pennsylvania.
- New coverage of the important Battle of King's Mountain, which was a decisive Patriot victory and another example of how the Revolution had turned into a violent civil war.
- A new segment on the Spanish-American alliance during the Revolutionary War that focuses on the Spanish general Bernardo de Gálvez, who organized a multicultural force of Spanish soldiers, Creole militiamen, Indians, free Blacks, and American volunteers and whose efforts helped compel the British to sign a peace treaty with the Americans guaranteeing their independence.

Chapter 6: Securing the Constitution and Union, 1783–1800

- New and expanded discussions on the Newburgh Conspiracy as a case study of the role of the military in a republic and how the Articles of Confederation laid the foundation for republicanism (representative democracy and majority rule).

Chapter 7: The Early Republic, 1800–1815

- Expanded biographical material about the achievements, contradictions, and legacy of Thomas Jefferson.
- New descriptions about the efforts of southerners to supply arms and ammunition to Haitian planters in hopes of quelling the uprisings of enslaved Haitians.
- Expanded discussions of the efforts of Tecumseh and his brother Tenskwatawa to forge an alliance of Native American nations to stop the influx of American settlers into their ancestral lands.

Chapter 8: The Emergence of a Market Economy, 1815–1850

- New and expanded discussions on innovations in travel and communications that grew out of the Industrial Revolution.
- New discussions describing the surge of Chinese immigrants to the West Coast during the California Gold Rush and the nativist attacks intended to deter the newcomers.

Chapter 9: Nationalism and Sectionalism, 1815–1828

- An expanded biography of President John Quincy Adams that discusses how his personality impacted his ability to govern.

Chapter 10: The Jacksonian Era, 1828–1840

- Expanded discussions of the origins of the Cherokee Nation and its first president, John Ross, and the story behind the signing of the Treaty of Echota and the Trail of Tears.

Chapter 11: The South and Slavery, 1800–1860

- New material about the centrality of slavery to the southern economy, the (mis)treatment of the enslaved on southern plantations, including the impact of separating and selling members of enslaved families, and the soaring profitability of new cotton plantations in the Gulf coast states of Alabama, Mississippi, Louisiana, and Texas.

Chapter 12: Religion, Romanticism, and Reform, 1800–1860

- Fresh biographical portraits of Peter Cartwright, one of the most famous frontier revivalist ministers, Joseph Smith, the founder of the Mormon faith, and Abigail Kelley, an early abolitionist and a fiery advocate of female suffrage (voting rights).

Chapter 13: Western Expansion and Southern Secession, 1830–1861

- Fresh insights into life on the overland trails to the Far West, including more discussions on the role of women and the impact of the high death and divorce rates triggered by the hardships of pioneering.
- A new profile of Juan Seguín, the son of a prominent Tejano family from San Antonio, who fought with the Anglos in the Texas War of Independence and was made a captain in the Texian army before going on to serve as the mayor of San Antonio.
- A new segment on the Cart War in Texas, which resulted in seventy-five Mexican-born wagon (cart) drivers being murdered by White Texan drivers.
- New discussions on the mistreatment of Mexican Americans and Native Americans following the Mexican-American War and the signing of the Treaty of Guadalupe.
- New portraits of freedom-seeking enslaved people Anthony Burns and Margaret "Peggy" Garner.

Chapter 14: The War of the Union, 1861–1865

- Revelation of the critical role played by Tejanos and Mexicans in the Civil War, both as soldiers serving in the Confederate and Union armies and as cowboys driving Texas longhorn steers to feed Confederate armies in the East.

Chapter 15: The Era of Reconstruction, 1865–1877

- Exploration of the Memphis race riot of 1866 and the massacre of African Americans.
- New coverage on how western states before and after the Civil War passed laws to keep Chinese immigrants from gaining U.S. citizenship.
- A new profile of Henrietta Wood, a freed enslaved person living in Ohio, who sued the slave trader who had sold her originally for $20,000. The Ohio Court ruled in her favor, awarding her $2,500, and in doing so established a legal foundation for reparations for the formerly enslaved.

Chapter 16: Business and Labor in the Industrial Era, 1860–1900

- A new vignette on Oliver Dalrymple, the "Wheat King of Minnesota," who created one of the first and largest bonanza farms worked by seasonal laborers from Mexico and Scandinavia.
- New discussions on how immigrant Chinese railroad laborers used work stoppages and strikes to demand better wages and treatment by their American bosses.

- A new segment focusing on the building of railroads in the Southwest and how developers set up recruiting centers in Mexico, leading to a 50 percent increase in the Mexican immigrant population in New Mexico from 1880 to 1900.

Chapter 17: The New South and the New West, 1865–1900

- New discussions on how the Duke family created the American Tobacco Company and other entrepreneurs joined the effort to industrialize the South after the Civil War.
- Expanded coverage of the Wilmington Insurrection.
- New discussions on how the Anglo cowboys learned how to ride horses and herd cattle from Mestizo Mexicans, called vaqueros, adopting their clothing, equipment, food, techniques, and terminology (*lasso, rodeo, rancho*).
- A new portrait of Callie Guy House, a former enslaved worker who launched a mass movement in the 1890s demanding pensions for former enslaved people.
- New discussions about the "Juan Crow" belt in south Texas where hundreds of Mexican Americans, many of them U.S. citizens, were lynched during the second half of the nineteenth century.
- New coverage of the Porvenir Massacre. Finally, Chapter 17 introduces to readers Las Gorras Blancas (the White Caps), who were Mexican American citizens in New Mexico who armed themselves to prevent Anglo settlers from seizing their land.

Chapter 18: Political Stalemate and the Rural Revolt, 1865–1900

- Enhanced coverage of nativist efforts on the West Coast to discriminate against Asian immigrants by urging new laws such as the Page Act and the Chinese Exclusion Act.

Chapter 19: Seizing an American Empire, 1865–1913

- Expanded discussions on American imperial expansion, including the colonization of Cuba and the writing of the new Cuban Constitution and the Platt Amendment, which gave the United States the right to intervene militarily as needed in Cuban affairs.
- New discussions on how many of the American colonies were designated as "unincorporated" so that their residents would not be protected by the U.S. Constitution.
- New coverage of the Plan of San Diego, a rebellion against the United States by Mexican anarchists living in south Texas.

Chapter 20: The Progressive Era, 1890–1920

- New and revised details on how the women's suffrage movement achieved the vote, especially the key role played by western states such as Wyoming in spearheading the movement.
- New discussions on philosopher John Dewey's vision of a pragmatic and socially engaged education for young people.
- New coverage on how the tragic Triangle Factory Fire in New York City led to a myriad of improvements in workers' rights and the wages paid to child laborers.

Chapter 21: America and the Great War, 1914–1920

- New data on the diverse ethnic and racial composition of American soldiers in the Great War, including 400,000 African Americans and 100,000 Hispanic Americans.
- New discussions on the Jones Act, which granted U.S. citizenship to Puerto Ricans and allowed them to enlist in the U.S. Army (20,000 did during the Great War).

Chapter 22: A Clash of Cultures, 1920–1929

- A new profile of Alain Locke, the guiding force behind the Harlem Renaissance.
- Fresh treatment of the significance of Albert Einstein's scientific theories and their contribution to cultural modernism.
- New coverage of the Immigration Act of 1924 that introduced the term *illegal aliens* and required Mexican American migrant workers to carry passports or visas before entering the United States to work.

Chapter 23: The Great Depression and the New Deal, 1933–1939

- New coverage of the "Cornbelt Rebellion" and how desperate farmers responded to the impact of the early stages of the Great Depression.
- A new segment about the massive deportation of Mexican workers and Mexican Americans in response to the soaring unemployment generated by the Great Depression.
- A refreshed biographical portrait of President Franklin D. Roosevelt.
- A new portrait of African American Mary McLeod Bethune, the first director of the National Youth Association.

Chapter 24: The Second World War, 1933–1945

- New insights into "Operation Barbarossa," the German invasion of the Soviet Union, including references to the Nazi "police" units that accompanied the invasion and murdered Russian Jews.

- A new vignette on A. Philip Randolph, the founder and head of the Brotherhood of Sleeping Car Porters, the largest African American labor union.
- A new profile of Harry T. Stewart, Jr., from Queens, New York, whose combat flights with the Tuskegee Airmen squadron earned him the Distinguished Flying Cross.
- Expanded treatment of the systematic prejudice against Jews working in the federal government during the war, and the role of the State Department in addressing the Holocaust in Europe.
- Expanded discussions on the fierce fighting in Pacific islands controlled by the Japanese during the Second World War, with special attention given to the Battle of Saipan Island and the "Unwanted Visit" to the homes of the many fallen American soldiers.

Chapter 25: The Cold War and the Fair Deal, 1945–1952

- New segments showing how Harry Truman's views on racism evolved over time and led to his decision to integrate the federal government, including the military branches.
- A new section on "Operation Wetback," the deportation of Mexican Americans during the presidency of Dwight Eisenhower.

Chapter 26: Affluence and Anxiety in the Atomic Age, 1950–1959

- New discussions on the "Lavender Menace," the effort by federal agencies to identify and fire gay and lesbian people from working for the government.
- A new vignette on Frank Kameny, who protested the discriminatory government efforts and became one of the nation's most prominent gay leaders in the 1950s.
- New discussion of *The Negro Motorist's Green Book*, a publication alerting African Americans to which motels and service stations served Blacks.
- New material on how women who were encouraged during the Second World War to work in defense plants were urged to resume their traditional roles as wives and mothers after the war.

Chapter 27: New Frontiers and a Great Society, 1960–1968

- A new segment on the Cold War and the race to the moon.
- Enhanced coverage of the Cuban Missile Crisis.
- Expanded discussions on the role of the Freedom Riders in propelling the civil rights movement into a national phenomenon.

- Expanded coverage of the civil rights march in Selma, Alabama, and how it prompted President Lyndon B. Johnson to insist that Congress pass the Voting Rights Act.
- Fresh coverage on Congressman John Lewis and his role in the civil rights movement.
- A new vignette on Fannie Lou Hamer and her role in the civil rights movement.

Chapter 28: Rebellion and Reaction, 1960s and 1970s

- A new segment about the Kerner Commission report on racism and urban violence.
- Expanded discussions of the feminist movement and the United Farm Workers movement with new biographical material on Cesar Chavez and Delores Huerta, its co-founders.
- New segments on Richard Nixon's Southern Strategy, his decision to expand the Vietnam War, the Kent State University shootings, and the controversy over the publication of the Pentagon Papers.

Chapter 29: Conservative Revival, 1977–2000

- A new biographical portrait of Mikhail Gorbachev, the leader of the Soviet Union.
- New treatment of the AIDS epidemic and the role of Larry Kramer in organizing the gay community to insist on more urgent government action to address the epidemic.
- New discussions of the impact of the Crime Bill of 1994 and the Illegal Immigration and Responsibility Act of 1996, which expanded the Border Patrol and the wall along the Mexican border.

Chapter 30: Twenty-First-Century America, 2000–Present

- A new framework for the Trump administration in the context of the ideological divide between supporters of economic nationalism and cooperative globalization and how this tension played out in the context of immigration policies, trade wars, and travel bans.
- New material on the COVID-19 pandemic, the Black Lives Matter movement, racial justice protests, the 2020 presidential election, the effort of pro-Trump rioters to storm the U.S. Capitol to prevent the certification of Joseph Biden as the new president, the second impeachment of Donald Trump, and the first 100 days of the Biden administration.

The new Twelfth Edition of *America: A Narrative History* also makes history an *immersive* experience through its innovative pedagogy and digital resources. InQuizitive—W. W. Norton's adaptive learning program—helps students better grasp the textbook's key topics and enables instructors to assess learning progress at the individual and classroom levels. For the first time, instructors will have access to a library of guided primary sources, plus a series of "Thinking Like a Historian" exercises for every chapter, inviting students to work with both primary and secondary sources. Online activities such as the History Skills Tutorials and "Thinking Like a Historian" exercises support the discipline's efforts to develop students' critical thinking and analytical skills that are applicable to this course as well as a career in virtually any field. An array of valuable support materials ranging from author videos and online document collections to lecture slides and test banks are available for download or integration into a campus learning management system. See pages xxx–xxxvii for information about student and instructor resources.

Finally, a note on terminology. History is a dynamic discipline: as time passes, it benefits not only from the discovery of new evidence and refined interpretations but also from being in conversation with our contemporary culture. After much analysis and discussion, we have joined other publishers, magazines, and newspapers in capitalizing group identity terms such as *Black* and *White*. While respecting the various and at times conflicting opinions on this matter, we feel our new approach is consistent with the goals of making "a more perfect union" where all people are treated equally and with dignity, including the language choices many use to identify themselves. In this effort, we have also shifted from using the word *slave* in the narrative to *enslaved* and from *fugitive slave* to *freedom seeker*. After all, people did not choose to become slaves; they were instead forcibly *enslaved*. Once enslaved, they yearned to be free again and often risked their lives to liberate themselves. Where the words *slave* and *fugitive slave* are used in historical quotations, we have retained their original form.

No single term can precisely encompass social groups. In the new edition's references to people with Spanish-speaking ancestors, we use identifying terms that are the most historically accurate and relevant for a given context, region, time period, or group of people—Spanish, Hispanic, Tejano, Californio, Mexican American, Chicano and Chicana, Cuban American, Puerto Rican American, and Latino, Latina, and Latinx. Not only is this approach more historically accurate, but it also better demonstrates the dynamism of group identities in America.

This new edition follows a similar strategy for other significant groups such as African Americans, Native Americans, Asian Americans, immigrants, and LGBTQ Americans. We recognize that there are several ways to deal with these sensitive issues and that the issue of group terminology remains a subject of robust discussion within classrooms, homes, communities, and politics. Our efforts in this edition represent a continuing commitment to remain current in our treatment of such shifting preferences.

MEDIA RESOURCES FOR INSTRUCTORS AND STUDENTS

America's digital resources are designed to develop successful readers, guiding students through the narrative while simultaneously developing their critical thinking and history skills.

The comprehensive support package features an award-winning adaptive learning tool, as well as new, innovative interactive resources, including the skill-building "Thinking Like a Historian" exercises, available for every chapter of the book, that encourage both primary and secondary source analysis. All of these resources are designed to help students master the Focus Questions in each chapter and continue to nurture their development as historians. To develop the resources, W. W. Norton is committed to partnering exclusively with subject-matter experts who teach the course. As a result, instructors have all the course materials needed to manage their U.S. history survey class, whether they are teaching face-to-face, online, or in a hybrid setting.

NEW! THINKING LIKE A HISTORIAN EXERCISES

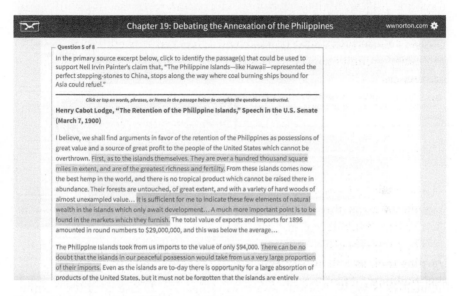

To strengthen students' history skills, *America* now offers a collection of new, assignable "Thinking Like a Historian" exercises for each chapter. Each online exercise highlights the foundational role of primary sources as the building blocks of history. A selection of exercises also includes secondary source document excerpts. Students examine a major historical debate or issue through the lens of primary source evidence and historians' differing interpretations of that evidence. A series of interactive questions with guiding feedback helps students dissect and compare the sources, building historical thinking skills throughout the semester. As a capstone assignment, follow-up short-answer writing prompts, delivered through the learning management system, encourage students to formulate their own interpretations about the historical debate in question.

InQuizitive

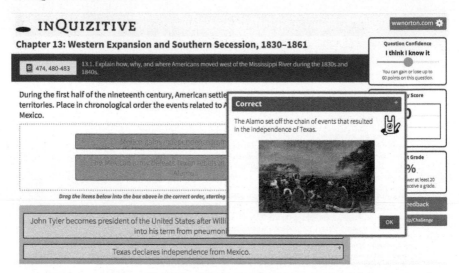

InQuizitive is W. W. Norton's award-winning, easy-to-use adaptive learning tool that personalizes the learning experience for students, helping them to grasp key concepts and achieve key learning objectives. Through a variety of question types, answer-specific feedback, and game-like elements such as the ability to wager points, students are motivated to keep working until they fully comprehend the concepts. As a result, students arrive better prepared for class, giving you more time for discussion and activities.

The InQuizitive course for *America* features over 1,500 engaging, interactive questions (approximately 20 percent of which are new or updated) tagged to each chapter's Focus Questions. Each activity ensures thorough coverage of the key concepts within the chapter reading, as well as questions that invite students to dig in and analyze maps, primary source excerpts, and other types of historical evidence such as artifacts, artworks, architecture, photographs, and more.

HISTORY SKILLS TUTORIALS

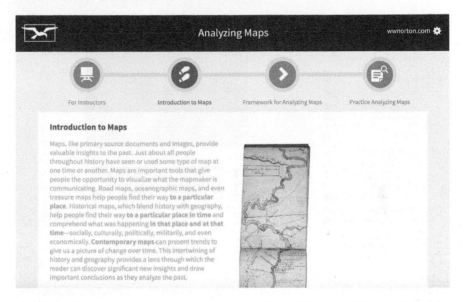

The History Skills Tutorials are interactive, online modules that support student development of the key skills for the American history survey course. The tutorials for *America* focus on the following:

- Analyzing secondary source documents (new to this edition)
- Analyzing primary source documents
- Analyzing images
- Analyzing maps

   With interactive practice assessments, helpful guiding feedback, and videos with author David Shi, these tutorials teach students the critical analysis skills that they will put to use in their academic and professional careers. These tutorials can be integrated directly into an existing learning management system, making for easy assignability and easy student access.

NORTON EBOOKS

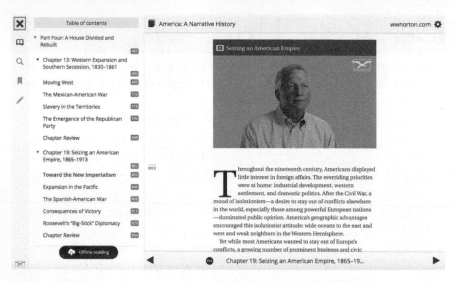

Norton Ebooks offer an enhanced reading experience at a fraction of the cost of a print textbook. They provide an active reading experience, enabling students to take notes, bookmark, search, highlight, and read offline. Instructors can even add notes that students can see as they are reading the text. Norton Ebooks can be viewed on all computers and mobile devices. The ebook for *America: A Narrative History* includes the following:

- Tool-tip key terms and definitions
- Clickable and zoomable maps and images
- Hundreds of embedded videos with author David Shi, including chapter overview videos that provide visual introductions to the key themes and historical developments students will encounter in each chapter

STUDENT SITE

A student website offers additional study and review materials for students to use outside of class. The resources include the following:

- An enhanced **Online Reader** featuring more than one hundred primary source documents and images, each with support materials such as brief headnotes and discussion prompts
- Hundreds of **Author Videos** featuring David Shi to help students understand the essential developments in the American History course
- **Flashcards** inviting students to review the key terms from the textbook
- **Chapter Outlines** giving students a detailed snapshot of the key topics of each chapter
- **iMaps** allowing students to view layers of information on various maps from the text
- **"What's It All About?" Infographics** employing the themes of continuity and change to frame visual overviews of important developments, such as the evolution of African Americans' legal status from the Civil War through Reconstruction

TEST BANK

The test bank features more than 2,500 questions—including multiple-choice, true/false, and short-answer—aligned to each chapter of the book. Questions are classified according to level of difficulty and Bloom's Taxonomy, providing multiple avenues for comprehension and skill assessment and making it easy to construct tests that are meaningful and diagnostic.

Norton Testmaker brings W. W. Norton's high-quality testing materials online. Create assessments for your course from anywhere with an Internet connection, without downloading files or installing specialized software. Search and filter test bank questions by chapter, type, difficulty, learning objectives, and other criteria. You can also customize test bank questions to fit your course. Easily export your tests or W. W. Norton's ready-to-use quizzes to Microsoft Word or Common Cartridge files for your LMS.

INSTRUCTOR'S MANUAL

The instructor's manual for *America: A Narrative History*, Twelfth Edition, is designed to help instructors prepare effective lectures. It contains chapter summaries, detailed chapter outlines, lecture ideas, in-class activities, discussion questions, and more.

RESOURCES FOR YOUR LMS

High-quality Norton digital media can be easily added to online, hybrid, or lecture courses. Get started building your course with our easy-to-use integrated resources; all activities can be accessed right within your existing learning management system. Graded activities are configured to report to the LMS course grade book. The downloadable file includes integration links to the following resources, organized by chapter:

- Ebook
- InQuizitive
- History Skills Tutorials
- Thinking Like a Historian exercises
- Thinking Like a Historian writing prompts
- Chapter outlines
- Flashcards

Instructors can also add customizable multiple-choice, true/false, and short-answer questions to their learning management system using Norton Testmaker.

CLASSROOM PRESENTATION TOOLS

- **Lecture PowerPoint slides:** Available for download, these PowerPoints feature bullet points of key topics, art, and maps—all sequentially arranged to follow the book. The Lecture PowerPoints also include lecture notes in the Notes section of each slide, perfect for use in both in-person and online courses. These slides are customizable in order to meet the needs of both first-time and experienced teachers.
- **Image files:** All images and maps from the book are available separately in JPEG and PowerPoint format for instructor use. Alt-text is provided for each item.

PRIMARY SOURCE READERS TO ACCOMPANY AMERICA: A NARRATIVE HISTORY

- **NEW!** Eighth Edition of *For the Record: A Documentary History of America*, by David E. Shi and Holly A. Mayer (Duquesne University), is the perfect companion reader for *America: A Narrative History.* It features over 250 primary source readings from diaries, journals, newspaper articles, speeches, government documents, and novels, including a noteworthy number of readings that highlight the role of Latino and Latina Americans in this new edition of *America.* If you haven't perused *For the Record* in a while, now would be a good time to take a look. The reader is now available as an ebook for the first time!

ACKNOWLEDGMENTS

This Twelfth Edition of *America: A Narrative History* has been a team effort. Several professors who have become specialists in teaching the introductory survey course helped create the instructor resources and interactive media:

David Cameron, Lone Star College–University Park

Brian Cervantez, Tarrant County College–Northwest Campus

Manar Elkhaldi, University of Central Florida

Christina Gold, El Camino College

Maryellen Harman, North Central Missouri College

David Marsich, Germanna Community College

Brian D. McKnight, University of Virginia's College at Wise

Lise Namikas, Baton Rouge Community College

Matthew Zembo, Hudson Valley Community College

The quality and range of the professorial reviews on this project were truly exceptional. The book and its accompanying media components were greatly influenced by the suggestions provided by the following instructors for both current and previous editions:

Milan Andrejevich, Ivy Tech Community College

Carol A. Bielke, San Antonio Independent School District

April Birchfield, Asheville-Buncombe Technical Community College

Carl Boschert, Hinds Community College

Kevin Brady, Tidewater Community College

Matt Brent, Rappahannock Community College

Sharon J. Burnham, John Tyler Community College

Michael Collins, Texas State University

Scott Cook, Motlow State
Community College
Carrie Coston, Blinn College
Nicholas P. Cox, Houston
Community College
Tyler Craddock, J. Sargeant
Reynolds Community College
Carl E. Creasman, Jr., Valencia
College
Stephen K. Davis, Texas State
University
Frank De La O, Midland College
Jim Dudlo, Brookhaven College
Jeffrey David Ewen, Ivy Tech
Community College
Robert Glen Findley, Odessa
College
Brandon Franke, Blinn College
Chad Garick, Jones County Junior
College
Christopher Gerdes, Lone Star
College–Kingwood and CyFair
Lanette Gonzalez, Ivy Tech
Community College
Abbie Grubb, San Jacinto College–
South Campus
Devethia Guillory, Lone Star
College–North Harris
Jennifer Heth, Tarrant County
College–South Campus
Justin Hoggard, Three Rivers College
Andrew G. Hollinger, Tarrant
County College
David P. Hopkins, Jr., Midland
College
Justin Horton, Thomas Nelson
Community College
David Houpt, University of North
Carolina, Wilmington

Bettye Hutchins, Vernon College
John Ivens, Glenville State College
Theresa R. Jach, Houston
Community College
Robert Jason Kelly, Holmes
Community College
Matthew Keyworth, Lone Star
College
Deborah Kruger, Butler
Community College
Jennifer Lang, Delgado Community
College
David W. Marsich, Germanna
Community College
Nina McCune, Baton Rouge
Community College
Adam Meredith, University of
Southern Indiana
Richard Randall Moore,
Metropolitan Community
College–Longview
Ken S. Mueller, Ivy Tech
Community College
Lise Namikas, Colorado State
University–Global
Brice E. Olivier, Temple College
Saul Panski, El Camino College
Candice Pulkowski, The Art
Institutes
Shane Puryear, Lone Star College–
Greenspoint and Victory Centers
Carey Roberts, Liberty University
John Schmitz, Northern Virginia
Community College–Annandale
Nancy Schurr, Chattanooga State
Community College
Donald Seals, Kilgore College
Greg Shealy, University of
Wisconsin–Madison

Wendy Shuffett, Jefferson State Community College

Steve Siry, Baldwin Wallace University

Thomas Summerhill, Michigan State University

Kevin Sweeney, Wayland Baptist University

Christopher Thomas, J. Sargeant Reynolds Community College

Tracy S. Uebelhor, Ivy Tech Community College

Scott M. Williams, Weatherford College

Laura Matysek Wood, Tarrant County College–Northwest

Crystal R. M. Wright, North Central Texas College

As always, my colleagues at W. W. Norton shared with me their dedicated expertise and their poise amid tight deadlines, especially Jon Durbin, Melissa Atkin, David Bradley, Allen Chen, Lily Gellman, Carson Russell, Rachel Mayer, Alexander Lee, Hillary Roegelein, Jennifer Jussel, Benjamin Reynolds, Sarah England Bartley, Janise Turso, Julie Sindel, Carrie Polvino, Elizabeth Trammell, Amla Sanghvi, Debra Morton-Hoyt, Lissi Sigillo, Hope Goodell Miller, Lisa Buckley, Jen Montgomery, Jenna Barry, Alicia Jimenez, Rose Paulson, Anna Marie Anastasi, Harry Haskell, Ellen Lohman, Marne Evans, and Kelly Minot Rafey. In addition, Jim Stewart, a patient friend and consummate editor, helped winnow my wordiness.

Finally, I have dedicated this Twelfth Edition of *America* to the incredible staff at W. W. Norton, a publisher whose dedicated employees are more interested in education than profit. I have been blessed to work with and learn from so many talented and dedicated professionals.

AMERICA

15 The Era of Reconstruction

1865–1877

Thomas Nast's *Emancipation* (1865) This wood engraving based on Thomas Nast's *Emancipation* represents his vision of an optimistic future for Blacks in the United States after emancipation, which would not outlast Reconstruction. The central scene of a joyous family contrasts with the background depicting enslavement and subordination prior to emancipation.

I n the spring of 1865, the terrible conflict finally ended. The United States was a "new nation," said an Illinois congressman, because it was now "wholly free." At a cost of some 750,000 lives and the destruction of the southern economy, the Union had won the war, and almost 4 million enslaved African Americans had seized their freedom.

Most civil wars, however, never end completely. Peace did not bring everyday equality or civil rights to people of color, nor did it end racism, in the South or the North. Many White Southerners opposed the decision of Confederate generals to surrender their armies, and many more bitterly resented the freeing of the enslaved. In the North, racism persisted too. The *New York Times* declared that African Americans, even if freed from slavery, had no more business voting than did women or Indians, and that it was "little short of insane" to think otherwise. The *Times* was also relieved to learn that most African Americans would stay in the South and would not "swarm to the North."

The defeated Confederates saw their world turned upside down. The ending of slavery, the disruptions to the southern economy, and the horrifying human losses and physical devastation had shattered the plantation system and upended racial relations in the South. "Change, change, indelibly stamped upon everything I meet, even upon the faces of the people!" sighed Alexander Stephens, vice president of the former Confederacy. His native region now had to adjust to a new order as the U.S. government set about "reconstructing" the South and using federal troops to police defiant ex-Confederates.

Formerly enslaved people felt just the opposite. Yankees were their liberators. No longer would enslaved workers be sold and separated from their families or prevented from learning to read and write or attending church. "I felt

focus questions

1. What major challenges did the federal government face in reconstructing the South after the Civil War?

2. How and why did the federal government's Reconstruction policies change over time?

3. In what ways did White and Black Southerners react to various Reconstruction programs and requirements?

4. What were the political and economic factors that helped end Reconstruction in 1877?

5. What was the significance of Reconstruction on the nation's future?

like a bird out of a cage," said Houston Holloway of Georgia, who had been sold to three different owners during his first twenty years. "Amen. Amen. Amen. I could hardly ask to feel any better than I did that day."

Many previously enslaved people rushed to change their names. Some only had a first name under slavery; others had used the same last name as their owners. Now, they could rename themselves as freedpeople. In Alabama, a freedman who had served in the Union army explained that after returning home after the war, "I was wearing the name of Lewis Smith, but I found that the negroes after freedom, were taking the names of their father like the white folks often did. So I asked my mother and she told me my father was John Barnett, a white man, and I took up the name of Barnett."

Many slaveowners defied emancipation until forced to comply by the arrival of Union soldiers. In South Carolina, violence against freedpeople was widespread. Federal troops found "the bodies of murdered Negroes" strewn in a forest. When a South Carolina White man caught an enslaved mother and her children running toward freedom, he "drew his bowie-knife and cut her throat; also the throat of her boy, nine years old; also the throat of her girl, seven years of age; threw their bodies into the river, and the live baby after them."

Such brutal incidents testified to the extraordinary challenges the nation faced in "reconstructing" a ravaged and resentful South while helping to transform formerly enslaved people into free workers and citizens. It would not be easy. The Rebels had been conquered, but they were far from being loyal Unionists, and few of them supported the federal effort to create a multiracial democracy in the former Confederacy.

The Reconstruction era, from 1865 to 1877, witnessed a complex debate about the role of the federal government in ensuring civil rights. Some Northerners wanted the former Confederate states returned to the Union with little or no changes. Others wanted Confederate leaders imprisoned or executed and the South rebuilt in the image of the rest of the nation. Still others cared little about reconstructing the South; they wanted the federal government to focus on promoting northern economic growth and westward expansion.

Although the Reconstruction era lasted only twelve years, it was one of the most challenging and significant periods in U.S. history. At the center of the debate over how to restore the Union were profound questions: Who is deserving of citizenship, and what does it entail? What rights should all Americans enjoy? What role should the federal government play in ensuring freedom and equality? Those questions are still shaping American life nearly 150 years later.

The War's Aftermath in the South

In the spring of 1865, Southerners were emotionally exhausted; a fifth of southern White males had died in the war; many others had been maimed for life. In 1866, Mississippi spent 20 percent of the state's budget on artificial limbs for Confederate veterans. The economy was also ravaged. Property values had collapsed. In the year after the war ended, eighty-one plantations in Mississippi were sold for less than a tenth of what they had been worth in 1860. Confederate money was worthless; personal savings had vanished; tens of thousands of horses and mules had been killed in the fighting; and countless farm buildings and pieces of agricultural equipment had been destroyed.

Many of the largest southern cities—Richmond, Atlanta, Columbia—were devastated. Most railroads and many bridges were damaged or destroyed, and Southerners, White and Black, were homeless and hungry. Along the path that General William T. Sherman's Union army had blazed across Georgia and the Carolinas, one observer reported in

Richmond after the Civil War Before evacuating the capital of the Confederacy, Richmond, Virginia, residents set fire to warehouses and factories to prevent their falling into Union hands. Pictured here is one of Richmond's burnt districts in April 1865. Women in mourning attire walk among the shambles.

1866, the countryside "looked for many miles like a broad black streak of ruin and desolation." Burned-out Columbia, South Carolina, said another witness, was "a wilderness of ruins"; Charleston, the birthplace of secession, had become a place of "vacant houses, of widowed women, of rotting wharves, of deserted warehouses, of weed-wild gardens, of miles of grass-grown streets, of acres of pitiful and voiceless barrenness."

Between 1860 and 1870, northern wealth grew by 50 percent while southern wealth dropped 60 percent. Emancipation wiped out almost $3 billion invested in the slave labor system, which had enabled the explosive growth of the cotton culture. Not until 1879 would the cotton crop again equal the record harvest of 1860. Tobacco production did not regain its prewar level until 1880. The sugar crop of Louisiana did not recover until 1893, and the rice economy along the coast of South Carolina and Georgia never regained its prewar levels of production or profit.

In 1860, just before the Civil War, the South had generated 30 percent of the nation's wealth; in 1870, it produced but 12 percent. Amanda Worthington, a planter's wife from Mississippi, assessed the damage: "None of us can realize that we are no longer wealthy—yet thanks to the Yankees, the cause of all unhappiness, such is the case."

Resentment in the South boiled over. Union soldiers were cursed and spat upon. A Virginia woman expressed a spirited defiance common among her Confederate friends: "Every day, every hour, that I live increases my hatred and detestation, and loathing of that race. They [Yankees] disgrace our common humanity. As a people I consider them vastly inferior to the better classes of our slaves." Fervent southern nationalists implanted in their children a similar hatred of Yankees and a defiance of northern rule.

Rebuilding the former Confederate states would not be easy, and the issues related to Reconstruction were complicated and controversial. For example, the process of establishing new state governments required first determining the legal status of the states that had seceded: Were they now conquered territories? If so, then the Constitution assigned Congress authority to re-create their state governments. But what if, as Abraham Lincoln argued, the Confederate states had never officially left the Union because the act of secession was itself illegal? In that circumstance, the president, not Congress, would be responsible for re-forming state governments.

Whichever branch of government—Congress or the Executive (presidency)—directed the reconstruction of the South, it would have to address the most difficult issue: What would be the political, social, and economic status of the freedpeople? They were free but by no means independent. Were they citizens? If not, what was their status?

What the former enslaved people most wanted was to become self-reliant, to be paid for their labor, to reunite with their family members, to gain education for their children, to enjoy full participation in political life, and to create their own community organizations and social life. Most southern Whites were just as determined to prevent that from happening.

BATTLES OVER POLITICAL RECONSTRUCTION

Reconstruction of former Confederate states actually began during the war and went through distinct phases, the first of which was called Presidential Reconstruction. In 1862, President Lincoln had named army generals to serve as temporary military governors for conquered Confederate areas. By the end of 1863, he had formulated a plan to reestablish governments in the former Confederate states.

LINCOLN'S WARTIME RECONSTRUCTION PLAN In late 1863, President Lincoln issued a Proclamation of Amnesty and Reconstruction, under which former Confederate states could re-create a Union government once a number equal to 10 percent of those who had voted in 1860 swore allegiance to the Constitution. Most Confederates received a presidential pardon acquitting them of treason. Certain groups, however, were denied pardons: Confederate government officials; senior officers of the Confederate army and navy; judges, congressmen, and military officers of the United States who had left their posts to join the rebellion; and those who had abused captured African American soldiers.

CONGRESSIONAL WARTIME RECONSTRUCTION PLANS A few conservative and most moderate Republicans supported Lincoln's "10 percent" program that immediately restored pro-Union southern governments. Radical Republicans, however, argued that Congress, not the president, should supervise Reconstruction. **Radical Republicans** favored a drastic transformation of southern society that would grant freedpeople full citizenship. Many Radicals believed that all people, regardless of race, were equal in God's eyes. They wanted no compromise with the "sin" of racism.

They also hoped to replace the White, Democratic planter elite with a new generation of small farmers. "The middling classes who own the soil, and work it with their own hands," explained Radical leader Thaddeus Stevens, "are the main support of every free government."

In 1864, with the war still raging, the Radicals tried to take charge of Reconstruction by passing the Wade-Davis Bill, named for two leading Republicans. In contrast to Lincoln's 10 percent Reconstruction plan, the Wade-Davis Bill required that a *majority* of White male citizens declare their allegiance to the Union before a Confederate state could be readmitted.

The bill never became law, however, for Lincoln vetoed it. In retaliation, Radicals issued the Wade-Davis Manifesto, which accused Lincoln of exceeding his constitutional authority. Unfazed by the criticism, Lincoln continued his efforts to restore the Confederate states to the Union. He also rushed assistance to the freedpeople in the South.

THE FREEDMEN'S BUREAU In early 1865, Congress approved the Thirteenth Amendment to the Constitution, officially abolishing slavery in the United States, and it became law in December. Yet what did freedom mean for the formerly enslaved, most of whom had no land, no home, no food, no jobs, and no education? "What is freedom?" asked Congressman James A. Garfield, a former Union general and a future U.S. president, in 1865. "Is it the bare privilege of not being chained? If this is all, then freedom is a bitter mockery, a cruel delusion." The debate over what freedom should entail became the central issue of Reconstruction. "Liberty has been won," Senator Charles Sumner noted. "The battle for Equality is still pending."

To address the complex issues raised by emancipation, Congress on March 3, 1865, created within the War Department the Bureau of Refugees, Freedmen, and Abandoned Lands (known as the **Freedmen's Bureau**) to assist the suffering "freedmen and their wives and children." It was the first federal effort to provide help directly to people rather than to states. And its task was daunting. When General William T. Sherman learned that his friend General Oliver O. Howard had been appointed to lead the Freedmen's Bureau, he warned: "It is not . . . in your power to fulfill one-tenth of the expectations of those who framed the Bureau."

Undeterred by such concerns, in May 1865 Howard declared that emancipated people "must be free to choose their own employers and be paid for their labor." He assigned army officers to negotiate labor contracts between freedpeople and White landowners, many of whom resisted. The Bureau also provided the now free African Americans with medical care, clothing, shelter, and food. By 1868, the Bureau had distributed more than 20 million meals. It also assisted former enslaved people in seeking justice in courts, managed abandoned lands, and helped formalize marriages and find relatives.

The Bureau also helped establish schools and colleges. A Mississippi freedman explained that education was his essential priority, for it "was the next best

Freedmen's School in Virginia As part of its effort to support formerly enslaved people in their transition to freedom, the Freedmen's Bureau established schools for the freedpeople across the southern states.

thing to liberty." By 1870, the Freedmen's Bureau was supervising more than 4,000 new schools serving almost 250,000 students in the former Confederate states. Bureau-created schools provided a crucial transition to conventional public schools that southern states eventually created. To staff its schools, the Bureau recruited thousands of teachers from the northern states. Charlotte Forten, an African American teacher, ventured south from Philadelphia after the war to be a volunteer teacher at a school for former enslaved people. She marveled at the passion for learning displayed by the students: "I never before saw children so eager to learn."

Yet the Freedmen's Bureau had significant limitations. It never had more than 900 agents across thirteen states to deal with 3.5 million former enslaved people spread across a million square miles, not nearly enough to implement the Bureau's broad goals. The number of Federal troops supporting the Freedmen's Bureau was also inadequate. As a Texas officer stressed, the Bureau agents were helpless "unless in the vicinity of our troops." Perhaps the most glaring weakness of the Bureau was its failure to redistribute land to formerly enslaved people.

SELF-SUSTAINING FREEDPEOPLE In July 1865, hundreds of African Americans gathered on St. Helena Island off the South Carolina coast. There, Martin Delaney, the highest-ranking Black officer in the U.S. Colored Troops, addressed them. Before the Civil War, he had been a prominent African American abolitionist in the North. Now, Major Delaney assured the gathering that slavery had indeed been "absolutely abolished." But abolition, he stressed, was less the result of Abraham Lincoln's leadership than it was the outcome of former enslaved people and free Blacks like him undermining the Confederacy. Slavery was dead, and freedom was now in their hands. "Yes, yes, yes," his listeners shouted.

Delaney then noted that many of the White planters in the area claimed that African Americans were lazy and "have not the intelligence to get on for yourselves without being guided and driven to the work by [White] overseers." Delaney dismissed such assumptions as lies intended to restore a system of forced labor resembling slavery. He then told the freedpeople that their best hope was to become self-sustaining farmers: "Get a community and get all the lands you can—if you cannot get any singly." He added that if they could not become economically self-reliant, they would find themselves enslaved again.

Several White planters attended Delaney's talk, and an army officer at the scene reported that they "listened with horror depicted in their faces." The planters predicted that such speeches would incite "open rebellion" among southern Blacks.

THE ASSASSINATION OF LINCOLN The possibility of lenient federal measures to "reconstruct" the Confederate states and restore them to the Union would die with Abraham Lincoln. The president who had yearned for a peace "with malice toward none, with charity for all" offered his last view of Reconstruction in the final speech of his life. On April 11, 1865, Lincoln rejected calls for a vengeful peace. He wanted "no persecution, no bloody work," no hangings of Confederate leaders, and no extreme efforts to restructure southern social and economic life.

Three days later, on April 14, Lincoln and his wife Mary Todd Lincoln attended a play at Ford's Theatre in Washington, D.C. With his trusted bodyguard called away to Richmond, Lincoln was defenseless as twenty-six-year-old John Wilkes Booth, a celebrated actor and rabid Confederate, slipped into the unguarded presidential box and shot the president behind the left ear. As Lincoln slumped forward, Booth pulled out a knife, stabbed the president's military aide, and jumped from the box to the stage, breaking his leg in the process. He then mounted a waiting horse and fled the city. Lincoln died nine hours later, the first president to be killed in office.

At the same time that Booth was shooting the president, other Confederate assassins were hunting Vice President Andrew Johnson and Secretary of State William H. Seward. Johnson escaped injury because his would-be assassin got drunk in the bar of the vice president's hotel. Seward and four others, including his son, however, suffered severe knife wounds when attacked at home.

The government was suddenly leaderless, and the nation was overwhelmed with shock, horror, and anguish. African American leader Frederick Douglass described Lincoln's murder as "an unspeakable calamity." In his view, Lincoln was "the black man's President: the first to show any respect for their rights as

Lincoln's Funeral Procession After Lincoln's assassination, his body was taken on a two-week-long funeral procession through five different states, allowing millions of people the chance to see his casket. This photograph was taken on April 25, when the procession passed through New York City.

men" by rising "above the prejudice of his times." Confederates had a different view. A seventeen-year-old South Carolina girl was giddy at the news. As she wrote in her diary, "Old Abe Lincoln has been assassinated!"

Vice President Andrew Johnson became the new president shortly after Lincoln was declared dead. Eleven days later, Union troops found John Wilkes Booth hiding in a northern Virginia tobacco barn. In his diary the night before, he had vowed never to be taken alive: "I have too great a soul to die like a criminal!" The soldiers set the barn on fire, and a few minutes later one of them shot and killed Booth. As he lay dying, the assassin whispered, "Tell my mother I died for my country." Three of Booth's collaborators were convicted by a military court and hanged, as was Mary Surratt, a middle-aged widow who owned the Washington boardinghouse where the assassination had been planned. Surratt and her extended family were ardent supporters of the Confederacy.

The outpouring of grief after Lincoln's death transformed the fallen president into a sacred symbol. Lincoln's body lay in state for several days in Washington, D.C., before being transported 1,600 miles for burial in Springfield, Illinois. In Philadelphia, 300,000 mourners paid their last respects; in New York City, 500,000 people viewed the president's body. On May 4, Lincoln was laid to rest.

JOHNSON'S RECONSTRUCTION PLAN President Lincoln's shocking death propelled Andrew Johnson of Tennessee, a pro-Union Democrat, into the White House. Johnson had been named as Lincoln's running mate in 1864 solely to help the president win reelection. Humorless, insecure, combative, and self-righteous, Johnson hated both the White southern elite and the idea of racial equality. He also had a weakness for liquor. At the inaugural ceremonies in 1865, a nervous and ill Johnson had fortified himself with so much whiskey ("I need all the strength I can get") that he took his vice-presidential oath of office in a state of slurring drunkenness.

Like Lincoln, Johnson was a self-made man, but he displayed none of Lincoln's dignity or eloquence. Born in 1808 in a log cabin near Raleigh, North Carolina, he lost his father when he was three and never attended school. His illiterate mother apprenticed him to a tailor to learn a trade. He ran away from home at thirteen and eventually landed in Greeneville, nestled in the mountains of East Tennessee, where he became a tailor. He taught himself to read, and his sixteen-year-old wife showed him how to write and do some basic arithmetic.

Over time, Johnson prospered and acquired five enslaved people, which he sold in 1863. A natural leader, he eventually served as the mayor, a state legislator, governor, congressional representative, and U.S. senator. A friend described the trajectory of Johnson's life as "one intense, unceasing, desperate upward struggle" during which he identified with the poor farmers and came to hate the "pampered, bloated, corrupted aristocracy" of wealthy planters.

During the Civil War, Johnson called himself a Jacksonian Democrat "in the strictest meaning of the term. I am for putting down the [Confederate] rebellion, because it is a war [of wealthy plantation owners] against democracy." Yet Johnson also shared the racist attitudes of most southern Whites. "Damn the negroes," he exclaimed during the war. "I am fighting those traitorous aristocrats, their masters," Impoverished Whites, Johnson maintained, were most hurt by the slave system, and he was an unapologetic White supremacist. "This is a country for White men," he exclaimed, "and by God, as long as I am president, it shall be a government for White men."

Andrew Johnson A Jacksonian Democrat from Tennessee, Johnson stepped into the role of president after Lincoln's assassination. He introduced a Restoration Plan that required southern states to ratify the Thirteenth Amendment and limited the political power of rich ex-Confederates.

Early in his presidency, Johnson stressed that he would continue Lincoln's policies in restoring the former Confederate states to the Union. **Johnson's Restoration Plan** included a few twists, however. In May 1865, Johnson issued a new Proclamation of Amnesty that excluded not only those ex-Confederates whom Lincoln had barred from a presidential pardon but also anyone with property worth more than $20,000. Johnson was determined to keep the wealthiest Southerners from regaining political power.

Surprisingly, however, by 1866 President Johnson had pardoned some 7,000 former Confederates and eventually pardoned most of the White "aristocrats" he claimed to despise. What brought about this change of heart? Johnson had decided that he could buy the political support of prominent Southerners by pardoning them, improving his chances of reelection.

Johnson appointed a Unionist as provisional governor in each southern state. Each governor was to call a convention of men elected by "loyal" (not Confederate) voters. Johnson's plan required that each state convention ratify the Thirteenth Amendment. The president also encouraged giving a few Blacks voting rights, especially those who had some education or had served in the military, so as to "disarm" the "Radicals who are wild upon" giving *all* African Americans the right to vote. Except for Mississippi, each former Confederate state held a convention that met Johnson's requirements but ignored his suggestion about voting rights for Blacks.

FREEDMEN'S CONVENTIONS Neither Lincoln nor Johnson saw fit to ask freedpeople in the South what they most needed. So the formerly enslaved—men and women—took matters into their own hands. They met and marched, demanding not just freedom but citizenship and full civil rights, land of their own, and voting rights. Especially in and around large cities such as New Orleans, Mobile, Norfolk, Wilmington, Nashville, Memphis, and Charleston, they organized regular meetings, chose leaders, protested mistreatment, learned the workings of the federal bureaucracy, and sought economic opportunities.

During the summer and fall of 1865, emancipated Southerners and free Blacks from the North ("missionaries") and South organized freedmen's

Freedmen's Convention In this 1868 woodcut, a group of southern freedpeople meet to discuss their political and social resolutions.

conventions (sometimes called Equal Rights Associations). Often led by ministers, the conventions met in state capitals "to impress upon the White men," as the Reverend James D. Lynch told the Tennessee freedmen's convention, "that we are part and parcel of the American republic." As such they were eager to counter the Whites-only state conventions being organized under Johnson's Reconstruction Plan. Virtually all the freedmen's conventions forged resolutions that stressed their desire for free public education, their need for paying jobs and their own land, and their insistence on full civil rights—especially voting rights.

The North Carolina freedmen's convention elected as its president James Walker Hood, a free Black from Connecticut. In his acceptance speech, he emphasized their goals: "We and the White people have to live here together. Some people talk of emigration for the Black race, some of expatriation, and some of colonization. I regard this as all nonsense. We have been living together for a hundred years and more, and we have got to live together still; and the best way is to harmonize our feelings as much as possible, and to treat all men respectfully." Hood then demanded three constitutional rights for African Americans: the right to testify in courts, serve on juries, and "the right to carry [a] ballot to the ballot box."

In sum, the freedmen's conventions demanded that their voices be heard in Washington and southern state capitals. As the Virginia freedmen's convention asserted, "Any attempt to reconstruct the states . . . without giving to American citizens of African descent all the rights and immunities accorded to white citizens . . . is an act of gross injustice."

THE RADICAL REPUBLICANS President Johnson's initial assault on the southern planter elite pleased Radical Republicans, but not for long. The most extreme Radical Republicans, led by Thaddeus Stevens of Pennsylvania and Charles Sumner of Massachusetts, wanted Reconstruction to provide social and political equality for Blacks.

Stevens and other Radicals resented Johnson's efforts to bring the South back into the Union as quickly as possible. Stevens argued that the Civil War had been fought to produce a *"radical revolution"* in southern life: The "whole fabric of southern society must be changed" to "revolutionize southern institutions, habits, and manners." The Confederate states were, in his view, "conquered provinces" to be readmitted to the Union by the U.S. Congress, not the president. Johnson, however, balked at such an expansion of federal authority. He was committed to the states' rights to control their affairs.

Former Confederates agreed with Johnson. After the war, most White Southerners could not accept Confederate defeat, and they resented and resisted the North's efforts to reconstruct their homeland. As a North Carolinian muttered in 1866, he felt the "bitterest hatred toward the North." He and others wanted to rebuild the new South as it had been before the war, the fabled "Old South," and they were determined to do so in their own way and under their own leadership. They saw no need for their beloved region to be "reconstructed" by outsiders. As a southern White woman lamented, "Think of all our sacrifices—of broken hearts, and desolated homes—or our *noble, glorious* dead—and say for what? *Reconstruction!* How the very word galls."

So when the U.S. Congress met in December 1865, for the first time since the end of the war, the new southern state governments looked remarkably like the former Confederate governments. Southerners had refused to extend voting rights to the newly freed African Americans. Instead, they had elected former Confederate leaders as their new U.S. senators and congressmen. Georgia, for example, had elected Alexander Stephens, former vice president of the Confederacy.

Across the South, four Confederate generals, eight colonels, six Confederate cabinet members, and several Confederate legislators were elected as new U.S. senators and congressmen. Outraged Republicans denied seats to all such "Rebel" officials and appointed a Joint Committee on Reconstruction to develop a new plan to bring the former Confederate states back into the Union.

Race Riots in Memphis, Tennessee In 1866, African Americans were murdered by White mobs in Memphis, Tennessee. Black neighborhoods, schools, and churches were destroyed. Forty-six African Americans were killed.

The Joint Committee discovered that White violence against Blacks was widespread. A freedman from Shreveport, Louisiana, testified that Whites still bullwhipped Blacks as if they were enslaved. He estimated that 2,000 freed-people had been killed in Shreveport in 1865. In 1866, White mobs murdered African Americans in Memphis and New Orleans. In Memphis, a clash between African American military veterans and city police triggered a race riot in which rampaging Whites raped and murdered Blacks before setting fire to their neighborhoods. Over two days, Black schools and churches were destroyed. Forty-six African Americans and two Whites were killed. Only the arrival of federal troops quelled the violence. Memphis authorities arrested no one responsible for the mayhem.

The racial massacres, Radical Republicans argued, resulted from Andrew Johnson's lenient policy toward White supremacists. Senator Charles Sumner asked, "Who can doubt that the President is the author of these tragedies?" The race riots helped spur the passage and ratification of the Fourteenth Amendment (1868), extending federal civil rights protections to African Americans.

BLACK CODES The violence against southern Blacks was triggered in part by Black protests over restrictive laws passed by the new all-White southern state legislatures in 1865 and 1866. These "**Black codes**," as a White Southerner explained, would ensure "the ex-slave was not a free man; he was a free Negro." A Northerner visiting the South observed that the new Black codes would guarantee that "the blacks at large belong to the whites at large."

Black codes varied from state to state. In South Carolina, African Americans were required to remain on their former plantations, forced to labor from dawn to dusk. Mississippi prohibited Blacks from hunting or fishing, making them even more dependent on their White employers.

Some Black codes recognized Black marriages but prohibited interracial marriage. The Mississippi codes stipulated that "no white person could intermarry with a freedman, free negro, or mulatto." Violators faced life in prison.

The codes also barred African Americans from voting, serving on juries, or testifying against Whites. They could own property, but they could not own farmland in Mississippi or city property in South Carolina. In Mississippi, every Black male over the age of eighteen had to be apprenticed to a White, preferably a former slave owner. Any Blacks not apprenticed or employed by January 1866 would be jailed as "vagrants." If they could not pay the vagrancy fine—and most of them could not—they were jailed and forced to work for Whites as convict laborers in "chain gangs."

In part, states employed this "convict lease" system as a means of increasing government revenue and cutting the expenses of housing prisoners. Many

"Slavery Is Dead (?)" Thomas Nast's 1867 cartoon argues that Blacks were still being treated as if they were enslaved despite the passage of the Fourteenth Amendment. This detail illustrates a case in Raleigh, North Carolina: a Black man was whipped for a crime despite federal orders specifically prohibiting such forms of punishment.

southern prisons were destroyed during the war, and states lacked the funds to rebuild them. Since most prisoners were Black (only in Texas were White prisoners a majority), the popular solution was to rent them out to White farmers and businesses.

At its worst, convict leasing—which was not outlawed until 1928—was one of the most exploitative labor systems in history, as people convicted of crimes, often African Americans who were falsely accused, were hired out by county and state governments to work for individuals and businesses—coal mines, lumber camps, brickyards, railroads, quarries, mills, and plantations. Convict leasing, in other words, was a thinly disguised form of slavery, and often more brutal. More than 10 percent of Black convicts died on the job. A southern planter explained that before the Civil War "we owned the negroes. If a man had a good negro he could afford to keep him. . . . But these convicts, we don't own 'em. [If] one dies, [we] get another."

The Black codes infuriated Republicans. "We [Republicans] must see to it," Senator William Stewart of Nevada resolved, "that the man made free by the Constitution of the United States is a freeman indeed." And that is what they set out to do.

JOHNSON'S BATTLE WITH CONGRESS   Early in 1866, the Radical Republicans openly challenged Andrew Johnson over Reconstruction policies. Johnson started the fight when he vetoed a bill renewing funding for the Freedmen's Bureau. The Republicans could not override the veto. Then, on February 22, 1866, Johnson criticized the Radical Republicans for promoting Black civil rights. Moderate Republicans thereafter deserted the president and supported the Radicals. Johnson had become "an alien enemy of a foreign state," Thaddeus Stevens declared.

In mid-March 1866, the Radical-led Congress passed the pathbreaking Civil Rights Act, the first federal law to define citizenship. It declared that "all persons born in the United States," including the children of immigrants, but excluding Native Americans, were citizens entitled to "full and equal benefit of all laws."

The Civil Rights Act infuriated Johnson. Congress, he fumed, could not grant citizenship to Blacks, who did not deserve it. Claiming that the proposed legislation trespassed on states' rights, Johnson vetoed it. This time, however, on April 6, 1866, Republicans overrode the veto. The government, said Senator Richard Yates of Illinois, never intended "to set 4 million slaves free . . . and at the same time leave them without the civil and political rights which attach to a free citizen."

It was the first time in history that Congress had overturned a presidential veto of a major bill. From that point on, President Johnson steadily lost both public and political support. A New Yorker noted in his diary that "the feud between Johnson and the 'Radicals' grows more and more deadly every day." General Ulysses S. Grant told his wife that Johnson had become "a national disgrace."

FOURTEENTH AMENDMENT   To remove all doubt about the legality of the new Civil Rights Act, Congress passed the **Fourteenth Amendment** to the U.S. Constitution in June 1866. It guaranteed citizenship not just to freedpeople but also to immigrant children born in the United States (known as birthright citizenship). The amendment gave the federal government responsibility for protecting (and enforcing) civil rights.

Taking direct aim at the Black codes, the amendment also prohibited any efforts to violate the civil rights of any "citizens"; to deprive any person "of life, liberty, or property, without due process of law"; or to "deny any person . . . the equal protection of the laws."

The Fourteenth Amendment was officially ratified by three quarters of the states in 1868. All states in the former Confederacy were required to ratify the amendment before they could be readmitted to the Union and to Congress.

President Johnson urged the southern states to refuse to ratify the amendment. He predicted that the Democrats would win the congressional elections in November and then nix the new amendment. But Johnson was steadily losing support in the North. New York newspaper editor Horace Greeley called Johnson "an aching tooth in the national jaw, a screeching infant in a crowded lecture room."

JOHNSON VERSUS THE RADICAL REPUBLICANS   To win votes for Democratic candidates in the 1866 congressional elections, Andrew Johnson went on a nineteen-day speaking tour during which he gave more than 100 speeches promoting his plan for reconstructing the South. He drew large crowds in Baltimore, Philadelphia, and New York City, where he denounced Radical Republicans as traitors who should be hanged. His partisan speeches backfired, however.

In Cleveland, Ohio, Johnson savaged Radical Republicans as "factious, domineering, tyrannical" men. When a heckler shouted that Johnson should hang Jefferson Davis as a war criminal, the thin-skinned president retorted, "Why not hang Thad Stevens?" Then a crowd member yelled, "Is this dignified?" Johnson shouted: "I care not for dignity."

The backlash was intense. One newspaper denounced Johnson's remarks as "the most disgraceful speech ever delivered" by a president. Even the pro-Johnson *New York Times* concluded that the president's boorish behavior was "compromising his official character."

Voters agreed. The 1866 congressional elections brought a devastating defeat for Johnson and the Democrats; in each house, Radical Republican candidates won more than a two-thirds majority, the margin required to override presidential vetoes. Congressional Republicans would now take over from the president the process of reconstructing the former Confederacy.

CONGRESS TAKES CHARGE OF RECONSTRUCTION In March 1867, Congress passed, over President Johnson's vetoes, three crucial laws that laid out the requirements for the former Confederate states to be readmitted to the Union: the Military Reconstruction Act, the Command of the Army Act, and the Tenure of Office Act.

The Military Reconstruction Act was the capstone of the Congressional Reconstruction plan. It abolished the governments "in the Rebel States" established under Johnson's lenient Reconstruction policies. In their place, Congress established military control over ten of the eleven former Confederate states. (Tennessee was exempted because it had already ratified the Fourteenth Amendment.) The ten states were divided into five "military districts," each commanded by an army general.

Yet only 10,000 federal troops, mostly African Americans, were dispatched to police those sprawling military districts. Between 1865 and 1871, the federal army shrank from more than a million men to 30,000, most of them stationed in the West to suppress Indian uprisings. There were never enough soldiers to enforce Congressional Reconstruction. The entire state of Mississippi, for instance, had fewer than 400 soldiers to ensure compliance.

The Military Reconstruction Act required each former Confederate state to write a new constitution that guaranteed all adult males the right to vote—Black or White, rich or poor, landless or property owners. Women—Black or White—were still not included as voters.

The act also stipulated that the new state constitutions were to be drafted by conventions elected by male citizens "of whatever race, color, or previous condition." Once a majority of voters ratified the new constitutions, the state legislatures had to ratify the Fourteenth Amendment; once the amendment became part of a new state constitution, the former Confederate states would be entitled to send representatives to Congress. Several hundred African American delegates participated in the constitutional conventions.

The second of the Reconstruction bills was called the Command of the Army Act. It required that the president issue all army orders through General in Chief Ulysses S. Grant. (The Radicals feared that President Johnson would appoint anti-Black generals to head the military districts, men who would be too lenient toward Whites who defied efforts to "reconstruct" the South.)

The third Reconstruction bill was the Tenure of Office Act. It stipulated that the Senate must approve any presidential effort to remove federal officials whose appointments the Senate had confirmed. Radicals intended this act to prevent Johnson from firing Secretary of War Edwin Stanton, the president's most outspoken critic in the cabinet.

Taken together, these laws came to represent what came to be called **Congressional Reconstruction**. It embodied the most sweeping peacetime legislation in American history to that point. It sought to ensure that freedpeople could participate in the creation of new state governments in the former Confederacy. As Thaddeus Stevens explained, the Congressional Reconstruction plan would create a "perfect republic" based on the principle of *equal rights* for all citizens. "This is the promise of America," he insisted. "No More. No Less."

IMPEACHING THE PRESIDENT The first two years of Congressional Reconstruction produced dramatic changes in the South, as new state legislatures rewrote their constitutions and ratified the Fourteenth Amendment. Radical Republicans were in control of Reconstruction, but one person still stood in their way—Andrew Johnson. During 1867 and early 1868, more and more Radicals decided that the president must be removed from office.

Johnson himself opened the door to impeachment (the formal process by which Congress charges the president with "high crimes and misdemeanors") when, in violation of the Tenure of Office Act, he suspended Secretary of War Edwin Stanton, who had refused to resign from the cabinet despite his harsh criticism of the president's Reconstruction policy. Johnson, who considered the act an illegal restriction of presidential power, soon decided that suspending Stanton was not sufficient. In February 1868, he fired the secretary of war. Stanton, however, refused to leave his office, claiming that his appointment was protected by the Tenure of Office Act. He then locked himself in the War

Department until the Senate voted to override President Johnson's firing of him. The Radicals now saw their chance. By removing Stanton without congressional approval, Johnson had violated the law.

On February 24, 1868, the Republican-dominated House of Representatives passed nine articles of impeachment (that is, specific charges against the president), most of which dealt with Stanton's firing. In reality, the essential grievance against the president was that he had opposed the policies of the Radical Republicans and in doing so had brought "disgrace, ridicule, hatred, contempt, and reproach" onto the Congress. According to Secretary of the Navy Gideon Welles, Radicals were so angry at Johnson that they "would have tried to remove him had he been accused of stepping on a dog's tail."

The first Senate trial of a sitting president began on March 5, 1868. The Republicans held a majority, but not the two-thirds required to convict. The trial was a dramatic spectacle before a packed gallery of journalists, foreign dignitaries, and political officials. Newspaper reporters clogged the halls. As the proceedings began, acid-tongued Stevens warned the president: "Unfortunate, unhappy man, behold your doom!"

The five-week trial came to a stunning end when the Senate voted 35–19 for conviction, only *one* vote short of the two-thirds needed for removal. Senator Edmund G. Ross, a young Republican from Kansas, cast the deciding vote in favor of acquittal. He later explained that despite tremendous pressure from his fellow Republicans, he decided that the evidence against Johnson was both insufficient for conviction and overtly partisan. Recent research, however, suggests that Ross secretly sold his vote for acquittal. After the impeachment trial ended, Ross asked the embattled president to get friends appointments to federal jobs, and Johnson agreed to every request. The president may also have given Ross cash from a $150,000 slush fund raised by Johnson's supporters.

In the end, the effort to remove Johnson was a grave political mistake, for it weakened public support for Congressional Reconstruction. The Richmond *Daily Dispatch* stressed that Johnson's acquittal was "a terrible rebuke on the Radical party." Nevertheless, the Radical cause did gain Johnson's private agreement to stop obstructing Congressional Reconstruction. (He would later break his word by turning a deaf ear to pleas for federal support in suppressing Ku Klux Klan violence.)

General Ulysses S. Grant, who replaced Edwin Stanton as secretary of war, urged Johnson to let him exert more federal force in the still-resistant South. To that end, he forwarded to the president a letter from a Tennessee legislator that documented gangs of Whites "scouring the country by night—causing

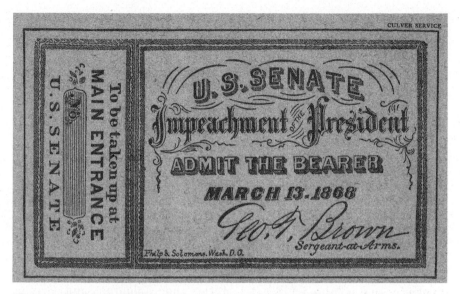

Ticket to the U.S. Senate Impeachment Trial of Andrew Johnson President Andrew Johnson's impeachment trial was the first in American history. To follow the trial's progress, spectators needed a ticket to gain admission into the U.S. Senate chambers.

dismay & terror to all—Our civil authorities are powerless." Johnson declared that it was a local issue. Federal troops should stay out of it.

Grant refused to take no for an answer. He continued to barrage Johnson with fresh evidence of White efforts to terrorize freedpeople. "If civil government fails to protect the citizen," Grant argued, "Military government should supply its place."

REPUBLICAN RULE IN THE SOUTH In June 1868, congressional Republicans announced that eight southern states could again send delegates to Congress. The remaining former Confederate states—Virginia, Mississippi, and Texas—were readmitted in 1870, with the added requirement that they ratify the **Fifteenth Amendment**, which would give voting rights to African American men. As the formerly enslaved Frederick Douglass had declared in 1865, "slavery is not abolished until the black man has the ballot."

The Fifteenth Amendment prohibited states from denying a citizen's right to vote on grounds of "race, color, or previous condition of servitude." Prior to its ratification, the individual states determined voting eligibility. But Susan B. Anthony and Elizabeth Cady Stanton, the determined leaders of the movement to secure voting rights for women, insisted that the amendment should have included women. As Anthony stressed in a famous speech, the U.S. Constitution refers to:

"We, the people; not we, the White male citizens; nor yet we, the male citizens; but we, the whole people, who formed the Union—women as well as men."

PREJUDICE AGAINST CHINESE AMERICANS Still another group ignored by the Fifteenth Amendment was Chinese Americans. In California, Nevada, and Oregon, state laws prevented them from voting. In *People v. Hall*, an 1857 California Supreme Court case, the justices described the Chinese as "a race of people whom nature has marked as inferior, and who are incapable of progress."

During Reconstruction, elected officials from the western states insisted that citizenship and voting rights were appropriate for Blacks but not Asians. The Chinese, asserted Senator Henry W. Corbett of Oregon, were "a different race entirely" and should not be allowed to vote. A Nevada congressman added that there were not "ten American citizens" in the Far West "who favor Chinese suffrage."

Continued Anti-Chinese Sentiment As new laborers to San Francisco, the Chinese had their belongings closely inspected by customs officers. Deemed culturally strange and racially inferior, the Chinese were not given voting rights despite the Fifteenth Amendment.

In the end, California and Oregon refused to ratify the Fifteenth Amendment because of the Chinese issue. Federal policies continued to bar Chinese Americans from citizenship and voting until 1943. In 1952, Asian Americans were made eligible for citizenship and voting. Native Americans were precluded from citizenship until 1924. Although the Fifteenth Amendment guaranteed every male the right to vote in federal elections, many states continued to deny state voting rights to African Americans and Chinese Americans until 1947.

Most men also remained opposed to voting rights for women. Radical Republicans tried to deflect the issue by declaring that it was the "Negro's hour." Anyway, argued Senator Richard Yates, allowing a woman to vote would be "destructive of her womanly qualities." Another Radical Republican, John M. Broomall, added that "the head of the family does the voting for the family." Women, both Black and White, would have to wait—another fifty years for voting rights, as it turned out.

BLACK SOCIETY UNDER RECONSTRUCTION

When a federal official asked Garrison Frazier, a freedman from Georgia, if he and others wanted to live among Whites, Frazier said that they preferred "to live by ourselves, for there is a prejudice against us in the South that will take years to get over." In forging new lives, Frazier and many other former enslaved people set about creating their own social institutions.

FREED BUT NOT EQUAL African Americans were active agents in affecting the course of Reconstruction. It was not an easy process, however, because Whites, both northern and southern, still embraced racism. A northern journalist traveling in the South after the war reported that the "whites seem wholly unable to comprehend that freedom for the negro means the same thing as freedom for them."

Once the excitement of freedom wore off, most southern Blacks realized that their best chance to make a living was by working for pay for their former owners. In fact, the Freedmen's Bureau and federal soldiers urged and even ordered them to sign labor contracts with local Whites. Many planters, however, conspired to control the amount of wages paid to freedmen. "It seems humiliating to be compelled to bargain and haggle with our own servants about wages," complained a White planter's daughter.

White Southerners also used terror, intimidation, and violence to suppress Black efforts to gain social and economic equality. In many respects, the war had not ended, as armed men organized to thwart federal efforts to reconstruct the South. In July 1866, a Black woman in Clinch County, Georgia, was arrested and given sixty-five lashes for "using abusive language" during an encounter with a White woman.

After emancipation, Union soldiers and northern observers often expressed surprise that the freed enslaved people did not leave the South. But why would they leave what they knew so well? As a group of African Americans explained, they did not want to abandon "land they had laid their fathers' bones upon." A Union officer noted that southern Blacks seemed "more attached to familiar places" than any other group in the nation.

Participation in the Union army or navy had given many freedmen training in leadership. Indeed, Black military veterans would form the core of the first generation of African American political leaders in the postwar South. Military service also gave many former enslaved people their first opportunities to learn to read and write and alerted them to new possibilities for economic advancement, social respectability, and civic leadership. In addition, fighting for the Union cause instilled a fervent sense of nationalism. A Virginia freedman explained that the United States was "now *our* country—made emphatically so by the blood of our brethren."

BLACK CHURCHES AND SCHOOLS African American religious life in the South was transformed during and after the war. Many former enslaved people identified with the biblical Hebrews, who were led out of slavery into the "promised land." Emancipation demonstrated that God was on *their* side. Before the war, Blacks who attended White churches were forced to sit in the back. After the war, with the help of many northern Christian missionaries, both Black and White, freedpeople established their own churches that became the crossroads for Black community life.

Ministers emerged as social and political leaders. One could not be a real minister, one of them claimed, without looking "out for the political interests of his people." Many African Americans became Baptists or Methodists, in part because these were already the largest denominations in the South, and in part because Baptists and Methodists reached out to the working poor. In 1866 alone, the African Methodist Episcopal (AME) Church gained 50,000 members. By 1890, more than 1.3 million African Americans in the South had become Baptists, nearly three times as many as had joined any other denomination.

The First African Church In June 1874, *Harper's Weekly* featured this illustration of the First African Church of Richmond, Virginia, on the eve of its move to a new building.

African American communities also rushed to establish schools. Starting schools, said a former slave, was the "first proof" of freedom. Before the Civil War, most plantation owners had denied Blacks an education to keep them from reading abolitionist literature and organizing uprisings. After the war, the White elite worried that education would distract poor Whites and Blacks from their work in the fields or encourage them to leave the South in search of better social and economic opportunities.

The opposition of southern Whites to education for Blacks made public schools all the more important to African Americans. South Carolina's Mary McLeod Bethune rejoiced in the opportunity: "The whole world opened to me when I learned to read." She walked five miles to school as a child, earned a scholarship to college, and went on to become the first Black woman to found a school that became a four-year college: Bethune-Cookman University, in Daytona Beach, Florida.

THE UNION LEAGUE The Fifteenth Amendment had enormous political consequences. No sooner was it ratified than northern Republicans, Black and White, sought to convince freedmen to join the party of Lincoln. To do so, they organized Union Leagues throughout the former Confederacy. Republicans had founded the Union League (also called the Loyal League) in 1862 to rally voters behind Lincoln, the war, and the party. By late 1863, the league claimed over 700,000 members in 4,554 councils across the nation.

In the postwar South, these Union League chapters were organized like fraternities, with formal initiations and rituals and secret meetings to protect the freedpeople from being persecuted by angry White Democrats. The leagues met in churches, schools, homes, and fields, often listening to northern speakers who traveled the South extolling the Republican party and encouraging Blacks to register and vote. By the early 1870s, the Union League in the South had become one of the largest Black social movements in history.

With the help of the Union Leagues, some 90 percent of southern freedmen registered to vote, almost all of them as Republicans, and they voted in record numbers (often 80–90 percent). Their doing so often required great courage, for most White Southerners were Democrats eager to deny freedmen the vote. "All the blacks who vote against my ticket shall walk the plank," threatened Howell Cobb, a Georgia Democrat who had been a Confederate general and former governor. Throughout the postwar South, angry Whites persecuted, evicted, or fired African American workers who "exercised their political rights," as a Union officer reported from Virginia.

Black Republicans were at times equally coercive. "The Negroes are as intolerant of opposition as the whites," a White South Carolina Democrat observed.

They shunned, expelled, and even killed any "of their own" who "would turn democrats." He added that freedwomen were as partisan as the men—and as intolerant of opposition: "[The] women are worse than the men, refusing to talk to or marry a renegade [Black Democrat], and aiding [men] in mobbing him."

Yet the net result of the Union Leagues was a remarkable mobilization of Blacks whose votes enabled men of color to gain elected offices for the first time in the states of the former Confederacy. Francis Cardozo, a Black minister who served as president of the South Carolina Council of Union Leagues, declared in 1870 that South Carolina had "prospered in every respect" as a result of the enfranchisement of Black voters enabled by the Union Leagues. "The fierce and determined opposition to us," he maintained, illustrated how powerful a force for equality the leagues had become.

POLITICS AND AFRICAN AMERICANS With many ex-Confederates denied voting rights, new African American voters helped elect some 600 Blacks—most of them former enslaved people—as state legislators under

African American Political Figures of Reconstruction As Blacks gained the right to vote, many ex-Confederate Whites were stripped of that right. As a consequence, several formerly enslaved men were elected to positions in government, such as Blanche K. Bruce *(left)* and Hiram Revels *(right)*, who served in the U.S. Senate. Between them is Frederick Douglass, who was a major figure in the abolitionist movement.

Congressional Reconstruction. In Louisiana, Pinckney Pinchback, a northern free Black and former Union soldier, was elected lieutenant governor. Several other African Americans were elected to high state offices. There were two Black senators in Congress, Hiram Revels and Blanche K. Bruce, both Mississippi natives who had been educated in the North, while fourteen Black congressmen served in the U.S. House of Representatives.

The election of Black politicians appalled most southern Whites. Democrats claimed that Radicals were trying to "organize a hell in the South" by putting "the Caucasian race" under the rule of "their own negroes." Southern Whites complained that emancipated Blacks were illiterate and had no civic experience or appreciation of political issues and processes. In this regard, however, Blacks were no different from millions of poor or immigrant White males who had been voting and serving in office for years. While Black political representation and influence did increase significantly, major obstacles remained within state legislatures. Only South Carolina's Republican state convention had a Black majority. Louisiana's was evenly divided racially, and in only two other state conventions were more than 20 percent of the members Black: Florida and Virginia.

Some freedmen frankly confessed their disadvantages. Beverly Nash, an African American delegate to the South Carolina convention of 1868, told his colleagues, "We are not prepared for this suffrage [the vote]. But we can learn. Give a man tools and let him commence to use them, and in time he will learn a trade. So it is with voting."

LAND, LABOR, AND DISAPPOINTMENT Many ex-enslaved people argued that what they needed most was land. A New Englander traveling in the postwar South noted that the "sole ambition of the freedman" was "to become the owner of a little piece of land, there to erect a humble home, and to dwell in peace and security at his own free will and pleasure."

In several southern states, former enslaved people had been given land by Union armies after they had taken control of Confederate areas during the war. Andrew Johnson, however, reversed such transfers of White-owned property to former enslaved people. In South Carolina, the Union general responsible for evicting former enslaved people urged them to "lay aside their bitter feelings, and become reconciled to their old masters." But the assembled freedmen shouted, "No, never!" and "Can't do it!"

They knew that ownership of land was the foundation of their freedom. They may have had no deeds or titles for the land they now worked, but it had been "earned by the sweat of *our* brows," said a group of Alabama freedmen. "Our wives, our children, our husbands, has been sold over and over again to purchase the lands we now locates on," a Virginia freedman noted. "Didn't we clear the land and raise de crops? We have a right to [that] land."

Thousands of former enslaved people were forced to return their farms to White owners. In addition, it was virtually impossible for former enslaved people to get loans to buy farmland because few banks were willing to lend to Blacks. Their sense of betrayal was profound. A formerly enslaved man in Mississippi said that he and others were left with nothing: "no *land,* no *house,* not so much as a place to lay our head."

As freedpeople were stripped of their land, they had little choice but to participate in a new labor system: **sharecropping**. It worked like this: White landowners would provide land, seed, and tools to poor laborers in exchange for a *share* of the crop. This essentially reenslaved the workers because, as a federal army officer said, no matter "how much they are abused, they cannot leave without permission of the owner." If they left, they would forfeit their portion of the crop. Workers who violated the terms of the contract could be evicted from the plantation, leaving them jobless and homeless—and subject to arrest as "vagrants." Across the former Confederacy, the rapid growth of sharecropping revealed that most White plantation owners and small farmers were determined to control African Americans as if they were still enslaved.

Sharecroppers This 1899 photograph by Frances Benjamin Johnston, one of the earliest female photojournalists, shows a sharecropping family outside their Virginia cabin.

And if bad weather or insects or disease stunted the harvest, it pushed the sharecropper only deeper in debt.

Many freed Blacks preferred sharecropping over working for wages, since it freed them from day-to-day supervision by White landowners. Over time, however, most sharecroppers, Black and White, found themselves trapped, deep in debt to the landowner, with little choice but to remain tied to the same discouraging system of dependence that, over the years, felt much like slavery. As a former slave acknowledged, he and others had discovered that "freedom could make folks proud but it didn't make 'em rich."

TENSIONS AMONG SOUTHERN BLACKS   African Americans in the postwar South were by no means a uniform community. They had their own differences and disputes, especially between the few who owned property and the many who did not. In North Carolina, for example, less than 7 percent of Black people owned land by 1870. Affluent northern Blacks and the southern free Black elite, most of whom were city dwellers and Mulattoes (people of mixed-racial parentage), often opposed efforts to redistribute land to the freedmen, and many insisted that political equality did not mean social equality. As an African American leader in Alabama stressed, "We do not ask that the ignorant and degraded shall be put on a social equality with the refined and intelligent." In general, however, unity prevailed, and African Americans focused on common concerns. "All we ask," said a Black member of the state constitutional convention in Mississippi, "is justice, and to be treated like human beings."

"CARPETBAGGERS" AND "SCALAWAGS"   White Southerners who resisted reconstruction called Whites who served in the new Republican southern state governments "carpetbaggers" or "scalawags." Carpetbaggers, critics argued, were the 30,000 scheming Northerners, mostly young men, who rushed south with their belongings in cheap suitcases made of carpeting ("carpetbags") to grab political power or buy plantations.

Some of the Northerners who migrated south were corrupt opportunists. However, most were Union military veterans drawn to the South by the desire to rebuild the region's wrecked economy. Many other so-called carpetbaggers were teachers, social workers, attorneys, physicians, editors, and ministers motivated by a genuine desire to help free Blacks and poor Whites improve their lives.

For example, Union general Adelbert Ames, who won the Medal of Honor, stayed in the South after the war because he felt a "sense of Mission with a large M" to help former enslaved people develop healthy communities. He served as the military governor of Mississippi before being elected a Republican U.S. senator in 1870.

Southern Democrats especially hated the scalawags, or southern White Republicans, calling them traitors to their region. A Nashville newspaper editor described them as the "merest trash." Most scalawags had been Unionists opposed to secession. They were prominent in the mountain counties of Georgia, Tennessee, and Alabama. Among the scalawags were several distinguished figures, including former Confederate general James Longstreet, who decided that the Old South must change its ways. He became a successful cotton broker in New Orleans, joined the Republican party, and supported Radical Reconstruction.

Another unlikely scalawag was Joseph E. Brown, the Confederate governor of Georgia, who urged Southerners to support Republicans because they were the only source of economic investment in the ravaged region. What the scalawags had in common was a willingness to work with Republicans to rebuild the southern economy.

SOUTHERN RESISTANCE   With each passing year during Reconstruction, African Americans suffered increasing exploitation and abuse. The Black codes created by White state governments in 1865 and 1866 were the first of many efforts to deny equality. As a former slave protested to President Johnson, the new state codes were "returning us to slavery again." Southern Whites used terror, intimidation, and violence to disrupt Black Republican meetings, target Black and White Republican leaders for beatings or killings, and, in general, prevent Blacks from exercising their political rights. Hundreds were killed across the South and many more injured in systematic efforts to "keep blacks in their place."

In Texas, a White farmer, D. B. Whitesides, told a formerly enslaved man named Charles Brown that his newfound freedom would do him "damned little good . . . as I intend to shoot you"—which he did, shooting Brown in the chest as he tried to flee. Whitesides then rode his horse beside Brown and asked, "I got you, did I Brown?" "Yes," a bleeding Brown replied. "You got me good." Whitesides yelled that the wound would teach "[Negroes like you] to put on airs because you are free."

Such ugly incidents revealed a harsh truth: the death of slavery did not mean the birth of true freedom for African Americans. For a growing number of southern Whites, resistance to Radical Reconstruction became more and more violent. Several secret terrorist groups, including the Ku Klux Klan, the Knights of the White Camelia, the White Line, and the White League, emerged to harass, intimidate, and even kill African Americans.

The **Ku Klux Klan** (KKK) was formed in 1866 in Pulaski, Tennessee. The name *Ku Klux* was derived from the Greek word *kuklos,* meaning "circle" or

A Visit from the Ku Klux Klan African Americans in the South lived in constant fear of racial violence, as this 1872 engraving from *Harper's Weekly*, published to elicit northern sympathy, illustrates.

"band"; *Klan* came from the English word *clan*, or family. The Klan, and other groups like it, began initially as a social club, with spooky costumes and secret rituals. But its members, most of them former Confederate soldiers, soon began harassing Blacks and White Republicans. General Philip Sheridan, who supervised the district that included Louisiana and Texas, said that Klansmen were terrorists intent on suppressing Black political participation.

These groups' motives were varied—anger over the Confederate defeat, resentment against federal soldiers occupying the South, complaints about having to pay Black workers, and an almost paranoid fear that freedmen might seek revenge against Whites. Klansmen marauded at night on horseback, spreading rumors, issuing threats, and burning schools and churches. "We are going to kill all the Negroes," a White supremacist declared during one massacre.

THE LEGACY OF CONGRESSIONAL RECONSTRUCTION

The widespread use of racial violence helped overturn Republican state governments. Yet they left behind an important accomplishment: the new constitutions they created remained in effect for years, and later constitutions incorporated many of their most progressive features.

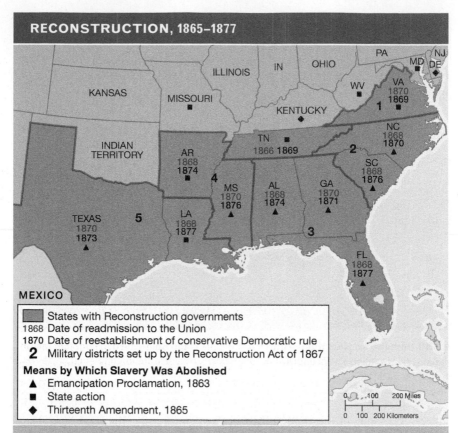

RECONSTRUCTION, 1865–1877

States with Reconstruction governments
1868 Date of readmission to the Union
1870 Date of reestablishment of conservative Democratic rule
2 Military districts set up by the Reconstruction Act of 1867

Means by Which Slavery Was Abolished
▲ Emancipation Proclamation, 1863
■ State action
◆ Thirteenth Amendment, 1865

- How did the Military Reconstruction Act reorganize governments in the South in the late 1860s and 1870s?
- What did the former Confederate states have to do to be readmitted to the Union?
- Why did "conservative" parties gradually regain control of the South from the Republicans in the 1870s?

Some of the significant innovations brought about by the Republican state governments protected Black voting rights and restructured legislatures to reflect shifting populations. More state offices were changed from appointed to elective positions to weaken the "good old boy" tradition of rewarding political supporters with state government jobs.

Given the hostile circumstances under which Republican state governments operated in the South, their achievements were remarkable. They provided free public schools for the first time in most southern counties, allowed women to keep their private property rather than transfer it to their husbands, and rebuilt an extensive railroad network destroyed during the war.

Southern Republicans also gave more attention to the poor and to orphanages, asylums, and institutions for the deaf and blind of both races. Much needed infrastructure—roads, bridges, and buildings—was repaired or rebuilt. African Americans achieved rights and opportunities that would repeatedly be violated in coming decades but would never completely be taken away, at least in principle, such as equality before the law and the rights to own property, attend schools, learn to read and write, enter professions, and carry on business.

Yet government officials also engaged in corrupt practices. Bribes and kickbacks, whereby companies received government contracts in return for giving government officials cash or stock, were commonplace. In Louisiana, a twenty-six-year-old carpetbagger, Henry Clay Warmoth, somehow turned an annual salary of $8,000 into a million-dollar fortune during his four years as governor. "I don't pretend to be honest," he admitted. "I only pretend to be as honest as anybody in politics." He was eventually impeached and removed from office.

As was true in the North and the Midwest, southern state governments awarded money to corporations, notably railroads, under conditions that invited shady dealings and outright corruption. Some railroad corporations received state funds but never built railroads, and bribery was rampant. But the Radical Republican regimes did not invent such corruption, nor did it die with them. Governor Warmoth recognized as much: "Corruption is the fashion" in Louisiana, he explained.

THE GRANT ADMINISTRATION

Andrew Johnson's crippled presidency created an opportunity for Republicans to elect one of their own in 1868. Both parties wooed Ulysses S. Grant, the "Lion of Vicksburg" credited by most with the Union victory in the Civil War. His differences with President Johnson, however, had pushed him toward the Republicans, who unanimously nominated him as their presidential candidate.

THE ELECTION OF 1868 The Republican party platform endorsed Congressional Reconstruction. More important, however, were the public expectations driving the candidacy of Ulysses S. Grant, whose slogan was "Let us have peace." Grant promised that, if elected, he would enforce the laws and promote prosperity for all.

Democrats shouted defiance. "This is a White man's country," they claimed, so "let White men rule." The Radical Republicans, Democrats charged, were subjecting the South "to military despotism and Negro supremacy." Democratic delegates nominated Horatio Seymour, the wartime governor of New York and a passionate critic of Congressional Reconstruction, who dismissed the Emancipation Proclamation as "a proposal for the butchery of women and children." His running mate, Francis P. Blair, Jr., a former Union general from Missouri who had served in Congress, was an avowed racist who wanted to "declare the reconstruction acts null and void" and withdraw all federal troops from the South. He attacked Grant for exercising military tyranny "over the eight millions of White people in the South, fixed to the earth with his bayonets." Blair denounced Republicans for promoting equality for "a semi-barbarous race" who sought to "subject the White women to their unbridled lust."

This belief that Black men were sexual predators lying in wait for White women was a false stereotype throughout the South with horrifying consequences: it was often used as a justification for lynchings. A Democrat later said that Blair's "stupid and indefensible" remarks cost Seymour a close election. Grant won all but eight states and swept the Electoral College, 214–80, but his popular majority was only a little more than 300,000 out of almost 6 million votes.

More than 500,000 African American voters, mostly in the South, accounted for Grant's margin of victory (he won only a minority of White votes nationwide), and many of them risked their lives supporting him. Klan violence soared during the campaigning, and hundreds of freedpeople paid with their lives. Still, the efforts of Radical Republicans to ensure voting rights for southern Blacks had paid off. As Frederick Douglass explained, "the Republican party is the ship and all else is the sea" as far as Black voters were concerned.

Grant, the youngest president up to that time (forty-six years old at his inauguration), had said during the Civil War that he was not "a politician, never was and never hope to be." Now he was the politician in chief. Although a courageous defender of Congressional Reconstruction and civil rights for Blacks, Grant has never been considered one of the greatest presidents. He later admitted that he took office "without any previous experience either in civil or political life. I thought I could run the government of the United States as I did the staff of my army. It was my mistake, and it led me into other mistakes."

Grant passively followed the lead of Congress and was often blind to the political forces and self-serving influence peddlers around him. He showed poor judgment in his selection of cabinet members, often favoring friendship, family, loyalty, and military service over integrity and ability.

During his two terms in office, Grant's seven cabinet positions changed twenty-four times. Some of the men betrayed his trust and engaged in criminal behavior. His former comrade in arms and close friend General William T. Sherman said he felt sorry for Grant because so many supposedly loyal Republicans used the president for their own selfish gains. Carl Schurz, a Union war hero who became a Republican senator from Missouri, expressed frustration that Grant was misled by cunning advisers who "prostituted" his administration.

Yet Grant excelled at bringing diversity to the federal government. He appointed more African Americans, Native Americans, Jews, and women than any of his predecessors, and he fulfilled his campaign pledge to bring peace to the divided nation.

"Let Us Have Peace" In the midst of the social and political turbulence of Reconstruction, Ulysses S. Grant's slogan, "Let us have peace"—as stamped on campaign coins like this one—struck a chord with voters.

THE BATTLE TO ENFORCE THE FIFTEENTH AMENDMENT

President Grant viewed Reconstruction of the South as the nation's top priority, and he doggedly insisted that freedpeople be allowed to exercise their civil rights without fear of violence. On March 30, 1870, Grant delivered a speech to Congress in which he celebrated the ratification of the Fifteenth Amendment, giving voting rights to African American men nationwide. "It was," he declared, ". . . the most important event that has occurred since the nation came into life . . . the realization of the Declaration of Independence."

To African American leader Frederick Douglass, the Thirteenth, Fourteenth, and Fifteenth Amendments seemed to ensure that Blacks would at last gain true equality. "Never was revolution more complete," Douglass announced in 1870. To President Grant, "more than any other man, the Negro owes his enfranchisement."

But Douglass and others were soon bitterly disappointed. The "revolution" turned out to be incomplete as the Fifteenth Amendment ignited a violent backlash in the South. In Georgia, White officials devised new ways to restrict Black voting, such as poll taxes and onerous registration procedures. Other states followed suit. "What is the use of talking about equality before the law," a freedman wrote as ex-Confederates took control of southern society. "There is none."

Four months after the Fifteenth Amendment became the law of the land, Congress also passed the Naturalization Act of 1870. For the first time, it extended the process whereby immigrants had gained citizenship to include "aliens of African nativity and to persons of African descent." Efforts to include Asians and Native Americans in the new naturalization law were defeated, however.

INDIAN POLICY   President Grant was almost as progressive in his outlook toward Native Americans as he was toward African Americans. In 1869, he appointed General Ely Parker, a Seneca chief trained as an attorney and engineer, as the new Commissioner of Indian Affairs, the first Native American to hold the position. Parker had served as Grant's military secretary during the war. Now, as commissioner, Parker faced formidable challenges in creating policies for the 300,000 Indians across the nation, many of whom continued to be pressured by White settlers, miners, railroads, and telegraph companies to give up their ancestral lands.

Working with Parker, Grant created a new Peace Policy toward Native Americans. "The Indians," he observed, "require as much protection from the Whites as the White does from the Indians." He did not want the army "shooting these poor savages; I want to conciliate them and make them peaceful citizens." His own experiences had shown that the "Indian problem" was in fact the result of "bad whites."

Grant believed that lasting peace could only result from Indians abandoning their nomadic tradition and relocating to government reservations, where federal troops would provide them "absolute protection." Even Lieutenant General William T. Sherman, no friend of the Indians, acknowledged the injustice of the situation. "The poor Indians are starving," he reported to his wife in 1868. "We kill them if they attempt to hunt," yet if they stay "within the reservation, they starve."

Grant also promised to end the chronic corruption whereby congressmen appointed cronies as licensed government traders with access to the Indian reservations. Many of the traders used their positions to swindle the Native Americans out of the federally supplied food, clothing, and other provisions intended solely for the reservations. One of the accused traders was the president's brother.

To clean up the so-called Indian Ring, Grant moved the Bureau of Indian Affairs out of the control of Congress and into the War Department. He also created a ten-man Board of Indian Commissioners, a new civilian agency whose mission was to oversee the operations of the Bureau of Indian Affairs to ensure that corruption was rooted out. Grant then appointed Quakers as reservation traders, assuming that their honesty, humility, and pacifism would improve the distribution of government resources. "If you can make Quakers out of the Indians," Grant told them, "it will take the fight out of them. Let us have peace." Yet Quakers proved no more able to manage Indian policy than government bureaucrats could.

Like other presidents, Grant discovered that there was often a gap between the policies he created and their implementation by others. Many of the officers and soldiers sent to the West to "pacify" Indian peoples in the Great Plains displayed an attitude toward Native Americans quite different from Grant's. For example, it was General Philip Sheridan who coined the infamous statement "The only good Indians I know are dead." He dismissed Indians as "the enemies of our race and of our civilization" and called for a campaign of "annihilation." Native Americans who refused to move to government-mandated reservations should be killed, he argued. General William T. Sherman agreed. He stressed to Sheridan that "the more [Indians] we kill this year, the less we would have to kill next year." Several members of Congress openly called for the "extermination" of the Indians.

Such attitudes led the abolitionist Wendell Phillips to ask why Indians were one of the only groups still denied citizenship. His answer was clear: "The great poison of the age is race hatred" directed at both African Americans and Native Americans. Most White Americans, however, did not care that racism was at work. "Wendell Phillips' new [Negro]," the editors of the *New York Herald* observed with disdain, "is the 'noble red man.'" Phillips responded, "We shall never be able to be just to other races . . . until we 'unlearn' contempt" for others different from us.

SCANDALS President Grant's naive trust in people, especially rich people, led his administration into a cesspool of scandal. Perhaps because of his own disastrous efforts as a storekeeper and farmer before the Civil War, Grant was awestruck by men of wealth. As they lavished gifts and attention on him, he was lured into their webs of self-serving deception.

In the summer of 1869, two unprincipled financial schemers, Jay Gould and James Fisk, Jr., both infamous for bribing politicians and judges, plotted with Abel Corbin, the president's brother-in-law, to "corner" (manipulate) the nation's gold market. They intended to create a public craze for gold by purchasing massive quantities of the precious metal to drive up its value.

The only danger to the complicated scheme lay in the possibility that the federal Treasury would burst the bubble by selling large amounts of its gold, which would deflate its market value. When Grant was seen in public with Gould and Fisk, people assumed that he supported their scheme. As the false rumor spread in New York City's financial district that the president endorsed the run-up in gold, its value soared.

On September 24, 1869—soon to be remembered mournfully as Black Friday—the Gould-Fisk scheme worked, at least for a while. Starting at $150 an ounce, the price of gold rose, first to $160, then to $165, leading more and more investors to join the stampede.

Then, around noon, Grant and his Treasury secretary realized what was happening and began selling government gold. Within fifteen minutes, the price plummeted to $138. Schemers lost fortunes amid the chaotic trading. Some ruined traders wept. One fainted, and still another felt the need to commit suicide. Soon the turmoil spread to the entire stock market, claiming thousands of victims. As Fisk noted, each man was left to "drag out his own corpse."

For weeks after the gold bubble collapsed, financial markets were paralyzed and business confidence was shaken. Congressman James Garfield wrote privately to a friend that President Grant had compromised his office by his "indiscreet acceptance" of gifts from Fisk and Gould and that any investigation of Black Friday would lead "into the parlor of the

Cornering the Gold Market In this political cartoon of the "Black Friday" gold scheme, Jay Gould attempts to manipulate the gold market, represented by caged and enraged bulls and bears. In the background, President Grant dashes from the U.S. Treasury to the scene, frantically trying to bring down the soaring price of gold.

President." One critic announced that U. S. Grant's initials actually stood for "uniquely stupid."

The plot to corner the gold market was only the first of several scandals that rocked the Grant administration. The secretary of war's wife, it turned out, had accepted bribes from merchants who traded with Indians at army posts in the West. And in St. Louis, whiskey distillers bribed federal Treasury agents in an effort to avoid paying excise taxes on alcohol. Grant's personal secretary participated in the scheme, taking secret payments in exchange for confidential information. Grant, spotlessly honest himself, urged Congress to investigate. "Let no guilty man escape," he stressed. "No personal considerations should stand in the way of performing a public duty."

When several congressional committees uncovered evidence of wrongdoing, Grant appointed the nation's first federal special prosecutor, but when his investigations got too close to the White House, President Grant fired him and appointed someone else who was less likely to focus on Grant. In the end, there was no evidence that the president was directly involved in the "whiskey ring," but again his choice of associates who proved corrupt earned him widespread criticism. Democrats scolded Republicans for their "monstrous corruption and extravagance" and reinforced public suspicion that elected officials were less servants of the people than they were self-serving bandits.

LIBERAL REPUBLICANS With the end of slavery, the Republican party lost its cohesion. Disputes over political corruption and the fate of Reconstruction helped divide Republicans into two warring factions: the Liberals (or Conscience Republicans) and Stalwarts (or Grant Republicans).

Liberal Republicans, led by Senator Carl Schurz, embraced free-enterprise capitalism and opposed any government regulation of business and industry, while championing gold coins as the only reliable currency. Liberal Republicans thirsted to oust the "tyrannical" Grant from the presidency and end what Schurz called "Negro supremacy" in the South. The "horror" of Reconstruction, Schurz insisted, must be stopped and federal troops withdrawn.

Schurz and other Liberal Republicans also sought to lower the tariffs lining the pockets of big corporations and promote "civil service reforms" to end the "partisan tyranny" of the "patronage system," whereby new presidents rewarded the "selfish greed" of political supporters with federal government jobs.

THE 1872 ELECTION In 1872, the Liberal Republicans, many of whom were elitist newspaper editors suspicious of the "working classes," held their own national convention in Cincinnati, during which they accused the Grant administration of corruption, incompetence, and "despotism." They then committed political suicide by nominating Horace Greeley, the editor of the *New York Tribune* and a longtime champion of causes ranging from abolitionism, socialism, vegetarianism, and spiritualism (communicating with the dead).

E. L. Godkin, the editor of the *Nation* magazine and a Liberal Republican sympathizer, could not imagine voting for Greeley, whom he dismissed as "a conceited, ignorant, half-cracked, obstinate old creature." Greeley's image as an eccentric who repeatedly reversed his political positions was matched by his record of hostility to Democrats, whose support the Liberal Republicans needed if they were to win.

Southern Democrats, however, liked Greeley's criticism of Reconstruction. His newspaper, for example, charged that "ignorant, superstitious, semi-barbarian" former enslaved people were "extremely indolent, and will make no exertion beyond what is necessary to obtain food enough to satisfy their hunger." Moreover, Radical Republicans had given the vote to "ignorant" former enslaved people whose "[Negro] Government" exercised "absolute political supremacy" in several states and was transferring wealth from the "most intelligent" and "influential" southern Whites to themselves.

In the 1872 balloting, Greeley carried only six southern states and none in the North. Grant won thirty-one states and tallied 3,598,235 votes to Greeley's 2,834,761. An exhausted Greeley confessed that he was "the worst beaten man who ever ran for high office." His wife died six days before the election, and he died three weeks later.

Grant was delighted that the "soreheads and thieves who had deserted the Republican party" were defeated, and he promised to avoid the "mistakes" he had made in his first term.

THE MONEY SUPPLY   Complex financial issues—especially monetary policy—dominated much of Ulysses S. Grant's first and second terms. Prior to the Civil War, the economy operated on a gold standard; state banks issued paper money that could be exchanged for an equal value of gold coins. So both gold coins and state bank notes circulated as currency. **Greenbacks** were issued by the federal Treasury during the Civil War to help pay for the war.

When a nation's supply of money grows faster than the economy itself, prices for goods and services increase (inflation). This happened when the greenbacks were issued. After the war, the U.S. Treasury assumed that the greenbacks would be recalled from circulation so that consumer prices would decline and the nation could return to a "hard-money" currency—gold, silver, and copper coins—which had always been viewed as more reliable in value than paper currency.

The most vocal supporters of a return to hard money were eastern creditors (mostly bankers and merchants) who did not want their debtors to pay them in paper currency. Critics of the gold standard tended to be farmers and other debtors. These so-called soft-money advocates opposed taking greenbacks out of circulation because shrinking the supply of money would bring lower prices (deflation) for their crops and livestock, thereby reducing their income and making it harder for them to pay their long-term debts. In 1868 congressional supporters of such a soft-money policy—mostly Democrats—forced the Treasury to stop withdrawing greenbacks.

President Grant sided with the hard-money camp. On March 18, 1869, he signed the Public Credit Act, which said that investors who purchased government bonds to help finance the war effort must be paid back in gold. The act led to a decline in consumer prices that hurt debtors and helped creditors. It also ignited a ferocious political debate over the merits of hard and soft money that would last throughout the nineteenth century—and beyond.

FINANCIAL PANIC President Grant's effort to withdraw greenbacks from circulation triggered a major economic collapse. During 1873, two dozen overextended railroads stopped paying their bills, forcing Jay Cooke and Company, the nation's leading business lender, to go bankrupt and close its doors on September 18, 1873.

The shocking news created a snowball effect as other hard-pressed banks began shutting down. A Republican senator sent Grant an urgent telegram from New York City: "Results of today indicate imminent danger of general national bank panic."

The resulting **Panic of 1873** caused a deep depression. Tens of thousands of businesses closed, 3 million workers lost jobs, and those with jobs saw their wages slashed. In major cities, the unemployed and homeless roamed the streets and formed long lines at soup kitchens. A quarter of New Yorkers were jobless.

The depression signaled that the maturing industrial economy was entering a long phase of instability punctuated by periods of soaring prosperity followed by desperate panics, bankruptcies, unemployment, recessions, and even prolonged depressions.

The Panic of 1873 led the U.S. Treasury to reverse course and begin printing more greenbacks to increase the nation's money supply. For a time, the supporters of paper money celebrated, but in 1874, Grant overruled his cabinet and vetoed a bill to issue even more greenbacks. His decision pleased bankers and other lenders but ignited a barrage of criticism. A Tennessee Republican congressman called the veto "cold-blooded murder," and a group of merchants in Indiana charged that Grant had sold his soul to those "whose god is the dollar."

Panic of 1873 The depression in 1873 left millions unemployed and destitute. In this contemporary woodcut, a line of somber men hugs the wall of a New York City hospice, where they hope to get a hot meal.

In the end, Grant's decision only prolonged what was then the worst depression in the nation's history. It also brought about a catastrophe for Republicans in the 1874 congressional elections, as Democrats blamed them for the economic hard times. In the House, Republicans went from a 70 percent majority to a 37 percent minority. They maintained control of the Senate but were placed on the defensive. As a result, the Republican effort to reconstruct the South ground to a halt.

DOMESTIC TERRORISM   President Grant initially fought to enforce federal efforts to reconstruct the postwar South, but southern resistance to "Radical rule" increased and turned brutally violent. In Grayson County, Texas, a White man and two friends murdered three former enslaved people because they wanted to "thin the [Negroes] out and drive them to their holes."

Klansmen focused their program of murder, violence, and intimidation on prominent Republicans, Black and White—elected officials, teachers in Black schools, state militias. In Mississippi, they killed a Black Republican leader in front of his family. Three White scalawag Republicans were murdered in Georgia in 1870, and that same year an armed mob of Whites attacked a Republican political rally in Alabama, killing four Black participants and wounding fifty-four. An Alabama Republican pleaded with President Grant to intervene. "Give us poor people some guarantee of our lives," G. T. E. Boulding wrote. "We are hunted and shot down as if we were wild beasts."

In South Carolina, White supremacists were especially violent. In 1871, some 500 masked men laid siege to the Union County jail and eventually lynched eight Black prisoners. In March 1871, Klansmen killed thirty African Americans in Meridian, Mississippi.

At Grant's urging, Republicans in Congress responded with three Enforcement Acts (1870–1871). The first of these measures imposed penalties on anyone who interfered with a citizen's right to vote. The second dispatched federal supervisors to monitor elections in southern districts where political terrorism flourished. The third, called the Ku Klux Klan Act (1871), outlawed various activities of the KKK—forming conspiracies, wearing disguises, resisting officers, and intimidating officials. It also allowed the president to send federal troops to any community where voting rights were being violated. When some Republicans balked at such federal intrusions into states' rights to police their elections, Grant appeared in person before Congress to urge passage of the Klan Act.

Once the legislation was approved, Grant sent Attorney General Amos Akerman, a Georgian, to recruit prosecutors and marshals to enforce it. The Klan, Akerman reported, "was the most atrocious organization that the civilized part of the world has ever known." Its violent acts "amount to war." In South Carolina alone, Akerman and federal troops and prosecutors convinced local juries to convict 1,143 Klansmen. By 1872, the Klan was effectively killed by Grant's stern actions.

In general, however, the Enforcement Acts were not consistently enforced. As a result, the violent efforts of southern Whites to thwart Reconstruction escalated. On Easter Sunday 1873 in the small Black Republican township of Colfax, Louisiana, a mob of 140 White vigilantes, most of them well-armed ex-Confederate soldiers led by Klansmen, used a cannon, rifles, and pistols to force a group of Black Republicans holed up in the courthouse to surrender. The Whites then called out the names of the African Americans, told them to step forward, and either shot them, slit their throats, or hanged them, slaughtering eighty-one and burning the building. When federal troops arrived, an officer reported that they found heaps of Black bodies being picked over by dogs and buzzards. "We were unable to find the body of a single White man," he said. Many of the dead "were shot in the back of the head and neck." Most had "three to a dozen wounds."

President Grant told the Senate that the "monstrous" Colfax Massacre was unprecedented in its "barbarity." He declared parts of Louisiana to be in a state of insurrection and imposed military rule. Federal prosecutors used the

Enforcement Acts to indict seventy Whites, but only nine were put on trial and just three were convicted—but of "conspiracy," not murder. None were sent to prison.

SOUTHERN "REDEEMERS" The Klan's impact on southern politics varied from state to state. In the Upper South, it played only a modest role in helping Democrats win local elections. In the Lower South, however, Klan violence had more serious effects. In overwhelmingly Black Yazoo County, Mississippi, vengeful Whites used terrorism to reverse the political balance of power. In the 1873 elections, for example, Republicans cast 2,449 votes and Democrats 638; two years later Democrats polled 4,049 votes, Republicans 7. Once Democrats regained power, they ousted Black legislators, closed public schools for Black children, and instituted poll taxes to restrict Black voting.

The activities of White supremacists disheartened Black and White Republicans alike. "We are helpless and unable to organize," wrote a Mississippi scalawag. We "dare not attempt to canvass [campaign for candidates], or make public speeches." At the same time, Northerners displayed a growing weariness with using federal troops to reconstruct the South. "The plain truth is," noted the *New York Herald*, "the North has got tired of the Negro."

President Grant, however, desperately wanted to use more federal force to preserve peace. He asked Congress to pass new legislation that would "leave my duties perfectly clear." Congress responded with the Civil Rights Act of 1875, which said that people of all races must be granted equal access to hotels and restaurants, railroads and stagecoaches, theaters, and other "places of public amusement."

Unfortunately for Grant, the new anti-segregation law provided little enforcement authority. Those who felt their rights were being violated had to file suit in court, and the penalties for violators were modest. In 1883, the U.S. Supreme Court, in an opinion arising from five similar cases, struck down the Civil Rights Act on the grounds that the Fourteenth Amendment focused only on the actions of state governments; it did not have authority over the policies of private businesses or individuals. Chief Justice Joseph Bradley added that it was time for Blacks to assume "the rank of a mere citizen" and stop being the "special favorite of the laws." As a result, the *Civil Rights Cases* (1883) opened the door for a wave of racial segregation that washed over the South during the late nineteenth century.

Republican political control in the South and public interest in protecting civil rights gradually loosened during the 1870s as all-White "conservative" parties mobilized the anti-Reconstruction vote. They called themselves conservatives to distinguish themselves from northern Democrats. Conservatives— the so-called **redeemers** who supposedly "saved" the South from Republican control and "Black rule"—used the race issue to excite the White electorate and threaten Black voters. Where persuasion failed to work, conservatives used trickery to rig the voting. As one conservative boasted, "The white and black Republicans may outvote us, but we can outcount them."

Republican political control ended in Virginia and Tennessee as early as 1869 and collapsed a year later in Georgia and North Carolina, although North Carolina had a Republican governor until 1876. Reconstruction lasted longest in the Lower South, where Whites abandoned Klan robes for barefaced intimidation in paramilitary groups such as the Mississippi Rifle Club and the South Carolina Red Shirts. The last Radical Republican regimes ended, however, after the elections of 1876, and the return of the old White political elite further undermined the country's commitment to Congressional Reconstruction.

THE SUPREME COURT   Key rulings by the U.S. Supreme Court further eroded Congressional Reconstruction by weakening the effects of the Thirteenth and Fourteenth Amendments. For instance, the *Slaughterhouse Cases* (1873) limited the "privileges or immunities" of U.S. citizenship as outlined in the recently ratified Fourteenth Amendment.

In 1869, the Louisiana legislature had granted a single company a monopoly of the livestock slaughtering business in New Orleans as a means of protecting public health. Competing butchers sued the state, arguing that the monopoly violated their "privileges" as U.S. citizens under the Fourteenth Amendment and deprived them of property without due process of law.

In a 5–4 decision, the Court ruled that the monopoly did not violate the Fourteenth Amendment because its "privileges and immunities" clause applied only to U.S. citizenship, not state citizenship. States, in other words, retained legal jurisdiction over their citizens, and federal protection of civil rights did not extend to the property rights of businesses.

Dissenting Justice Stephen J. Field argued that the Court's mistaken ruling rendered the Fourteenth Amendment a "vain and idle enactment" with little scope or authority. By designating the rights of state citizens beyond the jurisdiction of federal law, the *Slaughterhouse Cases* unwittingly opened the door for states to discriminate against African Americans.

Three years later, in *United States v. Cruikshank* (1876), the Supreme Court further eroded the protections of individuals embedded in the Fourteenth Amendment by overturning the convictions of William Cruikshank and two other White men who had led the Colfax Massacre. In doing so, the Court argued that the equal protection and due process clauses in the Fourteenth Amendment governed only state actions, not the behavior of individuals. Furthermore, the prosecution's failure to prove racial intent placed the convictions outside the reach of the equal protection clause of the Fourteenth Amendment.

In Chief Justice Morrison Waite's view, the duty to protect the "equality of the rights of citizens" had been "originally assumed by the States; and it still remains there." He and the other justices thus struck down the Enforcement Acts, ruling that the states, not the federal government, were responsible for protecting citizens from attack by other private citizens.

Taken together, the *Slaughterhouse* and *Cruikshank* cases so gutted the Fourteenth Amendment that freedpeople were left even more vulnerable to violence and discrimination. The federal government was effectively abandoning its role in enforcing Reconstruction as Northerners shifted their attention to corruption in Washington, D.C.

SEEKING RESTITUTION After the Civil War, a few resolute former enslaved people fought to be compensated for their years of forced labor. Henrietta Wood had grown up enslaved on a northern Kentucky plantation before being separated from her mother and sold several times. In 1848, the woman who owned Wood moved across the Ohio River to Cincinnati, where she freed Henrietta. Wood then worked at a boardinghouse cleaning rooms until one day in 1853 the owner, Rebecca Boyd, took her on a carriage ride to Kentucky. "I have some friends to see, and we can get back in time for supper," she assured Henrietta. Yet as they left the ferry on the Kentucky side of the river, Wood's employer handed her over to a slave-trading kidnapper who sold her to a Mississippi planter.

Eventually, Wood ended up enslaved on a Texas plantation so isolated that she did not learn of the Union victory in the Civil War until months after Robert E. Lee's surrender. Once freed, Wood returned in 1869 to Cincinnati with her young son, Arthur, who was likely the result of her having been raped by her Texas owner.

In 1870, a resilient, determined Henrietta Wood took slave trader Zebulon Ward to federal court in Cincinnati, arguing that she should be reimbursed $20,000 for the wages she had earned but never received after he reenslaved and sold her. Ward had grown wealthy in Arkansas after the war by leasing imprisoned Blacks to area farmers. After numerous delays, a jury of twelve White men ruled in favor of Wood in 1878. The judge, a former slaveowner himself, awarded her $2,500. It was the largest settlement of its kind, enabling her to buy a house and later send her son to college and law school. Wood's victory in court was the exception, but in part it would plant the idea to formerly enslaved people and their descendants to seek restitution for all their unpaid work when in bondage.

THE CONTESTED ELECTION OF 1876   President Grant wanted to run for an unprecedented third term in 1876, but many Republicans had lost confidence in his leadership. In the summer of 1875, he acknowledged the inevitable and announced that he would retire.

James Gillespie Blaine of Maine, former Speaker of the House, initially seemed the likeliest Republican to succeed Grant, but his candidacy crumbled when newspapers revealed that he had secretly promised political favors to railroad executives in exchange for shares of stock in the company.

The scandal led the Republican convention to select Ohio's favorite son, Rutherford B. Hayes. Orphaned at birth and raised by a single mother, he graduated first in his class at Kenyon College, then received a law degree from Harvard before becoming an anti-slavery attorney in Cincinnati. When the Civil War erupted, he joined the Union army and eventually became a major general; he was wounded four times. After the war, Hayes served three terms as governor of Ohio. He was a civil service reformer eager to reduce the number of federal jobs subject to political appointment. But his chief virtue was that he offended neither Radicals nor reformers. As a journalist put it, he was "obnoxious to no one."

The Democratic convention was uncharacteristically harmonious. On the second ballot, the nomination went to Samuel J. Tilden, a wealthy corporate lawyer and reform governor of New York.

The 1876 campaign avoided controversial issues. In the absence of strong ideological differences, Democrats highlighted the Republican scandals. Republicans responded by repeatedly waving "the bloody shirt," linking the Democrats to secession, civil war, and the violence committed against Republicans in the South. As Robert G. Ingersoll, the most celebrated Republican public speaker of the time, insisted: "The man that assassinated Abraham Lincoln was a Democrat. . . . Soldiers, every scar you have on your heroic bodies was given you by a Democrat!"

Early election returns pointed to a victory for Tilden. Nationwide, he out-polled Hayes by almost 300,000 votes, and by midnight following Election Day, Tilden had won 184 electoral votes, just 1 short of the total needed for victory. Overnight, however, Republican activists realized that the election hinged on 19 disputed electoral votes from Florida, Louisiana, and South Carolina.

The Democrats needed only one of the challenged votes to claim victory; the Republicans needed all nineteen. Republicans in the three states had engaged in election fraud, while Democrats had used violence to keep Black voters at home. All three states, however, were governed by Republicans who appointed the election boards, each of which reported narrow victories for Hayes. The Democrats immediately challenged the results.

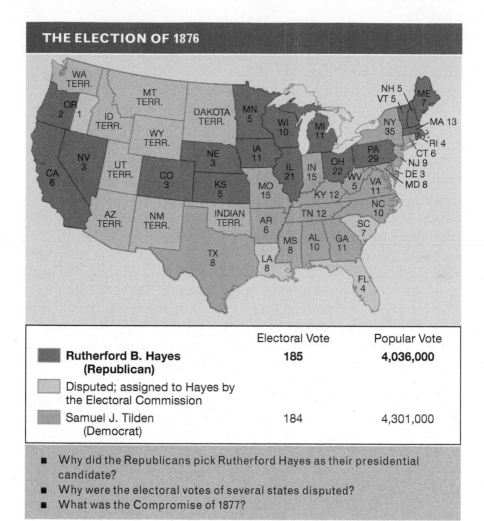

THE ELECTION OF 1876

	Electoral Vote	Popular Vote
■ Rutherford B. Hayes (Republican)	**185**	**4,036,000**
□ Disputed; assigned to Hayes by the Electoral Commission		
■ Samuel J. Tilden (Democrat)	184	4,301,000

- Why did the Republicans pick Rutherford Hayes as their presidential candidate?
- Why were the electoral votes of several states disputed?
- What was the Compromise of 1877?

In all three states, rival election boards submitted conflicting vote counts. Weeks passed with no solution. On January 29, 1877, Congress appointed an electoral commission to settle the dispute. Finally, on March 1, 1877, the commission voted 8–7 in favor of Hayes. The next day, the House of Representatives declared Hayes president by an electoral vote of 185–184.

Tilden decided not to protest the decision. His campaign manager explained that they preferred "four years of Hayes's administration to four years of civil war."

Hayes's victory hinged on the defection of key southern Democrats, who, it turned out, had made secret deals with the Republicans. On February 26, 1877, prominent Ohio Republicans and powerful southern Democrats had

Compromise of 1877 This illustration represents the compromise between Republicans and southern Democrats that ended Radical Reconstruction.

struck a private bargain—the **Compromise of 1877**—at Wormley's Hotel in Washington, D.C. The Republicans promised that if Hayes were named president, he would remove the last federal troops from the South.

For his part, President Grant was eager to leave the White House: "I never wanted to get out of a place as much as I did to get out of the Presidency." Others were sorry to see him leave. T. Jefferson Martin spoke for many African Americans when he wrote Grant upon his retirement: "As a colored man I feel in duty bound to return you my greatful [sic] and heartfelt thanks, for your firm, steadfast, and successful administrations of our country, both as military chieftain and civil ruler of this nation. . . . My dear friend of humanity."

THE END OF RECONSTRUCTION By 1877, Americans were no longer willing to pay the price to protect the newly won rights of African Americans. The Democrat-controlled House of Representatives refused to fund federal troops in the South after July, and President Hayes ordered U.S. soldiers in the South Carolina statehouse to return to their barracks. The state's Republican government collapsed soon thereafter.

In the congressional elections of 1878, Hayes admitted that the balloting in southern states was corrupted by "violence of the most atrocious character," but he would not send federal troops again. The Democrats controlling the

House went a step further and banned the use of federal troops to enforce civil rights in the former Confederacy. The news led a South Carolina African American to dread his future. "I am an unprotected freedman. O God save the Colored People."

Without the sustained presence of federal troops, African Americans could not retain their newly won civil rights. New White Democratic state governments rewrote their constitutions, ousted the "carpetbaggers, scalawags, and blacks," and cut spending. As the years passed, White supremacists found various ways to prevent Blacks from voting or holding office or even sharing the same railcar. State colleges and universities that had admitted Blacks now reversed themselves. In short, the North had won the Civil War but lost the peace. "The Yankees helped free us, so they say," a formerly enslaved North Carolinian named Thomas Hall remembered, "but [in 1877] they let us be put back in slavery again."

In an 1876 speech to the Republican National Convention, Frederick Douglass recognized that the party had won the Civil War, freed the enslaved, and passed amendments protecting their civil and voting rights, yet "what does it all amount to if the black man, after having been made free by the letter of your law, is unable to exercise that freedom . . . and is [again] to be subject to the slaveholder's shotgun?"

Reconstruction's Significance

Yet for all its unfulfilled promises, Congressional Reconstruction did leave an enduring legacy—the Thirteenth, Fourteenth, and Fifteenth Amendments. Taken together, they represented a profound effort to extend the principle of personal and political equality to African Americans. As Frederick Douglass proclaimed in 1870 after the passage of the Fifteenth Amendment, "We have all [that] we asked, and more than we expected."

If Reconstruction's experiment in interracial democracy failed to provide true social equality or substantial economic opportunities for African Americans, it did create the essential constitutional foundation for future advances in the quest for equality and civil rights—and not just for African Americans, but for women and other minority groups.

Until the pivotal Reconstruction era, the states were responsible for protecting citizens' rights. Thereafter, thanks to the Fourteenth and Fifteenth Amendments, Blacks had gained equal rights (in theory), and the federal government had assumed responsibility for ensuring that states treated Blacks equally. A hundred years later, the cause of civil rights would finally be embraced again by the federal government. "With malice toward none, with charity for all, with firmness in the right," as Abraham Lincoln urged in his second inaugural address, "let us strive to finish the work we are in, to bind up a nation's wounds, to . . . cherish a just and lasting peace." His vision for a reconstructed America retains its relevance and urgency today.

CHAPTER REVIEW

SUMMARY

- **Reconstruction Challenges**   With the defeat of the Confederacy and the passage of the Thirteenth Amendment, the federal government had to develop policies and procedures to address a number of difficult questions: What was the status of the defeated states, and how would they be reintegrated into the nation's political life? What would be the political status of the formerly enslaved people, and what would the federal government do to integrate them into the nation's social and economic fabric?

- **Reconstruction over Time**   Abraham Lincoln and his successor, Southerner Andrew Johnson, preferred a more lenient and faster *Restoration Plan* for the southern states. The *Freedmen's Bureau* attempted to educate and aid formerly enslaved people, negotiate labor contracts, and reunite families. Lincoln's assassination led many Northerners to favor the *Radical Republicans*, who wanted a more transformative plan designed to end the grasp of the old plantation elite on the South's society and economy. Southern Whites resisted and established *Black codes* to restrict the lives of formerly enslaved people. *Congressional Reconstruction* responded by stipulating that to reenter the Union, former Confederate states had to ratify the *Fourteenth Amendment* (1868) and *Fifteenth Amendment* (1870) to the U.S. Constitution to expand and protect the rights of African Americans. Congress also passed the Military Reconstruction Act, which used federal troops to enforce the voting and civil rights of African Americans.

- **Views of Reconstruction**   Many formerly enslaved people found comfort in their families and the independent churches they established, but land ownership reverted to the old White elite, reducing newly freed Black farmers to *sharecropping*. African Americans enthusiastically participated in politics, with many serving as elected officials. Along with White southern Republicans (scalawags) and northern carpetbaggers, they worked to rebuild the southern economy. Many White Southerners, however, blamed their poverty on formerly enslaved people and Republicans, and they supported the *Ku Klux Klan's* violent intimidation of the supporters of these Reconstruction efforts and the goal of "redemption," or White Democratic control of southern state governments.

- **Political and Economic Developments and the End of Reconstruction**   Scandals during the Grant administration involving an attempt to corner the gold market, plus the *Panic of 1873* and disagreement over whether to continue the use of *greenbacks* or return to the gold standard, eroded northern support for Reconstruction. Southern White *redeemers* were elected in 1874, successfully reversing the political progress of Republicans and Blacks. In the *Compromise of 1877*, Democrats agreed to the election of Republican Rutherford B. Hayes, who put an end to the Radical Republican administrations in the southern states.

- **The Significance of Reconstruction**   Southern state governments quickly renewed long-standing patterns of discrimination against African Americans, but the *Fourteenth* and *Fifteenth Amendments* remained enshrined in the Constitution, creating the essential constitutional foundation for future advances in civil rights. These amendments give the federal government responsibility for ensuring equal treatment and political equality within the states, a role it would increasingly assume in the twentieth century.

CHRONOLOGY

1865	Congress sets up the Freedmen's Bureau
April 14, 1865	Lincoln assassinated
1865	Johnson issues Proclamation of Amnesty
1865–1866	All-White southern state legislatures pass Black codes
1866	Ku Klux Klan organized
	Congress passes Civil Rights Act
1867	Congress passes Military Reconstruction Act
	Freedmen begin participating in elections
1868	Fourteenth Amendment is ratified
	The U.S. House of Representatives impeaches President Andrew Johnson; the Senate fails to convict him
	Grant elected president
	Eight former Confederate states readmitted to the Union
1869	Reestablishment of White Democratic rule ("redeemers") in former Confederate states
1870	Fifteenth Amendment ratified
	First Enforcement Acts passed in response to White terror in the South
1872	Grant wins reelection
1873	Panic of 1873 triggers depression
1877	Compromise of 1877 ends Reconstruction

KEY TERMS

Radical Republicans p. 705

Freedmen's Bureau p. 706

Johnson's Restoration Plan p. 711

Black codes p. 715

Fourteenth Amendment (1866) p. 717

Congressional Reconstruction p. 719

Fifteenth Amendment (1870) p. 721

sharecropping p. 728

Ku Klux Klan p. 730

greenbacks p. 740

Panic of 1873 p. 741

redeemers p. 744

Compromise of 1877 p. 749

🐰 INQUIZITIVE

Go to InQuizitive to see what you've learned—and learn what you've missed—with personalized feedback along the way.

part five

GROWING PAINS

The defeat of the Confederacy in 1865 restored the Union and helped accelerate America's transformation into an agricultural empire and an industrial powerhouse. During and after the Civil War, the Republican-led Congress pushed through legislation to promote industrial and commercial development as well as western expansion at the same time that it was "reconstructing" the former Confederate states. In the process of settling the continent, forcing Indians onto reservations, and exploiting the continent's natural resources, the

United States forged a dynamic new industrial economy serving an increasingly national and international market for American goods.

Fueled by innovations in mass production and mass marketing as well as advances in transportation and communications such as transcontinental railroads and transatlantic telegraph systems, huge corporations began to dominate the economy by the end of the nineteenth century. As the prominent social theorist William Graham Sumner remarked, the relentless process of industrial development "controls us all because we are all in it. It creates the conditions of our own existence, sets the limits of our social activity, and regulates the bonds of our social relations."

Late nineteenth-century American life drew much of its energy from the mushrooming industrial cities. "This is the age of cities," declared midwestern writer Hamlin Garland. "We are now predominantly urban." Yet the transition from an economy made up of mostly small local and regional businesses to one dominated by large-scale national and international corporations affected rural life as well. For more and more Americans during the so-called Gilded Age, their workday began with the shriek of a factory whistle rather than the crowing of a rooster.

The friction between the new forces of the national marketplace and the traditional folkways of small-scale family farming generated social unrest and political revolts (what one writer called "a seismic shock, a cyclonic violence") during the last quarter of the nineteenth century.

The clash between tradition and modernity, sleepy farm villages and bustling cities, peaked during the 1890s, one of the most strife-ridden decades in American history. A deep economic depression, political activism by farmers, and violent conflicts between industrial workers and employers transformed the presidential campaign of 1896 into a collision between rival visions of America's future.

The Republican candidate, William McKinley, campaigned on modern urban and industrial values. His opponent, William Jennings Bryan, the nominee of both the Democratic and the Populist parties, was an eloquent defender of America's rural past.

McKinley's victory proved to be a turning point in the nation's political and social history. By 1900, the United States had emerged as one of the world's greatest industrial powers, and it would thereafter assume a new leadership role in world affairs—for good and for ill.

16

Business and Labor in the Industrial Era

1860–1900

Carnegie Steel Company Steelworkers operate the dangerous yet magnificent Bessemer converters at Andrew Carnegie's huge steel mill in Pittsburgh, Pennsylvania.

Although the Civil War devastated the South, it provided a powerful stimulant to the northern economy. The need to supply Union armies with shoes, boots, uniforms, weapons, supplies, food, wagons, and railroads ushered in an era of unprecedented industrial development. As an Indiana congressman told business leaders in 1864, the war had sparked the development of "resources and capabilities such as you never before dreamed you possessed."

Between the end of the Civil War and 1900, the nation's population soared, agricultural production more than doubled, and manufacturing output grew *six* times over. In the thirty-five years after the Civil War, the United States achieved the highest rate of economic growth in world history, and by 1900, American industries and corporate farms dominated global markets in steel, oil, wheat, and cotton.

Such phenomenal growth led to profound social changes, the most visible of which was the sudden prosperity of large industrial cities such as Pittsburgh, Chicago, and Cleveland. In a wild scramble for wealth, millions of young adults left farms and villages to work in factories, mines, and mills, and to revel in city life. In growing numbers, women left the "cult of domesticity" and entered the urban-industrial workplace as clerks, typists, secretaries, teachers, nurses, and seamstresses.

The world of *Big Business*, a term commonly used to refer to the new giant corporations, was as untamed and reckless as the cow towns and mining camps of the West were. New technologies and business practices outpaced the ability of the legal system to craft new laws and fashion ethical norms to

focus questions

1. What factors stimulated the unprecedented industrial and agricultural growth in the late nineteenth century?

2. Who were the entrepreneurs who pioneered the growth of Big Business? What were their goals, and what strategies did they use to dominate their respective industries?

3. What role did the federal government play in the nation's economic development during this period?

4. In what ways did the class structure and lives of women change in the late nineteenth century?

5. How did workers use unions to promote their interests during this era?

govern the rapidly changing economy. Business owners took advantage of this lawless environment to build fortunes, destroy reputations, corrupt the political system, exploit workers and the environment, and gouge consumers. Yet out of the riotous quest for profits emerged an undreamed-of prosperity and a rising standard of living that became the envy of the world.

Along with great wealth came great poverty, however. In a capitalist economy, people with different talents, opportunities, and resources receive unequal rewards from their labors. In a capitalist democracy like America, the tensions between equal political rights and unequal economic status generate social instability. In the decades after the Civil War, the overwhelming influence exercised by the business tycoons provoked the formation of labor unions and farm associations. Increasingly, tensions erupted into violent clashes that required government intervention and produced class conflict.

The Elements of Industrial and Agricultural Growth

Technology drove the nation's economic growth and industrial development. Perhaps the most important achievement was the expansion of transportation systems—canals, steamboats, railroads, and the development of instantaneous communication networks enabled first by the telegraph and later by the telephone. These innovations created a national marketplace for the sale and distribution of goods and services.

In addition, the economy benefited from the continuing exploitation of the nation's vast natural resources: fertile soil, forests, minerals, oil, coal, water, and iron ore. At the same time, a rising tide of immigrants created an ever-growing army of low-wage, high-energy workers while expanding the pool of consumers eager to buy new products. Between 1865 and 1900, more than 15 million newcomers arrived in the United States.

Still another factor driving the Second Industrial Revolution was a new generation of outsized business leaders who spurred the transition to an urban-industrial society. Admirers called them captains of industry, while critics called them robber barons because they seized control of the flow of money and commerce. Whatever the label, these talented business leaders displayed keen intelligence, audacious planning, fierce ambition, bold ingenuity, and cutthroat determination. Their goal was not simply to generate profits but to dominate entire industries: steel, oil, sugar, meatpacking, and many others.

The post–Civil War tycoons strove to create large enterprises never before imagined. As proponents of free enterprise and self-reliance, they were convinced that what was good for their businesses was good for the country. Hated, feared, envied, or admired, they were the catalysts for a new America of cities and factories, prosperity amid poverty, and growing social strife and political corruption.

The promoters of Big Business ruthlessly improved efficiency and productivity, cut costs, bought politicians, and suppressed competition. When Cornelius Vanderbilt, a developer first of steamboats and then of railroads, learned that some rivals had tried to steal one of his properties, he penned a brief message: "Gentlemen: You have undertaken to cheat me. I will not sue you, for law takes too long. I will ruin you." And he did.

THE SECOND INDUSTRIAL REVOLUTION

The dramatic increases in economic productivity were driven by the **Second Industrial Revolution**, which began in the mid-nineteenth century and was centered in the United States and Germany. This revolution resulted from three related developments. The first was the creation of modern transportation and communication systems that gave farmers and factory owners access to national and international markets. The completion of transcontinental railroads and the development of larger, faster steamships helped expand markets worldwide, as did the laying of the telegraph cable under the Atlantic Ocean to connect the United States with Europe.

During the 1880s, a second breakthrough—the creation of electrical power—accelerated the pace of change in industrial and urban development. Electricity dramatically increased the power, speed, and efficiency of machinery. It accelerated urban growth by spawning the technologies needed to enable trolleys, subways, and streetlights, as well as elevators that allowed taller buildings.

The third major catalyst for the Second Industrial Revolution was the systematic application of scientific research to industrial processes. In laboratories staffed by graduates of new research universities and often funded by corporations or wealthy business owners, scientists (mostly chemists) and engineers discovered new ways to improve industrial processes. Researchers figured out, for example, how to refine kerosene and gasoline from crude oil, and how to manufacture steel more efficiently and in much larger quantities.

Using these improved processes, inventors developed new products—telephones, typewriters, phonographs, adding machines, sewing machines, cameras, zippers, farm machinery—which resulted in lower prices for an array of consumer items. These advances in turn expanded the scope and scale of industrial organizations. Capital-intensive industries, those requiring massive investments in specialized equipment, such as steel and oil, as well as processed food and tobacco, began emphasizing mass production and distribution across national and international markets. Serving customers across the nation and around the world required more sophisticated strategies of marketing and advertising, thus expanding those industries.

CORPORATE AGRICULTURE While the manufacturing sector was experiencing rapid growth, the agricultural economy was shifting to a large-scale industrial model of operation. Giant corporate-owned "bonanza farms," so called because of their huge size and profits, spread across the West. Comprising at least 3,000 acres, they were run like factories under the critical watch of professional, college-educated managers. Hundreds of migrant workers were hired to operate mechanized equipment to harvest crops—usually wheat or corn—destined for eastern or foreign markets.

Oliver Dalrymple, a graduate of Yale Law School who became the "wheat king of Minnesota," was one of the first to see the potential of bonanza farming. He agreed to manage several huge farms ("prairie plantations") in North Dakota. By the 1880s, he had gained ownership of one of the largest farms in the world—more than 100,000 acres.

Bonanza Farms Known as bonanza farms, these agricultural factories expanded food production dramatically and employed hundreds of Mexican and Scandinavian immigrant workers to harvest crops.

Dalrymple developed a system for managing wheat-growing bonanza farms that maximized their profits. He purchased the most efficient machinery, employed workers only when they were needed, and managed his fields for maximum fertility. He also developed systems of feeding and housing workers and livestock at the lowest possible cost.

The hundreds of seasonal laborers on bonanza farms, many of them Mexican migrant workers or Scandinavian or European immigrants, slept in military-like bunkhouses where drinking, smoking, and swearing were prohibited. They labored ten to thirteen hours a day for six days a week. Women, often the wives of foremen, were hired to do the cooking, cleaning, and washing.

The booming farm sector stimulated the industrial sector—and vice versa. In the West, bonanza farms using the latest machinery and scientific techniques became internationally famous for their productivity. On one bonanza farm in North Dakota, a single field of wheat encompassed 13,000 acres. For farmers in the High Plains, wheat became a perennial cash crop, and American-grown wheat was exported around the world. Another bonanza farm in South Dakota employed more than 1,000 migrant workers to tend 34,000 acres. Such agribusinesses were the wave of the future. By 1870, the United States had become the world's leading agricultural producer. With the growth of the commercial cattle industry, the process of slaughtering, packing, and shipping cattle, hogs, and sheep evolved into a major industry, especially in Chicago, the nation's fastest-growing city and home to the largest slaughterhouses and meatpacking plants in the world.

TECHNOLOGICAL INNOVATIONS America has always nurtured a culture of invention and innovation. Abraham Lincoln had often praised the nation's peculiar talent for "discoveries and inventions," which became especially evident in the decades after the Civil War. Inventors, scientists, research laboratories, and business owners developed labor-saving machinery and mass-production techniques that stimulated advances in efficiency and productivity, which increased the size of industrial enterprises.

Such innovations helped businesses turn out more products more cheaply, thus enabling more people to buy more of them. Technological advances created *economies of scale,* whereby larger business enterprises, including huge commercial farms, could afford expensive new machinery and large workforces that boosted their productivity.

After the Civil War, technological improvements led to phenomenal increases in industrial productivity. The U.S. Patent Office, which had recorded only 276 inventions during the 1790s, registered almost 235,000 new patents in the 1890s, many of them issued to women and African Americans. New

Yorker Beulah Louisa Henry accounted for almost fifty of those patents, most of them improvements on household goods, such as better sewing machines, typewriters, and umbrellas. Other innovations during the Gilded Age in the late nineteenth century included barbed-wire fencing, mechanical harvesters, refrigerated railcars, air brakes for trains, steam turbines, vacuum cleaners, ice cream churns, and electric motors.

Bell's Telephone Few inventions could rival the importance of the telephone. In 1875, twenty-eight-year-old Alexander Graham Bell began experimenting with the concept of a "speaking telegraph," or talking through wires. The following year, he developed a primitive "electric speaking telephone" that enabled him to send a famous message to his assistant in another room: "Mr. Watson, come here, I want to see you." In 1876, Bell patented his device and started the American Telephone and Telegraph Company (AT&T), to begin manufacturing telephones. Five years later, he perfected the long-distance telephone lines that revolutionized communication. By 1895, more than 300,000 telephones were in use in the United States. Bell's patent became the most valuable one ever issued.

Typewriters and Sewing Machines Other inventions changed the nature of work. Typewriters, for example, transformed the operations of business offices.

Office Typists Newly entrusted with typewriters, women occupied the secretarial positions at many offices, such as the Remington Typewriter Company, pictured here.

Because managers assumed that women had greater dexterity in their fingers and because women were paid less than men, they hired them to operate type-writers. Clerical positions soon became the fastest-growing job category for women working outside the home.

Likewise, the introduction of sewing machines for the mass production of clothing and linens opened new, though often exploitative, employment opportunities to women. So-called sweatshops emerged in the major cities, where large numbers of mostly young immigrant women worked long hours in cramped, stifling conditions.

Thomas Edison No American inventor was more influential or prolific than Thomas Alva Edison. As a boy in Michigan, he loved to daydream and "make things." His mother, Nancy, home-schooled him and allowed Thomas to perform what he called chemical "experiments." Edison later said his mother "let me follow my bent," which was toward telegraphy and electricity. He built his own telegraph set and dreamed of being a telegraph operator.

When Edison was twelve, he began working for the local railroad, selling newspapers, food, and candy. "Being poor," he explained, "I already knew that money is a valuable thing." One day he was late for the train and ran after it. A conductor reached down and lifted him aboard by his ears. Edison felt something snap in his head, and soon he was nearly deaf, which helps explain his adult preoccupation with sound-making inventions.

Despite having no formal scientific education, Edison became a mechanical genius famous for his inexhaustible energy. In January 1869, at the age of twenty-one, he announced that he would "hereafter devote his full time to bringing out his inventions." He moved to New York City to be closer

Thomas Edison Thomas Edison invented the electric lightbulb and devised a way to transmit electricity to illuminate an entire city. Now, work hours were no longer limited to available daylight. Here we see Thomas Edison *(left)*, participating at the Fiftieth Anniversary reenactment of the lighting of the first electric lightbulb in his workshop in Menlo Park, New Jersey, with Henry Ford *(middle)*, and President Herbert Hoover *(right)*.

to the center of America's financial world; there he developed dozens of new machines, including a "stock market ticker" to report the transactions on Wall Street in real time. Soon, job offers and what he referred to as "real money" flooded his way. The workaholic Edison, however, had a different goal: to become a full-time inventor.

In 1876, the compulsive tinkerer moved into what he called his invention factory designed for experiments in Menlo Park, New Jersey, twenty-five miles southwest of New York City. There, Edison demonstrated that the most fertile environment for innovation was to surround himself with a team of creative people. Genius, in other words, loves company.

At Menlo Park, he and his forty assistants created the phonograph in 1877 ("a miraculous talking machine") and a long-lasting electric lightbulb in 1879. He also improved upon the telephone, invented the formula for cement, and developed the world's largest rock crusher and tornado-proof house. He founded more than a hundred companies (including General Electric) and was awarded a record-setting 1,093 patents.

Altogether, Edison and his team invented or perfected hundreds of new devices and processes, including the storage battery, Dictaphone, mimeograph copier, electric motor, and motion picture camera and projector. Perhaps most important, however, was his design of an electrical transmission system that would illuminate and power an entire city.

One magazine saluted Edison as one of the "wonders of the world." No inventor did more to push society into modernity. Until Edison's inventions came along, the availability of daylight determined much about how people lived and worked. With the lightbulb, the distinction between night and day virtually disappeared.

George Westinghouse and Electric Power Before the 1880s, kerosene and gas lamps illuminated the nation after dark. All that changed in 1882, when the Edison Electric Illuminating Company launched the electric utility industry. Several companies that made lightbulbs merged into the Edison General Electric Company (later renamed General Electric) in 1888.

The use of direct electrical current, however, limited Edison's lighting system to a radius of about two miles. To cover greater distances required an alternating current, which could be transmitted at high voltage and then stepped down by transformers. After George Westinghouse, inventor of the railway air brake, developed the first alternating-current electric system in 1886, he set up the Westinghouse Electric Company to manufacture the equipment.

Edison resisted the new method as too risky, but the Westinghouse system won the "battle of the currents," and the Edison companies had to switch over to AC (alternating current) from DC (direct current). In 1887, a twenty-eight-year-old Croatian immigrant named Nikola Tesla, who had briefly worked with Thomas Edison before the two parted ways, set up laboratories in New York where he invented the alternating-current (AC) motor. He sold the plans for it to George Westinghouse, who improved it, and then he began selling dynamos (electric motors).

The invention of dynamos dramatically increased the power, speed, and efficiency of machinery. Electricity enabled factories and mills to be located anywhere; they no longer had to cluster around waterfalls and coal deposits to have a ready supply of energy. Electricity also encouraged urban growth by improving lighting, facilitating the development of trolley and subway systems, and stimulating the creation of elevators that enabled the construction of taller buildings.

THE RAILROAD REVOLUTION More than any new industry, railroads symbolized the impact of innovative technologies on industrial development. No other form of transportation played so large a role in the emergence of the interconnected national marketplace.

In 1888, William Cox, a Nebraska writer, reported that "a new railway has been commenced and completed" across the state, opening "up a great new artery of traffic, and bringing in its train joy and gladness for thousands of people." The new rail line was "building up three new villages along the way, and infusing new life and activity into a fourth." The railroads, he concluded, were providing America with a pathway to progress, profit, and modernity.

Every community wanted (and needed) a rail connection, and each year construction companies set new records of adding new tracks. In 1870, the nation was crisscrossed by 35,000 miles of railroad tracks; by 1900, the mileage exceeded 200,000. Such dramatic growth made the railroad the tangible symbol of America's remarkable industrial development. As railroads connected more towns and cities, they moved masses of people and goods faster, farther, and cheaper than any other form of transportation. The railroad network prompted the creation of uniform national and international time zones and popularized the use of wristwatches, for the trains were scheduled to run on time. Towns that had rail stations (depots) thrived; those that did not died.

Although the first great wave of railroad building occurred in the 1850s, the most spectacular growth took place after the Civil War. Alongside each mile of track, a network of telegraph poles and wires was installed. Transportation and communication thus combined to forge a truly national economy.

Railroads were America's first Big Business. The companies were the first beneficiaries of the great financial market known as Wall Street in New York

City, the nation's largest employers and the first industry to operate in several states, and the first to develop a large-scale management bureaucracy.

Railroads opened the West to economic development; transported federal troops to suppress Indian resistance; helped transform commercial agriculture, mining, cattle ranching, and forestry into major international industries. The rails delivered raw materials and livestock to factories and meatpacking plants while carrying finished goods to retailers. Railroads also stimulated basic industries through their massive purchases of iron and steel, coal, timber, leather (for seats), and glass. In addition, railroad companies were the nation's largest employers.

Railroads were expensive, however. Locomotives, railcars (called rolling stock), and the construction of track, trestles, and bridges required enormous investments. The railroad industry was the first to contract with "investment banks" to raise capital by selling shares of stock to investors.

As railroad companies laid tracks across sparsely populated western states and territories, they became the region's primary real estate developers. They transported millions of settlers from the East, many of them immigrants eager to gain free government homesteads. In 1872, Congress established Yellowstone National Park. Within ten years, railroads had brought a burgeoning tourist business to the nation's first national park in remote northwest Wyoming, then a territory. In the end, the railroads changed the economic, political, and physical landscapes of the nation and enabled the United States to emerge as a world power.

BUILDING THE TRANSCONTINENTALS For decades, visionaries had dreamed of the United States being the first nation to build railroad tracks spanning a continent. In the 1860s, the dream became reality as construction began on the first of four rail lines that would bridge the nation—and, as one promoter boasted, establish "our empire on the Pacific."

The transcontinental railroads were, in the words of General William T. Sherman, the "work of giants." Their construction required heroic feats by the surveyors, engineers, and laborers who laid the rails, built the bridges, and gouged out the tunnels through rugged mountains.

The first transcontinental railroads were much more expensive to build than the shorter "trunk" lines in the East. Because the western routes passed through vast stretches of unpopulated plains and deserts, construction materials as well as workers and supplies had to be hauled long distances. Locomotives, railcars, rails, ties, spikes, and much more were often transported by ships from the East Coast to San Francisco and then moved by train to the remote construction sites.

Congress helped fund the transcontinental lines. Through the Pacific Railway Acts of 1862 and 1864, the railroad construction companies received almost 13,000 acres of government-owned land per mile of track laid. The Central Pacific Railroad, for example, received tracts of land that in total were larger than the state of Maryland. In addition, the companies received $16,000 from the sale of government bonds for each twenty-mile section of track laid on the plains, and larger amounts for sections crossing the mountains.

The construction process was like managing a moving army. Herds of cattle, horses, mules, and oxen had to be fed and tended. Huge mobile camps, called "Hell on Wheels," were built to house the crews and moved with them as the tracks progressed. The camps even included tents for dance halls, saloons, gambling, and prostitution. Nightlife was raucous. As a British reporter wrote, "Soldiers, herdsmen, teamsters, women, railroad men, are dancing, singing, or gambling. There are men here who would murder a fellow-creature for five dollars. . . . Not a day passes but a dead body is found somewhere in the vicinity with pockets rifled of their contents."

The Pacific Railway Act (1862) Before the Civil War, construction of a transcontinental line from the Missouri River to California had been delayed because northern and southern congressmen clashed over the choice of routes. Secession and the departure of southern congressmen for the Confederacy in 1861 finally permitted Republicans in Congress to pass the Pacific Railway Act in 1862. It authorized construction along a north-central route by two competing companies: the Union Pacific Railroad (UP) westward from Omaha, Nebraska, across the prairie, and the Central Pacific Railroad (CP) eastward from Sacramento, California, through the Sierra Nevada range. Both companies began construction during the war, but most of the work was done after 1865.

Building a railroad across the continent entailed feats of daring, engineering, and construction. Laying rail around and through the mountains required extensive use of dynamite and required costly bridges and tunnels. Harsh weather led to frequent seasonal disruptions, and many workers were killed or injured over the course of construction. At times, some 15,000 people, mostly men, worked for each of the railroad companies as they raced each other to complete their tasks. The company that laid the most track in the shortest time would be awarded more money by Congress.

The competition led both companies to cut corners. Collis Huntington, one of the CP owners, confessed that his goal was to build "the cheapest road that I could . . . so that it moves ahead fast." If bridges or trestles collapsed under the weight of freight trains, they could be fixed later. Mark Hopkins, one of Huntington's partners, agreed, noting that his goal was to build as "poor a road as we can."

Railroad Workers The Union Pacific crews were largely young, unmarried, former Civil War soldiers—both Union and Confederate—along with ex-enslaved people and Irish and German immigrants. Ninety percent of the CP construction crews were young Chinese workers lured to America by the California gold rush or by railroad jobs. Thousands of Chinese immigrants gained passage on ships using what were called credit-tickets. American companies paid their fares in exchange for their agreeing to work for them for a certain number of years.

Chinese Railroad Workers Using horse-drawn carts, picks, shovels, and dynamite, Chinese laborers played a large role in constructing the transcontinental railroads.

Most of these single men, who were often referred to as "coolies," were eager to earn money to take back to China; less than 5 percent of the Chinese immigrants were women. The term *coolie* derived from the Hindu word for manual laborer, but in the western United States it became a derogatory term for workers willing to work for wages so low that they hurt all laborers. The immigrants' temporary status and dreams of a good life made them willing to endure the low pay, dangerous working conditions, and intense racial prejudice.

What distinguished Chinese from other laborers was their ability to work together in accomplishing daunting tasks. Mark Twain described them as "quiet, peaceable, tractable, free from drunkenness, and they are as industrious as the day is long. A disorderly Chinaman is rare, and a lazy one does not exist." Yet Chinese immigrants did not meekly accept their harsh working conditions. In late June 1867, the Chinese who were grading and digging tunnels put down their picks and shovels and staged a spontaneous strike. They demanded pay equal to Whites, shorter workdays, and better living and working conditions. They also resented having to pay for their lodging, food, and tools, while Whites received those benefits for free.

The eight-day strike ended when the owners of the Central Pacific cut off food, supplies, and transportation to the thousands of Chinese laborers living in work camps. The company made no concessions, but the Chinese had made their point: They should not be taken for granted.

Laying Track The process of building the rail lines involved a series of sequential tasks. First came the surveyors, who selected and mapped the routes and measured grade changes. Engineers then designed the bridges, trestles, tunnels, and snowsheds. Tree cutters and graders followed by preparing the rail beds. Wooden cross ties were then placed in the ground and leveled before thirty-foot-long iron rails weighing 560 pounds were laid atop them. Next came spikers, who used special hammers to wallop two-pound spikes attaching the rails to the ties. Finally, workers shoveled gravel between the ties to stabilize them.

This huge undertaking encountered constant interruptions: terrible weather, late deliveries of key items, accidents, epidemics, and Indian attacks. Arthur Ferguson, a supervisor who kept a journal, frequently noted the hazards of constructing the first transcontinental in 1868:

May 17—Two more men drowned in the river yesterday.
June 4—At about sunrise, were attacked by Indians and succeeded in shooting one.

June 21—Indians killed two men. Both had been horribly mutilated about the face by cuts made by a knife or a tomahawk.
June 30—Four men were killed and scalped today about two miles above camp.

It was not only Native American warriors doing the killing, however. Workers often fought and killed each other. On June 7, Ferguson recorded that "two men were shot this evening in a drunken row—one was instantly killed, and the other is not expected to live."

The Race to the Finish The drama of constructing the first transcontinental railroad seized the nation's imagination. Every major newspaper carried stories about the progress of the competing companies. Finally, on May 10, 1869, former California governor Leland Stanford, one of the owners of the Central Pacific, drove a gold spike to complete the line at Promontory Summit in the Utah Territory north of the Great Salt Lake. The Union Pacific had built 1,086 miles of track compared with the Central Pacific's 689, much of it mountainous. "In one sense," gushed the *Cincinnati Gazette,* the transcontinental railroad "is

The Union Pacific Meets the Central Pacific The celebration of the first transcontinental railroad's completion took place near Promontory Summit in the Utah Territory, in 1869.

as great an achievement as the war, and as grand a triumph." The golden spike used to connect the final rails symbolized the uniting of East and West.

Mexican Americans and Railroads During the last quarter of the nineteenth century, other railroad companies constructed more transcontinental lines across America. As prejudice against Chinese workers intensified, railroads throughout the West and Southwest turned to Native Americans and Mexican-born workers. As a railroad executive explained, Indians and Mexicans were "wonderfully adapted to the peculiar conditions under which they must live as laborers" in the Southwest.

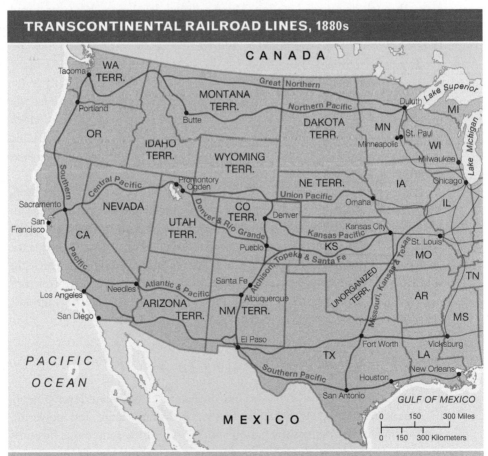

TRANSCONTINENTAL RAILROAD LINES, 1880s

- What was the route of the first transcontinental railroad, and why was it built in the North?
- Who built the railroads? How were they financed?
- In what ways did the railroads perpetuate inequalities in America?

Railroads in the Southwest, especially the Southern Pacific and the Santa Fe, needed so many track workers (*traqueros*) that they set up recruiting centers in Mexico. Between 1880 and 1900, the Mexican immigrant population in New Mexico increased some 50 percent.

Ethnic prejudice shaped wage levels. Track workers in Mexico were paid on average 25¢ a day; in the United States, they or Spanish-speaking Americans earned $1 a day. Irish-born workers, however, were paid $3 a day.

THE DOWNSIDE OF THE RAILROAD BOOM The railroads were spectacular engineering achievements that transformed the pace and focus of daily life. From the 1860s to the 1960s, most people entered or left a city through its railroad station. Many railroad developers, however, cared more about making money than safety. Accidents were all too common, and thousands of laborers were killed or injured.

Too many railroads were built; by the 1880s, there were twice as many as the economy could support. Some were poorly or even criminally managed and went bankrupt. Railroad lobbyists helped to corrupt state and federal legislators by "buying" the votes of politicians with cash or shares of stock in their companies. Charles Francis Adams, Jr., head of the Union Pacific Railroad, admitted, "Our method of doing business is founded upon lying, cheating, and stealing—all bad things."

Railroads also accelerated the displacement of Native Americans. In 1866, Red Cloud, the leader of the Sioux Nation, warned railroad surveyors in Wyoming to leave. "We do not want you here. You are scaring away the buffalo." When the railroad workers did not leave, the Indians attacked track crews and cut telegraph lines. But the railroads kept coming—and brought soldiers with them. In 1880, some 7,000 Whites settled in Indian Territory between Kansas and Texas. Nine years later, and five years after railroads crisscrossed the area, there were 110,000 White residents.

THE RISE OF BIG BUSINESS

The emergence of Big Business was one of the most significant developments in American history. Corporations grew increasingly large and powerful, transacting business across the nation and abroad. At the same time, business leaders exerted unprecedented influence and even bribery to gain the support of governors, legislators, Congress, and presidents.

THE GROWTH OF CORPORATIONS As businesses grew, they took one of several different forms. Some were owned by an individual;

others were partnerships involving several owners. Increasingly, however, large companies that served national and international markets were converted into corporations—legal entities that separate the *ownership* of an enterprise from the *management* of its operations.

Once a corporation was registered (chartered or incorporated) with a state government, it could raise money to operate (capital) by selling shares of stock—representing partial ownership of the company—to people not otherwise involved with it. Shareholders elected a board of directors who appointed and evaluated the corporation's executives (management). One of the most important benefits of a corporation was *limited legal liability*: stockholders shared in its profits but could not be held liable for its debts, although they could lose all their investment if it failed.

FIGHTING COMPETITION Competition is the great virtue of capitalism, since it forces businesses to produce better products at the lowest cost. As many businesses became giant corporations, however, some owners came to view competition as a burden. Financier J. Pierpont Morgan, for example, claimed that "bitter, destructive competition" always led to "destruction and ruin." To eliminate cutthroat competition and thereby stabilize production, wages, and prices, rival companies selling similar products often formed "pools" whereby they secretly agreed to keep production, prices, and wages at specified levels. Such pools rarely lasted long, however, because one or more participants usually violated the agreement. The more effective strategy for the most aggressive companies was to drive the weaker companies out of business—or buy them out.

The efforts of large corporations to eliminate competitors led critics to call the business titans "robber barons." When asked how people might react to the shady methods he used to build his network of railroads, William Henry Vanderbilt famously replied, "The public be damned!"

THE BARONS OF BUSINESS Most of the entrepreneurs who created large businesses in the late nineteenth century yearned to become rich and influential, and many religious leaders urged them on. "To secure wealth is an honorable ambition," stressed Russell Conwell, a prominent Baptist minister. "Money is power," he explained, and "every good man and woman ought to strive for power, to do good with it when obtained. I say, get rich! get rich!"

The industrial and financial leaders personified the values that Conwell celebrated. They were men of grit and genius who found innovative—and at times unethical and illegal—ways to increase production and eliminate competition. They were also mercilessly adept at cutting costs and lowering prices.

John D. Rockefeller The cofounder of Standard Oil Company, Rockefeller sought a monopoly over the oil industry.

Several business barons stood out for their extraordinary accomplishments: John D. Rockefeller and Andrew Carnegie for their innovations in organization, J. Pierpont Morgan for his development of investment banking, and Richard Sears and Alvah Roebuck for their creation of mail-order retailing.

John D. Rockefeller Born in New York in 1839, John D. Rockefeller moved as a child to Cleveland, Ohio. Raised by his mother, he developed a single-minded passion for systematic organization. As a young man, he decided to bring order and rationality to the new boom-and-bust oil industry. He was obsessed with precision, efficiency, tidiness—and money.

The railroad and shipping connections around Cleveland made it a strategic location for serving the booming oil fields of nearby western Pennsylvania. The first oil well in the United States began operating in 1859 in Titusville, Pennsylvania, and led to the Pennsylvania oil rush of the 1860s. Because oil could be refined into kerosene, which was widely used for lighting, heating, and cooking, the economic importance of the oil rush soon outstripped that of the California gold rush ten years earlier. Well before the end of the Civil War, oil refineries sprang up in Pittsburgh and Cleveland. Of the two cities, Cleveland had better rail service, so Rockefeller focused his energies there.

In 1870, Rockefeller teamed with his brother William and two other businessmen, Henry M. Flagler and Samuel Andrews, to establish the **Standard Oil Company** of Ohio. Although the company quickly became the largest oil refiner in the nation, John Rockefeller wanted to take control of the *entire* industry, in large part because he believed his competitors were inefficient.

During the 1870s, Rockefeller used various schemes to destroy his competitors. Early on, he pursued a strategy called horizontal integration, in which a dominant corporation buys or forces out most of its competitors. Rockefeller viewed competition as a form of warfare. In a few cases, he hired former competitors as executives, but only "the big ones," he said, "those who have already proved they can do a *big business*. As for the others, unfortunately they will have to *die*."

By 1879, Standard Oil controlled more than 90 percent of the nation's oil refining business. Still, Rockefeller's goal was a **monopoly**, a business so large that it controls an entire industry.

In pursuing a monopoly, Rockefeller methodically reduced expenses by improving productivity, squeezing suppliers to cut their prices, and eliminating any hint of waste. He was determined to avoid letting any of his suppliers earn "a profit" from him. Because Standard Oil shipped so much oil by rail, Rockefeller forced railroads to pay him secret rebates on the shipments, enabling him to spend less for shipping than his competitors did.

Most important, instead of depending upon the products or services of other firms, known as middlemen, Standard Oil eventually owned everything it needed to produce, refine, and deliver oil—from wells to the finished product. The company had its own pipelines, built factories to make its own wagons and storage barrels, did its own hauling, and owned its own storage tanks and tanker ships. In economic terms, this business strategy is called vertical integration.

During the 1870s, Standard Oil bought so many of its competitors that it developed nearly a complete monopoly over the industry. Many state legislatures responded by outlawing the practice of one corporation owning stock in competing ones. In 1882, Rockefeller tried to hide his efforts to gain a monopoly by organizing the Standard Oil Trust.

The Rise of Oil Crowding this Pennsylvania farm are wooden derricks that extracted crude oil.

A trust gives a corporation (the trustee) the legal power to manage another company. Instead of owning other companies outright, the Standard Oil Trust controlled more than thirty companies by having their stockholders transfer their shares "in trust" to Rockefeller and eight other trustees. In return, the stockholders received *trust certificates*, which paid them annual dividends from the trust's earnings. During the Gilded Age, however, Americans began to call any huge corporation a trust.

The formation of corporate trusts generated intense criticism. In 1890, Congress passed the Sherman Anti-Trust Act, which declared that efforts to monopolize industries and thereby "restrain" competition were illegal. But the bill's language was so vague, its regulations were toothless.

State laws against monopolies were more effective than the Sherman Act. In 1892, Ohio's Supreme Court ordered the Standard Oil Trust dissolved. Rockefeller then developed another way to maintain control of his companies: a **holding company**, which is a corporation that controls other companies by "holding" most or all of their stock certificates. A holding company produces nothing itself; it simply owns a majority of the stock in other companies.

Rockefeller was convinced that ending competition was a good thing for the nation. Monopolies, he insisted, were the natural result of capitalism at work. "It is too late," he declared in 1899, "to argue about the advantages of [huge] industrial combinations. They are a necessity." That year, Rockefeller brought his empire under the direction of the Standard Oil Company of New Jersey, a gigantic holding company. By 1904, Rockefeller controlled almost 85 percent of the petroleum industry.

Andrew Carnegie Like John D. Rockefeller, Andrew Carnegie, who created the largest steel company in the world, rose to wealth from poverty. Born in Scotland, the son of weavers, he migrated with his family in 1848 to western Pennsylvania. At age thirteen, he quit school and went to work twelve hours a day in a cotton mill where his father also worked. In 1853, he became personal secretary to Thomas Scott, then district superintendent of the Pennsylvania Railroad and later its president. When Scott was promoted, Carnegie became superintendent. During the Civil War, when Scott became assistant secretary of war in charge of transportation, Carnegie went with him to Washington, D.C., and helped develop a military telegraph system.

Carnegie worked his way up—from telegraphy to railroading to bridge building, and then to steelmaking and investments. In the early 1870s, he decided "to concentrate on the manufacture of iron and steel and be master in that." A tiny man (barely five feet tall), Carnegie wanted to tower over the steel industry, just as Rockefeller was doing with oil.

Until the mid-nineteenth century, steel, which is stronger and more flexible than iron, could be made only from wrought iron (expensive since it had to be imported from Sweden) and could only be manufactured in small quantities. Bars of wrought iron were heated with charcoal over several days to add carbon and produce steel. It took three tons of coke, a high-burning fuel derived from coal, to produce one ton of steel.

That changed in the 1850s, when England's Sir Henry Bessemer invented the Bessemer converter, a process by which high-quality steel could be produced more quickly by blasting oxygen through the molten iron in a furnace. In the early 1870s, Carnegie decided to concentrate on the manufacture of steel because Bessemer's process had made it so inexpensive to produce—and the railroad industry required massive amounts of it. As Carnegie exclaimed, "The day of iron is past! Steel is king!"

Andrew Carnegie An immigrant from Scotland, Carnegie overcame childhood poverty and established the Carnegie Steel Company.

As more steel was produced, its price dropped and its industrial uses soared. In 1860, the United States produced only 13,000 tons of steel. By 1880, production had reached 1.4 million tons annually. By 1900, the United States was producing more steel than Great Britain and Germany combined.

Between 1880 and 1900, Carnegie dominated the steel industry, acquiring competitors or driving them out of business by cutting prices and taking their customers. Carnegie insisted upon up-to-date machinery and equipment; he expanded production quickly and cheaply by purchasing struggling companies and preached continuous innovation to reduce operating costs. He also employed vertical integration to gain control of every phase of the steel business. He owned coal mines in West Virginia, bought vast deposits of iron ore in Michigan and Wisconsin, and transported the ore in his own ships across the Great Lakes and then by rail to his steel mills in Pittsburgh.

By 1900, the **Carnegie Steel Company**, with 20,000 employees, was the largest industrial company in the world. Carnegie's mills operated nonstop with

J. Pierpont Morgan Despite his privileged upbringing and financial success, Morgan was self-conscious about his deformed nose, caused by chronic skin diseases.

two daily twelve-hour shifts, the only exception being the Fourth of July. "The old nations of the world," Carnegie observed, "creep on at a snail's pace." America, however, "thunders past with the speed of an express [train]." Yet the frenzied pursuit of progress often made for dangerous working conditions. In a single month, seven workers were killed at Carnegie's mills. There were no safety regulations, only production goals.

J. Pierpont Morgan Unlike John D. Rockefeller and Andrew Carnegie, J. Pierpont Morgan was born to wealth in Connecticut. His father was a partner in a large English bank. After attending school in Switzerland and college in Germany, Morgan was sent in 1857 to work in New York City for a new enterprise started by his father, **J. Pierpont Morgan and Company**. The firm, under various names, invested European money with American businesses. It grew into a financial power by helping competing corporations merge and by purchasing massive amounts of stock in American companies and selling them at a profit.

Morgan, like Rockefeller and Carnegie, believed in freewheeling capitalism but hated competition. In his view, high profits required order and stability, and stability required consolidating competitors into trusts that he could own and manipulate.

Early on, Morgan recognized that railroads were essential to the nation's economy and growth, and by the 1890s, he controlled a sixth of the nation's railway system. But his crowning triumph was the consolidation of the steel industry. After a rapid series of mergers, he bought Carnegie's steel and iron holdings in 1901. Morgan added scores of related companies to form U.S. Steel Corporation, the world's first billion-dollar corporation, employing 168,000 people. It was the climactic event in the efforts of the great financial capitalists to reduce competition and forge monopolies. Between 1899 and 1904, Morgan and other investment bankers in New York City used mergers and purchases to consolidate 4,200 corporations into a mere 250 giants.

SEARS AND ROEBUCK After the Civil War, American inventors helped manufacturers produce a vast array of new products that made everyday life simpler and more convenient: electric stoves and lights, sewing machines, typewriters, washing machines, carpet sweepers, razors, rubber boots and shoes, zippers, ice boxes (predecessor to refrigerators), Kodak cameras, telephones, roller skates, bicycles, record players, tennis rackets, croquet sets, and board games.

The most important economic challenge was no longer how to invent and produce goods but how to enable Americans to become everyday consumers. To meet the need, huge downtown department stores emerged in the largest cities, while smaller "five-and-dime" stores were established to serve towns. Still, the millions of isolated farm families could not be regular consumers until businesses found a way to reach them—by mail.

Sears, Roebuck Catalog The Sears, Roebuck catalog provided rural Americans access to a variety of mail-order products previously only available to city dwellers.

A traveling salesman from Chicago named Aaron Montgomery Ward decided that he could reach more people by mail than on foot and thus eliminate the middlemen whose services increased the retail price of goods. Beginning in the early 1870s, Montgomery Ward and Company began selling goods at a 40 percent discount through mail-order catalogs.

By the end of the century, a new retailer had come to dominate the mail-order industry: Sears, Roebuck and Company, founded by two midwestern entrepreneurs, Richard Sears and Alvah Roebuck. The Sears, Roebuck catalog in 1897 was 786 pages long. It featured groceries, drugs, tools, furniture, household products, musical instruments, farm implements, shoes, clothes, books, and sporting goods. The company's ability to buy goods in high volume from wholesalers enabled it to sell items at prices below those offered in rural general stores. By 1907, Sears, Roebuck and Company, headquartered in Chicago, had become one of the largest businesses in the nation.

The Sears catalog helped transform the lives of millions of people. With the advent of free rural mail delivery in 1898, families on farms and in small towns and villages could purchase by mail the products that had been either prohibitively expensive or available only to city dwellers. By the turn of the century, 6 million Sears catalogs were being distributed each year, and the catalog had become the most widely read book in the nation after the Bible.

THE GOSPEL OF WEALTH The aggressive captains of industry were convinced that they benefited the public by accelerating America's transformation into an industrial colossus. In their eyes, it was a law of societal evolution (social Darwinism) that those most talented at producing wealth should accumulate enormous fortunes.

Some of them, however, insisted that great wealth brought great responsibilities. In his essay "The Gospel of Wealth" (1889), Andrew Carnegie argued that "not evil, but good, has come to the [Anglo-Saxon] race from the accumulation of wealth by those who have the ability and energy that produces it." Carnegie and John D. Rockefeller gave away much of their money, mostly to support education and medicine.

By 1900, Rockefeller had become the world's leading philanthropist. "I have always regarded it as a religious duty," he said late in life, "to get all I could honorably and to give all I could." He donated more than $500 million during his lifetime, including tens of millions to Baptist causes and $35 million to found the University of Chicago. His philanthropic influence continues today through the Rockefeller Foundation.

As for Carnegie, after retiring from business at age sixty-five, he declared that the "man who dies rich dies disgraced." He thereafter devoted himself to dispensing his $400 million fortune. Calling himself a "distributor" of wealth, he gave huge sums to numerous universities, built 2,500 public libraries, and helped fund churches, hospitals, parks, and halls for meetings and concerts, including New York City's Carnegie Hall.

THE ALLIANCE OF BUSINESS AND POLITICS

Most of the businesses developed by Andrew Carnegie, John D. Rockefeller, and others had cozy relationships with local, state, and federal government officials, a process of acquiring influence (lobbying) that continues to this day. Big Business has legitimate political interests, but at times it exercises a corrupt influence on government. Nowhere was this more evident than during the decades after the Civil War.

REPUBLICANS AND BIG BUSINESS During and after the Civil War, the Republican party and state and federal governments grew increasingly allied with Big Business. A key element of this alliance was tariff policy. Since 1789, the federal government had imposed tariffs—taxes on imported goods—to raise revenue and to benefit American manufacturers by penalizing foreign competitors. In 1861, as the Civil War was starting, the Republican-dominated Congress enacted the Morrill Tariff, which doubled tax rates on hundreds of imported items, to raise money for the war and reward businesses that supported the Republican party.

After the war, President Ulysses S. Grant and other Republican presidents and Congresses continued the party's commitment to high tariffs despite complaints that the tariffs increased consumer prices at home by restricting imports and thereby relieving American manufacturers of the need to keep prices down. Farmers in the South and Midwest especially resented tariffs because, while they had to sell their crops in an open world market, they had to buy manufactured goods whose prices were artificially high because of tariffs.

During the Civil War, Congress passed other key economic legislation. The Legal Tender Act of 1862 authorized the federal government to issue paper money (greenbacks) to help pay for the war. Having a uniform paper currency across the nation was essential to a modern economy. To that end,

Homesteaders An African American family poses outside their log-and-sod cabin in 1889.

the National Banking Act (1863) created national banks authorized to issue greenbacks, which discouraged state banks from continuing to print their own money.

Congress also took steps to tie the new western states and territories into the national economy. The U.S. government owned vast amounts of western land, most of it acquired from the Louisiana Purchase of 1803, the Oregon Treaty with Britain in 1846, and the lands taken from Mexico in 1848 after the Mexican-American War.

In the Homestead Act of 1862, Congress provided, for free, 160-acre (or even larger) western homesteads to male citizens, widows, single women, immigrants pledging to become citizens, and formerly enslaved people. The only requirement was that they "improve" the land for five years and build a residence. By encouraging western settlement, the Homestead Act created markets for goods and services and spurred railroad construction to connect scattered frontier communities with major cities. More than 1.5 million White families—both American-born and immigrant—eventually benefited from the program (about 5,000 homesteads were given to African Americans, most of whom settled in groups called colonies rather than as isolated individuals). Farming on the often drought-stricken plains was not easy, however. About half the homesteads failed within a few years.

The Morrill Land-Grant College Act of 1862 transferred to each state 30,000 acres of federal land for each member of Congress the state had. The sale of those lands provided funds for states to create colleges of "agriculture and mechanic arts," such as Iowa State University and Kansas State University. The land-grant universities were created specifically to support economic growth by providing technical training needed by farmers and rapidly growing industries such as mining, steel, petroleum, transportation, forestry, and construction (engineering).

LAISSEZ-FAIRE Equally important in propelling the postwar economic boom was what governments did *not* do. There were no sweeping investigations of business practices, no legislation to protect workers and consumers, and no effective regulatory laws or commissions. Elected officials deferred to business leaders.

In general, Congress and presidents opposed government regulation of business and accepted the traditional economic doctrine of **laissez-faire**, a French phrase meaning "let them do as they will." Business leaders spent time—and money—ensuring that government officials stayed out of their businesses. For their part, politicians were usually eager to help the titans of industry in exchange for campaign contributions—or bribes.

A CHANGED SOCIAL ORDER

Industrialization transformed not only the economy and the workplace, but also the nation's social life. Class divisions became more visible. The growing gap between rich and poor was like "social dynamite," said the Reverend Josiah Strong in 1885. Massachusetts reformer Lydia Maria Child reported that the rich "do not intermarry with the middle classes; the middle classes do not intermarry with the laboring class," nor did different classes "mix socially."

THE WAYS OF THE WEALTHY The financiers and industrialists who came to dominate social, economic, and political life in post–Civil War America amassed so much wealth and showed it off so publicly that the period is still called the Gilded Age. To "gild" something is to cover it with a thin layer of gold, giving it the appearance of having greater value than it warrants. The name derived from a popular novel by Mark Twain and Charles Dudley Warner, *The Gilded Age: A Tale of Today,* which mocked the crooked dealings of political leaders and the business elite.

In 1861, the United States had only a few dozen millionaires. By 1900, there were more than 4,000. Most of them were White Protestants who voted

Nouveaux Riche Upper-class members of New York City society pose for a photograph at the James Hazen Hyde Ball on January 31, 1905.

Republican. A few were women, including Madam C. J. Walker (born Sarah Breedlove, the daughter of former Louisiana enslaved people), who created specialized hair products for African Americans.

Many of the nouveaux riches (French for "newly rich") became hoggishly self-indulgent. They gloried in "conspicuous consumption," competing to host the fanciest parties and live in the most extravagant houses. One tycoon gave a lavish dinner to honor his dog and presented the mutt with a $15,000 diamond necklace. At a party at New York's Delmonico's restaurant, guests smoked cigarettes wrapped in $100 bills.

When not attending parties, the rich were relaxing in mansions overlooking the cliffs at Newport, Rhode Island, atop Nob Hill in San Francisco, along Chicago's Lake Shore Drive and New York City's Fifth Avenue, and down the "Main Line" in suburban Philadelphia. "Who knows how to be rich in America?" asked E. L. Godkin, a magazine editor. "Plenty of people know how to get money, but . . . to be rich properly is, indeed, a fine art. It requires culture, imagination, and character."

A GROWING MIDDLE CLASS   In addition to a growing number of millionaires, the Gilded Age witnessed the rise of a *middle class*. The term had become commonplace by the 1870s, as more and more Americans came to view themselves as members of a distinct social class between the ragged and the rich.

Most middle-class Americans working outside the home were salaried employees of large businesses who made up a new class of what would later be called "white-collar" professionals: editors, engineers, accountants, supervisors, managers, marketers, and realtors. Others, mostly unmarried women, were clerks, secretaries, salespeople, teachers, and librarians.

During the 1870s, the number of office clerks quadrupled, and the number of accountants and bookkeepers doubled. At the same time, the number of attorneys, physicians, professors, journalists, nurses, and social workers also rose dramatically, although it remained a tiny percentage of the total. The number of women working for wages outside the home tripled between 1870 and 1900, when 5 million women (17 percent of all women) held full-time jobs. This development led one male editor to joke that he was being drowned "by the rising tide of femininity."

MIDDLE-CLASS WOMEN   The growing presence of middle-class women in the workforce partly reflected the increasing number of women gaining access to higher education. Dozens of women's colleges were founded after the Civil War, and many formerly all-male colleges began admitting

College Women By the end of the century, women made up more than a third of all college students. Here, an astronomy class at New York's Vassar College is underway in 1880.

women. By 1900, a third of college students were women. "After a struggle of many years," a New York woman boasted, "it is now pretty generally admitted that women possess the capacity to swallow intellectual food that was formerly considered the diet of men exclusively."

To be sure, college women were often steered into "home economics" classes and "finishing" courses intended to perfect their housekeeping or social skills. Still, the doors of the professions—law, medicine, science, and the arts—were at least partially opened to women during the Gilded Age.

In this context, then, the "woman question" that created so much public discussion and controversy in the second half of the nineteenth century involved far more than the issue of voting rights; it also concerned the liberation of at least some women from the home and from long-standing limits on their social roles. "If there is one thing that pervades and characterizes what is called the 'woman's movement,'" E. L. Youmans, a prominent science writer, remarked, "it is the spirit of revolt against the home, and the determination to escape from it into the outer spheres of activity."

Jane Addams Social worker Jane Addams exemplified the rising number of women eager to develop careers outside the home. After graduating in 1881 from Rockford College in Illinois, she found few opportunities to use her degree and lapsed into a state of depression, during which she developed an intense "desire to live in a really *living* world."

Addams's desire to engage "real life" eventually led her to found Hull House in Chicago, one of the first of many "settlement houses" in large cities intended to help immigrants make the transition to life in America. There, she and other social workers helped immigrants adapt to American life and mentored young women to "learn of life from life itself." Addams and others helped convince many middle-class women to enter the "real" world. By 1890, *Arena* magazine would urge progressive-minded people to recognize the traditional view of "women as homebodies" for what it was: "hollow, false, and unreal."

The Ladies' Home Journal   Many women, however, identified more with the domestic life that was the focus of numerous mass-circulation magazines, the most popular of which was the *Ladies' Home Journal*. By 1910, it had almost 2 million subscribers, the largest circulation of any magazine in the world. The magazine provided a "great clearing house of information" to the rapidly growing urban middle class, including sections on sewing, cooking, religion, politics, and fiction.

The Ladies' Home Journal Focusing on domestic life, *The Ladies' Home Journal* was the most popular magazine for middle-class women.

Edward Bok became editor of the *Ladies' Home Journal* in 1889, at age twenty-six. Bok was no activist for gender equality; "my idea," he stressed, "is to keep women in the home." There, he believed, they would maintain a high moral tone for society, for women were better, purer, conscientious, and morally stronger than men. Bok saw the middle-class woman as the "steadying influence" between the "unrest among the lower classes and [the] rottenness among the upper classes."

Bok's view of the ideal life for a woman included "a healthful diet, simple, serviceable clothing, a clean, healthy dwelling-place, open-air exercise, and good reading." He preached contentment rather than conspicuous consumption, a message directed not just to middle-class readers but also to the working poor. In a Christmas editorial, though, Bok recognized that "it is a hard thing for those who have little to believe that the greatest happiness of life is with them: that it is not with those who have abundance."

THE WORKING CLASS Railroads, factories, mills, mines, slaughterhouses, and s   hops had growing needs for unskilled workers, which attracted new gr   to the workforce, especially immigrants and women and children. In add⁺ion, millions of rural folk, especially young people, formed a migratory stream from the agricultural regions of the South and Midwest to cities and factories across the country.

The factory and mill towns were filthy places to live. The sprawling Carnegie steel mill made the town of Homestead, near Pittsburgh, a case in point. The hilly streets were mostly mudholes, the tiny homes rotting shacks, the air polluted with soot and stench. A British visitor commented, "If Pittsburgh is hell with the lid off, Homestead is hell with the hatches on. Never was a place more egregiously misnamed. Here there is nothing but unrelieved gloom and grind."

Although wages rose during the Gilded Age, there was a great disparity in the pay received by skilled and unskilled workers. During the economic recessions and depressions that occurred about every six years, unskilled workers were the first to be laid off or to have their wages slashed. In addition, working conditions were difficult and often dangerous for those at the bottom of the occupational scale. The average workweek was fifty-nine hours, or nearly six 10-hour days.

American industry had the highest rate of workplace accidents and deaths in the world, and there were virtually no safety regulations. Few machines had safety devices; few factories, mills, or sweatshops had fire escapes. Respiratory diseases were common in mines, textile mills, and unventilated buildings. Between 1888 and 1894, some 16,000 railroad workers were killed and 170,000 maimed in on-the-job accidents. By the end of the nineteenth century, the United States was the only industrial nation with no insurance program to cover medical expenses for on-the-job injuries.

Working Women Mills, mines, sweatshops, factories, and large businesses needed far more unskilled workers than skilled ones. Employers often recruited women and children for the unskilled jobs because they were willing to work for lower wages than men. In addition to operating sewing machines or tending to textile machines spinning yarn or thread, women worked as maids, cooks, or nannies. In the manufacturing sector, women's wages averaged $7 a week, compared to $10 for unskilled men.

Child Labor Young people had always worked in America; farms required everyone to pitch in. In the late nineteenth century, however, millions of children took up work outside the home, sorting coal, stitching clothes, shucking oysters, peeling shrimp, canning food, blowing glass, tending looms, and operating other kinds of machinery. Child labor increased as parents desperate for income put their children to work. By 1880, one of every six children under age fourteen was working full-time; by 1900, the United States had almost 2 million child laborers.

In Pennsylvania, West Virginia, and eastern Kentucky, soot-smeared boys worked in the coal mines. In New England and the South, children labored in dusty textile mills where, during the night shift, they had water thrown in their faces to keep them awake. In the southern mills, a fourth of the employees were below age fifteen, and children as young as eight often worked twelve hours a day, six days a week. As a result, they received little or no education. Children, women, and immigrants created an abundant supply of workers that enabled business owners to keep wages low. It also meant that managers and foremen viewed workers as replaceable. "I regard my people," one manager

Children in Industry These four young boys performed the dangerous work of mine helpers in West Virginia around 1900.

admitted, "as I regard my machinery. So long as they can do my work for what I choose to pay them, I keep them, getting out of them all I can."

Factories, mills, mines, and canneries were especially dangerous for children, who suffered three times as many accidents as adult workers and higher rates of respiratory diseases. A child working in a southern textile mill was only half as likely to reach the age of twenty as a child who did not.

ORGANIZED LABOR

The efforts of the working poor to form unions to improve their pay and working conditions faced formidable obstacles during the Gilded Age. Many executives fought against unions. They retaliated against union organizers by circulating their names to keep them from being hired, fired labor leaders, and often hired "scabs" (nonunion workers) to replace workers who went on strike. Another factor impeding the growth of unions was that many workers were immigrants who spoke different languages and often distrusted people from other ethnic groups. Nonetheless, with or without unions, workers began to stage strikes that often led to violence.

THE MOLLY MAGUIRES During the early 1870s, violence erupted in the eastern Pennsylvania coalfields, when a secret Irish American group called the Molly Maguires took economic justice into their own hands. The Mollies took their name from an Irish patriot who had led the resistance against the British. Outraged by dangerous working conditions in the mines and the owners' brutal efforts to suppress union activity, the Mollies used intimidation, beatings, and killings to avenge the wrongs done to Irish workers.

Their terrorism reached its peak in 1874–1875, prompting mine owners to hire men from the Pinkerton Detective Agency (commonly referred to as Pinkertons) to stop the movement. One of the agents who infiltrated the Mollies uncovered enough evidence to have the leaders indicted for the coalfield murders. In 1876, twenty-four Molly Maguires were convicted by a non-Irish jury; ten were hanged.

THE GREAT RAILROAD STRIKE (1877) After the financial panic of 1873, the major rail lines, fearful of a recession, had slashed workers' wages by 35 percent. By 1876, the entire economy had settled into a paralyzing depression. In July 1877, the companies announced another 10 percent wage cut, which led most of the Baltimore and Ohio (B&O) railroad workers at Martinsburg, West Virginia, to walk off the job and prevent others from replacing them. Their efforts shut down rail traffic. Initially, John Garrett, the president of the B&O, was confident the protest would quickly subside. Because "labor lacked unity," he commented, "strikes had easily been broken and the men easily replaced."

Garrett was wrong. The railroad strike spread to hundreds of other cities and towns. In San Francisco, local grievances led raging trainmen, who blamed Asians for taking White jobs, to set fire to Chinese neighborhoods. Across the nation, tens of thousands of railroad workers walked off the job, and the subsequent violence left more than 100 people dead, hundreds wounded, and millions of dollars in damaged property.

In Pittsburgh, thousands of striking workers upset at the arrival of soldiers (state militiamen mobilized by the governor) burned 39 buildings and destroyed more than 1,000 railcars and locomotives. The strikers also assaulted workers who refused to join them. Hundreds of looters—men, women, and children—risked their lives to grab anything of value from the freight cars before they were put to the torch. A huge crowd filled nearby hillsides and cheered as the Pennsylvania Railroad, "that damned monopoly," went up in flames. Local militiamen threw down their rifles in support of the strikers.

The Great Railroad Strike of 1877 was the first nationwide labor uprising, and it revealed how polarized the relationship between the working poor and company executives had become. Governors mobilized state militia units to suppress the rioters.

In Philadelphia, the militia dispersed a crowd at the cost of twenty-six lives, but looting and burning continued until President Rutherford B. Hayes dispatched federal troops to put down the "insurrection." It was the first time federal troops in large numbers had suppressed civilian strikers. Eventually the disgruntled workers, lacking organized bargaining power, had little choice but to return to work.

The strike had failed, but for many it raised the possibility of what a Pittsburgh newspaper saw as "a great civil war in this country between labor and capital." Many workers felt that violence was their only option. "The working people everywhere are with us," a unionist told a reporter. "They know what it is to bring up a family on ninety cents a day, to live on beans and corn meal week in and week out . . . until you cannot get trusted any longer, to see the wife breaking down . . . and the children growing sharp and fierce like wolves day after day because they don't get enough to eat."

Equally disturbing to those in positions of corporate and political power was the presence of many women among the protesters. A Baltimore journalist noted that the "singular part of the disturbances is the very active part taken by the women, who are the wives and mothers of the [railroad] firemen."

President Hayes wrote in his diary, "The strikes have been put down by *force*. But now for the *real* remedy. Can't something be done by education of the strikers, by judicious control of the capitalists, by wise general policy, to end or diminish the evil?" It was a fair question that largely went unanswered.

THE SAND-LOT INCIDENT In California, the national railroad strike indirectly gave rise to a working-class political movement. In 1877, a meeting held in a sandy San Francisco vacant lot to express sympathy for the railroad strikers ended with White laborers attacking Chinese workers who were passing by. In the so-called Sand-Lot Incident, the 105,000 mostly male Chinese living in the Far West were easy scapegoats for frustrated Whites who believed the Asians had taken their jobs.

Such anti-Chinese sentiment soon drove an Irish immigrant deliveryman in San Francisco, Denis Kearney, to organize the Workingmen's Party of California, whose platform called for the United States to stop Chinese immigration. Kearney lectured about the "foreign peril" and blasted the railroad barons for exploiting the poor. Although Kearney failed to build a lasting movement, his anti-Chinese theme became a national issue. In 1882, Congress voted to prohibit Chinese immigration for ten years.

"The Chinese Must Go" In this advertisement for the Missouri Steam Washer, the American-made machine drives the stereotype of the Chinese laundryman back to China, playing on the growing anti-Chinese sentiments in the 1880s.

THE NATIONAL LABOR UNION As the size and power of corporations increased, efforts to build a national labor union movement gained momentum. During the Civil War, because of the increased demand for skilled labor, so-called craft unions made up of workers expert at a particular handicraft or trade grew in strength and number. Yet there was no overall connection among such groups until 1866, when the National Labor Union (NLU) convened in Baltimore.

The NLU was more interested in improving workplace conditions than in bargaining about wages. The group promoted an eight-hour workday, workers' cooperatives (in which workers, collectively, would create and own their own large-scale manufacturing and mining operations), "greenbackism" (the printing of paper money to inflate the currency and thereby relieve debtors), and equal voting rights for women and African Americans.

Like most such organizations in the nineteenth century, however, the NLU did not allow women as members. It also discriminated against African American workers, who were forced to organize unions of their own. W. E. B. Du Bois, a prominent Black civil rights activist, charged that the "white worker did not want the Negro in his unions, did not believe in him as a man."

After the NLU's head, William Sylvis, died suddenly in 1869, its support declined, and by 1872 the union had disbanded. It was, however, influential in persuading Congress to enact an eight-hour workday for federal employees and to repeal the 1864 Contract Labor Act, which had been passed to encourage the importation of laborers by allowing employers to pay for the passage of foreign workers to America. In exchange, the workers were committed to work for a specified number of years. Employers had taken advantage of the Contract Labor Act to recruit foreign laborers willing to work for lower wages than their American counterparts.

THE KNIGHTS OF LABOR In 1869, another national labor group emerged: the Noble Order of the **Knights of Labor**. Even as trade unions collapsed during the depression of the 1870s, it grew rapidly.

The Knights of Labor endorsed most of the reforms advanced by previous workingmen's groups, including the elimination of convict-labor competition, the establishment of the eight-hour day, and the greater use of paper currency. One reform the group pursued was equal pay for equal work by men and women.

The Knights of Labor wanted to transform capitalism. "We do not believe," a Knights leader explained, "that the emancipation of labor will come with increased wages and a reduction in the [working] hours of labor; we must go deeper than that, and this matter will not be settled until the wage system is abolished."

The Knights of Labor did not believe in organizing members according to their particular trade. The organization allowed as members all who had ever worked for wages, except lawyers, doctors, bankers, those who sold liquor, and the Chinese, whom they viewed as "coolies." By recruiting all types of workers, Black or White, men or women, the Knights became the nation's largest labor union, but they also struggled with internal tensions.

In 1879, Terence V. Powderly, the thirty-year-old mayor of Scranton, Pennsylvania, became head of the Knights of Labor. He stressed winning political control of the communities where union workers lived, and the Knights owed their greatest growth to strikes that occurred under his leadership. In the early 1880s, they increased their membership from about 100,000 to more than 700,000. As Powderly explained, the Knights were the "connecting link between all branches of honourable toil."

MOTHER JONES   One of the most colorful labor agitators was a remarkable woman known simply as Mother Jones. Dressed in matronly black dresses and hats, she was a tireless champion of the working poor who used fiery rhetoric to excite crowds and attract attention. She rallied crowds, led marches, dodged bullets, confronted business titans and police, and served several jail terms, explaining that "I can raise more hell in jail than out." In 1913, a district attorney called her the "most dangerous woman in America" because she labeled capitalists "cannibalistic plutocrats" and "pirates," and called John D. Rockefeller the "greatest murderer the nation had ever produced." Coal miners and steel workers adored her.

Born in Cork, Ireland, in 1837, Mary Harris was the second of five children in a poor Catholic family that fled the Irish potato famine at midcentury and settled in Toronto. In 1861, she moved to Memphis, Tennessee, and began teaching. There, as the Civil War was erupting, she met and married George Jones, an iron molder and staunch union member. They had four children, but in 1867, disaster struck. A yellow fever epidemic devastated Memphis, killing Mary's husband and children.

The grief-stricken thirty-year-old widow moved to Chicago and took

Mother Jones The Irish-born teacher turned celebrated union activist and progressive is pictured here campaigning for the rights of workers at the White House in 1924.

up dressmaking, only to see her shop, home, and belongings destroyed in the Great Fire of 1871. Having lost her family and her finances, and angry at the social inequality and injustices she saw around her, Mary Jones drifted into the labor movement and found a new family—of workers. She soon emerged as a passionate advocate of union membership. Chicago was, at the time, the seedbed of labor radicalism, and the union culture nurtured in her a lifelong dedication to the cause of wage workers and their families.

Declaring herself the "mother" of the fledgling labor movement, she joined the Knights of Labor as an organizer and public speaker. In the late 1880s she became an ardent advocate for the United Mine Workers (UMW), various other unions, and the Socialist party. For the next thirty years, she crisscrossed the nation, recruiting union members, supporting strikers (her "boys"), raising funds, walking picket lines, defying court injunctions, berating politicians, and spending time in prison. She became a living legend. By 1900, Jones was the most famous woman in the labor union movement. "Whenever trouble broke out against the miners," a union leader explained, "Mother Jones went there."

Wherever Mother Jones went, she promoted higher wages, shorter hours, safer workplaces, and restrictions on child labor. During a miners' strike in West Virginia, she was arrested, convicted of "conspiracy that resulted in murder," and sentenced to twenty years in prison. The outcry over her plight helped spur a Senate committee to investigate conditions in the coal mines. The governor set her free.

In 1903, Mother Jones organized a highly publicized weeklong march of child workers from Pennsylvania to the New York home of President Theodore Roosevelt. The children were physically stunted and mutilated, most of them missing fingers or hands from machinery accidents. Roosevelt refused to see them, but, as Jones explained, "Our march had done its work. We had drawn the attention of the nation to the crime of child labor." Shortly thereafter, the Pennsylvania state legislature raised the legal working age to fourteen.

Mother Jones's commitment never wavered. At age eighty-three, she was arrested and jailed after joining a miners' strike in Colorado. At her funeral, in 1930, a speaker urged people to remember her famous rallying cry: "Pray for the dead and fight like hell for the living."

ANARCHISM One of the many challenges facing the labor union movement during the Gilded Age was growing hostility from middle-class Americans who viewed unionized workers, especially those involved in clashes with police, as violent radicals or anarchists. Anarchists believed that powerful capitalists bribed elected officials to oppress the working poor. They dreamed of the elimination of government altogether; some were willing to use bombs and bullets to achieve their goal.

Many European anarchists, mostly Germans or Italians, immigrated to the United States during the last quarter of the nineteenth century. Although most disavowed violence, the terrorists among them ensured that the label "anarchist" provoked frightening images in the minds of many Americans. Anarchists dreamed of labor unions replacing governments, enabling workers to rule.

Labor-related violence increased during the 1880s as the gap between the rich and working poor widened. Between 1880 and 1900, some 6.6 million hourly workers participated in more than 23,000 strikes nationwide. Chicago was a hotbed of unrest and a magnet for immigrants, especially German and Irish laborers, some of whom openly endorsed violence to ignite a working-class uprising. The Chicago labor movement's foremost demand was for an eight-hour workday.

THE HAYMARKET RIOT (1886)

What came to be called the **Haymarket Riot** grew indirectly out of prolonged agitation for the eight-hour workday. In 1886, some 40,000 Chicago workers went on strike in support of an eight-hour workday. On May 3, violent clashes between strikers and nonunion scabs hired to replace them erupted outside the McCormick Harvesting Machine Company plant. The police arrived, shots rang out, and two strikers were killed. The killings infuriated leaders of the anarchist movement, who organized a mass protest at Haymarket Square, near Chicago's city center, the following night, May 4.

The rally was peaceful, but the speeches were not. After listening to speakers complain about low wages and long working hours, the crowd of angry laborers was beginning to break up when more than a hundred police

The Haymarket Riot A leaflet advertising the protest at Haymarket Square in Chicago, an event that would be remembered as the Haymarket Riot. That the leaflet was printed in German and English testified to the large number of immigrants involved.

arrived and ordered them to disperse. At that point, someone threw a bomb into the ranks of blue uniforms that left dozens maimed or killed. The police then fired into the fleeing crowd, resulting in more casualties. Four workers and seven policemen were killed, and over a hundred more were wounded in what journalists called America's first terrorist bombing.

The next day, Chicago's mayor banned all labor meetings, and city officials banned the printing of anarchist newspapers. "There are no good anarchists except dead anarchists," the *St. Louis Globe-Democrat* raged. One New York newspaper demanded stern punishment for "the few long-haired, wild-eyed, bad-smelling, atheistic, reckless foreign wretches" who promoted such unrest.

During the summer of 1886, seven anarchist leaders, all but one of them German-language speakers, were sentenced to death despite the lack of evidence linking them to the bomb thrower, whose identity was never determined. After being sentenced to be hanged, Louis Lingg declared that he was innocent but was "in favor of using force" to end the abuses of the capitalist system.

Lawyers for the anarchists appealed the convictions to the Illinois Supreme Court, and petitioners from around the world appealed for clemency. One of the petitioners was Samuel Gompers, the founding president of the American Federation of Labor (AFL). "I abhor anarchy," Gompers stressed, "but I also abhor injustice when meted out even to the most despicable being on earth."

On November 10, 1887, Lingg committed suicide in his cell, using a dynamite blasting cap hidden in a cigar. That same day, the governor commuted the sentences of two convicted conspirators to life imprisonment. The next day, the four remaining condemned men were hanged.

One of those executed was Albert Parsons, an Alabama-born socialist-anarchist journalist and labor organizer, the only English-speaker among those convicted. Orphaned at age five, he had been raised by an enslaved person named Esther before joining his older brother in Texas. As a fifteen-year-old, he enlisted in his brother's Confederate unit, the Lone Star Grays, and fought in the Civil War. After the war, he reversed himself and championed "the political rights of the negro people" and the Republican party. He later joined the Socialist party and published a militant newspaper, *The Spectator*. Doing so earned him "idolization" from African Americans and death threats from White Texans who called him a scalawag traitor. He was shot in the leg, beaten, and threatened with lynching.

Such violent acts led Parsons to move to Chicago in 1873 with his wife Lucy, a former enslaved person who had become a women's rights activist and union organizer. In Chicago, Parsons joined the Knights of Labor and published *The Alarm*, a newspaper aimed at the working poor.

During the early 1880s, Albert and Lucy Parsons embraced anarchism, explaining that the movement "believes in peace, but not at the expense of liberty." Albert denounced all "political laws as violations of the laws of nature, and the rights of men." From his prison cell in 1886, he penned a message to his friends and followers: "Lay bare the inequities of capitalism; expose the slavery of law; proclaim the tyranny of government; denounce the greed, cruelty, abominations of the privileged class who riot and revel on the labor of their wage-slaves."

Some 200,000 people lined the streets of Chicago as the caskets of Parsons and the other condemned men were paraded before burial. To labor militants around the world, the executed anarchists were working-class martyrs; to the police and the economic elite in Chicago, they were demonic assassins.

THE COLLAPSE OF THE KNIGHTS OF LABOR After the Haymarket Riot, tensions between workers and management reached a fever pitch across the nation. In 1886 alone, there were 1,400 strikes involving 700,000 workers. But the violence in Chicago also triggered widespread hostility to the Knights of Labor and labor groups in general. Despite his best efforts, union leader Terence Powderly could never separate in the public mind the Knights from the anarchists, since one of those convicted of conspiracy in the bombing was a member of the union.

Powderly clung to leadership until 1893, but after that the union evaporated. Yet the Knights did attain some lasting achievements, including an 1880 federal law providing for the arbitration of labor disputes, and the creation of the federal Bureau of Labor Statistics in 1884. Another of their successes was the Foran Act of 1885, which, though poorly enforced, penalized employers who imported immigrant workers. By their example, the Knights spread the idea of unionism and initiated a new type of organization: the industrial union, which included all skilled and unskilled workers within a particular industry.

SAMUEL GOMPERS AND THE AFL The craft (or trade) unions, representing skilled workers, generally opposed efforts to unite with industrial unions. Leaders of the craft unions feared that doing so would mean the loss of their identity and bargaining power. Thus, in 1886, delegates from twenty-five craft unions organized the **American Federation of Labor (AFL)**. It was a federation of many separate national unions, each of which was largely free to act on its own in dealing with business owners.

Samuel Gompers served as president of the AFL from its founding until his death in 1924. Born in England, he came to the United States as a teenager, joined the Cigar Makers' Union in 1864, and became president of his New York City local union in 1877. Unlike Terence Powderly and the Knights of

Labor, Gompers focused on concrete economic gains—higher wages, shorter hours, and better working conditions.

The AFL at first grew slowly, but by the turn of the century, it claimed 500,000 members. In 1914, it had 2 million, and in 1920, it reached a peak of 4 million. But even then, the AFL included less than 15 percent of the nation's nonagricultural workers. In fact, all unions, including the so-called railroad brotherhoods that were unaffiliated with the AFL, accounted for little more than 18 percent of the total workforce.

Organized labor's strongholds were in transportation and the building trades. Most of the larger manufacturing industries—including steel, textiles, tobacco, and meatpacking—remained almost untouched. Gompers never opposed industrial unions, and several became important affiliates of the AFL: the United Mine Workers, the International Ladies' Garment Workers, and the Amalgamated Clothing Workers.

Two incidents in the 1890s stalled the emerging industrial-union movement: the **Homestead Steel Strike** of 1892 and the **Pullman Strike** of 1894. These conflicts represented a test of strength for the organized labor movement. They also served to reshape the political landscape.

THE HOMESTEAD STEEL STRIKE The Amalgamated Association of Iron and Steel Workers, founded in 1876, was the nation's largest craft union. At the massive steel mill owned by Andrew Carnegie at Homestead, Pennsylvania, along the Monongahela River near Pittsburgh, the union had enjoyed friendly relations with management until Henry Clay Frick became chief executive in 1889 and the company's second largest shareholder. The gruff and grim Frick, prone to explosive rages, prided himself on being the most anti-labor executive in the nation.

A showdown was delayed until 1892, however, when the union contract came up for renewal. Carnegie, who had previously expressed sympathy for unions, now wanted to destroy the union so that he would no longer have to negotiate with workers over wages and working conditions. As the battle loomed, Carnegie embarked on a lengthy hunting trip in Scotland, intentionally leaving Frick to handle the difficult negotiations.

Carnegie knew what was in the works: a cost-cutting reduction in the number of highly paid skilled workers through the use of labor-saving machinery, even though the corporation was enjoying high profits. It was a deliberate attempt to smash the union. "Am with you to the end," Carnegie wrote to Frick. William Jones, the mill manager, opposed cutting wages because "our men are working hard and faithfully. . . . Now, mark what I tell you. Our labor is the cheapest in the country."

The Homestead Steel Strike When steel-mill owner Andrew Carnegie and his lieutenant Henry Frick set out to destroy the union, workers went on strike to negotiate improved wages and working conditions.

Jones's protests did little good. As negotiations dragged on, Frick, knowing that the union would reject the latest company offer, announced on June 25 that negotiations with the 3,800 workers would end in four days unless an agreement was reached. A strike—or, more properly, a lockout in which management closed down the mill to force the union to make concessions—would begin on June 29. Frick told journalists that he was determined to have "absolute control of our plant and business."

Frick ordered construction of a twelve-foot-high fence crowned with barbed wire around the plant and equipped it with watchtowers, searchlights, rifle slits, and high-pressure water cannons. He also hired a private army of 316 Pinkerton National Detective Agency agents to protect "Fort Frick."

Before dawn on July 6, 1892, the "Pinkertons," most of them untrained recruits, floated up the Monongahela River on two barges pulled by a tugboat. Thousands of unionists and their supporters, many of them armed, were waiting on shore. A fourteen-hour gun battle ensued. Seven workers, six of whom were immigrants, and four Pinkertons were killed, and dozens were wounded. Hundreds of women on shore shouted, "Kill the Pinkertons!"

In the end, the Pinkertons surrendered and were marched away to beatings and taunts from crowds lining the streets. The next day, the *St. Louis Post*

Dispatch reported that "capital and labor have clashed at Homestead, and the town is red with blood."

The celebrations among workers were short-lived, however. A week later, the Pennsylvania governor dispatched 8,500 National Guard troops to Homestead, where they surrounded the mill and dispersed the picketing workers. Frick then hired strikebreakers to operate the mill. He refused to resume negotiations: "I will never recognize the union, never, never!" By July 18, the tide had turned completely against the strikers. Martial law—"bayonet rule," as the *New York Times* called it—was in force.

The strike dragged on until November, but by then the union was dead and its leaders had been charged with murder and treason. The union cause was not helped when Alexander Berkman, a Lithuanian anarchist, tried to assassinate Frick in his office on July 23, shooting him twice in the neck and stabbing him three times. Despite his wounds, Frick fought back fiercely and, with the help of staff members, subdued the would-be assassin.

After that incident, much of the sympathy for the strikers evaporated. As a union leader explained, Berkman's bullets "went straight through the heart of the Homestead strike." Penniless and demoralized, the workers ended their walkout on November 20 and accepted the company's harsh wage cuts. Only a fifth of the strikers got their jobs back; the names of the others were sent to other steel mills with a request not to hire them.

Carnegie and Frick, with the support of local, state, and national officials, had eliminated the union. After the Homestead strike, none of Carnegie's steel plants employed unionized workers. Within a few years, Carnegie could confide to a friend that he was "ashamed to tell you" how large his profits were from the Homestead plant.

But his reputation was ruined. "Three months ago Andrew Carnegie was a man to be envied," wrote a St. Louis newspaper. "Today he is an object of mingled pity and contempt." The editor called him a "moral coward." A "single word from him [in Scotland] might have saved the bloodshed—but the word was never spoken."

With each passing year, Carnegie nursed regrets about how Frick had handled the Homestead strike. In the end, Frick split with Carnegie after learning that his boss had been telling lies about him and making "insults" about his character. Frick told Carnegie that he had grown "tired of your business methods, your absurd newspaper interviews and personal remarks and unwarranted interference in matters you know nothing about." When Carnegie sought to reconcile with his former lieutenant, Frick told the messenger: "You can say to Andrew Carnegie that I will meet him in hell where we are both going."

THE PULLMAN STRIKE (1894) The Pullman Strike of 1894 paralyzed the economies of the twenty-seven states and territories in the western half of the nation. It involved a dispute at Pullman, Illinois, a "model" industrial suburb of Chicago owned by the Pullman Palace Car Company, which made long-distance passenger train cars (called Pullmans or sleeping cars).

Upon Pullman's opening in 1881, visitors saluted it as a picture-book example of modern city planning. A London newspaper proclaimed it "the most perfect city in the world."

Over time, however, many workers came to resent living under the thumb of the company's stubborn and stingy owner, George Pullman. Union organizers were not allowed to enter the town. Drinking and gambling were prohibited, and only one church, which everyone was required to attend, was built to serve all denominations. The model town was, according to a British visitor, "a paternal despotism." One embittered worker agreed: "We are born in a Pullman house, fed from the Pullman shops, taught in the Pullman school, catechized in the Pullman Church, and when we die, we shall go to the Pullman Hell."

During the depression of 1893, Pullman laid off 3,000 of his 5,800 employees and slashed wages 25 to 40 percent for the rest, but he did not lower his enormous salary or the rents charged for company housing or the price of food in the company store. He also fired workers who complained about the situation. In the spring of 1894, desperate Pullman workers voted to strike and secretly joined the American Railway Union (ARU), founded the previous year by Eugene V. Debs, the most powerful labor leader in the nation.

Debs was a child of working-class immigrants in Indiana. He had quit school at age fourteen to work for an Indiana railroad before becoming a union organizer. After serving in the state legislature, he became a tireless spokesman for labor radicalism, and he worked to organize all railway workers—skilled or unskilled—into the American Railway Union, which soon became a powerful example of his idea of "One Big Union."

Debs was impossible to dislike. Even his enemies acknowledged that he was a truly good person. His essential goodness prompted him to intervene in the Pullman controversy. He urged the angry workers to obey the laws and avoid violence. After George Pullman fired three members of a workers' grievance committee, the workers went on strike on May 11, 1894.

In June, after Pullman refused Debs's plea for a negotiated settlement, the Railway Union workers stopped handling trains containing Pullman railcars. By the end of July, they had shut down most of the railroads in the Midwest and cut off all traffic through Chicago. Supplies of milk and produce ran short in the city. Livestock couldn't reach the Union Stock Yards, the nation's chief source of meat products. To get the trains running again, railroad executives

The Pullman Strike Federal troops guarding the railroads, 1894.

hired strikebreakers, and the U.S. attorney general, swore in 3,400 special deputies to protect them. Yet angry workers still assaulted strikebreakers and destroyed property.

Finally, on July 3, President Grover Cleveland sent thousands of federal troops to the Chicago area, claiming it was his duty to ensure delivery of the mail. Meanwhile, railroad attorney Richard Olney, whom President Cleveland had named U.S. attorney general, convinced a federal judge to sign an *injunction* (an official court decree) prohibiting the labor union from interfering.

On July 13, the union called off the strike. A few days later, a court cited Debs for violating the injunction and sentenced him to six months in prison. While jailed, Debs became a hero to the workers. Upon his release, some 100,000 people braved a pouring rain to welcome him back to Chicago. While a prisoner, Debs had become a Socialist; he would run for president five times as the nominee of the Socialist party.

In 1897, George Pullman died of a heart attack, and the following year, the Illinois Supreme Court ruled that a company town was "incompatible with the theory and spirit of our institutions."

THE WESTERN FEDERATION OF MINERS At the same time that Eugene Debs was mobilizing a socialist-based working-class movement, militant labor leaders in the West were organizing the Western Federation of Miners (WFM). The WFM represented smelter workers and "hard rock" miners who worked deep underground harvesting copper, gold, silver, and lead in Montana, Colorado, Idaho, Utah, and the Dakotas.

Almost from its birth in 1883 in Butte, Montana, the WFM was viewed as a radical labor union. The Western Federation was at the center of violent confrontations with unyielding mine operators who mobilized secret spies, private armies, state militias, and even federal troops against it.

That several dozen miners were killed in clashes with management helps explain why the WFM grew especially militant. At its 1901 convention, it was proclaimed that a "complete revolution of social and economic conditions" was "the only salvation of the working classes." WFM leaders demanded the abolition of the wage system. By the spring of 1903, the WFM was the most militant labor organization in the country.

The group's most outspoken leader was one-eyed William "Big Bill" Haywood. Born in Salt Lake City, Utah, he went to work in the Nevada silver mines at age nine. He later was a homesteader and surveyor before becoming a socialist miner and joining the union in 1896; by 1902, he was its primary spokesman, featuring a face "like a scarred battlefield."

Haywood and the WFM promoted industrial unionism, recruiting both skilled and unskilled workers. The organization also welcomed members of all races and ethnic groups—men and women. Perhaps most controversial was Haywood's advocacy of strikes over negotiations, a militant stance that few other unions adopted.

THE INTERNATIONAL WORKERS OF THE WORLD (IWW)

In 1905, Big Bill Haywood, Eugene Debs, Daniel De Leon (head of the Socialist Labor party), Mother Jones, Lucy Parsons, and two dozen other prominent socialists and union leaders met secretly in Chicago to form the International Workers of the World (IWW). It would be a giant global "revolutionary labor union" ("One Big Union") open to all workers, skilled or unskilled, man or woman, child or adult, native or immigrant, Black or White—as long as they renounced capitalism. Their purpose was to provide an alternative to the American Federation of Labor, which excluded unskilled laborers.

The "Wobblies," as IWW members were called, sought to destroy the capitalist system and replace it with workers' unions (syndicates) that would elect their workplace managers. De Leon argued that the IWW "must be founded on the class struggle" and "the irrepressible conflict between the capitalist class and the working class." The Wobblies were disproportionately members of the working poor: immigrants and migrant workers, the unskilled and unorganized, the unrepresented and the unwanted. Not surprisingly, the IWW generated intense criticism. The *Los Angeles Times,* for example, claimed that a "vast number of IWWs are non-producers. IWW stands for I won't work, and I want whisky. . . . The average Wobbly, it must be remembered, is a sort of half wild animal. He lives on the road, cooks his food in rusty tin cans . . . and sleeps in 'jungles,' barns, outhouses, freight cars. . . . They are all in all a lot of homeless men wandering about the country without fixed destination or purpose, other than destruction."

Like other radical groups, the IWW was split by sectarian disputes. Debs and De Leon withdrew because the IWW refused to affiliate with their rival socialist parties.

William "Big Bill" Haywood held the IWW together, recruiting tens of thousands of new members from lumberyards, farms, and factories. Tall and muscular, he commanded attention and respect. He despised the AFL and its conservative labor philosophy. Samuel Gompers, he claimed, was "a squat specimen of humanity" with "small snapping eyes, a hard cruel mouth," and a personality that was "vain, conceited, petulant and vindictive." Instead of following Gompers's advice to organize only skilled workers, Haywood persisted in his dream of an all-inclusive union dedicated to a socialism "with its working clothes on."

Haywood and the Wobblies, however, recruited members with the least power and influence, chiefly migrant workers in the West and immigrants

International Workers of the World Strike Members of the International Workers of the World union went on strike against a textile mill in Lawrence, Massachusetts, for wage increases and overtime pay in 1912.

in the East. Always ambivalent about diluting their revolutionary principles, Wobblies scorned the usual labor agreements even when they participated in them. They engaged in spectacular battles with employers but scored few victories while arousing hysterical opposition. They were branded anarchists, bums, and criminals.

The largest and most successful IWW strike was against a textile mill in Lawrence, Massachusetts, in 1912, when the owners announced an across-the-board cut in wages. Haywood and others, including young Elizabeth Gurley Flynn, the "Joan of Arc of the working class," forged an unlikely coalition of thousands of mostly immigrant women workers. Their ranks included Italians, Germans, French Canadians, Poles, Lithuanians, Russians, Greeks, as well as those from a dozen other countries. Representing almost half the mill's workforce, the strikers spoke as many as fifteen different languages.

The IWW organizers shrewdly captured public support by portraying the strike as a plea for basic human rights. As Flynn insisted, "Better to starve fighting than to starve working!" Striking mill girls carried picket signs announcing: "WE WANT BREAD AND ROSES TOO." The strikers won the fight, as the owners of the American Woolen Company agreed to wage increases, overtime pay, and other benefits. "Labor has seldom, if ever, won so complete a victory," journalist Lincoln Steffens wrote in the *New York Globe*.

ECONOMIC SUCCESS AND CORRUPTION   For all the stress and strain caused by swift industrialization and labor union responses, American productivity soared in the late nineteenth century. By 1900, the United States was producing a third of the world's goods, and millions of immigrants continued to risk all in hopes of chasing the American dream. Corporate empires generated enormous fortunes for a few and real improvements in the quality of life for many. The majority of workers now labored in factories and mines rather than on farms.

The urban-industrial revolution and the gigantic new corporations it created transformed the size, scope, and power of the American economy, for good and for ill. As the twentieth century dawned, an unregulated capitalist economy had grown corrupt and recklessly out of balance—and only government intervention could restore economic fairness and social stability.

CHAPTER REVIEW

SUMMARY

- **The Causes of Industrial and Agricultural Growth**   During the late nineteenth century, agricultural and industrial production increased sharply. The national railroad network increased to nearly 200,000 miles, the most of any nation in the world. Farmers and industrialists expanded their production for both national and international markets. The *Second Industrial Revolution* saw the expanded use of electrical power, the application of scientific research to industrial processes, and other commercial innovations that brought new products to market and improved methods for producing and distributing them.

- **The Rise of Big Business**   Many businesses transformed themselves into limited-liability corporations and grew to enormous size and power in this period, often ignoring ethics and the law in doing so. Leading entrepreneurs like John D. Rockefeller, Andrew Carnegie, and J. Pierpont Morgan were extraordinarily skilled at organizing and gaining control of particular industries. Companies such as Rockefeller's *Standard Oil* and *Carnegie Steel* practiced both vertical and horizontal integration. To consolidate their holdings and get around laws prohibiting *monopolies*, they created *trusts* and eventually *holding companies* in an effort to bring "order and stability" to the marketplace. *J. Pierpont Morgan and Company*, the largest of the new "investment banks," focused on raising capital to enable mega-mergers of large companies.

- **The Alliance of Business and Politics**   The federal government encouraged economic growth after the Civil War by imposing high tariffs on imported products, granting public land to railroad companies and settlers in the West, establishing a stable currency, and encouraging the creation of land-grant universities to spur technical innovation and research. Equally important, local, state, and federal governments made little effort to regulate the activities of businesses. This *laissez-faire* policy allowed entrepreneurs to experiment with new methods of organization but also created the conditions for rampant corruption and abuses.

- **A Changed Social Order**   The huge fortunes of the Gilded Age flowed to a few prominent families, and social class tensions worsened as productivity increased. Business owners and managers showed little concern for workplace safety, and accidents and work-related diseases were common. Industrialization and the rise of Big Business also increased the number of people considering themselves part of the middle class. Middle-class women increasingly went to college, took business and professional jobs, and participated in other public activities despite male resistance.

- **Organized Labor**   It was difficult for unskilled workers to organize effectively into unions, in part because of racial and ethnic tensions among laborers, language barriers, and the efforts of owners and supervisors to undermine unionizing efforts. Business owners often hired strikebreakers, usually immigrant workers who were willing to take jobs at the prevailing wage out of desperation. Business owners often relied on the support of political leaders, who would mobilize state and local militias and federal troops against strikers. Nevertheless, several unions did organize and advocate for workers' rights at a national level, including the *Knights of Labor*. After the violence associated with the *Haymarket Riot* (1886), the *Homestead Steel Strike* (1892), and the *Pullman Strike* (1894), many Americans grew fearful of unions and viewed them as politically radical. Craft unions made up solely of skilled workers became more successful at organizing, such as the *American Federation of Labor*.

CHRONOLOGY

1859	First well to strike oil in Titusville, Pennsylvania
1861	Congress creates the Morrill Tariff
1869	First transcontinental railroad is completed at Promontory Summit, Utah
1876	Alexander Graham Bell patents his telephone
1876	Thomas A. Edison invents the first durable incandescent lightbulb
1880s	Widespread use of electrical power begins
1882	John D. Rockefeller organizes the Standard Oil Trust
1886	Haymarket Riot
1886	American Federation of Labor is organized
1892	Homestead Steel Strike
1894	Pullman Strike
1901	J. Pierpont Morgan creates the U.S. Steel Corporation

KEY TERMS

Second Industrial Revolution p. 761

Standard Oil Company p. 776

monopoly p. 777

trust p. 778

holding company p. 778

Carnegie Steel Company p. 779

J. Pierpont Morgan and Company p. 780

laissez-faire p. 784

Knights of Labor p. 794

Haymarket Riot (1886) p. 797

American Federation of Labor p. 799

Homestead Steel Strike (1892) p. 800

Pullman Strike (1894) p. 800

INQUIZITIVE

Go to InQuizitive to see what you've learned—and learn what you've missed—with personalized feedback along the way.

17 The New South and the New West

1865–1900

The American West Cowboys, some of whom learned their herding skills from Spanish-speaking cowboys called vaqueros, working together to tame a small herd of wild horses.

A fter the Civil War, the devastated South and the untamed, undeveloped West were the most distinctive regions of the nation. Both eluded mapping or measuring, for they resided within powerful myths as much as physical regions. As southerners streamed across the Mississippi River into the Great Plains and Far West after the Civil War, they brought with them strongly held beliefs of White racial superiority, a male-dominated gender hierarchy, and the individual's "right" to resist federal government authority.

Both regions also provided enticing frontiers for personal enterprise and economic opportunity. The South had to be rebuilt, while the sparsely settled territories and states west of the Mississippi River were ripe for the development of farms, businesses, railroads, and towns. Bankers and financiers in America and Europe invested heavily in both regions, but the economic opportunities in the Far West—between the Mississippi River and California—were considered especially lucrative.

Many Americans had long viewed the Great Plains as suitable only for Indians. After 1865, however, the federal government encouraged western settlement and economic development in what was called Indian Country. Two thirds of Native Americans in 1865 still lived on the Great Plains. Free land and the possibility of finding gold or silver or starting a business or a farm

focus questions

1. In what ways did the "New South" emerge in the late nineteenth century?

2. What was the "crop-lien" system in the South? How did it shape the lives of poor farmers after the Civil War?

3. How and why did White southerners adopt Jim Crow segregation laws and take away African Americans' right to vote at the end of the nineteenth century?

4. Who were the various groups of migrants to the West after the Civil War? How and why did they move there?

5. What were the experiences of miners, farmers, ranchers, cowboys, women, and Mexican Americans in the West in the late nineteenth century?

6. How did the federal government's post–Civil War policies in the West affect Native Americans?

7. How did the South and West change by 1900?

lured millions westward. The western economy focused on farming, ranching, and extractive industries: mining, timber, and oil.

THE MYTH OF THE NEW SOUTH

While White conservatives in the postwar South were reasserting their political control and reinforcing White supremacy, novelists, poets, and former Confederate leaders were fashioning what came to be called the *Lost Cause* narrative, a sanitized version of history in which the romanticized Confederacy could do no wrong in the face of the "War of Northern Aggression."

Nostalgic apologists for secession glamorized the old plantation culture and insisted that secession and the Civil War had little to do with slavery and everything to do with a noble defense of states' rights and the efforts of southerners to stop the aggressions of tyrannical Republicans and abolitionists.

Idolizing the Confederacy Over 100,000 people assembled to celebrate the statue of General Robert E. Lee in Richmond, Virginia, at its unveiling on Memorial Day 1890.

The Lost Cause myth portrayed African Americans as preferring slavery over freedom. For example, a story written by a White southerner in 1893 featured a Black character named Little Mammy who "grieved, as she crept down the street, that she had never mounted the auctioneer's block" to be sold into blessed slavery. Likewise, as Jefferson Davis claimed in 1881, the enslaved had been "contented with their lot" in 1861. He went on to claim that President Abraham Lincoln, however, had hoodwinked those in bondage into believing they would be better off free and "sent them out to devastate their benefactors [owners]."

The Lost Cause myth also demonized abolitionists and idealized the leadership of Confederate generals Robert E. Lee ("the soldier who walked with God") and Stonewall Jackson, deifying them as chivalrous pillars of southern virtue who fought bravely and ethically against far larger Union armies led by ruthless outlaws such as Ulysses S. Grant and William T. Sherman.

To reinforce this reimagining of southern history, communities erected scores of monuments and memorials glorifying Confederate leaders. For example, on Memorial Day 1890, some forty years after the southern states seceded and formed the Confederacy, more than 100,000 people gathered in Richmond, Virginia, to celebrate the unveiling of a massive statue of General Lee seated on his celebrated warhorse, Traveller.

What the speakers at the event failed to mention was that Lee, before his death in 1871, had urged southerners *not* to create such memorials to a cause that was "lost" on the battlefields.

No region has inspired a more tenacious pride of place than the South. *Home* and *history* are two of the region's most revered words. Nineteenth-century southerners did not simply live in the present and dream of the future. They were forever glancing backward. As William Faulkner recognized in his novel *Intruder in the Dust* (1948), "the past for southerners isn't dead. It's not even past."

Some prominent southerners, however, rejected the mythology of the Lost Cause. They called for a *New South* to replace the dominant planter elite and slave-based agricultural economy of the Old South with a more demo-cratic society of small farms owned by Blacks and Whites. The New South envisioned by its promoters would also boast a growing industrial sector, and race relations would become harmonious.

The champion of the New South ideal was Henry Woodfin Grady, the powerful editor of the *Atlanta Constitution* newspaper. In 1886, Grady told a New York City audience he was glad that the Confederacy lost and that slavery was abolished. The Old South was dead, but there "is now a New South of union and freedom—that South, thank God, is living, breathing, and growing every hour."

Grady claimed that the New South was becoming "a perfect democracy" of small farms complemented by mills, mines, factories, and cities. The postwar South, he predicted, would no longer be dominated by the planter aristocracy or dependent upon cotton and the labor of the enslaved. No section of the nation "shows a more prosperous laboring population than the Negroes of the South; none in fuller sympathy with the employing and land-owning class." Without acknowledging his exaggeration, he insisted that the "relations of the Southern people with the Negro are close and cordial."

Many southerners shared Grady's progressive vision. The Confederacy, they concluded, had lost the war because it had relied too much on King Cotton—and slavery. In the future, the South needed to follow the North's example ("out-Yankee the Yankees") and develop a strong industrial sector to go with its agricultural foundation. New South advocates also stressed that more-efficient farming and widespread vocational training were urgently needed. At the same time, however, they asserted that Blacks would see faster economic progress if they accepted the tradition of White supremacy.

DEVELOPING A TEXTILE INDUSTRY The chief accomplishment of the New South's effort to industrialize was a dramatic expansion of the region's textile industry, which produced cotton thread, bedding, and clothing. From 1880 to 1900, the number of red-brick cotton mills in the South grew from 161 to 400, the number of mill workers (mostly Whites, with women and children outnumbering men) increased fivefold, and the demand for cotton products rose eightfold. By 1900, the South had surpassed New England as the largest producer of cotton fabric in the nation.

Thousands of dirt-poor farm folk—many of them children—rushed to take jobs in the mills. Seventy percent of mill workers were younger than twenty-one, and many were under fourteen. A dawn-to-dusk job in a mill paying 50¢ a day "was much more interesting than one-horse farming," noted one worker, "because you can meet your bills." Those bills were usually paid to the mill owner, who, like a feudal baron, provided housing, food, and supplies to the workers in his village—for a fee.

Over time, mill owners hired and paid the village schoolteachers, doctors, and ministers. They organized dances and concerts and created sports leagues. Their paternalistic social system was in part intended to create a sense of community so strong that workers would never be tempted to organize labor unions. By 1900, the South remained the least unionized region in the nation.

THE TOBACCO INDUSTRY Tobacco growing and cigarette production also soared. Essential to the rise of the tobacco industry was the Duke family of Durham, North Carolina. At the end of the Civil War, Washington Duke, a Confederate soldier, was released from a federal military prison in Richmond, Virginia, and taken to New Bern, on the North Carolina coast. Having no money or means of transport, he walked 135 miles to his farm near Durham.

There was no future in "dirt farming," Duke decided, so he began growing tobacco with the help of his two sons. After harvesting the tobacco, they dried it, hitched two mules to a wagon, and traveled across the state, selling tobacco in small pouches. By 1872, W. Duke & Sons was producing 125,000 pounds of tobacco annually. Now prosperous, Washington Duke moved his family to Durham and built a tobacco factory on Main Street, near the rail station.

Washington's son, James Buchanan "Buck" Duke, wanted even greater success, however. He focused on transforming tobacco into cigarettes, using immigrants from eastern Europe to roll each cigarette by hand. The best of them could roll four cigarettes a minute. Over time, however, that was not fast enough to keep up with demand, so Buck Duke perfected the mechanized mass production of cigarettes.

By 1885, W. Duke, Sons and Company was the leading cigarette producer in the country. Duke undersold competitors and cornered the supply of ingredients needed to make cigarettes. In 1890, he forced his four largest competitors to join him in creating the **American Tobacco Company**, which controlled nine tenths of the nation's cigarette production. The new enterprise came to be called the Tobacco Trust, because it exercised monopoly control of the tobacco industry.

Southern Smokes W. Duke, Sons & Company used its cigarette packaging as a form of advertisement to increase sales.

OTHER NEW SOUTH INDUSTRIES Effective use of other natural resources also helped revitalize the South. Along the Appalachian mountain chain from West Virginia to Alabama, coal production soared from 5 million tons in 1875 to 49 million tons by 1900. At the southern end of the mountains, Birmingham, Alabama, sprang up in large part because of the massive deposits of iron ore in the surrounding ridges, leading boosters to label the steelmaking city the "Pittsburgh of the South."

Urban and industrial expansion as well as rapid population growth created a need for housing. In response to the demand, logging and lumber production became the fastest-growing industry in the South after 1870. Northern investors bought vast forests of yellow pine and set about clear-cutting them and hauling the logs to new sawmills, where they were milled into lumber for the construction of homes and businesses.

By 1900, southern lumber had surpassed textiles in annual economic value. Still, for all its advances, the New South continued to lag behind the rest of the nation in industrial development, educational attainment, and per capita income.

THE REDEEMERS Henry Grady's vision of a New South celebrated the redeemers, the conservative, pro-business, White politicians in the Democratic party who had embraced the idea of industrial progress grounded in White supremacy. Their supporters referred to them as redeemers because they supposedly saved (redeemed) the South from Yankee domination, and what they called Black rule, during Reconstruction.

The redeemers included lawyers, merchants, railroad executives, and entrepreneurs who wanted a more diversified economy. They also sought cuts in state taxes and expenditures, including those for public-school systems started after the war. "Schools are not a necessity," claimed a Virginia governor. Black children, in particular, suffered from such cutbacks. The redeemers did not want educated African Americans. "What I want here is Negroes who can make cotton," explained a White planter, "and they don't need education to help them make cotton."

THE FAILINGS OF THE NEW SOUTH

Despite the development of mills, mines, and factories, the South in 1900 remained the least industrial, least urban, least educated, and least prosperous region in the nation. Per capita income in the South was only 60 percent of the national average. The typical southerner was less likely to be tending a textile loom or a steel furnace than, as the saying went, facing the eastern end of a westbound mule while plowing a field. The South was still dependent upon the North for investment capital and manufactured goods.

Cotton remained king after the Civil War, even though it never regained the huge profitability it had generated in the 1850s. By the 1880s, southern farmers, Black and White, were producing as much cotton as before the war, but they were earning far less money for it because the world price for cotton had declined sharply.

SOUTHERN POVERTY Henry Grady also hoped that growing numbers of southern farmers would own their own land by the end of the nineteenth century, but the opposite occurred. Many southern farmers *lost* ownership of the land they worked. The prolonged decline in crop prices made it more difficult than ever to buy and own land.

Because most southern communities had no banks after the Civil War, people had to find ways to operate with little or no cash. Many rural areas adopted a barter economy in which a local "crossroads" or "furnishing" merchant would provide food, clothing, seed, fertilizer, and other items to poor farmers "on credit" in exchange for a share (or lien) of their crops when harvested.

CROP-LIEN SYSTEM   Farmers, White and Black, who participated in the **crop-lien system** fell into three distinct categories: small farm owners, sharecroppers, and tenants. The farms owned by most southerners were small and did not generate much cash income. As a result, even those who owned farms had to pledge a portion of their future crop to the local merchant in exchange for supplies, clothing, and food purchased on credit.

Sharecroppers, poor Blacks and Whites who had nothing to offer a farm owner but their labor, worked the owner's land in return for shelter in a small cabin, seed, fertilizer, mules, supplies, and food. They also had to "share" a portion of their crop with the landowner. Share tenants, mostly White farmers who were barely better off than sharecroppers, might have their own mule or horse, a plow and tools, and a line of credit with the country store, but they still needed to rent land to farm. A few paid their rent in cash, but most, like sharecroppers, pledged a portion of the crop yield to the landowner. Usually, the tenant farmers were able to keep a larger share of the crop (about 60 percent) than the sharecroppers could, which meant that landowners often preferred to rent to "croppers" than to tenants.

"Free Slaves" African Americans painstakingly pick cotton while their White overseer observes them from atop his horse.

SHARECROPPING AND TENANCY, 1880–1900

Percentage of All Farmers, 1900
- Over 55 percent
- 40–55 percent
- 20–39 percent
- Under 20 percent

Increase in Percentage of Tenants and Sharecroppers between 1880 and 1900
- ● Over 10 percent
- ◗ 7–10 percent
- ◡ Under 7 percent
- ○ Decrease

- Why was there a dramatic increase in sharecropping and tenancy in the late nineteenth century?
- Explain why the South had more sharecroppers than other parts of the country.

Many African American sharecroppers worked for the same planter who had owned them when they had been enslaved. "The colored folks," said a Black Alabama sharecropper, "stayed with the old boss man and farmed and worked on the plantations. They were still slaves, but they were free slaves." Eighty percent of southern Blacks lived on farms in the late nineteenth century.

The crop-lien system was self-destructive. Its focus on planting cotton or tobacco year after year stripped the soil of its fertility and stability and led to disastrous erosion of farmland during rainstorms. Topsoil washed into nearby creeks, collapsing riverbanks and creating ever-deepening gullies. In addition, landowners required croppers and tenants to grow a "cash crop" exclusively, usually cotton or tobacco. By permitting only these cash crops, landowners prevented croppers and tenants from growing their own vegetable gardens; they had to get their food from the local merchant in exchange for promised cotton.

Because most farmers did not own the land they worked, the cabins they lived in, or the tools they used, they had little incentive to enrich the soil or maintain buildings and equipment. "The tenant," explained a study of southern agriculture in 1897 written by economist Matthew B. Hammond, "is interested only in the crop he is raising, and makes no effort to keep up the fertility of the land." The tenant system of farming, Hammond concluded, had been "more wasteful and destructive than slavery was anywhere."

The crop-lien system was a post–Civil War version of economic slavery for poor Whites as well as Blacks. The landowner or merchant (often the same person) decided what crop would be planted and how it would be cultivated, harvested, and sold. In good times, croppers and tenants barely broke even; in bad times, they struggled to survive. Sharecroppers and share tenants were among the poorest people in the nation. Most had little or no education, rarely enough food, and little hope for a better future.

Those who worked the farms developed an intense suspicion of their landlords, who often swindled them by not giving them their fair share of the crops. Landowners kept the books, handled the sale of crops, and gave the croppers or tenants their share of the proceeds after deducting for all the items supplied during the year, plus interest that ranged, according to one newspaper, "from 24 percent to grand larceny." Often, the cropper or tenant received nothing but a larger debt to be rolled over to the next year's crop. Over time, the high interest charged on the credit offered by the local store or landowner, coupled with sagging prices received for cotton and other crops, created a hopeless cycle of debt among small farmers, sharecroppers, and share tenants.

FALLING COTTON PRICES As cotton production soared during the last quarter of the nineteenth century, largely because of dramatic growth in Texas cultivation, the price paid for raw cotton fell steadily. "Have you all felt the effects of the low price of cotton?" Mary Parham of Amite, Louisiana, wrote to her father in 1892. "It nearly ruined us. I did not get my house built. The farmers are very blue here. But [they are] getting ready to plant cotton again." As the price of cotton dropped, desperate farmers planted even more cotton, which only accelerated the decline in price even more.

RACE RELATIONS DURING THE 1890S

The plight of southern farmers in the 1880s and 1890s affected race relations—for the worse. During the 1890s, White farmers and politicians demanded that Blacks be stripped of their voting rights and other civil rights. What northern observers called "Negrophobia" swept across the South and much of the nation.

In part, the resurgent wave of racism represented a revival of the idea that the Anglo-Saxon "race" of Whites, who originated in Germany and spread across western Europe and Great Britain, was intellectually and genetically superior to Blacks. Another reason was that many Whites had come to resent any signs of African American financial success and political influence. An Alabama newspaper editor reported that "our blood boils when the educated Negro asserts himself politically."

DISENFRANCHISING AFRICAN AMERICANS By the 1890s, a new generation of African Americans born and educated since the Civil War was determined to gain complete equality. They were more assertive and less patient than their parents. "We are not the Negro from whom the chains of slavery fell a quarter century ago, most assuredly not," a Black editor announced. A growing number of young White adults, however, were equally determined to keep all "Negroes in their place."

Mississippi took the lead in stripping Blacks of their voting rights. The so-called **Mississippi Plan (1890)**, a series of amendments to the state constitution, set the pattern of disenfranchisement that nine more southern states would follow. The Mississippi Plan of 1890 disenfranchised and disarmed most African Americans by erecting barriers to gun ownership as well as voter registration. Although written in race-neutral language, the new laws in practice were focused on Blacks.

The Mississippi Plan instituted a residence requirement for voting—two years in the state, one year in a local election district—aimed at African American tenant farmers who were in the habit of moving each year in search of better economic opportunities. Second, Mississippi disqualified residents from voting if they had committed certain crimes. Third, in order to vote, people had to have paid all taxes on time, including a so-called poll tax specifically for voting—a restriction that hurt both poor Blacks and poor Whites. Finally, all voters had to be able to read or at least "understand" the U.S. Constitution. White registrars decided who satisfied this requirement, and they frequently discriminated against Blacks.

Other states seeking to restrict Black voting had variations on the Mississippi Plan. In 1898, Louisiana inserted into its state constitution the "grandfather clause," which allowed illiterate Whites to vote if their fathers or grandfathers had been eligible to vote on January 1, 1867, when African Americans were still disenfranchised. By 1910, Georgia, North Carolina, Virginia, Alabama, and Oklahoma had incorporated the grandfather clause.

Every southern state created a Democratic primary process to select candidates. Most of the primaries excluded African American voters, and rarely was a Republican vote cast. Hence, the overwhelmingly Democratic region came to be called the Solid South.

When such "legal" means were not enough to ensure their political dominance, White Democratic candidates turned to fraud and violence. Benjamin Tillman, the White supremacist who served as South Carolina's governor from 1890 to 1894, maintained that his state's problems were caused by White farmers renting their land to "ignorant lazy negroes." African Americans, Tillman argued, "must remain subordinate or be exterminated."

Such openly racist comments gained Tillman the support of poor Whites. To ensure his election as governor, he and his followers effectively eliminated the Black vote. "We have done our level best [to prevent Black people from voting]," he bragged. "We stuffed ballot boxes. We shot them. We are not ashamed of it."

By the end of the nineteenth century, widespread racial discrimination—segregation of public facilities, political disenfranchisement, and vigilante justice—had elevated government-sanctioned bigotry to an official way of life in the South. The efforts of Tillman and other White supremacists to suppress the Black vote succeeded. In 1896, Louisiana had 130,000 registered Black voters; by 1900, it had only 5,320. In Alabama in 1900, the census data indicated that 121,159 Black men were literate; only 3,742, however, were registered to vote. By that year, the number of Blacks voting across the South had declined by 62 percent, the White vote by 26 percent.

THE SPREAD OF SEGREGATION While southern Blacks were being shoved out of the political arena, they were also being segregated socially. The symbolic first target was the railroad passenger car. In 1885, novelist George Washington Cable noted that in South Carolina, Blacks "ride in first-class [rail] cars as a right" and "their presence excites no comment." Likewise, in New Orleans a visitor was surprised to find that "white and colored people mingled freely." From 1875 to 1883, in fact, any local or state law requiring racial segregation violated the federal Civil Rights Act.

In 1883, however, the U.S. Supreme Court ruled that the Civil Rights Act of 1875 was unconstitutional. In an 8–1 opinion written by Justice Joseph P. Bradley, the Court declared that neither the Thirteenth nor the Fourteenth Amendment gave Congress the authority to pass laws dealing with racial discrimination by private citizens or businesses. The judges explained that individuals and organizations could engage in acts of racial discrimination because the Fourteenth Amendment specified only that "no State" could deny citizens equal protection of the law.

Justice John Marshall Harlan offered a famous dissent to the Court's decision. A Kentuckian who had once owned slaves but had served in the Union army, he had opposed the emancipation of slaves and the Fourteenth and Fifteenth Amendments. After the war, however, the violent excesses of the Ku Klux Klan had convinced him to rethink his attitudes. He became a Republican in 1868 and was named to the Supreme Court by President Rutherford B. Hayes in 1877.

Harlan now argued that the Thirteenth and Fourteenth Amendments, as well as the Civil Rights Act of 1875, were designed to ensure African Americans the same access to public facilities that White citizens enjoyed. The federal government, he insisted, had both the authority and the responsibility to protect citizens from any actions that deprived them of their civil rights. To allow private citizens and enterprises to practice racial discrimination would "permit the badges and incidents of slavery" to remain.

The Court's interpretation in what came to be called the Civil Rights Cases (1883) left as an open question the validity of city and state laws requiring racially segregated public facilities under the principle of "separate but equal," a slogan popular in the South referring to the argument that racial segregation laws were legal as long as the segregated facilities were equal in quality.

Plessy v. Ferguson (1896) In the 1880s, Florida, Tennessee, Texas, and Mississippi required railroad passengers to ride in racially segregated cars. After Louisiana followed suit in 1890 with a similar law, Blacks challenged it in the case of *Plessy v. Ferguson* (1896). The case originated in New Orleans when anti-segregation activists convinced Homer Adolph Plessy, an "octoroon" (a racist term for a person having *one-eighth* African ancestry), to refuse to leave a Whites-only railroad car. Plessy was convicted of violating the law.

In arguments presented to the U.S. Supreme Court, Plessy's attorney contended that the Louisiana law sought "to debase and distinguish against the inferior race." He then asked the justices to imagine a future dictated by such statutes: "Was there any limit to such laws? Why not require all colored people to walk on one side of the street and Whites on the other?" The Court disagreed, ruling that states had a right to create laws segregating public places such as schools, hotels, and restaurants.

The only justice to dissent was again John Marshall Harlan, who stressed that the Constitution is "color-blind, and neither knows nor tolerates classes among citizens. In respect of civil rights, all citizens are equal before the law." He argued that the *Plessy* ruling violated both the Thirteenth and Fourteenth Amendments. The former "not only struck down the institution of slavery" but also "any burdens or disabilities that constitute badges of slavery or servitude." The Fourteenth Amendment "added greatly to the dignity and glory of American citizenship, and to the security of personal liberty. . . . The arbitrary separation of citizens, on the basis of race . . . is a badge of servitude wholly inconsistent with the civil freedom and the equality before the law established by the Constitution. It cannot be justified on any legal grounds."

Harlan feared that the Court's ruling would plant the "seeds of race hate" under "the sanction of law." That is precisely what happened. The *Plessy* ruling endorsed racially "**separate but equal**" facilities in virtually every area of southern life. In 1900, the editor of the *Richmond Times* insisted that racial segregation "be applied in every relation of Southern life. God Almighty drew the color line, and it cannot be obliterated. The negro must stay on his side of the line, and the White man must stay on his side, and the sooner both races recognize this fact and accept it, the better it will be for both."

Jim Crow Segregation The new regulations came to be called Jim Crow laws. The name derived from "Jump Jim Crow," a song-and-dance caricature of African Americans made popular in the 1830s by Thomas D. Rice, a White New York songwriter/dancer and comedian who performed in blackface

The Lynching of Henry Smith Despite lack of evidence, Smith was convicted of murdering a White girl in Paris, Texas. A large crowd assembled to watch her family torture Smith from a platform labeled "Justice." After Smith was burned alive, the townspeople kept his charred teeth and bones as souvenirs.

makeup. By the 1890s, the term *Jim Crow* had become a satirical expression meaning "Negro." Signs reading "Whites Only" or "Colored Only" above restrooms and water fountains emerged as hallmarks of the Jim Crow system of racial segregation.

Racist customs dating to before the Civil War were revived. If Whites walked along a sidewalk, Blacks were expected to step aside and let them pass. There were racially separate funeral homes, cemeteries, churches, and water fountains. When a White deacon in a Mississippi church saw a Black man in the sanctuary, he asked: "Boy, what you doin' in there? Don't you know this is a white church?" The Black man replied: "Boss, I'm here to mop the floor." The White man paused and said, "Well, that's all right then, but don't let me catch you prayin.'"

Widespread violence accompanied the Jim Crow segregation laws. From 1890 to 1899, the United States averaged 188 lynchings per year, 82 percent of which occurred in the South. Lynchings usually involved a Black man (or men) accused of a crime, often rape. White mobs would seize, torture, and kill the accused, often in ghastly ways. Large crowds, including women and children, would watch amid a carnival-like atmosphere. Photographs of gruesome lynchings surrounded by laughing and smiling Whites were reproduced on postcards mailed across the nation. Mississippi governor James Vardamann declared that "if it is necessary that every Negro in the state will be lynched, it will be done to maintain white supremacy."

THE WILMINGTON INSURRECTION (1898) In the late 1890s, a violent wave of White supremacy spread across the South. In North Carolina's largest city, the prosperous coastal port of Wilmington, Whites toppled the multiracial government in 1898.

In 1894 and 1896, Black voters, a majority in the city, had elected African Americans and White Republicans to various municipal offices. This infuriated the White supremacist elite, all of whom were Democrats. "We will never surrender to a ragged rabble of Negroes led by a handful of white cowards," warned Alfred "Colonel" Waddell, a former congressman and Confederate officer.

On the day before elections in 1898, Waddell urged a mob of 1,500 armed ex-Confederates, militiamen, and prominent Democrats to "do your duty" as White men: "This city, county and state shall be rid of Negro domination, once and forever. Go to the polls tomorrow and if you find the negro out voting, tell him to leave the polls. And if he refuses, kill him! Shoot him down in his tracks."

The crowd did as ordered. Whites rampaged through the polling places, forcing Blacks out at gunpoint and stuffing ballot boxes to ensure that White supremacist candidates won. The rioters, armed with rifles, pistols, and even

Wilmington Insurrection (1898) A mob of White supremacists pose with their rifles before the demolished printing press of the *Daily Record*, an African American newspaper.

a machine gun, destroyed the offices of the *Daily Record*, the Black-owned newspaper, and then moved into African American neighborhoods, where they killed sixty, wounded dozens, and destroyed homes and businesses. An out-of-town reporter marveled at the audacity of the White assault on the city government: "What they did was done in broad daylight."

The mob stormed city hall, announced that "negro rule" was over, named Waddell mayor, and forced African American officials and their White Republican allies to resign. They then pushed prominent Blacks onto northbound trains, warning them never to return.

More than 2,000 African Americans fled the state or were forced out at gunpoint. The self-declared White supremacist city government issued a "Declaration of White Independence" that stripped Blacks of their jobs and voting rights. Desperate Blacks appealed to the governor and to President William McKinley, but they received no help. No one was ever convicted of the crimes committed against the African American community.

The **Wilmington Insurrection (1898)** marked the first—and only—time that an elected municipal government had been forcibly overthrown in the United States. Mayor Waddell boasted that his racist followers had "set the pace for the whole South on the question of white supremacy."

Waddell and others convinced the state legislature to amend the constitution to create a poll tax and literacy test designed to disenfranchise Black voters. "The chief object" of the proposed amendments, said a Democratic pamphlet, "is to eliminate the ignorant and irresponsible Negro vote." Such techniques worked better than anyone predicted. In 1896, there were 125,000 African Americans registered to vote in North Carolina. By 1902, there were only 6,000. The state legislature went on to pass the state's first Jim Crow laws, segregating train cars by race. Laws mandating separate public toilets, water fountains, theaters, and parks soon followed.

THE BLACK RESPONSE TO SEGREGATION By the end of the nineteenth century, the rule of White supremacy had triumphed across the South. Some African Americans chose to leave in search of greater safety, equality, and opportunity. Those who stayed and resisted White supremacy— even in self-defense—were ruthlessly suppressed. When a White woman, Mrs. Pines, struck her Black maid, Sarah Barnett, with a stick, Barnett fought back. Infuriated, Pines's husband shot Barnett through the shoulder. She survived, only to be convicted of assault and jailed. Another Black domestic servant, Ann Beston, stabbed and killed her abusive mistress in Rome, Georgia. A mob lynched her.

Most African Americans had no choice but to adjust to the realities of White supremacy and segregation. "Had to walk a quiet life," explained James Plunkett, a Virginian. "The least little thing you would do, they [Whites] would kill ya." Survival required Black people to wear a mask of deference and discretion and to behave in a "servile way" when shopping at White-owned stores. News of lynchings, burnings, and beatings sent chilling reminders of the dangers they constantly faced.

Black novelist Richard Wright remembered how in his native Mississippi the "sustained expectation of violence" at the hands of Whites induced a "paralysis of will and impulse" in him and others. It unconsciously affected his speech, movements, and manners around Whites. "The penalty of death awaited me if I made a false move."

Yet accommodation to White supremacy and segregation did not mean surrender. African Americans constructed their own lively culture. Churches continued to provide an anchor for Black communities and were often the only public buildings Blacks could use for large gatherings, such as club meetings, political rallies, and social events. For men especially, churches offered leadership roles and political status. Being a deacon was one of the most prestigious roles a Black man could achieve. As in many White churches, men preached and governed church affairs; the women often did everything else.

Religious life provided great comfort to a people worn down by the daily hardships and abuses associated with segregation. As the Reverend Benjamin Mays explained, he and his Black neighbors in South Carolina "believed that the trials and tribulations of the world would be all over when one got to heaven. Beaten down at every turn by the White man, as they were, Negroes could perhaps not have survived without this kind of religion."

One irony of Jim Crow segregation was that it created new economic opportunities for African Americans. Black entrepreneurs emerged to provide essential services to the Black community—insurance, banking, barbering, funerals, hair salons. Black people also formed their own social and fraternal clubs and organizations, all of which provided fellowship, mutual support, and opportunities for service.

Middle-class African American women organized a network of social clubs that served as engines of community service across the South and the nation. They cared for the aged, infirm, orphaned, and abandoned; they provided homes for single mothers and nurseries for working mothers; and they sponsored health clinics and classes in home economics.

In 1896, the leaders of women's clubs created the National Association of Colored Women. The organization's first president, Mary Church Terrell, told the members they had an obligation to serve the "lowly, the illiterate, and even the vicious to whom we are bound by the ties of race and sex, and put forth every effort to uplift and reclaim them." Courageous African American women declared that Black men were not providing sufficient leadership. An editorial in the *Woman's Era* called for "timid men and ignorant men" to step aside and let the women show the way.

Others pursued legal recourse to improve their quality of life. Tennessean Callie Guy House launched a mass movement in the 1890s demanding pensions for former slaves. In 1897, she helped found the National Ex-Slave Mutual Relief, Bounty and Pension Association. Its proposals were modeled after the military pensions being paid to Union military veterans. House and others crisscrossed the southern states promoting pensions as "reparation" for the sin of slavery. By 1900, some 300,000 people had joined the organization.

Federal officials, however, opposed the pension idea. At the same time, the U.S. Post Office and Pensions Bureau harassed House and other officers of the group, falsely accusing them of mail fraud. House was arrested, tried, and sentenced to ten months in a federal prison. No pensions were ever paid to any formerly enslaved person.

Ida B. Wells One of the most outspoken African American activists was Ida B. Wells. Born into slavery in 1862 in Mississippi, she attended a school staffed by White missionaries. In 1880, she moved to Memphis, Tennessee, where she taught in segregated schools and gained entrance to the social life of the African American middle class.

Ida B. Wells A journalist and outspoken advocate of racial equality, Wells was a cofounder of the National Association for the Advancement of Colored People.

In 1883, after losing her seat on a railroad car because she was Black, Wells became the first African American to file a lawsuit challenging such discrimination. The circuit court decided in her favor and fined the railroad, but the Tennessee Supreme Court overturned the ruling. Wells thereafter discovered "[my] first and [it] might be said, my only love"—journalism—which she used to fight for justice. She became the fearless editor of *Memphis Free Speech,* a newspaper that focused on African American issues.

In 1892, after three of her friends were lynched by a White mob, Wells launched a crusade against lynching. "The more the Afro-American yields and cringes and begs," Wells argued, "the more he is insulted, outraged, and lynched." She described Memphis as a White-governed "town which will neither protect our lives and property, nor give us a fair trial in the courts, but takes us out and murders us in cold blood."

Angry Whites responded by destroying her office and threatening to lynch her. Wells countered by purchasing a pistol, for she "felt one had better die fighting against injustice than to die like a dog or a rat in a trap." Later, Wells moved briefly to New York and then settled in Chicago, where she continued to criticize Jim Crow laws and fought for the restoration of Black voting rights. "Somebody must show that the Afro-American race is more sinned against than sinning," she explained, "and it seems to have fallen upon me to do so."

Wells helped found the National Association for the Advancement of Colored People (NAACP) in 1909 and worked for women's suffrage. In promoting racial equality, she often found herself in direct opposition to Booker T. Washington, the most influential African American leader in the nation.

Booker T. Washington Booker T. Washington was born a slave in Virginia in 1856, the son of a Black mother and a White father. At sixteen he enrolled at Hampton Normal and Agricultural Institute, one of several colleges

created during Reconstruction specifically for newly emancipated African
Americans. There he met the school's
founder, Samuel Chapman Armstrong,
who preached moderation and urged
the students: "Be thrifty and industrious," "Command the respect of your
neighbors by a good record and a good
character," "Make the best of your difficulties," and "Live down prejudice."
Washington listened and learned.

Nine years later, Armstrong received
a request from a group in northern
Alabama who were starting a Black college
called Tuskegee Institute. The college
needed a president, and Armstrong urged
them to hire Washington. Although only
twenty-five, he was, according to Armstrong, "a very capable mulatto, clear
headed, modest, sensible, polite, and a
thorough teacher and superior man."

Young Washington got the job and
quickly went to work. The first students had to help construct the institute's first buildings by making the
bricks themselves. As the years passed,
Tuskegee Institute became celebrated as a college dedicated to promoting
self-discipline in students and providing vocational training.

Booker T. Washington The founder and
first president of Tuskegee Institute, a
historically Black university, Washington
went on to become the nation's most
prominent African American leader,
championing individual education and
advancement while quietly financing
social justice efforts.

Over time, Washington became a skilled fund-raiser, gathering substantial
gifts from wealthy Whites, most of them northerners. The complicated racial
dynamics of the late nineteenth century required him to walk a tightrope
between being candid and being an effective college president. He learned to
act like a fox, masking his militancy to maintain the support of Whites. As the
years passed, the pragmatic Washington became a source of inspiration and
hope to millions of Blacks.

Washington's recurring message to Black students focused on the importance of gaining "practical knowledge." In part to please his White donors,
he argued that African Americans should not focus on fighting racial segregation. They should instead work hard and avoid stirring up trouble. Their
priority should be self-improvement rather than social change. Washington

told them to begin "at the bottom" as well-educated, hardworking farmers, not as social activists.

Yet Washington's emphasis on economic self-sufficiency did not satisfy many White racists. Thomas Dixon, a North Carolina Baptist minister, state legislator, and novelist, complained that Washington was teaching Black students "to be masters of men, to be independent, to own and operate their own industries," all of which would "destroy the last vestige of dependence on the white man for anything."

Washington ignored such critics. In a famous speech at the Cotton States and International Exposition in Atlanta in 1895, he urged the African American community not to migrate to northern states or to other nations but to "Cast down your [water] bucket where you are—cast it down in making friends . . . of the people of all races by whom we are surrounded. Cast it down in agriculture, mechanics, in commerce, in domestic service, and in the professions." Fighting for "social equality" and directly challenging White rule, Washington asserted, would be "the extremest folly," and any effort at "agitation" would, he warned, backfire. African Americans first needed to become self-sufficient economically. Civil rights would have to wait.

W. E. B. Du Bois Other African American leaders disagreed with Booker T. Washington's accommodationist strategy. W. E. B. Du Bois emerged as Washington's foremost rival. A native of Massachusetts, Du Bois recalled that he first experienced racial prejudice as a student at Fisk University in Nashville, Tennessee. He later studied in Germany before becoming the first African American to earn a doctoral degree from Harvard (in history and sociology). In addition to promoting civil rights, he left a distinguished record as a scholar, authoring more than twenty books.

In his most famous work, *The Souls of Black Folk,* Du Bois highlighted the "double consciousness" felt by African Americans: "One ever feels his two-ness—an American, a Negro; two souls, two thoughts, two unreconciled strivings; two warring ideals in one dark body, whose dogged strength alone keeps it from being torn asunder." Du Bois spent his career exploring this double consciousness and how it inevitably hindered Black progress. A young White visitor to Mississippi in 1910 noticed that nearly every Black person he met had "two distinct social selves, the one he reveals to his own people, the other he assumes among the Whites."

Trim and dapper, Du Bois had a flamboyant personality and a combative spirit. Not long after he began teaching at Atlanta University in 1897, he launched a public assault on Booker T. Washington's conservative strategy for improving the quality of life for African Americans. Du Bois called Washington's celebrated 1895 speech "the **Atlanta Compromise**" and said that he would not "surrender the leadership of this race to cowards" who, like Washington, "accepted the alleged inferiority of the Negro" so Blacks could "concentrate all their energies on industrial education, the accumulation of wealth, and the conciliation of the South." Du Bois stressed that the priorities should be reversed—that African American leaders should adopt a strategy of "ceaseless agitation" directed at ensuring the right to vote and winning civil equality. The education of Blacks, he maintained, should not be merely vocational but comparable to that enjoyed by the White elite, and it should help develop bold leaders willing to challenge Jim Crow segregation and discrimination. He demanded that disenfranchisement and legalized segregation cease immediately and that the laws of the land be enforced.

W. E. B. Du Bois A fierce advocate for Black education and civil rights through "ceaseless agitation," Du Bois challenged the tactics of Booker T. Washington, whose approach to racial equality was more publicly conciliatory.

For his part, Washington stressed that Du Bois, a New Englander, never understood the brutal dynamics of southern racism. A more militant strategy in the South would only have gotten more Blacks lynched. Nor did Du Bois or other critics know that Washington secretly worked to challenge segregation and disenfranchisement, stop brutal lynchings, increase funding for public schools, and finance legal efforts to oppose Jim Crow laws. He often acted privately because he feared that public activism would trigger violence against Tuskegee and himself. Such "quiet efforts," he noted, were more successful and realistic than the "brass band" approach championed by Du Bois.

The dispute between Washington and Du Bois exposed the tensions that would divide the twentieth-century civil rights movement: militancy versus conciliation, separatism versus assimilation, social justice versus economic opportunities. In the end, Washington wanted to engender in his students a confident faith in molding a better future. He counseled them to grasp hope rather than hate, and he told racist Whites that "you can't keep another man in the ditch without being in the ditch yourself." By 1915, when Washington died, the leadership of the nation's Black community was passing to Du Bois and others whose uncompromising efforts to gain true equality signaled the beginning of the civil rights century.

THE SETTLING OF THE NEW WEST

Like the South, the West has long been a region wrapped in myths and stereotypes, many of them reinforced even today by popular novels, movies, and television shows. The vast land west of the Mississippi River contains remarkable geographic extremes: majestic mountains, roaring rivers, deep-sculpted canyons, searing deserts, grassy plains, and dense forests.

For most western Americans—Indians, Mexicans, Asians, farmers, ranchers, trappers, miners, and Mormons scattered through the plains, valleys, and mountains—the Civil War and Reconstruction were remote events that hardly touched their lives or concerns. In the West, the relentless march of conquest, settlement, and exploitation continued, propelled by a special sense of "manifest destiny," a lust for land, a hope for quick fortunes, and a restless desire to improve one's lot in life.

Between 1870 and 1900, Americans settled more land in the West than they had on the entire continent in the centuries before 1870. By 1900, a third of the nation lived west of the Mississippi River. The post–Civil War West came to symbolize economic opportunity and personal freedom. On another level, however, the economic exploitation of the West was a story of irresponsible behavior and reckless abuse that scarred the land, decimated its wildlife, and nearly exterminated much of Native American culture—and Native Americans.

THE WESTERN LANDSCAPE   After midcentury, farmers and their families began spreading west across the Great Plains—western Kansas, Nebraska, Oklahoma, northern Texas, the Dakotas, eastern Colorado, Wyoming, and Montana. From California, miners moved eastward to Utah and Nevada, drawn by one new discovery after another. From Texas, nomadic cowboys drove herds of cattle northward each spring onto the plains and even across the Rocky Mountains into the Great Basin of Utah and Nevada and as far north as Montana. There the herds would fatten on the abundant grasslands before being shipped east by rail to Chicago for slaughter.

The western settlers encountered challenges markedly different from those they had left behind. The Great Plains had little rainfall and few rivers or trees, which rendered useless the familiar trappings of the pioneer—the axe, the log cabin, the rail fence—as well as traditional methods of tilling the soil.

For a long time, the region had been called the Great American Desert; in the minds of most Americans, it was unfit for human habitation, and, therefore, it was the perfect refuge for Indians determined to maintain their way of life. But the notion that the Great Plains region was inhospitable to settlement changed in the last half of the nineteenth century.

With the completion of the transcontinental railroads, the diminishing threat of Indian resistance, and a seemingly limitless supply of natural resources, the West came to be viewed as a place destined for prosperity. Capitalists made huge profits investing in western mines, cattle, railroads, buffalo hides, and commercial farms. Agriculture expanded westward as the development of new irrigation techniques made the Great American Desert fruitful, after all.

The Allure of the West A circular from 1872 advertising westward emigration. The idyllic image of the Nebraska prairie captures the freedom symbolized by the West, and the financial details underneath are meant to persuade Americans to think of emigration as an economic opportunity.

THE MIGRATORY STREAM During the second half of the nineteenth century, an unrelenting stream of migrants flowed into what had been the largely Indian and Hispanic West. Millions of Anglo-Americans, African Americans, Mexicans, South Americans, and European and Asian immigrants transformed the patterns of western society and culture. Most of the settlers were relatively prosperous White, native-born farm folk. Because of the expense of transportation, land, and supplies, the poor could not afford to relocate. Three quarters of the western migrants were men.

The largest number of foreign immigrants came from northern Europe and Canada. In the northern plains (the Dakotas, Minnesota, Montana, and Wyoming), Germans, Scandinavians, and Irish were especially numerous.

In Nebraska in 1870, a quarter of the 123,000 residents were foreign-born. In North Dakota in 1890, immigrants composed 45 percent of the residents.

Immigrants from China and Mexico were much less numerous but nonetheless significant. More than 200,000 Chinese arrived in California between 1876 and 1890, joining some 70,000 others who had come earlier to build railroads and work in mining communities. The Chinese were frequently discriminated against and denied citizenship rights—and they became scapegoats whenever there was an economic downturn.

THE AFRICAN AMERICAN MIGRATION After the collapse of federal reconstruction efforts in the postwar South, thousands of African Americans began migrating westward. Some 6,000 Black southerners arrived in Kansas in 1879, and as many as 20,000 followed the next year. They were called **Exodusters** because they were making their exodus from southern White supremacy in search of a haven from racism and poverty.

The foremost promoter of Black migration to the West was Benjamin "Pap" Singleton. Born a slave in Tennessee in 1809, he escaped and made his way to Michigan. After the Civil War, he returned to Tennessee and decided that African Americans could never gain equal treatment if they stayed in the former Confederacy. When he learned that land in Kansas was selling for $1.25 an acre, he led a party of 200 African American colonists to the state in 1878, bought 7,500 acres that had been an Indian reservation, and established the Dunlop community.

Nicodemus, Kansas By the 1880s, this colony had become a thriving town of Exodusters. Here, its residents are photographed in front of their First Baptist Church and general store.

Over the next several years, thousands of African Americans followed Singleton to Kansas, leading many southern leaders to worry about the loss of Black laborers. In 1879, White southerners closed access to the Mississippi River and threatened to sink all boats carrying Blacks to the West.

By the early 1880s, the exodus of Black southerners had petered out. Many were unprepared for the harsh living conditions on the western plains. Their Kansas homesteads were often not large enough to be self-sustaining, and most of the Black farmers were forced to supplement their income by hiring themselves out as laborers to White ranchers. Drought, grasshoppers, prairie fires, and dust storms led to frequent crop failures and bankruptcy.

The sudden influx of so many southern Blacks also taxed resources and patience. There were not enough houses, stores, or construction materials; few government services; and rarely enough water. Disappointed and frustrated, many African American pioneers in Kansas abandoned their land and moved to the few cities in the state. The frontier was not the "promised land" that they had been led to expect, but it was better than what they had experienced in the South. As an Exoduster minister stressed, "We had rather suffer and be free."

By 1890, some 520,000 African Americans lived west of the Mississippi River. As many as 25 percent of the cowboys who participated in the Texas cattle drives were African Americans, as were many federal horse soldiers in the West.

WESTERN MINING Valuable mineral deposits continued to lure people to the West after the Civil War. Every territory and state in the Far West developed a mining industry. The miners of the 1849 California gold rush (the forty-niners) had set the typical pattern, in which mobs of prospectors rushed to a new find, followed quickly by camp followers—peddlers, saloon keepers, prostitutes, gamblers, hustlers, and assorted desperadoes eager to "mine the miners." Lawlessness gave way first to vigilante rule as groups of miners created their own informal legal codes for the community and enforced penalties, including hangings, and, finally, to stable communities with municipal governments, sanitation, and law enforcement.

Along the South Platte River, not far from Pikes Peak in Colorado, a prospecting party found gold in 1858, and stories of success brought perhaps 100,000 "fifty-niners" into the area by the next year. New discoveries in Colorado kept occurring: near Central City in 1859, at Leadville in the 1870s, and at Cripple Creek in 1891 and 1894—the last important gold and silver strikes in the West. During those years, farming and grazing had given the economy a stable base, and Colorado, the Centennial State, entered the Union in 1876.

While the early miners were crowding around Pikes Peak in Colorado, the **Comstock Lode** was found near Gold Hill, Nevada, on the eastern slope of the Sierra Nevada Mountains near the California border. Henry Comstock, a Canadian-born fur trapper, talked his way into a share of a new discovery made by two other prospectors in 1859 and gave it his own name. The lode produced massive amounts of gold and silver. Within twenty years, it had yielded more than $300 million from shafts that reached thousands of feet into the mountainside.

The growing demand for orderly government in the West led to the hasty designation of new territories and eventually the admission of a host of new states. After Colorado's admission in 1876, however, there was a long pause because of party divisions in Congress: Democrats were reluctant to create states out of western territories that were heavily Republican. After the sweeping Republican victory in the 1888 legislative races, however, Congress admitted the Dakotas, Montana, and Washington in 1889 and Idaho and Wyoming in 1890. Utah entered the Union in 1896 (after the Mormons agreed to abandon the practice of polygamy) and Oklahoma in 1907; in 1912, Arizona and New Mexico rounded out the forty-eight contiguous states. (The final two states, Alaska and Hawaii, were added fifty years later.)

LIFE IN THE NEW WEST

In the 1880s, James H. Kyner, a railroad builder in Oregon, described "an almost unbroken stream of emigrants from horizon to horizon." These "hardy, optimistic folk" traveled in wagons, on horses, and on foot, "going west to seek their fortunes and to settle an empire." Most thought little about forcing out the Native Americans, Chinese workers, and Hispanic cowboys who were there first. Americans claimed a special destiny to settle, develop, and dominate the entire continent.

To encourage new settlers in the West, the federal government helped finance the construction of transcontinental railroads, dispatched federal troops to conquer Indians and relocate them to reservations, and sold government-owned land at low prices—or granted it to railroad companies as a means of rapidly populating areas served by trains. The transcontinental railroads received some 200 million acres of government land. Over time, the railroads sold much of the land to create towns and ranches. The arrival of trains was the lifeblood of the western economy.

The surge of western migration displayed some of the romantic qualities so often depicted in novels, films, and television shows. Those familiar yet often romanticized images tell only part of the story, however. Drudgery and tragedy were commonplace aspects of life on the western plains. In contrast to the Hollywood versions of the West, settlers were a diverse lot: they included women as well as men, African Americans, Hispanics, Asians, and European immigrants. The feverish quest for quick profits also helped fuel a boom-and-bust economic cycle that injected chronic instability into the society and politics of the region.

The abuse, displacement, and relocation of Native Americans and the rapidly shrinking buffalo herds coincided with a growing cattle industry in the West. Cattle were herded into the grasslands where buffalo once had roamed. For many years, wild cattle first brought to America by the Spanish had competed with buffalo in the borderlands of Texas and Arizona. Breeding them with Anglo-American domesticated cattle produced the hybrid Texas longhorn. Tough, lean, and rangy, longhorns were noted more for speed and endurance than for yielding choice steak. By the time the Confederacy surrendered, millions of longhorns were wandering freely across Texas. They had marginal economic value because the largest urban markets for beef were so far away—that is, until the railroads arrived.

THE CATTLE BOOM At the end of the Civil War, Kansas Pacific Railroad crews began laying rails westward across the state and eventually into Colorado. A few entrepreneurs began to imagine how the extension of the railroad might "establish a market whereby the Southern [cattle] drover and Northern buyer would meet upon an equal footing."

That meeting point was Abilene, in eastern Kansas, a "very small, dead place, consisting of about one dozen log huts." There, Joseph G. McCoy, an Illinois livestock dealer, recognized the possibilities of driving vast herds of cattle raised in Texas northward across the open range to Kansas. There they would be loaded onto freight cars and sent across the country.

In 1867, McCoy bought 250 acres in Abilene and built a stockyard, barn, office building, livestock scales, hotel, and a bank. He then sent an agent to Texas to convince the owners of herds bound north to go through Abilene. When various breeds of cattle reached Abilene in August 1867, they were loaded onto railcars and shipped to Chicago stockyards, where they were slaughtered and then sent (as sides of beef) around the nation.

Abilene flourished, and by 1871, an estimated 700,000 steers passed through the town every year. Moreover, the ability to ship large numbers of cattle by rail transformed ranching into a huge national industry as Americans shifted from eating pork to eating beef. In the process, Kansas became a major economic crossroads.

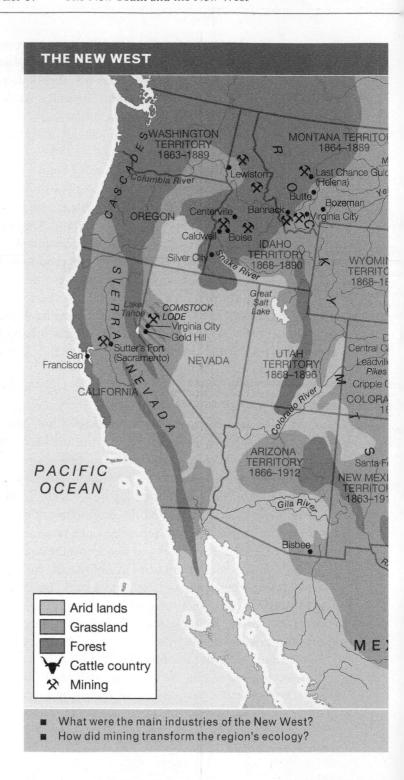

THE NEW WEST

WASHINGTON
TERRITORY
1863–1889

MONTANA TERRITORY
1864–1889

Columbia River

Lewiston

Last Chance Gulch
(Helena)

Butte

Bozeman

OREGON

Centerville

Bannack

Virginia City

Caldwell

Boise

IDAHO
TERRITORY
1868–1890

WYOMING
TERRITORY
1868–18

Silver City

Snake River

Great
Salt
Lake

CASCADES

SIERRA

Lake
Tahoe

COMSTOCK
LODE

Virginia City

Gold Hill

Central Ci

Leadvill

Pikes

San
Francisco

Sutter's Fort
(Sacramento)

NEVADA

UTAH
TERRITORY
1868–1896

CALIFORNIA

NEVADA

Cripple C

COLORA
18

Colorado River

ARIZONA
TERRITORY
1866–1912

Santa Fe

NEW MEXI
TERRITOR
1863–191

PACIFIC
OCEAN

Gila River

Bisbee

MEX

Arid lands
Grassland
Forest
Cattle country
Mining

- What were the main industries of the New West?
- How did mining transform the region's ecology?

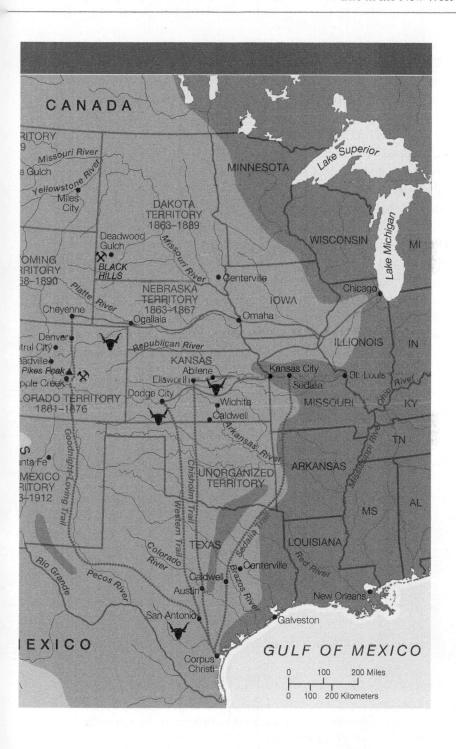

Other cattle towns sprouted along the rail line: Ellsworth, Wichita, Caldwell, Dodge City. But few of the cattle businesses lasted more than a few years. Once people bought farms nearby, they lobbied successfully to stop the Texas herds from coming through their area. Texas cattle brought with them a disease called tick fever that destroyed whole herds.

In response to efforts in Kansas to shut down the cattle drives, Texas ranchers developed new routes north to cow towns and rail hubs in Colorado, Wyoming, and Montana. Soon, those states had their own cattle ranches. By 1883, there were half a million cattle in eastern Montana alone, as the disappearing buffalo herds gave way to steers and sheep.

COWBOYS Centuries before cattle or cowboys appeared in the American West, Hispanics and Native Americans were herding livestock in Spanish Mexico. The Spanish-speaking cowboys, called vaqueros (from *vaca*, the Spanish word for cow), were accomplished riders and ropers adept at "busting broncos," lassoing steers with long ropes called lariats, and herding cattle.

As Americans (called Anglos because they spoke English) flooded into the Texas plains during the first half of the nineteenth century, they learned

The Original Cowboys A group of vaqueros, Spanish-speaking cowboys, who handed down their legendary herding skills to generations of settlers and immigrants to the American West.

the art of cattle ranching from *mestizo* Mexicans (people of mixed Native American and Spanish ancestry). They adopted the clothing, equipment, food, techniques, and terminology (lasso, rodeo, rancho) used by vaqueros. The vaqueros, wrote one American settler, "are universally acknowledged to be the best hands [workers]" dealing with cattle, horses, and other livestock.

Cowboys were mostly unmarried young men—the average age was twenty-four—willing to work seven days a week, often in bad weather. More than a third of them were Hispanic American, African American, or Native American. Texan Richard King, owner of what would become the nation's largest ranch, recruited 300 vaqueros to manage his herd of 65,000 longhorns because their skills were unsurpassed.

In Texas after the Civil War, being a cowboy was one of the few jobs open to men of color. Nat Love, a formerly enslaved Tennesseean-turned-Texas cowboy, recalled the comradeship he experienced on the trail with like-minded cowboys: "A braver, truer set of men never lived than those wild sons of the plains whose home was in the saddle and their couch, mother earth, with the sky for a covering."

Ranching was not without prejudice, however. Anglo cowboys were usually paid more than African Americans or those of Mexican descent. And vaqueros rarely rose to the ranks of foreman or trail boss. Rugged life on the trail occasionally helped break down racial barriers. Charles Goodnight, a former Confederate soldier who became a prosperous Texas cattleman, cherished his colleague and friend Bose Ikard, an African American cowboy who had been born enslaved in Mississippi before being sold to a Texan. After the Civil War, Ikard and Goodnight spent four years herding cattle from Texas to Colorado. Goodnight remembered that Ikard "never shirked a duty or disobeyed an order, rode with me in many stampedes, participated in three engagements with Comanches. Splendid behavior." Goodnight said he trusted Ikard "farther than any living man. He was my detective, banker, and everything else in Colorado, New Mexico, and the other wild country I was in."

FENCING IN THE OPEN RANGE Isolated cattle ranchers were forced to meet and develop their own code of laws and ways to enforce them. As cattle often wandered onto other ranchers' land, cowboys would "ride the line" to keep the animals in bounds. In the spring, the cowboys would "round up" the herds, which invariably got mixed up, and sort out ownership by identifying the distinctive ranch symbols "branded," or burned, into the cattle hides.

All that changed in 1873, when Joseph Glidden, an Illinois farmer, developed the first effective and inexpensive form of barbed-wire fencing. It transformed the West. Soon the open range, where a small rancher could graze his cattle anywhere there was grass, was no more. Barbed-wire fences triggered "range wars," where small ranchers fought to retain the open range and condemned barbed wire as "devil's rope." The widespread use of barbed wire also ravaged Native American culture by denying Indians access to their ancestral lands.

Fencing immediately converted free-range prairie into pastures, putting smaller-scale cattle ranchers out of business. Many former ranchers became cowboys working for wages. Cattle raising, like mining, evolved from a romantic adventure into a business dominated by "cattle barons" and large corporations. As one cowboy lamented, "times have changed." The advent of barbed-wire fencing and the continuing expansion of railroads ended the long cattle drives from Texas to cow towns in other states."

THE WESTERN METROPOLIS OF CHICAGO The rise of the cattle industry helped make Chicago the fastest-growing city in the nation in the decades after the Civil War. Located along Lake Michigan and served by several rivers and nine railroads in 1865, Chicago was where city and frontier intersected and was the gateway to the western economy. Its lumberyards, grain elevators, stockyards, and slaughterhouses became magnets for job-seeking immigrants, mostly Irish and Germans.

After a devastating fire swept across the city in 1871, killing some 300 people, destroying 18,000 buildings, and leaving a third of the residents homeless, Chicago experienced the greatest architectural boom in the nation's history. With no wooden structures allowed to be built downtown after the catastrophe, architect Louis Sullivan led an innovative steel-brick-and-stone skyscraper revolution in the city, enabled by the invention of elevators that allowed buildings to soar in height. Chicago was the catalyst for much of the West's development. "The Great Grey City, brooking no rival," wrote Frank Norris in his novel *The Pit* (1903), "imposed its dominion upon a reach of country larger than many a kingdom of the Old World. For thousands of miles beyond its confines its influence was felt."

The meatpacking industry in places like Cincinnati and Chicago had started not with cattle but with hogs, in part because pork could be preserved longer (with salt and smoking) than beef. Since colonial days, pork packing had been one of the earliest and most important frontier industries. Hogs reproduce much faster than cattle, and they thrive on corn. As a nineteenth-century economist explained, "What is a hog, but fifteen or twenty bushels of corn on four legs?"

In 1850, Chicago slaughterhouses butchered and packed 20,000 hogs. By contrast, Cincinnati (called "Porkopolis") processed 334,000 each year.

That changed as the federal government ordered vast quantities of pork for its armies. By 1862, Chicago had displaced Cincinnati as the world's largest pork-processing center. By the 1870s, thanks to the railroad connections, the city was processing more than 2 million hogs per year. The use of ice cut from frozen Lake Michigan and placed in freight trains enabled Chicago pork to be shipped all the way to the East Coast.

But there was no ice in the summer. This challenge led Gustavus F. Swift to begin experimenting with ways to "refrigerate" railcars year-round. Within a few years, Swift and his main competitor, Philip Armour, had developed refrigerated freight cars that enabled them to ship processed meat, rather than live hogs and cattle.

Refrigerated railcars allowed Chicago to add beef packing to its hog-processing operations. "The refrigerator car," announced Swift and Company, "is one of the vehicles on which the packing industry has ridden to greatness." By the end of the nineteenth century, the economies of scale enjoyed by the four dominant Chicago meatpacking corporations drove most local butchers across the nation out of business. Unfortunately, the meat-packers dumped all their waste—carcasses, blood, and manure—into the Chicago River, in direct violation of city ordinances.

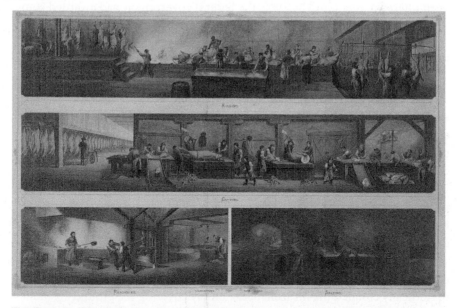

The Pork-Packing Industry An inside look into the pork-packing industry that shows labor divided across specific meat-processing tasks.

Swift and Armour became two of the richest men in the world. They soon branched out and became traders in grain—wheat and corn. They also built packing plants in cattle towns such as Kansas City, Omaha, and St. Louis. As production increased and the cost of beef and pork dropped, Americans became regular meat eaters. By the end of the century, meatpacking was the largest industrial employer in the nation.

FARMING ON THE PLAINS   Farming amid the unforgiving environment and harsh weather of the Great Plains was brutal. A New York newspaper publisher traveling to California described the region as "a treeless desert," scorching during daylight and "chill and piercing" cold at night. Still, people made the dangerous trek, lured by inexpensive federal land and misleading advertisements celebrating life on the plains. One woman said she was "glad to be leaving" her farm in Missouri: "We were going to a new land and get rich." Few got rich, however. "In plain language," concluded a study by the Department of Agriculture, "a farmer's wife, as a general rule, is a laboring drudge."

The first homesteaders in the Great Plains were mostly landless folk eager to try their hand at farming. Many of them had never used a hoe or planted a seed. "I was raised in Chicago without so much as a back yard to play in," said a Montana homesteader, "and I worked 48 hours a week for $1.25. When I heard you [a married couple] could get 320 acres just by living on it, I felt that I had been offered a kingdom." By 1900, the federal government had awarded some 270 million acres to 1.6 million people.

Yet these settlers faced a grim struggle. Although land was essentially free through the Homestead Act (1862), much of what was needed to make the property profitable—horses, livestock, wagons, wells, lumber, fencing, seed, machinery, and fertilizer—were expensive. Freight rates and interest rates seemed criminally high. As in the South, declining crop prices produced chronic indebtedness, leading strapped farmers to embrace virtually any plan to increase the money supply and thus pay off their debts with inflated currency.

The virgin land itself, although fertile, resisted planting; the heavy sod woven with tough grass roots broke many a plow. Since wood and coal were rare on the prairie, pioneer families initially had to use buffalo chips (dried dung from buffaloes and cattle) for fuel.

Farm families also fought a constant battle with the elements: tornadoes, hailstorms, droughts, prairie fires, blizzards, and pests. Swarms of locusts periodically clouded the horizon, occasionally covering the ground six inches deep. A Wichita newspaper reported in 1878 that the grasshoppers devoured "everything green, stripping the foliage off the bark and from the tender twigs of the fruit trees, destroying every plant that is good for food or pleasant to the eyes, that man has planted." In the late 1880s, a prolonged drought forced many homesteaders on the plains to give up. Thousands left, some in wagons whose canvas coverings read: "In God we trusted, in Kansas we busted." In the end, two thirds of the people who gained land under the Homestead Act failed to become self-sustaining farmers.

COMMERCIAL FARMING Eventually, as the railroads brought lumber from the East, farmers could upgrade their houses built of sod ("Kansas brick") into more-comfortable wood-framed dwellings. New machinery and equipment, for those who could afford them, improved productivity. In 1868, James Oliver, a Scottish immigrant living in Indiana, made a sturdy chilled-iron "sodbuster" plow that greatly eased the task of preparing land for planting. New threshing machines, hay mowers, seed planters, manure spreaders, and other equipment also lightened the burden of farm labor but often deepened the debts that farmers owed. By 1880, a steam-powered combine could do the work of twenty men.

Although the overall value of farmland and farm products increased, small farmers did not keep up. Their numbers grew in size but decreased in proportion to the population at large. Wheat in the western states, like cotton in the antebellum South, was the export crop that spurred economic growth. Few small farmers prospered, however, and by the 1890s, they were in open revolt against what they viewed as a "system" of corrupt processors (middlemen) and "greedy" bankers and railroaders who they believed conspired against them.

MINERS IN THE WEST As ranchers and farmers settled the plains, miners played a crucial role in the economic and social development of the Far West. Throughout the region, mining camps and towns sprouted in the second half of the century. Initially, the miners lived in crude tents and shacks they built themselves. They worked a nine- to ten-hour day, six days a week, and usually took Sunday off. As a camp grew, it became a town with cabins, stores, and saloons providing modern services and conveniences.

The first wave of prospectors focused on "placer" (surface) mining, using metal pans to sift gold dust and nuggets out of riverbeds. When the placer deposits were exhausted, however, miners had to use other methods, all of which required much larger operations and investments. As mining shifted from surface digging and panning to hydraulic mining, dredging, and deep-shaft hard-rock tunneling, mining ceased being an individual pursuit and became a big business. Only large-scale mining corporations financed by

American and European investors could afford the expensive specialized power equipment and blasting dynamite needed for such operations.

Many prospectors who had hoped to "strike it rich" turned into wage laborers working for mining corporations. Eventually, mine workers formed unions to represent their interests in negotiations with mine owners, in part because of low pay ($3 a day) and in part because deep-shaft mining was so dangerous. In the western hard-rock mines, on-the-job accidents disabled one out of every thirty miners and killed one out of eighty. Overall, some 7,500 workers were killed and 20,000 maimed in mine accidents during the late nineteenth century.

MINING AND THE ENVIRONMENT Hydraulicking, dredging, and shaft mining transformed vast areas of landscape and vegetation. Massive stamping mills driven by steam engines crushed mountains of rock. Huge hydraulic cannons shot enormous streams of water under high pressure, stripping the topsoil and gravel from hillsides and creating steep-sloped canyons that could not sustain plant life. The massive amounts of dirt and debris unearthed by the water cannons covered rich farmland downstream and created sandbars that clogged rivers and killed fish. All told, some 12 billion tons of earth were blasted out of the Sierra Nevada in California and washed down into local rivers.

MINING BOOMTOWNS Tombstone, Arizona, only thirty miles from the Mexican border, was the site of substantial silver mining in the 1870s. It was the fastest-growing boomtown in the Southwest. It boasted a bowling alley, four churches, an icehouse, a school, two banks, three newspapers, and an ice cream parlor along with 110 saloons, 14 gambling casinos, and numerous dance halls and brothels. Miners and cowboys especially enjoyed shows at the Bird Cage Theatre, the "wildest, wickedest night spot between Basin Street [in New Orleans] and the Barbary Coast [in San Francisco]," open twenty-four hours a day, 365 days a year.

Other large and famous mining boomtowns included Virginia City in Nevada, Cripple Creek and Leadville in Colorado, and Deadwood in the Dakota Territory. They were male-dominated communities with a substantial population of immigrants: Chinese, Chileans, Peruvians, Mexicans, French, Germans, Scots, Welsh, Irish, and English. In terms of ethnic diversity, the western mining cities were the most cosmopolitan communities in America.

Mining towns were violent places. The small gold-mining town of Belleville, California, had fifty murders in one year. In 1871, a visitor to Corinne, Utah, a town only four years old with 2,000 residents, noted that the streets "are full of white men armed to the teeth, miserable-looking Indians dressed in the ragged shirts and trousers furnished by the federal government, and yellow Chinese with a business-like air and hard, intelligent faces."

Ethnic prejudice was as common as violence in mining towns. Chinese, for example, were usually prohibited from working in the mines but were allowed to operate laundries and work in boardinghouses. Mexicans were often treated the worst. "Mexicans have no business in this country," a Californian insisted. "The men were made to be shot at, and the women were made for our purposes. I'm a white man—I am! A Mexican is pretty near black. I hate all Mexicans."

Most of the boomtowns, many of which were in remote mountainous areas, lasted only a few years, giving

Deadwood, Dakota Territory A gold-rush town in 1876, before the Dakotas became states, Deadwood was one of many mining boomtowns that sprang up across the West to support industrial mining.

rise to the phrase "boom and bust." Once the mines played out, the people moved on, leaving ghost towns behind. In 1870, Virginia City, then called the richest city in America, hosted a population of 20,000. Today it has fewer than 1,000 residents.

WOMEN IN THE WEST The West remained a largely male society. Most women in mining towns provided domestic services: cooking, cleaning, washing clothes. They were as valued as gold, since many mining towns had a male-to-female ratio as high as 9 to 1.

In both mining and farming communities, women were prized as spouses, in part because farming required everyone in a family to help. But women pioneers continued to face many of the same legal barriers and social prejudices prevalent in the East. Upon marriage, a wife's legal rights and obligations were transferred to her husband. A wife could not sell property without her husband's approval. Texas women could sue only for divorce, and they could not serve on juries, act as lawyers, or witness a will.

Over time, however, the constant fight for survival west of the Mississippi, however, made men and women there more equal partners than was

Women of the Frontier A woman and her family in front of their sod house. The difficult life on the prairie led to more egalitarian marriages than were found in other regions of the country because women had to play so many nontraditional roles.

typical in the East. Many women who lost their mates to the deadly toil of "sod busting" assumed responsibility for their farms. In general, women on the prairie became more independent than women leading domestic lives back East. A Kansas woman recalled "that the environment was such as to bring out and develop the dominant qualities of individual character. Kansas women of that day learned at an early age to depend on themselves—to do whatever work there was to be done, and to face danger when it must be faced, as calmly as they were able."

Perhaps the most common challenge to women on the plains was loneliness. Farms and ranches were widely scattered, usually a mile or two apart, and it took great effort to interact with others. Often, it was impossible. "Pioneer life always falls hardest on the women," explained Bell Harbert, president of the International Congress of Farm Women, for their lives on the prairie were "filled with loneliness and often rebellion."

It was not coincidental, then, that the new western territories and states were among the first to allow women to vote and hold office—in the hopes that by doing so, they would attract more women settlers. In 1890, Wyoming was admitted to the Union as the first state that allowed women to vote. Utah, Colorado, and Idaho followed soon thereafter.

THE HISPANIC SOUTHWEST   During the last quarter of the nine-teenth century, as prejudice against Chinese workers intensified, railroads throughout the West and Southwest turned to Native Americans and Mexi-can-born workers. As a railroad executive explained, Indians and Mexicans were "wonderfully adapted to the peculiar conditions under which they must live as laborers" in the Southwest.

Railroads in the Southwest, especially the Southern Pacific and the Santa Fe, needed so many track workers (*traqueros*) that they set up recruiting centers in Mexico. Between 1880 and 1900, the Mexican immigrant popula-tion in New Mexico increased some 50 percent. Ethnic prejudice shaped wage levels. Track workers in Mexico were paid on average 25¢ a day; in the United States, they or Spanish-speaking Americans earned $1 a day. Irish-born workers, however, were paid $3 a day. As an Arizona newspaper admitted, the "life of a Mexican is of no more moment than a mongrel dog."

The completion of the railroads created a continuing influx of Anglo Americans that ultimately overran the Mexican population in the Southwest. Mexican Americans soon found themselves outnumbered, outvoted, and—eventually—outcast. Sheriffs and judges discriminated against Mexican Amer-icans in land disputes, railroads, and mines, ranchers paid Mexican Americans less than Anglo Americans, and local governments passed laws intended to deter or end Mexican cultural traditions. Various "Sunday Laws," for example banned "noisy amusements" such as bullfights, cockfights, and other Hispanic recreations.

As in the post–Civil War South, segregation became the norm in south-western states. People of Mexican ancestry were not welcome in "White" res-taurants, churches, and parks. Spanish-speaking children were expected to attend "Mexican schools" separate from White children.

While White supremacists in the South were imposing Jim Crow laws and lynching African Americans, bigotry toward Mexican Americans flour-ished in Texas and other western states. In what historians are now calling the *Juan Crow* era, hundreds, perhaps thousands, of men, women, and children of Mexican descent, many of whom were U.S. citizens, were lynched. Most were hanged or shot. In 1910, Antonio Rodriquez, a twenty-year-old Mexican migrant worker accused of murdering a White Texan, was yanked from a jail cell in Rocksprings, Texas, tied to a tree, doused with kerosene, and burned alive.

In 1873, White vigilantes near Corpus Christi, Texas, hanged seven Mexican sheepherders. None of the killers was arrested. Four years later, forty Mexicans were killed by rampaging Whites in Nueces County, Texas, after a White man was murdered.

Violence against Mexican Americans Increased anti-Mexican sentiment led to violence between Anglo-Americans and Mexican Americans, in south Texas and areas along the Mexico and U.S. border.

One of the worst anti-Mexican incidents occurred in the remote farm village of Porvenir in West Texas. On January 28, 1918, four White ranchers, ten Texas Rangers, and forty U.S. Army cavalrymen descended on Porvenir in the dark of night, seized fifteen unarmed American-born men and boys of Mexican descent, marched them to a hill at the edge of the settlement, and killed them all. The group then burned the village, claiming, without evidence, that it was a community of "thieves, informers, spies, and murderers."

The remaining residents of Porvenir crossed the Rio Grande into Mexico and never returned. The Texas legislature investigated the massacre and several Texas Rangers were reassigned, but no one was ever charged with a crime.

The Porvenir massacre and similar acts of violence did produce one positive result: the founding of the League of United Latin American Citizens (LULAC) to promote and protect the civil rights of Mexican Americans.

LAS GORRAS BLANCAS (WHITE CAPS) Mexican American citizens at times rebelled against the efforts of Whites to seize their land. In 1889, in New Mexico, three brothers, Juan Jose, Pablo, and Nicanor Herrera, organized Las Gorras Blancas—the White Caps—to evict White "land grabbers" who had illegally created commercial ranches on property held in common by the citizens of New Mexico. The group's name derived from the hoods they wore to disguise their identity.

The White Caps, some 1,500 strong, declared themselves defenders of "the rights of all people in general, and especially the rights of poor people." They initially sought legal action to evict the often-wealthy squatters, but when that failed, they mobilized as night riders, cutting barbed wire fencing, destroying barns, railroad tracks, and telegraph lines, scattering livestock, and threatening trespassers.

The New Mexico governor denounced the White Caps as nothing more than a vigilante mob. Benjamin Butler, a prominent attorney and former Union general who claimed 400,000 acres in New Mexico, sent an investigator to the territory. In his report to Butler, he expressed the prevailing racism: "You must recollect that these are Mexicans; that the Mexicans in New Mexico, with the exception of perhaps five per cent, are the most ignorant people on the face of the earth."

As time passed, the White Caps grew frustrated that their vigilante tactics had failed to win improvements. The Herrera brothers then turned to political action, eventually gaining election to the state legislature. But their failure to garner widespread political support against the wealthy land grabbers brought an end to Las Gorras Blancas.

THE FATE OF WESTERN INDIANS

As settlers spread across the continent, some 250,000 Native Americans, many of them originally from east of the Mississippi River, were forced into what was supposed to be their last refuge, the Great Plains and mountain regions of the Far West. By signing the 1851 Fort Laramie Treaty in Wyoming, Plains Indians accepted tribal boundaries and allowed White pioneers to travel across their lands. Yet as the numbers of White settlers increased, fighting resumed.

INDIAN RELATIONS IN THE WEST   From the early 1860s until the late 1870s, the trans-Mississippi West, often called Indian Country, raged with the so-called **Indian wars**. Although the U.S. government had signed numerous treaties with Indian nations giving them ownership of reservation lands for "as long as waters run and the grass shall grow," those commitments were repeatedly violated by buffalo hunters, miners, ranchers, farmers, railroad surveyors—and horse soldiers. As General William T. Sherman explained, an Indian reservation was "a parcel of land inhabited by Indians and surrounded by [American] thieves."

In the 1860s, the federal government ousted numerous tribes from lands they had been promised would be theirs forever. A Sioux chieftain named Spotted Tail expressed the anger felt by many Indians when he asked, "Why does not the Great Father [U.S. president] put his red children on wheels so that he can move them as he will?"

In the two decades before the Civil War, the U.S. Army's central mission in the West was to protect pioneers traveling on the major Overland Trails.

During and after the war, the mission changed to ensuring that Native Americans stayed on the reservations and that settlers or miners did not trespass on Indian lands.

Emigrants, however, repeatedly violated the agreements. The result was simmering frustration punctuated by outbreaks of tragic violence. In the summer of 1862, an uprising by Sioux warriors in the Minnesota River Valley resulted in the deaths of 644 White traders, settlers, government officials, and soldiers. It was the first of many clashes between settlers and miners and the Indians living on reservations.

THE SAND CREEK MASSACRE   Two years later, a horrible incident occurred in Colorado as a result of the influx of White miners. After Indians murdered a White family near Denver, John Evans, the territorial governor, called on Whites to "kill and destroy" the "hostile Indians on the plains." At the same time, Evans persuaded "friendly Indians" (mostly Cheyenne and Arapaho) to gather at "places of safety" such as Fort Lyon, in southeastern Colorado near the Kansas border, where they were promised protection.

Despite that promise, at dawn on November 29, 1864, while most of the Indian men were off hunting, Colonel John M. Chivington's 700 militiamen attacked a camp of Cheyenne and Arapaho along Sand Creek, about forty miles

Sand Creek Massacre Southern Cheyenne illustration of Chivington's devastating attack on the Cheyenne and Arapaho in 1864. A small group of warriors rides toward a line of armed militiamen, who are firing at will.

from Fort Lyon. Chivington, a former abolitionist and Methodist minister, had ordered his men to murder Cheyenne "whenever and wherever found."

As the horse soldiers approached, Black Kettle, the Cheyenne chief, waved first an American flag and then a White flag, but the soldiers paid no heed. Over seven hours, they slaughtered, scalped, and mutilated 165 peaceful Indians— men, women, children, and the elderly. In his report to army officials, Chivington claimed a great victory against 1,000 entrenched Cheyenne warriors. He was greeted as a hero back in Denver. "Colorado soldiers have again covered themselves in glory," the *Rocky Mountain News* initially proclaimed.

Then the truth about Sand Creek began to come out. Captain Silas Soule had witnessed the massacre, but, along with his company of soldiers, had disobeyed orders to join the attack. "I refused to fire and swore [to my men] that none but a coward" would shoot unarmed women and children. Three weeks after the massacre, Soule wrote a letter to a superior officer revealing what had happened: "Hundreds of women and children were coming toward us, and getting on their knees for mercy," only to be murdered and "have their brains beat out by men professing to be civilized." Far from being a hero, Soule added, Chivington encouraged the slaughter through his *lack* of leadership: "There was no organization among our troops, they were a perfect mob—every man on his own hook." He predicted that "we will have a hell of a time with Indians this winter" because of the **Sand Creek Massacre**.

Congress and the army launched lengthy investigations, and Captain Soule was called to testify in January 1865. The eventual congressional report concluded that Chivington had "deliberately planned and executed a foul and dastardly massacre," murdering "in cold blood" Indians who "had every reason to believe they were under [U.S.] protection." An army general described the massacre as the "foulest and most unjustifiable crime in the annals of America."

Chivington resigned from the militia to avoid a military trial. He soon became the Denver sheriff. On April 23, 1865, Soule was shot and killed in Denver. One of his murderers—never prosecuted—was identified as one of Chivington's soldiers.

SPREADING CONFLICT The Sand Creek Massacre ignited warfare that raged across the central plains for the next three years, forcing the federal government to dispatch troops to the West. Arapaho, Cheyenne, and Sioux war parties attacked ranches and stagecoach stations, killing hundreds of White men and kidnapping many White women and children. The government responded by authorizing the recruitment of soldiers from among Confederate military prisoners (called "white-washed Rebels") and the creation of African American cavalry regiments.

In 1866, Congress passed legislation establishing two "colored" cavalry units and dispatched them to the western frontier. The Cheyenne nicknamed them "buffalo soldiers" because they "fought like a cornered buffalo; who, like a buffalo, had suffered wound after wound, yet had not died; and who, like a buffalo, had a thick and shaggy mane of hair."

The buffalo soldiers were mostly Civil War veterans from Louisiana and Kentucky. They built and maintained forts, mapped vast areas of the Southwest, strung hundreds of miles of telegraph lines, protected railroad construction crews, subdued hostile Indians, and captured outlaws and rustlers (horse and cattle thieves). Eighteen buffalo soldiers won Medals of Honor.

EVICTING INDIANS FROM THEIR ANCESTRAL LANDS   A congressional committee in 1865 gathered evidence on the Indian wars and massacres. Its 1867 "Report on the Condition of the Indian Tribes" led to the creation of an Indian Peace Commission charged with removing the causes of warfare.

Congress decided that this would be best accomplished by persuading nomadic Indians yet again to move to out-of-the-way federal reservations where they could take up farming that would "civilize" them. They were to give up their ancestral hunting lands in return for peace so that Whites could move in. In 1870, Native Americans outnumbered White people in the Dakota Territory by 2 to 1; by 1880, Whites, mostly gold prospectors, would outnumber Indians by more than 6 to 1. The U.S. government had decided it had no choice but to gain control of the region—by purchase if possible, by force if necessary.

In 1867, a conference at Medicine Lodge, Kansas, ended with the Kiowas, Comanches, Arapahos, and Cheyenne reluctantly agreeing to move to western Oklahoma. The following spring, the western Sioux (the Lakota) signed the Fort Laramie Treaty (1868). They agreed to settle within the huge Black Hills Reservation in southwestern Dakota Territory, in part because they viewed the Black Hills as sacred ground.

GRANT'S INDIAN POLICY   In his inaugural address in 1869, President Ulysses S. Grant urged Congress to adopt more-humane policies toward Native Americans: "The proper treatment of *the original inhabitants of this land*" should enable the Native Americans "to become *citizens* with all the rights enjoyed by every other American."

Grant's noble intentions, however, ran afoul of long-standing prejudices and the unrelenting efforts of miners, farmers, railroaders, and ranchers to trespass on Indian lands and reservations. The president recognized the challenges; Indians, he admitted, "would be harmless and peaceable if they were not put upon by whites." Yet he also stressed that protecting the new transcontinental railroad was his top priority. In the end, however, Grant told army officers that "it is much better to support a peace commission than a [military] campaign against Indians."

Periodic clashes brought demands for military action. William T. Sherman, commanding general of the U.S. Army, directed General Philip Sheridan, head of the military effort in the West, to "kill and punish the hostiles [Indian war parties], capture and destroy the ponies" of the "Cheyennes, Arapahos, and Kiowas."

Neither general agreed with Grant's peace policy. In their view, the president's naive outlook reflected the distance between the Great Plains and Washington, D.C. Sherman ordered Sheridan to force all "nonhostile" Indians onto federal reservations, where they would be provided land for farming, immediate rations of food, and supplies and equipment (a promise that was rarely kept). In 1867, however, after a brutal assault on American settlers by Lakota Sioux warriors, Sherman issued orders to "act with vindictive earnestness against the Sioux, even to their extermination, men, women, and children."

Some Native Americans refused to move. In the southern plains of New Mexico, north Texas, Colorado, Kansas, and Oklahoma, Native Americans, dominated by the Comanches, focused on hunting buffalo. Armed clashes occurred with increasing frequency until the Red River War of 1874–1875, when Sheridan's soldiers won a series of battles in the Texas Panhandle. The defeated Comanche, Cheyenne, Kiowa, and Arapaho were forced onto reservations.

CUSTER AND THE SIOUX Meanwhile, trouble was brewing again in the northern plains. White prospectors searching for gold were soon trespassing on Sioux hunting grounds in the Dakotas despite promises that the army would keep them out. Ohio senator John Sherman warned that nothing would stop the mass migration of pioneers across the Mississippi River: "If the whole Army of the United States stood in the way, the wave of emigration would pass over it to seek the valley where gold was found."

The massive gold rush convinced some Indians to make a last stand. As Red Cloud, a Sioux chief, said, "The white men have crowded the Indians back year by year, and now our last hunting ground, the home of my people, is to be taken from us. Our women and children will starve, but for my part I prefer to die fighting rather than by starvation." Another prominent Sioux war chief, Sitting Bull, told Indians living on the Black Hills reservation that "the whites may get me at last, but I will have good times till then."

In 1875, Lieutenant Colonel George Armstrong Custer, a Civil War hero and a veteran Indian fighter driven by headstrong ambition and reckless courage, led 1,000 soldiers into the Black Hills, where he announced the discovery of gold near present-day Custer, South Dakota. The news set off a massive gold rush, and within two years, the mining town of Deadwood overflowed with 10,000 miners.

The undermanned army units in the area could not keep the miners from violating the rights guaranteed to the Sioux by federal treaties. President Grant and federal authorities tried to convince the Sioux to sell the Black Hills to the government for $6 million. Sitting Bull told the American negotiator to tell "the Great Father [Grant] that I do not want to sell any land to the government."

With that news, Custer was sent back to the Black Hills, this time to find roving bands of Sioux and Cheyenne warriors and force them back onto reservations. If they resisted, he was to kill them. It would not be easy. As General William T. Sherman said, the Sioux were the "most brave and warlike Savages of this Continent."

The brash Custer, with his curly, golden hair and buckskin outfits, stood out among his soldiers. He never shied away from danger and was one of the few soldiers who fought for the fun of it; to him, war was "glorious." President Grant, however, was not impressed. He noted that Custer had graduated at the bottom of his class at West Point and was "not a very level-headed man."

During the Civil War, Custer had earned a battlefield promotion to brevet general (a way of honoring gallantry without conferring the actual rank) at the age of twenty-three, and the "Boy General" had played an important role in the Union victory at Gettysburg. Now he was preparing to attack the wandering bands of Sioux hunting parties, even though he recognized that intruding American miners had caused the renewal of warfare. As he told reporters, "We are goading the Indians to madness by invading their hallowed [hunting] grounds."

THE GREAT SIOUX WAR   What became the **Great Sioux War** was the largest military campaign since the end of the Civil War. The conflict lasted fifteen months and entailed fifteen battles in present-day Wyoming, Montana, South Dakota, and Nebraska. In the end, more soldiers than Indians were killed, but the Native Americans were defeated.

In June 1876, after several indecisive encounters, Custer found a large encampment of Sioux and their Northern Cheyenne and Arapaho allies on the Little Bighorn River in the southeast corner of the Montana Territory. Ignoring the warnings of his scouts, Custer split his force in two and attacked a Sioux village on June 25. "Hurrah boys, we've got them," he shouted, not

Battle of the Little Bighorn, 1876 Amos Bad Heart Bull, an Oglala Sioux artist and historian, painted this scene from the Battle of the Little Bighorn.

realizing how outnumbered the soldiers were. Within minutes, the horse soldiers were surrounded by 2,500 warriors led by the fierce Crazy Horse, who deemed it "a good day to fight, a good day to die!"

A Cheyenne chief remembered that "we swirled around the soldiers like water around a stone." After a half hour, the 261 soldiers, their ammunition exhausted, were all dead. Custer laughed as he fired his last bullet; he was then felled by shots to his head and heart. Cheyenne women pierced Custer's eardrums with sewing needles because he had failed to heed the warnings to stay out of their ancestral lands.

The Sioux had won their greatest battle but had ensured their ultimate defeat. Upon learning of the Battle of the Little Bighorn ("Custer's Last Stand"), President Grant and Congress abandoned the peace policy and dispatched more supplies and troops to the plains. General Philip Sheridan now planned for "total war." Former Confederates wrote to President Grant to offer their services.

Under Sheridan's aggressive leadership, the army quickly regained the offensive and relentlessly pursued the Sioux and Cheyenne across Montana. Warriors were slain, villages destroyed, and food supplies burned. Iron Teeth, a Cheyenne woman, recalled an attack by "white soldiers" in November 1876: "They killed our men, women, and children." She ran away with her three daughters, while her husband and two sons remained to fight. "My husband," she remembered, "was walking, leading his horse, and stopping

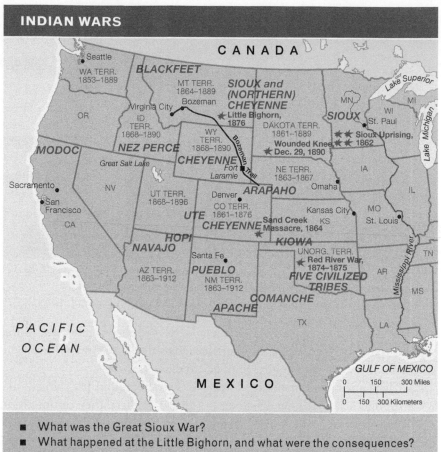

INDIAN WARS

- What was the Great Sioux War?
- What happened at the Little Bighorn, and what were the consequences?
- Why were hundreds of Native Americans killed at Wounded Knee?

at times to shoot. Suddenly, I saw him fall. I started to go back to him, but my sons made me go on." The last time she saw her husband, he was dead in the snow.

Forced back onto reservations, the remaining Native Americans soon were struggling to survive. Many died of starvation or disease. By the end of 1876, the chiefs living on the Dakota reservation agreed to sell the Black Hills to the U.S. government. "This was the country of the buffalo and the hostile Sioux only last year," Sheridan wrote in 1877. "There are no signs of either now, but in their place we find prospectors, emigrants, and farmers."

In the spring of 1877, Crazy Horse and his people surrendered. The Great Sioux War was over, but the fate of Native Americans remained uncertain. Two years later, President Rutherford Hayes journeyed by train to the western states and territories. In Larned, Kansas, he and General William T. Sherman gave speeches. Sherman noted that he was delighted to see the Indians gone, adding that "I don't care where they are gone to."

THE END OF THE BUFFALO The collapse of Indian resistance resulted as much from the decimation of the buffalo herds as from the actions of federal troops. In 1750, an estimated 30 million buffalo inhabited the plains. The herds were so vast that one traveler said they changed the color of the landscape, "blackening the whole surface of the country." By 1850, there were fewer than 10 million; by 1900, only a few hundred remained. (Today there are about 200,000.) What happened to them?

The conventional story focuses on intensive harvesting of buffalo by White commercial hunters after the Civil War. The construction of railroads through buffalo country brought hundreds of hunters who shipped huge numbers of hides to the East, where consumers developed a voracious demand for buffalo robes, buffalo leather, and trophy heads. The average commercial hunter killed 100 buffalo a day. "The buffalo," reported an army officer, "melted away like snow before a summer's sun." Army officers encouraged the slaughter. A colonel told a buffalo hunter: "Kill every buffalo you can! Every buffalo dead is an Indian gone."

The story is more complicated, however. A prolonged drought during the late 1880s and 1890s severely reduced the grasslands upon which the buffalo depended. At the same time, they had to compete for food with other grazing animals; by the 1880s, more than 2 million wild horses were roaming buffalo lands.

The Plains Indians themselves, empowered by horses and rifles and spurred by profits reaped from selling hides and meat to White traders, accounted for much of the devastation of the buffalo herds after 1840. If there had been no White hunters, the buffalo would have lasted only another thirty years because their numbers had been so greatly reduced by other factors. Whatever the reasons, the disappearance of the buffalo gave the Plains Indians little choice but to settle on government reservations.

THE LAST RESISTANCE In the Rocky Mountains and west to the Pacific Ocean, the story of courageous yet hopeless Native American resistance to White intruders was repeated again and again. Indians were the last obstacle to White western expansion, and they suffered as a result.

The Blackfeet and Crows had to leave their homes in Montana. In a war along the California-Oregon boundary, the Modoc held out for six months in 1871–1872 before they were overwhelmed. In 1879, the Utes were forced to give up their vast territories in western Colorado. In Idaho, the peaceful Nez

Perce bands refused to surrender land along the Salmon River, and prolonged fighting erupted there and in eastern Oregon.

In 1877, Joseph, a Nez Perce chief, led some 650 of his people on a 1,300-mile journey through Montana in hopes of finding safety in Canada. Just before reaching the border, they were caught by U.S. soldiers. As he surrendered, Joseph delivered an eloquent speech: "I am tired of fighting. Our chiefs are killed. . . . The old men are all dead. . . . I want to have time to look for my children, and see how many of them I can find. My heart is sick and sad. From where the sun now stands I will fight no more forever." The Nez Perce requested that they be allowed to return to their ancestral lands in western Idaho, but they were forced to settle in the Indian Territory.

A generation of Indian wars ended in 1886 with the capture of Geronimo, a powerful chief of the Chiricahua Apaches, who had outridden, outwitted, and outfought American forces in the Southwest for fifteen years. General Nelson A. Miles, commander of the soldiers who captured Geronimo, called him "one of the brightest, most resolute, determined-looking men that I have ever encountered."

THE GHOST DANCE The last major clash between Indians and American soldiers occurred near the end of the nineteenth century. Late in 1888, Wovoka (or Jack Wilson), a Paiute in western Nevada, fell ill. In a delirium, he imagined being in the spirit world, where he learned of a deliverer coming to rescue the Indians and restore their lands. To hasten their deliverance, he said, the Indians must perform a ceremonial dance wearing "ghost shirts" enlivened by sacred symbols that would make them bulletproof. The Ghost Dance craze fed upon old legends of the dead reuniting with the living and bringing prosperity and peace.

The **Ghost Dance movement** spread rapidly. In 1890, the western Sioux adopted the practice with such passion that it alarmed White authorities. "Indians are dancing in the snow and are wild and crazy," reported a government agent at the Pine Ridge Reservation in South Dakota. "We need protection and we need it now." The Bureau of Indian Affairs responded by banning the Ghost Dance ceremony on Lakota reservations, but the Indians defied the order.

On December 29, 1890, a bloodbath occurred at an Indian camp in South Dakota, along a frozen creek called Wounded Knee. U.S. soldiers ordered the Indians to surrender their weapons. "They called for guns and arms," remembered an Indian named White Lance, "so all of us gave the guns and they were stacked up in the center." Convinced that there were more weapons, the soldiers began searching in tipis. A medicine man began dancing the Ghost

Dance when a shot rang out. Overeager soldiers began firing indiscriminately into a group of Indians.

More than 150 unarmed Indian men, women, and children died in the Battle of Wounded Knee. Twenty-five soldiers were also killed, most by friendly fire. Major General Nelson A. Miles, the U.S. Army regional commander, wrote his wife that hopes for a peaceful settlement had dissolved into a "most abominable, criminal military blunder and a horrible massacre of women and children."

Miles ordered an inquiry into what had happened at Wounded Knee, for he was convinced that Colonel James W. Forsyth's actions as the senior officer at the site were "about the worst I have ever known." Yet the court of inquiry exonerated Forsyth and covered up the massacre, much to the chagrin of General Miles. Some twenty soldiers received the Medal of Honor for their role in the massacre.

A CENTURY OF DISHONOR   The Indian wars ended with characteristic brutality and misunderstanding. General Philip Sheridan, overall commander of U.S. troops, was acidly candid in summarizing how Whites had treated the Indians: "We took away their country and their means of support, broke up their mode of living, their habits of life, introduced disease and decay among them, and it was for this and against this that they made war. Could anyone expect less?"

Many politicians and religious leaders condemned the persistent mistreatment of Indians. In his annual message of 1877, President Rutherford B. Hayes joined the protest: "Many, if not most, of our Indian wars have had their origin in broken promises and acts of injustice on our part." Helen Hunt Jackson, a novelist and poet, focused attention on the Indian cause in *A Century of Dishonor* (1881), a book that powerfully detailed the sad history of America's exploitation of Native Americans.

In part as a reaction to Jackson's book, U.S. policies gradually improved but did little to enhance the Indians' difficult living conditions and actually fueled the destruction of their cultural traditions. The reservation policy inaugurated by the Peace Commission in 1867, though partly humanitarian in motive, also saved the government money; housing and feeding Indians on reservations cost less than fighting them.

Well-intentioned but biased White reformers sought to "Americanize" Indians by forcing them to become self-reliant farmers owning their own land rather than allowing them to be members of nomadic bands or tribes holding property in common. Such reform efforts produced the **Dawes Severalty Act of 1887** (also called the General Allotment Act), the most sweeping policy directed at Native Americans in U.S. history. Sponsored by Senator Henry L. Dawes of Massachusetts, it divided tribal lands and "allotted" them to individuals, granting 160 acres to each head of a family and lesser amounts to others.

The purpose of the policy was to convert the nomadic Indians into small farmers and landowners. Dawes complained that the traditional communal Indian culture in which land and food were shared was "communism."

Not surprisingly, most Indians balked. White Bear, a Kiowa chief, said that his people did "not want to settle down in houses you [the federal government] would build for us. I love to roam over the wild prairie. There I am free and happy." But his preferences were ignored. Between 1887 and 1934, Indians lost an estimated 86 million of their 130 million acres. As Henry Teller, a congressman from Colorado, pointed out, the allotment policy was designed solely to strip the "Indians of their lands and to make them vagabonds on the face of the earth."

THE END OF THE FRONTIER

The end of Native American resistance was one of several developments that suggested the New West was indeed different from the Old West. Other indicators of the region's transformation led some scholars to conclude that American society itself had reached a turning point by the end of the nineteenth century.

Frederick Jackson Turner The 1890 national census data indicated that the frontier era was over; Americans had spread across the entire continent. This news led Frederick Jackson Turner, a historian at the University of Wisconsin, to announce in 1893 his "frontier thesis." He argued that more than slavery or any other single factor, "the existence of an area of free land, its continuous recession, and the advance of American settlement westward, explain American development." The experience of taming and settling the frontier, he added, had shaped the national character in fundamental ways. It was

> to the frontier [that] the American intellect owes its striking characteristics. That coarseness and strength combined with acuteness and acquisitiveness; that practical, inventive turn of mind, quick to find expedients; that masterful grasp of material things, lacking in the artistic but powerful to effect great ends; that restless, nervous energy; that dominant individualism, working for good and for evil, and withal that buoyancy and exuberance which comes with freedom—these are traits of the frontier, or traits called out elsewhere because of the existence of the frontier.

Now, however, Turner stressed, "the frontier has gone and with its going has closed the first period of American history."

Turner's view of the frontier gripped the popular imagination. But the frontier experience that he described was in many respects a self-serving myth involving only Christian White men and devoid of towns and cities, which grew *along* with the frontier—not *after* it had been tamed. He virtually ignored the role of women, African Americans, Native Americans, Hispanics, and Asians in shaping the western United States. Moreover, Turner downplayed the vivid evidence of greed, exploitation, and frequent failure in the settling of the West.

He also implied that America would be fundamentally different after 1890 because the frontier experience was essentially over. In many respects, however, the West has retained the qualities associated with the rush for land, gold, timber, and water rights. The mining frontier, as one historian recently wrote, "set a mood that has never disappeared from the West: the attitude of every extractive industry—get in, get rich, get out."

DISCONTENTED FARMERS   By 1900, the South and West were quite different from what they had been in 1865. In both cases, changed economic conditions spurred the emergence of a New South and a New West.

In the West, mechanized commercial agriculture changed the dynamics of farming. By the end of the nineteenth century, many homesteaders had been forced to abandon their farms and become wage-earning laborers, migrant workers moving with the seasons to different states to harvest crops produced on large commercial farms or ranches. They were often treated as poorly as the White and Black sharecroppers in the South. One western worker complained that the landowner "looked at me, his hired hand, as if I was just another workhorse."

As discontent rose among farmers and farmworkers in the South and the West, many joined the People's Party, whose supporters were known as Populists, a grassroots social and political movement that was sweeping the poorest rural regions of the nation. In 1892, a Minnesota farm leader named Ignatius Donnelly told Populists at their national convention: "We meet in the midst of a nation brought to the verge of moral, political, and material ruin." He affirmed that Populism sought "to restore the Government of the Republic to the hands of the 'plain people' with whom it originated."

The Populist movement would tie the South and West together in an effort to wrest political control from Republicans in the Northeast and Midwest. That struggle would come to define the 1890s and determine the shape of twentieth-century politics.

CHAPTER REVIEW

SUMMARY

- **The New South** Many southerners embraced the vision of a New South, which called for a more diverse economy with greater industrialization, wider distribution of wealth, and more vocational training. The cotton textile industry grew, iron and steel manufacturing increased, and the *American Tobacco Company* became the world's largest manufacturer of cigarettes. But agriculture still dominated the southern economy, much as it had before the Civil War. Land remained concentrated in few hands, and the *crop-lien system* left much of the population, both Black and White, with little choice but to cultivate cotton for these large landholders.

- **Jim Crow Policies in the South** During the 1890s, southern states disenfranchised the vast majority of African American voters and instituted a series of policies known as Jim Crow laws segregating Blacks and Whites in all public facilities. Starting with the *Mississippi Plan* (1890), state governments used poll taxes, grandfather clauses, literacy tests, and residency requirements to virtually eliminate the African American vote. Disenfranchisement by the states was followed by legalized segregation ("*separate but equal*"), ruled constitutional by the Supreme Court in the 1896 *Plessy v. Ferguson* decision. African Americans who resisted were often the target of violence at the hands of Whites; the worst attacks were the organized lynchings. In one of the worst instances of racial violence, rampaging White supremacists overthrew the elected biracial government in the *Wilmington Insurrection* (1898). The African American response in the South was led by Booker T. Washington whose famous speech, the *Atlanta Compromise* (1895), encouraged southern Blacks to focus on vocational training and economic self-sufficiency. At the national level, leaders like Callie Guy House, Booker T. Washington, and W. E. B. Du Bois took on issues of segregation, racial violence, and reparations, while working to create more educational and economic opportunities for African Americans.

- **Western Migrants** Life in the West was often harsh and violent, but the promise of cheap land or wealth from mining drew settlers from the East. Although most westerners were White Protestant Americans or immigrants from Germany and Scandinavia, Mexicans, African Americans (the *Exodusters*), and Chinese, as well as many other nationalities, contributed to the West's diversity. About three fourths of those who moved to the West were men.

- **Miners, Farmers, Ranchers, Women, and Mexican Americans** Many migrants to the West were attracted by opportunities to mine, ranch, farm, or work on the railroads. Miners were drawn to the discovery of precious minerals such as silver at the *Comstock Lode* in Nevada in 1859. But most miners and cattle ranchers did not acquire wealth because mining and raising cattle, particularly after the development of barbed wire and the end of the open range, became large-scale enterprises run by corporations. Because of the economic hardship and the rugged isolation of life in the West, women there achieved greater equality in everyday life, including voting rights, than did most women elsewhere in the country. Mexican Americans made a significant contribution to the ranching culture and the building of the transcontinental railroads, yet they also were victims of violent ethnic prejudices.

- **Indian Wars and Policies** By 1900, Native Americans in the West were no longer free to roam. The prevailing attitude of most Whites in the West was to displace or exterminate the Native Americans. In 1864, for example, Colorado militiamen decimated a group of Indians—men, women, and children—at the *Sand Creek Massacre*. Instances of armed resistance, such as the *Great Sioux War*, were crushed. The *Indian wars* resulted in the collapse of armed Indian resistance to Western settlement. Initially, Indian tribes were forced to sign treaties and were confined to reservations. Beginning in 1887 with the *Dawes Severalty Act*, the American government's Indian policy shifted. It forced Indians to relinquish their traditional culture and adopt the "American way" of individual landownership. The *Ghost Dance movement* would emerge as a powerful new form of resistance and Native American religious expression to stop the expansion of settlement in the West.

- **The South and West in 1900** In 1893, Frederick Jackson Turner, a prominent historian, declared that the frontier had been the nation's primary source of democratic politics and rugged individualism. By 1900, however, the frontier era was over and the Populist movement had begun. The West resembled the South, where agricultural resources were concentrated in the hands of a few.

CHRONOLOGY

1859	Comstock Lode is discovered
1862	Congress passes the Homestead Act
1864	Sand Creek Massacre in Colorado
1873	Joseph Glidden invents barbed wire
1876	Battle of the Little Bighorn
1880s	Henry Grady spreads the New South idea
1886	Surrender of Geronimo marks the end of the Indian wars
1887	Congress passes the Dawes Severalty Act
1890	Battle of Wounded Knee; James B. Duke forms the American Tobacco Company
1893	Frederick J. Turner's "frontier thesis"
1895	The Atlanta Compromise speech
1896	*Plessy v. Ferguson* mandates "separate but equal" racial facilities
1898	The Wilmington Insurrection
1900	South surpasses New England in production of cotton fabric

KEY TERMS

American Tobacco Company p. 815
crop-lien system p. 817
Mississippi Plan (1890) p. 820
separate but equal p. 823
Wilmington Insurrection (1898) p. 825
Atlanta Compromise (1895) p. 831
Exodusters p. 834

Comstock Lode p. 836
Indian wars p. 851
Sand Creek Massacre (1864) p. 853
Great Sioux War p. 856
Ghost Dance movement p. 860
Dawes Severalty Act of 1887 p. 861

18 Political Stalemate and Rural Revolt

1865–1900

***New York,* 1911** This scene of early-twentieth-century life in New York City by George Wesley Bellows captures people of all walks of life converging on a busy, vibrant downtown intersection.

The Gilded Age, the period from the end of the Civil War to the beginning of the twentieth century, was noted for the widening social, economic, and political gap between the powerful and the powerless, the haves and have-nots. Writer Mark Twain sarcastically labeled it the Gilded Age—to "gild" something is to cover it with a thin layer of gold, giving it the appearance of having greater value than it warrants. It was an era marked by the greed of the newly rich as they flaunted their enormous personal wealth. Many of them would use their wealth to finance extensive political bribery and corporate corruption.

Between 1865 and 1900, millions of European and Asian immigrants, as well as masses of migrants from rural areas, streamed into rapidly growing cities, attracted by the jobs and excitements they offered. "We cannot all live in cities," cautioned Horace Greeley, the New York newspaper editor, "yet nearly all seem determined to do so."

The growth of cities brought an array of problems, among them widespread poverty, unsanitary living conditions, and new forms of political corruption. How to feed, shelter, and educate city dwellers taxed the imaginations and resources of government officials. Even more challenging was the development of neighborhoods divided by racial and ethnic background as well as social class and economic standing.

focus questions

1. What were the effects of urban growth during the Gilded Age? What problems did it create?

2. Who were the "new immigrants" of the late nineteenth century? How were they were viewed by American society?

3. How did urban growth and the increasingly important role of science influence leisure activities, cultural life, and social policy in the late nineteenth century?

4. How did the nature of politics during the Gilded Age contribute to political corruption and stalemate?

5. How effective were politicians in developing responses to the major economic and social problems in the aftermath of the Civil War?

6. Why did the money supply become a major political issue, especially for small farmers, during the Gilded Age? How did it impact American politics?

At the same time, researchers were making discoveries that improved human health, economic productivity, and communications. Advances in modern science stimulated public support for higher education but also created doubts about many long-accepted "truths" and religious beliefs, doubts that led to conflicts over whether or how Charles Darwin's controversial theory of evolution could be applied to human society.

Political life during the **Gilded Age** was shaped by three main factors: the balance of power between Democrats and Republicans, the high level of public participation in everyday politics, and the often corrupt alliance between business and political leaders at all levels of government. In 1873, Job Stephenson, an Ohio congressman, claimed that members of the House of Representatives were so often selling their votes to business lobbyists that the Capitol should have been renamed an "auction room."

The most important political issue of the Gilded Age was the growing tension between city and country, industry and agriculture. Millions of financially distressed farmers felt ignored or betrayed by a political system increasingly controlled by huge corporations. While industrialists and large commercial farmers prospered, small farmers struggled with falling crop prices, growing indebtedness to banks and railroads, and what they considered big-city greed and exploitation.

By the 1890s, discontented farmers would channel their frustrations into a movement to expand (inflate) the nation's money supply to relieve economic distress. The transformational election of 1896 centered on the issue of the money supply and symbolized the central conflict of the Gilded Age: the clashing cultural and economic values of two Americas, one small-scale and rural, and the other large, urban, and industrial.

AMERICA'S MOVE TO TOWN

Cities are perhaps the greatest human invention. By attracting people in large numbers, they also stimulate innovation and creativity, productivity and energy. "The greater part of our population must live in cities," announced Josiah Strong, a prominent Congregationalist minister, in 1898. "There was no resisting the trend."

After the Civil War, millions of Americans migrated from rural areas to cities. Many had been pushed off the land by new agricultural machinery that reduced the need for farmworkers. Four men could now perform the work that earlier had required fourteen.

Others were drawn to cities by plentiful jobs and new social and recreational opportunities. By the end of the nineteenth century, much of the settlement of the West was taking an urban form, with new towns forming around mines and railroad junctions. Still other migrants, bored by rural or small-town life, moved to cities in search of more excitement.

While the Far West had fewer cities, for example San Francisco and Denver, it had a higher proportion of urban dwellers compared to people living in the countryside; whereas the Northeast and Midwest still had significant numbers of people living in the countryside, and they had far more cities and far more people living in each of the huge cities—New York, Boston, Philadelphia, Pittsburgh, Chicago, Cincinnati, St. Louis, and others. Whether living in the east or west, most of these city dwellers had little or no money and nothing but their labor to sell.

GROWTH IN ALL DIRECTIONS Advances in technology helped city buildings hold their surging populations. In the 1870s, heating innovations such as steam radiators made the construction of much larger apartment buildings financially feasible, because expensive coal-burning fireplaces and chimneys were no longer required in each apartment. Before the 1860s, few structures had been more than five or six stories. During the 1880s, engineers developed cast-iron and steel-frame construction techniques that allowed for taller structures— "skyscrapers." When the Otis Elevator Company installed the first electric elevator in 1889, taller buildings became more practical to design and inhabit.

Cities grew out as well as up, as horse-drawn streetcars and commuter railways allowed people to live farther away from their downtown workplaces. In 1873, San Francisco became the first city to use cable cars that clamped onto a moving underground cable driven by a central power source. Some cities ran steam-powered trains on elevated tracks, but by the 1890s, electric trolleys were preferred. Mass transit received an added boost from underground subway trains built in Boston, New York City, and Philadelphia.

Commuter trains and trolleys allowed a growing middle class of business executives and professionals (accountants, doctors, engineers, salesclerks, teachers, store managers, and attorneys) to retreat from crowded downtowns to quieter, tree-lined "streetcar suburbs." But the working poor, many of them immigrants or African Americans, could rarely afford to leave the inner cities. As their populations grew, cities became dangerously congested and plagued with fires, violent crimes, and diseases. New York City, for instance, doubled in size between 1860 and 1890, so fast that basic services could not keep up.

CROWDS, DIRT, AND DISEASE The wonders of big cities—electric lights, streetcars, telephones, department stores, theaters, and many other attractions—lured rural dwellers bored by isolated farm life. Yet they often traded one set of problems for another. In New York City in 1900, some 2.3 million people—two thirds of the city's population—lived in overcrowded apartments called **tenements**, where residents, many of them immigrants, were packed like sardines in poorly ventilated and dimly lit buildings.

Tenement buildings were usually five to six stories tall, lacked elevators, and were jammed so tightly together that most of the apartments had little or no natural light or fresh air. The buildings typically housed twenty-four to thirty-two families, usually with lots of children who had few places to play except in the streets. On average, only one toilet (called a *privy*) served every twenty people. In one New York tenement apartment, twelve adults slept in a room of only thirteen square feet.

Late nineteenth-century cities were filthy and disease ridden. Most streets were unpaved and awash with horse urine and manure, and littered with dead animals—cats, dogs, and horses. Sidewalks were festooned with tobacco spit, which spread tuberculosis. Garbage and raw sewage were dumped into streets and waterways, causing epidemics of infectious diseases such as cholera, typhoid fever, and yellow fever. The child-mortality rate in tenements was as

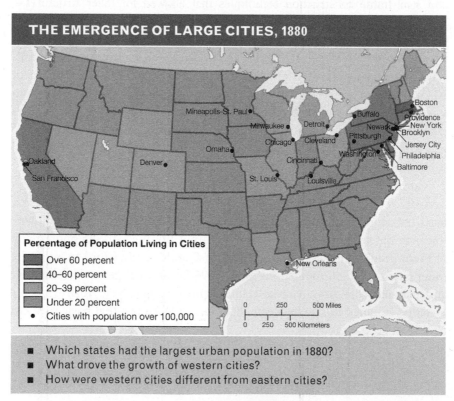

THE EMERGENCE OF LARGE CITIES, 1880

Percentage of Population Living in Cities
- Over 60 percent
- 40–60 percent
- 20–39 percent
- Under 20 percent
- • Cities with population over 100,000

- Which states had the largest urban population in 1880?
- What drove the growth of western cities?
- How were western cities different from eastern cities?

Urbanization and the Environment Starting in the late nineteenth century, trash in New York City was collected by garbage carts such as this one.

high as 40 percent. In one poor Chicago district at the end of the century, three of every five babies died before their first birthday.

So-called sanitary reformers—public health officials and engineers—eventually created cleaner conditions in tenements by enacting regulations requiring more space per resident as well as more windows and plumbing facilities. Reformers also pushed for modern water and sewage systems and for regular trash collection, which by 1900 had been adopted in most cities. The many animals in cities were a huge sanitary challenge. Reformers lobbied to ban slaughterhouses as well as the raising of hogs and cattle within city limits and to replace horse-drawn trolleys with electric-powered streetcars or trolleys.

The New Immigration

America's roaring prosperity and the promise of political and religious freedom attracted waves of immigrants from every part of the globe after the Civil War. By 1900, nearly 30 percent of city residents were foreign-born. Most of those newcomers were desperately poor people eager to pursue the American dream. They brought with them a distinctive work ethic. Working only to survive is often wretched. Working for a better life for oneself and one's

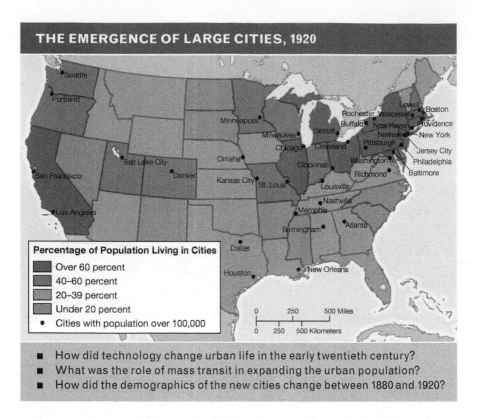

THE EMERGENCE OF LARGE CITIES, 1920

Percentage of Population Living in Cities

- Over 60 percent
- 40–60 percent
- 20–39 percent
- Under 20 percent
- Cities with population over 100,000

0   250   500 Miles
0   250   500 Kilometers

- How did technology change urban life in the early twentieth century?
- What was the role of mass transit in expanding the urban population?
- How did the demographics of the new cities change between 1880 and 1920?

children and grandchildren gives labor a fierce dignity. That dignity, infused with an optimistic energy and aspiration, endowed the new immigrants with resilience and determination. In providing much-needed labor for the growing economy, however, the influx of immigrants also sparked racial and ethnic tensions.

A SURGE OF NEWCOMERS   Immigration has always been one of the most powerful and controversial forces shaping American development. This was especially true between 1860 and 1900, as increasingly more foreigners, most of them young and poor, arrived from eastern and southern Europe. The number of immigrants rose from just under 3 million annually in the 1870s to more than 5 million per year in the 1880s. Nearly 9 million came to the United States annually in the first decade of the twentieth century. In 1890, four out of five New Yorkers were foreign-born, a higher proportion than in any city in the world. Chicago was not far behind.

Rapidly growing industries—including mines, railroads, mills, slaughterhouses, and factories—sought workers willing to accept long hours and low wages; they sent recruiters abroad to lure immigrants to the United States.

Under the Contract Labor Act of 1864, the federal government helped pay for immigrants' travel expenses to America. The law was repealed in 1868, but not until 1885 did the government stop companies from importing unskilled, low-wage foreign laborers, a practice that put immigrant workers under the control of their employers.

The so-called old immigrants were those who came to the United States before 1880; they were mainly Protestants and Roman Catholics from northern and western Europe. Germans were the single largest ethnic population in America by 1900, most of them eventually settling in the Midwest. By 1910, some 490 German-language newspapers were being published in the United States. The traditional pattern of immigration changed, however, as the proportion of immigrants from southern and eastern Europe, especially Russia, Poland, Greece, and Italy, rose sharply during the last quarter of the nineteenth century. After 1890, these "**new immigrants**" made up the majority of newcomers. Their languages and cultural backgrounds were markedly different from those of previous immigrants or of most native-born Americans. The dominant religions of the new immigrants, for example, were Judaism, Eastern Orthodoxy, and Roman Catholicism, whereas Protestants still formed a large majority of the U.S. population.

While many immigrants gravitated to large cities—New York, Boston, Philadelphia, Chicago—others headed west upon arriving in New York. By 1890, an estimated 45 percent of people living in North Dakota were foreign-born. In South Dakota, California, and Washington State, nearly 30 percent of residents were immigrants, and in virtually all the western states the foreign-born were over 20 percent of the population.

The South, however, remained unattractive to immigrants. Newcomers avoided the South because of its low wages, racial dynamics, and widespread poverty. The percentage of foreign-born residents in the states of the former Confederacy declined between 1860 and 1900. By 1910, only 2 percent of southerners were immigrants compared to the national average of 15 percent.

STRANGERS IN A NEW LAND Once on American soil, desperately poor immigrants needed to find jobs—quickly. Many were greeted at the docks by family and friends who had come over before them; others, by representatives of immigrant-aid societies or by company recruiters offering low-paying and often dangerous jobs in mines, mills, or sweatshops and on railroads. Since most immigrants knew little if any English and nothing about American employment practices, they were easy targets for exploitation. Many unwittingly lost a healthy percentage of their wages to unscrupulous hiring agents in exchange for a bit of whiskey and a job. Other companies eager for workers gave immigrants train tickets to inland cities such as Buffalo, Pittsburgh, Cleveland, Chicago, Milwaukee, Cincinnati, and St. Louis.

The influx of new immigrants generated widespread criticism and concern. The Reverend Josiah Strong acknowledged in 1885 that immigration brought "unquestioned benefits," but he believed it also was the primary cause of the nation's "most noxious" social problems. He described the typical "new immigrant" as a "European peasant" whose "horizon had been narrow, whose moral and religious training has been meagre or false, and whose ideas of life are low." Most of the newcomers from eastern and southern Europe were, he charged, destitute criminals. Many were Catholic or Jewish; others were socialists or anarchists. In his view, "there is no more serious menace to our civilization" than the "rabble" of "new immigrants."

By 1907, the concerns of Strong and others led Congress to appoint the Dillingham Commission to examine changes in immigration patterns. In its lengthy report, released in 1911, the commission concluded that immigrants from southern and eastern Europe posed a social and cultural threat to America's future. They were "far less intelligent than the old, approximately one-third of all those over 14 years of age when admitted being illiterate. Racially, they

Mulberry Street, 1900 This colorized photograph captures the many Italian immigrants who made Mulberry Street in downtown New York City their home at the turn of the century.

are for the most part essentially unlike the British, German, and other peoples who came during the prior period to 1880, and generally speaking they are actuated in coming by different ideals."

As strangers in a new land, most immigrants gravitated to neighborhoods populated by people from their homeland. The largest cities had vibrant immigrant districts with names such as Little Italy, Little Hungary, and Chinatown, where immigrants practiced their native religions and customs and spoke and read newspapers in their native languages. But they paid a price for such community solidarity. When new immigrants moved into an area, the previous residents often moved out, taking with them whatever social prestige and political influence they had achieved. Living conditions often deteriorated as tenement owners failed to abide by housing and sanitation codes.

THE NATIVIST RESPONSE   Then as now, many native-born Americans saw the newest immigrants as a threat to their jobs and way of life. These "nativists" were often racists who believed that "Anglo-Saxon" Americans—people of British or Germanic ancestry—were superior to the Slavic, Italian, Greek, and Jewish arrivals. A Stanford University professor, for instance, called immigrants from southern and eastern Europe "illiterate, docile, lacking in self-reliance and initiative, and not possessing the Anglo-Teutonic conceptions of law, order, and government." Throughout American history, Congress has passed immigration regulations with inconsistent goals and frequently rooted in racial and ethnic prejudice. During the late nineteenth century, such prejudice took an especially ugly turn against the Chinese, who suffered discrimination even beyond that leveled at the new immigrants from Europe. They were the first non-European and non-African group to migrate in large numbers to America.

The Chinese living in California were easy targets for discrimination. They were not White, few were Christians, and many could not read or write. Whites resented them for supposedly

Chinese Exclusion Act The caricature of John Chinaman, with his ironing board and opium pipe, is escorted out of America by Lady Liberty.

taking their jobs, although in many instances the Chinese were willing to do the menial work that Whites refused to do.

John Jeong, a young Chinese immigrant, arrived in San Francisco and quickly encountered ethnic persecution. As he and others made their way to the Chinatown neighborhood in an open carriage, "some white boys came up and started throwing rocks at us." Another Chinese newcomer experienced similar treatment. Whenever he and his friends strayed outside their own neighborhood, "whites would attack you with stones."

White Californians demanded an end to Chinese immigration. Until 1875, immigration policies had been left up to the states. In that year, however, Congress passed the Page Act, the first federal law intended to restrict "undesirable" immigration. Representative Horace F. Page, a California Republican, proposed the legislation to "end the danger of cheap Chinese labor and immoral Chinese women" coming into the country.

The Page Act barred "undesirable" immigrants, which meant *anyone* from East Asia who was recruited to the United States to be a forced laborer, *any* East Asian woman who might engage in prostitution, and *all* people who were convicts in their own country. The Page Act caused the number of Chinese women entering the United States to plummet. In 1882, when some 40,000 Chinese entered the country, only 136 of them were women.

Nativists then turned their anger toward Chinese men. In 1877, Dennis Kearney, an Irish immigrant in San Francisco, organized the Workingmen's Party of California, whose socialist platform called for the United States to revise the Page Act to stop ALL Chinese immigration, men and women. Five years later, in 1882, a bipartisan majority in Congress overwhelmingly passed two laws affecting immigration. The first excluded immigration by any criminals, prostitutes, lunatics, idiots, and paupers. The second, called the **Chinese Exclusion Act,** barred all Chinese laborers (disparagingly deemed the "yellow hordes") from entering the country for ten years. Thereafter it was periodically renewed. It also prohibited Chinese already in America from marrying Whites or African Americans, and it denied citizenship to Chinese immigrants. The Supreme Court, however, would rule in *U.S. v. Wong Kim Ark* (1898) that immigrant children born in the United States were citizens. The majority justices wrote that the Fourteenth Amendment "affirms the ancient and fundamental rule of citizenship by birth within the territory . . . including all children born of resident aliens."

With the Chinese Exclusion Act, the golden door welcoming foreigners to the United States began to close. It was the first federal law to restrict the immigration of people explicitly on the basis of race and class. Not until 1943 were barriers to Chinese immigration finally removed.

The Chinese were not the only group targeted. In 1887, Protestant activists in Iowa formed the American Protective Association (APA), a secret organization whose members pledged never to employ or vote for a Roman Catholic. Working often within local Republican party organizations, the APA quickly enlisted 2.5 million members and helped shape the 1894 election results in Ohio, Wisconsin, Indiana, Missouri, and Colorado.

In 1891, nativists in New England formed the Immigration Restriction League to, in their words, "save" the Anglo-Saxon "race" from being "contaminated" by "alien" immigrants, especially Roman Catholics and Jews. The League urged Congress to require that immigrants be given literacy tests to prove they could read and write. A powerful senator, Henry Cabot Lodge of Massachusetts, who helped found the Immigration Restriction League, confessed that he intended the literacy test to restrict particular groups from entering the United States. As Lodge admitted in 1907, "The races most affected by the . . . test are those whose emigration to this country has begun within the last twenty years and swelled rapidly to enormous proportions, races with which the English-speaking people have never hitherto assimilated, and who are most alien to the great body of the people of the United States."

Three presidents of both major parties vetoed bills requiring immigrants to pass a literacy test: Grover Cleveland in 1897, William H. Taft in 1913, and Woodrow Wilson in 1915 and 1917. The last time, however, Congress overrode the veto, and illiterate immigrants were banned—as well as immigrants from *all* Asian countries except for Japan and the Philippines.

As nativists were trying to "close the doors" to "new immigrants," the policies regarding all immigrants were changing. Congress directed that the federal government, rather than the states, assume responsibility for admitting immigrants. To do so, it created the Bureau of Immigration. In 1890, Congress appointed the first federal superintendent of immigration for the port of New York; he set about supervising the construction of the Ellis Island immigration inspection station on the Hudson River just a mile southwest of Manhattan. Opened in 1892, it was a gigantic facility, for New York City received more immigrants than all other cities combined.

The Ellis Island reception center could process as many as 5,000 people a day, thanks to an army of inspectors, translators, railroad ticket agents, baggage handlers, doctors, and nurses. But only the poorest of the poor—those who traveled in the cheapest "steerage" compartments in the lower decks— circulated through the reception center. Affluent immigrants were exempt from such bureaucratic processing.

The first immigrant to be processed at Ellis Island was seventeen-year-old Annie Moore from County Cork, Ireland, who had crossed the Atlantic with

Ellis Island To accommodate the soaring numbers of immigrants passing through New York City, Congress provided funds to build a huge reception center on Ellis Island, near the Statue of Liberty. It opened in 1892. Pictured here is its registry room, where immigrants awaited close questioning by officials.

her two younger brothers. They had understated their ages to gain lower fares, and they planned to reconnect with their parents and two siblings who had been in New York City for four years. A U.S. Treasury Department official and a Catholic chaplain welcomed Moore, and Ellis Island's commissioner gave her a $10 gold piece to mark the occasion. She confessed that it was the most money she had ever seen. (It represented a week's wages or a month's rent.)

Moore's new life in America was anything but easy, however. Three years after arriving at Ellis Island and already pregnant, she married Joseph Augustus "Gus" Schayer, a German American fish seller. Living in a series of shabby tenements in the Lower East Side of Manhattan, they had at least ten children, five of whom died of malnutrition before the age of three.

Ellis Island became known as the "island of hope, island of tears." Yet it provided far more hope than tears. Despite the increasingly stringent guidelines for accepting immigrants, few were denied entry. Of the 12 million people who passed through the doors of Ellis Island between 1892 and 1954, only 2 percent were deemed unfit to reside in the United States. Today, more than 40 percent of Americans can trace their ancestry through Ellis Island.

Changes in Culture and Thought

The flood of people into cities brought changes in daily life and increased opportunities for recreation and leisure. Middle- and upper-class families, especially those who had moved to the new suburban neighborhoods, often spent free time together at home, singing around a piano, reading, or playing games—cards, dominoes, backgammon, chess, and checkers. In congested urban areas, politics as a form of public entertainment attracted ever larger crowds, saloons became even more popular social centers for working-class men, and new forms of entertainment—movie theaters, music halls, vaudeville shows, art museums, symphony orchestras, and circuses—appealed to a broad cross-section of city residents.

Urbanization and technological progress also contributed to the prestige of modern science, whose impact increased enormously during the second half of the nineteenth century. By encouraging what one writer called a "mania for facts," scientists generated changes throughout social, intellectual, and cultural life. "I tell you these are great times," the writer and social critic Henry Adams wrote to his brother in 1862. "Man has mounted science and is now run away." Scientific research led to transformational technologies such as electrical power and lights, telephones, phonographs, motion pictures, bicycles, and automobiles.

URBAN LEISURE AND ENTERTAINMENT Although only men could vote in most states, both men and women flocked to hear candidates speak at political meetings. In the largest cities, membership in a political party offered many of the same benefits as belonging to a club or a college fraternity, as local political organizations provided social activities in addition to promoting new candidates. As labor unions became increasingly common, they too took on social roles for working-class men.

The sheer number of city dwellers also helped generate new forms of mass entertainment such as spectator sports and bicycle races. In the last quarter of the nineteenth century, college football and basketball and professional baseball began attracting many fans. In large cities, the new streetcar transit systems helped people gather easily for sporting events, and rooting for the home team helped unify a city's ethnic and racial groups and social classes. By the end of the century, sports of all kinds had become a crucial part of American popular culture.

Still, the most popular leisure destinations for urban working-class men were not athletic stadiums but saloons and dance halls. By 1900, the United States had more saloons (over 325,000) than grocery stores and

Vaudeville For as little as 1¢ a ticket, patrons could watch vaudeville shows aimed to please the tastes of their wildly diverse audience with a wide range of entertainment.

meat markets. New York City alone had 10,000 saloons, or 1 for every 500 residents.

The saloon served as the workingman's social club, offering fellowship to men who often worked ten hours a day, six days a week. In cities such as New York, Boston, Philadelphia, and Chicago, the customers were disproportionately Irish, German, and Italian Catholics, who tended to vote Democratic—partly because the "temperance" organizations that tried to close down saloons were led by Protestant Republicans.

Politics was often the topic of discussion in saloons; in fact, in New York City in the 1880s, saloons doubled as polling places, where patrons could cast their votes in local elections. One journalist called the saloon "the social and intellectual center of the neighborhood."

Besides drinking, socializing, and talking politics, men also went to saloons to check job postings, engage in labor union activities, cash paychecks, mail letters, read newspapers, and gossip. Patrons could play chess, billiards, darts, cards, dice, or even handball since many saloons included gymnasiums. Because saloons were heated and had restrooms, they served as refuges for the homeless, especially in the winter. Although the main barroom was for men only, women and children were allowed to enter through a side door to buy a pail of beer to carry home (a task called "rushing the growler"). Some

Coney Island Even members of the working class could afford the inexpensive rides at the popular Steeplechase Park in Coney Island, Brooklyn, New York.

saloons also provided "snugs," separate rooms for women customers. About a third of saloons, called "stall saloons," included "wine rooms" where prostitutes worked.

Married working-class women had even less leisure time than working-class men. Many were working for pay themselves, and even those who were not were frequently overwhelmed by housework and child-rearing responsibilities. As a social worker noted, "The men have the saloons, political clubs, trade-unions or [fraternal] lodges for their recreation . . . while the mothers have almost no recreation, only a dreary round of work, day after day, with occasionally doorstep gossip to vary the monotony of their lives." They often used the streets and alleys as their public space. Washing clothes, supervising children at play, or shopping at the local market provided opportunities for socializing with other women.

Single women, many of whom worked as domestic servants (maids) and had more time than working mothers for leisure and recreation, flocked to dance halls, theaters, amusement parks, and picnic grounds.

THE IMPACT OF DARWINISM Virtually every field of thought during the Gilded Age felt the impact of British natural scientist Charles Darwin's controversial book *On the Origin of Species* (1859), whose first edition sold out in one day. Basing his conclusions on extensive yet "imperfect" field research

Charles Darwin Scientist Darwin's controversial theories about the evolution of species influenced more than a century of political and social debate.

done around the world, Darwin showed how the chance processes of evolution give energy and unity to life. At the center of his concept was "natural selection." He demonstrated that most organisms produce many more offspring than can survive. Those offspring with certain favorable characteristics adapt and live, while others die from starvation, disease, or predators.

This "struggle for existence" in a crowded world drove the process of natural selection, Darwin said. Over many millions of years, modern species "evolved" from less complex forms of life; individuals and species that had characteristics advantageous for survival reproduced, while others fell by the wayside. As Darwin wrote, "the vigorous, the healthy, and the happy survive and multiply."

Darwin's theory of biological evolution was shocking because most people still embraced a literal interpretation of the biblical creation story, which claimed that God created all species at the same moment and they remained unchanged thereafter. Although Darwin had trained for the ministry and was reluctant to be drawn into religious controversy, his biological findings suggested to many, then and since, that there was no providential God controlling the universe. People were no different from plants and animals; they too evolved by trial and error rather than by God's purposeful hand. What came to be called *Darwinism* spelled the end of a God-given world.

These ideas generated heated arguments. Many Christians charged that Darwin's ideas led to atheism, a denial of the existence of God, while others found their faith severely shaken. Most of the faithful, however, came to reconcile science and religion. They decided that the process of evolutionary change occurring in nature must be God's doing.

Social Darwinism Although Charles Darwin's theory of evolution applied only to biological phenomena, many applied it to human society. Englishman

Herbert Spencer, a leading social philosopher, was the first major prophet of what came to be called **social Darwinism**.

Spencer argued that human society and its institutions, like the organisms studied by Darwin, evolved through the same process of natural selection. The "survival of the fittest," in Spencer's chilling phrase, was the engine of social progress. By encouraging people, ideas, and nations to compete with one another for dominance, society would generate "the greatest perfection and the most complete happiness."

Darwin dismissed Spencer's social theories as "unconvincing." He did not believe that the evolutionary process in the natural world had any relevance to human social institutions. Others, however, eagerly endorsed social Darwinism. If, as Spencer believed, society naturally evolved for the better through competition and conquest, then government interference with human rivalry in the marketplace was a serious mistake because it would help "unfit" people survive and thereby hinder societal progress.

Herbert Spencer and other social Darwinists thus called for hands-off, laissez-faire government policies; they argued against the regulation of business or of required minimum standards for sanitation and housing. To Spencer and many of his followers, the only acceptable charity was voluntary, and even that was of dubious value. Spencer warned that "fostering the good-for-nothing [people] at the expense of the good, is an extreme cruelty" to the health of civilization.

For Spencer and his many American supporters, successful businessmen and corporations provided proof of the concept of survival of the fittest. Oil tycoon John D. Rockefeller revealed his embrace of social Darwinism when he told his Baptist Sunday-school class that the "growth of a large business is merely a survival of the fittest. . . . This is not an evil tendency in business. It is merely the working-out of a law of nature and a law of God." In this way, the richest Americans justified the social and economic inequality on which their colossal fortunes were built.

Reform Darwinism Yale professor William Graham Sumner, Herbert Spencer's chief American supporter, used Darwinism to promote "rugged individualism" and oppose government regulation of business. For Sumner, it would be a mistake for governments to promote equality since to do so would interfere with the "survival of the fittest."

Others, however, strongly disagreed. What came to be called reform Darwinism found its major advocate in Lester Frank Ward, a government employee who fought his way up from poverty and never lost his empathy for the underdog.

Ward's book *Dynamic Sociology* (1883) singled out one aspect of evolution that both Darwin and Spencer had neglected: the human brain. True, as

Sumner claimed, people, like animals, compete. But, as Ward explained, people also collaborate. Unlike animals, people can plan for a distant future and are capable of shaping and directing social change. Far from being the helpless object of irresistible evolutionary forces, Ward argued, humanity could actively control social evolution through long-range planning.

Ward's reform Darwinism held that *cooperation,* not *competition,* would better promote social progress. Government, in Ward's view, should pursue two main goals: alleviating poverty, which impeded the development of the mind, and promoting the education of the masses. Intellect, informed by science, could foster social improvement. Reform Darwinism would prove to be one of the pillars of the progressive movement during the late nineteenth century and after.

REALISM IN LITERATURE AND ART Before the Civil War, Romanticism had dominated literature and painting. During the second half of the nineteenth century, however, writers and artists began to challenge the sentimentality and nature-worshipping focus of the Romantic tradition. A writer in *Putnam's Monthly* noted in 1854 a growing emphasis on "the real and the practical." This emphasis on *realism* matured into a full-fledged cultural force, as writers and artists focused on depicting the actual aspects of urban-industrial America: scientific research and technology, factories and railroads, cities and immigrants, labor unions and social tensions.

For many, the horrors of the Civil War had led to a more realistic view of life. An editor attending an art exhibition in 1865 sensed "the greater reality of feeling developed by the war. We have grown more sober, perhaps, and less patient of romantic idealism."

Another factor contributing to the rise of realism was the impact of science. The "stupendous power of Science," announced one editor, would rid thought of "every trace of old romance and art, poetry and romantic or sentimental feeling" and wash away the "ideal . . . and visionary."

Embracing realism, as writer Fanny Bates stressed, meant that stories and novels should be fed by facts and enlivened by textured social details. Authors should cast a roving eye on daily life and tell about life as it *is*. The tone of such writing and art appealed especially to people living in busy, swarming cities.

City streets, sidewalks, and parks provided countless scenes of *real* life to depict on canvas and in words. Novelist Henry James said that the urban scene unleashed a "flood of the real" to study and portray. John Sloan, a New York City painter, confided in his diary that he was addicted to "watching every bit of human life" through his windows and along the sidewalks.

Stag at Sharkey's (1909) New York painter George Bellows witnessed fierce boxing matches across the street from his studio, at the saloon owned by retired heavyweight boxer "Sailor" Sharkey. Bellows is one of the most famous artists from the Ashcan School, whose members were committed to capturing the gritty reality of the urban scene.

Others shared Sloan's "spectatorial" sensibility. "My favorite pastime," writer Theodore Dreiser remembered, "was to walk the city streets and view the lives and activities of others." In Dreiser's influential novel *Sister Carrie* (1900), Carrie Meeber uses her "gift of observation" to view strangers through the windows of shops, offices, and factories, imagining what "they deal with, how they labored, to what end it all came."

Just as scientists sought verifiable facts and transformed them into knowledge, cultural realists studied the world and expressed what they saw in art and literature. Like a gust of fresh air, they made Americans aware of the significance of all aspects of their everyday surroundings.

GILDED AGE POLITICS

The Gilded Age saw more political corruption than political innovation. A young college graduate in 1879, future president Woodrow Wilson, described the political system as having "no leaders, no principles." The real movers and shakers of the Gilded Age were not the men who sat in the White House or Congress but those who owned huge corporations. These "captains of industry," labeled "robber barons" by critics, regularly used their wealth to "buy" elections and favors from both major political parties and at all levels of government. Jay Gould, one of the most aggressive railroad giants, admitted that he elected "the [New York] legislature with [his] own money." Wilson's foremost critic, former president Theodore Roosevelt, agreed with him about the venality of Gilded Age politics. "When they call the roll in the Senate," he quipped, "the senators don't know whether to answer 'present' or 'not guilty.'"

The activities of "special interests," those businesses that bought illegal favors from government officials, dominated Gilded Age politics. As President Rutherford B. Hayes confessed, the "real difficulty" with the political system of his time was "the vast wealth and power in the hands of the few and unscrupulous who represent or control capital." By the end of the nineteenth century, however, new political movements and parties were pushing reforms to deal with the many excesses and injustices created by a political system that had grown corrupt in its support for the special interests of Big Business.

LOCAL POLITICS AND PARTY LOYALTIES Perhaps the most important feature of Gilded Age politics was its local focus. Most political activity occurred at the state and local levels. Unlike today, the federal government was an insignificant force in the daily lives of most citizens, in part because it was so small. In 1871, the entire federal civilian workforce totaled 51,000 (most of them postal workers), of whom only 6,000 actually worked in Washington, D.C. Not until the twentieth century did the importance of the federal government begin to surpass that of local and state governments.

Americans during the Gilded Age were intensely loyal to their chosen political party, which they joined as much for the fellowship and networking connections as for its positions on issues. Attending political speeches and gatherings was a major form of public recreation, and party loyalists eagerly read newspaper coverage of political issues and joined in rallies, picnics, and parades.

Unlike today, party members paid dues to join, and party leaders regularly demanded large campaign contributions from the captains of industry and finance. Collis Huntington, a California railroad tycoon, admitted that bribery in the form of campaign contributions was expected: "If you have to pay money to have the right thing done, then it is only just and fair to do it." Roscoe Conkling, a powerful Republican senator from New York, was equally candid: "Of course, we do rotten things in New York . . . Politics is a rotten business." Democrat Horatio Seymour, a presidential candidate in 1868,

"The Bosses of the Senate" This 1889 cartoon bitingly portrays the corrupt alliance between Big Business and legislators during the Gilded Age.

explained that "our people want men in office who will not steal, but who will not interfere with those who do."

In cities crowded with new immigrant voters, politics was usually controlled by "rings"—small groups who shaped policy and managed the nomination and election of candidates. Each ring typically had a powerful **party "boss"** who used his "machine"—a network of neighborhood activists and officials—to govern local politics.

The party in power expected the government employees it appointed to become campaign workers and to do the bidding of party bosses. Those bosses in "smoke-filled backrooms" often decided who the candidates would be and commanded loyalty and obedience by rewarding and punishing their party members.

Colorful figures such as New York City's William "Boss" Tweed ruled, plundered, and occasionally improved municipal government, often through dishonest and unethical means. Until his arrest in 1871, Tweed used the Tammany Hall ring to dole out contracts to business allies and jobs to political supporters. In the late 1870s, one of every twelve New York men worked for the city government. The various city rings and bosses were often corrupt, but they did bring structure, stability, and services to rapidly growing inner-city communities, many of them composed of immigrants newly arrived from Ireland, Germany, and, increasingly, from southern and eastern Europe.

Bosses like Tweed staged election parades, fireworks displays, and free banquets—with alcoholic beverages—for voters. They helped settle local disputes, provided aid for the needy, and excelled at **patronage**—the distribution of government jobs and contracts to loyal followers and corporate donors—the so-called spoils of office. As President Ulysses S. Grant's secretary told a Republican party boss, "I only hope you will distribute the patronage in such a manner as will help the Administration."

PARTISAN POLITICS AT THE NATIONAL LEVEL During the Gilded Age, national politics had a distinctive texture. Several factors contributed to make this political period unique. First, national political parties were much more powerful than they are today. Party loyalty was intense, often extending over generations in many families. A second distinctive element of Gilded Age politics at the national level was the close division between Republicans and Democrats in Congress, similar to the situation in the twenty-first century. Both parties avoided controversial issues or bold initiatives because neither was dominant. The third important aspect of post–Civil War politics was shaped by the intensity of voter involvement at all levels—local, state, and national. Voter turnout during the Gilded Age was commonly 70–80 percent. (By contrast, the turnout for the 2020 presidential election was over 65 percent, which was notable in its own right as it was the highest since 1908.)

Most voters cast their ballots for the same party year after year. Party loyalty was often an emotional choice. In the 1870s and 1880s, for example, people in the North and South continued to fight the Civil War during political campaigns. Republican candidates regularly "waved the bloody shirt," encouraging war veterans to "vote like you shot." They accused Democrats of having caused "secession and civil war," while Republicans took credit for abolishing slavery and saving the Union.

Democrats, especially in the South, where they monopolized political power after 1877, responded to such attacks by reminding voters that they stood for limited government, states' rights, and White supremacy. Republicans tended to favor high tariffs on imports, but many Democrats also supported tariffs if they benefited the dominant businesses in their districts or states. Third parties, such as the Greenbackers, Populists, and Prohibitionists, appealed to specific interests and issues, such as currency inflation, railroad regulations, or legislation to restrict alcohol consumption.

Party loyalties reflected religious, ethnic, and geographic divisions. After the Civil War, the Republican party remained strongest in New England, upstate

New York, Pennsylvania, Ohio, and the Midwest and weakest in the South. Republicans tended to be Protestants of English or Scandinavian descent. As the party of Abraham Lincoln (the Great Emancipator) and Ulysses S. Grant, Republicans could also rely upon the votes of African Americans in the South (until their ability to vote was suppressed or taken away by Jim Crow laws) and the support of a large bloc of Union veterans of the Civil War, who were organized into a powerful national interest group called the Grand Army of the Republic.

The Democrats, by contrast, were a more diverse and often unruly coalition of southern Whites, northern immigrants, Roman Catholics, Jews, freethinkers, and those repelled by the Protestant Republican "party of morality." As one Chicago Democrat explained, "A Republican is a man who wants you t' go t' church every Sunday. A Democrat says if a man wants to have a glass of beer on Sunday he can have it."

The mostly rural Republican Protestants considered saloons the social evil around which all others revolved, and they associated these evils with the ethnic groups that frequented saloons. Carrie Nation, the most colorful member of the Women's Christian Temperance Union (WCTU), became nationally known for attacking saloons with a hatchet. Saloons, she argued, stripped a married woman of everything by turning husbands into alcoholics: "Her husband is torn from her, she is robbed of her sons, her home, her food, and her virtue."

PRESIDENTIAL POLITICS   Between 1869 and 1913, from the first term of Ulysses S. Grant through the administration of William Howard Taft, Republicans monopolized the White House except for two nonconsecutive terms of New York Democrat Grover Cleveland. Otherwise, national politics was remarkably balanced. Between 1872 and 1896, *no* president won a majority of the popular vote. In each of those presidential elections, sixteen states invariably voted Republican and fourteen, including every southern state (referred to as the Solid South), voted Democratic. That left six "swing" (closely contested) states to determine the outcome. The votes from two of those states, New York and Ohio, decided the election of eight presidents from 1872 to 1908.

All presidents during the Gilded Age, both Republican and Democrat, deferred to their party leaders in the Senate and House of Representatives. They believed that Congress, not the White House, should formulate major policies that the president would implement. As Senator John Sherman of Ohio stressed, "The President should merely obey and enforce the law" as laid out by Congress.

CORRUPTION AND REFORM: HAYES TO HARRISON

While both political parties had their share of officials willing to buy and sell government jobs or legislative votes, each developed factions promoting honesty in government. The struggle for "clean" government became one of the foremost issues of the Gilded Age.

HAYES AND CIVIL SERVICE REFORM   President Rutherford B. Hayes brought to the White House in 1877 both a lingering controversy over the disputed election results (critics referred to him as "His Fraudulency" or "His Accidency") and a new style of uprightness, in sharp contrast to the scandals of Ulysses S. Grant's presidency. Hayes appointed a Democrat as postmaster general in an effort to clean up an agency infamous for trading jobs for political favors. The Ohioan Hayes was wounded four times in the Civil War. He went on to serve in Congress and as governor of Ohio. Stubbornly honest and conservative, he was, said a Republican journalist, a "third-rate nonentity."

Hayes had been the compromise presidential nominee of two factions fighting for control of the Republican party, the so-called Stalwarts and the Half-Breeds, led, respectively, by Senators Roscoe Conkling of New York and James Gillespie Blaine of Maine. The Stalwarts had been "stalwart" in their support of President Grant during the furor over the misdeeds of his cabinet members. Further, they had mastered the patronage (spoils) system of distributing political jobs to party loyalists. The Half-Breeds supposedly were only *half* loyal to Grant and *half* committed to reform of the spoils system. But in the end, the two factions existed primarily to advance the careers of Conkling and Blaine, who detested each other.

To his credit, President Hayes tried to stay above the petty bickering. He joined the growing public outrage over the era's astonishing corruption, admitting that his party "must mend its ways" by focusing on Republican principles rather than fighting over the spoils of office. It was time "for **civil service reform**." He appointed a committee to consider a merit system for hiring government employees. In a dramatic gesture, Hayes also fired Chester A. Arthur, a Stalwart Republican who ran the New York Customs House, because he had abused the patronage system in ways that promoted "ignorance, inefficiency, and corruption."

Hayes's commitment to cleaning up politics enraged Republican leaders. In 1879, Ohio congressman James Garfield warned Hayes that "if he wishes to hold any influence" with fellow Republicans, he "must abandon some of his notions of Civil Service reform." For his part, Hayes confessed that he had little hope of success because he was "opposed by . . . the most powerful men in my party."

On economic issues, Hayes held to a conservative line that would guide his successors—from both parties—for the rest of the century. His answer to demands for expansion of the nation's money supply (which would become one of the leading issues of the late nineteenth century) was a resounding no: he vetoed the Bland-Allison Act (1878), a bipartisan effort to increase the supply of silver coins. (More money in circulation was generally believed to raise farm prices and help those trying to pay off debts.) Hayes believed only in "hard money"—gold coins.

When the Democrat-controlled Congress convinced many Republicans to help overturn Hayes's veto, the president confided in his diary that he had become a president without a party. In 1879, with a year still left in his term, Hayes was ready to leave the White House. "I am now in my last year of the Presidency," he wrote a friend, "and look forward to its close as a schoolboy longs for the coming vacation."

GARFIELD, ARTHUR, AND THE PENDLETON ACT With Hayes choosing not to pursue a second term, the Republican presidential nomination in 1880 was up for grabs. In the end, the Stalwarts and Half-Breeds were forced to select a compromise candidate, Congressman James A. Garfield. Born in an Ohio log cabin, Garfield had been a minister, lawyer, professor, and college president before serving in the Civil War as a Union army general. In an effort to please the Stalwarts and also win the crucial swing state of New York, the Republicans named Chester A. Arthur, whom Hayes had fired as head of the New York Customs House, as their candidate for vice president.

The Democrats, as divided as the Republicans, selected Winfield Scott Hancock, a retired Union general who had distinguished himself at the Battle of Gettysburg but had done little since. In large part, the Democrats had selected Hancock to help deflect the Republicans' so-called bloody-shirt attacks on Democrats as the party of the Confederacy. Yet Hancock undermined that effort by supporting southern efforts to strip Blacks of voting rights.

In an election marked by widespread bribery, Garfield eked out a popular-vote plurality of only 39,000, or 48.5 percent out of some 9 million votes. He won a more comfortable margin of 214 to 155 in the Electoral College. Republicans took control of Congress as well. As the country entered the last decades of the century, Garfield would be the last president to have been born in a log cabin.

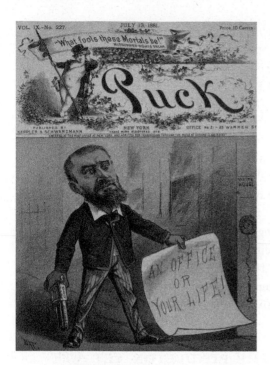

"A Model Office-Seeker" This cover of *Puck* magazine from July 1881 depicts Charles J. Guiteau, who was convicted of assassinating President James A. Garfield after being denied a job at the U.S. consulate. In one hand, he brandishes a pistol, and in the other, a paper that reads: "An office [job] or your life!"

A PRESIDENCY CUT SHORT

In his 1881 inaugural address, President Garfield gave an impassioned defense of civil rights, arguing that the "elevation of the negro race from slavery to the full rights of citizenship is the most important political change we have known since the adoption of the Constitution of 1787." The end of slavery, he said, "has added immensely to the moral and industrial forces of our people. It has liberated the master as well as the slave from a relation which wronged and enfeebled both." He also confirmed, however, that the Republicans had ended efforts to reconstruct the former Confederacy. Southern Blacks were on their own now; they had been "surrendered to their own guardianship."

Garfield would have no time to prove himself as president, however. On July 2, 1881, after only four months in office, he was walking through the Washington, D.C., railroad station when he was shot twice by Charles Guiteau, a thirty-nine-year-old Republican office-seeker. Guiteau had earlier visited Garfield to ask for a job in the U.S. consulate in Paris, only to be turned down. As a policeman wrestled Guiteau to the ground, the assassin shouted: "Yes! I have killed Garfield! [Chester] Arthur is now President of the United States. I am a Stalwart!" That declaration would eventually destroy the Stalwart wing of the Republican party.

On September 19, after seventy-nine days of struggle, Garfield died of infection resulting from inept medical care. "MURDERED BY THE SPOILS SYSTEM," exclaimed a *New York Tribune* headline.

THE CIVIL SERVICE COMMISSION Journalists saw little potential in the new president, Chester A. Arthur, who had been Roscoe Conkling's trusted lieutenant. Grant wrote an associate that he did not "expect much from this administration." Yet Arthur surprised most political observers by distancing himself from Conkling and the Stalwarts and becoming a civil service reformer. Throughout his presidency, he kept a promise not to remove any federal officeholder purely for political reasons. He also made cabinet appointments based on merit rather than partisanship.

In 1883, momentum against the spoils system generated by Garfield's assassination enabled George H. Pendleton, a Democratic senator from Ohio, to convince Congress to establish a Civil Service Commission, the first federal regulatory agency. Because of the Pendleton Civil Service Reform Act, at least 15 percent of federal jobs would now be filled based on competitive tests (the merit system) rather than political favoritism. In addition, federal employees running for office were prohibited from receiving political contributions from government workers.

The Pendleton Act was a limited first step in cleaning up the patronage process. It was sorely needed, in part because the federal government was expanding rapidly. By 1901, there would be 256,000 federal employees, five times the number in 1871. A growing portion of these federal workers were women, who by 1890 held a third of the government's clerical jobs.

THE CAMPAIGN OF 1884 Chester Arthur's efforts to clean up the spoils system might have attracted voters, but they did not please Republican leaders. So in 1884, the Republicans dumped the ailing Arthur (he had contracted a kidney disease) and chose as their nominee James Gillespie Blaine of Maine, the handsome, colorful secretary of state, former senator, and longtime leader of the Half-Breeds.

Corruption and a Sex Scandal Blaine was the consummate politician. He inspired the party faithful with his electrifying speeches and knew how to make backroom deals. One critic charged that Blaine "wallowed in spoils like a rhinoceros in an African pool."

Newspapers soon uncovered evidence of his corruption in the so-called Mulligan letters, which revealed that, as Speaker of the House, he had secretly sold his votes on measures favorable to a railroad corporation. There was no proof that Blaine had committed any crimes, but the circumstantial evidence was powerful: his senatorial salary alone could not have built either his mansion in Washington, D.C., or his palatial home in Augusta, Maine (which has since become the state's governor's mansion).

During the presidential campaign, more letters surfaced linking Blaine to shady deal making. In one of them, Blaine told the recipient: "Burn this letter!" For the reform element of the Republican party, this was too much, and many independent-minded Republicans refused to endorse Blaine's candidacy.

"We are Republicans but we are not slaves," said one of the independents. He insisted that the party of Lincoln must recommit itself to "retrenchment, purity and reform." Party regulars scorned such critics as "goo-goos"—the "good-government" crowd who were outraged by the corrupting influence of money in politics. The editor of a New York newspaper jokingly called the anti-Blaine Republicans **Mugwumps**, after an Algonquian Indian word meaning "big chief."

The Mugwumps, a self-appointed political elite dedicated to promoting honest government, saw the election as a "moral rather than political" contest. Centered in the large cities and major universities of the Northeast, the Mugwumps were mostly professors, editors, and writers. Like the Liberal Republicans before them, the Mugwumps sought to reform the patronage system by declaring that *all* federal jobs would be filled solely on the basis of merit. Their break with the Republican party testified to the depth of their convictions.

The rise of the Mugwumps, as well as growing national concerns about political corruption, prompted the Democrats to nominate New Yorker Grover Cleveland, a minister's son, as a reform candidate. A massive figure with a bull neck, strong jaw, and an overflowing moustache that made him resemble a walrus, Cleveland had first attracted national attention in 1881, when he was elected mayor of Buffalo on an anti-corruption platform. Elected governor of New York in 1882, he continued to build a reform record by fighting New York City's corrupt Tammany Hall ring. As mayor and as governor, he repeatedly vetoed bills that he felt served private interests at the expense of the public good. He supported civil service reform, opposed expanding the money supply, and preferred free trade rather than high tariffs.

Although Cleveland was known for his honesty and integrity, two personal issues hurt him: the discovery that he had paid for a substitute to take his place in the Union army during the Civil War, and a sex scandal that erupted when a Buffalo newspaper revealed that Cleveland, a bachelor, had seduced an attractive widow named Maria Halpin, who named him the father of her baby born in 1874. Cleveland had refused to marry her but had discreetly provided financial support for the child.

The escapades of Blaine and Cleveland inspired some of the most colorful battle cries in political history: "Blaine, Blaine, James G. Blaine, the continental liar from the state of Maine," Democrats chanted. Republicans countered with "Ma, ma, where's my Pa? Gone to the White House—Ha! Ha! Ha!"

Blunders of the Blaine Campaign Near the end of the nasty campaign, Blaine and his supporters committed two fateful blunders in the crucial state of New

York. The first occurred at New York City's fashionable Delmonico's restaurant, where Blaine went to a private dinner with 200 of the nation's wealthiest business leaders to ask them to help finance his campaign. Accounts of the unseemly event appeared in the newspapers for days afterward. One headline blared: "Blaine Hobnobbing with the Mighty Money Kings!" The article explained that the banquet was intended to collect contributions for a "Republican corruption fund."

Blaine's second blunder occurred when a Protestant minister visiting Republican headquarters in New York referred to the Democrats as the party of "rum, Romanism, and rebellion [the Confederacy]." Blaine, who was present, let pass the implied insult to Catholics—a fatal oversight, since he had cultivated Irish American support with his anti-English talk and repeated references to his mother being a Catholic. Democrats claimed that Blaine was, at heart, anti-Irish and anti-Catholic.

The two incidents may have tipped the election. The electoral vote was 219 to 182 in Cleveland's favor, but the popular vote ran far closer: Cleveland's plurality was fewer than 30,000 votes out of 10 million cast. Cleveland won New York by only 1,149 votes out of 1,167,169 cast. Blaine and his supporters charged that the Democrats had paid so many voters in New York that it had cost the Republican the White House. Yet Blaine refused to challenge the results, in part because the Republicans were buying votes too. Doing so, explained a journalist, "is considered a necessary part of 'practical politics,' and to be applauded in proportion to their success." By hook or by crook, a Democrat was back in the White House.

CLEVELAND'S REFORM EFFORTS

During his first few months in office, President Cleveland struggled to keep Democratic leaders from reviving the corrupt patronage system. In a letter to a friend, the new president reported that he was living in a "nightmare," that "dreadful, damnable, office-seeking hangs over me and surrounds me," and that it made him "feel like resigning." Democratic newspapers heaped scorn on him for refusing to award federal

"Another Voice for Cleveland" A political cartoon from 1884 depicts Grover Cleveland, with the ironic label "Grover the Good" hanging from his jacket, plugging his ears to drown out the cry of his illegitimate child.

jobs to his supporters. One accused Cleveland of "ingratitude" toward those who had "delivered the vote." Despite the president's best efforts, about two thirds of the 120,000 federal jobs went to Democrats as patronage during his administration.

Cleveland also opposed federal favors to Big Business. He held to a strictly limited view of government's role in both economic and social matters, a philosophy illustrated by his 1887 veto of a congressional effort to provide desperate Texas farmers with seeds in the aftermath of a terrible drought. "Though the people support the government, the government should not support the people," Cleveland asserted. During his administration, he would veto more acts of Congress than any previous president.

Railroad Regulation Despite his commitment to limited government, President Cleveland urged Congress to adopt an important new policy to enable the federal government to regulate the freight rates charged by interstate railroads (those whose tracks crossed state lines) to ship goods, crops, or livestock. He believed with many others that railroads were charging too much, especially in communities served by only one railroad. States had passed laws regulating railroads since the late 1860s, but in 1886 the Supreme Court declared in *Wabash v. Illinois* that no state could regulate the rates charged by railroads engaged in interstate traffic. Because most railroads crossed state lines, Cleveland urged Congress to close the loophole.

Congress followed through, and in 1887, President Cleveland signed an act creating the **Interstate Commerce Commission (ICC)**, the first federal agency designed to regulate business activities. The law empowered the ICC's five members to ensure that railroad freight rates were "reasonable and just." But one senator called the new agency "a delusion and a sham" because its members tended to be former railroad executives. Moreover, the commission's actual powers were weak when challenged by railroads in the courts. Over time, the ICC came to be ignored, and the railroads continued to charge high rates while making secret pricing deals with large shippers.

Tariff Reform and the Election of 1888 President Cleveland's most dramatic challenge to Big Business focused on **tariff reform**. During the late nineteenth century, the government's high-tariff policies, shaped largely by the Republican party, had favored American manufacturers by effectively shutting out foreign imports, thereby enabling U.S. corporations to dominate the marketplace and charge higher prices for their products. Tariffs on some 4,000 imported items had also brought in more revenue from foreign manufacturers than the federal government spent. As a result, the tariff revenues were producing an annual government surplus, which proved to Cleveland and the Democrats that the rates were too high.

In 1887, Cleveland argued that Congress should reduce both the tariff rates ("the vicious, inequitable and illogical source of unnecessary taxation . . . [and] a burden upon the poor") and the number of imported goods subject to tar- iffs, which would enable European companies to compete in the American marketplace (and bring down prices for consumers). His outspoken stance set the stage for his reelection campaign in 1888.

To oppose Cleveland, the Republicans, now calling themselves the GOP (Grand Old Party) to emphasize their longevity, turned to the obscure Benjamin Harrison, a Civil War veteran whose greatest attributes were his availability and the fact that he was from Indiana, a pivotal state in presiden- tial elections. The grandson of President William Henry Harrison, he had a modest political record; he had lost a race for governor and had served one term in the U.S. Senate (1881–1887). Stiff and formal, Harrison was labeled the "human iceberg."

"COMING OUT" FOR HARRISON.
Protected Monopolist.—Chuck in your votes there, and don't forget that you 're "working for—Kane!"

"'Coming Out'—For Harrison" This 1888 cartoon depicts efforts by employers to force the working class to vote for the Republican party ticket, including presidential nominee Benjamin Harrison.

The Republicans accepted Cleveland's challenge to make tariffs the chief issue in the campaign. To fend off the president's efforts to reduce the tariff, business executives contributed generously to the Republican cause. Still, the outcome was incredibly close. Cleveland won the popular vote by the thinnest of margins—5,540,329 to 5,439,853—but Harrison carried crucial New York State and the Electoral College, 233 to 168. "Providence," said the new president, "has given us the victory." Matthew Quay, the powerful Republican boss of Pennsylvania who managed Harrison's campaign, knew better. Harrison, he muttered, "ought to know that Providence hadn't a damned thing to do with it! [A] number of men were compelled to approach the penitentiary to make him President."

REPUBLICAN ACTIVISM UNDER HARRISON The Republicans took advantage of their control of Congress to pass a cluster of significant legislation in 1890, specifically, the Sherman Anti-Trust Act; the Sherman Silver Purchase Act; and the McKinley Tariff Act. Congress admitted Idaho and Wyoming into the Union that same year, following on the heels of North and South Dakota, Montana, and Washington becoming states in 1889.

The Sherman Anti-Trust Act, named for Ohio senator John Sherman, prohibited powerful corporations from "conspiring" to establish monopolies or "restrain trade" in their industries. It made the United States the first nation in the world to outlaw monopolistic business practices.

Though badly needed, the Sherman Anti-Trust Act was rarely enforced. Critics called it the "Swiss Cheese Act" because it had so many holes in its language, especially its vague definitions of *trusts* and *monopolies*. As the *New York Times* recognized in 1890, the "so-called Anti-Trust law" was passed "to deceive the people," so that party spokesmen "might say 'Behold! We have attacked the trusts. The Republican Party is the enemy of all such rings.'" From 1890 to 1901, only eighteen lawsuits were instituted, four of which were filed against labor unions rather than corporations.

As for tariff policy, Republicans viewed their electoral victory as a mandate to reward the support of large corporations by raising tariff rates even higher. Piloted through Congress by Ohio representative William McKinley, the McKinley Tariff Act of 1890 raised duties (taxes) on imported manufactured goods to their highest level in history and added many agricultural products to the tariff list to appease farmers. Its passage encouraged many businesses to raise prices, because their European competitors were now effectively shut out of the U.S. market. The *New York Times* expressed the indignation of many voters when it charged in a huge headline: "MCKINLEY'S PICKPOCKETS [WERE] PAYING A PARTY DEBT" to large corporate donors by passing the new tariff bill.

The Republican efforts to reward Big Business backfired, however. In the November 1890 congressional elections, Democrats regained control of the House by a 3 to 1 margin. William McKinley, who had sponsored the tariff bill, lost his seat (although the following year he would be elected Ohio's governor). In the Senate, the Republican majority was reduced to four. Republicans were "astounded and dazed" by their election losses. Even more worrisome was the emergence of the Populists, a new political party representing disgruntled farmers and wage laborers. Revolution was in the air.

Unhappy Farmers and the "Money Problem"

Even more than with tariffs, trusts, and the efforts to clean up political corruption, national politics during the Gilded Age was preoccupied with complex monetary issues. The nation's money supply had not grown along with the expanding economy and population of the late nineteenth century. From 1865 to 1890, the amount of money in circulation (both coins and paper currency) actually *decreased* about 10 percent at the same time that the economy and population were dramatically expanding.

Such currency deflation raised the cost of borrowing money as the shrinking money supply enabled lenders to hike interest rates on loans. Creditors— bankers and others who loaned money—supported a "sound money" policy limiting the currency supply as a means of increasing their profits. By contrast, farmers, ranchers, miners, and others who constantly had to borrow money to make ends meet claimed that the sound money policy had the deflationary effect of lowering prices for their crops and herds, driving them deeper into debt. Farmers in the Midwest, Great Plains, and South and miners in the West demanded more paper money and the increased coinage of silver, which would inflate the currency supply, raise commodity prices, and provide them with more income.

A VICIOUS CYCLE OF DEPRESSED PRICES AND DEBT

Since the end of the Civil War, farmers in the South and the Great Plains had suffered from worsening economic conditions. The basic source of their problems was a decline in prices earned for their crops, a deflationary trend caused by overproduction and growing international competition in world food markets, as well as the inadequate money supply.

The vast new lands brought under cultivation in the plains poured an ever-increasing supply of farm products into world markets, driving prices down. Meanwhile, farmers, especially small farmers in the South and West, had become increasingly indebted to "greedy" local banks or merchants who loaned them money to buy seed, fertilizer, tools, and other supplies. As prices for wheat, cotton, and corn dropped, however, so did the income the farmers received, thus preventing them from paying their debts on time.

In response, most farmers had no choice but to grow even more wheat, cotton, or corn, creating a vicious cycle: as still more grains and cotton were harvested and sold, the increased supply drove down prices and farmers' incomes even further. High tariffs on imported goods also hurt farmers because they blocked foreign competition, allowing U.S. companies to raise the prices of manufactured goods needed by farm families. Farmers, however, had to sell their crops in open world markets unprotected by tariffs, where competition lowered prices.

Besides bankers, merchants, and high tariffs, struggling farmers also blamed the railroads, warehouse owners, and food processors, the so-called middlemen who helped get their products to market. They especially resented that railroads, most of which had a monopoly over the shipping of grains and livestock, charged such high rates to ship their farm products.

SILVER AND INFLATION   Among the factors distressing farmers, the nation's inadequate money supply emerged as the source of greatest frustration. In 1873, the Republican-controlled Congress had declared that only gold, not silver, could be used for coins.

This decision (called "the Crime of '73" by critics) occurred just when silver mines in the western states had begun to increase their production. Hard-pressed farmers in the South and Midwest demanded increased coinage of silver, which would inflate the currency and thereby raise commodity prices, providing farmers with more income with which to pay their annual debts.

They found allies among legislators representing the new western states. All six states admitted to the Union in 1889 and 1890 had substantial silver mines, and their new congressional delegations—largely Republican—wanted the federal government to buy more silver for coins.

The so-called silver delegates shifted the balance in Congress enough to pass the Sherman Silver Purchase Act (1890), which required the Treasury to purchase 4.5 million ounces of silver each month with new paper money. Such inflationary policies helped set the stage for the currency issue to eclipse all others during the financial panic that would sweep the country in 1893.

In the 1890 midterm elections, voters rebelled not only against the McKinley Tariff but also in support of the militant new farm protests. People used the term *revolution* to describe the swelling grassroots support for the Populists, a new third party focused on the needs of miners and small farmers, many of whom did not own the land they worked. In drought-devastated Kansas, Populists won five congressional seats from Republicans. The result was that Democrats outnumbered Republicans in the new House of Representatives by almost 3 to 1; in the Senate, the Republican majority was reduced to eight. In early 1891, the newly elected Populists and Democrats took control of Congress just as an acute economic crisis appeared on the horizon: farmers' debts were mounting as crop prices plummeted.

THE GRANGER MOVEMENT The overwhelming victory of the Democrats and Populists in the congressional midterm elections of 1890 shocked many voters, but the seeds for their win were planted over two decades earlier.

When the Department of Agriculture sent Oliver H. Kelley on a tour of the South in 1866, he was struck by the social isolation of people living on small farms. To address the problem, Kelley helped found the National Grange of the Patrons of Husbandry, better known as the Grange (an old word for places where crops were stored).

In the next few years, the **Granger movement** mushroomed, reaching a membership of 1.5 million by 1874. It offered social events and educational programs for farmers and their families, but as it grew, it began to promote *cooperatives* where farmers could join together to store and sell their crops to avoid the high fees charged by brokers and other middlemen.

In five midwestern states, Grange chapters persuaded legislatures to pass "Granger laws" establishing state commissions to regulate the prices charged by railroads and grain warehouses (called elevators). Farmers rented space in the grain elevators to store their harvested crop before it was sold and shipped by railroads. Many elevator operators were corrupt, however. They secretly conspired with their competitors to "fix" the storage rates they charged farmers. Railroads also squeezed the farmers. Since they usually had a monopoly in a given agricultural community, railroads could charge whatever they wanted to ship grain, and they discriminated in favor of the largest farms.

To address the concerns of grain growers, the Illinois legislature in 1871 established regulations prohibiting railroads from charging different freight rates and establishing rates for grain-elevator storage. The state created a Board of Railroad and Warehouse Commissioners to enforce the new regulations. Other states passed similar laws.

Railroad and warehouse owners challenged and often defied the laws, arguing that efforts to regulate them were forms of socialism. In *Munn v. Illinois* (1877), however, the Supreme Court ruled 7–2 that the Constitution sanctioned regulation of businesses that operated in the public interest. In

"I Feed You All!" (1875) This Granger-inspired poster celebrates the farmer as the cornerstone of society. Without the food he produces, Americans could not perform their jobs—including the very railroad magnate *(left)* and warehouse owners who try to exploit farmers.

response to the Court's decision, Chicago grain elevators lowered their storage fees. Nine years later, however, the Court threw out the *Munn* ruling, finding in *Wabash v. Illinois* that only Congress, not states, could regulate industries involved in *interstate* commerce.

FARMERS' ALLIANCES The Granger movement failed to address the foremost concerns of struggling farmers: declining crop prices and the inadequate amount of money in circulation. As a result, people shifted their allegiance to new regional organizations that taken together were called the **Farmers' Alliances**. Like the Grange, the Farmers' Alliances organized social and recreational activities for small farmers and their families while also emphasizing political action and economic cooperation to address the hardships caused by chronic indebtedness, declining crop prices, and droughts.

Emerging first in Texas, the Southern Alliance movement swept across the South, Kansas, Nebraska, and the Dakotas. By 1890, the White Alliance movement had about 1.5 million members nationwide. The Southern Alliance refused to allow Blacks to join, not only because of racism but also because most Black farmers were tenants and sharecroppers rather than landowners. Although many landless farmers supported the Alliances, the majority of members were landowners who sold their crops in the marketplace. In 1886, a White minister in Texas responded to the appeals of African American farmers by organizing the Colored Farmers' National Alliance. By 1890, it would claim more than 1 million members.

The Alliances welcomed rural women and men over sixteen years of age who displayed a "good moral character," believed in God, and demonstrated "industrious habits." A North Carolina woman relished the "grand opportunities" the Alliance provided women to emerge from household drudgeries. One Alliance publication made the point explicitly: "The Alliance has come to redeem woman from her enslaved condition and place her in her proper sphere." Many women assumed key leadership roles in the "grand army of reform."

In the states west of the Mississippi River, political activism intensified after record blizzards in 1887, which killed most of the cattle and hogs across the northern plains, and a prolonged drought two years later that destroyed millions of acres of corn, wheat, and oats. Distressed farmers lashed out against what they considered to be a powerful conspiracy of eastern financial and industrial interests, which they variously called "monopolies," "the money power," or "Wall Street." As William Jennings Bryan, a Democratic congressman from Nebraska, explained: "We simply say to the East: take your hands out of our pockets and keep them out."

The Alliances called for the federal government to take ownership of the railroads and create a permanent income tax on the wealthiest citizens. They also organized economic *cooperatives* to bind together their collective strength in negotiations with warehouse operators and railroads. In 1887, Charles W. Macune, the Southern Farmers' Alliance president, explained that "the Alliance is the people and the people are together." He exhorted Texas farmers to create their own Alliance Exchange to free themselves from dependence on commercial warehouses, grain elevators, and banks. Members of the Alliance Exchange would act collectively, pooling their resources to borrow money from banks and purchase their goods and supplies from a new corporation created by the Alliance in Dallas. The exchange would also build warehouses to store members' crops. With these crops as collateral, members would receive loans to buy household goods and agricultural supplies. Once the farmers sold their crops, they would pay back the loans provided by the Alliance warehouse. But the cooperatives died when banks refused to finance them.

The failure of the cooperatives convinced many farm leaders that they needed more political power to secure needed reforms.

NEW THIRD PARTIES The Alliances, frustrated that few Democrats or Republicans embraced their cause, decided to form new political parties. In 1890, farm activists in Colorado joined with miners and railroad workers to form the Independent party, and Nebraska farmers formed the People's Independent party. Across the South, however, White Alliance members hesitated to leave the Democratic party, seeking instead to control it. Both the third-party and the southern approaches produced startling success.

The Populists supported increased government intervention in the economy, for only the U.S. Congress could expand the money supply, counterbalance the power of Big Business, and provide efficient national transportation networks to support the agricultural economy. Third parties also took control of one house of the Kansas legislature and both houses in Nebraska. In the South Dakota and Minnesota legislatures, Populists won enough seats to control the balance of power between Republicans and Democrats.

In the South, the Alliance movement elected four Democratic supporters as governors, forty-four as congressmen, and several as U.S. senators; Alliance supporters also gained control of seven state legislatures.

Among the most respected of the Southern Alliance leaders was red-haired Thomas E. Watson of Georgia. The son of prosperous slaveholders who had lost everything after the Civil War, Watson became a successful lawyer and speaker on behalf of the Alliance cause. He took the lead in urging African American tenant farmers and sharecroppers to join White farmers in ousting the political elite. "You are kept apart," he told Black and White farmers, "that you may be separately fleeced of your earnings." He insisted on cooperation by Black and White farmers to resist the power of the wealthy political elite in the South.

Mary Elizabeth Lease One of the first female attorneys in Kansas, Lease was a charismatic leader in the farm protest movement.

In Kansas, Mary Elizabeth Lease emerged as a fiery speaker for the farm protest movement. Born in Pennsylvania to Irish immigrants, Lease migrated to Kansas, taught school, raised a family, and failed at farming in the mid-1880s. She then studied law, "pinning sheets of notes above her wash tub," and became one of the state's first female attorneys.

A proud, tall, and imposing woman with a magical voice, Lease began giving public speeches during the 1890s on behalf of struggling farmers that drew attentive audiences. "The people are at bay," she warned in 1894; "let the bloodhounds of money beware." She urged angry farmers to take control "with the ballot if possible, but if not that way then with the bayonet."

Like so many Alliance supporters, Lease viewed eastern financiers as the enemy. "Wall Street owns the country. It is no longer a government of the people, by the people, and for the people, but a government of Wall Street, by Wall Street, and for Wall Street. The great common people of this country are slaves, and monopoly is the master." The two political parties "lie to us" in blaming farmers for overproduction, "when 10,000 little children starve to death every year in the United States."

THE 1892 ELECTION In 1892, Alliance leaders organized a convention in Omaha, Nebraska, at which they formed the **People's party (Populists)**. Their platform was truly radical for its time. It called for unlimited coinage of silver, a *progressive* income tax whose rates would rise with income levels, and federal ownership of the railroads and telegraph systems. The Populists also endorsed the eight-hour workday and new laws restricting "undesirable" immigration, for fear that the "pauper and criminal classes of the world" were taking Americans' jobs. "We meet in the midst of a nation brought to the verge of moral, political, and material ruin," the Populists announced. "The fruits of toil of millions are boldly stolen to build up colossal fortunes for a few." They called for the "power of government" to be expanded to assault "oppression, injustice, and poverty."

The Populist party's platform turned out to be more exciting than its presidential candidate: Iowa's James B. Weaver, a former Union army officer who had headed the Greenback party ticket twelve years earlier. The major parties renominated the same candidates who had run in 1888: Democrat Grover Cleveland and Republican president Benjamin Harrison. Each major candidate received more than 5 million votes, but Cleveland won a majority of the Electoral College. Weaver received more than 1 million votes and carried Colorado, Kansas, Nevada, and Idaho. Alabama was the banner Populist state of the South, with 37 percent of its vote going to Weaver.

THE DEPRESSION OF 1893 AND THE "FREE SILVER" CRUSADE While farmers were funneling their discontent into politics, a fundamental weakness in the economy was about to cause a major collapse and a social rebellion. Just ten days before Grover Cleveland was inaugurated in the winter of 1893, the Philadelphia and Reading Railroad declared bankruptcy, setting off a national financial crisis, now called the **Panic of 1893**. It grew into the worst depression the nation had ever experienced.

Other overextended railroads collapsed, taking many banks with them. European investors withdrew their funds from America. By the fall of 1893, more than 600 banks had closed and 15,000 businesses had failed. Farm foreclosures soared in the South and West, and by 1900, a third of all American farmers rented their land rather than owned it. A quarter of unskilled urban workers lost their jobs, and many others had their wages cut. By 1894, the nation's economy had reached bottom. But the depression lasted another four years, with unemployment hovering at 20 percent. In New York City, the jobless rate was close to 35 percent, and 20,000 homeless people camped out at police stations and other makeshift shelters.

President Cleveland's response to the economic catastrophe was to convince Congress to return the nation's money supply to a gold standard by repealing the Sherman Silver Purchase Act of 1890, a move that made the depression worse. The weak economy needed *more* money in circulation, not *less*. Investors rushed to exchange their silver dollars for gold, further constricting the money supply.

A wave of labor unrest symbolized the fracturing of the social order; in 1894, some 750,000 workers went on strike. One protest group, called Coxey's Army, was led by "General" Jacob S. Coxey, a wealthy Ohio quarry owner turned Populist who demanded that the federal government coin more silver dollars and provide the unemployed with meaningful work. Coxey, his wife, and their son, Legal Tender Coxey, rode in a carriage ahead of some 120 protesters, more than 40 reporters, and a band with bugler—all who traveled by foot the hundreds of miles to Washington, D.C. When they arrived, Coxey was arrested for trespassing on the Capitol lawn. Although the ragtag army dispersed peacefully, the march, as well as the growing strength of Populism, struck fear into the hearts of many conservatives, including President Grover Cleveland.

In this climate of class warfare and social anxiety, the 1894 congressional elections devastated President Cleveland and the Democrats, who were blamed for the economic crisis. Republicans portrayed Populists as "tramps" and "hayseed socialists" whose election would endanger the capitalist system. The Populists responded by charging that Americans were divided into "tramps and millionaires."

In the final results, the Republicans gained 118 seats in the House, the largest increase ever. Only in the solidly Democratic South did the party retain its advantage. The Populists, who emerged with six senators and seven representatives, expected the festering discontent in rural areas to carry them to national power in 1896. Their hopes would be dashed, however.

SILVERITES VERSUS GOLDBUGS President Cleveland's decision to repeal the Sherman Silver Purchase Act created an irreparable division in his party. One embittered pro-silver Democrat labeled the president a traitor. Politicians from western states with large silver mines increased their demands for the "unlimited" coinage of silver, presenting a strategic dilemma for Populists: should the party promote the long list of reforms it had originally advocated, or should it try to ride the silver issue into power?

The latter seemed more likely to succeed. Although flooding the economy with silver currency would probably not have provided the benefits its advocates claimed, the "free silver" crusade had taken on powerful symbolic overtones.

Over the protests of more-radical members, Populist leaders decided to hold their 1896 nominating convention after the two major-party conventions, confident that the Republicans and Democrats would at best straddle the silver issue and enable the Populists to lure away pro-silver advocates from both.

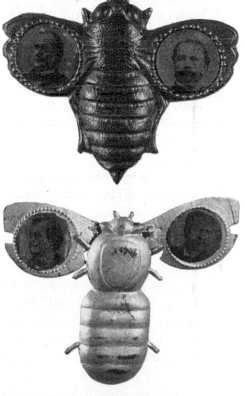

Contrary to those expectations, the major parties took opposite positions on the currency issue. The Republicans, as expected, nominated William McKinley, a former congressman and governor of Ohio, on a platform committed to gold coins as the only form of currency. After the convention, a friend told McKinley that the "**money question**" would determine the election. He was right.

The Democratic convention in the Chicago Coliseum was one of the great turning points in American political history. The pro-silver, largely rural delegates surprised the party leadership and the "Gold Democrats," or "goldbugs," by capturing the convention for their inflationary crusade.

Presidential Campaign Badges On the left wings of the "goldbug" and "silverite" badges are McKinley *(top)* and Bryan *(bottom)*, with their running mates on the right.

William Jennings Bryan Bryan's "Cross of Gold" speech at the 1896 Democratic Convention roused the delegates and secured him the party's presidential nomination.

WILLIAM JENNINGS BRYAN
Thirty-six-year-old William Jennings Bryan of Nebraska gave the final speech at the Democratic convention before the presidential balloting began. A fiery evangelical moralist, Bryan was a two-term congressman who had lost a race for the Senate in 1894, when Democrats by the dozens were swept out of office. In the months before the convention, he had traveled throughout the South and West, speaking passionately for the unlimited coinage of silver, attacking Cleveland's "do-nothing" response to the depression, and endorsing both Democrats and Populists who embraced the cause of "free silver."

Bryan was a magnetic public speaker with a booming voice, a crusading preacher in the role of a Populist politician. At the 1896 convention, he was only a "dark horse" candidate—that is, a little-known long shot—for the presidential nomination. He felt compelled to take a calculated risk: he would be intentionally provocative and disruptive.

In his well-rehearsed "Cross of Gold" speech, which became so famous that Bryan recorded it several times in later years, he claimed that two ideas about the role of government were competing for the American voter. The Republicans, he said, believed "that if you just legislate to make the well-to-do prosperous, that their prosperity will leak through on those below." The Democrats, by contrast, believed "that if you legislate to make the masses prosperous their prosperity will find its way up and through every class that rests upon it." For his part, Bryan spoke for the "producing masses of this nation" against the eastern "financial magnates" who had "enslaved" them by manipulating the money supply to ensure high interest rates.

As Bryan brought his electrifying twenty-minute speech to a climax, he fused Christian imagery with Populist anger:

> I come to speak to you in defense of a cause as holy as the cause of liberty—
> the cause of humanity. . . . We have petitioned, and our petitions have

been scorned. . . . We have begged, and they have mocked when our calamity came. We beg no longer; we entreat no more; we petition no more. We defy them!

Sweeping his fingers across his forehead, he shouted: "You shall not press down upon the brow of labor this crown of thorns. You shall not crucify mankind upon a cross of gold!"—at which point he extended his arms straight out from his sides, as if he were being crucified.

Bryan's riveting performance worked better than even he himself had anticipated. As he strode triumphantly off the stage, the delegates erupted in wild applause. "Everybody seemed to go mad at once," reported the *New York World*. For their part, the Republicans were not at all amused by Bryan's antics. A Republican newspaper observed that no political movement had "ever before spawned such hideous and repulsive vipers."

The next day, Bryan won the presidential nomination on the fifth ballot, but in the process the Democratic party was fractured. Disappointed pro-gold Democrats who had supported Grover Cleveland dismissed Bryan as a fanatic and a socialist. They were so alienated by his positions and his rhetoric that they walked out of the convention and nominated their own candidate, Senator John M. Palmer of Illinois. "Fellow Democrats," Palmer announced, "I will not consider it any great fault if you decide to cast your vote for William McKinley."

When the Populists gathered in St. Louis for their presidential nominating convention two weeks later, they faced an impossible choice. They could name their own candidate and divide the pro-silver vote with the Democrats, or they could endorse Bryan and probably lose their identity as an independent party. In the end, they backed Bryan but chose their own vice-presidential candidate, Thomas E. Watson, and invited the Democrats to drop their vice-presidential nominee. Bryan refused the offer.

THE ELECTION OF 1896 The election of 1896 was a turning point in American history, in part because of the striking contrast between the candidates and in part because the terrible economic depression made the stakes so high. One observer said that the campaign "took the form of religious frenzy." Indeed, Bryan campaigned like the evangelist he was. He was the first major candidate since Andrew Jackson to champion the poor, the discontented, and the oppressed against the financial and industrial elite. He excited struggling farmers, miners, and union members. And he was the first leader of a major party to call for the expansion of the federal government to help the working and middle classes.

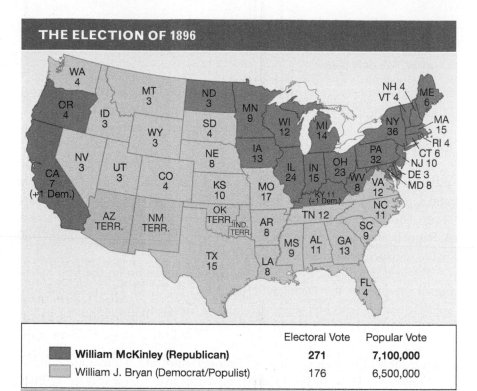

THE ELECTION OF 1896

	Electoral Vote	Popular Vote
William McKinley (Republican)	**271**	**7,100,000**
William J. Bryan (Democrat/Populist)	176	6,500,000

- How did Bryan's "Cross of Gold" speech divide the Democratic party?
- How did McKinley's campaign strategy differ from Bryan's?
- Why was Bryan able to carry the West and the South but unable to win in cities and the Northeast?

Candidate Bryan crisscrossed the country like a man on a mission, delivering hundreds of impassioned speeches on behalf of the "producing masses"—workers, farmers, miners, and small-business owners. His populist crusade was for Whites only, however. Like so many otherwise progressive Democratic leaders, Bryan never challenged the practices of racial segregation and violence against Blacks in the solidly Democratic South. And he alienated many working-class Catholics in northern states by supporting prohibition of alcoholic beverages.

McKinley, meanwhile, stayed at home in Ohio and kept his mouth shut, letting other Republicans speak for him. He knew he could not compete with Bryan as a speaker, so he conducted a "front-porch campaign," welcoming some 750,000 supporters who came to his home in Canton, Ohio, during the campaign. He gave only prepared statements to the press, most of which warned middle-class voters of the perils of Bryan's "dangerous" ideas. McKinley's brilliant campaign manager, Mark Hanna, shrewdly portrayed Bryan as a

"Popocrat" (Populist Democrat), a radical whose "communistic spirit" would ruin the capitalist system and stir up a class war. Hanna convinced the Republican party to declare that it was "unreservedly for sound money"—meaning gold coins.

By appealing to such fears, the Republicans raised vast sums from corporations and wealthy donors to finance an army of 1,400 speakers who traveled the country promoting McKinley. It was the most sophisticated—and expensive—presidential campaign in history to that point. In the end, Bryan won the most votes of any candidate in history thus far—6.5 million—but McKinley won even more: 7.1 million. The better-organized and better-financed Republicans won the Electoral College vote by 271 to 176. Two million more voters cast ballots than in 1892.

Bryan carried most of the West and all the South but found little support in the North and East. In the crucial Midwest, from Minnesota and Iowa eastward to Ohio, he did not win a state. His evangelical Protestantism repelled many Roman Catholic voters, who were normally drawn to the Democrats. Farmers in the Northeast, moreover, were less attracted to radical reform than were farmers in the West and South. Workers in the cities found it easier to identify with McKinley's focus on reviving the industrial economy than with Bryan's farm-based, free-silver evangelism. Of the nation's twenty largest cities, Bryan won only New Orleans.

Although Bryan lost, he launched the Democratic party's shift from pro-business conservatism to its eventual twentieth-century role as a party of liberal reform. The Populist party, however, virtually disintegrated. Having won a million votes in 1896, it collected only 50,000 in 1900. Conversely, McKinley's victory climaxed a generation-long struggle for political control of an industrialized urban America. The Republicans would be dominant for sixteen years.

By 1897, when McKinley was inaugurated, prosperity was returning. Economic recovery came in part from the inflation of U.S. currency, which bore out the arguments of the Greenbackers and silverites that the nation's money supply had been inadequate during the Gilded Age. Inflation came, however, not from the influx of more greenbacks or silver dollars but from a flood of gold discovered in South Africa, northwest Canada, and Alaska. In 1900, Congress passed, and McKinley signed, a bill affirming that the nation's money supply would be based only on gold.

Even though the Populist movement faded after William Jennings Bryan's defeat, most of the ideas promoted by Bryan Democrats and Populists, dismissed as too radical in 1896, would be implemented over the next two decades by a more diverse coalition of Democrats and Republicans who would call themselves "progressives." The volcanic turmoil of the 1890s set the stage for the twentieth century's struggles and innovations.

CHAPTER REVIEW

SUMMARY

- **America's Move to Town**   America's cities grew in all directions during the *Gilded Age* (1860–1896). Electric elevators and new steel-frame construction allowed architects to extend buildings upward, and mass transit both above- and belowground enabled the middle class to retreat to suburbs. Crowded *tenements* bred disease and crime and created an opportunity for *party bosses* to gain power, in part by distributing to the poor the only relief that existed.

- **The New Immigration**   By 1900, nearly 30 percent of Americans living in major cities were foreign-born, with the majority of *new immigrants* arriving from eastern and southern Europe rather than western and northern Europe, like most immigrants of generations past. Their languages, culture, and religion were quite different from those of native-born Americans. They tended to be Catholic, Eastern Orthodox, or Jewish rather than Protestant. Beginning in the 1880s, nativists advocated restrictive immigration laws and won passage of the *Chinese Exclusion Act* (1882).

- **Changes in Culture and Thought**   Many areas of American life underwent profound changes during the *Gilded Age*. The growth of large cities led to the popularity of vaudeville and Wild West shows and the emergence of football, baseball, and basketball as spectator sports. Saloons served as local social and political clubs for men, despite the disapproval of anti-liquor groups. Charles Darwin's *On the Origin of Species* shocked people who believed in a literal interpretation of the Bible's account of creation. Herbert Spencer and William Graham Sumner were proponents of *social Darwinism*, which applied Darwin's theory of evolution to human society by equating economic and social success with the "survival of the fittest." In contrast, Lester Frank Ward supported reform Darwinism, which held that humans should promote social progress with cooperation, not competition.

- **Gilded Age Politics**   The politics of the time was dominated by huge corporations and the money they used to buy political influence. Political power was still concentrated at the state and local levels. Americans were intensely loyal to the two major parties, whose local "bosses" and "machines" won votes by distributing *patronage* jobs and contracts to members as well as charitable relief. Party loyalties reflected regional, ethnic, and religious differences.

- **Corruption and Reform: Hayes to Harrison**   In addition to the *money question*, national politics in this period focused on *tariff reform* (1887), the regulation of corporations, and *civil service reform*. The passage of the Pendleton Civil Service Reform Act in 1883 began the professionalization of federal workers. In the 1884 presidential election, Republicans favoring reform, the *Mugwumps*, helped elect Democrat Grover Cleveland. Cleveland signed the 1887 act creating the *Interstate Commerce Commission (ICC)*, intended to regulate interstate railroads. In 1890, under President Benjamin Harrison, Republicans passed the Sherman Anti-Trust Act, the Sherman Silver Purchase Act, and the McKinley Tariff Act.

- **Inadequate Currency Supply and Unhappy Farmers** Over the course of the late nineteenth century, the *money question* had become a central political issue. The supply of money had not increased as the economy had grown. This deflationary trend increased the value of money, which was good for bankers and creditors who could charge higher interest rates on loans, but bad for farmers who faced both more expensive mortgages and declining prices for their products, especially after the devastating *Panic of 1893* and the ensuing depression. As a result, farmers banded together economically and increased their participation in politics through groups like the *Farmers' Alliance* and the *Granger movement* and helped fuel the growth of a major third party, the *People's party (Populists)*.

CHRONOLOGY

1859   Charles Darwin's *On the Origin of Species* is published

1873   San Francisco begins using cable cars for mass transit

1873   Congress ends silver coinage

1877   Rutherford B. Hayes is inaugurated president

1881   President James A. Garfield is assassinated

1882   Congress passes the Chinese Exclusion Act

1883   Congress passes the Pendleton Civil Service Reform Act

1886   Supreme Court issues *Wabash, St. Louis, and Pacific Railroad Company v. Illinois* decision

1887   Interstate Commerce Commission is created

1889   Otis Elevator Company installs the first electric elevator

1890   Congress passes the Sherman Anti-Trust Act, the Sherman Silver Purchase Act, and the McKinley Tariff Act

1891   Basketball is invented

KEY TERMS

Gilded Age (1860–1896) p. 868

tenements p. 870

new immigrants p. 873

Chinese Exclusion Act (1882) p. 876

social Darwinism p. 883

party boss p. 887

patronage p. 888

civil service reform p. 890

Mugwumps p. 894

Interstate Commerce Commission (ICC) (1887) p. 896

tariff reform (1887) p. 896

Granger movement p. 901

Farmers' Alliances p. 902

People's party (Populists) p. 905

Panic of 1893 p. 906

money question p. 907

🐇 INQUIZITIVE

Go to InQuizitive to see what you've learned—and learn what you've missed—with personalized feedback along the way.

19

Seizing an American Empire

1865–1913

The Charge of the Rough Riders on San Juan Hill **(1898)** Before Frederic Remington
became a celebrated artist, he had been a hunter, rancher, and saloon owner in the
American West. His intimacy with the western way of life, his technical skill, and
his keen sense of observation were not lost on Theodore Roosevelt, who invited
Remington to travel with the Rough Riders during the Spanish-American War and
publicize their efforts.

Throughout the nineteenth century, few Americans displayed much interest in foreign affairs. The overriding priorities were at home: industrial development, western settlement, and domestic politics. After the Civil War, a mood of isolationism—a desire to stay out of conflicts elsewhere in the world, especially those among powerful European nations—dominated public opinion. America's geographic advantages encouraged this isolationist attitude: wide oceans to the east and west, and weak neighbors in the Western Hemisphere.

Yet while most Americans wanted their nation to avoid getting involved in Europe's conflicts, a growing number of prominent business and civic leaders urged U.S. officials to acquire territory outside North America. The old idea of "manifest destiny" from the 1840s—that God wanted the United States (it was destined) to expand its territory westward across the North American continent—now focused on expanding control over other regions of the Western Hemisphere, and even in the Pacific and Asia.

Armed with this concept of a destiny made manifest (revealed) to people by what they saw as the obvious superiority of their way of life, Americans sought distant territories as "colonies" with no intention of their becoming states. The new manifest destiny, in other words, became a justification for imperialism. For the United States to survive and prosper, expansionists argued, it had to keep pushing beyond its current borders. During the late nineteenth century, manifest destiny also took on racial meaning as many Americans agreed with Theodore Roosevelt that the United States needed to expand around the world "on behalf of the *destiny* of the [Anglo-Saxon] race."

focus questions

1. What factors motivated America's new imperialism after the Civil War?

2. How and why did the United States expand its influence in the Pacific before the Spanish-American War?

3. What were the causes of the Spanish-American War? What were its major events?

4. What were the consequences of the Spanish-American War for American foreign policy?

5. What was behind Theodore Roosevelt's rapid rise to the presidency? What were the main elements of his foreign policies?

In more practical terms, prominent political and business leaders argued that America's rapid industrial development required the addition of foreign territories—by conquest, if necessary—to gain easier access to vital raw materials such as rubber, tin, copper, palm oil, and various dyes. At the same time, American manufacturers and commercial farmers had become increasingly dependent upon international trade, a dependence that required an expanded naval force to protect its merchant vessels as they crisscrossed the globe. And a modern, steam-powered navy needed bases in the Pacific where its ships could replenish their supplies of coal and water.

For these and other reasons, the United States during the last quarter of the nineteenth century expanded its territorial possessions both within and beyond the Western Hemisphere. During just a few crucial months in 1898, a nation born in a revolution against British colonial rule would itself become an imperial ruler of colonies around the world. Motivated by a mixture of moral and religious idealism, assumptions of "Anglo-Saxon" racial superiority, and naked greed, the expansionist impulse also generated strong opposition. But most Americans sided with future president Theodore Roosevelt, who in his 1896 book *The Winning of the West*, declared that the conquest of the "backward peoples" of the world, like the defeat of the Indians in the American West, benefited "civilization and the interests of mankind."

TOWARD THE NEW IMPERIALISM

In 1902, the British economist J. A. Hobson announced that imperialism was "the most powerful factor in the current politics of the Western world." The United States was a latecomer to the **imperialism** long practiced by European nations. Beginning in the 1880s, the British, French, Belgians, Italians, Dutch, Spanish, and Germans had conquered most of Africa and Asia. Often competing with one another for territories, they had established colonial governments to rule over the native populations and exploited the colonies economically. Each of the imperial nations, including the United States, dispatched Christian missionaries to convert conquered peoples.

During the late nineteenth century, a small yet influential group of American officials aggressively encouraged expansion beyond North America. They included powerful senators Albert J. Beveridge of Indiana and Henry Cabot Lodge of Massachusetts; as well as the assistant secretary of the navy, Theodore Roosevelt; and naval captain Alfred Thayer Mahan, president of the U.S. Naval War College in Rhode Island.

In 1890, Mahan published *The Influence of Sea Power upon History, 1660–1783*, in which he argued that Great Britain had demonstrated that national greatness flowed from naval power. Mahan insisted that modern economic development required a powerful navy centered on huge battleships, foreign commerce, colonies to provide raw materials and new markets for American products, and global naval bases. A self-described imperialist, he urged Americans to "look outward" beyond the continental United States.

Mahan championed America's "destiny" to control the Caribbean Sea, build a Central American canal to connect the Atlantic and Pacific Oceans, and spread Christian civilization across the Pacific. His ideas were widely circulated within political and military circles in the United States as well as Great Britain and Germany, and by 1896 the United States had built eleven new steel battleships, making America's navy the third most powerful in the world behind those of Great Britain and Germany.

Claims of racial superiority reinforced the new imperialist spirit. During the late nineteenth century, many Americans assumed that the Anglo-Saxon "race" was dominant and others (Native Americans, Africans) were clearly inferior. Such traditional notions justifying racism were given new "scientific" authority by researchers at universities throughout Europe and America. At the Johns Hopkins University in Baltimore, Professor James K. Hosmer claimed that "the primacy of the world will lie with us" because of the superior qualities of the Anglo-Saxon civilization.

Prominent Americans used the arguments of Social Darwinism to justify economic exploitation and territorial conquest abroad and racial segregation at home. Among nations as among individuals, they claimed, only the strongest survived. John Fiske, a Harvard historian and popular lecturer on Darwinism, proclaimed in 1885 the superior character of Anglo-Saxon institutions and peoples. The English-speaking "race," he asserted, was destined to dominate the globe and transform the institutions, traditions, language, and even the blood of the world's "backward" races.

Fiske Flying the Evolution Kite This cartoon printed in the *Daily Graphic* in 1874 depicts John Fiske flying a kite labeled "The Doctrine of Evolution." Fiske and many of his contemporaries insisted that Anglo-Saxons were the superior "race," therefore justifiably dominant.

All these factors helped excite imperialist fervor in the United States during the late nineteenth century. As a Kentucky newspaper editor proclaimed in 1893, the United States was "the most advanced and powerful" nation in the world, an "imperial Republic" destined to shape the "future of the world." The *Washington Post* agreed: "The taste of Empire is in the mouth of the people."

EXPANSION IN THE PACIFIC

For John Fiske and other imperialists, Asia offered an especially attractive target. In 1866, Secretary of State William H. Seward had predicted that the United States must inevitably impose its economic domination "on the Pacific Ocean, and its islands and continents." To take advantage of the Asian mar-

"Our New Senators" Mocking the Alaska Purchase, this political cartoon shows President Andrew Johnson and Secretary of State William H. Seward welcoming two new senators from Alaska: an Eskimo and a seal.

kets, Seward believed that the United States first had to remove foreign powers from its northern Pacific coast and gain access to the region's valuable ports. To that end, Seward tried to acquire British Columbia, sandwiched between Russian-owned Alaska and the Washington Territory.

Late in 1866, while encouraging British Columbia to consider becoming a U.S. territory, Seward learned of Russia's desire to sell Alaska. He leaped at the opportunity, thinking the purchase might influence British Columbia to join the United States. In 1867, the United States bought Alaska for $7.2 million, thus removing the threat of Russian imperialism in North America. Critics scoffed at "Seward's folly," but the Alaska Purchase proved to be the best bargain since the Louisiana Purchase, in part because of its vast deposits of gold and oil.

Seward's successors at the State Department sustained his expansionist vision. Their major focus was acquiring key Pacific Ocean ports. Two island groups occupied especially strategic positions: Samoa and Hawaii (the Sandwich Islands). Both had major harbors, Pago Pago and Pearl Harbor, respectively. In the years after the Civil War, American interest in those islands deepened.

SAMOA In 1878, the Samoans granted the United States a naval base at Pago Pago and extraterritoriality for Americans (meaning that in Samoa, Americans remained subject only to U.S. law), exchanged trade concessions, and called for the United States to help resolve any disputes with other nations. The following year, the German and British governments worked out similar arrangements with other islands in the Samoan group. There matters rested until civil war broke out in Samoa in 1887. A peace conference in Berlin in 1889 established a protectorate over Samoa, with Germany, Great Britain, and the United States in an uneasy partnership administering the island nation.

HAWAII The Hawaiian Islands, a unified kingdom since 1795, had a sizable population of American Christian missionaries and a profitable crop, sugarcane. In 1875, Hawaiian officials had signed a trade agreement allowing its sugar to enter the United States duty free in exchange for a promise that none of its territory would be leased or granted to a third power. This agreement led to a boom in sugar production based on cheap immigrant labor, mainly Chinese and Japanese workers, and American sugar planters soon formed an economic elite. By the 1890s, the native Hawaiian population had been reduced to a minority by smallpox and other diseases, and Asian immigrants had become the largest ethnic group.

Beginning in 1891, Queen Liliuokalani, the Hawaiian ruler, tried to restore "Hawaii for the Hawaiians" by restricting the political power exercised

Queen Liliuokalani The Hawaiian queen sought to preserve her nation's independence but was thwarted by the wealthy *Haole* (White) planters who pushed for annexation.

by U.S. planters in the islands. Two years later, however, Hawaii's White population (called *Haoles*) revolted and overthrew the monarchy when John L. Stevens, the U.S. ambassador, brought in marines to support the coup in January 1893. The queen surrendered "to the superior force of the United States," leading Stevens to report that the "Hawaiian pear is now fully ripe, and this is the golden hour for the United States to pluck it." Within a month, a committee representing the haoles asked the U.S. government to annex the islands. President Benjamin Harrison sent an annexation treaty to the Senate just as he was leaving the presidency in early 1893.

To investigate the situation, the new U.S. president, Grover Cleveland, sent a special commissioner to Hawaii, who reported that the Americans in Hawaii had acted improperly and that most native Hawaiians opposed annexation. Cleveland tried to restore the queen to power but met resistance from the haoles. On July 4, 1894, the government they controlled created the Republic of Hawaii, which included in its constitution a provision for American annexation. In 1897, when Republican William McKinley became president, he sought an excuse to annex the islands. "We need Hawaii," he claimed, "just as much and a good deal more than we did California. It is [America's] manifest destiny." The United States took control of Hawaii in the summer of 1898, over the protests of native Hawaiians who resented their nation being annexed without "the consent of the people of the Hawaiian Islands."

THE SPANISH-AMERICAN WAR

The annexation of Hawaii set in motion efforts to create a much larger American presence in Asia. Ironically, this imperialist push originated in Cuba, a Spanish colony ninety miles southeast of Florida. Even more ironically, the chief motive for intervention in Cuba was outrage at Spain's brutal imperialism.

THE CUBAN INDEPENDENCE MOVEMENT Throughout the second half of the nineteenth century, Cubans had repeatedly revolted against Spanish rule, only to be ruthlessly suppressed. As one of Spain's oldest colonies, Cuba was a major market for Spanish goods. Powerful American sugar and mining companies had also invested heavily in Cuba. In fact, the United States traded more with Cuba than Spain did, and American owners of sugar plantations in Cuba had grown increasingly concerned about the security of their investments.

On February 24, 1895, Cubans again rebelled against Spanish troops. During what became the Cuban War for Independence (1895–1898), at least 95,000 Cuban peasants died of combat wounds as well as disease and starvation in Spanish detention camps.

Americans followed the conflict through the daily newspapers. Two of the largest publications, William Randolph Hearst's *New York Journal* and Joseph Pulitzer's *New York World*, were then locked in a fierce competition for readers. Each strove to outdo the other with sensational headlines about Spanish atrocities, real or invented.

Hearst believed that newspapers should not simply report on events but should also shape public opinion and legislation. Newspapers, he boasted, had the power to "declare wars" by their sensational story making. Editors sent their best reporters to Cuba and encouraged them to distort, exaggerate, or even make up stories to attract more readers. Such sensationalist reporting came to be called **yellow journalism**. In addition to boosting the *Journal*'s circulation, Hearst wanted a war against Spain to propel the United States to world-power status. Once war was declared, he took credit for it; one headline blared, "HOW DO YOU LIKE THE *JOURNAL*'S WAR?" Many Protestant ministers and publications also campaigned for war, in part because of antagonism toward Catholic Spain.

THE POLITICAL PATH TO WAR At the outset of the Cuban War for Independence, President Grover Cleveland tried to avoid military involvement. After his inauguration in March 1897, President William McKinley continued the policy of neutrality while taking a sympathetic stance toward the rebels. Later that year, Spain offered Cubans autonomy (self-government without formal independence) in return for ending the rebellion, but the Cuban rebels rejected the offer.

Early in 1898, two events pushed Spain and the United States into a war that neither wanted. On January 25, the **U.S. battleship *Maine*** anchored in Havana, the Cuban capital, supposedly on a courtesy call. In fact, however, McKinley had sent the warship to protect "American life and property."

Then on February 9, the *New York Journal* released the text of a letter from Dupuy de Lôme, Spanish ambassador to the United States. In the **de Lôme letter**, which had been stolen from the post office by a Cuban spy, the Spanish diplomat called McKinley "weak and a bidder for the admiration of the crowd, besides being a would-be politician who tries to leave a door open behind himself while keeping on good terms with the jingoes [warmongers] of his party." Although the Spanish government recalled de Lôme and apologized for his indiscretions, McKinley responded that he had lost his patience with Spanish bungling in Cuba.

Soon after, a tragic disaster made war much more likely. On February 15, the *Maine* exploded without warning. Within minutes, its ruptured hull filled with water. Many sailors, most of whom were asleep, drowned as the ship sank. Of the 354 on board, 266 died. (Half of the sailors were foreign-born immigrants.) Years later, the sinking was ruled an accident resulting from an on-board coal explosion, but in 1898, those eager for war were convinced that the Spanish had sunk the ship. The headline in the *New York Journal* screamed: "WHOLE COUNTRY THRILLS WITH WAR FEVER."

Theodore Roosevelt called the sinking "an act of dirty treachery on the part of the Spaniards" and told a friend that he "would give anything if President McKinley would order the fleet to Havana tomorrow." The United States, he insisted, "needs a war."

Congress authorized $50 million to prepare for combat, but McKinley, who assumed that the sinking was an accident, resisted demands for war while negotiating with the Spanish. He also avoided interacting with Roosevelt, who he said was "too pugnacious."

As the days passed, Roosevelt, an imperialist and war lover, told his friends that McKinley was too timid; he "has no more backbone than a chocolate éclair." With Roosevelt's encouragement, the public's antagonism toward Spain grew, stirred by the popular saying "Remember the *Maine*, to Hell with Spain!"

In the weeks following the sinking, the Spanish government agreed to every major demand by the American government regarding its rule over Cuba. But the weight of outraged public opinion and the influence of Republican "jingoists" (war-loving patriots) such as Roosevelt and the president's closest friend, Senator Henry Cabot Lodge, eroded McKinley's neutrality.

"We are all jingoes now," trumpeted the *New York Sun*, "and the head jingo is the Hon. William McKinley." On April 11, McKinley asked Congress for authority to use the armed forces to end the fighting in Cuba. On April 20, Congress responded by demanding the withdrawal of Spanish forces. The Spanish government quickly broke diplomatic ties with the United States. After U.S. ships began blockading Cuban ports, Spain declared war on April 24,

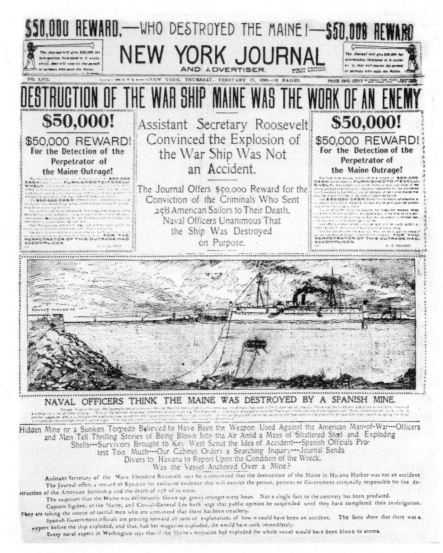

"$50,000 Reward!" As if the news of the *Maine* sinking were not disturbing enough, the *New York Journal* sensationalized the incident by offering a $50,000 reward for the perpetrator—the equivalent of $1.3 million today.

1898. The next day, Congress passed its own declaration of war. The **Teller Amendment** to the war resolution denied any U.S. intention to annex Cuba.

President McKinley called for 125,000 volunteers to supplement the 28,000 men already serving in the U.S. Army. Among the first to enlist was Theodore Roosevelt, who resigned from his government post and told his tailor to make him a dashing army uniform. To him, combat would help America reclaim "the stern and manly qualities which are essential to the well-being of a masterful race."

Never has an American war, so casually begun and so enthusiastically supported, generated such unexpected and far-reaching consequences as did the conflict against Spain. Although McKinley had gone to war reluctantly, he soon saw an opportunity to acquire overseas territories. "While we are conducting war and until its conclusion," he wrote privately, "we must keep all we get; when the war is over, we must keep what we want." A war to free Cuba thus became a way to gain an empire.

"A SPLENDID LITTLE WAR" The war with overmatched Spain lasted only 114 days, but it set the United States on a course that would transform its role in the world. The conflict was barely under way before the U.S. Navy produced a spectacular victory 7,000 miles away, at Manila Bay in the Philippine Islands, a colony controlled by Spain for more than 300 years. Just before war was declared, Roosevelt, who was still assistant secretary of the navy, ordered Commodore George Dewey, commander of the U.S. Asiatic Squadron, to engage Spanish warships in the Philippines in case the United States went to war in Cuba.

Commodore Dewey arrived at Manila Bay on April 30 with six modern warships, which quickly destroyed or captured the outdated Spanish vessels there. An English reporter called it "a military execution rather than a real contest." News of Dewey's victory set off wild celebrations in the United States. Commodore Dewey was now in awkward possession of Manila Bay, but without any soldiers to go onshore. While he waited for reinforcements, German and British warships cruised offshore like watchful vultures, ready to seize the Philippines if the United States did not.

In the meantime, Emilio Aguinaldo, leader of the Filipino nationalist movement, declared the Philippines independent from Spain on June 12, 1898. With Aguinaldo's help, Dewey's augmented forces entered Manila on August 13 and accepted the surrender of the Spanish troops, who had feared for their lives if they surrendered to the Filipinos.

News of the American victory sent President McKinley scurrying to find a map to locate "those darned islands" now occupied by U.S. soldiers and sailors. Senator Lodge was delighted with the news from the Philippines: "We hold the other side of the Pacific," he bragged, "and the value to this country is almost beyond imagination. We must on no account let the [Philippine] islands go," for they provided access to "the vast markets furnished by the millions of people in the East." As a result of the American victory, Aguinaldo's dream of Filipino independence and self-rule would soon be crushed by U.S. forces. As the writer

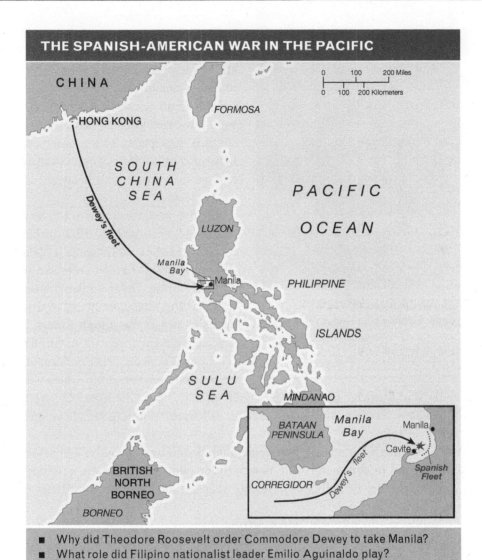

THE SPANISH-AMERICAN WAR IN THE PACIFIC

- Why did Theodore Roosevelt order Commodore Dewey to take Manila?
- What role did Filipino nationalist leader Emilio Aguinaldo play?
- Why were many Americans opposed to the acquisition of the Philippines?

Mark Twain would explain, "There must be two Americas: one that sets the captive free, and one that takes a once-captive's new freedom away from him."

THE CUBAN CAMPAIGN While Commodore Dewey was defeating the Spanish in the Philippines, the fighting in Cuba reached a surprisingly quick climax. At the start of the war, the Spanish army in Cuba was five times as large as the entire U.S. Army. President McKinley's call for volunteers, however, inspired nearly a million men to enlist, and some 200,000 were accepted.

African American Troops in Cuba Soldiers stand in formation wearing old wool uniforms unsuited to Cuba's tropical heat.

Among the new recruits were an estimated 10,000 African American soldiers, mostly northerners determined to "show our loyalty to our land." In the Jim Crow South, however, Blacks were less eager to enlist because, as a Virginia newspaper editor observed, they suffered "a system of oppression as barbarous as that which is alleged to exist in Cuba."

In the meantime, the U.S. Navy blockaded the Spanish fleet inside Santiago Harbor while some 17,000 American troops hastily assembled at Tampa, Florida. The most flamboyant unit was the First Volunteer Cavalry, better known as the **Rough Riders**, a special regiment made up of former Ivy League athletes; Irish policemen; ex-convicts; cowboys from Oklahoma and New Mexico; Texas Rangers; gold miners; and Cherokee, Choctaw, Chickasaw, Pawnee, and Creek Indians. All were "young, good shots, and good riders."

The Rough Riders are best remembered because Theodore Roosevelt was second in command. One Rough Rider said that Roosevelt was "nervous, energetic, virile [manly]. He may wear out some day, but he will never rust out."

When the 578 Rough Riders, accompanied by a gaggle of reporters and photographers, landed on June 22, 1898, at the undefended southeastern tip of Cuba, chaos ensued. Except for Roosevelt's horse, most of the unit's horses and mules had been mistakenly sent elsewhere, leaving the Rough Riders to become the "Weary Walkers." Nevertheless, land and sea battles around Santiago quickly broke Spanish resistance.

On July 1, about 7,000 U.S. soldiers took the fortified village of El Caney. While a much larger force attacked San Juan Hill, a smaller unit, led by Roosevelt on horseback and including the Rough Riders on foot, prepared to seize nearby Kettle Hill. Situated in a field of tall grass, the frustrated Americans were being shot at by Spanish snipers while waiting to attack. Captain Bucky O'Neill decided to boost morale by strolling among the men while smoking a cigarette. When one of them shouted, "Captain, a bullet is sure to kill you," O'Neill replied, "Sergeant, the Spanish bullet ain't made that will kill me"—whereupon a Spanish bullet struck him in the jaw, killing him instantly.

O'Neill's death prompted Roosevelt to mount his horse and order his men to charge the Spaniards. Although shot in the arm, Roosevelt kept moving, and his headlong gallop toward the Spanish defenders, wearing a blue polka-dot bandana, made him a home-front legend. The *New York Times* reported that he had led the charge with "bulldog ferociousness." Roosevelt boasted that nobody "else could have handled this regiment quite as I handled it." He may have been bragging, but what he said was true.

Roosevelt crowed that he had "killed a Spaniard with my own hand—like a jack rabbit." Unburdened by humility, he requested a Congressional Medal of Honor for his exploits. It did not come. (President Bill Clinton finally awarded the medal posthumously in 2001.)

While Colonel Roosevelt was basking in the glory of battle, other U.S. soldiers were less enthusiastic about modern warfare. Walter Bartholomew, a private from New York, reported that the war "in all its awfulness" was so "much more hideous than my wildest imagination that I have not yet recovered from the shock." A soldier standing beside him had "the front of his throat torn completely off" by a Spanish bullet. As Bartholomew's unit was charging up San Juan Hill, they "became totally disorganized and thrown into utter

Colonel Roosevelt With one hand on his hip, Roosevelt rides with the Rough Riders in Cuba. Most of this regiment was culled from Arizona, New Mexico, and Texas because the southwestern climate resembled that of Cuba.

confusion" amid the intense shooting. He discarded all he carried except for his rifle "in the mad scramble to get out of the valley of death." While stopping to shoot, he saw the 24th Regiment of Colored Infantry racing up the hill and decided to follow their lead. He was "so excited that I forgot to fire my gun, and I actually charged clean up to the top of the hill without shooting, in as great panic as if I had been retreating."

SPANISH DEFEAT AND CONCESSIONS On July 3, the Spanish navy trapped at Santiago attempted to evade the American fleet blockading the harbor. The outgunned Spanish ships were quickly destroyed by the more modern American fleet; 474 Spaniards were killed or wounded, while the Americans suffered only two casualties. Spanish officials surrendered on July 17. On July 25, an American force moved into Spanish-held Puerto Rico, meeting only minor resistance as it took control of that island.

The next day, the Spanish government sued for peace. A cease-fire agreement was signed on August 12. In Cuba, the Spanish formally surrendered to the U.S. commander and sailed for home. Excluded from the ceremony were the Cubans, for whom the war had supposedly been fought.

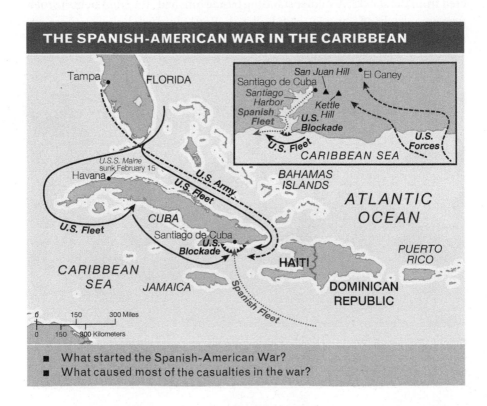

THE SPANISH-AMERICAN WAR IN THE CARIBBEAN

■ What started the Spanish-American War?
■ What caused most of the casualties in the war?

On December 10, 1898, the United States and Spain signed the Treaty of Paris. Under its terms, Cuba was to become independent and the United States was to annex Puerto Rico and Guam (a Spanish-controlled island between Hawaii and the Philippines) as new American territories. The United States would continue to occupy Manila, pending a transfer of power to the U.S. government in the Philippines.

With the Treaty of Paris, the Spanish Empire in the Americas initiated by the voyages of Christopher Columbus some four centuries earlier came to a humiliating end. The United States was ready to create its own empire.

During the four-month Spanish-American War, more than 60,000 Spanish soldiers and sailors died of wounds or disease—mostly malaria, typhoid, dysentery, or yellow fever. Some 10,500 Cubans died. Among the 274,000 Americans who served in the war, 5,462 died, but only 379 in battle; most died from unsanitary conditions in the army camps. At such a cost, the United States was launched onto the world scene as a great power, with all the benefits—and burdens—of managing a colonial empire.

Halfway through the conflict in Cuba, John Hay, the U.S. ambassador to Great Britain who would soon become secretary of state, wrote a letter to Roosevelt, his close friend. In acknowledging Roosevelt's trial by fire, Hay called the conflict "a splendid little war, begun with the highest motives, carried on with magnificent intelligence and spirit, favored by that fortune which loves the brave."

CONSEQUENCES OF VICTORY

Victory in the Spanish-American War boosted American self-confidence and reinforced the self-serving belief that the United States had a manifest destiny to reshape the world in its own image. In 1885, the Reverend Josiah Strong had written a best-selling book titled *Our Country* in which he used a Darwinian argument to strengthen the appeal of manifest destiny. The "wonderful progress of the United States," he boasted, was itself an illustration of Charles Darwin's concept of "natural selection." After all, Americans had demonstrated that they were the world's "superior" civilization, "a race of unequaled energy" who represented "the largest liberty, the purest Christianity, the highest civilization" in the world, a race of superior people destined to "spread itself over the earth," to Central and South America, and "out upon the islands" in the Pacific and beyond to Asia.

Strong asserted that the United States had a Christian duty to expand American influence around the world. International trade, he noted, would grow directly out of America's missionary evangelism and racial superiority. "Can anyone doubt," he asked, "that this race . . . is destined to dispossess many weaker races, assimilate others, and mold the remainder until . . . it has Anglo-Saxonized mankind?"

Europeans agreed that the United States had now made an impressive entrance onto the world stage. The *Times* of London announced that the American victory over Spain must "effect a profound change in the whole attitude and policy of the United States. In the future, America will play a part in the general affairs of the world such as she has never played before." America's acquisition of its first imperial colonies created a host of long-lasting moral and practical problems, from the ethical dilemmas of imposing U.S. rule by force on native peoples to the challenge of defending far-flung territories around the globe.

TAKING THE PHILIPPINES The United States soon substituted its own imperialism for Spain's. If the war had saved many lives by ending the insurrection in Cuba, it had also led the United States to take many lives in suppressing the anti-colonial insurrection in the Philippines.

The Treaty of Paris dismantled most of the Spanish Empire but left the political status of the Philippines unresolved. American business leaders wanted the United States to keep the area's 400 inhabited islands so that they could more easily penetrate the markets of nearby China and reach its huge population. As Mark Hanna, President McKinley's top adviser, stressed, controlling the Philippines would enable the United States to "take a large slice of the commerce of Asia."

American missionary organizations, mostly Protestant, also favored annexation; they viewed the Philippines as a base from which to bring Christianity to "the little brown brother." After the United States took control, American authorities ended the Roman Catholic Church's status as the Philippines' official religion and made English the official language, thus opening the door for Protestant missionaries to begin evangelical activities across the region.

These factors helped convince President McKinley of the need to annex the Philippines. He claimed to have agonized over the issue, walking "the floor of the White House night after night" until finally he got down on his knees and prayed "for light and guidance." Then,

> one night late it came to me this way—I don't know how it was, but it came: (1) that we could not give them back to Spain—that would be cowardly and dishonorable; (2) that we could not turn them over to France or Germany—our commercial rivals in the Orient—that would be bad business and discreditable; (3) that we could not leave them

to themselves—they were unfit for self-government—and they would soon have anarchy and misrule over there worse than Spain's was; and (4) that there was nothing left for us to do but to take them all, and to educate the Filipinos, and uplift and civilize and Christianize them, and by God's grace do the very best we could by them, as our fellow-men for whom Christ also died. And then I went to bed, and went to sleep and slept soundly.

In this one brief statement, McKinley summarized the motivating ideas of American imperialism: (1) national glory, (2) expanding commerce, (3) racial superiority, and (4) Christian evangelism.

American negotiators in Paris finally offered Spain $20 million for the Philippines, Puerto Rico, and Guam, the last of which would serve as a coaling station for ships headed across the Pacific to Asia.

Meanwhile, in addition to annexing Hawaii in 1898, the United States also claimed Wake Island, between Guam and Hawaii, which would become a vital link in a future transpacific telegraph cable. In 1899, Germany and the United States agreed to divide the Samoa Islands.

"Well, I hardly know which to take first!" With a growing appetite for foreign territory, Uncle Sam browses his options: Cuba Steak, Puerto Rico Pig, Philippine Floating Islands, and others. An expectant President McKinley waits to take his order.

DEBATING THE TREATY By early 1899, the Senate had yet to ratify the Treaty of Paris with Spain because of growing domestic opposition to a global American empire. Anti-imperialists argued that annexing the former Spanish colonies would violate the long-standing American principle embodied in the Constitution that people should be self-governing rather than colonial subjects. Massachusetts senator George Hoar warned that approving the treaty would "make us a vulgar, commonplace empire, controlling subject races . . . in which one class must forever rule and other classes must forever obey."

Emilio Aguinaldo As the first president of the Philippines, Aguinaldo led the *insurrectos* in their war against American forces, who refused his appeal for a truce.

Treaty opponents also noted the moral inconsistency of liberating Cuba and annexing the Philippines. Senator Albert Beveridge of Indiana, however, openly championed U.S. imperialism. He argued that the ideal of democracy "applies only to those who are capable of self-government." In his view as a White supremacist, the Filipinos were incapable of governing themselves. His friend Theodore Roosevelt expressed the widespread racism of the time more bluntly. The Filipinos, he declared, were "wild beasts" who would benefit from American-imposed discipline: "There must be control! There must be mastery!"

The opposition might have killed the treaty had not the most prominent Democratic leader, William Jennings Bryan, argued that endorsing the treaty would open the way for the future independence of the Philippines. His change of position convinced just enough Senate Democrats to support the treaty. On February 6, 1899, it passed by the narrowest of margins: only one vote more than the necessary two-thirds majority.

President McKinley, however, had no intention of granting independence to the Philippines. He insisted that the United States take control of the islands as an act of "benevolent assimilation" of the native population. A California newspaper gave a more candid explanation, however. "Let us be frank," the editor exclaimed. "WE DO NOT WANT THE FILIPINOS. WE WANT THE PHILIPPINES."

The Filipinos themselves had a different vision. In early 1899, rebels again declared independence and named twenty-nine-year-old Emilio Aguinaldo president. The following month, an American soldier outside Manila fired on Aguinaldo's nationalist forces, called *insurrectos*, killing two, who may have been unarmed. The following day, the Filipino rebels acknowledged that the fighting had begun accidentally. They asked for an immediate cease-fire. The U.S. commander, however, rejected the request, replying that the "fighting, having begun, must go on to the grim end."

On June 2, 1899, the Philippine Republic declared war against the United States. America now found itself in an even more costly conflict than the war with Spain—this one to suppress the Filipino independence movement. Since the *insurrectos* controlled most of the Philippine islands, what followed was largely a war of conquest at odds with the founding principle of the United States: that people have the right to govern themselves. The war would rob the Filipinos of the chance to be their own masters.

THE PHILIPPINE-AMERICAN WAR (1899–1902) The grisly American effort to crush Filipino nationalism lasted three years, involved some 126,000 U.S. troops, and took the lives of hundreds of thousands of Filipinos (most of them civilians) and 4,234 American soldiers. It was a brutal conflict in which both sides used torture and committed massacres.

While Whites in southern states were lynching African Americans, a similarly vicious form of racism spurred numerous atrocities by U.S. troops. Soldiers burned villages, tortured and executed prisoners, and imprisoned civilians in overcrowded concentration camps. A reporter for the *Philadelphia Ledger* noted that U.S. soldiers had "killed to exterminate men, women, children, prisoners and captives, active insurgents and suspected people from lads of ten up, the idea prevailing that the Filipino as such was little better than a dog." One U.S. soldier from Indiana celebrated the slaughter of an entire village in retaliation for the murder of an American: "I am in my glory when I can sight my gun on some dark skin and pull the trigger."

Both sides used torture to gain information. A favorite method employed by Americans was the "water cure," a technique to simulate drowning developed in the Spanish Inquisition during the sixteenth century. (Today it is called waterboarding and is considered a war crime.) A captured insurgent would be placed on his back on the ground. While soldiers stood on his outstretched arms and feet, they pried his mouth open and poured salt water into the captive's mouth and nose until his stomach was bloated, whereupon they would stomp on his abdomen, forcing the water, now mixed with gastric juices, out of his mouth. They repeated the process until the captive told the soldiers what they wanted to know—or died. "It is not civilized warfare," wrote the *Philadelphia Ledger*, "but we are not dealing with civilized people."

Thus did the United States set out to destroy a revolutionary movement modeled after America's own struggle for independence from Great Britain. Organized Filipino resistance collapsed by the end of 1899, but sporadic clashes continued for months thereafter. On April 1, 1901, Aguinaldo swore an oath accepting the authority of the United States over the Philippines and pledging his allegiance to the U.S. government.

Against the backdrop of this nasty guerrilla war, a great debate over imperialism continued in the United States. In 1899, several groups combined to form the **American Anti-Imperialist League**. Andrew Carnegie financed the League and even offered $20 million to buy independence for the Filipinos.

"The Water Cure" American soldiers torture a Filipino prisoner during the Philippine-American War.

Other prominent anti-imperialists included Mark Twain, college presidents Charles Eliot of Harvard and David Starr Jordan of Stanford, and social reformer Jane Addams. Even former presidents Grover Cleveland and Benjamin Harrison urged President McKinley to withdraw U.S. forces from the Philippines. The conflict to suppress Filipino independence had become "a quagmire," said Mark Twain, and the United States should "not try to get them under our heel" or intervene "in any other country that is not ours." Harvard philosopher William James was even more emphatic, arguing that the nation's imperialism in Asia had caused the United States to "puke up its ancient soul." Of the Philippine-American War, James asked, "Could there be any more damning indictment of that whole bloated ideal termed 'modern civilization'?"

Senator Hoar, one of the few surviving founders of the Republican party, led the opposition to annexation in the Senate. Under the Constitution, he pointed out, "no power is given the Federal government to acquire territory to be held and governed permanently as colonies" or "to conquer alien people and hold them in subjugation."

Many ministers denounced imperialism as unchristian. Charles Ames, a prominent Unitarian leader, predicted that embracing imperialism would "put us into a permanent attitude of arrogance, testiness, and defiance towards other nations. . . . We shall be one more bully among bullies."

ORGANIZING THE FORMER SPANISH TERRITORIES In the end, the imperialists won the debate over the status of the territories acquired from Spain. Senator Albert J. Beveridge boasted in 1900: "The Philippines are ours forever. And just beyond the Philippines are China's illimitable markets. . . . The power that rules the Pacific is the power that rules the world." He added that the U.S. economy was producing "more than we can consume, making more than we can use. Therefore we must find new markets for our produce." American-controlled colonies would make the best new markets. Without acknowledging it, Beveridge and others were using many of the same arguments that English officials had used in founding the American colonies in the seventeenth century.

On July 4, 1901, the U.S. military government in the Philippines gave way to civilian control, and William Howard Taft became the governor. In 1902, Congress passed the Philippine Government Act, which in essence, transformed the Philippines into an American-controlled *colony*, not a territory eligible for statehood. (In 1917, the Jones Act affirmed America's intention to grant the Philippines independence, but that would not happen until 1946.)

Closer to home, Puerto Rico had been acquired in part to serve as a U.S. outpost guarding the Caribbean Sea. On April 12, 1900, the Foraker Act

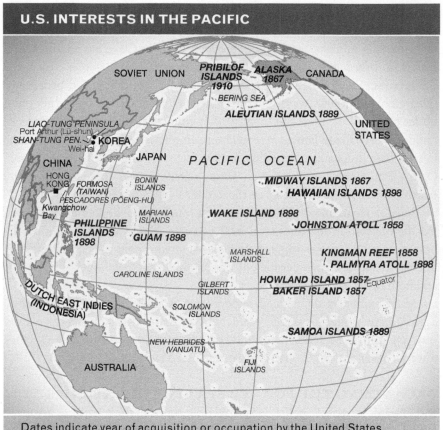

U.S. INTERESTS IN THE PACIFIC

SOVIET UNION

PRIBILOF ISLANDS 1910

ALASKA 1867

CANADA

BERING SEA

ALEUTIAN ISLANDS 1889

LIAO-TUNG PENINSULA
Port Arthur (Lü-shun)
SHAN-TUNG PEN. KOREA
Wei-hai

UNITED STATES

CHINA

JAPAN

PACIFIC OCEAN

HONG KONG FORMOSA (TAIWAN)
PESCADORES (PÖENG-HU)
Kwangchow Bay

BONIN ISLANDS

MIDWAY ISLANDS 1867
HAWAIIAN ISLANDS 1898

MARIANA ISLANDS

WAKE ISLAND 1898

JOHNSTON ATOLL 1858

PHILIPPINE ISLANDS 1898
GUAM 1898

MARSHALL ISLANDS

KINGMAN REEF 1858
PALMYRA ATOLL 1898

CAROLINE ISLANDS

GILBERT ISLANDS

HOWLAND ISLAND 1857 Equator
BAKER ISLAND 1857

DUTCH EAST INDIES (INDONESIA)

SOLOMON ISLANDS

SAMOA ISLANDS 1889

NEW HEBRIDES (VANUATU)

FIJI ISLANDS

AUSTRALIA

Dates indicate year of acquisition or occupation by the United States.
- Why was President McKinley eager to acquire territory in the Pacific and the Caribbean?
- What kind of political system did the U.S. government create in Hawaii and in the Philippines?
- How did Filipinos and Hawaiians resist the Americans?

established a government on the island, and its residents were declared citizens of the Commonwealth of Puerto Rico, not Spain; they were made dual citizens of the United States 1917.

In Cuba, the United States finally fulfilled the promise of independence after restoring order, organizing schools, and improving sanitary conditions. The problem of widespread disease prompted the work of Dr. Walter Reed. Named head of the Army Yellow Fever Commission in 1900, he proved that mosquitoes carry yellow fever. The commission's experiments led the way to effective control of the disease worldwide. In 1900, on President McKinley's order, Cubans drafted a constitution modeled on that of the United States. The following year, however, the Platt Amendment, added to an army appropriations bill, sharply restricted the Cuban government's independence by requiring that the Cuban government never sign a treaty with a third power and that it acknowledge the right of the United States to intervene in Cuba's affairs whenever it saw fit. Finally, Cuba had to sell or lease to the United States lands to be used for coaling or naval stations, a stipulation that led to a U.S. naval base at Guantánamo Bay that still exists today. American troops remained in control of the rest of Cuba until 1902 and returned several times later (1912, 1917, and 1920) to suppress insurrections.

"UNINCORPORATED TERRITORIES"   Until 1900, the U.S. government granted territories the protection of the Constitution and a path to statehood. The acquisition of Puerto Rico, Guam, and the Philippines, however, led to a new policy. In 1900, William McKinley won reelection on a platform that celebrated America's new overseas empire and referred to residents of the newly acquired territories as "rescued peoples." His successor, Theodore Roosevelt, hailed "the expansion of the peoples of white, or European, blood" into the lands of "mere savages."

The U.S. Supreme Court clarified the rights of the newly acquired territories in *Downes v. Bidwell* (1901). The justices declared that America's territories were either "incorporated" with the United States or "unincorporated." Only the "incorporated" territories—at that time Alaska, Arizona, Hawaii, Oklahoma, and New Mexico—received the full protections of the Constitution. The "unincorporated" territories—Guam, the Philippines, Puerto Rico, and Samoa—were, according to the justices, "inhabited by alien races" incapable of appreciating America's constitutional values.

IMPERIAL RIVALRIES IN EAST ASIA   While the United States was suppressing the Filipino independence movement, other nations were threatening to carve up China. After Japan defeated China in the First Sino-Japanese War (1894–1895), European nations began to exploit the weakness of the virtually defenseless nation. By the end of the century, Russia, Germany, France, and Great Britain had each established spheres of influence in China—territories that they controlled but did not formally annex.

In 1898 and again in 1899, the British asked the American government to join them in preserving the territorial integrity of China against further imperialist actions. Both times, however, the Senate rejected the request because the United States had no strategic investment in the region. The American outlook changed with the defeat of Spain and the acquisition of the Philippines. Instead of acting jointly with Great Britain, however, the

U.S. government decided to act alone (unilaterally) in implementing the British policy.

What came to be known as the **Open Door policy** was outlined in Secretary of State John Hay's Open Door Note, dispatched in 1899 to his European counterparts. Without consulting the Chinese, Hay announced that China should remain an "open door" to European and American trade and that other nations should not try to take control of Chinese ports or territory. None of the European powers except Britain accepted Hay's principles, but none rejected them, either. So, Hay announced that all major powers involved in China had accepted the policy.

The Open Door policy was rooted in the desire of American businesses to exploit and ultimately dominate Chinese markets. It also appealed to those who opposed imperialism because it pledged to keep China from being carved up by powerful European nations. The policy had little legal standing, however. When the Japanese became concerned about growing Russian influence in Manchuria (in northeast China) and asked how the United States intended to enforce the policy, Hay replied that America was "not prepared . . . to enforce these views." So the situation would remain for forty years, until continued Japanese military expansion in China would bring about a diplomatic dispute with America that would lead to war in 1941.

Intervention in China After quelling the Boxer Rebellion, U.S. troops march in the Forbidden Palace, the imperial palace in the Chinese capital of Peking.

THE BOXERS A new Asian crisis arose in 1900 when Chinese nationalists known to the Western world as Boxers—they called themselves the "Fists
of Righteous Harmony"—rebelled against foreign involvement in China, especially Christian missionary efforts, and laid siege to foreign embassies in Peking
(now known as Beijing). An expedition of British, German, Russian, Japanese,
and American soldiers was organized to rescue the international diplomats and
their staffs. Hay, fearful that the intervention might become an excuse for other
nations to carve up China into separate colonies, took the opportunity to refine
the Open Door policy. The United States, he said, sought a solution that would
"preserve Chinese territorial and administrative integrity" as well as "equal
and impartial trade with all parts of the Chinese Empire." Six weeks later, the
foreign military expedition reached Peking and ended the Boxer Rebellion.

Roosevelt's "Big-Stick" Diplomacy

Theodore Roosevelt transformed the role of the United States abroad. The
nation had emerged from war in Cuba as a world power with major new international responsibilities. To ensure that Americans accepted their new global
role, Roosevelt stretched both the Constitution and executive power to the
limit. In the process, he pushed a reluctant nation onto the center stage of
international events.

RISE TO NATIONAL PROMINENCE Born in 1858, Roosevelt had
grown up in New York City in a cultured, wealthy family. He visited Europe
as a child, spoke German fluently, and graduated from Harvard with honors
in 1880. From a sickly, nearsighted boy with chronic asthma, he built himself
into a barrel-chested man of almost superhuman energy and hyperactivity.

A boxer, wrestler, mountain climber, hunter, and all-around outdoorsman,
the robust Roosevelt also displayed extraordinary intellectual curiosity. He
became a voracious reader in several languages, a natural scientist, a historian, and a zealous moralist. He wrote thirty-eight books on a wide variety of
subjects. Roosevelt's zest for life and his combative spirit were contagious, and
he was ever eager to express an opinion on any subject. After young Roosevelt
participated in a buffalo hunt in the Dakotas, one of the cowboys said: "There
goes the most remarkable man I ever met. Unless I am badly mistaken, the
world is due to hear from him one of these days."

Within two years of graduating from Harvard, Roosevelt won election to
the New York legislature. "I rose like a rocket," he later observed. He could not
be bought, nor did he tolerate the excesses of the spoils system. "Though I am

a strong party man," he warned, "if I find a corrupt public official, I would take off his head."

With the world at his feet, however, disaster struck. In 1884, Roosevelt's mother, Mittie, only forty-eight years old, died of typhoid fever. Eleven hours later, his "bewitchingly pretty," twenty-two-year-old wife, Alice, died in his arms of kidney failure, having given birth to their only child just two days earlier. The "light has gone out of my life," Roosevelt noted in his diary. The double funeral service for his wife and mother was so emotional that the officiating minister wept throughout his prayer.

Shaken by his "strange and terrible fate," Roosevelt turned his newborn daughter over to his sister, quit his political career, sold the family house, and moved to a cattle ranch in the Dakota Territory, where he stayed for two years. He threw himself into becoming a cowboy: roping and branding steers, shooting buffaloes and bears, capturing outlaws, fighting Indians (whom he called a "lesser race"), and reading novels by the campfire. He was, by his own admission, a poor shot, a bad roper, and an average rider, but he loved his western life. He would write in his memoirs that "I owe more than I can express to the West."

Back in New York City, Roosevelt remarried and ran unsuccessfully for mayor in 1886. He later served as a U.S. Civil Service commissioner and as head of the city's police commissioners. Roosevelt lusted to be "one of the governing class," so he took full advantage of the celebrity he had gained with the Rough Riders in Cuba to win the governorship of New York in 1898. By then, he had become the most prominent rising Republican leader in the nation. Two years later, Republican leaders were urging him to become the vice-presidential running mate for McKinley, who was hoping for a second presidential term.

FROM VICE PRESIDENT TO PRESIDENT   In the 1900 presidential contest, the Democrats turned once again to William Jennings Bryan, who wanted to make American imperialism the "paramount issue" of the campaign. The Democratic platform condemned the conflict with Filipino nationalists as "an unnecessary war" that had placed the United States "in the false and un-American position of crushing with military force the efforts of our former allies to achieve liberty and self-government."

The Republicans renominated McKinley and named Roosevelt, now known as "Mr. Imperialism," their candidate for vice president. Roosevelt, who dismissed Bryan as a dangerous "radical," crisscrossed the nation on behalf of McKinley, speaking in opposition to Bryan's "communistic and socialistic doctrines" promoting higher taxes and the unlimited coinage of silver. At one stop, Roosevelt claimed that Bryan's supporters were "all the lunatics, all the idiots, all the knaves, all the cowards." In the end, McKinley and Roosevelt won by 7.2 million to 6.4 million popular votes and 292 to 155 electoral votes. Bryan even lost Nebraska, his home state.

Less than a year later, however, McKinley's second term ended abruptly and tragically. On September 6, 1901, while the president was visiting the Pan-American Exposition in Buffalo, New York, Leon Czolgosz (pronounced chol-GOSH), a twenty-eight-year-old unemployed anarchist, approached with a concealed gun and fired twice at point-blank range. "I done my duty!" Czolgosz screamed.

The president's coat button and breastbone deflected one bullet, but the other tore through his abdomen and lodged in his back. McKinley urged police not to "hurt" his assailant; he is "just some poor misguided fellow."

For several days, doctors issued optimistic reports about McKinley's condition, but after a week, the president knew he was dying. "It is useless, gentlemen," he told the doctors. "I think we ought to have a prayer." Then

Big-Stick Diplomacy President Theodore Roosevelt wields "the big stick," symbolizing his aggressive diplomacy. As he stomps through the Caribbean, he drags a string of American warships behind him.

he said, "Goodbye, goodbye to all." Czolgosz was convicted of murder and executed in an electric chair, a new invention.

The combustible Theodore Roosevelt was suddenly the new president. "Now look," exclaimed Mark Hanna, "that damned cowboy is President of the United States!"

Six weeks short of his forty-third birthday, Roosevelt, known affectionately as TR, was the youngest man to become president. But he had more experience in public affairs than most new presidents, and perhaps more vitality than any. One observer compared his boundless personality and energy to Niagara Falls—"both great wonders of nature." TR's glittering spectacles, glistening teeth, and overflowing enthusiasm were like divine gifts to political cartoonists, as was his motto, an old African proverb: "Speak softly, and carry a big stick."

Roosevelt was the first truly activist president. The presidency was, as he put it, a "bully pulpit"—an inviting platform for delivering fist-pumping speeches on the virtues of honesty, courage, and civic duty.

Nowhere was President Roosevelt's forceful temperament more evident than in his handling of foreign affairs. Like many of his political friends and associates, Roosevelt was convinced that the "civilized" and "barbarian" peoples of the world faced inevitable conflict, not unlike the fate of the Native Americans pushed off their ancestral lands by settlers and soldiers. In 1899, he argued that the United States needed to conquer other regions of the world to bring "law, order, and righteousness" to "backward peoples." He believed that American imperialists would be missionaries of civic virtue, spreading the merits of their "race" to "savages."

THE PANAMA CANAL After the Spanish-American War, one issue overshadowed every other in the Caribbean: the proposed Panama Canal. By enabling ships to travel from the Pacific Ocean directly into the Gulf of Mexico, such a canal would cut the travel distance between San Francisco and New York City by almost 8,000 miles.

The nation of Panama had been a major concern of Americans since the late 1840s, when it became an important overland link in the sea route from the East Coast to the California goldfields. From 1881 to 1887, a French company led by Ferdinand de Lesseps, who had engineered the Suez Canal in Egypt, had already spent nearly $300 million and some 20,000 lives to dig a canal a third of the way across Panama, which was still under Colombian control. The company asked the American government to purchase its partially completed canal.

In return for acquiring a canal zone six miles wide, the United States agreed to pay Colombia $10 million, but the Colombian Senate held out for $25 million. As President Roosevelt raged against the "foolish and homicidal corruptionists in Bogotá," the Panamanians revolted against Colombian rule. President Roosevelt aided the Panamanian rebels and signed a treaty with the newly independent nation that extended the Canal Zone from six to ten miles wide.

For a $10 million down payment and $250,000 a year, the United States received "in perpetuity the use, occupation and control" of the fifty-mile-long Canal Zone. Not everyone applauded the president's actions. A Chicago newspaper attacked him for his "rough-riding assault upon another republic over the shattered wreckage of international law. Roosevelt later explained, "I took the Canal Zone and let Congress debate [about the legitimacy of his actions]; and while the debate goes on the [construction of the] Canal does also."

Building the Panama Canal was one of the greatest engineering feats in history. Over ten years, some 60,000 mostly unskilled workers from Europe, Asia, and the Caribbean, as well as U.S. engineers and managers, used dynamite and steam shovels to gouge out the canal from dense jungle. Almost a third of the workers died from malaria or yellow fever. "People get killed and injured almost every day," a worker reported in his journal. "And all the bosses want is to get the canal built." With great fanfare, however, the canal opened on August 15, 1914, two weeks after the outbreak of the Great War in Europe.

Digging the Land President Theodore Roosevelt stands on a steam shovel during his visit to the Panama Canal, having secured U.S. rights to use and control the canal in perpetuity.

U.S. INTERESTS IN THE CARIBBEAN

UNITED STATES

☐ United States and its possessions
☐ Occupied by or a protectorate of the United States

GULF OF MEXICO

CUBA
Occupied
1898–1902,
1906–1909,1912
1917,1922
Protectorate
1898–1934

Havana

BAHAMA ISLANDS

DOMINICAN REPUBLIC
Occupied 1916–1924
Protectorate 1905–1941

•Veracruz

Guantánamo
(U.S. naval base)

MEXICO
Occupied 1914

BRITISH HONDURAS

JAMAICA

PUERTO RICO
Annexed 1898

GUATEMALA   HONDURAS

HAITI
Occupied 1915–1934
Protectorate 1915–1936

EL SALVADOR

Proposed route for Nicaraguan canal

VIRGIN ISLANDS
Acquired from Denmark 1917

NICARAGUA
Occupied 1912–1925
1926–1939

PANAMA CANAL ZONE
Leased from Panama 1903

COSTA RICA

VENEZUELA

0   250   500 Miles
0   250 500 Kilometers

PANAMA
Protectorate 1903–1939

COLOMBIA

■ Why did America want to build the Panama Canal?
■ How did the U.S. government interfere with Colombian politics in an effort to gain control of the canal zone?
■ What was the Roosevelt Corollary?

INTERVENING IN LATIN AMERICA Theodore Roosevelt's "theft" of the Panama Canal Zone created decades of ill will toward the United States throughout Latin America. Constant interference from both the United States and European countries only aggravated tensions. A frequent excuse for intervention was to promote a safe and stable environment for American businesses, including the collection of debts owed by Latin American governments. The Latin Americans responded with the Drago Doctrine (1902), named after Argentinian foreign minister Luis María Drago, which prohibited armed intervention by other countries to collect debts.

In December 1902, however, German and British warships blockaded Venezuela to force the repayment of debts in defiance of both the Drago Doctrine and the Monroe Doctrine, the U.S. policy dating to 1823 that prohibited European intervention in the Western Hemisphere. Roosevelt decided that if the United States were to keep European nations from intervening militarily in Latin America, "then sooner or later we must keep order [there] ourselves." In 1904, a crisis over the debts of the Dominican Republic prompted Roosevelt to send two warships to the island nation and issue what came to be known as the **Roosevelt Corollary** to the Monroe Doctrine: the principle, in short, that in certain circumstances, the United States was justified in intervening militarily in Latin America to prevent Europeans from doing so. "Chronic wrongdoing," Roosevelt asserted, would justify U.S. exercise of "an international police power" in the region. Thereafter, Roosevelt and other U.S. presidents repeatedly used military force to ensure that Latin American nations paid their debts to U.S. and European banks.

RELATIONS WITH JAPAN While wielding a "big stick" in Latin America, Roosevelt was playing the role of peacemaker in East Asia. In 1904,

Japanese Immigration Japanese immigrants arrive at Angel Island, a major immigration processing center in the San Francisco Bay. By the early 1900s, ethnic tensions on the West Coast prompted the U.S. Congress and President Theodore Roosevelt to adopt new policies regarding Asian immigrants.

the rivalry between Russia and Japan flared into the Russo-Japanese War over Japan's attempts to expand its influence in China and Korea. On February 8, Japanese warships devastated the Russian fleet. The Japanese then occupied the Korean peninsula and drove the Russians back into Manchuria.

When the Japanese signaled that they would welcome a negotiated settlement, Roosevelt sponsored a peace conference in Portsmouth, New Hampshire. In the Treaty of Portsmouth, signed on September 5, 1905, Russia acknowledged Japan's "predominant political, military, and economic interests in Korea." (Japan would annex the kingdom in 1910.) Both powers agreed to leave Manchuria. Japan's show of strength raised concerns among U.S. leaders about the security of the Philippines. During the Portsmouth talks, Roosevelt sent William Howard Taft to meet with the Japanese foreign minister. They negotiated the Taft-Katsura Agreement of July 29, 1905, in which the United States accepted Japanese control of Korea in exchange for Japan acknowledging U.S. control of the Philippines. Three years later, the Root-Takahira Agreement, negotiated by Secretary of State Elihu Root and the Japanese ambassador to the United States, reinforced the Open Door policy by supporting "the independence and integrity of China" and "the principle of equal opportunity for commerce and industry in China."

Behind the outward appearances of goodwill, however, lay distrust. For many Americans, the Russian threat in East Asia gave way to concerns about the "yellow peril." Racial conflict on the West Coast, especially in California, helped sour relations with Japan. In 1906, San Francisco's school board ordered students of Asian descent to attend a separate public school from "Americans." When the Japanese government protested, President Roosevelt persuaded the school board to change its policy, but only after making sure that Japanese authorities would stop encouraging unemployed Japanese laborers to go to America. This "Gentlemen's Agreement" of 1907 halted the influx of Japanese immigrants to California.

THE "GREAT WHITE FLEET"   After Theodore Roosevelt's election to a full term as president in 1904, he decided to showcase to the world America's rise as a world power. In 1907, without consulting Congress or his cabinet, he sent the entire U.S. fleet of warships, by then second in strength only to Britain's Royal Navy, on a fourteen-month world tour to demonstrate America's emerging power and to show that "the Pacific is as much our home waters as the Atlantic."

At every port of call—down the Atlantic coast of South America, then up the Pacific coast, out to Hawaii, and down to New Zealand and Australia—the "Great White Fleet" of eighteen gleaming battleships, eight armored cruisers, and assorted support ships, received a rousing welcome. The triumphal procession continued to Japan, China, and the Philippines, then to Egypt, through the Suez Canal and across the Mediterranean Sea—a total distance of 46,000 miles—before steaming back to Virginia in early 1909, just in time to close Roosevelt's presidency.

Roosevelt's success in expanding U.S. power abroad would have mixed consequences, however, because it enmeshed America in global conflicts and tensions that otherwise could have been avoided. Moreover, underlying Roosevelt's imperialism was a militantly racist view of international relations. Roosevelt and others among his circle of powerful friends and advisers believed that the world included "civilized" societies, such as the United States and the nations of Europe, and those they described as "barbarous," "backward," or "impotent." It was the responsibility of the "civilized" nations to exercise control of the "barbarous" peoples, by force if necessary.

The "Great White Fleet" In an act of pride and power, Roosevelt dispatched the entire U.S. Navy on a worldwide tour. No sooner had the "Great White Fleet" returned than the ships were all repainted in military gray.

WILLIAM HOWARD TAFT'S "DOLLAR DIPLOMACY"
Republican William Howard Taft, who succeeded Roosevelt as president in 1909, continued to promote America's economic interests abroad, practicing what Roosevelt called "**dollar diplomacy.**" Taft used the State Department to help American companies and banks invest in foreign countries, especially East Asia and the less developed nations of Latin America and the Caribbean. To ensure the stability of those investments, Taft did not hesitate to intervene in nations experiencing political and economic turmoil. In 1909, he dispatched U.S. Marines to support a revolution in Nicaragua. Once the new government was formed, Secretary of State Philander C. Knox helped U.S. banks negotiate loans to prop it up. Two years later, Taft again sent American troops to restore political stability. This time they stayed for more than a decade.

WOODROW WILSON'S INTERVENTIONISM In 1913, the new Democratic president, Woodrow Wilson, attacked dollar diplomacy as a form of economic imperialism. He promised to treat Latin American nations "on terms of equality and honor." Yet Wilson, along with William Jennings Bryan, his secretary of state, soon engaged in what might be called moral imperialism. Determined to make other nations behave as they saw fit, they dispatched American military forces to Latin America more often than Taft and Roosevelt combined.

Like Roosevelt, Wilson argued that the United States must intervene to stabilize weak governments in the Western Hemisphere to keep European nations from doing so. He said it was "reprehensible" to allow European governments to take control of these "weak and unfortunate republics."

During his two presidential terms, Wilson sent U.S. troops into Cuba once, Panama twice, and Honduras five times. In 1915, when the Dominican Republic refused to sign a treaty that would have given the United States a "special" role in governing the island nation, Wilson sent Marines to establish a military government and suppress anti-American rebels. That same year, Wilson intervened in Haiti, next door to the Dominican Republic. He admitted that his actions were "high-handed" but argued that they were justified because the "necessity for exercising control there is immediate, urgent, imperative." Others disagreed. As the *New York Times* charged, Wilson's frequent interventions made Taft's dollar diplomacy look like "ten cent diplomacy."

THE UNITED STATES IN MEXICO Mexico was a much thornier problem for Woodrow Wilson. In 1910, Mexicans had revolted against the dictatorship of Porfirio Díaz, who had given foreign corporations a free rein in developing the nation's economy. After occupying Mexico City in 1911, the victorious rebels began squabbling among themselves. The leader of the rebellion, Francisco Madero, was overthrown by his chief of staff, General Victoriano Huerta, who assumed power in early 1913 and then had Madero and thirty other political opponents murdered.

President Wilson refused to recognize "a government of butchers." Huerta ignored the criticism and established a dictatorship. Wilson decided that Huerta must be removed and ordered U.S. warships to halt shipments of foreign weapons to the new government. "I am going to teach the South American republics to elect good men," Wilson vowed. Meanwhile, several rival revolutionary Mexican armies, the largest of which was led by Francisco "Pancho" Villa, began trying to unseat Huerta.

On April 9, 1914, nine American sailors were arrested in Tampico, Mexico, while trying to buy supplies. Mexican officials quickly released them and apologized to the U.S. naval commander. There the incident might have ended, but the imperious U.S. admiral demanded that the Mexicans fire a twenty-one-gun salute to the American flag. After they refused, Wilson sent U.S. troops ashore at Veracruz on April 21, 1914. They forcibly occupied the city at a cost of 19 American lives; at least 300 Mexicans were killed or wounded. Latin Americans saw the U.S. military intervention as another example of hemispheric imperialism.

Intervention in Mexico American marines enter Veracruz, Mexico, in 1914.

The use of U.S. military force in Mexico played out like many previous interventions in the Caribbean and Central America. Congress readily supported the decision, and the naive Wilson believed that most Mexicans would welcome America's intervention since his intentions were so "unselfish."

But the arrival of U.S. troops in Veracruz backfired. Instead of welcoming the Americans as liberators, Mexicans viewed them as invaders. Newspapers in Mexico shouted for "Vengeance! Vengeance! Vengeance!" For seven months, the Americans governed Veracruz. They left in late 1914 after Huerta was overthrown by Venustiano Carranza.

Still, the troubles south of the U.S. border continued as various factions engaged in ongoing civil wars. In 1916, the colorful rebel leader, Pancho Villa, launched raids into south Texas and New Mexico in a deliberate attempt to trigger U.S. intervention and reinforce his anti-American credentials. On March 9, he and his men attacked Columbus, New Mexico, just three miles across the border. With Villa shouting, "Kill all the Gringos!" his army of 500 peasant revolutionaries looted stores, burned the town, and killed seventeen Americans, both men and women.

A furious Wilson sent General John J. Pershing to Mexico with 6,000 U.S. soldiers to capture Villa and destroy his army. For nearly a year, Pershing's troops chased Villa's army through the rugged mountains of northern Mexico. As Pershing muttered, "It's like trying to chase a rat in a cornfield." In 1917, the American troops were ordered home. The elusive Villa, meanwhile, named his mule "President Wilson."

THE PLAN OF SAN DIEGO The turbulence of the Mexican Revolution spilled over into the United States. A million Mexicans sought refuge in the southwestern states of Texas, New Mexico, Arizona, and California. While many of the refugees eventually returned to Mexico, the number of Mexicans living in the United States tripled between 1910 and 1930, half of them settling in Texas. In most cases, the refugees faced discrimination, segregation, exploitation, and violence, particularly in what one Mexican American called the "savage state of Texas."

A small group of anarchists among the Mexican American ranchers living in the southern tip of Texas decided to incite a revolution in the United States. In 1915, a sheriff in McAllen, Texas, arrested a twenty-four-year-old Mexican revolutionary named Basilio Ramos, Jr. He was carrying documents that included the "Plan of San Diego," drafted by Mexican rebels. The plan called for the formation of an army in the southwestern states made up of all races and ethnicities. Its mission was to overthrow U.S. government control and establish an independent republic made up of the five states bordering

Mexico. Most shocking among the Plan of San Diego's instructions was that "every North American over sixteen years of age shall be put to death" along with any prisoners of war. Mexican Americans who refused to participate in the plan were also to be killed.

Once in Texas, Ramos tried to recruit others (*sediciosos*) to his cause. Soon, however, he was arrested by federal authorities, who then requested military assistance should the planned revolution erupt into violence, which it did in 1915. Beginning in early July, hundreds of Mexican Americans raided stores, post offices, farms, ranches, and railroads, killing dozens of Whites (Anglos). Panic spread across south Texas. In response, heavily armed Texas Rangers (statewide police on horseback), local law enforcement officers, and civilian vigilantes launched what one newspaper called a vengeful "war of extermination" against Mexicans.

The Plan of San Diego became one of the bloodiest episodes of racial and cultural violence in U.S. history. Thousands of Mexican Americans were killed, and south Texas verged on a race war. Often the Rangers did not distinguish between Mexican insurgents and Mexican Americans as they unleashed their fury. Their campaign of retribution included mass lynchings of immigrants and Tejanos (people of Mexican ancestry born in Texas). Thousands of Tejanos fled Texas for Mexico, never to return. By July 1916, however, the Plan of San Diego uprising had petered out. The war in south Texas was over, just as America became embroiled in the much larger war in Europe.

CHAPTER REVIEW

Summary

- **Toward the New Imperialism**   Near the end of the nineteenth century, the popular idea that America had a "manifest destiny" to expand its territory abroad and industrialists' desire for new markets for their goods helped to fuel America's new *imperialism*. The racist ideology of social Darwinism was used to justify the colonization of less developed nations.

- **Expansion in the Pacific**   Business leaders hoped to extend America's commercial reach across the Pacific. The United States purchased the vast Alaska territory from Russia in 1867. In 1894, Hawaii's minority White population, led by American planters, overthrew the native Hawaiian queen, declared a republic, and requested that Hawaii be annexed by the United States.

- **The Spanish-American War**   When Cubans revolted against Spanish colonial rule in 1895, many Americans supported their demand for independence. *Yellow journalism* sensationalizing the harsh Spanish suppression of the revolt further aroused Americans' sympathy. Early in 1898, the publication of the *de Lôme letter*, followed by the mysterious explosion sinking the *U.S. battleship Maine* in Havana Harbor, helped propel America into war with Spain. Under the Treaty of Paris ending the war, Cuba became independent and the United States annexed Puerto Rico, which it had occupied. In the Spanish colony of the Philippine Islands, America's Pacific naval fleet defeated the Spanish fleet in the Battle of Manila Bay and took control of the capital, Manila.

- **Consequences of Victory**   A vicious guerrilla war in the Philippines followed when Filipinos who favored independence rebelled against U.S. control. American soldiers eventually suppressed the rebellion, and President McKinley announced that the United States would annex the Philippines. The *American Anti-Imperialist League* and others argued that acquiring overseas territories violated American principles of self-determination and independence. But in the end, the imperialists won the debate, and Congress set up a government in the Philippines as well as in Puerto Rico. In Cuba, the United States imposed significant restrictions on the new government after U.S. forces left the island. In the Pacific region, the United States also annexed Hawaii, Guam, Wake Island, and some of the Samoa Islands during or shortly after the Spanish-American War. In East Asia, Secretary of State John Hay promoted the *Open Door policy* (1899) of preserving China's territorial integrity and equal access by all nations to trade with China. There were no plans made for most of these newly acquired territories to ever become states.

- **Roosevelt's "Big-Stick" Diplomacy**   After succeeding to the presidency upon McKinley's assassination in 1901, Theodore Roosevelt pursued an imperialist foreign policy that confirmed the United States' new role as a world power. He helped negotiate the treaty that ended the Russo-Japanese War, oversaw diplomatic and military actions leading to the U.S. construction and control of the Panama Canal, and sent the navy's fleet of new battleships around the world as a symbol of American might. He also proclaimed the *Roosevelt Corollary* (1904) to the Monroe Doctrine, asserting that the United States would intervene in Latin America as necessary in order to prevent European intervention. The U.S. interventions typically took the form of what Theodore Roosevelt called *dollar diplomacy,* which involved the U.S. government fostering American investments in less developed nations and then using U.S. military force to protect those investments.

CHRONOLOGY

1867	The United States purchases Alaska from Russia
1880s	European nations create colonial empires in Asia and Africa
1890	Alfred Mahan publishes *The Influence of Sea Power upon History, 1660–1783*
1894	Republic of Hawaii is proclaimed
1895	Cuban insurrection of Spanish rule
1898	U.S. battleship *Maine* explodes in Havana Harbor
	The Spanish-American War
	United States annexes Hawaii
1899	U.S. Senate ratifies the Treaty of Paris, ending the Spanish-American War
1899–1902	Insurgents resist U.S. conquest of the Philippines
1901	President McKinley assassinated; Theodore Roosevelt becomes president
1903	Panamanians revolt against Colombia
1904–1905	Russo-Japanese War
1907–1909	U.S. "Great White Fleet" circles the globe
1914	Panama Canal opens
1909–1917	U.S. military interventions in Mexico and Latin America

KEY TERMS

imperialism p. 916

The Influence of Sea Power upon History, 1660–1783 p. 916

yellow journalism p. 921

U.S. battleship *Maine* p. 921

de Lôme letter (1898) p. 922

Teller Amendment (1898) p. 923

Rough Riders p. 926

American Anti-Imperialist League p. 934

Open Door policy (1899) p. 938

Roosevelt Corollary (1904) p. 945

dollar diplomacy p. 948

🔖 InQUIZITIVE

Go to InQuizitive to see what you've learned—and learn what you've missed—with personalized feedback along the way.

part six

MODERN AMERICA

The United States entered the twentieth century on a wave of unrelenting change. The nation teetered on the threshold of modernity, which both excited and scared Americans. Old truths and beliefs clashed with unsettling scientific discoveries and social practices. People debated the legitimacy of Darwinism, the existence of God, the dangers of jazz, and the federal effort to prohibit the sale of alcoholic beverages.

The advent of automobiles and airplanes helped shrink time and distance, and communication innovations such as radio and movies helped strengthen the sense that America now had a national culture. William McKinley was the first president to ride in an automobile, appear in motion pictures, and use the telephone to plot political strategy.

The outbreak of the Great War in Europe in 1914 posed a dangerous challenge to America's tradition of nonintervention. The prospect of a German victory over the French and British threatened the balance of power in Europe, which had long ensured the security of the United States. By 1917, it appeared that Germany might triumph and begin to menace the Western Hemisphere. When German submarines began sinking U.S. merchant ships, President Woodrow Wilson's patience ran out, and in April 1917, the United States entered the Great War, later called the First World War.

Wilson's crusade to impose his idealistic principles on international affairs dislodged American foreign policy from its isolationist moorings. It also spawned a prolonged debate about the nation's role in the world—a debate that the Second World War would resolve (for a time) on the side of internationalism.

While the United States was becoming a formidable military power, cities and factories were sprouting across the nation, and an abundance of jobs and affordable farmland attracted millions of foreign immigrants. They were not always welcomed, nor were they readily assimilated. Ethnic and racial strife grew, as did labor agitation promoting the rights and demands of the working class.

Amid such social turmoil and unparalleled economic development, reformers addressed the worst excesses of urban-industrial development—corporate monopolies, child labor, political corruption, hazardous working conditions, urban ghettos. During the Progressive Era (1890–1920), local, state, and federal officials sought to rein in industrial capitalism and develop more rational and efficient policies designed to promote the public interest.

A conservative Republican resurgence during the 1920s challenged the notion of the new regulatory state, and free enterprise and corporate capitalism enjoyed a revival. But the stock market crash of 1929 helped propel the United States and the world into the worst economic downturn in history. The severity of the Great Depression renewed demands for federal programs to protect those struggling for survival. The New Deal initiatives and agencies instituted by President Franklin Delano Roosevelt and his Democratic administration created the framework for the federal government providing much greater assistance to people in need, a framework that has since served as the basis for much of American public policy.

The New Deal revived public confidence and put people back to work, but it took World War II to end the Great Depression and restore full employment.

Mobilizing the nation to support the global war also accelerated the growth of the federal government, and the unparalleled scope of the war helped catapult the United States into a leadership role in world politics. The development of atomic bombs ushered in a new era of nuclear diplomacy that held the fate of the world in the balance. For all the new creature comforts associated with modern  life, Americans in 1945 found themselves celebrating victory in a horrific war while struggling with an array of new anxieties.

20 The Progressive Era

1890–1920

"Votes for Us When We Are Women!" Parades organized by women's suffrage groups brought together women of all ages and social classes. Here, from a patriotically outfitted automobile, young suffragists ask spectators for "votes for us when we are women."

Theodore Roosevelt's emergence as a national leader coincided with the onset of what historians have labeled the Progressive Era (1890–1920), a period of extraordinary social activism and political innovation during which insistent public issues forced profound changes in the role of government and presidential leadership.

Millions of progressives believed that modern America was experiencing a crisis of democracy because of problems created by the urban-industrial revolution. Inner-city poverty, children laboring long hours in unregulated mines and factories, tainted food and unsanitary apartments, miserable working conditions and low pay, progressives insisted, required bold action by churches, charitable organizations, experts, and individuals—and an expanded role for local, state, and federal governments.

To improve the quality of life, progressives demanded that governments foster social harmony, moral uplift, and economic fairness. If the rich grew richer while workers grew poorer, if women were treated as second-class citizens, then the nation would never fulfill its potential as the world's greatest democracy.

Rampant political corruption was one of the major concerns of progressive reformers. They particularly targeted the self-serving influence powerful corporations wielded to affect the political process and Congress. As New Yorker Amos Pinchot said, corruption was "destroying our respect for government, uprooting faith in political parties, and causing every precedent and convention of the old order to strain at its moorings."

focus questions

1. What were the motives of progressive reformers?

2. Which sources of thought and activism contributed to the progressive movement?

3. What were the specific goals of progressive reformers, and how did they advance them?

4. What contributions did Presidents Theodore Roosevelt and William Howard Taft make to the progressive movement? How and why did these men come to disagree about the best ways to advance progressive ideals?

5. Which policies of President Woodrow Wilson were influenced by the progressive movement? How and why did they differ from the policies of Roosevelt and Taft?

By the 1890s, the gap between rich and poor had become a chasm. Walter Weyl, a progressive economist, insisted that "political equality is a farce and a peril unless there is at least some measure of economic equality." Rapid industrial growth had produced a new class of super-wealthy industrialists and financiers, a prosperous middle class, and a vastly expanded class of unskilled wage workers. Hourly workers had no legal rights to limit their working hours, set minimum wage levels, or provide financial compensation if they were killed or injured on the job. The United States had the highest rate of workplace accidents in the world, yet it was the only industrialized nation without insurance for on-the-job injuries.

Urban squalor was a third major concern. In the rapidly growing cities, basic social services—food, water, housing, education, sanitation, transportation, and medical care—could not keep pace with population growth. Progressive reformers attacked all these issues and more. By the beginning of the twentieth century, progressivism had become the most dynamic social and political force in the nation.

THE PROGRESSIVE IMPULSE

Progressives were liberals, not revolutionaries. They believed that local, state, and federal governments must regulate the behavior of big businesses and ensure public welfare. They wanted to reform and regulate capitalism, not destroy it. Most were Christian moralists who felt that politics had become a contest between good and evil, honesty and corruption. What all progressives shared was the assumption that governments must become more active in addressing the problems created by rapid urban and industrial growth. Chicago's Jane Addams, a leading progressive reformer, reported that charities and churches were "totally inadequate to deal with the vast numbers of the city's disinherited." The "real heart of the [progressive] movement," declared another reformer, was to expand the role of government "as an agency of human welfare."

Unlike Populism, whose grassroots appeal centered on farming regions in the South and Midwest, progressivism was a national movement. Progressive activists came in all stripes: men and women; Democrats, Republicans, Populists, and socialists; labor unionists and business executives; teachers, engineers, editors, and professors; social workers, doctors, ministers, and journalists; farmers and homemakers; Whites and Blacks; clergymen, atheists, and agnostics. Their combined efforts led to significant social reforms and government regulation of businesses.

Theodore Roosevelt called progressivism the "forward movement" because it was led by people "who stand for the cause of progress, for the cause of the uplift of humanity and the betterment of mankind." Progressives, he stressed, "fight to make this country a better place to live in for those who have been harshly treated by fate."

To make governments more efficient and businesses more honest, progressives drew upon the new "social sciences"—sociology, political science, psychology, public health, and economics. The progressive approach was to appoint social scientists to "investigate, educate, and legislate." Activist Florence Kelley voiced the era's widespread belief that once people knew "the truth" about social ills, "they would act upon it."

Like every social reform movement, progressivism had flaws, inconsistencies, blind spots, and hypocrisies. The "do-good" perspective animating progressivism was often corroded by racial and ethnic prejudices, as well as by social and intellectual snobbery. The goals of upper-class White progressives rarely included racial equality, for example. Many otherwise progressive people, including Theodore Roosevelt and Woodrow Wilson, believed in the supremacy of the "Anglo-Saxon race" and assumed that the forces shaping modern society were too complicated for the "ignorant" masses to understand, much less improve, without direction by those who knew better.

THE VARIED SOURCES OF PROGRESSIVISM

During the last quarter of the nineteenth century, progressives began to attack corrupt political bosses and irresponsible corporate barons. They sought a more honest and efficient government, more-effective regulation of big businesses ("the trusts"), and better living and working conditions for the laboring poor. Only by expanding the scope of local, state, and federal governments, they believed, could these goals be attained.

ECONOMIC DISCONTENT AND POPULISM The devastating economic depression of the 1890s ignited the progressive spirit of reform. The economic downturn brought massive layoffs; nearly a quarter of adults lost their jobs. Although the United States boasted the highest per capita income in the world, it also had some of the highest concentrations of poverty. In 1900, the U.S. population numbered 82 million, of which an estimated 10 million were living in poverty. The devastating effects of the depression prompted many urban reformers—lawyers, doctors, executives, social workers, teachers, professors, journalists, and college-educated women—to organize efforts to help those in need and to keep them from becoming social revolutionaries or anarchists.

Populism was another thread in the fabric of progressivism. The People's party (Populist) platforms of 1892 and 1896 included reforms intended to give more power to the people, such as the "direct" election of U.S. senators by voters rather than by state legislatures. Although William Jennings Bryan's loss in the 1896 presidential campaign ended the Populist party as a political force, many reforms pushed by Populists were implemented by progressives.

MUGWUMPS AND SOCIALISTS The Mugwumps—"gentlemen" reformers who had fought the patronage system and insisted that government jobs be awarded on the basis of merit—supplied progressivism with another key goal: the "honest government" ideal. Over the years, the good-government movement expanded to address persistent urban issues such as crime, unequal access to electricity, clean water and municipal sewers, mass transit, and garbage collection.

The Socialist Party of America, supported mostly by militant farmers and German and Jewish immigrants, was the radical wing of progressivism. Socialists focused on improving working conditions and closing the income gap between rich and poor through progressive taxation, whereby tax rates would rise with income. Most progressives, however, rejected the extremes of both socialism and laissez-faire individualism, preferring a new, regulated capitalism "softened" by humanitarianism.

Fire on Hell Street This photograph by Jacob Riis revealed the cramped and unsanitary living conditions faced by many immigrants living in tenements on New York City's lower East Side.

MUCKRAKING JOURNALISM Progressivism depended upon the press—newspapers and magazines—to inform the public about corruption and social problems. The so-called **muckrakers** were America's first investigative journalists, and they were at the heart of progressivism. Their aggressive reporting educated readers about political and corporate wrongdoing and revealed "how the other half lives," a description drawn from the title of an influential exposé of the terrible living conditions experienced by immigrants in New York City, written by photojournalist Jacob Riis, a Danish immigrant.

The muckrakers got their nickname from Theodore Roosevelt, who said that crusading journalists who raked through the "muck" of social ills were "often indispensable to . . . society." Roosevelt, both as governor of New York and as president of the United States, frequently used muckrakers to drum up support for his policies and to help shape public opinion.

The golden age of muckraking began in 1902, when Samuel S. McClure, owner of *McClure's* magazine, recruited idealistic journalists to expose corruption in politics and corporations. McClure maintained that the "vitality of democracy" depended upon educating the public about "complex questions." *McClure's* and other muckraking magazines investigated corporate monopolies and crooked political machines while exposing the miserable conditions in which the working poor lived and labored.

Muckrakers Lincoln Steffens, Ray Stannard Baker, and Ida Tarbell led the way in promoting reforms of all sorts. Steffens focused on political corruption while Baker concentrated on rail-road abuses. In *The Shame of the Cities* (1904), Steffens concluded that "the typical businessman is a bad citizen. . . . He is a self-righteous fraud." For her part, Ida Tarbell spent years investigating the unethical and illegal shenanigans by which John D. Rockefeller had built his gigantic Standard Oil Trust. At the end of her series of nineteen articles in *McClure's* investigating the abuses of the Standard Oil Company, she asked readers: "And what are we going to do about it?" It was "the people of the United States, and nobody else," she stressed, "[who] must cure whatever is wrong in the industrial situation."

Without the muckrakers, progressivism would never have achieved widespread popular support. Investigative journalism became such a powerful force for change that one editor said that Americans were benefiting from "Government by Magazine."

Ida Tarbell An author, teacher, and pioneer of investigative journalism in the United States, Tarbell wrote a series of nineteen exposés of Rockefeller's Standard Oil Trust.

RELIGIOUS ACTIVISM AND SOCIAL RESPONSIBILITY Still another element of progressivism was religious activism directed at achieving social justice—the idea that Christians and Jews had an ethical obligation to help the poorest and most vulnerable members of society. A related ideal was the **social gospel**, the belief that religious institutions and individual Christians must help bring about the "Kingdom of God" on earth.

In many respects, in fact, the progressive movement represented a Christian spiritual revival, an energetic form of public outreach focused not so much on individual conversion and salvation as on social reform. "Christian socialism" offered hope for unity among all classes. "Every religious and political question," said George Herron, a religion professor at Grinnell College, "is fundamentally economic." The solution to economic tensions was social responsibility and solidarity. "We believe," as the Religious Education Association explained, "that the age of sheer individualism is past, and the age of social responsibility has arrived."

During the last quarter of the nineteenth century, many churches and synagogues began emphasizing community service to address the needs of the unfortunate. New organizations made key contributions to the movement. The Young Men's Christian Association (YMCA) and a similar group for women, the YWCA, both entered the United States from England in the 1850s and grew rapidly after 1870. The Salvation Army, founded in London in 1878, came to the United States a year later.

During the late nineteenth century, the YMCA and YWCA—both known as "the Y"—combined nondenominational evangelism with social services and fitness training in community centers, which were segregated by race and gender. Intended to provide low-cost housing and exercise in a "safe Christian environment" for young men and women from rural areas or foreign countries, the YMCA/YWCA centers often included libraries, classrooms, and kitchens. "Hebrew" counterparts—YMHAs and YWHAs—provided many of the same facilities in cities with large Jewish populations. At the same time, Salvation Army centers offered "soup kitchens" to feed the poor and day nurseries for the children of working mothers.

The major forces behind the social gospel movement were Protestants and Catholics who charged that Christianity had become too closely associated with the upper and middle classes. In 1875, Washington Gladden, a pastor in Springfield, Massachusetts, published *Working People and Their Employers* (1876), which argued that true Christianity was based on the principle that "thou shalt love thy neighbor as thyself." Gladden rejected the view of social Darwinists that the poor and disabled deserved their fate and should not be helped. He argued that helping the poor was an essential element of the

Christian faith. To that end, he became the first prominent religious leader to support the rights of workers to form unions. He also condemned racial segregation and discrimination against immigrants.

Gladden's efforts helped launch a new era in which churches engaged with the problems created by a rapidly urbanizing and industrializing society. He and other social gospelers reached out to the working poor who lived in grossly substandard housing, lacked the legal right to form unions, and had no insurance for on-the-job accidents.

Walter Rauschenbusch, a German-born Baptist minister serving immigrant tenement dwellers in the Hell's Kitchen neighborhood of New York City, became the greatest champion of the social gospel. In 1907, he published *Christianity and the Social Crisis,* in which he argued that "whoever uncouples the religious and social life has not understood Jesus." The Christian emphasis on personal salvation, he added, must be linked with an equally passionate commitment to social justice. Churches must embrace "the social aims of Jesus," for Christianity was intended to be a "revolutionary" faith.

In Rauschenbusch's view, religious life needed the social gospel to revitalize it and make it socially relevant: "We shall never have a perfect social life, yet we must seek it with faith." Like the muckrakers, Rauschenbusch sought to expose the realities of poverty in America and convince public officials to deal with the crisis. His message resonated with Theodore Roosevelt, Woodrow Wilson, and many other progressives in both political parties. Years later, Reverend Martin Luther King, Jr. spoke for three generations of radicals and reformers when he said that *Christianity and the Social Crisis* "left an indelible imprint on my thinking."

SETTLEMENT HOUSES   Among the most visible soldiers in the social gospel movement were those who volunteered in innovative community centers called settlement houses. Hull House was a dilapidated two-story red-brick mansion converted in 1889 into a settlement house in a shabby immigrant Chicago neighborhood. Two college-educated women from privileged Illinois backgrounds, Jane Addams and Ellen Gates Starr, organized a progressive reform community there to address the needs of the unskilled working poor, especially newly arrived European immigrants. Some 50,000 working poor circulated through Hull House in its first year. By 1940, the annual number was 320,000.

Addams and Starr were driven by an "impulse to share the lives of the poor" and to make social service "express the spirit of Christ." Besides a nursery for the infant children of working mothers, Hull House also sponsored health clinics, lectures, music lessons and art studios, men's clubs, an

Settlement Houses Jane Addams, the co-founder of Hull House, is photographed alongside a group of young women inside the settlement house. Addams championed immigrants and the working class, and her social work expanded from the settlement house movement to political reform.

employment bureau, job training, a gymnasium, a coffeehouse, a savings bank, and a public bath. Classes were offered in acting, weaving, carpentry, art history, philosophy, and music. All residents were treated as equals. By the early twentieth century, there were hundreds of settlement houses in cities across the United States, most of them in the Northeast and Midwest.

Addams and other settlement house leaders soon realized, however, that their work was like bailing out the ocean with a teaspoon. They thus added political reform to their agenda and began lobbying for city parks and play-grounds, neighborhood cleanup days, and laws and regulations to improve living conditions in poor neighborhoods.

A graduate of Cornell University and Northwestern University School of Law, Florence Kelley served as a staff member at Hull House and played a key role in the arena of polit-ical reform. As a researcher for the Illinois Bureau of Labor Statistics, she visited Chicago's tenements and sweatshops to document the exploita-tion of desperately poor women and children. Her pathbreaking book *Hull-House Maps and Papers* (1895) contained her research results as well as essays by social scientists. The book supplemented tenement tours that Kelley organized for state legislators and inspired new city ordinances and workplace regulations.

As her influence grew in Chicago, Jane Addams served on governmental and community boards, focusing her radiant personality and powerful convic-tions on improving public health and food safety. She pushed for better street lighting and police protection in poor neighborhoods and sought to reduce the misuse of narcotics. An ardent pacifist and outspoken advocate for *suffrage* (voting rights) for women, Addams would become the first American woman to win the Nobel Peace Prize.

THE WOMEN'S SUFFRAGE MOVEMENT After the Civil War, women active in the suffrage movement had hoped that the Fifteenth Amendment, which guaranteed voting rights for African American men, would aid their efforts to gain the vote. Such arguments made little impression on the majority of men, however, who still insisted that women stay out of politics. A Mississippi Democrat was blunt about his opposition: "I would rather die and go to hell," he claimed, "than vote for woman's suffrage."

Yet women reformers were on the march. From 1880 to 1910, the number of women employed outside the home tripled from 2.6 million to 7.8 million. As college-educated women became more involved in the world of work and wages, the suffrage movement grew as more and more women demanded equal rights.

Susan B. Anthony and Elizabeth Cady Stanton founded the National Woman Suffrage Association (NWSA) in 1869 to promote a **women's suffrage** amendment to the Constitution. They condemned both the Fourteenth and Fifteenth Amendments for limiting voting rights to males only. The NWSA agitated for more than the right to vote. Its members also campaigned for higher pay for working women and for laws helping abused wives secure divorces.

Other suffrage activists insisted that pursuing multiple issues hurt their cause. In 1869, Julia Ward Howe and Lucy Stone formed the American Woman Suffrage Association (AWSA). Based in Boston, it focused single-mindedly on voting rights and included men among its leaders.

Many women did not support the suffrage movement. Women opposed to voting rights argued that they were not ready to be voters because they did not understand many issues. They also feared that they would *lose* their traditional political influence if they were voters because they would inevitably lose their nonpartisan neutrality and become aligned with one of the political parties.

The so-called "antis" testified before state legislators, published newsletters, and organized conferences—all in an effort stop the suffrage movement. In 1911, anti-suffrage activists met in the New York City apartment of Josephine Dodge to found the National Association Opposed to Woman Suffrage (NAOWS). By 1919, NAOWS boasted a half million members.

In 1890, Wyoming was admitted as a state, the first that gave full voting rights for women in national, as well as state and local, elections. When the territorial government had initially applied for statehood, Congress responded that it would first have to stop letting women vote. Wyoming responded, "We will remain out of the Union one hundred years rather than come in without the women."

It was in the territories and states west of the Mississippi River that the suffrage movement had its earliest successes. In those areas, where Populism

East Meets West San Francisco suffragists marched across the country in 1915 to deliver to Congress an amendment petition with more than 500,000 signatures. Along the way, they were warmly received by other suffragists, like those of New Jersey, pictured here.

found its strongest support, women were more engaged in grassroots political activities than they were in the East. In addition, the early settlers in the western territories were mostly men, so they hoped that allowing women to vote would encourage more women to settle in the territories. For these reasons and others, the West was the region most supportive of women's rights. Between 1890 and 1896, the suffrage cause won three more victories in western states—Utah, Colorado, and Idaho.

In the early twentieth century, however, the national suffrage movement remained in the doldrums until proposals for voting rights easily won in Washington State in 1910 and then carried California by a close majority in 1911. The following year three more states west of the Mississippi—Arizona, Kansas, and Oregon—joined to make a total of nine western states with full suffrage. In 1913, Illinois granted women voting rights in presidential and municipal elections. Not until New York acted in 1917 did a state east of the Mississippi River allow women to vote in all elections.

The advocates of women's suffrage put forth several arguments for their position. Many said that the right to vote and hold office was a matter of simple justice: women were just as capable as men of exercising the rights and responsibilities of citizenship. Others insisted that women were morally superior to men, and therefore their participation would raise the quality of the political

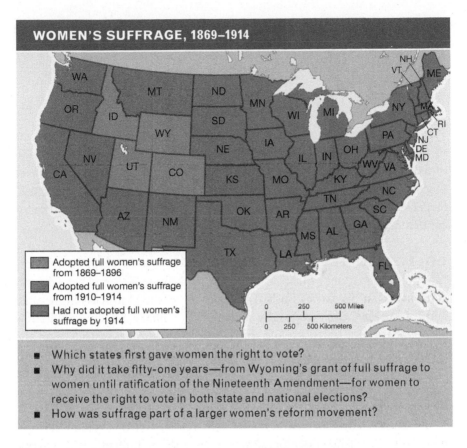

WOMEN'S SUFFRAGE, 1869–1914

Adopted full women's suffrage from 1869–1896

Adopted full women's suffrage from 1910–1914

Had not adopted full women's suffrage by 1914

- Which states first gave women the right to vote?
- Why did it take fifty-one years—from Wyoming's grant of full suffrage to women until ratification of the Nineteenth Amendment—for women to receive the right to vote in both state and national elections?
- How was suffrage part of a larger women's reform movement?

process and reduce the likelihood of future wars, corruption, and scandals. Women voters and politicians, advocates argued, would promote the welfare of society as a whole rather than partisan or selfish goals, so allowing women to participate in politics would create a great engine for progressive social change. One activist explicitly linked women's suffrage with the social gospel, declaring that women followed the teachings of Christ more faithfully than did men; if women were elected to public office, they would "far more effectively guard the morals of society and the sanitary conditions of cities."

Yet the women's suffrage movement was not free from the social, ethnic, and racial prejudices of its time. Carrie Chapman Catt, who became president of the National American Woman Suffrage Association in 1900, echoed the fears of many middle- and upper-class women when she warned that poverty-stricken male voters and "ignorant" immigrant voters would distort the political process. She added that the nation with "ill-advised haste" had given immigrants and Black men the vote but still withheld it from educated White women. In the South, one suffragist claimed that giving White women the vote would help "insure immediate and durable white supremacy." Throughout the country, most suffrage organizations excluded African American women.

PROGRESSIVES' AIMS AND ACHIEVEMENTS

Progressivism set in motion the two most important political developments of the twentieth century: the rise of direct democracy and the expansion of federal power. In his monthly articles in *McClure's* magazine, muckraker Lincoln Steffens regularly asked: "Will the people rule? Is democracy possible?" Steffens and other progressives often stressed that the way to improve America's democracy was to make it even more democratic.

POLITICAL REFORMS To empower citizens to clean up the corrupt political system, which was driven by backroom deals and rigged party conventions, progressives pushed to make the political process more open and transparent. One proposal was the *direct primary*, which would allow all members of a party to vote on the party's nominees, rather than the traditional practice in which an inner circle of party leaders chose the candidates, often behind closed doors. In 1896, South Carolina became the first state to adopt a statewide primary. Within twenty years, nearly every state had done so.

Progressives developed other ways to increase public participation in the political process (direct democracy) so as to curb the influence of corporate bosses on state legislatures. In 1898, South Dakota became the first state to adopt the *initiative* and *referendum*, procedures that allowed voters to create laws directly rather than having to wait for legislative action. Citizens could sign petitions to have a proposal put on the ballot (the initiative) and then vote it up or down (the referendum). Still another progressive innovation was the *recall*, whereby corrupt or incompetent elected officials could be removed by a public petition and vote. By 1920, nearly twenty states had adopted the initiative and referendum, and nearly a dozen had sanctioned the recall procedure.

Progressives also fought to change how U.S. senators were elected. Under the Constitution, state legislatures elected senators, a process frequently corrupted by lobbyists and vote buying. In 1900, for example, Senate investigators revealed that a Montana senator had given more than $100,000 in secret bribes to members of the legislature that chose him. In 1913, thanks to the efforts of progressives, the **Seventeenth Amendment**, providing for the direct election of senators, was ratified and became law.

THE EFFICIENCY MOVEMENT IN BUSINESS AND GOVERNMENT

A second major theme of progressivism was the "gospel of efficiency." Its champion was Frederick Winslow Taylor, an industrial engineer who became a celebrated business consultant, helping factory owners implement "scientific management."

The nation's first "efficiency expert," Taylor showed employers how to cut waste and improve productivity. By breaking down work activities (filling a wheelbarrow, driving a nail, shoveling coal) into a sequence of mechanical steps and using stopwatches to measure the time it took each worker to perform each step, Taylor established detailed performance standards (and cash rewards) for each job classification, specifying how fast people should work and when they should rest. His book *The Principles of Scientific Management* (1911) influenced business organizations for decades.

The goal of what came to be called **Taylorism** was to usher in a "mental revolution" in business management that would improve productivity and profits, raise pay for the most efficient workers, and reduce the likelihood of worker strikes. As Taylor wrote, "Men will not do an extraordinary day's work for an ordinary day's pay."

Many workers, however, resented Taylor's innovations, seeing them as just tools to make people work faster at monotonous tasks. "We object to being reduced to a scientific formula," an Iowa machinist thundered. Yet Taylor's controversial system of industrial management became one of the most important contributions to capitalist economies in the twentieth century. It brought solid, measurable improvements in productivity. "In the future," Taylor predicted in 1911, "the system [rather than the individual workers] will be first."

Political progressives applied Taylorism to the operations of government by calling for the reorganization of state and federal agencies to eliminate duplication, to establish clear lines of authority, and to replace political appointees with trained specialists. By the early twentieth century, many complex functions of government had come to require specialists with technical expertise. As Woodrow Wilson wrote, progressive ideals could be achieved only if government agencies at all levels were "informed and administered by experts." Many cities set up "efficiency bureaus" to identify government waste and apply more cost-effective "best practices."

Municipal Reform   Two Taylorist ideas to reform city and county governments emerged in the first decade of the new century. One, the commission system, was first adopted in 1901 by the city of Galveston, Texas, after the local government collapsed following a devastating hurricane and tidal wave that killed more than 8,000 people—the largest natural disaster in American history.

The commission system placed ultimate authority in a board composed of commissioners who combined both legislative and executive powers in heading up city departments (sanitation, police, utilities, and so on). By 1911, over sixty cities had adopted the commission system of government.

Even more popular was the city-manager plan, under which an appointed administrator ran a city or county government in accordance with policies set by the elected council and mayor. Staunton, Virginia, adopted the first city-manager plan in 1908. Five years later, the inadequate response of municipal officials to a flood led Dayton, Ohio, to become the first large city in the nation to adopt the plan.

Yet the efforts to make local governments more "businesslike" and professional had a downside. Shifting control from elected officials representing individual neighborhoods to at-large commissioners and nonpartisan specialists separated local government from party politics, which for many working-class voters had been their primary civic activity. In addition, running a city like a business led commissioners and managers to focus on reducing expenses rather than expanding services, even when such expansion was clearly needed.

The Wisconsin Idea   At the state level, the ideal of efficient government run by nonpartisan experts was pursued most notably by progressive Republican governor Robert M. La Follette of Wisconsin. In 1901, "Fighting Bob" La Follette

Friends of the Workingman Lincoln Steffens (*left*) was a muckraker who exposed political corruption, while Robert M. La Follette (*right*) pioneered the "Wisconsin idea" to promote a bipartisanship in government.

declared war on "vast corporate combinations" and political corruption by creating a nonpartisan state government that would become a "laboratory for democracy." He established a Legislative Reference Bureau, which provided elected officials with nonpartisan research, advice, and help in drafting legislation. La Follette used the bureau's reports to enact such reforms as the direct primary, stronger railroad regulation, the conservation of natural resources, and workmen's compensation programs to support people injured on the job. The "Wisconsin idea" was widely copied by other progressive governors.

REGULATION OF BUSINESS Of all the problems facing American society, one towered above all: how to regulate giant corporations. The threat of corporate monopolies increased during the depression of the 1890s as struggling companies were gobbled up by larger ones. Between 1895 and 1904, some 157 new holding companies gained control of 1,800 different businesses. Almost 50 of these giant holding companies controlled more than 70 percent of the market in their respective industries. In 1896, fewer than a dozen companies other than railroads were worth $10 million or more. By 1903, that number had soared to 300. The explosive growth of Big Business changed the nature of business life. "We have come upon a very different age from any that preceded us," New Jersey governor Woodrow Wilson observed. People now worked "not for themselves" but "as employees of great corporations."

Concerns over the concentration of economic power in trusts and other forms of monopolies had led Congress to pass the Sherman Anti-Trust Act in 1890, but it proved ineffective. In addition, government agencies responsible for regulating businesses were often headed and staffed by men who had worked in the very industries they were appointed to regulate. Congress, for instance, named retired railroad executives to the Interstate Commerce Commission (ICC), which had been created to regulate railroads. The issue of regulating the regulators has never been fully resolved.

JOHN DEWEY AND PROGRESSIVE EDUCATION The progressive emphasis on efficiency and reform dovetailed with a dynamic educational reform movement led by John Dewey, a Vermont-born philosopher who first taught at the University of Chicago and then Columbia University in New York City. Dewey believed that America's educational system should focus on producing good citizens. This required a profound transformation in educational philosophy. "If we teach today's students as we taught yesterday's," Dewey asserted, "we rob them of tomorrow."

Learning, Dewey believed, should be applied to real social problems rather than remain focused on abstract "book learning." He wanted schools to promote "a genuine form of active community life, instead of [being] a place apart in which to learn lessons."

Schools, Dewey concluded, were to become laboratories for progressive social reform. They "should take an active part in directing social change, and share in the construction of a new social order." In other words, progressive education highlighted "pragmatic" knowledge and useful skills to remedy pressing social problems and benefit the common good after students finished their schooling. "The goal of education," Dewy concluded, was lifelong learning. He wanted people "to continue their education" throughout their lives, and he yearned to see educated people apply their learning to the nation's most pressing social problems.

PROMOTION OF SOCIAL JUSTICE

The progressive movement also sought to promote social justice for the working poor, the jobless, and the homeless. In addition to their work in settlement houses and other areas, many progressives formed advocacy organizations such as the National Consumers' League, led by Florence Kelley, which promoted safer and less exploitative working conditions for women and children by educating consumers about suffocating sweatshop factories and dangerous mines, canneries, and textile mills. Driven by a fiery sense of indignation, Kelley and the League organized consumer boycotts against companies that refused to embrace workplace reforms or increase wages.

Other grassroots progressive organizations, such as the General Federation of Women's Clubs, insisted that civic life needed the humanizing effect of female leadership. Women's clubs across the country sought to clean up slums by educating residents about personal and household hygiene (what women reformers called "municipal housekeeping"), urging construction of sewer systems, and launching public-awareness campaigns about the connection between unsanitary tenements and disease. Women's clubs also campaigned for child-care centers and kindergartens; government inspection of food processing plants; stricter housing codes; laws protecting women in the workplace; and more social services for the poor, sick, disabled, and abused. Still others focused on prostitution and alcohol abuse.

THE CAMPAIGN AGAINST DRINKING Middle-class women were the driving force behind efforts to stop the sale and consumption of alcoholic beverages. Founded in Cleveland, Ohio, in 1874, the Women's Christian Temperance Union (WCTU) became the largest women's group in the nation, boasting 300,000 members. While some members were motivated by

Protestant beliefs that consuming alcohol was a sin, most saw excessive drinking, especially in saloons, as a threat to social progress and family stability.

Initially, WCTU members met in churches to pray and then marched to saloons to try to convince their owners to close. They promoted *temperance*—the reduction of alcohol consumption. But they also urged individuals to embrace *abstinence* and refuse to drink any alcoholic beverages. By attacking drunkenness and closing saloons, temperance reformers hoped to (1) improve family life by preventing domestic violence, (2) reduce crime in the streets, and (3) remove one of the worst tools of corruption—free beer on Election Day, which was used to "buy" votes among the working class. As a Boston sociologist concluded, the saloon had become "the enemy of society because of the evil results produced upon the individual."

Frances Willard The founder and president of the WCTU, Willard lobbied for a range of progressive reforms, prohibition being chief among them.

Frances Willard, the dynamic president of the WCTU between 1879 and 1898, greatly expanded the goals and scope of the organization. Under her leadership, it began promoting legislation to ban alcohol (referred to as prohibition) at the local, state, and federal levels. Willard also pushed the WCTU to lobby for other progressive reforms important to women, including a nationwide eight-hour workday, the regulation of child labor, government-funded kindergartens, the right to vote for women, and federal inspections of the food industry.

The battle against alcoholic beverages took on new strength in 1893 with the formation of the Anti-Saloon League, an organization based in churches that pioneered the strategy of the single-issue political pressure group. The bipartisan league, like the WCTU, initially focused on closing down saloons rather than abolishing alcohol altogether. Eventually, however, it decided to force the prohibition issue into the forefront of state and local elections. At its "Jubilee Convention" in 1913, the league endorsed an amendment to the Constitution prohibiting the manufacture and sale of alcoholic beverages, which Congress approved in 1917 and the states finally ratified in 1919.

LABOR LEGISLATION In addition to the efforts to reduce alcohol consumption, other progressive reformers pushed legislation to improve working conditions in mills, mines, and factories—and on railroads. In 1890, almost half of wage workers toiled up to twelve hours a day—sometimes seven days a week—in unsafe, unsanitary, and unregulated conditions for extremely low wages. Workplace accidents were appallingly common and frequently ignored. During the construction of the New York City subway system, fifty-four workers were killed. Legislation to ensure better working conditions and limit child labor was perhaps the most significant reform to emerge from the drive for progressive social justice.

The Triangle Fire It took a stunning tragedy, however, to spur meaningful government regulation of dangerous workplaces. On March 25, 1911, a raging fire broke out at the ten-story Asch Building in New York City. Its top three

Triangle Fire (1911) After a raging fire, the Triangle Shirtwaist factory was left in ruins. This tragedy killed 146 garment workers and prompted new safety and labor regulations and reforms.

floors hosted the Triangle Shirtwaist factory (shirtwaists were gauzy white cotton blouses then popular with women), where some 500 workers, mostly teenage women, almost all Jewish, Italian, or Russian immigrants, toiled at sewing machines twelve hours a day.

As the fire roared out of control, escape routes were limited because the owners kept one of the two stairway doors locked to prevent theft. In the end, after thirty minutes of sheer horror, 146 garment workers died. All but 23 of them were young women.

Most of the dead succumbed to suffocation but more than 50 leaped to their deaths from the ninth story. Fire trucks arrived quickly, but their ladders only reached the sixth floor, and the safety nets held by firemen collapsed under the weight of the plunging bodies. Heaps of bodies were found against the locked emergency exit and on the flimsy fire escape that crashed from too much weight. Some of the victims held each other's hands as they jumped to their deaths.

In the days after the fire, press coverage fed public indignation. Demand for reforms soared with every graphic article and poignant photograph of mangled and charred bodies lined up on the sidewalk outside the factory and on an East River pier-turned-morgue.

Frances Perkins, the thirty-year-old executive secretary of the National Consumers' League, a nonprofit organization devoted to improving workplaces, was among the hundreds who witnessed the Triangle fire. She and others soon organized a mass meeting to turn the tragedy into "some kind of victory" for workers.

Their efforts resulted in dozens of new city and state regulations dealing with fire hazards, working conditions, women workers' rights, and child labor. Twenty years later, President Franklin D. Roosevelt would appoint Frances Perkins his secretary of labor, making her the first female cabinet member in history.

Regulating Child Labor and Working Conditions for Women Legislation to limit child labor was perhaps the most significant reform to emerge from the drive for progressive social justice. At the end of the nineteenth century, fewer than half of working families lived solely on the husband's earnings. Everyone in the family who could work did so. Many married women did "homework"—making clothes, selling flower arrangements, preparing food for others, and taking in boarders. Children of poor families frequently dropped out of school and went to work in factories, shops, mines, mills, canneries, and on farms. In 1900, some 1.75 million children between ten and fifteen years old were working outside the home.

PRODUCTS OF THE TENEMENT WORKSHOP

Chiffon Applique

Glove Finishing

Infants Dress (D)

National Consumers' League Exhibit To raise awareness about labor reform, everyday objects are displayed at a New York exhibition in 1908 alongside descriptions of the poor working conditions and exploitation that went into their manufacture.

Progressives argued that children, too, had rights in a democracy. In southern textile mills, a third of the workers were children. In several southern states, children worked sixty-six hours a week. "I regard my employees," a manager said, "as I regard my machinery. So long as they can do my work for what I choose to pay them, I keep them, getting out of them all I can." The National Child Labor Committee, organized in 1904, campaigned for laws prohibiting the employment of children. Most states passed such laws, although some were lax in enforcing them.

Reformers also sought to regulate the length of the workday for women, in part because some working mothers were pregnant and others had children at home with inadequate supervision. Spearheaded by Florence Kelley, progressives convinced many state governments to ban the hiring of children below a certain age, and to limit the hours that women and children could work. With more children staying at home and going to school, reformers also demanded that cities build more parks and playgrounds to encourage healthy activities.

The Supreme Court was inconsistent in its rulings on state labor laws. In *Lochner v. New York* (1905), the Court declared that a state law limiting bakers to a sixty-hour workweek was unconstitutional because it violated workers' rights to accept any job they wanted, no matter how bad the working conditions or how low the pay.

Three years later, in *Muller v. Oregon* (1908), the Court changed its mind. Based on evidence that long working hours increased the chances of health problems, the Court approved an Oregon law restricting the workday to no more than ten hours for women. In *Bunting v. Oregon* (1917), the Court accepted a state law allowing no more than a ten-hour workday for both men and women. For twenty more years, however, the nation's highest court held out against state laws requiring a minimum wage.

THE "PROGRESSIVE" INCOME TAX   Progressives also promoted social justice by addressing growing economic inequality. One way to redistribute wealth was through the creation of a "progressive" federal income tax—so called not because of the idea's association with the progressive movement, but because the tax rates were based on a sliding scale—that is, the rates "progress" or rise as income levels rise, thus forcing the rich to pay more. Such a graduated, or progressive tax system, was the climax of the progressive movement's commitment to a more equitable distribution of wealth.

The progressive income tax was an old idea. In 1894, William Jennings Bryan had persuaded Congress to approve a 2 percent tax on corporations and individuals earning more than $4,000 a year (the equivalent of $123,199 today). Soon after the tax became law, however, the Supreme Court, in *Pollock v. Farmers' Loan Company* (1895), declared it unconstitutional, claiming that only the states could levy income taxes.

Still, progressives continued to believe that a graduated income tax would help slow the concentration of wealth in the hands of the richest Americans. In 1907, President Theodore Roosevelt announced his support. Two years later, his successor, William Howard Taft, endorsed a constitutional amendment allowing such a tax, and Congress agreed. This taxation became law in 1913 with state ratification of the **Sixteenth Amendment**.

PROGRESSIVISM UNDER ROOSEVELT AND TAFT

In the late nineteenth century, most progressive policies originated at the state and local levels. Federal reform efforts began in earnest only when Republican Theodore Roosevelt ("TR") became president in 1901 after the assassination of William McKinley. Roosevelt had grown more progressive with each passing year. "A great democracy," he said, "has got to be *progressive* or it will soon cease to be great or a democracy."

TR was relentlessly energetic, and he thrived on confrontation. He was a force of nature, an American original blessed with a triumphant grin and an oversized intellect and ego. He hated indecision or inaction. And he loved what he called "strenuosity." In the White House, the ever-boyish Roosevelt invited male guests to wrestle and box with him or to fight with wooden swords or climb trees. His contradictions were maddening, but his exuberance, charm, energy, and humor made up for them. Woodrow Wilson confessed after meeting Roosevelt, "You can't resist the man."

Like Andrew Jackson, Roosevelt greatly increased the power of the presidency in the process of enacting his progressive agenda. On his first day in the White House, Roosevelt announced his intention to use the presidency as his "bully pulpit." He would educate Americans about the new realities facing their society at the beginning of the new century. He tackled his duties with self-described "strenuosity."

Roosevelt loved power, for he was certain that he knew best how to lead the nation. Congress, he had decided, had grown too dominant and too corrupt. He therefore abandoned the Gilded Age tradition in which presidents had deferred to Congress. In his view, the problems caused by explosive industrial growth required substantial responses, and he was unwilling to wait for Congress to act. "I believe in a strong executive [president]," he asserted. "I believe in power."

During Roosevelt's administration, the president, not Congress, became the primary source of policy making. His friend and successor, William Howard Taft, continued Roosevelt's progressive effort to regulate corporate trusts, but he proved neither as energetic nor as wide ranging in his role as a reformer president—a difference that led to a fateful break between the two men.

TAMING BIG BUSINESS Theodore Roosevelt was the first president to use executive power to rein in Big Business. As governor of New York, he had pushed for legislation to regulate sweatshops, institute state inspections of factories and slaughterhouses, and limit the workday to eight hours. He believed in capitalism and the accumulation of wealth, but he was willing to adopt radical methods to ensure that the social unrest caused by the insensitivity of business owners to the rights of workers and the needs of the poor did not mushroom into a revolution.

CURBING THE TRUSTS In outlining his progressive agenda, Roosevelt applauded the growth of industrial capitalism but declared war on corruption and on "cronyism"—the awarding of political appointments, government contracts, and other favors to politicians' personal friends and donors. He endorsed a **"Square Deal"** for "every man, great or small, rich or poor."

TR's Square Deal program featured what was called the "Three Cs": greater government *control* of corporations, enhanced *conservation* of natural resources, and new regulations to protect *consumers* against contaminated food and medicines.

Early in 1902, President Roosevelt ordered the attorney general to use the Sherman Anti-Trust Act (1890) to rein in huge corporations engaged in illegal activities. In his view, some big businesses were bad not because they were big but because their executives acted unethically or unfairly. From his youth, Roosevelt had developed a firm commitment to "fair play" in sports, in business, and in politics, and his version of progressivism centered on a commitment to equal opportunity.

In 1902, only five months into his presidency, Roosevelt stunned financiers when he ordered the U.S. attorney general to break up the Northern Securities Company, a vast network of railroads and steamships run by J. Pierpont Morgan that monopolized transportation in several regions of the country. Shocked that Roosevelt would try to dismantle his corporation, Morgan rushed from New York to the White House and told the president: "If I have

Square Deal This 1906 cartoon likens Roosevelt to the Greek legend Hercules, who as a baby strangled snakes sent from hell to kill him. Here, the serpents are pro-corporation senator Nelson Aldrich and Standard Oil's John D. Rockefeller.

done anything wrong, send your man to my man and they can fix it up."

The U.S. attorney general, who was also at the meeting, told Morgan: "We don't want to 'fix it up.' We want to stop it." Morgan then asked Roosevelt if he planned to attack his other trusts, such as U.S. Steel and General Electric. "Certainly not," Roosevelt replied, "unless we find out that . . . they have done something wrong." In 1904, the Supreme Court ruled 5–4 that the Northern Securities Company was indeed a monopoly and must be dismantled.

Altogether, Roosevelt approved about twenty-five anti-trust suits against oversized corporations. He also sought stronger regulation of the railroads. In 1903, at his behest, Congress passed the Elkins Act, making it illegal for railroads to give secret rebates (cash refunds) on freight charges to favored high-volume customers. That same year, Congress created a Bureau of Corporations to monitor the activities of big businesses. When the Standard Oil Company refused to turn over its records, Roosevelt launched an anti-trust suit that led to the breakup of the powerful company in 1911. The Supreme Court also ordered the American Tobacco Company dismantled because it had monopolized the cigarette industry.

THE 1902 COAL STRIKE In everything Roosevelt did, he acted forcefully. On May 12, 1902, more than 100,000 members of the United Mine Workers (UMW) labor union walked off the job at coal mines in Pennsylvania and West Virginia. The overworked and underpaid miners were seeking a 20 percent wage increase and a shorter nine-hour workday, reduced from the present ten-hour shifts. The union organization also sought official recognition by the mine owners—but they refused to negotiate and instead chose to shut down the coal mines.

The owners closed the mines to starve out the miners, many of whom were immigrants from eastern Europe. One owner expressed the ethnic prejudices shared by many of his colleagues when he proclaimed, "The miners don't suffer—why, they can't even speak English."

By October, the lengthy shutdown had caused the price of coal to soar, and hospitals and schools reported empty coal bins as winter approached. In many northern cities, poor households had run out of coal. "The country is on the verge of a vast public calamity," warned Walter Rauschenbusch. The Reverend Washington Gladden led a petition drive urging Roosevelt to mediate the strike.

The president took the bold step of inviting leaders of both sides to a conference in Washington, D.C. Never had a president shown such initiative. Roosevelt appealed to the leaders' "patriotism, to the spirit that sinks personal considerations and makes individual sacrifices for the public good." The mine owners, however, refused to speak to the UMW leaders.

Roosevelt was so infuriated by what he called the "extraordinary stupidity" of the "wooden-headed" and "arrogant" owners that he wanted to grab their spokesman "by the seat of his breeches" and "chuck him out" a window. Instead, he threatened to declare a national emergency so that he could take control of the mines and use soldiers to run them. When a congressman questioned the constitutionality of such a move, Roosevelt roared, "To hell with the Constitution when the people want coal!"

The president's threat worked; the strike ended on October 23. The miners won a nine-hour workday and a 10 percent wage increase. Roosevelt was the first president to use his authority to referee a dispute between management and labor—believing that both sides deserved a fair hearing. In contrast, his predecessors had instead responded to strikes by sending federal troops to shoot union activists.

ROOSEVELT'S SECOND TERM Theodore Roosevelt's forceful leadership won him friends and enemies. As he prepared to run for reelection

Roosevelt's Duality Theodore Roosevelt depicted as an "apostle of prosperity" *(top)* and as a Roman tyrant *(bottom)*. Roosevelt's energy, self-righteousness, and impulsiveness elicited conflicting reactions.

in 1904, he acknowledged that the "whole Wall Street crowd" would do all they could to defeat him. Nevertheless, he won the Republican nomination. The Democrats, having lost twice with William Jennings Bryan, essentially gave the election to Roosevelt and the Republicans by nominating the virtually unknown Alton B. Parker, chief justice of the New York Supreme Court. Parker was the dullest—and most forgettable—presidential candidate in history. One journalist dubbed him "the enigma from New York." The most interesting item in Parker's campaign biography was that he had trained his pigs to come when called by name.

In the election, the Democrats suffered their worst defeat in thirty-two years. After sweeping to victory by an electoral vote of 336 to 140, Roosevelt told his wife that he was "no longer a political accident." He now had a popular mandate to do great things. On the eve of his inauguration in March 1905, Roosevelt announced: "Tomorrow I shall come into office in my own right. Then watch out for me!" He was ready to become the leader of the progressive movement.

PROGRESSIVE REGULATION Theodore Roosevelt launched his second term with an even stronger commitment to regulating corporations and their corrupt owners who exploited workers and tried to eliminate competition. His comments irked many of his corporate contributors and congressional Republican leaders. Said Pittsburgh steel baron Henry Frick, "We bought the son of a bitch, and then he did not stay bought."

To promote the "moral regeneration of business," Roosevelt first took aim at the railroads. In 1906, he persuaded Congress to pass the Hepburn Act, which gave the federal Interstate Commerce Commission (ICC) the power to set maximum freight rates for the railroad industry.

Under Roosevelt's Square Deal programs, the federal government also assumed oversight of key industries affecting public health: meat-packers, food processors, and makers of drugs and patent medicines. Muckraking journalists had revealed all sorts of unsanitary and dangerous activities in the preparation of food and drug products.

Perhaps the most powerful blow against these abuses was struck by Upton Sinclair's novel *The Jungle* (1906), which told the story of a Lithuanian immigrant working in a filthy Chicago meatpacking plant:

> It was too dark in these storage places to see well, but a man could
> run his hand over these piles of meat and sweep off handfuls of
> the dried dung of rats. These rats were nuisances, and the packers
> would put poisoned bread out for them, they would die, and

then rats, bread, and meat would go into the hoppers [to be ground up] together.

After reading *The Jungle*, Roosevelt urged Congress to pass the Meat Inspection Act of 1906. It required the Department of Agriculture to inspect every hog and steer whose carcass crossed state lines. The Pure Food and Drug Act (1906), enacted the same day, required the makers of prepared food and medicines to host government inspectors—and label the ingredients in their products.

ENVIRONMENTAL CONSERVATION One of the most enduring legacies of Theodore Roosevelt's leadership was his energetic support for environmental conservation, one of the pillars of his Square Deal. Roosevelt, an avid outdoorsman, naturalist, and amateur scientist, championed efforts to manage and preserve natural resources (which he called "wild places") for the benefit of future generations. He created fifty federal wildlife refuges, approved five new national parks and fifty-one federal bird sanctuaries, and designated eighteen national monuments, including the Grand Canyon.

In 1898, Vice President Roosevelt had endorsed the appointment of his friend Gifford Pinchot, the nation's first professionally trained forest manager, as head of the Department of Agriculture's Division of Forestry. Pinchot, like Roosevelt, believed in economic growth as well as environmental preservation. Pinchot said that the conservation movement promoted the "greatest good for the greatest number for the longest time."

Yosemite Valley A couple playfully poses atop Glacier Point Rock in Yosemite National Park in 1902.

Roosevelt and Pinchot used the Forest Reserve Act (1891) to protect 172 million acres of federally owned forests from loggers. The owners of lumber companies were furious, but the president held firm, declaring, "I hate a man who skins the land." Overall, Roosevelt set aside more than 234 million acres of federal land for conservation purposes and created forty-five national forests in eleven western states. As Pinchot recalled, "Launching the conservation movement was the most significant achievement of the TR Administration, as he himself believed."

ROOSEVELT AND RACE   Roosevelt's most significant failure as a progressive was his refusal to confront racism. Like Populists, progressives worked to empower "the people" against the entrenched "special interests." In the view of most of them, however, "the people" did not include African Americans, Native Americans, Mexican Americans, or some immigrant groups. Most White progressives ignored or even endorsed the passage of Jim Crow laws in the South that prevented Blacks from voting and subjected them to rigid racial separation in schools, housing, parks, and playgrounds.

By 1901, nearly every southern state had prevented most African Americans from voting or holding political office by disqualifying or terrorizing them. During the Progressive Era, hundreds of African Americans were lynched each year across the South, where virtually no Blacks were allowed to serve on juries or work as sheriffs or policemen. A White candidate for governor in Mississippi in 1903 announced that he believed "in the divine right of the white man to rule, to do all the voting, and to hold all the offices, both state and federal." The South, wrote W. E. B. Du Bois, then a young Black sociologist at Atlanta University, "is simply an armed camp for intimidating Black folk."

At the same time, few progressives questioned the many informal patterns of segregation and prejudice in the North and West. In New York City, for example, African American doctors could not practice at public hospitals, and Black teachers were not employed by the Board of Education until 1895. "The plain fact is," the muckraking journalist Ray Stannard Baker admitted in 1909, "most of us in the North do not believe in any real democracy between white and colored men."

Theodore Roosevelt himself shared such prejudices. He confided to a friend in 1906 his belief that "as a race and in the mass" African Americans "are altogether inferior to whites."

Yet on occasion the president made exceptions. On October 16, 1901, Roosevelt invited Booker T. Washington, then the nation's most prominent Black leader, to the White House for dinner. Upon learning of the meeting, White southerners exploded with

Theodore Roosevelt and Booker T. Washington Roosevelt addresses the National Negro Business League in 1900 with Washington seated to his left.

fury. The *Memphis Scimitar* newspaper screamed that Roosevelt's allowing a [Negro] to dine with him was "the most damnable outrage that has ever been perpetrated by a citizen of the United States."

Roosevelt found such violent reactions "inexplicable," but in the end he gave in to the criticism. Never again would he host an African American leader. During a tour of the southern states in 1905, he pandered to Whites by highlighting his own southern ancestry (his mother was from Georgia) and expressing his admiration for the Confederacy and Robert E. Lee. His behavior, said a Black leader, was "national treachery to the Negro."

The Brownsville Riot   Worse was to come, however. In 1906, a violent racial incident occurred in Brownsville, Texas, where a dozen or so members of an African American army regiment shot several Whites who had been harassing them outside a saloon. One White bartender was killed, and a police officer was seriously wounded. Both sides claimed the other started the shooting. An investigation concluded that the soldiers were at fault, but no one could identify any of the shooters, and none of the soldiers was willing to talk about the incident.

Roosevelt responded to their silence by dishonorably discharging the entire regiment of 167 soldiers, several of whom had been awarded the Congressional Medal of Honor for their service in Cuba during the Spanish-American War. None of them received a hearing or a trial. Critics of Roosevelt's harsh action flooded the White House with angry telegrams. Secretary of War William H. Taft urged the president to reconsider, but Roosevelt refused to show any mercy to "murderers, assassins, cowards, and comrades of murderers." (Sixty years later, the U.S. Army "cleared the records" of the Black soldiers.)

THE TRANSITION FROM ROOSEVELT TO TAFT   After his 1904 election victory, Theodore Roosevelt had said he would not run for president again, in part because he did not want to be the first president to serve the equivalent of three terms. "No president has ever enjoyed himself as much as I enjoyed myself," he reflected. "I have used every ounce of power there was in the office, and I have not cared a rap for the criticisms of those who spoke of my 'usurpation of power.'" The strength of the United States depended upon having a "strong central executive," he declared. In 1909, he was ready to leave the White House and go hunting for big game in Africa.

Unlike most retiring presidents, however, Roosevelt would leave with regret, for he was loved by his party, who gave him a roaring ovation at the 1908 Republican nominating convention. When the cheers subsided, he urged the delegates to nominate his longtime friend, Secretary of War William Howard Taft, which they did on the first ballot.

Taft, who had no stomach for campaigning, reluctantly agreed to run and promised to continue Roosevelt's policies. The Democrats again chose William Jennings Bryan. The Democratic platform echoed the Republican emphasis on regulation of business but called for a lower tariff. Bryan struggled to attract national support and was defeated for a third time, as Taft swept the Electoral College, 321 to 162.

A LIFE OF PUBLIC SERVICE On paper, William Howard Taft was superbly qualified to be president. Born in Cincinnati in 1857, the son of a prominent attorney who had served in President Grant's cabinet, Taft had graduated second in his class at Yale University and became a leading legal scholar, serving on the Ohio Supreme Court. In 1900, President McKinley appointed him the first American governor-general of the Philippines, and three years later Theodore Roosevelt named him secretary of war. Taft supervised the construction of the Panama Canal and organized the relief effort after the San Francisco earthquake of 1906.

William Howard Taft The twenty-seventh president, Taft served in the shadow of Roosevelt, and freely admitted a dislike of politics.

Until becoming president, Taft had never held elected office, nor was he ever sure he wanted to be chief executive. His preference was to be a justice on the U.S. Supreme Court. Running for president, he once confessed, was "a nightmare," for politics "makes me sick." Unlike the robust, athletic Roosevelt, Taft struggled most of his life with obesity, topping out at 332 pounds and earning the nickname "Big Bill." Roosevelt, Taft explained, "loves the woods; he loves hunting; he loves roughing it, and I don't." His primary sin, he confessed, was laziness. He often fell asleep at public events.

Although good-natured and easygoing, Taft as president never managed to escape the shadow of his charismatic predecessor. "When I hear someone say 'Mr. President,'" he confessed, "I look around expecting to see Roosevelt."

Taft was a conservative progressive who vowed to preserve capitalism by protecting "the right of property" and the "right of liberty." In practice, this meant that he was even more determined than Roosevelt to support "the spirit of commercial freedom" against monopolistic trusts, but he was not interested in pushing for additional reforms.

Taft was no crusader; he viewed himself as a judge-like administrator, not an innovator. He said he "hated politics" and was reluctant to exercise presidential authority (after leaving the White House, he got the job he had always wanted, chief justice of the U.S. Supreme Court).

TAFT AND THE TARIFF   After taking office, President Taft displayed his credentials as a progressive Republican by supporting lower tariffs on imports; he even called a special session of Congress to address the matter. But he proved less skillful than Roosevelt in dealing with legislators and lobbyists. Taft confessed that he did not know how to use the "bully pulpit," which Roosevelt had perfected.

In the end, the Payne-Aldrich Tariff (1909) made little change in federal tariff policies. Some rates went down while others went up, but overall, tariff policies continued to favor the industrial Northeast over the rest of the nation. Taft's failure to gain real reform and his lack of a "crusading spirit" like Roosevelt's angered the progressive, pro-Roosevelt wing of the Republican party, whom Taft dismissed as "assistant Democrats."

Roosevelt was not happy; nor were other Republican progressives. William Allen White, a prominent newspaper editor in Kansas, concluded that Taft, a "genial, chuckling, courteous, kindly gentleman," was at heart "a deep-dyed political and economic conservative, and bull-headed at that."

THE BALLINGER-PINCHOT CONTROVERSY   In 1910, the split between the conservative and progressive Republican factions was widened into a chasm by the Ballinger-Pinchot controversy. President Taft's secretary of the interior, Richard A. Ballinger, opened to commercial development millions of acres of federal lands that Roosevelt had ordered protected. Chief of forestry Gifford Pinchot, TR's close friend, complained about the "giveaway," but Taft refused to intervene, calling Pinchot a "radical and a crank." When Pinchot made his opposition public early in 1910, the president fired him. In doing so, Taft ignited a feud with Roosevelt that would eventually end their friendship—and cost him reelection.

THE TAFT-ROOSEVELT FEUD In 1909, soon after Taft became president, Roosevelt and his son Kermit had sailed to Africa, where they would spend nearly a year trophy hunting big game. (When business tycoon J. Pierpont Morgan heard about the extended safari, he expressed the hope that "every lion would do its duty" by devouring Roosevelt.) Roosevelt had left the White House assuming that Taft would continue to promote a progressive agenda. But by filling the cabinet with corporate lawyers and firing Gifford Pinchot, Taft had, in Roosevelt's view, failed to "carry out my work unbroken."

Roosevelt's rebuke of Taft was in some ways undeserved. Taft had at least attempted tariff reform, which Roosevelt had never dared. Although Taft had fired Pinchot, he had replaced him with another conservationist. Taft's administration actually preserved more federal land in four years than Roosevelt's had in nearly eight, and it filed twice as many anti-trust suits, including one that led to the breakup of the Standard Oil Company in 1911. Taft advanced other progressive causes as well. In 1910, with his support, Congress passed the Mann-Elkins Act, which extended the authority of the ICC beyond railroads to telephone and telegraph companies. Taft established a federal Children's Bureau (1912) to promote the welfare of youth and a Bureau of Mines (1910) to oversee that huge industry. Taft also supported women's suffrage and ensuring that workers had the right to join unions.

None of that satisfied Roosevelt, however. On August 31, 1910, the former president, eager to return to the political spotlight, gave a speech at Osawatomie, Kansas, in which he announced his new platform, called "New Nationalism." Roosevelt explained that he wanted to go beyond ensuring a Square Deal in which corporations were forced to "play by the rules"; he now promised to "change the rules" to force large corporations to promote social welfare and serve the needs of working people.

To save capitalism from the threat of a working-class revolution, Roosevelt called for tighter federal regulation of "arrogant" corporations that too often tried to "control and corrupt" politics; for a federal income tax (the Sixteenth Amendment had still not become law); and for federal laws regulating child labor. "What I have advocated," he explained, "is not wild radicalism. It is the highest and wisest kind of conservatism."

Encouraged by public reaction to his ideas, on February 24, 1912, Roosevelt announced that he would challenge Taft for the Republican presidential nomination. He dismissed the "second-rate" Taft as a "hopeless fathead" and "flubdub" who had "sold the Square Deal down the river." Taft responded by calling Roosevelt a "dangerous egotist" and a "demagogue." Thus began a bitter war in which Roosevelt had the better weapons, not the least of which was his love of a good fight.

By 1912, a dozen or so states were letting citizens vote for presidential candidates in party primaries instead of following the traditional practice in which party leaders chose the nominee behind closed doors. Roosevelt decided that if he won big in the Republican primaries, he could claim to be "the people's choice." Yet even though he won all but two primaries, including the one in Taft's home state of Ohio, his popularity was no match for Taft's authority as party leader. In the thirty-six states that chose candidates by conventions dominated by party bosses, the Taft Republicans prevailed. At the Republican National Convention, Taft won easily.

Roosevelt was furious. He denounced Taft and his supporters as thieves and stormed out of the Chicago convention hall along with his delegates— mostly social workers, teachers, professors, journalists, and urban reformers, along with a few wealthy business executives.

THE PROGRESSIVE PARTY   Some 150 disappointed Roosevelt delegates marched the short distance from the Chicago Coliseum to Orchestra Hall. Hundreds more joined them. "The crowd of people wanting to get into the hall extended for blocks in a line four deep," a reporter noted. "Thousands failed to get in the building."

At TR's urging, the pro-Roosevelt crusaders launched a new political party that would promote the most advanced ideas of the era. He assured them that he felt "fit as a bull moose," leading journalists to nickname the new Progressive party the "Bull Moose party."

Progressives adored Roosevelt because he showed what a government dedicated to the public good might achieve. When Roosevelt closed his acceptance speech by saying, "We stand at Armageddon [the climactic encounter between Christ and Satan], and we battle for the Lord," the delegates stood and began singing the hymn "Onward, Christian Soldiers." One reporter wrote that the "Bull Moose" movement was not so much a party as it was a political crusade, and Roosevelt was its leading evangelist.

The **Progressive party** platform, audacious for its time, revealed Roosevelt's growing liberalism. It supported a minimum "living wage" for hourly workers; an eight-hour workday; women's suffrage and "an equal voice with women in every phase of party management"; campaign finance reform; and a system of "social security" insurance to protect people against sickness, unemployment, and disabilities. It also pledged to end the "boss system" governing state and local politics and destroy the "unholy alliance between corrupt business and corrupt politics." Conservative critics called Roosevelt a socialist, a revolutionist, and a "monumental egotist."

Roosevelt charged that President Taft was not a progressive because he had tried to undo land conservation efforts and had failed to fight for social justice or against the special interests. Instead, Roosevelt said that Taft had aligned himself with the privileged political and business leaders who steadfastly opposed "the cause of justice for the helpless and the wronged."

Roosevelt and the organizers of the new party announced that they would return to Chicago in six weeks to host their first presidential convention. As state organizers prepared to elect delegations to attend the party's national convention in Chicago, controversy arose in the South over the role of African Americans in the new party. Benjamin Franklin Fridge, a Roosevelt activist from Mississippi, told supporters of the new third party in his home state that "this is strictly a white man's party, the movement is led by white men, and we expect only white men in our organization."

As the dispute over Black delegates exploded in the national press, Roosevelt urged a middle ground, arguing that northern states with large numbers of African American voters would be allowed to send biracial delegations to the party convention while the segregated southern states would send all-White representatives. Many observers found Roosevelt's stance hypocritical. "Bars Southern Negro," the *Baltimore Sun* said in a front-page headline, "But 'T. R.' Welcomes Blacks in States Where Vote Is Factor."

Jane Addams, the celebrated Chicago social reformer, expressed the disgust of many progressives with Roosevelt's cynical stance: "Some of us are very

Sideshow Ted This 1912 cartoon criticizes the Bull Moose party for being just a sideshow (with suffragists selling lemonade outside) and points out TR's menacing ego.

disturbed that this Progressive Party, which stands for human rights, should even appear not to stand for the rights of the negroes," she said. In the end, Roosevelt won the battle but lost the war. Disappointed African Americans from southern states were not allowed among their "lily white" delegations, and many of them now publicly denounced Roosevelt and his candidacy.

WOODROW WILSON: A PROGRESSIVE SOUTHERNER

The fight between William Howard Taft and Theodore Roosevelt gave hope to the Democrats, whose presidential nominee, New Jersey governor Woodrow Wilson, had enjoyed remarkable success in his brief political career. Until his election as governor in 1910, Wilson had been a college professor and then president of Princeton University, where he had become a popular speaker promoting progressive political reforms and government regulation of corporations.

Like Taft, Wilson had never run for political office or worked in business. He was a man of books and ideas, with a keen intellect and a "first class mind" bolstered by an analytical temperament, a tireless work ethic, an inspiring speaking style, and a strong conviction that he knew what was best for the nation.

TO SERVE HUMANITY Born in Staunton, Virginia, in 1856, the son, grandson, nephew, and son-in-law of Presbyterian ministers, Thomas Woodrow Wilson had grown up in Georgia and the Carolinas during the Civil War and Reconstruction. The South, he once said, was the only part of the nation where nothing had to be explained to him.

Tall and slender, with a long, chiseled face, he developed an unquestioning religious faith. Convinced that

Woodrow Wilson Wilson was the only president to hold a Ph.D. degree, and his intellect and idealism compensated for his lack of political experience.

God had selected him to serve humanity, he often displayed an unbending self-righteousness that would prove to be his undoing as president. As Ray Stannard Baker observed, Woodrow Wilson was "a lonely man, outwardly cold and remote, inwardly molten passion, and with an unparalleled tenacity of faith, an unequaled constancy of courage."

Wilson graduated from Princeton in 1879. After law school at the University of Virginia, he briefly worked as an attorney before enrolling at Johns Hopkins University to study history and political science. He earned one of the nation's first doctoral degrees, became an expert in constitutional government, and served as a popular professor at several colleges before becoming president of Princeton in 1902.

Eight years later, Wilson accepted the support of New Jersey Democrats for the gubernatorial nomination. He harbored higher ambitions, however. If he could become governor, he said, "I stand a very good chance of being the next President of the United States." Like Roosevelt, Wilson was intensely ambitious and idealistic; he felt destined to preside over America's emergence as the greatest world power.

After winning the governorship by a landslide, Wilson persuaded the state legislature to adopt an array of progressive reforms to curb the power of party bosses and corporate lobbyists. "After dealing with college politicians," he joked, "I find that the men who I am dealing with now seem like amateurs."

Wilson soon attracted national attention. At the 1912 Democratic convention, he faced stiff competition from several veteran party leaders for the presidential nomination. With the support of William Jennings Bryan, however, he won on the forty-sixth ballot.

THE 1912 ELECTION The 1912 presidential campaign was one of the most exciting in history. It involved four strong candidates: Democrat Woodrow Wilson, Republican William Howard Taft, Socialist Eugene V. Debs, and Progressive Theodore Roosevelt. For all their differences, the candidates shared a basic progressive assumption that modern social problems could be resolved only through active governmental intervention.

No sooner did the formal campaign open than Roosevelt's candidacy almost ended. While on his way to deliver a speech in Milwaukee, Wisconsin, he was shot at close range by John Schrank, a deranged New Yorker who believed that any president seeking a third term should be killed. The bullet went through Roosevelt's overcoat, a steel eyeglasses case, and his fifty-page speech, then fractured a rib before nestling just below his right lung, an inch from his heart.

THE ELECTION OF 1912

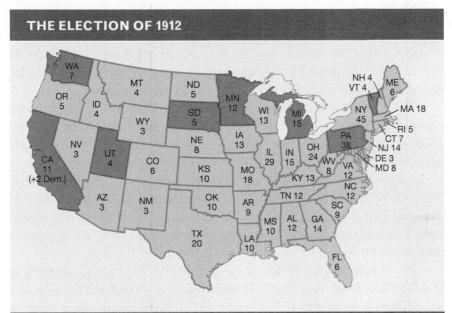

	Electoral Vote	Popular Vote
Woodrow Wilson (Democratic)	**435**	**6,300,000**
Theodore Roosevelt (Progressive)	88	4,100,000
William H. Taft (Republican)	8	3,500,000

- Why was Taft so unpopular?
- How did the division between Roosevelt and Taft give Wilson the presidency?
- Why was Wilson's victory in 1912 especially significant?

Refusing medical attention, Roosevelt insisted on delivering his eighty-minute speech to 10,000 supporters. In a dramatic gesture, he showed the audience his bloodstained shirt and punctured text, explaining that "the bullet is in me now, so I cannot make a very long speech." Then, grinning, he vowed, "It takes more than this to kill a bull moose. I will make this speech or die." When finished, Roosevelt went directly to a hospital, where he stayed for a week.

As the campaign developed, Taft quickly lost ground and essentially gave up. "There are so many people in the country who don't like me," he lamented. The contest settled into a debate over Theodore Roosevelt's New Nationalism and Woodrow Wilson's **New Freedom**. The New Freedom favored small government and states' rights, arguing that federal intervention in society should be a last resort. It aimed to restore economic competition by eliminating *all* trusts rather than just those that misbehaved. Where Roosevelt believed that bigness in business was inevitable, Wilson insisted that huge, "heartless" industries needed to be broken up.

On Election Day, Wilson won handily, collecting 435 electoral votes to 88 for Roosevelt and just 8 for Taft, who said he had only one consolation: "No candidate was ever elected ex-President by such a large majority."

After learning of his election, Wilson told the chairman of his campaign committee, "I owe you nothing. God ordained that I should be the next president of the United States. Neither you nor any other mortal could have prevented that."

Had the Republicans not divided their votes between Taft and Roosevelt, however, Wilson would have lost. His was the victory of a minority candidate over a divided opposition. Since all four candidates called themselves progressives, however, the president-elect expressed his hope "that the thoughtful progressive forces of the nation may now at last unite."

The election profoundly altered the character of the Republican party, as the defection of the Bull Moose Progressives had weakened its progressive wing. Upon returning to power in the 1920s, its platform would be more conservative in tone and temperament.

EUGENE DEBS   The real surprise of the 1912 election was the strong showing of the Socialist party candidate, Eugene V. Debs, running for the fourth time. The tall, blue-eyed idealist had devoted his career to fighting the "monstrous system of capitalism" on behalf of the working class, first as a labor union official, then as a socialist looking forward to the day when workers of all kinds would unite as a class to promote government ownership of railroads and the sharing of profits with workers.

Debs promoted a brand of socialism that was flexible rather than rigid, Christian rather than Marxist, democratic rather than totalitarian. He believed in political transformation, not violent revolution. As one of his supporters said, "That old man with the burning eyes actually believes that there can be such a thing as the brotherhood of man. And that's not the funniest part of it. As long as he's around I believe it myself."

Debs became the symbol of a diverse movement that united West Virginia coal miners, Oklahoma sharecroppers, Pacific Northwest lumberjacks, and immigrant workers in New York City sweatshops. One newspaper described "The Rising Tide of Socialism" in 1912, as some 1,150 Socialist party candidates won election to local and state offices across the nation, including eighteen mayoral seats.

To many voters, the Socialist party, whose 118,000 dues-paying members in 1912 were double the number from the year before, offered the only real alternative to a stalemated political system in which the two major parties had few real differences. A business executive in New York City explained that he had become a Socialist "because the old parties [Democrats and Republicans] were flimflamming us all the time." Fear of socialism was also widespread, however. Theodore Roosevelt warned that the rapid growth of the Socialist party was "far more ominous than any Populist or similar movement in the past."

In 1912, with very few campaign funds, Debs crisscrossed the nation giving fiery speeches. He dismissed Roosevelt as "a charlatan, mountebank [swindler], and fraud" whose progressive promises were nothing more than "the mouthings of a low and utterly unprincipled self-seeker and demagogue." Debs's untiring efforts brought him over 900,000 votes, an astonishing total for a Socialist, more than twice as many as he had received four years earlier.

A Burst of Reform Bills

On March 4, 1913, a huge crowd surrounded the Capitol in Washington, D.C., to watch Woodrow Wilson's inauguration. In his speech, the new president declared that it was not "a day of triumph" but "a day of dedication." Blessed with Democratic majorities in the House and Senate, Wilson promised to lower "the stiff and stupid" Republican tariff, create a new national banking system, strengthen anti-trust laws, and establish an administration "more concerned about human rights than about property rights."

Wilson worried about being compared to Roosevelt: "He appeals to their imagination; I do not. He is a real, vivid person. . . . I am a vague, conjectural [philosophical] personality, more made up of opinions and academic prepossessions than of human traits and red corpuscles."

Roosevelt had been a strong president by force of personality; Wilson became a strong president by force of conviction. "I have a strong instinct for leadership," he stressed, and he sincerely believed he was being directed by God.

Despite their differences, Wilson and Roosevelt, both progressive presidents, shared a belief that national problems demanded national solutions. Together they set in motion the modern presidency, expanding the scope of the executive branch at the expense of Congress. As Wilson had written in his doctoral dissertation, the U.S. president "is at liberty both in law and conscience to be as big as he can."

As a political scientist, Wilson was an expert at the processes of government. During his first two years, he pushed through Congress more new bills than any previous president. Like "most reformers," however, Wilson "had a fierce and unlovely side," according to the president of Harvard University. The president found it hard to understand—much less work with—people who disagreed with him.

His victory, coupled with majorities in the House and Senate, gave Democrats effective national power for the first time since the Civil War—and also gave southerners a significant national role for the first time since the war. Five of Wilson's ten cabinet members were born in the South.

COLONEL HOUSE Wilson's closest adviser, however, held no government position. "Colonel" Edward M. House of Texas was a skilled political operator, and he and Wilson developed the most famous political partnership of the twentieth century. The president described House as "my second personality. He is my independent self. His thoughts and mine are one."

Colonel House told Wilson that the theme of his presidency should be a form of Christian democracy. The "strong should help the weak, the fortunate should aid the unfortunate, and business should be conducted upon a higher and more humane plane." House helped steer Wilson's proposals through a Congress in which southerners, by virtue of their seniority, held the lion's share of committee chairmanships. As a result, much of the progressive legislation of the Wilson era would bear the names of southern Democrats.

THE TARIFF AND THE INCOME TAX Like Taft, Wilson pursued tariff reform, but with greater success. By 1913, the federal tariff included hundreds of taxes on different imported goods, from oil to nails. The president believed that U.S. corporations were misusing the tariff to keep out foreign competitors and to create monopolies that held consumer prices artificially high.

To lower tariff rates and thereby lower consumer prices, Wilson summoned Congress to a special session. The new tariff bill passed the House easily. The crunch came in the Senate, where swarms of lobbyists grew so thick, Wilson said, "a brick couldn't be thrown without hitting one of them." By publicly criticizing the "industrious and insidious" tariff lobby, Wilson finally convinced Congress to support his approach.

The Underwood-Simmons Tariff Act (1913) lowered tariff rates on almost 1,000 imported products. To compensate for the reduced tariff revenue, the bill created the first income tax allowed under the newly ratified Sixteenth Amendment: the initial tax rates were 1 percent on income more than $3,000 ($4,000 for married couples) up to a top rate of 7 percent on annual income of $500,000 or more. Most workers paid no income tax because they earned less than $3,000 a year.

THE FEDERAL RESERVE ACT No sooner did the new tariff pass than the administration proposed the first major banking reform since the Civil War. Ever since Andrew Jackson had killed the Second Bank of the United States in the 1830s, the nation had been without a central bank. Instead, the money supply was chaotically "managed" by thousands of local and state banks.

Such a decentralized system was unstable and inefficient. During financial panics, fearful depositors eager to withdraw their money would create "runs" that often led to the failure of smaller banks because they would run out of cash. The primary reason for a new central bank was to prevent such panics, which had occurred five times since 1873. President Wilson believed the banking system needed a central reserve agency that, in a crisis, could distribute emergency cash to stressed banks. Any new system, however, must be overseen by the government rather than by bankers themselves (the "money power"). He wanted a central bank that would benefit the entire economy, not just the large banks headquartered on Wall Street in New York City.

After much dickering, Congress passed the **Federal Reserve Act** on December 23, 1913. It created a national banking system with twelve regional districts, each of which had its own Federal Reserve Bank owned by member banks in the district. All nationally chartered banks had to be members of the Federal Reserve System. State-chartered banks—essentially unregulated—did not. (Indeed, two thirds of the nation's banks chose not to become members of the Federal Reserve System). The twelve regional Federal Reserve banks were supervised by a central board of directors in Washington, D.C.

The overarching purpose of the Federal Reserve System was to adjust the nation's currency supply to promote economic growth and ensure the stability and integrity of member banks. When banks ran short of cash, they could borrow from the Federal Reserve. Each of the new regional banks issued Federal Reserve notes (paper currency) to member banks in exchange for their loans. By doing so, the Fed, as the system came to be called, promoted economic growth and helped preserve the stability of banks during panics. The Federal Reserve Board required member banks to have a certain percentage of their total deposits in cash on hand (on reserve) at all times.

One conservative Republican called the Federal Reserve Act "populistic, socialistic, half-baked, destructive, and unworkable." The system soon proved its worth, however, and the criticism eased. The Federal Reserve Act was the most significant new program of Wilson's presidency.

ANTI-TRUST ACTIONS While promoting tariff and banking reforms, Woodrow Wilson made "trust-busting" the focus of his New Freedom program. Giant corporations had continued to grow despite the Sherman Anti-Trust Act

(1890) and the Bureau of Corporations, the federal watchdog agency created by Theodore Roosevelt. Wilson decided to make a strong **Federal Trade Commission (FTC)** the cornerstone of his anti-trust program. Created in 1914, the five-member FTC replaced Roosevelt's Bureau of Corporations and assumed powers to define "unfair trade practices" and issue "cease and desist" orders when it found evidence of such practices. Wilson explained that the purpose of the FTC was to "destroy monopoly and maintain competition as the only efficient instrument of business liberty." His goal was to prevent monopolistic trusts, not to regulate them.

Like Roosevelt, Wilson also supported efforts to strengthen and clarify the Sherman Anti-Trust Act. Henry D. Clayton, a Democrat from Alabama, drafted an anti-trust bill in 1914. The **Clayton Anti-Trust Act** declared that labor unions were not to be viewed as "monopolies in restraint of trade," as courts had treated them since 1890, and revived the Populists' demand that companies, such as railroads, be prohibited from charging different prices to different customers. It also prohibited corporate directors from serving on the boards of competing companies and further clarified the meaning of various "monopolistic" activities.

PROGRESSIVES' DISAPPOINTMENTS WITH WILSON

In November 1914, just two years after his election, President Wilson announced that he had accomplished the major goals of progressivism. Through his effective leadership, he had fulfilled his audacious promises to lower the tariff, create a national banking system, and strengthen the anti-trust laws. The New Freedom was now complete, he wrote, for he had no desire to continue increasing the power of the federal government. "The history of liberty," he stressed, "is the history of the limitation of governmental power, not the increase of it." As the *New York Times* acknowledged, "this Congress has a President on its back, driving it pitilessly. . . . Never were Congressmen driven so, not even in the days of [TR] and the 'big stick.'"

Wilson's victory declaration bewildered many progressives, especially those who had long advocated additional social-justice legislation that the president had earlier supported. Herbert Croly, editor of the *New Republic* magazine, wondered how the president could assert "that the fundamental wrongs of a modern society can be easily and quickly righted as a consequence of [passing] a few laws." Wilson's about-face, he concluded, "casts suspicion upon his own sincerity [as a progressive] or upon his grasp of the realities of modern social and industrial life."

PROGRESSIVISM FOR WHITES ONLY African Americans were also disappointed by Wilson's racism. Like many other progressives, Wilson showed little interest in addressing the daily discrimination and violence that African Americans and Mexican Americans faced. In fact, he shared many of the racist attitudes common at the time. As a student at Princeton, he had dismissed African Americans as "an ignorant and inferior race." He was the first president since the Civil War who openly endorsed discrimination against African Americans.

Wilson rarely consulted Black leaders and largely avoided associating with them in public or expressing support for them. That he refused to create a National Race Commission was a great disappointment to the Black community, as were his cabinet appointments of White southerners who were outspoken racists.

New Freedom, Old Rules Wilson and the First Lady ride in a carriage with African American drivers.

Josephus Daniels, a North Carolina newspaper editor who became Wilson's secretary of the navy, was a White supremacist who wrote that "the subjection of the negro, politically, and the separation of the negro, socially, are paramount to all other considerations in the South." For Daniels and other southern progressives, including Woodrow Wilson, "progress" was possible only if Blacks were "kept in their place."

Daniels and other cabinet members racially segregated the employees in their agencies; Secretary of State William Jennings Bryan supported such efforts to create racially separate offices, dining facilities, restrooms, and water fountains. President Wilson claimed that racial segregation "is not humiliating but a benefit." After visiting Washington, D.C., in 1913, Booker T. Washington reported that he had "never seen the colored people so discouraged and bitter." In November 1914, a delegation of African American leaders met with Wilson in the White House to ask how a "progressive" president could adopt such "regressive" racial policies.

Wilson responded that segregating the races in federal offices eliminated "the possibility of friction." William Trotter, a Harvard-educated African American newspaper editor who had helped found the National Association for the Advancement of Colored People (NAACP), scolded the president: "Have you a 'new freedom' for White Americans, and a new slavery for 'your Afro-American fellow citizens' [a phrase Wilson had used in a speech]? God forbid." A furious Wilson then told Trotter and the other visitors to leave, saying, "Your tone, sir, offends me."

THE VOTE FOR WOMEN Activists for women's suffrage were also disappointed in President Wilson. Despite having two daughters who were suffragists, he insisted that the issue of giving women voting rights should be left to the states rather than embodied in a constitutional amendment.

Wilson's lack of support led some leaders of the suffrage movement to revise their tactics. In 1910, Alice Paul, a New Jersey–born Quaker social worker who had earned a doctoral degree in political science from the University of Pennsylvania, urged activists to picket state legislatures, target, and "punish" politicians who failed to endorse suffrage, chain themselves to public buildings, incite police to arrest them, and undertake hunger strikes.

In 1913, Paul organized thousands of suffragists, women and men, who converged on Washington, D.C., to protest Woodrow Wilson's presidential inauguration. Spectators "taunted, spat upon, and roughed up" the marchers. The War Department dispatched a cavalry unit to restore order. Wilson ordered his driver to avoid the rally, for he could not stand hearing "women speak in public."

Ida Wells, the outspoken African American crusader against lynching, helped to integrate the suffrage movement at the Washington march. Alice Paul and other leaders had made the pragmatic decision to place African American marchers at the rear of the group so as not to risk alienating southern voters needed to ratify the constitutional amendment. "As far as I can see," Paul explained, "we must have a White procession, or a Negro procession, or no procession at all."

When Wells learned of the decision to hide African American women in the rear of the parade, she initially refused to participate. Yet as the march began, she emerged from the huge crowd of bystanders and took her place at the head of the Illinois delegation, walking between two White supporters.

Alice Paul In this photo, Paul sews a suffrage flag—orange and purple, with stars—that she and other suffragists often waved during strikes and protests.

A few days later, Paul and three other suffragists met with Wilson. They warned that if he continued to oppose a voting rights amendment, thousands of progressive women would campaign against his reelection. "If they did that," Wilson replied, "they would not be as intelligent as I believe they are."

Four years later, having formed the National Woman's Party, Paul urged suffragists to do something even more dramatic: picket the White House. Beginning on January 11, 1917, from 10 A.M. to 5 P.M., five days a week, amid rain, sleet, and snow, Paul and her followers (the "Silent Sentinels") took turns carrying signs reading: "MR. PRESIDENT! HOW LONG MUST WOMEN WAIT FOR LIBERTY?"

They picketed for six months, until Wilson ordered their arrest. Some sixty middle-class suffragists were jailed. At their trials, the women found their voices. Florence Bayard Hilles, daughter of a former secretary of state, expressed the outrage felt by all suffragists: "What a spectacle it must be to the thinking people of this country to see us urged to go to war for democracy in a foreign land and to see women thrown into prison who plead for the same cause at home."

Paul was sentenced to seven months in prison. She went on a hunger strike, leading prison officials to force-feed her raw eggs through a rubber tube inserted in her nose. She recalled, "It was shocking that a government of men could look with such extreme contempt on a movement that was asking nothing except such a simple little thing as the right to vote." Buffeted by negative press coverage and public criticism, Wilson pardoned Paul and the other activists.

PROGRESSIVE RESURGENCE By 1916, the need to create a winning political coalition in the upcoming presidential election—which required courting Republican as well as Democratic progressives—had pushed Wilson back onto the road of reform. The president scored progressive points when he nominated Bostonian Louis D. Brandeis, the "people's attorney," to the Supreme Court. Brandeis was not just a famed defender of unions against big businesses; he would also be the first Jewish member of the Supreme Court. Progressives viewed the nomination as a "landmark in the history of American democracy." Others disagreed. Former president Taft dismissed Brandeis as "a muckraker, an emotionalist for his own purposes, a socialist . . . who is utterly unscrupulous." The Senate, however, confirmed Brandeis's appointment. Justice Oliver Wendell Holmes Jr., the leading figure on the court, sent Brandeis a one-word telegram: "WELCOME."

Farm Legislation President Wilson also urged Congress to pass the first federal legislation directed at assisting farmers. Because farmers continued to suffer from a shortage of capital available for lending, Wilson supported a proposal to set up special rural banks to provide long-term farm loans. The Federal Farm Loan Act became law in 1916. Under the control of the Federal Farm Loan Board, twelve Federal Land banks offered loans to farmers for five to forty years at low interest rates.

At about the same time, a dream long advocated by Populists—federal loans to farmers on the security of their crops stored in warehouses—finally came to fruition when Congress passed the Warehouse Act of 1916. These crop-security loans were available to sharecroppers and tenant farmers as well as to farmers who owned the land they worked.

Farmers also benefited from the Smith-Lever Act of 1914, which provided programs to educate farmers about new machinery and new ideas related to agricultural efficiency, and the Smith-Hughes Act (1917), which funded agricultural and mechanical education in high schools. Farmers with newfangled automobiles had more than a passing interest as well in the Federal Highways Act of 1916, which helped finance new roads, especially in rural areas where farmers needed to get their harvests to market as quickly as possible.

Labor Legislation The progressive resurgence of 1916 broke the logjam on workplace reforms as well. One of the long-standing goals of progressive Democrats was a federal child-labor law. When Congress passed the Keating-Owen

Act in 1916, prohibiting employers from hiring workers under fourteen years of age, Wilson expressed doubts about its constitutionality but eventually signed it. The act was later ruled unconstitutional by the Supreme Court on the grounds that child labor was outside the bounds of Congress's authority to regulate interstate commerce. Effective action against child labor abuses had to wait until the 1930s.

Another landmark law was the eight-hour workday for railroad workers, a measure that the Supreme Court upheld. The Adamson Act of 1916 resulted from a threatened strike by railroad unions demanding an eight-hour day. The Adamson Act required time-and-a-half pay for overtime work beyond eight hours and appointed a commission to study working conditions in the railroad industry.

THE LIMITS OF PROGRESSIVISM

Progressivism reached its peak during Wilson's two terms as president. People grew optimistic about the economy and an improving society. After two decades of political upheaval and social reform, progressivism had shattered the traditional laissez-faire notion that government had no role in regulating the economy or in improving the quality of life.

The courage and compassion displayed by progressives demonstrated that people of good will could make a difference in improving social conditions for all. Progressivism awoke people to the evils and possibilities of modern urban-industrial life. Most important, progressives established the principle that governments—local, state, and federal—had a responsibility to ensure that Americans were protected from abuse by powerful businesses and corrupt politicians. As a Texas progressive said in 1910, most Americans now acknowledged that governments must protect "the weak against the encroachments of the strong."

Yet even though it had succeeded in accomplishing most of its goals, progressivism still fell short of its supporters' hopes and ideals. Child labor would not be addressed on a national level until the Great Depression in the 1930s. It would also take the shock of the Depression to gain passage of a national minimum wage and the creation of a government-administered pension program for retirees and disabled workers (Social Security).

Finally, progressivism faded because international crises pushed aside domestic concerns. By 1916, the optimism about social progress disappeared in the face of the distressing slaughter occurring in Europe in the Great War.

The twentieth century, which had dawned with such bright hopes for social progress, held in store episodes of unprecedented brutality that led people to question whether governments could be trusted to serve the public interest or that progress was even possible anymore.

CHAPTER REVIEW

SUMMARY

- **The Progressive Impulse**   Progressives believed that industrialization and urbanization were negatively affecting American life. They were mostly middle-class idealists who promoted reform and government regulation in order to ensure social justice. They also called for legislation to end child labor, promote safety in the workplace, ban the sale of alcoholic beverages, regulate or eliminate trusts and other monopolies, and grant *women's suffrage.*

- **The Varied Sources of Progressivism**   Progressivism grew out of many sources going back several decades. The depression in the 1890s led many urban middle-class people to pursue reforms to aid the working class and the poor. *Muckrakers*—investigative journalists who exposed significant political and corporate corruption—further fueled the desire of progressive reformers to address abuses of power in American society. Many religious reformers, such as those involved in the *social gospel* movement, had urged their fellow Christians to reject social Darwinism and do more to promote a better life for the urban poor. The settlement house movement spread through urban America as educated middle-class women formed community centers in poverty-stricken neighborhoods.

- **Progressives' Aims and Achievements**   To address corruption in politics, progressives implemented political reforms such as the direct primary; initiative, referendum, and recall at the state level; and the direct election of senators through the *Seventeenth Amendment* (1913). They also focused on incorporating new modes of efficiency into government administration through *Taylorism*. Many middle-class women reformers targeted what they saw as the social evils of alcohol consumption, prostitution, and poor living and working conditions. Social justice reformers also fought successfully for a progressive income tax with the passage of the *Sixteenth Amendment* (1913).

- **Progressivism under Roosevelt and Taft**   The administrations of Theodore Roosevelt and William H. Taft increased the power of the president and the federal government to regulate corporate power. Roosevelt promoted his progressive *Square Deal* program, which included the arbitration of the 1902 coal strike, and Pure Food and Drug Acts. After severe criticism of his White House meeting with Booker T. Washington, he made no further gestures toward racial harmony or equality. Choosing not to seek reelection in 1908, Roosevelt endorsed Taft, who easily won the election. But Taft's inability to bring about major tariff reduction with the Payne-Aldrich Tariff Act, among other failings, led Roosevelt to run again for president, promoting his New Nationalism vision. Unable to defeat Taft for the Republican nomination, Roosevelt formed a *Progressive party*. This split the Republican vote, allowing Democrat Woodrow Wilson, another progressive reformer, to win the office.

- **Woodrow Wilson's "Southern" Progressivism**   Wilson's *New Freedom* program promised less federal intervention in business and a return to traditional Democratic policies that supported low tariffs and anti-trust regulation. Wilson followed through on his promises with the Underwood-Simmons Tariff Act and the *Federal Reserve Act* (1913) and by beginning a rigorous anti-trust program with the passage of the *Clayton Anti-Trust Act* (1914) and the creation of the *Federal Trade Commission* (1914). To rally Republican progressives to his side for the 1916 reelection, he endorsed greater regulation of child labor and railroad corporations, particularly through the Adamson Act. He also helped ensure passage of two bills to allow farmers to get federal loans, a longtime goal of the Populist movement. Wilson, however, balked at giving women the vote and promoting racial equality.

CHRONOLOGY

1889	Hull House opens in Chicago
1901	William McKinley is assassinated; Theodore Roosevelt becomes president
	Governor Robert La Follette creates the "Wisconsin idea"
1902	Roosevelt attempts to arbitrate a coal strike
	Northern Securities Company breakup
1903	Congress passes the Elkins Act
1904	National Child Labor Committee formed
1906	Upton Sinclair's *The Jungle* is published
	Congress passes the Meat Inspection Act and the Pure Food and Drug Act
1909	William Howard Taft inaugurated
1911	Triangle Shirtwaist factory fire
	Frederick Taylor's *The Principles of Scientific Management* published
1912	Woodrow Wilson elected president
1913	5,000 suffragists protest Wilson's inauguration
	Sixteenth and Seventeenth Amendments ratified
	Underwood-Simmons Tariff and Federal Reserve Act passed
1914	Congress passes the Clayton Anti-Trust Act
1916	Congress passes the Adamson Act

KEY TERMS

muckrakers p. 962
social gospel p. 964
women's suffrage p. 967
Seventeenth Amendment (1913) p. 970
Taylorism p. 971
Sixteenth Amendment (1913) p. 979
Square Deal p. 980

Progressive party p. 991
New Freedom p. 995
Federal Reserve Act (1913) p. 999
Federal Trade Commission (FTC) (1914) p. 1000
Clayton Anti-Trust Act (1914) p. 1000

21 America and the Great War

1914–1920

Make American History In this U.S. Navy recruiting poster in New York City, a sailor encourages a young man to play a patriotic role in the Great War and gestures toward warships in the distance.

T hroughout the nineteenth century, the Atlantic Ocean had protected America from wars fought in Europe. During the early twentieth century, however, the nation's global isolation ended. Ever-expanding world trade entwined U.S. interests with the international economy. In addition, the development of steam-powered ships and submarines meant that foreign navies could directly threaten U.S. security.

At the same time, the election of Woodrow Wilson in 1912 brought to the White House a self-righteous moralist determined to impose his standards on what he saw as renegade nations. This made the startling outbreak of the "Great War" in Europe in 1914 a profound crisis for the United States. The first world war would become the defining event of the early twentieth century.

For almost three years, President Wilson maintained America's stance of "neutrality" toward the war while providing increasing amounts of food and supplies to Great Britain and France. In 1917, however, German submarine attacks on U.S. ships forced Congress to declare war.

Once America entered the war, almost 5 million men joined the military, including 400,000 African Americans and 150,000 Hispanics, mostly Mexicans and Puerto Ricans. A quarter of the draftees in 1918 were recent immigrants, including Germans who still spoke their native language. Immigrants continued to view military service as a pathway to citizenship and respect. Overall, U.S. soldiers spoke forty-nine languages. During one battle in France, German troops close enough to hear American soldiers talking to one another assumed they were Italians. They were instead Italian immigrants from Manhattan.

focus questions

1. What caused the outbreak of the Great War, and why did the United States join the conflict? What was distinctive about the fighting on the Western Front?

2. How did the Wilson administration mobilize the home front? How did these mobilization efforts affect American society?

3. What were the major events of the war after the United States entered the conflict? How did the American war effort contribute to the defeat of the Central Powers?

4. How did Wilson promote his plans for a peaceful world order as outlined in his Fourteen Points?

5. What were the consequences of the war at home and abroad?

The departure of so many men from civilian life opened new jobs for men and women. Recruited by businesses and lured by the prospect of higher-paying jobs, some 1.6 million—mostly rural African Americans—moved to cities outside the South to work in defense industries in what was called the Great Migration. Blacks were eager to escape the violent racism and rigid Jim Crow segregation they endured in the southern states.

The Great War was so vast and destructive that it transformed the course of modern history, redrawing the map of Europe and elevating the United States to great power status. It also introduced a brutal new era in which advances in military firepower, especially submarines, machine guns, massive cannons, tanks, and warplanes, greatly increased the number of killed and wounded.

AN UNEASY NEUTRALITY

Woodrow Wilson once declared that he had "a first-class mind." He was indeed intelligent, thoughtful, principled, and courageous, but Wilson had no experience or expertise in international relations. "It would be an irony of fate," he confessed, "if my administration had to deal chiefly with foreign affairs." Ironic or not, when the "dreadful conflict" erupted in Europe in 1914, he shifted his attention from progressive reforms to foreign affairs.

Lasting more than four years, from 1914 to 1918, the Great War (a future generation would call it the First World War) would involve more nations and cause greater destruction than any previous conflict: 20 million military and civilian deaths, and 21 million more wounded. The global conflict would topple monarchs, destroy empires, create new nations, and set in motion a series of events that would lead to an even costlier war in 1939.

THE GREAT WAR The Great War resulted from long-simmering national rivalries and ethnic and religious conflicts in Europe. Germany's determination to have its "place in the sun" at the expense of Great Britain was only one of several threats to peace and stability.

Great Britain, France, Germany, Austria-Hungary, and Russia had long been competing for global colonies and markets. Such competition triggered a furious arms race that led to the creation of competing military alliances: the **Triple Alliance** (called the Central Powers during the war)—consisting of Germany, Austria-Hungary, Bulgaria, and Turkey (the Ottoman Empire)—and the **Triple Entente** (later called the **Allied Powers**)—composed of France, Great Britain, Russia, and, later, Italy.

The members of these two alliances pledged to come to the defense of their partners should they be attacked, thus dividing Europe into two armed camps. In May 1914, President Woodrow Wilson had sent his closest adviser, Colonel Edward House, to Europe to take the pulse of the rival nations. "The situation is extraordinary," House reported to the president. It is jingoism [extreme nationalism] run stark mad. . . . There is too much hatred, too many jealousies."

At the core of the tensions was the "powder keg of Europe," the Austro-Hungarian (Habsburg) Empire, an unstable collection of eleven nationalities whose leaders were determined to suppress Serbia, their southern neighbor and long-standing enemy. Serbian nationalists (Pan-Slavists) had long hoped to create "Yugoslavia," a nation encompassing all ethnic Slavic peoples from throughout the Austro-Hungarian Empire. Russia, home to millions of Slavs, supported the Pan-Slavic movement.

A recklessly militaristic Germany, led by Kaiser (Emperor) Wilhelm II, had been a latecomer to industrialization and nationalism, having become a united nation only in 1871. Its leaders yearned to catch up with Great Britain and France.

Germany had created its own colonial empire in Africa and Asia while building a navy powerful enough to challenge British supremacy and an army capable of defeating its old enemies, the Russian Empire and France.

These factors—militarism, alliances, imperialism, and nationalism—created a combustible situation. All that was needed to ignite it was a spark.

The Balkan Peninsula, a volatile region of southeastern Europe on the southern border of the Austro-Hungarian Empire, provided that spark. There, for centuries, the Austrian and Russian monarchies had competed with the Turkish-led Ottoman Empire for control. Six years before, in 1908, Austria had annexed Bosnia from the Ottoman Empire, infuriating Serbian nationalists.

On June 28, 1914, the heir to the Austro-Hungarian throne, Archduke Franz Ferdinand, and his pregnant wife, Sophie, paraded through Sarajevo (the capital of Austrian-controlled Bosnia) in an open car. When the arch-duke's driver took a wrong turn and was forced to back the car down a crowded street, Gavrilo Princip, a half-mad nineteen-year-old Serbian nationalist, shot and killed the imperial couple.

To avenge the murders, Austria-Hungary, with Germany's approval, resolved to bring Serbia under its control—or destroy it. Kaiser Wilhelm was willing to risk a massive war in the belief that it was best to strike before the Russians could build up their military power.

With the "blank check" of German support, Austria-Hungary issued deliberately unreasonable ultimatums. Serbia agreed to most of them,

THE GREAT WAR IN EUROPE, 1914

Legend:
- Central Powers (Triple Alliance)
- Allied Powers (Triple Entente)
- Neutral countries

0   250   500 Miles
0   250   500 Kilometers

- How did the European system of military alliances spread conflict across Europe?
- How was the Great War different from previous wars?
- How did the war in Europe lead to ethnic tensions in the United States?

but Austria-Hungary mobilized for war anyway. A flurry of diplomacy failed to break the deadlock, and on July 28, Austria-Hungary declared war on Serbia.

Russia responded by mustering its army to defend Serbia, triggering reactions by other members of the rival European military alliances. "It will be a hopeless struggle," predicted the head of Austria's armed forces, "but it must be pursued, because so old a monarchy and so glorious an army cannot go down ingloriously."

German leaders had a different outlook. Expecting a limited war and quick victory, they declared war on Russia on August 1, 1914, and on France two days later. German troops then invaded neutral Belgium to get at France, murdering or deporting thousands of civilians in the process. The "rape of Belgium" brought Great Britain into the war on August 4 on the **Western Front**, the battle line in northern France and Belgium.

On the sprawling Eastern Front, Russian armies clashed with German and Austro-Hungarian forces as well as those of the Turkish (Ottoman) Empire. Within five weeks of the assassination in Sarajevo, a "great war" was threatening the stability of the entire world order.

AN INDUSTRIAL WAR The Great War was the first industrial war, fought between nations using new weapons that dramatically increased the war's scope and destruction. Machine guns, submarines, aerial bombing, poison gas, flame throwers, land mines, mortars, long-range artillery, and armored tanks changed the nature of warfare and produced appalling casualties and widespread destruction, a slaughter on a scale unimaginable to this day. Of the approximately 70 million soldiers and sailors who fought on both sides, more than half were killed, wounded, imprisoned, or unaccounted for. It was the mechanized weaponry that made possible such mass killing on an "industrial" scale—the same scale on which items were mass-produced in an industrial economy. Mass mobilization of economies and civilians was required to assemble such vast armies and achieve such unprecedented levels of industrial production.

TRENCH WARFARE In the early weeks of the war, German armies swept quickly across Belgium and northeastern France, only to bog down in nightmarish **trench warfare** that came to symbolize a brutal war of futility. Both sides dug in and fought a grinding war of attrition, gaining little territory in the process. The U.S. ambassador in London cabled President Wilson that the "horror" of the conflict "outruns all imagination."

During 1914–1915, the two sides built a sprawling network of zigzagging trenches from the coast of Belgium some 460 miles across northeastern France to the border of Switzerland. The trenches could measure up to forty feet deep and were frequently carpeted with mud and infested with rats and lice. "When all is said and done," grumbled an English infantry officer, "the war was mainly a matter of holes and ditches."

Soldiers often ate, slept, lived, and died without leaving their underground dugouts. A French soldier described life in the trenches as a "physical, almost animal" existence in which "the primitive instincts of the race have full sway: eating, drinking, sleeping, fighting—everything but loving."

The object of trench warfare was not so much to gain ground as it was to inflict death and destruction on the enemy until its resources were exhausted. In one assault against the Germans in Belgium, the British lost 13,000 men

Trench Warfare German soldiers prepare for attack.

in three hours—and gained only 100 yards. As the war ground on, both sides found themselves using up their available men, resources, courage, and cash. The Great War, mourned a German soldier, had become the "grave of nations."

Throughout 1914, both sides talked about the "glory" and "glamour" of war. Captain Julian Grenfell, a poet, was giddy after his first combat. "I adore war," he wrote his parents. "It is like a big picnic. . . . I've never been so well or so happy. The fighting-excitement vitalizes everything, every sight and action. One loves one's fellow man so much more when one is bent on killing him." Five months later, a piece of shrapnel hit Grenfell in the head; he died thirteen days later.

As the casualties soared, notions of romantic glory died with them. British poet Wilfred Owen called the idealization of combat "the old Lie." (He would be killed in action in 1918, just a week before the war ended.) The traditional glorification of military combat disintegrated as soldiers died like cattle in a slaughterhouse, killed often at such long distances that they never saw their opponents.

What the military leaders failed to envision was the scale of devastation that new weaponry enabled. Long-range artillery, machine guns, grenades, poison gas, tanks, warplanes, and more accurate and rapid-firing rifles created killing zones ("No Man's Land") more than a thousand yards deep, across which attacking soldiers were ordered to advance. From 1914 to 1918, the opposing armies in northeastern France attacked and counterattacked along the Western Front, gaining little ground while casualties soared into the millions. Time and again, inept generals sent their troops "over the top," climbing out of waterlogged trenches carrying sixty pounds of gear. They then had to slog across the cratered "No Man's Land." Their lives depended on navigating through webs of barbed wire, devastating fire from machine guns and high-powered rifles, and constant artillery shelling.

During the Battle of Verdun in northeastern France, which lasted from February to December 1916, some 32 *million* artillery shells streaked across the landscape—1,500 shells for every square yard of the battlefield. Such massive firepower produced horrifying casualties and widespread destruction. On August 22, 1914, for example, the French army lost 27,000 men. An average of 900 French and 1,300 German soldiers died *every* day on the Western Front.

The hellish nature of trench warfare posed extraordinary psychological challenges for the combatants on both sides. Hundreds of thousands of soldiers fell victim to "shell shock," now known as post–traumatic stress disorder. "It was a horrible thing," explained a nurse. "They became quite unconscious, with violent shivering and shaking."

In 1916, a British officer ordered his unit to "fix bayonets" and prepare to charge out of the trenches when he sounded his whistle. One of his men recalled standing "beside a young chap called Lucas, and he was a bundle of nerves. . . . He could hardly hold his rifle, never mind fix [attach] his bayonet. So I fixed mine and then I said, 'Here you are, Lucas,' and I fixed it for him." They then clambered out of the trench and began moving forward. "There were shell-holes everywhere . . . and there were lads falling all over the place" as German machine guns mowed them down. "Lucas went down."

An English private tried to explain in a letter to his mother what he had experienced during the Battle of the Somme: "We had strict orders not to take prisoners, no matter if wounded. My first job . . . was to empty my magazine on three Germans that came out of one of their deep dugouts, bleeding badly [in order] to put them out of their misery. They cried for mercy, but I had my orders. . . . It makes my head jump to think about it."

An American journalist reported that the massive casualties changed the way men viewed war. In earlier conflicts, soldiers were eager to fight and confident they would return unscathed. Now, the new recruits seemed to have "left hope behind" and were confident that they were "going to their death."

In 1917, George Barnes, a British official whose son had been killed in the war, went to speak at a military hospital in London, where injured soldiers were being fitted with artificial limbs. At the appointed hour, the men, in wheelchairs and on crutches, all with empty sleeves or pants, arrived to hear the speaker. Yet when Barnes rose to talk, he found himself speechless—literally. As the minutes passed, tears rolled down his cheeks. Finally, without having said a word, he simply sat down. What the mutilated soldiers heard was not a war-glorifying speech but the muted pity of grief. The war's mindless horrors had come home.

The unprecedented firepower deployed during the Great War ravaged the land, obliterating nine villages and turning farmland and forests into cratered wastelands. Some 162,000 French soldiers died at Verdun; the Germans lost 143,000. Amid the senseless killing in the muck and slime of the trenches, the innocence about the true nature of warfare died, too. Charles de Gaulle, a young French lieutenant who forty years later would become his nation's president, said the conflict had become a "war of extermination."

INITIAL AMERICAN REACTIONS   When war erupted in Europe, American officials were stunned. One of President Wilson's cabinet members remembered that "the end of things had come. I stopped in my tracks, dazed and horror-stricken." But shock mingled with relief that a wide ocean stood between America and the killing fields. President Wilson, an avowed pacifist, maintained that the United States "was too proud to fight" in Europe's war, "with which we have nothing to do, whose causes cannot touch us." He repeatedly urged Americans to remain "neutral in thought as well as in action." Privately, however, he sought to ensure that the United States could provide Great Britain and France as much financial assistance and supplies as possible.

That most Americans wanted the nation to stay out of the fighting did not keep them from choosing sides. More than a third of the nation's citizens were first- or second-generation immigrants still loyal to their homelands. Nine million German-born Americans lived in the United States in 1914, and there were more than 500 German-language newspapers across the country. Most of the 4.5 million Irish-born Americans detested England, which had ruled Ireland for centuries. For the most part, these groups supported the Central Powers, while others, largely of British origin, supported the Allied Powers.

One of the few issues that Woodrow Wilson and former president Theodore Roosevelt agreed on was the need to stamp out what they called "Hyphenism" and replace it with "100 Percent Americanism." The one way to destroy America, Roosevelt charged, would be to "permit it to become a tangle of squabbling nationalities, an intricate knot of German-Americans, Irish-Americans, English-Americans, French-Americans, Scandinavian-Americans, or Italian-Americans, each preserving its separate nationality, each at heart feeling more sympathy with Europeans of that nationality, than with the other citizens of the American Republic." There is no such thing as "a hyphenated American," he argued, "who is a good American."

Supporting the Allies By the spring of 1915, the Allied Powers' need for food, supplies, and weapons had generated an economic windfall for U.S. businesses, bankers, and farmers. Exports to France and Great Britain quadrupled from 1914 to 1916, and America's manufacturing capacity soon surpassed that of Great Britain, the world's leader. Farm income soared 25 percent. The Allies, especially Britain and France, needed loans from U.S. banks and "credits" from the U.S. government, which would allow them to pay for their purchases later.

Early in the war, Secretary of State William Jennings Bryan, a strict pacifist, took advantage of President Wilson's absence from Washington following the death of the First Lady to tell J. Pierpont Morgan, the world's richest banker, that loans to any nations at war were "inconsistent with the true spirit of neutrality."

Upon his return to the White House, an angry Wilson reversed Bryan's policy by removing all restrictions on loans to the warring nations. The president was determined that America avoid the war's horrors while reaping its economic benefits.

Banks and other investors would eventually send more than $2 billion to the Allies before the United States entered the fighting, while offering only $27 million to Germany. What Bryan feared, and what Wilson did not fully realize, was that the more Britain and France borrowed and purchased, the harder it became for America to remain neutral. As Senator Robert La Follette, a progressive Republican from Wisconsin, asked in 1915, "How long can we maintain a semblance of real neutrality while we are supplying the Allies with the munitions of war and money to prosecute the war?"

Despite the disproportionate financial assistance provided to the Allies, the Wilson administration maintained its stance of neutrality for thirty months.

"The Sandwich Man" To illustrate America's hypocritical brand of neutrality, this political cartoon shows Uncle Sam wearing a sandwich board that advertises the nation's conflicting desires to remain out of the war while profiting from it.

In particular, Wilson tried valiantly to defend the age-old principle of "freedom of the seas," arguing that the ships of neutral nations had the right to trade with warring nations without fear of being attacked.

On August 6, 1914, Bryan urged the warring countries to respect the rights of neutral nations to ship goods across the Atlantic. The Central Powers agreed, but the British refused. In November, the British ordered the ships of neutral nations to submit to searches to discover if cargoes were bound for Germany. A few months later, the British announced that they would seize any ships carrying goods bound to Germany.

AMERICAN VOLUNTEERS The United States provided more than material aid to the Allies. Thousands of men and women volunteered in the British, Canadian, and French militaries, the French Foreign Legion, the American Ambulance Field Corps, military hospitals, and various refugee relief organizations. In October 1914, the first American Red Cross ship arrived in France, carrying 170 doctors and nurses.

Some volunteers sought adventure or glory. Others were eager to fight German imperialism, and still others sought to repay France for its support for America during the Revolutionary War. Almost 300 volunteers served as pilots in an all-American aviation unit in France called the Lafayette Escadrille. Some 4,000 Native Americans, still not granted citizenship in the United States, volunteered in the Canadian Expeditionary Force. Theodore Roosevelt's son Kermit used his father's help to gain a commission as a captain in the British Expeditionary Force in France. By 1916, some 45,000 Americans were serving as volunteers in Allied hospitals in France and England, or as soldiers or pilots on the Western Front.

Poet Alan Seeger, a Harvard graduate living in Paris when the war started, volunteered in the French Foreign Legion. He did so for "a chance to live life free from stain and that rare privilege of dying well." After months of living and fighting in disgusting trenches, however, Seeger saw little glory in the conflict. As a "poor common soldier," he wrote, his role was "simply to dig himself a hole in the ground and to keep hidden in it as tightly as possible. Continually under the fire of the opposing [artillery] batteries, he is yet never allowed to get a glimpse of the enemy. Exposed to all the dangers of war, but with none of its enthusiasms or splendid *élan* [spirit], he is condemned to sit like an animal in its burrow and hear the shells whistle over his head and take their little daily toll from his comrades."

While awaiting combat, Seeger wrote his famous poem "I Have a Rendezvous with Death," with its oft-quoted lines: "I have a rendezvous with death / On some scarred slope or battered hill / When Spring comes round again this year / And the first meadow-flowers appear." On July 4, 1916, Seeger died well, as the romantic he was, "smiling and without regret," at the Battle of the Somme in northern France.

NEUTRAL RIGHTS AND SUBMARINE ATTACKS With its warships bottled up by a British blockade of its ports, the German government announced a "war zone" around the British Isles. All ships in those waters would be attacked by submarines, the Germans warned, and "it may not always be possible to save crews and passengers."

The German use of submarines, or **U-boats** (*Unterseeboote* in German), violated the long-established wartime custom of stopping an enemy vessel and allowing the passengers and crew to board lifeboats before sinking it. During 1915, German U-boats sank 227 British ships in the Atlantic Ocean and North Sea.

President Wilson warned German leaders that he would hold them to "strict accountability" for the loss of any American lives and property. Then, on May 7, 1915, a German submarine off the Irish coast fired a single torpedo that sank the British passenger ship *Lusitania*, the largest, fastest, and most luxurious ocean liner in the world. Of the 1,198 persons on board who died, 128 were Americans. Fifty of the dead were infants.

The sinking of the *Lusitania*, asserted Theodore Roosevelt, called for an immediate declaration of war. Wilson, however, urged patience: "There is such a thing as a man being too proud to fight. There is such a thing as a nation being so right that it does not need to convince others by force that it is right."

Wilson's earlier threat of "strict accountability" now required a tough response. On May 13, Secretary of State Bryan demanded that the Germans stop unrestricted submarine warfare, apologize, and pay the families of those

Remembering the *Lusitania* The sinking of the *Lusitania* in 1915 sparked the widespread anger expressed in propaganda posters such as this, urging Americans to join the Allied forces.

killed on the *Lusitania*. The Germans countered that the ship was armed (which was false) and secretly carried thousands of cases of rifles and ammunition (which was true); they further declared it was transporting hundreds of Canadian soldiers (which was true). On June 9, Wilson dismissed the German claims and reiterated that the United States was "contending for nothing less high and sacred than the rights of humanity." Bryan resigned as secretary of state in protest of Wilson's pro-British stance despite his claim of neutrality.

Stunned by the global outcry over the *Lusitania* sinking, the German government told its U-boat captains to stop attacking passenger vessels. Despite the order, however, a German submarine sank the British liner *Arabic*, and two Americans on board were killed. The Germans paid a cash penalty to the families of the deceased and issued what came to be called the *Arabic* Pledge on September 1, 1915: "Liners will not be sunk by our submarines without warning and without safety of the lives of non-combatants, provided that the liners do not try to escape or offer resistance."

In early 1916, Wilson again sent Colonel Edward House to London, Paris, and Berlin in hopes of stimulating peace talks, but the mission failed. So the killing continued. On March 24, 1916, a U-boat sank the French passenger ferry *Sussex*, killing eighty passengers and injuring two Americans. After Wilson threatened to end relations with Germany, its leaders again promised not to sink merchant and passenger ships. The *Sussex* Pledge implied the virtual abandonment of submarine warfare. Colonel House noted in his diary that Americans were "now beginning to realize that we are on the brink of war and what war means."

PREPARING FOR WAR The expanding scope of the Great War and the attacks by German submarines generated a growing demand in the United States for a stronger army and navy. On December 1, 1914, champions of the "preparedness" movement, including Theodore Roosevelt, had organized the National Security League to promote increased military spending. After the *Lusitania* sinking, Wilson asked the War and Navy Departments to develop plans for a $1 billion military expansion.

Many Americans—pacifists, progressives, and midwestern Republicans—opposed the preparedness effort, seeing it as simply a propaganda campaign to benefit businesses that made weapons and other military equipment. Some of them charged that Wilson was secretly plotting to get the nation into the war. A popular song in 1916 reflected such views: "I Didn't Raise My Boy to Be a Soldier."

Despite substantial opposition among Republicans, Congress in 1916 passed the National Defense Act, which provided for the expansion of the U.S.

Army from 90,000 to 223,000 men over the next five years. While some complained that Wilson wanted to "drag this nation into war," the president told an aide that he was determined not to "be rushed into war, no matter if every damned congressman and senator stands up on his hind legs and proclaims me a coward."

Opponents of preparedness insisted that the expense of military expansion should rest upon the wealthy munitions makers who were profiting from trade with the Allies. Congress decided to use the income tax as its weapon to deter war-related profiteering. The Revenue Act of 1916 doubled the income tax rate from 1 to 2 percent, created a 12.5 percent tax on munitions makers, and added a new tax on "excessive" corporate profits. The new taxes were the culmination of the progressive legislation that Wilson had approved to strengthen his chances in the upcoming presidential election. Fearing that Theodore Roosevelt would be the Republican presidential candidate, Colonel House believed that the "Democratic Party must change its historic character and become the progressive party in the future."

THE 1916 ELECTION As the 1916 election approached, Theodore Roosevelt hoped to become the Republican nominee. But his decision in 1912

Peace with Honor A car decked out in pro-Wilson advertisements proclaims the president's promise of peace, prosperity, and preparedness. Wilson's neutrality policies proved popular in the 1916 campaign.

to run as a third-party candidate had alienated many powerful members of his party, and his eagerness to enter the war scared many voters. So instead, the Republicans nominated Supreme Court Justice Charles Evans Hughes, a progressive who had served as governor of New York from 1907 to 1910.

The Democrats, staying with Wilson, adopted a platform centered on social-welfare legislation and prudent military preparedness. The peace theme, refined in the slogan "He kept us out of war," became the campaign's rallying cry, although the president acknowledged that the nation could no longer refuse to play the "great part in the world which was providentially cut out for her. . . . We have got to serve the world." Colonel House was more blunt. He told Secretary of State Robert Lansing that they "could not permit the Allies to go down in defeat, for if they did, we would follow."

The two candidates were remarkably similar. Both Wilson and Hughes were sons of preachers; both were attorneys and former professors; both had been progressive governors; both were known for their integrity. Hughes called for higher tariffs, attacked Wilson for being hostile to Big Business, and implied that Wilson was not neutral enough in responding to the war. Roosevelt called the bearded Hughes a "whiskered Wilson." Wilson, however, proved to be the better campaigner—barely.

By midnight on election night, Wilson went to bed assuming that he had lost. Roosevelt was so sure Hughes had won that he sent him a congratulatory telegram. At 4 A.M., however, the results from California showed that Wilson had eked out a victory in that state by only 4,000 votes, and thus had become the first Democrat to win a second consecutive term since Andrew Jackson in 1832. His pledge of "peace, prosperity, and progressivism" won him the western states, Ohio, and the solidly Democratic South.

AMERICA GOES TO WAR After his close reelection, Woodrow Wilson again urged the warring nations in Europe to negotiate a "peace without victory," but to no avail. A French official spoke for many European leaders when he said that Wilson's notion of peace without victory was like "bread without yeast."

On January 31, 1917, German military leaders ordered that unrestricted submarine warfare in the Atlantic be renewed on February 1, for they had come to believe that victory depended on their cutting off the trans-Atlantic supply lines from America and Canada to the European allies. Now, all American vessels headed for Britain, France, or Italy could be sunk without warning. "This was practically ordering the United States off the Atlantic," said William McAdoo, Wilson's secretary of the Treasury.

Germany's decision, Colonel House wrote in his journal, left Wilson "sad and depressed," for the president knew it meant war. For their part, the German leaders underestimated the American reaction. The United States, the German military newspaper proclaimed, "not only has no army, it has no artillery, no means of transportation, no airplanes, and lacks all other instruments of modern warfare." When his advisers warned that German submarines might cause the United States to enter the war, Kaiser Wilhelm scoffed, "I don't care."

THE ZIMMERMANN TELEGRAM On February 3, President Wilson informed Congress that he had formally ended diplomatic relations with the German government to preserve the "dignity and honor of the United States." Three weeks later, on February 25, he learned that the British had intercepted a coded telegram from Germany's foreign minister, Arthur Zimmermann, to the German ambassador in Mexico City. The telegram said that Germany would begin "unrestricted submarine warfare on February 1." If war erupted with the United States, the ambassador was instructed to offer the Mexican government an alliance: If the United States entered the war in Europe, Mexican forces would invade the United States. In exchange, Germany would return to Mexico its "lost territory in Texas, New Mexico, and Arizona."

On March 1, newspapers broke the news of the notorious **Zimmermann telegram**. The Mexican government immediately disavowed any support for the Germans, but the German attempt to recruit Mexico as an ally so infuriated Americans that many called for war. A New York newspaper said the Zimmermann telegram was "final proof that the German government has gone stark mad."

AMERICA ENTERS THE WAR In March 1917, German submarines torpedoed five U.S. ships in the North Atlantic. For Wilson, this was the last straw. On April 2, he called on Congress to declare war against the German Empire and its allies.

In one of his greatest speeches, Wilson acknowledged that it was "a fearful thing to lead this great peaceful people into war," but "the world must be made safe for democracy." He warned that winning the war would require mobilizing "all the material resources of the country" and millions of military recruits to bolster the armed forces. The nation's motives, he insisted, were pure. The United States was entering the war not so much to defend its honor as to lead a "great crusade" for the "ultimate peace of the world and for the liberation of its peoples."

Congress erupted with approval. Wilson told an aide how surreal it was to watch the legislators stand and applaud the decision for war. "My message today was a message of death for our young men. How strange it seems to

Wake Up America! Political cartoonist James Montgomery Flagg created this poster featuring actress Mary Arthur in response to the United States entering the Great War.

applaud that." He then sat down and sobbed. Two days later, the Senate passed the war resolution by a vote of 82 to 6. The House followed, 373 to 50, and Wilson signed the measure on April 6.

Opposing the war resolution were thirty-two Republicans, sixteen Democrats, one Socialist, and one independent. Among the "no" voters was Republican Jeannette Rankin of Montana, the first woman elected to the House of Representatives. "Peace is a woman's job," she explained. "You can no more win a war than you can win an earthquake. I want to stand by my country, but I cannot vote for war."

Like Rankin, Wilson had doubts about joining the war. The president feared—accurately, as it turned out—that waging war and stamping out dissent would destroy the ideals and momentum of progressivism: "Every reform we have made will be lost if we go into this war." Yet in the end, he saw no choice. America's long embrace of isolationism was over. The nation had reached a turning point in its relations with the world that would test the president's political and diplomatic skills—and his stamina.

MOBILIZING FOR WAR

In April 1917, the U.S. Army remained small, untested, and poorly armed. With just 127,000 men, it was ranked as only the seventeenth-largest army in the world. Now the Wilson administration needed to recruit, equip, and train an army of millions and transport them across an ocean infested with German submarines. On May 18, 1917, Congress passed the Selective Service Act, which instructed local boards to register men ages twenty-one to thirty for the draft (later expanded to eighteen to forty-five years old). Community draft boards were supposed to be impartial; many were not. An Atlanta board exempted 526 out of 815 White men but only 6 out of 202 Black men.

Many men did not wait to be drafted; they rushed to enlist. Twenty percent of those who joined the army were immigrants. Some 31 percent of them were illiterate. The challenge of training recruits who spoke different languages led the army to create the Foreign-Speaking Soldier Subsection to bridge the communication gap. An army officer said the foreign-born recruits "obeyed orders better and were less complaining than the native-born Americans."

MANAGING THE HOME FRONT

Mobilizing the nation for war led to an unprecedented expansion of federal authority. Congress passed the Lever Act, which gave the president authority to manage the nation's supplies of food and fuels (oil and gasoline), and to take over factories, railroads, mines, warehouses, and telephone and telegraph systems. Federal agencies could also set prices for wheat and coal.

Soon after the United States declared war, President Wilson called for complete economic mobilization on the home front and created new federal agencies to coordinate the effort. The War Industries Board (WIB) soon became the most important of all the federal mobilization agencies. Bernard Baruch, a brilliant financier, headed the WIB, which had unprecedented authority to ration raw materials, construct factories, and set prices.

WARTIME PROPAGANDA On April 14, 1917, eight days after the declaration of war, President Wilson established the Committee on Public Information (CPI) to help ensure public support for the war effort. Its executive director, George Creel, organized a public relations campaign to explain the Allies' war aims to the people and,

FOOD WILL WIN THE WAR
You came here seeking Freedom
You must now help to preserve it
WHEAT is needed for the allies
Waste nothing
UNITED STATES FOOD ADMINISTRATION

The Immigrant Effort This Food Administration poster emphasizes that "wheat is ... for the allies," urging consumers to conserve more so that grains could be shipped to the Allied nations.

above all, to the enemy, where it might help sap their morale. Creel organized the CPI into four divisions. The Speaking Division recruited 75,000 public lecturers known as "Four-Minute Men" for their ability to compress the war's objectives into a few words. They gave some 7.5 million speeches to civic groups, churches, synagogues, fraternal lodges, union halls, colleges, and schools. The Film Division produced short films with titles such as *Pershing's Crusaders* and *America's Answer*, all celebrating the U.S. war effort.

THE FOOD ADMINISTRATION   Wilson appointed business magnate Herbert Hoover to lead the new Food Administration, whose slogan was "Food will win the war." The bureau's purpose was to increase agricultural production while reducing civilian food consumption, because Great Britain and France needed massive amounts of corn and wheat. Hoover organized a huge group of volunteers who fanned out across the country to urge families and restaurants to participate in "Wheatless" Mondays, "Meatless" Tuesdays, and "Porkless" Thursdays and Saturdays. In crises such as war, Hoover declared, democracies must show "a willingness to yield to dictatorship."

FINANCING THE WAR   The Great War would cost the U.S. government $30 billion, which was more than thirty times the federal budget in 1917. In addition to raising taxes to finance war efforts, the Wilson administration launched a nationwide campaign to sell "liberty bonds," government certificates that guaranteed the purchaser a fixed rate of return. The government recruited dozens of celebrities to promote bond purchases, arguing that a liberty bond was both patriotic and a smart investment. Even the Boy Scouts and Girl Scouts sold bonds, using advertising posters that said, "Every Scout to Save a Soldier." By war's end, the government had sold more than $20 billion in bonds, most of which were purchased by banks and investment houses rather than by individuals.

A NEW LABOR FORCE   Removing millions of men from the workforce to serve in the armed forces created an acute labor shortage across the United States during 1917. It was made worse because the European war shut off the flow of immigration to the United States. To address the shortfall of workers, the government and businesses encouraged women to take jobs that had been held mostly by men. One government poster shouted: "Women! Help America's Sons Win the War: Learn to Make Munitions." Another said, "For Every Fighter, a Woman Worker."

Initially, most women supported the war effort in traditional ways. They helped organize fundraising drives, donated canned food and war-related materials, volunteered for the Red Cross, and joined the army nurse corps.

At the Munitions Factory The government urged women to play crucial roles in the war effort, from building airplanes to cooking for soldiers overseas. Here, women use welding torches to make shells.

As the scope of the war widened, however, women were recruited to work on farms, loading docks, and railway crews, as well as in the armaments industry, machine shops, steel and lumber mills, and chemical plants. "At last, after centuries of disabilities and discrimination," noted a speaker at a Women's Trade Union League meeting in 1917, "women are coming into the labor [force] and festival of life on equal terms with men."

The changes turned out to be limited and brief, however. About a million women participated in "war work," but most were young, single, and already working outside the home. Most returned to their previous jobs once the war ended. In fact, after the war, male-dominated unions encouraged women to go back to domestic roles. The Central Federated Union of New York insisted that "the same patriotism which induced women to enter industry during the war should induce them to vacate their positions after the war."

MINORITIES AND THE WAR The Great War also generated dramatic changes for many minority groups. The need for millions of soldiers and sailors diversified the armed forces. The 23,000 soldiers in the 77th "Melting Pot" Division, for example, included New York City draftees representing fifty nationalities and forty-three languages, most of them immigrants: Jews, Chinese, Poles, Italians, Irish, Greeks, Armenians, Russians, Scandinavians, Mexicans, Puerto Ricans, and Germans. The division's insignia patch featured the image of the Statue of Liberty.

Once Congress declared war, African American leader W. E. B. Du Bois urged Blacks to join the war effort: "Let us, while this war lasts, forget our special grievances and close our ranks shoulder to shoulder with our white fellow citizens and the allied nations that are fighting for democracy."

So many African Americans heeded the call that the War Department had to stop accepting Black volunteers because the quotas were filled. Eventually, more than 400,000 Blacks joined the army or navy (they were not allowed in the marines), where they were required to serve in racially segregated units commanded by White officers.

Puerto Ricans also served in the armed forces during the Great War. Just a month before the United States entered the conflict, Congress passed a law granting U.S. citizenship to the inhabitants of Puerto Rico, an island territory a thousand miles southeast of Florida that had been seized from Spain at the end of the nineteenth century.

The Jones Act created a bill of rights for Puerto Rico, separated its government into executive, legislative, and judicial branches, and made English its

Segregation in the Military Most African American recruits served in technical and supply units because Whites believed them unfit for combat, despite Black military contributions since the Revolution. Here, combat personnel of the 92nd Infantry Division (one of the few "colored" divisions sent overseas) march in Verdun, France.

official language. Yet it did not allow Puerto Ricans to vote in U.S. elections or give them representation in Congress. The Jones Act did, however, allow Puerto Rican men to be drafted into the military. Some 20,000 eventually served during the Great War. They were attached to either Black or White units, depending on their skin color.

Many Mexican Americans hoped military service would improve their status in their adopted country. Between 1917 and 1920, more than 100,000 job-seeking Mexicans crossed the border into the United States. Some joined the military. David Barkley Hernandez had to drop his last name when he enlisted in San Antonio, Texas, because the local draft board was not accepting Mexicans. In 1918, just two days before the war ended, he died in France while returning from a dangerous mission behind German lines. Hernandez became the first person of Mexican descent in the U.S. Army to win the Congressional Medal of Honor.

THE GREAT MIGRATION The most significant development in African American life during the early twentieth century was the **Great Migration** northward from the South. The mass movement accelerated in 1915–1916, when rapidly expanding war industries needed new workers. It continued throughout the twenties, as almost a million African Americans, mostly sharecroppers, boarded trains bound for what they called the "promised land" up north.

Many landed in large cities—New York City, Chicago, Detroit, Cleveland, Washington, D.C., Philadelphia, and others. In 1900, only 740,000 African Americans lived outside the South, just 8 percent of the nation's Black population. By 1970, more than 10.6 million African Americans lived outside the South, 47 percent of the nation's total.

They were lured by what writer Richard Wright called the "warmth of other suns": better living conditions and better-paying jobs. In the North, for the most part, African Americans were able to speak more freely and were treated better than in the South, and educational opportunities for children were much better. Collectively, Blacks gained more political leverage by settling in populous states like New York, Pennsylvania, Ohio, and Illinois, with their larger numbers of electoral votes. The political effects of the Great Migration were evident in 1928 when a Chicago Republican, Oscar De Priest, became the first Black elected to Congress since Reconstruction and the first ever from a northern district.

The difficult decision to leave their native South ended one set of troubles for African Americans but created others. "Never in history," said Richard Wright, "has a more utterly unprepared folk wanted to go to the city." They were strangers in a strange land, and in densely populated northern cities, Blacks who moved into established neighborhoods sometimes clashed with local ethnic groups, especially Irish and Italians who feared that the newcomers would take their jobs. Many southern Blacks, ignorant of city ways, were swindled by White landlords, realtors, and bankers; they were often forced into substandard and segregated housing and received lower wages than Whites.

Northern discrimination, however, still paled beside the injustices of the segregated South. Poet Langston Hughes spoke for many Blacks when he wrote that he was "fed up / With Jim Crow laws, / People who are cruel / And afraid, / Who lynch and run, / Who are scared of me / And me of them."

Over time, the transplanted African Americans built new lives, new churches, new communities, new families, and new cultural activities.

A LOSS OF CIVIL LIBERTIES Once the United States entered the war, many Americans equated anything German with disloyalty. Towns, streets, businesses, and even families with German names were renamed. Berlin, Iowa, became Lincoln, and East Germantown, Indiana, became Pershing, in honor of the military leader. Many quit drinking beer because German Americans owned most of the breweries. Orchestras refused to perform music by Bach and Beethoven, schools canceled German-language classes, hyperpatriots burned German books, and grocers renamed *sauerkraut* "liberty cabbage." Mobs killed several German Americans accused of spying. Dozens of others were tarred and feathered.

President Wilson had predicted as much. "Once [we] lead this people into war," he said, "they'll forget there ever was such a thing as tolerance." What Wilson did not say was that he would lead the effort to suppress civil liberties, for, as he claimed, subversive forces in a nation at war must be "crushed out." The Wilson administration recruited 250,000 informers to form the American Protective League to identify people suspected of treason.

In passing the Espionage and Sedition Acts, Congress gave the Wilson administration extraordinary authority to punish critics of the war effort. The Espionage Act of 1917 stipulated that anyone who helped the enemy, encouraged insubordination, disloyalty, or refusal of duty in the armed services, or interfered with the war effort in other ways, could be imprisoned for up to twenty years.

A year later, Congress amended the Espionage Act with the Sedition Act. It outlawed saying, writing, or printing anything "disloyal, profane, scurrilous, or abusive" about the American form of government, the Constitution, or the army and navy. The effort to squelch free speech provoked sharp criticism. Senator George Norris, a progressive Republican from Nebraska, wondered why the nation should fight a war for democracy abroad if Congress were going to interfere "with the very fundamental principles of human liberty and human freedom on which our great Commonwealth is founded."

The Supreme Court upheld the constitutionality of the Espionage and Sedition Acts in two rulings issued after the war ended. *Schenck v. United States* (1919) reaffirmed the conviction of Charles T. Schenck, head of the Socialist party, for circulating anti-war leaflets among members of the armed forces. Justice Oliver Wendell Holmes wrote the unanimous opinion that freedom of speech did not apply to words that represented "a clear and present danger to the safety of the country." In *Abrams v. United States* (1919), the Court upheld the conviction of a man who had distributed pamphlets opposing military intervention in Russia to thwart the Communist revolution.

During the U.S. involvement in the war, courts convicted 1,055 people

Keep Out Of It In this 1918 war poster, the kaiser—with his famous moustache and spiked German helmet—is characterized as a spider, spinning an invisible web to catch the stray words of Allied civilians.

under the Espionage Act, not one of whom was a spy. Most were simply critics of the war. On June 16, 1918, Socialist leader Eugene V. Debs, the sixty-three-year-old pacifist who had run against Wilson in 1912, gave a speech in Canton, Ohio, in which he stressed that the war was inherently unfair. It was, he said, "the working class who fight all the battles, the working class who make the supreme sacrifices, the working class who freely shed their blood and furnish the corpses, have never yet had a voice in either declaring war or making peace. It is the ruling class that invariably does both. They alone declare war and they alone make peace."

Government agents recorded the speech, and two weeks later they arrested Debs. After being convicted of violating the Espionage Act for expressing sympathy for men jailed for encouraging others to avoid the draft, he was sentenced to ten years in prison. He told the court he was exercising his rights of free speech under the First Amendment and would always criticize wars imposed by the "master" class: "While there is a lower class, I am in it. While there is a criminal element, I am of it. While there is a soul in prison, I am not free." In 1919, the Supreme Court unanimously upheld Debs's conviction. In 1920, the Socialist party nominated the imprisoned Debs for the fifth time as its presidential candidate. He would receive more than 900,000 votes.

THE "POISON OF DISLOYALTY" President Wilson was equally resolute in prosecuting immigrants who supported America's enemies. From colonial days, Americans had always recruited, yet feared, immigrants. Now, fear took over. As Wilson warned, "there are citizens of the United States, I blush to admit, born under other flags . . . who have poured the poison of disloyalty into the very arteries of our national life. . . . Such creatures of passion, disloyalty, and anarchy must be crushed out."

Others were determined to shut off immigration altogether, especially from southern and eastern Europe. In 1916, Madison Grant, a New York attorney,

The Immigration Act of 1917 This law placed new restrictions on immigration, including the requirement of a literacy test for immigrants over sixteen years old to demonstrate basic reading ability.

published a hugely influential book, *The Passing of the Great Race*. Grant was a fervent eugenicist (a believer in the pseudoscience of racial breeding). During the early twentieth century, the popularity of eugenics prompted thirty states to pass laws requiring compulsory sterilization of the insane, the "feebleminded," the "dependent," and the "diseased."

Grant, like his friend Theodore Roosevelt, claimed that racial purity was the foundation of great nations. Yet America's once-dominant Nordic stock, he warned in *The Passing of the Great Race*, was committing "race suicide" by interbreeding with African Americans and an "increasing number of the weak, the broken, and the mentally crippled of all the races drawn from the lower stratum of the Mediterranean basin and the Balkans, together with hordes of the wretched, submerged populations of the Polish

Ghettos." He railed against "the maudlin sentimentalism" that welcomed these "worthless race types" from Europe, for they were "sweeping the nation toward a racial abyss."

Such notions led Congress in 1917 to revive the idea of requiring immigrants to pass a literacy test. Three times before, Congress had passed similar legislation, only to see Presidents Cleveland, Taft, and Wilson (1915) veto it. Now, in response to theories of racial superiority and pleas from labor union leaders concerned about an influx of unskilled "aliens," overwhelming majorities in both the House and Senate overrode Wilson's veto of the first widely restrictive immigration law. (Wilson had argued that literacy had nothing to do with a person's character.)

The Immigration Act of 1917 required immigrants over sixteen years old to take a literacy test to demonstrate basic reading ability in any language. The act also increased the "head tax" immigrants paid upon arrival to $8 (about $160 today) and allowed immigration officials to exercise more discretion in excluding newcomers. It specifically denied entry to "idiots, imbeciles, feeble-minded persons, epileptics, insane persons, paupers, beggars, vagrants, alcoholics, prostitutes, persons afflicted with disease, criminals, polygamists, and anarchists."

More restrictive than the 1882 Chinese Exclusion Act, the Immigration Act of 1917 excluded *all* Asians except Japanese and Filipinos. In 1907, the Japanese Government had voluntarily limited Japanese immigration to the United States in the so-called Gentlemen's Agreement with President Roosevelt. Because the Philippines was a U.S. colony, its citizens were U.S. nationals and could travel freely to the United States.

WAGING WAR ON LABOR RADICALS President Wilson grew concerned about the loyalty of Americans affiliated with "radical" groups. Hundreds of local and state officials belonged to the Socialist party, which opposed U.S. involvement in the war. And thousands of wage workers were "Wobblies," members of the radical Industrial Workers of the World (IWW), who supported the battle between labor and management, not the war in Europe.

Once the United States declared war, the IWW opposed the conflict, urging young men: "Don't be a soldier, be a man!" The IWW was devastated by the Great War, when hundreds of Wobblies were jailed, beaten, shot, and tortured for opposing the conflict. Federal agents raided forty-eight IWW offices across the country. They confiscated filing cabinets filled with correspondence and records and arrested 165 Wobblies. A hundred were eventually tried for sedition, and all were convicted and imprisoned.

THE AMERICAN ROLE IN THE WAR

In 1917, America's war strategy focused on helping the struggling French and British armies on the Western Front. The Allied leaders stressed that they needed at least a million U.S. troops, but it would take months to recruit, equip, and train that many new soldiers. A shortage of troop ships further delayed the process of getting American troops to Europe.

On December 21, 1917, French premier Georges Clemenceau urged the Americans to rush their army, called the American Expeditionary Force (AEF), to France. "A terrible blow is imminent," he told a journalist about to leave Paris. "Tell your Americans to come quickly." Clemenceau was referring to the likelihood of a massive German attack, made more probable by the end of the fighting on the Eastern Front following the Bolshevik Revolution in Russia in November 1917.

THE BOLSHEVIK REVOLUTION Among the many unexpected developments of the Great War, none was more significant than the Bolshevik Revolution and the destruction of the Russian Empire and its monarchy. Russia was the first nation to crack under the prolonged strain of the war. On March 2, 1917, Nicholas II, having presided over a war that had ruined his nation's economy and transportation system, abdicated his throne after a week of worker protests in the streets of major Russian cities, ending 300 years of rule by the Romanov dynasty. The tsar turned the nation over to the Provisional Government led by Alexander Kerensky. Within months, Russia was a republic committed to continuing the war.

The republic did not last long. In the fall of 1917, the Germans helped an exiled Russian Marxist radical named Vladimir Ilyich Lenin board a train to Russia from Switzerland. For years, Lenin had been biding his time, waiting for the war to devour the Russian monarchy. The Germans hoped that Lenin, maniacally obsessed with fomenting revolution, would cause turmoil in his homeland. He did much more than that.

On the night of April 16, 1917, the forty-seven-year-old Lenin, a man of iron will, arrived in Petrograd eager for revenge—and power. A huge crowd welcomed him. Climbing atop an armored car, Lenin pledged to withdraw Russia from the devastating war and to eliminate private property. "The people," he shouted, "need peace, the people need bread, the people need land."

As Lenin observed, power in war-weary Russia was lying in the streets, waiting to be picked up. To grab that power, he mobilized the Bolsheviks, a small but determined group of ruthless Communist revolutionaries who, during the night of November 6–7, seized authority from the provisional government and established a dictatorship.

Lenin banned political parties and organized religions (atheism became the official Communist belief); eliminated civil liberties and the free press; and killed or imprisoned opposition leaders, including the tsar and his family.

After the Bolshevik takeover, Tsar Nicholas urged the British and then the French to give him and his family asylum, but both countries refused. Lenin then placed the royal family under house arrest. After midnight on July 17, 1918, Bolshevik secret police awakened the Romanov family and ordered them and their four servants to the cellar, telling them it was for their own safety. Once in the cellar, they were shot, clubbed, and stabbed. All the servants and the seven Romanovs—the tsar, his wife, and five children—were dead, as was the Russian monarchy.

When Woodrow Wilson was alerted to the murders at a dinner party, he stood up and rushed off, saying over his shoulder, "A great menace to the world has taken shape."

THE RUSSIAN CIVIL WAR The Bolshevik Revolution triggered a prolonged civil war throughout Russia in which the United States and its allies worked to overthrow the Communists. Wilson sent 20,000 American soldiers to Siberia to support the anti-Communist Russian forces, an effort that proved unsuccessful. Lenin declared that the world would be freed from war only by a global revolution in which capitalism would be replaced by communism. To that end, he wanted to get Russia out of the Great War as soon as possible.

On March 3, 1918, Lenin signed a humiliating peace agreement with Germany, the Treaty of Brest-Litovsk. The treaty forced Russia to transfer vast territories to Germany and its ally Turkey and to recognize the independence of the Ukraine region. In addition, Russia had to pay $46 million to Germany. Lenin was willing to accept such a harsh peace because he needed to concentrate on his many internal enemies in the ongoing civil war.

Walter Lippmann, editor of the *New Republic* magazine, warned Wilson that he should stick to his original position of "no interference in Russia's internal affairs" and not embroil U.S. troops in the Russian civil war. Yet Wilson intervened anyway. After nineteen months of unsuccessful military efforts against the Bolsheviks, U.S. troops returned to America in April 1920. Thereafter, Russian Communists steadfastly believed that America had tried to smash their revolution.

AMERICA BOLSTERS THE WESTERN FRONT In March 1918, the Germans began the first of several offensives in France and Belgium designed to win the war before the American Expeditionary Force arrived in force. By May, the Germans had advanced to the Marne River, within fifty

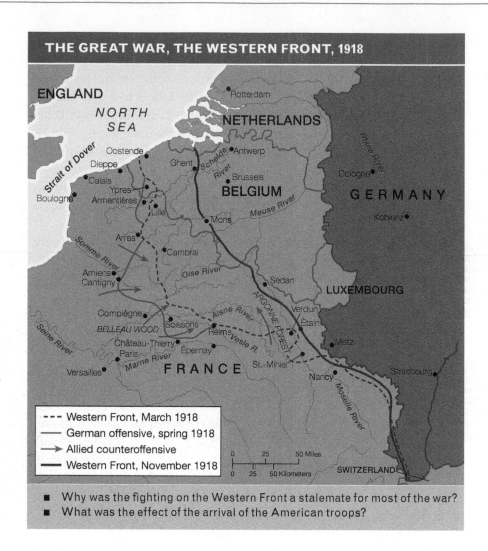

THE GREAT WAR, THE WESTERN FRONT, 1918

- - - Western Front, March 1918
—— German offensive, spring 1918
→ Allied counteroffensive
—— Western Front, November 1918

0   25   50 Miles

0   25   50 Kilometers

■ Why was the fighting on the Western Front a stalemate for most of the war?
■ What was the effect of the arrival of the American troops?

miles of Paris. In May, French and British leaders pressed Wilson to get the U.S. troops to France as soon as possible. By the end of the month, some 650,000 American soldiers were in Europe.

In June 1918, at the Battle of Belleau Wood, U.S. forces commanded by General John J. "Black Jack" Pershing joined the French in driving the Germans back. During the battle, a French officer urged an American unit to retreat. In a famous exchange, U.S. Marine captain Lloyd W. Williams refused the order, saying: "Retreat? Hell, we just got here."

The crucial American role in the fighting occurred with a massive Allied offensive begun on September 26, 1918. American troops joined British and French armies in a drive toward Sedan, France, and its strategic railroad, which supplied the German army. With 1.2 million U.S. soldiers involved, including some 180,000 African Americans, it was the largest American action of the war, and it resulted in 117,000 U.S. casualties, including 26,000 dead.

Along the entire French-Belgian front, however, the outnumbered Germans were in desperate retreat eastward across Belgium during the early fall of 1918. "America," wrote German general Erich Ludendorff, "became the decisive power in the war."

An American Hero: Alvin York Among the soldiers in France, one stood out: Sergeant Alvin York, an American originally from a deeply religious, dirt-poor family in the Tennessee mountains.

When the United States entered the war, York, a devout Christian pacifist, wanted no part of it. Yet over several weeks, he changed his mind: "I begun to understand that no matter what a man is forced to do, so long as he is right in his own soul, he remains a righteous man. I knowed I would go to war."

In France, York's unit became embroiled in the forty-seven-day-long offensive in the Argonne Forest. His platoon was told to assault three dozen German machine guns perched along a ridge. A storm of bullets stymied the Americans, killing or wounding every officer and leaving York in charge of seven privates who were trapped in "No Man's Land."

York, a crack shot, began to return fire. Every time a German helmet popped up, he shot with deadly accuracy. Finally, a German officer and five soldiers rose from a trench twenty-five yards away and charged York, who dropped his rifle and pulled out a pistol. He shot the last man first, then the next farthest from him, and the next, just like "the way we shoot wild turkeys at home." York killed all six, which led others to surrender.

Sergeant Alvin Cullum York Sergeant York was one of the most decorated American soldiers of the Great War.

By the end of the day, York had killed twenty-one Germans using only twenty shots, one of which killed two men. He and his surviving comrades marched their prisoners to the rear, capturing and killing more Germans along the way. When a lieutenant counted the prisoners, the number was 132.

Word spread quickly that York had singlehandedly "captured the whole damned German army." The Allied nations showered him with their highest military honors, and the United States awarded him the Congressional Medal of Honor.

THE END OF THE WAR Woodrow Wilson was determined to ensure that the Great War would be the last world war. To that end, during 1917, he appointed a group of experts, called the Inquiry, to draft a peace plan. With their advice, Wilson developed what would come to be called the **Fourteen Points**, a comprehensive list of provisions intended to shape the peace treaty and reshape the postwar world.

On January 8, 1918, Wilson presented his Fourteen Points to a joint session of Congress. He described his proposal "as the only possible program" for peace. The first five points called for the open conduct of diplomacy, the recognition of neutral nations' right to continue maritime commerce in time of war ("freedom of the seas"), the removal of international trade barriers (free trade), the reduction of armaments, and the transformation of colonial empires into independent nations.

Most of the remaining points dealt with territorial claims: Wilson called on the Central Powers to evacuate occupied lands and urged the victors to follow the difficult principle of "self-determination" in redrawing the map of Europe, allowing overlapping nationalities and ethnic groups to develop their own independent nations.

Point 13 created a new nation for the Poles, a people dominated by the Russians on the east and the Germans on the west for the previous 123 years. Point 14, the capstone of Wilson's postwar scheme, called for a "league of nations" to preserve global peace. When the Fourteen Points were made public, African American leaders asked the president to add a fifteenth point: an end to racial discrimination. Wilson did not respond.

British and French leaders accepted the Fourteen Points as a basis of peace negotiations but with two significant reservations: the British insisted on limiting freedom of the seas, since their powerful navy was the key to their security, and the French demanded reparations (payments) from Germany and Austria for war damages.

Meanwhile, by the end of October 1918, Germany was on the verge of collapse. Millions were fed up with the war, and thousands were starving. Revolutionaries rampaged through the streets. Sailors mutinied.

***Armistice Night in New York* (1918)** George Luks, known for his vivid paintings of urban life, captured the outpouring of patriotism and joy that extended through the night of Germany's surrender.

On November 9, the German kaiser resigned, and a republic was proclaimed. Then, on November 11 at 5:00 A.M., the nations at war reached an armistice (cease-fire agreement).

Six hours later, at the eleventh hour of the eleventh day of the eleventh month, and after 1,563 days of terrible warfare, the guns fell silent. From Europe, Colonel House sent a telegram to President Wilson: "Autocracy [government by an individual with unlimited power] is dead; long live democracy and its immortal leader [Wilson]."

The end of fighting led to wild celebrations throughout the world as fear and grief gave way to hope. "The nightmare is over," wrote African American activist W. E. B. Du Bois. "The world awakes. The long, horrible years of dreadful night are passed. Behold the sun!"

President Wilson was not as joyful. The Great War, he said, had dealt a grievous injury to civilization "which can never be atoned for or repaired."

During its nineteen months of combat in the Great War, the United States had lost 53,000 servicemen in combat. Another 63,000 died of various diseases, especially the influenza epidemic that swept through Europe and around the world in 1918–1919. Germany's war dead totaled more than 2 million, including civilians. France lost nearly 1.4 million combatants; Great Britain, 703,000; and Russia, 1.7 million. The new Europe would be quite different from the prewar version: much poorer, more violent, more polarized, more cynical, less sure of itself, and less capable of decisive action. The United States, for good or ill, emerged from the war as the world's dominant power.

THE POLITICS OF PEACE

On June 25, 1918, Colonel House wrote Woodrow Wilson from France, urging him to take charge of the peacemaking process. "It is one of the things with which your name should be linked during the ages." House was right. Wilson and the peace agreement ending the Great War would be forever linked, but not in the positive light they assumed.

In the making of the peace agreement, Wilson showed himself both at his best and worst. The Fourteen Points embodied his vision of a better world governed by fair principles. In promoting his peace plan, he felt guided "by the hand of God." A peacekeeping "League of Nations" was, in his view, the key element to a "secure and lasting peace" and the "most essential part of the peace settlement."

If the diplomats gathering to draft the peace treaty failed to follow his plans to reshape the world in America's image, he warned, "there will be another world war" within a generation. In the end, however, Wilson's grand efforts at global peacemaking failed—not abroad—but at home, and because of his own faults.

WILSON'S KEY ERRORS   Whatever the merits of President Wilson's peace plan, his efforts to implement it proved clumsy and self-defeating. He made several decisions that would come back to haunt him. First, against the advice of his staff and of European leaders, he decided to attend the peace conference in Paris that opened on January 18, 1919. Never before had a president left the United States for such a prolonged period (six months). During his time abroad, Wilson lost touch with political developments at home.

His second mistake involved politics. In the congressional election campaign of 1918, Wilson defied his advisers and political tradition by urging voters to elect a Democratic Congress as a sign of their approval of his policies in handling the war—and the peace. He "begged" the public not to "repudiate" his leadership.

Republicans, who for the most part had backed Wilson's war measures, were not pleased. Theodore Roosevelt called Wilson's self-serving appeal "a cruel insult to every Republican father or mother whose sons have entered the Army or Navy."

Voters were not impressed either, especially western farmers upset with government price ceilings placed on wheat. In the elections, the Republicans won control of both houses of Congress. It was a bad omen for Wilson's peace-making efforts, since any treaty to end the war would have to be approved by at least two thirds of the Senate. Roosevelt said that Wilson could no longer claim "to speak for the American people." The former president and his friend Henry Cabot Lodge thereafter did their best to undermine Wilson's negotiating strength with the Allies.

Meanwhile, Wilson had dispatched Colonel House and several aides to Europe to begin convincing Allied leaders to embrace the Fourteen Points. The lopsided losses in the elections, said House, "made his difficulties enormously greater." Gordon Auchincloss, House's son-in-law who assisted him in Europe, displayed the brash confidence of many American diplomats when he boasted that "before we get through with these fellows over here, we will teach them how to do things and to do them quickly." It would not be so easy.

Wilson's efforts were further weakened when he refused to appoint a prominent Republican to the peace delegation. House had urged him to appoint Roosevelt—or Lodge, the president's archenemy, and the leading Republican in Congress—but Wilson refused. In the end, he appointed Harry White, an

Fit for a Messiah A triumphant President Wilson rode down the Champs-Élysées in Paris as the crowds showered him with flower petals and cheered, "*Vive Wilson! Vive l'Amérique! Vive la liberté!*"

obscure Republican. Former president William Howard Taft groused that Wilson's real intention in going to Paris was "to hog the whole show."

Wilson's participation in the Paris Peace Conference would be an opportunity for him to convince Europe to follow him in creating a very different postwar world. As Wilson prepared to head for Europe, muckraking journalist Ray Stannard Baker wrote that the president "has yet to prove his greatness. The fate of a drama lies in its last act, and Wilson is now coming to that."

Initially, Wilson's entrance on the European stage in December 1918 was triumphant. Millions of grateful Europeans greeted him as an almost mystical hero, even as their savior. An Italian mayor described Wilson's visit as the "second coming of Christ." Others hailed him as the "God of peace."

From such a height, there could only be a fall. Although popular with the European people, Wilson had to negotiate with tough-minded, wily statesmen who resented his efforts to forge a peace settlement modeled on American values. That Wilson had not bothered to consult them about his Fourteen Points proposal before announcing it to the world did not help. In the end, the European leaders would force the American president to abandon many of his ideals. In some cases, Wilson's stances were hardly idealistic. When the Japanese delegation suggested that racial equality should be a guiding principle of the peace treaty, the U.S. president vetoed the idea.

THE PARIS PEACE CONFERENCE The Paris Peace Conference lasted from January to June 1919. The participants had no time to waste. The German, Austro-Hungarian, and Ottoman Empires were in ruins. Across much of the European continent, food was scarce and lawlessness rampant. The threat of revolution loomed over Central Europe as Communists in the defeated nations threatened to take control of governments in chaos.

The peace conference dealt with immensely complex and controversial issues (including the need to create new nations and redraw the maps of Europe and the Middle East) that required both political statesmanship and technical expertise. The British delegation alone included almost 400 members, many of them specialists in political geography or economics.

The Big Four From the start, the Paris Peace Conference was controlled by the Big Four: the prime ministers of Britain, France, and Italy, and the president of the United States. Neither Germany nor its allies participated. Communist Russia was also not invited. Although combat had ended, the Allies continued to blockade Germany's ports, which created a life-threatening shortage of food and medical supplies.

The Big Four David Lloyd George, Vittorio Orlando, Georges Clemenceau, and President Woodrow Wilson *(from left to right)* stand outside the palace at Versailles during a break in the treaty negotiations.

Georges Clemenceau, the seventy-seven-year-old French premier known as "the Tiger," had little patience with President Wilson's idealistic preaching. In response to Wilson's claim that "America is the only idealistic nation in the world," Clemenceau grumbled that talking with Wilson was like talking to Jesus Christ. "God gave us the Ten Commandments and we broke them," the French leader sneered. "Wilson gave us the Fourteen Points—we shall see."

The Big Four fought in private and in public. The French and British, led by Prime Minister David Lloyd George, insisted that Wilson agree to their proposals to weaken Germany economically and militarily, while Vittorio Orlando, prime minister of Italy, focused on gaining territories from defeated Austria.

The League of Nations Although suffering from chronic health issues, including hypertension and blinding headaches, Wilson lectured the other statesmen about the need to embrace his proposed **League of Nations**, which he insisted must be the "keystone" of any peace settlement. He believed that a world peace organization would abolish war by settling international disputes and mobilizing united action against aggressors. Article X of the League of Nations charter, which Wilson called "the heart of the League," allowed member nations to impose military and economic sanctions, or penalties, against those that engaged in aggression. The league, Wilson assumed, would exercise enormous moral influence, making military action unnecessary. These unrealistic expectations became, for Wilson, a self-defeating crusade.

On February 14, 1919, Wilson presented the final draft of the league charter to the Allies and left Paris for a ten-day visit home, where he faced growing opposition among Republicans. The League of Nations, Theodore Roosevelt complained, would revive German militarism and undermine American morale. "To substitute internationalism for nationalism," Roosevelt argued, "means to do away with patriotism."

Henry Cabot Lodge, powerful chair of the Senate Foreign Relations Committee, who despised Wilson, also opposed the League of Nations because, he claimed, it would potentially involve sending U.S. troops to foreign conflicts without Senate approval. "I have always loved one flag," Lodge explained, "and I cannot share that devotion with a mongrel banner created for a League."

On March 3, 1919, Lodge presented a resolution on the Senate floor that the "League of Nations in the form as now proposed . . . should not be accepted by the United States." He then announced that thirty-seven Republicans endorsed his resolution—more than enough to block ratification of Wilson's treaty.

THE TREATY OF VERSAILLES Henry Cabot Lodge's preemptive action undermined President Wilson's leverage with the British and French. So, too, did a potent virus and the strain of overwork that weakened Wilson physically. When he returned to Paris in the spring of 1919, his European colleagues maneuvered him into concessions that mocked his ideals. For example, the U.S. leader yielded to French demands that Germany transfer territory to France on its west and to Poland on its east and north.

In other territorial matters, Wilson had to abandon his lofty but impractical and ill-defined principle of national self-determination. As Secretary of State Robert Lansing correctly predicted, preaching self-determination would only "raise hopes which can never be realized." (Wilson himself later told the Senate that he wished he had never said that "all nations have a right to self-determination.")

In their efforts to allow for some degree of ethnic self-determination in multiethnic regions, the statesmen at Versailles transformed Europe from a continent of empires to one of nations. They created Austria, Hungary, Poland, Yugoslavia, and Czechoslovakia in Central Europe and four new nations along the Baltic Sea: Finland, Estonia, Lithuania, and Latvia.

The victorious Allies, however, did not create independent nations out of the colonies of the defeated and now defunct European empires. Instead, they assigned the former German colonies in Africa and the Turkish colonies in the Middle East to France and Great Britain for an unspecified time, while Japan took control of the former German colonies in the Pacific.

The bitterest arguments among the diplomats in Paris focused on efforts to make Germany pay for the expenses of the war. The British and the French (on whose soil much of the war was fought) wanted Germany to pay the *entire* financial cost of the war, including the lifetime pensions they would pay to their military veterans.

On this point, Wilson made perhaps his most fateful concessions. Although initially opposed to reparations, he eventually agreed to a crucial clause that forced Germany to accept responsibility for the war and its entire expense. The "war guilt" clause so offended Germans that it became a major factor in the rise of Adolf Hitler and the Nazi party during the 1920s. Wilson himself privately admitted that if he were a German, he would refuse to sign the treaty.

Colonel Edward House privately blamed Wilson for many problems associated with the treaty, saying that the president "speaks constantly of teamwork but seldom practices it." Wilson was "becoming stubborn and angry, and he never was a good negotiator."

On May 7, 1919, the victorious powers presented the treaty to the German delegates, who returned three weeks later with 443 pages of criticism. Among other things, they noted that Germany would lose 13 percent of its territory, 10 percent of its population, and all its colonies in Asia and Africa. The German president called the treaty's terms "unrealizable and unbearable." He resigned rather than sign it.

A few minor changes were made, but when the Germans still balked, the French threatened to launch a new military attack. Finally, on June 28, 1919, the Germans gave up and signed the treaty in the glittering Hall of Mirrors at Versailles, the magnificent palace built by King Louis XIV in the late seventeenth century. Thereafter, the agreement was called the **Treaty of Versailles**. It was signed exactly five years after the assassination of Archduke Franz Ferdinand.

None of the peacemakers was fully satisfied with the treaty. As France's Georges Clemenceau observed, "it was not perfect," but it was, after all, the "result of human beings. We did all we could to work fast and well." British diplomat Harold Nicolson predicted that historians would "come to the conclusion that we were very stupid men [in creating the Versailles Treaty]. I think we were."

When Adolf Hitler, then a German soldier, learned of the treaty's provisions, he vowed a ghastly and pitiless revenge, launching a determined effort

EUROPE AFTER THE TREATY OF VERSAILLES, 1919

.... 1914 boundaries
New nations
Plebiscite areas
Occupied area

■ Why was self-determination so difficult to apply in Central Europe?
■ How did territorial concessions weaken Germany?

to seize control of German's future. "We need a dictator who is a genius," he claimed, referring to himself. And he used public resentment over the treaty to mobilize support. "It cannot be that two million Germans have fallen in vain," he screamed during a speech in Munich in 1922. "We demand vengeance!"

A treaty intended to make wars irrelevant would bring on another world war in less than twenty years. The Japanese also insisted that the treaty include a clause asserting the equality of all races and nations. This demand reflected Japanese indignation at the way California and other western states were discriminating against Japanese immigrants. Woodrow Wilson refused the Japanese request.

THE TREATY RATIFICATION DEBATE On July 8, 1919, Woodrow Wilson arrived back in Washington, D.C., to promote Senate approval of the treaty. Before leaving Paris, he had assured a French diplomat that he would not allow changes to the treaty: "The Senate must take its medicine." Thus began one of the most bitterly partisan disputes in American history.

On July 10, Wilson was the first president to deliver in person a treaty to be voted on in the Senate. He called upon both parties to accept their "great duty" and ratify the treaty, whose language had been guided "by the hand of God." Breathing defiance, Wilson then grew needlessly confrontational. He dismissed critics of the League of Nations as "blind and little provincial people." The whole world, he claimed, was relying on the United States to sign the Versailles Treaty: "Dare we reject it and break the heart of the world?"

Yes, answered Senate Republicans, who had decided that Wilson's commitment to the League of Nations was a reckless threat to America's independence. Henry Cabot Lodge denounced the treaty's "scheme of making mankind suddenly virtuous by a statute or a written constitution." Lodge's strategy was to delay a vote on the treaty in hopes that public opposition would grow. To do so, he took six weeks to read aloud the text of the treaty to the Foreign Relations Committee. He then organized a parade of expert witnesses, most of whom opposed the treaty, to appear at the hearings on ratification.

In the Senate, a group of "irreconcilables," fourteen Republicans and two Democrats, refused to support U.S. membership in the League. They were mostly western and midwestern isolationists who feared that the United States would lose its right to decide which wars it entered.

Lodge belonged to a larger group called the "reservationists," who insisted upon limiting American participation in the League of Nations in exchange for approving the rest of the treaty. The only way to get Senate approval was for Wilson to agree to revisions, the most important of which was the requirement that Congress authorize any American participation in a league-approved war.

Colonel Edward House urged the president to "meet the Senate in a conciliatory spirit." Wilson scoffed that he had long ago decided that you "can never get anything in this life that is worthwhile without fighting for it." House courageously disagreed, reminding Wilson that American civilization was "built on compromise." It was the last time the two men would speak to or see each other.

Wilson was temperamentally incapable of compromising. He refused to negotiate, declaring that "if the Treaty is not ratified by the Senate, the War will have been fought in vain."

LET THE PEOPLE DECIDE In September 1919, after a summer of fruitless debate, an exhausted Wilson decided to take his case directly to the voters. On September 2, against doctor's orders and the advice of his wife

President Wilson on Tour In a last-minute effort to save his struggling treaty, President Wilson set out on a national tour to win over the American people.

and aides, he boarded a train and left Washington for a grueling three-week tour through the Midwest to the West Coast. He planned to visit twenty-nine cities and deliver nearly 100 speeches on behalf of the treaty.

No president had ever made such an effort to win public support. Enormous crowds greeted him in Columbus, Kansas City, Des Moines, Omaha, and other stops. In St. Louis, Wilson said that he had returned from Paris "bringing one of the greatest documents of human history," which was now in danger of being rejected by the Senate. He pledged to "fight for a cause . . . greater than the Senate. It is greater than the government. It is as great as the cause of mankind."

Onward through Nebraska, South Dakota, Minnesota, North Dakota, Montana, Idaho, and Washington, Wilson traveled by rail, speaking to large crowds several times a day, despite suffering from pounding headaches. It did not help his morale to learn that his secretary of state, Robert Lansing, had said that the League of Nations was "entirely useless."

By the time Wilson's train reached Spokane, Washington, the president was visibly fatigued. But he kept going, heading south through Oregon and California. Some 200,000 people greeted him in Los Angeles. By then, he had covered 10,000 miles in twenty-two days and given thirty-two major speeches.

Then disaster struck. After delivering an emotional speech on September 25, 1919, in Pueblo, Colorado, Wilson collapsed from severe headaches. His left side was paralyzed, and one side of his face was palsied, limp, and expressionless. "I seem to have gone to pieces," he sighed. The presidential train, its blinds drawn, raced back to Washington, D.C.

A STRICKEN PRESIDENT Four days after returning to the White House, President Wilson suffered a stroke (cerebral hemorrhage) that left him paralyzed on his left side and partially blind; he could barely speak. Only his secretary, his doctor, and his wife, Edith, knew his true condition. For five months, Wilson lay in bed while his doctor issued reassuring medical bulletins to reporters. Wilson's physical decline hardened his stubbornness; he refused to listen to anyone. The president "lived on, but oh, what a wreck of his former self!" sighed a White House staffer. "He had changed from a giant to a pygmy." If a document needed his signature, his wife guided his hand, leading one senator to complain that the nation now had a "petticoat government."

Secretary of State Robert Lansing urged the president's aides to declare him disabled and appoint Vice President Thomas Marshall in his place. They angrily refused. Soon thereafter, Wilson replaced Lansing. With each passing week, Wilson became more emotionally unstable and began displaying signs of paranoia. A visitor found the president bitter and brooding, full of self-pity and anger. For the remaining seventeen months of Wilson's second term, his wife, along with aides and trusted cabinet members, kept him isolated from all but the most essential business. When a group of Republican senators visited the White House, one of them said: "Well, Mr. President, we have all been praying for you." Wilson replied, "Which way, Senator?"

THE TREATY UNDER ATTACK   In the vacuum created by Wilson's physical collapse, Henry Cabot Lodge pushed through the Senate fourteen changes (the number was not coincidental) in the Treaty of Versailles. Wilson rejected them all; the Senate must endorse *his* treaty or there would be *no* treaty.

The final Senate vote in 1920 on Lodge's revised treaty was 39 in favor and 55 against. On the question of approving the original treaty without changes, the irreconcilables and the reservationists, led by Lodge, combined to defeat ratification, with 38 for and 53 against.

Woodrow Wilson's grand effort at global peacemaking had failed miserably. (He did receive the Nobel Peace Prize for his efforts.) When told of the final Senate vote, he said it "would have been better if I had died last fall." A Connecticut senator concluded after the treaty defeat that Wilson had "strangled his own child." The United States would never join the League of Nations.

After refusing to ratify the treaty, Congress tried to declare an official end to the war by a joint resolution on May 20, 1920, which Wilson vetoed. It was not until July 2, 1921, four months after he had left office and almost eighteen months after the fighting had stopped, that another joint resolution officially ended the state of war with Germany and Austria-Hungary. Separate peace treaties with Germany, Austria, and Hungary were ratified on October 18, 1921. By then, Republican Warren G. Harding was president.

The U.S. failure to ratify the Versailles Treaty was a defining moment in world history, for it helped trigger a chain of events that would contribute to a second world war twenty years later. The chaos created by the Great War allowed for the rise of communism in Russia, Nazism in Germany, and fascism in Italy. With Great Britain and France too exhausted and too timid to keep Germany weak and isolated, a dangerous power vacuum would emerge in Europe, one that Adolf Hitler and the Nazis would fill.

STUMBLING FROM WAR TO PEACE

In America, celebrations over the war's end soon gave way to widespread inflation, unemployment, labor unrest, socialist and Communist radicalism, race riots, terrorist bombings, and government tyranny. With millions of servicemen returning to civilian life, war-related industries shutting down, and wartime price controls ending, unemployment and prices for consumer goods spiked.

Bedridden by his stroke, President Wilson became increasingly distant and depressed, so emotionally fragile that he was incapable of making sound decisions. His administration was in disarray, and he had never been so unpopular. The Democratic party was floundering along with him.

THE SPANISH FLU PANDEMIC Beginning in 1918, the world confronted an infectious enemy that produced far more casualties than the war itself. Like the COVID-19 pandemic in 2020, the influenza virus quickly spread around the globe and altered the course of world history. The virus became known as the "Spanish" influenza, not because it originated there but because Spain, which had remained neutral during the war, was one of the few countries whose newspapers honestly reported the number of cases and deaths.

The disease appeared suddenly in January 1918 at an overcrowded Kansas army camp and spread quickly to Europe with the U.S. troops. By June, the pandemic stretched from Algeria to New Zealand, India, and the Pacific islands. Its initial outbreak lasted a year and killed between 50 million and 100 million people worldwide. In the United States alone, it infected 26 million people, some 670,000 of whom died, more than ten times the number of U.S. combat deaths in France. The public health system was strained to the breaking point. Hospitals ran short of beds, nurses, and doctors; funeral homes ran out of coffins.

Fear seized the population. Schools and churches closed, and people ignored desperate appeals for hospital volunteers for fear of becoming infected themselves. In Goldsboro, North Carolina, Dan Tonkel remembered, "We were actually almost afraid to breathe. You were afraid to go out. The fear was so great people were actually afraid to leave their home . . . afraid to talk to one another."

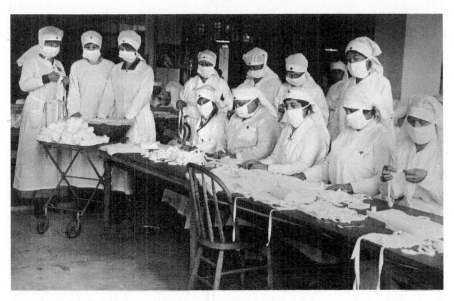

The Spanish Flu Pandemic Red Cross volunteers made white gauze face masks in response to the mandatory masking protocol during the pandemic in 1918.

By the spring of 1919, the pandemic had run its course, ending as suddenly—and as inexplicably—as it had begun. Although another outbreak occurred in the winter of 1920, people had grown more resistant to it. No disease in human history—indeed, no war, famine, or natural catastrophe—had killed so many in such a short time.

The pandemic had long-lasting social effects. People blamed immigrants and foreigners for the virus, and after the war Congress would greatly restrict the flow of newcomers. At the same time, because the pandemic killed more men than women, it, along with the war, skewed gender ratios for years afterward.

WOMEN'S SUFFRAGE AT LAST   As the first outbreak of the Spanish flu was ending, women finally gained a constitutional guarantee of their right to vote. After six months of delay, debate, and failed votes, Congress passed the **Nineteenth Amendment** in the spring of 1919 and sent it to the states for ratification.

Tennessee's legislature was the last of thirty-six state assemblies to approve the amendment, and it did so in dramatic fashion. "The entire world," said one legislator, "has cast its eyes on Tennessee."

As thousands of supporters and opponents mobilized in Knoxville, the state capital, the outcome was uncertain. Bribes were offered; threats were made. Many southerners, both women and men, opposed the Nineteenth Amendment because they feared the impact of giving African American women the vote.

The initial vote on extending the suffrage to women was 48–48. Then a twenty-four-year-old Republican legislator named Harry T. Burn changed his no vote to yes at the insistence of his strong-willed mother, Phoebe Ensminger Burn. She had written her son a note admonishing him to be a "good boy" and vote for suffrage. "Don't keep them in doubt!" He did as she directed, and the Nineteenth Amendment became official on August 18, 1920, making the United States the twenty-second nation to allow women's suffrage. Josephine Pearson, the most vocal Tennessee anti-suffragist, labeled Burn a "traitor to manhood's honor."

Women's suffrage, the culmination of generations of activism, was the climactic achievement of the Progressive Era. Suddenly, 9.5 million women were eligible to vote in national elections; in the 1920 presidential election, they would make up 40 percent of the electorate. "The greatest thing to come out of the war," said suffragist Carrie Chapman Catt, "was the emancipation of women, for which no man fought."

Many women of color, however, never got to exercise their new voting rights. African American women in the South faced the same Jim Crow tactics that had long denied African American men access to the vote. And Native Americans were still not considered citizens and therefore could not vote. Not until 1924 did Congress pass the Indian Citizenship Act.

Their First Votes Women of New York City's East Side vote for the first time in the presidential election of 1920.

ECONOMIC TURBULENCE As consumer prices rose after the war, discontented workers, released from wartime controls on wages, grew more willing to go on strike. In 1919, more than 4 million hourly wage workers, 20 percent of the workforce, participated in 3,600 strikes. Most wanted nothing more than higher wages and shorter workweeks, but their critics linked them with the worldwide Communist movement. After a general strike in Seattle, the mayor, Ole Hanson, claimed the strikers were seeking a "revolution" under Bolshevik influence, and a Seattle newspaper declared that "this is America—not Russia."

Such charges of a Communist conspiracy were greatly exaggerated, however. In 1919, fewer than 70,000 people nationwide belonged to the Communist party. The Seattle strike lasted only five days, but public resentment of the strikers damaged the cause and image of unions across the country.

The most controversial labor dispute was in Boston, where police went on strike on September 9, 1919. Massachusetts governor Calvin Coolidge mobilized the National Guard to maintain order. After four days during which looters panicked the city, the striking police offered to return, but Coolidge ordered that they all be fired. When labor leaders appealed for their reinstatement, Coolidge responded in words that made him an instant national hero: "There is no right to strike against the public safety by anybody, anywhere, any time."

RACE RIOTS The end of the Great War brought fresh hopes that African Americans might gain full equality. John M. Ross, a Black army officer, stressed that fighting the war had given him "a greater feeling of pride in the achievements of my race, and a hope that this great country of ours will give every man in it a square deal, no matter what his race or color may be." Others were more skeptical. Herbert Seligmann, a journalist who served on the board of the NAACP, maintained that the war "has meant a vital change in the position of the Negro and in his own feeling about the position." Yet Seligmann warned that "if the White man tries to 'show the [Negro] man his place' by flogging and lynching him, the Negro, when the government does not defend him, will purchase arms to defend himself."

Seligmann's greatest fear was realized. The end of the war brought a violent backlash by southern Whites against African Americans, including Black war veterans. A Louisiana newspaper denounced Black soldiers for having returned from France with "more exalted ideas of their station in life than really exists" and urged readers "to show them what will and will not be permitted."

African Americans were subjected to a wave of racist assaults in the months after the war ended. Black soldier Chris Lewis returned home from France to Tyler Station, Kentucky. On December 15, 1918, a police officer stormed into Lewis's cabin and accused him of robbery. Lewis, still wearing his uniform, proclaimed his innocence and fled. He was soon captured. His attempted escape, however, prompted local Whites to "teach him a lesson." After midnight, more than a hundred masked men stormed the jail, pulled Lewis outside, tied a rope around his neck and hanged him. A New York newspaper reported that "every loyal American negro who has served with the colors [flag] may fairly ask: 'Is this our reward for what we have done?'"

In 1919 alone, eighty-three Blacks, including nine military veterans, were lynched. What African American leader James Weldon Johnson called the "Red Summer" (*red* signifying blood) began in July, when a mob of Whites invaded the Black neighborhood in Longview, Texas, angry over rumors of interracial dating. They burned shops and houses and ran several Black residents out of town. A week later, in Washington, D.C., false reports of Black assaults on White women stirred up White mobs, and gangs of rioters waged a race war in the streets until soldiers and driving rains ended the fighting.

In late July, 38 people were killed and 537 injured in five days of rioting in Chicago, where some 50,000 African Americans, mostly migrants from the South, had moved during the war, leading to tensions with local Whites over jobs and housing. White unionized workers especially resented Black workers who were hired as strikebreakers.

Safe, Briefly Escorted by a police officer, an African American family moves its belongings from its home, likely destroyed by White rioters, into a protected area of Chicago.

In September, African American sharecroppers in Elaine, Arkansas, gathered in a church to organize a labor union. Some were armed, fearing that they might be attacked. That fear proved all too real when a group of White men fired into the church. The sharecroppers shot back, killing one of the attackers.

Word of the killing spread rapidly, as did false rumors about a "[Negro] insurrection." The Arkansas governor called for some 600 federal soldiers and local police to arrest the "heavily-armed negroes." Nearly a thousand White vigilantes also joined the effort. The soldiers were ordered to shoot anyone who resisted arrest. They went well beyond that, killing more than 200 African Americans—men, women, and children—in what came to be called the Elaine Massacre. None of the rampaging Whites were convicted of any crimes.

Twelve Black men were accused of murder and hastily convicted. Attorneys from around the country volunteered to appeal their convictions, and in 1923 the U.S. Supreme Court ruled in favor of the African American defendants, pointing out in *Moore v. Dempsey* that the all-White jury and the judge's decision to deny them the opportunity to testify violated their civil right to legal "due process" under the Fourteenth Amendment. For the first time, the Supreme Court sided with poor Blacks against White supremacists.

Altogether, twenty-six race riots erupted in the summer of 1919. In August, the National Association for the Advancement of Colored People (NAACP) sent President Wilson a telegram "respectfully enquiring how long the Federal Government under your administration intends to tolerate anarchy in the United States?" The White House chose not to reply.

The riots were indeed a turning point for many African Americans, but not a happy one. "We made the supreme sacrifice," a Black veteran told poet-journalist Carl Sandburg. "Now we want to see our country live up to the Constitution and the Declaration of Independence." Another ex-soldier noted how much the war experience had changed the outlook of Black people: "We were determined not to take it anymore."

Many blamed the riots on socialist and Communist agitators. "Reds Try to Stir Negroes to Revolt," and "Radicals Inciting Negro to Violence," cautioned the *New York Times* in July 1919. The *New York Tribune* followed suit, announcing that a "Plot to Stir Race Antagonism in United States Charged to Soviets." By December 1919, the *Times* had decided that "no element in this country is so susceptible to organized propaganda . . . as the least informed class of Negroes." It warned that "Bolshevist[s] . . . are winning many recruits among the colored races."

THE FIRST RED SCARE With so many people convinced that the strikes and riots were inspired by Communists and anarchists (two different groups that shared a hatred for capitalism), a New York journalist reported that Americans were "shivering in their boots over Bolshevism, and they are far more scared of [Vladimir] Lenin than they ever were of the [German] Kaiser. We seem to be the most frightened victors the world ever saw."

Fears of revolution led to what came to be called the **First Red Scare** (another would occur in the 1950s). In early 1919, the Secret Service discovered a plot by Spanish anarchists to kill President Wilson and other government officials. In April 1919, postal workers intercepted nearly forty homemade mail bombs addressed to government officials. One mail bomb, however, blew off the hands of a Georgia senator's maid.

In June, a twenty-four-year-old Italian anarchist named Carlo Valdinoci used a suitcase filled with dynamite to blow up Attorney General A. Mitchell Palmer's home in Washington, D.C. The bomb exploded prematurely when Valdinoci tripped and fell as he approached the house. A neighbor, Assistant Secretary of the Navy Franklin Roosevelt, was walking with his wife Eleanor when the bomb exploded. The blast shattered windows and knocked neighbors out of their beds. Valdinoci's collarbone landed on the Roosevelts' front steps, and his scalp ended up on their roof. Valdinoci had become the nation's first suicide bomber.

The bombing transformed Attorney General Palmer. "I remember . . . the morning after my house was blown up, I stood in the middle of the wreckage of my library with Congressmen and Senators, and without a dissenting voice they called upon me in strong terms to exercise all the power that was possible . . . to run to earth the criminals who were behind that kind of outrage."

At the same time, other anarchist bombers were setting off explosives in New York City, Boston, Pittsburgh, Philadelphia, Cleveland, and Washington, D.C. Palmer, who had ambitions to succeed Wilson as president, concluded that a "Red Menace," a Communist "blaze of revolution," was "sweeping over every American institution of law and order."

In August 1919, Palmer appointed a twenty-four-year-old attorney named J. Edgar Hoover to lead the new General Intelligence Division within the Justice Department to collect information on radicals. Hoover and others in the Justice Department worked with a network of 250,000 informants in 600 cities, all of them members of the American Protective League, which had been founded during the war to root out "traitors" and labor radicals.

On November 7, 1919, in what came to be called the "Palmer raids," federal agents rounded up 450 alien "radicals," most of whom were law-abiding Russian immigrants. All were deported to Russia without a court hearing. On January 2, 1920, federal agents and police in dozens of cities arrested 5,000 more suspects. In 1919, novelist Katharine Fullerton Gerould announced in *Harper's Magazine* that America "is no longer a free country in the old sense."

Panic about possible foreign terrorists and American radicals erupted across the nation. Vigilantes, driven by fear, prejudice, and ignorance, took matters into their own hands. At a patriotic pageant in Washington, D.C., a sailor shot a spectator who refused to rise for "The Star-Spangled Banner"; the crowd cheered. In Hammond, Indiana, a jury took two minutes to acquit a man who had murdered an immigrant for yelling, "To hell with the U.S." In Waterbury, Connecticut, a salesman was sentenced to six months in jail for saying that Lenin was "one of the brainiest" of the world's leaders.

By the summer of 1920, the Red Scare had begun to subside. But it left a lasting mark by strengthening the conservative crusade for "100 percent Americanism" and new restrictions on immigration.

EFFECTS OF THE GREAT WAR The extraordinary turbulence in 1919 and 1920 revealed how the Great War had changed the shape of modern history: the conflict was a turning point after which little was the same. The Great War had destroyed old Europe—its cities, people, economies, and four grand empires. The war also changed Europe's self-image as the admired center of civilized Western culture. Winston Churchill, the future British prime minister, called postwar Europe "a crippled, broken world."

Peace did not bring stability; the trauma of the war lingered long after the shooting stopped. Most Germans and Austrians believed they were the *victims* of a harsh peace, and many wanted revenge, especially a hate-filled German war veteran named Adolf Hitler.

At the same time, the war had hastened the already simmering Bolshevik Revolution, which caused Russia to exit the war, abandon its western European allies, and, in 1922, reemerge as the Union of Soviet Socialist Republics (USSR). Thereafter, Soviet communism would be one of the most powerful forces shaping the twentieth century.

Postwar America was a much different story. For the first time, the United States had decisively intervened in a major European war. The economy had emerged from the conflict largely unscathed, and bankers and business executives were eager to fill the vacuum created by the destruction of the major European economies.

The United States was now the world's dominant power. In 1928, ten years after the end of the Great War, a British official declared that Great Britain now faced "a phenomenon for which there is no parallel in our modern history." The United States, he explained, was "twenty-five times as wealthy, three times as populous, twice as ambitious, almost invulnerable, and at least our equal in prosperity, vital energy, technical equipment, and industrial strength." What came to be called the "American Century" was well under way.

CHAPTER REVIEW

SUMMARY

- **An Uneasy Neutrality**   In 1914, a system of military alliances divided Europe in two. Britain, France, and the Russian Empire had formed the *Triple Entente*, later called the *Allied Powers*. The *Triple Alliance (Central Powers)* was composed of Germany, Austria-Hungary, Bulgaria, and Turkey (the Ottoman Empire). Italy would switch sides in 1915 and join the *Allied Powers*. In the summer of 1914, the assassination of the heir to the Austro-Hungarian throne by a Serbian nationalist triggered a chain reaction involving these alliances that erupted into the Great War. On the *Western Front*, troops primarily engaged in *trench warfare*. New weapons such as machine guns, long-range artillery, and poison gas resulted in unprecedented casualties. The Wilson administration initially declared the United States neutral but allowed American businesses to extend loans to the Allies. Americans were outraged by the German *U-boat* warfare, especially after the 1915 sinking of the British passenger liner *Lusitania*. In 1917, the publication of the *Zimmermann telegram* led the United States to enter the Great War.

- **Mobilizing a Nation**   The Wilson administration drafted millions of young men and created new agencies, such as the War Industries Board and the Food Administration, to coordinate industrial and agricultural production. As White workers left their factory jobs to join the army, hundreds of thousands of African Americans migrated from the rural South to the urban North, a massive relocation known as the *Great Migration*. Many southern Whites and Mexican Americans also migrated to industrial centers. One million women worked in defense industries. The federal government severely curtailed civil liberties during the war. The Espionage and Sedition Acts of 1917 and 1918 criminalized public opposition to the war.

- **The American Role in the War**   In 1918, the arrival of millions of fresh American troops turned the tide of the war, rolling back a final desperate German offensive. German leaders sued for peace, and an armistice was signed on November 11, 1918. Woodrow Wilson insisted that the United States entered the war to help ensure a new, more democratic Europe. His *Fourteen Points* (1918) speech outlined his ideas for smaller, ethnically based nation-states to replace the empires. A *League of Nations*, he believed, would promote peaceful resolutions to future conflicts.

- **The Politics of Peace**   At the Paris Peace Conference, Wilson was only partially successful in achieving his goals. The *Treaty of Versailles* (1919) did create the *League of Nations* but included a *war guilt* clause that forced Germany to pay massive reparations for war damages to France and Britain. In the United States, the fight for Senate ratification of the treaty pitted supporters against those who feared that involvement in a league of nations would hinder domestic reforms and require U.S. participation in future wars. Wilson's refusal to compromise and the alienation of Republican senators resulted in the failure of Senate ratification.

- **Stumbling from War to Peace**   The Bolsheviks established a Communist regime in the old Russian Empire in 1917. The German and Austro-Hungarian Empires were dismantled and replaced by smaller nation-states. The "war guilt" clause fostered

German bitterness and contributed to the subsequent rise of the Nazis. The United States struggled with its new status as the leading world power and with changes at home. As wartime industries shifted to peacetime production, wartime wage and price controls were ended, and millions of former soldiers reentered the workforce. Unemployment rose and consumer prices increased, provoking labor unrest in many cities. Many Americans believed the labor strikes were part of a Bolshevik plot to gain power in the United States. Several incidents of domestic terrorism fueled these fears and provoked the *First Red Scare* (1919–1920). Race riots broke out as resentful White mobs tried to stop African Americans from exercising their civil rights. The summer of 1919 also saw the passage of the *Nineteenth Amendment*; ratified in 1920, it gave women throughout the country the right to vote.

CHRONOLOGY

1914	The Great War (World War I) begins in Europe
1915	The British liner *Lusitania* is torpedoed by a German U-boat; 128 Americans are killed
1916	Congress passes the National Defense Act and the Revenue Act
February 1917	Germany announces unrestricted submarine warfare
March 1917	Zimmermann telegram
April 1917	United States enters the Great War
November 1917	Bolshevik Revolution in Russia
January 1918	Woodrow Wilson delivers his Fourteen Points
November 11, 1918	Peace armistice signed
1919	Paris Peace Conference convenes; Germany signs the Treaty of Versailles; Race riots during the Red Summer
1919–1920	First Red Scare; Boston police strikers fired.
1920	Senate rejects the Treaty of Versailles; Nineteenth Amendment is ratified

KEY TERMS

Triple Alliance (Central Powers) p. 1010
Triple Entente (Allied Powers) p. 1010
Western Front p. 1013
trench warfare p. 1013
U-boat p. 1019
Lusitania p. 1019
Zimmermann telegram p. 1023

Great Migration p. 1029
Fourteen Points p. 1038
League of Nations p. 1043
Treaty of Versailles p. 1045
Nineteenth Amendment (1920) p. 1051
First Red Scare (1919–1920) p. 1056

INQUIZITIVE

Go to InQuizitive to see what you've learned—and learn what you've missed—with personalized feedback along the way.

22 A Clash of Cultures

1920–1929

***Interpretation of Harlem Jazz I* (ca. 1915–1920)** During the Great Migration, many African Americans in the South migrated to northern cities in quest of jobs related to the war effort. In Harlem, a densely populated neighborhood of northern Manhattan in New York City, a vibrant African American cultural movement known as the Harlem Renaissance emerged in the 1920s. This abstract piece by German American artist Winold Reiss depicts African Americans dancing to jazz music.

The 1920s most iconic labels—the Jazz Age and the Roaring Twenties—describe a period that was, as a writer in the *New York Times* declared in 1923, "the greatest era of transition the human race has ever known. Old institutions are crumbling, old ideals are being battered into dust; the shock of the most cataclysmic war in history has left the world more disorganized than ever."

The twenties experienced an economic boom fueled by the impact of transformational technologies (automobiles, trucks, tractors, airplanes, radios, movies, electrical appliances, indoor plumbing) that enhanced the standard of living for most Americans. Between 1922 and 1927, the nation's economic output grew by an astounding 7 percent a year.

At the same time, significant social and political changes signaled what many called a "New Era" in American life. The Eighteenth Amendment (1919) outlawed the production and sale of alcoholic beverages ("Prohibition"), but many Americans defied the law. By some accounts, more people drank, and drank more, than before the ban. The seventy-year struggle for women's suffrage finally ended with the ratification of the Nineteenth Amendment (1920), which allowed women to vote (although most African American women—and men—in the South were prevented from doing so). During the twenties, women claimed many freedoms previously limited to men.

Another disruptive force resulted from startling new scientific theories developed by physicist Albert Einstein and psychiatrist Sigmund Freud. Their

focus questions

1. Assess the impact of the consumer culture that emerged in America during the 1920s. What contributed to its growth?

2. What were the other major new social and cultural trends and movements that became prominent during the twenties? How did they challenge traditional standards and customs?

3. What does "modernism" mean in intellectual and artistic terms? How did the modernist movement influence American culture in the early twentieth century?

4. How did reactionary conservatism during the 1920s manifest itself in social life and governmental policies?

5. To what extent did the policies of the Republican party dominate the federal government during the twenties? In what ways were these policies a rejection of progressivism?

findings undermined many traditional assumptions about God, the universe, and human behavior.

Such new ideas and sweeping social changes created what one historian called a "nervous generation" of Americans "groping for what certainty they could find." Mabel Dodge Luhan, a leading promoter of modern art and literature, said that the literary and artistic rebels who emerged during the Great War were determined to overthrow "the old order of things."

Much of the cultural conflict grew out of tensions between rural and urban ways of life and notions of morality. For the first time, more Americans lived in cities than in rural areas. While urban economies prospered, farmers suffered as Europe no longer needed record amounts of wheat, corn, and cotton. Depressed crop prices spurred 4 million people to move from farms to cities, bringing their different cultural values with them. Given this population shift and the nation's growing ethnic and religious diversity, fights erupted over evolutionary theory, Prohibition, and other charged issues.

Both major political parties still included "progressive" wings, but they were shrinking. Woodrow Wilson's losing fight over the Treaty of Versailles, coupled with his administration's savage crackdown on dissenters and socialists during and after the war, had weakened an already fragmented progressive movement. As reformer Amos Pinchot bitterly observed, Wilson had "put his enemies in office and his friends in jail." By 1920, many disheartened progressives had withdrawn from public life. Reformer Jane Addams lamented that the twenties, dominated by a Republican party devoted to the interests of Big Business, were "a period of political and social sag."

The desire to restore traditional values and social stability led voters to elect Republican Warren G. Harding president in 1920. He promised to end progressivism and return America to "normalcy." The demand for honest, efficient government and public services remained strong; the impulse for social reform, however, shifted into a drive for moral righteousness and social conformity. In sum, postwar life in America and Europe was fraught with turbulent changes, contradictory impulses, superficial frivolity, and seething tensions.

A "New Era" of Consumption

During the twenties, the U.S. economy became the envy of the world. Following the brief recession in 1920–1921, Americans benefited from the fastest economic growth in history. Between 1922 and 1928, industrial production soared by 70 percent. Jobs were plentiful, inflation was low, and income rose steadily. The nation's total wealth almost doubled between 1920 and 1930, while wage workers enjoyed a whopping 30 percent increase in income, the sharpest rise in history. By 1929, the United States had the highest standard of living in the world.

Construction led the economic recovery. By 1921, a building boom was under way that would last throughout the decade. Technology boosted mass production through the moving assembly-line process. New machines (electric motors, steam turbines, dump trucks, tractors, bulldozers, steam shovels) and more efficient ways of operating farms, factories, plants, mines, and mills generated dramatic increases in productivity. In 1920, the nation's factories produced 5,000 electric refrigerators; in 1929, they produced almost a million.

In the late nineteenth century, commercial agriculture and large-scale industrial production spurred the building of railroads and bridges, the manufacturing of steel, and the construction of housing and businesses in cities.

During the twenties, such industrial production continued, but the dominant aspect of the economy involved an explosion of new consumer goods made available through a national marketplace. The success of mass production made mass consumption more critical than ever.

THE FLORIDA LAND RUSH While production and consumption were soaring, so were get-rich-quick schemes, the most outlandish of which was the Florida real estate boom. One of the least developed states on the Atlantic coast suddenly became the nation's fastest-growing state, in part because it was the only state without an income tax or inheritance tax, and in part because widespread ownership of automobiles made it possible for masses of people to vacation in the "winter playground of America."

Like prospectors during the California gold rush, speculators and developers swooped into the "Land of Flowers" and bought, cleared, tamed, subdivided, and sold parcels of land so fast they could not keep up with the paperwork. Miami, the "Magic City," was the fastest-growing community in the nation. From 1,700 residents in 1900, its population mushroomed to 111,000 by 1925. One reporter gushed that Miami was "growing so fast it creaks." A beachfront property that sold for $35,000 went for $1 million just three years later.

An advertisement for Florida made it sound like Shangri-la: "Florida is bathed in passionate caresses of the southern sun. It is laved by the limpid waves of the embracing seas, wooed by the glorious Gulf Stream. . . . Florida is an emerald kingdom . . . clothed in perpetual verdure and lapt in the gorgeous folds of the semi-tropical zone."

By the end of 1925, some 20 million parcels were for sale in Florida, enough for every adult in the nation. Hundreds of thousands of people, mostly northerners, invested in Florida real estate sight unseen, but what they were told was prime property often turned out to be swamp land. Fraudulent sales made people hesitant to join the stampede. Soon, analysts predicted the Florida land bubble would burst. "The rise in Florida [land values] will continue as long as northern money is sent to Florida," said the Ohio state commerce director, "and the end will be that of every boom, where few prosper and many hold the bag at the end."

As he predicted, in mid-1926, the Florida real estate bubble imploded. Too much growth too fast had caused unexpected problems. Railroads struggling to supply food to the state's rapidly growing population announced they were no longer transporting construction supplies, leaving thousands of homes unfinished. In July, *The Nation* magazine reported: "The world's greatest poker game, played with building lots instead of chips, is over. And the players are now cashing in or paying up." A devastating hurricane that roared across South Florida in September only deepened the pain.

By 1928, much of Florida was a wasteland. A journalist described the damage: "Dead subdivisions line the highway, their pompous names half-obliterated on crumbling stucco gates. Lonely, white-way lights stand guard over miles of cement sidewalks, where grass and palmetto [trees] take the place of homes that were to be. . . . Whole sections of outlying subdivisions are composed of unoccupied houses, through which one speeds on broad thoroughfares as if traversing a city in the grip of death." The collapse of the Florida land boom proved to be but an audition for the great stock market bubble that would burst at the end of 1929.

A GROWING CONSUMER CULTURE

Perhaps the most visible change during the twenties was the emergence of a powerful "**consumer culture**" in which mass production and consumption of nationally advertised products dictated much of social life and social status. "A change has come over our democracy," a 1920 newspaper editorial insisted. "It is called consumptionism." The American's "first importance to his country is no longer that of citizen but that of consumer. Consumption is a new necessity."

Old virtues such as hard work, plain living, and prudent money management were challenged by new values celebrating leisure, self-expression, and self-indulgence. "During the war," a journalist noted in 1920, "we accustomed ourselves to doing without, to buying carefully, to using economically. But with the close of the war came reaction. A veritable orgy of extravagant buying is going on. Reckless spending takes the place of saving, waste replaces conservation."

To stimulate such spending, businesses focused on two crucial innovations: marketing and advertising. "Layaway" plans and installment buying encouraged consumers to "buy now, pay later." As a result, consumer debt almost tripled during the twenties. At the same time, advertising began driving the mass-production/mass-consumption economy. President Calvin Coolidge declared that advertising had become "the most potent influence in adopting and changing the habits and modes of life, affecting what we eat, what we wear, and the work and play of the whole nation."

The visibility of ads helped shape how people behaved, what they purchased, and how they pursued happiness. Zelda Sayre Fitzgerald, the spirited wife of celebrated novelist F. Scott Fitzgerald, recalled that "we grew up founding our dreams on the infinite promises of American advertising." In a 1923 interview, she embraced the culture of consumption: "I don't mean that money means happiness, necessarily. But having things, just things, objects, makes a woman happy. The right kind of perfume, the smart pair of shoes." Her husband chimed in: "Women care for 'things,' clothes, furniture, for themselves . . . and men [do too], in so far as they contribute to their vanity."

Advertisers targeted women, who purchased two-thirds of consumer goods, and sponsored new weekday radio programs (popular with middle-class homemakers) that were funded by "commercials" promoting laundry detergent and hand soap—hence the term *soap operas*.

Electricity became a revolutionary new force influencing everyday life and the consumer culture. In 1920, only 35 percent of homes had electricity; by 1930, the number was 68 percent. Similar increases occurred in the number of households with indoor plumbing, washing machines, and automobiles.

A Modern Home This 1925 Westinghouse advertisement urges homemakers to buy its "Cozy Glow, Jr." heater and "Sol-Lux Luminaire" lamp, among other new electrical appliances that "do anything for you in return."

Moderately priced creature comforts and conveniences, such as flush toilets, electric irons and fans, handheld cameras, wristwatches, cigarette lighters, vacuum cleaners, and linoleum floors, became more widely available, especially among the rapidly growing urban middle class.

THE RISE OF MASS CULTURE

Mass advertising, mass production, and the mass media combined to create a mass culture: Americans read the same magazines, listened to the same radio programs, watched the same movies, and drove the same cars. They saw the same ads and shopped at the same national retail stores. By the 1920s, Woolworth's, for example, had 1,500 stores across the country; Walgreen's had 525. National retailers bought goods in such large quantities that they were able to get discounted prices that they passed on to consumers.

A LOVE AFFAIR WITH MOVIES In 1896, a New York City audience viewed one of the first moving-picture shows. By 1924, there were 20,000 theaters nationwide showing 700 new "silent" films a year with captions to show the dialogue, making movies the primary form of mass entertainment. Hollywood, California, emerged as the international center of movie production, grinding out Westerns, crime dramas, murder mysteries, and the comedies of Mack Sennett's Keystone Company, in which a raft of slapstick comedians, notably London-born Charlie Chaplin, perfected their art, transforming it into a form of social criticism.

Charlie Chaplin An English-born actor who rose to international fame as the "Tramp," Chaplin is pictured above in the 1921 silent film *The Kid.*

Movie attendance during the 1920s averaged 80 million people a week. It surged even more after 1927 with the appearance of movies with sound ("talkies"). Americans spent ten times as much on movies as they did on tickets to baseball and football games. Movies did much more than entertain, however. They helped expand the consumer culture by setting standards and tastes in fashion, music, dancing, and hairstyles.

THE RADIO CRAZE Radio broadcasting experienced even more spectacular growth. Between 1922 and 1930, the number of families owning a radio soared from 60,000 to nearly 14 million. Almost two-thirds of homes had at least one radio. The radio changed the patterns of everyday life. At night after dinner, families gathered to listen to music, speeches, news broadcasts, weather forecasts, and comedy shows. One ad claimed that the radio "is your theater, your college, your newspaper, your library." President Calvin Coolidge's monthly radio talks paved the way for Franklin Delano Roosevelt's influential "fireside chats" during the thirties.

The radio networks transformed jazz music into a national craze. Big band leaders Paul Whiteman, Guy Lombardo, Duke Ellington, Glenn Miller, and Tommy and Jimmy Dorsey regularly performed live over the radio. Country music also developed a national following as a result of radio broadcasts. In 1925, WSM, a station in Nashville, Tennessee, began offering a weekly variety show, *The Grand Ole Opry*, which featured an array of country music stars.

TAKING TO THE AIR Advances in transportation were as significant as the impact of commercial radio and movies. In 1903, Wilbur and Orville Wright, owners of a bicycle shop in Dayton, Ohio, had built and flown the first airplane at Kitty Hawk, North Carolina, flying only a few hundred feet at 34 miles per hour.

Airplane technology advanced slowly until the outbreak of war in 1914, after which Europeans rapidly adapted the airplane as a military weapon. When the United States entered the war, it had no combat planes; American pilots flew British or French warplanes. An American aircraft industry arose during the war but collapsed in the postwar demobilization. Under the Kelly Act of 1925, however, the federal government began to subsidize the industry through airmail delivery contracts. The Air Commerce Act of 1926 provided federal funds for the advancement of air transportation and navigation, including the construction of airports.

The aviation industry received a huge psychological boost in May 1927 when twenty-six-year-old Charles A. Lindbergh Jr., a St. Louis–based pilot blessed with extraordinary courage and endurance, won a $25,000 prize (and a Medal of Honor) by making the first *solo* nonstop transatlantic flight. He traveled from New York City to Paris in thirty-three and a half hours through thunderstorms, ice clouds, and blinding fog.

A handsome, daring college dropout, Lindbergh oversaw a fanatical effort to reduce the weight of his plane to accommodate the 2,500 pounds of fuel—heavier than the plane itself—needed for the crossing. He used a wicker basket for a seat, removed the radio, and modified the tail section to make the plane hard to control so as to ensure he did not fall asleep.

When Lindbergh, known as the "Lone Eagle," landed in France, some 150,000 people greeted him with thunderous cheers. The New York City parade honoring his accomplishment surpassed the celebration of the end of the Great War. A new dance, the Lindy Hop, was named for him, and a popular song, "Lucky Lindy," celebrated his "peerless, fearless" feat. Lindbergh's flight redefined the potential of "flying machines" to transform transportation and compress distance.

No sooner did Lindbergh return to America than promoters began looking for a female pilot to equal his feat. Women had finally gained the right to vote in 1920, but they still had to fight for equal rights in most aspects of life. The first women who tried flying were dismissed as "petticoat pilots" or "flying flappers" who risked killing themselves—and others. Various aeronautic organizations sought to ban women from cockpits. A group of female pilots responded, "Women have the same inherent right to be killed in airplane races as men have."

Amelia Earhart The pioneering aviator would tragically disappear during her 1937 attempt to fly around the world.

In June 1928, Kansas-born Amelia Earhart, who had dropped out of college during the Great War to nurse wounded soldiers, joined two male pilots in being the first woman to cross the Atlantic in an airplane—as a passenger. "Stultz did all the flying — had to," she said. "I was just baggage, like a sack of potatoes. Maybe someday I'll try it alone." Thereafter, Earhart launched a national organization of female pilots, solo-piloted a plane nonstop coast to coast across the United States, and set several speed records for women pilots. In 1932, Earhart climbed into her candy-apple-red Lockheed Vega and equaled Lindbergh by flying solo from Canada to Northern Ireland in fifteen hours, thereby becoming one of the most famous women in the world. In 1937, Earhart set out with a male navigator to fly around the globe at the equator, long before radar was developed. They would use the sun and stars to guide them the 30,000 miles. Just before taking off, she told reporters, "I won't feel completely cheated if I fail to come back." Tragically, while crossing the South Pacific, she lost radio contact and was never heard from again.

THE CAR CULTURE The most significant economic and social development of the early twentieth century was the widespread ownership of automobiles. The motor car came to symbolize the mechanization of modern life. In 1924, when asked about the changes transforming American life, a resident of Muncie, Indiana, replied: "I can tell you what's happening in just four letters: A-U-T-O."

The first motorcars had been manufactured for sale in the late nineteenth century, but the founding of the Ford Motor Company in 1903 revolutionized the infant industry. The first cars were handmade, expensive, and designed for the wealthy. Henry Ford changed all that by pledging to build "a car for the multitude." He vowed "to democratize the automobile. When I'm through, everybody will be able to afford one, and about everyone will have one."

Ford's Model T, cheap and durable, appeared in 1908 at a price of $850 (about $22,000 at today's prices). By 1924, Ford's increasingly efficient production techniques enabled him to sell the same car for $290. The Model T changed little from year to year. Ford ads assured buyers that they "could have any color [they] want, as long as it is black." Selling millions of identical cars at a small profit allowed Ford to keep prices low and wages high—the perfect formula for a mass-consumption economy.

Other automakers followed Ford's production model. In 1916, the total number of cars and trucks in the United States passed 1 million; by 1920, more than 8 million were registered, and in 1929 there were more than 23 million. The automobile revolution was in part propelled by the discovery of vast oil fields in Texas, Oklahoma, Wyoming, and California. By 1920, the United

States produced two-thirds of the world's oil and gasoline. By 1930, an estimated 10 percent of America's workforce was producing automobiles.

The automobile industry also became the leading example of modern, mechanized, mass-production techniques. Ford's Highland Park plant outside Detroit, where 68,000 workers were employed, was the largest factory in the world. It increased output dramatically by creating a moving assembly line rather than having a crew of workers assemble each car in a fixed position. With conveyors pulling the parts along feeder lines and the chassis moving steadily down an assembly line, each worker performed a single task, such as installing a fender or a wheel. This system could produce a new car in ninety-three minutes. Such efficiency enabled Ford to lower car prices, thereby increasing the number of people who could afford them.

Just as the railroad helped transform the pace and scale of life in the late nineteenth century, the automobile changed social life during the twentieth century. A car not only provided greater mobility; it offered *freedom*. In the words of one male driver, young people viewed the car as "an incredible engine of escape" from parental control and a safe place to "take a girl and hold hands, neck, pet, or . . . go the limit."

Highland Park Plant, 1913 The Ford Motor Company led the way in efficiency and cost-cutting production methods. Here, gravity slides and chain conveyors move each automobile chassis down the assembly line.

Cars and networks of new roads enabled people to live farther away from their workplaces, thus encouraging suburban sprawl. Cars also helped fuel the economic boom of the 1920s by creating tens of thousands of new jobs and a huge demand for steel, glass, rubber, leather, oil, and gasoline. The ever-expanding car culture stimulated road construction, sparked a real estate boom in Florida and California, and dotted the landscape with gasoline stations, traffic lights, billboards, and motels. By 1929, the federal government was constructing 10,000 miles of paved highways each year.

SPECTATOR SPORTS Automobile ownership and rising incomes changed the way people spent their leisure time. During the 1920s, Americans fell in love with spectator sports; people in cities could drive into the countryside, visit friends and relatives, and go to ballparks, stadiums, or boxing rings.

Baseball had become the "national pastime." With larger-than-life heroes such as New York Yankee legends George Herman "Babe" Ruth and Henry Louis "Lou" Gehrig, baseball teams attracted intense interest and huge crowds.

Babe Ruth This star pitcher, outfielder, and slugger won the hearts of Americans with the Boston Red Sox, the New York Yankees, and finally the Boston Braves. Here, he autographs bats and balls for military training camps.

Ruth may well have been the most famous athlete of all time. In 1920, more than a million spectators attended his games.

Two years later, the Yankees moved into a new stadium, dubbing it the "House That Ruth Built." They went on to win World Series championships in 1923, 1927, and 1928. More than 20 million people attended professional games in 1927, the year that Ruth, the "Sultan of Swat," set a record by hitting an astonishing sixty home runs. Yet for all its popularity, baseball would remain a racially segregated sport for another twenty years; the so-called Negro Leagues provided playing opportunities for African Americans.

Football, especially at the college level, also attracted huge crowds. It, too, benefited from outsized heroes such as running back Harold Edward "Red" Grange of the University of Illinois, the first athlete to appear on the cover of *Time* magazine. In a 1924 game against the University of Michigan, the "Galloping Ghost" scored touchdowns the first four times he carried the ball. After Illinois won, students carried him on their shoulders for two miles across the campus. When Grange signed a contract with the Chicago Bears in 1926, he single-handedly made professional football competitive with baseball as a spectator sport.

What Ruth and Grange were to their sports, William Harrison "Jack" Dempsey was to boxing. In 1919, he won the world heavyweight title from Jess Willard, a giant of a man weighing 300 pounds and standing six and a half feet tall. Dempsey knocked him down seven times in the first round. Willard gave up in the fourth round, and Dempsey became a dominant force in boxing. The "Manassa Mauler" was especially popular with working-class men, for he had been born poor and lived for years as a hobo, wandering the rails in search of work and challenging toughs in bars to fight for money.

Dempsey was more than a champion; he was a hero to millions. In 1927, when James Joseph "Gene" Tunney defeated Dempsey, more than 100,000 people attended, including 1,000 reporters, 10 state governors, and numerous Hollywood celebrities. Some 60 million people listened to the fight over the radio.

THE "JAZZ AGE"

During the twenties, many young people launched a social and cultural rebellion—trying new fads and fashions, new music, new attitudes, and new ways of having fun. F. Scott Fitzgerald became the self-appointed "voice of his generation" after publishing his best-selling first novel, *This Side of Paradise* (1920). It portrayed rowdy student life at Princeton University, which he had attended.

"No one else," Fitzgerald announced with self-confident bravado, "could have written so searchingly the story of the youth of our generation." He fastened upon the "**Jazz Age**" as the evocative label for the rebelliousness, spontaneity, and sensuality during the "greatest, gaudiest spree in history."

Fitzgerald and his wife Zelda, a precocious, spoiled southern belle and "wild girl," fashioned a "fairy tale" marriage full of longing and passion, heartbreak and betrayal. They became exemplars of the extravagant, frenzied, carefree, boozing emphasis of the Jazz Age. Scott and Zelda ricocheted from New York to Paris to the French Riviera, caught up in a heedless quest for the good life. They danced on tables at the Waldorf Hotel, rode on the roofs of taxis down Fifth Avenue, walked in fountains, passed out at parties, and greeted the dawn at all-night cafes.

Predictably, they paid a price for their pleasure-seeking. "Nothing could have saved our life," Zelda reflected. "All I want to be is very young always and very irresponsible and to feel that my life is my own to live and be happy and die in my own way to please myself." Scott would die

The Beautiful and the Damned The wayward daughter of a strict Alabama judge, Zelda Fitzgerald famously lived up to husband Scott's description of her as the "First American Flapper." In an outfit typical of flappers, Zelda Fitzgerald poses with her husband on the Riviera in 1926.

of a heart attack at forty-four, and Zelda would die at age forty-seven in a fire that swept through the sanatorium where she had been committed for fourteen years.

THE BIRTH OF JAZZ F. Scott Fitzgerald's "Jazz Age" label referred to the popularity of jazz music, a dynamic blend of several musical traditions. It had first emerged as piano-based "ragtime" at the end of the nineteenth century. Thereafter, African American musicians such as Jelly Roll Morton, Duke Ellington, Louis Armstrong, and Bessie Smith (known as the "Empress of the Blues") combined the energies of ragtime with the emotions of the blues to create *jazz*, originally an African American slang term meaning sexual intercourse. With its improvisations, variations, and sensual spontaneity, jazz appealed to people of all ethnicities and ages because it celebrated pleasure and immediacy. In 1925, an African American journalist announced that jazz had "absorbed the national spirit, that tremendous spirit of go, the nervousness, lack of conventionality and boisterous good-nature characteristic of the American, white or black."

Louis Armstrong, an inspired trumpeter with a unique, froggy voice, was the Pied Piper of jazz, an inventive and freewheeling performer who reshaped the American music scene. Born in a New Orleans shack in 1900, the grandson of slaves, he was abandoned by his father and raised by his prostitute mother, who was just fifteen when he was born. As a youth, he experienced the mean and ugly side of America. "I seen everythin' from a child comin' up," he said once. "Nothin' happen I ain't never seen before." Then he found music, using his natural genius to explore the fertile possibilities of jazz. As a teen, he sneaked into music halls to watch Joe "King" Oliver and other early jazz innovators. In 1922, Armstrong moved to Chicago, where he delighted audiences with his passionate trumpet performances and open-hearted personality. He

Duke Ellington Jazz emerged in the 1920s as an American expression of the modernist spirit. African American artists bent musical conventions to give freer rein to improvisation and sensuality.

radiated a joy that reflected his faith in the power of music and laughter to promote racial harmony.

The culture of jazz quickly spread from its origins in New Orleans, Kansas City, Memphis, and St. Louis to the African American neighborhoods of Harlem in New York City and Chicago's South Side. Large dance halls met the demand for jazz music and the dances it inspired, like the Charleston and the Black Bottom, whose sexually provocative movements shocked traditionalists. Affluent Whites flocked to the dance halls as well as to "black" nightclubs and "jazz joints." People spoke of "*jazzing* something up" (invigorating it) or "jazzing around" (acting youthfully and energetically).

A REVOLUTION IN MANNERS AND MORALS Many old-timers were shocked by the revolution in manners and morals among young people, especially those on college campuses: wild parties, skinny-dipping, and "petting" in automobiles on lovers' lanes. A promotional poster for the 1923 silent film *Flaming Youth* asked: "How Far Can a Girl Go?" Other ads claimed the movie appealed especially to "neckers, petters, white kisses, red kisses, pleasure-mad daughters, [and] sensation-craving mothers."

THE IMPACT OF SIGMUND FREUD The increasingly frank treatment of sex during the twenties resulted in part from the spreading influence of Sigmund Freud, the founder of modern psychoanalysis. Freud, an Austrian trained physician, changed the way people understood their behavior and feelings by insisting that the mind is mysteriously "conflicted" by unconscious efforts to control or repress powerful irrational impulses and sexual desires ("libido"). Freud created a new vocabulary for mapping the inner lives of people, explaining the complex dynamics of the ego, the id, and, after 1914, the superego.

By 1909, when Freud first visited the United States to lecture at Clark University in Massachusetts, he was

Sigmund Freud Freud founded modern psychoanalysis. His writings on the subconscious, dreams, and latent sexual yearnings captured the attention of many Americans, especially young adults.

surprised to find himself famous "even in prudish America." It did not take long for his ideas to penetrate society at large. Psychoanalysis soon became the most celebrated—and controversial—technique for helping troubled people come to grips with their psychic demons. Through "talk therapy," patients discussed their inner frustrations and revealed their suppressed fears and urges as part of getting to know their hidden selves. Freud believed that psychoanalysis, not religion, could provide the answers to the fundamental questions: How should we live? Why does happiness elude us? What really matters? By 1916, there were some 500 psychoanalysts in New York City alone.

For many young Americans, Freud provided scientific justification for rebelling against social conventions and indulging in sex. Some oversimplified his theories by claiming that sexual pleasure was essential for emotional health, that all forms of sexual activity were good, and that all inhibitions—feelings of restraint—about sex were bad. Traditionalists, on the other hand, were shocked at the scandalous behavior of rebellious young women who claimed to be acting out Freud's theories. "One hears it said," complained a Baptist magazine, "that the girls are actually tempting the boys more than the boys do the girls, by their dress and conversation."

WOMEN IN THE 1920S Young women emboldened by gaining the right to vote sought other freedoms as well. The empowered "new women" of the twenties discarded the confining wardrobe of their "frumpy" mothers—pinched-in corsets, choking girdles, layers of petticoats, and floor-length dresses—in favor of more daring attire.

In 1919, skirts were typically six inches above the ground; by 1927, they were at the knee. The shortest ones were worn by the so-called **flappers**, young women who—in defiance of "proper" standards—drove automobiles; "bobbed" their hair (cut it short, requiring the invention of the "bobby pin"); and wore minimal underclothing, gauzy fabrics, sheer stockings, and plenty of makeup, especially brightly colored rouge and lipstick and smoky mascara. They also joined young men in smoking cigarettes, (illegally) drinking and gambling, and shaking and shimmying to the sensual energies of jazz music.

Self-consciously outrageous and outlandish, flappers wanted more out of life than marriage and motherhood. Their carefree version of feminism—fun-loving, defiant, and self-indulgent—aroused furious criticism. A Catholic priest in Brooklyn complained that the feminism of the 1920s had provoked a "pandemonium of powder, a riot of rouge, and a moral anarchy of dress." In discussing the flapper phenomenon, a newspaper columnist reported that "the world is divided into those who delight in her, those who fear her, and those who try pathetically to take her as a matter of course."

MARGARET SANGER AND BIRTH CONTROL The most controversial women's issue of the Jazz Age was birth control. Christians—both Protestants and Catholics—opposed it as a violation of God's law. Other crusaders viewed it differently. Margaret Sanger, a nurse and midwife in the working-class tenements of Manhattan, watched many young mothers struggle to provide for their large families. One of eleven children born to Irish immigrants, she had experienced the poverty often faced by immigrants. "Our childhood," she remembered, "was one of longing for things that were always denied."

In her work as a midwife, Sanger witnessed the consequences of unwanted pregnancies, miscarriages, and alleyway abortions. To her, the problems had an obvious solution: *birth control*, a term she and friends coined in 1914. Birth control devices, she argued, provided the best alternative to abortions and "enforced, enslaved maternity."

In 1911, Sanger and her husband joined the Socialist party, and their home became a gathering place for journalists, anarchists, labor leaders, and reformers. The party hired Sanger to promote women's suffrage, but she decided that birth control was more important to poor women than the vote. In 1912, she began to distribute birth-control information to working-class women and resolved to spend the rest of her life helping women take charge of their bodies. "Every child a wanted child" became the slogan for her campaign.

In 1914, Sanger launched a feminist magazine called *Woman Rebel* in which she promoted women's suffrage, workers' rights, and contraception. In the magazine's first issue, Sanger declared that every woman had a fundamental right to be "absolute mistress of her own body," including the right to practice birth control.

In 1916, Sanger opened the nation's first birth-control clinic, in Brooklyn. In just its first nine days of operation, the clinic served 464 clients before police shut it down and arrested Sanger. She served thirty days in jail but emerged even more determined to continue her contraception crusade.

In 1921, Sanger organized the American Birth Control League, which in 1942 would change its name to Planned Parenthood. The Birth Control League distributed contraceptive information to doctors, social workers, women's clubs, the scientific community, and thousands of women. Sanger, however, alienated supporters of birth control by endorsing sterilization for the mentally incompetent. Birth control, she stressed, was "the most constructive and necessary of the means to racial health."

Although Sanger failed to legalize the distribution of contraceptives and contraceptive information through the mail, she laid the foundation for such efforts. In 1936, a federal court ruled that physicians could prescribe

Margaret Sanger An American sex educator, nurse, and birth control activist, Margaret Sanger founded the American Birth Control League, later renamed Planned Parenthood, and devoted her life to securing women the right to use contraceptives.

contraceptives. Before Sanger died in 1966 at the age of eighty-seven, the U.S. Supreme Court, in *Griswold v. Connecticut* (1965), declared that women had a constitutional right to use contraceptives as a form of birth control.

NOT-SO-"NEW" WOMEN Most women in the 1920s were not rebels like Margaret Sanger or flappers like Zelda Fitzgerald, however. Lillian Symes, a longtime activist, stressed that her "generation of feminists" had little in common with the "spike-heeled, over-rouged flapper of today." Although more middle-class women attended college in the 1920s than ever before, a higher percentage of them married soon after graduation than had been the case in the nineteenth century.

Women were discouraged from enrolling in coeducational colleges and universities, however. Male doctors warned that mixed-gender classrooms hindered childbearing potential in women by "forcing their blood to nourish their brain instead of their ovaries." Prolonged academic study made women "mannish."

The conservative political mood helped steer women who had worked for the war effort back into their traditional roles as homemakers, and college curricula began to shift accordingly. At Vassar College, an all-women's school outside New York City, students still took domestic courses such as "Husband and Wife," "Motherhood," and "The Family as an Economic Unit."

At the same time, fewer college-educated women pursued careers outside the home. The proportion of physicians who were women fell during the twenties, and similar reductions occurred among dentists, architects, and chemists. A student at all-female Smith College in Massachusetts expressed frustration "that a woman must choose between a home and her work, when a man may have both. There must be a way out, and it is the problem of our generation to find the way."

As before, most women who worked outside the home labored in unskilled, low-paying jobs. Only 4 percent of working women were salaried professionals. Some moved into new roles, such as accounting assistants and department-store clerks. The number of beauty shops soared from 5,000 in 1920 to 40,000 in 1930, creating jobs for hair stylists, manicurists, and cosmeticians.

African American and Latina women faced the stiffest challenges. As a New York City newspaper observed, they did the "work which white women will not do." Women of color usually worked as maids, laundresses, or dressmakers, or on farms.

Racism also continued to limit the freedom of women. For example, in 1919, an interracial couple from Ayer, Massachusetts, Mabel Puffer, a wealthy college graduate, and Arthur Hazzard, a handyman, decided to get married in Concord, New Hampshire. When applying for a marriage license, they were told that there was a five-day waiting period. The mayor of Concord agreed to perform the service.

When news of the interracial couple strolling the streets of Concord reached the Boston newspapers, the headline in the *Boston Traveler* read: "Will Marry Negro in 'Perfect Union': Rich Ayer Society Woman Determined to Wed Servant Although Hometown Is Aflame with Protest." Suddenly, the mayor of Concord announced he could not perform the wedding. The betrothed couple, after being turned down several times, finally found a minister willing to marry them. But the night before the wedding, the Ayer police chief arrested Hazzard on a charge of "enticement" and took Puffer into custody because she had been deemed "insane." The nation remained an unsafe place for those bold enough to cross the color line.

Most women during the twenties remained either full-time wives and mothers or household servants. The growing availability of electrical appliances—vacuum cleaners, toasters, stoves, refrigerators, washing machines, irons—made housework easier. Likewise, "supermarkets" offered year-round access to fruits, vegetables, and meats, which greatly reduced the traditional tasks of food preparation—canning, baking bread, and plucking chickens.

THE HARLEM RENAISSANCE As their Great Migration from the segregated South continued into the twenties, African Americans found new freedoms in northern settings; they also gained leverage as voters by settling in high-population states with many electoral votes. With these new opportunities came a bristling spirit of protest known as the **Harlem Renaissance**, the nation's first self-conscious Black literary and artistic movement.

The movement started among the fast-growing African American community in the Harlem neighborhood of northern Manhattan in New York City. The "great, dark city" of Harlem, as poet Langston Hughes called it, contained more Blacks per square mile than any other urban neighborhood in the nation. Their numbers generated a sense of common identity, growing power, and distinctive self-expression that soon made Harlem the cultural capital of African American life. James Weldon Johnson, a poet, lawyer, and civil rights activist, coined the term *Aframerican* to designate Americans with African ancestry, whom he called "conscious collaborators" in the creation of American society and culture.

Dotted with raucous nightclubs where writers and painters discussed literature and art while listening to jazz and drinking bootleg alcohol, Harlem became what journalists called the "Nightclub Capital of the World."

African American Art *Into Bondage* (1936), a painting by Aaron Douglas *(left)*, exemplifies how Black artists in the Harlem Renaissance used their African roots and collective history as inspiration. The sculpture *Realization (right)*, by Augusta Savage, reflects her mission to challenge negative views of African Americans. After having been rejected for an arts fellowship abroad because of her race, Savage spoke out and became a pillar of the artistic community in Harlem.

The Harlem Renaissance writers celebrated African American culture, especially jazz and the blues. As Langston Hughes wrote, "I am a Negro—and beautiful. . . . The night is beautiful. So [are] the faces of my people." He loved Africa and its cultural heritage but declared, "I was not Africa. I was Chicago and Kansas City and Broadway and Harlem."

Harvard graduate Alain Locke, the first Black Rhodes scholar, was the guiding spirit of the "new" African American culture. Tiny in stature—he was less than five feet tall and weighed ninety-five pounds—Locke played a herculean role as the champion of the Harlem Renaissance. In 1925, for example, he announced that the Harlem Renaissance was led by a self-confident "New Negro" who no longer felt subservient to White culture or paralyzed by a sense of grievance against the Jim Crow system of White supremacy. Blacks, he argued, could shape their future by using a cultural flowering to transform their present.

Women were active in the Harlem Renaissance. In January 1925, a thirty-four-year-old African American woman named Zora Neale Hurston arrived in Harlem from Eatonville, an all-Black community in rural Florida. An aspiring writer and inventive storyteller, she became the first African American to enroll at Barnard College, the women's college of Columbia University, where she majored in cultural anthropology.

Hurston had mastered the art of survival by learning to reinvent herself as the need arose. Motherless at nine and a runaway at fourteen, she became a calculating opportunist blessed with remarkable willpower. She came to Harlem to immerse herself in the "clang and clamor" of city life.

Within a few months, Hurston was behaving, in her words, as the queen of the Harlem Renaissance, writing short stories and plays about the "Negro furthest down" while positioning herself at the center of the community's raucous social life. Her outspokenness invited controversy, as when she claimed that she "did not belong to the sobbing school of Negrohood who hold that nature somehow has given them a lowdown dirty deal and whose feelings are all hurt about it." Hurston went on to become an anthropologist, folklorist, and novelist, expert at describing the ways in which African Americans in the Lower South forged cohesive communities in the face of White bigotry and violence. She also spoke out on behalf of poor African Americans who, "having nothing, still refused to be humble."

By 1930, the Harlem Renaissance writers had produced dozens of novels and volumes of poetry; several Broadway plays; and a flood of short stories, essays, and films. A people capable of producing such great art and literature, Johnson declared, should never again be "looked upon as inferior."

MARCUS GARVEY The celebration of Black culture found much different expression in what came to be called Black nationalism, which promoted Black separatism from mainstream American life. Its leader was Marcus Mosiah Garvey, who claimed to speak for all 400 million Blacks worldwide. In 1916, Garvey brought to Harlem the headquarters of the Universal Negro Improvement Association (UNIA), which he had started in his native Jamaica two years before.

Garvey insisted that Blacks had *nothing* in common with Whites. "The black skin," he stressed, "is not a badge of shame, but rather a glorious symbol of national greatness." Garvey urged African Americans to cultivate Black solidarity and "Black power."

The UNIA grew quickly after the Great War ended. By 1923, Garvey claimed the UNIA had as many as 4 million members served by 800 offices. His goal was to build an all-Black empire in Africa. "Back to Africa" became his rallying cry. To that end, he called himself the "Provisional President of Africa," raised funds to send Americans to Africa, and expelled any UNIA member who married a White.

Garvey's message of Black nationalism and racial solidarity mushroomed into the largest Black mass movement in American history. It appealed both to poor Blacks in northern cities and across the rural South.

Garveyism, however, appalled most Black leaders, for they viewed relocating African Americans to Africa as another form of colonization. Even worse in their view was Garvey's praise for the Ku Klux Klan and its opposition to racial mixing. W.E.B. Du Bois labeled Garvey "the most dangerous enemy of the Negro race. . . . He is either a lunatic or a traitor."

Garvey's crusade collapsed in 1923 when a jury convicted him of fraud for overselling shares of stock in a steamship corporation, the Black Star Line, which he had founded to transport American Blacks to Africa. Sentenced to five years in prison, he was pardoned in 1927 by President Calvin Coolidge on the condition that he be deported to Jamaica. Garvey died in obscurity in 1940, but the memory of his movement and its emphasis on Black pride would reemerge in the 1960s under the slogan "Black power."

THE NAACP A more lasting force for racial equality during the twenties was the **National Association for the Advancement of Colored People (NAACP)**, founded in 1910 by Black activists and White progressives. African American NAACP leaders came mainly from the Niagara Movement, a group that had met each year since 1905 at places associated with the anti-slavery movement and issued defiant statements against discrimination. Within a few years, the NAACP had become a broad-based national organization. It embraced the progressive idea that the solution to social problems begins with education, by informing people about the harsh realities of social problems. W.E.B. Du Bois became the organization's director of publicity and research and the editor of its journal, *Crisis*.

The NAACP focused its political strategy on legal action to bring the Fourteenth and Fifteenth Amendments back to life. One early victory came with *Guinn v. United States* (1915), in which the Supreme Court struck down Oklahoma's efforts to deprive African Americans of the vote. In 1919, the NAACP launched a national campaign against lynching, still a common form of vigilante racist violence. An anti-lynching bill to make mob murder a federal crime passed the House in 1922, but White southerners in the Senate blocked its passage.

THE MODERNIST REVOLT

"The world broke in two in 1922 or thereabouts." So wrote author Willa Cather. She meant that during the twenties, cultural modernists and their traditionalist critics engaged in a civil war.

Modernism appeared first in the capitals of Europe—London, Paris, Berlin, and Vienna—in the 1890s. By the second decade of the twentieth century, cultural modernism had spread to the United States, especially New York City and Chicago.

Modernists were rebellious intellectuals, writers, and artists who viewed conventional Christian morality as the greatest obstacle to artistic creativity and personal freedom. They engaged in a relentless search for new and even scandalous modes of expression and behavior.

Modernism did not simply drop out of the sky in 1922. It had been years in the making. Modernism reflected a widespread recognition that Western civilization was experiencing bewildering changes. New technologies, modes of transportation and communication, and startling scientific discoveries were transforming the nature of everyday life and the way people "saw" the world.

Since the eighteenth-century Enlightenment, conventional wisdom had held that the universe was governed by basic laws of time and energy, light and motion. This rational world of order and certainty disintegrated in the early twentieth century, thanks to the discoveries of European physicists.

SCIENCE AND MODERNISM: EINSTEIN AND RELATIVITY

In the first decade of the twentieth century, Albert Einstein, a young German physicist, published several research papers that changed how scientists viewed the world—and the universe. Einstein used his intuition, imagination,

Albert Einstein One of the most influential scientists of the twentieth century, Einstein received a Nobel Prize in 1921.

and analytical skill to conduct what he called thought experiments. "Imagination," he said, "is more important than knowledge." He happily left it to others to test his mind-bending conclusions.

Einstein first asserted that unseen and unmeasurable atoms and sub-atomic particles do exist and constitute the building blocks of all solids, liquids, and gases.

Second, he demonstrated through the famous equation $E=mc^2$ (in which E stands for energy, m for mass, and c^2 the speed of light multiplied by itself) that matter and energy are different forms of the same thing and that splitting the atoms within even small amounts of matter (mass) has the potential to release titanic amounts of energy. That is why nuclear power plants and atomic and hydrogen bombs are so powerful.

Third, Einstein predicted that nothing could travel faster than light and that light was not a continuous wave of energy, as had long been believed, but a stream of tiny particles, called *quanta* (now called *photons*) that emit light in bursts. This breakthrough would provide the theoretical basis for quantum physics and lead to new technologies such as television, laser beams, and semiconductors used to make computers and cell phones.

Einstein's most controversial discovery overturned traditional notions of the universe by introducing his "special theory of relativity." It explained that no matter how fast one is moving toward or away from a source of light, the speed of that light beam will remain a constant 186,282 miles per second.

Space and time, however, *will* change *relative* to the constant speed of light. So, if a train were traveling at the speed of light, time would slow down from the perspective of those watching, and the train itself would get shorter and heavier. Weird, yes, but true. Space and time, in other words, are not independent of one another. They instead form the fabric of space-time within which the universe resides.

Einstein took ten more years to devise his mind-boggling gravitation theory, which he called a *general theory of relativity*. It built upon his earlier insights while focusing on the role of gravity. Instead of being an invisible force that attracts objects to one another, gravity in Einstein's view represents a curving or warping of space. The more massive an object, the more gravity it exerts to warp the space around it.

Imagine placing a bowling ball in the center of a trampoline. The heavy ball would press down into the fabric, causing it to dimple. A marble rolled around the edge of the trampoline would spiral inward toward the bowling ball, pulled in much the same way that the gravity of a planet pulls objects toward it. Like the speed of light, this gravitational force also distorts time—clocks run slower in a strong gravitational field than they do in empty space.

Einstein revolutionized notions of time, space, and light. Although few understood the details of his theories, many began to embrace the idea that there were no absolute standards or fixed points of reference in the world. During the twenties, the idea of "relativity" gradually emerged in popular discussions of decidedly nonscientific topics such as sexuality, the arts, and politics; there was less faith in absolutes, not only of time and space but also of truth and morality.

In 1920, the year before Einstein was awarded the Nobel Prize, an American journalist said that his theories had moved physics into the region of "metaphysics, where paradox and magic take the place of solid fact . . . and common sense." As scientists reached farther out into the universe and probed deeper into the microscopic world of the atom, traditional certainties dissolved.

MODERNIST ART AND LITERATURE

The scientific breakthroughs associated with Sigmund Freud, Albert Einstein, and others helped to inspire and shape a "modernist" cultural revolution. The horrors of the Great War accelerated and expanded the appeal of modernism. To be modern was to take chances, violate artistic rules and moral restrictions, and behave in deliberately shocking ways. "Art," said a modernist painter, "is meant to disturb."

Modernism thrived on three unsettling assumptions: (1) God did not exist; (2) reality was not rational, orderly, or obvious; and, in the aftermath of the Great War, (3) social progress could no longer be taken for granted. These premises led writers, artists, musicians, designers, and architects to rebel against good taste, old-fashioned morals, and old-time religion.

Modernists refused to be conventional. Poet Ezra Pound, a militant propagandist for the modernist movement, believed that he and other cultural rebels were "saving civilization" from the dictatorship of tradition: "We are restarting civilization." Pound provided the slogan for modernism when he exclaimed, "Make It New!"

Like many previous cultural movements, modernism involved a new way of *seeing* the world, led by an intellectual and cultural elite determined to capture and express the hidden realm of imagination and dreams. Doing so, however, often made their writing, art, music, and dance difficult to understand, interpret, or explain. "The pure modernist is merely a snob," explained a British writer.

But for many modernists, being misunderstood was a badge of honor. American experimentalist writer Gertrude Stein, for example, declared that a novel "which tells about what happens is of no interest." Instead of depicting real life or telling recognizable stories in books such as *Three Lives* and *Tender Buttons*, she was interested in playing with language. Words, not people, are the characters in her writings.

***Russian Ballet* (1916)** Jewish American artist Max Weber's painting is a modernist view of a traditional subject. Splicing the scene of the performance into planes of jarring colors, this painting exemplifies the impact of psychoanalysis and the theory of relativity on the arts.

Until the twentieth century, most writers and artists had taken for granted an accessible, identifiable world that could be readily observed, scientifically explained, and accurately represented in words or paint or even music. Modernists, however, applied Einstein's ideas about relativity to a world in which reality no longer had an objective or recognizable basis. They agreed with Freud that reality was an intensely inward and subjective experience—something deeply personal that was to be imagined and expressed by one's innermost being. Walter Pach, an early champion of modern art, explained that modernism resulted from the discovery of "the role played by the unconscious in our lives."

For modernists such as Spanish painter Pablo Picasso and Irish writer James Joyce, art involved an unpredictable journey into the realm of individual fantasies and dreams, exploring and expressing the personal, the unknown, the primitive, the abstract.

In the early-twentieth-century art world, modernists discarded literal representation of recognizable subjects in favor of vibrant color masses, simplified forms, or geometric shapes. American artist Marsden Hartley reported from Paris that his reading of Freud and other "new psychologists" had led him to quit painting objects from "real life" and instead paint "intuitive abstractions."

THE ARMORY SHOW The efforts to bring European-inspired modernism to the United States reached a climax in the Armory Show of 1913, the most controversial event in the history of American art. Mabel Dodge, one of the organizers, wrote to Gertrude Stein that the exhibition would cause "a riot and revolution and things will never be the same afterwards."

To house the 1,200 works of modern art collected from more than 300 painters and sculptors in America and Europe, the two dozen young painters who organized the show leased the vast 69th Army Regiment Armory in New York City. The Armory Show, officially known as the International Exhibition of Modern Art, opened on February 17, 1913. As Dodge had predicted, it created an immediate sensation.

For many who toured the Armory Show, modern art became the thing that they loved to hate. Modernism, growled a prominent art critic, "is nothing else than the total destruction of the art of painting." The *New York Times* warned visitors who shared the "old belief in reality" that they would enter "a stark region of abstractions" at the "lunatic asylum" show that was "hideous to our unaccustomed eyes."

The experimentalist ("*avant-garde*") artists whose works were on display (including paintings by Vincent Van Gogh, Paul Gaugin, and Henri Matisse as

The Armory Show, 1913 Celebrated by some and hated by others, the controversial Armory Show brought widespread attention to the modernist movement in the arts.

well as Cezanne and Picasso) were "in love with science but not with objective reality," the *Times* critic complained, adding that they had produced paintings "revolting in their inhumanity."

Yet the Armory Show also generated excitement. "A new world has arisen before our eyes," announced an art magazine. "To miss modern art," a critic stressed, "is to miss one of the few thrills that life holds." From New York, the show went on to Chicago and Boston, where it aroused similarly strong responses and attracted overflow crowds. A quarter-million people viewed the exhibition in the three cities.

After the Armory Show, modern art became one of the nation's favorite topics of debate. Many artists, writers, and critics adjusted to the shock of modernism and found a new faith in the disturbing powers of art. "America in its newness," predicted Walt Kuhn, a painter who helped organize the exhibition, "is destined to become the coming center" of modernism. Indeed, the Museum of Modern Art, founded in New York City in 1929, came to house the world's most celebrated collection of avant-garde paintings and sculpture.

POUND, ELIOT, AND STEIN The leading American champions of modernist art and literature lived in England and Europe: Idaho-born Ezra Pound and St. Louis–born T. S. Eliot in London, and Californian Gertrude Stein in Paris. They were self-conscious revolutionaries concerned with creating strange, new, and often beautifully difficult forms of expression, and they found more inspiration and more receptive audiences in Europe than in the United States.

As the foreign editor of the Chicago-based *Poetry* magazine, Pound became the cultural promoter of modernism. In bitter poems and earnest essays denouncing war and commercialism, he displayed an uncompromising urgency to transform the literary landscape. An English poet called him a "solitary volcano." Eliot claimed that Pound was single-handedly responsible for the modernist movement in poetry.

Pound recruited, edited, published, and reviewed the best young talents among the modernist writers, improving their writing, bolstering their courage, and propelling their careers. In his own poetry, he expressed the feeling of many that the Great War had wasted a generation of young men who died in defense of a "botched civilization."

One of the young American writers Pound took under his wing was T. S. Eliot, who had recently graduated from Harvard. Within a few years, Eliot surpassed Pound to become the leading American modernist. Eliot's epic 433-line poem *The Waste Land* (1922), which Pound edited, became a monument of modernism. It expressed a sense of postwar disillusionment and melancholy that had a powerful effect on other writers. As a poet and critic for the *Criterion,* a poetry journal that he founded in 1922, Eliot became the arbiter of modernist taste in Anglo-American literature.

Gertrude Stein was the self-appointed champion of the American modernists living in Paris. An uninhibited eccentric, she sought to capture in words the equivalent of abstract painting and its self-conscious revolt against portraying recognizable scenes from real life. Stein also hosted an effervescent cultural salon in Paris that became a gathering place for American and European modernists. On any night, she and her lifelong partner, Alice B. Toklas, might be hosting her "charmed circle" of literary stars and painters—James Joyce, Ernest Hemingway, F. Scott Fitzgerald, Ezra Pound, Henri Matisse, and Pablo Picasso—surrounded by her fabled collection of modern art.

THE "LOST GENERATION" In addition to modernism, the arts and literature of the twenties were also greatly influenced by the horrors of the

The Lost Generation Following the Great War's atrocities, American writers found themselves in cynical conversations about disillusionment. Gertrude Stein, pictured here in her studio apartment in Paris, characterized Ernest Hemingway and his comrades who served in the war as "the lost generation," underlining a loss of innocence.

Great War. F. Scott Fitzgerald wrote in *This Side of Paradise* (1920) that the younger generation of Americans, the "sad young men" who had fought in Europe to "make the world safe for democracy," had "grown up to find all Gods dead, all wars fought, all faiths in man shaken." Cynicism had displaced idealism in the wake of the war's horrific senselessness. As Fitzgerald asserted, "There's only one lesson to be learned from life anyway. . . . That there's no lesson to be learned from life."

Hemingway, Fitzgerald, and other young modernists came to be labeled the Lost Generation—those who had lost faith in the values and institutions of Western civilization and were frantically looking for new gods to worship. In 1921, Gertrude Stein told Hemingway that he and his dissolute friends who had served in the war as soldiers or ambulance drivers "are a lost generation." When Hemingway objected, she held her ground. "You are [lost]. You have no respect for anything. You drink yourselves to death."

In his first novel, *The Sun Also Rises* (1926), Hemingway used the phrase "lost generation" in the book's opening quotation. The novel centers on Jake Barnes, a young American castrated by a war injury. His impotence leads him to wander the cafes and nightclubs of postwar Europe with his often-drunk friends, who acknowledge that they are all wounded and neutered in their own way. They have lost their innocence, their illusions, and their motivation to do anything with their lives.

Hemingway sought "in all my stories to get the feeling of the actual life across—not just to depict life—but to actually make it alive. So that when you have read something by me you actually experience the thing."

Hemingway's friend and rival, Fitzgerald, shared a similar goal. He was the self-appointed chronicler of the Lost Generation. Like his fictional characters, Fitzgerald blazed up brilliantly, delighted in the heavy-drinking, party-going pace of the Jazz Age, and then flickered out in a fog of drunkenness. (He would die in 1940 at age forty-four.) A fellow writer called Fitzgerald "our darling, our genius, our fool." He used his writings to depict the frivolity of the "upper tenth" social elite and to reveal his own shortcomings and failures, guilt and shame.

In 1924, while drafting *The Great Gatsby*, Fitzgerald announced his intention to "write a novel better than any novel ever written in America." The novel dealt with the misfortunes of the fortunate: self-indulgent and self-destructive wealthy people who drank and partied as a means of medicating themselves to the pointlessness of their shallow lives.

Jay Gatsby, the main character, is a self-created hero, a tycoon with a crooked past who excels at selling con-man illusions: he seduces the gullible wealthy with his gaudy mansion, mysterious charm, jazz parties, flashy cars, and genius for deceit. As a stylish fraud, Gatsby symbolizes America itself during the twenties: a nation overflowing with wealth and excess but hollow at its core, as it pursues the empty materialism of the American Dream.

What gave depth to the best of Fitzgerald's stories was what a character in *The Great Gatsby* called "a sense of the fundamental decencies" amid all the superficial merriment and fanatical materialism—and a sense of impending doom in a world that had lost its meaning through the disorienting discoveries of modern science and the horrors of war.

Just six months after the stock market crashed in October 1929, Zelda Fitzgerald experienced the first of several nervous breakdowns triggered by schizophrenia and punctuated by attempted suicide. She and Scott, drinking heavily and fighting viciously, experienced the "crack up" of their hopes and sanity just as the world careened into the Great Depression.

The gaiety of the Jazz Age, F. Scott Fitzgerald noted, "leaped to a spectacular death in October 1929" with the collapse of the stock market and the ensuing Great Depression. The title of Fitzgerald's early novel, *The Beautiful and the Damned*, seemed to have predicted the collapse of the Jazz Age amid its hollowness and aimlessness. In 1931, he recalled that the Roaring Twenties "was an age of miracles, an age of art, it was an age of excess, and it was an age of satire." Fitzgerald said he looked back on the decade with nostalgia. It "bore him up, flattered him and gave him more money than he had dreamed of, simply for telling people that he felt as they did, that something had to be done with all the nervous energy stored up and unexpended in the War."

To be sure, the twenties roared primarily for a small group of affluent Americans, but those years involved something soon inconceivable— the belief in freedom at all costs; freedom for the sake of nothing but the enjoyment of one's freedom; freedom that endowed life with vitality, ingenuity, and openness to new experience, a sense of unparalleled freedom that had defined the myth of being an American since colonial days.

THE REACTIONARY TWENTIES

The pleasure-seeking excesses of the Lost Generation and the frivolities associated with the Jazz Age made little sense to most Americans. They were not disillusioned, self-destructive, or defiantly modernist. Most people still led traditional lives. They aggressively defended established values, old certainties, and the comfort of past routines, and they were shocked by the decade's social turmoil and cultural rebelliousness.

In national politics, a country-versus-city backlash fed on irrational fears— of immigrants plotting revolution, of liberal churches embracing evolution, of young people rejecting traditional notions of moral behavior. These cultural tensions mirrored Republican efforts to reverse the progressivism of Theodore Roosevelt and Woodrow Wilson.

By 1920, the progressive political coalition that reelected Wilson in 1916 had fragmented. The growing middle class became preoccupied less with reform than with enjoying America's economic prosperity, the outcome of increased mass production, mass consumption, and labor-saving electrical appliances.

Many Americans traced the germs of dangerous radicalism (the Red Scare) to cities teeming with immigrants and foreign ideas such as socialism, communism, anarchism, and labor union militancy. Others feared the erosion of traditional religious beliefs in the face of secular modernism. People were convinced that dangers from abroad and at home must be vigorously resisted.

This reactionary conservatism of the 1920s fed on the popularity of **nativism**—prejudice against immigrants from countries outside of western Europe—and a militant Protestant fundamentalism that sought to restore the primacy of traditional Christian morality.

REACTIONARY CONSERVATISM AND IMMIGRATION RESTRICTION The Red Scare of 1919 and a postwar surge of immigration helped generate a new wave of anti-immigrant hysteria. After the end of the Great War, masses of people emigrated from Europe to the United States.

Between 1919 and 1924, more than 800,000 Europeans, many of them Italians, Jews, Poles and Russians, entered the United States. At the same time, some 150,000 Mexicans crossed the American border, most of them settling in the Southwest and California. In the early 1920s, more than half of the White men and a third of the White women working in mines, mills, and factories were immigrants. Some harbored a passion for socialism or anarchism—as well as a willingness to use violence to achieve their political goals.

White Protestant nativists alarmed by the surge in immigration from Asia and eastern and southern Europe decided that federal officials were not excluding enough newcomers. Racism and fears of an invasion of foreign radicals, especially Communists and anarchists, led Congress to pass the Emergency Immigration Act of 1921, which limited *total* annual immigration to 150,000 people from outside the Western Hemisphere. Even more important, it restricted newcomers by "national origin"; the annual quota from each European country was limited to 3 percent of the total number of that nationality represented in the 1910 census.

Three years later, Congress responded to continuing complaints that too many eastern and southern Europeans were still being admitted by passing the **Immigration Act of 1924** (the National Origins Act). The bill reduced the number ("quota") of visas from 3 to 2 percent of the total number of people of each nationality in the United States as of the 1890 rather than the 1910 national census, since there were far fewer eastern and southern Europeans in the nation in 1890. It also banned most immigrants from Asia and introduced a new category—"illegal alien."

The purpose of placing a numerical ceiling or quota on immigrants was to shrink the total number of newcomers, to favor immigrants from northern and western Europe, and to reduce those coming from southern and eastern Europe, especially Jews, Italians, Poles, Turks, and Russians. The intent was openly racist. Congressman Fred S. Purnell of Indiana urged legislators to stop the "stream of irresponsible and broken wreckage that is pouring into the lifeblood of America the social and political diseases of the Old World."

Senator Ellison D. "Cotton Ed" Smith, a South Carolina Democrat, likewise asserted that it was long past time "to shut the door. We have been called the melting pot of the world . . . we had allowed influences to enter our borders that were about to melt the pot in place of us being the melting pot. Americanize what we have and save the resources of America for the natural increase of our population."

H. L. Mencken, the celebrated columnist for the *Baltimore Evening Sun*, attacked the Immigration Act because its primary purpose was "to hobble and cage the citizen of newer [racial] stocks in a hundred fantastic ways." Immigrants from southern and eastern Europe were being treated as domestic enemies, he charged, even though they were benefiting the nation. "The fact that they increase [in number] is the best hope of civilization in America. They shake the old race out of its spiritual lethargy and introduce it to disquiet and experiment. They make for a free play of ideas."

Such arguments had no effect on President Calvin Coolidge. "America," he emphasized, "must be kept American." He readily signed the immigration restriction bill, which remained in force until 1965. Its impact was immediate. Under the quota system, more than 50,000 Germans could enter the nation annually, while fewer than 4,000 Italians were allowed, compared to the more than 2 million Italians who had arrived between 1910 and 1920.

The Immigration Act of 1924, however, placed no quota on immigrants from countries in the Western Hemisphere. Between 1890 and 1920, some 1.5 million Mexicans had entered the United States. Up to that point, they were not required to apply for legal entry. By the 1920s, many employers in the western states had grown dependent on Mexican workers, and they pressured Congress to ensure an adequate supply of low-paid laborers from Mexico, Puerto Rico, and Cuba.

While not restricting the number of Latin Americans, Congress did require them for the first time to have passports and visas before entering the United States. Otherwise, they would be charged as "illegal aliens." Congress created the U.S. Border Patrol to enforce the new requirements. An unexpected result of the 1924 Immigration Act was that people of Latin American descent became the fastest-growing ethnic minority during the twenties.

The number of Mexicans living in Texas increased tenfold between 1900 and 1930 in response to the needs of Texas farmers for "stoop" laborers hired to harvest cotton and other crops. "Cotton picking suits the Mexican," was the common assertion among Texas growers. Because migrant workers were less

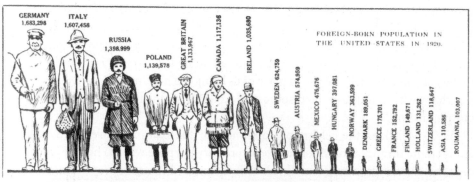

Immigration Act of 1924 This immigration chart illustrates the nationalities of the foreign-born population in the United States in 1920, which formed the basis of the quota system introduced in the Johnson-Reed Act.

likely to have established "roots" in the United States and because they were willing to move with the seasons, farm owners came to prefer them over Black or Anglo tenants and farm laborers.

SACCO AND VANZETTI The most celebrated criminal case of the 1920s reinforced the connection between European immigrants and political radicalism. On May 5, 1920, two Italian immigrants who described themselves as revolutionary anarchists eager to topple the American government were arrested outside Boston, Massachusetts.

Shoemaker Nicola Sacco and fish peddler Bartolomeo Vanzetti were accused of stealing $16,000 from a shoe factory and killing the paymaster and a guard. Both men carried loaded pistols when arrested, both lied to the police, both were identified by eyewitnesses, and both had flimsy alibis. The stolen money, however, was never found, and several people claimed that they were with Sacco and Vanzetti far from the scene of the crime when it occurred.

The **Sacco and Vanzetti case** erupted at the height of Italian immigration to the United States and against the backdrop of numerous terror attacks by anarchists, some of which Sacco and Vanzetti had participated in. The charged atmosphere, called "the Red hysteria" by one journalist, ensured that their trial would be a public spectacle.

In July 1921, Sacco and Vanzetti were convicted and sentenced to death. Their legal appeals lasted six years before they were electrocuted on August 23, 1927, still claiming innocence. To millions around the world, Sacco and Vanzetti were victims of capitalist injustice. People still debate their guilt.

THE NEW KLAN The most violent of the reactionary conservative movements during the twenties was a revived Ku Klux Klan, the infamous post–Civil War group of White racists that had re-created itself in 1915 in conjunction with the widely popular film *The Birth of a Nation*. Produced and directed by D. W. Griffith, son of a Confederate army officer, the movie was set during Reconstruction and based on a novel, *The Clansman: An Historical Romance of the Ku Klux Klan* (1905), written by Thomas Dixon, a Princeton classmate of Woodrow Wilson. President Wilson hosted a special showing of the film at the White House and was reported to have said, "It is like writing history with lightning. And my only regret is that it is all so terribly true."

Thanks in part to Wilson's endorsement, *The Birth of a Nation* became the most popular movie up to that time. The film rewrote southern history, portraying Klansmen as crusading heroes and newly freed slaves as working with unprincipled carpetbaggers and scalawags to corrupt state governments.

During the film's ballyhooed opening in Atlanta, William J. Simmons, a traveling salesman turned Methodist preacher, announced the founding of the second Ku Klux Klan. This new version was, by 1920, a *nationwide* organization devoted to "the maintenance of White Supremacy" and "100 percent Americanism." Only "natives"—meaning white, "Anglo-Saxon," evangelical Protestants born in the United States—could be members. At its peak in 1924, the new Klan numbered more than 4 million members, making it the largest far-right movement in history. (It is no coincidence that 1924 was the same year in which numerous states erected memorial statues celebrating Confederate generals such as Robert E. Lee.)

Shrouded in secrecy and costumed in White sheets and spooky hats, the Klan was both bizarre and mainstream, sponsoring baseball teams, college fraternities, and county fairs. It even hosted beauty pageants where young women competed to be "Miss 100 Percent America." The new Klan included a women's auxiliary group called the Kemellia, and whole families attended Klan gatherings, "klasping" hands while listening to inflammatory speeches, watching fireworks, and burning crosses. Most Klan members were small farmers, sharecroppers, or wage workers, but the organization also attracted clergymen, engineers, doctors, lawyers, accountants, business leaders, teachers, judges, mayors, sheriffs, state legislators, six governors, and three U.S. senators.

Klan leader Hiram Wesley Evans explained that the organization embodied "an idea, a faith, a purpose, an organized crusade" against "that which is corrupting and destroying the best in American life." The Klan embraced militant patriotism, restrictions on immigration and voting, and strict personal morality. It opposed illegal ("bootleg") liquor and labor unions and preached hatred against African Americans, Roman Catholics, Jews, immigrants, Communists, atheists, prostitutes, and adulterers.

The Klan became infamous for its blanket assaults on various categories of Americans. As a member stressed, "Every criminal, every gambler, every thug . . . every wife beater . . . every moonshiner, every crooked politician . . . is fighting the Klan." The United States was no melting pot, shouted William Simmons: "It is a garbage can! . . . When the hordes of aliens walk to the ballot box and their votes outnumber yours, then that alien horde has got you by the throat."

In the Southwest, Klansmen directed their anger at Mexicans; in the Pacific Northwest, people of Japanese ancestry were the enemy; in New York, the targets were primarily Jews and Catholics. Klan members were elected governor in Oregon, Texas, and Colorado; others were mayors in Portland, Oregon, and Portland, Maine.

In Texas, Klan members used harassment, intimidation (often in the form of burning crosses), beatings, and "tar and feathers" to discipline alcoholics, gamblers, adulterers, and other sinners. In the spring of 1922 alone, the Dallas Klan flogged sixty-eight men.

The reborn Klan, headquartered in Atlanta and calling itself the "Invisible Empire," grew rapidly, especially in the rural Midwest. During the twenties, 40 percent of its "Anglo-Saxon" members were in three midwestern states: Illinois, Indiana, and Ohio. Only 16 percent of registered Klansmen were in the former Confederate states. Recruiters, called Kleagles, were told to "play upon whatever prejudices were most acute in a particular area."

African Americans grew increasingly concerned about Klan violence. The Chicago *Defender*, the African American newspaper with the widest circulation in the nation, urged its readers to fight back against Klansmen trying to "win what their fathers [in the Civil War] lost by fire and sword."

The Grand Dragon of Indiana, a con man named David C. Stephenson, grew so influential in electing local and state officials (the "kluxing" of America, as he called it) that he boasted, "I am the law in Indiana!" Klan-endorsed candidates won the Indiana governorship and controlled the state legislature.

Ku Klux Klan Rally In 1925, the KKK held a massive march down Pennsylvania Avenue in Washington, D.C.

At the 1924 Republican State Convention, Stephenson patrolled the aisles with a pistol and later confessed that he "purchased the county and state officials." Stephenson, who had grown wealthy by skimming from the dues he collected from Klan members as well as selling robes and hoods, planned to run for president of the United States.

In August 1925, some 25,000 Klansmen paraded down Pennsylvania Avenue in the nation's capital, dressed in their white-hooded regalia. But the Klan's influence, both in Indiana and nationwide, crumbled after Stephenson was sentenced to life in prison in 1925 for kidnapping and raping a twenty-eight-year-old woman who then committed suicide. Stephenson assumed the governor would pardon him. When that did not happen, he told police about the widespread political bribery he had engaged in. As a result, the governor, the Indianapolis mayor, the county sheriff, congressmen, and other officehold-ers were indicted. Many ended up in prison.

News of the scandal caused Klan membership to tumble. More than a dozen Klan offices and meeting places across the country were bombed, burned, or blasted by shotguns. At the same time, several states passed anti-Klan laws and others banned the wearing of masks. By 1930, nationwide mem-bership had dwindled to 100,000, mostly southerners. Yet the bigoted impulse underlying the Klan lived on, fed by deep-seated fears and hatreds that have yet to disappear.

FUNDAMENTALISM

While the Klan saw a threat mainly in the "alien menace," many defenders of "old-time religion" felt threatened by ideas circulating in "progressive" Protes-tant churches, especially the idea that the Bible should be studied in the light of modern scholarship (the "higher criticism") or that it should accommo-date Darwinian theories of biological evolution. In response to such "modern" notions, conservative Protestants embraced a militant new fundamentalism, which was distinguished less by a shared faith than by a posture of hostility toward "liberal" beliefs and its insistence on the literal truth of the Bible.

In a famous 1922 sermon titled "Shall the Fundamentalists Win?" Harry Emerson Fosdick, the progressive pastor at New York City's First Presbyte-rian Church, dismissed biblical fundamentalism as "immeasurable folly." The Bible, he explained, was not literally the "word of God" but a representation of God's wonders. Christianity had nothing to fear from Darwinian evolution or modern science, he argued, for liberal Christianity "saves us from the necessity of apologizing for immature states in the development of the biblical reve-lation." Fosdick, an outspoken critic of racism and social injustice, outraged fundamentalists, who launched an effort to "try" him for heresy. He decided to resign instead.

Among national leaders, however, only the "Great Commoner," William Jennings Bryan, the former Democratic congressman, secretary of state, and three-time presidential candidate, had the support, prestige, and eloquence to transform fundamentalism into a popular crusade. Bryan was a strange bird, a liberal progressive and pacifist Populist in politics and a right-wing religious crusader who believed in the literal Bible.

Bryan supported new state laws banning the teaching of evolution in public schools. He passionately denounced Darwin's theory of evolution, insisting that "all the ills from which America suffers can be traced back to the teaching of evolution." "Darwinism is not science at all," he maintained. "It is guesses strung together."

THE SCOPES TRIAL The dramatic climax of the fundamentalist war on Darwinism came in Tennessee, where in 1925 the legislature outlawed the teaching of evolution in public schools and colleges. In the tiny mining town of Dayton, in eastern Tennessee, civic leaders eager for publicity persuaded John T. Scopes, a twenty-four-year-old high-school science teacher, to become a test case against the new law.

Scopes used a textbook that taught Darwinian evolution, and police arrested him for doing so. The town boosters succeeded beyond their wildest hopes: the **Scopes Trial** received worldwide publicity—but it was not flattering to Dayton.

Before the start of the twelve-day "monkey trial" on July 10, 1925, the narrow streets of Dayton swarmed with evangelists, atheists, hot-dog and soda-pop peddlers, and hundreds of newspaper and radio reporters. A man tattooed with Bible verses preached on a street corner while a live monkey was paraded about town.

The stars of the show pitting science against fundamentalism were both national celebrities: William Jennings Bryan, a true believer in the literal Bible, volunteered his services to the prosecution, and Clarence Darrow, the nation's most famous trial lawyer, a tireless defender of hopeless causes who championed the rights of the working class, offered to defend Scopes and evolution.

Temperatures surpassed 100 degrees as the trial began. Bryan insisted that the trial was not about Scopes but about a state's right to determine what was taught in the public schools, and he announced that the "contest between evolution and Christianity is a duel to the death." Darrow countered: "Scopes is not on trial. Civilization is on trial." His goal was to prevent "bigots and ignoramuses from controlling the education of the United States" by proving that

America was "founded on liberty and not on narrow, mean, intolerable and brainless prejudice of soulless religio-maniacs."

On July 20, the seventh day of the trial, the defense called Bryan as an expert witness on biblical interpretation. Darrow began by asking him about biblical stories. Did he believe that Jonah was swallowed by a whale and that Joshua made the sun stand still? Yes, Bryan replied, as beads of sweat streamed down his face. All things are possible with God. Darrow pressed on relentlessly. What about the great flood and Noah's ark? Was Eve really created from Adam's rib? Bryan hesitated, and the crowd grew uneasy as the hero of fundamentalism crumpled in the heat. Bryan appealed to the judge, claiming that the Bible was not on trial, only to have Darrow yell: "I am examining you on your fool ideas that no intelligent Christian on earth believes." A humiliated Bryan claimed that Darrow was insulting Christians. Darrow, his thumbs clasping his colorful suspenders, shot back: "You insult every man of science and learning in the world because he does not believe in your fool religion." At one point, the men lunged at each other, prompting the judge to adjourn court for the day.

Scopes Monkey Trial In this snapshot of the courtroom, John Scopes *(far left)* clasps his face in his hands and listens to his attorney *(second from right)*. Clarence Darrow *(far right)* listens, too, visibly affected by the sweltering heat and humidity.

As the trial ended, the judge ruled that the only issue before the jury was whether John T. Scopes had taught evolution, and no one had denied that he had done so. Eager to get on with their lives and get the peach harvest in, the jurors did not even sit down before deciding that Scopes was guilty. But the Tennessee Supreme Court, while upholding the anti-evolution law, waived Scopes's $100 fine on a technicality. Both sides claimed victory.

Five days after the trial ended, William Jennings Bryan died of a heart condition aggravated by heat and fatigue. Scopes left Dayton to study geology at the University of Chicago; he became a petroleum engineer. Meanwhile, the Scopes Trial only sharpened the national debate between fundamentalism and evolution that continues today.

PROHIBITION William Jennings Bryan died knowing that one of his other religious crusades had succeeded: alcoholic beverages had been out-lawed nationwide. The movement to prohibit beer, wine, and liquor forged an unusual alliance between rural and small-town Protestants and urban political progressives—between believers in "old-time religion," who considered drink-ing sinful, and social reformers, mostly women, who were convinced that **Prohibition** would reduce divorces, prostitution, spousal abuse, and other alcohol-related violence. "There would not be any social evil," insisted Ella Boole of the Women's Christian Temperance Union, "if there was no saloon evil."

Elizabeth Tilton, a Bostonian active in efforts to ban alcohol, claimed that alcohol was "directly and indirectly responsible for 42 percent of broken homes, 45 percent of children cruelly deserted, 50 percent of crime, 25 percent of our poverty, not to mention feeble mindedness and insanity."

What connected the two groups to each other and to nativist movements were the ethnic and social prejudices that many members shared. The head of the Anti-Saloon League, for example, declared that German Americans "eat like gluttons and drink like swine." For many anti-alcohol crusaders, in fact, the primary goal of Prohibition seemed to be policing the behavior of the foreign-born, the working class, the poor, and Blacks.

During the Great War, both houses of Congress had finally responded to the efforts of the Anti-Saloon League and the Women's Christian Temperance Union. The wartime need to use grain for food rather than for making booze, combined with a grassroots backlash against beer brewers because so many had German backgrounds, transformed the cause of Prohibition into a vir-tual test of American patriotism. On December 18, 1917, Congress sent to the states the Eighteenth Amendment. Ratified on January 16, 1919, it banned "the manufacture, sale, and transportation of intoxicating liquors," effective one year later.

Prohibition was thus the law during the 1920s—but it was not widely followed. As the most ambitious social reform ever attempted in the United States, it proved to be a colossal and costly failure. It was too sweeping for the government to enforce and too frustrating for most Americans to respect, and it had many unforeseen consequences.

The loss of liquor taxes, for example, cost the federal government almost 30 percent of its annual revenue. The closing of breweries, distilleries, and saloons eliminated thousands of jobs. Even more troubling was the huge number of Americans who broke the law and the enormous boost that Prohibition gave to police corruption and to organized crime.

The Volstead Act (1919), which outlined the rules and regulations needed to enforce the Eighteenth Amendment, had so many loopholes that it guaranteed failure. For example, the law allowed individuals and organizations to keep and use any liquor owned on January 16, 1919, when the amendment was officially ratified. Not surprisingly, people stocked up before the law took effect. The Yale Club in Manhattan stored enough liquor to supply itself for the entire thirteen years that Prohibition was enforced.

Thousands of people set up home breweries, producing 700 million gallons of beer in 1929 alone. Wine was made just as easily, and "bathtub gin" was the simplest of all, requiring little more than a one-gallon still and some fruit, grain, or potatoes. Two-thirds of illegal liquor came from Canada, with most of the rest from Mexico or overseas. Yet this bootleg alcohol became notoriously dangerous. Tens of thousands were killed or disabled by deadly batches of illegal liquor, whose alcohol content usually exceeded that in wine and beer.

Many of the activities associated with the Roaring Twenties were fueled by bootleg liquor supplied by organized crime and sold in illegal saloons called "speakeasies," which were often ignored by local police corrupted by bribes. New York City's police commissioner estimated that there were 32,000 speakeasies in the city in 1929, compared with 15,000 saloons in 1919. Popular singer Bessie Smith openly proclaimed, "Any bootlegger sure is a pal of mine."

President Warren G. Harding and members of Congress displayed the ironies and hypocrisies associated with Prohibition. While the president was lambasting the "national scandal" of noncompliance with Prohibition, he regularly drank and served bootleg liquor in the White House, explaining that he was "unable to see this as a great moral issue."

Congress never supplied adequate funding to implement the Volstead Act. The Prohibition Unit, a new agency within the U.S. Treasury Department, had 3,000 employees to police the nation, five times the number at the new Federal Bureau of Investigation. Yet their numbers were not nearly enough to enforce Prohibition. New York's mayor said it would require 250,000 police officers in

All Fair in Drink and War Torpedoes filled with illegal malt whiskey were discovered in the New York harbor in 1926, an elaborate attempt by bootleggers to smuggle alcohol during Prohibition. Each "torpedo" had an air compartment so it could be floated to shore.

his city alone. In working-class and ethnic-rich Detroit, the bootleg industry was second in size only to the auto industry. In Virginia, jails could not contain the 20,000 Prohibition-related arrests each year.

The efforts to defy Prohibition generated widespread police corruption and boosted organized crime. Well-organized crime syndicates controlled the entire stream of liquor's production, pricing, distribution, and sales. As a result, the Prohibition era was a thirteen-year orgy of unparalleled criminal activity. By 1930, more than one-third of federal prisoners were Prohibition violators.

Although total alcohol consumption did decrease during the twenties, as did the number of deaths from alcohol abuse, in many cities drinking actually *increased* during Prohibition.

Al Capone and Organized Crime Prohibition turned many Americans into criminals and supplied organized crime with a source of enormous new income. The most ruthless Prohibition-era gangster was Alphonse Gabriel "Al" Capone. Born in Brooklyn in 1899, the son of Italian immigrants, he was expelled from school for hitting a female teacher. Capone then aligned himself with organized crime gangs. During a fight at a brothel, he suffered a knife wound on his cheek that gave him his lifelong nickname: "Scarface."

Capone moved to Chicago and worked his way up in the city's most notorious organized crime family. By age twenty-six, Capone was in charge. In 1927, his Chicago-based bootlegging, prostitution, and gambling empire involved 700 gangsters, extended from Canada to Florida, and brought in $60 million a year (over $1 billion in today's dollars), much of which he spent bribing police officials, judges, and politicians.

Capone loved flashy clothes, gaudy jewelry, and fancy cars yet fancied himself a modern "Robin Hood," a friend of the poor and jobless, dispensing wads of cash to soup kitchens throughout Chicago. Yet he was also utterly ruthless. When he learned that two of his henchmen were planning to turn him in to the police, Capone invited them to dinner and then bludgeoned them to death with a baseball bat.

Capone frequently insisted that he was merely giving the public the goods and services it demanded: "They say I violate the Prohibition law. Who doesn't?" He neglected to add that he had ordered the execution of dozens of rival criminals.

"Al" Capone In this photo from 1931, Capone *(right)* meets with his attorney, Abraham Teitelbaum, unfazed by the prospect of federal imprisonment.

Capone's Mafia empire grew so large that he attracted the attention of President Herbert Hoover, who in March 1929 asked Andrew Mellon, his Treasury secretary, "Have you got this fellow Capone yet? I want that man in jail." Mellon decided that the best hope for prosecuting the notorious mobster was to prove that he never paid taxes on his ill-gotten gains.

Federal law-enforcement officials, led by a dynamic agent named Eliot Ness, smashed Capone's bootlegging operations in 1929. Soon thereafter, Ness, having refused bribes from Capone, charged the crime boss with tax evasion. Tried and found guilty in 1931, Capone spent most of the next thirteen years in federal prison. Bankrupt and helpless, he died in 1947 of degenerative syphilis contracted years before in one of his own brothels.

REPUBLICAN RESURGENCE

After the Great War, most Americans had endured enough of President Woodrow Wilson's crusading idealism and spurned any leader who promoted sweeping reforms. Wilson, who despite his poor health wanted a third presidential term, recognized the shifting public mood. "It is only once in a generation," he remarked, "that a people can be lifted above material things. That is why conservative government is in the saddle two-thirds of the time."

Progressivism lost its momentum for several reasons. For one thing, its leaders were no more. Theodore Roosevelt died in 1919, just as he was beginning to campaign for the Republican presidential nomination, and Wilson's stroke had left him broken physically and mentally.

In addition, organized labor resented the Wilson administration's crackdown on striking workers in 1919–1920. Farmers in the Great Plains and West thought wartime price controls had discriminated against them. Liberal intellectuals became disillusioned with grassroots democracy because of popular support for Prohibition, the Ku Klux Klan, and religious fundamentalism.

Progressivism did not disappear, however. Progressive Republicans and Democrats occupied key leadership positions in Congress during much of the 1920s. The progressive impulse for honest, efficient government and regulation of business remained strong, especially at the state and local levels, where efforts to improve public education, public health, and social-welfare programs gained momentum. At the national level, however, conservative Republicans returned to power eager to reduce the size and scope of the federal government—and the presidency.

WARREN HARDING AND "NORMALCY"

In 1920, Republican leaders turned to a likeable mediocrity as their presidential candidate: Warren G. Harding, a dapper, silver-haired U.S. senator from the small village of Blooming Grove, Ohio. One Republican senator explained that the party chose Harding not for his abilities or experience (which were minimal) but because he was from a key state and looked presidential. Harding, he said, was "the best of the second-raters." Harding admitted as much. When he asked his campaign manager, Harry Daugherty, if he had the abilities to be president, Daugherty laughed: "The day of giants in the presidential chair is passed."

Harding set a conservative tone of his campaign when he pledged to "safeguard America first . . . to exalt America first, to live for and revere America first." America, Harding concluded, needed not "heroics, but healing; not nostrums, but normalcy; not revolution, but restoration; not agitation, but adjustment; not surgery, but serenity; not the dramatic, but the dispassionate."

At their convention, the Democrats quickly rejected Woodrow Wilson's desire for a third term and chose Ohioan James Cox, a former newspaper publisher and three-term governor of the state. For vice president, they selected New Yorker Franklin Delano Roosevelt, who as assistant secretary of the navy occupied the same position his Republican cousin Theodore Roosevelt had once held. Handsome, vigorous, and a stirring speaker, he would deliver more than 1,000 speeches during the campaign.

Cox's campaign was disorganized and underfunded, however, and the Democrats struggled against the conservative postwar mood. In the words of progressive journalist William Allen White, Americans were "tired of issues, sick at heart of ideals, and weary of being noble."

Harding won big, getting 16 million votes to 9 million for Cox, and the Republicans increased their majority in both houses of Congress. Harding's victory led Clarence Darrow to quip that he had grown up hearing that "anybody can become president. I'm beginning to believe it." Franklin Roosevelt predicted that the Democratic party could not hope to return to power until the Republicans led the nation "into a serious period of depression and unemployment." He was right.

The one-sided election was significant in another way: it was the first presidential contest in which women voted in all forty-eight states. (In the 1916 presidential election, about thirty states had permitted women to participate.) Still, not all women found voting easy. In North Carolina, Blanche Benton remembered that many men "said if their wives voted, they would leave them. Even my mother didn't want to vote the first time." She told the

Charlotte Observer that many women voted like their husbands or fathers in the beginning, but she voted her conscience. "My husband, he said to vote the way I wanted, and he would vote the way he wanted."

HARDING'S PERSONALITY AND ASSOCIATES Harding's vanilla promise of a "**return to normalcy**" reflected his unexceptional background and limited abilities. A farmer's son and newspaper editor, Harding described himself as "just a plain fellow" who was "old-fashioned and even reactionary in matters of faith and morals" and had pledged "total abstinence" from alcohol.

In fact, however, Harding drank outlawed liquor in the White House, smoked and chewed tobacco, hosted twice-weekly poker games, had numerous affairs, and even fathered children with women other than his domineering wife, Florence Harding, whom he called "the Duchess." The president's dalliances brought him much grief, however. One of his mistresses blackmailed him, demanding money for her silence—which she received. Another, after his death in 1923, wrote a tell-all account of their affair titled *The President's Daughter*. The public, however, saw Harding as a handsome, charming politician who looked the part of a leader.

Harding in office had much in common with Ulysses S. Grant. His cabinet, like Grant's, mixed some of the "best minds" in the party with a few of the worst. Charles Evans Hughes, like Grant's Hamilton Fish, became a

The Ohio Gang President Warren Harding *(third from right)* surrounded himself with a cluster of questionable friends, known as the "Ohio gang," often appointing them to public office despite inferior credentials and questionable morals.

distinguished secretary of state. Herbert Hoover in the Commerce Department, Andrew W. Mellon in the Treasury, and Henry C. Wallace in the Agriculture Department made policy on their own. Other cabinet members and administrative appointees, however, were not so conscientious. The secretary of the interior landed in prison, and the attorney general narrowly escaped serving time. Many lesser offices went to members of the "Ohio gang," a group of Harding's drinking buddies.

Harding was no reformer. He set out to reverse the progressive activism of Woodrow Wilson and Theodore Roosevelt and reassert the primacy of Congress over the presidency. He and his lieutenants dismantled or neutralized many progressive regulatory laws and agencies. His four Supreme Court appointments were all conservatives, including Chief Justice William Howard Taft, who announced that he had been "appointed to reverse a few decisions." During the 1920s, the Taft-led court struck down a federal child-labor law and a minimum-wage law for women, issued numerous injunctions against striking unions, and passed rulings limiting the powers of federal agencies that regulated big businesses.

ANDREW MELLON AND THE ECONOMY The Harding administration also inherited a slumping economy burdened by high wartime taxes and a national debt that had ballooned from $1 billion in 1914 to $27 billion in 1920 because of the expenses associated with the war. Unemployment was at nearly 12 percent.

To generate economic growth, Secretary of the Treasury Andrew Mellon, at the time the third-richest man in the world behind John D. Rockefeller and Henry Ford, developed the Mellon plan, which called for reducing federal spending and lowering tax rates. To implement the plan, Mellon persuaded Congress to pass the landmark Budget and Accounting Act of 1921, which created a Bureau of the Budget to streamline the process of preparing an annual federal budget to be approved by Congress. The bill also created a General Accounting Office to audit spending by federal agencies. The act fulfilled a long-held progressive desire to bring greater efficiency and nonpartisanship to the budget preparation process.

The brilliant but cold Mellon (his son described him as a "thin-voiced, thin-bodied, shy and uncommunicative man") also proposed sweeping tax reductions. By 1918, the wartime tax rate on the highest income bracket had risen to 73 percent. Mellon believed the high rates were pushing wealthy Americans to avoid paying taxes by investing their money in foreign countries or tax-free government bonds. His policies systematically reduced tax rates while increasing tax revenues. He convinced Congress to cut the top rate from

73 percent in 1921 to 24 percent in 1929, and rates for individuals with the lowest incomes were also cut substantially, helping the working poor. By 1929, barely 2 percent of American workers had to pay any income tax.

At the same time, Mellon helped Harding reduce the federal budget. Government expenditures fell, as did the national debt, and the economy soared. Unemployment plummeted to 2.4 percent in 1923. Mellon's supporters labeled him the greatest Treasury secretary since Alexander Hamilton in the late eighteenth century.

The Republican economic program also sought to dismantle or neutralize many progressive regulatory laws and agencies. President Harding appointed commissioners to federal agencies who would promote "regulatory capitalism" and policies "friendly" to business interests. Republican senator Henry Cabot Lodge, who influenced Harding's choices to lead the regulatory agencies, boasted that "we have torn up Wilsonism by the roots."

RACIAL PROGRESS In one area, however, conservative Warren G. Harding abandoned his conventional views and proved to be more progressive than Woodrow Wilson. He reversed Wilson's segregationist policy of excluding African Americans from federal government jobs. He also spoke out against the racist lynchings that had flared up across the country during and after the war.

In his first speech to a joint session of Congress in 1921, Harding insisted that the nation must deal with the festering "race question." He attacked the Ku Klux Klan for fomenting "hatred and prejudice and violence" and urged Congress "to wipe the stain of barbaric lynching from the banners of a free and orderly, representative democracy." Harding supported an anti-lynching bill that passed the House but was killed by southern Democrats in the Senate.

In October 1921, Harding became the first president to deliver a speech in the former Confederacy focused on race. In Birmingham, Alabama, to celebrate the city's fiftieth anniversary, the president shocked the 100,000 in attendance by demanding complete economic and political rights for African Americans: "I say let the black man vote when he is fit to vote; prohibit the white man voting when he is unfit to vote." As Whites in the segregated audience responded with icy silence, Harding abandoned his prepared text and lectured them: "Whether you like it or not, our democracy is a lie unless you stand for that equality." He then stressed that he did not endorse "social equality" for Blacks and Whites, by which he meant intermarriage and the desegregation of schools, restaurants, hotels, and other public places: "Racial amalgamation can never come in America."

After reading the text of the president's speech, Marcus Garvey, president of the Universal Negro Improvement Association, sent a telegram to Harding in which he applauded his speech "on behalf of four hundred million negroes of the world." Garvey added that "all true negroes are against social equality, believing that all races should develop on their own social lines. Only a few selfish members of the negro race believe in the social amalgamation of black and white." Harding's unprecedented speech also delighted W. E. B. Du Bois, head of the NAACP. Writing in *The Crisis*, he stressed that Harding's address, "like sudden thunder in blue skies, ends the hiding and drives us all into the clear light of truth."

Few southerners agreed, however. Pat Harrison, a Democratic senator from Mississippi, warned that if Harding's speech "were carried to its ultimate conclusion, that means that the Black man can strive to become president of the United States!" Likewise, Senator J. Thomas Heflin of Alabama reminded the president that White southerners "hold to the doctrine that God Almighty has fixed the limits and boundaries between the two races, and no Republican living can improve upon His work."

SETBACKS FOR UNIONS Urban workers shared in the affluence of the 1920s. "A workman is far better paid in America than anywhere else in the world," a French visitor wrote in 1927, "and his standard of living is enormously higher." Nonfarm workers gained about 30 percent in real wages between 1921 and 1928, but farm income rose only 10 percent, and organized labor suffered. Although President Harding endorsed collective bargaining and tried to reduce the twelve-hour workday and six-day workweek to give the working class "time for leisure and family life," he ran into stiff opposition in Congress. After the war, the Red Scare and the violent strikes of 1919 led many people to equate labor unions with radicalism.

Between January 1920 and August 1921, the national unemployment rate jumped from 2 percent to 14 percent, and industrial production fell by 23 percent. The brief postwar depression so weakened unions that in 1921 business groups in Chicago designated the **open shop** to be the "American plan" of employment. Although the open shop in theory implied only an employer's right to hire anyone, whether a union member or not, in practice it meant discrimination against unionists and a refusal by companies to negotiate with unions even when most of the workers belonged to one.

To suppress unions, employers often required new workers to sign "yellow-dog" contracts, which forced them to agree not to join a union. Owners also used spies, blacklists, and intimidation to keep their workers from organizing unions. Some employers, such as Henry Ford, tried to kill the unions with kindness by introducing programs of "industrial democracy" guided by company-sponsored unions or various schemes of "welfare capitalism," such as profit sharing, bonuses, pensions, health programs, and recreational activities.

Such anti-union efforts paid off for employers. Union membership dropped from about 5 million in 1920 to 3.5 million in 1929 as industrial production soared and joblessness fell to 3 percent. But the anti-union effort, led by businesses that wanted to keep wages low and unions weak, unwittingly helped create a "purchasing crisis" whereby the working poor were not earning enough to buy the goods being churned out by increasingly productive industries. In fact, large groups of hourly workers, such as miners and textile mill hands, saw their income *drop*. Executives used company profits to pay dividends to stockholders, invest in new equipment, and increase their own salaries, while doing little to help wage earners. In 1929, corporate executives, an estimated 5 percent of the nation's workforce, received one-third of the nation's income.

In other words, the much-trumpeted "new economy" was not benefiting enough working-class Americans to be sustainable. Wage levels did not give the masses enough purchasing power to sustain economic growth. This would be a major cause of the Great Depression, as the Republican formula of high tariffs, low and stagnant wages, low taxes, little regulation, and anti-unionism would eventually implode.

ISOLATIONISM IN FOREIGN AFFAIRS The desire to stay out of foreign wars did not mean that the United States could ignore its expanding global interests. The Great War had made the United States the world's chief banker, and American investments and loans enabled foreigners to purchase U.S. exports. Yet the degree of American involvement in world affairs remained a source of political controversy.

European War Debts Nothing did more to heighten America's isolationism— and anti-American feelings among Europeans—than the complex issue of paying off war debts. In 1917, when France and Great Britain ran out of money to pay for desperately needed military supplies, the U.S. government had advanced them massive loans, first for the war effort and then for postwar reconstruction projects.

Most Americans expected the wartime debts to be repaid, but Europeans thought differently. The French and British had held off the German invasion at great cost while the United States was raising an army in 1917. The British also noted that after the American Revolution, the newly independent United States had repudiated old debts to British investors. The French likewise pointed out that they had never been repaid for helping the Americans win the Revolution.

Throughout the 1920s, the British and French were in a complex financial bind. To get U.S. dollars with which to pay their war-related debts, European nations had to sell their goods to the United States. However, soaring American tariff rates made imported European goods more expensive for U.S. consumers, so the war-related debts became harder to pay. The French and British insisted that they could repay their debts only if they could collect the $33 billion in reparations owed them by Germany. The German economy, however, was in shambles.

Twice during the 1920s, the financial strain on Germany brought the structure of international payments to the verge of collapse. Both times the international Reparations Commission called in private American bankers to work out rescue plans. Loans provided by U.S. banks thus propped up the German economy so that Germany could pay its reparations to Britain and France, thereby enabling them to pay their debts to the United States.

Attempts at Disarmament After the Great War, many American officials decided that the best way to keep the peace was to limit the size of armies and navies. The United States had no intention of maintaining a large army after 1920, but under the shipbuilding program begun in 1916, it had constructed a powerful navy second only to that of Great Britain. Although neither the British nor the Americans wanted a naval armaments race, both were worried about the growth of Japanese power in Asia and the Pacific.

To address the problem, President Harding in 1921 invited diplomats from eight nations to the Washington Naval Conference in Washington, D.C., at which Secretary of State Charles Evans Hughes made a blockbuster proposal.

Washington Naval Conference International powers convene in Washington, D.C., to negotiate the world's first disarmament treaty.

The only way out of an expensive naval arms race, he declared, "is to end it now" by eliminating scores of existing warships. He pledged that America would junk thirty battleships and cruisers, and then named thirty-six British and Japanese warships that would also be destroyed. The stunned audience stood and roared its approval. In less than fifteen minutes, one journalist reported, Hughes had destroyed more warships "than all the admirals of the world have sunk in a cycle of centuries."

The delegates at the Washington Naval Conference (1921–1922) spent months ironing out the final details of the agreement. Delegates from the United States, Britain, Japan, France, and Italy signed the Five-Power Treaty (1922), which limited the size of their navies. It was the first disarmament treaty in history. The agreement also, in effect, divided the world into spheres of influence: U.S. naval power became supreme in the Western Hemisphere, Japanese power in the western Pacific, and British power from the North Sea to Singapore.

With these disarmament agreements in hand, Harding could boast of what seemed to be a brilliant diplomatic coup. But the Five-Power Treaty set limits only on "capital" ships (battleships and aircraft carriers); the race to build cruisers, destroyers, submarines, and other smaller craft continued. Japan withdrew from the agreement in 1934, and by then the Soviet Union and Germany, which had been excluded from the conference, were building up their navies as well. Thus, twelve years after the Washington Naval Conference, the dream of naval disarmament died.

The Kellogg-Briand Pact During and after the Great War, many Americans embraced the fanciful idea of abolishing war with a stroke of a pen. In 1921, a wealthy Chicagoan founded the American Committee for the Outlawry of War. "We can outlaw this war system just as we outlawed slavery and the saloon," said an enthusiastic convert.

The seductive notion of simply abolishing war culminated in the signing of the Kellogg-Briand Pact. In 1927, French foreign minister Aristide Briand proposed to U.S. Secretary of State Frank B. Kellogg that the two countries agree never to go to war against each other.

Kellogg countered with a plan to have *all* nations sign the pact. The General Treaty for Renunciation of War as an Instrument of National Policy, or the Kellogg-Briand Pact, signed on August 27, 1928, declared that the signatories renounced war "as an instrument of national policy." Eventually, sixty-two nations, including all the great powers, signed the pact, but all reserved the right of "self-defense." The U.S. Senate ratified the agreement by a vote of 85 to 1.

A senator who voted for "this worthless, but perfectly harmless peace treaty" wrote a friend later that he feared it would "confuse the minds of many good people who think that peace may be secured by polite professions of neighborly and brotherly love." In a more pointed assessment, British writer George Orwell said that outlawing war was one of those "ideas so absurd only an intellectual could believe them."

The treaty went into effect July 24, 1929, after which Japan invaded Manchuria (1931); Italy invaded Ethiopia (1935); Japan invaded China (1937); Germany invaded Poland (1939); the Soviet Union invaded Finland (1939); Germany invaded Denmark, Norway, Belgium, the Netherlands, Luxembourg, and France, and attacked Great Britain (1940); and Japan attacked the United States (1941), culminating in a global war that resulted in more than 60 million deaths. All these nations had signed the Kellogg-Briand Pact. So much for outlawing war.

The World Court The isolationist mood in the United States was no better illustrated than in the repeated refusal by the Senate to approve American membership in the World Court, formally called the Permanent Court of International Justice, at The Hague in the Netherlands. Created in 1921 by the League of Nations, the World Court was intended to arbitrate disputes between nations. During the 1920s, Presidents Harding, Coolidge, and Hoover had each asked the Senate to approve American membership in the World Court, but the legislative body refused, for the same reasons that it had refused to sign the Versailles Treaty: it did not want the United States to be bound in any way by an international organization.

THE HARDING SCANDALS As time passed, President Harding found himself increasingly distracted by scandals within his administration. Early in 1923, the head of the Veterans Bureau resigned when faced with an investigation for stealing medical and hospital supplies intended for former servicemen. A few weeks later, the legal adviser to the bureau killed himself.

Soon thereafter, it was revealed that Jesse Smith, a colleague of Attorney General Harry M. Daugherty, was illegally selling federal paroles, pardons, and judgeships from his Justice Department office. When Harding learned of his escapades, he called Smith to the Oval Office and dressed him down. The next day, Smith killed himself in Daugherty's apartment. Then, Daugherty was accused of selling, for his personal gain, German assets seized after the war. When asked to testify about the matter, he refused on the grounds that doing so might incriminate him.

The Teapot Dome Scandal The most serious controversy was the **Teapot Dome Scandal**. The Teapot Dome was a government-owned oil field in Wyoming managed by the Department of the Interior. Secretary of the Interior Albert B. Fall, deeply in debt and eight years overdue in paying his taxes, began selling the oil to close friends who were executives of petroleum companies. In doing so, Fall took huge bribes from two oil tycoons. It was, in the words of Thomas J. Walsh, the senator whose committee hearings blew the lid off the teapot, "the most stupendous piece of thievery known to our annals, or perhaps to those of any other country."

Convicted of conspiracy and bribery and sentenced to a year in prison, Fall was the first former cabinet official to serve time because of misconduct in office. It was later revealed that

Teapot Dome Scandal In this 1924 political cartoon, Washington officials attempt to outrun the Teapot Dome Scandal, represented by a giant steamrolling teapot, on an oil-slicked highway.

the same oil barons had given $1 million to Harding's presidential campaign in exchange for Fall being named secretary of the interior.

How much Harding knew of the scandals is unclear, but he knew enough to be troubled. "My God, this is a hell of a job!" he confided to a journalist, "I have no trouble with my enemies; I can take care of my enemies all right. But my damn friends, my God-damn friends. . . . They're the ones that keep me walking the floor nights!"

In 1923, Harding left on what would be his last journey, a trip to the West Coast and the Alaska Territory. Along the way, he asked Herbert Hoover, the secretary of commerce, what he should do about the Fall scandal. Hoover gave the correct response: "Publish it, and at least get credit for integrity on your side." Before Harding had time to act, he suffered an attack of food poisoning in Seattle. After showing signs of recovering, he died in San Francisco. He was fifty-seven years old.

Because of Harding's corrupt associates, his administration came to be viewed as one of the worst in history. Even Hoover admitted that Harding was not "a man with either the experience or the intellectual quality that the position needed."

More recent assessments, however, suggest that the scandals obscured Harding's accomplishments. He led the nation out of the turmoil of the post-war years and helped create the economic boom of the 1920s. He endorsed diversity and civil rights and was a forceful proponent of women's rights. Yet even Harding's foremost scholarly defender admits that he lacked good judgment and "probably should never have been president."

COOLIDGE CONSERVATISM

The news of President Harding's death reached Vice President Calvin Coolidge when he and his wife were visiting his father in Plymouth Notch, Vermont. "Guess we'd better have a drink," said Coolidge upon being awakened to learn the news. At 2:47 A.M. on August 3, 1923, Colonel John Coolidge, a farmer, merchant, and notary public, issued the presidential oath of office to his son by the light of a kerosene lamp.

Calvin Coolidge, born on the fourth of July in 1872, was a throwback to an earlier era. A puritan in his personal life, he was horrified by the jazzed-up Roaring Twenties. He believed in the ideals of personal integrity and devotion to public service, and, like Harding, he was an evangelist both for capitalism and for minimal government regulation of business.

A DO-NOTHING PRESIDENT—BY DESIGN   Although Coolidge had won every political race he had entered, he had never loved the limelight. Shy and awkward, he was a man of famously few words—hence his nickname, "Silent Cal." After being reelected president of the Massachusetts State Senate in 1916, he gave a four-sentence inaugural address that concluded with "above all things, be brief." He later explained that he had "never been hurt by what he had not said."

Voters liked Coolidge's uprightness, his straight-talking style, and his personal humility. He was a simple, direct man of strong principles and intense patriotism who championed self-discipline and hard work. Alice Roosevelt Longworth, the outspoken daughter of Theodore Roosevelt, said the atmosphere in the Coolidge White House compared to that of Harding was "as different as a New England front parlor is from the back room in a speakeasy." Coolidge, she quipped, looked like he had been "weaned on a pickle."

Coolidge was determined *not* to be an activist president. He noted that his greatest accomplishment was "minding [his] own business." Unlike Theodore Roosevelt and Woodrow Wilson, he had no exaggerated sense of self-importance; he knew he was "not a great man." Nor did he have an ambitious program to push through Congress. "Four-fifths of our troubles," Coolidge professed, "would disappear if we would sit down and keep still." Coolidge insisted on twelve hours of sleep *and* a lengthy afternoon nap. H. L. Mencken claimed that Coolidge "slept more than any other president." His idea of a great day was one during "which nothing happened."

Even more than Harding, Coolidge sought to reduce the size and scope of the federal government. "If the federal government were to go out of existence," he predicted, no one would notice. He also linked the nation's welfare with the success of Big Business. "The chief business of the American people is business," he preached. "The man who builds a factory builds a temple. The man who works there worships there." Coolidge famously claimed that "wealth is the *chief* end of man."

Calvin Coolidge "Silent Cal" was so reticent that when he died in 1933, American humorist Dorothy Parker remarked, "How could they tell?"

Where Harding had tried to balance the interests of labor, agriculture, and industry, Coolidge focused on promoting industrial development.

He reduced federal regulations of business and, with the help of Treasury secretary Mellon and Republican congresses, continued to lower income tax rates. Coolidge was also "obsessed" with reducing spending, even to the point of issuing government workers only one pencil at a time—and only after they turned in the stub of the old pencil. "I am for economy" in government spending, he stressed. "After that, I am for more economy." When a South African mayor sent the president two lion cubs as a present, Coolidge named them "Tax Reduction" and "Budget Bureau." His fiscal frugality and pro-corporate stance led the *Wall Street Journal* to rejoice: "Never before, here or anywhere else, has a government been so completely fused with business."

America also had too many laws, Coolidge insisted, and it was "much more important to kill bad bills than to pass good ones." True to his word, he vetoed fifty acts of Congress. As a journalist said, "In a great day of yes-men, Calvin Coolidge was a no-man."

THE ELECTION OF 1924 Calvin Coolidge restored the dignity of the presidency while holding warring Republican factions together. He easily gained the party's 1924 presidential nomination. Soon thereafter, he invited reporters to the White House. One reporter asked, "Have you any statement on the campaign?" Coolidge said, "No." Another reporter tried: "Can you tell us about the world situation?" Again the president said, "No." After some-one asked about Prohibition, the reply was the same: "No." As the frustrated reporters left, Coolidge yelled, "Now remember—don't quote me."

Meanwhile, the Democratic party's nominating convention in New York City illustrated the deep divisions between urban and rural America. One of the leading contenders, lawyer William McAdoo, Woodrow Wilson's son-in-law, was endorsed by the Ku Klux Klan. The other front-runner, New York governor Al Smith, was an Irish Catholic who led the party's anti-Klan, anti-Prohibition wing.

Neither McAdoo nor Smith could gain the nomination. The fragmented Democrats took a record 103 ballots over sixteen broiling summer days before deciding on a compromise candidate: John W. Davis, a little-known lawyer from West Virginia who could nearly outdo Coolidge in his conservatism.

While the Democrats bickered, rural Populists and urban progressives decided to abandon both major parties, as they had done in 1912. Reorganizing the old Progressive party, they nominated Wisconsin's Robert M. "Fighting Bob" La Follette. As a Republican senator, La Follette had voted against the 1917 decla-ration of war against Germany and its allies. Now, in addition to the progressives, he won the support of the Socialist party and the American Federation of Labor.

In the 1924 election, Coolidge swept both the popular and electoral votes. Davis and the Democrats took only the southern states, and La Follette car-ried only Wisconsin, his home state. The popular vote went 15.7 million for Coolidge, 8.4 million for Davis, and 4.8 million for La Follette—the largest popular vote ever polled by a third-party candidate up to that time. Coolidge viewed his landslide as a mandate to continue his efforts to shrink the federal government. If it disappeared, he predicted, most voters "would not detect the difference."

Coolidge's victory represented the height of postwar political conserva-tism. Business executives interpreted the election results as an endorsement of their influence on government policy, and Coolidge saw the economy's surging prosperity as confirmation of his support of Big Business. The United States, he proclaimed in his 1925 inaugural address, had reached "a state of content-ment seldom before seen." His duty was to do nothing that might undermine such contentment.

THE RISE OF HERBERT HOOVER

During the twenties, the drive for industrial efficiency, which had been a prominent theme among progressives, powered the wheels of mass produc-tion and consumption and became a cardinal belief of Republican leaders.

Herbert Hoover, secretary of commerce in the Harding and Coolidge cabinets, embodied the dream of organizational efficiency, for he himself was a remarkable success story.

Born into a devout Quaker family in Iowa in 1874, he was orphaned at age nine, and raised by stern uncles in Iowa and Oregon. He was a shy "loner" who studied geology and mechanical engineering at Stanford University, where he determined that he was smarter, more energetic, and more disciplined than others. After graduating, he became a world-renowned mining engineer, harvesting gold in Australia, coal in China, and zinc in Burma. He went on to prosper as an oil tycoon and financial wizard, becoming a multimillionaire before the age of forty.

Hoover's business success and ruthless genius for managing difficult operations bred in him a self-confidence verging on conceit. In his twenties, he began planning to be president of the United States.

A PROGRESSIVE CONSERVATIVE With the outbreak of war in 1914, Herbert Hoover exchanged his career in private business for one in public service. He organized the evacuation of tens of thousands of Americans stranded in Europe by the German invasion of France, then led a massive program to provide food to 7.5 million starving civilians in German-occupied Belgium.

The "Great Humanitarian" also applied his managerial skills to the Food Administration during the war and served with the U.S. delegation at the Versailles peace conference. Hoover idolized Woodrow Wilson and supported American membership in the League of Nations. Franklin Roosevelt, then assistant secretary of the navy, stood in awe of Hoover. In 1920, Roosevelt said that Hoover was "certainly a wonder [boy], and I wish we could make him President of the United States. There would not be a better one."

Hoover, however, soon disappointed Roosevelt by declaring himself a Republican "progressive conservative." In a book titled *American Individualism* (1922), Hoover said he wanted to promote a "rugged individualism" directed at promoting the greater good, not selfishness. He wanted government officials to encourage business leaders to forgo "cutthroat competition" and engage in "voluntary cooperation" by forming trade associations that would share information and promote standardization—all intended to increase efficiency and productivity.

As secretary of commerce during the 1920s, Hoover transformed the small department into the government's most dynamic agency. He looked for new markets for business, created a Bureau of Aviation to promote the new airline industry, and established the Federal Radio Commission. When the Mississippi

River flooded in 1927, devastating much of the Midwest and Gulf states, Hoover organized the massive recovery effort, despite President Coolidge's indifference.

THE 1928 ELECTION: HOOVER VERSUS SMITH On August 2, 1927, while on vacation in the Black Hills of South Dakota, President Coolidge announced, "I do not choose to run for President in 1928." Coolidge's decision cleared the way for Herbert Hoover to win the Republican nomination. The party's platform took credit for the nation's longest period of sustained prosperity, the government's cost cutting, debt and tax reduction, and the high tariffs ("as vital to American agriculture as . . . to manufacturing") designed to "protect" American businesses from foreign competition.

The Democrats nominated four-term New York governor Alfred E. Smith, called the "Happy Warrior" by Franklin D. Roosevelt in his nominating speech. The candidates presented sharply different images: Hoover, the successful businessman and bureaucratic manager from an Iowa farm, and Smith, a professional Irish American politician from New York City's Lower East Side. To working-class Democrats in northern cities, Smith was a hero, the poor grandson of Irish Catholic immigrants who had become governor of the most populous state. His outspoken criticism of Prohibition also endeared him to the Irish, Italians, Germans, and others.

On the other hand, as the first Roman Catholic nominated for president by a major party, a product of New York's machine-run politics, and a "wet" on Prohibition (in direct opposition to his party's platform), Smith represented all that was opposed by southern and western rural Democrats—as well as most rural and small-town Republicans. A Kansas newspaper editor declared that the "whole puritan civilization, which has built a sturdy, orderly nation, is threatened by Smith." The Ku Klux Klan issued a "Klarion Kall for a Krusade" against him, mailing thousands of postcards proclaiming that "Alcohol" Smith, the Catholic New Yorker, was the Antichrist. While Hoover stayed above the fray, Smith was forced to deal with constant criticism.

No Democrat could have beaten Hoover in 1928, however. The nation was prosperous and at peace, and Hoover seemed the best person to sustain the good times. He was perhaps the best-trained economic mind ever to run for president, and he was widely viewed as a brilliant engineer and humanitarian, a genius "who never failed." He promised that soon "poverty will be banished from this earth."

On Election Day, Hoover, the first Quaker to be president, won in a landslide, with 21 million popular votes to Smith's 15 million and an electoral college majority of 444 to 87. Hoover even penetrated the Democrats' Solid South, winning Virginia, North Carolina, Tennessee, Florida, and Texas. Republicans also kept control of both houses of Congress.

Hidden in the results, however, was a glimmer of hope for Democrats. Overall, Smith's vote total, especially strong in the largest cities, doubled that of John Davis four years earlier. In 1932, Franklin D. Roosevelt would build upon that momentum to win back the presidency for the Democrats.

Calvin Coolidge was skeptical that Hoover could sustain the good times. He quipped that the "Wonder Boy" had offered him "unsolicited advice for six years, all of it bad." Coolidge's doubts about Hoover's political abilities would prove accurate, as the new president would soon confront an economic earthquake that would test his considerable skills—and expose his weaknesses.

CHAPTER REVIEW

SUMMARY

- **A "New Era" of Consumption**   During the 1920s, the American economy grew at the fastest rate in history, while consumer debt tripled. Innovations in production, advertising, and financing, combined with a jump in the use of electricity, enabled and encouraged millions of Americans to purchase automobiles, radios, and other electrical household appliances. The new *consumer culture* valued leisure, self-expression, and self-indulgence. More and more Americans purchased national brand-name items from retail chain stores, listened to the same radio shows, and watched the same movies.

- **The "Jazz" Age**   New social and cultural movements challenged the traditional order. The carefree attitude of the 1920s, perhaps best represented by the frantic rhythms of jazz music, led writer F. Scott Fitzgerald to call the decade the *Jazz Age*. Though *flappers* emerged to challenge gender norms, most women remained full-time housewives or domestic servants. As the Great Migration continued, African Americans in northern cities felt freer to speak out against racial injustice and express pride in their race. The *Harlem Renaissance* gave voice to African American literature and arts. Racial separatism and Black nationalism grew popular under Marcus Garvey, while the *National Association for the Advancement of Colored People (NAACP)* made efforts to undo racism through education and legislation.

- **The Modernist Revolt**   Many artists and intellectuals were attracted to *modernism*, which drew upon Einstein's theory of relativity and Freud's psychological explorations. For modernists, the world was no longer governed by reason, but rather something created and expressed through one's highly individual consciousness. To be "modern" meant to break free of tradition, to violate restrictions, and to shock and confuse the public.

- **The Reactionary Twenties**   Retaliating against these challenges to convention, various movements fought to uphold their traditional ideas of what America was and how it should remain. In reaction to a renewed surge of immigration after the Great War and the Red Scare, Americans again embraced *nativism*. The 1921 *Sacco and Vanzetti case*, which resulted in the conviction and death sentence of two Italian immigrants who were self-professed anarchists, reinforced the fear that immigrants were too often troublemakers. Nativists persuaded Congress to restrict future immigration with the *Immigration Act of 1924*. A revived Ku Klux Klan gained a large membership and considerable political influence across the nation. Fundamentalist Protestants campaigned against teaching evolution in public schools, arguing instead for the literal truth of the Bible. Their efforts culminated in the 1925 *Scopes Trial*. Progressive reformers and conservative Protestants supported the nationwide *Prohibition* of alcoholic beverages that started in 1920.

- **Republican Resurgence**   Union membership declined as businesses adopted new anti-labor techniques such as the *open shop*. Disillusionment with the Great War turned the public against progressivism and in favor of disarmament and isolationism. The Republican Party benefited from this shift in the public mood. Warren G. Harding's call for a *return to normalcy* brought about his landslide presidential victory in 1920. His administration followed the Mellon Plan, which succeeded in reviving the economy. Despite numerous scandals that plagued the Harding administration, including the *Teapot Dome Scandal* (1923), the progressive goal of efficiency through better management remained a part of many Republican initiatives, such as the Budget and Accounting Act.

CHRONOLOGY

1903	Wright Brothers fly first motorized airplane; Ford Motor Company is founded
1910	National Association for the Advancement of Colored People (NAACP) is founded
1913	Armory Show brings modern art to America
1916	Marcus Garvey brings Universal Negro Improvement Association to New York
1920	Prohibition begins; Warren G. Harding is elected president
1921	Sacco and Vanzetti trial; Five-Power Treaty
	Congress passes Emergency Immigration Act
1923	Teapot Dome Scandal; Harding dies
1924	Congress passes Immigration Act; Calvin Coolidge is reelected president
1925	Scopes "monkey trial"
1927	Charles A. Lindbergh, Jr., makes first solo transatlantic airplane flight
	Sacco and Vanzetti are executed
1928	Herbert Hoover is elected president

KEY TERMS

consumer culture p. 1064

Jazz Age p. 1073

flappers p. 1076

Harlem Renaissance p. 1080

National Association for the Advancement of Colored People (NAACP) p. 1082

modernism p. 1083

nativism p. 1092

Immigration Act of 1924 p. 1093

Sacco and Vanzetti case (1921) p. 1095

Scopes Trial (1925) p. 1099

Prohibition (1920–1933) p. 1101

return to normalcy p. 1107

open shop p. 1110

Teapot Dome Scandal (1923) p. 1114

INQUIZITIVE

Go to InQuizitive to see what you've learned—and learn what you've missed—with personalized feedback along the way.

23 The Great Depression and the New Deal

1933–1939

***Construction of a Dam* (1939)** One of the most famous and controversial of the artists commissioned by the New Deal's Works Progress Administration was William Gropper, who painted this mural in the Department of the Interior building in Washington, D.C. Based on his observations of dam construction on the Columbia and Colorado Rivers, Gropper illustrates the triumph and brotherhood that emerged from America's grand construction projects during the Great Depression.

The milestone year 1929 dawned with high hopes. Rarely had a new president entered office with greater expectations. In fact, Herbert Hoover, the "Great Engineer," was worried that people viewed him as "a superman; that no problem is beyond my capacity." Hoover was right to be concerned. Voters referred to him as "the man who had never failed"—a dedicated public servant whose engineering genius and business savvy would ensure continued prosperity. In 1929, more Americans were working than ever before and earning record levels of income. But that was about to change in unexpected ways.

The Great Depression, which began at the end of 1929, generated widespread human misery. Never had a business slump been so deep, so long, or so painful. By 1932, one out of four Americans was unemployed; in many large cities, nearly half the adults were out of work. Some 500,000 people had lost homes or farms because they could not pay their mortgages. Thousands of banks had failed; millions of people lost their life savings.

Jobless, homeless, and hungry people grew desperate. A man noted in his diary that "hold-ups and killings are becoming more frequent, and it becomes dangerous to walk the streets." Worst of all, many Americans lost hope. As former president Calvin Coolidge acknowledged in 1932, "In other periods of depression, it has always been possible to see some things which were solid and upon which you could base hope . . . but as I look about, I now see nothing to give ground to hope."

What made the Great Depression so severe and so enduring was its global nature. In 1929, the economies of Europe were still reeling from the Great War. Once the American economy tumbled, it sent shock waves throughout Europe and elsewhere.

focus questions

1. What were the major causes of the Great Depression?

2. How did the Great Depression impact the American people?

3. In what ways did the Hoover administration fail to address the human distress caused by the Great Depression?

4. What were the goals and accomplishments of the First New Deal?

5. What were the major criticisms of the First New Deal?

6. How did the New Deal transform the role of the federal government in American life?

The suffering was worldwide when Franklin Delano Roosevelt was elected in 1932 to lead an anxious nation mired in the third year of an unprecedented economic downturn. Within days of becoming president, Roosevelt, often called FDR, took dramatic steps that forever transformed the scope and role of the federal government. He and a supportive Congress adopted bold measures to relieve the human suffering and promote economic recovery.

Roosevelt was not an ideologue; rather, he was a pragmatist willing to try different approaches. As he once explained, "Take a method and try it. If it fails, admit it frankly and try another." Roosevelt's program for recovery, the New Deal, was therefore a series of trial-and-error actions rather than a comprehensive scheme. None of Roosevelt's well-intentioned but often poorly planned initiatives worked perfectly, and in fact some of them failed miserably. But their combined effect was to restore hope and energy to a nation paralyzed by fear and uncertainty.

The Causes of the Great Depression

Herbert Hoover's election led Wall Street investors to assume that the celebrated "Great Bull Market" would continue unabated. Since 1924, the prices of stock shares invested in U.S. companies had steadily risen. Beginning in 1927, prices soared further on wings of reckless speculation. In 1919, some 317 million shares of stock had changed hands; in 1929, the number was more than a billion, driven by a mass madness comparable to the nineteenth-century gold rush. By 1928, stock market speculation was driving the economy.

Treasury Secretary Andrew W. Mellon's tax reductions had given people more money, and much of it went into the stock market. In April 1929, however, Hoover voiced concern about the "orgy of mad speculation" and urged investors to be more cautious—while privately telling his broker to sell many of his stock holdings. He saw disaster coming.

THE ROARING STOCK MARKET OF THE 1920S What made it so easy for so many to invest in stocks was the common practice of buying shares "on margin." An investor could make a small cash down payment (the "margin") and borrow the rest from a stockbroker, who held the stock certificates as security in case the share price plummeted. If stock prices rose, as they did in 1927, 1928, and most of 1929, the investor made enough profits to pay for the "margin loan" and reinvest the rest.

If the stock price declined and the buyer failed to pay off the broker's loan, the broker could sell the stock at a much lower price to cover the loan. By

August 1929, stockbrokers were lending investors more than two thirds of the face value of the stocks they were buying. Yet few people seemed concerned, for stock prices kept rising.

There had been signs that the economy was weakening. By 1927, steel production, residential construction, and automobile sales were slowing, as was the rate of consumer spending. By mid-1929, industrial production, employment, and other measures of economic activity were also declining. Still, the stock market rose.

Then, in early September 1929, the market fell sharply and continued to stall, sputter, and surge. By the middle of October, world exchanges had gone into a steep decline. Still, most investors remained upbeat. The nation's foremost economist, Irving Fisher of Yale University, told investors on October 17, "Stock prices have reached what looks like a permanently high plateau."

THE CRASH   The next week, however, stock market values wobbled, then tumbled again, triggering a wild scramble among terrified investors. As they rushed to sell their shares, the decline in stock prices accelerated. On what came to be called Black Tuesday, October 29—the worst day in stock market

Black Tuesday On October 29, 1929, the stock market fell lower than it ever had before. In this photo, a crowd of shareholders and investors gather outside the Wall Street Stock Exchange in a panic, many of them facing enormous losses.

history—prices went into free fall, and brokers found themselves flooded with stocks they could not sell. From October 23 to November 13, the market lost almost 40 percent of its value.

Fear and uncertainty began to spread like a virus across the nation and the world. Investors who had borrowed heavily to buy stocks were now forced to sell their holdings at huge losses so they could pay their debts.

Some stockbrokers and investors committed suicide. In New York, the president of a bankrupt cigar company jumped off a hotel window ledge, and two business partners joined hands and leaped to their deaths from the Ritz Hotel. Room clerks in Manhattan hotels started asking registering guests if they wanted a room for jumping or sleeping.

The entire economy began to sputter. In 1930, more than 25,000 businesses shut down; even more failed the following year. Treasury Secretary Andrew Mellon wrote his son that the "depression in business" had "gone further than anyone believed possible, and the prospects indicate a long period of readjustment."

The collapse of the stock market did not *cause* the **Great Depression**, however. Rather, it revealed that the prosperity of the 1920s had been built on weak foundations. As F. Scott Fitzgerald observed in *Echoes of the Jazz Age* (1931), the twenties were an "age of excess" that could not last.

The stock market crash also created a psychological panic that accelerated the economic decline. Frightened of losing everything, people rushed to remove their money from banks and the stock market. This only made things worse. By 1932, more than 9,000 banks had closed.

WHY THE ECONOMY COLLAPSED What were the underlying *causes* of the Great Depression? Most economic historians emphasize a combination of interrelated elements. The economy had actually begun to fall into a recession months *before* the crash because of *overproduction* and *underconsumption*. During the twenties, manufacturing production increased 43 percent, but the purchasing power of consumers did not keep pace. The economy was turning out more products than consumers could buy.

At the same time, many business owners had taken large profits while denying wage increases to employees. As Herbert Hoover lamented, "the only trouble with capitalism is capitalists; they're too damn greedy." By plowing profits into business expansion, executive salaries, and stock dividends, corporate leaders created an imbalance between production and consumption. Because union membership had plummeted, organized labor lost the leverage to convince management to provide wage increases. Two thirds of families in 1929 earned less than $2,000 annually. Inequality thus skyrocketed during the twenties.

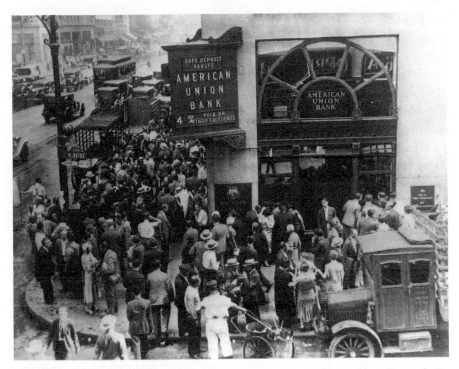

Bank Run As news of the Great Crash spread across the world, people rushed to their banks to withdraw their deposits, and some banks, such as the American Union Bank in New York City, were forced to close their doors when they ran out of cash.

As the stock market was crashing, factories were reducing production or shutting down altogether. From 1929 to 1933, U.S. economic output dropped 27 percent. At the same time, the farm sector stagnated. Farm incomes had soared during the Great War because European nations needed American grains, beef, and pork. Eager to sustain their prosperity, farmers borrowed money to buy more acreage or equipment to boost output. However, without European demand, increased production during the twenties led to *lower* prices for grains and livestock. To make matters worse, record harvests in the summer and fall of 1929 caused prices for corn, wheat, and cotton to fall precipitously, pinching the income of farmers who had taken on mounting debts. A bushel of wheat that brought a farmer $2.94 in 1920 brought only 30¢ by 1932.

GOVERNMENT'S ACTION AND THE ECONOMY Faulty government policies also contributed to the Depression. Like most Republican presidents, Herbert Hoover supported raising tariffs to keep foreign products from competing with American producers. The Smoot-Hawley Tariff of 1930, authored by Republicans Reed Owen Smoot and Willis C. Hawley, sought to help the farm sector by raising tariffs on agricultural imports. A swarm of corporate lobbyists convinced Congress to add thousands of nonagricultural items to the tariff bill, and the average tariff rate jumped from an already high 25 percent to 50 percent, making it the highest in history.

More than 1,000 economists petitioned Hoover to veto the tariff because its logic was flawed. By trying to "protect" farmers from foreign competition, it would raise prices on most raw materials and consumer products for Americans. On June 17, 1930, however, Hoover signed the bill, which caused another steep drop in the stock market.

As predicted, the Smoot-Hawley Tariff prompted other countries to retaliate by passing tariffs of their own, thereby making it more difficult for American farms and businesses to sell their products abroad. U.S. exports plummeted along with international trade in general, worsening the Depression.

Still another factor contributing to the Great Depression was the stance of the Federal Reserve Board, the government agency that manages the nation's money supply and interest rates. Instead of expanding the money supply to generate growth, the Federal Reserve tightened it out of concern for possible inflation in consumer prices. Between 1929 and 1932, the money supply shrank by a third, leading almost 10,000 small banks to close—and take millions of depositors with them into bankruptcy.

THE IMPACT OF EUROPE A final cause of the Depression was the chaotic state of the European economy, which had never fully recovered from the shock of the Great War. During the late 1920s, Great Britain, France, Spain, and Italy reduced their purchases of American goods as their shattered economies, slowly recovering from the devastation of the war, were finally able to produce more goods of their own. Meanwhile, the important German economy continued to flounder.

A related factor was the continuing inability of European nations to pay their debts to each other—and to the United States—that they had incurred during the war. The U.S. government insisted that the $11 billion it loaned to the Allies be repaid, but nations such as Great Britain and France had no money to send to Washington, D.C. They were forced to borrow huge sums ($5 billion) from U.S. banks, which only increased their indebtedness.

After the stock market crash in October 1929, American banks could no longer prop up the European economies. Germany's economy, which had grown dependent upon loans from American banks, was devastated as American money dried up. Then the Smoot-Hawley Tariff made it even more difficult for European nations to sell their products in the United States, which meant that those countries had less money with which to buy American goods. So as the European economy sputtered, it dragged the American economy deeper into depression.

THE HUMAN TOLL OF THE DEPRESSION

The Great Depression generated record levels of unemployment and widespread human distress. By 1932, perhaps a quarter of the entire population could not afford housing or adequate food. Grassroots protests erupted as the Depression worsened. In many cities, hungry people looted grocery stores. Angry mobs stopped local sheriffs from foreclosing on farms; others threatened to lynch judges at bankruptcy hearings.

Frustrated Iowa farmers formed the Farmers' Holiday Association to make their case for government assistance. If their demands were not met, they threatened to go on strike ("holiday"), withholding their crops, milk, and livestock from markets. Before the association could mobilize, however, scattered groups of farmers took direct action, in what became known as the Cornbelt Rebellion, blockading roads and preventing the movement of milk and grains. "There was anger and rebellion among a few," recounted an Iowa farmer, but most people lived in "helpless despair and submission."

Some people talked of revolution. "Folks are restless," Mississippi governor Theodore Bilbo told reporters in 1931. "Communism is gaining a foothold. . . . In fact, I'm getting a little pink myself."

The Grapes of Wrath **(1939)** A first edition of John Steinbeck's best seller, which told the story of the Joads, a family of tenant farmers struggling to survive during the Great Depression.

RISING UNEMPLOYMENT AND DEMANDS FOR RELIEF As the economy spiraled downward, unemployment soared to record levels: 4 million in 1930, 8 million in 1931, and 12 million by 1932. As always, unemployment especially hurt the most vulnerable:

the young, the elderly, the unskilled and undereducated, African Americans, immigrants, and Mexican Americans. Unemployed city dwellers became street-corner merchants. Some 6,000 jobless New Yorkers sold apples on street corners to survive. Their motto was, "Buy an apple a day and eat the Depression away."

Many hard-pressed business executives and professionals—lawyers, doctors, dentists, accountants, stockbrokers, teachers, nurses, and engineers—went without food and medical care to avoid the humiliation of "going on relief" (seeking assistance from churches, charitable organizations, and soup kitchens). The sense of shame cut across class lines. In *The Grapes of Wrath* (1939), John Steinbeck's novel about the victims of the Depression, a poor but proud woman is disgraced by accepting "charity" from the Salvation Army: "We was hungry. They made us crawl for our dinner. They took our dignity."

HUNGER Struggling families went without fruit and most vegetables, eating mainly beans and soup. Surveys of children in the nation's public schools in 1932 showed that one quarter suffered from malnutrition. In a rural school in Appalachia, a teacher told a sickly child to go home and get something to eat. "I can't," she replied. "It's my sister's turn to eat." In 1931, New York City hospitals reported about 100 cases of actual starvation, where people died solely from the lack of food. Hungry people by the millions lined up at soup kitchens where minimal amounts of food and water were distributed; others rummaged through trash cans behind restaurants. In Detroit, "we saw the city at its worst," wrote Louise V. Armstrong. "One vivid, gruesome moment of those dark days we shall never forget. We saw a crowd of some fifty men fighting over a barrel of garbage which had been set outside the back door of a restaurant. American citizens fighting over scraps of food like animals!"

HOMELESSNESS The contraction of the economy squeezed homeowners who had monthly mortgages to pay. A thousand per day lost their homes to foreclosure, and millions were forced to move in with relatives or friends. At first, the homeless were placed in almshouses, also called *poorhouses* or *workhouses*.

By 1933, however, the swelling numbers of homeless people overwhelmed public facilities. People were forced to live on the street, in culverts, under bridges, on park benches, and in doorways and police stations.

Millions of homeless people, mostly men, took to living on the road or the rails. These hobos, or tramps, as they were called, walked, hitchhiked in cars, or sneaked onto empty railway cars and rode from town to town. One railroad, the Missouri Pacific, counted 200,000 people living in its empty boxcars in 1931.

Chicago Shantytown In response to the economic devastation of the Great Depression, numerous shantytowns emerged in cities across the country to house the recently homeless; here, a man reads a newspaper outside his makeshift dwelling in Chicago.

In New York City, hundreds of homeless people lived on subway trains. One of them, Karl Monroe, an unemployed reporter, discovered that he could pay a nickel and ride the subway all night, sleeping in his seat. "A good corner seat" on a subway train, he explained, "gives the rider a chance to get a fair nap, and the thing can be repeated endlessly."

DESPERATE RESPONSES What could be done? Some women's magazines urged working women to give unemployed men their jobs. A Texas congressman suggested deporting all immigrants so that "real" Americans could have their jobs. Theodore Bilbo, soon to be a U.S. senator from Mississippi, urged that the nation's 12 million Blacks be shipped back to Africa. A retired army officer recommended killing people who had grown so feeble that they were "of no use to themselves or anyone else."

Desperate conditions led desperate people to do desperate things. Crime soared, as did begging, homelessness, and prostitution. Although the divorce rate dropped, in part because couples could not afford to live separately or pay legal fees, many jobless husbands simply deserted their wives and children. "You don't know what it's like when your husband's out of work," a woman told a reporter. "He's gloomy and unhappy all the time. Life is terrible. You must try all the time to keep him from going crazy."

With their future so uncertain, fewer people married, and those who did often decided not to have children. Birth rates plummeted, and many parents sent their children to live with relatives or friends. Some 900,000 children simply left home and joined the growing army of homeless wanderers. During the Great Depression, for the first time ever, more people left the United States than arrived as immigrants.

THE PLIGHT OF WORKING WOMEN The Depression put women in a peculiar position. By 1932, an estimated 20 percent of working women were unemployed, a slightly lower percentage than men. Because women held a disproportionate number of the lowest-paying jobs, they were often able to keep them.

Applying for a Job In October 1938, the government advertised six custodian positions and 15,000 African American women started lining up overnight to turn in their applications. Pictured here is a policeman leaping over a hedge to administer some crowd control.

As the Depression deepened, however, married women became the primary targets of layoffs. Twenty-six states passed laws prohibiting their employment, the reasoning being that a married woman should not "steal" a job from a husband and father. Three fourths of the nation's public-school systems fired women teachers who got married. As a legislator commented, the working woman in Depression-era America was "the first orphan in the storm."

It was considered acceptable for single White women to find jobs that were considered "women's work": salesgirls, beauticians, schoolteachers, secretaries, cooks, maids, and nurses.

AFRICAN AMERICANS   Most African Americans during the Depression still lived in the eleven southern states of the former Confederacy and earned their livelihood from farming as tenants and sharecroppers. Pervasive racial discrimination kept Blacks out of the few labor unions in the South and consigned them to the most menial, lowest-paying jobs.

They also continued to be victims of violence and intimidation. Jim Crow laws still excluded most African Americans from voting, and public places remained segregated. Some 3 million rural southern Blacks lived in cramped cabins without electricity, running water, or bathrooms.

In the mills, factories, mines, and businesses of the North, Black workers who had left the South to take northern factory jobs were among the first to be laid off; this group had the highest rate of joblessness in the early years of the Great Depression. "At no time in the history of the Negro since slavery," reported the Urban League, "has his economic and social outlook seemed so discouraging."

MEXICAN AMERICANS   As the Depression worsened, frustrated people looked for scapegoats, and immigrants were an easy target. In California, Texas, and other western states, residents blamed Mexican Americans for taking jobs from Whites and for placing an unsustainable burden on social welfare programs and charities.

President Hoover targeted Mexican Americans. He used a racially coded slogan, "American jobs for real Americans," to justify what came to be called the Mexican repatriation, arguing that "those people" would be better off with "their own kind."

In 1931, Hoover directed the secretary of labor, William Doak, to organize a series of raids by Bureau of Immigration agents and local police. Officials rounded up anyone with a Mexican-sounding name and demanded that they show proof of legal entry and citizenship. Those who failed to do so were detained without due process and then loaded on trains, buses, or flatbed trucks that took them deep into Mexico, where they were left to fend for themselves. Many of those deported were U.S. citizens. Doak also encouraged local communities to pass ordinances forbidding government employment of *anyone* of Mexican heritage, even legal permanent residents and citizens born in the United States.

Estimates vary widely, but at least 350,000 people, mostly factory laborers or farm workers and their families, were exiled to Mexico in the early 1930s. Texas alone sent 132,000 across the Rio Grande. An unknown number were American-born U.S. citizens who did not speak Spanish.

In 2005, the California state legislature "apologized" to the thousands sent to Mexico during the Great Depression "for the fundamental violations of their

Mexican Repatriation Amid fears of job scarcity during the Great Depression, Mexicans and Mexican Americans were targeted by the U.S. government to relocate to Mexico by train.

basic civil liberties and constitutional rights committed during the period of illegal deportation and coerced emigration."

DUST BOWL MIGRANTS Everywhere one looked in the early 1930s, people were suffering. City, county, and state governments proved incapable of managing the misery. As Americans turned to the federal government for answers, Herbert Hoover struggled to provide any, in large part because he never acknowledged the severity of the crisis.

In the southern plains of the Midwest and the Mississippi River Valley, a terrible drought during the 1930s created a catastrophe known as the **Dust Bowl**. Colorado, New Mexico, Kansas, Nebraska, Texas, Arkansas, and Oklahoma were the states hardest hit. Crops withered and income plummeted. Strong winds swept across the treeless plains, scooping up millions of tons of parched topsoil into billowing dark clouds that floated east across entire states, engulfing farms and towns in what were called black blizzards. By 1938, over 25 million acres of prairie land had lost topsoil.

Okies on the Run A sharecropping family reaches its destination of Bakersfield, California, in 1935, after they "got blowed out in Oklahoma."

Human misery paralleled the environmental devastation. Parched-land farmers could not pay their debts, and banks foreclosed on their property. Suicides soared. Many farmers and their families from the South and the Midwest headed toward California, where jobs were said to be plentiful.

Frequently lumped together as "Okies" or "Arkies," most of the Dust Bowl refugees were from cotton belt communities in Arkansas, Texas, Missouri, and Oklahoma. During the 1930s and 1940s, some 800,000 people, mostly Whites, left those four states and headed to the Far West.

Most people uprooted by the Dust Bowl went to California's urban areas—Los Angeles, San Diego, or San Francisco. Others moved into the San Joaquin Valley, the state's agricultural heartland. They discovered that rural California was no paradise. Only a few Dust Bowl migrants could afford to buy land. Living in tents or crude cabins and frequently on the move, the migrant workers suffered from exposure to the elements, poor sanitation, and social abuse. As an Okie reported, when the big farmers "need us they call us *migrants*, and when we've picked their crop, we're *bums* and we got to get out."

FROM HOOVERISM TO THE NEW DEAL

The Great Depression revealed Herbert Hoover to be a brilliant mediocrity. His initial response to the crisis was denial; all that was needed, he and others in his administration argued, was to let the economy cure itself. The best policy, Treasury Secretary Andrew Mellon advised, would be to "liquidate labor, liquidate stocks, liquidate the farmers, liquidate real estate." He wanted wages, stocks, production, and land values to bottom out so that recovery could spontaneously begin. Letting events run their course, he claimed, would "purge the rottenness out of the [capitalist] system" and force people to "work harder, [and] lead a more moral life." This time, however, a do-nothing approach did not work.

HOOVER'S EFFORTS AT RECOVERY

As the months passed, President Hoover proved less willing than Andrew Mellon to let events take their course. He decided that the government had a responsibility to "cushion the situation," which to him meant trying to bolster public confidence and shore up failing banks and businesses. He invited business, labor, government, and agricultural leaders to a series of conferences in which he urged companies to maintain employment and wage levels, asked unions to end strikes, and pleaded with state governors to accelerate planned construction projects to keep people working.

President Hoover also tried to boost public morale, but he was an ineffective cheerleader. "If you put a rose in Hoover's hand," wrote an observer, "it would wilt." In early May 1930, the president told the U.S. Chamber of Commerce that he was "convinced we have passed the worst and with continued effort we shall rapidly recover." A few weeks later, Hoover assured a group of bankers that the "depression is over." His administration also circulated upbeat slogans such as "Business IS Better" and "Keep Smiling." Uplifting words were not enough, however.

SHORT-SIGHTED TAX INCREASES   The Great Depression was the greatest national emergency since the Civil War, and the nation was woefully unprepared to deal with it. As personal income plummeted, so did the tax revenues needed to fund local, state, and federal governments. Hundreds of towns could not pay teachers or garbage collectors. Schools closed and discarded food and rubbish rotted in the streets. President Hoover insisted on trying to balance the federal budget by raising taxes and cutting budgets—precisely the wrong prescription for reversing a depression. He pushed through Congress the Revenue Act of 1932, the largest—and most poorly timed—peacetime tax

Hooverville *(Left)* Of the many Hoovervilles set up in Seattle alone, this shantytown near the shipyards was the largest and lasted nine years. *(Right)* A pair of toddlers beg for change in one of the Bonus Army camps.

increase in history, raising the top rate from 24 percent to 63 percent. Taking money out of consumers' pockets meant that they had less to spend when what the economy most needed was increased consumer spending.

HOOVER'S RESPONSE TO THE SOCIAL CRISIS   By the fall of 1930, many city governments were buckling under the strain of lost revenue and growing human distress. The federal government had no programs to deal with homelessness and joblessness. State and local governments cut spending, worsening the economic situation. Across the country, shantytowns sprouted in vacant lots where people erected shacks out of cardboard and scrap wood and metal. There they shivered and suffered, calling their makeshift villages Hoovervilles in criticism of the president. To keep warm during the winter, the homeless wrapped themselves in newspapers, dubbing them Hoover blankets. As the suffering deepened, more and more people called for governments to step in to deal with the emergency of homeless, starving people. Frustrated by his critics, Hoover dismissed the concerns of "calamity mongers and weeping men."

President Hoover refused to provide any federal programs to help the needy for fear that the nation would be "plunged into socialism." His governing philosophy, rooted in his commitment to rugged individualism, self-reliance, and free enterprise, set firm limits on emergency government action, and he was unwilling to set that philosophy aside even to meet an unprecedented national emergency. The president still trumpeted the virtues of "self-reliance" and individual initiative, claiming that government assistance would be the very worst thing for a nation in crisis, for it would rob people of the desire to help themselves.

Hoover hoped that the "natural generosity" of the American people and local charitable organizations and churches would be sufficient to handle the crisis, and he believed that volunteers (the backbone of local charity organizations) would relieve the social distress caused by the Depression. Hoover's faith in traditional "voluntarism" was misplaced, however. Although most Americans tried to get jobs to earn a living, there simply were no jobs, even for industrious people. The magnitude of the social crisis overwhelmed the resources of local and state relief agencies. Churches and charitable organizations like the Salvation Army and the Red Cross were swamped with needy people.

RISING CRITICISM OF HOOVER

That the economic collapse was so unexpected and intense made people more insecure and anxious, and Herbert Hoover increasingly became the target of their frustration. The *New York Times* reported in the summer of 1930 that public opinion "is turning rather heavily against the Hoover administration."

The Democrats shrewdly exploited the president's predicament, calling the crisis the "Hoover Depression." In November 1930, Democrats won a majority in the House and a near majority in the Senate. Instead of seeing the elections as a warning, Hoover grew more resistant to calls for federal intervention. The *New York Times* concluded that he had "failed as a party leader. He has failed as an economist. . . . He has failed as a business leader. . . . He has failed as a personality because of [his] awkwardness of manner and speech and lack of mass magnetism." When Hoover asked Treasury Secretary Andrew Mellon for a nickel to phone a friend, the secretary replied, "Here are two nickels—call all of them."

CONGRESSIONAL INITIATIVES With a new Congress in session in 1932, demands for federal action forced President Hoover to do more. That year, Congress approved his request to create the **Reconstruction Finance Corporation (RFC)** to make emergency loans to banks, life insurance companies, and railroads. It helped shore up several faltering businesses. Yet the RFC also aroused criticism. If the federal government could provide cash to help huge banks and railroads, asked New York Democratic senator Robert F. Wagner, why not "extend a helping hand to that forlorn American, in every village and every city of the United States, who has been without wages since 1929?" Hoover, however, signed only the Emergency Relief Act (1932), which authorized the RFC to make loans to states for infrastructure projects. Critics called the RFC a "breadline" for businesses while the unemployed went hungry.

VETERANS IN PROTEST   Fears of organized revolt arose when thousands of unemployed military veterans converged on the nation's capital in the spring of 1932. The **Bonus Expeditionary Force**, made up of members of the American Expeditionary Force that fought in France in the Great War, pressed Congress to pay the cash bonus owed to nearly 4 million veterans. The House passed a bonus bill, but when the Senate voted it down to avoid a tax increase, most of the veterans went home. The rest, along with their wives and children, having no place to go, camped in vacant federal buildings and in a shantytown at Anacostia Flats, within sight of the Capitol building.

Eager to remove the homeless veterans, Hoover persuaded Congress to pay for their train tickets home. More left, but others stayed even after Congress adjourned, hoping at least to meet with the president. Late in July, President Hoover ordered the government buildings cleared. In doing so, a policeman panicked, fired into the crowd, and killed two veterans. The secretary of war then dispatched 700 soldiers to remove the "Bonus Army."

The soldiers, commanded by the army chief of staff, General Douglas MacArthur, removed the veterans from government buildings. MacArthur, however, then disobeyed Hoover's directive to leave their makeshift camp

Assault on the Bonus Army   Unemployed military veterans of the Bonus Expeditionary Force clash with Washington, D.C., police at Anacostia Flats in July 1932.

alone. His soldiers rampaged through the unarmed veterans and their families, burning their flimsy shelters, terrorizing women, killing a baby, and bayoneting a boy chasing a rabbit. Fifty-five veterans were injured and 135 arrested.

The brutal attack on veterans and their families was a public relations disaster and led even more people to view Hoover and the Republicans as heartless. The Democratic governor of New York was horrified as he read newspaper accounts of the army's violent assault on the Bonus Army. "Well," Franklin Roosevelt told an aide, "this elects me" as the next president.

HOOVER'S PREDICAMENT   The stress of trying to manage the economic crisis sapped Herbert Hoover's health and morale. When aides urged him to be more of a public leader, he replied, "I have no Wilsonian qualities." He hated giving speeches, and when he did his words came across as cold and uncaring. He also got along badly with journalists, who highlighted his sour demeanor. Hoover, who had promised Americans "permanent prosperity," became a laughingstock. Unemployment continued to rise, wage levels continued to fall, and millions struggled simply to survive. In the end, Hoover's efforts failed because he never understood or acknowledged the seriousness of the nation's economic problems and social distress.

THE 1932 ELECTION   In June 1932, glum Republicans gathered in Chicago to nominate Herbert Hoover for a second term. By contrast, the Democrats arrived in Chicago a few weeks later confident that they would nominate the next president. Fifty-year-old New York governor Franklin Delano Roosevelt ("FDR") won on the fourth ballot.

Roosevelt—charming, witty, energetic, and eloquent—traveled to Chicago to accept the nomination in person. No candidate had ever done so. He told the cheering delegates that "this generation of Americans has a rendezvous with destiny." The nation must fight to save democracy both "for ourselves and for the world," but winning the fight against the depression would require unprecedented measures. "I pledge myself," Roosevelt promised, "to a *new deal* for the American people" that would create a new, enlightened administration "of competence and courage."

Throughout the campaign, Roosevelt stressed the need for "bold, persistent experimentation" to deal with the crisis of the Depression. "Above all," he pledged to "try something" new and bold to get the economy going again. There were "many ways of going forward," but "only one way of standing still."

In contrast, Hoover lacked vitality and vision. He warned that Roosevelt's proposals for unprecedented government action "would destroy the very foundations of our American system." The election, he said, was a battle "between

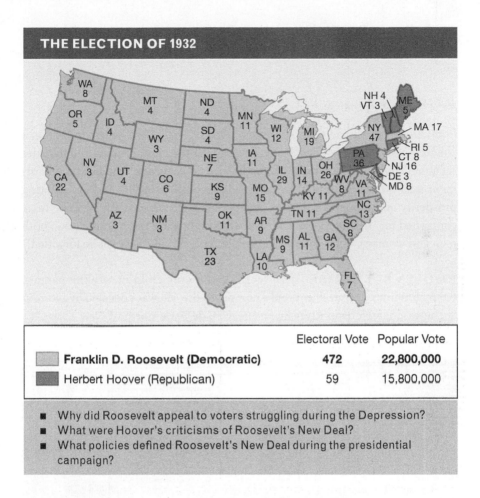

THE ELECTION OF 1932

	Electoral Vote	Popular Vote
Franklin D. Roosevelt (Democratic)	472	22,800,000
Herbert Hoover (Republican)	59	15,800,000

- Why did Roosevelt appeal to voters struggling during the Depression?
- What were Hoover's criticisms of Roosevelt's New Deal?
- What policies defined Roosevelt's New Deal during the presidential campaign?

two philosophies of government" that would decide "the direction our nation will take over a century to come."

On Election Day, voters swept Roosevelt into office, 23 million to 16 million.

MOBILIZING THE NEW DEAL Franklin Roosevelt sought to save American capitalism by transforming it from within. Like his cousin and hero, Theodore Roosevelt, he believed that the basic problem was the excessive power of large corporations. Only the federal government and an active president could regulate corporate capitalism for the public benefit because Big Business had grown *so* big.

FDR overflowed with cheerfulness, strong convictions, and an unshakable confidence in himself and in the resilience of Americans. He was affable, cool under pressure, and expert at the art of persuasion, but at heart he was a private person who revealed little about himself even to his closest friends and family. Frances Perkins, his secretary of labor, said Roosevelt was "the most complicated human being I ever knew."

ROOSEVELT'S NEW DEAL

Franklin Roosevelt had promised voters a "New Deal." Now he had to fashion a concrete one. Within hours of being inaugurated, the new president and his aides set about creating a "new order of competence and courage." The federal government assumed responsibility for national economic planning and for restoring prosperity and ensuring social security—for all. Roosevelt claimed to be most concerned for the "forgotten man" (by which he meant the working poor, both men and women). Those Americans, he pledged, would no longer be forgotten.

ROOSEVELT'S RISE Born in 1882, the only child of wealthy parents, young Franklin Roosevelt enjoyed a pampered life. He was educated by tutors at Springwood, a Hudson River manor near Hyde Park, north of New York City.

Franklin Delano Roosevelt This photo captures Roosevelt preparing to deliver the first of his popular radio "fireside chats," in which he discussed measures to reform the American banking system.

At age fourteen, he boarded his father's private railroad car and traveled to Massachusetts, where he enrolled in the exclusive Groton School. He then attended Harvard College and Columbia University Law School, where he did not earn a degree. While a law student in 1905, he married Anna Eleanor Roosevelt, his distant cousin and the favorite niece of President Theodore Roosevelt. Eleanor's father, Elliott, was Theodore's alcoholic brother.

In 1910, twenty-eight-year-old Franklin Roosevelt won a Democratic seat in the New York State Senate. Tall, handsome, and athletic, blessed with a keen intellect, sparkling personality, and infectious smile, he quickly impressed Democratic leaders. In 1913, President Woodrow Wilson appointed him assistant secretary of the navy. Seven years later, Roosevelt became James Cox's vice-presidential running mate on the Democratic ticket that lost to Republican Warren G. Harding.

Then a tragedy occurred. In 1921, at age thirty-nine, Franklin Roosevelt contracted polio, an infectious neuromuscular disease that left him permanently disabled, unable to stand without braces. Roosevelt fought back, however. For seven years, aided by his remarkable wife, Eleanor, he strengthened his body to compensate for his disability. The long battle for recovery transformed Roosevelt. He became less arrogant, less superficial, more focused, and more interesting. A friend recalled that Roosevelt's struggle with polio left him "completely warm-hearted, with a new humility of spirit" that led him to identify with the poor and the suffering.

In 1928 and 1930, Roosevelt won the governorship of New York. The child of wealth had developed the common touch as well as a great talent for public relations, but he also was vain and calculating, a clever manipulator of others. In other words, he was a skilled politician.

1933 INAUGURATION Inaugurated in March 1933, Franklin Delano Roosevelt assumed leadership during a profound national crisis that threatened the very fabric of American capitalism and unleashed the possibility of widespread civil unrest. "The situation is critical, Franklin," journalist Walter Lippmann warned. "You may have to assume dictatorial powers"—as had happened in Germany, Italy, and the Soviet Union.

Roosevelt did not become a dictator, but he did take extraordinary steps while assuring Americans "that the only thing we have to fear is fear itself." He confessed in his inaugural address that he did not have all the answers, but he did know that "this nation asks for action, and action now." He asked Congress for "a broad Executive power to wage a war against the emergency" just as "if we were in fact invaded by a foreign foe." Roosevelt's uplifting speech won rave reviews. Nearly 500,000 Americans wrote letters to the new president, and even the pro-Republican *Chicago Tribune* praised his "courageous confidence."

FDR was neither a masterful administrator, like Herbert Hoover, nor a deep thinker, like Woodrow Wilson. One of his closest aides said the president never "read a serious book." He did, however, love talking to voters and reporters, and he was determined to help those struggling Americans who could not help themselves. Colonel Edward House, the veteran Democratic counselor, explained that Woodrow Wilson "liked humanity as a whole and disliked people individually." Roosevelt, by contrast, was "genuinely fond of people and shows it."

THE FIRST HUNDRED DAYS In March 1933, President Roosevelt confronted four major challenges: reviving the industrial economy, addressing the needs of record numbers of jobless and homeless Americans, rescuing the ravaged farm sector, and reforming the defects of the capitalist system that had contributed to the Depression. He admitted that he would try several different "experiments." Some would succeed, and others would fail, but the important thing was to do something bold—and fast.

To advise him, Roosevelt assembled a "brain trust" of specialists—professors, journalists, economists, social workers, and others. "I'm not the smartest fellow in the world," Roosevelt admitted, "but I sure can pick smart colleagues."

The president and his advisers settled on a three-pronged strategy to revive the economy and help those in need. First, they would tackle the banking crisis and provide short-term emergency relief for the jobless. Roosevelt said, "Our greatest primary task is putting people to work." Second, the New Dealers—men and women who swarmed to Washington during the winter of 1933–1934—would encourage agreements between management and unions designed to keep businesses from failing. Third, the federal government would raise depressed commodity prices (corn, cotton, wheat, beef, pork, etc.) by paying farmers "subsidies" to *reduce* the sizes of their crops and herds so that prices would *rise* and thereby increase farm income over time, even if it meant higher food prices for consumers. From March 9, when the session opened, to June 16, the so-called First Hundred Days, Congress approved fifteen major pieces of legislation proposed by Roosevelt. Several of these programs comprised what came to be called the **First New Deal** (1933–1935).

SHORING UP THE FINANCIAL SYSTEM

Money is the lubricant of capitalism, and by 1933, money was fast disappearing from circulation. Since the stock market crash of 1929, panicky depositors had been withdrawing their money from banks and the stock market—and hoarding gold. Taking so much money out of circulation worsened the Depression and brought the banking system to the brink of collapse. Throughout the twenties, an average of about 700 banks had failed annually nationwide, most of them small, rural institutions in the South and Midwest weakened by the collapse of crop prices after the Great War. But after 1929, the number of bank failures soared.

BANKING REGULATION On March 5, 1933, his first full day in office, Franklin Roosevelt called on Congress to convene in emergency session. He asked the legislators to pass the Emergency Banking Relief Act, which declared a four-day bank holiday to allow the financial panic to subside. (A sulking Herbert Hoover criticized the move as a "reckless" step toward "gigantic socialism.") For the first time, all U.S. banks closed their doors.

The Galloping Snail A vigorous Roosevelt drives Congress to action in this *Detroit News* cartoon from March 1933.

Roosevelt's financial experts drafted the Emergency Banking Relief Act of 1933 to restore confidence in banks and inject $2 billion of new cash into the economy. On March 12, in the first of his many radio "fireside chats" to the nation, the president assured his 60 million listeners that it was safer to "keep your money in a reopened bank than under the mattress." The following day, people began taking their money back to the banks. "Capitalism was saved in eight days," said one of Roosevelt's advisers.

On June 5, 1933, Roosevelt shocked the financial world and earned the scorn of many bankers by taking the United States off the gold standard, whereby the amount of dollars in circulation was governed by the amount of gold stored in government vaults. Dropping the gold standard enabled the president to increase the currency supply and ward off deflation while encouraging the public to spend, which would foster economic growth. As it turned out, the sooner countries abandoned the gold standard, the more quickly their economies recovered. By 1936, most nations had done so.

On June 16, Roosevelt signed the Glass-Steagall Banking Act of 1933. It created the **Federal Deposit Insurance Corporation (FDIC)**, which insured customer bank accounts up to $2,500, thus reducing the likelihood of future panics. The Glass-Steagall Act also called for the separation of commercial banking from investment banking to prevent banks from investing the savings of depositors in the risky stock market. Only banks that specialized in investment could trade shares in the stock market after 1933. In addition, the Federal Reserve Board was given more authority to intervene in future financial emergencies. These steps effectively ended the banking crisis.

REGULATING WALL STREET Before the Great Crash in 1929, there was little government oversight of the securities (stocks and bonds) industry. In 1933 and 1934, President Roosevelt's administration developed two important pieces of legislation intended to regulate the operations of the stock market and eliminate fraud and abuses.

The Securities Act of 1933 was the first major federal legislation to regulate the sale of stocks and bonds. It required every corporation that issued stock for public sale to disclose all relevant information about the operations and management of the company so that investors could know what they were buying. The second bill, the Securities Exchange Act of 1934, established the **Securities and Exchange Commission (SEC)** to enforce the new laws and regulations governing the issuance and trading of stocks and bonds.

THE FEDERAL BUDGET As part of the breathless pace of the First Hundred Days, FDR convinced Congress to pass the Economy Act. This law allowed the president to cut government workers' salaries, reduce payments to military veterans for non-service-connected disabilities, and reorganize federal agencies. These policies were all designed to reduce government expenses and help the new president fulfill a promise to voters to balance the federal budget. Roosevelt then took the dramatic step of calling for an end to Prohibition; he did this for several reasons: because the law was so widely violated, because most Democrats wanted to end it, and because he wanted to regain the federal tax revenues from the sale of alcoholic beverages. The Twenty-First Amendment, ratified on December 5, 1933, ended Prohibition.

HELPING THE UNEMPLOYED AND HOMELESS

Another top priority was relieving the human distress caused by joblessness and homelessness. Herbert Hoover had stubbornly refused to help the unemployed and homeless, since he assumed that individual self-reliance and charitable organizations like the Red Cross, churches, and "city missions" would be sufficient.

The Roosevelt administration, however, knew that the numbers of people in need far exceeded the capacity of charitable organizations and local agencies. With a sense of urgency that Herbert Hoover had never summoned, President Roosevelt pushed through a series of programs that created what came to be called the "welfare state." He did not believe that the government should give suffering people cash (called a "dole"), but he insisted that the federal government help the unemployed and homeless by providing them with jobs. For the first time, the federal government took responsibility for assisting the most desperate Americans.

PUTTING PEOPLE TO WORK The Federal Emergency Relief Administration (FERA), headed by Harry L. Hopkins, was Roosevelt's first effort to deal with massive unemployment. It sent money to the states to spend on the unemployed and homeless. After the state-sponsored programs proved inadequate, Congress created the Civil Works Administration (CWA) in November 1933. It marked the first large-scale *federal* effort to put people directly on the government payroll at competitive wages: 40¢ an hour for unskilled workers, $1 for skilled.

The CWA, also headed by Hopkins, provided 4 million federal jobs during the winter of 1933–1934 and organized a variety of useful projects: repairing 500,000 miles of roads, laying sewer lines, constructing or improving more than 1,000 airports and 40,000 public schools, and providing 50,000 teaching jobs that helped keep small rural public schools open. When journalists marveled at how fast Hopkins put unemployed men and women to work, he replied, "Hunger is not debatable." When the program's cost soared to over $1 billion,

Federal Relief Programs Civilian Conservation Corps enrollees in 1933, on a break from work. Directed by army officers and foresters, the CCC adhered to a semi-military discipline.

however, Roosevelt ordered the CWA dissolved. By April 1934, 4 million workers were again unemployed.

THE CCC The most successful New Deal jobs program was the Civilian Conservation Corps (CCC), managed by the War Department. It built 2,500 camps in forty-seven states to house up to half a million unemployed, unmarried young men ages seventeen to twenty-seven. They worked as "soil soldiers" in national forests, parks, and recreational areas, and on soil-conservation projects. The CCC also recruited 150,000 jobless military veterans and 85,000 Native Americans.

Congress passed the CCC bill only after Oscar De Priest, an African American legislator from Illinois, introduced an amendment requiring that the agency not discriminate on account of race, color, or creed. Women were excluded from working in the CCC; African Americans and Native Americans were housed in segregated facilities.

Over the next nine years, the almost 3 million CCC enrollees were provided shelter in barracks, and given uniforms, food, and a small wage of $30 a month ($25 of which had to be sent home to their families). The young men could also earn high school diplomas. Critics charged that the CCC would undermine wage gains made by the labor union movement, but Roosevelt responded that the young men selected for the program would be those who "have no chance to get a job."

CCC workers cleared brush; constructed roads, bridges, campgrounds, fire towers, fish hatcheries, and 800 parks; planted 3 *billion* trees; taught farmers how to control soil erosion; built 13,000 miles of hiking trails, including the Appalachian Trail from Georgia to Maine; and fought forest fires. Roosevelt, a dedicated conservationist, saw the New Deal as an opportunity to reinvigorate the movement to preserve America's natural resources. He believed that a "nation that destroys its soils destroys itself. Forests are the lungs of our land, purifying the air and giving fresh strength to our people."

SAVING HOMES In 1933, an estimated 1,000 homes or farms were foreclosed upon each day because people could not pay their monthly mortgages. President Roosevelt convinced Congress to create the Home Owners' Loan Corporation, which helped people refinance their mortgages at lower interest rates. In 1934, Roosevelt created the Federal Housing Administration (FHA), which offered mortgages of much longer duration (twenty years) to reduce monthly payments. Prior to that, typical home mortgages had terms of less than ten years.

REVIVING THE INDUSTRIAL SECTOR The centerpiece of the New Deal's efforts to revive the industrial economy was the National Industrial Recovery Act (NIRA) of 1933. It created massive public-works construction projects funded by the federal government. The NIRA started the Public Works Administration (PWA), granting $3.3 billion for the construction of government buildings, roads, highways, bridges, dams, port facilities, airports, and sewage plants. Among its noteworthy projects were the Blue Ridge Parkway in North Carolina, the Skyline Drive in Virginia, and the Grand Coulee Dam in Washington State. The PWA also built forty-seven public housing projects for low-income Americans, all of them segregated by race to satisfy the demands of southern Democrats.

A second, more controversial part of the NIRA created the **National Recovery Administration (NRA)**, headed by Hugh S. Johnson, a hard-drinking retired army general known for his administrative expertise. The NRA represented a radical shift in the federal government's role in the economy. Never before in peacetime had Washington bureaucrats taken charge of setting prices, wages, and standards for working conditions.

The primary purpose of the NRA was to promote economic growth by waiving the anti-trust laws and allowing large corporations to create detailed "codes of fair competition" among themselves, including the setting of prices on an array of products. At the same time, the NRA codes also included "fair-labor" policies long sought by unions and social progressives: a national forty-hour workweek, minimum weekly wages of $13 ($12 in the South, where living costs were lower), and a ban on the employment of children under the age of sixteen. The NRA also guaranteed the right of workers to organize unions.

For a time, the downward spiral of wages and prices subsided. As soon as economic recovery began, however, small business owners complained that the NIRA's price-fixing robbed small producers of the chance to compete with large corporations. As one small business owner explained, the "big boys in the industry" dictated the codes and the "little fellows weren't being consulted." And because NIRA wage codes excluded agricultural and domestic workers (at the insistence of southern Democrats), few African Americans derived any benefit. When the Supreme Court declared the NIRA unconstitutional in *Schechter Poultry Corp. v. United States* in May 1935 for assigning lawmaking powers to the NIRA in violation of the Constitution's allocation of such authority only to Congress, few regretted its demise.

Despite being declared unconstitutional, some NRA policies that remained in place had lasting effects. New workplace standards, such as the forty-hour workweek, a national minimum wage, and restrictions that ended child labor were part of the NRA legacy. Its endorsement of collective bargaining spurred the growth of unions. Yet, as 1934 ended, industrial recovery was still feeble.

AGRICULTURAL ASSISTANCE   In addition to rescuing the banks and providing jobs to the unemployed, Franklin Roosevelt created the Farm Credit Administration to help farmers deal with their debts and lower their mortgage payments to avoid bankruptcy. The **Agricultural Adjustment Act** of 1933 created the Agricultural Adjustment Administration (AAA), which sought to raise prices for crops and herds by paying farmers to cut production. The money came from a tax on the businesses that processed food crops and certain agricultural commodities—cotton gins, flour mills, and slaughterhouses.

By the time the AAA was created, however, spring planting was underway. The prospect of another bumper cotton crop forced the AAA to pay farmers to "plow under" the sprouting seeds in their fields. To destroy a growing crop was a "shocking commentary on our civilization," Agriculture Secretary Henry A. Wallace admitted. "I could tolerate it only as a cleaning up of the wreckage from the old days of unbalanced production." Moreover, in an effort to raise pork prices, some 6 million baby pigs were slaughtered and buried. By the end of 1934, the AAA efforts had worked. Wheat, cotton, and corn production had declined, and prices for those commodities had risen. Farm income increased by 58 percent between 1932 and 1935.

A NEW ROLE FOR GOVERNMENT   At the end of the First Hundred Days of Franklin Roosevelt's presidency, the principle of an *activist* federal government had been established. While journalists characterized the AAA, NRA, CCC, CWA, and other New Deal programs as "alphabet soup," and conservative critics warned that Roosevelt was leading America toward fascism or communism, the president had become the most popular man in the nation.

THE TENNESSEE VALLEY AUTHORITY   Early in his presidency, Franklin Roosevelt declared that the "South is the nation's number one economic problem." Indeed, since the end of the Civil War, the economy and quality of life in the southern states had lagged far behind the rest of the nation. That gap only widened during the Great Depression. Nationwide, some 70 percent of Americans lived in homes with electricity. In the rural South, only 10 percent of households had electricity, even fewer in poverty-ravaged Appalachia. In fact, 75 percent of Appalachian households did not have running water or indoor plumbing.

To help, Roosevelt created one of the most innovative programs of the First New Deal: the Tennessee Valley Authority (TVA), which brought electrical

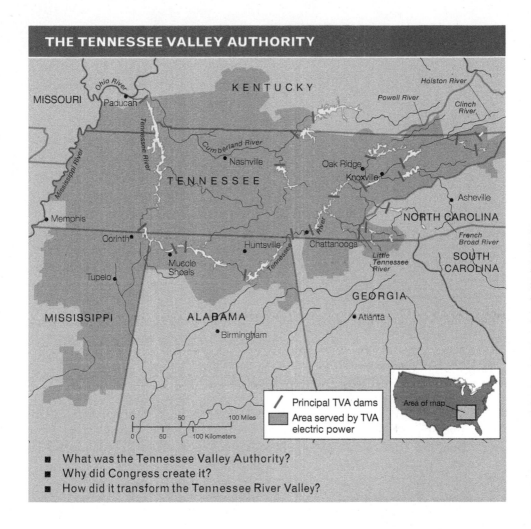

THE TENNESSEE VALLEY AUTHORITY

Principal TVA dams
Area served by TVA electric power
Area of map

- What was the Tennessee Valley Authority?
- Why did Congress create it?
- How did it transform the Tennessee River Valley?

power, flood control efforts, and jobs to Appalachia, the desperately poor mountainous region that stretched from West Virginia through western Virginia and North Carolina, Kentucky, eastern Tennessee, and northern Georgia and Alabama.

By 1940, the TVA, a multipurpose public corporation, had constructed twenty-one hydroelectric dams that created the "Great Lakes of the South" in Kentucky, Tennessee, North Carolina, Georgia, and Alabama, and produced enough electricity to power the entire region, at about half the average national rate. The TVA also dredged rivers to allow for boat and barge traffic, promoted soil conservation and forestry management, attracted new industries, and improved schools and libraries. It provided 1.5 million isolated farms with electricity and indoor plumbing.

Norris Dam The massive dam in Tennessee, completed in 1936, was essential to creating jobs and expanding power production under the TVA.

Progress often comes at a cost. Many New Deal programs helped some people and hurt others. Tough choices had to be made. The construction of huge dams in Appalachia and the subsequent lakes they created displaced thousands of residents from homes and villages that were destroyed to make way for progress. "I don't want to move," said an elderly East Tennessee woman. "I want to sit here and look out over these hills where I was born. My folks are buried down the road a piece, and our babies are over there on the hill under the cedars."

Yet overall, the First New Deal programs—and Roosevelt's leadership—had given Americans a renewed faith in the future. A government field-worker in the Carolinas reported that "every house I visited—mill worker or unemployed—had a picture of the President." Voters showed their appreciation in the congressional elections of 1934: Democrats increased their dominance in Congress with an almost unprecedented midterm victory for a party in power.

ELEANOR ROOSEVELT

One of the main reasons for FDR's popularity was his energetic wife, Eleanor, who would prove to be one of the most influential leaders of the twentieth century. Never had a First Lady been so engaged in public life or so widely beloved. She was her husband's moral compass, prodding him about social-justice issues while steadfastly supporting his political ambitions and policies.

Born in 1884 in New York City, Eleanor married her distant cousin Franklin in 1905, only to learn that his domineering mother, Sara Delano Roosevelt, would always be the most important woman in his life. (Sara once had workers erect a ladder to Franklin's boarding school window so that she could climb up and care for him during an illness.) "He might have been happier with a wife who was completely uncritical," Eleanor wrote later. "That I was never able to be, and he had to find it in other people."

Eleanor was dedicated to humanitarian causes from an early age. Before her marriage to Franklin, she was an energetic progressive: she worked in the Rivington Street settlement house in Manhattan and joined the National Consumers League. After the Great War, she participated in the International Congress of Working Women and the Women's International League for Peace and Freedom, endorsing efforts to address widespread poverty among women around the world. She joined the League of Women Voters in 1920.

Eleanor Roosevelt Intelligent, principled, and a political figure in her own right, Eleanor Roosevelt is pictured here addressing the Red Cross Convention in 1934.

While raising six children, she worked tirelessly on behalf of women, African Americans, and youth, giving voice to the voiceless and hope to the hopeless. Her compassion resulted in large part from the self-doubt and loneliness she had experienced as the ignored child of an alcoholic father and an aloof mother. Throughout her life, she fought a paralyzing fear of being unloved.

In September 1918, the Roosevelts' marriage changed forever when Eleanor, while unpacking Franklin's suitcase after a trip, discovered love letters he had exchanged with Lucy Mercer, her friend and personal secretary. As Eleanor read the letters, "the bottom dropped out" of her world. Eleanor offered Franklin a divorce, but he knew that would end his political future since divorce was not a socially accepted practice at the time. So they decided to maintain their marriage as a political partnership. As their son James said, the relationship became an "armed truce"—more a merger than a marriage. Eleanor later observed that she could "forgive, but never forget," but she never truly forgave or forgot.

Franklin and Eleanor were both concerned for each other's happiness while acknowledging their inability to provide it. In the White House, they lived apart, rarely seeing each other except for formal occasions and public events. As Eleanor confided to a friend, "There is no fundamental love to draw on," no passion or intimacy, "just respect and affection." Over time, Eleanor developed an independent "life of my own" and formed "special friendships" with men and women.

March 7, 1933

Eleanor Roosevelt and Lorena Hickok
While covering the First Lady for a campaign story, journalist Lorena "Hick" Hickok and Eleanor Roosevelt fell in love. Their close work and personal relationship lasted the better part of six years.

Journalist Lorena "Hick" Hickok, the only female reporter on Franklin's 1932 "Roosevelt Special" campaign train, had asked the Associated Press to assign her to cover the First Lady. Within weeks, the women fell in love, and Eleanor proudly wore an emerald ring Hick had given her. "Remember," Eleanor told Hick in early 1933, "no one is just what you are to me."

By then, Hickok had quit her job to become Eleanor's traveling companion. When separated, they wrote letters, more than 3,000 of them during their thirty-year relationship. "I wish I could lie down beside you tonight & take you in my arms," Eleanor wrote Hick. Eleanor convinced Hickok to move into the White House and assume a post in the Federal Emergency Relief Administration, but in fact she served as Eleanor's primary aide and adviser. It was Hickok who suggested that Eleanor hold regular news conferences catering especially to women journalists. Two years later, however, Eleanor ended the relationship, which had grown suffocating.

While redefining the role of the First Lady, Eleanor Roosevelt became more adored than her husband. She was an outspoken and relentless activist: the first woman to address a national political convention, write a nationally syndicated newspaper column, and hold press conferences (348 of them). She crisscrossed the nation, speaking in support of the New Deal, meeting with African American leaders, supporting equal access for women in the workforce and in labor unions, and urging Americans to live up to their humanitarian ideals. She helped convince her husband to reverse Woodrow Wilson's policy segregating federal government agencies and offices, which had remained in place during the Republican administrations during the 1920s.

In 1933, Eleanor convened a White House conference on the emergency needs of women. It urged the Federal Emergency Relief Administration (FERA) to ensure that "women are employed wherever possible." Within six months, some 300,000 women were at work on various federal government projects. The First Lady had become, said a journalist, "the most influential woman of our times." A popular joke claimed that the president's nightly prayer was: "Dear God, please make Eleanor a little tired." In fact, however, he was deeply dependent on his wife. She was the impatient agitator dedicated to what *should* be done; he was the calculating politician concerned with what *could* be done.

THE NEW DEAL UNDER FIRE

By 1934, Franklin Roosevelt was loved because he believed in and fought for the common people, for the "forgotten man" (and woman). The president, said a southern White tenant farmer, "is as good a man as ever lived." A textile mill worker reinforced the point by declaring that Roosevelt "is the biggest-hearted man we ever had in the White House." Where Herbert Hoover received an average of 400 letters a day as president, Roosevelt got more than ten times as many.

Voters also appreciated what a French leader called his "glittering personality." Roosevelt, with his famously arched eyebrows, upturned chin, and twinkling eyes, radiated personal charm, joy in his work, courage in a crisis, and optimism for the future. "Meeting him," said British prime minister Winston Churchill, "was like uncorking a bottle of champagne." Roosevelt, he added, was "the greatest man I have ever known."

Roosevelt was the most visible and accessible of all U.S. presidents. Twice a week he held press conferences, explaining new legislation, addressing questions and criticisms, and winning over most journalists while befuddling his opponents. Huey Long, a Democratic senator from Louisiana and one of Roosevelt's harshest critics, complained that the president could charm a snake: "You go in there [the White House] and see FDR wanting to tear him apart. You come out whistling 'Dixie.'"

But even Roosevelt's charm had its limits. He was despised by business leaders and political conservatives who believed the New Deal and the higher taxes it required were moving America toward socialism. Some called Roosevelt a "traitor to his [aristocratic] class."

Others, on the left, hated him for not doing enough to end the Depression. By the mid-1930s, the early New Deal programs had helped stop the economy's downward slide, but prosperity remained elusive. "We have been patient and long suffering," said a farm leader. "We were promised a New Deal. . . . Instead, we have the same old stacked deck."

In many respects, the contrasting opinions of Roosevelt reflected his own divided personality and erratic management style. He was both a man of idealistic principles and a practical politician prone to snap judgments, capable of both compromise and contradictory actions. He once admitted to an aide that to implement the New Deal he had to "deceive, misrepresent, leave false impressions . . . and trust to charm, loyalty, and the result to make up for it. . . . A great man cannot be a good man."

CONTINUING HARDSHIPS

Economic growth during FDR's first term averaged 9 percent, a peacetime record, but extensive suffering persisted. As late as 1939, some 9.5 million workers (17 percent of the labor force) remained unemployed.

IMMIGRATION AND THE GREAT DEPRESSION   There was no New Deal for immigrants. Hard times had always provoked anti-immigration feelings, and the Great Depression was no exception. Nativist prejudices prevailed as people blamed "aliens" for taking "American jobs." In 1935, the *New York American* newspaper declared that "existing immigration laws ought to be strengthened not weakened."

Congressman Martin Dies of Texas, a powerful Democrat, blamed the Depression itself on immigration. "If we had refused admission to the 16,500,000 foreign-born who are living in this country today, we would have no unemployment problem to distress and harass us." Dies was an ardent nativist who viewed immigration as the nation's greatest threat. "There is no middle ground or compromise" on the issue, he argued. "Either we are for or against America. If we are for America, we must be for the exclusion of these new-seed immigrants and the deportation of those unlawfully here."

Opposing such efforts was Congressman Vito Marcantonio, the son of Italian immigrants whose New York City district was filled with immigrants from Italy and Puerto Rico. "Let us legislate not by hysteria but with common sense," he told the House of Representatives. Marcantonio expressed his sorrow and disbelief that congressmen "would dare talk disparagingly about any racial group in the United States where, after all, we are all of alien stock." His strenuous opposition to "anti-immigrant bills" prevented their passage during the mid-1930s, a development made more remarkable by the failure of Franklin Roosevelt to speak out on the issue. Fearful of losing Democratic support in the South, he refused to take political risks by protecting immigrants.

AFRICAN AMERICANS AND THE NEW DEAL   The New Deal also had blind spots. Franklin Delano Roosevelt was never as progressive on social issues as most people assumed. FDR showed little interest in the plight of African Americans, even as Black voters were shifting from the Republicans (the "party of Lincoln") to the Democrats.

Roosevelt and the New Dealers failed to confront racism in the South for fear of angering powerful conservative southern Democrats who held almost half the congressional seats and controlled the key committee chairmanships. As a result, Roosevelt and his staff repeatedly had to make devil's bargains with southern segregationist senators, letting them force discriminatory provisions into New Deal legislation. As Mary White Ovington, treasurer of the National Association for the Advancement of Colored People (NAACP), stressed, the racism in any agency "varies according to the White people chosen to administer it, but always there is discrimination."

For example, the payments from the AAA to farm owners to take land *out* of production to raise prices for farm products forced hundreds of thousands of tenant farmers and sharecroppers, both Black and White, off the land. Such farm laborers were omitted from the progressive provisions of the NIRA and the Social Security Act (1935). In addition, FHA refused to guarantee mortgages on houses purchased by African Americans in White neighborhoods, and both the CCC and the TVA practiced racial segregation within their facilities.

The disproportionate political power of southern legislators imposed other costs as well. Twice, civil rights activists proposed bills to make lynching a federal crime. Twice, southern Democrats blocked them. Each time, President Roosevelt did nothing, even though his support may have changed the outcome.

Others did act, however. The NAACP waged an energetic campaign against racial prejudice throughout the 1930s. So did Eleanor Roosevelt, who helped convince her husband to appoint more African Americans to significant government positions than had any of his predecessors.

One of the most visible of those appointments was Mary McLeod Bethune. In 1935, President Roosevelt named her director of the Division of Negro Affairs within the National Youth Administration, an agency that provided jobs to unemployed youth. The fifteenth of seventeen children born to formerly enslaved people in South Carolina, Bethune had founded a school for African American girls in Daytona Beach, Florida. In the 1920s, she had headed the NAACP. Now, as the highest-ranking African American in the federal government, she convened the "Black Cabinet," a group of Black administrative officials who lobbied FDR to end racial discrimination in the federal workforce. The president assured her that he would do what he could. (In 1941, he would sign an executive order creating the Fair Employment Practice Committee to ensure that African Americans had a fair chance at federal government jobs.)

COURT CASES AND CIVIL LIBERTIES Racial prejudice remained widespread in the United States during the Great Depression, and it was especially vicious in the South. In 1931, an all-White Alabama jury, on flimsy, conflicting testimony, convicted nine Black males, ranging in age from thirteen to twenty-one, of raping two young White women mill workers while riding a freight train. Eight of the "Scottsboro Boys" were sentenced to death as White spectators cheered. In his award-winning novel *Native Son* (1940), African American writer Richard Wright recalled the "mob who surrounded the Scottsboro jail with rope and kerosene."

The injustice of the Scottsboro case sparked protests throughout the world. Many called the verdict a "legal lynching." The two White women, it turned out, were prostitutes who had been selling sex to White and Black teens on the train. One of the women eventually recanted and began appearing at rallies on behalf of the defendants.

No case in legal history produced as many trials, appeals, reversals, and retrials as the Scottsboro case. Further, it prompted two important rulings. In *Powell v. Alabama* (1932), the U.S. Supreme Court overturned the original convictions and ordered new trials because the judge had not ensured that the accused were provided competent defense attorneys. In *Norris v. Alabama* (1935), the Court ruled that the systematic exclusion of African Americans from Alabama juries had denied the Scottsboro defendants equal protection under the law—a principle that had widespread impact on state courts by opening juries to African Americans.

Scottsboro Case Heywood Patterson *(center)*, one of the defendants in the case, is seen here with his attorney, Samuel Leibowitz *(left)*, in Decatur, Alabama, in 1933.

Although Alabama eventually dropped the charges against the four youngest Scottsboro defendants and granted paroles to the others, their lives were ruined. The last defendant left prison in 1950. The Scottsboro cases thereafter came to symbolize continuing racial injustice in the South.

NATIVE AMERICANS AND THE DEPRESSION The Great Depression also ravaged Native Americans. Some were initially encouraged by President Roosevelt's appointment of John Collier as commissioner of the Bureau of Indian Affairs (BIA). Collier steadily increased the number of Native Americans employed by the BIA and ensured that all Indians gained access to New Deal relief programs.

Collier's primary objective, however, was passage of the Indian Reorganization Act. Designed to reinvigorate Native American cultural traditions by restoring land to tribes, the proposed law would have granted them the right to start businesses, establish self-governing constitutions, and receive federal funds for vocational training and economic development. The act that Congress passed, however, was a much-diluted version of the original proposal, and the "Indian New Deal" brought only partial improvements. It did, however, spur several tribes to revise their constitutions to give women the right to vote and hold office.

Cultural Life during the Depression

One might have expected the onset of the Great Depression to have deepened the despair of the writers, artists, and intellectuals during the 1920s who were known as the Lost Generation. Instead, it brought them a renewed sense of militancy and affirmation. By the summer of 1932, even the "golden boy" of the Lost Generation, F. Scott Fitzgerald, had declared that "to bring on the revolution, it may be necessary to work within the Communist party."

During the 1930s, membership in the Communist party of the United States of America (CPUSA) grew from 7,500 to 55,000. The CPUSA promoted the civil rights of African Americans, sought to improve the wages and working conditions of the laboring class, and lobbied for greater government assistance to the unemployed and homeless. The CPUSA played a crucial role in financing the legal appeals of the Scottsboro Boys.

Few Americans remained members of the Communist party for long, however. Most writers rebelled at demands to hew to a shifting party line, and many abandoned communism by the end of the decade upon learning that Soviet leader Josef Stalin practiced a tyranny more horrible than that of the Russian czars.

LITERATURE AND THE DEPRESSION Among the writers who addressed themes of social significance during the 1930s, two deserve special notice: John Steinbeck and Richard Wright. To capture the ordeal of the Depression in *The Grapes of Wrath* (1939), Steinbeck traveled with some of the 3.5 million "Okies" driven from the Dust Bowl to chase the false rumor that good jobs were to be had for the taking in the fields of California's Central Valley.

This firsthand experience of people struggling to maintain their lives and dignity amid grinding poverty allowed Steinbeck to create an epic tale of the Joad family's migration, hope, disappointment, and resilience. "Rich fellas come up an' they die, an' their kids ain't no good an' they die out," says Ma Joad. "But we keep a'comin'. We're the people that live. They can't wipe us out; they can't lick us. We'll go on forever, Pa, cause we're the people." The solidarity of struggling migrant farm workers was Steinbeck's theme. As Tom Joad promises, "Wherever there's a fight so hungry people can eat, I'll be there." Critics smeared Steinbeck as a Communist, and officials in California banned the novel.

Among the most talented novelists to emerge in the 1930s was African American Richard Wright. The grandson of formerly enslaved people and the son of a Mississippi sharecropper who deserted his family, Wright ended his formal schooling with the ninth grade (as valedictorian of his class). He then worked in Memphis and devoured books he borrowed on a White friend's library card, all the while saving to go north. In Chicago, his period as a Communist, from 1934 to 1944, gave him an intellectual framework for his powerful novels that examined the quest for social justice.

Native Son (1940), Wright's masterpiece, focuses on the forgotten Americans at the bottom of the heap. It tells the story of twenty-year-old Bigger Thomas, a Black pool shark and petty thief imprisoned in a Chicago ghetto by virtue of his birth. "Bigger, sometimes I wonder why I birthed you," his God-fearing mother tells him. "Honest, you the most no-countest man I ever seen in all my life."

Bigger fears and envies Whites. "Every time I get to thinking about me being Black and they being White, me being here and they being there," he explains, "I feel like something awful's going to happen to me."

And something awful does happen. An accidental murder and its cover-up lead him to more heinous crimes, all of which, Wright suggests, resulted from the racism in American society. "I just can't get used to it," Bigger tells one of his poolroom buddies. "I swear to God I can't. . . . Every time I think about it [White oppression] I feel like somebody's poking a red-hot iron down my throat."

At Bigger's trial for murder, his attorney, Mr. Max, pleads for African Americans in general: "They are not simply twelve million people; in reality they constitute a separate nation, stunted, stripped and held captive *within* this nation." Many of them are overflowing with "balked longing for some kind of fulfilment and exultation"; and their seething futility is "what makes our future seem a looming image of violence."

POPULAR CULTURE While many writers and artists dealt with the suffering and social tensions aroused by the Great Depression, the more popular cultural outlets, such as radio programs and movies, provided a welcome escape. In 1930, more than 14 million families owned a radio set—more than 40 percent of the population; by the end of the decade the percentage was 83 percent.

Movies were transformed by the introduction of sound. "Talkies" made movies the most popular form of entertainment during the 1930s, and the introduction of double features in 1931 and the construction of outdoor drive-in theaters in 1933 boosted interest and attendance. More than 60 percent

"There's No Way Like the American Way" Margaret Bourke-White's famous 1937 photograph of desperate people waiting in a disaster-relief line in Louisville, Kentucky, captures the continuing racial divide of the era and the elusiveness of the "American dream" for many minorities.

of the population—70 million people—paid a quarter to see at least one movie each week.

The movies rarely dealt directly with hard times. People wanted to be entertained, uplifted, and distracted. In *Stand Up and Cheer!* (1934), featuring child star Shirley Temple, President Roosevelt appoints a Broadway producer to his cabinet as Secretary of Amusement. His goal is to use entertainment to distract people from the ravages of the Depression.

Most feature films transported viewers into the escapist realms of adventure, spectacle, and fantasy. *Gone with the Wind* (1939), based on Margaret Mitchell's Pulitzer Prize–winning novel, was a good example, as were *The Wizard of Oz* (1939) and Walt Disney's Mickey Mouse cartoons. Moviegoers also relished shoot-'em-up gangster films, extravagant musicals (especially those starring dancers Fred Astaire and Ginger Rogers), "screwball" romantic comedies like *It Happened One Night* (1934), *My Man Godfrey* (1936), and *Mister Deeds Goes to Town* (1936), and horror films such as *Dracula* (1931), *Frankenstein* (1931), *The Mummy* (1932), *King Kong* (1933), *The Invisible Man* (1933), and *Werewolf of London* (1935).

Perhaps the best way to escape the Depression was to watch the zany comedies of the Marx Brothers. As one Hollywood official explained, the movies of the 1930s were intended to "laugh the big bad wolf of the depression out of the public mind." *The Cocoanuts* (1929), *Animal Crackers* (1930), *Monkey Business* (1931), *Horse Feathers* (1932), and *Duck Soup* (1933) introduced moviegoers to the anarchic antics of Chico, Groucho, Harpo, and Zeppo Marx, who combined slapstick humor with verbal wit to create masterpieces of irreverent satire.

CRITICS ASSAULT THE NEW DEAL

For all their criticisms of racially biased New Deal programs, Native Americans and African Americans still voted in large majorities for Franklin Roosevelt. Other New Deal critics, however, hated Roosevelt and his policies. The head of the Communist party, Earl Browder, claimed in 1934 that Roosevelt's "program is the same as finance capital the world over. . . . It is the same as [Adolf] Hitler's program." Many Republican business executives were so angered by the president's promotion of a welfare state and support for labor unions that they refused to use his name, calling him instead "that man in the White House."

HUEY LONG Others criticized President Roosevelt for not doing enough to help the common people. The most potent of the president's "populist" opponents was Huey Pierce Long Jr., a flamboyant Democratic senator from Louisiana. A short, colorful hillbilly with rowdy, curly hair and a flair for the ridiculous, Long was a classic demagogue, a theatrical politician who appealed to the raw emotions of his supporters, earning him the title "Messiah of the Rednecks." The son of a backwoods farmer, he sported pink suits and pastel shirts, red ties, and two-toned shoes. Long claimed to be leading a crusade to serve the poor, arguing that Louisiana would be a place where "every man [is] a king, but no one wears a crown."

First as Louisiana's governor, then as its U.S. senator, Long had taxed the rich to benefit the poor, winning him the adoration—and votes—of the masses. His popularity, however, went to his head, and he came to view the state as his personal kingdom. He bribed and threatened his way to power. Reporters called him the "dictator of Louisiana." True, he reduced state taxes, improved roads and schools, built charity hospitals, and provided better public services. But he used threats, intimidation, and blackmail to get his way.

In 1933, Long swaggered into Washington as a supporter of Roosevelt and the New Deal, but he quickly grew suspicious of the National Recovery Administration's efforts to cooperate with Big Business. Having developed presidential aspirations, he also became jealous of Roosevelt's popularity.

To launch his presidential candidacy, Long devised a simplistic plan called the Share-the-Wealth Society. He proposed to raise taxes on the wealthiest Americans and redistribute the money to "the people"—giving every poor family $5,000 and every wage worker an annual income of $2,500, providing pensions to retirees, reducing the workweek to thirty hours, giving four-week annual vacations to everyone, paying bonuses to military veterans, and enabling every qualified student to attend college or vocational school.

It did not matter that his plan would have spent far more money than his proposed taxes would have raised. As Long told a group of Iowa farmers, "Maybe somebody says I don't understand it [government finance]. Well, you don't have to. Just shut your damn eyes and believe it. That's all."

By early 1935, Long claimed to have enough support to unseat Roosevelt: "He's scared of me. I can outpromise him, and he knows it. People will believe me, and they won't believe him." Long's popularity forced the Roosevelt administration to pursue more progressive programs, and his antics led Roosevelt to declare that the Louisiana senator was "one of the two most dangerous men in the country." (The other was U.S. Army Chief of Staff Douglas MacArthur.)

THE TOWNSEND PLAN   Another critic of Roosevelt who championed a form of populist capitalism was Francis E. Townsend, a retired California doctor. Shocked by the sight of three elderly women digging through garbage cans for food scraps, he began promoting the Townsend Recovery Plan in 1934. He wanted the federal government to pay $200 a month to every American

Roosevelt's Critics Dr. Francis E. Townsend, Reverend Gerald L. K. Smith, and Father Charles E. Coughlin *(left to right)* attend the Townsend Recovery Plan convention in Cleveland, Ohio.

over age sixty who agreed to quit working. The recipients would have to spend the money each month.

Townsend claimed that his plan would create jobs for young people by giving older people the means to retire, and it would energize the economy by enabling retirees to buy more products. But like Long's Share-the-Wealth scheme, the numbers in Townsend's plan did not add up. It would have paid retirees, only 9 percent of the population, more than half the total national income. Townsend, like Long, didn't care about his plan's cost. Not surprisingly, it attracted great support among Americans sixty years and older. Advocates flooded the White House with letters urging Roosevelt to enact it.

FATHER COUGHLIN A third outspoken critic of FDR and the New Deal was Father Charles E. Coughlin, a Canadian-born Roman Catholic "radio priest" in Detroit, Michigan. In fiery weekly broadcasts that attracted as many as 40 million listeners nationwide, he assailed President Roosevelt as "anti-God" and claimed that the New Deal was a Communist conspiracy. Coughlin wanted to put all banks, utilities, oil companies, and "our God-given natural resources" under government control.

During the 1930s, as fascism and Nazism gained power in Europe, Coughlin became rabidly anti-Semitic, claiming that Roosevelt was a tool of "international Jewish bankers" and relabeling the New Deal the "Jew Deal." He praised Adolf Hitler and the Nazis for killing Jews because, he claimed, they were all Communists. During the 1940 presidential campaign, Coughlin gave a Nazi salute and bragged, "When we get through with the Jews in America, they'll think the treatment they received in Germany was nothing."

Such threats finally galvanized groups across the country, both Jewish and non-Jewish. They exerted enough pressure to force radio stations to drop Coughlin's weekly broadcast. By late 1940, his radio program went off the air.

In the mid-thirties, however, Coughlin was at the peak of his influence. He, Francis Townsend, and Huey Long formed a powerful threat to Roosevelt's reelection. A 1935 poll showed that Long could draw more than 5 million votes as a third-party candidate for president, perhaps enough to prevent Roosevelt's reelection. General Hugh S. Johnson, head of the NRA, warned corporate executives, "You can laugh at Father Coughlin. You can snort at Huey Long—but this country was never under a greater menace."

MOVING LEFT Franklin Roosevelt decided to "steal the thunder" from his three most visible critics by instituting an array of progressive programs. "I'm fighting Communism, Huey Longism, Coughlinism, Townsendism," he told a reporter in early 1935. He explained that he needed "to save our system, the capitalist system," from such "crackpot ideas." Doing so, wrote Interior Secretary Harold Ickes in his diary, would require Roosevelt to "move further to the left in order to hold the country." The alternative, Ickes feared, would be social revolution.

OPPOSITION FROM THE SUPREME COURT The growing opposition to the New Deal came from all directions. By the mid-1930s, businesses were filing lawsuits against various elements of the New Deal, and some of them made their way to the U.S. Supreme Court.

On May 27, 1935, as noted earlier, the Supreme Court killed the National Industrial Recovery Act (NIRA) by a unanimous vote. In *Schechter Poultry Corporation v. United States*, the justices ruled that Congress had given too much authority to the president when the National Recovery Administration (NRA) brought business and labor leaders together to create "codes of fair competition" for their industries—an activity that violated federal anti-trust laws.

On January 6, 1936, in *United States v. Butler*, the Supreme Court declared that the Agricultural Adjustment Act's tax on "middle men," the companies that processed food crops and warehoused commodities like cotton, was unconstitutional. In response, the Roosevelt administration convinced Congress to pass the Agricultural Adjustment Act of 1938, which reestablished the earlier crop-reduction payment programs but left out the tax on processors. Although the AAA helped boost the overall farm economy, conservatives criticized the sweeping powers granted under the new program.

By the end of its 1935–1936 term, the Supreme Court had ruled against New Deal programs in seven of nine major cases. Similar conservative judicial reasoning, Roosevelt warned, might endanger other New Deal programs—if he did not prevent it.

THE SECOND NEW DEAL

To rescue his legislative program from judicial and political challenges, President Roosevelt launched in January 1935 the **Second New Deal**, much more radical than the First New Deal. He explained that "social justice . . . has become a definite goal" of his administration. In his effort to undermine Long's appeal, the president called on Congress to pass legislation that included another federal construction program to employ the jobless; banking reforms; higher taxes on the wealthy; and "social security" programs to protect people during unemployment, old age, and illness. Roosevelt's closest aide, Harry L. Hopkins, told the cabinet: "Boys—this is our hour. We've got to get everything we want—a [public] works program, social security, wages and hours, everything—now or never."

THE WPA In the first three months of 1935, dubbed the Second Hundred Days, Roosevelt convinced Congress to pass most of the Second New Deal's "must" legislation. The Second New Deal (1935–1939) would transform American life.

The first major initiative was the $4.8 billion Emergency Relief Appropriation Act. The largest peacetime spending bill in history to that point, it included an array of job programs managed by a new agency, the **Works Progress Administration (WPA)**.

The WPA, headed by Harry Hopkins, quickly became the nation's largest employer, hiring an average of 2 million people annually over four years. WPA workers, mostly men with little formal education, built 650,000 miles of highways and roads; created 8,000 parks; constructed 78,000 bridges; restored the St. Louis riverfront; and employed a wide range of writers, artists, actors, and musicians in new cultural programs such as the Federal Theatre Project, the Federal Art Project, the Federal Music Project, and the Federal Writers' Project.

The National Youth Administration (NYA), also under the WPA, provided part-time employment to students and aided jobless youths. Two future presidents were among the beneficiaries: Twenty-seven-year-old Lyndon B. Johnson directed an NYA program in Texas, and Richard M. Nixon, a Duke University law student, found work through the NYA at 35¢ an hour.

African Americans benefited greatly from the WPA programs. Horace Cayton, a Black sociologist who assessed the impact of the New Deal on minorities, remembered that "the WPA came along and Roosevelt came to be [viewed as] a god. . . . You worked, you got a paycheck, and you had some dignity."

Federal Art Project A group of WPA artists at work on *Building the Transcontinental Railroad*, a mural celebrating the contributions of immigrants that adorned the dining hall on Ellis Island, the immigrant receiving center near New York City.

THE WAGNER ACT Another major element of the Second New Deal was the National Labor Relations Act, often called the **Wagner Act** in honor of the New York senator, Robert Wagner, who drafted it and convinced Roosevelt to support it. The Wagner Act guaranteed workers the right to organize unions and bargain directly with management about wages and other issues. It also created a National Labor Relations Board to oversee union activities and ensure that management bargained with them in good faith.

SOCIAL SECURITY The Great Depression hit the oldest Americans and those with disabilities especially hard. To address these problems, FDR proposed the **Social Security Act** of 1935. Social Security, he announced, was the "cornerstone" and "supreme achievement" of the New Deal.

The basic concept of government assistance to the elderly was not new. Progressives during the early 1900s had proposed a federal system of social security for the aged, poor, disabled, and unemployed, and other nations had already enacted such programs. The hardships caused by the Great Depression

Social Security The federal government distributed posters such as this one to educate the public about the new Social Security Act.

revived the idea, and Roosevelt masterfully guided the legislation through Congress.

The Social Security Act, designed by Secretary of Labor Frances Coralie Perkins, the first woman cabinet member in history, included three major provisions. Its centerpiece was a federal retirement fund for people over sixty-five. Beginning in January 1937, workers and employers contributed payroll taxes to establish the fund, and the first payments were made to recipients. Most of the collected taxes funded pension payments to retirees; the rest went into a trust fund for the future.

Roosevelt stressed that Social Security would not guarantee everyone a comfortable retirement. Rather, it would supplement other sources of income and protect the elderly from destitution. Not until the 1950s did voters and politicians come to view Social Security as the *primary* source of retirement income for working-class Americans.

The Social Security Act also set up a shared federal-state unemployment insurance program, financed by a payroll tax paid by employers. In addition, it committed the national government to a broad range of social-welfare activities based upon the assumption that "unemployables"—people who were unable to work—would remain a state responsibility while the national government would provide work relief for the able-bodied. To that end, the Social Security Act provided federal funding for three state-administered programs—old-age assistance, aid to dependent children, and aid for the blind—and further aid for maternal, child-welfare, and public health services.

When compared with similar programs in Europe, the U.S. Social Security system was—and remains—conservative. It is the only government-managed retirement program in the world financed by taxes on the earnings of workers; most other countries fund such programs out of general government revenues.

The Social Security payroll tax was also a regressive tax because it used a single withholding tax *rate* for everyone, regardless of income level. It thus pinched the poor more than the rich and hurt efforts to revive the economy because it removed from circulation a significant amount of money.

In addition, the Social Security system, at the insistence of southern Democrats, *excluded* nearly half the national workforce, some 9.5 million workers who most needed it: low-paid farm laborers, domestic workers (maids and cooks), and the self-employed, a disproportionate percentage of whom were African Americans.

Roosevelt regretted the Social Security Act's limitations, but he saw them as necessary compromises to gain congressional approval and withstand court challenges. As he told an aide who criticized funding the program out of employee contributions:

> I guess you're right on the economics, but those taxes were never a problem of economics. They are politics all the way through. We put those payroll contributions there so as to give the contributors a moral, legal, and political right to collect their pensions and their unemployment benefits. With those taxes in there, no damn politician can ever scrap my Social Security program.

FDR also preferred that workers fund their own Social Security pensions because he wanted Americans to view their retirement checks as an *entitlement*— as something that they had paid for and deserved.

Conservatives condemned the Social Security Act as another "tyrannical" expansion of government power. The head of the National Association of Manufacturers told Congress that Social Security would lead to "ultimate socialist control of life and industry." Former President Herbert Hoover refused to apply for a Social Security card because of his opposition to the "radical" program. He received a Social Security number anyway.

TAXING THE RICH Another major bill in the second phase of the New Deal was the Revenue Act of 1935, sometimes called the Wealth-Tax Act but popularly known as the "soak-the-rich" tax. It raised tax rates on annual income above $50,000, in part because of stories that many wealthy Americans were not paying taxes. The powerful banker J. P. Morgan, for example, confessed to a Senate committee that he had created fictitious sales of stock to his wife that enabled him to pay no taxes.

Morgan and other business leaders fumed over Roosevelt's tax and spending policies. Newspaper tycoon William Randolph Hearst growled that the wealth tax was "essentially communism." Roosevelt countered, stressing that "I am fighting communism. . . . I want to save our system, the capitalistic system." Yet he added that saving capitalism and "rebalancing" its essential elements required a more equal "distribution of wealth." Like his cousin Theodore, Franklin Roosevelt did not hate capitalism; he hated capitalists who engaged in "unfair" or illegal behavior.

A NEW DIRECTION FOR UNIONS   The New Deal reinvigorated the labor union movement. When the National Industrial Recovery Act (NIRA) demanded that industry fairness codes affirm workers' rights to organize, unionists quickly translated it to mean "the president wants you to join the union." John L. Lewis, head of the United Mine Workers (UMW), was among the first to capitalize on the pro-union spirit of the NIRA. He rebuilt the UMW from 150,000 members to 500,000 within a year.

Encouraged by Lewis's success, Sidney Hillman of the Amalgamated Clothing Workers of America and David Dubinsky of the International Ladies' Garment Workers' Union organized clothing industry workers into an industrial union (composed of all types of workers, skilled and unskilled). Opposing them were the smaller craft unions (composed of skilled male workers only, with each union serving just one trade).

"100 Sit Down Strike—'Don't Scab'"   Unionized automobile workers, striking in 1937, hang effigies of stool pigeons (police informants) from the windows of their factory.

In 1935, with the passage of the Wagner Act, industrial unions formed a Committee for Industrial Organization (CIO) to represent their interests. In 1936, the much larger American Federation of Labor (AFL) expelled the CIO unions, in part because of different views on the calling of strikes. The Committee for Industrial Organization then formed a permanent structure of its own called the Congress of Industrial Organizations (also known by the initials CIO). The rivalry between the two organizations spurred both groups to greater efforts.

The Congress of Industrial Organizations focused on organizing the automobile and steel industries. Companies used various forms of intimidation to fight the unions. Early in 1937, automobile workers tried a new tactic, the "sit-down strike," in which they refused to leave a workplace until employers had granted them collective-bargaining rights.

Led by the fiery Walter Reuther, thousands of employees at the General Motors plant in Flint, Michigan, stopped production and locked themselves in the plant. "She's ours," yelled one worker participating in the sit-down strike. Company officials responded by turning off the heat to the plant, called in police to harass the strikers with tear gas and cut off their food supply, and threatened to fire the workers. They also pleaded with President Roosevelt to dispatch federal troops. He refused but expressed his displeasure with the strike.

The standoff lasted more than a month before the company relented and signed a contract recognizing the United Automobile Workers (UAW) as a legitimate union. Dubbed the "strike heard round the world," the successful takeover of automobile plants inspired workers and led many to join unions. In the year following the strike, the UAW's membership soared from 30,000 to 500,000.

ROOSEVELT'S SECOND TERM   On June 27, 1936, Franklin Delano Roosevelt accepted the Democratic party's nomination for a second term as president. The Republicans chose Governor Alfred M. Landon of Kansas, a progressive who had endorsed many New Deal programs. "We cannot go back to the days before the depression," Landon scolded conservative Republicans. "We must go forward, facing our new problems."

The Republicans hoped that the followers of Huey Long, Charles E. Coughlin, Francis E. Townsend, and other Roosevelt critics would combine to draw enough Democratic votes away from the president to give Landon a winning margin. That possibility faded, however, when Dr. Carl Weiss, upset about the way Long had treated Weiss's father-in-law, shot and killed the forty-two-year-old senator in 1935.

In the 1936 election, Roosevelt proved himself an unrivaled political force. He carried every state except Maine and Vermont, with a popular vote of 28 million to Landon's 17 million, the largest winning margin in any election to that point. Democrats would also dominate the new Congress, by 77 to 19 in the Senate and 328 to 107 in the House.

Roosevelt had forged a new electoral coalition that would dominate national politics for years to come. While holding the support of most traditional Democrats, North and South, he made strong gains in the West. In the northern cities, he held on to the ethnic groups helped by New Deal welfare policies. Many middle-class voters flocked to support him, as did intellectuals stirred by the ferment of new ideas. The revived labor union movement also threw its support to Roosevelt, and, in the most meaningful shift of all, a majority of African Americans voted for a Democratic president. "My friends, go home and turn Lincoln's picture to the wall," a Pittsburgh journalist told Black voters. "That debt has been paid in full."

THE COURT-PACKING PLAN   President Roosevelt's landslide victory emboldened him to pursue even more extensive efforts to end the Great Depression. One major roadblock stood in the way: the conservative Supreme Court. In Roosevelt's view, it had become an outdated court made up of what a newspaper columnist called "nine old men" (average age: seventy-one) determined to thwart Roosevelt's attempts to expand executive authority to deal with the economic crisis.

Lawsuits challenging the constitutionality of the Social Security and Wagner Acts were pending before the Court. Given the conservative bent of the justices and their earlier anti–New Deal rulings, Roosevelt feared that the Second New Deal was in danger of being nullified by a handful of judges.

For that reason, he directed Homer Cummings, the attorney general, to suggest ways to make the Court more supportive of the New Deal. Cummings proposed reforming the Supreme Court by enlarging it. Congress, not the Constitution, determines the size of the Court, which over the years had numbered between six and ten justices. In 1937, the number was nine. On February 5, 1937, without having consulted his cabinet, legislative leaders, or justices of the Court, Roosevelt told reporters he was going to ask Congress to name up to six new justices, one for each of the current justices over seventy years old, explaining that the aging members of the Court were falling behind in their work and needed help.

The Court-packing plan, as opponents labeled the scheme, backfired, however, and ignited a profound debate among the three branches of government—executive, legislative, and judicial. For the next 168 days, the nation was preoccupied with the constitutionality of Roosevelt's proposal, officially called the Judicial Reorganization Act. Journalist Walter Lippmann charged that Roosevelt had become "drunk with power." A Democratic senator dismissed the plan as "mentally unsound, undemocratic, and reactionary in principle."

As it turned out, several Supreme Court decisions during the spring of 1937 *upheld* disputed provisions of the Wagner and Social Security Acts. In addition, a conservative justice resigned, and Roosevelt replaced him with a New Dealer, Senator Hugo Black of Alabama.

Still, Roosevelt insisted on forcing his Court-packing bill through Congress. "The people are with me," he insisted; "I know it." But the Senate Judiciary Committee described the judicial reorganization bill as "a measure which should be so emphatically rejected that its parallel will never again be presented to the free representatives of the free people of America." On July 22, 1937, the Senate overwhelmingly voted it down.

The Court-packing scheme was the worst blunder of Roosevelt's career. The episode damaged the president's prestige and fractured the Democratic party, as anti–New Deal Democrats, mostly southerners, thereafter openly opposed Roosevelt's leadership. The bill's defeat, however, preserved the institutional integrity of the Supreme Court and of the nation's constitutional foundation, the chief genius of which is its system of checks and balances among the three branches of government.

A SLUMPING ECONOMY During 1935 and 1936, the economy finally began showing signs of revival. By the spring of 1937, industrial output had risen above the 1929 level before the stock market crash. In 1937, however, President Roosevelt, worried about federal budget deficits and rising inflation, ordered sharp cuts in government spending.

The result was not what he or his "brain trust" expected. The economy quickly stalled, then slid into a slump nearly as deep as that of 1929 after the Wall Street crash. In only three months, unemployment rose by 2 million. The "recession is more remarkable than the depression," noted *Time* magazine, highlighting the 35 percent drop in industrial production from the previous summer as "the swiftest decline in the history of U.S. business and finance." Like Herbert Hoover before him, Roosevelt now decided that doing nothing was the best strategy. "Everything will work out if we just sit tight and keep quiet," he told the cabinet.

When the spring of 1938 failed to bring recovery, however, Roosevelt reversed himself and asked Congress for a new federal spending program. Congress approved $3.3 billion in new expenditures. The increase in government spending helped, but only during the Second World War would employment again reach pre-1929 levels.

The Court-packing fight, the sit-down strikes, and the 1937 recession all undercut Roosevelt's prestige and power. When the 1937 congressional session ended, the only major New Deal initiatives were the Wagner-Steagall National Housing Act and the Bankhead-Jones Farm Tenant Act. The Housing Act, developed by Senator Robert F. Wagner, set up the United States Housing Authority within the Department of Interior. It extended long-term loans to cities to build high-rise public housing projects in blighted neighborhoods and provide subsidized rents for low-income residents. Later, during the Second World War, it would finance housing for employees working in new defense plants.

The Farm Tenant Act created the Farm Security Administration (FSA), which provided loans to keep farmers from losing their land to bankruptcy. It also made loans to tenant farmers to enable them to purchase farms. In the end, however, the FSA did little more than tide a few farmers over during difficult times. A more effective answer to the sluggish economy eventually arrived in the form of national mobilization for war, which landed many struggling tenant farmers in military service or the defense industry, broadened their horizons, and taught them new skills.

In 1938, Congress enacted the Fair Labor Standards Act. It replaced many of the provisions that had been in the NIRA, which were deemed unconstitutional. Like the NIRA, it established a minimum wage of 40¢ an hour and a maximum workweek of forty hours. The act, which applied only to businesses engaged in *interstate* commerce, also prohibited the employment of children under the age of sixteen.

SETBACKS FOR THE PRESIDENT   During the late 1930s, Democrats in Congress increasingly split into two factions, with conservative southerners on one side and liberal northerners on the other. Many southern Democrats balked at the party's growing dependence on the votes of northern union members and African Americans. Senator Ellison "Cotton Ed" Smith of South Carolina and several other southern delegates walked out of the 1936 Democratic party convention, with Smith declaring that he would not support any party that views "the Negro as a political and social equal." Other critics believed that President Roosevelt was exercising too much power and spending too much money. Some southern Democrats began to work with conservative Republicans to block proposed New Deal programs.

The congressional elections of November 1938 handed the administration another setback when the Democrats lost 7 seats in the Senate and 80 in the House. In his State of the Union message in 1939, Roosevelt for the first time spoke of the need "to *preserve* our reforms" rather than add to them. The conservative coalition of Republicans and southern Democrats had stalemated him.

A HALFWAY REVOLUTION The New Deal's political momentum petered out in 1939 just as a new world war was erupting in Europe and Asia. What, then, was its impact? In hindsight, it had more energy than coherence. Many New Deal programs failed or were poorly conceived and implemented, victims of bureaucratic infighting and inefficient management, but others were changing American life for the better: Social Security, federal regulation of stock markets and banks, minimum wage levels for workers, federally insured bank accounts, and government-sanctioned labor unions.

The greatest triumph of the New Deal, however, was its demonstration that American democracy could, through governmental lawmaking and presidential leadership, cope with the collapse of capitalism. A self-proclaimed "preacher president," Franklin Roosevelt raised the nation's spirits and its income through his relentless optimism and unprecedented activism. As a CCC worker recalled late in life, Roosevelt "restored a sense of confidence and morale and hope—hope being the greatest of all." New Deal programs provided stability for tens of millions of people. "We aren't on relief anymore," one woman noted with pride. "My husband is working for the government."

Roosevelt changed the role of the federal government and the presidency in national life. During the 1930s, for the first time in peacetime, the federal government assumed responsibility for planning and managing the economy and intervening to ensure social stability. By the end of the 1930s, the power and scope of the national government were vastly larger than in 1932. Landmark laws expanded federal powers by establishing regulatory agencies and laying the foundation of a social welfare system.

The enduring reforms of the New Deal entailed more than just a bigger federal government, an activist president, and revived public confidence; they also constituted a significant change from the progressivism of Theodore Roosevelt and Woodrow Wilson. Those reformers had assumed that the function of progressive government was to use aggressive *regulation* of industry and business to ensure that people had an equal opportunity to pursue the American dream.

Franklin Roosevelt and the New Dealers went beyond the progressive concept of regulated capitalism by insisting that the government provide at least a minimal level of support for all Americans. On June 27, 1936, Roosevelt gave a speech accepting the Democratic party nomination for a second presidential term. In it, he articulated his concern for ordinary Americans: "Governments can err, Presidents do make mistakes, but the immortal Dante tells us that divine justice weighs the sins of the cold-blooded and the sins of the warmhearted in different scales." The true test of the nation's progress, he asserted, "is not whether we add to the abundance of those who have much; it is whether we provide enough for those who have little."

Roosevelt's New Deal created for most Americans a powerful sense of belonging, of having rights and opportunities they'd never had before. That civic sense was evident among the industrial working class, where the wearing of union buttons became a source of pride. A similar sense of dignity and hope swept through ethnic communities that had long been dismissed as being less than American. And despite the racial injustices imposed on the New Deal by southern Democrats, the same new sense of national belonging amid a determined quest for equal rights took hold in African American communities, too.

The greatest failure of the New Deal was its inability to restore prosperity and end record levels of unemployment. In 1939, some 10 million Americans—nearly 17 percent of the workforce—remained jobless. Only the prolonged crisis of the Second World War and its attendant military and industrial needs would at last bring full employment to the United States.

Roosevelt was an idealist without illusions. Energetic pragmatism was his greatest strength—and weakness. He admitted that he often acted out of conflicting convictions. "I am a juggler," he explained. "I never let my right hand know what my left hand does." He sharply increased the regulatory powers of the federal government and laid the foundation for what would become an expanding system of social welfare programs.

The result was both revolutionary and conservative. New Deal initiatives left a legacy of unprecedented innovations: a joint federal-state system of unemployment insurance; a compulsory, federally administered retirement system; financial support for families with dependent children; maternal and child-care programs; and several public health programs. The New Deal also improved working conditions and raised wage levels for millions.

Roosevelt, however, was no socialist, as Republican critics charged; he sought to preserve the basic capitalist economic structure while providing protection to the nation's most vulnerable people. In this sense, the New Deal represented a "halfway revolution" that permanently altered the nation's social and political landscape. "During the ten years between 1929 and 1939," marveled an appreciative social worker in 1940, "more progress was made in public welfare and relief than in the three hundred years after this country was first settled." In a time of peril, Roosevelt created for Americans a more secure future.

CHAPTER REVIEW

SUMMARY

- **The Causes of the Great Depression**   The 1929 stock market crash revealed the structural flaws in the economy, but it was not the only cause of the *Great Depression* (1929–1941). During the twenties, business owners did not provide adequate wage increases for workers, resulting in the overproduction of many goods by the end of the decade. The nation's agricultural sector also suffered from overproduction. Government policies—such as high tariffs and the reduction of the nation's money supply—further reduced the nation's consumption and exacerbated the emerging economic depression.

- **The Human Toll of the Depression**   Thousands of banks and businesses closed, while millions of homes and jobs were lost. By the early 1930s, many people were homeless and hopeless. The *Dust Bowl* of the 1930s compounded the hardship for rural Americans. Discrimination against married women, African Americans, Native Americans, Mexican Americans, and Asian Americans in hiring was widespread.

- **Hoover's Failure**   The first phase of federal response to the Great Depression included President Hoover's attempts at increasing public works and exhorting unions, businesses, and farmers to revive economic growth. In 1932, Congress created the *Reconstruction Finance Corporation* to help banks and corporations avoid bankruptcy, but Hoover's philosophy of voluntary self-reliance prevented him from using federal intervention to relieve the suffering of American citizens. When thousands of out-of-work veterans of the Great War, the *Bonus Expeditionary Force*, protested in Washington, D.C., their efforts ended in violence. In March 1933, the economy was shattered. Millions more Americans were without jobs, basic necessities, and hope.

- **The First New Deal**   During the early months of the administration, Congress and President Roosevelt enacted the *First New Deal* (1933–1935), which propped up the banking industry with the *Federal Deposit Insurance Corporation* (1933), provided short-term emergency work relief, promoted industrial recovery with the *National Recovery Administration* (1933), raised agricultural prices with the *Agricultural Adjustment Act* (1933), and enforced new laws and regulations on Wall Street with the *Securities and Exchange Commission* (1934). In this second phase of the federal response, most of the early New Deal programs helped end the economy's downward spiral but still left millions unemployed and mired in poverty.

- **The New Deal under Fire**   The Supreme Court ruled that several of the First New Deal programs were unconstitutional violations of private property and states' rights. Many conservatives criticized the New Deal for expanding the scope and reach of the federal government so much that it was steering the nation toward socialism. By contrast, other critics did not think the New Deal went far enough. African American critics decried the widespread discrimination in New Deal policies and agencies.

- **The Second New Deal and the New Deal's Legacy**   Roosevelt responded to the criticism and the continuing economic hardship with a third phase, the *Second*

New Deal (1935–1938), which sought to reshape the nation's social structure by expanding the role of the federal government. Many of its programs, such as the *Works Progress Administration* (1935), the *Wagner Act* (1935), and the *Social Security Act* (1935) aimed to achieve greater social justice by establishing new regulatory agencies and laying the foundation of a federal social welfare system. The Second New Deal reformed business, industry, and banking with provisions such as unemployment pay, a minimum hourly wage, old-age pensions, and bank-deposit insurance. The New Deal established the idea that the federal government should provide a baseline quality of life for all Americans.

CHRONOLOGY

1929	Herbert Hoover inaugurated as president in March; stock market crashes in late October
1930	Congress passes the Smoot-Hawley Tariff
1932	Congress sets up the Reconstruction Finance Corporation Bonus Expeditionary Force heads to Washington, D.C. Franklin D. Roosevelt is elected president
March–June 1933	First Hundred Days of Roosevelt's presidency
December 1933	Twenty-First Amendment repeals Prohibition
1935	Roosevelt creates the Works Progress Administration Supreme Court finds National Industrial Recovery Act unconstitutional; Congress passes the Wagner Act
1936	President Roosevelt is reelected in a landslide
1937	Social Security goes into effect; Roosevelt attempts Court-packing scheme

KEY TERMS

Great Depression (1929–1941) p. 1128
Dust Bowl p. 1136
Reconstruction Finance
Corporation (RFC) (1932) p. 1140
Bonus Expeditionary Force (1932)
p. 1141
First New Deal (1933–1935) p. 1146
Federal Deposit Insurance
Corporation (FDIC) (1933) p. 1147
Securities and Exchange
Commission (SEC) (1934) p. 1148

National Recovery Administration
(NRA) (1933) p. 1151
Agricultural Adjustment Act (1933)
p. 1152
Second New Deal (1935–1938) p. 1168
Works Progress Administration
(WPA) (1935) p. 1168
Wagner Act (1935) p. 1169
Social Security Act (1935) p. 1169

🐰 INQUIZITIVE

Go to InQuizitive to see what you've learned—and learn what you've missed—with personalized feedback along the way.

24 The Second World War

1933–1945

***Raising the Flag on Iwo Jima* (February 23, 1945)** Six members of the U.S. Marine Corps raise the flag on Mount Suribachi during the Battle of Iwo Jima. Three of these marines would die within days of this photograph, which later earned photographer Joe Rosenthal the Pulitzer Prize. A bronze statue of this scene is the centerpiece of the Marine Corps War Memorial in Virginia.

When Franklin Roosevelt became president in 1933, he shared with most Americans a determination to stay out of international disputes. So-called isolationists insisted that there was no justification for America to become embroiled in international affairs, much less another major war. With each passing year during the 1930s, however, totalitarian governments in Germany, Italy, and Japan threatened the peace and stability of Europe and Asia.

Roosevelt strove to keep the United States out of what he called the "spreading epidemic of world lawlessness" as fascist dictatorships in Germany and Italy and ultranationalist militarist leaders in Japan launched invasions against neighboring countries. By the end of the thirties, Roosevelt had decided that the only way for the United States to avoid getting embroiled in another war was to offer all possible military equipment to Great Britain, France, and China.

Roosevelt's efforts to stop what he called "aggressor nations" ignited a fierce debate between isolationists and interventionists that ended on December 7, 1941, when Japan launched a surprise attack against U.S. warships and military bases at Pearl Harbor in Hawaii. With that shocking event, America again entered a world war. It would become the most significant event of the twentieth century, engulfing five continents and leaving few people untouched around the world.

The Japanese attack on U.S. military targets in Hawaii unified the country as never before. Men and women rushed to join the armed forces. Eventually, 16.4 million Americans would serve in the military during the war, including

focus questions

1. What gave rise to fascism in Europe after the Great War? How did authoritarian leaders gain control in Germany, Italy, and Japan?

2. How did President Roosevelt and Congress respond to the events leading to the early stages of wars in Europe and Asia between 1933 and 1941?

3. What were the effects of the Second World War on American civilians?

4. What major factors enabled the United States and its allies to win the war in Europe?

5. How were the Japanese defeated in the war in the Pacific?

6. How did President Roosevelt and the Allies try to reshape the postwar world?

350,000 women. The massive government spending required to wage total war boosted industrial production, ended unemployment, and wrenched the economy out of the Great Depression.

In 1945, the United States and its allies emerged victorious in the most destructive war in history. More than 50 million people were killed between 1939 and 1945—perhaps 60 percent of them civilians, including millions of Jews and other ethnic and social minorities killed in Nazi death camps and Soviet concentration camps. The war uprooted and cast adrift millions of refugees. Cities were flattened, treasures of art and architecture were destroyed, and much of the history and heritage of Europe and Asia were lost—forever.

The Second World War transformed America's role in the world. Isolationism gave way to internationalism. By 1945, America was the world's most powerful nation, with new international interests and responsibilities. Instead of bringing peace, however, the end of the fighting led to a lengthy "cold war" between two former allies, the United States and the Soviet Union.

THE RISE OF FASCISM IN EUROPE

In 1917, Woodrow Wilson had led the United States into the Great War to make the world "safe for democracy." In fact, though, democracy was in retreat after 1919, while Soviet communism and European fascism were on the march. **Fascism** was a radical form of totalitarian government in which a dictator employed hateful lies against minority groups to gain power and popularity. Once achieving power, fascists used brute force to seize control of all aspects of national life—the economy, armed forces, legal and educational systems, and media. Fascism in Germany and Italy thrived on a violent patriotism and almost hysterical emotionalism built upon claims of racial superiority and the simmering resentments spawned by defeat in the Great War.

At the same time, halfway around the world, the Japanese government fell under the control of expansionists eager to conquer China and much of Asia. Japanese leaders were convinced that theirs was a "master race" with a mission to lead a resurgent Asia, just as Adolf Hitler claimed that Germany's mission was to use its supposed racial supremacy to dominate Europe. By 1941, there would be only a dozen or so democratic nations left around the world.

ITALY AND GERMANY In 1922, politician and journalist Benito Mussolini and 40,000 of his black-shirted supporters seized control of Italy, taking advantage of an inept government incapable of dealing with widespread unemployment, runaway inflation, mass strikes, and fears of communism.

Democracies were unstable, inefficient, and slow to act, Mussolini claimed. He pledged to show Italians the decisiveness of a forceful ruler, for he was, in his own words, a *great man* who would exercise absolute power on behalf of the people.

By 1925, Prime Minister Mussolini was wielding dictatorial power as "Il Duce" (the Leader). He called his version of antisocialist totalitarian nationalism *fascism*. He eliminated all political parties except the Fascists and ordered many of his political opponents murdered. Yet there was something clownish about the strutting, chest-thumping Mussolini, who claimed that "my animal instincts are always right," when in fact he was at best a mediocre statesman.

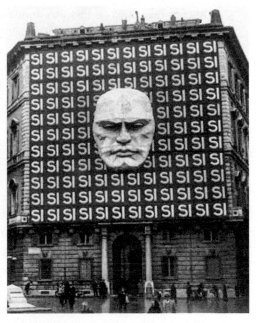

Fascist Propaganda Mussolini's headquarters in Rome's Palazzo Braschi; the building bore an oversized reproduction of his leering face and 132 *si*'s (Italian for "yes") in 1934.

There was nothing amusing, however, about his German counterpart, the Austrian-born Adolf Hitler, whom Mussolini privately described as "an aggressive little man . . . probably a liar, and certainly mad." Hitler's transformation during the 1920s from social misfit to head of the National Socialist German Workers' (Nazi) party startled the world. Many observers continued to underestimate Hitler and his appeal. As late as 1930, a German magazine editor dismissed Hitler as a "half-insane rascal," a "pathetic dunderhead," and a "nowhere fool" whose Nazi organization had "no future at all."

Yet Hitler used his talent for demagoguery, lying, and showmanship to organize a grassroots movement through nativist appeals to the masses. The objective of fascism was to replace diversity with unity: "one people, one state, one leader," in the words of the Nazi slogan. Hitler and the Nazis claimed to represent a German "master race" whose "purity and strength" were threatened by liberals and other "inferior" peoples: Jews, socialists, Romani (gypsies), Communists, and homosexuals.

"Democracy must be destroyed," Hitler thundered. Jews, he claimed, were subhuman, "a spiritual pestilence, worse than the Black Death [bubonic plague]." In the name of genetic purity and the fashioning of a "super race," Hitler and the Nazis even had disabled citizens killed to make way for the master race. And all this was done ruthlessly, pitilessly, with no misgivings or second thoughts.

Hitler had little patience with conventional political processes. To enforce his rise to power, he recruited 2 million street-brawling thugs ("storm troopers") to intimidate his opponents. "We are barbarians!" Hitler shouted. "We want to be barbarians! It is an honorable title. We shall rejuvenate the world!"

Hitler was appointed chancellor on January 30, 1933, five weeks before Franklin Roosevelt was first inaugurated. Like Mussolini, he quickly declared himself absolute leader, or *Führer*, banned all political parties except the Nazis, created a secret police force known as the *Gestapo*, and stripped enemies of their voting and civil rights. There would be no more labor unions or strikes.

During the mid-1930s, Hitler's brutal Nazi police state cranked up the engines of tyranny and terrorism, propaganda, and censorship. Brown-shirted Nazi storm troopers fanned out across the nation, burning books and persecuting, imprisoning, and murdering Communists, Jews, and their sympathizers.

Most Germans gloried in Hitler's anti-Semitism and his ruthless aggressiveness. At a famous rally in Nuremburg, his supporters screamed: "We want one leader! Nothing for us! Everything for Germany!" President Roosevelt confided to the French ambassador to the United States that Hitler was "a madman."

Adolf Hitler Hitler performs the Nazi salute at a rally. The giant banners, triumphant music, powerful oratory, and expansive military parades were all designed to stir excitement and allegiance among the public.

EXPANDING AGGRESSION As the 1930s unfolded, a series of catastrophic events sent the world hurtling toward disaster. In 1931–1932, some 10,000 Japanese troops occupied Manchuria, in northeast China. It was a territory rich in raw materials; mineral deposits, including iron ore and coal; and farmland needed for Japanese expansion. At the time, China was fragmented by civil war between Communists led by Mao Zedong and Nationalists led by Chiang Kai-shek. The Japanese took advantage of China's weakness to proclaim Manchuria's independence, renaming it the "Republic of Manchukuo."

While Japan was expanding its control in Asia, Benito Mussolini was on the march. In 1935, he launched a reconquest of Ethiopia, a nation in eastern Africa that Italy had controlled until 1896. When the League of Nations retaliated by imposing economic sanctions on Italy, Mussolini expressed surprise that European leaders would prefer a "horde of barbarian Negroes" in Ethiopia over Italy, the "mother of civilization."

In 1935, Hitler, in flagrant violation of the Versailles Treaty, began rebuilding Germany's armed forces. He reinstated compulsory military service and started building an air force. The next year, Hitler again defied the terms of the treaty when he sent 3,000 soldiers into the Rhineland, the demilitarized buffer zone between France and Germany created after the Great War. In a staged vote, 99 percent of the Germans living in the Rhineland approved Hitler's action. The failure of France and Great Britain to counter these moves convinced Hitler that the western democracies were cowards and would not try to stop him.

The year 1936 also witnessed the outbreak of the Spanish Civil War, which began when Spanish troops (the Nationalists) loyal to General Francisco Franco, with the support of the Roman Catholic Church, revolted against Spain's fragile new democratic government (the Republicans, or Loyalists). Hitler and Mussolini rushed troops (called "volunteers" to disguise their purpose), warplanes, and military and financial aid to support Franco's fascist insurgency. Some 2,800 American volunteers joined the Abraham Lincoln Battalion in defense of Spain's Republican government, supported by weapons from the Soviet Union. Eventually, the conflict would cost 600,000 lives and result in another totalitarian regime in Europe, this one led by Franco.

While peace in Europe was unraveling, the Japanese government fell under the control of aggressive militarists. On July 7, 1937, Japanese and Chinese soldiers clashed at China's Marco Polo Bridge, near Beijing. The incident quickly escalated into the Second Sino-Japanese War, with Japanese troops spreading across northern China before moving south.

By December, the Japanese had captured the Nationalist Chinese capital of Nanjing. For the next six weeks, they looted the city; executed prisoners of war; and raped, tortured, and murdered as many as 300,000 civilians—men, women, and children—in what came to be called the Rape of Nanjing, one of the worst atrocities of the twentieth century. Thereafter, the Sino-Japanese War bogged down into a stalemate.

From Isolationism to Intervention

Most Americans responded to the mounting world crises by deepening their commitment to isolationism. In his 1933 inaugural address, President Franklin Roosevelt announced that he would continue to promote what Woodrow Wilson had earlier called "the good neighbor policy" in the Western Hemisphere, declaring that no nation "has the right to intervene in the internal or external affairs of another. The nation's isolationist mood was reinforced by a Senate inquiry into the role of bankers and businesses in the American government's decision to enter the Great War in 1917. Chaired by Senator Gerald P. Nye of North Dakota, the "Nye Committee" concluded that weapons makers and bankers (the "merchants of death") had spurred U.S. intervention and were continuing to "help frighten nations into military activity."

U.S. NEUTRALITY In 1935, *Christian Century* magazine declared that "ninety-nine Americans out of a hundred would today regard as an imbecile anyone who might suggest that, in the event of another European war, the United States should again participate in it." Such strongly felt isolationism led President Roosevelt to sign the first of several "**neutrality laws**" to help avoid involvement in another war.

The Neutrality Act of 1935 prohibited American manufacturers from selling weapons to nations at war ("belligerents") and banned citizens from traveling on ships owned by belligerents. In 1936, Congress revised the Neutrality Act by banning loans to warring nations.

Roosevelt, however, was not convinced that the United States could or should remain neutral in a world of growing conflict. In October 1937, he delivered a speech in Chicago, the heartland of isolationism, in which he called for international cooperation to "quarantine the aggressors" responsible for disturbing world peace, especially the Japanese who had assaulted China. But his appeal for a more active American role in world affairs fell flat in Congress and across the nation.

American Neutrality A 1938 cartoon shows U.S. foreign policy entangled by the serpent of isolationism.

The Neutrality Act of 1937, however, allowed the president to sell nonmilitary goods to warring nations on a "cash-and-carry" basis—that is, a nation would have to pay cash and then transport the U.S.-made goods in its own ships. This would preserve America's profitable trade with warring nations without running the risk of being drawn into the fighting.

THE AXIS ALLIANCE In 1937, Japan joined Germany and Italy in establishing the Rome-Berlin-Tokyo **"Axis" alliance** because they claimed that all other nations would be forced to revolve around the "axis" created by those three dominant nations. Hitler and Mussolini vowed to create a "new order in Europe," while Japanese imperialists pursued their "divine right" to control East Asia by creating what they called the Greater East Asia Co-Prosperity Sphere. Hitler was not concerned that the United States would try to impede his aggressions. "Because of its neutrality laws," he said, "America is not dangerous to us."

HITLER TAKES AUSTRIA Adolph Hitler's madness broke over Europe in dark waves. In March 1938, he forced the *Anschluss* (union) of Austria with Germany. His triumphant return to his native country delighted crowds in Vienna waving Nazi flags and tossing flowers. Soon, "Jews Not Wanted" signs appeared in Austrian cities. Socialists and Jews were beaten and humiliated and forced to clean street gutters and public toilets. When British and French diplomats protested Hitler's takeover of Austria, he shouted that it was none of their business. When Mussolini congratulated Hitler for his daring move, the German dictator told his Italian partner that he would "never forget him for this. Never, never, never—whatever happens."

A month later, after arresting more than 70,000 anti-Nazis, German leaders announced that 99.75 percent of Austrian voters had "approved" the forced union with Germany. (In fact, it was a sham election, since some 400,000 Austrians, mostly liberals and Jews, were prevented from voting.) Soon the Nazi government in Austria began arresting or murdering opponents and imprisoning or exiling Jews, including the famed psychiatrist Sigmund Freud. Again, no nation stepped up to oppose Hitler, in part because it was so hard to assess the German leader's motives, predict his moves, and understand his ambition—or his lunacy.

THE MUNICH PACT (1938)   Hitler turned next to the Sudeten territory (Sudetenland), a mountainous region in western Czechoslovakia along the German border where more than 3 million ethnic Germans lived. It was also where the Czechs had positioned their defensive positions in the event of a war with Germany. Hitler threatened to ignite a European war unless the Czechs gave the Sudetenland to Germany. In response, timid British and French leaders tried to "appease" Hitler, hoping that if they agreed to his demands for the Sudeten territory, he would stop his aggressions.

On September 30, 1938, the British prime minister, Neville Chamberlain, and the French prime minister, Édouard Daladier, joined Mussolini and Hitler in signing the notorious Munich Pact, which transferred the Sudetenland to Germany. Even though Chamberlain had earlier described Hitler as "the bully of Europe" and a "lunatic," he mistakenly decided to trust the German tyrant. Chamberlain and Daladier were so determined to avoid another world war that they were willing to give Hitler whatever he wanted, in large part because they had little military leverage; they had allowed their armed forces to deteriorate after the Great War.

In Prague, the capital, Czechs listened to the official announcement of the Munich Pact with the excruciating sadness of people too weak to preserve their own independence, which they had gained from Austria-Hungary in 1918 as a result of the Great War. As pawns in the chess game of European politics, the Czechs now faced a grim future. President Roosevelt privately grumbled that Britain and France had left Czechoslovakia "to paddle its own canoe" and predicted that they would "wash the blood from their Judas Iscariot hands."

The naive Chamberlain claimed that the Munich treaty had provided "peace for our time. Peace with honor." Winston Churchill, a member of the British Parliament who would become prime minister in May 1940, strongly disagreed. In a speech to the House of Commons, he claimed that "England has been offered a choice between war and shame. She has chosen shame, and will get war. . . . This is only the beginning of the reckoning."

Churchill was right. Hitler never intended to honor the Munich Pact. Although the Nazi tyrant had promised that the Sudetenland would be his last territorial demand, he scrapped his pledge in March 1939 and sent German tanks and soldiers to conquer the remainder of the multinational and multi-ethnic Czech Republic. The European democracies continued to cower in the face of his seemingly unstoppable military advances.

After German troops seized Czechoslovakia on March 15, 1939, Hitler called it "the greatest day of my life." He immediately set about oppressing the 263,000 Jews living in Czechoslovakia, lumping them together with "thieves, criminals, swindlers, insane people, and alcoholics." By the end of May, the Nazis were filling prisons with Czechs who resisted or resented the German occupation. Hitler's conquest of Czechoslovakia convinced Roosevelt that fascism and Nazism must be stopped. Hitler and Mussolini were "madmen" who "respect force and force alone." Throughout late 1938 and 1939, Roosevelt tried to convince Americans, as well as British and French leaders, that the growing menace of fascism must be stopped. He also persuaded Congress to increase military spending in anticipation of a possible war.

THE CONQUEST OF POLAND   In mid-1939, Hitler, having decided that he had "the world in my pocket," turned to Poland, Germany's eastern neighbor. Conquering Poland would give the German army a clear path to invade the Soviet Union, especially the fertile Ukraine region, where much of the world's grains were grown.

To ensure that the Soviets did not interfere, Hitler camouflaged his intentions. On August 23, 1939, he shocked the world by signing the Nazi-Soviet Nonaggression Pact with Josef Stalin, the brutish, anti-fascist Soviet premier. Stalin had become the Soviet leader after Vladimir Lenin's death in 1924. Soon after, he had launched a Great Purge, in which some 8 million "critics" of his iron-fisted rule were executed and millions more exiled to forced-labor camps. Two thirds of the Communist party leadership and some 35,000 army officers were victims of Stalin's reign of terror.

When Hitler learned that Stalin had agreed to the deal, he was ecstatic: "This will strike like a bomb. Now Europe is mine. The others can have

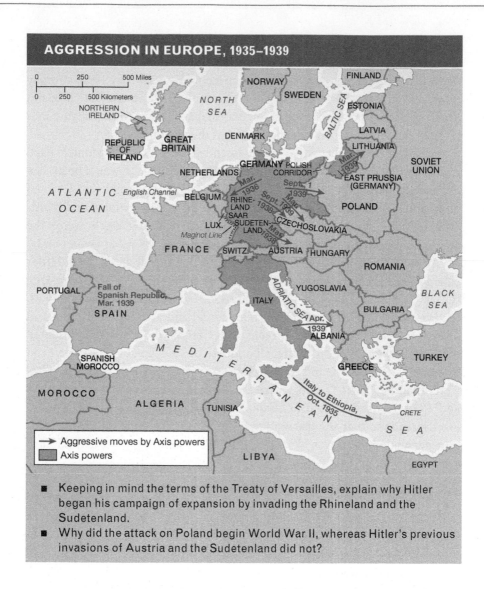

AGGRESSION IN EUROPE, 1935–1939

Aggressive moves by Axis powers

Axis powers

- Keeping in mind the terms of the Treaty of Versailles, explain why Hitler began his campaign of expansion by invading the Rhineland and the Sudetenland.
- Why did the attack on Poland begin World War II, whereas Hitler's previous invasions of Austria and the Sudetenland did not?

Asia." The announcement of the Nazi-Soviet treaty surprised a world that had assumed fascists and Communists were mortal enemies. Yet Stalin and Hitler had secretly agreed to divide northern and eastern Europe between them. The Germans took most of Poland, and the Soviet Union claimed a "sphere of interest" in Estonia, Latvia, Finland, and a portion of Lithuania.

Just nine days later, at dawn on September 1, 1939, an estimated 1.5 million German troops invaded Poland from the north, south, and west. Hitler ordered them "to kill without mercy men, women, and children of the

Polish race or language." He also directed that all terminally ill German patients in hospitals be killed to make room for Nazi soldiers wounded in Poland.

The invasion of Poland was the final straw for the western democracies. A second world war had begun. Two days later, on September 3, Great Britain and France declared war against Germany. The nations making up the British Empire and Commonwealth—the United Kingdom, Canada, India, Australia, New Zealand—joined the war as Americans watched in horror. "This nation," declared Franklin Roosevelt, "will remain a neutral nation, but I cannot ask that every American remain neutral in thought as well. Even a neutral cannot be asked to close his mind or conscience."

Sixteen days after German troops stormed across the Polish border, the Soviet Union invaded Poland from the east. Pressed from all sides, 700,000 poorly equipped Polish soldiers surrendered after a few weeks. On October 6, 1939, the Nazis and Soviets divided Poland between them.

Hitler's goal was to obliterate Polish civilization, especially the large Jewish population, and to Germanize the country. For his part, Stalin wanted to recapture Polish territory lost during the Great War. Over the next five years, millions of Poles were arrested, deported, enslaved, and murdered. In April and May 1940, the Russians executed some 22,000 Polish military officers, government officials, and intellectuals to ensure that its conquered neighbor would never mount a rebellion.

In late November 1939, the Soviets invaded neighboring Finland, leading President Roosevelt to condemn their "wanton disregard for law." Outnumbered five to one, Finnish troops held off the invaders for three months before being forced to negotiate a treaty that gave the Soviet Union a tenth of Finland.

REVISING THE NEUTRALITY ACT With war erupting in Europe, President Roosevelt decided that the United States must do more to stop "aggressor" nations. He summoned Congress into special session to revise the Neutrality Act so that the United States could aid Great Britain and France. "I regret that Congress passed the Act," the president said. "I regret equally that I signed the Act."

After six weeks of hot-blooded debate, Congress approved the president's proposed revisions. The Neutrality Act of 1939 lifted the arms embargo and put all trade with warring nations under the terms of "cash-and-carry." The ban on loans remained in effect, and U.S. ships were barred from transporting goods to ports of nations at war. It was, said Roosevelt, the best way "to keep us out of war." Public opinion supported such measures as long as other nations did the fighting.

"PHONY WAR" IN EUROPE The war in Europe settled into a three-month stalemate during early 1940, as Hitler's generals waited out the winter. American newspapers called it a "phony war" since no fighting occurred. Then, at dawn on April 9, Germany attacked again, invading Denmark and landing troops along the Norwegian coast. German paratroopers, the first used in warfare, seized Norway's airports. Denmark fell in a day, Norway within a few weeks. On May 10, German forces invaded the Low Countries—Belgium, Luxembourg, and the Netherlands (Holland). Luxembourg fell the first day, the Netherlands three days later. Belgium held out until May 28.

A few days later, German tanks roared into northern France. "The fight beginning today," Hitler declared, "decides the fate of the German nation for the next thousand years!" His **blitzkrieg** ("lightning war") strategy centered on speed. Columns of tanks, motorized artillery, and truck-borne infantry, all supported by warplanes and paratroopers, moved so fast they stunned their opponents. Winston Churchill called the Allied performance "a colossal military disaster."

Winston Churchill The prime minister of Great Britain, Churchill led the nation during the Second World War.

A British force sent to help the Belgians and French fled along with French troops toward the coast, with the Germans in hot pursuit. On May 26, Churchill organized a desperate week-long evacuation of British, Belgian, Canadian, and French soldiers from the beaches at Dunkirk. Despite attacks by German warplanes, some 338,000 soldiers escaped in 700 warships and an array of privately owned vessels volunteered for the emergency: fishing trawlers, barges, yachts, and other pleasure craft. The fleeing troops left behind vast stockpiles of vehicles, weaponry, and ammunition. "Wars are not won by evacuations," observed Churchill, "but there was a victory inside this deliverance."

While the Dunkirk evacuation was unfolding, German forces decimated the remaining French armies. Tens of thousands of panic-stricken French civilians and soldiers clogged the roads to Paris. Mussolini also declared war on France and Great Britain, which he dismissed as "the reactionary democracies of the West."

On June 14, 1940, German soldiers marched unopposed through the streets of Paris, a city now of lost hopes, of gloom, and grave despair. Eight days later, French leaders officially surrendered, whereupon the Germans established a puppet fascist government for southern France in the city of Vichy.

The rapid fall of France astonished the world. In the United States, complacency about the Nazis turned to fear and even panic as people realized that the Germans, who now ruled most of western Europe, could eventually assault America. Great Britain stood alone against Hitler's relentless military power. "The war is won," an ecstatic Hitler bragged to Mussolini. "The rest is only a matter of time." The German leader turned his attention to the conquest of Great Britain. "The Battle of France is over," Churchill told the House of Commons. "I expect the Battle of Britain is about to begin."

PREPARING AMERICA FOR WAR As Germany celebrated triumph after triumph, the United States was in no condition to wage war. After the First World War (there now being a Second World War), the U.S. Army was reduced to a small force; by 1939, it numbered only 175,000. By contrast, Germany had almost 5 million soldiers. In May 1940, President Roosevelt called for increasing the size of the army and adding a phenomenal 50,000 warplanes.

Roosevelt also responded to Winston Churchill's repeated requests for assistance by increasing military shipments to Great Britain and promising to provide all possible "aid to the Allies short of war." Churchill, whose mother was an American, focused on one strategic objective: to convince, coax, bluff, seduce, or frighten the United States into entering the war.

THE MANHATTAN PROJECT Adding to President Roosevelt's concerns was the possibility that Germany might have a secret weapon. The famous physicist Albert Einstein, who had renounced his German citizenship in 1933 before emigrating to America, joined other European physicists in alerting Roosevelt that the Germans were trying to create atomic bombs. In June 1940, Roosevelt established the National Defense Research Committee to coordinate a top-secret effort—the Manhattan Project—to develop an atomic bomb before the Germans did. Almost 200,000 people worked on the Manhattan Project, including Dr. J. Robert Oppenheimer, who led the team of scientists scattered among thirty-seven secret facilities in thirteen states.

THE BATTLE OF BRITAIN   Having conquered western Europe, Hitler began preparing to invade Great Britain (Operation Sea Lion). In May 1940, he launched the Battle of Britain, as the Germans first sought to destroy the Royal Air Force (RAF). Over the next twelve months, the Nazis deployed some 2,500 warplanes, outnumbering the RAF two to one. "Never has a nation been so naked before its foes," Winston Churchill admitted.

Churchill and his stirring radio speeches became the symbol of British tenacity and resilience. With his bulldog face, ever-present cigar, and "V for Victory" gesture, he urged Britons to make the defense of their homeland "their finest hour." He breathed defiance as the British built fortifications, laid mines, dug trenches, and mobilized to stop a German invasion. The British, Churchill pledged, would greet Hitler's invaders with "blood, toil, tears, and sweat." They would "never surrender."

In July and August 1940, the German air force (the *Luftwaffe*) launched raids against military targets across southeast England. RAF pilots employed radar, a secret new technology, to fend off the assault, ultimately destroying 1,700 German warplanes.

A frustrated Hitler then ordered his bombers to target civilians and cities (especially London) in relentless night raids designed to terrorize civilians and force a surrender. In what came to be called "the Blitz" during September and October 1940, German bombers destroyed a million homes and killed

The London "Blitz"   An aerial photograph of the aftermath in London after the heavy German bombing raids in 1940. Winston Churchill responded, "We shall never surrender."

40,000 civilians. No place was safe; churches and cathedrals, museums, libraries, and hospitals were all targeted. So many people were killed that there was no more wood for coffins; the dead were buried in cardboard. "The last three nights in London," reported the U.S. ambassador to Great Britain on September 10, "have been simply hell."

The Blitz, however, enraged rather than demoralized the British, who mustered extraordinary resolve in the face of massive attacks. A London newspaper headline summarized the nation's courage and mood: "Is That the Best You Can Do, Adolf?" Over the next nine months, the British success in the air proved decisive. In May 1941, Hitler scrapped his invasion plans and turned his attention to the Soviet Union. It was the first battle he had lost, and it was Britain's finest hour. By blunting Hitler's momentum, the British convinced many Americans to support increased aid to their ally.

"ALL AID SHORT OF WAR"   During the Battle of Britain, Franklin Roosevelt received a telegram from Winston Churchill that described Britain as being "in mortal danger" of collapse. German submarines (U-boats) were sinking too many freighters and tankers bringing crucial arms and supplies from the United States. In response, Roosevelt began an urgent campaign to convince Americans that isolationism was impractical and even dangerous. "Never before," he told the nation, "has our American civilization been in such danger as now." Hitler and the Nazis were determined "to enslave all of Europe." To stop them, he planned to give Great Britain "all aid short of war," for the best chance to keep the United States out of the war was to ensure that the British were not defeated.

A SAVAGE DEBATE   The world crisis transformed Franklin Roosevelt. Having been stalemated for much of his second term by congressional opposition to the New Deal, he was revitalized by the need to stop Nazism. Yet his efforts outraged isolationists. A prominent Democrat later remembered that the dispute between isolationists and so-called interventionists was "the most savage political debate during my lifetime." FDR predicted it would be "a dirty fight," and it was. Convinced that isolationists were a major threat to the nation, the president authorized secret FBI investigations of his opponents.

Isolationists, mostly midwestern and western Republicans, formed the America First Committee in 1940 to oppose "military preparedness." Within a year, the organization had 800,000 members. Charles Lindbergh, the first man to fly solo across the Atlantic Ocean, led the effort. Openly racist and anti-Semitic and an admirer of Hitler and Nazism as the best barrier against Soviet communism, Lindbergh charged that Roosevelt's efforts to help Britain were driven by powerful Jews who owned "our motion pictures, our press, our radio, and our government." Were it not for the Jews in America, Lindbergh claimed, "we would not be on the verge of war today." He assured Americans that Britain was doomed and that they should join hands with Hitler: "Democracy as we know it is a thing of the past," and "one of the first steps must be to disenfranchise the Negro."

ROOSEVELT'S THIRD TERM   Charles Lindbergh and other isolationists sought to make the 1940 presidential campaign a debate about the European war. The Republicans nominated Wendell L. Willkie of Indiana, a plainspoken corporate lawyer and former Democrat who had voted for FDR in 1932.

Now, however, Willkie called Roosevelt a "warmonger" and predicted that "if you re-elect him, you may expect war in April, 1941." Roosevelt responded that he had "said this before, but I shall say it again and again and again: Your boys are not going to be sent into any foreign wars." When Willkie heard that statement, he gasped, "That hypocritical son-of-a-bitch! This is going to beat me."

Roosevelt was especially concerned about a German invasion of the British Isles. "It is now most urgent," Prime Minister Churchill cabled Roosevelt, "that you let us have the destroyers" needed to stop such an invasion. The backlash among isolationists opposed to the military draft was so intense that Roosevelt predicted he would lose his reelection effort in November.

In the end, however, Roosevelt won an unprecedented third term by 27 million votes to Willkie's 22 million and by an even more decisive margin, 449 to 82, in the Electoral College. Winston Churchill wrote Roosevelt that he had "prayed for your success and I am truly thankful for it."

THE LEND-LEASE ACT (1941)   Once reelected, Roosevelt found an ingenious way to provide more aid to Britain, whose cash was running out. The **Lend-Lease Act** (officially "An Act to Promote the Defense of the United States"), introduced in Congress on January 10, 1941, allowed the president to lend or lease military equipment to "any country whose defense the President deems vital to the defense of the United States." It was a bold challenge to the isolationists. As Senator Hiram Johnson of California claimed, "This bill is war."

Roosevelt told critics that "no nation can appease the Nazis. No man can turn a tiger into a kitten by stroking it." The United States, he added, would provide everything the British needed while doing the same for China in its war against Japan, all in an effort to keep Americans from going to war themselves. "We must be the great arsenal of democracy," Roosevelt explained. Churchill

Lend-Lease Act Members of the isolationist "Mother's Crusade," urging defeat of the lend-lease program, kneel in prayer in front of the Capitol in Washington, D.C. They feared the program aiding America's allies would bring the United States into the wars in Europe and Asia.

shored up the president's efforts by announcing that Britain did not need American troops to defeat Hitler: "Give us the tools and we will finish the job."

In early March 1941, Congress approved the Lend-Lease Act, a decision hailed by the *New York Times* as marking "the day when the United States ended the great retreat [from world leadership] which began with the Senate rejection of the Treaty of Versailles and the League of Nations." Isolationism, the editors added, had failed. "Let not the dictators of Europe or Asia doubt our unanimity now," Roosevelt declared.

Between 1941 and 1945, the lend-lease program would ship $50 billion worth of supplies to Great Britain, the Soviet Union, France, China, and other Allied nations. Churchill called it the most generous "act in the history of any nation."

GERMANY INVADES THE SOVIET UNION While Americans continued to debate President Roosevelt's efforts to help Great Britain, the

European war expanded in unexpected ways. In the spring of 1941, German troops joined Italian armies in Libya, forcing the British army in North Africa to withdraw to Egypt. In April 1941, Nazi armies overwhelmed Yugoslavia and Greece. With Hungary, Romania, and Bulgaria also under Nazi control, Hitler ruled most of Europe. His ambition was unbounded, however, and he remained dangerously unpredictable.

On June 22, 1941, Hitler massed 3.6 million soldiers—mostly Germans but also Italians, Finns, Hungarians, and Romanians—to launch Operation Barbarossa, a reckless invasion of the Soviet Union, his supposed ally. It was the largest military assault in history, and it took Josef Stalin by surprise. The Soviet army would suffer millions of casualties (killed or wounded) in the next six months.

The objectives of Germany's invasion of the Soviet Union were to destroy communism (his long-standing obsession), enslave the vast population of the Soviet Union, and acquire new lands and their natural resources for Germans to manage. Behind the advancing German troops were "police" units whose mission was to kill all Russian Jews. In most of the massacres, Jews—men, women, and children—were marched to an isolated execution site, ordered to undress, and then killed.

The Nazi invasion of the Soviet Union was the defining moment of the European war, for it proved disastrous for Hitler. He had gambled on a quick victory, but a series of military blunders and his own blindness to battlefield realities undermined the Nazi effort. At first, however, the invasion seemed a great success, as entire Soviet armies and cities were destroyed. During the second half of 1941, an estimated 3 million Soviet soldiers—50 percent of the Soviet army—were captured. For four months, the Soviets retreated in the face of the German blitzkrieg while suffering appalling losses.

During the summer of 1941, German forces surrounded Leningrad (now called St. Petersburg) and laid siege to the city. Food and supplies became scarce; hunger alone would kill 800,000 Russians. Desperate people ate cats, dogs, rats, and even sawdust. As a bitterly cold winter set in, corpses were left to freeze in the snow. Still, Leningrad held out and became known as the city that refused to die. By December 1941, other German armies had reached the suburbs of Moscow, 1,000 miles east of Berlin.

To American isolationists, Germany's invasion of Russia confirmed that the United States should stay out of the war and let the two dictatorships bleed each other to death. Roosevelt, however, insisted on including the Soviet Union in the lend-lease agreement. He and Churchill were determined to keep the Russians fighting Hitler so that the Nazis could not concentrate their forces on Great Britain.

The fear that Germany might win the war led Churchill and Roosevelt to declare their support for the Soviet Union as "true allies in the name of the peoples of Europe and America." This was the beginning of what came to be called the Grand Alliance. A steady stream of agreements and periodic meetings between leaders of the three countries formalized the alliance. In 1941 alone, America sent thousands of trucks, tanks, guns, and warplanes to the Soviet Union, along with food (especially Spam) and enough blankets, shoes, and boots to clothe every Soviet soldier.

Gradually, Josef Stalin slowed the Nazi advance by forcing the Russian people to fight—or be killed. During the Battle of Moscow, Soviet defenders executed 8,000 civilians charged with "cowardice." Stalin ordered that Soviet soldiers who surrendered be classified as traitors and their families killed. In 1941, when the Germans captured Stalin's eldest son, Yakov, Stalin had his son's wife arrested, separated from her three-year-old daughter, and imprisoned for two years as punishment for her husband's "cowardice" in surrendering. "There are no prisoners of war," Stalin explained, "only traitors to their homeland." While still a prisoner of war, Yakov committed suicide in 1943 by throwing himself onto an electric fence.

By the winter of 1941–1942, Hitler's generals were learning the same bitter lesson that the Russians had taught Napoléon and the French in 1812: invading armies must contend not only with Russia's ferocious fighters and enormous population but also vast distances, deep snow, and subzero temperatures. Russia soon became the graveyard of the Nazi's best soldiers. Hitler had catastrophically underrated Soviet powers of resistance and overrated the German economy's ability to sustain a protracted campaign in Russia.

THE ATLANTIC CHARTER (1941) By late summer 1941, the United States was no longer behaving like a neutral nation as the scope of the war in Europe widened. In August, Roosevelt and Churchill met on a warship off the Canadian coast and drew up a joint statement of "common principles" known as the **Atlantic Charter**. The agreement pledged that after the "final destruction of the Nazi tyranny," the victors would promote the self-determination of all peoples, economic cooperation, freedom of the seas, and a new multination system of international security to be called the United Nations. Within weeks, eleven anti-Axis nations, including the Soviet Union, had endorsed the Atlantic Charter.

BATTLE OF THE ATLANTIC The Lend-Lease Act sending supplies to Great Britain and the Soviet Union was hampered by German submarines prowling like "wolfpacks" in the North Atlantic. Hundreds of U-boats were

WORLD WAR II MILITARY ALLIANCES, 1942

- Axis
- Axis-controlled
- Allies
- Neutral

- What was the Atlantic Charter?
- Compare and contrast the alliances in the First World War with those in the Second World War.
- How were the Germans able to seize most of Europe so quickly?

sinking British ships laden with American weapons and supplies faster than they could be replaced.

The Germans were willing to fire the first shot. On September 4, 1941, the U.S. warship *Greer* was tracking a German U-boat off the coast of Iceland when it was attacked, but not hit. In response, Roosevelt began an undeclared war in the Atlantic by ordering warships to protect shipping convoys all the way to Iceland and "shoot on sight" any German submarines. Six weeks later, on October 17, 1941, a U-boat sank the U.S. warship *Kearny*. Eleven sailors died. Two weeks later, the *Reuben James* was torpedoed and sunk while escorting a convoy near Iceland, with a loss of 115 seamen.

Step by step, the United States was engaging in naval warfare against Nazi Germany. Still, Americans hoped to avoid all-out war and remain technically neutral.

The Storm in the Pacific

If the war in Europe and the Atlantic was not enough to challenge President Roosevelt's statesmanship, Japan and the United States were moving closer to war in the Pacific. Roosevelt pursued two strategies to slow Japanese efforts to control East Asia. First, he sent military supplies to China. Second, he tried to slow Japanese aggression by cutting off strategic resources that the United States had been supplying, especially oil and aviation gasoline. As an island nation, Japan depended on imports for most of its essential raw materials. Some 85 percent of its oil came from the United States.

Hitler's efforts to conquer Great Britain and the Soviet Union stalled by late 1941, but U.S. relations with Japan were worsening. In 1940, Japan and the United States began a series of moves that pushed them closer to war. Japan built airfields in northern Indochina and shut down rail service into south China. The United States responded with the Export Control Act of July 2, 1940, which authorized President Roosevelt to restrict the export of military supplies and other strategic materials crucial to Japan.

THE TRIPARTITE PACT (1940) On September 27, 1940, the imperial Japanese government signed a Tripartite Pact with Nazi Germany and fascist Italy, by which each pledged to declare war on any nation that attacked any of them. Roosevelt called the pact an "unholy alliance" designed to force the United States to remain neutral by threatening it with the prospect of fighting a two-ocean war. He responded by cutting off all steel shipments to Japan. Several weeks later, the United States expanded its trade embargo to include iron ore, copper, and brass, deliberately leaving oil as the remaining bargaining chip in the ongoing tension between the two nations, for it was the commodity Japan most needed to sustain its war against China.

In July 1941, Japan sent 40,000 troops to take control of French Indochina and thereby gain access to the raw materials denied it by the United States. Roosevelt responded by restricting oil exports to Japan. *Time* magazine claimed that Roosevelt was "waging the first great undeclared war in U.S. history."

THE ATTACK ON PEARL HARBOR (1941) On October 16, 1941, Hideki Tōjō became the Japanese prime minister. He ordered a fleet of Japanese warships to prepare for a surprise attack on Hawaii's Pearl Harbor, the most important U.S. military base in the Pacific. The Japanese naval commander, Admiral Isoroku Yamamoto, knew that his country could not defeat the United States in a long war. Its only hope was "to decide the fate of the war on the very first day" by launching a "fatal attack."

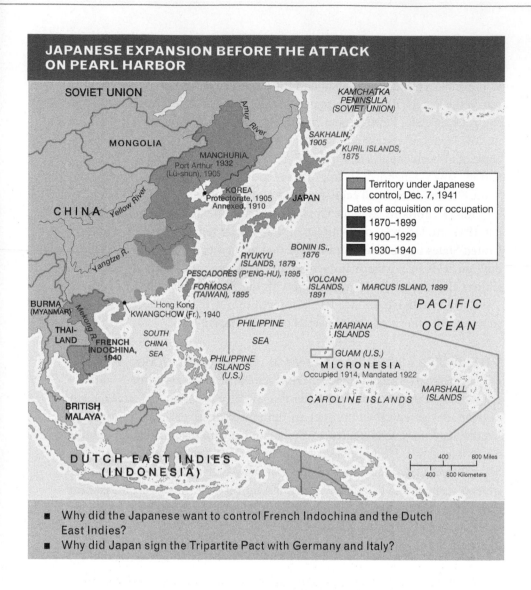

JAPANESE EXPANSION BEFORE THE ATTACK ON PEARL HARBOR

SOVIET UNION

KAMCHATKA PENINSULA (SOVIET UNION)

Amur River

MONGOLIA

MANCHURIA, 1932
Port Arthur (Lü-shun), 1905

SAKHALIN, 1905

KURIL ISLANDS, 1875

KOREA
Protectorate, 1905
Annexed, 1910

JAPAN

CHINA   Yellow River

Yangtze R.

RYUKYU ISLANDS, 1879

BONIN IS., 1876

PESCADORES (P'ENG-HU), 1895

FORMOSA (TAIWAN), 1895

VOLCANO ISLANDS, 1891

MARCUS ISLAND, 1899

BURMA (MYANMAR)

Mekong R.

Hong Kong
KWANGCHOW (Fr.), 1940

PACIFIC OCEAN

THAI-LAND   FRENCH INDOCHINA, 1940

SOUTH CHINA SEA

PHILIPPINE SEA

MARIANA ISLANDS

GUAM (U.S.)

PHILIPPINE ISLANDS (U.S.)

MICRONESIA
Occupied 1914, Mandated 1922

BRITISH MALAYA

CAROLINE ISLANDS

MARSHALL ISLANDS

DUTCH EAST INDIES (INDONESIA)

	Territory under Japanese control, Dec. 7, 1941

Dates of acquisition or occupation

	1870–1899
	1900–1929
	1930–1940

0   400   800 Miles
0   400   800 Kilometers

- Why did the Japanese want to control French Indochina and the Dutch East Indies?
- Why did Japan sign the Tripartite Pact with Germany and Italy?

On November 5, 1941, Japanese diplomats asked the Roosevelt administration to end its embargo or "face conflict." At a White House meeting on November 25, Secretary of War Henry Stimson said the focus of discussion was "how we could maneuver them into the position of firing the first shot without showing too much danger to ourselves."

The next day, Secretary of State Cordell Hull told Japan that it must remove its troops from China before the United States would lift its embargo. The Japanese government then secretly ordered a fleet of warships to begin steaming toward Hawaii. By this time, political and military leaders on both sides

Explosion of the USS *Shaw* The destroyer exploded after being hit by Japanese warplanes at Pearl Harbor. It was repaired shortly thereafter and went on to earn eleven battle stars in the Pacific campaign.

considered war inevitable. Yet Hull continued to meet with Japanese diplomats in Washington, privately dismissing them as being as "crooked as a barrel of fish hooks."

Roosevelt and others expected the Japanese to strike Singapore or the Philippines. The U.S. Navy Department sent an urgent message to its commanders in the Pacific: "Negotiations with Japan . . . have ceased, and an aggressive move by Japan is expected within the next few days."

Yet none of the U.S. commanders expected an assault on Hawaii. Early Sunday morning, December 7, 1941, Japanese planes began bombing the unsuspecting U.S. fleet at **Pearl Harbor**. All eight battleships moored there were sunk or disabled, along with eleven other ships. Some 180 U.S. warplanes were destroyed, most of them on the ground. The raid, which lasted less than two hours, killed more than 2,400 civilians and servicemen (mostly sailors), and wounded nearly 1,200 more. At the same time, the Japanese assaulted U.S. military facilities in the Philippines and on Guam and Wake Island in the Pacific, as well as attacking British bases in Singapore, Hong Kong, and Malaya.

The shocking attack on Pearl Harbor fell short in two important ways, however. First, the Japanese bombers ignored the maintenance facilities and oil storage tanks that supported the U.S. fleet, without which the surviving ships might have been forced back to the West Coast. Second, the Japanese missed the U.S. aircraft carriers that had left port a few days earlier. In the naval war to come, aircraft carriers, not battleships, would prove to be decisive.

In a larger sense, the attack on Pearl Harbor was a spectacular miscalculation, for it destroyed the American isolationist movement. As the Japanese admiral who planned the attack said, "I fear that we have only succeeded in awakening a sleeping tiger." After learning of the Japanese attack, Winston Churchill, who desperately wanted the United States to enter the war, later wrote that he "slept the sleep of the saved and thankful," for America's entry into the war would ensure victory: "Hitler's fate was sealed! Mussolini's fate was sealed! As for the Japanese, they would be ground to powder."

At half past noon on December 8, President Roosevelt delivered his war message to Congress: "Yesterday, December 7, 1941—a date which will live in infamy—the United States of America was suddenly and deliberately attacked by naval and air forces of the Empire of Japan." He asked Congress to declare a "state of war." The Senate approved the resolution twenty-five minutes after Roosevelt finished speaking; the House followed immediately thereafter.

Three days later, on December 11, Germany and Italy declared war on what Hitler called the "half Judaized and the other half Negrified" United States. After learning of the attack on Pearl Harbor, Hitler shouted that "it is impossible for us to lose the war." The separate wars in Asia, Europe, and Africa had now become one global conflict. A few weeks later, in his State of the Union address, Roosevelt vowed: "The militarists of Berlin and Tokyo started this war, but the massed, angered forces of common humanity will *finish* it."

MOBILIZATION AT HOME

With the declaration of war, millions of men and women chose not to wait to be drafted but instead began enlisting in the armed services. The average male soldier or sailor was twenty-six years old, stood five feet eight, and weighed 144 pounds, an inch taller and eight pounds heavier than the typical recruit in the First World War. Only one in ten had attended college, and only one in four had graduated from high school.

Among those who enlisted after the attack on Pearl Harbor were all nine sons of Hiram and Elizabeth Bond, from Fond du Lac, Wisconsin. The Bond brothers survived the war, but not without some close calls. One spent the rest of his life with a limp because of a German bullet in his hip. Another was shot in the thigh and hip before being captured by German soldiers in France. Still another, Russell Bond, served as a radio operator in the Army Air Corps (there was no separate air force during the Second World War). Flying in a bomber from England to Germany and back, he wrote, "was no picnic." After one mission, his B-24 Liberator returned with 1,800 holes from German anti-aircraft guns and fighter planes. None of the Bond brothers thought of themselves as heroes. Every young man, it seemed, recalled wife Marilyn Bond, "went into the service. It was just to keep our country safe, so that's what they did."

ARSENAL OF DEMOCRACY

After the attack on Pearl Harbor, President Roosevelt told Congress that the nation's "powerful enemies must be outfought and outproduced." In 1940, Adolf Hitler had scoffed at the idea that the United States could produce 50,000 warplanes a year, claiming that America was nothing but "beauty queens, millionaires, and Hollywood." By the end of 1942, however, U.S. war production had doubled the *combined* output of Germany, Japan, and Italy, an incredible achievement enabled by government planning, business enterprise, and the cooperation of labor unions.

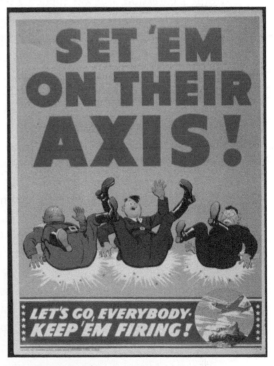

The **War Production Board**, created by Roosevelt in 1942, directed the conversion of industries to war production. In 1941, more than 3 million automobiles were manufactured; only 139 were built during the next four years, as automobile plants were reorganized to produce huge numbers of tanks, jeeps, trucks, and warplanes. "Something is happening that Hitler doesn't understand," announced *Time* magazine in 1942. "It is the Miracle of production."

War Production Board This 1942 poster features caricatures of Mussolini, Hitler, and Tōjō who—according to the poster—will fall on their "axis" if American civilians continued their relentless production of military equipment.

FINANCING THE WAR To cover the war's huge cost (more than $3 trillion in today's values), Congress passed the Revenue Act of 1942 (Victory Tax), which required most workers to begin paying taxes. In 1939, only about 4 million people (about 5 percent of the workforce) earned enough to file tax returns; by the end of the war, 90 percent of workers were paying income tax. Tax revenues covered about 45 percent of military costs from 1939 to 1946; the government borrowed the rest, mostly by selling $185 billion worth of government war bonds, which paid interest to purchasers. By the end of the war, the national debt was six times what it had been at the start.

The size of the federal government soared. More than a dozen new federal agencies managed the war effort, and the number of civilian federal workers quadrupled to 4 million. Jobs were suddenly plentiful, as millions quit work to join the military. The unemployment rate plummeted from 14 percent in 1940 to 2 percent in 1943. People who had long lived on the margins of the economic system, especially women, now entered the labor force in large numbers.

For most civilians, especially those who had lost their jobs and homes in the Depression, the war spelled a better life. Some 24 million Americans moved during the war to take advantage of new job opportunities in different parts of the country. Many headed to the West Coast, where shipyards and airplane factories were hiring nonstop.

ECONOMIC CONTROLS The United States not only had to equip and feed its military forces but also needed to provide massive amounts of food, clothing, and weapons to its allies. This created shortages at home that caused sharp price increases in consumer goods. In 1942, Congress ordered the Office of Price Administration to set price ceilings. With prices frozen, basic goods had to be allocated through rationing, with coupons doled out for limited amounts of sugar, coffee, gasoline, automobile tires, and meat.

The government promoted patriotic conservation with a massive public relations campaign that circulated posters with slogans such as "Use it up, wear it out, make it do, or do without," and it urged every family to become a "fighting unit on the home front." People collected scrap metal, tin foil, rubber, and cardboard for military use. Businesses and workers often grumbled about the wage and price controls, but the system succeeded. By the end of the war, consumer prices had risen about 31 percent, far less than the increase of 62 percent during the First World War.

THE DISRUPTIVE EFFECTS OF WORLD WAR

The Second World War transformed life at home as it was being fought abroad. Housewives went to work as welders and riveters (workers who connected sheets of metal together with metal pins) at aircraft factories and defense plants.

Some 3.5 million rural southerners left farms for cities outside the South. The federal government paid for a national day-care program for young children to enable their mothers to work full-time. The dramatic changes affected many areas of social life, and their impact would last long after the war's end.

WOMEN IN THE WAR The war marked a watershed in the status of women. Nearly 350,000 women served in the U.S. armed forces. They enlisted in the **Women's Army Corps (WAC)**; the Navy's equivalent, called the Women Accepted for Volunteer Emergency Service (WAVES); and in the Marine Corps, the Coast Guard, and the Army Air Force.

More than 6 million women entered the civilian workforce during the war, an increase of more than 50 percent overall (110 percent in manufacturing alone). To help recruit women for traditionally male jobs, the government launched a promotional campaign featuring the story of "Rosie the Riveter," a woman named Rosina Bonavita, who excelled as a worker at an airplane factory.

Many men opposed women taking traditionally male jobs. A disgruntled male legislator asked: "Who will do the cooking, the washing, the mending,

Women of the Workforce, 1942 At the Douglas Aircraft Company in Long Beach, California, three women assemble the tail fuselage of a Boeing B-17 Flying Fortress bomber.

the humble homey tasks to which every woman has devoted herself; who will rear and nurture the children?" Many women, however, were eager to escape the grinding routines of domestic life and earn good wages. A female welder remembered that her wartime job "was the first time I had a chance to get out of the kitchen and work in industry and make a few bucks. This was something I had never dreamed would happen."

AFRICAN AMERICANS DURING THE WAR   Although Americans found themselves fighting the racial bigotry celebrated by fascism and Nazism, the war did not end racism in the United States. The Red Cross, for example, initially refused to accept blood donated by African Americans, and the president of North American Aviation announced that "we will not employ Negroes." Black workers were often limited to the lowest-paid, lowest-skilled jobs. Mississippi senator James Eastland spoke for racists everywhere when he declared at the start of the war that Blacks "are an inferior race. They will not work. They will not fight."

Some courageous Black leaders fought back. In 1941, A. Philip Randolph, the founder and head of the Brotherhood of Sleeping Car Porters (railroad baggage handlers/valets), the largest African American labor union, organized the March on Washington Movement to recruit 100,000 people to demand an end to racial discrimination in defense industries, whose labor force included only 3 percent African Americans.

To fend off the march, the Roosevelt administration struck a bargain. Randolph called off the demonstration in return for Roosevelt issuing an executive order requiring equal treatment in the hiring of workers. Within a year, African Americans were working at high-paying jobs in aircraft factories and arms plants.

More than a half-million African Americans left the South for better opportunities during the war years, and more than a million Blacks joined the industrial workforce for the first time, lured by jobs and higher wages in plants and factories retooled for military production. Many African Americans from Texas, Oklahoma, Arkansas, and Louisiana headed to the states along the Pacific coast, where the dramatic expansion of defense-related jobs had significant effects on the region's population. During the war years, the number of African Americans rose sharply in cities such as Chicago, Detroit, Seattle, Portland, and Los Angeles.

At the same time, the construction of military bases and the influx of new personnel provided a boon to southern textile mills responding to the war effort through the manufacture of military uniforms and blankets. Manufacturing jobs led tens of thousands of "dirt poor" sharecroppers and tenant farmers, many of them African Americans, to leave the land for steady work in new mills and factories. Sixty of the hundred new army camps created during the war were in southern states, further transforming local economies. Throughout the United States during the Second World War, the rural population decreased by 20 percent.

RACIAL TENSION IN THE MILITARY The most volatile social issue ignited by the war was African American participation in the military. Although the armed forces were still racially segregated in 1941, African Americans rushed to enlist after the attack on Pearl Harbor. As Joe Louis, the heavyweight boxing champion, explained, "Lots of things [are] wrong with America, but Hitler ain't going to fix them." Altogether, about a million African Americans—men and women—served in the armed forces during the war.

Once in uniform, however, African Americans experienced the same kinds of prejudice they had known as civilians. Most were relegated to menial duties: loading ships, driving trucks, digging latrines, serving food, washing dishes, working in warehouses, and sorting mail. Military leaders intentionally assigned White officers from the South to supervise Black units on the mistaken assumption that southerners better understood African Americans.

African American officers could not command White soldiers or sailors. Henry L. Stimson, the secretary of war, claimed that "leadership is not embedded in the negro race." Military bases had segregated facilities to prevent the "intermingling" of "colored and white" troops.

A remarkable number of African Americans in the armed forces rebelled at the idea of fighting for democracy abroad while racism reigned at home. "I just as soon die fightin' for democracy right here in Georgia," a recruit explained, "as go all the way to Africa or Australia."

In late 1944, however, the need for more troops led the government to revisit its racial policies. General Dwight Eisenhower, commander of U.S. forces in Europe, agreed to let Black volunteers fight in all-Black fifty-man platoons commanded by White officers. A Black officer said the decision was "the greatest" for African Americans "since enactment of the constitutional amendments following the Civil War."

Black soldiers became known as fierce fighters. The same was true of nearly a thousand African American pilots trained in Tuskegee, Alabama, site of the only airfield that allowed Black trainees. One of them was Harry T. Stewart Jr., from Queens, New York. As a child, he had dreamed of becoming a pilot. In 1944, his dream came true when he and his squadron began escorting U.S. bombers over Europe. During one raid over Austria, Stewart shot down three German warplanes, earning him the Distinguished Flying Cross.

Home Front versus Frontlines *(Left)* The Tuskegee Airmen were the first African American military pilots. Here, the first graduates are reviewed at Tuskegee, Alabama, in 1941. *(Right)* Though tasked with protecting an African American man from further violence in the Detroit Riots of 1943, the police officers do nothing when a White thug reaches out to strike him.

Stewart and the other **Tuskegee Airmen** flew more than 15,000 missions, and their undeniable excellence spurred military and civilian leaders to desegregate the armed forces after the war. At war's end, however, the U.S. Army reimposed segregation. It would be several more years before the military was truly integrated. After leaving the military in 1949, Stewart applied to fly for Pan American and Trans World Airlines. Both companies rejected him. Why? He was Black.

THE DOUBLE V CAMPAIGN In 1942 the editors of the *Pittsburgh Courier*, the Black newspaper with the largest national circulation, urged African Americans to support the war effort while fighting for civil rights and racial equality at home. It was called the "Double V" campaign because the newspaper published two interlocking Vs with the theme "Democracy: Victory at Home, Victory Abroad."

The Double V campaign also demanded that African Americans who were risking their lives abroad receive full citizenship rights at home. As the newspaper explained, the campaign represented a "two-pronged attack" against those who would enslave "us at home and those who abroad would enslave us. WE HAVE A STAKE IN THIS FIGHT. . . . WE ARE AMERICANS TOO!"

The editors stressed that no one should interpret their "militant" efforts "as a plot to impede the war effort. Negroes recognize that the first factor in the survival of this nation is the winning of the war. But they feel integration of Negroes into the whole scheme of things 'revitalizes' the U.S. war program."

The response among the nation's Black community was "overwhelming." The *Courier* was swamped with telegrams and letters of support, and

Double V clubs sprouted across the nation. Other Black-owned newspapers joined the effort to promote the values at home that American forces were defending abroad.

Still, African Americans continued to face discrimination and violence during the war. During the summer of 1943 alone, there were 274 race-related incidents in almost fifty cities. In Detroit, racial tensions escalated into a full-fledged riot. Fighting raged for two days until federal troops arrived. Twenty-five Blacks and nine Whites were killed, and more than 700 people were injured.

MEXICAN AMERICANS DURING THE WAR   As rural dwellers moved west, many farm counties experienced a labor shortage. Commercial farms were most eager to find laborers who would work for low wages and not go on strike. In an ironic about-face, local and federal authorities who before the war had forced migrant laborers back across the Mexican border now recruited them to harvest crops on American farms. The Mexican government would not consent to provide the laborers, however, until the United States promised to ensure them decent working and living conditions.

The result was the creation in 1942 of the Emergency Farm Labor Program, soon dubbed the **bracero program** (for a Spanish word meaning manual laborer). Under the program, Mexico agreed to provide 168,000 seasonal

Off to Court Latinos dressed in zoot suits are loaded onto a Los Angeles County Sheriff's bus for a court appearance in June 1943.

farmworkers, virtually all males, on year-long contracts between 1942 and 1945. At least that many more crossed the border as undocumented workers.

California and twenty-five other states took advantage of the program. The braceros were not considered immigrants since they were supposed to return to Mexico when the war ended. Bracero babies born in the United States, however, were citizens. The success of the program led to its extension after the war, and the annual numbers of seasonal migrant workers soared.

Even though some 300,000 Mexican Americans served in the war and earned a higher percentage of Medals of Honor than any other minority group, racial prejudice against Mexicans and other Latinos persisted, especially in the Far West. In southern California, for example, there was constant conflict between White servicemen and Mexican American gang members and teenage "zoot-suiters." (Zoot suits were flamboyant clothing worn by some young Mexican American men.) In 1943, several thousand off-duty sailors and soldiers, joined by hundreds of Whites, rampaged through Los Angeles, assaulting Latinos, African Americans, and Filipinos. The weeklong violence came to be called the "Zoot Suit Riots."

NATIVE AMERICANS IN THE MILITARY Native Americans supported the war effort more fully than any other group. Almost a third of age-eligible Native American men served in the armed forces. Unlike their African American counterparts, Indian servicemen were integrated into regular units with Whites. Many others worked in defense-related industries, and thousands of Indian women volunteered as nurses or joined the WAVES. As was the case with African Americans, Native Americans benefited from the experiences afforded by the war by gaining vocational skills they would transfer to civilian jobs once it ended.

Why did so many Native Americans fight for a nation that had stripped them of their land and ravaged their heritage? Some felt that they had no choice. Mobilization for the war ended many New Deal programs that had provided them with jobs. At the same time, many viewed the Nazis and Japanese as threats to their own homeland.

Whatever their motivations, Indians distinguished themselves in the military. Perhaps their most distinctive role was serving as "code talkers." As had occurred during the First World War, every military branch used Native Americans, especially Navajos, to encode and decipher messages using Indian languages unknown to the Germans and Japanese.

DISCRIMINATION AGAINST JAPANESE AMERICANS After the attack on Pearl Harbor, widespread fear of a Japanese attack on the U.S.

Navajo Code Talkers The complexity of the Navajo language made it impossible for the Axis Powers to decode American messages. Here, a code talker relays messages for the U.S. Marines in the Battle of Bougainville in the South Pacific in 1943.

mainland fueled a hunger for vengeance against the Nisei—people of Japanese descent living in the United States. "A Jap's a Jap," declared Lieutenant General John L. DeWitt, head of West Coast defense efforts. "It makes no difference whether he's an American [citizen] or not." The Japanese, he insisted, were "an enemy race" regardless of where they were living. Many westerners shared his bigoted views. Storefront signs appeared declaring, "No Japs Wanted." Banks stopped cashing the checks of Japanese Americans, and grocers refused to sell them food.

Such bigotry helps explain why the U.S. government sponsored one of the worst violations of civil liberties in history when armed soldiers forcibly removed more than 120,000 Nisei from their homes, about 80,000 of whom were U.S. citizens. Allowed to take only what they could carry, they were loaded onto trucks, buses, and trains and transported to ten "**war relocation camps**" in western states. The bleak camps were hastily constructed tent cities in remote areas that were essentially internment camps guarded by sentry towers and soldiers with machine guns.

President Roosevelt initiated the incarceration of Japanese Americans, 70 percent of whom were already U.S. citizens, when he issued Executive Order 9066 on February 19, 1942. There were no trials, no due process, no concerns about violations of civil rights. Roosevelt called the program a "military necessity," although not a single incident of espionage involving Japanese Americans was proved. Only later did government documents reveal that the motive for the mass removal of Japanese Americans was to quell fears among the general public after the attack on Pearl Harbor.

On Evacuation Day, Burt Wilson, a White schoolboy in Sacramento, California, was baffled as soldiers ushered the Nisei children out of his school:

> We wondered what had happened. They took somebody out of eighth grade, a boy named Sammy, who drew wonderful cartoons. He was my friend, and one day he was there and the next day he was gone. And that was very difficult for us to understand because we didn't see Sammy or any Japanese American—at least I didn't—as the enemy.

Some 39,000 Japanese Americans served in the U.S. armed forces during the war, and others worked as interpreters and translators.

A Farewell to Civil Rights U.S. troops escorted Japanese Americans by gunpoint to remote war relocation camps, some of which were horse racing tracks, where the stables served as housing.

Not until 1983 did the U.S. government acknowledge the injustice of the incarceration policy. Five years later, Congress issued a formal apology for the internment and the Civil Liberties Act granted the 82,000 Nisei still living $20,000 each in compensation, a minor sum relative to what they had lost during four years of confinement. "The internment of Americans of Japanese ancestry," explained President George H. W. Bush in 1991, "was a great injustice, and it will never be repeated."

THE ALLIED DRIVE TOWARD BERLIN

By mid-1942, Americans began to hear good news from the war in Europe. U.S. naval forces had become increasingly successful at destroying German U-boats off the Atlantic coast. Up to that point, German submarines had sunk hundreds of Allied cargo vessels, killing 2,500 sailors. Stopping the submarine attacks was important because the Grand Alliance—Great Britain, the United States, and the Soviet Union—called for the defeat of Germany first. Defeating the Japanese could wait.

WAR AIMS AND STRATEGY

As Franklin Roosevelt and his military leaders plotted a strategy to win the war, the military situation in early 1942 was grim. Japan's armies had swept across the Pacific and Southeast Asia with the same speed that Adolf Hitler had conquered most of western Europe. By mid-March, Japanese forces had conquered Hong Kong, Guam, Wake Island, Singapore, Malaya, Java, and Borneo, and landed an invasion force on the beaches of New Guinea.

In Europe, Hitler had fulfilled his pledge to ignite "a world in flames." German submarines were sinking huge numbers of ships crossing the Atlantic from the United States to Great Britain, and the German effort to conquer the Soviet Union, while blunted by Russian resistance, continued.

During 1942, British and American pilots, flying from bases in England, began bombing military and industrial targets in German-occupied western Europe, and in Germany itself. At the same time, a major consideration for Allied military strategy was to help the Soviets survive the massive German invasion. The Soviet population—by far—bore the brunt of the war against the Nazis, leading Josef Stalin to insist that the Americans and British attack the Germans in western Europe, thereby forcing Hitler to pull soldiers, tanks, and warplanes away from Russia.

Franklin Roosevelt and Winston Churchill agreed that only by allying with Stalin and creating a second front could they ensure victory over Nazi Germany, but American and British strategists could not agree on the timing or location of an invasion of German-controlled France.

U.S. planners wanted to attack before the end of 1942. The British, however, were wary of moving too fast. An Allied defeat on the French coast, Churchill warned, was "the only way in which we could possibly lose this war." Finally, Roosevelt decided to accept Churchill's proposal for a joint Anglo-American invasion of North Africa, which was then controlled by German and Italian armies not nearly as strong as those in Europe.

THE NORTH AFRICA CAMPAIGN   On November 8, 1942, 100,000 American and British troops landed in Morocco and Algeria on the North African coast (Operation Torch). U.S. general Dwight D. Eisenhower led the assault. After the Americans lost badly in early battles, Eisenhower, soon known as "Ike," found a brilliant field commander in General George Patton, who exemplified the old saying, "When the going gets rough, they call on the sons of bitches." He was an aggressive commander who could not stand the word *retreat*.

Brimming with bravado, Patton showed American troops how to fight a modern war of speed and daring. On May 12, 1943, some 250,000 Germans and Italians surrendered, leaving North Africa in Allied control. The "continent had been redeemed," said Winston Churchill.

THE CASABLANCA CONFERENCE (1943)   Five months earlier, in January 1943, Franklin Roosevelt, Winston Churchill, and the Anglo-American military chiefs had met at a seaside resort near Casablanca in French Morocco. It was a historic occasion for Roosevelt. No U.S. president had ever flown overseas while in office, and none had ever visited Africa. Stalin chose to stay in the Soviet Union, but he again urged the Allies to invade Nazi-controlled western Europe to relieve the pressure on the Russians.

At the conference, the British convinced the Americans to assault the Italian island of Sicily. Roosevelt and Churchill also decided to step up the bombing of German cities. Finally, they agreed to increase shipments of military supplies to the Soviet Union and the Nationalist Chinese forces fighting the Japanese.

Before leaving the conference, Roosevelt announced, with Churchill's blessing, that the war would end only with the "unconditional surrender" of all enemy nations. This decision was designed to ease Soviet suspicions that the Americans and British might negotiate separately with Hitler to end the war in western Europe. The announcement also reflected Roosevelt's determination that "every person in Germany should realize that this time Germany is a defeated nation."

Whatever its impact on Soviet morale or enemy resistance, however, the decision to require unconditional surrender ensured the destruction of Germany and Japan that would create power vacuums along the western and eastern borders of the Soviet Union.

THE CLIMAX OF THE BATTLE FOR THE ATLANTIC While fighting raged in North Africa, the Battle of the Atlantic reached its climax. Great Britain desperately needed more food and military supplies from the United States, but German submarines were sinking more and more British freighters and tankers. By July 1942, some 230 Allied ships and almost 5 million tons of war supplies had been lost. "The only thing that ever frightened me during the war," recalled Churchill, "was the U-boat peril."

By the end of 1942, however, the British and Americans had cracked the German naval radio codes, enabling Allied convoys to steer clear of U-boats or hunt them down with warplanes (called subchasers) and new, more effective anti-submarine weapons deployed on warships. New technology also helped, as sonar and radar allowed Allied ships and warplanes to track submarines.

In May 1943, the Allies destroyed fifty U-boats. Thereafter, Allied shipping losses fell significantly—just as hundreds of thousands of American troops and equipment were being transported across the Atlantic to prepare for the invasion of German-occupied France. Victory in the Atlantic enabled the Allies to win the war, for had Hitler's submarines been able to sever the lifeline of American goods and troops headed to Great Britain, Germany would have won.

SICILY AND ITALY On July 10, 1943, following the Allied victory in North Africa, about 250,000 British and American troops landed on the coast of Sicily. General Eisenhower called it the "first page of the liberation of the European continent." The successful assault brought an end to Benito Mussolini's twenty years of fascist rule in Italy.

On July 25, 1943, two weeks after the Anglo-American invasion, the Italian king dismissed Mussolini as prime minister and had him arrested. The new Italian government then startled the Allies when it offered to switch sides in the war. Hitler responded by sending German armies into Italy to prevent such a possibility.

The Italian campaign thereafter became a series of stalemated battles. Winter came early to southern Italy, making life even more miserable for the soldiers.

The Germans positioned themselves behind formidable defenses and rugged terrain that enabled them to slow the Allied advance to a crawl. "Italy was one hill after another," said a U.S. soldier, "and when it was wet, you were either going up too slow or down too fast, but always the mud. And every hill had a German [machine] gun on it." Allied casualties soared.

By February 1944, the two sides were, in the words of U.S. commander Mark W. Clark, like "two boxers in the ring, both about to collapse." Mussolini, plucked from prison by a daring German airborne commando raid, became head of a fascist government in northern Italy as Allied forces finally took control of the rest of the country. On June 4, 1944, the U.S. Fifth Army entered Rome, just two days before D-day on the coast of France. "We were woken by trucks moving through the street," one overjoyed Italian remembered. "At first I thought it was the Germans, but then I heard American accents. . . . By dawn people were lining the streets. I cried."

THE TEHRAN CONFERENCE (1943) Late in the fall of 1943, in Tehran, Iran, Winston Churchill and Franklin Roosevelt had their first joint meeting with Josef Stalin. Their discussions focused on the planned invasion of Nazi-controlled France and a simultaneous Russian offensive across eastern Europe. The three leaders agreed to create an international organization—the United Nations (UN)—to maintain world peace after the war. By the end of the conference, Roosevelt told a cabinet officer that he had grown to like Stalin and had forged a close working relationship with the Soviet leader. Stalin knew this, too, for he had told his secret police to bug Roosevelt's rooms.

Upon arriving back in the United States, Roosevelt confided to Churchill that he still distrusted Stalin, saying that it was a "ticklish" business keeping the "Russians cozy with us" because of the ideological tension between communism and capitalism. As General Eisenhower stressed, however, the fate of Britain and the United States depended on the Soviets' survival as an ally against Nazi Germany. "The prize we seek," he said in 1942, "is to keep 8 million Russians [soldiers] in the war."

THE STRATEGIC BOMBING OF HITLER'S EUROPE Months of meticulous preparation went into the Allied invasion of German-occupied France. While waiting for D-day (the day the invasion would begin), the U.S. Army Air Force tried to pound Germany into submission. Although the air offensive, while killing 350,000 civilians, failed to shatter German morale or war-related production, it did force the Germans to commit precious resources to air-raid defense and eventually wore down their air force. With Allied air supremacy assured by 1944, the much-anticipated invasion of Hitler's "Fortress Europe" could move forward.

PLANNING AN INVASION In early 1944, Dwight D. Eisenhower arrived in London with a new title: Supreme Commander of the Allied Expeditionary Force (AEF). A West Point graduate from Kansas, he faced the daunting task of planning **Operation Overlord**, the daring assault on Hitler's "Atlantic Wall," an array of mines, machine guns, barbed wire, and jagged obstacles along the French coastline. The planned invasion gave Churchill nightmares: "When I think of the beaches . . . choked with the flower of American and British youth . . . I see the tides running red with their blood. I have my doubts. I have my doubts."

For months, Eisenhower, neither an experienced strategist nor a combat commander, dedicated himself to detailed planning for the risky invasion and managing the complex political and military rivalries among the Allied leaders. Well-organized and efficient, he was a high-energy perfectionist, impatient and often short-tempered with his staff. He attended to every detail, including the amassing of 5 million tons of military equipment and munitions and thousands of warplanes and ships.

The seaborne invasion would be the greatest gamble and most complex military operation in history. "I am very uneasy about the whole operation," admitted Sir Alan Brooke, head of British forces. "It may well be the most ghastly disaster of the whole war." Eisenhower was so concerned that he carried in his wallet a note to be circulated if the Allies failed. It read: "If any blame or fault attaches to the attempt, it is mine alone."

General Dwight D. Eisenhower Eisenhower visiting with U.S. paratroopers before they launch the nighttime airborne assault in Operation Overlord.

D-DAY AND AFTER Operation Overlord succeeded in part because it surprised the Germans. The Allies positioned British decoy troops and made misleading public statements to fool the Nazis into believing that the invasion would come at Pas-de-Calais, on the French-Belgian border, where the English Channel was narrowest. Instead, the landings would actually occur along 50 miles of shoreline in northern Normandy, a French coastal region almost 200 miles south.

On the blustery evening of June 5, 1944, General Eisenhower visited some of the 16,000 U.S. paratroopers preparing to board some 800 planes that would drop them behind German lines. The soldiers, noticing Eisenhower's concerned demeanor, tried to lift his spirits. "Now quit worrying, General," one of them said, "we'll take care of this thing for you." A sergeant said, "We ain't worried. It's Hitler's turn to worry."

After the planes took off, Eisenhower confided to an aide: "I hope to God I know what I'm doing." Others were concerned too. As he got into bed that night, Winston Churchill, with tears running down his cheeks, asked his wife: "Do you know that by the time you wake up in the morning, 20,000 men may have been killed?"

As the planes carrying the paratroopers arrived at their drop points, thick clouds and German anti-aircraft fire disrupted the formations. Some soldiers were dropped miles from their landing sites, some were dropped far out at sea, and some were dropped so low that their parachutes never opened. Yet those among the U.S. 82nd and 101st Airborne Divisions who landed safely outfought three German divisions during the night and prepared the way for the main invasion by destroying bridges and capturing artillery positions and key road junctions.

Donald Burgett, a nineteen-year-old paratrooper in the 101st Airborne Division, recalled dropping into France in the dark of night and being alone: "My throat went dry and I swallowed, but nothing went down. My heart pounded, sending blood throbbing through my temples and causing a weak-feeling in the pit of my stomach." But he had no time for fear. As he stumbled upon others who had survived the landing, they soon found themselves embroiled in combat.

THE NORMANDY LANDINGS As the gray, misty light of dawn broke on D-day, June 6, 1944, the largest invasion fleet in history—some 5,300 Allied ships carrying 370,000 soldiers and sailors—filled the horizon off the Normandy coast. Sleepy German soldiers awoke to the breathtaking array of ships. "I saw an armada like a plague of locusts," said a German officer. "The number of ships was uncountable."

The Landing at Normandy D-day, June 6, 1944. Before they could huddle under a seawall and begin to dislodge the Nazi defenders, U.S. soldiers on Omaha Beach had to cross a fifty-yard stretch that exposed them to machine gun fire from protected concrete bunkers.

Eisenhower was lucky on D-day, for the Germans misinterpreted the Normandy landings as a diversion for the "real" attack at Pas-de-Calais. It helped that the German commander, Field Marshal Erwin Rommel, assuming that the weather was too rough for an invasion, had gone home to Germany to celebrate his wife's June 6 birthday. "How stupid of me," Rommel said when he heard the news. "How stupid of me!" By one o'clock in the afternoon, he was racing back to France.

When Hitler learned of the Allied landings, he boasted that "the news couldn't be better. As long as they [the Allied armies] were in Britain, we couldn't get at them. Now we have them where we can destroy them." In the United States, word that the long-anticipated liberation of Nazi Europe had begun captured the nation's attention. Businesses closed, church bells tolled, and people prayed in the streets.

During the first day of Operation Overlord, foul weather and rough seas caused injuries and seasickness and capsized dozens of the boxy, flat-bottomed landing craft. More than 1,000 soldiers, weighed down by seventy pounds of equipment, drowned as they stepped into water above their heads. Some of the landing craft delivered their often seasick troops to the wrong locations. "We have landed in the wrong place," shouted fifty-six-year-old Brigadier General Theodore Roosevelt Jr. (son of the former president), who would receive the Medal of Honor for his courage that day. "But we will start the war from here."

The noise was deafening as shells exploded across the beaches and in the surf. Bodies piled up amid wrenching cries for help. "As our boat touched sand and the ramp went down," Private Harry Parley remembered, "I became a visitor to Hell."

The first U.S. units ashore at Omaha Beach, beneath 130-foot-tall cliffs defended by German machine guns and mortars, lost more than 90 percent of their men. Officers struggled to rally the troops. "Two kinds of men are staying on this beach," shouted cigar-smoking Colonel George Taylor. "The dead and those who are going to die. Get up! Move in! Goddammit! Move in and die! Get the hell out of here!"

Inch by inch, U.S. troops pushed across the beaches and up the cliffs. By nightfall, 170,000 Allied soldiers—57,000 of them Americans—were scattered across fifty miles of the windswept Normandy coastline. So too were the bodies of 10,724 dead or wounded Allied soldiers.

On June 13, a week after the Normandy landings, Erwin Rommel told his wife that the "battle is not going at all well for us." Within three weeks, the Allies had landed more than a million troops, 566,000 tons of supplies, and 171,000 vehicles. "Whether the enemy can still be stopped at this point is questionable," German army headquarters near Paris warned Hitler. "The enemy air superiority is terrific and smothers almost every one of our movements. . . . Losses in men and equipment are extraordinary."

Operation Overlord was the greatest seaborne invasion in the history of warfare, but it was small when compared with the offensive launched by the Soviet army a few weeks later. Between June and August 1944, the Soviets killed, wounded, or captured more German soldiers (350,000) than were stationed in all of western Europe.

Still, the Normandy invasion was a turning point in the war. With the beachhead secured, the Allied leaders knew that final victory was just a matter of time, as Hitler's armies were caught between the Soviets advancing from the east and the Allied forces from the west and south. "What a plan!" Churchill exclaimed to the British Parliament.

THE LIBERATION OF PARIS It would take seven more weeks and 37,000 more lives for the Allied troops to gain control of Normandy. The Germans lost more than twice that many, and some 19,000 French civilians were killed. Then, on July 25, American armies headed east from Normandy

WORLD WAR II IN EUROPE AND AFRICA, 1942–1945

Legend:
- ✳ Major battle
- Axis Powers at outbreak of the war
- Maximum extent of Axis military power
- → Allied offensives
- ⋯⋯ Inside limit of German U-boat operations

- What was the Allied strategy for dislodging Italian and German forces in North Africa, and why was it important for the invasion of Italy?
- Why did Eisenhower's plan for the D-day invasion succeed?
- What was the role of strategic bombing in the war? Was it effective?

toward Paris. On August 15, a joint American-French force landed on the Mediterranean coast and raced up the Rhone Valley in eastern France.

German resistance collapsed after only ten weeks. On D-day, one German unit, the 21st Panzer Division, boasted 12,000 men and 127 tanks; ten weeks later, having retreated across France, it had just 300 men and 10 tanks left. A division of the Free French Resistance, aided by American units, liberated Paris on August 25. As U.S. soldiers marched through the cheering crowds, a reporter said that he had never "seen in any place such joy as radiated from the people of Paris this morning"

By mid-September, most of France and Belgium had been cleared of German troops. Meanwhile, the Soviet army moved relentlessly westward along a 1,200-mile front, pushing the fleeing Germans out of Russia. Between D-day and the end of the war in Europe a year later, 1.2 million German soldiers were killed or wounded.

ROOSEVELT'S FOURTH TERM In 1944, war or no war, the calendar required another presidential election. This time the Republicans nominated New York governor Thomas E. Dewey, who argued that it was time for a younger man to replace the "tired" Democratic leader.

Franklin Roosevelt was not only tired; he was seriously ill, suffering from high blood pressure, heart failure, and clogged arteries. In March, the president's physician predicted that Roosevelt would not survive another four years in office. The next day, the president, determined to guide the nation to victory and create a stable postwar world, announced that he would accept his party's nomination for a fourth term. The public knew nothing about his failing health. On November 7, 1944, Roosevelt won yet again, this time by a popular vote of 25.6 million to 22 million and an electoral vote of 432 to 99.

The End of the War in Europe

By the time Franklin Roosevelt was reelected, Allied armies were approaching the German border from the east and the west. Winston Churchill was worried that if the Soviets arrived first in Berlin, the German capital, Josef Stalin would control the postwar map of Europe. Churchill urged Eisenhower to beat the Soviets to Berlin. Eisenhower, however, decided it was not worth the estimated 100,000 American casualties such an operation would cost.

GERMAN COUNTERATTACK: THE BATTLE OF THE BULGE As the Anglo-American armies approached the German border in mid-December 1944, a desperate Hitler sprang a surprise. He dispatched most of his army's reserves and 1,800 tanks to the Ardennes Forest in Belgium, where they launched a brazen counterattack intended to split the Allied advance and retake the Belgian port of Antwerp. "This battle is to decide whether we shall live or die," Hitler told his officers. "The battle must be fought with brutality, and all resistance must be broken in a wave of terror."

What came to be called the Battle of the Bulge was America's largest battle ever. It involved a million combatants and almost changed the course of the war. Initially, the counterattack surprised Allied commanders, punched a hole in the overstretched Allied lines, and drove the British and U.S. forces back fifty miles, thus creating the "bulge" on the map that gave the battle its name. Eight days of brutal winter weather complicated matters, as frigid temperatures,

Battle of the Bulge Two U.S. soldiers stand out sharply against snow-covered ground and a night sky illuminated by a barrage of artillery fire.

blinding snow, winter fog, and thick clouds prevented Allied warplanes from supporting the troops. With temperatures averaging twenty degrees, thousands of soldiers suffered frostbite.

General Eisenhower remained calm. He saw the massive assault as "an opportunity" to destroy much of the German army. The heaviest fighting centered on the town of Bastogne, where seven key roads converged. There, some 18,000 U.S. infantry and paratroopers found themselves hopelessly surrounded. For more than a week, as they ran low on supplies, they held off a much larger force of Germans as General George S. Patton's Third Army, some ninety miles away, raced to the rescue with 250,000 soldiers. Patton, too, saw the German counterattack as an opportunity to shorten the war. Hitler, he claimed, "had stuck his head into a meat grinder, and this time I've got the handle."

On December 22, the German commander encircling Bastogne sent his American counterpart, General Anthony McAuliffe, a demand to surrender within two hours or be "annihilated." McAuliffe's one-word reply ("Nuts!") confused the Germans. An American officer then explained to the German representative that "Nuts" meant the same as "Go to Hell." And, he added, "We will kill every goddamned German who tries to break into the city."

The weather cleared the next morning, enabling U.S. planes to bring desperately needed supplies to the units trapped in Bastogne. A few days later, the advance guard of Patton's relief force arrived. Bastogne was no longer surrounded. For three more weeks, the Germans repeatedly tried to take the town, but without success. Throughout the region, wave after wave of American and British warplanes assaulted German forces in what one observer called "a great slaughter."

Hitler's great gamble had failed. The Germans at the Battle of the Bulge lost more than 100,000 men—killed, wounded, or captured. American casualties were also high—89,000—but it was clear that Germany was teetering toward defeat. "Now," Patton wrote in his diary, "we are going to attack until the war is over."

THE YALTA CONFERENCE (1945) As the Allied armies converged on Berlin, Josef Stalin hosted Franklin Roosevelt and Winston Churchill at Yalta, a resort on the Black Sea. At the **Yalta Conference** (February 4–11, 1945), the "Big Three" agreed that, once Germany surrendered, the Soviets would occupy eastern Germany, and the Americans and British would control western Germany. Berlin, the German capital within the Soviet zone, would be subject to joint occupation.

The Yalta Conference Churchill, Roosevelt, and Stalin (with their respective foreign ministers behind them) confer on postwar plans in February 1945.

Roosevelt had two goals at Yalta: First, to convince Stalin and the Soviets to join the new United Nations organization and, second, to ensure that the Soviets joined the fight against Japan, since all assumed at that point that the cost would be high to force a Japanese surrender.

Stalin's goals were to retrieve former Russian territory transferred to Poland after the First World War and impose Soviet control over eastern and central Europe. Churchill and Roosevelt urged Stalin to allow Poland, then occupied by the Red Army, to become a self-governing democracy. Stalin refused, explaining that Soviet control of Poland was more important to him than participation in the United Nations, Roosevelt's proposed international peacekeeping organization.

Stalin also knew that the Americans needed Soviet support in the ongoing war with Japan. Military analysts estimated that Japan could hold out for eighteen months after the defeat of Germany unless the Soviets joined the war in Asia. Stalin agreed to do so, but the price was high: he demanded territories from Japan and China.

As a face-saving gesture, Roosevelt and Churchill convinced Stalin to sign the Yalta Declaration of Liberated Europe, which called for free and open elections in the liberated nations of eastern Europe. Nevertheless, Stalin would renege on his promises. When the Soviet Red Army "liberated" Hungary, Romania, Bulgaria, Czechoslovakia, Poland, and eastern Germany, it plundered and sent back to Russia anything of economic value, dismantling thousands of factories and mills and rebuilding them in the Soviet Union. To ensure control over eastern Europe, the Soviets shipped off to prison anyone who questioned the new Communist governments they created.

At Yalta, the three leaders agreed to hold organizational meetings for the United Nations beginning on April 25, 1945. Like Woodrow Wilson, Roosevelt was determined to replace America's "outdated" isolationism with an engaged internationalism. But to get Stalin's approval of the UN, Roosevelt gave in to the Soviet leader's demands for territory held by Japan in northeast Asia.

Roosevelt's critics, then and since, claimed that the president "gave away" eastern Europe to Stalin. Yet the United States could not have dislodged the Soviet army from its control of eastern Europe. The course of the war shaped the outcome at Yalta, and the United States had no real leverage. As a U.S. diplomat admitted, "Stalin held all the cards." Roosevelt agreed. "I didn't say the result was good," Roosevelt said after returning from the Yalta Conference. "I said it was the best I can do for Poland at this time." As always for FDR, politics was the art of the possible; he focused on deals that could be made.

DEATH OF A PRESIDENT By early 1945, Nazi Germany was on the verge of defeat, but sixty-three-year-old Franklin Roosevelt would not live to join the victory celebrations. In the spring of 1945, he went to the "Little White House" in Warm Springs, Georgia. On April 12, 1945, just eighty-two days into his fourth term, he complained of a headache but seemed to be in good spirits. It was nearly lunchtime when he said to an artist painting his portrait, "Now we've got just about 15 minutes more to work." Then, while reading some documents, Roosevelt groaned, saying that he had "terrific pain" in the back of his head. He slumped over, fell into a coma, and died two hours later.

On hand to witness the president's death was Lucy Mercer Rutherford, the woman with whom Roosevelt had had an affair thirty years before. Eleanor Roosevelt was in Washington, D.C., when Franklin died, unaware of the president's guest. Although Franklin had promised in 1918 to end all communications with Mercer, he had in fact secretly stayed in touch, even enabling her to attend his presidential inauguration in 1933.

Roosevelt's death shocked and saddened the world. Even his sharpest critics were devastated. Ohio senator Robert Taft, known as "Mr. Republican," said, "The President's death removes the greatest figure of our time at the very climax of his career. . . . He dies a hero of the war, for he literally worked himself to death in the service of the American people."

THE COLLAPSE OF NAZISM   Adolf Hitler's Nazi empire collapsed less than a month later. In Berlin on April 28, as Soviet troops entered the German capital, Hitler married his mistress, Eva Braun, in an underground bunker. That same day, Italian freedom fighters captured Mussolini. Despite his plea to "Let me live, and I will give you an empire," Mussolini and his mistress were shot and hung by their heels from a girder above a Milan gas station. On April 30, Hitler and his wife retired to their underground bedroom, where she poisoned herself and he put a bullet in his head. Their bodies were taken outside, doused with gasoline, and burned.

On May 2, Berlin fell to Soviet soldiers. Axis forces in Italy surrendered the same day. Five days later, on May 7, the chief of staff of the German armed forces surrendered unconditionally. So ended the Nazi domination of Europe, just over twelve years after Hitler had proclaimed his "Thousand-Year Reich."

May 8, V-E day (Victory in Europe), witnessed massive celebrations across the free world. In Paris, an American bomber pilot flew his plane through the arch of the Eiffel Tower. In New York City, 500,000 people celebrated in the streets. The elation, however, was tempered by the ongoing war against Japan and the immense challenges of helping Europe rebuild. The German economy had to be revived, a new democratic government had to be formed, and millions of displaced Europeans had to be clothed, housed, and fed.

THE HOLOCAUST   The end of the war in Europe revealed to the world the horrific extent of the **Holocaust**, Hitler's systematic program to destroy Jews and other minority groups he deemed unfit to live. In 1941, a German soldier wrote his wife: "The Jews are being completely exterminated." He reminded her not to tell their son about such atrocities.

It took longer for the rest of the world to learn of the Holocaust. Reports of the Nazis' methodical slaughter of Jews had appeared as early as 1942, but

MAY 8, 1945 The celebration in New York City's Times Square on V-E day was just one of many massive events held around the world to cheer the end of World War II.

the ghastly stories of millions killed in gas chambers seemed beyond belief until the Allied armies liberated the Nazi death camps in central and eastern Europe. There the Germans had imposed their "Final Solution": the wholesale extermination of at least 6 million Jews, and many millions more non-Jewish peoples. Winston Churchill called the Holocaust the "most horrible crime ever committed in the history of the world."

The Allied troops were shocked at what they discovered in the extermination camps, where as many as 24,000 Jews a day had been killed. Bodies were piled as high as buildings; survivors were living skeletons wrapped in skin. General Eisenhower reported that the "things I saw beggar description." Everywhere, the "starvation, cruelty, and bestiality were so overpowering as to leave me a bit sick. In one room, where they were piled up twenty or thirty naked men, killed by starvation, [General] George Patton would not even enter. He said that he would get sick if he did so. I made the visit deliberately, in order to be in a position to give first-hand evidence of these things if ever, in the future, there develops a tendency to charge these allegations merely to 'propaganda.'"

American army officers forced neighboring German villagers to tour the death camps so that there could be no denying what had gone on there. After doing so, the mayor of Dachau and his wife hanged themselves.

American officials had dragged their feet in acknowledging the Holocaust for fear that relief efforts for Jewish refugees might stir up anti-Semitism at home. At the same time, several key figures in the State Department proved to be anti-Semitic themselves, and they balked at bringing more Jewish refugees to America.

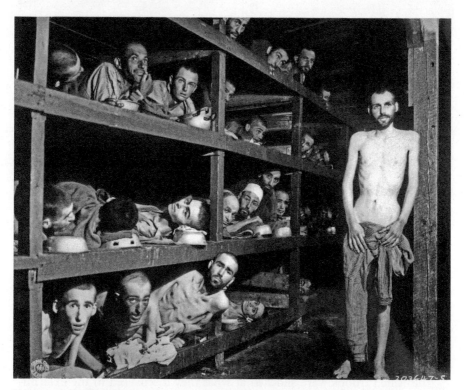

Holocaust Survivors American troops liberate survivors of the Buchenwald concentration camp in April 1945. Among the prisoners is Elie Wiesel *(second row from the bottom, seventh from the left)*, who went on to become an author, professor, political activist, and recipient of the Nobel Peace Prize.

Robert Reynolds, a Democratic senator from North Carolina, expressed the prevailing view when he roared in a Senate speech that "if I had my way I would today build a wall about the United States so high and so secure that not a single alien or foreign refugee from any country upon the face of the earth could possibly scale or ascend it."

In 1942, the Nazi-controlled Romanian government had offered to spare 70,000 Jews in death camps for a ransom of fifty dollars each. The State Department had declined, prompting a young Treasury Department official, Josiah E. Du Bois Jr., to write a letter of protest. "One of the greatest crimes in history, the slaughter of the Jewish people in Europe, is continuing unabated," he revealed. Du Bois charged that anti-Semitic members of the State Department were covering up Nazi atrocities.

Prejudice against Jews was not limited to the State Department; it was widespread across the United States. In 1938, a national poll asked, "What kind of people do you object to?" Jews were named most often. The nation's best colleges and universities applied quotas to Jewish applicants, prestigious country clubs barred them from joining, and marriages between Jews and Christians were discouraged.

Under pressure from Jewish groups and his wife, Roosevelt had created a War Refugee Board early in 1944 to rescue European Jews at risk of extermination. The War Refugee Board managed to rescue about 200,000 European Jews and some 20,000 other refugees.

The Roosevelt administration, however, refused appeals from Jewish leaders to bomb the concentration camp at Auschwitz, Poland, arguing that doing so would kill many Jews, be ineffective (the Nazis would simply build another one), and distract resources from the priority of defeating Hitler's war machine.

THE PACIFIC WAR

For months after the attack on Pearl Harbor at the end of 1941, the news from the Pacific was "all bad," as President Roosevelt acknowledged. With stunning speed, the Japanese had captured numerous territories in Asia, including the British colonies of Hong Kong, Burma, Malaya, and Singapore, and the French colony of Indochina.

THE PHILIPPINES In the Philippines, U.S. forces and their Filipino allies were overwhelmed. On April 10, 1942, the Japanese gathered some 12,000 captured American troops along with 66,000 Filipinos and forced them to march sixty-five miles in six days up the Bataan peninsula. Already underfed and ravaged by disease, the prisoners were brutalized in what came to be known as the Bataan Death March. Those who fell out of line were bayoneted or shot. Others were beaten, stabbed, or shot for no reason. More than 10,000 prisoners died along the way. News of the Bataan Death March outraged Americans and contributed to the Pacific war's emotional intensity and mutual atrocities.

By the summer of 1942, Japan was on the verge of assaulting Australia when its naval leaders succumbed to what one admiral called "victory disease." Intoxicated with easy victories and lusting for more, they pushed into the South Pacific, intending to isolate Australia and strike again at Hawaii.

CORAL SEA AND MIDWAY During the spring of 1942, U.S. forces in the Pacific finally had some success. In the Battle of the Coral Sea (May 2–6), U.S. warplanes forced a Japanese invasion fleet headed toward the island of New Guinea to turn back after sinking an aircraft carrier and destroying seventy planes.

A few weeks later, Admiral Yamamoto steered his main Japanese fleet of eighty-six warships and 700 warplanes toward Midway, a tiny island in the central Pacific Ocean, some 1,300 miles northwest of Honolulu, Hawaii. The Japanese hoped to launch another air strike from Midway on Pearl Harbor. This time, however, the Japanese were the ones who were surprised. In a crucial breakthrough, Americans had cracked the Japanese military radio code, allowing Admiral Chester Nimitz, commander of the U.S. central Pacific fleet, to learn where Yamamoto's fleet was heading.

The Japanese hit Midway hard on June 4, 1942, but at the cost of about a third of their warplanes. American planes then struck back, sinking four of the six Japanese aircraft carriers that had launched the attack on Pearl Harbor.

The **Battle of Midway** was the first major defeat for the Japanese navy in 350 years and a turning point of the Pacific war. The American victory blunted Japan's military momentum, eliminated the threat to Hawaii, and bought time for the United States to organize its massive industrial productivity for a wider war.

GENERAL MACARTHUR'S PACIFIC STRATEGY American and Australian forces were jointly under the command of General Douglas MacArthur, an egotistical military genius who irritated his superiors with his "unpleasant personality" and constant self-promotion. MacArthur had retired in 1937 but was called back into service in mid-1941. In 1942, he assumed command of the Allied forces in the southwest Pacific and masterminded the American effort to strike back at the Japanese.

On August 7, 1942, some 19,000 marines landed on Guadalcanal Island, where the Japanese had an air base. Savage fighting lasted through February 1943, but it resulted in the Japanese army's first defeat, with a loss of 20,000 men compared to 1,752 Americans. Said a marine, "These people refuse to surrender." Another wished "we were fighting against Germans. They are human beings, like us. . . . But the Japanese are like animals."

The suicidal intensity of the Japanese led MacArthur and Admiral Chester Nimitz to adopt a "leapfrogging" or "island-hopping" strategy whereby they liberated the most important islands and bypassed the others, leaving isolated Japanese bases to "wither on the vine," as Nimitz put it.

BATTLES IN THE CENTRAL PACIFIC On June 15, 1944, U.S. forces liberated Tinian, Guam, and Saipan in the Mariana Islands. The battle for control of Saipan was one of the most brutal and deadly in the Pacific. It was strategically important because it allowed the new American B-29 "Super-fortress" bombers to strike Japan itself.

Fanatical Japanese resistance made an inferno of every beachhead as American forces assaulted the dug-in defenders. U.S. marines and army soldiers, including African Americans in combat for the first time in the war, were pushed to the limit.

The struggle for Saipan lasted three weeks because the 30,000 well-prepared Japanese defenders, twice as many as the Americans expected, commanded the heights overlooking the beaches where the U.S. troops landed. As he observed the 600 American ships positioned offshore unloading U.S. marines, a Japanese commander muttered, "Hell is upon us."

But hell has no favorites. Both sides experienced hellish conflict as the invasion unfolded. A marine officer described the four miles of beach where the landings occurred: "All around us was the chaotic debris of bitter combat. Japanese and marine bodies lying in mangled and grotesque positions, . . . the acrid smell of high explosives; the shattered trees; and the churned-up sand littered with discarded equipment."

Once off the beach, the Americans had to slog through brutal jungle terrain that gave the defenders a tactical advantage: ravines, caves, cliffs and hills, earned nicknames such as Hell's Pocket, Death Valley, and Purple Heart Ridge. Five soldiers and marines received the Medal of Honor.

The Battle of Saipan culminated on July 7, when the besieged Japanese launched the largest Banzai ("suicide") attack in the Pacific war, in which large numbers of Japanese soldiers would charge American troops in a horde-like fashion with the officers swishing their swords over their heads with soldiers firing rapidly behind them shouting, "Banzai." Every available American, whether a senior officer, cook, medic, or radio operator, grabbed a weapon to help stop the relentless assault. Japanese bodies piled up so high that the Americans had to move their machine guns to gain a field of fire. The Americans were eventually able to stand their ground and systematically kill or wound every attacker.

Some 20,000 Japanese defenders were killed compared to 3,100 Americans, making Saipan the costliest campaign in the Pacific to date. But as many as 7,000 more Japanese soldiers committed suicide upon the order of their commanding general, Yoshitsugu Saito, who killed himself after being wounded.

THE UNWANTED VISIT   As combat involving U.S. forces in the Pacific grew more intense and widespread, casualties mounted. Families dreaded receiving the telegram or hearing the knock on the door that meant a husband or a son had been killed.

In January 1943, Thomas Sullivan was preparing to go to work in Waterloo, Iowa, when three U.S. Navy officers appeared at his door. All five of Sullivan's sons—George, Madison, Albert, Francis, and Joseph—had enlisted after the Japanese attack on Pearl Harbor. They had insisted on serving on the same ship. Now, Thomas Sullivan asked the visitors which of his sons had been killed. "All of them," an officer replied.

Their ship, the USS *Juneau,* had been sunk by a Japanese submarine in the Pacific. Three Sullivan brothers had died after the initial explosion; the two others scrambled into life rafts but died while waiting for rescue. A new warship was named for them.

RETURN TO THE PHILIPPINES   General MacArthur's forces invaded the Japanese-controlled Philippines on October 20, 1944. The Japanese, knowing that the loss of the Philippines would cut them off from essential raw materials, brought in warships from three directions to defend the islands they had controlled since 1942. They were unaware that they were steaming into a carefully prepared American trap. On October 23, 1944, the jaws of the trap closed.

The four naval and air battles fought over three days in the Philippine Sea, known collectively as the Battle of Leyte Gulf, marked the largest naval engagement in history and the worst Japanese defeat of the war. Some 216 U.S. warships converged to engage 64 Japanese ships. By the end of the colossal battle, 36 Japanese warships, including 4 aircraft carriers, had been destroyed. The once invincible Japanese Imperial Navy died in Leyte Gulf.

As MacArthur waded ashore with the U.S. troops liberating the Philippines, he reminded reporters of his 1942 pledge—"I shall return"—when

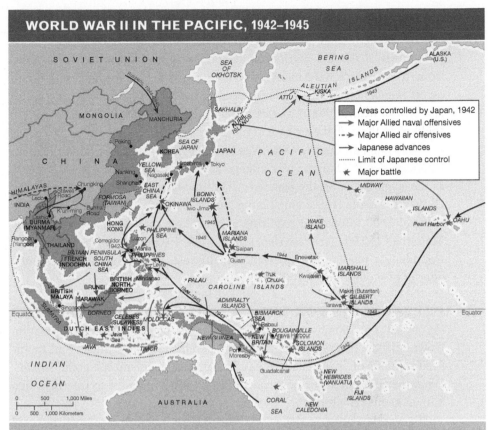

WORLD WAR II IN THE PACIFIC, 1942–1945

Areas controlled by Japan, 1942
→ Major Allied naval offensives
·-▸ Major Allied air offensives
→ Japanese advances
········ Limit of Japanese control
★ Major battle

- What was General MacArthur's "leapfrogging" strategy in the western Pacific? Why were the battles in the Marianas a major turning point in the war?
- What was the significance of the Battle of Leyte Gulf?
- How did the battle at Okinawa affect both Japanese and American military strategies?

he was evacuated in the face of the Japanese invasion. Now he announced: "People of the Philippines, I have returned! The hour of your redemption is here. . . . Rally to me."

The massive battle featured the first Japanese *kamikaze* ("divine wind") attacks, in which pilots deliberately crashed their bomb-laden planes into American warships (Japanese warplanes carried only enough fuel to reach their targets). From the fall of 1944 to the war's end in the summer of 1945, an estimated 4,000 kamikaze pilots died on such suicide missions. "Kamikazes just poured at us, again and again," a sailor remembered. "It scared the shit out of us."

THE BATTLE OF OKINAWA The closer the Allied forces got to Japan, the fiercer the resistance they encountered. While fighting continued in the Philippines, 30,000 U.S. marines landed on Iwo Jima, a volcanic atoll 760 miles from Tokyo, which the Americans wanted as an air base for fighter planes to escort bombers over Japan. It took almost six weeks to secure the tiny island at a cost of nearly 7,000 American lives—and 21,000 of the 22,000 Japanese soldiers. In the end, the air base never materialized.

The assault on Okinawa was even bloodier. Only 360 miles from the main Japanese islands, Okinawa was strategically important because it would serve as the staging area for the planned Allied invasion of Japan. The conquest of Okinawa was the largest amphibious operation of the Pacific war, involving some 300,000 troops and requiring almost three months of brutal fighting. More than 150,000 Japanese were killed; some 49,000 Americans were killed, wounded, or missing, a 35 percent casualty rate. A third of U.S. pilots and a quarter of submariners lost their lives.

PREPARATION FOR THE INVASION OF JAPAN As the fighting raged on Okinawa, Allied commanders began planning Operation Downfall—the invasion of Japan itself. The Japanese government had mobilized millions of civilians into a national militia to defend the home islands. What they did not know was that military leaders intended to use them in a human kamikaze effort.

To weaken Japanese defenses, destroy their war-related industries, and erode civilian morale, the Allied command stepped up bombing raids in the summer of 1944. Then, in early 1945, General Curtis Lemay, head of the U.S. Bomber Command, ordered devastating "firebomb" raids upon Japanese cities: "Bomb and burn 'em till they quit."

On March 9, some 300 B-29 bombers dropped napalm bombs on Tokyo. The attack incinerated sixteen square miles of the city and killed some 100,000 people while rendering a million people homeless. By then, American military leaders had lost all moral qualms about targeting Japanese civilians. The kamikaze attacks, the Japanese savagery toward prisoners of war, the burning of Manila that killed 100,000 civilians, and the brutal treatment of Chinese civilians had eroded almost all sympathy.

By August 1945, sixty-six Japanese cities had been firebombed. Secretary of War Henry Stimson called the lack of public outcry in the United States over the raids "appalling."

THE ATOMIC BOMB Still, Japanese military leaders preferred national suicide over surrender. In early 1945, Harry S. Truman, the vice president who became president upon Roosevelt's death on April 12, learned of the first successful test of an atomic bomb in New Mexico. Now that military planners knew the bomb would work, they selected two Japanese cities as targets. The first was **Hiroshima**, a port city and army headquarters in southern Japan. On July 25, 1945, Truman, who knew nothing about the devastating effects of radiation poisoning, ordered that the atomic bomb be dropped if Japan did not surrender before August 3.

Although an intense debate emerged over the decision (General Eisenhower argued that the "Japanese were ready to surrender," and he "hated to see our country be the first to use such a weapon"), Truman later recalled, "We faced half a million casualties trying to take Japan by land. It was either that or the atom bomb, and I didn't hesitate a minute, and I've never lost any sleep over it since."

To Truman and others, the use of atomic bombs seemed a logical next step to end the war. Some 85 percent of Americans surveyed agreed with the decision to use atomic bombs. As it turned out, scientists greatly underestimated the bomb's power. Their prediction that 20,000 people would be killed proved much too low.

In mid-July 1945, the Allied leaders met in Potsdam, Germany, near Berlin. Josef Stalin demanded, according to Truman, that the United States and Great Britain "recognize the new puppet governments" the Soviets had created in Romania, Bulgaria, and Hungary. Truman responded that the United States would do so only after the Soviets allowed "free access" to them and adopted "democratic" processes. Until that happened, America would veto efforts to allow such Soviet-dominated nations to participate in the new United Nations.

The conference deadlocked over the issue of Soviet control of eastern Europe. The Allies did issue the Potsdam Declaration, which demanded that Japan surrender by August 3 or face "prompt and utter destruction." Truman left Potsdam optimistic about postwar relations with the Soviet Union. "I can deal with Stalin," he wrote. "He is honest—but smart as hell." (Truman would soon change his mind about Stalin's honesty.)

The deadline calling for Japan's surrender passed, and on August 6, 1945, a B-29 bomber piloted by Colonel Paul Tibbets (the plane was named *Enola Gay* after Tibbets's mother) took off at 2:00 A.M. from the island of Tinian, headed for Hiroshima. At 8:15 A.M., flying at 31,600 feet, the bombardier aboard the *Enola Gay* released the five-ton, ten-foot-long uranium bomb nicknamed "Little Boy."

Forty-three seconds later, the bomb exploded at an altitude of 1,900 feet, creating a blinding flash of light followed by a fireball towering to 40,000 feet. The tail gunner on the *Enola Gay* described the scene: "It's like bubbling molasses down there . . . the mushroom is spreading out . . . fires are springing up everywhere . . . it's like a peep into hell."

The bomb's shock wave and firestorm initially killed some 78,000 people, including thousands of Japanese soldiers and 23 American prisoners of war. By the end of the year, the death toll would reach 140,000, as more people died of injuries or radiation poisoning. In addition, the bomb destroyed 76,000 buildings.

President Truman was returning from the Potsdam conference when news arrived that the atomic bomb had been dropped. "This is the greatest thing in history!" he repeatedly exclaimed. In the United States, Americans greeted the news with similar joy. "No tears of sympathy will be shed in America for the Japanese people," the *Omaha World-Herald* predicted. "Had they possessed a comparable weapon at Pearl Harbor, would they have hesitated to use it?" Others reacted by pointing to the implications of atomic warfare. "Yesterday," journalist Hanson Baldwin wrote in the *New York Times*, "we clinched victory in the Pacific, but we sowed the whirlwind."

Two days after the Hiroshima bombing, an opportunistic Soviet Union entered the war in the Pacific by sending hundreds of thousands of troops

The Aftermath of "Little Boy" A photograph of the wasteland that remained after the atomic bomb "Little Boy" decimated Hiroshima, Japan, on August 6, 1945.

into Japanese-occupied Manchuria, along the border between China and the Soviet Union. Truman and his aides, frustrated by the refusal of Japanese leaders to surrender and fearful that the Soviet Union's entry would complicate negotiations, ordered a second atomic bomb ("Fat Man") to be dropped.

On August 9, the city of Nagasaki, a shipbuilding center, experienced the same nuclear devastation that had destroyed Hiroshima. An estimated 71,000 people were killed in the city of some 240,000 residents. Although Japanese military leaders wanted to fight on, the emperor decided that defending the homeland against such ghastly new bombs was impossible, and he ordered the military government to surrender. The formal surrender ceremony occurred on an American warship in Tokyo Bay on September 2, 1945, a date quickly known as V-J day.

Bombing of Nagasaki A 20,000-foot-tall mushroom cloud shrouded the city of Nagasaki following the atomic bombing on August 9, 1945.

A New Age Is Born

The Second World War was the costliest conflict in terms of human life and property destroyed in history. The Soviet Union suffered 20 million deaths, China 10 million, Germany 5.6 million, and Japan 2.3 million. The United States suffered 292,000 battle deaths and 114,000 noncombat deaths. In proportion to its population, however, the United States suffered far fewer losses than did the other Allied nations or their enemies. For every American killed in the Second World War, for example, some 59 Soviets died.

The war was the pivotal event of the turbulent twentieth century. It engulfed five continents, leveled cities, reshaped entire societies, transformed international relations, and destroyed German and Italian fascism as well as Japanese militarism. It set in motion the fall of China to communism in 1949 and the outbreak of the Korean War a year later. The colonial empires in Africa and Asia governed by European nations rapidly crumbled as the changes wrought by the war unleashed independence movements. In 1947, for example, the new nations of India and Pakistan liberated themselves from British control. The Soviet Union emerged as a new global superpower, while the United States, as Winston Churchill told the House of Commons, stood "at the summit of the world."

WHY DID THE ALLIES WIN? Many factors contributed to the Allied victory in the Second World War. The American and British leaders—Roosevelt and Churchill—were better at coordinating military efforts and maintaining national morale than were Hitler, Mussolini, and the Japanese emperor, Hirohito. By 1944, Hitler had grown increasingly unstable and unpredictable in his decision making and more withdrawn from the German people, especially after a failed attempt by high-ranking officers to assassinate him that July by placing a bomb under his desk. The blast shattered Hitler's eardrums, riddled his body with wooden splinters, and caused a nervous breakdown that left him paranoid, anxious, and addicted to cocaine injections.

In the end, however, what turned the tide was the awesome productivity of American industry and the ability of the Soviet Union to absorb the massive German invasion and push the Nazis back all the way to Berlin. By the end of the war, Japan had run out of food and Germany had run out of fuel. By contrast, the United States was churning out more of everything. As early as 1942, just a few weeks after the Japanese attack on Pearl Harbor, Fritz Todt, a Nazi engineer, told Hitler that the war against the United States was already lost because of America's ability to outproduce all the other warring nations combined.

THE TRANSFORMATION OF AMERICAN LIFE The war transformed American life by ending the Great Depression and launching a period of unprecedented prosperity. Big businesses during the war grew into gigantic corporations as they benefited from huge government contracts for military weapons, equipment, and supplies. New technologies and products developed for military purposes—radar, computers, electronics, plastics and synthetics, jet engines, rockets, atomic energy—began to transform the private sector, as did new consumer products resulting from war-related innovations. And new opportunities for women as well as for African Americans, Mexican Americans, and other minorities set in motion major social changes that would culminate in the civil rights movement and the feminist movement two decades later.

The expansion of the federal government spurred by the war effort continued after 1945. Presidential authority increased enormously at the expense of congressional and state power. The isolationist sentiment in foreign relations that had been so powerful in the 1920s and 1930s evaporated, as the United States assumed new global responsibilities and economic interests.

In August 1945, President Truman told the nation that the United States had "emerged from this war the most powerful nation in this world—the most powerful nation, perhaps, in all history." But the Soviet Union, despite its profound human losses and physical destruction, had gained much new territory, built massive armed forces, and enhanced its international influence, making it the greatest power in Europe and Asia. A little over a century after Frenchman Alexis de Tocqueville had predicted that Europe would eventually be overshadowed by the United States and Russia, his prophecy had come to pass.

CHAPTER REVIEW

SUMMARY

- **Fascism in Europe**   In Italy, *fascism* took hold under Benito Mussolini, who assumed control of the government in 1922 by promising law and order. Adolf Hitler rearmed Germany in defiance of the Treaty of Versailles and aimed to unite all German speakers in a "Greater Germany." Civil war in Spain and the growth of the Soviet Union under Josef Stalin contributed to a precarious balance of power in Europe during the 1930s. On September 27, 1940, the leaders of Germany, Italy, and Japan signed the Tripartite Pact, which became known as the *Axis alliance*, an agreement to divide the world into spheres of influence they each would conquer and control.

- **From Isolationism to Intervention**   By March 1939, Nazi Germany had annexed Austria and seized Czechoslovakia. Hitler then invaded Poland with the *blitzkrieg* strategy in September 1939, after signing a nonaggression pact with the Soviet Union. At last, the British and French governments declared war. The United States issued "*neutrality laws*" to keep the nation out of war, but with the fall of France in 1940, Roosevelt accelerated military aid to Great Britain through the *Lend-Lease Act* (1941). That year, the United States and Great Britain signed the *Atlantic Charter*, announcing their aims in the war. When Japan announced its intention in July 1941 to take control of French Indochina, President Roosevelt froze Japanese assets in the United States and restricted oil exports to Japan. The frustrated Japanese decided to launch a surprise attack at *Pearl Harbor*, Hawaii, in hopes of destroying the U.S. Pacific Fleet.

- **Mobilization at Home**   The war ended unemployment and the Great Depression. Farmers, too, recovered from hard times, supported by Mexican labor through the *bracero program*. The federal government, through agencies like the *War Production Board*, took control of managing the economy for the war effort. Many women took nontraditional jobs, some in the *Women's Army Corps*. About 1 million African Americans served in the military in segregated units such as the *Tuskegee Airmen*. More than 100,000 Japanese Americans were forced into *war relocation camps*.

- **The Allied Drive to Berlin**   By 1943, the Allies had defeated the German and Italian armies occupying North Africa, then launched attacks on Sicily and the mainland of Italy. Stalin demanded an Allied attack on the Atlantic coast of France, but *Operation Overlord* was delayed until 1944. Invaded from the west and the east, German resistance slowly crumbled. Allied leaders Roosevelt, Churchill, and Stalin met at the *Yalta Conference* in February 1945, where they decided to divide a conquered Germany into occupation zones. In May, Soviet forces captured Berlin and Germany surrendered. After the war, Allied forces discovered the extent of the *Holocaust*—the Nazis' systematic attempt to exterminate the Jews.

- **The Pacific War**   The Japanese advance across the Pacific was halted in June 1942 when the U.S. Navy destroyed much of the Japanese fleet in the *Battle of Midway*. The United States fought costly battles in New Guinea and Guadalcanal before dislodging the Japanese from the Philippines in 1944. Fierce Japanese resistance at Iwo Jima and Okinawa and refusal to surrender led the new president, Harry S. Truman, to drop atomic bombs on the Japanese cities of *Hiroshima* and Nagasaki.

- **A New Age Is Born** The Soviet Union and the United States emerged from the war as global superpowers. Military production had brought America out of the Great Depression and new military technologies changed industrial and private life. The opportunities for women and minorities during the war also increased their aspirations and would contribute to the emergence of the civil rights and feminist movements.

CHRONOLOGY

1933	Hitler becomes chancellor of Germany
1935	Italy invades Ethiopia
1936–1939	Spanish Civil War
1937	Japan launches war against China
1938	Hitler forces the *Anschluss* (union) of Austria and Germany
1939	Soviet Union agrees to a nonaggression pact with Germany
September 1939	German troops invade Poland
1940	Battle of Britain
September 1940	Germany, Italy, and Japan sign the Tripartite Pact
June 1941	Germany invades Soviet Union
August 1941	United States and Great Britain sign the Atlantic Charter
December 7, 1941	Japanese launch surprise attack at Pearl Harbor, Hawaii
June 1942	Battle of Midway
July 1943	Allied forces land on Sicily
June 6, 1944	D-day in France
February 1945	Yalta Conference
May 7, 1945	Nazi Germany surrenders unconditionally
August 1945	Atomic bombs dropped on Hiroshima and Nagasaki

KEY TERMS

fascism p. 1184

neutrality laws p. 1188

Axis alliance p. 1189

blitzkrieg (1940) p. 1194

Lend-Lease Act (1941) p. 1198

Atlantic Charter (1941) p. 1201

Pearl Harbor (1941) p. 1205

War Production Board p. 1207

Women's Army Corps p. 1209

Tuskegee Airmen p. 1212

bracero program (1942) p. 1213

war relocation camps p. 1215

Operation Overload p. 1221

Yalta Conference (1945) p. 1228

Holocaust p. 1230

Battle of Midway p. 1234

Hiroshima (1945) p. 1239

🐰 INQUIZITIVE

Go to InQuizitive to see what you've learned—and learn what you've missed—with personalized feedback along the way.

part seven

THE AMERICAN AGE

As the Second World War was ending in 1945, President Franklin D. Roosevelt, like Woodrow Wilson before him, staked his hopes for a peaceful future on a new international organization, this time called the United Nations rather than the League of Nations. On April 25, 1945, two weeks after Roosevelt's death and two weeks before the German surrender, delegates from fifty nations at war with Germany and Japan met in San Francisco to draw up the Charter of the United Nations. The charter gave the UN Security Council "primary responsibility for the maintenance of international peace and security."

1247

The Security Council included five *permanent* members: the United States, the Soviet Union (replaced by the Russian Federation in 1991), Great Britain, France, and the Republic of China (replaced by the People's Republic of China in 1971). Each permanent member could *veto* any proposed action by the United Nations. It quickly became evident, however, that two members of the Security Council, the United States and the Soviet Union, had such intense differences of opinion about international policies that the United Nations was largely impotent in dealing with the Cold War that shaped postwar politics. As a consequence, the postwar period witnessed neither war nor peace but a constant state of tension.

The United States emerged from the Second World War as the world's greatest military and economic power, the only nation with atomic weapons. While much of Europe and Asia struggled to recover from the human misery and physical devastation of the war, including an acute shortage of working men, the United States was virtually unscathed, its economic infrastructure intact and operating at peak efficiency. Jobs that had been scarce in the 1930s were now available for the taking. By 1955, the United States, with only 6 percent of the world's population, was producing half the world's goods. American capitalism became a dominant cultural force around the world, too. In Europe, Japan, South Korea, and elsewhere, American products, fashion, and forms of entertainment and popular culture attracted excited attention. Henry Luce, the publisher of *Time* and *Life* magazines, proclaimed that the twentieth century had become the "American century."

Yet a deepening "cold war" between the democratic and Communist nations cast a cloud of concern over the postwar world. The ideological combat with the Soviet Union produced numerous foreign crises and sparked a witch hunt for Communists in the United States. After 1945, Republican and Democratic presidents aggressively sought to "contain" the spread of communism around the world. At the same time, the United States and the Soviet Union took advantage of the collapse of European overseas empires in Africa, the Middle East, and Asia to launch a ruthless competition to secure new markets, natural resources, and geopolitical influence in the so-called developing nations.

This containment strategy embroiled the United States in costly wars in Korea and in Southeast Asia. A backlash against the Vietnam War (1964–1973) also inflamed a youth rebellion at home in which militant young idealists not only opposed the war but also provided much of the energy for many overdue social reforms, including racial equality, gay rights, feminism, and environmentalism. The anti-war movement destroyed Lyndon Johnson's presidency in 1968 and provoked a conservative counterattack. President Richard Nixon's paranoid reaction to his critics led to the Watergate affair and the destruction of his presidency.

Through all this turmoil, however, the expanding role of the federal government that Franklin Roosevelt and his New Deal programs had initiated remained essentially intact. With only a few exceptions, both Republicans and Democrats after 1945 acknowledged that the federal government must assume greater responsibility for the welfare of individuals. Even President Ronald Reagan, a sharp critic of federal social welfare programs during the 1980s, recognized the need for the government to provide a "safety net" for those who could not help themselves.

Yet this fragile consensus on public policy and the Cold War had collapsed by the late 1980s amid stunning international developments and social changes at home. The surprising implosion of the Soviet Union in 1989 and the disintegration of European communism left the United States as the only superpower. After forty-five years, U.S. foreign policy was no longer focused on a single adversary. During the early 1990s, East and West Germany reunited; racial segregation (*apartheid*) in South Africa ended; and Israel and the Palestinians, long-standing foes, signed a treaty ending hostilities—at least for a while.

The end of the Cold War and the dissolution of the Soviet Union into Russia and fourteen separate nations lowered the threat of nuclear war and reduced public interest in foreign affairs. Yet numerous ethnic, nationalist, and separatist conflicts brought constant tensions and instability at the end of the twentieth century and into the twenty-first. The United States found itself drawn into political and military crises in faraway lands such as Bosnia, Somalia, Afghanistan, Iraq, Ukraine, and Syria.

Throughout the 1990s, the United States waged a difficult struggle against many groups engaged in organized terrorism. The challenges facing intelligence agencies in tracking the movements of foreign terrorists became tragically evident in 2001. At 8:46 on the morning of September 11, 2001, the world watched in horror as a hijacked commercial airplane slammed into the North Tower of the World Trade Center in New York City. Seventeen minutes later, a second hijacked plane hit the South Tower. While the catastrophe was unfolding in New York City, a third hijacked airliner crashed into the Pentagon in

Washington, D.C., while a fourth, presumably headed for the White House or the Capitol, missed its mark when passengers assaulted the four terrorists, sending the plane out of control and crashing to the ground near Shanksville, Pennsylvania, killing all forty-five people on board.

Within hours of the hijackings, officials identified the nineteen hijackers as members of Al Qaeda (Arabic for "the Base"), a well-financed worldwide network of Islamic terrorists, led by a wealthy Saudi renegade, Osama bin Laden. The new president, Republican George W. Bush, responded by declaring a "war on terror." With the passage of the so-called Patriot Act, Congress gave the president new authority to track down and imprison terrorists at home and abroad. The war on terror began with assaults first on terrorist bases in Afghanistan and then on Saddam Hussein's dictatorship in Iraq (Operation Iraqi Freedom). Yet terrorism proved to be an elusive and resilient foe, and the war in Iraq and the ensuing U.S. military occupation were much longer, more expensive, and less successful than Americans had expected.

The 9/11 terrorist attacks generated a wave of patriotism in the United States, but divisive issues remained. A huge federal debt, rising annual budget deficits, and soaring health-care costs threatened to bankrupt an America that was becoming top-heavy with retirees as the baby boom generation born during and after the Second World War entered its sixties. The "graying of America" had profound social and political implications. It made the tone of political debate more conservative (because older people tend to be more conservative) and exerted increasing stress on health-care costs, nursing-home facilities, and the Social Security system.

The surprising victory of Barack Obama in the 2008 presidential election resulted from people embracing his theme of "hope and change." He pledged to end the wars in Iraq and Afghanistan, unite a divided nation, create a health-care system directed at the uninsured, and provide jobs to the growing numbers of unemployed. As the first African American president, Obama symbolized the societal changes transforming national life in the twenty-first century. Yet no sooner was Obama inaugurated than he inherited the worst economic slowdown since the Great Depression of the 1930s. What came to be called the Great Recession dominated the Obama presidency and, indeed, much of American life, bringing with it a prolonged sense of uncertainty and insecurity. For all its economic power and military might, the United States in the twenty-first century has not eliminated the threat of terrorism or unlocked the mystery of sustaining prosperity in an era of globalization.

That many Americans did not share in the economic recovery and were frustrated by the continuing influx of immigrants, especially Mexicans and Central Americans, and the inability of the politicians in Washington, D.C., to work together to solve problems helps explain the remarkable presidential candidacy of brash real-estate developer Donald Trump. As a self-described "disruptive" political force, he seized control of the 2016 presidential campaign by turning conventional assumptions of America's role abroad and its priorities at home topsy-turvy.

Donald Trump lived up to his pledge to be a disruptive president. He discarded traditional norms of behavior with Congress and the media, and he used executive authority to bypass a Democrat-controlled House of Representatives. He greatly restricted the admission of immigrants and refugees, lowered taxes, appointed conservative justices to the Supreme Court and lower courts, and forged friendships with foreign dictators, from Russia's Vladimir Putin to North Korea's Kim Jong-un.

During Trump's presidency, a series of incidents in which police in various cities killed unarmed Blacks set off massive protest marches across the nation and the world. The demonstrations against police brutality reinvigorated the Black Lives Matter (BLM) movement and triggered counterprotests by White supremacists. That President Trump expressed mixed messages about the legitimacy of White nationalist groups such as the Proud Boys only made a volatile situation more incendiary.

Early in 2020, President Trump and his administration were slow to respond to the onset of the coronavirus pandemic that swept across the world in 2020. Within just a few months, the United States had the highest number of cases and the highest death toll in the world, in large part because President Trump decided it was more important to reopen the U.S. economy than to follow the advice of public health officials in fighting the spread of the virus. Medical experts urged the president and governors to slow the spread of the contagion by closing schools, colleges, and businesses; banning spectator sports and all large gatherings; and requiring the universal wearing of face masks along with the practice of "social distancing," whereby people were asked to stay six feet apart from one another.

More than anything, these two events—the surging coronavirus pandemic and the protests against police brutality—explain why Democrat Joe Biden was able to defeat Donald Trump's bid for a second term in 2020. Biden won the fiercely contested election and immediately set about accelerating the distribution of vaccines to immunize Americans against the coronavirus and pushing through Congress a massive economic stimulus bill intended to revive the sluggish economy.

25 The Cold War and the Fair Deal

1945–1952

Duck and Cover A "duck-and-cover" air-raid drill in 1951 that was commonplace in schools during the Cold War. The drills began in 1949, when the Soviet Union set off its first nuclear weapon. Pictured here are American schoolchildren practicing how to respond to a nuclear attack in February 1951.

N o sooner did the Second World War end than a prolonged "cold war" began between East and West. The awkward wartime alliance between the capitalist United States and the Communist Soviet Union collapsed during the spring and summer of 1945. With the elimination of Nazism, their common enemy, the two strongest nations to emerge from the war became intense ideological rivals who could not bridge their differences over the basic issues of human rights, individual liberties, democratic elections, and religious freedom. Mutual suspicion and a race to gain influence over the "nonaligned" nations of the world in Asia, Africa, the Middle East, and Central and South America further distanced the two former allies. The defeat of Japan and Germany had created power vacuums in Europe and Asia that sucked the Soviet Union and the United States into an unrelenting war of words fed by clashing strategic interests and political ideologies.

The postwar era also saw an eruption of anti-colonial liberation movements in Asia, Africa, and the Middle East that would soon strip Great Britain, France, the Netherlands, and the United States of their global empires. The Philippines, for example, gained its independence from America in 1946. The next year, Great Britain withdrew from Hindu-dominated India after carving out two new Islamic nations, Pakistan and Bangladesh (originally called East Pakistan). The emergence of Communist China (the People's Republic) in 1949 further complicated global politics and the dynamics of the Cold War.

The postwar world was thus an unstable one in which international tensions shaped domestic politics as well as foreign relations. The advent

focus questions

1. Why and how did the Cold War between the United States and the Soviet Union develop?

2. What was the impact of U.S. efforts to contain the Soviet Union and the growth of global communism during Harry Truman's presidency?

3. How did Truman expand the New Deal? How effective was his Fair Deal agenda?

4. What were the major international developments during 1949–1950, and how did they alter U.S. foreign policy?

5. How did the Red Scare emerge? How did it impact American politics and society?

of atomic weapons was both a blessing and a curse. Such weapons of mass destruction made the very idea of warfare unthinkably horrific, which in turn made national leaders more cautious to avoid letting disputes get out of hand. Yet even the mere possibility of nuclear holocaust cast a cloud of anxiety over the postwar era.

TRUMAN AND THE COLD WAR

In April 1945, less than three months after Harry S. Truman had begun his new role as vice president, Eleanor Roosevelt calmly informed him, "Harry, the President is dead." When Truman asked how he could help her, the First Lady replied: "Is there anything we can do for *you*? For you are the one in trouble now."

Michigan's Arthur Vandenberg, a leading Republican senator, noted in his diary after learning of Roosevelt's death, "The gravest question-mark in every American heart is about Truman. Can he swing the job?" He answered his own question: "I believe he can."

Born in 1884 in western Missouri, Truman grew up in Independence, near Kansas City. During the First World War, he served in France as captain of an artillery battery. After the war, he and a partner started a clothing business, but it failed and left him in debt for twenty years. Truman, the only twentieth-century president who did not attend college, then entered politics as a Democrat. In 1934, Missouri voters sent him to the U.S. Senate.

There was nothing extraordinary about Harry Truman except his integrity, decisiveness, and courage. Neither charming nor brilliant, he was impulsive and quick to take offense at critics. Truman was a poor public speaker devoid of eloquence and charisma. He was so nearsighted that he never took his eyes off his text when giving a speech.

When informed that Roosevelt had chosen him as his running mate in 1944, Truman gasped, "Oh, shit!" On his first full day as president, he had a similar reaction, "Boys, if you

Harry S. Truman The successor to Franklin Roosevelt who led the United States through the final phase of World War II.

ever pray, pray for me now," he told reporters. "I don't know whether you fellows ever had a load of hay fall on you, but when they told me yesterday what had happened, I felt like the moon, the stars and all the planets had fallen on me."

Although Washington politicos had low expectations for the new president, Truman did better than anyone expected. He rose above his limitations and never pretended to be something he was not. During a visit to America in 1952, British leader Winston Churchill confessed to Truman that initially he had held him "in very low regard. I loathed your taking the place of Franklin Roosevelt. I misjudged you badly. Since that time, you, more than any other man, have saved Western civilization."

What Churchill saw in Truman was an ordinary man placed in an extraordinary position who succeeded because of his simple faith in the common-sense wisdom of the people.

ORIGINS OF THE COLD WAR Historians have long debated the unanswerable question: Was the United States or the Soviet Union more responsible for starting the Cold War? The conventional view argues that the Soviets, led by Josef Stalin, set out to dominate the globe after 1945, and the United States had no choice but to defend democratic capitalist values.

Historians critical of this explanation insist that the United States unnecessarily antagonized the Soviet Union. Instead of continuing Franklin Roosevelt's collaborative efforts with the Soviets, Truman pursued a confrontational foreign policy that focused on stopping the spread of communism, a policy that only aggravated tensions. For example, the United States in 1947 and 1948 secretly intervened in elections in France and Italy to ensure that Communist candidates were defeated. American agents gave bags of money to anti-Communist candidates, provided campaign advisers, and publicly threatened to cut off aid to the governments if Communists were elected.

In retrospect, the onset of the Cold War seems to have been an unavoidable result of the ideological competition between democratic capitalism and totalitarian communism and their opposing views of what the postwar world should become. America's commitment to free-enterprise capitalism, political self-determination, and religious freedom conflicted with the Soviet Union's preference for controlling its neighbors, ideological conformity, and prohibiting religious practices.

Insecurity drove much of Soviet behavior. Russia, after all, had been invaded by Germany twice in the first half of the twentieth century, and some 23 million people died as a result. Soviet leaders were determined to dominate nations on their borders and in their region, just as the United States had been doing for decades in Central and South America.

The people of Eastern Europe were caught in the middle, and the Cold War soon came to dominate global politics. It was not simply a traditional contest between rival great powers; it was also a global war of ideas, worldviews, and political systems. President George H. W. Bush would later call the Cold War a struggle "for the soul of mankind." Americans are still living in its shadow.

CONFLICTS WITH THE SOVIETS   The wartime military alliance against Nazism disintegrated after 1945 as the Soviet Union violated the promises it had made at the Yalta Conference. Instead of allowing the people living in Eastern European nations—Albania, Bulgaria, Czechoslovakia, Hungary, Poland, Romania—to vote in democratic elections to choose their governments, the Soviets imposed military control and a Communist political system on the nations of Eastern Europe that it had liberated from Nazi control. On May 12, 1945, four days after victory in Europe, Winston Churchill asked Harry Truman: "What is to happen about [Eastern] Europe? An **iron curtain** is drawn down upon [the Russian] front. We do not know what is going on behind [it]." Churchill and Truman wanted to lift the iron curtain and help those nations develop democratic governments. Events during the second half of 1945, however, dashed those expectations.

Beginning in the spring of 1945 and continuing for the next two years, the Soviet Union systematically imprisoned half the European continent and installed puppet governments across Central and Eastern Europe. The Soviets eliminated all political parties except the Communists; created secret police forces; took control of intellectual and cultural life, including the mass media; and organized a process of ethnic cleansing whereby whole populations— 12 million Germans, as well as Poles and Hungarians—were relocated, usually to West Germany or to prisons. Anyone who opposed the Soviet-installed regimes was exiled, silenced, imprisoned, or executed.

Stalin's promise at the Yalta Conference to allow open elections in the nations controlled by Soviet armies had turned out to be a lie. In a fit of candor, he admitted that "a freely elected government in any of these countries would be anti-Soviet, and that we cannot allow."

U.S. secretary of state James F. Byrnes tried to use America's monopoly on the atomic bomb to pressure the Soviets. In April 1945, he suggested to President Truman that nuclear weapons "might well put us in position to dictate our own terms [with the Soviets] at the end of the war." The Soviets, however, paid little attention, in part because their spies had kept them informed of what U.S. scientists had been doing, and in part because they were developing their own atomic bombs.

In April 1945, a few days before the opening of the conference to organize the United Nations, Truman met with Soviet foreign minister Vyacheslav

Molotov. Truman directed Molotov to tell Stalin that the United States expected the Soviet leader to live up to his agreements. "I have never been talked to like that in my life," Molotov angrily replied. "Carry out your agreements," Truman snapped, "and you won't get talked to like that."

That July, when Truman met Stalin at the Potsdam conference, he wrote that he had never seen "such pig-headed people as are the Russians." He later acknowledged that they broke their promises "as soon as the unconscionable Russian Dictator [Stalin] returned to Moscow!" Truman added, with a note of embarrassment, "And I liked the little son of a bitch."

THE CONTAINMENT POLICY

By the beginning of 1947, relations with the Soviet Union had grown ice cold. In February 1946, Stalin had proclaimed the superiority of the Soviet Communist system of government and declared that peace with the United States was impossible "under the present capitalist development of the world economy."

Stalin's provocative statement led the State Department to ask for an analysis of Soviet communism from George Frost Kennan, the best-informed expert on the Soviet Union, who was then working in the U.S. embassy in Moscow.

Kennan responded on February 22, 1946, with a famous 8,000-word "Long Telegram" in which he described the roots of Russian history, the pillars of Soviet policy, Stalin's "neurotic view of world affairs," and Russia's historic determination to protect its western border with Europe. Kennan explained that the Soviet Union was founded on a rigid ideology (Marxism-Leninism) that saw a fundamental conflict between the Communist and capitalist nations. Stalin and other Soviet leaders, he added, could not imagine

George F. Kennan A specialist in the history and values of the Soviet Union, diplomat George Kennan developed the rationale for the containment strategy at the heart of the Truman Doctrine.

"permanent peaceful coexistence" with the capitalist nations. The Soviet goal was to build military strength while promoting tensions between the capitalist democracies and subverting their stability by all possible means.

The best way for the United States to deal with such an ideological foe, Kennan advised, was not military confrontation. Instead, he called for patient, persistent, and firm "strategic" efforts to "contain" Soviet expansionism over the long term, without resorting to war. Creating such "unalterable counterforce," he predicted, would eventually cause "either the breakup or the gradual mellowing of Soviet power" because communism, in Kennan's view, was an unstable system that would eventually collapse if Americans were patient and helped postwar Europe rebuild its economies.

New Secretary of State George C. Marshall, the distinguished commander of the U.S. armed forces during the war, was so impressed by Kennan's analysis that he put him in charge of the State Department Policy Planning office. No other diplomat at the time forecast so accurately what would happen to the Soviet Union some forty years later.

In its broadest dimensions, Kennan's call for the "firm and vigilant **containment** of Russian expansive tendencies" echoed the outlook of Truman and his advisers and would guide U.S. foreign policy for decades. Kennan's careful analysis, however, was vague on several key issues: How exactly were the United States and its allies to "contain" the Soviet Union's expansionist tendencies? How should the United States respond to specific acts of Soviet aggression around the world?

Kennan was an analyst, not a policy maker. He left the task of containing communism to President Truman and his advisers, most of whom, unlike Kennan, viewed containment as a *military* doctrine rather than a *political* strategy. As Truman insisted, "Unless Russia is faced with an iron fist and strong language, another war is in the making." In his view, Stalin and the Soviets only understood one language: the language of military power. "I'm tired of babying the Soviets."

In 1946, civil war broke out in Greece between the monarchy backed by the British and a Communist-led insurgency supported by the Soviets. On February 21, 1947, the British informed the U.S. government that they could no longer provide economic and military aid to Greece and would withdraw their 40,000 troops in five weeks. Truman quickly conferred with congressional leaders. One of them, Senator Aurthur Vandenberg, a powerful Republican from Michigan, warned the president that he would need to "scare the hell out of the American people" about the menace of communism to gain public support for any new aid program.

THE TRUMAN DOCTRINE On March 12, 1947, President Truman responded to the crisis in the eastern Mediterranean by asking Congress to provide $400 million for economic and military assistance to Greece and Turkey. More important, the president announced what came to be known as the **Truman Doctrine**. Because the Communist challenge was worldwide, he declared, it had to be confronted everywhere around the globe. Like a row of dominoes, Truman predicted, the fall of Greece to communism would spread to the other nations of the Middle East, then to Western Europe. To prevent such a catastrophe, he said, the United States must "support free peoples who are resisting attempted subjugation by armed minorities or by outside pressures."

In this single sentence, Truman established the foundation of U.S. foreign policy for the next forty years. In his view, shared by later presidents, the assumptions of the "domino theory" made an aggressive containment strategy against communism a necessity.

Truman's speech generated widespread public support. The *New York Times* said that his message was clear: "The epoch of isolation is ended. It is being replaced by an epoch of American responsibility." At the State Department, Secretary Marshall announced that "we are now concerned with the peace of the entire world."

Still, the secretary of state and others privately feared that the "flamboyant anticommunism" in Truman's speech was unnecessarily provocative. Marshall believed that the president was overstating the Soviet threat. Others expressed concern about the scope and vagueness of the Truman Doctrine. George Kennan cringed at the president's "grandiose" commitment to contain communism *everywhere*. In Kennan's view, Truman's "militarized view of the Cold War" was a foolish crusade that knew no limits. Such efforts needed to be selective rather than universal, political and economic rather than military in nature. For all its power, he noted, the United States could not intervene in every "hot spot" around the world.

Kennan saw no need to provide military aid to Turkey, where no Communist threat existed. And he preferred that economic assistance, not weapons, be provided to Greece. In his view, the Soviet threat was primarily political, not military, in nature.

Truman and his advisers rejected such concerns. In 1947, Congress approved the president's request for aid to Greece and neighboring Turkey. The Truman Doctrine marked the beginning of a contest that the former presidential adviser Bernard Baruch named in a 1947 speech to the legislature of South Carolina: "Let us not be deceived—today we are in the midst of a *cold war*."

THE MARSHALL PLAN In the spring of 1947, postwar Europe remained broke, shattered, and desperate. Factories had been bombed to rubble; railroads and bridges had been destroyed. People were starving for food and for jobs, and political unrest was growing. By 1947, Socialist and Communist parties were emerging in many European nations struggling to recover after the war, including Italy, France, and Belgium. The crisis in postwar Europe required bold action.

While giving a graduation speech at Harvard University in May, Secretary of State George C. Marshall, building upon suggestions given to him by George Kennan, called for a massive U.S. program to provide financial and technical assistance to rescue Europe, as well as the Soviet Union. What came to be known as the **Marshall Plan** was "directed not against country or doctrine, but against hunger, poverty, desperation, and chaos."

The Marshall Plan sought to reconstruct the European economy, neutralize Communist insurgencies, and build up secure foreign markets for American products. As Truman said, "The American [capitalist] system can survive only if it is part of a world system." The Marshall Plan was about more than economics, however. It was also part of Truman's effort to contain the expansionist tendencies of the Soviet Union by reestablishing a strong Western Europe anchored in American values. The Americans, said a British official, "want an integrated Europe looking like the United States of America."

In December 1947, Truman submitted Marshall's proposal to a special session of Congress, saying that "if Europe fails to recover" from the war's devastation, voters might be won over by Communist parties, which would deal a "shattering blow to peace and stability." Initially, Republican critics dismissed the plan as "New Dealism"

All Our Colors to the Mast As part of the Marshall Plan, thirteen European nations participated in the Intra-European Poster Competition in 1950. Organized around the theme "Intra-European Cooperation for a Better Standard of Living," this poster by Dutch artist Reyn Dirksen was selected as the winner out of 10,000 submissions.

for Europe. However, two months later, on February 25, 1948, a Communist-led coup in Czechoslovakia, the last nation in Eastern Europe with a democratic government, ensured congressional passage of the Marshall Plan, for it seemed to confirm the immediate Communist threat to Western Europe.

The Marshall Plan exceeded all expectations. From 1948 until 1951, the plan provided $13 billion to sixteen European nations to revive their war-ravaged economies. The Soviet Union, however, refused to participate, calling it "dollar imperialism," and forced the Eastern European countries under its control to refuse as well. The Marshall Plan returned prosperity to Europe. By 1951, Western Europe's industrial production had soared to 40 percent above prewar levels, and its farm output was larger than ever. England's *Economist* magazine called the Marshall Plan "an act without peer in history."

THE BERLIN BLOCKADE The Marshall Plan drew the nations of Western Europe closer together, but it increased tensions with the Soviet Union, for Josef Stalin saw the American effort to rebuild the European economy as a way to weaken Soviet influence in the region.

The breakdown of the wartime alliance between the United States and the Soviet Union also left the problem of postwar Germany unsettled. In 1945, Berlin, the German capital, had been divided into four sectors, or zones, each governed by one of the four principal allied nations—the United States, France, Great Britain, and the Soviet Union.

The German economy languished, requiring the U.S. Army to provide food and supplies to millions of civilians. Slowly, the German occupation zones evolved into functioning governments. In 1948, the British, French, and Americans united their three administrative zones into one and developed a common currency for West Germany and West Berlin, a city of 2.5 million people, which was more than 100 miles inside the Soviet occupation zone of East Germany. The West Germans also organized state governments and began drafting a federal constitution.

The political unification and economic recovery of West Germany infuriated Stalin, and the status of divided Berlin had become a flash point for both sides. In March 1948, Stalin prevented the new West German currency from being used in Berlin. Then, on June 23, he stopped all road, rail, and water traffic into West Berlin. He hoped the blockade would force the United States and its allies to leave the divided city.

The Americans interpreted Stalin's aggressive blockade as a tipping point in the Cold War. "When Berlin falls," predicted General Lucius D. Clay, the U.S. Army commander in Germany, "western Germany will be next. Communism will run rampant." The United States thus faced a dilemma fraught with dangers: risk a third world war by using force to break the Soviet blockade or begin a humiliating retreat from West Berlin.

Truman, who prided himself on his decisiveness, made clear his stance: "We stay in Berlin—period." In response to the Soviet blockade, he announced an embargo against all goods exported from Soviet-controlled eastern Germany. To provide West Berliners with desperately needed food and supplies, the United States and its allies organized a massive air lift of material into West Berlin. Their doing so brought them to the edge of conflict with the Soviet Union. Truman noted solemnly in his diary: "We are very close to war."

By October 1948, the U.S. and Allied air forces were landing cargo planes every few minutes at the Berlin airport, flying in 7,000 tons of food, fuel, medicine, coal, and equipment each day. The **Berlin airlift** went on daily for 321 days without any shots being fired. Finally, on May 12, 1949, the Soviets lifted the blockade, in part because bad Russian harvests made them desperate for food grown in western Germany.

The Berlin airlift was the first major "victory" for the West in the Cold War, and the unprecedented efforts of the United States, Great Britain, and France to supply West Berliners transformed most of them into devoted allies. In May 1949, the Federal Republic of Germany (West Germany) was founded. In October,

Family Reunion A girl gives her grandmother a kiss through the barbed-wire fence that divided the Dutch-German frontier in 1947.

Through the Iron Curtain German children greet a U.S. cargo plane with waves and cheers as it prepares to land in West Berlin to drop off much-needed food and supplies.

the Soviet-controlled German Democratic Republic (East Germany) came into being.

FORMING ALLIANCES The Soviet blockade of Berlin convinced the United States and its allies that they needed to act together to stop further Communist expansion into Western Europe. On April 4, 1949, representatives of twelve nations met in Washington, D.C., to sign the North Atlantic Treaty: the United States, Great Britain, France, Belgium, the Netherlands, Luxembourg, Canada, Denmark, Iceland, Italy, Norway, and Portugal. Greece and Turkey joined the alliance in 1952, West Germany in 1955, and Spain in 1982.

The **North Atlantic Treaty Organization (NATO)**, the largest defensive alliance in the world, declared that an attack against any of the members would be an attack against all. The creation of NATO marked the high point of efforts to contain Soviet expansion. By joining NATO, the United States committed itself to go to war on behalf of its allies. Isolationism was dead.

REORGANIZING THE MILITARY The onset of the Cold War and the emergence of nuclear weapons led President Truman to sign the **National Security Act** (1947), which reorganized the armed forces and intelligence agencies. It renamed the War Department the Department of Defense led by a new cabinet officer, the secretary of defense. The act also created a Joint Chiefs

THE OCCUPATION OF GERMANY AND AUSTRIA

- How did the Allies divide Germany and Austria at the Yalta Conference?
- What was the "iron curtain"?
- Why did the Allies airlift supplies to Berlin?

of Staff to oversee the three military branches—the army, navy, and the newly created air force; and it established the National Security Council (NSC), a group of top specialists in international relations appointed to advise the president. The act also established the Central Intelligence Agency (CIA) to coordinate global intelligence-gathering activities. The following year, the NSC gave the CIA permission to launch covert operations abroad to undermine governments that threatened American interests.

A NEW JEWISH NATION: ISRAEL At the same time that the United States was forming new alliances, it was helping to form a new nation.

Palestine, the biblical Holy Land, had been a British protectorate since 1919. For hundreds of years, Jews throughout the world had dreamed of returning to their ancestral Israeli homeland and its ancient capital Zion, a part of Jerusalem. Many Zionists—Jews who wanted a separate Jewish nation—had migrated there. More arrived during and after the Nazi persecution of European Jews. Hitler's effort to exterminate Jews convinced many that their only hope for a secure future was to create their own nation.

Late in 1947, the United Nations voted to divide (partition) Palestine into separate Jewish and Arab states. The Jews agreed to the partition, but the Arabs opposed it. Palestine was their ancestral home, too; Jerusalem was as holy to Muslims and Christians as it was to Jews.

Arabs viewed the creation of a Jewish nation in Palestine as an act of war, and they attacked Israel in early 1948. Hundreds were killed before the Haganah (Jewish militia) won control of most of Palestine. When British oversight of Palestine officially expired on May 14, 1948, David Ben-Gurion, the Jewish leader in Palestine, proclaimed Israel's independence. President Harry Truman officially recognized the new Israeli nation within minutes, and the Soviet Union did so soon thereafter.

The creation of Israel deepened and complicated America's involvement in the Middle East. No solution to the Palestine question would satisfy both parties. Supporting the Jews risked alienating Arab leaders whose countries contained the bulk of the world's oil deposits. Secretary of State George C. Marshall adamantly opposed Truman's decision, arguing that the creation of an Israeli nation would ignite war in the Middle East. Marshall believed that Truman acted as he did to gain Jewish votes in the 1948 presidential election. He told the president in early May 1948, "If you [recognize the state of Israel] and if I were to vote in the election, I would vote against you."

Marshall's objections made no difference to the 1 million Jews, most of them European immigrants, who now had their own nation. Early the next morning, however, as Secretary of State Marshall predicted, the Arab League nations—Lebanon, Syria, Iraq, Jordan, and Egypt—invaded Israel. Mediators from the United Nations gradually worked out a truce, restoring an unstable peace by May 11, 1949, when Israel joined the United Nations. Israel kept all its conquered territories, including the whole Palestine coast.

The Palestinian Arabs lost everything. Most became stateless refugees who scattered into neighboring Lebanon, Jordan, and Egypt. Stored-up resentments and sporadic warfare between Israel and the Arab states have festered since, complicating U.S. foreign policy, which has tried to maintain friendships with both sides but has usually tilted toward Israel.

EXPANDING THE NEW DEAL

For the most part, Republicans and Democrats in Congress cooperated with President Harry Truman on issues related to the Cold War. On domestic issues, however, Truman faced widespread opposition, as cost-cutting Republicans hoped that they could end the New Deal programs created by Franklin Roosevelt. As a brand-new president, Truman thought otherwise as he guided the nation's "complicated and difficult" transition from war to peace.

FROM WAR TO PEACE   In September 1945, Truman called Congress into a special emergency session at which he presented a twenty-one-point program to guide the nation's "reconversion" from wartime to peacetime. His greatest challenge was to ensure that the peacetime economy absorbed the millions of men and women who had served in the armed forces and were now seeking civilian jobs.

That would not be easy. The day after the war with Japan ended, the federal government canceled 100,000 contracts for military supplies and weaponry. Within hours, the Springfield Armory in Massachusetts, which had manufactured weapons for the army, fired every worker. Other military-dependent companies also announced layoffs.

The nation faced a crisis as some 12 million men and women left military service and returned to an economy careening into recession. The end of the war initially wreaked havoc with the economy. Many women who had been recruited to work in wartime defense industries were shoved out as men took off uniforms and looked for jobs. At a shipyard in California, a foreman gathered the women workers and told them to go welcome the troop ships as they pulled into port from Asia. "We were thrilled. We all waved," recalled one of the women. Then, the next day, the women were laid off to make room for male veterans.

Still, several shock absorbers cushioned the economic impact of demobilization. They included federal unemployment insurance (and other Social Security benefits) and the Servicemen's Readjustment Act of 1944, known as the GI Bill of Rights, under which the federal government provided $13 billion for military veterans to use for education, vocational training, medical treatment, unemployment insurance, and loans for building houses and starting new businesses.

With the war over, veterans eagerly returned to colleges, jobs, wives and husbands. Marriage rates soared. So, too, did population growth, which had dropped off sharply in the 1930s. Americans born in the two decades after 1945 composed what came to be called the baby boom generation, a disproportionately large group that would shape the nation's social and cultural life throughout the second half of the twentieth century and after.

Truman's program to ensure a smooth transition to a peacetime economy included proposals for unemployment insurance to cover more workers, a higher minimum wage, the construction of massive low-cost public housing projects, regional development projects modeled on the Tennessee Valley Authority to put military veterans to work, and much more. A powerful Republican congressman named Joseph W. Martin was stunned by the scope of Truman's proposals. "Not even President Roosevelt," he gasped, "ever asked for so much at one sitting."

Truman's primary goal was to "prevent prolonged unemployment" while avoiding the "bitter mistakes" made after the First World War that had produced wild inflation in consumer prices and a recession. To do so, he also wanted to retain, for a year or so, the wartime controls on wages, prices, and rents, as well as the rationing of scarce food items.

On-the-Job Training An advertisement aimed at young veterans promotes the GI Bill of Rights' professional resources, intended to help military veterans enter the civilian workforce.

Congress responded by approving the Employment Act of 1946, which authorized the federal government "to promote maximum employment, production, and purchasing power."

Yet other than the Employment Act, most of Truman's proposed programs did not gain congressional approval. Throughout 1946, Republicans and conservative southern Democrats in Congress balked at the president's efforts to revive or expand New Deal programs. Liberals were disappointed by Truman's inability to win over skeptical legislators. "Alas for Truman," said the *New Republic*, there was "no bugle note in his voice" to rally public opinion. "What one misses," said journalist Max Lerner, "is the confident sense of direction that Roosevelt gave, despite all the contradictions of his policy."

WAGES, PRICES, AND LABOR UNREST The most acute economic problem Harry Truman faced was the postwar spike in prices for consumer goods. During the war, the government had frozen wages and prices—and banned strikes by labor unions. Truman's decision in June 1946 to remove wartime controls on wages and consumer prices caused consumer prices to spike, which led labor unions to demand pay increases. When management balked at providing higher wages, more than 4,000 strikes at automobile plants, steel mills, coal mines, and railroads erupted in 1945–1946, involving some 5 million workers. Never before or since had so many employees walked off the job in one year.

Like Theodore Roosevelt before him, Truman grew frustrated with the stubbornness of both management and labor leaders. He took federal control of the coal mines, whereupon the mine owners agreed to union demands. Truman also seized control of the railroads and won a five-day postponement of a strike. When the union leaders refused to make further concessions, however, the president decried their "obstinate arrogance" and threatened to draft striking railroad workers into the armed forces. A few weeks later, the unions backed down and returned to work, having won healthy improvements in wages and benefits. By taking such a hard line, however, Truman lost the support of unionists, a key constituency within the Democratic party coalition.

The backlash over postwar inflation led Truman to restore government controls on particular consumer items such as meat. This only led to more complaints. Ranchers were so upset that they refused to sell their cattle for slaughter. Suddenly, there was a "beefsteak" crisis as consumers complained that the supply of food was worse than it had been during the war. *Time* magazine's Washington-based political reporter alerted his editor that Truman was so unpopular "he could not carry Missouri now."

POLITICAL COOPERATION AND CONFLICT During the congressional election campaigns in 1946, Republicans adopted a simple, four-word slogan: "Had Enough? Vote Republican!" Using loudspeakers, Republicans drove through city streets saying, "Ladies, if you want meat, vote Republican." Others quipped, "To err is Truman."

At the same time, wage workers rebelled against the president. A labor union leader tagged Truman "the No. 1 Strikebreaker," while much of the public, upset by the unions, price increases, food shortages, and scarcity of automobiles and affordable housing, blamed the strikes on the White House.

Labor unions had emerged from the war with more power than ever, for blue-collar workers were essential to military victory. The National Labor Relations Act (NLRA) of 1935 had also helped ensure the rights of workers to form and join unions. As a consequence, by 1945 some 14.5 million workers, more than a third of the manufacturing workforce, were unionized. Members had tended to vote Democratic, but not in the 1946 elections, for union members viewed Truman as their enemy. Their votes gave the Republicans majorities in both houses of Congress for the first time since 1928. Even many Democrats had soured on Truman, circulating a slogan that expressed their frustration: "I'm just Mild about Harry."

The new Republican-controlled Congress that convened in early 1947 sought to curb the power of unions by passing the **Taft-Hartley Labor Act** (officially called the Labor-Management Relations Act). The law gutted many of the provisions of the NLRA by allowing employers to campaign against efforts to form unions, and outlawing unions from coercing workers to join or refusing to negotiate grievances.

The Taft-Hartley Act also required union leaders to take "loyalty oaths" declaring that they were not members of the Communist party; banned strikes by federal government employees; and imposed a "cooling-off" period of eighty days on any strike that the president deemed dangerous to the public welfare. Yet the most troubling element of the new bill for unions was a provision that allowed state legislatures to pass "right-to-work" laws that ended the practice of forcing all workers to join a union once a majority voted to unionize. William Green, the president of the American Federation of Labor (AFL), proclaimed that the true purpose of the Taft-Hartley Act was "to destroy unions and to wreck collective bargaining."

Truman vetoed the Taft-Hartley Act, denouncing it as "bad for labor, bad for management, and bad for the country." Working-class Democrats were delighted. Many unionists who had voted Republican in 1946 now returned to the Democrats. Journalist James Wechsler reported that "Mr. Truman has

Fight for Desegregation Demonstrators led by African America activist A. Philip Randolph *(left)* picket the Democratic National Convention on July 12, 1948, calling for racial integration of the armed forces.

reached the crucial fork in the road and turned unmistakably to the left." Congress, however, overrode the president's veto, and Taft-Hartley became law, largely because southern Democrats overwhelmingly supported it. Southern conservatives adamantly opposed the formation of unions. They feared that unions would disrupt the profitability of the southern textile industry and exert pressure against the tradition of racial segregation.

The number of strikes dropped sharply as a result of the Taft-Hartley Act, as representatives of management and labor were forced to work together. By 1954, fifteen state legislatures, mainly in the South and West, had used the Taft-Hartley Act to pass right-to-work laws deterring the formation of unions. Those states thereafter recruited industries to relocate because of their low wages and nonunion policies. As the Republicans celebrated, however, they did not realize that the Taft-Hartley Act would cause most union members to vote Democratic in 1948.

CIVIL RIGHTS DURING THE 1940S AND 1950S Another of Truman's challenges in postwar labor relations was the bigotry faced by returning African American soldiers. When one Black veteran arrived home in a uniform decorated with medals, a White neighbor yelled, "Don't you forget . . . that you're still a [Negro]." Another Black veteran was yanked off a bus in South Carolina and beaten so badly in a jail cell that he was blinded.

The Second World War, however, did improve America's overall racial landscape. As a *New York Times* editorial explained in early 1946, "This is a particularly good time to campaign against the evils of bigotry, prejudice, and race hatred because we have witnessed the defeat of enemies who tried to found a mastery of the world upon such cruel and fallacious policy."

African Americans had fought to overthrow the Nazi regime of government-sponsored racism, and many returning Black veterans were unwilling to put up with racial abuse at home. The Cold War also gave political leaders added incentive to improve race relations. The Soviets often compared racism in the United States to the Nazis' brutalization of Jewish people. In the ideological contest against capitalism, Communists highlighted examples of racism to win influence among newly emerging African nations.

Harry Truman was an unlikely civil rights crusader. As a Missouri farm boy raised by Confederate sympathizers, he grew up surrounded by racism, and both sets of his grandparents owned slaves. In 1911, Truman revealed his bigotry in a letter to his girlfriend and future wife, Bess Wallace:

> I think one man is just as good as another so long as he's honest and
> decent and not a [Negro] or a Chinaman. Uncle Will says that the Lord

made a White man from dust, a [Negro] from mud, and then threw what was left and it came down a Chinaman. He does hate Chinese and [Japanese]. So do I. It is race prejudice I guess. But I am strongly of the opinion that negroes ought to be in Africa, yellow men in Asia, and White men in Europe and America.

Yet Truman's outlook on racial issues evolved with the times—and with his growing desire to court African American voters once in office.

Black veterans often risked their lives when protesting racial bigotry. In 1946, a White mob in rural Georgia gunned down two African American couples. One of the murderers explained that George Dorsey, one of the victims, was "a good [Negro]" until he went into the army. "But when he came out, he thought he was as good as any white people."

In the fall of 1946, a delegation of civil rights activists urged President Truman to condemn the Ku Klux Klan and the lynching of African Americans. The delegation graphically described incidents of torture and intimidation against Blacks in the South. Truman was horrified: "My God! I had no idea that it was as terrible as that! We've got to do something."

Such horrific racial incidents so shocked Truman that he appointed a Committee on Civil Rights to investigate violence against African Americans and strengthen and safeguard their civil rights. Southern Democrats were infuriated. A Mississippi congressman claimed that Truman "had seen fit to run a political dagger into our backs" by intervening in southern race relations.

A year later, in 1947, the committee issued a report, *To Secure These Rights*, which called for a federal anti-lynching bill, abolition of the poll tax designed to keep poor Blacks from voting, a voting rights act, an end to racial segregation in the armed forces, and a ban on racial segregation in public transportation. Truman declared that the federal government under his leadership would become "a friendly, vigilant defender of the rights and equalities of all Americans." When the president finished his public remarks about the committee's report, he turned to a Black leader and said, "I mean every word of it—and I am going to prove that I do mean it." The leading African American magazine, *The Crisis*, called Truman's remarks the best speech on civil rights by an American president.

On July 26, 1948, Truman took a bolder step by banning racial discrimination throughout the federal government. Four days later, he issued an executive order ending racial segregation in the armed forces. Desegregating the military was, Truman claimed, "the greatest thing that ever happened to America." White southerners disagreed. Democratic Mendel Rivers, the powerful South Carolina congressman, boasted that Truman "is a dead bird" as far as being reelected. "We in the South are going to see to that."

JACKIE ROBINSON Meanwhile, racial segregation was being dismantled in a much more public area than the federal government: professional baseball. In April 1947, the Brooklyn Dodgers roster included the first African American to play major league baseball in the modern era: Jack Roosevelt "Jackie" Robinson. He was born in 1919 in a Georgia sharecropper's cabin, the grandson of slaves. Six months later, his father left, never to return. Robinson's mother moved the family to Pasadena, California, where Jackie became a marvelous all-around athlete. At UCLA, Robinson was the first student in school history to letter in four sports: baseball, basketball, football, and track. After serving in the army during World War II, he began playing professional baseball in the so-called Negro Leagues. Major league scouts reported that he could play in the big leagues.

Branch Rickey, president and general manager of the Brooklyn Dodgers, interviewed Robinson for three hours on August 28, 1945. Rickey asked Robinson if he could face racial abuse without losing his temper. Robinson was shocked: "Are you looking for a Negro who is afraid to fight back?" Rickey replied that he needed a "Negro player [with] guts enough *not* to fight back." Robinson assured him he was the best candidate to integrate baseball.

Jackie Robinson Robinson's unfaltering courage and skill prompted the integration of other sports, drawing African American and Latino spectators to the games. Here, he greets his Dominican fans at Trujillo High School in Santo Domingo.

After signing Robinson to a contract for $600 a month, Rickey explained to his critics that he had found a terrific player of incomparable courage capable of looking the other way when provoked. And Robinson was often provoked—on the field and on the road. Soon after Robinson arrived for preseason practice, many of his White teammates refused to take the field with him. Manager Leo Durocher told the team, "I don't care if the guy is yellow or black, or if he has stripes. . . . I'm the manager of this team, and I say he plays."

During the 1947 season, teammates and opposing players viciously baited Robinson. Pitchers hit him, baserunners spiked him, and spectators booed him and even threatened to kill him. Hotels refused him rooms, and restaurants denied him service. Hate mail arrived by the bucketful. One sportswriter called Robinson "the loneliest man I have ever seen in sports." On the other hand, Black spectators loved Robinson's courageous example and turned out in droves to watch him play. A headline in a Boston newspaper expressed the prevailing sentiment: "Triumph of Whole Race Seen in Jackie's Debut in Major League Ball."

As time passed, Robinson won over many fans and players with his courage, wit, grit, and talent. Sportswriter Red Smith observed that Robinson was an example of "the unconquerable doing the impossible." During his first season with the Dodgers, Robinson led the National League in stolen bases and was named Rookie of the Year. Between 1949 and 1954, he had a batting average of .327, among the best in baseball. Robinson's very presence on the field forced spectators sitting in racially divided bleachers to confront the hypocritical reality of segregation. Other teams soon began signing Black players. In 1947, Robinson was voted the second most popular American, behind singer Bing Crosby. "My life," Robinson remembered, "produced understanding among whites, and it gave black people the idea that if I could do it, they could do it, too, that blackness wasn't subservient to anything." Robinson eventually became the highest paid Brooklyn Dodger in history.

MEXICAN AMERICANS In the Far West, Mexican Americans (often grouped with other Spanish-speaking immigrants as *Hispanics* or *Latinos*) continued to experience ethnic prejudice after the war. Schools in Arizona, New Mexico, Texas, and California routinely segregated Mexican American children from Whites. The 500,000 Hispanic military veterans were especially frustrated that their efforts in the armed forces did not bring equality at home. "We had paid our dues," said one war veteran, yet nothing had changed. Hispanics were frequently denied access to educational, medical, and housing benefits made available to White veterans. Some mortuaries even denied funeral services to Mexican Americans killed in combat. As a funeral director

Hector Perez Garcia Photographed alongside President Ronald Reagan, Garcia attends the American GI Forum in El Paso, Texas. He advocated education and equal treatment of all Americans, eventually earning the Presidential Medal of Freedom.

in Texas explained, "The Anglo people would not stand for it."

To fight such prejudicial treatment, Mexican American veterans led by Dr. Hector Perez Garcia, a U.S. Army major who had served as a combat surgeon, organized the American GI Forum in Texas in 1948, with branches throughout Texas and across the nation. Garcia, born in Mexico in 1914 and raised in Texas, stressed the importance of formal education to Mexican Americans. The new organization's motto proclaimed: "Education Is Our Freedom and Freedom Should Be Everybody's Business." At a time when Mexican Americans in Texas averaged no more than a third-grade education, Garcia and five of his siblings were exceptional, each having completed medical school and become a physician. Yet upon Major Garcia's return from the war, he encountered "discrimination everywhere. We had no opportunities. We had to pay [poll taxes] to vote. We had segregated schools. We were not allowed to go into public places."

Garcia and the GI Forum initially focused on veterans' issues but soon expanded the organization's scope to include fostering equal treatment for all people. The GI Forum lobbied to end poll taxes, sued for the right of Latinos to serve on juries, and developed schools for jobless veterans. In 1984, President Ronald Reagan bestowed on Garcia the Presidential Medal of Freedom, the nation's highest civilian honor.

"OPERATION WETBACK" (1954) Anti-Mexican sentiment simmered throughout the postwar era until it boiled over in 1955, during the Eisenhower presidency. Texas residents fastened onto the racial slur "wetbacks" to refer to Mexicans who entered the United States illegally by crossing the Rio Grande. Although employing undocumented immigrants was technically illegal, authorities often turned a blind eye to violations. Texan Harlon Carter, head of the Border Patrol, who as a youth had killed a Mexican teen after an argument, convinced President Eisenhower to launch a massive effort—"Operation Wetback"—to capture and deport undocumented Mexicans.

Led by General Joseph Swing, head of the Immigration and Naturalization Service (INS), the operation was planned like a military assault. Some 750 Border Patrol agents swept through factories, farms, ranches, restaurants, and other workplaces employing Mexicans, arresting some 300,000 undocumented workers and trucking them to detention camps for deportation.

American officials arranged with the Mexican government to transport the detainees by train or truck to southern Mexico, hundreds of miles from the American border. Because most of the deportees were not from southern Mexico, they were left stranded, without food or water, and without friends or families to take them in. Scores of them died.

Harlon Carter bragged that Operation Wetback was "the biggest drive against illegal aliens in history." Swing and the INS called the massive dragnet a great success and announced that the U.S.-Mexican border "had been secured." Like the similar federal effort during the 1930s, however, Operation Wetback involved frequent violations of civil rights and wrongly deported many U.S. citizens in the process. Journalists depicted the ruthless side of Operation Wetback,

"Operation Wetback" President Eisenhower launched "Operation Wetback" in 1954 to capture and deport undocumented Mexicans. The racial slur "wetbacks" referred to Mexicans who illegally entered the United States by crossing the Rio Grande. Some 300,000 Mexicans were transported by train or truck to Mexico.

showing detained men herded into crude holding pens in city parks before being loaded on buses and trains and sent back to Mexico.

During congressional hearings about Operation Wetback, the following exchange occurred between Senator Lyndon Baines Johnson of Texas and General Swing:

> Senator Johnson: General, do you have a Mexican maid?
> General Swing: I certainly do.
> Senator Johnson: Was she recruited through the Immigration Service?
> General Swing: [She] is a Mexican maid who was serving in a restaurant in Juarez, and while I was on one of my inspection trips down in El Paso, I said to the district director, "It is hard to get a maid in Washington! Wondering if there is any little Mexican girl over in Juarez who would like to immigrate and come over and go to work for me."

General Swing's "little Mexican girl" comment reflected the widespread condescension displayed toward Mexicans by government officials.

SHAPING THE FAIR DEAL   By early 1948, after three years in the White House, President Truman had yet to shake the widespread impression that he was a hapless successor to the celebrated Franklin Roosevelt. The editors of *Time* magazine reflected the national sentiment when they wrote, "Mr. Truman has often faced his responsibilities with a cheerful, dogged courage. But his performance was almost invariably awkward, uninspired, and above all, mediocre." Voters, they added, believed that Truman "means well, but he doesn't do well."

Most political analysts assumed that the president would lose his race to win a second term in November. The *New York Times* reported in April 1948 that Truman's "influence is weaker than any president's in modern history." That the Democratic party was splitting in two did not help his reelection chances: southern conservatives resented Truman's outspoken support of civil rights, while the left wing of the party criticized his firing of Secretary of Commerce Henry A. Wallace in September 1946 for openly criticizing the administration's anti-Soviet policies.

Virtually everyone predicted a Truman defeat in 1948. "Never was there such a mess," Truman told his mother. "The President," predicted the *United States News*, "is a one-termer." When asked how he planned to deal with an Eightieth Congress dominated by Republicans, Truman said he intended to do "as I damn please for the next two years and to hell with them."

Predictions of a Truman defeat in 1948 did not faze the combative president. He mounted an intense campaign. His first step was to shore up the major elements of the New Deal coalition of working-class voters: farmers, labor unionists, and African Americans. In his 1948 State of the Union message, Truman announced that the programs he would later call his "**Fair Deal**" (to distinguish his new domestic program from Roosevelt's New Deal) would offer something to nearly every group the Democrats hoped to attract as voters. The first goal, Truman said, was to ensure civil rights for all Americans. He added proposals to increase federal aid to education, expand unemployment and retirement benefits, create a system of national health insurance, enable more rural people to connect to electricity, and increase the minimum wage.

THE SURPRISE ELECTION OF 1948   The Republican-controlled Congress dismissed President Truman's proposals, an action it would later regret. At the Republican convention, moderate New York governor Thomas E. Dewey, who had lost to Roosevelt in 1944, won the presidential nomination on the third ballot. While the party's platform endorsed most New Deal reforms and approved the administration's bipartisan

Birth of the Dixiecrats Alabama delegates boo Truman's announcement of his civil rights platform before walking out of the 1948 Democratic National Convention.

foreign policy, Dewey promised to run things more efficiently and promote civil rights for all.

In July, glum Democrats gathered in Philadelphia. A reporter wrote that they behaved "as though they [had] accepted an invitation to a funeral." At the convention, some party leaders, including Franklin Roosevelt's son James, a California congressman, tried to convince Dwight Eisenhower to accept the Democratic nomination. The popular war hero declined all offers.

Delegates who expected to do little more than go through the motions of nominating Truman were doubly surprised, first by the battle on the convention floor over civil rights and then by Truman's endorsement of civil rights in his acceptance speech. Liberal Democrats led by Minnesota's Hubert Humphrey commended Truman "for his courageous stand" and declared that the "time has arrived for the Democratic party to get out of the shadow of civil rights." White delegates from Alabama and Mississippi walked out in protest. The solidly Democratic South had fractured over race.

On July 17, a group of rebellious southern Democrats organized their own convention in Birmingham, Alabama. While waving Confederate flags and singing "Dixie," they nominated South Carolina's segregationist governor, Strom Thurmond, on a States' Rights Democratic party ticket, whose members were quickly dubbed the "**Dixiecrats**."

Thurmond, a cocky White supremacist, had secretly fathered a child with a Black housekeeper. He later paid hush money to his biracial daughter, denounced Truman's civil rights initiatives, and championed states' rights against federal efforts to change the tradition of White supremacy in the South. He warned that there were "not enough troops in the U.S. Army to force the Southern people to . . . admit the Negro race into our theaters, into our swimming pools, into our homes and into our churches." As the editor of the *Atlanta Journal* noted, the Dixiecrat party was "really the anti-Negro party."

On July 23, militant liberals abandoned the Democrats to form a new third party—the Progressives—and nominated Henry A. Wallace, FDR's former vice president, whom Truman had fired as secretary of commerce. Wallace charged that both major parties were recklessly provoking a confrontation with the Soviet Union.

The splits in the Democratic ranks seemed to spell doom for Truman, but he refused to give in. He aroused the faithful by promising, "I will win this election and make the Republicans like it!" He pledged to bring Congress into special session and demand that it confront the housing crisis and boost the minimum wage.

Within days, Truman set out on a 22,000-mile transcontinental train tour, making 351 speeches scolding the "do-nothing, good-for-nothing"

THE ELECTION OF 1948

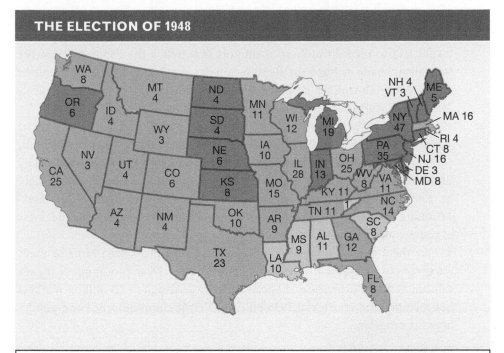

	Electoral Vote	Popular Vote
Harry S. Truman (Democrat)	**303**	**24,200,000**
Thomas E. Dewey (Republican)	189	22,000,000
J. Strom Thurmond (States' Rights Democrat)	39	1,200,000

- Why did the political experts predict a Dewey victory?
- Why was civil rights such a divisive issue at the Democratic Convention?
- How did the candidacies of Strom Thurmond and Henry Wallace end up helping Truman win the presidency?

Republican-controlled Congress. The plain-talking president attracted huge crowds. The Republicans, he charged, "have the propaganda and the money, but we have the people, and the people have the votes. *That's* why we're going to win." Friendly audiences loved his fighting spirit and dogged courage, shouting, "Pour it on, Harry!" and "Give 'em hell, Harry." Truman responded: "I don't give 'em hell. I just tell the truth and they think it's hell."

The polls predicted a sure win for Thomas Dewey, but on Election Day, Harry Truman pulled off the biggest upset ever, taking 24.2 million votes (49.5 percent) to Dewey's 22 million (45.1 percent) and winning a thumping margin of 303 to 189 in the Electoral College. Democrats also regained control of both houses of Congress. Thurmond and Wallace each received more than a million votes. The president was helped by Black voters who, angered by the Dixiecrats, turned out in record numbers to support him, while the Progressive party's radicalism made it hard for Republicans to tag Truman as a Communist sympathizer. Thurmond carried only four southern states (South Carolina, Mississippi, Alabama, and Louisiana).

THE FAIR DEAL REJECTED Harry Truman viewed his victory in 1948 as a mandate for expanding the social welfare programs established by Franklin Roosevelt. "Every segment of our population and every individual," he declared, "has a right to expect from our government a *fair deal*." Truman's Fair Deal promised "greater economic opportunity for the mass of the people."

Yet there was little new in Truman's Fair Deal proposals. Most of them were simply extensions or enlargements of New Deal programs: a higher minimum wage, expansion of Social Security coverage to 10 million workers not included in the original 1935 bill, and a large slum-clearance and public-housing program.

"Dewey Defeats Truman" Truman's victory in 1948 was such a surprise that this early edition of the *Chicago Daily Tribune* reported that Dewey had won.

Despite enjoying Democratic majorities in Congress, however, Truman ran up against the same alliance of conservative southern Democrats and Republicans who had worked against Roosevelt in the late 1930s. The bipartisan conservative coalition rejected several civil rights bills, national health insurance, federal aid to education, and a new approach to subsidizing farmers. It also turned down Truman's request to repeal the anti-union Taft-Hartley Act. Yet the Fair Deal was not a complete failure. It laid the foundation for programs that the next generation of reformers would promote a decade later.

THE COLD WAR HEATS UP

As was true during Truman's first term, global concerns during his second term again distracted him from domestic issues. In his 1949 inaugural address, Truman called for a vigilant anti-Communist foreign policy resting on three pillars: the United Nations, the Marshall Plan, and NATO. None of them could help resolve the civil war in China, however.

"LOSING" CHINA One of the thorniest postwar problems, the Chinese civil war, was fast coming to a head. Chinese Nationalists, led by the corrupt Chiang Kai-shek, had been fighting Mao Zedong and the Communists since the 1920s. After the Second World War, the Communists won over most of the peasants. By the end of 1949, the Nationalist government was forced to flee to the island of Formosa, which it renamed Taiwan.

President Truman's critics—mostly Republicans—asked, "Who lost China to communism?" What they did not explain was how Truman could have prevented a Communist victory without a massive U.S. military intervention, which would have been risky, unpopular, and expensive. After 1949, the United States continued to recognize the Nationalist government

Mao Zedong Chairman of the Chinese Communist Party and founder of the People's Republic of China, Mao led the Communists to victory against the Chinese Nationalists in 1949.

on the island of Taiwan as the official government of China, delaying formal relations with the People's Republic of China ("Red China") for thirty years.

THE SOVIETS DEVELOP ATOMIC BOMBS As the Communists gained control of China in 1949, news that the Soviets had detonated a nuclear bomb led Truman to accelerate the design of a hydrogen "superbomb," far more powerful than the atomic bombs dropped on Japan. That the Soviets now possessed atomic weapons intensified every Cold War confrontation. "There is only one thing worse than one nation having an atomic bomb," said Nobel Prize–winning physicist Harold C. Urey, who helped develop the first atomic bomb. "That's two nations having it."

NSC-68 In January 1950, President Truman grew so concerned about the Soviets possessing atomic weapons that he asked the National Security Council to assess America's readiness to contain communism. Four months later, the Council submitted a top-secret report, *NSC-68*, which called for an even more robust effort and revealed the major assumptions that would guide U.S. foreign policy for the next twenty years: "The issues that face us are momentous,

Fallout Shelter The interior view of an underground fallout shelter designed to protect against a nuclear attack, equipped with crates of canned food and water for the couple and their three children.

involving the fulfillment or destruction not only of this Republic but of civilization itself."

NSC-68 endorsed George Kennan's containment strategy. But where he had focused on political and economic counterpressure, the report called for a massive military buildup and "a policy of calculated and gradual coercion" against Soviet expansionism—everywhere.

Paul Nitze, Kennan's successor as director of policy planning for the State Department, wrote *NSC-68*. He claimed that the Soviets were becoming increasingly "reckless" and would invade Western Europe by 1954, by which time they would have enough nuclear weapons to destroy the United States. *NSC-68* became the guidebook for future American policy, especially as the United States became involved in an unexpected war in Korea that ignited the smoldering animosity between communism and capitalism around the world.

WAR IN KOREA

By the mid-1950s, tensions between the United States and the Soviet Union in Europe had temporarily eased as a result of the "balance of terror" created by both sides having atomic weapons. In Asia, however, the situation remained turbulent. Communists had gained control of mainland China and were threatening to destroy the Chinese Nationalists, who had taken refuge on Taiwan. Japan, meanwhile, was experiencing a dramatic recovery from the devastation caused by the Second World War. Douglas MacArthur showed deft leadership as the consul in charge of U.S.-occupied Japan. He oversaw the disarming of the Japanese military, the drafting of a democratic constitution, and the nation's economic recovery, all of which were turning Japan into America's friend.

To the east, however, tensions between North and South Korea threatened to erupt into civil war. The Japanese had occupied the Korean Peninsula since 1910, but after they were defeated and withdrew in 1945, the victorious Allies had faced the difficult task of creating an independent Korean nation.

A DIVIDED KOREA   Complicating that effort was the presence of Soviet troops in northern Korea. They had accepted the surrender of Japanese forces above the 38th parallel, which divides the Korean Peninsula, while U.S. forces had overseen the surrender south of the line. The Soviets quickly organized a Communist government, the Democratic People's Republic of Korea (North Korea). The Americans countered by helping to establish a democratic government in the more populous south, the Republic of Korea (South Korea). By the end of 1948, Soviet and U.S. forces had withdrawn, and some 2 million North Koreans had fled to South Korea.

WAR ERUPTS On June 20, 1950, Secretary of State Dean Acheson gave a speech in which he said he was often asked, "Has the State Department got an Asian policy?" He stressed that the United States had assumed "the necessity of . . . the military defense of Japan." Acheson then added that America had created a "defensive perimeter" running along the Aleutian Islands off the coast of Alaska to Japan to the Ryukyu Islands to the Philippines. Where "other areas in the Pacific are concerned," Acheson added, "it must be clear that no person can guarantee these areas against military attack."

Acheson's statement came back to haunt him. On June 24, 1950, he telephoned President Truman to report, "The North Koreans have invaded South Korea." With the encouragement of the Soviet Union and Communist China, the Soviet-equipped North Korean People's Army—135,000 strong—had sent the South Korean defenders reeling into a headlong retreat. Within three days, Seoul, the South Korean capital, was captured, and only 22,000 of the 100,000 South Korean soldiers were still capable of combat. People then and since have argued that Acheson's clumsy reference to the limits of the "defensive perimeter" in Asia may have convinced the North Koreans and Soviets that the United States would not resist an invasion of South Korea.

When reporters asked Truman how he would respond, the president declared: "By God, I'm going to let them have it!" Without consulting the Joint Chiefs of Staff or Congress, he decided to wage war through the backing of the United Nations rather than by seeking a declaration of war from Congress, which the Constitution requires. He feared that a congressional debate would take so long that, once finished, it might then be too late to stop the Communists from seizing control of South Korea.

An emergency meeting of the UN Security Council in late June 1950 censured the North Korean "breach of peace." By sheer coincidence, the Soviet delegate, who held a veto power, was at the time boycotting the council because it would not seat Communist China in place of Nationalist China. On June 27, the Security Council called on UN members to "furnish such assistance to the Republic of Korea as may be necessary to repel the armed attack and to restore international peace and security in the area."

Truman then ordered U.S. air, naval, and ground forces into action and appointed seventy-year-old Douglas MacArthur supreme commander of the UN forces. The attack on South Korea, Truman said, made "it plain beyond all doubt that the international Communist movement is prepared to use armed invasion to conquer independent nations." Truman's decisive steps gained strong bipartisan approval, but neither the nation nor the administration was united on the objectives of the war or how it was to be conducted.

Fight and Flight U.S. soldiers brush shoulders with Korean refugees as they march into the Nakdong River region in the south.

The Korean conflict was the first military action fought under the banner of the United Nations, and some twenty other nations participated along with the United States. For the first time, soldiers fought under an international flag. America provided the largest contingent by far, some 330,000 troops. The defense of South Korea set a worrisome precedent: war by order of a president—rather than by a vote of Congress. Truman dodged the issue by calling the conflict a "police action" rather than a war. Critics labeled it "Mr. Truman's War."

For most Americans, the North Korean invasion confirmed what Truman had been saying: communism was on a ruthless march to world domination. In fact, however, the Korean War was largely a civil war between two factions vying for control of a new nation. Blinded by anticommunism, U.S. leaders plunged into a conflict that they never truly tried to understand.

TURNING THE TABLES The Korean War featured brutal combat in terrible conditions punctuated by heavy casualties and widespread destruction. For the first three months, the fighting went badly for the Republic of

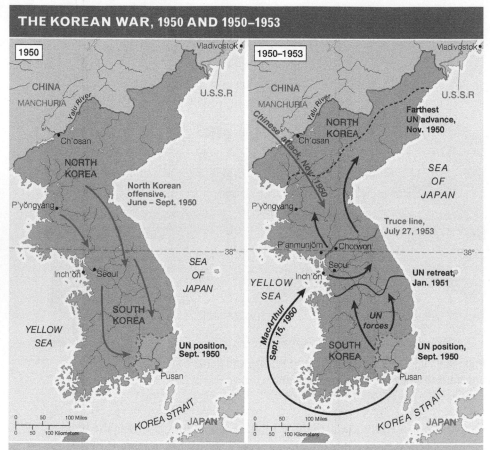

THE KOREAN WAR, 1950 AND 1950–1953

■ How did the 1945 surrender of the Japanese in Korea set up the conflict between Soviet-influenced North Korea and U.S.-influenced South Korea?
■ What was General MacArthur's strategy for winning the Korean conflict?
■ Why did President Truman remove General MacArthur from command?

Korea (ROK) and the UN forces. By September 1950, South Korean troops were barely hanging on at Pusan, at the southeast corner of the Korean Peninsula. Then, in a brilliant maneuver on September 15, General MacArthur staged a surprise amphibious landing behind the North Korean lines at Inchon, the port city for Seoul, some 150 miles north of Pusan. United Nations' troops drove a wedge through the North Korean army; only a quarter of the North Koreans, some 25,000 soldiers, managed to flee across the border. Days later, South Korean troops recaptured Seoul.

At that point, an overconfident MacArthur persuaded Truman to allow the U.S. troops to push north and eliminate the Communists in Korea.

Containment of communism was no longer enough; MacArthur now hatched a grandiose plan to rid North Korea of the "red menace," even if this meant expanding the war into China in order to prevent the Chinese from resupplying their North Korean allies. Truman foolishly approved MacArthur's request to advance into North Korea so as to destroy its armies and enable the unification of both Koreas. He told the White House physician that the "son-of-bitch" MacArthur would probably "get us involved in a war with China."

THE CHINESE INTERVENE By October 1950, UN forces were about to capture the North Korean capital, P'yŏngyang. President Truman, concerned that General MacArthur's move would provoke Communist China to enter the war, repeatedly asked the U.S. commander to meet with him, only to be rebuffed. Finally, the president flew 7,000 miles to Wake Island to meet with MacArthur, who contemptuously refused to salute his commander in chief. For his part, Truman had decided that MacArthur was "a supreme egoist, who regards himself as something of a god."

At the meeting on October 15, MacArthur dismissed Chinese threats to intervene, even though they had massed troops on the Korean border. That same day, the Chinese Communist government announced that it "cannot stand idly by" as its North Korean allies were humiliated. On October 20, UN forces entered the North Korean capital, and six days later, advance units reached Ch'osan on the Yalu River, North Korea's border with China.

MacArthur predicted total victory by Christmas. He could not have been more wrong. On the night of November 25, some 500,000 Chinese "volunteers" crossed into Korea and sent surprised U.S. forces scrambling in retreat. A shaken MacArthur cabled the White House that the American forces confronted "an entirely new war." He urgently requested reinforcements of the "greatest magnitude" and suggested that several dozen atomic weapons be used on China. A shellshocked Truman wrote in his diary that it "looks like World War III is here."

By January 15, the Communist Chinese and North Koreans had recaptured Seoul, the South Korean capital. "We ran like antelopes," said one American soldier. "We lost everything we had." What had started as a defensive war against North Korean aggression had become an unlimited war against the North Koreans and China's People's Liberation Army.

MACARTHUR CROSSES THE LINE In late 1950, the UN forces rallied. By January 1951, they had secured their lines below Seoul and launched a counterattack. When President Truman began negotiations with North Korea to restore the prewar boundary, General MacArthur undermined him by issuing an ultimatum for China to make peace or suffer an attack. On April 5, on the floor of Congress, the Republican minority leader read a letter from MacArthur that criticized the president and said that "there is no substitute for victory."

Such public insubordination and MacArthur's refusal to follow numerous orders left Truman only two choices: He could accept MacArthur's aggressive demands or fire him. Secretary of State Dean Acheson warned Truman that "if you relieve MacArthur, you will have the biggest fight of your administration."

SACKING A HERO On April 11, 1951, with civilian control of the military at stake, Truman removed General MacArthur and replaced him with General Matthew B. Ridgway, who better understood how to conduct a modern war in pursuit of limited objectives. "I believe that we must try to limit the war to Korea," Truman explained in a speech to Congress. "A number of events have made it evident that General MacArthur did not agree with that policy. I have therefore considered it essential to relieve General MacArthur so that there would be no doubt or confusion as to the real purpose and aim of our policy."

Firing of MacArthur In this 1951 cartoon by L. J. Roche, President Truman, Secretary of State Dean Acheson, and the Pentagon dance in the American public's proverbial frying pan for the removal of General Douglas MacArthur from his post as the supreme commander of UN forces in Korea.

Truman's decision to sack the army's only five-star general created a firestorm. "Seldom had a more unpopular man fired a more popular one," *Time* magazine reported. Senator Joseph McCarthy called the president a "son of a bitch," and an editorial in the *Chicago Tribune* demanded that Truman "be impeached and convicted." Sixty-nine percent of Americans initially opposed Truman's decision.

Douglas MacArthur was greeted by adoring crowds upon his return to the United States, but Truman stood firm: "I fired him because he wouldn't respect the authority of the President. I didn't fire him because he was a dumb son of a bitch, although he was, but that's not against the law for generals. If it was, half to three-quarters of them would be in jail." That all of the top military leaders supported Truman's decision deflated much of the criticism. "Why, hell, if MacArthur had had his way," the president warned, "he'd have had us in the Third World War and blown up two-thirds of the world."

A CEASE-FIRE On June 24, 1951, the Soviet representative at the United Nations proposed a cease-fire in Korea along the 38th parallel, the original dividing line between North and South. Secretary of State Acheson accepted the cease-fire (armistice) with the consent of the United Nations. China and North Korea responded favorably.

Truce talks that started on July 10, 1951, dragged on for two years while sporadic fighting continued. The chief snags were exchanges of prisoners (many captured North Korean and Chinese soldiers did not want to go home) and South Korea's insistence on unification of the two Koreas. By the time a truce was reached, on July 27, 1953, Dwight D. Eisenhower had succeeded Truman as president. No peace treaty was ever signed, and Korea, like Germany, remained divided. The inconclusive war cost the United States more than 33,000 battle deaths and 103,000 wounded or missing. South Korean casualties were about 2 million, and North Korean and Chinese casualties were an estimated 3 million.

THE IMPACT OF THE KOREAN WAR The Korean War influenced U.S. foreign policy in significant ways. To most Americans, the North Korean attack on South Korea provided concrete proof that there was an international Communist conspiracy guided by the Soviet Union to control the world. Harry Truman's assumption that Josef Stalin and the Soviets were behind the invasion of South Korea deepened his commitment to stop communism elsewhere. Fearful that the Soviets would use the Korean conflict as a diversion to invade Western Europe, he ordered a major expansion of U.S. military forces around the world. Truman also increased assistance to French troops fighting a Communist independence movement in the French colony of Indochina (which included Vietnam), starting America's military involvement in Southeast Asia. Finally, the Korean War demonstrated how important a role Japan would play in America's military presence in Asia.

ANOTHER RED SCARE

The Korean War sparked another Red Scare at home, as people grew fearful that Soviet-directed Communists were infiltrating American society. Since 1938, the **House Committee on Un-American Activities (HUAC)** had claimed that Communist agents had infiltrated the federal government. On March 21, 1947, just nine days after he announced the Truman Doctrine, President Truman sought to blunt conservative Republicans' attacks on the patriotism of left-wing Democrats by signing an executive order (known as the Loyalty Order). It required all 2 million federal government workers to undergo a background investigation to ensure they were not Communists or even associated with Communists (as well as other "subversive" groups).

The president knew that the "loyalty program" violated the civil liberties of government workers, but he felt he had no choice. He was responding to pressure from FBI director J. Edgar Hoover and Attorney General Tom Clark, both of whom believed that there were numerous spies working inside the federal government. Truman was also eager to reduce criticism by Republicans that he was not doing enough to ensure that Soviet sympathizers were not working in government.

Privately, however, Truman insisted that concerns about Communist spies were exaggerated. "People are very much wrought up about the communist 'bugaboo,'" he wrote to Pennsylvania governor George Earle, "but I am of the opinion that the country is perfectly safe so far as Communism is concerned." By early 1951, the federal Civil Service Commission had cleared more than 3 million government workers, while only 378 had been dismissed for doubtful loyalty. In 1953, President Eisenhower revoked the Loyalty Order.

THE HOLLYWOOD TEN In May 1947, charges that the Hollywood movie industry was a "hotbed of communism" led the HUAC to launch a full-blown investigation. The committee subpoenaed dozens of prominent actors, producers, and directors to testify at hearings held in Los Angeles in October. Ten witnesses refused to answer questions about their political activities, arguing that such questions violated their First Amendment rights. When asked if he was a member of the Communist party, screenwriter Ring Lardner Jr. replied: "I could answer, but I would hate myself in the morning." Another member of the so-called Hollywood Ten, screenwriter Dalton Trumbo, shouted as he left the hearings, "This is the beginning of an American concentration camp." All ten were cited for contempt of Congress, given prison terms, and blacklisted (banned) from the film industry.

The witch hunt launched by the HUAC inspired Arthur Miller, who himself was banned, to write *The Crucible*, an award-winning play produced in 1953. His dramatic account of the witch trials in Salem, Massachusetts, at the end of the seventeenth century was intended to alert audiences to the dangers of anti-Communist hysteria.

ALGER HISS The spy case most damaging to the Truman administration involved Alger Hiss, president of the Carnegie Endowment for International Peace. Whittaker Chambers, a former Soviet spy who reversed himself and became an informer testifying against supposed Communists in the government, told the HUAC in 1948 that Hiss had given him secret documents ten years earlier, when Chambers was spying for the Soviets and Hiss was working in the State Department. Hiss sued Chambers for libel, and Chambers produced microfilm of the State Department documents that he said Hiss had passed to him. Although Hiss denied the accusation, he was convicted in 1950. The charge was perjury, but he was convicted of lying about espionage, for which he could not be tried because the statute of limitations on the crime had expired.

More cases of Communist infiltration surfaced. In 1949, eleven top leaders of the Communist party of the United States were convicted under the Smith Act of 1940, which outlawed any conspiracy to advocate the overthrow of the government. The Supreme Court upheld the law under the doctrine of a "clear and present danger," which overrode the right to free speech.

ATOMIC SPYING In 1950, the FBI discovered a British-American spy network that had secretly passed information about the development of the atomic bomb to the Soviet Union. The disclosure led to the widely publicized arrest of Klaus Fuchs, a German-born English physicist who had worked in the United States during the war, helping develop the atomic bomb.

As it turned out, a New York couple, former Communists Julius and Ethel Rosenberg, were part of the same Soviet spy ring. Their claims of innocence were undercut by Ethel's brother, who admitted he was a spy along with his sister and brother-in-law.

The convictions of Fuchs and the Rosenbergs fueled Republican charges that Truman's administration was not doing enough to hunt down Communist agents who were stealing American military secrets. The Rosenberg case, called the crime of the century by J. Edgar Hoover, also heightened fears that a vast Soviet network of spies and sympathizers was operating in the United States—and now had "given" Stalin the secret of building atomic weapons. Irving Kaufman, the federal judge who sentenced the Rosenbergs to death, explained that "plain, deliberate murder is dwarfed . . . by comparison with the crime you have committed." They were the first Americans ever executed for spying.

JOSEPH MCCARTHY'S WITCH HUNT Evidence of Soviet spying encouraged politicians to exploit fears of the Communist menace at home.

Early in 1950, a little-known Republican senator, Joseph R. McCarthy of Wisconsin, surfaced as the most ruthless manipulator of the nation's anti-Communist anxieties.

An intelligent, determined, but unethical man thirsty for media attention, McCarthy took up the cause of anti-Communism with a fiery speech to a Republican women's club in Wheeling, West Virginia, on February 9, 1950. He charged that the State Department was infested with Communists—and he claimed to have their names, although he never provided them.

"Joe" McCarthy's reckless charges created a media sensation. As the *New York Times* said, "It is difficult, if not impossible, to ignore charges made by Senator McCarthy just because they are usually proved exaggerated or false." During the next four years, McCarthy made more irresponsible accusations, initially against Democrats, whom he attacked as "dupes" or "fellow travelers" of the "Commies," then against just about everyone, including officers in the U.S. Army.

Truman privately denounced McCarthy as "just a ballyhoo artist who has to cover up his shortcomings with wild charges," but McCarthy grew into a formidable figure. He enjoyed the backing of fellow Republicans eager to hurt Democrats in the 1950 congressional elections by claiming they were "soft on communism." Senator Lyndon B. Johnson of Texas said McCarthy was "the sorriest senator" in Washington. "But he's riding high now, he's got people scared to death."

By the summer of 1951, what had come to be called **McCarthyism** had gotten out of control. McCarthy outrageously accused George Marshall, the former secretary of state and war hero, of making "common cause with Stalin." Concerns about truth or fair play did not faze McCarthy. He refused to answer critics or provide evidence; his goal was to use groundless accusations to create a reign of terror.

Despite his outlandish claims and bullying style, McCarthy never uncovered a single Communist agent within the federal government. Yet his smear campaign, which tarnished

Joseph R. McCarthy A photo from 1954 of McCarthy, the crusading senator who was determined to "sweep" the Communists out of the federal government and beyond.

many lives and reputations and had a chilling effect on free speech, went largely unchallenged until the end of the Korean War. During the Red Scare, thousands of left-wing activists were banned from employment because of past political associations, real or rumored. Movies with titles like *I Married a Communist* fed the hysteria, and magazine stories warned of "a Red under every bed."

THE MCCARRAN ACTS   Fears of Soviet spies working with American sympathizers led Congress in 1950 to pass, over President Truman's veto, the McCarran Internal Security Act, which made it unlawful "to combine, conspire, or agree with any other person to perform any act which would substantially contribute to . . . the establishment of a totalitarian dictatorship." The legislation, proposed by the conservative Democratic senator Pat McCarran (Nevada), required Communist organizations to register with the Justice Department. Immigrants who had belonged to totalitarian parties in their home countries were barred from entering the United States, and during any future national emergencies, Communists were to be herded into concentration camps. The McCarran Internal Security Act, Truman said in his veto message, would "put the government into the business of thought control."

Concerns about Communist infiltration also shaped immigration policy. In 1952, Senator McCarran pushed through the Immigration and Nationality Act of 1952 (the McCarran-Walter Act). It gave immigration officials extraordinary powers to search, seize, and deport undocumented immigrants ("aliens"). While reducing the number of immigrants admitted each year, it renewed the national-origins quota system established by the Immigration Act of 1924, which favored newcomers from northern and western Europe. As a result, the act allocated 85 percent of the 154,277 annual visas to people from northern and Western European nations. It also introduced a system of preferences based on skills and family ties and removed the ban on Asian immigrants. Yet the number of Asians allowed into the United States remained small (only 100 per year). Finally, it barred suspected "subversives" and the "immoral," including gays and lesbians. Truman vetoed the bill, but Congress overrode him again.

ASSESSING THE RED SCARE AND HARRY TRUMAN   The Red Scare ended up violating the civil liberties of innocent people. President Truman may have erred in 1947 by creating a government loyalty program that aggravated the anti-Communist hysteria. His attorney general, Tom Clark, contended that there were "so many Communists in America" that they "were everywhere—in factories, offices, butcher shops, on street corners, in private businesses—and each carries with him the germs of death for society."

Truman also overstretched resources when he pledged to "contain" communism everywhere. Containment itself proved hard to contain amid the ideological posturing of Soviet and American leaders. Its chief theorist, George F. Kennan, later confessed that he had failed to clarify the limits of the containment policy and to stress that the United States needed to prioritize its responses to Soviet adventurism.

The years after the Second World War were unlike any other postwar period. Having taken on global burdens after the war, the United States became committed to a permanently large military establishment, along with the attendant creation of shadowy new government agencies such as the National Security Council (NSC), the National Security Agency (NSA), and the Central Intelligence Agency (CIA).

The federal government—and the presidency—grew larger, more powerful, and more secretive during the Cold War, fueled by the actions of both major political parties as well as by the intense lobbying efforts of what Dwight D. Eisenhower would later call the *military-industrial complex*—defense contractors, lobbyists, and influential legislators.

Fears of communism at home grew out of legitimate concerns about a Soviet spy network in the United States but mushroomed into politically motivated paranoia. As had been true during the first Red Scare, after the First World War, long-standing prejudices against Jews fed the anti-Communist hysteria; indeed, many Communist sympathizers were Jews from Eastern Europe.

The Red Scare also provided a powerful tool for Republicans eager to attack the Truman administration and the Democratic party, claiming that Democrats were "soft on communism." One of the worst effects of the Red Scare was to encourage widespread conformity of thought and behavior in the United States. By 1950, it had become dangerous to criticize anything associated with the "American way of life."

On March 30, 1952, Harry Truman announced that he would not seek another presidential term, in part because it was unlikely he could win. Less than 25 percent of voters surveyed thought he was doing a good job, the lowest presidential approval rating in history. Although Americans applauded Truman's integrity and courage, they were disheartened that some members of his administration were revealed to be inept and even corrupt. The unrelenting war against communism, at home and abroad, led people to question Truman's strategy. Negotiations to end the war in Korea had bogged down for many months, the "Red-baiting" of McCarthyism was expanding across the nation, and conservative southern Democrats, members of Truman's own party, had defeated most of the president's Fair Deal proposals in Congress. The war in Korea had also brought higher taxes and higher prices for consumers, many of whom blamed Truman for their frustrations. Only years later would the American people (and historians) fully appreciate how effective Truman had been in dealing with so many complex problems.

To the end of his presidency, Truman viewed himself as an ordinary person operating in extraordinary times. "I have tried my best to give the nation everything I have in me," Truman told reporters at one of his last press conferences. "There are a great many people . . . who could have done the job better than I did it. But I had the job and had to do it." And it was not a simple job, by any means. At the end of one difficult day in the White House, Truman growled: "They [his critics] talk about the power of the President, how I can just push a button to get things done. Why, I spend most of my time kissing somebody's . . . butt."

By the time a frustrated Truman left the White House in early 1953, the Cold War against communism had become an accepted part of the American way of life. But fears of Soviet and Chinese communism were counterbalanced by the joys of unexpected prosperity. Toward the end of Truman's presidency, during the early fifties, the economy began to grow at the fastest rate in history, transforming social and cultural life and becoming the marvel of the world. The booming economy brought with it the "nifty" fifties.

CHAPTER REVIEW

Summary

- **The Cold War** The Cold War was an ideological contest between the Western democracies (especially the United States) and the Communist nations (especially the Soviet Union). At the end of the Second World War, the Soviet Union established "friendly" (puppet) governments in the Eastern European countries it occupied behind an *iron curtain*, violating promises that Stalin had made at the Yalta Conference. The United States and the Soviet Union, former allies, differed openly on issues of human rights, individual liberties, self-determination, and religious freedoms. As mutual hostility emerged, the two nations and their allies competed to shape the postwar global order.

- **Containment** President Truman responded to the Soviet occupation of Eastern Europe with *containment*, a policy to halt the spread of communism by opposing it wherever it emerged around the world. With the *Truman Doctrine* (1947), the United States provided economic and military aid to countries facing Communist insurgencies, such as Greece and Turkey. The *National Security Act* (1947) reorganized the U.S. armed forces and created National Security Council and the Central Intelligence Agency. It also merged the War Department and Navy Department into a single Department of Defense under the secretary of defense, who also directed the newly created Department of the Air Force. The *Marshall Plan* (1948) offered postwar redevelopment aid to all European nations. In 1948–1949, the United States withstood a Soviet blockade of supplies to West Berlin with the *Berlin airlift* and, in 1949, became a founding member of the *North Atlantic Treaty Organization (NATO)*.

- **Truman's Fair Deal** The *Fair Deal* (1949) sought to expand the New Deal in the face of intense Republican opposition in Congress. While he could not stop the Republican-backed, anti-union *Taft-Hartley Labor Act* (1947), Truman successfully expanded Social Security, desegregated the military, and banned racial discrimination in the hiring of federal employees. In his second term, he proposed what he called his *Fair Deal* programs that included a civil rights bill, national health insurance, federal aid to education, and new farm subsidies. However, conservative majorities of Republicans and southern Democrats (*Dixiecrats*) defeated most of these proposals.

- **The Korean War** While containment policies halted Soviet expansion in Europe, they proved less effective in East Asia as Communists won a long civil war in China in 1949 and ignited a war in Korea. In response, Truman authorized *NSC-68* (1950), a study that proposed a dramatic increase in military spending and nuclear arms. When North Korean troops invaded South Korea in June 1950, Truman quickly decided to go to war under the auspices of the United Nations, thus bypassing Congress's authority to declare war. After three years of war, a truce established a demilitarized zone in Korea on either side of the 38th parallel. Truman also began assisting French efforts to subdue a Communist insurgency in its Southeast Asian colony of Indochina.

- **The Red Scare** The onset of the Cold War inflamed another Red Scare. After the Second World War, investigations by the *House Committee on Un-American Activities (HUAC)* sought to find "subversives" within the federal government. Starting in 1950, Senator Joseph R. McCarthy exploited American fears of Soviet infiltration of the U.S. government. *McCarthyism* flourished in the short term because the threat of a world dominated by Communist governments seemed all too real to many Americans.

CHRONOLOGY

1944	Congress passes the GI Bill of Rights
April 1945	Fifty allied nations sign the UN Charter; Soviet Union begins installing puppet Communist regimes in Eastern Europe
February 1946	George Kennan issues his "Long Telegram"
March 1947	President Truman announces the Truman Doctrine
May 1947	Secretary of State George Marshall proposes the Marshall Plan
June 1947	Congress passes Taft-Hartley Labor Act
July 1947	National Security Council (NSC) is established
May 1948	Israel is proclaimed an independent nation
July 1948	Truman issues an executive order ending segregation in the U.S. armed forces
August 1948	Alger Hiss accused of having been a Soviet spy before the HUAC
October 1948	Berlin airlift begins
April 1949	North Atlantic Treaty Organization (NATO) is created
October 1949	China "falls" to communism; Soviet Union tests an atomic bomb
February 1950	McCarthy's Red Scare begins
June 1950–July 1953	The Korean War

KEY TERMS

iron curtain p. 1256
containment p. 1258
Truman Doctrine (1947) p. 1259
Marshall Plan (1948) p. 1260
Berlin airlift (1948–1949) p. 1262
North Atlantic Treaty Organization (NATO) p. 1263
National Security Act (1947) p. 1263

Taft-Hartley Labor Act (1947) p. 1269
Fair Deal (1949) p. 1277
Dixiecrats p. 1278
NSC-68 (1950) p. 1282
House Committee on Un-American Activities (HUAC) p. 1289
McCarthyism p. 1292

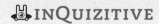 INQUIZITIVE

Go to InQuizitive to see what you've learned—and learn what you've missed—with personalized feedback along the way.

26 Affluence and Anxiety in the Atomic Age

1950–1959

American Consumerism The United States experienced unprecedented prosperity after the Second World War, enabling many Americans in the 1950s to engage in carefree consumption and personal indebtedness.

In the summer of 1959, most Americans believed that a nuclear war with the Soviet Union was "likely." Such fears led newlyweds Melvin and Maria Mininson to spend their honeymoon in an underground bomb shelter in their Miami backyard. Weighing twenty tons, the steel-and-concrete bunker held enough food and water to survive an atomic attack.

The image of a young couple seeking shelter from nuclear terror symbolized how the Cold War with the Soviet Union cast a frightening shadow over everyday life. Still, most Americans had emerged from the Second World War proud of their country's military strength, international stature, and industrial might. As the editors of *Fortune* magazine proclaimed in 1946, "This is a dream era. . . . The Great American Boom is on."

So it was, at least for White, middle-class Americans. During the late 1940s and throughout the 1950s, the United States enjoyed unprecedented economic growth, and surveys revealed that most people were content with their lives. Divorce and homicide rates fell, and people lived longer, on average, thanks in part to medical breakthroughs, including the vaccine invented by Dr. Jonas Salk that ended the menace of polio. The idealized image of America in the fifties as an innocent, prosperous nation awash in good times and enlivened by teenage energies contains a kernel of truth. But life was actually much more complicated—even contradictory and hypocritical at times, as it always is.

focus questions

1. What were President Eisenhower's political philosophy and priorities?

2. What factors contributed to America's postwar prosperity? To what extent did Americans benefit from it?

3. What were the criticisms of postwar society and culture? What were the various forms of dissent and anxiety?

4. What were the goals and strategies of the civil rights movement during the fifties? What was its impact?

5. What were President Eisenhower's foreign policy priorities? What was his influence on global affairs?

MODERATE REPUBLICANISM: THE EISENHOWER YEARS

Dwight David Eisenhower dominated politics during the 1950s. He was the nation's most famous figure, a model of moderation, modesty, stability, and optimism, a war hero celebrated for his genial personality and irresistible grin. He was a soldier who hated war, a politician who hated politics. If forced to choose, he preferred golf over governance. Committed to what he called **moderate Republicanism**, President Eisenhower promised to balance the federal budget, cut government spending, restore the authority of state and local governments, and restrain the federal government from engaging in the kind of political and social "engineering" represented by Franklin Roosevelt and the New Deal.

"TIME FOR A CHANGE" By 1952, the Truman administration had become the target of growing public criticism. The conflict in Korea had stalled

Dwight D. Eisenhower As a reflection of the consumer culture's impact on politics, Eisenhower's many supporters wore "I Like Ike" hats, pins, and even nylon stockings to demonstrate their political support.

and the economy was sputtering. People were tired of strikes and rising prices. The disclosure that corrupt lobbyists had rigged military contracts related to the Korean War put Truman on the defensive. The scandal led him to fire nearly 250 Internal Revenue Service employees, but doubts lingered that he would ever finish that housecleaning. Critics charged that the slogan for his administration was "plunder at home, blunder abroad."

It was, Republicans claimed, "time for a change," and public sentiment turned their way as the 1952 election approached. Beginning in the late 1940s, both Republican and Democratic leaders, including Truman, recruited Eisenhower to be their presidential candidate. Eisenhower, known as "Ike," had displayed remarkable organizational and diplomatic skills in coordinating the Allied invasion of Nazi-controlled Europe in 1944. Eight years later, after serving as president of Columbia University, he had moved to Paris to become supreme commander of NATO forces in

Europe. His decision to run for president as a Republican was wildly popular. Bumper stickers announced, "I Like Ike."

At the 1952 Republican presidential convention, Eisenhower was nominated on the first ballot. Party leaders named as his running mate Richard M. Nixon, a thirty-nine-year-old California senator known for his shrewd opportunism and combative temperament. Nixon was an aggressive anti-Communist; his dogged pursuit of the Alger Hiss spying case had brought him national prominence. The Republican platform declared that the Democratic emphasis on "containing" communism was "negative, futile, and misguided." If elected, Eisenhower would bring "genuine independence" to the oppressed people of Eastern Europe.

THE ELECTION OF 1952 The presidential campaign featured contrasting personalities. Dwight Eisenhower was an international figure and a man of readily acknowledged decency and integrity. He pledged to clean up "the mess in Washington" by eradicating the "Left-wingish, pinkish influence in our life." He also promised to travel to Korea to secure "an early and honorable" end to the prolonged war.

Illinois governor Adlai Stevenson, the Democratic candidate, was virtually unknown outside his home state. Although brilliant and witty, he came across as more an aloof intellectual than a leader. Republicans labeled him an "egghead" (meant to suggest a balding professor with more intellect than common sense). Even Harry Truman grumbled that Stevenson "was too busy making up his mind whether he had to go to the bathroom or not."

Stevenson was outmatched against Eisenhower. On election night, "Ike" triumphed in a landslide, gathering nearly 34 million votes to Stevenson's 27 million. The electoral vote was more lopsided: 442 to 89. Stevenson even failed to win his home state of Illinois. More important, by securing four southern states, Eisenhower had cracked the solidly Democratic South.

Yet voters liked Eisenhower more than they liked other Republican candidates. In the 1952 election, Democrats kept control of most governorships, lost control in the House by only eight seats, and broke even in the Senate, where only the vote of the vice president gave Republicans the slimmest majority. The congressional elections two years later would further weaken the Republican grip on Congress, and Eisenhower would have to work with a Democratic Congress throughout his last six years in office.

A "MIDDLE WAY" PRESIDENCY Dwight Eisenhower was the first professional soldier elected president since Ulysses S. Grant in 1868. During his campaign, he appealed to the "middle-of-the-road voter" and progressive

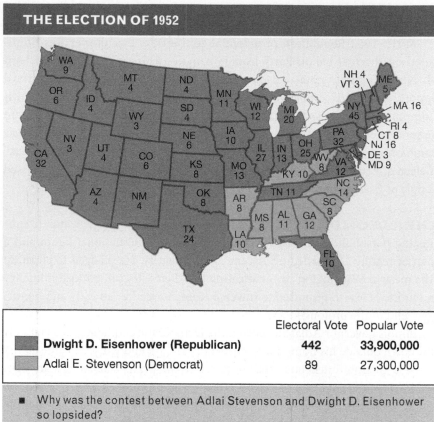

THE ELECTION OF 1952

	Electoral Vote	Popular Vote
Dwight D. Eisenhower (Republican)	**442**	**33,900,000**
Adlai E. Stevenson (Democrat)	89	27,300,000

■ Why was the contest between Adlai Stevenson and Dwight D. Eisenhower so lopsided?

■ Why was Eisenhower's victory in several southern states remarkable?

moderates. Once elected, he promised to pursue a "middle way" between conservatism and liberalism. He was a pragmatist who liked to be called a "responsible progressive." Rather than dismantle all the New Deal and Fair Deal programs, he wanted to end the "excesses" resulting from twenty years of Democratic control of the White House.

Eisenhower's cautious personality and genial public face fit the prevailing public mood. He inspired trust, sought consensus, and avoided confrontation. He pledged to shrink the federal bureaucracy and make it more efficient while restoring the balance between the executive and legislative branches. He also promised to reduce the national debt and military expenses, balance the federal budget, and cut taxes. At the same time, however, he insisted that workers had a right to form unions and bargain with management. He added that employees needed to be paid enough to afford the comforts of a good life. "We all—workers and farmers, foremen and financiers, technicians and builders—all must produce, produce more, and produce yet more," he said.

World peace, Eisenhower believed, should be maintained "not by weapons of war but by wheat and cotton, by milk and wool, by meat and by timber and by rice." He hated the arms race because "every gun that is made, every warship launched, every rocket fired signifies, in the final sense, a theft from those who hunger and are not fed, those who are cold and are not clothed."

"DYNAMIC CONSERVATISM" AT HOME President Eisenhower labeled his domestic program "dynamic conservatism," by which he meant being "conservative when it comes to money and liberal when it comes to human beings." He kept intact the basic structure of the Democrats' New Deal, even convincing Congress to establish a federal Department of Health, Education, and Welfare and to extend Social Security benefits to millions of workers formerly excluded: white-collar professionals, housekeepers and sales clerks, farmworkers, and members of the armed forces. Eisenhower also approved increases in the minimum wage and additional public-housing projects for the poor.

Conservative Republicans charged that Eisenhower was being too liberal. He told his brother Edgar in 1954 that if the "stupid" right wing of the Republican party tried "to abolish Social Security and eliminate labor laws and farm programs, you would not hear of that party again in our political history."

TRANSPORTATION IMPROVEMENTS Under Dwight Eisenhower, the federal government launched two huge construction projects: the St. Lawrence Seaway and the interstate highway system, both of which resembled the public works projects constructed under the New Deal during the 1930s. The St. Lawrence Seaway project (in partnership with Canada) opened the Great Lakes to oceangoing ships.

The **Federal-Aid Highway Act** (1956) created a network of interstate highways modeled after the German *autobahnen* (limited-access national highways) to serve the needs of commerce and defense, as well as the public. The $32 billion interstate highway system, funded largely by federal gasoline taxes, took twenty-five years to construct and was the largest federal project in history. It stretched for 47,000 miles and required 55,512 bridges.

Highway construction generated what economists call "multiplier effects." It created jobs; stimulated economic growth; and spurred the tourism, motor hotel (motel), billboard, fast-food, and long-haul trucking industries. Interstates transformed the way people traveled and where they lived, while creating a new form of middle-class leisure—the family vacation by car. In 1956, writer Bernard De Voto exclaimed that "a new highway is not only a measure of progress, but a true index of our culture."

THE CAR CULTURE   The second great age of the automobile had arrived after the war. Thanks to the interstate highway system, President Eisenhower said, cars would provide "greater convenience, greater happiness, and greater standards of living." In 1948, only 60 percent of families had owned a car; by 1955, some 90 percent owned a car, and many households had two. "The American," novelist William Faulkner observed in 1948, "really loves nothing but his automobile."

Americans had always cherished personal freedom and mobility and masculine force. Automobiles embodied all these qualities and more. Cars were much more than a form of transportation; they provided social status, freedom, and a wider range of choices—where to travel, where to work and live, where to seek pleasure and recreation. The "car culture" prompted the creation of "convenience stores," drive-in movies, and fast-food restaurants. Even more important, the interstate highway system and the car culture weakened public transit systems (buses and subways), accelerated the movement of White people from cities to suburbs, and caused a surge in environmental pollution.

1950's Car Culture In this 1954 advertisement for a Volvo 444, a family gets ready to enjoy a picnic lunch in the countryside.

THE "LAVENDER MENACE" The anti-Communist crusade after 1945 expanded to include an anti-homosexual crusade. For many gay men and women, the Second World War had been a liberating experience. Service in the armed forces surrounded recruits with people of their own gender. For some, their military experience provided a way of living and loving they had already embraced. Others were introduced for the first time to men and women with similar feelings.

After the war ended, gays and lesbians grew more visible, although most communities still classified gayness as a crime, a mental illness, and a "sexual perversion." Underground gay bars emerged in the nation's largest cities, and a lesbian subculture coalesced. Two national organizations, the Mattachine Society (which derived its name from male medieval dancers who performed in masks to allow for greater freedom of expression) and the Daughters of Bilitis (named for a famous collection of lesbian poems), were formed in 1950 and 1955 to protect the civil rights of gays and lesbians.

Amid the anxieties of the Cold War, however, gayness became equated with Communist subversion. Psychologists mistakenly reported that gays, lesbians, and Communists displayed similar characteristics: moral corruption, psychological immaturity, and a crafty ability to live undetected in mainstream society.

In 1948, Indiana University sex researcher Dr. Alfred Kinsey published *Sexual Behavior in the Human Male* (1948), the first of several books about American sexual behavior. His most controversial finding was that 37 percent of males and 13 percent of females had engaged in gay or lesbian behavior. Such data shocked social conservatives, for in their eyes sexual "deviancy" and Communist subversion were mutually reinforcing perversions. Roman Catholic leaders in Indiana announced that Kinsey's findings would "pave the way for people to believe in communism."

Concerns about gay and lesbian people working in government agencies came to be called the "lavender menace," a phrase derived from the slang expression "lavender lads" used to denigrate gay men. Anti-Communists believed that it was especially problematic for gays and lesbians to work at the State Department or serve in the armed forces, since Soviet agents could use sexual blackmail to gain access to important documents or information.

In 1950, the Senate issued the results of its "investigation" into gays and lesbians in government service. The report, titled *Employment of Homosexuals and other Sex Perverts in Government*, stressed that gay and lesbian people were social "outcasts" who lacked "the emotional stability of normal Americans" and therefore could not be trusted with government positions. Although staff researchers did not find a single gay or lesbian person who had betrayed secrets to the Soviets, they concluded that gays had a "corrosive influence" on their fellow employees. "One homosexual can pollute a government office," the Senate report concluded.

Critics of the Truman administration seized on the report to claim that there were numerous gay and lesbian people working in federal agencies. Instead of fighting the charges, President Truman acquiesced. Thereafter, State Department officials launched a campaign to root out "immoral," "scandalous," and "dangerous" government employees—people whose personal conduct supposedly put the nation at risk. The department fired 54 alleged gays in 1950, 119 in 1951, and 134 in 1952.

During the early 1950s, with the aid of the FBI and its dictatorial director, J. Edgar Hoover, Senator Joseph McCarthy and his staff collected—illegally—gossip, rumor, hearsay, and slander against anyone who did not conform to their view of red-blooded Americanism. One of Hoover's agents, William Sullivan, later admitted: "We were the ones who made the McCarthy hearings possible. We fed McCarthy all the material he was using."

McCarthy was as determined to root out gay and lesbian people as he was to uncover Communists, for in his view they were all "subversives" intent on undermining the "American way of life." McCarthy claimed that America's leading diplomats in the State Department were wealthy elitists, "sexual perverts," and "unmanly degenerates."

McCarthy's "witch hunt" against gays led President Eisenhower in 1953 to issue Executive Order 10450. It required all federal agencies to fire gay and lesbian employees on the grounds of "sexual perversion." The armed forces immediately discharged thousands of men and women, accusing many of them only of displaying gay and lesbian "tendencies."

FRANKLIN KAMENY, GAY HERO Franklin Kameny, a combat veteran of World War II, had earned a Ph.D. in astronomy from Harvard before taking a job with the Army Map Service within the Defense Department. After only a few months on the job, however, he was fired for being gay. Unlike most others in his situation, Kameny fought back. He appealed his firing all the way up to President Eisenhower, although in the process he remained jobless and barely able to pay his rent, subsisting on a daily diet of baked beans and food donated by friends.

None of the appeals worked. Kameny thereafter became a brash, tenacious crusader for gay rights, giving more than 100 speeches a year and becoming a founding member of the Mattachine Society of Washington, the precursor to gay, lesbian, trans, and queer rights organizations. In 1961, he petitioned the U.S. Supreme Court, arguing that gays and lesbians were suffering "a persecution and discrimination not one whit more warranted or justified than those against . . . other minority groups."

Franklin Kameny Former combat veteran Franklin Kameny was fired by the Defense Department for being gay. When his appeals for wrongful termination failed, Kameny took to the streets in protest of the government's homophobic policies.

Four years later, inspired by the civil rights movement, Kameny organized the first gay demonstration at the White House. In 1968, he would coin the slogan "Gay is good." Three years later, he would become the first openly gay candidate for Congress. As a scientist, he was especially effective at challenging the prevailing assumption that being gay or lesbian was a mental disease and played a major role in convincing the American Psychiatric Association to stop classifying homosexuality as a mental disorder. In 2009, the federal government would formally apologize for his firing in 1957.

THE END OF McCARTHYISM Republicans thought their presidential victory in 1952 would curb the often-unscrupulous efforts of Wisconsin senator Joseph R. McCarthy to ferret out Communist spies in the federal government. Instead, the publicity-seeking senator's behavior grew even more outlandish, in part because reporters loved his theatrics and in part because he became a master at telling outrageous lies. President Eisenhower despised McCarthy but refused to criticize him in public, explaining that he did not want to "get into a pissing contest with that skunk."

McCarthy finally overreached when he made the absurd charge that the U.S. Army itself was "soft" on communism. For thirty-six days in the spring of 1954, a congressional committee conducted what were called the Army-McCarthy hearings. The televised hearings captivated 45 million viewers. The unkempt McCarthy was at his worst, browbeating high-ranking officers, shamelessly promoting himself, and producing little evidence to back up his charges. "You are a disgrace to the uniform," he told General Ralph Zwicker. "You're shielding Communist conspirators. You're not fit to be an officer. You're ignorant. You are going to be put on public display."

McCarthy was finally outwitted by the deliberate, reasoned counterattacks of the army's legal counsel, Joseph Welch. When McCarthy tried to smear one of Welch's associates, the attorney exploded: "Until this moment, Senator, I think I never really gauged your cruelty or your recklessness. . . . Have you no sense of decency, sir, at long last?" When the audience burst into applause, the confused senator was reduced to whispering, "What did I do?"

On December 2, 1954, the Senate voted 67 to 22 to "condemn" McCarthy for his reckless tactics. Soon thereafter, his political influence collapsed. His savage crusade against Communists had catapulted him into the limelight and captured the nation's attention, but also revealed that he had trampled upon civil liberties. His rapid demise helped the Democrats capture control of both houses of Congress in the 1954 elections. In 1957, at the age of forty-eight, he died of liver inflammation brought on by years of alcohol abuse.

A PEOPLE OF PLENTY

What most distinguished the United States from the rest of the world after the Second World War was what one journalist called America's "screwball materialism." The economy soared to record heights as businesses shifted from wartime production to the construction of new housing and the manufacture of mass-produced consumer goods. The quarter century from 1948 to 1973 witnessed the highest rate of sustained economic growth in history. In 1957, *U.S. News and World Report* magazine declared that "never had so many people, anywhere, been so well off." Magazines and television commercials featured beaming couples buying new homes, cars, and appliances. America had become, said historian David Potter, a "people of plenty." By 1960, some 90 percent of American families owned a car and 87 percent had a television set.

POSTWAR PROSPERITY Several factors led to the nation's extraordinary prosperity. First, huge federal expenditures during the Second World War and Korean War propelled the economy out of the Great Depression. Unemployment was virtually nonexistent. High government spending continued in the 1950s, thanks to the construction of highways, bridges, airports, and ports, and the global arms race. Military spending after 1945 represented 60 percent of the national budget and was by far the single most important stimulant to the economy.

The superior productivity of American industries also contributed to economic growth. No sooner was the war over than the government transferred many federal defense plants to civilian owners who retooled them for peacetime manufacturing. Military-related research helped stimulate new glamour industries: chemicals (including plastics), electronics, and aviation. By 1957, the aircraft industry was the nation's largest employer.

The economy also benefited from the emergence of new technologies, including the first generation of computers. Factories and industries became increasingly automated. At the same time, the oil boom in Texas, Wyoming, and Oklahoma continued to provide low-cost fuel to heat buildings and power cars and trucks.

Another reason for the record-breaking economic growth was the lack of foreign competition. Most of the other major industrial nations—Great Britain, France, Germany, Japan, and the Soviet Union—had been physically devastated during the Second World War, leaving U.S. manufacturers with a virtual monopoly on international trade that lasted well into the 1950s.

THE COLD WAR CONSUMER CULTURE What differentiated the postwar era from earlier periods of prosperity was the large number of

Postwar Consumerism Booming chain stores, such as this Super Giant grocery store, began to dot the new suburbs, offering an outlet for the carefree consumerism of the postwar years.

people who shared in the rising standard of living. *Consumerism* became America's secular religion. Most Americans had money to spend during the fifties, and they did so with gusto. Between 1947 and 1960, the average income for the working class increased by as much as it had in the previous *fifty* years. Increasingly, more blue-collar Americans, especially unionized automotive and steel workers, moved into the middle class. George Meany, the leading union spokesman during the 1950s, declared in 1955 that his members "never had it so good." A marketing consultant stressed that the new economy required "that we convert the buying and use of goods into [religious] rituals, that we seek our spiritual satisfaction, our ego satisfaction, in consumption."

A BUYING SPREE Americans engaged in a prolonged buying spree, aided by financing innovations that made it easier to buy things. The first credit card appeared in 1949; soon, "buying with plastic" had become the new norm. Personal indebtedness doubled, and frugality became unpatriotic. A handbook for newlyweds published by *Brides* magazine explained that purchasing brand-name appliances and household goods was "vital" to "our whole American way of living."

What most Americans wanted to buy was a new house. In 1945, only 40 percent of Americans owned homes; by 1960, the number had increased to

Family, Modified The dynamics of family life changed with the onslaught of new products. In this 1959 advertisement for TV dinners, the family eats out of disposable containers in front of the enticing television set.

60 percent. New homes featured the latest electrical appliances—refrigerators, ovens, dishwashers, garbage disposals, washing machines, vacuum cleaners, mixers, carving knives, even shoe polishers.

The use of electricity tripled, in part because of the popularity of television, which displaced listening to the radio and going to the movies as the most popular way to spend free time. Between 1946 and 1960, the number of homes with TV sets soared from 8,000 to 46 million. In 1954, grocery stores began selling frozen "TV dinners" to be heated and consumed while watching popular shows such as *Father Knows Best, I Love Lucy, Leave It to Beaver,* and *The Adventures of Ozzie and Harriet,* all of which idealized the child-centered world of suburban White families.

The popularity of television provided a powerful medium for advertisers to promote a new phase of the consumer culture that reshaped the contours of postwar life: the nature of work, where people lived and traveled, how they interacted, and what they valued. It also affected class structure, race relations, and gender roles. The amount spent on advertising doubled between 1950 and 1960, and "ad-men" on Madison Avenue in Manhattan ("Mad-Men") emerged as some of the most powerful people shaping American tastes and values.

THE GI BILL OF RIGHTS   As World War II neared its end, fears that a sudden influx of veterans into the workforce would produce widespread unemployment led Congress in 1944 to pass the Servicemen's Readjustment Act, nicknamed the **GI Bill of Rights**. ("GI" meant "government issue," a phrase stamped on military uniforms and equipment that became slang for "serviceman.")

Between 1944 and 1956, the GI Bill boosted upward social mobility. The GI Bill's package of benefits for veterans included unemployment pay for one year, preference to those applying for federal government jobs, loans for home construction or starting a business, access to government hospitals, and generous subsidies for education. Some 5 million veterans bought homes with the assistance of GI Bill mortgage loans, which required no down payment. Almost 8 million took advantage of GI Bill benefits to attend college or enroll in job-training programs.

Before the Second World War, about 160,000 Americans had graduated from college each year. By 1950, the figure had risen to 500,000. In 1949, veterans accounted for 40 percent of college enrollments, and the United States could boast the world's best-educated workforce, largely because of the GI Bill. For African American veterans, however, most colleges and universities remained racially segregated and refused to admit Blacks; those that did often discriminated against people of color.

African American students at White colleges or universities were barred from playing on athletic teams, attending social events, and joining fraternities or sororities. Even with GI Bill mortgage loans, Black veterans were often prevented from buying homes in White neighborhoods by the practice of "redlining," whereby banks would refuse to provide mortgages to homebuyers based on their race or ethnicity. Although women veterans were eligible for the GI Bill, there were so few of them that the program had the unintended effect of widening the income gap between men and women, since the much more numerous male veterans had greater access to education and housing.

COOLING THE SUBURBAN FRONTIER The second half of the twentieth century brought a mass migration to a new frontier—the suburbs. An acute postwar housing shortage prompted Whites to move from inner cities to sprawling suburbs emerging in the countryside, just outside of city or town limits. Of the 13 million homes built between 1948 and 1958, more than 11 million were in the new suburbs. Many among the exploding middle-class White population moved to what were called the Sun Belt states—California, Arizona, Florida, Texas—as well as to the Southeast, where rapid population growth and new highways generated an economic boom.

A crucial factor in the exploding growth of the Sun Belt was the emergence of air conditioning. The first air-conditioning system was designed in 1902 by inventor Willis Carrier. The earliest home unit was installed in 1914, but it utilized hazardous chemicals and was too bulky, noisy, and expensive to become widely applicable. Advances in technology eventually produced the more convenient window air conditioner in the late 1930s, though it remained too costly for most residents.

Most Americans first encountered air conditioning while sitting in movie theaters and walking through department stores. In 1951, inexpensive window units were invented, and soon thousands of homes featured dripping, humming metal boxes hanging out bedroom windows.

As air conditioning spread across the Sun Belt, the appeal of living in warmer climates soared. California led the way. In 1940, it was the fifth most-populous state; by 1963, it held first place. And by 1960, for the first time since the Civil War, more people moved into the South than moved out.

SUBURBAN CULTURE The new suburban communities ("**suburbia**") met an acute need—affordable housing—and fulfilled a common dream—personal freedom and family security within commuting distance of cities. In the half century after the Second World War, the suburban "good life" included

Levittown Identical, mass-produced houses in Levittown, New York, and other suburbs across the country provided military veterans and their families with affordable homes.

a big home with a big yard on a big lot accessed by a big car—or two. By 1970, more people lived in suburbs than in cities.

William Levitt, a brassy New York real estate developer, led the suburban revolution. Between 1947 and 1951, on 6,000 acres of Long Island farmland east of New York City, he built 17,447 small (750 square feet), sturdy, two-bedroom homes (bungalows) to house more than 82,000 mostly lower-middle-class residents. Levitt believed he was enabling the American dream of home ownership and personal mobility and thereby helping to win the Cold War. "No man who owns his own lot and his own house can be a communist," he said.

Levitt's first planned suburban community, called Levittown, symbolized the American Dream of upward mobility. The men tended to be war veterans who had become prosperous blue-collar workers aspiring to become members of the middle class, which to most Americans meant being neither rich nor poor but having a secure job and the confidence that their children would prosper even more. As a journalist reported, Levittown was a "one-class community" that included schools, parks, swimming pools, shopping centers, and playing fields.

William Levitt encouraged and even enforced uniformity and conformity in Levittown. The look-alike houses came in three styles—the Cape Cod, the

Rancher, and the Colonial. All sold for the same low price—$6,990, with no down payments for veterans—and featured the same floor plan and accessories. Each had a living room with a picture window and a television set, a bathroom, two bedrooms, and a kitchen equipped with an electric refrigerator, oven, and washing machine. Homeowners were required to cut their grass once a week and prohibited from erecting fences or hanging laundry on outside clotheslines on weekends.

When the first houses in Levittown went on sale, military veterans received first priority, and they stood in long lines to buy starter homes. The impatient demand for housing led Levitt to build three more Levittowns in Pennsylvania, New Jersey, and Puerto Rico. They and other planned suburban communities benefited greatly from government assistance. Federal and state tax codes favored homeowners over renters, and local governments paid for the infrastructure the subdivisions required: roads, water and sewer lines, fire and police protection. By insuring loans for up to 95 percent of the value of a house, the Federal Housing Administration (FHA) made it easy for builders to construct low-cost homes and for people to purchase them.

Levitt and other suburban developers created lily-white communities. Initially, the contracts for houses in the Levittown communities specifically excluded "members of other than the Caucasian race." When asked about this "racial covenant," Levitt blamed prevailing prejudices: "If we sell one house to a Negro family, then 90 to 95 percent of our white customers will not buy into the community." His policy was: "We can solve a housing problem or we can try to solve a racial problem. But we can't combine the two."

In 1948, the U.S. Supreme Court ruled in *Shelley v. Kraemer* that such racial restrictions were unconstitutional. The Court's ruling, however, did not end segregated housing practices; it simply made them more discreet. In 1953, when the original Levittown's population reached 70,000, it was the largest community in the nation without an African American resident. Although Jewish himself, Levitt discouraged Jews from living in his communities. "As a Jew," he explained, "I have no room in my heart for racial prejudice. But the plain fact is that most whites prefer not to live in mixed communities. This attitude may be wrong morally, and someday it may change. I hope it will."

Other developers soon mimicked Levitt's efforts, building all-White suburban communities with rustic names such as Lakewood, Streamwood, Elmwood, Cedar Hill, Park Forest, and Deer Park. In 1955, *House and Garden* magazine declared that suburbia had become the "national way of life." By 1960, however, only 5 percent of African Americans lived in suburbs.

PEOPLE OF COLOR ON THE MOVE

The mass migration of rural southern Blacks to cities in the North, Midwest, and West after the Second World War was much larger than the migration after the First World War, and its social consequences were even more dramatic. After 1945, more than 5 million Blacks left the South in search of better jobs and housing, higher wages, and greater civil rights.

By 1960, for the first time in history, more African Americans were living in urban than in rural areas. As people of color moved into cities, however, many White residents left for the suburbs. Between 1950 and 1960, some 3.6 million Whites left the nation's largest cities for suburban neighborhoods (referred to as White flight), while 4.5 million Blacks and thousands of Puerto Ricans moved into large cities.

The increasing mobility of African Americans revealed how deeply entrenched White racism and Jim

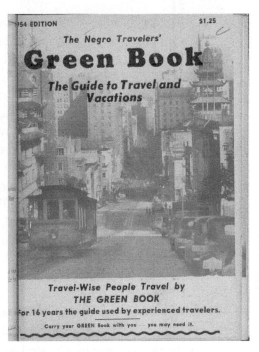

The Green Book Postal employee Victor Green published this essential travel guidebook for Black travelers beginning in 1936 to identify which businesses, especially motels and restaurants, served African Americans.

Crow segregation had become across the United States. Black travelers, whether by car, bus, train, or airplane, could not visit most White-owned restaurants or hotel/motels. If traveling in automobiles, they could not get gasoline at most service stations. In addition, Blacks traveling at night could not enter "sundown" towns, all-White communities that banned Blacks after dark. African Americans often drove all night because no motels would take them in. Along the way, Blacks encountered racist billboards and signs. In rural Greenville, Texas, for example, visitors were greeted by a banner proclaiming, "Greenville: The Blackest land, the Whitest people."

The lack of roadside businesses willing to serve African Americans prompted Victor Green in 1936 to publish *The Negro Traveler's Green Book*, an essential guidebook for Black travelers that listed the mostly Black-owned eateries, service stations, hotels, nightclubs, and other businesses willing to serve African Americans. The book appeared in new editions for thirty years.

It ceased publication in 1966, after the civil rights movement and new federal laws prohibited racial segregation in public facilities.

Through organizations such as the National Association for the Advancement of Colored People (NAACP), the Congress of Racial Equality (CORE), and the National Urban League, Blacks during the fifties sought to change the hearts and minds of their White neighbors. However, for all the racism that Black migrants encountered nationwide, most of them preferred their new lives outside the South to the enforced segregation and often violent abuse in their native region.

Just as African Americans were on the move, so, too, were Mexicans and Puerto Ricans. Congress renewed the bracero program, begun during the Second World War, which enabled Mexicans to work as wage laborers in the United States, often as migrant farmworkers. Mexicans streamed across the nation's southwest border. By 1960, Los Angeles had the largest concentration of Mexican Americans in the nation.

Mexican Americans, Puerto Ricans, and other Latinos who served in the military also benefited from the GI Bill. Many of them—and their families— were able to relocate to the mainland United States because of the educational and housing programs provided veterans through the federal government. Between 1940 and 1960, nearly a million Puerto Ricans, mostly small farmers and agricultural workers, moved into American cities, especially New York City. By the late 1960s, more Puerto Ricans (who enjoy dual citizenship of the Commonwealth of Puerto Rico and the United States) lived in New York City than in San Juan, the capital of Puerto Rico.

SHIFTING WOMEN'S ROLES   During the Second World War, millions of women had assumed traditionally male jobs in factories and mills. After the war, the influx of men returning to the civilian workforce led many employers to push working women back into traditional homemaking roles. A 1945 article in *House Beautiful* magazine informed women that the returning war veteran was "head man again. . . . Your part in the remaking of this man is to fit his home to him, understanding why he wants it this way, forgetting your own preferences."

Throughout the postwar period, women were urged to be satisfied housewives and mothers, letting their husbands be the "breadwinner." Democratic presidential nominee Adlai Stevenson told the graduating class at all-female Smith College in 1955 that they should embrace "the humble role of housewife." To be a single woman in the fifties, however, was to be sentenced to a joyless and lonely life, according to most women's magazines. At Mount Holyoke College, an all-female school in Massachusetts, 330 of the 350 seniors in 1949 married immediately after graduation.

Hollywood Homemakers TV shows, movies, and plays in the fifties were outlets for homemakers' anxieties and fantasies. *(Left) Leave it to Beaver* (1957) was a popular comedy about a young boy and his happy-go-lucky family living in one of the many lookalike suburbs. *(Right)* Domestic bliss was often out of reach for African American female characters. In *Porgy and Bess* (1959), Dorothy Dandridge plays an addict so lost in the vice of New Orleans that even her self-sacrificing disabled lover (Sidney Poitier) cannot save her.

Few women questioned such priorities. "I got a little secretarial job after college," recalled Bonnie Carr. "Education, work, whatever you did before marriage, was only a prelude to your real life, which was marriage." In 1940, some 69 percent of the population was married; by 1950, the number had risen to 77 percent, and by 1960 to 80 percent. During the fifties, half of brides married before the age of nineteen.

In 1950, some 721,000 women were enrolled in colleges, compared to 2.26 million men. A common sexist joke was that women went to college to get an "M.R.S. degree"—that is, a husband. Marriage was "all I thought about in college," recalled Joy Wilner. "Life was not concerned with work, but with men and dating." When Cassandra Dunn told her parents she wanted to become a lawyer, her father exploded, "If you do this, no man will ever want you."

Despite this "modern" version of the nineteenth century's cult of domesticity, many women did work outside the home. In 1950, women accounted for 29 percent of the workforce, and that percentage rose steadily throughout the decade. Some 70 percent of employed women worked in clerical positions—as secretaries, bank tellers, or sales clerks—or on assembly lines or in the service industry (as waitresses, laundresses, housekeepers). Less than 15 percent were employed in a professional capacity (teachers, nurses, accountants, social workers). Women represented only 3.5 percent of attorneys and 6 percent of physicians. African American and other women of color had even fewer vocational choices and were mostly relegated to low-paying domestic service jobs such as maids and cooks.

THE CHILD-CENTERED FIFTIES The fifties witnessed a record number of marriages—and births. The decade was an ideal time to be a child. The horrors of the Second World War were over, the economy was surging, and social life centered on children—because there were so many of them. Between 1946 and 1964, the birth of 76 million Americans created a demographic upheaval whose repercussions are still being felt.

The "**baby boom**" peaked in 1957, when a record 4.3 million births occurred, one every seven seconds. Most brides during the fifties were pregnant within seven months of their wedding, and they didn't stop at just one child. Large families were typical. From 1940 to 1960, the number of families with three children doubled and the number of families having a fourth child quadrupled. Dr. Benjamin Spock's *The Common Sense Book of Baby and Child Care* sold more than a million copies a year during the fifties.

Children's needs drove economic growth. Postwar babies created a surge in demand for diapers, washing machines, and baby food, then required the construction of thousands of new schools—and the hiring of teachers to staff them.

A special issue of *Life* magazine in 1956 featured the "ideal" middle-class woman: a thirty-two-year-old "pretty and popular" White suburban housewife, mother of four, who had married at age sixteen. She was described as an excellent wife, mother, volunteer, and "home manager." She made her own clothes, hosted dozens of dinner parties each year, sang in her church choir, and was devoted to her husband. "In her daily round," *Life* reported, "she attends club or charity meetings, drives the children to school, does the weekly grocery shopping, makes ceramics, and is planning to study French."

The soaring birthrate reinforced the notion that a woman's place was in the home. "Of all the accomplishments of the American woman," *Life* magazine proclaimed, "the one she brings off with the most spectacular success is having babies." Carol Freeman described her life in a new California suburb as "a warm, boring, completely child-centered culture. We sat around in each other's kitchens and backyards and drank a lot of coffee and smoked a million cigarettes and talked about our children."

A RELIGIOUS NATION After the Second World War, Americans joined churches and synagogues in record numbers. In 1940, less than half the

Roadside Service Drive-in churches offered participants the convenience of listening to Sunday church services from their cars. Here, the pastor of New York's Tremont Methodist Church greets a member of his four-wheeled congregation.

adult population belonged to a church; by 1960, more than 65 percent were members. Sales of Bibles soared, as did the demand for books, movies, and songs with religious themes.

The Cold War provided a stimulant to Christian evangelism. A godly nation, it was assumed, would better withstand the march of "godless" communism. Communism, explained the Reverend Billy Graham, the most famous evangelist of the fifties, was "a great sinister anti-Christian movement masterminded by Satan" that must be fought wherever it emerged around the world.

President Eisenhower promoted a patriotic religious crusade during the fifties. "Recognition of the Supreme Being," he declared, "is the first, the most basic, expression of Americanism. Without God, there could be no American form of government, nor an American way of life." In 1954, Congress added the phrase "[one nation] under God" to the Pledge of Allegiance. In 1956, it made the statement "In God We Trust" the nation's official motto, and Eisenhower ordered it displayed on all currency. "Today in the United States," *Time* magazine claimed in 1954, "the Christian faith is back at the center of things." The prevailing tone of the religious revival was upbeat and soothing. As the Protestant Council of New York City explained to its radio and television presenters, their on-air broadcasts "should project love, joy, courage, hope, faith, trust in God, goodwill. . . . In a very real sense we are 'selling' religion, the good news of the Gospel."

The best salesman for this "good news" was the Reverend Norman Vincent Peale. No speaker was more in demand, and no writer was more widely read. Peale's book *The Power of Positive Thinking* (1952) was a phenomenal best seller—and for good reason. It offered a simple how-to course in personal happiness, which Peale called Practical Christianity. "Flush out all depressing, negative, and tired thoughts," he advised. "Start thinking faith, enthusiasm, and joy." By following this simple formula, he pledged, each American could become "a more popular, esteemed, and well-liked individual." At the height of Peale's popularity, he was reaching 30 million people each week through radio, television, and his weekly newspaper columns.

CRACKS IN THE PICTURE WINDOW

In contrast to the "happy days" image of the fifties, there was also anxiety, dissent, and diversity. In *The Affluent Society* (1958), economist John Kenneth Galbraith attacked the prevailing notion that sustained economic growth would solve all major social problems. He reminded readers that the nation had yet to eradicate poverty, especially among minorities in inner cities, female-led households, Mexican American migrant farmworkers, Native Americans, and rural southerners—both Black and White.

POVERTY AMID PROSPERITY Uncritical praise for the "throwaway" culture of consumption during the 1950s masked the chronic poverty amid America's much-celebrated plenty. In 1959, a quarter of the population had *no* financial assets, and more than half had no savings accounts or credit cards. Poverty afflicted nearly half of African Americans, compared to only a quarter of Whites. True, by 1950, Blacks were earning on average more than four times their 1940 wages, but they and other minorities lagged well behind Whites in their *rate* of improvement. At least 40 million people—Whites and people of color—remained "poor" during the 1950s, but their plight was largely ignored amid the wave of middle-class White consumerism.

As was true after the First World War, many southerners migrated during the Second World War and after to northern cities where they hoped to find higher-paying jobs in manufacturing. The "promised land" in the North was not perfect, for migrating Whites or people of color. Because those who left the South were often undereducated, poor, and Black, they were regularly denied access to good jobs, good schools, and good housing. Although states in the North, Midwest, and Far West were not as blatantly discriminatory as in the South, African Americans still encountered racism and discrimination.

LITERATURE AS SOCIAL CRITICISM Many critics, writers, and artists rejected America's social complacency and worship of consumerism. Playwright Thornton Wilder labeled young adults of the fifties the "Silent Generation" because of their self-centered outlook. Everyone in the new middle-class White suburbs, a social critic claimed, "buys the right car, keeps his lawn like his neighbor's, eats crunchy breakfast cereal, and votes Republican."

The most powerful novels of the postwar period emphasized the individual's struggle for survival amid the smothering forces of mass society. Books such as James Jones's *From Here to Eternity* (1951), Ralph Ellison's *Invisible Man* (1952), Saul Bellow's *Seize the Day* (1956), J. D. Salinger's *Catcher in the Rye* (1951), William Styron's *Lie Down in Darkness* (1951), and John Updike's *Rabbit, Run* (1961) feature restless, tormented souls who can find neither contentment nor respect in a superficial world.

The upper-middle-class White suburbs and the culture of comfortable conformity they created were frequent literary targets. Writer John Cheever located most of his brilliant short stories in suburban neighborhoods outside of New York City—"cesspools of conformity," where the life he witnessed was mindless and hollow. In his vicious satire of affluent suburbia, *The Crack in the Picture Window* (1956), John Keats charged that "miles of identical boxes are spreading like gangrene" across the

Ralph Ellison Ellison is best remembered for his 1952 novel, *Invisible Man*. His writings criticized many of the social and cultural changes sweeping through postwar America.

nation, producing "haggard" businessmen, "tense and anxious" housewives, and "the gimme kids" who, after unwrapping the last Christmas gift, "look up and ask whether that is all." He dismissed Levittowns as residential "developments conceived in error, nurtured by greed, corroding everything they touch. They destroy established cities and trade patterns, pose dangerous problems for the areas they invade, and actually drive mad myriads of housewives shut up in them."

THE BEATS A small but highly controversial group of young writers, poets, painters, and musicians rejected the consumer culture and the traditional responsibilities of middle-class life. They were known as the **Beats**. To be "beat" was likened to being "on the beat" in "real cool" jazz music. But the Beats also liked the name because it implied "weariness," being "exhausted" or "beaten down," qualities that none of them actually exhibited.

Art Ache The Beat community fostered a frenzied desire to experience life in all its intensity, spontaneity, and zaniness. In this 1959 photograph, poet Tex Kleen reads verse in a bathtub at Venice Beach, California, while artist Mad Mike paints trash cans.

Jack Kerouac, Allen Ginsberg, William Burroughs, Neal Cassady, Gary Snyder, and other Beats rebelled against conventional literary and artistic expression and excelled at often purposeless and even criminal behavior. In nurturing their alienation from mainstream life, the mostly male Beats were nomadic seekers, restless and often tormented souls who stole cars and cash and sought solace in booze, mind-altering drugs, carefree sex, and various forms of risk-taking behavior. A drunk Burroughs, for example, tried to shoot a glass off his wife's head and missed, killing her.

The Beats emerged from the bohemian underground in New York City's Greenwich Village. An anarchic boys club, the Beats were masters at outrageous behavior who viewed women as second-class accessories. Throughout the fifties, the Beats seemed in perpetual cross-country motion, crisscrossing the continent in a feverish search for ecstasy. They were, as Jack Kerouac wrote, "mad to live, mad to talk, mad to be saved." During three feverish weeks, Kerouac typed nonstop on a continuous roll of teletype paper the manuscript of his remarkable novel *On the Road* (1957), an account of a series of frenzied cross-country trips he and others made between 1948 and 1950.

The Beats were as much a force for social change as they were a cultural movement. Many Beats, notably Allen Ginsberg and his lifelong partner, poet Peter Orlovsky, were openly gay or bisexual during an era when being so continued to be scorned as "deviant" behavior. Ginsberg and Orlovsky termed their relationship a marriage, and by doing so the two men were social pioneers, the first gay "married" couple that many people had ever encountered. They remained partners for more than forty years, until Ginsberg's death in 1997.

ROCK 'N' ROLL The raucous rebelliousness of the Beats set the stage for the more widespread youth revolt of the 1960s and the flowering of the "hippies." The millions of children making up the first wave of "baby boomers" became adolescents in the late 1950s. People began calling them *teenagers*, and a distinctive teen subculture began to emerge, as did a wave of juvenile delinquency. By 1956, more than a million teens were being arrested each year. One contributing factor was access to automobiles, which enabled them to escape parental control and, in the words of one journalist, provided "a private lounge for drinking and for petting [embracing and kissing] or sex episodes."

Many blamed teen delinquency on *rock 'n' roll*, a new form of music. Alan Freed, a Cleveland disc jockey, coined the term in 1951. He had noticed that White teenagers buying rhythm and blues (R&B) records preferred the livelier recordings by African Americans and Latino Americans. Freed began playing R&B songs on his radio show, but he called the music rock 'n' roll (a phrase used in African American communities to refer to dancing and sex). By 1954, Freed had moved to New York City, where his rock 'n' roll radio show helped bridge the gap between "White" and "Black" music.

African American singers such as Chuck Berry, Little Richard, and Ray Charles, along with Latino American performers such as Ritchie Valens (Richard Valenzuela), captivated young, White, middle-class audiences. At the same time, Sam Phillips, a disk jockey in Memphis, Tennessee, was searching for a particular type of pop singer. "If I could find a white man with a Negro sound," Phillips said, "I could make a billion dollars."

Elvis Presley Star-struck fans grab at him from all angles, but the "King of Rock and Roll" stays cool while performing in Miami, 1956.

He found him in Elvis Presley, the lanky son of poor Mississippi farmers. In 1956, the twenty-one-year-old Presley, by then a regional star famous for his long, unruly hair, sullen yet sensual sneer, and swiveling hips, released his smash-hit recording "Heartbreak Hotel." Over the next two years, Elvis emerged as one of the most popular musicians in American history, carrying rock 'n' roll across the race barrier and assaulting the bland conformity of fifties culture. Presley's gyrating performances (his nickname was "Elvis the Pelvis") and incomparable voice drove young people wild and earned him millions of fans. His movements on stage, said one music critic, "suggest, in a word, sex."

Although Presley claimed to neither smoke nor drink and said daily prayers, cultural conservatives urged parents to destroy his records. One observer reported that Presley's live performances were "strip-teases with clothes on . . . not only suggestive but downright obscene." A Roman Catholic official denounced Presley as practicing a "creed of dishonesty, violence, lust and degeneration." Patriotic groups claimed that rock 'n' roll music was part of a Communist plot to corrupt America's youth. Writing in the *New York Times*, a psychiatrist characterized rock music as a "communicable disease." A U.S. Senate subcommittee warned that Presley was promoting "open revolt against society. The gangster of tomorrow is the Elvis Presley type of today."

Yet rock 'n' roll flourished in part because it was so controversial. It gave teenagers a sense of belonging to a tribal social group. More important, it brought together, on equal terms, musicians (and their audiences) of varied races and backgrounds. The composer Leonard Bernstein, conductor of the New York Philharmonic orchestra, said Elvis Presley was "the greatest cultural force in the twentieth century."

THE EARLY YEARS OF THE CIVIL RIGHTS MOVEMENT

Soon after the Cold War began, Soviet diplomats began to use America's widespread racism as a propaganda tool to illustrate the defects of the capitalist nation's way of life. Under the Jim Crow system in southern states, Blacks still risked being lynched if they registered to vote. They were forced to use separate facilities—restrooms, hotels, theaters, parks—and attend segregated schools. In the North, discrimination was not officially sanctioned by local and state laws as it was in the South, but it was equally real, especially in housing and employment.

EISENHOWER AND RACE President Eisenhower had an opportunity to exercise transformational leadership in race relations; his unwillingness to do so was his greatest failure. As *Time* magazine noted in 1958, Eisenhower "overlooked the fact that the U.S. needed [his] moral leadership in fighting segregation." The president had entered the White House committed to civil rights in principle, and he pushed for improvements in some areas. During his first three years, public facilities (parks, playgrounds, libraries, restaurants) in Washington, D.C., were desegregated, and he intervened to end discrimination at military bases in Virginia and South Carolina. Beyond that, however, he refused to make civil rights for African Americans a moral crusade.

Like many Whites, Eisenhower failed to recognize until it was too late the depth of African American anger and frustration. He also was cowed by the determination of southern Whites to resist any effort to end segregation.

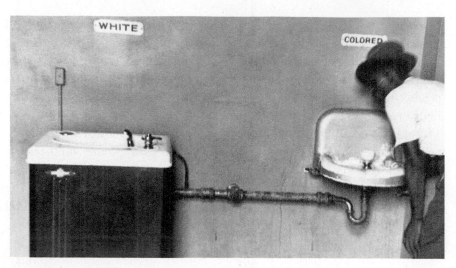

Fountains of Truth This iconic image taken by Elliot Erwitt in North Carolina in 1950 powerfully depicts the injustice of segregation.

Pushing the former Confederate states too hard, Eisenhower believed, would "raise tempers and increase prejudices."

Two aspects of Eisenhower's political philosophy limited his commitment to racial equality: his preference for state or local action over federal involvement and his doubt that laws could change deeply embedded racist attitudes. His passivity meant that governmental leadership on civil rights would come from the judiciary more than from the executive or legislative branches.

In 1953, Eisenhower appointed Republican Earl Warren, former governor of California, as chief justice of the U.S. Supreme Court, a decision he later said was the "biggest damn fool mistake I ever made." Warren, who had seemed safely conservative while in elected office, displayed a social conscience as chief justice. Under his leadership (1953–1969), the Supreme Court became a powerful force for social and political change.

AFRICAN AMERICAN ACTIVISM   The most crucial leaders of the early civil rights movement came from those groups whose rights were most often violated: African Americans, Latino Americans, Asian Americans, and others. Courageous Blacks were in the forefront of what would become the most important social movement in twentieth-century America. They fought in the courts, at the ballot box, and in the streets.

Although many African Americans had moved to the North and West, a majority remained in the South, where they still faced a rigidly segregated society. In the 1952 presidential election, for example, only 20 percent of eligible African Americans were registered to vote. And although the public schools, especially in the South, were racially separate but supposedly equal in quality, many all-Black schools were actually underfunded, understaffed, and overcrowded.

In the mid-1930s, the National Association for the Advancement of Colored People (NAACP) challenged the **separate-but-equal** judicial doctrine that had preserved racial segregation since the *Plessy* decision by the Supreme Court in 1896. It took almost fifteen years, however, to convince the courts that racial segregation must end. Finally, in *Sweatt v. Painter* (1950), the Supreme Court ruled that a separate Black law school in Texas was *not* equal in quality to the state's Whites-only law schools. The Court ordered Texas to remedy the situation. It was the first step toward dismantling America's tradition of racial segregation.

THE *BROWN* DECISION (1954) By the early 1950s, civil rights activists were challenging state laws requiring racial segregation in the public schools. Five such cases, from Kansas, Delaware, South Carolina, Virginia, and the District of Columbia—usually cited by reference to the first, ***Brown v. Board of Education*** *of Topeka, Kansas*—were bundled together and considered by the Supreme Court in 1952. President Eisenhower gutlessly told the attorney general that he hoped the justices would postpone dealing with the case "until the next Administration took over." When it became obvious that the Court was moving forward, Eisenhower urged Chief Justice Warren to side

Separate, but Not Equal African American children pose outside their segregated schoolhouse in Selma, Alabama, in 1965.

with segregationists. Warren was not swayed: "You mind your business," he told the president, "and I'll mind mine."

Warren wrote the pathbreaking unanimous opinion, delivered on May 17, 1954, in which the Court declared that "in the field of public education the doctrine of 'separate but equal' has no place." The justices used a variety of sociological and psychological findings presented by civil rights attorneys to show that even if racially separate schools were equal in quality, the very practice of separating students by race caused feelings of inferiority among Black children. A year later, the Court directed that racial *integration* should move forward "with all deliberate speed."

No longer, it seemed, could racially segregated schools claim they were simply obeying the old "separate but equal" law. The Court's ruling in *Brown*, said the *Chicago Defender*, a leading African American newspaper, was "a second emancipation proclamation . . . more important to our democracy than the atomic bomb or the hydrogen bomb." President Eisenhower refused to endorse or enforce the Court's ruling. In private, he grumbled that "the Supreme Court decision set back progress in the South at least fifteen years."

Eisenhower even refused to condemn the 1955 lynching of fourteen-year-old Emmett Till, an African American from Chicago who was visiting relatives in Tallahatchie, Mississippi. While buying bubble gum in Bryant's Grocery and Meat Market in the small town, Till supposedly winked or whistled at the White woman who owned the store with her husband. A few nights later, several White men found Till at his relatives' home, dragged him out of bed, and took him into the woods where they beat and tortured him before shooting him. They then used barbed wire to tie a 75-pound cotton-gin fan around his neck before throwing his naked body into the Tallahatchie River. His body was so mutilated that the mortician urged his mother not to have an open casket at the funeral in Chicago. No, she replied, leave his casket open "so all the world could see what they did to my son." More than 100,000 people viewed and mourned Emmett Till's mutilated body. The men who were tried for Till's murder were found not guilty by the all-White jury, though they later admitted they had killed him.

William Faulkner, the Nobel Prize–winning Mississippi novelist, reacted to news of the Emmett Till lynching by writing, "If we in America have reached that point in our desperate culture when we must murder children, no matter for what reason or what color, we don't deserve to survive, and probably won't."

"MASSIVE RESISTANCE" The senseless violence in Mississippi revealed yet again how difficult it would be to dislodge White supremacy in southern society. While token racial integration began as early as 1954 in northern states and the border states of Kentucky and Missouri, hostility mounted in the Lower South and Virginia. The Alabama State Senate and the Virginia legislature both passed resolutions "nullifying" the Supreme Court's school integration decision, arguing that racial integration was an issue of states' rights. Arkansas governor Orval Faubus insisted that the "federal government is a creature of the states. . . . We must either choose to defend our rights or else surrender."

In 1954, Harry F. Byrd, a Virginia senator and former governor, called for **"massive resistance"** against federal efforts to enforce integration in the South. Senator James O. Eastland of Mississippi, a state where African Americans made up 45 percent of the population, pledged that "integration will never come to Mississippi." A plantation owner and notorious racist whose father had lynched a Black couple, Eastland denounced the *Brown* decision as an "illegal, immoral, and sinful doctrine." He told the Senate that "the Negro race is an inferior race" and that the South was determined to maintain White supremacy. He blamed the *Brown* decision on Communists. "The Negroes," he claimed, "did not themselves instigate the agitation against segregation. They were put up to it by radical busybodies who are intent upon overthrowing American institutions."

The grassroots opposition among southern Whites to the *Brown* case was led by newly formed Citizens' Councils, middle-class versions of the Ku Klux Klan that spread quickly and eventually enrolled 250,000 members. The Councils, which used economic coercion against Blacks who crossed racial boundaries, grew so powerful in some communities that membership became almost a necessity for an aspiring White politician.

In 1956, more than a hundred members of Congress signed a Declaration of Constitutional Principles ("Southern Manifesto"), deploring the *Brown* decision as "a clear abuse of judicial power" that had created an "explosive and dangerous condition" in the South. Only three southern Democrats refused to sign. One of them, Senator Lyndon B. Johnson of Texas, would become president seven years later. In six southern states at the end of 1956, two years after the *Brown* ruling, no Black children attended school with Whites. By 1960, only 765 of 6,676 school districts in the South had desegregated.

THE MONTGOMERY BUS BOYCOTT While mobilizing White resistance, the *Brown* case also inspired many Black (and White) activists by suggesting that the federal government was finally beginning to confront racial discrimination. Yet the essential role played by the NAACP and the courts in the civil rights movement often overshadows the courageous contributions of individual African Americans who took great risks to challenge segregation.

For example, in Montgomery, Alabama, on December 1, 1955, Mrs. Rosa Parks, a forty-two-year-old seamstress who was a veteran activist for racial justice, boarded the Cleveland Avenue bus and sat in the third row. As White passengers boarded, the White driver, James Blake, told Parks she had to move to the back, as the city required Blacks to do. She refused. Blake then demanded, "Why don't you stand up?" Parks calmly replied, "I don't think I should have to stand up." When the driver told her that "'Negroes' must move back" or be arrested, she replied, "You may do that." She was "tired of giving in," she recalled. She had been "pushed as far as I could stand to be pushed." Police then arrested her. In holding her ground, Parks had unwittingly launched the modern civil rights movement.

The night Rosa Parks was arrested, Jo Ann Robinson, an English professor at Alabama State College, circulated 50,000 flyers across town that read, "Another Negro woman has been arrested and thrown into jail because she refused to get up out of her seat on the bus for a White person to sit down. Don't ride the buses." The next night, Black community leaders met at Dexter Avenue Baptist Church to organize a long-planned boycott of the city's bus system, most of whose riders were African Americans. The **Montgomery bus boycott** had begun.

MARTIN LUTHER KING JR. In the Dexter Avenue church's twenty-six-year-old pastor, Martin Luther King Jr., the boycott movement found a brave and charismatic leader. The grandson of a slave and son of a prominent minister, King was an eloquent speaker. "We must use the weapon of love," he told supporters. "We must realize so many people are taught to hate us that they are not totally responsible for their hate."

Nonviolent Civil Disobedience *(Left)* Rosa Parks is fingerprinted by a Montgomery police officer on February 22, 1956, along with about 100 other protesters who joined the bus boycott. *(Right)* Martin Luther King Jr. is arrested for "loitering" in 1958. He would be arrested thirty times in his life for defying racist laws.

To his foes, King warned, "We will soon wear you down by our capacity to suffer, and in winning our freedom we will so appeal to your heart and conscience that we will win you in the process." He preached **nonviolent civil disobedience,** the tactic of defying unjust laws through peaceful actions, but he also valued militancy, for without crisis and confrontation there would be no progress.

The Montgomery bus boycott was a stunning success. For 381 days, African Americans, women and men, organized carpools, used Black-owned taxis, hitchhiked, or simply walked. White supporters also provided rides. The unprecedented mass protest infuriated many Whites; police harassed and ticketed Black carpools, and White thugs attacked Black pedestrians. Ku Klux Klan members burned Black churches and bombed houses.

In trying to calm an angry Black crowd eager for revenge against their White tormentors, Martin Luther King urged restraint: "Don't get panicky. Don't get your weapons. We want to love our enemies." King himself was arrested twice. "The eyes of Alabama, the South, and now the nation," reported the *Washington Post*, "are on Montgomery."

On December 20, 1956, the Montgomery boycotters won a federal case they had initiated against racial segregation on public buses. The Supreme Court affirmed that "the separate but equal doctrine can no longer be safely followed as a correct statement of the law." The next day, King and other African Americans boarded the city buses. They showed that well-coordinated, nonviolent Black activism could trigger major changes. Among African Americans, hope replaced resignation, and action supplanted passivity. The boycott also catapulted King into the national spotlight.

And what of Rosa Parks? She and her husband lost their jobs. Hate mail, death threats, and fire bombings forced them to leave Alabama eight months after her arrest. They moved to Detroit, where they remained fully engaged in the evolving civil rights movement. "Freedom fighters never retire," she explained.

THE CIVIL RIGHTS ACTS OF 1957 AND 1960 In 1956, hoping to exploit divisions between northern and southern Democrats and reclaim some of the Black vote for Republicans, congressional leaders agreed to support what became the Civil Rights Act of 1957.

The first civil rights law enacted since 1875, it was passed, after a year's delay, with the help of majority leader Lyndon B. Johnson, a Texas Democrat who knew that he could never be elected president if he was viewed as just another racist White southerner. The bill was intended to ensure that all Americans, regardless of race or ethnicity, were allowed to vote. Johnson won southern acceptance of the bill by watering down its enforcement provisions.

The Civil Rights Act established the Civil Rights Commission and a new Civil Rights Division in the Justice Department intended to prevent interference with the right to vote. Yet by 1959, not a single southern Black voter had been added to the rolls. The Civil Rights Act of 1960, which provided for federal courts to register African Americans to vote in districts where there was a "pattern and practice" of racial discrimination, also lacked teeth and depended upon vigorous presidential enforcement to achieve any tangible results.

DESEGREGATION IN LITTLE ROCK A few weeks after the Civil Rights Act of 1957 was passed, Arkansas's Democratic governor, Orval Eugene Faubus, a rabid segregationist, called a special session of the state legislature. He asked the legislators to pass a series of bills designed to give him sweeping powers to close public schools threatened with integration; he also requested authority to transfer funds from public schools facing federally enforced integration to private "segregation academies."

"Lynch Her!" A determined Elizabeth Eckford endures the hostile screams of White students and parents as she tries to enter all-White Central High School in Little Rock, Arkansas.

In the fall of 1957, Faubus defied a federal court order by using the state's National Guard to prevent nine Black students from enrolling at Little Rock's Central High School. When one of the students, fifteen-year-old Elizabeth Eckford, tried to enter the school, National Guardsmen barred the door. Alone, she headed back to the bus stop, only to be confronted by a mob of jeering White mothers and schoolgirls shrieking, "Lynch her! Lynch her!" Eckford recalled, "They moved closer and closer. . . . I tried to see a friendly face somewhere in the crowd—someone who maybe could help. I looked into the face of an old woman and it seemed a kind face, but when I looked at her again, she spat at me."

The mayor of Little Rock frantically urged Eisenhower to send federal troops, and he reluctantly dispatched 1,000 army paratroopers to protect the brave Black students as they tried to enter the school. "Mob rule," he told the nation, "cannot be allowed to overrule the decisions of our courts."

It was the first time since the 1870s that federal troops had been sent to the South to protect African Americans. With television cameras sending dramatic images across the country, paratroopers used bayonets and rifle butts to disperse the angry crowd. The nine courageous, dignified Black students attended their first classes with soldiers patrolling the halls. The soldiers stayed in Little Rock through the school year.

To a man, unyielding southern governors and congressmen furiously lashed out at President Eisenhower, charging that he was violating states' rights. The president had "lit the fires of hate," claimed Senator James Eastland. Eisenhower, who had grown up in an all-White Kansas town and spent his military career in a segregated army, stressed that his use of federal troops had little to do with "the integration or segregation question" and everything to do with maintaining law and order. Although Eisenhower favored equality of opportunity, he explained to an aide that equality did not mean "that a Negro should court my daughter."

In Eisenhower's view, the federal troops in Little Rock showed that the United States government was based on the rule of law, that the Constitution remained the supreme law of the land, and that the U.S. Supreme Court was the final interpreter of the Constitution. Martin Luther King Jr. forced the president to take decisive action. He told Eisenhower that the "overwhelming majority of southerners, Negro and white, stand behind your resolute action to restore law and order in Little Rock."

In the summer of 1958, Governor Faubus closed the Little Rock high schools rather than allow racial integration. The governor of Virginia did the same. Their actions led Jonathan Daniels, editor of the Raleigh (North Carolina) *News & Observer*, to write that closing public schools is "something beyond secession from the Union; [it] is secession from civilization."

Court proceedings in Arkansas dragged into 1959 before the schools reopened. Resistance to integration in Virginia collapsed when state and federal courts struck down state laws that had cut off funds to integrated public schools. Thereafter, massive resistance to racial integration was confined mostly to the Lower South, where five states—from South Carolina westward through Louisiana—still opposed even token integration. Not a single pupil in those states attended an integrated school. Orville Faubus went on to serve six terms as governor of Arkansas.

SOUTHERN CHRISTIAN LEADERSHIP CONFERENCE After the confrontation in Little Rock, progress toward greater civil rights seemed agonizingly slow. The widespread sense of disappointment gave Martin Luther

King's nonviolent civil rights movement even greater visibility. As King explained, "We were confronted with blasted hopes, and the dark shadow of a deep disappointment settled upon us. So we had no alternative except that of preparing for direct action, whereby we would present our very bodies as a means of laying our case before the conscience of the local and national community."

On January 10, 1957, King invited sixty Black ministers and leaders to Ebenezer Church in Atlanta. Their goal was to form an organization to promote nonviolent civil disobedience as a method of desegregating bus systems across the South. As a result of their meetings, a new organization emerged: the **Southern Christian Leadership Conference (SCLC)**, with King as its president. Unlike the NAACP, which recruited individual members, the SCLC coordinated activities on behalf of a cluster of organizations, mostly individual churches or community groups. Because King pushed for direct action, only a few African American ministers were initially willing to affiliate with the SCLC, for fear of a White backlash.

King persisted, however, and over time the SCLC grew into a powerful organization. The activists knew that violence awaited them. Roy Wilkins, head of the NAACP, noted that "the Negro citizen has come to the point where he is not afraid of violence. He no longer shrinks back. He will assert himself, and if violence comes, so be it."

Thus began the second phase of the civil rights movement. It would come to fruition in the 1960s as African American activists showed the courage to resist injustice, the power to love everyone, and the strength to endure discouragement and opposition. They did so without the president's support. As Wilkins asserted: "President Eisenhower was a fine general and a good, decent man, but if he had fought World War II the way he fought for civil rights, we would all be speaking German today."

Christian faith was the bedrock of the early civil rights movement. As John Lewis, one of the most heroic civil rights leaders, stressed, "the movement was built on deep-seated religious convictions, and the movement grew out of a sense of faith—faith in God and faith in one's fellow human beings." Lewis remembered that frustrated Blacks met to discuss tactics "we would ask questions about what would Jesus do."

Foreign Policy in the Fifties

The Truman administration's commitment to contain communism focused on the Soviet threat to Western Europe. During the 1950s, members of the Eisenhower administration, especially Secretary of State John Foster Dulles, determined that containment was no longer enough; instead, the United States must develop a "dynamic" foreign policy that would "roll back" communism around the world.

Dulles's goal was to "liberate" people under Communist rule rather than merely contain its expansion. "For us," he said, "there are two kinds of people in the world. There are those who are Christians and support free enterprise, and there are the others." He soon discovered, however, that the complexities of world affairs and the realities of Soviet and Communist Chinese power made his moral commitment to manage the destiny of the world unrealistic—and costly.

CONCLUDING AN ARMISTICE President Eisenhower's first priority in foreign affairs was to end the Korean conflict, a war that neither side wanted to prolong but neither wanted to lose. Alas, he acknowledged, there "was no simple formula for bringing a swift, victorious end" to the stalemate. Eisenhower faced two choices: increase the war effort or pursue a negotiated settlement. He chose to do both.

In May 1953, Eisenhower took the bold step of intensifying the aerial bombardment of North Korea. He let it be known that he would use nuclear weapons if a truce were not forthcoming. Thereafter, negotiations moved quickly toward an armistice (cease-fire agreement) on July 26, 1953. It ended "all acts of armed force" and reaffirmed the historical border between the two Koreas just above the 38th parallel until both sides could arrive at a "final peaceful settlement." Other factors in bringing about the armistice were China's rising military losses in the conflict and the spirit of uncertainty felt by Soviet Communists after the death of Josef Stalin on March 5, 1953. Whatever the reasons for ending the war, Eisenhower was delighted that "three years of heroism, frustration, and bloodshed were over."

The Korean War was the first in which helicopters were used in combat, and it ushered in the era of jet fighters. It transformed the United States into the world's police officer by convincing American political and military leaders that communism was indeed a global threat. As President Eisenhower declared, the battle between democratic capitalism and tyrannical communism was a fight to the death: "Freedom is pitted against slavery; lightness against dark."

Within a few years, the United States would create scores of permanent military bases around the world and organize a national security apparatus in Washington to manage its new responsibilities—not the least of which was a growing stockpile of nuclear weaponry.

DULLES AND "MASSIVE RETALIATION" The architect of the Eisenhower administration's efforts to "roll back" communism was Secretary of State John Foster Dulles. Like Woodrow Wilson, Dulles was a Presbyterian minister's son, a self-righteous statesman with immense energy and intelligence who believed that the United States was "born with a sense of destiny and mission" to defeat communism and lead the world. (His British counterparts, however, were not impressed with his sermonizing monologues, calling them "dull, duller, Dulles.")

Dulles (and Eisenhower) insisted that containing communism was "immoral and futile" because it did nothing to free people from oppression. America, he argued, should work toward the liberation of the "captive peoples" of Eastern Europe and China. When State Department analyst George F. Kennan, architect of the containment doctrine, dismissed Dulles's rhetoric as lunacy, Dulles fired him. Eisenhower, however, understood Kennan's objections. He stressed that the so-called liberation doctrine would not involve military force. Instead, he would promote the removal of Communist control "by every peaceful means, but only by peaceful means." Yet he did nothing to temper Dulles's rhetoric and praised his secretary of state's moral fervor.

"Don't Be Afraid—I Can Always Pull You Back" In this political cartoon, Secretary of State John Foster Dulles pushes a reluctant America to the brink of war as a means of creating diplomatic leverage.

Dulles and Eisenhower knew they could not win a ground war against the Soviet Union or Communist China, whose armies had millions more soldiers than did the United States. Nor could the administration afford—politically or financially—to sustain military expenditures at the levels required during the Korean War. So they crafted a strategy that came to be called **"massive retaliation,"** which meant using the threat of nuclear warfare to prevent Communist aggression. The strategy, they argued, would provide a "maximum deterrent at bearable cost," or "more bang for the buck." In a 1954 speech, Secretary of

State Dulles called for "the deterrent of massive retaliatory power . . . by means and at times of our own choosing."

The massive retaliation strategy had major weaknesses, however. By the mid-1950s, both the United States and Soviet Union had developed hydrogen bombs that were 750 times as powerful as the atomic bombs dropped on Japan in 1945. A single hydrogen bomb would have a devastating global impact, yet war planners envisioned using hundreds of them. "The necessary art," Dulles explained, was in the *brinkmanship*, "the ability to get to the verge without getting into war. . . . If you are scared to go to the brink, you are lost." Yet the massive retaliation strategy meant that it escalated every global dispute into a possible war of annihilation. The *Milwaukee Journal* found Dulles's brink-manship strategy terrifying: "It is like saying that the closer you get to war the better you serve peace. It is like saying that the destiny of the human race is something to gamble with."

THE CIA'S FOREIGN INTERVENTIONS   While publicly promoting the liberation of Communist nations and massive retaliation as a strategy against the Soviets, President Eisenhower and Secretary of State Dulles were secretly using the **Central Intelligence Agency (CIA)** to manipulate world politics in covert ways—propaganda, bribery, assassinations—that produced unintended consequences—all of them bad.

The anti-colonial independence movements unleashed by the Second World War led to nationalist groups around the globe revolting against British and French involvement in their affairs. In May 1951, the Iranian parliament seized control of the nation's British-run oil industry. The following year, prime minister Mohammed Mossadegh cut diplomatic ties with Great Britain and insisted that Iran, not Britain, should own, sell, and profit from Iranian oil. Dulles predicted that Iran was on the verge of falling under Communist control. The CIA and the British intelligence agency, MI6, then launched Operation Ajax to oust Mossadegh.

The CIA bribed Iranian army officers and hired Iranian agents to arrest Mossadegh, who was then convicted of high treason. Thereafter, in return for access to Iranian oil, the U.S. government provided massive support for the anti-Communist (and increasingly authoritarian) regime of the shah (king) of Iran, Mohammad Reza Pahlavi, who seized power in 1953. The Iranians would not forget that the Americans had put the hated shah in power.

The success of the CIA-engineered coup emboldened Eisenhower to authorize other secret operations to undermine "unfriendly" government regimes, even if it meant aligning with corrupt dictatorships. In 1954, the target was the democratically elected government of Guatemala, a poor Central American country led by Colonel Jacobo Arbenz Guzman. Arbenz's decision to take over U.S.-owned property and industries convinced Dulles that Guatemala was falling victim to "international communism." Dulles persuaded Eisenhower to approve a CIA operation to organize a secret Guatemalan army in Honduras. On June 18, 1954, aided by CIA-piloted warplanes, 150 CIA-paid "liberators" forced Arbenz into exile in Mexico. The United States then installed a new ruler in Guatemala who eliminated all political opposition.

By secretly overthrowing elected governments to ensure that they did not join the Soviet bloc, however, the CIA destabilized Iran and Guatemala and created resentments in the Middle East and Central America that would eventually come back to haunt the United States.

THE INDOCHINA WAR During the 1950s, the United States also became embroiled in Southeast Asia. Indochina, a French colony created out of the old kingdoms of Cambodia, Laos, and Vietnam, offered a distinctive case of anti-colonial nationalism. During the Second World War, after Japanese troops had occupied the region, the Viet Minh (League for the Independence of Vietnam) waged a guerrilla resistance movement led by Ho Chi Minh, a seasoned revolutionary and passionate nationalist.

"Uncle Ho," a wispy man weighing barely 100 pounds, had a single goal for his country: independence. At the end of the war against Japan, the Viet Minh controlled part of northern Vietnam. On September 2, 1945, Ho Chi Minh proclaimed the creation of a Democratic Republic of Vietnam, with its capital in Hanoi.

The French underestimated the determination of the Vietnamese nationalists to maintain their independence. In 1946, the First Indochina War erupted when Ho's fighters resisted French efforts to restore the colonial regime. French forces quickly regained control of the cities, while the Viet Minh controlled the countryside. Ho predicted that his forces would absorb more losses, but the French would give in first.

When the Korean War ended, the United States continued its efforts to strengthen French control of Vietnam. By the end of 1953, the Eisenhower administration was paying nearly 80 percent of the cost of the French military effort. In December 1953, some 12,000 French soldiers parachuted into **Dien Bien Phu**, a cluster of villages in a valley ringed by mountains in northwestern Vietnam. Their plan was to lure Viet Minh guerrillas into the open and then overwhelm them with superior firepower. The French assumed that the surrounding forested ridges were impassable. Their strategy, however, backfired. More than 55,000 Viet Minh fighters took up positions atop the ridges overlooking the French base. They then laboriously dug trenches and tunnels

Dien Bien Phu Viet Minh soldiers march captured French soldiers to a prisoner-of-war camp near Dien Bien Phu on May 7, 1954.

down into the valley and slowly drew a noose around the French garrison. By March 1954, the French found themselves surrounded—and trapped.

As the weeks passed, the French government pleaded with the United States to relieve the pressure on Dien Bien Phu. The National Security Council—John Foster Dulles, Vice President Richard Nixon, and the chairman of the Joint Chiefs of Staff—urged President Eisenhower to use atomic bombs to aid the French. Eisenhower snapped back: "You boys must be crazy. We can't use those awful things against Asians for the second time in less than ten years. My God!" The president opposed U.S. intervention unless the British joined the effort. When they refused, Eisenhower told the French that U.S. military action was "politically impossible." He repeated his concern at a press conference, stressing that he could not "conceive of a greater tragedy for America than to get heavily involved now in an all-out war" in Indochina.

On May 7, 1954, the Viet Minh fighters overwhelmed the last French resistance. The catastrophic defeat signaled the end of French colonial rule in Asia. On July 20, 1954, representatives of France, Britain, the Soviet Union,

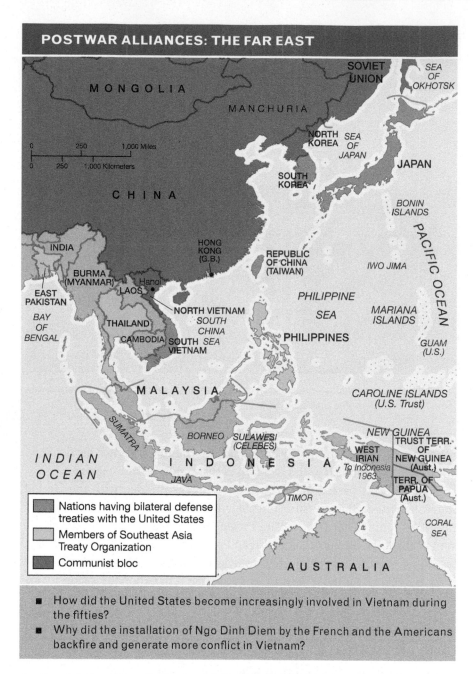

POSTWAR ALLIANCES: THE FAR EAST

- Nations having bilateral defense treaties with the United States
- Members of Southeast Asia Treaty Organization
- Communist bloc

■ How did the United States become increasingly involved in Vietnam during the fifties?

■ Why did the installation of Ngo Dinh Diem by the French and the Americans backfire and generate more conflict in Vietnam?

the People's Republic of China, and the Viet Minh signed the Geneva Accords, which gave Laos and Cambodia their independence and divided Vietnam at the 17th parallel of latitude. The Viet Minh Communists were given control in the North, with the French remaining south of the line until nationwide elections in 1956. Ho Chi Minh took charge of the government in North Vietnam, executing thousands of Vietnamese he deemed opponents.

In South Vietnam, power gravitated to a new premier chosen by the French at American urging: Ngo Dinh Diem, a Catholic nationalist who had opposed both the French and the Viet Minh. In 1954, Eisenhower began providing military and economic aid to Diem. Yet Diem's autocratic efforts to eliminate all opposition played into the hands of the Communists, who found eager recruits among the discontented South Vietnamese. By 1957, Communist guerrillas known as the **Viet Cong** were launching attacks on the Diem government. As the warfare intensified, the Eisenhower administration concluded that its only option was to "sink or swim with Diem."

Eisenhower had used what he called the **"falling-domino" theory** to explain why the United States needed to fight communism in Vietnam: "You have a row of dominos set up, you knock over the first one, and what will happen to the last one is the certainty that it will go over very quickly." If South Vietnam were to fall to communism, he predicted, the rest of Southeast Asia would soon follow.

The domino analogy assumed that communism was a global movement directed by Soviet leaders in Moscow. Yet anti-colonial insurgencies resulted more from nationalist motives than from Communist ideology. The domino analogy thus informed policy decisions to the point that the United States had to police the entire world. As a consequence, *every* insurgency mushroomed into a strategic crisis.

REELECTION AND FOREIGN CRISES

As a new presidential campaign unfolded in 1956, Dwight Eisenhower still enjoyed widespread public support. James Reston, a political reporter for the *New York Times*, noted that the president's popularity "has got beyond the bounds of reasonable calculation and will have to be put down as a national phenomenon, like baseball." Americans had developed a "love affair" with Eisenhower, but the president's health was beginning to deteriorate. In September 1955, he had suffered a heart attack, the first of three major illnesses that would affect the rest of his presidency. The sixty-five-year-old Eisenhower explained to a friend that "no president had ever reached his seventieth year in the White House," and he might not make it either.

The Republicans, however, eagerly renominated Eisenhower. The party platform endorsed the president's moderate Republicanism, meaning balanced budgets, reduced government intervention in the economy, and an internationalist foreign policy. The Democrats turned again to the liberal Illinois leader, Adlai Stevenson.

REPRESSION IN HUNGARY   During the last week of the presidential campaign, fighting erupted along the Suez Canal in Egypt and in the streets of Budapest, Hungary. On October 23, 1956, Hungarian nationalists, encouraged by American propaganda broadcasts through the Radio Free Europe network created in 1951 by the U.S. government to encourage resistance to Soviet control, revolted against Communist troops. The Soviets responded by sending troops and tanks to quash the uprising. They killed some 40,000 Hungarian freedom fighters and forced nearly 200,000 more to flee before installing a new puppet government. The revolution had been crushed in twelve days.

The brutal Soviet suppression of the Hungarian uprising stunned the world and revealed the tyrannical energy behind communism. Yet the U.S. government received its share of criticism, too. Eisenhower's strategy in dealing with such crises was, as he later said, "Take a hard line—and bluff."

In Hungary, the Soviets instead called the Eisenhower administration's bluff. The Hungarian freedom fighters, having been led to expect U.S. support, paid with their lives. Vice President Nixon cynically reassured Eisenhower that the Soviet crackdown would be beneficial in showing the world the ruthlessness of communism. The president felt guilty about failing to support the rebels, but Secretary of State Dulles showed little concern, reminding the president that "we always have been against violent rebellion."

THE SUEZ WAR   President Eisenhower was more successful in handling an unexpected crisis in Egypt. In 1952, Egyptian army officer Gamal Abdel Nasser had overthrown King Farouk and set out to become the leader of the Arab world. To do so, he promised to destroy the new Israeli nation, created in 1948, and to end British and French imperialism in the region. Nasser, with Soviet support, first sought to take control of the Suez Canal, the crucial international waterway in Egypt connecting the Mediterranean and the Red Sea flowing into the Indian Ocean.

The canal had opened in 1869 as a joint French–Egyptian venture. From 1882 on, British troops had protected it as the British Empire's "lifeline" to oil in the Middle East and to India and its other Asian colonies. When Nasser's regime pressed for the withdrawal of the British forces, an Anglo-Egyptian treaty provided for their withdrawal within twenty months.

In 1955, Nasser, adept at playing both sides, announced a huge arms deal with the Soviet Union. The United States countered by offering to help Egypt finance a massive hydroelectric dam at Aswan on the Nile River. In 1956, when Nasser increased trade with the Soviet bloc and recognized the People's Republic of China, Secretary of State John Foster Dulles abruptly canceled the Aswan dam offer.

The Suez Canal A crucial international waterway in Egypt connecting the Mediterranean and Red Seas, the Suez Canal became a site of maritime warfare. Egyptian president Gamal Abdel Nasser ordered the sinking of forty international ships in the canal.

Unable to retaliate directly against the United States, Nasser seized control of the French-owned Suez Canal Company and denied Israel-bound ships access through the canal. For Egyptians, this was their declaration of independence from European colonialism. The British and French were furious, for two thirds of Europe's oil came through the canal, but they needed a pretext that warranted military action. Israel soon provided one.

On September 30, 1956, Israeli, British, and French officials secretly hatched a full-scale invasion plan: Israel would attack Egypt from the east and race west to the Suez Canal. The French and British would then send troops to the canal zone, posing as peacekeepers.

On October 29, 1956, Israeli paratroopers dropped into Egypt. The British and French then issued an ultimatum demanding that the fighting cease. When Egypt rejected the ultimatum, British warplanes began bombing Egyptian airfields. On November 5, British and French soldiers invaded the canal zone. Nasser responded by sinking all forty international ships then in the

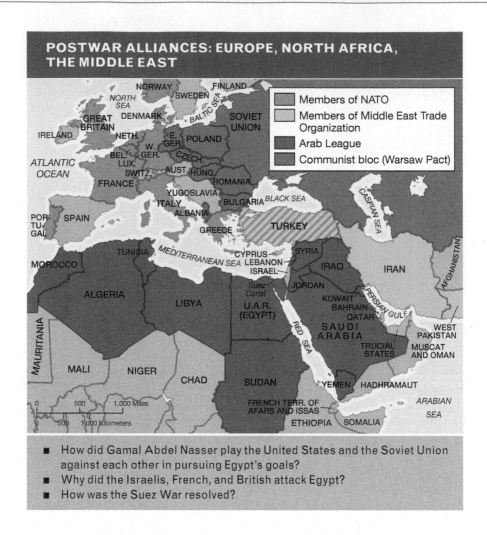

POSTWAR ALLIANCES: EUROPE, NORTH AFRICA, THE MIDDLE EAST

- Members of NATO
- Members of Middle East Trade Organization
- Arab League
- Communist bloc (Warsaw Pact)

- How did Gamal Abdel Nasser play the United States and the Soviet Union against each other in pursuing Egypt's goals?
- Why did the Israelis, French, and British attack Egypt?
- How was the Suez War resolved?

Suez Canal. A few days later, Anglo-French commandos and paratroopers took control of the canal.

The attack on Egypt by Britain, France, and Israel almost destroyed the NATO alliance. Eisenhower was furious that the three nations had attacked Egypt without informing the American government. He resolved to put a stop to the invasion, for he believed the Egyptians had the right to control the Suez Canal, since it was entirely within their boundaries. Eisenhower criticized the military action as a revival of the "old-fashioned gunboat diplomacy" associated with colonial imperialism. "How could we possibly support Britain and France," he asked, "if in doing so we lose the whole Arab world?"

To defuse the crisis, Eisenhower adopted a bold stance. He put America's armed forces on alert around the world and warned Soviet diplomats that the

United States would go to war if the Communist superpower tried to intervene. Then the president shocked Americans by demanding that the British and French withdraw their troops from the Suez Canal and that the Israelis evacuate the Sinai Peninsula—or face severe economic sanctions. That the three aggressor nations grudgingly complied with a cease-fire agreement on November 7 testified to Eisenhower's strength, influence, and savvy in dealing with military matters.

The **Suez crisis** had profound and lasting effects on international relations. Nationalists throughout Africa and Asia realized the British and French could not withstand international pressure to dismantle their global empires. The Suez debacle led to the resignation of British prime minister Anthony Eden and hastened the process of independence among Great Britain's remaining colonies. British influence on world affairs has steadily declined since 1957. But perhaps its major result was that the British government realized the risk of acting independently of the United States. Egypt reopened the Suez Canal, and, as Eisenhower had predicted, operated it in a professional, nonpolitical manner.

The Suez crisis and the Hungarian revolt led Democrat Adlai Stevenson to declare the Eisenhower administration's foreign policy "bankrupt." Most Americans, however, reasoned that the crises actually affirmed the nation's status as *the* global superpower. Voters handed Eisenhower an even more lopsided victory in 1956 than in 1952. In carrying Louisiana, Eisenhower became the first Republican to win a Lower South state since Reconstruction; nationally, he carried all but seven states and won the electoral vote by 457–73. Eisenhower's decisive victory, however, failed to swing a Republican majority in either the Senate or the House of Representatives.

SPUTNIK On October 4, 1957, the Soviets shocked the world when they announced the launch of the first satellite, called *Sputnik* ("traveling companion"). Only twenty-three inches in diameter, Sputnik was a shiny aluminum sphere weighing just 184 pounds. It was equipped with two radio transmitters sending continuous signals back to Earth.

Americans panicked at the news. If the Soviets could put a satellite traveling in orbit at 18,000 miles per hour, many feared, they could also fire a rocket with a nuclear warhead across the Pacific Ocean and detonate it on the west coast of the United States. Senator Lyndon B. Johnson warned that the Russians would soon be "dropping bombs on us from space like kids dropping rocks on cars from freeway overpasses."

The unexpected Soviet success in space also dealt a severe blow to the prestige of American science and technology and changed the military balance of power. No event since the Japanese attack on Pearl Harbor created such fear and hysteria. Democrats in Congress charged that the Soviets had "humiliated" the United States and opened a congressional investigation to assess the new threat. *Life* magazine called the Sputnik coup a "major American defeat" and asked, "Why Did the U.S. Lose the [Space] Race?"

President Eisenhower initially played down the Soviet achievement, stressing that it was German scientists (former Nazis) in the Soviet Union, not Russian scientists, who enabled the Sputnik launch. The news of Sputnik, he claimed, did not bother him "one iota." His explanation, however, did not reassure nervous Americans.

"*Sputnik*-mania" eventually led Congress to increase defense spending and enhance science education. In 1958, President Eisenhower convinced Congress to create the National Aeronautics and Space Administration (NASA) to coordinate research and development related to outer space. The same year, Congress, with President Eisenhower's support, enacted the National Defense Education Act (NDEA), which authorized large federal grants to colleges and universities to enhance education and research in mathematics, science, and modern languages, as well as for student loans and fellowships.

THE EISENHOWER DOCTRINE In the aftermath of the Suez crisis, President Eisenhower decided that the United States must replace Great Britain and France as the guarantor of Western interests in the Middle East. In 1958, Congress approved what came to be called the Eisenhower Doctrine, which promised to extend economic and military aid to Arab nations and to use armed force if necessary to assist any such nation against Communist aggression. When Lebanon appealed to the United States to help fend off an insurgency, Eisenhower dispatched 5,000 marines into the country. In October 1958, once the situation had stabilized, U.S. forces (up to 15,000 at one point) withdrew.

CRISIS IN BERLIN The unique problem of West Berlin, an island of Western capitalism deep in Soviet-controlled East Germany, boiled over in the late 1950s. Since the end of the Second World War, West Berlin had served as a "showplace" of Western democracy and prosperity, a listening post for Western intelligence gathering, and a funnel through which news and propaganda from the West penetrated what British leader Winston Churchill had labeled the "iron curtain." Although East Germany had sealed its western frontiers, refugees could still pass from East to West Berlin.

On November 10, 1958, Soviet leader Nikita Khrushchev threatened to give East Germany control of East Berlin and of the air lanes into West Berlin.

After the deadline he set (May 27, 1959), Western authorities would have to deal with the Soviet-controlled East German government or face the possibility of another blockade of the city.

Eisenhower told Khrushchev that he "would hit the Russians" with every weapon in the American arsenal if they persisted in their efforts to intimidate West Berlin. At the same time, however, Eisenhower sought a settlement. The negotiations distracted attention from the May 27 deadline, which passed almost unnoticed. In September 1959, Khrushchev and Eisenhower agreed to a summit meeting.

Nikita Khrushchev The fiery Soviet premier addresses the United Nations in 1960.

THE U-2 SUMMIT The summit meeting literally crashed and burned, however, when on Sunday morning, May 1, 1960, a Soviet rocket brought down a U.S. spy plane (called the U-2) flying at 70,000 feet over the Soviet Union. Khrushchev, embarrassed by the ability of U.S. spy planes to enter Soviet airspace, then sprang a trap on Eisenhower. The Soviets announced only that the plane had been shot down. The U.S. government, not realizing that the Soviets had captured the pilot, lied about the incident and claimed that it was missing a weather-monitoring plane over Turkey. Khrushchev then announced that the Soviets had American pilot Francis Gary Powers "alive and kicking" and also had the photographs Powers had taken of Soviet military installations.

On May 11, Eisenhower took personal responsibility for the spying program, explaining that such illegally obtained intelligence information was crucial to national security. At the testy summit in Paris five days later, Khrushchev lectured Eisenhower for forty-five minutes before walking out because the U.S. president refused to apologize. Later, in 1962, Powers would be exchanged for a captured Soviet spy.

COMMUNIST CUBA President Eisenhower's greatest embarrassment was Fidel Castro's new Communist regime in Cuba, which came to power on January 1, 1959, after two years of guerrilla warfare against the U.S.-supported dictator, Fulgencio Batista. The bearded, cigar-smoking Castro embraced Soviet support as he systematically imprisoned hundreds of opponents, canceled elections, and staged public executions. A CIA agent predicted, "We're

Fidel Castro Castro *(center)* became Cuba's Communist premier in 1959 upon overthrowing the Batista regime after three years of guerrilla warfare.

going to take care of Castro just like we took care of Arbenz [in Guatemala]." The Soviets warned that American intervention in Cuba would trigger a military response.

One of Eisenhower's last acts as president, on January 3, 1961, was to suspend diplomatic relations with Cuba. He also authorized a secret CIA operation to train a force of Cuban refugees to oust Castro, but the final decision on the use of the invasion force would rest with the next president, John F. Kennedy.

EVALUATING THE EISENHOWER PRESIDENCY During President Eisenhower's second term, Congress added Alaska and Hawaii as the forty-ninth and fiftieth states (1959), while the nation experienced its worst economic slump since the Great Depression. Volatile issues such as civil rights, defense policy, and corrupt aides compounded the administration's troubles. The president's desire to avoid divisive issues led him at times to value harmony and popularity over justice. One observer called the Eisenhower years "the time of the great postponement," during which the president left domestic and foreign policies "about where he found them in 1953."

Opinion of Eisenhower's presidency has improved with time, however. He presided with steady self-confidence over a prosperous nation. In dealing with crises, he displayed good judgment and firmness of purpose. He fulfilled his pledge to end the war in Korea, refused to intervene militarily in Indochina, and maintained the peace in the face of explosive global tensions.

Eisenhower's greatest decisions were the wars he chose to avoid. After the truce in Korea, not a single American soldier died in combat during his two presidential terms, something no president since has achieved. For the most part, he acted with poise, restraint, and intelligence in managing an increasingly complex Cold War.

If Eisenhower refused to take the lead in addressing social and racial problems, he did balance the budget while sustaining the major reforms of the New Deal. If he tolerated unemployment of as much as 7 percent, he saw to it that inflation remained minimal. Even Adlai Stevenson admitted that Ike's victory in 1952 had been good for America. "I like Ike, too," he said.

Still, it is fair to ask what might have happened if Eisenhower had invested his enormous prestige and popularity in the civil rights movement. Because he did not, his successors were forced to try to improve race relations in a much more volatile political and social climate.

Eisenhower's January 17, 1961, farewell address focused on the threat posed to government integrity by "an immense military establishment and a large arms industry." It was striking for Eisenhower, a celebrated military leader, to highlight the dangers of a large "military-industrial complex" exerting "unwarranted influence" in Congress and the White House.

Eisenhower confessed that his greatest disappointment was that he could affirm only that "war has been avoided," not that "a lasting peace is in sight." The heroic military leader of the Second World War pledged to "do anything to achieve peace within honorable means. I'll travel anywhere. I'll talk to anyone." His successors would not be as successful in keeping war at bay.

CHAPTER REVIEW

SUMMARY

- **Moderate Republicanism: The Eisenhower Years**   As president, Dwight Eisenhower promoted what he called *moderate Republicanism* or "dynamic conservatism." He expanded Social Security coverage and launched ambitious public works programs, such as the *Federal-Aid Highway Act* (1956), which constructed the interstate highway system. He opposed large budget deficits, however, and cut spending on national defense and an array of domestic programs.

- **Growth of the U.S. Economy**   High levels of federal government spending, begun before the war, continued during the postwar period. The *GI Bill of Rights* (1944) boosted home buying and helped many veterans attend college and enter the middle class. Consumer demand for homes, cars, and household goods that had been unavailable during the war; additional product demand created by the *baby boom*; and the new ability to finance purchases with credit cards all fueled the economy. After the Second World War, with the growth of *suburbia*, corporations, and advertising, America's mass culture displayed what critics called a bland sameness. A large majority of Americans, including many in the working class, experienced unprecedented rising living standards during the 1950s. But discrimination continued against African Americans, Hispanics, and women.

- **Critics of Mainstream Culture**   The *Beats* rebelled against what they claimed was the suffocating conformity of middle-class life in the fifties, as did many other writers and artists. Adolescents rebelled through acts of juvenile delinquency and a new form of sexually provocative music called rock 'n' roll. Pockets of chronic poverty persisted despite record-breaking economic growth, and minorities did not prosper to the extent that White Americans did.

- **The Early Years of the Civil Rights Movement**   During the early 1950s, the NAACP mounted legal challenges in federal courts to states requiring racially segregated public schools. In the most significant case, *Brown v. Board of Education* (1954), the U.S. Supreme Court nullified the *separate-but-equal* doctrine. Many White southerners adopted a strategy of *massive resistance* against court-ordered desegregation. In response, civil rights activists, both Blacks and Whites, used *nonviolent civil disobedience* to force local and state officials to allow integration, as demonstrated in the *Montgomery bus boycott* in Alabama and the forced desegregation of public schools in Little Rock, Arkansas. Martin Luther King Jr. organized the *Southern Christian Leadership Conference (SCLC)* to rally civil rights opposition after White violence against activists in Little Rock. In 1957, the U.S. Congress passed a Civil Rights Act intended to stop discrimination against Black voters in the South, but it was rarely enforced.

- **Foreign Policy in the 1950s**   Eisenhower's first major foreign-policy accomplishment was to end the fighting in Korea. Thereafter, Eisenhower relied on *Central Intelligence Agency (CIA)* intervention, financial and military aid, and threats of *massive retaliation* to stem the spread of communism. Though American aid was not enough to save the French at *Dien Bien Phu*, Eisenhower's belief in the *"falling-domino" theory* deepened U.S. support for the government in South Vietnam in its war with North Vietnam and the Communist *Viet Cong* insurgents. He came closest to ordering military intervention in the *Suez crisis* (1956) but was able to mediate a solution. Closer to home, however, he approved a secret CIA operation to overthrow Fidel Castro, Cuba's Communist leader.

CHRONOLOGY

1949	The first credit card is introduced
1952	Eisenhower wins the presidency
July 1953	Armistice is reached in Korea
	CIA organizes the overthrow of Mohammed Mossadegh in Iran and Jacobo Arbenz Guzman in Guatemala
1954	*Brown v. Board of Education*
July 1954	Geneva Accords adopted
December 1955	Montgomery, Alabama, bus boycott begins
1956	Elvis Presley releases "Heartbreak Hotel"
	Congress passes the Federal-Aid Highway Act
	Soviets suppress Hungarian revolt
	In Suez War, Israel, Britain, and France attack Egypt
1957	Desegregation of Central High School in Little Rock, Arkansas
	Soviet Union launches Sputnik satellite
	Baby boom peaks
1959	Fidel Castro seizes power in Cuba
1960	The U-2 incident

KEY TERMS

moderate Republicanism p. 1300
Federal-Aid Highway Act (1956)
p. 1303
GI Bill of Rights (1944) p. 1311
suburbia p. 1312
baby boom p. 1318
Beats p. 1322
separate-but-equal p. 1327
Brown v. Board of Education
(1954) p. 1327
massive resistance p. 1329

Montgomery bus boycott p. 1330
nonviolent civil disobedience p. 1331
Southern Christian Leadership
Conference (SCLC) p. 1334
massive retaliation p. 1336
Central Intelligence Agency (CIA)
p. 1337
Dien Bien Phu p. 1338
Viet Cong p. 1341
"falling-domino" theory p. 1341
Suez crisis (1956) p. 1345

🐰 INQUIZITIVE

Go to InQuizitive to see what you've learned—and learn what you've missed—with personalized feedback along the way.

27 New Frontiers and a Great Society

1960–1968

March on Washington Marchers hold aloft picket signs calling for "INTEGRATED SCHOOLS NOW!," "EQUAL RIGHTS," "JOBS FOR ALL," and "CIVIL RIGHTS LAWS NOW." They were among the more than 250,000 people nationwide who joined the March on Washington for Jobs and Freedom on August 28, 1963. The televised march showcased Martin Luther King Jr.'s landmark "I Have a Dream" speech. At the time, it was the largest protest ever held in the nation's capital.

For those who considered the fifties dull, the following decade provided a striking contrast. The sixties were years of extraordinary social turbulence and liberal activism, tragic assassinations and painful trauma, cultural conflict and youth rebellion, civil rights and civil unrest. Assassins killed four of the most important leaders of the time: John F. Kennedy, Malcolm X, Martin Luther King Jr., and Robert F. Kennedy.

The "politics of expectation" that a British journalist said shone brightly in John Kennedy's short tenure as president did not die with him in November 1963. Instead, his idealistic commitment to improving the nation's quality of life—for everyone—was given new meaning by his successor, Texan Lyndon B. Johnson, whose War on Poverty and Great Society social programs outstripped Franklin Roosevelt's New Deal in their scope and promises, expense and controversy.

Lyndon Johnson's energy and legislative savvy created a blizzard of new programs as many social issues that had been ignored or postponed for decades—civil rights for people of color, equality for women, gay and lesbian rights, medical insurance, federal aid to the poor—forced their way to the forefront of national concerns. In the end, however, Johnson promised too much. His Great Society social programs fell victim to unrealistic hopes, poor execution, and the nation's expanding involvement in the Vietnam War. The deeply entrenched assumptions of the Cold War led the United States into the longest, most controversial, and least successful war in its history to that point.

focus questions

1. How did President John F. Kennedy try to contain communism abroad and address civil rights and other social programs at home?

2. What were the strategies and achievements of the civil rights movement in the 1960s? What divisions emerged among its activists?

3. What were President Lyndon B. Johnson's major War on Poverty and Great Society initiatives? How did they impact American society?

4. What were Kennedy's and Johnson's motivations for deepening America's military involvement in the Vietnam War?

5. What issues propelled Richard Nixon to victory in the 1968 presidential election?

The New Frontier

In his speech accepting the 1960 Democratic presidential nomination, John F. Kennedy showcased the muscular language that would characterize his campaign and his presidency: "We stand today on the edge of a **New Frontier**—the frontier of unknown opportunities and perils—a frontier of unfulfilled hopes and threats." He wanted Americans to explore "science and space, unsolved problems of peace and war, unconquered pockets of ignorance and prejudice, unanswered questions of poverty and surplus." Kennedy and his staff fastened upon the frontier metaphor as the label for their proposed domestic programs because they believed Americans had always been eager to conquer and exploit new frontiers. Kennedy promised to be more aggressive in waging the Cold War with the Soviet Union than Dwight Eisenhower had been.

KENNEDY VERSUS NIXON The 1960 presidential election featured two candidates—Vice President Richard M. Nixon and Massachusetts senator John F. Kennedy—of similar ages and life experiences. Both were elected to Congress in 1946, both were navy veterans, and both preferred foreign affairs over domestic issues.

In fact, however, they were more different than alike. Although Nixon was Dwight Eisenhower's vice president for two terms, Eisenhower had grave misgivings about him. When asked by reporters to name a single major accomplishment of his vice president, Ike replied: "If you give me a week, I might think of one." The two Republican leaders had long had a testy relationship. Nixon once called Eisenhower "a goddamned old fool," while the president dismissed his vice president as a man who couldn't "think of anything but politics." On more than one occasion, Eisenhower had sought to dump Nixon in favor of other Republicans whom he respected.

A native of California, the forty-seven-year-old Nixon had fought to be a success, first as an attorney, then as a congressman. He had come to Washington after the Second World War eager to reverse the tide of New Deal liberalism. His visibility among Republicans rose when he played a prominent role in the anti-Communist hearings in the House of Representatives during the McCarthy hysteria.

Nixon—graceless, awkward, and stiff—proved to be one of the most complicated political figures in American history. By 1960, he had become known as "Tricky Dick," a cunning deceiver who concealed his real ideas and bigoted attitudes. Kennedy told an aide that "Nixon doesn't know who he is . . . so every time he makes a speech he has to decide which Nixon he is, and that will be very exhausting."

The Kennedy-Nixon Debates Nixon's decision to debate Kennedy on television backfired when 70 million Americans tuned in and saw a sick, sweaty Nixon outshone by his young, charismatic opponent.

Unlike Nixon, the forty-three-year-old Kennedy lit up a room with his smile, charm, and zest for life. He was handsome, articulate, and blessed with youthful energy and wit. Coolly analytical and dangerously self-absorbed, he was a contradictory and elusive political celebrity. But John "Jack" Kennedy had a bright, agile mind; a Harvard education; a record of heroism in the Second World War; a rich and powerful Roman Catholic family; and a beautiful and accomplished young wife. In the words of a southern senator, Kennedy combined "the best qualities of Elvis Presley and Franklin D. Roosevelt"—a combination that played well in the first-ever televised presidential debate.

Some 70 million people tuned in to watch. They saw an uncomfortable Nixon, ill with a virus and perspiring heavily; he looked pale and haggard, and, as many viewers described, even somewhat menacing. By contrast, Kennedy looked tanned, poised, and confident. He offered crisp answers that made him appear qualified for the nation's highest office. The morning after the debate, his approval ratings skyrocketed. The *Chicago Daily News* asked, "Was Nixon Sabotaged by TV Makeup Artists?"

Kennedy's political rise owed much to the public relations campaign engineered by his wealthy father, Joseph Kennedy, a self-made tycoon with a genius for promotion who believed that *image* was much more important than substance. "Can't you get it into your head," he told his son John, "that it's not important what you *really* are? The only important thing is what people *think* you are." To ensure that people thought well of his son, the elder Kennedy hired talented writers to produce John's two books, paid a publisher to print them, purchased thousands of copies to make them "best sellers," and helped engineer his son's elections to the House of Representatives and Senate.

The momentum that Kennedy gained from the first debate with Nixon was not enough to ensure his victory, however. The Democratic candidate was a relentless presidential campaigner, traveling 65,000 miles, visiting twenty-five states, and making more than 350 speeches. In an address to Protestant ministers in Texas, he neutralized concerns about his being a Roman Catholic by stressing that the pope would never "tell the President—should he be a Catholic—how to act."

Kennedy focused on criticizing the Eisenhower administration. The United States, he claimed, was falling behind the Soviet Union in scientific research, missile development, and worldwide prestige. It was time, he repeatedly said, "to get this country moving again."

Although Kennedy worked to increase voter registration among African Americans, his response to the growing civil rights movement was ambivalent. Like Eisenhower, Kennedy believed racial unrest needed to be handled with caution. To him, racial justice was less an urgent moral crusade than a potential barrier to his election. He understood the injustices of bigotry and segregation, but he needed the votes of southern Whites to win the presidency.

During the campaign, Kennedy won the hearts of many Black voters by helping to get Martin Luther King Jr. discharged from a Georgia prison. King had been convicted and jailed for trespassing in an all-White restaurant in a downtown department store, where he and members of the Student Non-violent Coordinating Committee (SNCC) had organized a sit-in. Kennedy's efforts led King's father to change his opinion on the election. "I had expected to vote against Senator Kennedy because of his religion," the elder Reverend King explained. "Now he can be my president, Catholic or whatever he is." On the Sunday before Election Day, a million leaflets describing Kennedy's effort on King's behalf were distributed in African American churches across the nation.

Kennedy and his running mate, Texas senator Lyndon B. Johnson, won one of the closest presidential elections in history. Their margin was only 118,574 votes out of more than 68 million cast, a record turnout. Nixon won more

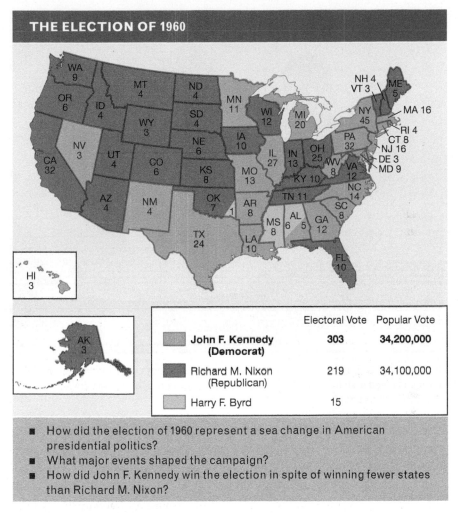

THE ELECTION OF 1960

		Electoral Vote	Popular Vote
	John F. Kennedy (Democrat)	303	34,200,000
	Richard M. Nixon (Republican)	219	34,100,000
	Harry F. Byrd	15	

- How did the election of 1960 represent a sea change in American presidential politics?
- What major events shaped the campaign?
- How did John F. Kennedy win the election in spite of winning fewer states than Richard M. Nixon?

states, but Kennedy captured 70 percent of the Black vote, which proved decisive in at least three key states. Nixon convinced himself that the Democrats had stolen the election through chicanery in Illinois and Texas, but recounts confirmed the vote totals.

A VIGOROUS NEW ADMINISTRATION   John F. Kennedy (often referred to as JFK) was the youngest man and the first Roman Catholic elected president. At times, he seemed self-assured to the point of cockiness. "Sure it's a big job," he told a reporter. "But I don't know anybody who can do it any better than I can." That he had been elected by the narrowest of margins and had no working majority in Congress did not faze him. In his mind, he was destined to be a great president.

Jack and Jackie Young, refined, and attractive, the Kennedys were instant celebrities. Women teased their hair into the First Lady's famous hairdo, while men craved JFK's effortless cool.

Kennedy's inauguration ceremony on a cold, sunny, blustery January afternoon introduced the world to his elegance and flair. He focused his inaugural address almost entirely on foreign affairs, which he thought were all that really mattered. He accepted the responsibility of "defending freedom in its hour of maximum danger" and promised to keep America strong while seeking to reduce friction with the Soviet Union: "Let us never negotiate out of fear, but let us never fear to negotiate."

Kennedy claimed "that the torch has been passed to a new generation of Americans—born in this century, tempered by war, disciplined by a hard and bitter peace." He dazzled listeners with uplifting words: "Let every nation know, whether it wishes us well or ill, that we shall pay any price, bear any burden, meet any hardship, support any friend, oppose any foe, to assure the survival and success of liberty. And so, my fellow Americans: ask not what your country can do for you—ask what *you* can do for your country."

Such steely optimism heralded a presidency of fresh promise and new beginnings. Kennedy was brimming with energy and addicted to excitement.

Nearly everything he did was injected with urgency. Yet Kennedy lacked the seriousness of purpose found in most great leaders, and much of the glamour surrounding him was cosmetic.

Despite Kennedy's athletic interests and robust appearance, he suffered from serious medical issues: gastrointestinal problems, ulcers, Addison's disease (a rare and dangerous disorder triggered by the withering of the adrenal glands), venereal disease, chronic back pain, and fierce fevers. He daily took a powerful cocktail of prescription medicines and painkillers to manage a degenerative bone disease, to deal with anxiety, to help him sleep, and to control his allergies. (The medications gave Kennedy the perpetual tan that the public interpreted as a sign of good health.) Between 1955 and 1957, Kennedy had been hospitalized nine times.

Kennedy and his associates hid both his physical ailments and his reckless sexual couplings in the White House with a galaxy of women, including actress Marilyn Monroe and Judith Campbell Exner, the girlfriend of a Chicago mob boss. The handsome president was a compulsive womanizer and partier, confident that no one would reveal his brazen behavior.

Kennedy represented a new wave of political figures who had fought in the Second World War. Known as the "pragmatic generation," they were decisive, bold, and prized courage and conviction in the face of the Cold War and the threat of nuclear conflict. Kennedy fully embraced the conviction that "the enemy is the Communist system itself—implacable, insatiable, increasing its drive for world domination." The Cold War, he asserted, was "a struggle for supremacy between two competing ideologies: freedom under God versus ruthless, godless tyranny."

A CONTRARY CONGRESS   President Kennedy had a difficult time launching his New Frontier domestic program, in part because he was not skilled at pushing legislation through Congress. Conservative southern Democrats joined Republicans in blocking Kennedy's efforts to increase federal aid to education, provide medical insurance for the aged, and establish a cabinet-level department of urban affairs and housing to address inner-city poverty. In his first year, Kennedy submitted 355 legislative requests; Congress approved only half of them. He complained that he "couldn't get a Mother's Day resolution through the goddamned Congress."

Legislators did approve the president's requests for increasing the minimum wage; a Housing Act that earmarked nearly $5 billion for new public-housing projects in poverty-stricken inner-city areas; the Peace Corps, which recruited idealistic young volunteers who would provide educational and technical service abroad; and the Alliance for Progress, a financial assistance program to Latin American countries intended to blunt the appeal of communism. In 1963, Kennedy also signed the Equal Pay Act, which required that women performing the same jobs as men be paid the same. But his efforts to provide more assistance for educational programs and for medical care for the elderly faltered.

News that the Soviets had launched the first manned space flight in 1961 prompted Kennedy's greatest legislative success. He convinced Congress to commit $40 billion to put an American on the moon within ten years. (The goal was achieved in 1969.) Such an audacious project, he believed, would demonstrate that American technological savvy was greater than that of the Soviet Union. America could not afford to become "second in space," because "space has too many implications militarily, politically, psychologically."

KENNEDY AND CIVIL RIGHTS   The most important developments affecting domestic life during the sixties occurred in civil rights. Throughout the South, racial segregation remained firmly in place. Signs outside public restrooms distinguished between "Whites" and "colored"; signs in restaurants declared "Colored Not Allowed" or "Colored Served Only in Rear." Stores prohibited African Americans from trying on clothes before buying them. Witnesses in courtrooms were sworn in with their hands placed on different Bibles, depending on their race. Despite the *Brown v. Board of Education* ruling in 1954, most public schools across the South remained segregated and unequal in quality.

Kennedy was reluctant to challenge conservative southern Democrats on the explosive issue of racial integration. As he told the African American baseball star Jackie Robinson, "I don't know much about the problems of colored people since I come from New England." Both he and his brother Robert had to be dragged into supporting the civil rights movement. After appointing Harris Wofford, a White law professor and campaigner for racial equality, as the special presidential assistant for civil rights, President Kennedy told him "to make substantial headway against . . . the nonsense of racial discrimination," but to do so with "minimum civil rights legislation [and] maximum Executive action."

CATASTROPHE IN CUBA   Kennedy's performance in foreign relations was spectacularly mixed. Although he had told a reporter that he wanted to "break out of the confines of the Cold War," he quickly found himself reinforcing its ideological assumptions. While still a senator, Kennedy had blasted President Eisenhower for not being tough enough with the Soviets and for allowing Communist Fidel Castro and his followers to take over Cuba, just ninety miles from the southern tip of Florida.

A Failed Invasion Anti-Castro Cubans are marched into captivity after the misguided attack at the Bay of Pigs.

Soon after his inauguration, Kennedy learned that Eisenhower had approved a secret CIA operation to train some 1,500 anti-Castro Cubans to invade their homeland in hopes of triggering a mass uprising against Castro. U.S. military leaders assured Kennedy that the plan was feasible; CIA analysts and the Joint Chiefs of Staff naively predicted that news of the invasion would inspire anti-Castro Cubans to rebel. Secretary of Defense Robert McNamara, National Security Advisor McGeorge Bundy, and Attorney General Robert "Bobby" Kennedy endorsed the plan, as did the new president.

The ragtag group of 1,543 Cuban exiles, trained by the CIA on a Guatemalan banana plantation and transported on five rusty freighters, landed before dawn at the **Bay of Pigs** on Cuba's south shore on April 17, 1961. Having been tipped off by spies, Castro had 20,000 soldiers waiting. When Kennedy realized the operation was failing, he refused pleas from the trapped rebels for support from U.S. warplanes that he had promised. General Lyman Lemnitzer, chair of the Joint Chiefs of Staff, said that Kennedy's "pulling out the rug [on the Cuban invaders] was . . . almost criminal." More than a hundred of the Cuban exiles were killed and some 1,200 were captured. (Kennedy later approved paying $53 million for their release.)

The failed operation humiliated Kennedy and elevated Castro in the eyes of the world. A *New York Times* columnist wrote that the Americans "looked like fools to our friends, rascals to our enemies, and incompetents to the rest." In Moscow, Soviet leader Nikita Khrushchev asked if Kennedy could "really be that indecisive."

To his credit, Kennedy admitted that the Bay of Pigs invasion was a "colossal mistake." Only later did he learn that the CIA planners had assumed that he would commit American forces if the invasion effort failed. He said that after the initial disastrous reports from the Bay of Pigs, "we all looked at each other and asked, 'How could we have been so stupid?'" He never again trusted his military advisers.

Afterward, Kennedy met with Eisenhower and discussed the Bay of Pigs fiasco. The former president recalled that Kennedy seemed "more than a little bewildered." The new president admitted that "you don't know how tough this job is until you have it." In reference to the failed invasion, Eisenhower told Kennedy that there was "only one thing to do when you go into this kind of thing. It must be a success."

THE VIENNA SUMMIT MEETING Just weeks after the Bay of Pigs invasion, President Kennedy met Soviet premier Khrushchev at a summit conference in Vienna, Austria. Khrushchev badgered Kennedy, bragged about the superiority of communism, and threatened to take full control of Berlin, the divided city inside Communist East Germany. Kennedy confided to a journalist that the summit "was awful. Worst thing of my life. He rolled right over me—he thinks I'm a fool—he thinks I'm weak. . . . He treated me like a little boy." When asked what he planned to do to raise his stature, Kennedy replied: "I have to confront them [the Soviets] someplace to show that we're tough." Kennedy, in fact, during the summit was heavily medicated because of chronic back pain.

The first thing Kennedy did upon returning to the White House was to request an estimate of how many Americans might be killed in a nuclear war with the Soviet Union. The answer was chilling: 70 million. Kennedy, desperate not to appear weak in the face of Khrushchev's aggressive actions in Germany, asked Congress for additional spending on defense and called up 156,000 members of the Army Reserve and National Guard to protect West Berlin. He also ordered an armed military convoy to travel from West Germany across East Germany to West Berlin to show the Soviets that he would use force to protect the city. "West Berlin," he declared, "has become . . . the great testing place of Western courage and will."

The Soviets responded on August 13, 1961. They first stopped all traffic between East and West Berlin and began erecting the twenty-seven-mile-long **Berlin Wall** to prevent thousands of refugees from fleeing communism each week by crossing into West Berlin. For the United States, the concrete wall and its 500 watch towers became a powerful propaganda weapon in the Cold War. As Kennedy said, "Freedom has many difficulties and democracy is not perfect, but we have never had to put up a wall to keep our people in."

The Berlin Wall demonstrated the Soviets' willingness to challenge American resolve in Europe. In response, Kennedy gave a televised address alerting the nation to the significance of the Berlin crisis. Then, he and Secretary of Defense Robert McNamara embarked upon the most intensive arms race in history. The administration increased the number of nuclear missiles fivefold, added 300,000 men and women to the armed forces, and created the U.S. Special Forces (Green Berets), an elite group of army commandos who specialized in guerrilla warfare and could provide a "more flexible response" to hot spots around the world.

In contrast to the Eisenhower-Dulles emphasis of "massive retaliation" to deter Soviet misbehavior around the world, Kennedy sought more military flexibility: "We intend to have a wider choice than humiliation or all-out war." He and McNamara also launched a civil defense program focused on the construction of nuclear fallout shelters. Secretly, they commissioned an analysis of the implications of launching a full-scale nuclear strike against the Soviet Union in response to any effort to invade West Berlin.

A RACE TO THE MOON In April 1961, twenty-six-year-old Soviet cosmonaut Yuri Gagarin became the first person to orbit the Earth in a spacecraft. The *New York Times* headline read: "Soviets Put Man in Space: Spokesman Says U.S. Asleep at the Wheel."

An embarrassed President Kennedy directed Vice President Lyndon Johnson to assess which space mission the Americans had the best chance of winning. He wanted something that "promises dramatic results." Before Johnson could make his recommendation, the United States launched its first astronaut into space. In May 1961, Alan Shepard rose to an altitude of 116 miles for a fifteen-minute suborbital flight before landing in the ocean near Bermuda.

First American in Space In response to the Soviet Union sending the first person to space, the United States quickly followed, selecting astronaut Alan Shepard as the first American to soar into space.

The space race with the Soviets became an obsession for Kennedy because he viewed it as a major battle in the Cold War. In a White House meeting with NASA executives, he explained, "All over the world, we are judged by how well we do in space. Therefore, we've got to be first. That's all there is to it."

On May 25, 1961, twenty days after Alan Shepard's flight, Kennedy told Congress that "these are extraordinary times, and we face an extraordinary challenge." The United States and the Soviet Union were competitors in a "contest of will and purpose as well as force and violence, a battle for minds and souls as well as lives and territory. And in that contest, we cannot stand aside." It was time, he explained, "for this nation to take a clearly leading role in space achievement" by landing a man on the moon and returning him "safely to Earth." No single space project, he added, "will be more impressive to mankind" than the race to the moon, "and none will be so difficult or expensive to accomplish."

THE CUBAN MISSILE CRISIS In the fall of 1962, Nikita Khrushchev and the Soviets decided to challenge President Kennedy again. To protect Communist Cuba from another U.S. coup attempt and show critics that he was not afraid of the Americans, Khrushchev approved the secret installation of 160 Soviet missiles on the island nation along with some 40,000 Soviet troops. The Soviets felt justified in doing so because Kennedy, after the Bay of Pigs

The Cuban Missile Crisis Photographs taken from a U.S. surveillance plane on October 14, 1962, revealed both Soviet missile launchers and missile shelters near San Cristóbal, Cuba.

invasion, had ordered that U.S. missiles with nuclear warheads be installed in Turkey, along the Soviet border and within range of Moscow.

On October 16, 1962, Kennedy learned that photos taken by U.S. spy planes showed some forty Soviet missile sites and twenty-five jet bombers in Cuba. "We have some big trouble," he alerted his brother Bobby by phone. Somehow, the president had to convince the Soviets to remove the missiles. But how? As the air force chief of staff told Kennedy, "You're in a pretty bad fix, Mr. President." From the start, Kennedy explained, he was seeking a response that "lessens the chances of a nuclear exchange, which obviously is the final failure."

Over the next thirteen days, Kennedy and the National Security Council (NSC) considered several responses. Initially, the choices centered on military action: an air strike to destroy the missiles; a broader attack on airfields, warplanes, and storage areas; or a full-scale amphibious invasion.

At that point, the world came closer to a nuclear war than ever before or since. Kennedy and the NSC discussed in some detail the unthinkable possibility of a nuclear war, even estimating the damage that atomic bombs might inflict on major cities. Eventually, however, the group narrowed the options to a choice between a "surgical" air strike on the missiles that would be followed, if necessary, by an invasion, and a naval blockade of Cuba, in which U.S. warships would stop Soviet vessels and search them for missiles. Although the military advisers urged bombing the missile sites followed by an invasion of the island, Kennedy chose the naval blockade, which was carefully disguised by calling it a *quarantine*, since a *blockade* is technically an act of war.

Kennedy feared that an American attack on Cuba would give the Soviets an excuse to take control of West Berlin. What he did not know was that Soviet military units were prepared to use tactical nuclear weapons if the U.S. invaded Cuba.

On October 22, Kennedy, cool, rational, and willing to compromise, delivered a televised speech of the "highest national urgency." He announced that the U.S. Navy was establishing a quarantine of Cuba to prevent Soviet ships from delivering more weapons. Kennedy added that he had "directed the armed forces to prepare for any eventuality." Forcing the Soviets to remove missiles from Cuba, he stressed, was "a difficult and dangerous effort. . . . No one can foresee precisely what course [the crisis] will take or what costs or casualties will be incurred. Many months of sacrifice and self-discipline lie ahead." The president closed by urging the Soviets to stop the "reckless and provocative threat to world peace" and "move the world back from the abyss of destruction." Newscasters talked of atomic warfare, and some 200,000 U.S. soldiers made their way to southern Florida.

Khrushchev replied that Soviet ships would ignore the quarantine and accused Kennedy of "an act of aggression propelling humankind into the abyss of a world nuclear-missile war." Despite such confrontational rhetoric, however, on Wednesday, October 24, five Soviet ships, presumably with more missiles aboard, stopped well short of the quarantine line. Two days later, Khrushchev, knowing that the United States enjoyed a 5 to 1 advantage in nuclear weapons, offered a deal. Neither he nor Kennedy wanted to be the first to launch nuclear missiles, and both leaders were frantically searching for a way to defuse the crisis.

In the end, the Soviets agreed to remove the missiles in Cuba in return for a *public* pledge by the United States never to invade Cuba—and a *secret* agreement to remove the fifteen U.S. missiles with nuclear warheads from Turkey. Kennedy accepted the proposal, but insisted that the Soviets never reveal his willingness to remove the missiles in Turkey. Kennedy was determined that Americans view him as the cool and courageous winner of the Cold War showdown. As Secretary of State Dean Rusk stressed to a newscaster, "Remember, when you report this, [say] that eyeball to eyeball, they [the Soviets] blinked first."

In the aftermath of the **Cuban missile crisis**, Cold War tensions subsided, in part because of several symbolic steps: an agreement to sell the Soviet Union surplus American wheat, the installation of a "hotline" telephone between Washington and Moscow to provide instant contact between the heads of government, and the removal of U.S. missiles from Turkey, Italy, and Britain.

"PEACE FOR ALL TIME" Teetering on the brink of nuclear war convinced President Kennedy and others in the administration to soften their Cold War rhetoric and pursue other ways to reduce the threat of atomic warfare. As Kennedy told his advisers at a White House meeting, "It is insane that two men, sitting on opposite sides of the world, should be able to decide to bring an end to civilization." Later, Kennedy told an audience at American University on June 10, 1963, that his new goal was "not merely peace in our time, but peace for all time."

Soon thereafter, he began discussions with Soviet and British leaders to reduce the risk of nuclear war. The discussions resulted in the Limited Nuclear Test Ban Treaty, ratified in September 1963, which banned the testing of nuclear weapons in the atmosphere. It was the first joint agreement of the Cold War and an important move toward improved relations with the Soviet Union. As Kennedy put it, using an ancient Chinese proverb: "A journey of a thousand miles begins with one step."

KENNEDY AND VIETNAM As tensions with the Soviet Union eased, events in Southeast Asia were moving toward what would become the greatest American foreign-policy calamity of the century. Throughout the 1950s, U.S. officials increasingly came to view the preservation of anti-Communist South Vietnam as the critical test of American willpower in waging the Cold War. As a senator in 1956, John F. Kennedy described South Vietnam as the "cornerstone of the free world in Southeast Asia."

Yet the situation in South Vietnam had worsened under the corrupt leadership of Premier Ngo Dinh Diem and his family. Diem had reneged on promised social and economic reforms, and his efforts to repress dissent, directed not only against Communists but also against the Buddhist majority and other critics, played into the hands of his enemies.

President Eisenhower had provided more than 80 percent of the funding for the French military efforts against the Vietnamese Communists and $1 billion in aid to Diem's government during the late fifties. Initially, Kennedy sent more weapons, money, and some 16,000 military "advisers" to South Vietnam to help shore up the government. (They were called advisers to avoid the impression that U.S. soldiers were doing the fighting.) "If I tried to pull out," Kennedy explained, "we would have another Joe McCarthy red scare on our hands," with Republicans accusing him of "losing" Vietnam to communism. To withdraw "would be a great mistake."

By 1963, Kennedy was receiving sharply conflicting reports from South Vietnam. U.S. military analysts expressed confidence in the Army of the Republic of Vietnam. Journalists, however, predicted civil turmoil as long as Diem remained in power. By midyear, frequent Buddhist demonstrations against Diem ignited widespread discontent. The spectacle of Buddhist monks setting themselves on fire in public squares to protest government tyranny stunned Americans.

In the rice paddies and jungles of South Vietnam, the National Liberation Front (NLF), a left-wing nationalist movement backed by Communist North Vietnam, had launched a violent insurgency in which guerrilla fighters known as the Viet Cong (VC) were winning the fight against the South Vietnamese government. American military advisers began relocating Vietnamese peasants to "strategic hamlets"—new villages ringed by barbed wire—where the VC could not receive assistance.

By the fall of 1963, Kennedy acknowledged that Premier Diem was "out of touch with his people" and had to be removed. On November 1, Vietnamese generals, with the approval of U.S. officials and CIA agents in Saigon, seized control of the government. They then took a step that Kennedy had neither intended nor expected: they murdered Diem and his brother on November 2, 1963.

However ineffective Diem had been for nine years, his successors were worse. The South Vietnamese generals who engineered Diem's death soon began fighting one another, leaving Vietnam even more vulnerable to the Communist insurgency. For several years, South Vietnam essentially became an American colony. The United States put Vietnamese generals in power, gave them orders, and provided massive financial support, much of which was diverted into the hands of corrupt politicians and their families. The war grew steadily more intense but never moved closer to a U.S. victory.

By September 1963, Kennedy had developed doubts about his ability to defend the South Vietnamese. "In the final analysis," he told aides, "it's their war. . . . We can help them as advisers but they have to win it." Yet only a week later, in a televised interview, Kennedy reiterated the domino theory endorsed by Presidents Truman and Eisenhower, saying that if South Vietnam fell to communism, the rest of Southeast Asia would follow. He stressed that "we should stay [in South Vietnam]. We should use our influence in as effective a way as we can, but we should not withdraw." Yet the president told his closest advisers that he intended to withdraw U.S. forces if he won a second presidential term. "So we had better make damned sure that I am reelected," he told special assistant Kenneth O'Donnell.

KENNEDY ASSASSINATED By the fall of 1963, John F. Kennedy had matured as president. He had come to see the Cold War as a more complex challenge than he had believed during his first year in office. What Kennedy would have done thereafter in dealing with the Soviet Union has remained a matter of endless discussion.

Kennedy never made it to the 1964 election. While preparing to leave Washington for a speech in Dallas, he warned his wife, "We're heading into nut country today." More than thirty Texans had threatened his life. Kennedy told Jacqueline that "if somebody wants to shoot me from a window with a rifle, nobody can stop it, so why worry about it?"

At noon on November 22, 1963, the Kennedys were riding with Texas governor John Connally and his wife in an open convertible through Dallas as thousands of cheering spectators crowded the sidewalks. Connally looked back over his shoulder and told Kennedy, "You can't say Dallas doesn't love you, Mr. President." Just seconds later, Kennedy was shot and killed by Lee Harvey Oswald, a twenty-four-year-old ex-marine turned Communist who was positioned at a window on the sixth floor of the Texas Book Depository overlooking the street. Oswald had earlier defected to the Soviet Union. He idolized Fidel Castro and hated the United States. After shooting Kennedy, he also killed a Dallas policeman.

President Shot Dead Stunned New York City commuters read the news of President Kennedy's assassination on November 22, 1963.

Debate still swirls about whether Oswald acted alone or as part of a conspiracy, because he did not live long enough to tell his story. As Oswald was being transported to a court hearing, Jack Ruby, a Dallas nightclub owner with Mafia ties, shot and killed him at police headquarters as a nationwide television audience watched.

Kennedy's assassination and heartrending funeral enshrined the president in the public imagination as a martyred leader cut down in the prime of life. He came to have a stronger reputation after his death than he enjoyed in life. "That debonair touch, that shock of chestnut hair, that beguiling grin, that shattering understatement—these are what we shall remember," wrote newspaper columnist Mary McGrory.

Kennedy's thousand-day presidency had flamed up and out like a comet hitting the earth's atmosphere. Yet all the transformational events of the later 1960s— the Vietnam War, the civil rights revolution, and the youth rebellion—were set in motion during his brief time in the White House. With his death, Americans wept in the streets, the world was on edge, and Lyndon B. Johnson was now president.

Expansion of the Civil Rights Movement

After the Montgomery bus boycott of 1955–1956, Martin Luther King Jr.'s philosophy of militant nonviolence stirred others to challenge the deeply entrenched patterns of racial segregation in the South. During the sixties,

King became the face and heart of the civil rights movement. His goal was integration and equality, and he was an uplifting example of fortitude and dignity in confronting brutality and oppression. By nature, he was inspirational and courageous, with an astonishing capacity for forgiveness and a deep understanding of the dynamics of political power and social change. Yet he was also immensely complicated and contradictory, even hypocritical, as the FBI discovered by subjecting him to relentless electronic surveillance and even extortion.

King was neither a genius nor a saint, but his shortcomings pale into insignificance when compared to his achievements that earned him a Nobel Peace Prize and selection as *Time* magazine's "Man of the Year." He was one of the world's most inspiring examples of courage, conviction, and dignity in the face of violent prejudice and persecution. Even King's enemies acknowledged his remarkable courage despite constant threats and violent attacks. A deranged woman stabbed him, and he suffered repeated assaults while leading protest marches. He was hit by rocks, stung by tear gas, and beaten by police. Yet with the help of those he led and inspired, King changed the trajectory of American history—for the better.

SIT-INS The civil rights movement gained added momentum when four African American freshmen from North Carolina Agricultural and Technical College ordered coffee and doughnuts at an "all-White" Woolworth's lunch counter in Greensboro, North Carolina, on February 1, 1960. One of them, seventeen-year-old Joseph McNeil, said, "Segregation makes me feel that I'm unwanted. I don't want my children exposed to it." He recruited three friends to join him at the segregated lunch counter. As expected, the White waitress refused to serve them, explaining that "we don't serve colored here." Blacks had to eat standing up or take their food outside.

The Greensboro Four, as the students came to be called, returned the next day with two dozen more students. As they sat for hours, fruitlessly waiting to be served, some read Bibles; others read Henry David Thoreau's famous essay on civil disobedience. They returned every day for a week, patiently tolerating the hostility of White hooligans. The White mayor of nearby Raleigh, the North Carolina state capital, admonished the students for "endangering" race relations by "seeking to change a long-standing custom in a manner that is all but destined to fail." The "sit-in," however, did not fail. In fact, it helped propel the civil rights movement into the nation's top priorities.

The sit-in movement spread quickly to six more towns in the state, and within two months, similar sit-ins—involving 50,000 Blacks and Whites, men and women, young and old—had occurred in over 100 cities in thirteen states.

Civil Rights and Its Peaceful Warriors The Greensboro Four—*(from left)* Joseph McNeil, Franklin McCain, Billy Smith, and Clarence Henderson—await service on day two of their sit-in at a Woolworth's lunch counter. Their orders were never taken.

Black comedian Dick Gregory participated in several sit-ins. When the managers told him, "We don't serve Negroes," he replied: "No problem, I don't eat Negroes." Some 3,600 people were arrested nationwide, but the sit-ins worked. By the end of July 1960, officials in Greensboro lifted the Whites-only policy. The civil rights movement had found an effective new, nonviolent tactic against segregation.

In April 1960, some 200 student activists, Black and White, converged in Raleigh, North Carolina, to form the **Student Nonviolent Coordinating Committee** (SNCC—pronounced "snick"). The goal of what they came to call "the movement" was to intensify the effort to dismantle segregation. One of the organizers, the self-effacing Ella Baker, granddaughter of an enslaved person and perhaps the most prominent female leader within the civil rights movement, sought to build the self-confidence of young activists. She urged them not to adopt a "leader-centered orientation." As she explained, "strong people don't need strong leaders."

SNCC expanded the sit-ins to include "kneel-ins" at all-White churches and "wade-ins" at segregated public swimming pools. In many communities, demonstrators were pelted with rocks, burned with cigarettes, and even killed by White racists. As a Florida hog farmer named Holstead "Hoss" Manucy told a journalist, "I ain't got no bad habits. Don't smoke. Don't cuss. My only bad habit is fightin' [Negroes]."

The young activists who participated in sit-ins across the South found courage in their religious convictions. African American congressman John Lewis recalled that in preparing for the sit-ins in Nashville, "we felt that the message was one of love—the message of love in action: don't hate. If someone hits you, don't strike back. Just turn the other side. Be prepared to forgive. That's not anything any Constitution say[s] . . . about forgiveness. It is straight from the Scripture: reconciliation."

FREEDOM RIDES In 1961, civil rights leaders focused on integrating public transportation, namely buses and trains. Their larger goal was to force President Kennedy to embrace the cause of civil rights in the South. On May 4, the New York–based Congress of Racial Equality (CORE), led by James Farmer, decided to put "the civil rights movement on wheels" when a courageous group of thirteen Black and White men and women called **Freedom Riders** boarded two buses traveling from Washington, D.C., through the Lower South to New Orleans. They included ministers, college students, and civil rights activists.

The Freedom Riders wanted to test a recent federal court ruling that banned racial segregation on buses and trains, and in terminals. They knew

Freedom Riders On May 14, 1961, a White mob assaulted a Freedom Bus, flinging firebombs into its windows and beating the activists as they emerged. Here, the surviving Freedom Riders rest outside the burnt shell of their bus.

there would be confrontations and probably violence. Many of them hastily wrote wills before boarding the buses. "We felt we could count on the racists of the South to create a crisis," Farmer recalled, "so that the federal government would be compelled to enforce the law." The travelers described their departing meal at a Chinese restaurant in Washington as "The Last Supper." No one wanted to die, but their willingness to risk their lives was essential to the quest for justice. Farmer warned Attorney General Robert F. Kennedy that the bus riders would probably be attacked as they traveled through the South.

The warning was well founded, for on May 14, a mob of White racists in rural Alabama, many of them Klansmen, surrounded the buses carrying the Freedom Riders. Local police had told them they would not be arrested if they attacked the riders. After throwing a firebomb into one of the buses, the Whites barricaded its door. "Burn them alive," one yelled. The riders were able to escape the bus, only to be battered with metal pipes, chains, and clubs.

A few hours later, Freedom Riders on a second bus were beaten by Whites with baseball bats and chains after entering the Whites-only waiting room at a terminal in Birmingham, Alabama. Journalists and photographers covering the incident were also attacked. The city police, it turned out, had encouraged the assaults. The brutality, displayed on television, caused national outrage. The Freedom Riders wanted to continue their trip, but the bus drivers refused out of fear for their own safety.

When Diane Nash, a Black college student and SNCC organizer in Nashville, Tennessee, heard about the violence in Birmingham, she recruited new riders among the Nashville Student Movement, which she had helped found to organize sit-ins at local restaurants. President Kennedy called her, warning that she could "get killed if you do this." Her response: "It doesn't matter if we're killed. Others will come—others will come."

John Lewis, a friend of Nash, was one of the original thirteen Freedom Riders. One of ten children of Alabama sharecroppers, he grew up in a tiny house with no electricity or running water. He spent Sundays with his great-grandfather, who was born into slavery. His dream was to become a minister, and he practiced by preaching to the family's chickens.

While attending seminary in Nashville, however, Lewis experienced a political awakening that convinced him to confront racial injustice with nonviolent resistance. In April 1960, someone bombed the home of an African American civil rights attorney and city councilman in Nashville. Lewis and Nash led thousands of people who walked in silence to city hall to confront Nashville mayor Ben West.

On May 17, 1961, Nash and ten other college students took a bus to Birmingham to link up with the Freedom Riders. Upon arriving, they were arrested. While in jail, they sang "freedom songs," many of which were versions of old gospel hymns or spirituals: "We'll Never Turn Back," "Ain't Gonna Let Nobody Turn Me Around," "We Shall Overcome." Their joyous rebelliousness so frustrated Eugene "Bull" Connor, the city's racist police chief, that he drove them in the middle of the night to the Tennessee state line and dropped them off to walk home. Instead of going back to Nashville, however, the students returned to Birmingham.

President Kennedy feared that the Freedom Riders would inflame southern segregationists, divide the Democratic party, and paralyze his ability to get legislation through Congress. He called them "publicity seekers" who were trying to embarrass him and the United States on the eve of his summit meeting with Soviet leader Nikita Khrushchev. Kennedy ordered Harris Wofford, his special assistant on civil rights, to end the freedom rides: "Can't you get your goddamned friends off those buses? Stop them!" The activists finally forced the president to provide another bus, which enabled them to renew the journey to New Orleans. When the new group of Riders reached Montgomery, the capital of Alabama, hundreds of White racists, men, women, and children, attacked them.

"It was madness. It was unbelievable," Rider John Lewis recalled. He was knocked cold when someone smashed his head with a Coca-Cola crate. His self-possessed suffering revealed his foes as the monsters they were. "I thought I was going to die," he remembered. "But you keep going. You see something that is so necessary, so right. And I say to my brothers and sisters in the movement that you have to be hopeful, you have to be optimistic, be hopeful, keep going! Don't get lost in a sea of despair."

The Montgomery police chief had assured Floyd Mann, Alabama's public safety director, that there would be no violence. Yet when Mann arrived at the bus station, Klansmen armed with clubs and baseball bats were pummeling the Freedom Riders. Realizing that he had been double-crossed, Mann rushed inside, fired his revolver into the air, and yelled, "There'll be no more killing here today." When a Klansman raised a baseball bat to hit a Black bus rider, Mann put his gun to the attacker's head. "One more swing," he threatened, and "you're dead."

The next night, civil rights activists, including Martin Luther King, Jr., gathered at a Montgomery church to honor the Freedom Riders, but their meeting was interrupted by a mob of Whites armed with rocks and firebombs.

Ministers made frantic appeals to the White House. Kennedy responded by urging the Alabama governor to intervene. After midnight, national guardsmen arrived. The Freedom Riders continued into Mississippi, where they were jailed. Yet they persisted, finally reaching New Orleans by plane.

Over the next several months, 436 people participated in more than sixty Freedom Rides.

The courage and principled resistance of the Freedom Riders—along with that of federal judges whose rulings supported integration efforts—prompted the Interstate Commerce Commission (ICC) in September 1961 to order that all interstate transportation facilities be integrated. Equally important, the Freedom Riders kindled the rapid growth of civil rights groups. Widespread media coverage showed the nation that the nonviolent protesters were prepared to die for their rights rather than continue to endure racist assaults on their dignity.

Despite the court rulings, White segregationists remained violently opposed to racial equality. In Birmingham in September 1962, King was speaking at the meeting of the Southern Christian Leadership Conference when a White member of the American Nazi party jumped on the stage and punched him in the face. King simply dropped his hands and allowed the man to hit him again. "Don't touch him," King yelled. "We have to pray for him." King was determined, as an aide said, to "love segregation to death." His home was bombed three times, and he was arrested fourteen times, yet he kept telling people to use "the weapon of nonviolence, the breastplate of righteousness, the armor of truth, and just keep marching."

JAMES MEREDITH In the fall of 1962, James Meredith, an African American air force veteran whose grandfather had been enslaved, tried to enroll at the all-White University of Mississippi in Oxford. Ross Barnett, the governor of Mississippi, refused to allow Meredith to register and defiantly vowed "to rot in jail" rather than "let one Negro ever darken the sacred threshold of our white schools."

U.S. attorney general Robert F. Kennedy dispatched 300 federal marshals to enforce the law, but when they were assaulted by a mob of 2,000 Whites shouting "Go to Hell, JFK," the president sent 23,000 National Guard troops to Oxford. Their arrival ignited rioting that left a reporter and a bystander dead and hundreds injured, most of them federal marshals. Once the violence subsided, Meredith was registered at the university. "Only in America," a reporter noted, "would the federal government send thousands of troops to enforce the right of an otherwise obscure citizen to attend a particular university."

BIRMINGHAM Several months later, in early 1963, in conjunction with the celebration of the hundredth anniversary of Abraham Lincoln's Emancipation Proclamation, Martin Luther King Jr. announced that he and other civil rights activists were fed up "with tokenism and gradualism and

Bull's Dogs Eugene "Bull" Connor ordered Birmingham police to unleash their dogs on civil rights demonstrators in May of 1963.

see-how-far-you've-comeism. We can't wait any longer. Now is the time." He then defied the wishes of President Kennedy by organizing a massive series of demonstrations against segregation in Birmingham, Alabama, a state presided over by a feisty new racist governor—George Wallace—who had vowed to protect "segregation now, segregation tomorrow, segregation forever!" King knew that demonstrations in Birmingham would likely provoke violence, but a hard-won victory there, he felt, would build national support and "break the back of segregation all over the nation" by revealing southern "brutality openly—in the light of day—with the rest of the world looking on" through television cameras.

The Birmingham campaign began with sit-ins at restaurants, picket lines at segregated businesses, and a march on city hall. The police jailed hundreds of activists. Each day, however, more demonstrators, Black and White, joined the efforts. As thousands marched through the streets on May 7, the all-White police force led by "Bull" Connor used snarling dogs, tear gas, electric cattle prods, and high-pressure fire hoses on the protesters.

Americans were outraged when they saw the ugly confrontations on television. "The civil rights movement," President Kennedy observed, "owes Bull

Connor as much as it owes Abraham Lincoln." More than 3,000 demonstrators were arrested, including King and several White ministers. In his cell, King wrote a "Letter from Birmingham Jail," a stirring defense of **nonviolent civil disobedience** that has become a classic document of the civil rights movement. "We know from painful experience," he stressed, "that freedom is never voluntarily given by the oppressor; it must be demanded by the oppressed." Still, he refused to condone violence. "One who breaks an unjust law," King stressed, "must do so openly, lovingly, and with a willingness to *accept the penalty.*"

In a reference to President Kennedy's timid support, King wrote that the most perplexing foe of equal justice was not the southern White bigot but "the White moderate, who is more devoted to 'order' than to justice . . . who constantly says, 'I agree with you in the goal you seek, but I cannot agree with your methods.'" King believed that Kennedy had "the understanding and the political skill" to embrace the civil rights movement, but lacked the necessary "moral passion."

King's efforts prevailed when Birmingham officials finally agreed to end their segregationist practices. But throughout 1963, Whites in the Lower South continued to defy efforts at racial integration, while Black and White activists organized demonstrations across the nation. One angry Alabaman sent a letter to King: "This isn't a threat but a promise—your head will be blown off as sure as Christ made green apples." The "gradualism" that Kennedy preferred, King concluded, "is little more than escapism and do-nothingism, which ends up in stand-stillism."

By 1963, Alabama was the only state where Black and White students did not attend the same schools or colleges. On June 11, 1963, Alabama governor George Wallace theatrically blocked the door at the University of Alabama as African American students tried to register for classes. Wallace finally stepped aside in the face of insistent federal marshals.

That night, President Kennedy finally decided he needed to lead. The South, he told his brother Robert, "will never reform." In a hastily arranged televised speech, Kennedy announced that he would soon submit to Congress a major new civil rights bill that would remove race as a consideration "in American life or law." He stressed that "a great change is at hand," and he was determined to make "that change, that [civil rights] revolution," peaceful and constructive. "We are confronted primarily with a moral issue," the president said in language King had been urging him to invoke for years. "It is as old as the Scriptures and is as clear as the American Constitution. The heart of the question is whether all Americans are to be afforded equal rights and equal opportunities." He asked "every American, regardless of where he lives," to "stop and examine his conscience," for America, "for all its hopes and all its boasts, will not be fully free until all its citizens are free."

That night, in Mississippi, a thirty-seven-year-old African American activist, Medgar Evers, a World War II combat veteran, listened to the president's speech in his car. Kennedy's remarks so excited Evers that he turned around and went home so that he could discuss the speech with his children. When he arrived at his house in Jackson at midnight, he was shot and killed by a White racist.

The killing of Medgar Evers aroused the nation's indignation and reinforced Kennedy's commitment to make civil rights America's most pressing social issue. The president hosted his first meeting of civil rights leaders in the White House and helped spur plans for a massive demonstration on the Mall in Washington, D.C. On June 18, Kennedy declared that "race has no place in American life or law" and asked Congress to pass a comprehensive civil rights bill. "There comes a time when a man needs to take a stand," Kennedy told congressional Democrats.

"I HAVE A DREAM!" For weeks, southern Democrats in the House of Representatives blocked President Kennedy's civil rights bill. The standoff led African American leaders to take a bold step. On August 28, some 250,000 Blacks and Whites, many of them schoolchildren brought in on buses, marched arm in arm down the Mall in Washington, D.C., chanting "Equality Now!" and singing "We Shall Overcome."

The **March on Washington** for Jobs and Freedom was the largest political demonstration in American history. "When you looked at the crowd," remembered a U.S. Park Service ranger, "you didn't see Blacks or Whites. You saw America." The organizers, primarily civil rights veterans Bayard Rustin and A. Philip Randolph, never imagined that so many people would participate. For almost six hours, prominent entertainers sang protest songs and civil rights activists gave speeches calling for racial justice. John Lewis vowed "to splinter the segregated South into a thousand pieces and put them back together in the image of God and democracy."

Then something remarkable happened. On the steps of the Lincoln Memorial, thirty-four-year-old Martin Luther King Jr. came to the podium, welcomed by a huge roar from the crowd. He began awkwardly. Noticing his nervousness, someone on the podium urged him to "tell 'em about the dream, Martin."

As if suddenly inspired, King set aside his prepared remarks and delivered an extraordinary sermon in the form of a call for action, using righteousness and passion to inspire his listeners to action. He started slowly and picked up

"I Have a Dream" Martin Luther King Jr. is photographed before delivering his now-famous speech at the March on Washington while the huge crowd of supporters listen.

speed, as if he were speaking at a revival, giving poetic voice to the hopes of millions as he stressed the "fierce urgency of now" and the unstoppable power of "meeting physical force with soul force."

King then shared his dream for an America in which equality would be realized:

> In spite of the difficulties and frustrations of the moment, I still have a *dream*. It is a *dream* deeply rooted in the American dream. I have a *dream* that one day this nation will rise up and live out the true meaning of its creed: 'We hold these truths to be self-evident; that all men are created equal.' I have a *dream* that one day . . . the sons of former slaves and the sons of former slaveowners will be able to sit together at the table of brotherhood.

As if at a massive church service, many in the crowd began shouting "Amen!" as King summoned a flawed nation to justice: "So let freedom ring!" he shouted, for "when we allow freedom to ring from every town and every hamlet, from every state and every city, we will be able to speed up the day when *all* God's children—Black men and White men, Jews and Gentiles, Protestants and Catholics—will be able to join hands and sing in the words of the old Negro spiritual, *Free at last, free at last, thank God Almighty, we are free at last!*"

As King finished, there was a startling hush, then a deafening ovation. The crowd spontaneously joined hands and began singing "We Shall Overcome." "I have never been so proud to be a Negro," said baseball superstar Jackie Robinson. "I have never been so proud to be an American." President Kennedy, who had tried to convince organizers to call off the march, was watching on TV at the White House, just a mile away. As King spoke, the president told an aide that "he's damn good."

But King's dream remained just that—a dream deferred. Eighteen days later, four Klansmen in Birmingham detonated a bomb in a Black church, killing four young girls. The murders sparked a new wave of indignation across the country and the world. The editors of the *Milwaukee Sentinel* stressed that the bombing "should serve to goad the conscience. The deaths . . . in a sense are on the hands of each of us."

THE WARREN COURT The civil rights movement depended as much on the courts as it did on the leadership of Martin Luther King, Rosa Parks, John Lewis, Ella Baker, and others. Federal judges kept pressuring states and localities to integrate schools and other public places. Under Chief Justice Earl Warren, the U.S. Supreme Court also made landmark decisions in other areas of American life.

In 1962, the Court ruled in *Engel v. Vitale* that a school prayer adopted by the New York State Board of Regents violated the constitutional prohibition against government-supported religion. Alabama governor George Wallace condemned the ruling: "They have put Negroes in the schools. And now they have taken God out."

In *Gideon v. Wainwright* (1963), the Court required that those charged with a felony be provided a lawyer regardless of their ability to pay. In 1964, the Court ruled in *Escobedo v. Illinois* that a person accused of a crime must be allowed to consult a lawyer before being interrogated by police.

Two years later, in *Miranda v. Arizona*, the Court ordered that an accused person in police custody must be informed of certain basic rights: the right to remain silent; the right to know that anything said to authorities can be used against the individual in court; and the right to have an attorney present during interrogation. These requirements have come to be known as *Miranda* rights. In addition, the Court established rules for police to follow in telling suspects of their legal rights before questioning could begin.

FREEDOM SUMMER During late 1963 and throughout 1964, the civil rights movement continued to grow. Racial segregation, however, remained entrenched in the Lower South. White officials kept African Americans from voting by charging them poll taxes, forcing them to take difficult literacy tests, making the application process inconvenient, and intimidating them through arson, beatings, and lynchings.

In early 1964, soft-spoken Robert "Bob" Moses, a Black New Yorker who had resigned from his work as a schoolteacher to head the Student Nonviolent Coordinating Committee (SNCC) office in Mississippi. There he decided it would take "an army" to force the state to give voting rights to Black people. So he set about recruiting Black and White volunteers who would live with poor, illiterate, rural African Americans, teach them in "freedom schools," and help thousands of them register to vote. Racist Whites did not appreciate Moses's efforts. They knifed and shot at him, yet he always displayed extraordinary composure in the face of horrific violence.

Most of the 800 volunteers that Moses helped recruit for what came to be called Freedom Summer were idealistic White college students, many of them Jewish, and all of them willing to work without pay. A third of them were women. Mississippi's White leaders prepared for "the [Negro]-Communist invasion" by doubling the state police force and stockpiling tear gas, electric cattle prods, and shotguns.

In mid-June, the volunteer activists met at an Ohio college to learn about southern racial history, nonviolent civil disobedience, and the likely abuses they would suffer. On the final evening of training, Moses pleaded with anyone who feared heading to Mississippi to go home; several did. The next day, the volunteers boarded buses and headed south.

In all, forty-one freedom schools taught thousands of Mississippi children math, writing, and history. They also tutored Black adults about the complicated process of voter registration. Stokely Carmichael, an African American student from Trinidad studying at Howard University, wrote that Black Mississippians "took us in, fed us, instructed and protected us, and ultimately civilized, educated, and inspired the smartassed college students."

Forty-six-year-old Fannie Lou Hamer was one of the local Black activists who worked with the SNCC volunteers. The youngest in a household of twenty children, she had spent most of her life working on cotton plantations. During the Freedom Summer of 1963 and after, she led gatherings of volunteers in freedom songs and excelled as a lay preacher. "God is not pleased," she said, "at all the murdering, and all the brutality, and all the killings for no reason at all. God is not pleased at the Negro children in the State of Mississippi, suffering from malnutrition. God is not pleased because we have to go raggedy each day. God is not pleased because we have to go to the field and work from ten to eleven hours for three lousy dollars."

The Ku Klux Klan, local police, and other White racists harassed, arrested, and assaulted many of the volunteers. During Freedom Summer, there were

Fannie Lou Hamer Civil rights activist Fannie Lou Hamer gained prominence as a skilled volunteer organizer and preacher, drawing on freedom songs to energize activists over issues like police brutality toward African Americans and widespread hunger in Black communities.

thirty-five shootings, thirty bombings, and eighty beatings. The worst incident occurred on June 21, 1964, when three young SNCC workers—James Earl Chaney, Andrew Goodman, and Michael "Mickey" Schwerner—disappeared after going to investigate the burning of an African American church. Their decomposed, bullet-riddled bodies were found two months later buried in a dam at a cattle pond. They had been abducted and murdered by Klan members, two of whom were the county sheriff and his deputy.

Eventually, the county sheriff, his deputy, and seventeen other Klansmen were charged with "conspiracy" to deprive the three murdered men of their civil rights. In 1967, seven of the defendants were convicted. Two were sentenced to ten years in prison; the others drew lesser sentences. When questioned about the light sentences, the openly racist judge, who called African Americans "chimpanzees," replied that those convicted had "killed one [Negro], one Jew, and a White man. I gave them what I thought they deserved."

Meanwhile, a growing number of activists, especially young Blacks associated with SNCC, were beginning to question Martin Luther King's strategy of Christian nonviolence. "The only way we gonna stop them White men from whuppin' us is to take over," declared Stokely Carmichael. "We been saying freedom for six years, and we ain't got nothin'." Years later, President Jimmy

Carter, a Georgian, stressed that "Martin Luther King didn't integrate the South. SNCC integrated the South."

BLACK POWER Racism was not limited to the South. By the mid-1960s, about 70 percent of the nation's African Americans were living in blighted urban areas, and many young Blacks were losing faith in the strategy of Christian nonviolence. Inner-city poverty and frustration cried out for its own social justice movement.

The fragmentation of the civil rights movement was tragically evident on August 11, 1965, when Watts, the largest and poorest Black neighborhood in Los Angeles, exploded in response to another incident of racist police brutality. Over the course of six chaotic nights, the rioting, burning, and looting left 34 dead, almost 4,000 in jail, and caused widespread damage. The Watts riots dumbfounded President Lyndon Johnson. "How is it possible," he asked, "after all we've accomplished? How could it be? Is the world topsy-turvy?"

The spreading inner-city violence revealed the growing war within the civil rights movement. As Gil Scott-Heron, a Black musician, sang: "We are tired of praying and marching and thinking and learning / Brothers want to start cutting and shooting and stealing and burning." What came to be called "Black power" began to compete with the integrationist, nonviolent philosophy espoused by Martin Luther King and the Southern Christian Leadership Conference.

MALCOLM X AND BLACK POWER The most visible spokesman for the **Black Power movement** was Malcolm X, born in 1925 in Omaha, Nebraska, as Malcolm Little. His father, a Baptist minister, and his West Indian mother had supported Marcus Garvey's crusade for Black nationalism in the 1920s, and their home was burned to the ground by White racists. His father was killed when Malcolm was six, perhaps by White supremacists. Afterward, Malcolm's mother suffered a breakdown and was institutionalized for the rest of her life. Young Malcolm was placed in foster care, but after being expelled from school in the ninth grade, he drifted from Detroit to New York City to Boston.

By age nineteen, Malcolm, now known as Detroit Red, had become a thief, drug dealer, and pimp. He spent seven years in Massachusetts prisons, where he joined a small Chicago-based anti-White religious sect, the Nation of Islam (NOI), whose members were called Black Muslims.

The organization had little to do with Islam and everything to do with its domineering leader, Elijah Muhammad. Muhammad dismissed Whites as "devils" and championed Black nationalism, racial pride, self-respect, and

Malcolm X The Black Power movement's most influential spokesman, Malcolm X, promoted a militant message that conflicted with Martin Luther King, Jr.'s emphasis on nonviolence.

self-discipline. By 1953, a year after leaving prison, Malcolm Little was calling himself Malcolm X in tribute to his lost African name, and he had become a full-time NOI minister famous for electrifying speeches attacking White racism and Black powerlessness. He insisted that Blacks call themselves *African Americans* as a symbol of pride and as a spur to learn more about their history.

Malcolm X dismissed Martin Luther King and other mainstream civil rights leaders as "nothing but modern Uncle Toms" who "keep you and me in check, keep us under control, keep us passive and peaceful and nonviolent." He insisted that there "was no such thing as a nonviolent revolution." African Americans, he argued, had a right to meet police brutality with force. His righteous fury inspired thousands of mostly urban Blacks to join the Nation of Islam and to use what he called "any means necessary" to gain equality, justice, and dignity. "Our enemy is the White man!" he thundered.

Malcolm X expressed the emotions and frustrations of the inner-city African American working poor. Yet at the peak of his influence, and just as he was moderating his militant message, he became embroiled in a conflict with Elijah Muhammad that proved fatal. NOI assassins killed Malcolm X in Manhattan on February 21, 1965. He was 39.

Black militancy did not end with Malcolm X, however. By 1966, "Black power" had become a rallying cry for many young militants. When Stokely Carmichael became head of the Student Nonviolent Coordinating Committee, he ousted Whites from the organization. "When you talk of Black power," Carmichael shouted, "you talk of bringing this country to its knees, of building a movement that will smash everything Western civilization has created." Having been beaten by Whites and having seen fellow volunteers killed, Carmichael rejected the nonviolent philosophy of the civil rights movement.

THE BLACK PANTHER PARTY Stokely Carmichael spoke to the seething rage displayed by the young Black underclass. Soon he and others would embrace the Black Panther Party for Self Defense (BPP). The Black Panthers were a group of revolutionaries founded in 1966 by Huey P. Newton and Bobby Seale in Oakland, California. Newton and Seale formed the BPP after San Francisco police killed Matthew Johnson, an unarmed Black teen. The BPP, which never had more than 2,000 members, called for an end to "police terrorism," full employment for African Americans, decent housing, and the release of all Black men from prison.

Wearing black berets, leather coats, and sunglasses and armed with rifles and shotguns, cartridge belts, a menacing swagger, and a clenched-fist Black power salute, Black Panthers rejected the integrationist philosophy of Martin Luther King Jr. in favor of revolutionary violence. "We do not believe in passive and nonviolent tactics," Newton explained. "They haven't worked for us Black people. They are bankrupt" in the inner cities of America. "Force, guns, and arms are the real political arena." The "racist" police "in our communities are not there to protect us. They are here to contain us, to oppress us, to brutalize us."

The Black Panthers intended to "police the police" in their communities while addressing the challenges of inner-city life by creating self-governing communities. To that end, they organized Free Breakfast for Children programs, offered job-training programs, and created free community health clinics. Soon, more than forty Black Panther chapters emerged in cities across America: New York, Los Angeles, Chicago, Boston, Philadelphia, and Seattle, among others.

The Black Panthers insisted that they had a right to defend themselves from police harassment and brutality. A gun battle with police in which an officer was shot and killed landed Newton in jail. Between 1967 and 1969, nine police officers and ten Black Panthers were killed in shootouts. FBI Director J. Edgar Hoover labeled the Black Panthers terrorists who constituted the "greatest threat to the internal security of the country." To meet that threat of "Black nationalist hate groups," he organized a comprehensive program to undermine the Black Panther party. The efforts of the FBI, along with infighting and drug abuse among the members, destroyed the Black Panthers by 1982.

By then, the handsome, eloquent Huey Newton had become a drug addict and alcoholic. He spent three years in prison for shooting a policeman. Afterwards, he became a tyrant, expelling co-founder Bobby Seale from the BPP and beating him with a bullwhip. In 1989, a drug dealer shot and killed him.

For all their violent and self-destructive behavior, the Black Panthers infused the civil rights movement with powerful insights and constructive

Panther Power Promising to bring power to the people, the Black Panthers built community through local initiatives centered on food, health, and jobs. In addition to improving their material conditions, they fervently denounced police brutality.

beliefs. They affirmed that the necessary first step for African Americans seeking true equality was to learn to love oneself and then to love and protect each other, regardless of age, gender, or sexual preference.

Audre Lorde, a powerful New York writer, the child of West Indian immigrants who described herself as a Black lesbian feminist, mother, warrior, and poet, credited the Black Panthers with helping to expand the civil rights movement to include other "disenfranchised" groups such as women and gays/lesbians. Huey Newton, for example, urged the BPP "to form a working coalition with the Gay Liberation and Women's Liberation groups."

Lorde emphatically agreed, noting that people "don't lead single-issue lives." Creating a truly powerful movement for social change thus required connecting organizations that speak to different constituencies. Activists must learn "how to take our differences and make them strengths."

The young men who founded the Black Panther party proclaimed themselves "the cream of Black Manhood" who would protect and defend "our Black community." Initially, the role of female Panthers was to "stand behind Black men" and be supportive. Yet despite such masculine bravado, the majority of Black Panthers were women. "The women who were drawn to the Black Panther Party were all feminists," explained Ericka Huggins, a leader of the organization. By 1969, the Black Panther Party newspaper declared that men and women were now equal members of the organization and instructed male members to treat women as equals.

Alabama-born Angela Davis, a Phi Beta Kappa graduate of Brandeis University who earned a doctoral degree in philosophy from Humboldt University in Germany and taught at the University of California at Los Angeles (UCLA), was a radical feminist aligned with SNCC, the Black Panthers, and the Communist Party. California governor Ronald Reagan ordered the Board of Regents to fire Davis for using "inflammatory language," for she repeatedly referred to police officers as "pigs."

A formidable speaker, Davis became an outspoken activist for an array of causes. She opposed the Vietnam War, racism, sexism, and the "prison-industrial complex." She also supported gay/lesbian rights and other social justice movements. "I am no longer accepting the things I cannot change," she declared. "I am changing the things I cannot accept."

BLACK POWER IN RETROSPECT   Although widely covered in the media, the Black Power movement never attracted more than a small minority of African Americans. Still, it forced Martin Luther King and other mainstream civil rights leaders to shift their focus from the rural South to inner-city neighborhoods in the North and West. Between 1965 and 1968, King urged an end to U.S. involvement in Vietnam and promoted social justice and economic equality. Integration was no longer enough.

The time had come, King declared while launching his "Poor People's Campaign" in December 1967, for radical new measures "to provide jobs and income for the poor." As he and others stressed, the war in Vietnam was taking funds away from federal programs serving the poor, and Black soldiers were dying in disproportionate numbers in Southeast Asia. He wanted America to be the "moral example to the world," but it had instead become "the greatest purveyor of violence in the world."

The Black Power movement also motivated African Americans to take greater pride in their racial heritage by demanding Black studies programs in schools and colleges, the celebration of African cultural and artistic traditions, the organizing of inner-city voters to elect Black mayors, laws forcing landlords to treat Blacks fairly, and the creation of grassroots organizations and community centers in Black neighborhoods.

LYNDON BAINES JOHNSON AND THE GREAT SOCIETY

Stronger federal support for civil rights came from an unlikely source: the White Texan who succeeded John F. Kennedy in the White House. Lyndon B. Johnson, known as LBJ, took the presidential oath on board the plane that brought Kennedy's body back to Washington from Dallas. Kennedy's widow, Jacqueline Kennedy, stood beside the new president, still wearing her blood-stained pink wool suit. Fifty-five years old and six feet four inches tall, Johnson had spent twenty-six years in Washington and served nearly a decade as one of

The Oath of Office Less than an hour and a half after Kennedy's death, Vice President Lyndon Johnson took the presidential oath aboard *Air Force One*, standing between his wife, Lady Bird *(left)*, and Jacqueline Kennedy *(right)*, before flying out of Dallas for Washington, D.C.

the most powerful Democratic leaders ever in the Senate. Now he was the first southern president since Woodrow Wilson, a legislative magician who had excelled as Senate majority leader.

Johnson's transition to the presidency was not easy. John and Bobby Kennedy despised him and his hardscrabble Texas background. JFK had warned aides that Johnson was "a very insecure, sensitive man with a huge ego," and he had directed them to "kiss his ass from one end of Washington to the other." Not surprisingly, Johnson had come to hate the Kennedys, for they had all but ignored him as vice president, often lampooning him as "Uncle Cornpone."

Johnson's rise to the presidency was a rags-to-riches story. He had worked his way out of rural Texas poverty during the Great Depression to become one of the Senate's dominant figures.

LBJ's personality largely shaped his successes and failures. His ego and insecurities were as massive as his vanity and ambition. He could not stand being alone, and he insisted on always being the center of attention. At press conferences he referred to "my Vietnam policy," "my Security Council," "my Cabinet," "my legislation," and "my boys" fighting in Southeast Asia. He personalized the war in Vietnam, pledging that "I am not going to lose Vietnam." Thereafter, for many Americans, the deepening commitment in Southeast Asia became "Johnson's War."

George Reedy, Johnson's press secretary, described the president as a "man of too many paradoxes." Ruthless and often bullying, Johnson was rabidly impatient with anyone who dissented or diverged from his agenda. His temperamental outbursts became legendary.

The product of a domineering mother and moody father, Johnson became famous for his rants and dramatic mood swings: he was either very up or very down. His press secretary said he "walked on air" one minute and then was ready to "slash his wrists" the next. The imperious and even cruel Johnson often berated his aides with profanity and belittling humor. "There's only two kinds at the White House," he told the staff. "There's elephants and there's pissants. And I'm the only elephant."

Those who viewed Johnson as a stereotypical southern conservative failed to appreciate his long-standing admiration for Franklin D. Roosevelt, the depth of his concern for the poor, and his bold support for the cause of civil rights (in part because he needed to win over the northern wing of the Democratic party). "I'm going to be the best friend the Negro ever had," Johnson bragged to a member of the White House staff soon after becoming president.

Johnson's commitment to civil rights was in part motivated by politics, in part by his desire to bring the South into the mainstream of American life, and in part by his life experiences. His first teaching job after college was at an elementary school in Texas serving Mexican American children. Teaching Mexican Americans created in him a lifelong desire to help "those poor little kids. I saw hunger in their eyes and pain in their bodies. Those little brown bodies had so little and needed so much." He grew determined to "fill their souls with ambition and interest and belief in the future."

Unlike the politically cautious Kennedy, Johnson had Texas-sized ambitions and audacity. Few presidents had ever dreamed as big as Lyndon Johnson. He was determined to be the greatest president, the one who did the most good for the most people. He promised to "help every child get an education, to help every Negro and every American citizen have an equal opportunity, to help every family get a decent home, and to help bring healing to the sick and dignity to the old."

POLITICS AND POVERTY

Lyndon Johnson had unrivaled get-it-done energy. He maneuvered legislation through Congress better than any previous president. He was a genius at working the levers of political power and a consummate wheeler-dealer.

In 1964, he took advantage of widespread public backing in the aftermath of John F. Kennedy's death to push through Congress the fallen president's stalled measures for tax reductions and civil rights. The Revenue Act of 1964 provided a 20 percent reduction in tax rates. (The top rate was then a whopping 91 percent, compared to 37 percent today.) It was intended to give consumers more money to spend so as to boost economic growth and create new jobs—and it worked even better than expected. Unemployment fell from 5.2 percent in 1964 to 4.5 percent in 1965, and to 3.8 percent in 1966.

THE CIVIL RIGHTS ACT (1964)   Long thwarted by southern Democrats in Congress, the **Civil Rights Act of 1964** finally became law on July 2. It guaranteed equal treatment for *all* Americans and outlawed

Down with Segregation A worker removes a sign from a public restroom at Montgomery Municipal Airport that reads: "WHITE MEN."

discrimination in public places—theaters, restaurants, parks, hotels, sports arenas, libraries, museums, playgrounds, and other venues—on the basis of race, sex, or national origin. It also prohibited racial discrimination in the buying, selling, and renting of housing—called redlining—as well as in the hiring and firing of employees.

With an urgent sense of purpose, Johnson pushed and even bullied members of Congress to pass the Civil Rights Act. He lobbied key legislators over drinks and cigarettes in his office, flattering, threatening, and bargaining with them to vote his way. One senator said that the president would "twist your arm off at the shoulder and beat your head with it" if you did not agree to vote as he wanted.

Soon after becoming president, Johnson hosted Georgia senator Richard Russell, his close friend and an arch-segregationist. Over lunch, the president warned Russell that "you've got to get out of my way. I'm going to run over you" to pass the Civil Rights Act. "You may do that," Russell replied. "But by God, it's going to cost you the South and cost you the election of 1964." Johnson would not be bullied. "If that's the price I've got to pay," he replied, "I'll pay it gladly." Soon thereafter, Johnson told Congress that "we have talked long enough in this country about equal rights. . . . It is time now to write the next chapter, and to write it in the book of law." He added that it would be the best way to honor Kennedy's memory.

People from all walks of life helped Johnson convince Congress to pass the Civil Rights Act—congressional committee chairs (both Republicans and Democrats), labor unions, church leaders, and civil rights organizations. Their efforts produced what is arguably the most important piece of legislation in the twentieth century. Its passage marked one of those extraordinary moments when the ideals of democracy, equal opportunity, and human dignity were affirmed.

The Civil Rights Act dealt a major blow to racial segregation while giving the federal government new powers to bring lawsuits against organizations or businesses that violated constitutional rights. It also established the Equal Employment Opportunities Commission to ensure that employers treated job applicants equally, regardless of race, gender, or national origin.

WAR ON POVERTY In addition to fulfilling President Kennedy's legislative priorities that had stalled in Congress, Lyndon Johnson launched an elaborate legislative program of his own, declaring "unconditional war on poverty in America." Elected officials had "rediscovered" poverty in 1962 when social critic Michael Harrington published a powerful exposé, *The Other America,* in which he argued that more than 40 million people were mired in an invisible "culture of poverty" in which residents of ghetto neighborhoods developed attitudes, behaviors, and self-concepts that constrict their ability to improve their quality of life. Poverty led to poor housing conditions, which in turn led to poor health, poor attendance at school or work, alcohol and drug abuse, unwanted pregnancies, and single-parent families. Harrington added that such entrenched poverty was more extensive than people realized because much of it was hidden from view in isolated rural areas or inner-city slums. He pushed for a "comprehensive assault on poverty."

President Kennedy had read Harrington's book and had asked his advisers in the fall of 1963, just before his assassination, to investigate the problem and suggest solutions. Upon becoming president, Lyndon Johnson announced that he wanted an anti-poverty legislative package "with real impact." He was determined to help the "one-fifth of families with incomes too small to even meet their basic needs."

Johnson knew that the "war" on poverty would be long and costly. He did not expect to "wipe out poverty" in "my lifetime. But we can minimize it, moderate it, and in time eliminate it." His War on Poverty would not give people handouts but open "the door of opportunity" for those struggling to put food on the table. The primary weapons in this war would be "better schools and better health and better homes and better training and better job opportunities."

War on Poverty In 1964, Johnson visited Tom Fletcher, a father of eight children living in a tar-paper shack in rural Kentucky. Fletcher became a "poster father" for the War on Poverty, though, as it turned out, his life improved little as a result of its programs.

OPPORTUNITY ACT OF 1964 The **Economic Opportunity Act of 1964** was the primary weapon in Johnson's War on Poverty. It created an Office of Economic Opportunity (OEO) to administer eleven new community-based programs, many of which still exist. They included a Job Corps training program for the long-term unemployed; an Upward Bound program to excite inner-city youth about attending college; a Head Start educational program for disadvantaged preschoolers; a Legal Services Corporation to provide free legal assistance for low-income Americans; financial-aid programs for low-income college students; grants to small farmers and rural businesses; loans to businesses that hired the chronically unemployed; the Volunteers in Service to America program (VISTA) to combat inner-city poverty; and the Community Action Program, which would allow the poor "maximum feasible participation" in organizing and directing their own neighborhood programs. In 1964, Congress also approved the Food Stamp Act to help the poor afford groceries.

THE 1964 ELECTION President Johnson's successes aroused a conservative Republican counterattack. Arizona senator Barry Goldwater, a wealthy department-store owner and self-proclaimed frontiersman, emerged as the square-jawed, blunt-talking leader of the growing right wing of the Republican party. He was one of only six Republican senators to vote against the Civil Rights Act and warned that the bill would lead to a "federal police state."

Campaign Buttons, 1964 A button for and against Barry Goldwater from the election campaigns of 1964.

In his best-selling book *The Conscience of a Conservative* (1960), Goldwater had called for ending the income tax and drastically reducing federal entitlement programs such as Social Security. Conservatives controlled the Republican National Convention when it gathered in San Francisco in the early summer of 1964, and they ensured Goldwater's nomination. "I would remind you," Goldwater told the delegates, "that extremism in the defense of liberty is no vice." He later explained that his objective was like that of Calvin Coolidge in the 1920s: "to reduce the size of government. Not to pass laws, but to repeal them."

Goldwater was refreshingly candid. He was quick to smile and easy to like, but he was out of his depth as a presidential candidate. He frightened many voters by arguing that President Kennedy should have torn down the Berlin Wall and invaded Fidel Castro's Cuba. He also urged wholesale bombing of North Vietnam and suggested the use of atomic weapons. He criticized Johnson's War on Poverty as a waste of money, told college students that the federal government should not provide funds for education, and opposed the nuclear test ban treaty. To Republican campaign buttons that claimed, "In your heart, you know he's right," Democrats responded, "In your guts, you know he's nuts."

Johnson, by comparison, portrayed himself as a responsible centrist. He chose as his running mate Hubert H. Humphrey of Minnesota, a prominent liberal senator who had long promoted civil rights, and pledged that he was "not about to send American boys nine or ten thousand miles from home to do what Asian boys ought to be doing for themselves."

The election was not close. Johnson won 61 percent of the popular vote and dominated the electoral vote, 486 to 52. Goldwater captured only Arizona and five states in the Lower South. In the Senate, the Democrats increased their majority by two (68 to 32) and in the House by thirty-seven (295 to 140).

But Goldwater's success among White voters in the Lower South accelerated the region's shift to the Republican party, and his candidacy proved to be a turning point in the development of the national conservative movement by inspiring a generation of young activists and the formation of conservative organizations that would transform the dynamics of American politics during the 1970s and 1980s. Their success would culminate in the presidency of Ronald Reagan, the Hollywood actor who co-chaired the "California for Goldwater" campaign in 1964.

THE GREAT SOCIETY

Lyndon Johnson misread his lopsided victory in 1964 as a mandate for massive changes. He knew, however, that his popularity could quickly fade. "Every day I'm in office," he told his aides, "I'm going to lose votes. I'm going to alienate somebody. . . . We've got to get this legislation fast. You've got to get it during my honeymoon."

As Johnson's War on Poverty gathered momentum, his outsized ambitions grew even bolder. In May 1964, he launched an array of new programs intended to create a "**Great Society**" that would end poverty and racial injustice and provide "abundance and liberty for all."

That was a magisterial goal, but it "was just the beginning," Johnson insisted, given that the United States had the resources to do much more than assault poverty. "We have the opportunity to move not only toward the rich society and the powerful society, but upward to the Great Society." He did not explain precisely what he meant by a "great society," but it soon became clear that Johnson viewed the federal government as the magical lever for raising the quality of life for all Americans—rich and poor. He would surpass his hero Franklin Roosevelt in expanding the goals and scope of the federal government to ensure that Americans were a people of plenty.

When Johnson became president in November 1963, Social Security was America's only nationwide social program. That soon changed. He convinced the Democrat-controlled Congress to approve a torrent of legislative requests focused on education, health care, civil rights, urban renewal, rural poverty, transportation, and even cultural offerings such as government-funded public television and radio programming. The Great Society also featured initiatives to enhance the environment, including an Air Quality Act, a Water Quality Act, a Wilderness Act, an Endangered Species Act, a Scenic Rivers Act, and a National Trails Act.

HEALTH INSURANCE, HOUSING, AND HIGHER EDUCATION

Lyndon Johnson's first priorities among his Great Society programs were federal health insurance and aid for young people to pursue higher education— proposals that had first been suggested by President Truman in 1945 but were rejected by conservative southern Democrats and Republicans in Congress. For twenty years, the steadfast opposition of the American Medical Association (AMA) had stalled a comprehensive medical-insurance program. Now that Johnson and the Democrats had the votes, however, the AMA joined Republicans in supporting a bill serving only those over age sixty-five.

The act created not just a **Medicare** health insurance program for the elderly but also a **Medicaid** program of federal grants to states to help cover medical expenses for the poor of all ages. Johnson signed the bill on July 30, 1965, in Independence, Missouri, with eighty-one-year-old Harry Truman looking on.

The Higher Education Act of 1965 increased federal grants to universities, created scholarships for low-income students, provided low-interest loans for students, and established a National Teacher Corps. "Every child," Johnson asserted, "must be encouraged to get as much education as he has the ability to take."

The momentum generated by the Higher Education and Medicare bills helped carry many more Great Society bills through Congress. Among them was the Appalachian Regional Development Act of 1966, which allocated $1 billion for programs in impoverished mountain areas. The Housing and Urban Development Act of 1965 provided $3 billion for urban renewal projects in inner cities. Funds to help low-income families pay their rent followed in 1966, and the same year a new Department of Housing and Urban Development was established, headed by Robert C. Weaver, the first African American cabinet member.

In implementing his Great Society programs, Lyndon Johnson had, in the words of one Washington reporter, "brought to harvest a generation's backlog of ideas and social legislation." People were amazed by Johnson's energy, drive, and legislative skills. He never seemed to stop or slow down. A woman in Hawaii noted that Johnson "is a mover of men. Kennedy could inspire men, but he couldn't move them."

THE IMMIGRATION ACT (1965) Little noticed in the stream of Great Society legislation was the **Immigration and Nationality Services Act of 1965** (also called the Hart-Celler Act), which President Johnson signed in a ceremony at the base of the Statue of Liberty. It was the most sweeping revision in immigration policies in decades, and both Democrats and Republicans supported its provisions ending discriminatory ethnic restrictions. In his speech, Johnson stressed that the law would redress the wrong done to those "from southern and eastern Europe" and the "developing continents" of Asia, Africa, and Latin America.

The old system, dating to 1924, favored immigrants from Great Britain and the countries of western and northern Europe over those from southern and Eastern Europe, Asia, and Africa. The new law ended national-origins quotas and created hemispheric ceilings on visas issued: 170,000 for persons from outside the Western Hemisphere, 120,000 for persons from within. It also stipulated that no more than 20,000 people could come annually from any one country, including Mexico. The new law thus had the unintended effect of making it much more difficult for Mexicans to enter the United States legally, despite the aggressive efforts of commercial farms to recruit them. Johnson explained that the new law "repairs a deep and painful flaw in the fabric of

American life. . . . The days of unlimited immigration are past. But those who come will come because of what they are—not because of the land from which they sprung."

Johnson's insistence that the new law was not "revolutionary" has been proven wrong. During the 1960s and since, Europeans dropped to less than 10 percent of the total immigrants while the number of Asian and Latin American immigrants soared. In the 350 years before 1965, some 43 million people had come to America; since 1965, more than 80 million immigrants have come to America, most of them from Mexico, the Philippines, Cuba, South Korea, China, Vietnam, and Taiwan.

VOTING RIGHTS LEGISLATION   The civil rights movement accelerated its efforts during the mid-1960s. Building upon the successes of Freedom Summer, Martin Luther King Jr. organized an effort in early 1965 to register the 3 million unregistered African American voters in the South. That effort bore fruit on February 6, 1965, when the White House announced that it would urge Congress to enact a voting rights bill to ensure that all Americans who wanted to vote could do so.

Weeks later, civil rights activists converged on Selma, Alabama, where only 250 of the 15,000 Blacks of voting age were registered voters. Martin Luther King targeted Selma because he knew its White residents would respond violently to a civil rights demonstration. He told his staff on February 10 that to get the voting rights bill passed, "we need to make a dramatic" statement.

Bloody Sunday While leading a peaceful march from Selma, Alabama, future congressman John Lewis and 600 other nonviolent protesters were assaulted by law enforcement officers. Here, Lewis *(center)* is held down and beaten by a state trooper.

A week later, Reverend C. T. Vivian, one of King's senior aides, was helping to register Black voters at the Selma courthouse when he compared the city's notorious sheriff, a White supremacist named Jim Clark, to Adolf Hitler. Television cameras then captured Clark punching Vivian in the face. An unflappable Vivian yelled back, "We're willing to be beaten for democracy!"

On Sunday, March 7, hundreds of Black and White civil rights activists assembled near the Edmund Pettus Bridge over the Alabama River to begin a fifty-four-mile march to Montgomery, where the Confederate flag still flew above the state capitol (the bridge was named for Edmund Pettus, a Confederate army officer who, after the Civil War, became a Grand Dragon of the Alabama Ku Klux Klan).

Before reaching the bridge, the 600 marchers were assaulted by helmeted state troopers using clubs, tear gas, and bullwhips. In what came to be called "Bloody Sunday," the violence initiated by the troopers was televised for all to see. Five women were knocked unconscious, seventy marchers were hospitalized, and a White Unitarian minister from Boston was beaten to death.

John Lewis, the twenty-five-year-old chairman of the Student Non-violent Coordinating Committee helped lead the march and sustained a fractured skull after a state trooper beat him to the ground with a nightstick. The militant yet gentle Lewis, a man of extraordinary courage and undying faith and hope, would later serve in Congress for more than three decades.

The horrific violence of "Bloody Sunday" in Selma prompted President Johnson to summon Alabama governor George Wallace to the White House. His goal was to get the defiant defender of segregation to welcome federal troops to protect the civil rights marchers.

Ushered into the Oval Office, Governor Wallace sat down on the soft sofa and sank down into its cushions. Johnson pulled up a rocking chair so that he towered over the much shorter Wallace. Leaning in, he told the feisty governor he must let African Americans exercise their constitutional right to vote. "Oh yes, there's no quarrel with that," Wallace replied. "Well then, why don't you let them vote?" Johnson asked. "I don't have that power," the governor claimed. "That belongs to the county registrars in the state of Alabama."

Wallace was lying, and Johnson knew it. Johnson asked Wallace how he wanted to be remembered in Alabama: "Now, in 1985, George, what do you want left behind? Do you want a great big marble monument that says 'George Wallace: He Built'? Or do you want a little piece of scrawny pine . . . that says 'George Wallace: He Hated'?"

After three hours and seventeen minutes of the famous "Johnson treatment," Wallace agreed to ask for federal troops to protect the civil rights demonstrators. One observer described the governor as having been reduced to "a quivering mass of flesh." He later admitted as much. "Hell," he said, "if I'd stayed in there much longer, he'd have me coming out for civil rights."

Martin Luther King, torn between congressional appeals to call off the march in Alabama and the demands of militants that it continue, announced that a second march would be organized. A federal judge agreed to allow the marchers to continue once President Johnson agreed to provide soldiers and federal marshals for their protection.

At the same time, Johnson told Attorney General Nicholas Katzenbach: "I want you to write the goddamnedest toughest Voting Rights Act you can devise." On March 15, the president urged Congress to "overcome the crippling legacy of bigotry and injustice" by making the cause of civil rights "our cause too." He concluded by slowly speaking the words of the movement's anthem of social protest: "And we *shall* overcome."

The resulting **Voting Rights Act of 1965** was a momentous legislative accomplishment. It ensured *all* citizens the right to vote and authorized the attorney general to send federal officials to register voters in areas that had long experienced racial discrimination. The act banned the various methods, like requiring literacy tests, which local officials had used to keep Black and Latino citizens from voting. By the end of the year, some 250,000 African Americans were newly registered to vote in several southern states.

By 1968, an estimated 53 percent of Blacks in Alabama were registered, compared to only 14 percent in 1960. In this respect, the Voting Rights Act was even more important than the Civil Rights Act because it empowered Black voters in the South, thereby transforming the White-dominated politics in the region by making possible the election of Black public officials. Yet by enabling southern Blacks—most of whom preferred Democratic candidates—to vote, it also helped turn the once-solidly Democratic South into a Republican stronghold, as many White voters switched parties.

ASSESSING THE GREAT SOCIETY   As an accidental president following a tragic assassination, Lyndon B. Johnson sought to give Americans a sense of forward movement in troubled times and show them that he could overcome their fears of a divided America and create a "Great Society" whereby people of all colors would be "more concerned with the quality of their goals than the quantity of their goods." Franklin Roosevelt had pushed through Congress fifteen major bills in his First Hundred Days, Johnson told an aide in 1966, whereas he had "passed two hundred in the last two years." A *New York Times* columnist joked that LBJ was "getting everything through the Congress but the abolition of the Republican party, and he hasn't tried that yet."

The scope of Lyndon Johnson's Great Society programs exceeded Franklin Roosevelt's New Deal in part because of the nation's booming prosperity during the mid-1960s. "This country," Johnson proclaimed, "is rich enough to do anything it has the guts to do and the vision to do and the will to do."

That proved *not* to be the case, however. As *Time* magazine reported, "No matter how much Lyndon gets, he asks for more." Soon there was no more money to spend. In 1966, Johnson warned that if taxes were not raised, the economy would suffer a "ruinous spiral of inflation" and "brutally higher interest rates."

The Great Society and War on Poverty did not end urban blight or rural poverty or stubborn social problems, in part because the Vietnam War soon took priority and siphoned away funding, and in part because neither Johnson nor his congressional supporters understood the complexity of chronic poverty.

The Great Society, however, did include several triumphs for low-income Americans. Infant mortality has dropped, college completion rates have soared, malnutrition is significantly lower, and far fewer elderly Americans are living below the poverty line and without access to health care. The federal guarantee of civil rights and voting rights remains in place. Medicare and Medicaid have become two of the most appreciated—and expensive—government programs. Consumers now have a federal agency, the Bureau of Consumer Protection, safeguarding them from business abuses. Head Start programs providing preschool enrichment activities for poor students have produced long-term benefits. The federal food stamp program has improved the nutrition and health of children living in poverty. Finally, the scholarships provided to low-income college students have been immensely valuable in enabling young people to gain access to higher education.

Several of Johnson's most ambitious programs, however, were ill-conceived, others were vastly underfunded, and many were mismanaged and even corrupt. Some of the problems they were meant to address actually worsened. Medicare, for example, removed incentives for hospitals to control costs, thereby contributing to skyrocketing medical bills. In addition, food stamp fraud occurred as people took advantage of a Great Society program intended to ensure healthy nutrition among the poorest Americans. A final example has been the challenge of single-parent households. In 1965, about 10 percent of children were born to single mothers. Today, the number has soared to 30 percent, the highest in the world. Why is the number so high in the United States? Many factors are at work, including a general decline in the percentage of Americans who are married, increased premarital sex, financial instability, and the availability of government-funded child support.

Overall, Great Society programs helped reduce poverty from 19 percent in 1964 to 10 percent in 1973, but they did so largely by providing federal welfare payments, not by finding people jobs. In 1966, middle-class resentment over the cost and excesses of the Great Society programs generated a conservative backlash that fueled a Republican resurgence. In the congressional elections of 1966, only thirty-eight of the seventy-one Democrats elected to the House in 1964 won reelection.

THE TRAGEDY OF VIETNAM

In foreign affairs, Lyndon Johnson was, like Woodrow Wilson, a novice. He admitted that he was "not temperamentally equipped to be commander in chief." And, again like Wilson, his presidency would become a victim of his crusading idealism. In June 1964, Johnson telephoned Senator Richard Russell to discuss the deteriorating situation in Vietnam. "I don't believe the American people ever want me to run [away]," he told Russell. "If I lose it [Vietnam], I think they'll say, I've lost." Russell replied with peculiar foresight: "It would take half a million [U.S.] men. They'd be bogged down there for ten years." As they were.

Johnson inherited a long-standing U.S. commitment to prevent a Communist takeover in Vietnam. Beginning with Harry S. Truman, U.S. presidents had done just enough to avoid being charged with having "lost" Vietnam. Johnson initially sought to do the same. His path, how-ever, took the United States into a deeper military commitment. When John F. Kennedy was assassinated in November 1963, there were 16,000 U.S. military "advisers" in South Vietnam. Officially, they were not to engage in combat but instead "advise" the South Vietnamese army. As vice president, Johnson had been a believer in the domino theory of Communist takeovers. As he told President Kennedy, "If we don't stop the Reds in South Vietnam, tomorrow they will be in Hawaii, and next week they will be in San Francisco."

Johnson, however, soon came to doubt that South Vietnam was worth more extensive military involvement. In May 1964, he told his national security adviser, McGeorge Bundy: "It looks to me like we are getting into

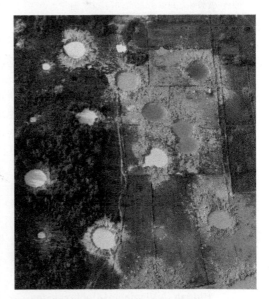

U.S. Air Strikes Sustained bombing of Vietnam left thirty- to fifty-foot-wide craters that can still be seen today.

another Korea. . . . I don't think it's worth fighting for. And I don't think we can get out. It's just the biggest damned mess that I ever saw." Yet Johnson's fear of appearing weak in the face of communism outweighed his misgivings. He was convinced that the "loss" of South Vietnam to communism would "shatter my presidency." By the end of 1965, there were 184,000 U.S. troops in Vietnam; in 1966, there were 385,000; and by 1969, at the height of the American war effort, 542,000.

ESCALATION IN VIETNAM The official justification for the military *escalation*—a Defense Department term—was the **Tonkin Gulf Resolution**, passed by the Senate on August 7, 1964. On that day, President Johnson, unknowingly acting on false information provided by Secretary of Defense Robert McNamara, told a national television audience that on August 2 and 4, North Vietnamese torpedo boats had attacked two American warships, the U.S.S. *Maddox* and the U.S.S. *C.*

Hidden A Vietnamese mother hides her son near the village of Le My in 1965 while U.S. Marines clear the area of Viet Cong forces.

Turner Joy, in the Gulf of Tonkin, off the coast of North Vietnam. McNamara called it "naked aggression on the high seas." That statement was later shown to be false and misleading because the U.S. ships had actually fired first. They had been supporting South Vietnamese attacks against two North Vietnamese islands—attacks planned by American advisers. (Whether the American warships were actually fired upon remains in dispute.)

But the facts didn't matter. Congress had given the president what he wanted, a "blank check" to wage war without officially declaring war. The Tonkin Gulf Resolution empowered Johnson to "take all necessary measures" to protect U.S. forces and "prevent further aggression." Surveys revealed that a sizable majority of Americans approved of the undeclared war.

It would be no small war, however. Soon after his landslide victory over Barry Goldwater in November 1964, Johnson committed America to full-scale war in Vietnam. On February 5, 1965, Viet Cong guerrillas attacked a U.S. military base near Pleiku, in South Vietnam, killing and wounding more than 100 Americans. More attacks led Johnson to approve "Operation Rolling Thunder," the first sustained U.S. bombing of North Vietnam. Thereafter, there were essentially two fronts in the war: one in North Vietnam, where U.S. warplanes conducted a massive bombing campaign, and the other in South Vietnam, where nearly all the ground combat occurred.

In March 1965, the U.S. commander, General William C. Westmoreland, greeted the first American combat troops in Vietnam. His strategy was to wage a war of attrition, using overwhelming U.S. firepower to produce so many casualties that the Viet Cong and North Vietnamese would give up.

Soon, U.S. forces launched "search and destroy" operations against Communist guerrillas throughout South Vietnam. But the Viet Cong, both men and women, wore no uniforms and dissolved by day into the villages, hiding among civilians. Their elusiveness exasperated American soldiers, most of whom were not trained for such unconventional warfare in Vietnam's dense jungles and intense heat and humidity.

The escalating war brought rising U.S. casualties (the number of killed, wounded, and missing), which were announced each week on television news programs. Criticism of the war grew, but LBJ stood firm. "We will not be defeated," he told the nation. "We will not grow tired. We will not withdraw." Johnson viewed the war as a test of his manliness. He vowed to an aide that he was not going to let a "raggedy-ass little fourth-rate country" like North Vietnam push him around.

Yet LBJ greatly underestimated the tenacity and ingenuity of the North Vietnamese, as did virtually everyone at the White House, the State Department, and the Pentagon. On July 20, 1965, Robert McNamara told Johnson that "the situation in South Vietnam is worse than a year ago (when it was worse than the year before that)." The South Vietnamese army had proved inept, and the U.S. bombing campaign was ineffective.

McNamara posed three options: (1) "cut our losses and withdraw," (2) "continue about the present level," or (3) "expand promptly and substantially the U.S. pressure." LBJ chose the third option, and the American buildup in Vietnam began. What the public did not know was that Johnson never thought the war was winnable. He told his wife Lady Bird in July 1965 that escalating the war was "like being in an airplane and I have to choose between crashing the plane or jumping out. I do not have a parachute."

THE STAKES OF WAR President Johnson's decision to "Americanize" the war flowed directly from the mistaken assumptions that had long guided

U.S. foreign policy during the Cold War. The commitment to contain the spread of communism everywhere guided Johnson as well. "Why are we in Vietnam?" the president asked during a speech in 1965. "We are there because we have a promise to keep. . . . To leave Vietnam to its fate would shake the confidence of all these people in the value of American commitment."

Johnson's military advisers also believed that U.S. military force would defeat the Viet Cong. Yet the president insisted that the war effort not reach levels that would cause the Chinese or Soviets to become involved—which meant, as it turned out, that a military victory was never possible. Johnson committed the United States to fighting a limited war against the Vietnamese Communists, who were fighting a revolutionary war that for them had no limits. The United States was not fighting to "win" but to prevent the North Vietnamese and Viet Cong from winning and, eventually, to force them to sign a negotiated settlement. This meant that the United States would have to maintain a military presence as long as the enemy retained the will to fight.

RESISTANCE GROWS   As the futile war ground on, opposition grew fierce. In 1965, college campuses began hosting "teach-ins" critical of the war effort. Professors gathered with students to discuss "a better policy" in Vietnam. In April 1965, some 20,000 students converged on Washington, D.C., where they picketed the White House before moving to the Washington Monument, where they carried signs saying: GET OUT OF SAIGON AND INTO SELMA, FREEDOM NOW IN VIETNAM, WAR ON POVERTY NOT PEOPLE. The crowd then went to the Capitol, where it demanded that Congress "end, not extend, the war in Vietnam."

The following year, Senator J. William Fulbright of Arkansas, the Democratic chairman of the Senate Foreign Relations Committee, began congressional investigations into American policy in Vietnam. George F. Kennan, the former State Department diplomat, told the committee that the containment doctrine he helped inspire was appropriate for Europe but not for Southeast Asia, which he did not consider a region vital to American security. President Johnson disagreed. He labeled his political critics and anti-war protesters "Communists" and used government agencies to punish them. Other political leaders agreed. California Republican governor Ronald Reagan dismissed student militants as "those bastards at UC-Berkeley" who loved to indulge in "sex, drugs, and treason."

Still, the resistance grew. By 1967, anti-war demonstrations were commonplace, and their chant was personal: "Hey, hey, LBJ, how many kids did you kill today [in Vietnam]?" Americans began dividing into "hawks" who supported the war effort and "doves" who opposed it. Nightly television accounts of the fighting—Vietnam was the first war to receive extended television coverage

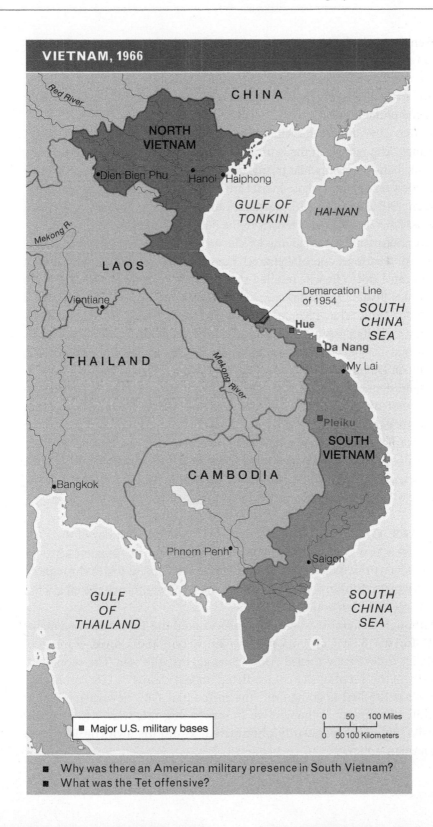

and hence was dubbed the "living-room war"—called into question the accuracy of statements by military and government officials claiming the Americans were winning. Journalists called it a "credibility crisis." But Johnson insisted that there would be no withdrawal as he desperately looked for "light at the end of the tunnel."

By May 1967, however, even Secretary of Defense Robert McNamara was wavering: "The picture of the world's greatest superpower killing or injuring 1,000 civilians a week, while trying to pound a tiny backward nation into submission on an issue whose merits are hotly disputed, is not a pretty one." Between 1965 and 1968, U.S. warplanes dropped more bombs on Vietnam than had fallen on all enemy targets in the Second World War.

As criticism of the war mounted, Johnson grew more frustrated and deeply depressed. "I can't get out [of Vietnam]. I can't finish it with what I got. So what the hell can I do?" His wife recalled that Vietnam became a "hell of a thorn stuck in his throat. It wouldn't come up; it wouldn't go down. . . . It was pure hell." White House aides became so concerned about Johnson's mental stability that they consulted psychiatrists.

Johnson became preoccupied with the day-to-day conduct of the war, insisting on giving the final approval to bombing targets, fretting over logistical details, demanding information about enemy movements. As Westmoreland requested more and more soldiers, Johnson found it impossible to turn him down, explaining that doing so would be like "hearing the call from the Alamo for help and answering that we're not coming." Yet spending so much time dealing with the war was bitterly frustrating to Johnson. How could he be expected to win the War on Poverty if the war in Vietnam kept siphoning away the nation's resources?

THE TET OFFENSIVE On January 31, 1968, the first day of the Vietnamese New Year (Tet), some 70,000 Viet Cong and North Vietnamese troops unleashed surprise attacks on U.S. and South Vietnamese forces throughout South Vietnam. Within a few days, American firepower turned the tables, but the damage had been done.

Although General Westmoreland proclaimed the **Tet offensive** a major defeat for the Viet Cong, its *political* impact in the United States was dramatic; it decisively turned Americans against the war. The scope and intensity of the Tet offensive contradicted upbeat claims by U.S. commanders. "What the hell is going on?" the influential CBS newscaster Walter Cronkite demanded. "I thought we were winning this war." After the Tet offensive, Johnson's popularity plummeted, as did his own confidence in his Vietnam policy.

Equally disturbing to LBJ was General Westmoreland's unexpected request for 206,000 additional U.S. troops. The request stunned Clark Clifford, who had replaced Robert McNamara as defense secretary in March 1968. Clifford told the president that the military leaders "don't know what they're talking about." Instead of winning the war, he added, the United States had become mired in a sinkhole with "no end in sight."

Civil rights leaders and social activists felt betrayed as federal funds earmarked for domestic programs were gobbled up by the war. By 1967, the United States was spending some $2 billion each month in Vietnam, about $322,000 for every VC killed. Anti-poverty programs at home received only $53 per person. Martin Luther King Jr. pointed out that "the bombs in Vietnam explode at home—they destroy the hopes and possibilities for a decent America."

Whose War? President Johnson lowers his head in disappointment as he listens to a commander's report from Vietnam in 1968.

Senator Eugene McCarthy of Minnesota took advantage of the consternation caused by the Tet Offensive to ramp up his anti-war challenge to Johnson in the Democratic presidential primaries. With students rallying to his "Dump Johnson" candidacy, McCarthy polled a stunning 42 percent of the vote to Johnson's 48 percent in New Hampshire's March primary. "Dove bites Hawk," a reporter quipped.

McCarthy's success in New Hampshire convinced Lyndon Johnson's long-time critic Robert F. Kennedy, now a New York senator, to launch his own presidential bid. Kennedy called the war in Vietnam a ghastly "horror" and lamented that a whole generation of young people had become alienated from their own government—and president. His campaign, he announced, "would end the bloodshed in Vietnam and in our cities."

That members of Johnson's own Democratic party were opposing his reelection devastated the beleaguered president. The growing public opposition to the Vietnam War was an even worse blow. During a private meeting with military leaders, Johnson acknowledged that "the country is demoralized. . . . Most of the press is against us. . . . We have no support for the war." Johnson had also grown concerned about his own health. Lady Bird told him to think about retiring after one term.

On March 31, 1968, Johnson appeared on national television to announce a limited halt to the bombing of North Vietnam to enable a negotiated cease-fire agreement with the Communists. Then, he made an astounding announcement: "I shall not seek, and I will not accept, the nomination of my party for another term as your President." As his daughter explained, the "agony of Vietnam" had engulfed her father. Johnson, a flawed giant, had promised far more than he could accomplish, raising false hopes and stoking violent resentments. He ended up losing two wars—the one in Vietnam and the one against poverty. Although U.S. troops would remain in Vietnam for five more years, the quest for military victory ended with Johnson's presidency. Among other things, the war revealed that the capabilities of the United States, including its military power, were limited; the nation could not simply have its way around the world.

Now there were three candidates for the Democratic nomination: McCarthy, Robert Kennedy, and Vice President Hubert Humphrey. Many antiwar Democrats expected McCarthy to drop out in favor of Kennedy, but the Minnesota senator, buoyed by his success and convinced of his moral superiority, refused to leave the race. For his part, Kennedy, with his long hair and boyish faith, appealed to the idealism of America's youth: "Some men see things as they are and ask, why? I dream things that never were and say, why not?"

THE TURMOIL OF THE SIXTIES

By the late 1960s, traditional notions of authority were under attack throughout the United States and in Europe. The spirit of resistance was especially evident among disaffected youth who called into question not only the Vietnam War and the credibility of the Johnson administration but virtually every aspect of mainstream life, including the traditional family structure, the middle-class work ethic, universities, religion, and the nonviolent integrationist philosophy underpinning the civil rights movement. Many alienated young people, often lumped together as "hippies," felt that they were part of "the Revolution" that would overthrow a corrupt and outdated way of life.

A TRAUMATIC YEAR   All the turbulent elements affecting American life came to a head in 1968, the most traumatic year in a traumatic decade. As *Time* magazine reported, "Nineteen sixty-eight was a knife blade that severed past from future." It was "one tragic, surprising, and perplexing thing after another."

On April 4, four days after LBJ withdrew from the presidential race, Dr. Martin Luther King Jr. was in Memphis to assist striking garbage collectors, most of whom were African Americans. He promised them his support, even if it meant giving his life. "I've seen the Promised Land," he shouted. "I may not get there with you. But I want you to know tonight that we, as a people, will get to the Promised Land."

The next night, King arrived at a Memphis motel after speaking in support of the sanitation workers. Waiting for him was James Earl Ray, a thirty-nine-year-old petty thief, drifter, and White racist who had escaped from a Missouri prison. As King and several aides stood on a balcony outside his motel room, Ray shot and killed the civil rights leader. Ray had earlier vowed that he was going "to get the big [Negro]."

King's murder stunned the world, rendered people speechless, left many in tears, and drove some to violence. Riots erupted in more than 100 cities, but the damage was especially devastating in Chicago, Baltimore, and Washington. Forty-six people were killed, all but five of them African Americans. Some 20,000 army soldiers and 34,000 National Guard troops eventually helped stop the violence across the country, and 21,000 people were arrested.

The night that King died, Robert Kennedy was in Indianapolis, Indiana. Upon hearing the news, he spoke to a grieving crowd of African Americans. "Those of you who are Black can be filled with hatred, with bitterness and a desire for revenge," he said. "We can move toward further polarization. Or we can make an effort, as Dr. King did, to understand, to reconcile ourselves and to love."

Kennedy won all but one of the presidential primaries he entered. Two months after King's death, after midnight on June 6, 1968, he appeared at the Ambassador Hotel in Los Angeles to celebrate his victory over Eugene McCarthy in the California primary. Kennedy closed his remarks by pledging that "we can end the divisions within the United States, end the violence."

After the applause subsided, Kennedy walked through the hotel kitchen on his way to the press room for interviews. Along the way, a mentally unstable, twenty-four-year-old Palestinian-born militant named Sirhan Sirhan, angered by the senator's strong support of Israel, pulled out a pistol and fired eight shots, hitting Kennedy in the head and wounding five others. Kennedy died the next morning. At his funeral in New York City, his younger brother, Edward "Ted" Kennedy, asked that his brother "be remembered simply as a good and decent man, who saw wrong and tried to right it, saw suffering and tried to heal it, saw war and tried to stop it." Only forty-two years old, Robert

Kennedy was buried beside his brother John in Arlington National Cemetery outside of Washington, D.C.

The assassinations of the Kennedys, Martin Luther King, and Malcolm X framed the chaos of the sixties, a decade of blasted hopes and rising fears. With their deaths, a wealth of idealism died too—the idealism that Bobby Kennedy had hoped would put a fragmented America back together again. Having lost the leading voices for real change, a growing number of young people lost hope in democracy and turned to radicalism and violence—or gave up on society and dropped out.

CHICAGO AND MIAMI In August 1968, the nation's social unrest came to a head at the **Chicago Democratic National Convention**, where delegates gathered to nominate Lyndon Johnson's faithful vice president, Hubert H. Humphrey, as the party's candidate for president. LBJ had endorsed Humphrey as his successor despite criticizing him in private as "all heart and no balls." He had also ordered the FBI to tap the vice president's phone to learn if Humphrey was truly loyal to Johnson. The Democratic leadership decided not to invite Johnson to the convention, leading a foreign journalist to write that LBJ had been chased out of the party "like a wounded bear fleeing hounds."

On August 28, outside the convention hall, almost 20,000 police officers and National Guardsmen confronted thousands of anti-war protesters who taunted them with obscenities. Richard J. Daley, Chicago's autocratic Democratic mayor, warned that he would not tolerate disruptions. Nonetheless, riots broke out and were televised nationwide. The Chicago police went berserk, removing their badges and yelling "Kill, kill, kill," while using clubs to pummel everyone they encountered, including passersby, reporters, and doctors and nurses helping the injured. It was as if the police were the rioters. All the while, demonstrators chanted for the TV cameras, "The whole world is watching. The whole world is watching." The *New York Times* reported, "Those were our children in the streets, and the Chicago police beat them up." Nationally, the Democratic party began to fragment as a result of the chaos in Chicago.

Three weeks earlier, the Republicans had gathered in Miami Beach to nominate Richard Nixon. In 1962, after losing the California governor's race, Nixon had vowed never again to run for public office. He gracelessly snarled to reporters, "You won't have Nixon to kick around anymore, because, gentlemen, this is my last press conference." By 1968, however, he had changed his mind and become a self-appointed spokesman for the conservative values of "middle America." He and the Republicans claimed they would "end the war" in Vietnam and "win the peace" while bringing their version of "law and order" to the nation's streets.

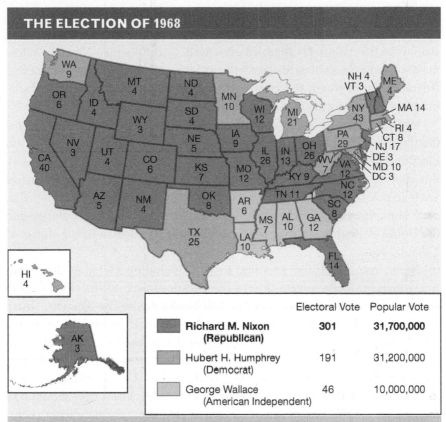

THE ELECTION OF 1968

	Electoral Vote	Popular Vote
Richard M. Nixon **(Republican)**	301	31,700,000
Hubert H. Humphrey (Democrat)	191	31,200,000
George Wallace (American Independent)	46	10,000,000

- How did the riots at the Chicago Democratic National Convention affect the 1968 presidential campaign?
- What does the electoral map reveal about the support base for each of the three major candidates?
- How was Richard Nixon able to win enough electoral votes in such a close three-way presidential race?
- What was Governor George Wallace's appeal to 10 million voters?

Nixon appealed to what he called the "**silent majority**" of working- and middle-class Americans, who viewed the "rabble rousing" protesters with contempt. In accepting the nomination, Nixon pledged to listen to "the voice of the great majority of Americans, the forgotten Americans, the non-shouters, the non-demonstrators, that are not racists or sick, that are not guilty of the crime that plagues the land."

Former Alabama governor George Wallace, an outspoken segregationist, ran for president in 1968 on the American Independent party ticket. The combative Wallace, a former boxer, mounted a crusade on behalf of "common folks" against Blacks, political elites, and "little pinkos [Communists]."

In his view, the "liberals, intellectuals, and long hairs have run the country for too long." He promised to get tough on "scummy anarchists" and bring stability to the nation. He appealed even more forcefully than Nixon to White male working-class voters' disgust with anti-war protesters, the mushrooming federal welfare system, the growth of the federal government, forced racial integration, and rioting in the inner cities.

Wallace displayed a savage wit, once saying that the "only four-letter words that hippies did not know were w-o-r-k and s-o-a-p." He predicted that on Election Day, the nation would realize that "there are a lot of rednecks in this country." His candidacy generated considerable appeal outside his native South, especially among White working-class communities. Wallace hoped to deny Humphrey and Nixon an electoral majority and throw the choice into the House of Representatives, which would have provided a fitting climax to a chaotic year.

Nixon resolved to do anything to win, including violating the Logan Act, which prohibits private citizens from communicating with foreign governments about controversial issues. Just weeks before the election, Nixon ordered aide H. R. Haldeman to "monkey wrench" President Johnson's last-minute efforts to end the Vietnam War. He feared that if Johnson succeeded in pulling off a last-minute deal to end the Vietnam War, it would give Hubert Humphrey's campaign a boost sufficient to win the election. Nixon used an intermediary to let South Vietnamese leaders know they should stall the negotiations because Nixon, if elected, would provide them better terms. They agreed to halt the peace talks.

When President Johnson learned, through CIA surveillance, of Nixon's efforts to scuttle the negotiations, he was furious, shouting that Nixon had committed "treason." But he did not have enough proof to share with the public.

While it remains an open question whether Johnson could have negotiated a deal to end the war before the election, Nixon's most recent biographer, John A. Farrell, concluded that "of all of Richard Nixon's actions in a lifetime of politics, this was the most reprehensible," for he chose winning an election over the possibility of ending a war. In what one journalist called an "uncommon act of political decency," Humphrey decided not to make Nixon's efforts to sabotage the peace a last-minute election issue.

RICHARD NIXON TRIUMPHANT   On November 5, 1968, Richard Nixon and Governor Spiro Agnew of Maryland, his acid-tongued running mate, eked out a narrow victory of some 500,000 votes, a margin of about 1 percentage point. The electoral vote was more decisive: 301 for Nixon and

191 for Hubert Humphrey; the 46 electoral votes for George Wallace all came from the Lower South.

Embedded in the election returns was a sobering development for Democrats, although they retained majority control in both the House and the Senate. White wage workers, the backbone of the party since FDR and the New Deal, were shifting to the Republicans. Both Ohio and New Jersey, traditional Democratic strongholds, went for Nixon. And more southern Whites voted Republican than Democrat, a trend that has continued to this day.

So at the end of 1968, the century's most turbulent year, a divided society looked to Richard Nixon to fulfill his promises to bring "peace with honor" in Vietnam and to "bring us together" as a nation. Nixon privately admitted that he was a polarizing figure who saw political enemies everywhere. In his first week in the White House, he told an aide that "I've got to put on my nice-guy hat . . . but let me make it clear that's not my nature."

CHAPTER REVIEW

SUMMARY

- **The New Frontier**   President John F. Kennedy promised a *New Frontier* in 1961, but many of his domestic policies stalled in Congress. The *Bay of Pigs* (1961) fiasco led the Soviet premier, Nikita Khrushchev, to erect the *Berlin Wall* and install nuclear-armed missiles in Cuba, provoking the *Cuban missile crisis* (1962). Kennedy ordered a naval "quarantine" of Cuba and succeeded in forcing Khrushchev to withdraw the missiles. During his presidency, Kennedy also deepened America's anti-Communist commitment in Vietnam.

- **Expansion of the Civil Rights Movement**   At the beginning of the sixties, growing numbers of African Americans and Whites staged acts of *nonviolent civil disobedience* to protest discrimination in the South. In 1960, activists formed the *Student Nonviolent Coordinating Committee (SNCC)* to intensify efforts to dismantle segregation. In 1961, courageous *Freedom Riders* attempted to integrate southern bus and train stations. Martin Luther King Jr. delivered his famous "I Have a Dream" speech at the *March on Washington* (1963). But King and other leaders did little to address the concerns of the inner cities. The *Black Power movement* emphasized militancy, Black pride, separatism, and, often, violence.

- **Lyndon Baines Johnson and the Great Society**   Early in his presidency, Johnson shepherded through Congress the *Civil Rights Act of 1964* and, as part of his "War on Poverty," the *Economic Opportunity Act of 1964*. After his resounding presidential victory in 1964, he pushed his *Great Society* programs through Congress— hundreds of initiatives that expanded federal authority into new areas, such as the *Voting Rights Act of 1965*, *Medicare,* and *Medicaid*. Still another important policy change urged by President Johnson was the *Immigration and Nationality Services Act of 1965*. It ended the National Origins Formula, which had governed immigration since the 1920s. The act halted discrimination against Southern and Eastern Europeans, Asians, as well as the other non-Northwestern European ethnic groups.

- **The Tragedy of Vietnam**   In 1964, President Johnson used the Tonkin Gulf incident off the coast of Vietnam to push through Congress the *Tonkin Gulf Resolution* (1964), which gave the administration the power to wage war in Southeast Asia without a congressional declaration of war. By 1968, over 500,000 U.S. military personnel were in South Vietnam. Claims that the American effort was winning the war were upended by the North Vietnamese *Tet offensive* (1968), which led many Americans to decide that the war could not be won. Thereafter, resistance to "Johnson's War" steadily increased.

- **The Turmoil of the Sixties**   In early 1968, Johnson shockingly chose not to seek reelection. Anti-war Democrats rallied around Senators Eugene McCarthy and Robert Kennedy. In April, Martin Luther King Jr. was assassinated, setting off a series of violent riots in impoverished urban neighborhoods across the country. Robert Kennedy was assassinated in June. Ultimately, the Democrats selected Johnson's loyal vice president, Hubert Humphrey, as their nominee, provoking angry protests by anti-war demonstrators at the 1968 *Chicago Democratic National Convention*. The Republicans nominated former candidate Richard Nixon, who claimed to represent the *silent majority*. The segregationist former governor of Alabama, George Wallace, ran as an independent candidate and also appealed to the silent majority. In the end, Nixon narrowly beat Humphrey and Wallace.

CHRONOLOGY

February 1960	Greensboro Four stage a sit-in
April 1960	Student Nonviolent Coordinating Committee (SNCC) formed
November 1960	John F. Kennedy elected president
April 1961	Bay of Pigs invasion fails
May 1961	Freedom Rides begin
August 1961	Soviets erect the Berlin Wall
October 1962	Cuban missile crisis
August 1963	March on Washington for Jobs and Freedom
November 1963	John F. Kennedy assassinated in Dallas, Texas
June 1964	Congress passes the Civil Rights Act
August 1964	Congress passes the Tonkin Gulf Resolution
November 1964	Lyndon B. Johnson elected to a full term
February 1965	Malcolm X assassinated
June–August 1965	Congress passes immigration reform, Medicare and Medicaid, the Voting Rights Act
August 1965	Race riots in Watts, California
January 1968	Viet Cong stage the Tet offensive
April 1968	Martin Luther King Jr. assassinated
June 1968	Robert Kennedy assassinated
August 1968	Democratic National Convention in Chicago
November 1968	Richard Nixon elected president

KEY TERMS

New Frontier p. 1354

Bay of Pigs (1961) p. 1361

Berlin Wall p. 1362

Cuban missile crisis (1962) p. 1366

Student Nonviolent Coordinating Committee (SNCC) p. 1371

Freedom Riders p. 1372

nonviolent civil disobedience p. 1377

March on Washington (1963) p. 1378

Black Power movement p. 1383

Civil Rights Act of 1964 p. 1390

Economic Opportunity Act of 1964 p. 1393

Great Society p. 1395

Medicare and Medicaid p. 1395

Immigration and Nationality Services Act of 1965 p. 1396

Voting Rights Act of 1965 p. 1399

Tonkin Gulf Resolution (1964) p. 1402

Tet offensive (1968) p. 1406

Chicago Democratic National Convention p. 1410

silent majority p. 1411

28 Rebellion and Reaction

1960s and 1970s

Rebels with a Cause Established in 1967, the Vietnam Veterans against the War group grew quickly during the sixties and seventies. Here, a former marine throws his service uniform jacket and medals onto the steps of the Capitol on April 23, 1971, as part of a five-day protest against the U.S. invasion of Laos, an outgrowth of the Vietnam War.

As Richard M. Nixon entered the White House in early 1969, the nation's social fabric was in tatters. The traumatic events of 1968 had revealed how divided American society had become and how difficult a task Nixon faced in carrying out his campaign pledge to restore social harmony.

Ironically, many of the forces that had contributed to the complacent prosperity of the fifties—the baby boom, the Cold War, and the growing consumer culture—helped generate the social upheaval of the sixties and early seventies. The civil rights movement inspired efforts to ensure equal treatment for other minorities—from African Americans to women, gays and lesbians, bisexuals, Native Americans, Latinos, the elderly, and people with disabilities. At the same time, intense opposition to the Vietnam War helped launch an unprecedented countercultural "youth revolt" that encompassed a unique blend of idealism, opportunism, irreverence, and goofiness.

Despite Nixon's promise to restore the public's faith in the integrity of its leaders, he ended up aggravating the growing cynicism about the motives and methods of government officials. During 1973 and 1974, the Watergate scandal resulted in the greatest constitutional crisis since the impeachment of President Andrew Johnson in 1868, and it ended with the first resignation of a U.S. president.

focus questions

1. In what ways did the origins of the youth revolt shape the New Left and the counterculture?

2. How did the youth revolt and early civil rights movement influence other protest movements? How did new protest movements affect social attitudes and public policy?

3. Describe how the political environment of the late sixties influenced Richard Nixon's election strategy and domestic policy?

4. How and why did Nixon and Henry Kissinger change military and political strategies to end America's involvement in the Vietnam War?

5. What was the international strategy brought about by Nixon's and Kissinger's diplomacy and foreign policy during the 1970s?

6. How did the Watergate scandal unfold? What was its political significance?

"Forever Young": The Youth Revolt

The sit-in at a segregated Woolworth's lunch counter in Greensboro, North Carolina, in 1960 launched a decade of civil rights activism. Rennie Davis, a sophomore at Ohio's Oberlin College in 1960, remembered that the Greensboro African American activists inspired him and many others: "Here were four students from Greensboro who were suddenly all over *Life* magazine. There was a feeling that they were us and we were them, and a recognition that they were expressing something we were feeling as well."

The sit-ins, marches, protests, and sacrifices associated with the civil rights movement inspired many other groups to demand justice, freedom, and equality. As Bob Dylan sang in 1963, "How many times can a man turn his head / And pretend that he just doesn't see?"

Many idealistic young people decided that they could no longer ignore the widespread injustice and inequality staining the American dream, and the result was a full-fledged youth revolt. *Time* magazine acknowledged the social significance of the younger generation when it announced that its "Man of the Year" in 1967 was not an individual but a generation: "Twenty-Five and Under."

By 1970, more than half of Americans were under thirty. These baby boomers—who, unlike their parents—had experienced neither an economic depression nor the Second World War, were now attending colleges and universities in record numbers; enrollment quadrupled between 1945 and 1970.

Many universities had become dependent upon huge research contracts from corporations and the federal government, especially the Defense Department. As these "multiversities" grew larger and more bureaucratic, they became targets for students wary of what President Dwight D. Eisenhower had labeled "the military-industrial complex." As criticism of U.S. military involvement in Vietnam mounted, disillusioned young people flowed into two distinct yet frequently overlapping movements: the New Left and the counterculture.

THE NEW LEFT The political arm of the youth revolt originated in 1960 with the formation of Students for a Democratic Society (SDS). Two years later, Tom Hayden and Alan Haber, two University of Michigan students, convened a meeting of sixty SDS activists at Port Huron, Michigan. Their goal was ambitious: to quit reading history in order to *make* history, and to remake the United States into a more democratic society. Several participants were the children of former leftists or Communists; even more were Jewish.

At the gathering, Hayden, a veteran of the civil rights struggle in the South, drafted an impassioned document known as the "Port Huron Statement." The manifesto began: "We are the people of this generation, bred in at least moderate comfort, housed in universities, looking uncomfortably to the world we inherit." Only by giving "power to the people," the manifesto insisted, could America restore its founding principles. Inspired by African American civil rights activists, Hayden declared that college campuses would become the crossroads of social change. College students would snatch "control of the educational process from the administrative bureaucracy."

Hayden and others adopted the term **New Left** to distinguish their efforts at grassroots democracy from those of the "Old Left" of the 1930s, whose members had embraced an orthodox Marxism. Hayden's proposed revolution would be energized by hope and change, not abstract economic theories. Within a few years, more than 1,000 campuses hosted SDS chapters, and the organization began publishing an underground newspaper, *The Rag*.

In the fall of 1964, students at the University of California at Berkeley took Hayden's New Left program to heart. Several had spent the summer working with the Student Nonviolent Coordinating Committee's (SNCC) voter-registration project in Mississippi ("Freedom Summer"), where three volunteers had been killed by Klansmen and many others had been arrested or harassed. When the university's chancellor announced that campus political

The Free-Speech Movement Mario Savio, a founder of the FSM, speaks at a rally at the University of California at Berkeley.

demonstrations were banned, thousands of students staged a sit-in. After a thirty-two-hour standoff, the administration relented, lifting the ban on political demonstrations. Student groups then formed the free-speech movement (FSM) led by Mario Savio.

The FSM denounced what Savio called the "depersonalized, unresponsive bureaucracy" stifling free speech on many campuses. The students' grievances were directed at those older than them. "Never trust anyone over 30," Jack Weinberg, one of the militant students, famously said. In 1964, Savio led hundreds of students into Sproul Hall, UC Berkeley's administration building, and organized another sit-in. At 4 A.M., 600 state police arrested the demonstrators. A few hours later, some 7,000 students filled Sproul Plaza, circulating leaflets and joining folk singer Joan Baez in singing "We Shall Overcome," the informal anthem of the civil rights movement. Finally, the faculty and university administration gave in and lifted all restrictions on political activity.

Anti-War Demonstrations Demonstrative of anti-war attitudes, the National Mobilization Committee to End the War in Vietnam organized a large protest in Washington, D.C., to stop violence abroad and bring American troops home.

ANTI-WAR PROTESTS During the mid-1960s, the ideals and tactics of the free-speech movement spread across the country. FSM served as the bridge between the college students who participated in the civil rights movement and those who fueled the anti-war movement.

By 1965, the growing U.S. involvement in Vietnam had changed the New Left's agenda as millions of young men suddenly faced the prospect of being drafted to fight in the increasingly unpopular conflict. The Vietnam War was primarily a poor man's fight. Most college students were able to postpone military service until they received their degree or reached the age of twenty-four. From 1965 through 1966, college students made up only 2 percent of military inductees. Of the 1,200 men in Harvard's class of 1970, only fifty-six served in the military, and just two of them went to Vietnam. African Americans and Latinos were twice as likely to be drafted as Whites.

As the war dragged on, opposition to U.S. involvement exploded. Some 200,000 young men ignored their draft notices, and some 4,000 served prison sentences for doing so. Another 56,000 qualified for conscientious objector (CO) status, meaning that they presented evidence to officials authenticating their moral, ethical, or religious opposition to war and/or the military. If their petition was granted, COs had to perform alternative civilian service, often in hospitals or clinics. Others defied the draft by burning their draft cards while shouting, "Hell no, we won't go!" Still others fled to Canada or Sweden to avoid military service or found creative ways to flunk the physical examination.

In the fall of 1967, some 70,000 people protesting the war marched from the Lincoln Memorial in Washington, D.C., across the Potomac River to the Pentagon, where they taunted hundreds of U.S. marshals and soldiers. That many of the middle-class protesters wanted to be arrested or even beaten revealed the intensity of the burgeoning anti-war movement. Like earlier civil rights activists, they wanted the world to see how brutal "the system" enforcing misguided government policies could be. Hundreds were arrested, and the mass protest garnered headlines across the country. The war at home had begun.

"TWO SOCIETIES, ONE BLACK, ONE WHITE—SEPARATE AND UNEQUAL" Throughout 1967 and 1968, inner-city neighborhoods in Cleveland, Detroit, Newark, and other large urban areas exploded in flames fanned by racial injustice. Frustration over discrimination in employment, housing, and mistreatment by police, as well as staggering rates of joblessness among inner-city African American youths, ignited the rage.

In July 1967, President Lyndon Johnson had appointed a blue-ribbon commission to analyze the causes of the nation's growing "civil disorder." When the Kerner Commission, named for its chair, Illinois governor Otto Kerner, issued its report in early 1968, President Johnson was so infuriated by the results that he canceled a White House ceremony intended to share the report with the nation.

Why such anger? After visiting several cities ravaged by rioting, the commissioners concluded that the fundamental cause of urban violence was the nation's oldest and most explosive problem: White racism. "What white Americans have never fully understood—but what the Negro can never forget—," the report stressed, "is that white society is deeply implicated in the [black] ghetto." After all, the commission found, "white institutions created it, white institutions maintain it, and white society condones it." In the report's most quoted statement, it warned that "our nation is moving toward two societies, one black, one white—separate and unequal."

The Kerner Commission report went on to highlight the elements creating such a racially split society—including widespread police brutality against African Americans. "Almost invariably," the commission found, "the incident that ignites disorder arises from [inappropriate] police action." Within a few weeks of its publication, however, the Kerner report was drowned out by a nation in turmoil.

COMING APART AT THE SEAMS—1968 In 1968, the nation seemed to be unraveling. During the spring—when Lyndon Johnson announced that he would not run for reelection and Martin Luther King Jr. and Robert F. Kennedy were assassinated—campus unrest boiled over. The disorder reached a climax at Columbia University, where SDS student radicals and Black militants occupied the president's office and classroom buildings. They renamed the administration building Malcolm X Hall.

Mark Rudd, the campus SDS leader, called his parents to report, "We took a building." His father, Jacob Rudd, a retired army officer and a real estate investor, replied, "Well, give it back." After a failed attempt to negotiate an end to

Columbia Riots Mark Rudd, leader of SDS at Columbia University, speaks to the media during student protests in April 1968.

the takeover, the university's president canceled classes and called in the New York City police. More than 100 students were injured, 700 were arrested, and the leaders of the uprising were expelled. President Richard Nixon declared that the rebellion was "the first major skirmish in a revolutionary struggle to seize the universities."

Part of the problem with SDS and other militant organizations was that they were much more effective at criticizing the status quo than they were at creating a blueprint for an alternative future. "If there is a road to power," SDS president Todd Gitlin acknowledged, "we have no map for it."

The events at Columbia inspired similar clashes at Harvard, Cornell, and San Francisco State, among others. Vice President Spiro Agnew dismissed the militants as "impudent snobs who characterize themselves as intellectuals" and condemned the "circuit-riding, Hanoi-visiting . . . caterwauling, riot-inciting, burn-America-down" anti-war protesters, whom he labeled "thieves and traitors." He scorned journalists as "nattering nabobs of negativism."

THE WEATHER UNDERGROUND A small group of radical militants called the Revolutionary Youth Movement (RYM) emerged during the summer of 1969. They wanted to move political radicalism from "protest to resistance." At the SDS convention in Chicago on June 18, 1969, RYM members distributed a position paper titled "You don't need a weatherman / To know which way the wind blows," a line from Bob Dylan's 1965 song "Subterranean Homesick Blues."

The document called for a "White fighting force" to take the youth revolution from campuses to the streets. They would ally with the Black Panthers and others to destroy "U.S. imperialism and achieve a classless world: world communism." By embracing revolutionary violence, however, the so-called Weathermen essentially killed SDS by abandoning the pacifist principles that had given the movement moral legitimacy.

At the urging of the Revolutionary Youth Movement, members of the Weather Underground took to the streets of Chicago in October 1969 to launch what they called the "Days of Rage." Their goal was "to lead White kids into armed revolution." Wearing jackboots and helmets, carrying clubs and metal pipes, they ran riot in the streets, looking for police to assault. Almost 300 were arrested.

Between September 1969 and May 1970, the notorious Weathermen bombed 250 draft board offices, ROTC buildings (for military training on university campuses), federal government facilities, and corporate headquarters. In March 1970, three members of the Weather Underground in New York City died when a bomb they were making exploded prematurely.

The Weathermen and other radical groups were forced underground by the aggressive efforts of federal law enforcement agencies. But they remained determined to overthrow America's capitalistic society. Spokesperson Bernardine Dohrn issued a "Declaration of War" in which she insisted that "revolutionary violence is the only way" to address "the frustration and impotence that comes from trying to reform this system."

Yet the appeal of revolutionary violence diminished as President Nixon ended the draft and systematically began withdrawing U.S. troops from Vietnam. Mark Rudd, one of the Weathermen organizers, later confessed that they intended to destroy SDS "because it wasn't revolutionary enough for us. I am not proud of this history."

Rudd's conversion to revolutionary violence, he explained, "had something to do with an exaggerated sense of my own importance. I wanted to prove myself as a man—a motive exploited by all armies and terrorist groups." Rudd later regretted his embrace of revolutionary violence, calling the intentional destruction of SDS by the Weathermen a "crime." It weakened "the larger antiwar movement and demoralized many good people." Blowing things up "got us isolated" by the media and "smashed" by the FBI.

THE COUNTERCULTURE

Looking back over the 1960s, Tom Hayden, the founder of SDS, recalled that most of the youthful rebels "were not narrowly political. Most were not so interested in attaining [elected] office but in changing lifestyles." Hayden acknowledged that the shocking events of 1968 led hippies to embrace the **counterculture**, an unorganized and leaderless rebellion against mainstream institutions, values, and behavior that focused more on cultural change, personal exploration, and tribal intimacy than political activism. (The term was coined by Theodore Roszak in his 1969 book, *The Making of a Counter Culture.*)

In pursuing personal liberation, hippies strove to exceed limits, trespass across boundaries, and heighten sensibilities. They rejected the pursuit of wealth and careers and embraced plain living, authenticity, friendship, peace, and, especially, *freedom*. In a 1967 cover story, the editors of *Time* magazine suggested that "in their independence of material possessions and their emphasis on peacefulness and honesty, hippies lead considerably more virtuous lives than the great majority of their fellow citizens. . . . In the end, it may be that the hippies have not so much dropped out of American society as given it something to think about."

Both the counterculture and the New Left rejected the status quo, but most hippies preferred to "drop out" of mainstream society rather than mobilize to change the political system. They had no desire to take control of society or redirect it toward new goals. They showed little interest in reforming the society they lived in since many of its values were irrelevant to them. They instead pursued a much easier goal: changing what was inside their heads. Self-exploration and self-expression were their goals, not taking over campuses and assaulting police. Their preferred slogan was "Make Love, Not War."

Like the Beats of the 1950s, hippies created their own subculture. Defiant, innocent, egalitarian, optimistic, and pleasure-seeking, they rejected the authority of the nation's core institutions: the family, government, political parties, corporations, the military, and colleges and universities. "Do Your Own Thing" became their unofficial motto.

The counterculture lifestyle included an array of ideals and activities: peace, love, harmony, rock music, mystical religions, illicit drugs, casual sex, yoga, vegetarianism, organic food, and communal living. Hippie fashion featured long hair for both women and men and casual clothing that was striking, unusual, and more comfortable than traditional clothing: flowing cotton dresses, granny gowns, ragged bell-bottom blue jeans, tie-dyed T-shirts, love beads, Tibetan bells, peace symbols, black boots, and sandals. Young men grew beards and women stopped wearing makeup as badges of difference

Flower Power Hippies let loose at a 1967 love-in, gatherings that celebrated peace, free love, and nontheological spirituality, often as a protest against mainstream society.

(or indifference). Defying parental control and the law became central to the counterculture. "Half the fun of marijuana and LSD," explained a hippie to an interviewer, "is that they're illegal."

Underground newspapers celebrating the counterculture appeared in every large city, many of them with defiant names such as *Fuck You: A Magazine of the Arts*. The *Berkeley Barb* attracted more than 100,000 subscribers. A hippie magazine called *Avatar* asked, "Who is the underground?" Its answer: "You are, if you think, dream, work, and build towards the improvements and changes in your life, your social and personal environments, towards the expectations of a better existence. . . . Think, look around, maybe in a mirror, maybe inside."

TIMOTHY LEARY: "DO YOUR OWN THING" The countercultural rebels were primarily middle-class Whites alienated by the Vietnam War, racism, political corruption, and parental authority. In their view, a superficial materialism was suffocating mainstream life. They chose another path to the good life by embracing the pathway to freedom popularized by former Harvard clinical psychology professor Timothy Leary: "Tune in, turn on, drop out." Leary added that "your only hope is dope [marijuana or opiates]." If it had not been for marijuana, said one hippie, "I'd still be wearing a crew cut and saluting the flag."

Leary, the self-styled high priest of the psychedelic revolution, had been dismissed by Harvard in 1963 for using students in experiments with hallucinatory drugs. (After ingesting LSD, one student tried to eat the bark off a tree.) Leary was convinced that LSD (lysergic acid diethylamide—nicknamed "acid") was a magic potion that took users on a spiritual journey away from Western rationality and the superficial materialism of the consumer culture to Eastern mysticism. In 1966, the same year that Congress

Timothy Leary Countercultural rebel and former Harvard psychology professor Timothy Leary championed the use and even abuse of hallucinatory drugs amid national chaos. Convicted of possessing marijuana, Leary fled the United States but was captured. Pictured here in London, Leary is returning to imprisonment in California.

banned LSD, Leary formed the League of Spiritual Discovery (LSD) to lobby for decriminalization of mind-altering drugs. He promised his mostly young supporters that "proper drugs and rock music can make everybody young forever." He assured audiences that he had "a blueprint [for a new mind-altering religion], and we're going to change society in the next ten years."

Leary's crusade on behalf of expanded consciousness frightened most Americans, for LSD ruined many young people, some of whom committed suicide under its influence. A psychiatrist reported that one of his LSD-using patients "thinks he's an orange, and that if anybody touches him, he'll squirt juice." Others also experienced remarkable hallucinations. The celebrated rock guitarist Jimi Hendrix revealed that during his first "acid trip," he looked in the mirror and saw not his own face but that of actress Marilyn Monroe (both Monroe and Hendrix died young of drug overdoses). In Los Angeles, four teens high on LSD rammed a house with their car, killing a three-year-old child. The driver was jailed, where he tried to climb the cell wall, yelling, "I'm a graham cracker—oops, my arm crumpled off."

President Richard Nixon called Timothy Leary "the most dangerous man in America." Leary responded by announcing his candidacy for the governorship of California. John Lennon of the Beatles wrote Leary's campaign song, "Come Together."

Soon thereafter, Leary was convicted in California of possessing marijuana. The judge called him "an insidious menace" to society and a "pleasure-seeking, irresponsible, Madison Avenue advocate of the free use of LSD." Six months later, however, Leary pulled off a dramatic penitentiary escape and, with the help of friends, left the country. He was ultimately captured in Afghanistan and returned to prison in California, where he was a cellmate of mass murderer Charles Manson.

"EIGHT MILES HIGH" As Timothy Leary hoped, illegal drugs—marijuana, amphetamines, cocaine, peyote, hashish, heroin, and LSD, the "acid test"—became commonplace within the counterculture. Said SDS leader Todd Gitlin, "More and more, to get access to youth culture" in the late 1960s, "you had to get high." The Byrds sang about getting "Eight Miles High," and Bob Dylan proclaimed that "everybody must get stoned!"

Getting stoned was the goal of those who participated in the 1967 "Summer of Love," a series of nationwide cultural and social festivals protesting the Vietnam War and celebrating the youth revolt. In San Francisco, more than 100,000 hippies (a.k.a. flower children) converged in the Haight-Ashbury neighborhood in search of tribal intimacy and anarchic freedom. They included runaways, delinquents, seekers, and mere followers of fashion.

Author P. J. O'Rourke recalled, "I believed love was all you need. . . . I believed drugs could make you a better person. I believed I could hitchhike to California with 35 cents and people would be glad to feed me. . . . I believed the Age of Aquarius was about to happen. . . . With the exception of anything my parents said, I believed everything."

The members of the loosely organized "Council for the Summer of Love" intended the gatherings to be the first step in a grassroots revolution opposing the war in Vietnam by celebrating "hippiedom" and other alternative lifestyles. Yet the psychedelic paradise eventually turned into a horror drama as hippie enclaves grew crowded with dysfunctional young people preoccupied with "getting stoned" and vulnerable to "bad trips," sexually transmitted diseases, and criminal behavior.

THE YIPPIES The countercultural alternative to SDS and the New Left was the Youth International Party, whose members called themselves the Yippies. The facetious organization was founded in New York City in 1967 at a New Year's Eve party when a half dozen stoned revelers led by two impudent pranksters, Jerry Rubin and Abbie Hoffman, announced, "We declare ourselves to be the Youth International Party—YIP!"

The Yippies were countercultural comedians bent on thumbing their noses at the "absurdity" of conventional laws and traditional behavior and mocking capitalism and the consumer culture. Utterly alienated from mainstream life, they wanted "to offer the people an alternative lifestyle. Something to do other than conform or die." Their notion of community was modeled after their superficial understanding of Native American culture: "a whole bunch of people living together, having children, none of them married."

Hoffman explained that their "conception of revolution is that it's fun." They wanted to form an alliance between hippies and Weathermen, a "blending of pot and politics," and overthrow the power structure through outrageous acts of silliness. Rubin claimed that "the first part of the Yippie program is to kill your parents," since they are "our first oppressors." He added that the use of psychedelic drugs "signifies the total end of the Protestant ethic: screw work, we want to know ourselves."

The Yippie platform called for peace in Vietnam, absolute personal freedom, free birth control and abortions, and the legalization of marijuana and LSD. Hoffman had no interest in making the Yippies a traditional political organization. "We shall not defeat *Amerika* by organizing a political party," he declared. "We shall do it by building a new nation—a nation as rugged as the marijuana leaf."

The anarchic Yippies organized marijuana "smoke-ins," threw pies at political figures, nominated a squealing pig ("Pigasus") for the presidency, passed out brownies laced with marijuana, urged voters to cast their ballots for "None of the Above," and threatened to run naked in the streets and put LSD in Chicago's water supply during the 1968 Democratic National Convention. When asked what being a Yippie meant, Hoffman replied, "Energy–fun–fierceness–exclamation point!"

COUNTERCULTURAL COMMUNES For some, the counterculture involved experimenting with alternative living arrangements, especially "intentional communities" or "communes." Communal living in urban areas such as San Francisco's Haight-Ashbury district, New York's Greenwich Village, Chicago's Uptown, and Atlanta's 14th Street neighborhood were popular for a time, as were rural communes. Thousands of young runaways headed to the countryside, eager to live in harmony with nature, coexist in love and openness, deepen their sense of self, and forge authentic community ties. "Out here," one of the rural communalists reflected, "we've got the earth and ourselves and God above. . . . We came for simplicity and to rediscover God."

Yet all but a handful of the back-to-the-land experiments quickly collapsed. Few participants knew how to sustain a farm, and many were unwilling to do the hard work that living off the land required. "The hippies will not change America," a journalist predicted, "because change means pain, and the hippie subculture is rooted in the pleasure principle."

In 1968, *Newsweek* magazine reported "Trouble in Hippieland," noting that most flower children were "seriously disturbed youngsters" incapable of sustaining an alternative to mainstream life. In a candid reflection, a young hippie confessed that "we are so stupid, so unable to cope with anything practical."

Communal Living This photograph of the members of the Family of the Mystic Arts commune in Oregon appeared on the cover of *Life* magazine's July 18, 1969 edition.

A resident of Paper Farm in northern California, a commune started in 1968 only to fold a year later, said of its participants: "They had no commitment to the land—a big problem. All would take food from the land, but few would tend it. . . . We were entirely open. We did not say no [to anyone]. We felt this would make for a more dynamic group. But we got a lot of sick people."

WOODSTOCK   The sixties counterculture thrived on music—initially folk "protest" songs and later psychedelic rock. During the early sixties, Pete Seeger; Joan Baez; Bob Dylan; and the trio Peter, Paul, and Mary, among others, produced powerful songs intended to spur the civil rights and social reform movements. In Dylan's "The Times They Are a-Changin'," he warns: "Come mothers and fathers / Throughout the land / And don't criticize / What you can't understand. / Your sons and your daughters / Are beyond your command / Your old road is rapidly agin'/ Please get out of the new one if you can't lend your hand /For the times they are a-changin'."

Bob Dylan Born Robert Allen Zimmerman, Dylan came to the New York folk music scene by way of northern Minnesota, penning the anti-war movement anthem, "Blowin' in the Wind."

The hippies' favorite performers were those under the influence of mind-altering drugs, especially the San Francisco–based "acid rock" bands: Jefferson Airplane, Big Brother and the Holding Company, and the Grateful Dead. "Rock 'n roll was the tribal telegraph," remembered Jann Wenner, founder of *Rolling Stone* magazine. His colleague, Jon Landau, added that rock music "was an essential component of a 'new culture,' along with drugs and radical politics." The Jefferson Airplane spoke for many when they sang, "We are forces of chaos and anarchy / Everything they say we are we are / And we are very / Proud of ourselves." Only later did Jorma Kaukonen, the band's lead guitarist, confess that he and his multimillionaire bandmates, while eagerly indulging in psychedelic drugs, shared little else with their flower children fans: "My colleagues and I were not hippies; we were affluent, and our problems were upper-class ones."

Huge outdoor concerts—music-infused psychedelic campouts—were wildly popular. The largest and most publicized was the Woodstock Music and Art Fair ("Aquarian Exposition"). In mid-August 1969, more than 400,000 mostly young people converged on an alfalfa farm near the tiny rural town of Bethel, New York, for what was billed as the world's "largest happening," three days "of peace and music."

The festival boasted a cast of all-star musicians, among them Jimi Hendrix, Jefferson Airplane, Big Brother and the Holding Company (featuring Janis Joplin), the Grateful Dead, Santana, the Who, Joan Baez, and Crosby, Stills and Nash. For three days amid broiling heat, rainstorms, and rivers of mud, the flower children "grooved" on music, beer and booze, marijuana, and casual sex. Baez described Woodstock as a "technicolor, mud-splattered reflection of the 1960s."

The petite but fierce Joplin, the Texas-born "queen" of rock and roll, with her raw, raspy, sultry voice, untamed red hair, and unrivaled intensity, was an American original, the first female rock star. She once explained the difference between the folk protest movement and her distinctive "blues rock" when she said, "My music isn't supposed to make you riot. It's supposed to make you fuck."

Yet Joplin also confessed that the supposedly glamorous life of a rock star was a charade. "Onstage," she explained, "I make love to 25,000 people, then I go home alone." Perhaps that is what led her on a hellbent quest for uninhibited fulfillment. "I'd rather have ten years of superhypermost than live to be seventy sitting in some goddamn chair watching TV." She got her wish. In 1970, she died of a heroin overdose, utterly alone in a rundown motel room at age 27. As she once said, "I love being a star more than life itself." Three weeks earlier, Jimi Hendrix had also died of an overdose. He too was 27. Several months later, Jim Morrison, the iconic singer for The Doors, died of an overdose at age 27. They lived fast and died young. Their explosive music, however, lives forever. Woodstock's carefree "spirit of love" was short-lived too.

Four months later, when concert promoters tried to replicate the Woodstock festival experience at the Altamont Speedway Festival near San Francisco, the counterculture fell victim to the drug-addled criminal culture. The Rolling Stones foolishly hired the local Hells Angels motorcycle gang to provide "security" for their show. During the band's performance of "Under My Thumb," an eighteen-year-old African American named Meredith Hunter pulled a gun in front of the stage to protect himself against the out-of-control bikers. He was outmanned, however. One of the leather-clad Angels stabbed Hunter five times while others beat him senseless. He died at the scene. Three other spectators were also killed. As news of the deaths and chaos spread, much of the vitality and innocence of the counterculture died too.

After 1969, the hippie phenomenon began to fade as the spirit of liberation ran up against the hard realities of poverty, drug addiction, crime, and mental and physical illness among the flower children. As Jon Landau confessed, "We tell ourselves we are a counterculture. And yet are we really so different from the culture against which we rebel?" The frantic search for self-fulfillment among alienated young people generated illusions of gratification and liberation that often yielded more self-destruction than it did social justice.

Still, several authentic strands of the counterculture survived the sixties: the popularity of ecology and environmental awareness; yoga; meditation; "health foods," organic farming, and food co-ops; craft guilds; and promoting connectedness, sharing, and collaboration.

SOCIAL ACTIVISM SPREADS

The same liberationist ideals that prompted young people to revolt against mainstream values and protest the Vietnam War led many of them to embrace other causes. The civil rights movement inspired women, Latinos, and Native Americans, gays and lesbians, the elderly, and people with physical and mental disabilities to demand equal opportunities and equal rights. Still others joined the emerging environmental movement or groups working on behalf of consumers.

THE NEW FEMINISM

The first wave of the women's movement in the late nineteenth and early twentieth centuries had focused on gaining the right to vote. The second wave, in the sixties and seventies, challenged the conventional ideal of female domesticity and worked to ensure that women gained equal treatment in the workplace and on college campuses.

Many women in the early 1960s, however, did not view gender equality as possible or even desirable. In 1962, more than two thirds of women surveyed agreed that the most important family decisions "should be made by the man of the house." Although the Equal Pay Act of 1963 had made it illegal to pay women less than men for doing the same job, discrimination and harassment continued. Women, who comprised 51 percent of the nation's population and held 37 percent of the jobs, were paid 42 percent less than men on average.

Betty Friedan, a forty-two-year-old mother of three from Peoria, Illinois, who supplemented her husband's income by writing articles for women's magazines, emerged as one of the leaders of the postwar **women's movement**. As a student at all-female Smith College in Massachusetts, she had edited the campus newspaper, arguing for America to stay out of the Second World War and for the right of campus housekeepers to form a union. After the war, she wrote for progressive publications promoting labor unions. In her articles, Friedan called for equal pay for equal work and an end to gender- and race-based discrimination in hiring and housing.

Then, in 1963, Friedan published her searing first book, *The Feminine Mystique*, which helped launch the second phase of the feminist movement (although the book never used the word *feminism*). Rarely has a single book exercised such influence.

Friedan argued that her generation of upper- and middle-class college-educated White mothers and wives (she did not discuss working-class women, women of color, or women without husbands or suburban homes) had actually lost ground after the Second World War, when many left wartime employment and settled in suburbia as full-time wives and mothers. They suffered, she said, from the "happy homemaker" syndrome that undermined their intellectual capacity and public aspirations while handcuffing them to boring household duties. "A century earlier," she wrote, "women had fought for higher education; now girls went to college to get a husband."

Friedan blamed the "enforced domesticity" of postwar America on a massive propaganda campaign by advertisers and women's magazines that brainwashed women to embrace the "feminine mystique," in which personal fulfillment came only with marriage and motherhood. Women, Friedan claimed, "were being duped into believing home-making was their natural destiny."

The Feminine Mystique, an immediate best seller, forever changed American society by defining "the problem that has no name." Friedan inspired many well-educated, unfulfilled middle- and upper-class White women who felt trapped by household drudgery.

Betty Friedan Author of *The Feminine Mystique* and the first president of NOW, Friedan directed her feminism mainly at middle- and upper-class White women, seeking to empower them to aspire beyond female domesticity.

Moreover, Friedan discovered that there were far more married women working outside the home than she had assumed. Many were frustrated by the demands of holding "two full-time jobs instead of just one—underpaid clerical worker and unpaid housekeeper." Perhaps most important, Friedan helped empower women to achieve their "full human capacities"—in the home, in schools, in offices, on college campuses, and in politics.

In 1966, Friedan and other activists founded the National Organization for Women (NOW). They chose the acronym NOW because it was part of a popular civil rights chant: "What do you want?" protesters yelled. "FREEDOM!" "When do you want it?" "NOW!" The new organization promoted "true equality for all women in America . . . as part of the worldwide revolution of human rights now taking place." It sought to end gender discrimination in the workplace and spearheaded efforts to legalize abortion and obtain federal and state support for child-care centers. Change came slowly, however. By 1970, there was still only one woman in the U.S. Senate, ten in the House of Representatives, and none on the Supreme Court or in the president's cabinet.

RADICAL FEMINISM   During the late sixties, a new wave of younger and more radical feminists emerged to challenge everything from women's economic, political, and legal status to sexual double standards for men and women. They sought "women's liberation" from all forms of "sexism" (also called "male chauvinism" or "male oppression"), not simply equality in the workplace.

The new generation of feminists, often called "women's libbers," was more militant than Betty Friedan and others who had established NOW. Many younger feminists were veterans of the civil rights movement and the antiwar crusade who had come to realize that male revolutionaries could be sexists, too. They began meeting in small groups to discuss their opposition to the war and racism, only to discover at such "consciousness-raising" sessions that what bound them together were their shared grievances as women operating in a "man's world." Gaining true liberation, many of them decided, required exercising "sexual politics" whereby women would organize themselves into a political movement based on women's common problems and goals. The writer Robin Morgan captured this newly politicized feminism in the slogan "The personal is political," a radical notion that Betty Friedan rejected. When lesbians demanded a public role in the women's movement, Friedan deplored the "lavender menace" of lesbianism, calling it a divisive distraction that would only enrage their opponents. By 1973, however, NOW had endorsed gay rights.

Friedan's criticisms failed to dampen or deflect the energies of the younger generation of women activists, just as Martin Luther King Jr. had failed to suppress the Black Power movement. The goal of the women's liberation movement, said Susan Brownmiller, a self-described "radical feminist," was to "go beyond a simple concept of equality. NOW's emphasis on legislative change left the radicals cold." She dismissed Friedan as "hopelessly bourgeois." For women to be truly equal, Brownmiller and others believed, required transforming *every* aspect of society: child rearing, entertainment, domestic duties, business, and the arts. Lesbianism, she and others argued, should be celebrated rather than hidden.

Radical feminists also took direct action, such as picketing the 1968 Miss America Pageant, burning copies of *Playboy* and other men's magazines, tossing their bras and high-heeled shoes into "freedom cans," and assaulting gender-based discrimination in all its forms.

GLORIA STEINEM The women's movement received a boost from the energetic leadership provided by Gloria Steinem, who founded, with others, *Ms.* magazine in 1971. It was the first feminist periodical with a national readership. Its first edition of 300,000 copies sold out in eight days, and at the end of the first year it enjoyed half a million subscribers. By writing scores of hard-hitting essays in *Ms.* and other national magazines, Steinem expanded the scope of feminism beyond what Betty Friedan and others had started.

Born in Toledo, Ohio, in 1934, Steinem grew up in a poor, dysfunctional family. By age ten, she became her family's primary caregiver. Gloria did not spend a full year in school until she was twelve, but by then she was reading a book a day on her own. To supplement her family's meager finances, she performed as a tap dancer and salesclerk before earning a scholarship to Smith College, where she majored in government and political affairs. She graduated with honors in 1956 and earned a two-year fellowship for study in India.

Upon her return to America, Steinem began a career as a hard-nosed freelance investigative journalist living in New York City. In 1963, *Show* magazine hired her to go undercover as a scantily clad "Bunny" at the New York City Playboy Club. The resulting article ("I Was a Playboy Bunny") detailed the degrading treatment and inequitable wages she and others received as sex objects wearing rabbit ears and cottontails. It also made Steinem famous. In 1968, she helped found *New York* magazine, which enabled her, the only woman on the staff, to write about political topics and progressive social issues.

A year later, in 1969, Steinem attended an event in Greenwich Village sponsored by the Redstockings, a radical feminist group, at which women stood and recounted their experience with abortion. Having had an illegal abortion in London at age twenty-two on her way to India, Steinem stood and told her story to the group of strangers. "Why should each of us," she asked, "be made to feel criminal or alone?"

That event proved to be life changing, as Steinem sensed "a great blinding lightbulb" flashing in her head. That night she committed herself to advancing the women's liberation movement through advocacy journalism that gave voice to the voiceless. She resolved to engage in "outrageous acts and everyday rebellions."

Steinem thereafter became a prolific writer, fundraiser, and speaker, addressing numerous rallies, sit-ins, demonstrations, corporations, and organizations. She donated half her speaking fees to women's organizations and insisted on sharing the lectern with at least one woman of color to demonstrate that the women's liberation movement encompassed many diverse feminisms. "For twenty years," she recalled, "not a week went by when I wasn't on a plane" headed to give another public address. Steinem testified before a Senate committee in 1970 on behalf of the Equal Rights Amendment, and was co-founder of the Women's Action Alliance, and the National Women's Political Caucus.

Steinem soon became the public face and voice of the women's liberation movement—its celebrity diva and the icon of feminism. She was usually the first choice of reporters eager for provocative interviews and comments. As feminist scholar Rebecca Traister explained, Steinem was "young and White and pretty, and she looked great on magazine covers. I'm not deriding her. She tells this story about herself."

Steinem joined with fellow journalists Patricia Carbine and Letty Cottin Pogrebin to launch *Ms.* magazine in December 1971 because there was "nothing for women to read that

Gloria Steinem Gloria Steinem was a progressive feminist journalist who helped found *Ms.* and *New York* magazines. Through her writing and activism, she became one of the most prominent leaders of the women's liberation movement.

was controlled by women." The masthead of the first issue listed the editors alphabetically so as not to imply a hierarchy, because hierarchies were male inventions and hence undesirable. The first issue included stories titled "Sisterhood," "Raising Kids without Sex Roles," and "Women Tell the Truth about Their Abortions." Just a few months later, *Ms.* shocked the publishing world in 1972 when it revealed the names of women who admitted to having had an abortion when the procedure was still illegal in most states.

Unlike other women's magazines, *Ms.* focused on controversial topics such as gender bias, sexual harassment, abortion, pornography, workplace equality, same-sex marriage, and college curricula. "We need Women's Studies courses just as much as Black Studies," Steinem insisted in 1971. The famous magazine was not without its own internal controversies. The much-celebrated African American writer Alice Walker, an early *Ms.* contributor, resigned from the staff because the magazine covers featured too many Whites and not enough Blacks. Steinem persevered in the face of attacks from all sides. She was a gifted conciliator who always sought common ground in dealing with her critics.

FEMINIST VICTORIES In the early 1970s, Gloria Steinem joined members of Congress, the Supreme Court, and NOW in advancing the cause of gender equality. A major victory occurred with the congressional passage of Title IX of the Educational Amendments of 1972. It barred gender discrimination in any "education program or activity receiving federal financial assistance." Most notably applied to athletics, Title IX spurred female participation in high school sports to increase nearly tenfold and to almost double at the college level.

At the same time, the feminist movement was largely responsible for the decision of hundreds of all-male colleges and universities to admit women between 1969 and 1974. Yale and Princeton began the process, and within a few years, there were only three all-male colleges left: Hampden-Sydney, Morehouse, and Wabash. To be sure, the decisions to go co-ed were controversial. Many alumni vigorously opposed the change. In 1970, a Dartmouth grad wrote the board chair of the college: "For God's sake, for Dartmouth's sake, and for everyone's sake, keep the women out." Coeducation, a Princeton alumnus predicted, would dilute the college's "sturdy masculinity with disconcerting, mini-skirted young things cavorting on its playing fields."

The motives leading college boards of trustees to embrace coeducation were mixed. Many all-male colleges were witnessing a decline in applications because fewer young men wanted to attend a single-sex college. They needed women students to improve their quality and rankings.

Congress advanced the feminist movement when it overwhelmingly approved an equal-rights amendment (ERA) to the U.S. Constitution in 1972, which, if ratified by the states, would have required equal treatment for women throughout society and politics. By mid-1973, twenty-eight states had approved the amendment, ten short of the thirty-eight needed for approval.

The U.S. Supreme Court decided an even more controversial case in 1973. Using the pseudonym Jane Roe (the female equivalent of John Doe), Norma McCorvey, a homeless, jobless woman who been forced to give birth to an unwanted child, filed suit against the state of Texas for banning abortions. Feminist organizations rallied to her support during the three years it took the case to make its way to the Supreme Court.

In 1973, the justices ruled 7–2 that states must allow women, married or single, to have abortions before the twelfth week of pregnancy. Women, the justices wrote, have a fundamental "right to choose" whether to bear a child or not, since pregnancy necessarily affects a woman's health and well-being. The *Roe v. Wade* (1973) decision, and the ensuing success of NOW's efforts to liberalize local and state abortion laws, generated a powerful conservative backlash, especially among Roman Catholics and evangelical Protestants, who mounted a "right-to-life" crusade that helped fuel the conservative political resurgence in the seventies and thereafter.

By the mid-1990s, Norma McCorvey had dramatically switched sides and become a born-again Christian and an antiabortion crusader. Just before her death in 2007, however, she confessed that right-wing Christian evangelical groups had paid her $450,000 to reverse her public stance. They even coached her to deliver the appropriate antiabortion statements.

FRACTURED FEMINISM By the end of the seventies, sharp disputes between moderate and radical feminists had fractured the women's movement in ways similar to the fragmentation experienced by civil rights organizations a decade earlier. The movement's failure to broaden its appeal much beyond White, middle-class, heterosexual women also caused reform efforts to stall.

Ratification of the Equal Rights Amendment ("Equality of rights under the law shall not be denied or abridged by the United States or by any State on account of sex") was stymied in several state legislatures by conservative groups led by Phyllis Schlafly's STOP (Stop Taking Our Privileges) ERA organization (see fuller discussion on Schlafly and STOP in the next chapter on "The Rise of the New Right"). By 1982, it had died, three states short of the thirty-eight needed for ratification. Conservatives saw the defeat of the ERA as a triumph. They drew much of their strength from the backlash against changing social attitudes about women's roles.

What Women Want *(Left)* The Women's Strike for Equality brought tens of thousands of women together on August 26, 1970, to march for gender equality and celebrate the fiftieth anniversary of the Nineteenth Amendment (1920), which gave voting rights to women. *(Right)* The anti-feminist campaign STOP ERA ("Stop Taking Our Privileges, Equal Rights Amendment") found its most outspoken activist in Phyllis Schlafly, a constitutional lawyer and staunch conservative.

Yet the successes of the women's movement endured. The women fighting for equal rights during the 1970s focused on several basic issues: gender discrimination in the workplace; equal pay for equal work; an equal chance at jobs traditionally reserved for men; the availability of high-quality, government-subsidized child-care centers; and easier access to birth-control devices, prenatal care, and abortion. Feminists also helped win improvements in divorce laws. In 1970, only 40 percent of women favored fighting for equal rights; by 2020, the number was 96 percent.

Feminists called attention to issues long hidden or ignored. In 1970, for example, 36 percent of the nation's "poor" families were headed by women, as were most urban families dependent on federal welfare services. Nearly 3 million poor children needed access to day-care centers, but there were places for only 530,000.

The feminist movement helped women achieve mass entry into the labor market and enjoy steady improvements toward equal pay and treatment. In 1960, some 38 percent of women were working outside the home; by 1980, an estimated 52 percent were doing so (In 2020, the percentage was 57.4).

A growing presence in the labor force brought women a greater share of economic and political influence. By 1976, more than half of married women, and nine of ten female college graduates, were employed outside the home;

a development that one economist called "the single most outstanding phenomenon of this century." Women also enrolled in graduate and professional schools in record numbers. During the 1970s, more women began winning elected offices at the local, state, and national levels.

THE SEXUAL REVOLUTION AND THE PILL The feminist movement coincided with the so-called sexual revolution as Americans became more tolerant of premarital sex, and women became more sexually active. Between 1960 and 1975, the number of college women engaging in heterosexual sexual intercourse doubled, to 50 percent.

Enabling this change, in large part, was the birth-control pill, approved for public use by the Food and Drug Administration in 1960. Widespread access to "the pill" gave women a greater sense of sexual freedom and led to more-open discussion of birth control, reproduction, and sexuality in general. Although the pill contributed to a rise in sexually transmitted diseases, many women viewed it as an inexpensive, nonintrusive way to gain better control over their bodies, their careers, and their futures. "It was a savior,"

YOU CAN DECIDE HOW MANY CHILDREN YOU WANT

PLANNED PARENTHOOD CAN HELP
...with information on birth control and infertility services

CALL 421-2290

PLANNED PARENTHOOD OF NEW YORK CITY 29 WEST 51 ST. NEW YORK, 10019

Birth Control To spread the word about birth-control options, Planned Parenthood in 1967 displayed posters like this one in New York City buses.

recalled Eleanor Smeal, president of the Feminist Majority Foundation. "The whole country was waiting for it. I can't even describe to you how excited people were."

THE RISE OF IDENTITY AND GROUP POLITICS

The activism of student revolts, the civil rights movement, and the crusade for women's rights soon spread to various ethnic groups. Everywhere, it seemed, long oppressed minority groups asserted their right to be treated equally and fairly.

LATINO RIGHTS The word *Latino*, referring to people who trace their ancestry to Spanish-speaking Latin America, came into use after 1945 in conjunction with efforts to promote economic and social justice.

Labor shortages during the Second World War had led defense industries to offer Latino Americans their first significant access to skilled-labor jobs. And as with African Americans, service in the military helped to heighten an American identity among Latino Americans and increase their desire for equal rights and social opportunities.

Social equality, however, remained elusive as Latinos still faced widespread discrimination in hiring, housing, and education. Latino activists denounced segregation; called for improved public schools; and struggled to increase their political influence, economic opportunities, and visibility in the curricula of schools and colleges.

Latino civil rights leaders faced an awkward dilemma: what should they do about the stream of undocumented Mexican workers flowing across the border into the United States? Many Latinos argued that their hopes for economic advancement and social equality were threatened by the influx of Mexican laborers willing to accept low-paying jobs. In 1964, Latino leaders helped end the *bracero* program, which trucked in contract day laborers from Mexico during harvest season.

CESAR CHAVEZ AND THE UNITED FARM WORKERS In the early 1960s, impoverished Mexican American farmworkers formed their own civil rights organization, the **United Farm Workers (UFW)**. Its founder was the charismatic Cesar Chavez. Born in 1927 in Yuma, Arizona, the son of Mexican immigrants, Chavez spent his youth shuttling with his family to various farm camps. The family often earned only a dollar a day as fruit pickers. Chavez and his siblings went barefoot and attended forty different schools. After the eighth grade, he dropped out to work in the fields, picking peas in winter, cherries in spring, and cotton in the fall. During the Second World War, he served in the U.S. Navy. Afterward, he was a migrant laborer and a tireless, self-educated community organizer focused on registering Latinos to vote in California. "My motivation comes from my personal life," Chavez explained. "It grew from anger and rage . . . when people of my color were denied the right to see a movie or eat at a restaurant."

In 1962 Chavez formed the Farm Workers' Association. Like the earlier farm alliances, it was more than a union. It was *La Causa*, a broad social movement intended to enhance the solidarity and dignity of migrant farm workers, most of whom traced their ancestry to Mexico.

Like Martin Luther King Jr., Chavez viewed his efforts to organize migrant workers as a religious crusade for social justice. His life was a public prayer for a life of suffering. "I am convinced," he explained, "that the truest act of courage, the strongest act of manliness, is to sacrifice ourselves for others in a totally non-violent struggle for justice. To be a man is to suffer for others. God help us to be men."

Chavez's relentless energy and deep Catholic faith, his insistence upon nonviolent tactics, his reliance upon college-student volunteers, his skillful alliance with organized labor and religious groups, and his simple lifestyle attracted popular support in a strike that would last five years.

By 1965, Chavez and Dolores Huerta, a former teacher who would receive the Presidential Medal of Honor in 2012, converted the Farm Workers' Association into the United Farm Workers, a union for migrant lettuce workers and grape pickers, many of them undocumented immigrants who could be deported at any time. "I couldn't tolerate seeing kids come to class hungry and needing shoes," Huerta remembered. "I thought I could do more by organizing farm workers than by trying to teach their hungry children."

Over the next ten years, Chavez and Huerta led some of the poorest workers in the nation in a series of nonviolent protest marches, staged hunger strikes, and managed nationwide boycotts. Workers were spellbound by their humility, integrity, and dedication to improving the quality of their lives. Chavez and Huerta became the most famous Mexican Americans of the era.

The United Farm Workers gained national attention in September 1965 when it joined with Filipino migrant workers in organizing a strike (*la huelga*) and nationwide consumers' boycott against commercial grape growers in California's San Joaquin Valley, home to some of the richest farmland in the nation. Their grievance focused on wages; they earned about $1,350 a year. As Huerta explained, "We have to get farmworkers the same type of benefits, the same type of wages, and the respect that they deserve because they do the most sacred work of all. They feed our nation every day."

In 1968, Chavez began a twenty-five-day hunger strike to raise national attention for their efforts. On the day he broke his fast, the first to greet him was Robert F. Kennedy, then campaigning for the Democratic presidential nomination. "The world must know, from this time forward, that the migrant farm worker, the Mexican-American, is coming into his own rights," Kennedy declared, adding that the farmworkers were gaining "a special kind of citizenship. . . . You are winning it for yourselves—and therefore no one can ever take it away."

Finally, in 1970, the grape growers agreed to raise wages, offer health benefits, and improve working conditions. Chavez then turned his attention to political activism, organizing voter registration drives and advocating laws to protect the civil rights of migrant workers. In doing so, however, he unwittingly let the United Farm Workers wither.

As Chavez recognized, the chief strength of the civil rights movement in the western states lay in the rapid growth of the Hispanic American population. From 1970 to 2019, their numbers grew from 9 million (4.8 percent of the total population) to 60 million, making them the nation's largest ethnic group (17 percent). The increased population of Hispanics in key electoral states has given them significant political clout.

Cesar Chavez and Delores Huerta
Pictured here in front of posters of other civil rights figures Robert F. Kennedy and Mahatma Gandhi, labor activists Cesar Chavez and Delores Huerta worked as a team to improve the working conditions for migrant farmers. Their collaborative advocacy resulted in higher wages and health benefits.

NATIVE AMERICANS' QUEST FOR EQUALITY American Indians—many of whom began calling themselves Native Americans—also emerged as a political force in the late 1960s. Two conditions combined to make Indian rights a priority. First, many Whites felt guilty for the destructive actions of their ancestors toward a people who had, after all, been here first. Second, Indian unemployment was ten times the national rate, life expectancy was twenty years lower than the national average, and the suicide rate was a hundred times higher than the rate for Whites.

Although President Lyndon Johnson attempted to funnel federal anti-poverty-program funds to reservations, many Native American activists grew impatient. Those promoting "**Red Power**" organized protests and demonstrations against local, state, and federal agencies.

On November 20, 1969, fourteen Red Power activists occupied Alcatraz Island near San Francisco. The island had been the site of a federal prison, but it was closed in 1963, and the federal government then declared the island surplus government property, leading Red Power activists to stake a claim on it. In late 1969, hundreds of other supporters, mostly students, joined the occupiers. The Nixon administration responded by cutting off electrical service and telephone lines to the island. Stranded without power and fresh water, most of the protesters left. Finally, on June 11, 1971, the government removed the remaining fifteen Native Americans.

In 1968, the year before the Alcatraz occupation, George Mitchell and Dennis Banks, two Chippewas (or Ojibwas) living in Minneapolis, founded the American Indian Movement (AIM). In October 1972, AIM organized the Trail of Broken Treaties caravan, which traveled by bus and car from the West coast to Washington, D.C., to draw attention to the federal government's broken promises. When Nixon administration officials refused to meet with them, the protesters barged into the offices of the Bureau of Indian Affairs. The sit-in ended when government negotiators agreed to renew discussions of Native American grievances.

In 1973, AIM led 200 Sioux in the occupation of the tiny South Dakota village of Wounded Knee, where the U.S. Seventh Cavalry had massacred an entire Sioux village in 1890. Outraged by the light sentences given a group of local Whites who had killed a Sioux just a year earlier, the organizers sought to draw attention to the plight of Native Americans and took eleven hostages.

Federal marshals and FBI agents surrounded the encampment. When AIM leaders tried to bring in food and supplies, a shoot-out erupted, with two activists killed and a U.S. marshal shot and paralyzed. The confrontation ended with a government promise to reexamine Indian treaty rights.

Indian protesters subsequently discovered a more effective tactic: they went into federal courts armed with copies of old treaties and demanded that the documents become the basis for financial restitution for the lands taken from them. In Alaska, Maine, South Carolina, and Massachusetts, the groups won substantial settlements that officially recognized their tribal rights and helped to upgrade the standard of living on several reservations.

The chronic need for additional revenue at cash-starved reservations led tribal leaders to create gambling casinos during the late 1970s and 1980s. Bingo parlors emerged first in California, Florida, New York, and Wisconsin, before

Standoff at Wounded Knee After occupying the hamlet of Wounded Knee on the Pine Ridge Indian reservation in South Dakota and taking eleven hostages, members of the American Indian Movement and the Oglala Sioux stand guard outside the town's Sacred Heart Catholic Church.

spreading to many other states. The success of revenue-generating bingo led to the construction of large casinos that featured diverse games of chance: slot machines, blackjack, craps, and roulette. The revenues from the Indian gaming industry now exceed $22 billion annually.

GAY AND LESBIAN RIGHTS The liberationist impulses of the sixties also encouraged lesbian, gay, bisexual, transgender, and queer people (LGBTQ), long defamed as sinful or mentally ill, to assert their right to be treated as equals. Throughout the 1960s, this diverse population of outcasts had continued to suffer social and institutional discrimination. Many local ordinances and state laws deemed non-heterosexual behavior a vice crime, meaning an activity was illegal because it "offended" the moral standards of the community.

At 3 A.M. on June 28, 1969, a New York City Police Department vice squad raided the Stonewall Inn, the most popular gay/transgender club in Greenwich Village. There had been police raids before, but this time the cops were determined to shut down the club—for good. "Line up. Get your IDs out," shouted a policeman. With their identities confirmed, those customers who were not "minors" were shooed out the door. Instead of dispersing, however, the patrons stood on the sidewalk and began applauding and cheering as each customer emerged.

The crowd grew as passersby joined in the festival-like atmosphere. "Queers were usually very docile," a policeman involved in the raid remembered. Not that night, however. As the cops handcuffed patrons, some began to resist arrest. "The crowd became explosive," a reporter wrote. The surging crowd, led by transgender women of color, drag queens, and street people, fought back with pent-up anger brought to a roiling rage. The outnumbered police took shelter inside the bar.

Outraged customers threw whatever they could find—rocks, bricks, bottles, beer cans, pennies—and then torched the building. "I had been in combat situations before," one of the police officers recalled, but "I never felt more scared than that night." For several nights thereafter, crowds returned to the Stonewall Inn, chanting "Gay Power!" and "We Want Freedom Now!" One participant described the clash with police as "a public assertion of real anger by gay people that was just electric."

The **Stonewall Uprising** lasted six nights and involved thousands of people—not only gays, but transsexuals, people of color, militants, street youth,

Gay Pride in the Seventies Gay rights activists march in the Fifth Annual Gay Pride Day demonstration, commemorating the anniversary of the Stonewall Uprising (1969) that jump-started the gay rights movement in the United States.

and sex workers. In the end, four policemen were injured, thirteen patrons were arrested, and the New York City police commissioner issued a public apology to the LGBTQ community.

The Stonewall Uprising was a turning point in the LGBTQ movement. Although there had been many protests and demonstrations before, the week-long riots crystallized the quest for gay legitimacy. The widely publicized event helped many gays and transsexuals "come out of the closet," and it helped many others see the gay/lesbian/trans liberation movement as interwoven with the struggle for civil rights. Stonewall also injected greater militancy into the tactics of the gay liberation movement. Government and police were put on notice," said one activist, "that homosexuals won't stand being kicked around."

The Stonewall Uprising prompted the founding of two organizations, the Gay Liberation Front and the Gay Activists' Alliance, both of which focused on ending discrimination and harassment against gay, lesbian, bisexual, and transgender people. (In 2016, President Barack Obama declared the rebuilt Stonewall Inn a national monument.)

As news of the Stonewall rebellion spread, the gay rights movement grew in size and visibility. By 1973, almost 800 organizations supporting sexual orientation and gender identification rights had emerged. That year, the board of the American Psychiatric Association voted unanimously to remove "homosexuality" from its official diagnostic manual of mental disorders. Colleges and universities began offering courses and majors in Gay and Lesbian Studies (also called Queer Studies), and groups began lobbying for government recognition of same-sex marriages. As with the civil rights and women's movements, however, the campaign for gay and lesbian rights soon witnessed internal divisions over inclusiveness, definitions, tactics, and goals; it also sparked a conservative counterattack.

"THE EAGLE HAS LANDED" During the turbulent sixties, one event briefly united both the country and the world. On July 16, 1969, some 600 million people around the globe watched on television as U.S. astronauts Neil Armstrong, Edwin "Buzz" Aldrin, and Michael Collins set off atop a Saturn V rocket on the long-awaited Apollo 11 space mission to land people on the moon. They almost did not make it. As the lunar module descended toward its designated landing site, the astronauts saw that they were headed toward a crater strewn with boulders that could destroy the lander.

Armstrong quickly overrode the automatic pilot, took control of the module, and frantically searched for a smoother landing site. The problem was that these unplanned maneuvers were using up precious fuel needed to fire the rockets to leave the moon.

Moon Landing With the world watching, astronauts Neil Armstrong, Edwin Aldrin, and Michael Collins landed on the moon. Together they planted an American flag and were the first people to walk on the moon's surface.

The engineers at Mission Control in Houston relayed their sense of urgency to Armstrong: he had only sixty seconds of fuel left. "There ain't no gas stations on the moon," a flight controller reminded the astronauts. At that moment, the NASA technician in Houston monitoring the radar system scanning the landing site fainted.

Yet the lunar lander, named *Eagle*, was still a hundred feet from the surface. "Thirty seconds of fuel left," yelled mission control. Armstrong's heart rate soared to 156 beats per minute. Finally, Aldrin reported: "Contact!" Then Armstrong followed with, "Houston, the *Eagle* has landed"—with just twenty seconds of fuel to spare.

Armstrong became the first human to walk on the moon's surface; he famously described the moment as "one small step for man, one giant leap for mankind." Soon thereafter, Aldrin joined him to plant an American flag, organize several experiments, and collect moon rocks.

The nation and the world rejoiced. What had begun as a Cold War challenge had evolved over eight years into something much more significant. The mission itself became both the goal and the inspiration—for those working on it and for everyone else around the world. A Soviet official remembered,

"Everyone forgot that we were all citizens of different countries on Earth. That moment really united the human race."

President Nixon claimed that the moon landing was "the greatest event in the history of the world," and he proudly presided over five more Apollo moon landing missions before the program ended in 1972.

NIXON AND THE REVIVAL OF CONSERVATISM

The turmoil of the sixties spawned a cultural backlash among what President Richard Nixon called the "great silent majority" of middle-class Americans who had propelled him to victory in 1968. He had been elected as the representative of middle America—voters fed up with student radicals, hippies, radical feminism, gay and lesbian rights, and **affirmative-action** programs that gave preferential treatment to people of color and women to atone for past injustices.

THE CONSERVATIVE BACKLASH Alabama's Democratic governor, George Wallace, led the conservative White backlash. "Liberals, intellectuals, and long hairs," he shouted, "have run the country for too long." He repeatedly attacked "welfare queens," unmarried African American mothers who he claimed "were breeding children as a cash crop" to receive federal child-support checks. Wallace became the voice for many working-class Whites fed up with political liberalism and social radicalism.

All in the Family, the most popular television show in the 1970s, showcased the decade's culture wars. In the sitcom, the Bunker family lived in a working-class suburb of New York City. Semiliterate Archie Bunker (played by Carroll O'Connor), a Polish American loading-dock worker, was the gruff head of the family, a proud Richard Nixon supporter and talkative member of the silent majority who railed against Blacks, Jews, Italians, gays, feminists, hippies, and liberals (including his live-in daughter and her hippie husband). At one point, he said: "I ain't no bigot. I'm the first guy to say, 'It ain't your fault that youse are colored.'"

The producer of the series, Norman Lear, sought to provoke viewers to question their own prejudices. In fact, however, many of the 50 million people watching each Saturday night identified *with* Archie's values and bigotries.

"LAW AND ORDER" Richard Nixon courted working- and middle-class Whites who feared that America was being corrupted by permissiveness, anarchy, and the tyranny of the rebellious minority. He explicitly appealed to voters "who did not break the law, people who pay their taxes and go to work, people who send their children to school, who go to their churches, people who are not haters, people who love this country." Above all, he promised to restore "law and order," by "cracking down" on anti-war protesters, civil rights demonstrators, and activists who challenged traditional gender roles.

A grocer's son from Whittier, California, Nixon was a humorless man of fierce ambition and extraordinary perseverance. Raised in a family that struggled with poverty ("I wore my brother's shoes"), he nursed a deep resentment of "privileged" people who had enjoyed an easier time (the "moneyed class"). Like Lyndon Johnson, Nixon was a paradoxical character. He was smart and cunning, a tireless worker and shrewd strategic thinker, and he was doggedly determined to succeed in politics—at all costs. Cold and calculating, he relished political combat. He saw enemies, real and perceived, around every corner and allowed his paranoia and ruthless vengefulness to isolate him from political reality—and from his family.

Nixon was a pathological loner who fed on resentments. Socially awkward and even graceless, Nixon was stiff and formal even when he didn't have to be; he wore a necktie with his pajamas and donned dress shoes while walking on the beach. Once, he visited his mother to wish her happy birthday, followed by a camera crew, and when she came to the door, he shook her hand. Nixon and his wife, Pat, had separate bedrooms for most of their marriage, and he wrote sterile memos to her with the formal salutation, "To Mrs. Nixon, from the President."

Nixon displayed violent mood swings (punctuated by alcohol binges), raging temper tantrums, frequent profanity, and anti-Semitic and anti-feminist outbursts. As he once told an aide, "I'm not for women frankly, in any job. I don't want any of them around. Thank God we don't have any in the Cabinet." Critics nicknamed him "Tricky Dick" because he excelled at deceit. In his speech accepting the Republican nomination in 1968, Nixon pledged "to find the truth, to speak the truth, and live with the truth." In fact, however, he often did the opposite. One of his presidential aides admitted that "we did often lie, mislead, deceive, try to use [the media], and to con them."

NIXON'S APPOINTMENTS In his first term, Nixon selected for his cabinet and staff only White men who would blindly carry out his orders. John Mitchell, the gruff attorney general, was his closest confidant. H. R. "Bob" Haldeman, a former Los Angeles advertising executive, served as chief of staff. Nixon called him his "chief executioner." As Haldeman explained, "Every President needs a son of a bitch, and I'm Nixon's." John Ehrlichman, a Seattle attorney and college schoolmate of Haldeman, was chief domestic-policy adviser. John W. Dean III, an associate deputy in the Office of the U.S. Attorney General, became the White House legal counsel.

Nixon tapped as secretary of state his friend William Rogers, who had served as attorney general under Dwight D. Eisenhower. The president, however, virtually ignored Rogers while forging an unlikely partnership with Dr. Henry Kissinger, a brilliant German-born Jew and Harvard political scientist who had become one of the nation's leading foreign-policy experts. Kissinger's thick accent, owlish appearance, and outsized ego had helped to make him an international celebrity, courted by presidents of both parties. In 1969, Nixon named Kissinger his national security adviser, and in 1973 Kissinger became secretary of state.

Both Nixon and Kissinger were outsiders who preferred operating in secret; both were insecure and even paranoid at times; and each mistrusted and envied the other's power and prestige. For his part, Kissinger lavished praise on Nixon in public, but in private he dismissed the president as an insecure man with a "meatball mind" and an alcohol problem. (To his aides, Kissinger referred to Nixon as "our drunken friend.") Yet for all their differences, Nixon and Kissinger worked well together on foreign policy initiatives, in part because they both loved intrigue, power politics, and diplomatic flexibility, and in part because of their shared vision of a multipolar world order that was beginning to replace the bipolar Cold War.

NIXON'S SOUTHERN STRATEGY   A major reason for Nixon's election victories in 1968 and 1972 was his shrewd strategy for converting the Democratic South into a Republican region. Rising crime, civil disobedience, and urban riots had changed the context of national politics. Nixon forged a new voting majority by nurturing the fears, resentments, and racism of working-class Whites and middle-class suburbanites in the South (and in conservative Catholic ethnic neighborhoods in the Midwest).

Most White southern voters were religious and patriotic, fervently anti-Communist and anti-union, and skeptical of "liberal" social welfare programs benefiting people of color. Nixon and his campaign advisers realized that White southerners were ripe for abandoning the increasingly liberal Democratic party that had dominated the region since the end of the Civil War.

In the 1970s, the South's population was growing by 40 percent, a rate more than twice the national average. The region's warm climate, low cost of living, absence of labor unions, low taxes, and state government incentives for economic development convinced waves of businesses to relocate there. During the 1970s, job growth in the South was seven times greater than in New York and Pennsylvania. Southern "redneck" culture suddenly became the rage as the nation embraced stockcar racing, cowboy boots, pickup trucks, barbecue, and country music.

Rapid population growth—and the continuing spread of air-conditioning—brought the Sunbelt states of the South, the Southwest, and California more congressional seats and more electoral votes. Nixon's favorite singer, country star Merle Haggard, crooned in his smash hit "Okie from Muskogee": "We don't smoke marijuana in Muskogee / We don't take our trips on LSD / We don't burn our draft cards down on Main Street / We like livin' right and bein' free."

Like Nixon, Haggard's working-class fans bristled at anti-war protesters, hippies, rising taxes, social welfare programs, and civil rights activism. The alienation of many blue-collar Whites from the Democratic party, the demographic changes transforming Sunbelt states, and the White backlash against court-ordered integration created a fertile opportunity to gain southern votes that the Republican party eagerly exploited.

In the 1968 presidential campaign, Nixon won over traditionally Democratic White working-class voters. He cleverly "played the race card," assuring White conservatives that he would appoint justices to the Supreme Court who would undermine federal enforcement of civil rights laws, such as mandatory school busing to achieve racial integration and affirmative-action programs that gave women and people of color priority in hiring decisions and the awarding of government contracts. Nixon also appealed to the economic concerns of middle-class southern Whites by promising lower tax rates and reduced government regulation.

In the 1972 election, Nixon easily carried every southern state. The Republican takeover of the once Solid South was the greatest realignment in American politics since Franklin D. Roosevelt's election in 1932. It was also an unlikely coalition, for it brought together traditional "country club" Republicans—corporate executives, financiers, and investors—with poor, rural, fundamentalist southerners who had always voted for segregationist Democrats. What they shared was a simmering hatred for what the Democratic party had become.

NIXON'S DOMESTIC AGENDA   As president, Richard Nixon shared with his predecessors John Kennedy and Lyndon Johnson an urge to increase presidential power. All three believed that the presidency had become the central source of governmental action, that foreign policy should be managed from the White House rather than the State Department, and that the president had the authority to wage war without a congressional declaration of war. Nixon was less a rigid conservative ideologue than a crafty politician. Forced to deal with a Congress controlled by Democrats throughout his presidency, he chose his battles carefully and showed surprising flexibility, leading journalist Tom Wicker to describe him as "at once liberal and conservative, generous and begrudging, cynical and idealistic, choleric and calm, resentful and forgiving."

During his first term, Nixon focused on developing policies and programs that would please conservatives and ensure his reelection. To recruit conservative Democrats, he touted his New Federalism, which sent federal money to state and local governments to spend as they saw fit. He also disbanded the core agency of Lyndon Johnson's war on poverty—the Office of Economic Opportunity—and cut funding to several Great Society programs.

At the same time, Democrats in Congress passed significant legislation that Nixon chose to sign rather than veto: the right of eighteen-year-olds to vote in national elections (1970) and in all elections under the Twenty-Sixth Amendment (1971); increases in Social Security benefits and food-stamp funding; the Occupational Safety and Health Act (1970) to ensure safer workplace environments; the Clean Air Act (1970) to mitigate pollution; and the Federal Election Campaign Act (1971), which modified the rules governing corporate financial donations to political campaigns.

NIXON AND CIVIL RIGHTS

During his first term, President Nixon followed through on campaign pledges to blunt the momentum of the civil rights movement. He appointed no African Americans to his cabinet and refused to meet with the all-Democratic Congressional Black Caucus. "We've had enough social programs: forced integration, education, housing," he told his chief of staff. "People don't want more [people] on welfare. They don't want to help the working poor, and our mood needs to be harder on this, not softer."

He also launched a concerted effort to block congressional renewal of the Voting Rights Act of 1965 and to delay implementation of federal court orders requiring the desegregation of school districts in Mississippi. Sixty-five lawyers

Off to School Because of violent protests against desegregation, school buses in South Boston are escorted by police in October 1974.

in the Justice Department signed a letter protesting Nixon's stance. The Democratic-controlled Congress extended the Voting Rights Act over his veto.

The Supreme Court also thwarted Nixon's efforts to slow desegregation. In its first decision under new Chief Justice Warren Burger—a Nixon appointee—the Court ordered the racial integration of the Mississippi public schools in *Alexander v. Holmes County Board of Education* (1969). During Nixon's first term, more schools were desegregated under court order than in all the Kennedy and Johnson presidencies combined.

The Burger Court also ruled unanimously in *Swann v. Charlotte-Mecklenburg Board of Education* (1971) that school systems must bus students out of their neighborhoods if necessary to achieve racially integrated schools. Protests over busing erupted in the North, the Midwest, and the Southwest, as White families denounced the destruction of "the neighborhood school." Angry White parents in Pontiac, Michigan, were so determined to stop mandatory busing that they boycotted the schools and firebombed ten empty school buses.

NIXON AND ENVIRONMENTAL PROTECTION　During the seventies, dramatic increases in the price of oil and gasoline fueled a major energy crisis that coincided with a surging public interest in protecting the natural environment from pollution and abuse by corporations. Spiking gasoline prices spooked many consumers who had long benefited from low energy prices compared to most other nations. Nixon also recognized that the burgeoning environmental movement was growing more popular with voters. In addition, the Democratic majorities in the House and Senate had shifted in favor of greater federal environmental protections, especially after two widely publicized environmental disasters in 1969.

The first was a massive oil spill off the coast of Santa Barbara, California, when a slick of crude oil contaminated 200 miles of California beaches, killing thousands of sea birds and marine animals. Six months later, on June 22, 1969, the Cuyahoga River, an eighty-mile-long stream that slices through Cleveland, Ohio, spontaneously caught fire. Fouled with oil and grease, bubbling with subsurface gases, and littered with debris, the river burned for five days. The images of the burning Ohio river and oil-stained California beaches helped raise environmental awareness. A 1969 survey of college campuses by the *New York Times* revealed that many young people were transferring their idealism from the anti-war movement to the environmental movement.

Nixon knew that if he vetoed legislative efforts to improve environmental quality, the Democratic majorities in Congress would overrule him, so he chose not to stand in the way. Soon after becoming president, the president told adviser John Ehrlichman, "Just keep me out of trouble on environmental issues." In late 1969, he signed the amended Endangered Species Preservation Act and the National Environmental Policy Act. The latter became effective on January 1, 1970, the year that environmental groups established an annual Earth Day celebration. In 1970, Nixon signed the Clean Air Act and an executive order that created two federal agencies, the **Environmental Protection Agency (EPA)** and the National Oceanic and Atmospheric Administration (NOAA). Two years later, he vetoed a new clean water act, only to see Congress override him. He also undermined many of the new environmental laws he signed by refusing to spend money appropriated by Congress to fund them.

Environmental Awareness A group of Clark College students wearing gas masks as part of an Earth Day demonstration to highlight the dangers of air pollution.

"**STAGFLATION**" The major domestic development during the Nixon administration was a floundering economy. The accumulated expense of the Vietnam War and the Great Society programs helped quadruple the annual inflation rate from 3 percent in 1967 to 12 percent in 1974. Meanwhile, unemployment, at only 3.3 percent when Nixon took office, hit 6 percent by the end of 1970.

Economists coined the term "**stagflation**" to describe the simultaneous problems of stalled economic growth (stagnation), rising inflation, and high unemployment. Consumer prices usually increased with a rapidly growing economy and rising employment. This was just the reverse, and there were no easy ways to fight the unusual combination of recession and inflation.

Stagflation had at least three causes. First, the Johnson administration had financed both the Great Society social welfare programs and the Vietnam War without a major tax increase, thereby generating large federal deficits, a major expansion of the money supply, and price inflation. Second, U.S. companies were facing stiff competition from West Germany, Japan, and other emerging international industrial powers. Third, America's prosperity since 1945 had resulted in part from the ready availability of cheap sources of energy. No other nation was more dependent upon the automobile, and no other nation was more wasteful in its use of fossil fuels. During the seventies, however, oil and gasoline became scarcer and costlier. High energy prices and oil shortages took their toll on the economy.

Just as America's domestic petroleum reserves began to dwindle and dependence upon foreign sources increased, the Organization of Petroleum Exporting Countries (OPEC) decided to use its huge oil supplies as a political and economic weapon. In 1973, the United States sent massive aid to Israel after a devastating Syrian-Egyptian attack that was launched on Yom Kippur, the holiest day on the Jewish calendar. OPEC responded by announcing that it would not sell oil to the United States and other nations supporting Israel in the so-called Yom Kippur War and that it was raising its oil prices by 400 percent (see the later section, "Shuttle Diplomacy," for a full discussion of the Yom Kippur War). President Nixon alerted Americans to a stark new fact: "We are heading toward the most acute shortage of energy since the Second World War." He asked the airlines to reduce their flights, lowered the maximum speed limit on federal highways to 55 mph, halted plans to convert electricity-generating plants from coal to oil, and urged all Americans to conserve energy.

The Arab oil embargo, called by some an "economic Pearl Harbor," caused gasoline shortages and skyrocketing prices. Motorists suddenly faced mile-long lines at gas stations. "These people are like animals foraging for food," said a gas station owner. "If you can't sell them gas, they threaten to beat you up, wreck your station, or run you over with a car." To manage the crisis, the federal government created a gas-rationing program: service stations would be open on alternate days to drivers with license plates ending in odd or even numbers.

Another condition leading to stagflation was the flood of new workers—mainly baby boomers and women—into the labor market. From 1965 to 1980, the workforce grew by almost 30 million workers, a number greater than the total labor force of France or West Germany. The number of new jobs could not keep up with the growth of the workforce, leaving many unemployed.

The Nixon administration responded erratically and ineffectively to stag-flation, trying old remedies for a new problem. First, the president sought to reduce the federal deficit by raising taxes and cutting the budget. When the Democratic Congress refused to cooperate, he encouraged the Federal Reserve Board to reduce the nation's money supply by raising interest rates. The stock market immediately nosedived, and the economy plunged into the "Nixon recession."

A sense of desperation about the stagnant economy seized the White House. In 1969, when asked about the possibility of imposing government caps on wages and prices, Nixon had been clear: "Controls. Oh, my God, no! . . . We'll never go to controls." In 1971, however, he reversed himself. He froze all wages and prices for ninety days, arguing that doing so would generate a "new prosperity: more jobs, more incomes, more profits, without inflation and without war." It did not work out that way as the economy remained sluggish.

"Peace with Honor": Ending the Vietnam War

By the time Richard Nixon entered the White House in January 1969, he and Henry Kissinger had developed a comprehensive vision of a new world order. The result of their collaboration was a dramatic transformation of U.S. foreign policy. Since 1945, the United States had lost its monopoly on nuclear weapons, its overwhelming economic dominance, and much of its geopolitical influence. The rapid rise of competing power centers in Europe, China, and Japan further complicated international relations and the Cold War.

Nixon and Kissinger envisioned defusing the Cold War by pursuing peaceful coexistence with the Soviets and Chinese Communists. Preoccupied with secrecy, they bypassed the State Department and Congress in their efforts to take advantage of shifting world events.

Their immediate task was to end the war in Vietnam. Until all U.S. troops had returned home, the social harmony that Nixon had promised would remain elusive. Privately, he had decided by 1969 that "there's no way to win the war," so he sought what he and Kissinger called "peace with honor." That is, the United States needed to withdraw in a way that upheld the credibility of its military alliances around the world. Peace, however, was long in coming, not honorable, and shockingly brief.

GRADUAL WITHDRAWAL The Vietnam policy implemented by Richard Nixon and Henry Kissinger moved along three fronts in 1969. First, U.S. negotiators in Paris demanded the withdrawal of Viet Cong forces from South Vietnam and the preservation of the U.S.-backed government of President Nguyen Van Thieu. The North Vietnamese and Viet Cong negotiators insisted on retaining a Communist military presence in the south and reunifying the Vietnamese people under a government dominated by the Communists. There was no common ground. Hidden from public awareness and from America's South Vietnamese allies were secret meetings between Kissinger and the North Vietnamese.

On the second front, Nixon tried to quell domestic unrest. He labeled the anti-war movement a "brotherhood of the misguided, the mistaken, the well-meaning, and the malevolent." He sought to defuse the anti-war movement by steadily reducing the number of U.S. troops in Vietnam, justifying the reduction as the natural result of "**Vietnamization**"—the equipping and training of South Vietnamese soldiers and pilots to assume the burden of combat. From a peak of 560,000 troops in 1969, U.S. combat forces returned home at a steady pace. By 1973, only 50,000 troops remained in Vietnam.

In 1969, Nixon also established a draft lottery whereby the birth dates of nineteen-year-old men were randomly selected and assigned a number between 1 and 366 in order of their selection. Those with low lottery numbers, from 1 to 160, would be the first drafted into military service. The lottery system eliminated many inequities and clarified the likelihood of being drafted. Four years later, in 1973, the president ended the draft altogether by creating an all-volunteer military.

Those initiatives, coupled with the troop withdrawals from Vietnam, defused the anti-war movement. Opinion polls showed strong public support for Nixon's policies related to the Vietnam War. "We've got those liberal bastards on the run now," the president gloated, "and we're going to keep them on the run." Nixon had much less success in forcing concessions from the North Vietnamese negotiators.

On the third front, while steadily reducing the number of U.S. combat troops in Southeast Asia, Nixon and Kissinger greatly expanded the U.S. bombing of North Vietnam in hopes of pressuring the Communist leaders to end the war. Kissinger felt that "a fourth-rate power" like North Vietnam must have a "breaking point" at which it would decide it was suffering too much damage. Nixon agreed, suggesting that they let the North Vietnamese leaders know that he was so "obsessed about Communism" that he might use the "nuclear button" if necessary.

In March 1969, Nixon approved a secret fourteen-month-long bombing campaign aimed at Communist Vietnamese forces that were using neighboring Cambodia as a base for raids into South Vietnam. Congress did not learn of the air strikes until 1970, although the total tonnage of bombs dropped was four times that dropped on Japan during World War II. Still, Hanoi's leaders did not flinch; they decided to let Nixon's domestic critics undermine his presidency. Then, on April 30, 1970, Nixon announced an "incursion" into "neutral" Cambodia by U.S. troops to "clean out" hidden Vietnamese Communist military bases. Privately, Nixon told Kissinger, who strongly endorsed the decision to extend the fighting into Cambodia, "If this doesn't work, it'll be your ass, Henry." Nixon knew that sending troops into Cambodia would reignite the anti-war movement. Secretary of State Rogers predicted, "This will make the [anti-war] students puke."

COLLAPSE OF MILITARY MORALE Another factor supporting withdrawal from Vietnam was the collapse of military morale. Discipline among the troops eroded and drug use soared; in 1971, four times as many troops were hospitalized for drug overdoses as for combat-related wounds. Hundreds of disgruntled soldiers tried to kill or injure their officers. More than a million went AWOL (absent without leave) during the war, and almost a half million left military service with a less-than-honorable-discharge.

Revelations of atrocities committed by U.S. soldiers caused even the staunchest supporters of the war to wince. Late in 1969, the My Lai Massacre exposed the country to the tale of William L. "Rusty" Calley, a twenty-six-year-old army lieutenant who ordered the murder of 347 Vietnamese civilians in the village of My Lai in 1968. Calley himself killed some 50 unarmed Vietnamese. One soldier described it as "point-blank murder, and I was standing there watching it."

Newsmagazines published gruesome photos of the massacre, and Americans debated the issues it raised. A father in northern California grumbled that Calley "would have been a hero" in the Second World War. His son shot back: "Yeah, if you were a Nazi." Twenty-five army officers were charged with complicity in the massacre and subsequent cover-up, but only Calley was convicted. Nixon later granted him parole.

My Lai Massacre This wartime atrocity became a turning point in the Vietnam War. When the public learned that 347 unarmed Vietnamese civilians were killed in the village of My Lai by American soldiers, anti-war sentiment skyrocketed.

DIVISIONS AT HOME Just as Nixon had expected, the escalation of the air war in Vietnam and the extension of the war into Cambodia triggered widespread anti-war demonstrations. By late 1969, the diverse groups and individuals making up the anti-war movement had crystallized around a national effort known as the Moratorium to End the War in Vietnam. The effort centered on a national work stoppage that would enable huge numbers of people to engage in protest marches.

On October 15, 1969, the Moratorium mobilized marches in 200 cities by 2 million people. Wearing black armbands, they participated in nonviolent rallies, demonstrations, and candlelight vigils designed to force Nixon to remove U.S. forces sooner. Some 500,000 people crowded into the Washington Mall, where folk singer Pete Seeger led them in singing John Lennon's "Give Peace a Chance." It was the largest single demonstration in American history.

That night, 100,000 demonstrators participated in a candlelight march past the White House. Nixon, however, was unmoved by the behavior of such "bums." As he gruffly explained, "We expect it; however, under no circumstances will I be affected whatever by it."

KENT STATE AND JACKSON STATE In the spring of 1970, news of the secret Cambodian "incursion" by U.S. forces set off explosive protests on college campuses and across the nation. In Ohio, the governor sent the National Guard to Kent State University to control campus rioting. The poorly trained guardsmen panicked and opened fire on rock-throwing demonstrators, killing four student bystanders.

The widely publicized killings at Kent State added new fury to the anti-war and anti-Nixon movement. That spring, demonstrations occurred on more than 350 campuses. A presidential commission charged with investigating the shootings concluded that they were "unnecessary and unwarranted." Not all agreed, however. A resident of Kent told a reporter, "Anyone who appears on the streets of a city like Kent with long hair, dirty clothes, or barefooted deserves to be shot. . . . It would have been better if the Guard had shot the whole lot of them."

Singer/songwriter Neil Young had a different view. Shortly after the killings, he composed a song called "Ohio": "Tin soldiers and Nixon's coming. / We're finally on our own. / This summer I hear the drumming. / Four dead in Ohio." The Ohio governor banned radio stations from playing the song, which only made it more popular.

Eleven days after the Kent State tragedy, on May 15, Mississippi highway patrolmen riddled a dormitory at predominantly Black Jackson State College with bullets, killing two student protesters and wounding twelve others. In

New York City, anti-war demonstrators who gathered to protest the student deaths and the invasion of Cambodia were attacked by conservative "hard-hat" construction workers, many of them shouting "All the way, USA" and "America: Love it or leave it." They forced the protesters to disperse and then marched on City Hall to raise the U.S. flag, which had been lowered to half-staff in mourning for the Kent State victims. "Thank God for the hard hats," Nixon exclaimed.

It was later discovered that the Nixon White House had urged a New York labor union to recruit the 200 burly workers to confront the thousand protestors. Three weeks after the "Hard Hat Riot," Peter Brennan, head of the New York union of construction workers, visited the White House and gave Nixon a hard hat. In 1973, President Nixon named Brennan the new U.S. secretary of labor.

THE PENTAGON PAPERS In June 1971, the *New York Times* began publishing excerpts from *The History of U.S. Decision-Making Process on Vietnam Policy*, a secret Defense Department study commissioned by Robert McNamara before his resignation as Lyndon Johnson's secretary of defense in 1968. The so-called Pentagon Papers, leaked to the press by Daniel Ellsberg, a former marine and thereafter a Defense Department official, confirmed what many critics of the war had long suspected: Congress and the public had not received the full story on the Gulf of Tonkin incident of 1964. Plans for U.S. entry into the war were being drawn up even as President Johnson was promising that combat troops would never be sent to Vietnam.

Although the Pentagon Papers dealt with events only up to 1965, the Nixon administration blocked their publication, arguing that release of the classified information would endanger national security and would prolong the war. By a vote of 6–3, the Supreme Court ruled against the government. Newspapers throughout the country began publishing the controversial documents the next day.

WAR WITHOUT END During 1972, mounting social divisions at home and the approach of the presidential election influenced the negotiations in Paris between the United States and representatives of North Vietnam. In the summer of 1972, Henry Kissinger renewed private meetings with the North Vietnamese negotiators in Paris. He dropped his insistence upon the removal of all North Vietnamese troops from South Vietnam before the withdrawal of the remaining U.S. troops. On October 26, a week before the U.S. presidential election, a jubilant Kissinger announced that "peace is at hand."

As it turned out, however, Kissinger's announcement was a cynical ploy to win votes for Nixon's reelection bid. Several days earlier, the Thieu regime in South Vietnam had rejected the cease-fire plan, fearful that allowing North Vietnamese troops to remain in the south would guarantee a Communist victory. The peace talks broke off on December 16, and two days later the newly reelected Nixon ordered massive bombings of Hanoi and Haiphong, the two largest cities in North Vietnam. "The bastards have never been bombed like they're going to be this time," Nixon pledged.

The so-called Christmas bombings and the simultaneous U.S. decision to place underwater mines in North Vietnam's Haiphong harbor to prevent ships from offloading their cargoes aroused worldwide protests. The air strikes stopped on December 29, and the talks in Paris soon resumed. A month later on January 27, 1973, the United States, North and South Vietnam, and the Viet Cong signed an "agreement on ending the war and restoring peace in Vietnam," known as the Paris Peace Accords.

In fact, however, the agreement, which the U.S. Senate never ratified, was a carefully disguised surrender that enabled the United States to end its combat role. While Nixon and Kissinger claimed that the massive bombings had brought North Vietnam to its senses, in truth the North Vietnamese never altered their basic stance; they kept 150,000 troops in South Vietnam while forcing the United States to remove all its troops. What had changed was the willingness of the South Vietnamese leaders, who had not been allowed to participate in the negotiations, to accept the agreement based on Nixon's private pledge that the United States would respond "with full force" to any Communist violation of the agreement.

Between the time Nixon took office in 1969 and the signing of the Paris Peace Accords in 1973, another 20,000 American troops had died in Vietnam; the morale of the U.S. military had been shattered and millions of Southeast Asians had been killed, wounded, or displaced. Fighting soon broke out again in both Vietnam and Cambodia. In the end, the diplomatic efforts gained nothing the president could not have accomplished in 1969 by ending the war on similar terms.

THE COLLAPSE OF SOUTH VIETNAM On March 29, 1973, the last U.S. combat troops left Vietnam. The same day, the North Vietnamese released almost 600 U.S. prisoners of war. Within months, however, the cease-fire collapsed, the war resumed, and Communist forces gained the upper hand. In Cambodia (renamed the Khmer Republic after a 1970 military coup) and Laos, where fighting had been sporadic, a Communist victory seemed inevitable.

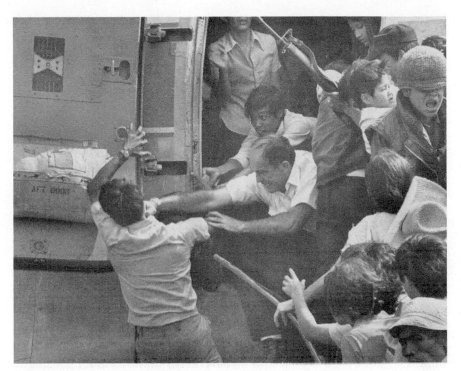

Leave with Honor Hundreds of thousands of South Vietnamese tried to flee the Communist forces with evacuating Americans. Here, a U.S. official punches a Vietnamese man attempting to join his family in an overflowing airplane at Nha Trang in April 1975.

In 1975, the North Vietnamese launched a full-scale invasion of South Vietnam, creating headlong panic. President Thieu appealed to Washington for the U.S. military assistance that Nixon had secretly promised him. But Congress, weary of spending dollars and lives in Vietnam, refused. On April 21, Thieu resigned and flew to Taiwan.

In the end, "peace with honor" had given the United States just enough time to remove itself before the collapse of the South Vietnamese government. On April 30, 1975, Americans watched on television as North Vietnamese tanks rolled into Saigon, soon to be renamed Ho Chi Minh City, and military helicopters airlifted U.S. embassy and South Vietnamese officials and their families to warships offshore.

The longest, most controversial, and least successful war in American history to that point was finally over. It left a bitter legacy. During the period of U.S. involvement, the combined death count for combatants and civilians reached nearly 2 million. North Vietnam absorbed incredible losses—some 600,000 soldiers and countless civilians. South Vietnam lost 240,000 soldiers, and more than 500,000 Vietnamese became refugees in the United States. More than 58,000 Americans died; another 300,000 were wounded, 2,500 were declared missing, and almost 100,000 returned missing one or more limbs. The United States spent more than $699 billion on the war.

The Vietnam War was the defining life event for the baby boomers, the generation that provided most of the U.S. troops as well as most of the anti-war protesters. The controversial war divided them in ways that would be felt for years. The "loss" of the war, combined with news of atrocities committed by American soldiers, eroded respect for the military so thoroughly that many young people came to regard military service as corrupting and dishonorable.

Vietnam veterans (average age nineteen, compared to twenty-six in the Second World War) had "lost" a war in which their country had lost interest. When they returned, many found even their families unwilling to talk about what the soldiers had experienced, or they themselves were embarrassed about their involvement in the war. "I went over there thinking I was doing something right and came back a bum," said Larry Langowski from Illinois. "I came back decked with medals on my uniform, and I got spit on by a hippie girl."

The Vietnam War, initially described as a crusade for democratic ideals, revealed that America's form of democracy was not easily transferable to regions of the world that lacked democratic traditions. And, as critics noted, imposed democracy is not democratic. Fought to contain the spread of communism, the war instead fragmented the national consensus that had governed U.S. foreign affairs since 1947, when President Truman developed policies to contain communism around the world.

As opposition to the war undermined Lyndon B. Johnson's presidency, it also created enduring fractures within the Democratic party. Said George McGovern, the anti-war senator and 1972 Democratic presidential nominee, "The Vietnam tragedy is at the root of the confusion and division of the Democratic party. It tore up our souls."

Not only had a decade of American effort in Vietnam proved costly and futile, but the Khmer Rouge, the insurgent Cambodian Communist movement, had also won a resounding victory over the U.S.-backed Khmer Republic, plunging the country into a horrific bloodbath. The maniacal Khmer Rouge leaders renamed the country Kampuchea and organized a campaign to destroy all their opponents, killing almost a third of the total population.

The Nixon Doctrine and a Thawing Cold War

Richard Nixon greatly preferred foreign policy to domestic policy (which he compared to building "sewer projects"), and his greatest successes were in international relations. Nixon was an expert in foreign affairs, and he benefited greatly from the strategic vision of Henry Kissinger. Their grand design for U.S. foreign policy after the Vietnam War centered on developing friendly relations with the Soviet Union and Communist China while using the CIA to intervene in the politics of less developed nations. Kissinger said they wanted to "improve the possibilities of accommodations with each as we increase our options with both," enabling all three superpowers to reduce the cost of the arms race while minimizing the possibility of nuclear war.

THE CIA IN CHILE Henry Kissinger pressed for a return to an Eisenhower-era approach to foreign policy that entailed using the Central Intelligence Agency to pursue America's strategic interests covertly while reducing large-scale military interventions.

After Fidel Castro and his supporters gained control of Cuba in 1959, American presidents had been determined to prevent any more Communist insurgencies in the Western Hemisphere. In 1970, Salvador Allende, a Socialist party leader, friend of Castro, and critic of the United States, was a leading presidential candidate in Chile. Kissinger and President Nixon knew that, if elected, Allende planned to take control of Chilean industries owned by U.S. corporations, just as Fidel Castro had done after seizing power in Cuba in 1959.

Nixon urged the CIA to do anything necessary to prevent an Allende presidency. Although CIA agents provided campaign funds to his opponents, Allende was democratically elected on October 24, 1970. The CIA then encouraged Chilean military leaders to oust him. In September 1973, the army took control, Allende either committed suicide or was murdered, and General Augusto Pinochet, a ruthless dictator supposedly friendly to the United States, declared himself head of the government. Within a few months, Pinochet had taken over dozens of U.S.-owned businesses in Chile. For the next sixteen years, Pinochet kept Chile in a grip of authoritarian terror. Thousands of his political opponents were rounded up, tortured, and never heard from again.

It was yet another example of the United States being so obsessed by anti-communism and protecting American business interests that it was willing to interfere in the democratic process of other nations. Kissinger, now secretary of state, told Nixon that the CIA "didn't do it," but "we helped" put Pinochet in office by creating the conditions that made the coup possible.

THE NIXON DOCTRINE In July 1969, while announcing the first troop withdrawals from Vietnam, President Nixon unveiled what came to be called the Nixon Doctrine. Unlike John F. Kennedy, who had declared that the United States would "pay any price, bear any burden" to win the Cold War, Nixon explained that "America cannot—and will not—conceive *all* the plans, design *all* the programs, execute *all* the decisions, and undertake *all* the defense of the free nations of the world." Other nations had to do more. Under the Nixon Doctrine, the United States would support "proxy warfare," providing weapons and money to fend off Communist insurgencies, but not American troops.

At the same time, Nixon announced that he would pursue partnerships with Communist countries in areas of mutual interest. That Nixon, with his history of rabid anti-communism, would embrace such a policy of **détente** (a French word meaning "easing of relations") shocked many and demonstrated yet again his pragmatic flexibility.

THE PEOPLE'S REPUBLIC OF CHINA Richard Nixon had an exquisite gift for doing the unexpected. In 1971, the president told Henry Kissinger, his national security advisor, to make a secret trip to Beijing to explore the possibility of U.S. recognition of Communist China, the most populous nation in the world, with over 800 million people. Kissinger was flabbergasted. He told his staff that "our leader has taken leave of reality. He thinks this is the moment to establish normal relations with Communist China."

Since 1949, when Mao Zedong's revolutionary movement established control of China, the United States, with Nixon's hearty support, had refused even to recognize the People's Republic of China, preferring to regard Chiang Kai-shek's exiled regime on Taiwan as the legitimate Chinese government.

Now, however, Nixon felt the time was ripe for a bold renewal of ties. Both the United States and Communist China were exhausted from domestic strife (anti-war protests in America, the Cultural Revolution in China), and both were eager to resist Soviet expansionism. Most of all, Nixon relished the shock effect of his action, which he told senior aide John Ehrlichman would "discombobulate" the "god-damned liberals."

Nixon's announcement on July 15, 1971, that Kissinger had just returned from Beijing and that the president himself would be going to China the following year, stunned the world and began the slow process of normalizing relations with Communist China. Nixon became the first U.S. president to publicly use the term *People's Republic of China*, a symbolic step in normalizing relations. The Nationalist Chinese on the island of Taiwan felt betrayed by Nixon's actions, and the Japanese, historic enemies of China, were furious.

Nixon Goes to China President Nixon and Chinese premier Zhou Enlai raise a toast to each other at the lavish farewell banquet in Shanghai that rounded off the historic visit.

In October 1971, the United Nations voted to admit the People's Republic of China and expel Taiwan.

On February 21, 1972, during the "week that changed the world," Nixon arrived in Beijing. Americans watched on television as the president shook hands and drank toasts with Prime Minister Zhou Enlai and Communist party chairman Mao Zedong. In one simple but astonishing initiative, Nixon and Kissinger had ended two decades of diplomatic isolation of the People's Republic of China.

During the president's week-long visit, the two nations agreed to scientific and cultural exchanges and outlined steps toward resuming trade. Nixon also secretly assured the Chinese leaders that the U.S. would support the eventual reunification of Taiwan with the mainland. A year later, "liaison offices" that served as unofficial embassies were established in Washington and Beijing. In 1979, diplomatic recognition was officially formalized.

Nixon's bold transformation of relations with Communist China virtually ensured his reelection, transformed superpower politics, opened China to the outside world, and dazzled the media. As a conservative anti-Communist, Nixon had accomplished a diplomatic feat that his Democratic predecessors could not have attempted for fear of being branded "soft" on communism. Nixon's and Kissinger's daring move gave them leverage with the Soviet Union, which was understandably nervous about a U.S.-Chinese alliance. Nixon had grown convinced that the last third of the twentieth century would be "an era of negotiation rather than confrontation" among the superpowers.

EMBRACING THE SOVIET UNION   China welcomed the breakthrough with America in part because of tensions with the Soviet Union, with which it shared a long but contested border. By 1972, the Chinese had become more fearful of the Soviet Union than of the United States.

The Soviets were also eager to ease tensions with the Americans. In 1972, President Nixon again surprised the world by announcing that he would visit Moscow for discussions with Leonid Brezhnev, the Soviet premier. The high drama of the China visit was repeated in Moscow, with toasts and dinners attended by world leaders who had previously regarded each other as incarnations of evil.

Nixon and Brezhnev signed the pathbreaking **Strategic Arms Limitation Treaty (SALT I)**, which negotiators had been working on since 1969. The agreement did not end the nuclear arms race, but it did limit the number of missiles with nuclear warheads and prohibited the construction of missile-defense systems. The Moscow summit also produced new trade agreements, including an arrangement whereby the United States sold almost a quarter of its wheat crop to the Soviets at a favorable price.

The Moscow summit resulted in a dramatic easing of tensions. As Nixon told Congress upon his return, "never before have two adversaries, so deeply divided by conflicting ideologies and political rivalries, been able to limit the armaments upon which their survival depends." Over time, détente with the Soviet Union would help end the Cold War by lowering Soviet hostility to Western influences, which in turn slowly eroded Communist rule from the inside.

Taken together, the Nixon-Kissinger efforts to pursue détente with the Soviet Union and official recognition of Communist China were the harmonizing halves of a bold new geopolitical strategy to replace the Cold War against communism with an American effort to play the two largest Communist nations against one another. As Kissinger said to Nixon, they should use "China as a counterweight to Russia."

SHUTTLE DIPLOMACY   The long-standing American commitment to the security of Israel continued to infuriate Arab nations eager to engineer the Jewish nation's destruction. In late May 1967, Israeli intelligence services discovered that Egypt, Jordan, Iraq, and Palestinian forces were preparing an attack. On June 5, Israeli forces launched a preemptive air strike, destroying most of Egypt's and Syria's warplanes. Israeli tanks and infantry then captured the Gaza Strip, much of Egypt's Sinai Peninsula, the West Bank of the Jordan River, and East Jerusalem.

After just six days of fighting, the Arab nations requested a cease fire, which the United Nations helped to negotiate. Egypt, Syria, and Jordan had suffered more than 18,000 killed or wounded, compared with 700 for Israel.

The lopsided Six-Day War had long-range consequences, as the Israelis took control of strategic Syrian and Egyptian territories that almost doubled the nation's size. More important, the war launched a new phase in the perennial conflict between Israel and the nationless Palestinians. The brief conflict uprooted hundreds of thousands of Palestinian refugees and brought more than 1 million Palestinians in the occupied territories under Israeli rule.

The Nixon-Kissinger initiatives in the Middle East were less dramatic and less conclusive than those in China and the Soviet Union, but they showed that the United States at last recognized the legitimacy of Arab interests in the region and America's dependence upon Middle Eastern oil.

But the Arab-Israeli conflict continued to ignite periodic warfare. On October 6, 1973, Syria and Egypt, backed by Saudi Arabia and armed with Soviet weapons, attacked Israel, triggering what became the Yom Kippur War. It created the most dangerous confrontation between the United States and the Soviet Union since the Cuban missile crisis. When the Israeli army, with weapons supplied by the United States, launched a fierce counterattack that threatened to overwhelm Egypt, the Soviets prepared to intervene militarily.

As the crisis unfolded, Nixon was bedridden because he was drunk, according to Henry Kissinger and other aides, so Kissinger, as secretary of state, presided over a National Security Council meeting that placed America's military forces on full alert.

On October 20, Kissinger flew to Moscow to meet with Soviet premier Brezhnev. Kissinger skillfully negotiated a cease-fire agreement and exerted pressure on the Israelis to prevent them from taking additional Arab territory. Then, to broker a lasting settlement, he made numerous flights among the capitals of the Middle East. His "shuttle diplomacy" won acclaim from all sides, although he failed to find a comprehensive formula for peace. He did, however, lay the groundwork for an important treaty between Israel and Egypt in 1977.

WATERGATE

Richard Nixon's foreign policy achievements allowed him to stage the presidential campaign of 1972 as a triumphal procession. Early on, the main threat to his reelection came from George Wallace, who had the potential as a third-party candidate to deprive the Republicans of conservative southern votes and thereby throw the election to the Democrats. That threat ended, however, on May 15, 1972, when Wallace, while campaigning in Maryland, was shot by a twenty-one-year-old drifter named Arthur Bremer. Although Wallace survived the assassination attempt, he was left paralyzed below the waist and had to withdraw from the campaign. Nixon ordered aides to plant a false story that Democrats had orchestrated Wallace's assassination.

The Democratic candidate was Senator George McGovern of South Dakota, an anti-war liberal who had been a World War II bomber pilot. "George is the most decent man in the Senate," Robert Kennedy had said. "As a matter of fact, he is the only decent man." Decency does not win elections, however. McGovern was a poor campaigner, and many dismissed him as a left-wing extremist when he announced his simplistic plan to give every American $1,000 to help close the growing gap between rich and poor. Nixon also defused the Vietnam War as the central issue in the campaign, emphasizing that he had brought more than 500,000 troops home from Vietnam. By Election Day, only 20,000 U.S. military personnel remained in South Vietnam.

In the 1972 election, Nixon won the greatest victory of any Republican presidential candidate in history, capturing 520 electoral votes to only 17 for McGovern. The popular vote was equally decisive: 46 million to 28 million, a proportion of the total vote (60.8 percent) second only to Lyndon Johnson's victory over Barry Goldwater in 1964. McGovern later wrote that political pundits dismissed his failed candidacy as "'graceless,' 'bumbling,' 'a debacle,' 'a disaster,' and 'a catastrophe,'" all of which were accurate descriptors. The only downside for the Republicans was that the Democrats maintained control of Congress.

For all of Nixon's abilities and accomplishments, however, he remained chronically insecure. He later admitted that he was a "paranoiac" who had become "almost a basket case" by 1972. He told Henry Kissinger that the young radicals protesting in the streets "hate us, the country, themselves, their wives, everything they do—these liberals are a lost generation. They have no reason to live anymore."

More than most presidents, Nixon nursed grudges and took politics personally, and he could be ruthless—even criminal—in attacking his opponents. As president, he began keeping a secret "enemies list" and launched numerous efforts to embarrass and punish those on the list. He also approved illegal plans to break into the offices of his opponents. Little did Nixon know that such behavior would bring his second term crashing down around him.

THE NIXON ADMINISTRATION AND "DIRTY TRICKS"

White House aide John Ehrlichman continued to oversee the secret team of "dirty tricksters" who performed absurd pranks and various acts of partisan sabotage, such as falsely accusing Democratic senators Hubert H. Humphrey and Henry Jackson of sexual improprieties, forging press releases, setting off stink bombs at Democratic campaign events, planting spies on George McGovern's campaign plane, ordering illegal wiretaps on Nixon's opponents (as well as on his own aides), and trying to coerce the Internal Revenue Service to intimidate Democrats. Charles "Chuck" Colson, one of the most active "dirty tricksters," admitted that "we did a hell of a lot of things and never got caught." But he had no regrets. He said he would "walk over his grandmother" if it would help Nixon stay in power.

Others, however, were caught. On June 17, 1972, police in Washington, D.C., captured five burglars breaking into the Democratic National Committee headquarters in the sprawling **Watergate** hotel-apartment-office complex. The burglars were all former CIA agents; four were Miami-based Cuban exiles, and the other, James W. McCord, was the Nixon campaign's security director. Two others—Gordon Liddy and E. Howard Hunt—were arrested while directing the break-in from a hotel across the street. The purpose of the break-in was to plant illegal listening devices on phones in the Democratic party offices.

Nixon and his staff dismissed the incident as a "third-rate burglary." The president denied any involvement, but he was lying; he told Alexander Haig, then his national security adviser, that "we will cover up [the Watergate burglary] until hell freezes over."

To protect Nixon, White House aides secretly provided $350,000 in "hush money" to the jailed burglars, only to learn that they demanded $1 million. Nixon responded that "they have to be paid." The president and his aides also discussed using the CIA to derail the Justice Department's investigation of the burglary. Bob Haldeman, Nixon's chief of staff, told the FBI to quit investigating the incident, falsely claiming that it involved a secret CIA operation. Meanwhile, White House spokesmen lied to journalists and destroyed evidence.

Nixon encouraged the cover-up, stressing that his "main concern is to keep the White House out of it." In August 1972, he told reporters that his own investigation into the Watergate incident had confirmed that no one in the White House or the administration was involved—when in fact, there was no such investigation.

UNCOVERING THE COVER-UP During the trial of the accused Watergate burglars in January 1973, relentless questioning by federal judge John J. Sirica, a Nixon supporter and hard-nosed jurist with the nickname "Maximum John" because of his reputation for issuing harsh sentences, led one of the accused to tell the full story. James W. McCord, security chief of the

Committee to Re-Elect the President (CREEP), was the first in what would become a long line of informers to reveal Nixon's systematic efforts to create an "imperial presidency." By the time of the Watergate break-in, money to finance such dirty tricks was being illegally collected through CREEP and controlled by the White House staff.

The trail of evidence was pursued first by Judge Sirica, then by a grand jury, then by the *Washington Post*, and finally by a Senate committee headed by Democrat Samuel J. Ervin Jr. of North Carolina. The investigations led directly to what White House legal counsel John Dean called a "cancer close to the Presidency." By this point, Nixon was using his presidential powers to block the investigation. He ordered the CIA to keep the FBI off the case and coached his aides on how to lie under oath. Most alarming, as it turned out, the Watergate burglary was merely part of a larger pattern of corruption and criminality sanctioned by the White House.

The cover-up crumbled as people involved began to cooperate with prosecutors. James McCord admitted to Sirica that the White House had provided the burglars' hush money and that witnesses had lied at the trial. He then provided names of those orchestrating the cover-up, including Attorney General John Mitchell and Nixon's chief of staff, Bob Haldeman. This led other White House aides to confess their role in the burglary and the cover-up. At the same time, two reporters for the *Washington Post*, Carl Bernstein and Bob Woodward, relentlessly pursued the story, eventually making it a compelling topic of national conversation. Still, Nixon continued to lie, telling Americans that he condemned "any attempt to cover up this case."

The cover-up unraveled further in 1973 when L. Patrick Gray, acting director of the FBI, resigned after confessing that he had destroyed incriminating documents at the behest of the president. On April 30, Ehrlichman and Haldeman also resigned (they would later serve time in prison), as did Attorney General Richard Kleindienst. A few days later, Nixon nervously assured the public in a television address, "I am not a crook." Then John Dean, the White House legal counsel whom Nixon had dismissed because of his cooperation with prosecutors, shocked the nation. He told the Ervin committee that there had been a White House cover-up approved by the president himself. Suddenly, Dean became the Ervin Committee's star witness, for he knew all the Watergate secrets. He provided damning testimony in exchange for a reduced prison sentence for obstruction of justice.

Nixon thereafter behaved like a cornered lion. He refused to provide Senator Ervin's committee with documents it requested, citing "executive privilege" to protect national security. Then, in another shocking disclosure, a White House aide told the committee that Nixon had installed a secret taping system in the White House, meaning that many of the conversations about the Watergate burglary and cover-up had been recorded. Haldeman explained to Ehrlichman that Nixon wanted his conversations recorded to prove that he, not Henry Kissinger, was the architect of the administration's foreign policy successes.

The bombshell news of the secret recordings set off a feverish legal battle for the "Nixon tapes." The Watergate affair was no longer about a burglary but a struggle over recorded evidence of Nixon's efforts to obstruct justice. Harvard law professor Archibald Cox, whom Nixon's new attorney general, Elliot Richardson, had appointed as special prosecutor to investigate the Watergate case, took the president to court in October 1973 to obtain the tapes. Nixon refused to release the recordings and ordered Cox fired.

On October 20, in what became known as the "Saturday Night Massacre," Richardson and his deputy, William Ruckelshaus, resigned rather than fire Cox. (Solicitor General Robert Bork finally fired him.) Cox's dismissal produced a firestorm of public indignation. Numerous newspapers and magazines, as well as a growing chorus of legislators, called for the president to resign or be impeached for obstructing justice. A Gallup poll revealed that Nixon's approval rating had plunged to 17 percent, the lowest in presidential history. John Chancellor, the NBC News anchor, announced on air that "the

Watergate Scandal A demonstration outside the White House calls on Congress to impeach President Nixon for his illegal actions.

country tonight is in the midst of what may be the most serious constitutional crisis in its history."

Still, Nixon pledged neither to resign nor turn over the tapes. The new special prosecutor, Leon Jaworski, a prominent Texas attorney, also took the president to court to get the Oval Office recordings. In March 1974, the Watergate grand jury indicted Ehrlichman, Haldeman, and former attorney general John Mitchell for obstruction of justice and named Nixon an "unindicted co-conspirator."

On April 30, Nixon, still refusing to turn over the tapes, released 1,254 pages of transcribed recordings that he had edited himself, often substituting the phrase "expletive deleted" for his vulgar language and rants about Jews and Blacks. ("People said my language was bad," Nixon later rationalized, "but Jesus, you should have heard LBJ!") The transcripts revealed a president whose conversations were so petty, self-serving, bigoted, and profane that they degraded the presidency. At one point in the transcripts, the president told his aides to have frequent memory lapses when testifying.

THE NIXON TAPES   By the summer of 1974, Nixon was in full retreat. He became alternately combative, melancholy, and petty, and his efforts to orchestrate the cover-up obsessed, unbalanced, and unhinged him. Henry Kissinger found him increasingly unstable and drinking heavily. After meeting with the president, Senator Barry Goldwater reported that Nixon "jabbered incessantly, often incoherently." He seemed "to be cracking."

On July 24, 1974, the Supreme Court ruled unanimously that the president must surrender *all* the tape recordings. A few days later, the House Judiciary Committee voted to recommend three articles of impeachment: obstruction of justice through the payment of hush money to witnesses and the withholding of evidence; abuse of power through the use of federal agencies to deprive citizens of their constitutional rights; and defiance of Congress by withholding the tapes. The president, chief of staff Alexander Haig confided to White House aides, was "guilty as hell." He then told Nixon that he did not "see how we can survive this one."

Before the House of Representatives could vote on impeachment, Nixon grudgingly handed over the tapes. The drama continued, however, when investigators learned that segments of several recordings were missing, including eighteen minutes of a damning conversation in June 1972 during which Nixon first mentioned the Watergate burglary.

The president's loyal secretary took the blame for the erasure, claiming that she had accidentally pushed the wrong button, but technical experts later concluded that the missing segments had been intentionally deleted. The other recordings, however, provided more than enough evidence of Nixon's involvement in the cover-up. At one point, he had yelled at aides who were asking what they and others should say to Watergate investigators: "I don't give a shit what happens. I want you all to stonewall it, let them plead the Fifth [Amendment], cover up or anything else."

The incriminating recordings led Republican leaders to decide that the embattled president must resign for the good of the country rather than face a Senate impeachment trial. "There are only so many lies you can take and now there has been one too many," Senator Barry Goldwater concluded. "Nixon should get his ass out of the White House—today."

V for "Victory" Before boarding the White House helicopter following his resignation, Nixon flashes a bright smile and his trademark V for Victory sign to the world on August 9, 1974.

On August 9, 1974, Nixon did just that. He resigned from office, the only president to do so.

Nixon had begun his presidency promising to heal a fractured America. He left the White House having orchestrated the most pervasive corruption in American political history. A London newspaper explained that America had digressed "from George Washington, who could not tell a lie, to Richard Nixon, who could not tell the truth."

Nixon never understood why the Watergate affair could have ended his presidency; in his view, his only mistake was getting caught. Nixon claimed that a president's actions could not be "illegal." He was wrong. The Watergate affair's clearest lesson was that not even a president is above the law. But while the system worked by calling a president to justice, many Americans lost faith in the credibility of elected officials. The *New York Times* reported that people "think and feel differently from what they once did" as a result of the Watergate crisis. "They ask questions, they reject assumptions, they doubt what they are told."

WATERGATE AND THE PRESIDENCY If there was a silver lining in the dark cloud of Watergate, it was the vigor and resilience of the institutions that had brought a rogue president to justice—the press, Congress, the courts, and public opinion. In the aftermath of the scandal, Congress passed several pieces of legislation designed to curb executive power. Nervous about possible efforts to renew military assistance to South Vietnam, the Democratic Congress passed the **War Powers Act (1973)** over President Nixon's veto. It requires a president to inform Congress within forty-eight hours if U.S. troops are deployed in combat abroad and to withdraw them after sixty days unless Congress specifically approves their stay or passes a declaration of war.

Then, to correct abuses in the use of campaign funds, Congress enacted legislation in 1974 that set new ceilings on political campaign contributions and expenditures. And in reaction to the Nixon claim of "executive privilege" as a means of withholding evidence, Congress strengthened the 1966 Freedom of Information Act to require prompt responses to requests for information from government files and to place on government agencies the burden of proof for classifying information as secret.

AN UNELECTED PRESIDENT   During Richard Nixon's last year in office, the Watergate crisis so dominated national politics that major domestic and foreign problems received little attention.

Vice President Spiro Agnew had himself been forced to resign in October 1973 for accepting bribes from Maryland contractors before and during his term in office. The vice president at the time of Nixon's resignation was Gerald Rudolph Ford, a square-jawed, plain-speaking former House minority leader from Michigan whom Nixon had appointed to succeed Agnew under the provisions of the Twenty-Fifth Amendment.

On August 9, 1974, Ford, an honest, amiable, and decent man who held a law degree from Yale, was sworn in as the nation's chief executive, the only person in history to serve as both vice president and president without having been elected to those offices. "I am acutely aware that you have not elected me as your President by your ballots," Ford said in a televised address. "So I ask you to confirm me as your President with your prayers." He then assured the nation that "our long national nightmare [Watergate] is over. Our Constitution works!"

But less than a month after taking office, Ford reopened the wounds of Watergate by issuing Nixon a "full, free, and absolute pardon" for any crimes he may have committed while in office.

Ford's pardon unleashed a storm of controversy. "Jail Ford!" yelled protesters outside the White House. A House subcommittee grilled the new president, wanting to know whether Nixon had made a secret deal for the pardon. Ford vigorously denied the charge, but others wondered why he had pardoned someone who had not been charged with a crime. The *Washington*

Post declared that Ford's decision was "nothing less than the continuation of a cover-up," while the *New York Times* dismissed the pardon as "profoundly unwise, divisive, and unjust."

The controversial pardon hobbled Ford's presidency. Ford stated that he had issued the pardon so that the country could move forward and heal, but doing what he had thought was the best thing for the country made him suspect in the eyes of many voters. His approval rating plummeted from 71 percent to 49 percent in one day, the steepest drop ever recorded. His press secretary resigned in protest of the "Nixon pardon."

THE FORD PRESIDENCY As president, Gerald Ford continued the role he had developed as minority leader in the House of Representatives: nay-saying leader of the opposition who believed the federal government exercised too much power. In his first fifteen months as president, Ford vetoed thirty-nine bills passed by the Democratic-controlled Congress, outstripping Herbert Hoover's all-time veto record in less than half the time.

By far the most important issue during Ford's brief presidency was the struggling economy. In the fall of 1974, the nation entered its deepest recession since the Great Depression. Unemployment jumped to 9 percent in 1975, the rate of inflation reached double digits, and the federal budget deficit hit a record. Ford announced that inflation had become "Public Enemy No. 1," but instead of taking bold action, he launched a timid public relations campaign featuring lapel buttons that simply read WIN, symbolizing the administration's determination to "Whip Inflation Now." The WIN buttons became a national joke. Alan Greenspan, chair of the Federal Reserve Board, dismissed the WIN campaign as a silly publicity stunt. The millions of WIN buttons left in warehouses became embarrassing symbols of Ford's ineffectiveness.

Gerald Ford The thirty-eighth president dealt with rising rates of unemployment and inflation in 1974.

In his State of the Union address in 1975, Ford conceded that "the state of the union is not good." The economic recession was now his greatest concern, not inflation. In March 1975, Ford signed a tax-reduction bill that failed to stimulate economic growth. The federal budget deficit grew from $53 billion in 1975 to $74 billion in 1976.

In foreign policy, Ford retained Henry Kissinger as secretary of state (while stripping him of his dual role as national security adviser). He continued to pursue Nixon's goals of stability in the Middle East, friendly relations with China, and détente with the Soviet Union. Kissinger's tireless Middle East diplomacy produced an important agreement: Israel promised to return to Egypt most of the Sinai territory captured in the 1967 war, and the two nations agreed to rely on diplomacy rather than force to settle future disagreements.

These limited but significant achievements, however, were drowned in the criticism over the collapse of the South Vietnamese government in the face of the North Vietnamese invasion. In early 1975, President Ford, just days after giving a speech at Tulane University in which he declared that the Vietnam War "is finished as far as America is concerned," asked Congress for more military assistance for a desperate South Vietnam, only to be turned down by the Senate. In April, North Vietnamese tanks and soldiers captured Saigon, the South Vietnamese capital. There would now be only one Vietnam—a Communist one.

At the same time, conservative Republicans led by Ronald Reagan lambasted Ford and Kissinger for their policy of détente toward the Soviet Union. Reagan argued that the efforts of Nixon, Kissinger, and Ford were helping to ensure the continued existence of the Soviet Union rather than accelerating its self-destruction.

THE 1976 ELECTION Both political parties were in disarray as they prepared for the 1976 presidential election. Gerald Ford had to fend off a challenge from the darling of the Republican party's growing conservative wing, Ronald Reagan, a former two-term California governor and Hollywood actor. In the end, Ford narrowly won the nomination, whereupon he invited Reagan to join him at the podium in a show of party unity. Reagan, however, seized the microphone to deliver a fiery speech preparing the party for his seeking the nomination in 1980.

The Democrats chose a little-known candidate, James "Jimmy" Carter Jr., who had served one term as governor of Georgia. When Carter told his mother he was running for president, she replied: "President of *what*?" Tip O'Neill, the Democratic Speaker of the House, dismissed Carter as "a complete unknown."

Yet Carter did have several assets. A former naval officer and engineer turned peanut farmer who had been raised in a farmhouse with no electricity or running water, he was one of several southern Democratic governors who sought to move their party away from its traditional "tax and spend" liberalism. The federal government, Carter charged, was a "horrible, bloated, confused . . . bureaucratic mess." The Great Society social welfare programs created by LBJ were a "failure" that were in "urgent need of a complete over-haul." He supported the death penalty, opposed abortion rights and the use of busing to achieve racially integrated schools, and showed little sympathy for labor unions. "I was never a liberal," he explained. "I am and have always been a conservative."

Carter capitalized on post-Watergate cynicism about Washington politicos by promising that he would "never tell a lie to the American people." He also trumpeted his status as a political "outsider," and reporters covering the campaign marveled at a Southern Baptist candidate who was a "born again" Christian.

A poll found that voters viewed Gerald Ford as "a nice guy," but "not . . . very smart about the issues the country is facing." Ford reinforced that impression during a televised debate with Carter when he mistakenly claimed that "there is no Soviet domination of Eastern Europe."

Carter revived the New Deal voting alliance of southern Whites, Blacks, urban labor unionists, and ethnic groups such as Jews and Latinos to eke out a narrow win, receiving 41 million votes to Ford's 39 million. A heavy turnout of African Americans in the South enabled Carter to sweep every state in the region except Virginia. He also benefited from the appeal of Walter F. Mondale, his liberal running mate and a favorite among blue-collar workers and the urban poor. Ford was the first president to lose his bid for reelection since Herbert Hoover in 1932.

The most significant story of the election, however, was the low voter turn-out. Almost half the eligible voters chose to sit out the election, the lowest turnout since the Second World War.

In explaining why he had not cast a vote, one man noted that he was "a three-time loser. In 1964 I voted for the peace candidate—Johnson—and got war. In '68 I voted for the law-and-order candidate—and got crime. In '72 I voted for Nixon again, and we got Watergate." Such an alienated voter was not a good omen for a new Democratic president about to begin his first term as head of the nation.

CHAPTER REVIEW

Summary

- **Youth Revolt**   Civil rights activism inspired a heightened interest in social causes during the 1960s, especially among the youth. Students for a Democratic Society (SDS) embodied the *New Left* ideology, and their ideas and tactics spread to many campuses. By 1970, a distinctive *counterculture* had emerged among disaffected youth and attracted hippies, many of whom used mind-altering drugs, lived on rural communes, and refused conventional life, which they viewed as corrupt and constricting.

- **The Inspirational Effects of the Civil Rights Movement**   The civil rights movement inspired many other social reform movements, including the *women's movement*, the *Red Power* movement, and the *United Farm Workers (UFW)*. In 1973, women's lives were transformed when the Supreme Court in *Roe v. Wade* struck down state laws banning abortions during the first trimester of a pregnancy, ruling that women had a "right to choose" whether to bear a child. The 1969 *Stonewall Uprising* marked a militant new era in the crusade for gay rights.

- **Reaction and Domestic Agenda**   Richard Nixon's "southern strategy" took advantage of the backlash against these liberal politics and cultural movements to win election in 1968 with the conservative southern vote. As president, he sought to slow the momentum of *affirmative-action* programs intended to benefit minorities, but in 1970 he created the *Environmental Protection Agency (EPA)*. Both the Nixon and Ford administrations were unable to overcome *stagflation*.

- **End of the Vietnam War**   In his 1968 campaign, Nixon pledged to secure "peace with honor" in Vietnam, but years would pass before the war ended. He did change the military strategy in Vietnam by implementing *Vietnamization*: increasing aid to South Vietnam and aggressively bombing North Vietnam, while attempting to negotiate a cease-fire with North Vietnam. North and South Vietnam agreed to a cease-fire called the Paris Peace Accords. In 1975, the South Vietnamese government collapsed after a massive North Vietnamese invasion. The Communist victors forcibly reunited the North and South.

- **Détente**   Nixon's greatest accomplishments were in foreign policy. As an aggressive anti-Communist, he shocked the world by opening diplomatic relations with Communist China and pursuing *détente* with the Soviet Union, focusing on areas of shared agreement with the 1972 *Strategic Arms Limitation Treaty (SALT I)*.

- **Watergate**   During the 1972 presidential campaign, the Committee to Re-Elect the President (CREEP) was implicated in the *Watergate* burglary. In *United States v. Richard M. Nixon* (1974), the Supreme Court ruled that Nixon had to surrender the recordings of White House meetings dealing with the scandal. Nixon resigned in 1974 to avoid impeachment. Democrats in Congress passed the *War Powers Act* (1973), designed to limit the ability of presidents to wage war in the absence of a congressional declaration of war.

CHRONOLOGY

1960	Students for a Democratic Society (SDS) founded
1963	Betty Friedan's *The Feminine Mystique* published
1965	United Farm Workers (UFW) established
	Forced integration of Mississippi schools
1966	National Organization for Women (NOW) founded
1967–1968	Inner-city riots; student sit-ins on college campuses
1968	Riots at the Democratic National Convention
	American Indian Movement (AIM) founded
	Richard M. Nixon elected president
March 1969	U.S. warplanes bomb Cambodia
June 1969	Stonewall Uprising in New York City
August 1969	Woodstock music festival attracts more than 400,000 people
1970	Kent State and Jackson State shootings
	EPA created; Clean Air Act
1971	Pentagon Papers published
1972	Nixon visits China and the Soviet Union, signs the Strategic Arms Limitation Talks (SALT I) treaty
1972–1974	Watergate scandal unfolds
1973	Sioux occupation of Wounded Knee, South Dakota
	U.S. troop withdrawal from Vietnam completed
	Roe v. Wade allows abortion
1974	Nixon resigns; Gerald Ford becomes president
April 1975	Saigon falls to the North Vietnamese
1976	Jimmy Carter elected president

KEY TERMS

New Left p. 1419

counterculture p. 1424

women's movement p. 1432

Roe v. Wade (1973) p. 1438

United Farm Workers (UFW) p. 1441

Red Power p. 1444

Stonewall Uprising (1969) p. 1446

affirmative action p. 1449

Environmental Protection Agency (EPA) p. 1455

stagflation p. 1455

Vietnamization p. 1458

détente p. 1466

Strategic Arms Limitation Treaty (SALT I) p. 1468

Watergate (1972–1974) p. 1471

War Powers Act (1973) p. 1476

INQUIZITIVE

Go to InQuizitive to see what you've learned—and learn what you've missed—with personalized feedback along the way.

29 Conservative Revival

1977–2000

Feels Good to Be Right This proud Republican and Reagan supporter lets her decorated top hat adorned with campaign buttons speak for her at the 1980 Republican National Convention. Held in Detroit, Michigan, the convention nominated former California governor Ronald Reagan, who promised to "make America great again."

D uring the seventies, the United States lost much of its self-confidence. The failed Vietnam War; the sordid revelations of the Watergate scandal; and the spike in oil prices, interest rates, and consumer prices revealed the limits of the nation's power, prosperity, and virtue. Surveys showed that Americans felt defensive and dispirited about their nation and its prospects in what journalists were calling a new "age of limits." For a nation long accustomed to economic growth and spreading prosperity, the persistence of stagflation and gasoline shortages exasperated Americans used to being a people of plenty. Even in July 1976, as the United States celebrated the bicentennial of its independence, many people were downsizing their expectations of the American dream.

President Jimmy Carter took office in 1977 promising a government that would be "competent" as well as "decent, open, fair, and compassionate." After four years as president, however, Carter had little to show for his efforts. The economy remained sluggish, consumer prices continued to increase at historic levels, and failed efforts to free Americans held hostage in Iran prompted critics, including Democrats, to denounce the administration as being indecisive and inept. In the end, Carter's call for "a time of national austerity" revealed both his ineffective legislative skills and his misreading of the public mood.

The Republicans capitalized on the public frustration with Jimmy Carter by electing Ronald Reagan president in 1980. Where Carter had denounced the evils of unregulated capitalism, Reagan promised to revive the capitalist

focus questions

1. Why did Jimmy Carter have such limited success as president?

2. What factors led to the election of Ronald Reagan, the rise of the modern conservative movement, and the resurgence of the Republican party?

3. What is "Reaganomics"? What were its effects on American society and economy?

4. How did Reagan's Soviet strategy help end the Cold War?

5. What economic and social issues and innovations emerged during the 1980s?

6. What was the impact of the end of the Cold War and the efforts of President George H. W. Bush to create a post–Cold War foreign policy?

7. What were the accomplishments and setbacks of Bill Clinton's presidency?

spirit, restore national pride, and regain international respect. He did all that and more. During his two-term presidency in the 1980s, he transformed the political landscape. Reagan accelerated the conservative resurgence in politics and set in motion the forces that would cause the collapse of the Soviet Union and the end of the Cold War.

The Carter Presidency

James "Jimmy" Earl Carter Jr. won the close 1976 election over Gerald Ford because he convinced voters that he was an incorruptible political "outsider," a born-again Christian of pure motives who would restore integrity and honesty to the presidency in the aftermath of the Watergate scandal. A former Georgia governor (1971–1975), he represented a new generation of moderate southern Democrats who were committed to restraining "big-government" spending.

In his 1977 inaugural address, Carter confessed that he had no grand "vision" of the future. Unlike his predecessors, he highlighted America's limitations rather than its potential: "We have learned that 'more' is not necessarily 'better,' that even our great nation has its recognized limits, and that we can neither answer all questions nor solve all problems." That may have been true, but retrenchment was not what many voters wanted to hear. Carter later admitted that his remarks about dialing back national expectations were "politically unpopular," for "Americans were not accustomed to limits—on natural resources . . . or on the power of our country to . . . control international events."

Jimmy Who?

Jimmy Carter's public modesty masked a complex and, at times, contradictory personality. No modern president was as openly committed to his Christian faith as Carter. At the same time, few presidents were as tough on others as Carter was.

Carter, who came out of nowhere to win the presidency ("Jimmy Who?"), displayed an "almost arrogant self-confidence," as *Time* magazine described it. All his life he had shown a fierce determination to succeed, and he expected those around him to show the same tenacity. "I am pretty rigid," Carter admitted. He and his closest aides ("the Georgia Mafia") arrived in Washington, D.C., convinced that they would clean up the "mess" made by career politicos and bureaucrats within the federal government. Congress, Carter noted in his diary, "was disgusting." Yet his naive dismissal of Congress would prove to be his downfall.

Carter, the former naval officer, nuclear engineer, efficiency expert, and business executive, wanted to be a "strong, aggressive president," who would make the federal government run more smoothly at less expense to taxpayers by eliminating waste and providing expert management. Yet he had little ability to inspire people to follow his lead. Democratic senator Eugene McCarthy described Carter as an "oratorical mortician," while a journalist stressed that "there's no music in him." He was, as he acknowledged, a manager rather than a visionary.

Voters expected Carter to restore U.S. stature abroad, cure the prolonged economic recession, and reduce both unemployment and inflation at a time when industrial economies around the world were struggling. He was also expected to lift the national spirit in the wake of the Watergate scandal.

The Carters After his 1977 inauguration, President Jimmy Carter broke tradition and chose not to ride in the presidential limousine. He instead walked down Pennsylvania Avenue with his wife, Rosalynn.

Such expectations were daunting, and while Carter displayed a sunny smile and flinty willpower, he was no miracle worker, and no one accused him of being charismatic or charming.

EARLY SUCCESS During the first two years of his presidency, Jimmy Carter enjoyed several successes, both symbolic and real. To demonstrate his frugality with taxpayers' money, he took the symbolic step of selling the presidential yacht, cut the White House staff by a third, told cabinet officers to give up their government cars, and installed solar panels on the White House roof to draw attention to the nation's need to become energy independent. His administration included more African Americans and women than any before.

He fulfilled a campaign pledge by offering amnesty (forgiveness) to the thousands of young men who had fled the country rather than be drafted to serve in Vietnam. He also reorganized the executive branch and created two new cabinet-level agencies, the Departments of Energy and Education. Carter pushed several significant environmental initiatives through the Democratic-controlled Congress, including stricter controls over the strip-mining of coal, the creation of a $1.6 billion "Superfund" to clean up toxic chemical waste sites, and a bill protecting more than 100 million acres of Alaskan land from development. He also deregulated the trucking, airline, and financial industries in an effort to restore competition. At the end of his first 100 days in office, Carter enjoyed a 75 percent public approval rating.

CARTER'S LIMITATIONS Yet Jimmy Carter's successes were short-lived. By nature, he was less an inspiring leader than a compulsive microman-ager (he even insisted on scheduling the use of the White House tennis court). During his first two years in the White House, Carter chose to serve as his own chief of staff, with disastrous results, for he was so busy handling mundane tasks like his daily calendar that he failed to establish an uplifting vision for the nation's future. Instead of focusing on a few priorities, he tried to do too much too fast, and his inexperienced team of senior aides was often more a burden than a blessing. The chief of staff he finally appointed, Hamilton Jordan, spent much of his time drinking, chasing women, and alienating members of Con-gress. Worst of all, Carter, the self-proclaimed "outsider" president, saw little need to consult with Democratic congressional leaders, which helps explain why many of his legislative requests got nowhere.

Ultimately, Carter's inability to revive the economy crippled his presi-dency. He first attacked unemployment, authorizing some $14 billion in fed-eral spending to trigger job growth while cutting taxes by $34 billion. His actions helped generate new jobs but also caused a spike in consumer prices from 5 percent when he took office to as much as 13 percent during 1980. The result was a deepening recession and rising unemployment, and growing crit-icism of the president. Liberal Democrats complained that Carter was doing nothing to address spreading poverty and inner-city decline. He responded with a lecture that sounded more like a conservative Republican president: "Government cannot solve our problems. It cannot eliminate poverty, or provide a bountiful economy, or reduce inflation, or save our cities, or cure illiteracy, or provide energy."

What made Carter's efforts to restore prosperity more challenging was the worsening "energy crisis." A dedicated environmentalist, he claimed that America was the "most wasteful nation on earth." Since the Arab oil embargo in 1973, the price of imported oil had doubled, while U.S. dependence on for-eign oil had grown from 35 to 50 percent of its annual needs. In April 1977, Carter presented Congress with a comprehensive energy proposal designed to cut oil consumption. Legislators, however, turned down most of the bill's key elements, in part because of Carter's poor relationship with Democrats in Congress. The final energy bill, the National Energy Act of 1978, was so gutted by oil, gas, and automobile industry lobbyists that one presidential aide said it looked like it had been "nibbled to death by ducks."

In 1979, the energy crisis grew more troublesome when Islamic fundamentalists seized the government of oil-rich Iran. They shut off the supply of Iranian oil to the United States, creating gasoline shortages and higher prices. Warning that the "growing scarcity in energy" supplies would paralyze the U.S. economy, Carter asked Congress for a more comprehensive energy bill, but again the legislators rejected its energy conservation measures.

A "CRISIS OF CONFIDENCE" By July 1979, President Carter had grown so discouraged with the nation's tepid efforts to reduce U.S. oil consumption that for eleven days he holed up at Camp David, the presidential retreat in the Maryland mountains. There he met privately with some 150 representatives from business, labor, education, politics, religion, even psychiatrists—all the while keeping the media at bay.

Then on July 15, he returned to the White House and delivered a televised speech in which he sounded more like an angry preacher than a president. A "crisis of confidence," he claimed, was paralyzing the nation. The people had lost confidence in his leadership and with legislators, and America had become rudderless, with no "sense of purpose" other than "to worship self-indulgence and consumption." He repeatedly blamed the citizenry for the nation's problems. "All the legislation in the world can't fix what's wrong with America," Carter stressed. Americans had become preoccupied with "owning and consuming things" at the expense of "hard work, strong families, close-knit communities, and our faith in God."

The nation was at a crossroads, Carter concluded. Americans could choose continued self-indulgence and political stalemate, or they could commit themselves to simpler lives by reviving traditional values such as thrift, mutual aid, frugality, and spirituality. "We can take the first step down that path as we begin to solve our energy problem. Energy will be the immediate test of our ability to unite this nation."

Carter failed that test, however. An Arizona newspaper grumbled that "the nation did not tune in Carter to hear a sermon. It . . . wanted answers. It did not get them." Even Democrats lambasted the speech. Arkansas governor Bill Clinton said that Carter was behaving more like a "17th century New England Puritan than a 20th century Southern Baptist."

It did not help when, two days after the speech, Carter asked more than thirty government officials, including his entire cabinet, to resign. He accepted the resignations of five cabinet officers. In doing so, he reinforced the public image of a rudderless White House in chaos.

Carter's inept legislative relations ensured that his energy proposals got nowhere in Congress. By the fall of 1979, his poll ratings were among the lowest in history. Former president Gerald Ford observed that if Nixon had created "an imperial presidency," Carter had fashioned "an imperiled presidency."

CARTER'S FOREIGN POLICY

Jimmy Carter's crowning achievement, which even his most bitter critics applauded, was his dogged effort to negotiate a 1978 peace agreement between Prime Minister Menachem Begin of Israel and President Anwar Sadat of Egypt. When the two foreign leaders arrived at Camp David, Maryland, they refused to be in the same room together, so Carter shuttled back and forth with various versions of a settlement. After twelve days, his strenuous efforts paid off when the parties signed two landmark treaties, thereafter called the **Camp David Accords**.

The Camp David Accords Egyptian president Anwar el-Sadat *(left)*, Jimmy Carter *(center)*, and Israeli prime minister Menachem Begin *(right)* at the announcement of the Camp David Accords, September 1978.

The first of the treaties provided the framework for an eventual peace agreement. The Israelis pledged to end their military occupation of the Sinai region of Egypt, and the Egyptians promised to restore Israeli access to the Suez Canal. The second treaty called for a comprehensive settlement based on Israel's willingness to allow the Palestinians living in the Israeli-controlled West Bank and Gaza Strip to govern themselves.

Sadat's willingness to recognize the legitimacy of the Israeli nation and sign the two treaties sparked violent protests across the Arab world. The Arab League, representing twenty-two Arab nations, expelled Egypt and announced an economic boycott, and the Israelis later backtracked on their initial willingness to have the Palestinian authority replace Israeli security forces in the occupied territories. President Sadat, however, paid the highest price, as Islamist extremists assassinated him in 1981. Still, President Carter's high-level diplomacy made another war between Israel and the Arab world less likely.

HUMAN RIGHTS President Carter stumbled again, however, when he vowed that "the soul of our foreign policy" should be an absolute "commitment to human rights" abroad, drawing a direct contrast between his international "idealism" and the geopolitical "realism" practiced by Richard Nixon and Henry Kissinger. Carter created an Office of Human Rights within the State Department and selectively cut off financial assistance to some repressive governments around the world. "America did not invent human rights," he stressed. "In a very real sense, human rights invented America."

Critics noted that the United States had its own human rights issues, including the plight of Native Americans and African Americans, and that Carter ignored frequent human rights abuses committed by key allies, such as the shah of Iran and brutal governments like Argentina, Ethiopia, Pakistan, and Uruguay. Others asserted that the president's definition of human rights was so vague and sweeping that few nations could meet its benchmark. Critics on the right argued that the president was sacrificing America's global interests to promote an impossible standard of international moral purity, while critics on the left highlighted his seeming hypocrisy in pursuing human rights in a few selected nations but not everywhere.

THE PANAMA CANAL Similarly, President Carter's decision to turn over control of the ten-mile-wide Panama Canal Zone to the Panamanian government aroused intense criticism. He argued that Panama's deep resentment of America for taking control of the Canal Zone during the presidency of Theodore Roosevelt left him no choice.

Conservatives blasted Carter's "giveaway" of a major strategic asset. In Ronald Reagan's view, "We bought it, we paid for it, it's ours." Legal scholars and the Panamanian government disagreed, however. No Panamanian had signed the 1903 document granting the United States perpetual control of the strategic waterway. The new agreement called for the Canal Zone to be transferred to Panama at the end of 1999. Carter said the exchange reflected the American belief that "fairness, not force, should lie at the heart of our dealings with the world."

AFGHANISTAN   In late December 1979, President Carter faced another crisis when 100,000 Soviet soldiers invaded Afghanistan, a remote, mountainous country where a faltering Communist government was being challenged by Islamist jihadists ("holy warriors") and ethnic warlords. It was the first Soviet army deployment outside Europe since the Second World War, and the invaders soon found themselves mired in what some called the Soviet Vietnam.

Carter responded to the Soviet invasion with a series of steps. In January 1980, he refused to sign a Strategic Arms Limitation Talks (SALT II) treaty with the Soviets, suspended U.S. grain shipments to the Soviet Union, began using the CIA to supply Afghan "freedom fighters" with weapons to use against Soviet troops, requested large increases in U.S. military spending, required all nineteen-year-old men to register for the military draft, and called for an international boycott of the 1980 Olympic Games, which were to be held that summer in Moscow. Some sixty nations joined the United States in the boycott. Still, the Soviets persisted in their Afghan intervention for nine years before giving up. It ultimately cost 15,000 Soviet lives.

The Soviet invasion of Afghanistan also prompted Carter to announce what came to be called the Carter Doctrine, in which he threatened to use military force to prevent any nation from gaining control of the Persian Gulf waterways, through which most of the oil from the Middle East made its way to foreign ports, including those in the United States.

Unfortunately, Carter's doctrine set in motion an endless U.S. military presence in the Middle East, as future presidents, both Democrats and Republicans, relied on armed force and technological firepower as the primary instruments of foreign policy in that strategic yet fractured and fractious region.

CRISIS IN IRAN   Then came the **Iranian hostage crisis**, a series of dramatic events that illustrated the inability of the United States to control world affairs. In January 1979, Islamist revolutionaries had ousted the pro-American government led by the hated ruler of Iran, Shah Mohammad Reza Pahlavi. The rebel leaders executed hundreds of the shah's former officials. Thousands more Iranians were imprisoned, tortured, or executed for refusing to abide by strict Islamist social codes. The turmoil led to a sharp drop in oil production, driving up gasoline prices worldwide. By the spring of 1979, Americans were again waiting in long lines for limited amounts of high-priced gasoline.

In October, despite the warnings of U.S. diplomats, the Carter administration allowed the now deposed shah of Iran to come to the United States to receive medical treatment for cancer. The president's "humanitarian" decision incensed Iranian revolutionaries.

On November 4, 1979, an Iranian mob stormed the U.S. embassy in Teh-

Ayatollah Khomeini Religious figure and leader of the Iranian Revolution that overthrew the Iranian monarchy in 1979.

ran and seized sixty-six diplomats, marines, and staff, including fifty-two American citizens. Iranian leader Ayatollah Ruhollah Khomeini demanded the return of the hated shah (and all his wealth) in exchange for the release of the American hostages. Nightly television coverage in the United States generated a near obsession with the fate of the hostages.

Angry Americans, including many in Congress, demanded a military response. Fearful that any military action would result in the hostages being killed, Carter appealed to the United Nations to help resolve the crisis, but Khomeini scoffed at UN efforts to free the hostages. Carter then froze all Iranian financial assets in America and asked Europe to join in a trade embargo of Iran. But because America's allies were not willing to lose access to Iranian oil, the trade restrictions were only partially effective.

As the crisis continued and gasoline prices rose to record levels, Carter authorized a risky rescue attempt by U.S. commandos on April 24, 1980. (His secretary of state, Cyrus Vance, resigned in protest because he thought the military action would be counterproductive.) As it turned out, the raid had to be aborted when several helicopters developed mechanical problems; the operation ended with the loss of eight U.S. soldiers when a helicopter collided with a transport plane in the Iranian desert.

A King's Ransom An Iranian militant holds a group of U.S. embassy staff members hostage in Tehran, Iran, in 1979.

The Iranian hostage crisis would continue for fourteen months, paralyzing Carter's ability to lead the nation. Newspaper headlines captured the growing concern about the president's ineptitude: "Error and Crisis: A Foreign Policy Against the Ropes," said the *Washington Post*, while the *New York Times* announced, "A U.S. Foreign Policy in Deep Disarray." For many, the standoff with Iran became a symbol of Carter's failed presidency.

The Iranian crisis finally ended after 444 days, on January 20, 1981, when Carter, just hours before leaving office, released several billion dollars of Iranian assets to ransom the hostages.

THE RISE OF RONALD REAGAN

No sooner had Jimmy Carter been elected in 1976 than conservative Republicans (the "New Right") began working to ensure that he would not win a second term. Their plans centered on Ronald Reagan, the handsome actor, two-term California governor, and prominent political commentator. An outspoken patriot and champion of conservative principles, Reagan believed that Americans had put too much faith in the government to solve their problems. Over time, runaway government spending had produced inflation, incompetence, and corruption. He promised to roll back the federal government.

THE ACTOR TURNED PRESIDENT

Born in Tampico, Illinois, in 1911, the son of an often-drunk, Irish Catholic shoe salesman and a devout, Bible-quoting mother, Ronald Reagan earned a football scholarship to attend tiny Eureka College during the Great Depression; he washed dishes in the dining hall to pay for his meals. After graduation, Reagan worked as a radio sportscaster before starting a movie career in Hollywood. He served three

Ronald Reagan The "Great Communicator" flashes his charming, trademark smile.

years in the army during the Second World War, making training films. At that time, as he recalled, he was a Democrat, "a New Dealer to the core" who voted for Franklin Delano Roosevelt four times.

After the war, Reagan became president of the Screen Actors Guild (SAG), where he honed his negotiating skills and fended off efforts by Communists to infiltrate the union. Reagan supported Democrat Harry S. Truman in the 1948 presidential election, but during the fifties he decided that federal taxes were too high. In 1960, he campaigned as a Democrat for Richard Nixon, and two years later he joined the Republican party, explaining that he "didn't leave the Democratic party, the Democratic party left me."

Reagan achieved political stardom in 1964 when he delivered a rousing speech on national television on behalf of Barry Goldwater's presidential candidacy. Wealthy admirers convinced him to run for governor of California in 1966, and he won by a landslide.

THE CANDIDATE OF HOPE AND OPTIMISM As the Republican presidential nominee in 1980, Reagan set about contrasting his optimistic vision of America's future with Jimmy Carter's bleak outlook and "mediocre leadership." President Carter, he claimed, kept saying that "our nation has passed its zenith. My fellow citizens, I utterly reject that view." Reagan insisted that there was "nothing wrong with the American people" and that there were "simple answers" to the complex problems facing the country, although they were not *easy* answers. He pledged to slash many social welfare programs, increase military spending to "win" the Cold War, dismantle the "bloated" federal bureaucracy, restore states' rights, reduce taxes and government regulation of businesses, and appoint conservative judges to the federal courts. He also promised to affirm old-time religious values by banning abortions and restoring prayer in public schools.

Reagan's popularity resulted in part from his skill as a speaker (journalists dubbed him the "Great Communicator") and his commitment to a few basic principles and simple themes. Blessed with a reassuring baritone voice and a wealth of entertaining stories, he rejected Carter's assumption that Americans needed "to start getting along with less, to accept a decline in our standard of living." He instead promised boundless economic expansion and endless prosperity. By reducing taxes and easing government regulations of businesses, he pledged, the engine of free-enterprise capitalism would spread wealth to everyone.

The Rise of the New Right

By 1980, social developments had made Reagan's anti-liberal stance a major asset. An increase in the number of senior citizens, a group that tends to be more politically and socially conservative, and the steady migration of people—especially older Americans—to the conservative Sun Belt states were shifting the political balance of power. Fully 90 percent of the nation's population growth during the 1980s occurred in southern or western Sun Belt states, while the Northeast and industrial states of the Midwest—Ohio, Michigan, Illinois, Indiana, Pennsylvania, and West Virginia (called the Rust Belt states)—experienced economic decline, factory closings, and population losses.

A related development was a growing tax revolt. As consumer prices and home values rose, so did property taxes. In California, Ronald Reagan's home state, skyrocketing property taxes threatened to force many working-class people from their homes. This spurred efforts to cut back on the size and cost of government to enable reductions in property taxes. In June 1978, tax rebels, with Reagan's support, succeeded in putting an initiative known as Proposition 13 on the state ballot. An overwhelming majority of voters approved the measure, which slashed property taxes by 57 percent and amended the state constitution to make it more difficult to raise taxes. The "Prop 13" tax revolt soon spread across the nation, leading the *New York Times* to call it a "modern Boston Tea Party."

THE CHRISTIAN RIGHT The California tax revolt fed into a national conservative resurgence led by the rapidly growing "**Christian Right**." Religious conservatives promoting a faith-based political agenda formed the strongest grassroots movement of the late twentieth century. By the 1980s, Catholic conservatives and Protestant evangelicals owned television and radio stations, operated their own schools and universities, and organized "megachurches" from which "televangelists" such as the Reverend Jerry Falwell launched a cultural crusade against the "demonic" forces of liberalism at home and communism abroad.

In 1979, Falwell formed the Moral Majority (later renamed the Liberty Alliance) to campaign for the political and social goals of the religious right: The economy should operate without "interference" by the government, which should be reduced in size; the Supreme Court decision in *Roe v. Wade* (1973) legalizing abortion should be reversed; Darwinian evolution should be replaced in school textbooks by the biblical story of creation; daily prayer should return to public schools; women should submit to their husbands; and communism should be opposed as a form of pagan totalitarianism.

Look on the Right Side The rise of the Christian Right saw protests against Supreme Court rulings that reinforced the separation of church and state. Here, in a 1984 protest organized by the Moral Majority, students chant "Kids need to pray!" in support of a proposed constitutional amendment to reinstate prayer in public schools.

That Ronald Reagan became the hero of the Christian Right was a tribute to his political skills, for he rarely attended church and had no strong religious affiliations. Jimmy Carter, though famous as a born-again Baptist Sunday school teacher, lost the support of religious conservatives because he was not willing to ban abortions or restore prayers in public schools. His push for state ratification of the Equal Rights Amendment (ERA) also cost him votes among conservatives.

ANTI-FEMINIST BACKLASH By the late 1970s, a well-organized, well-financed backlash against the feminist movement reinforced the rise of the New Right. Republican Phyllis Schlafly, a formidable Catholic attorney from Illinois who had created the Eagle Forum in 1972 to give voice to conservative women, became a powerful activist for conservative values. Many argued that she singlehandedly stopped the Equal Rights Amendment from being ratified by the required thirty-eight states.

Schlafly's STOP (Stop Taking Our Privileges) ERA organization recruited an army of militant conservative women to lobby against the amendment. She warned that the ERA would destroy the two-parent family unit, allow husbands to abandon their wives, force women into military service, and give gay "perverts" the right to marry. She and others stressed that the gender equality promised by the proposed amendment violated biblical teachings about women's "God-given" roles as nurturers and helpmates. By the end of the decade, the national effort to gain ratification of the ERA had stalled, largely because no states in the conservative South and West had ratified it.

Many of Schlafly's anti-ERA supporters also participated in the growing anti-abortion, or "pro-life," movement. The National Right to Life Committee denounced abortion as murder, and the emotional intensity of the issue made it a powerful political force. Reagan highlighted his support for traditional "family values," gender roles, and the "rights" of the unborn, which helped persuade many northern Democrats—mostly working-class Catholics—to switch parties and support Reagan.

FINANCING CONSERVATISM The business community had also become a source of conservative activism. In 1972, leaders of the nation's largest corporations formed the Business Roundtable to promote their interests in Congress. Within a few years, many of them had created political action committees (PACs) to distribute money to pro-business political candidates. Corporate donations also helped fund conservative "think tanks," such as the American Enterprise Institute, the Cato Institute, and the Heritage Foundation. By 1980, the conservative insurgency had become a potent political movement with substantial financial resources, carefully crafted ideas, and grassroots energy, all of which helped explain Ronald Reagan's presidential victory.

THE ELECTION OF 1980 Ronald Reagan's supporters loved his simple solutions and genial, upbeat personality, and they responded passionately to his recurring question: "Are you better off than you were four years ago?" Their answer was a resounding "No!" Jimmy Carter had not been able to gain the release of the Americans held hostage in Iran prior to Election Day, nor had he improved the economy. His approval ratings had sunk below those of Richard Nixon. On Election Day 1980, Reagan swept to a lopsided victory, with 489 electoral votes to 49 for Carter, who carried only six states. It was the second-worst defeat for an incumbent president in the twentieth century, behind William Howard Taft in 1912. The popular vote was 44 million (51 percent) for Reagan to Carter's 35 million (41 percent), with 7 percent

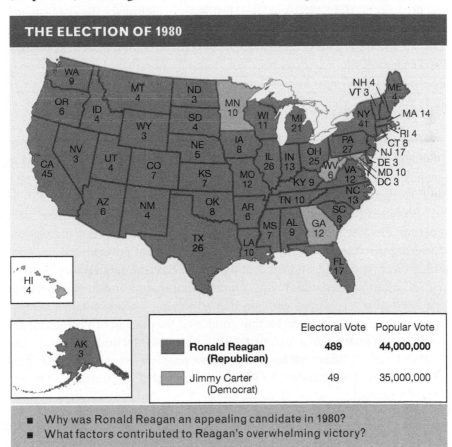

THE ELECTION OF 1980

	Electoral Vote	Popular Vote
Ronald Reagan (Republican)	**489**	**44,000,000**
Jimmy Carter (Democrat)	49	35,000,000

- Why was Ronald Reagan an appealing candidate in 1980?
- What factors contributed to Reagan's overwhelming victory?

going to John Anderson, a moderate Republican who ran as an independent. Reagan's victory signaled a major realignment of voters in which many so-called Reagan Democrats—conservative White southern Protestants and blue-collar northern Catholics—crossed over to the Republican party.

THE REAGAN REVOLUTION

Those Democrats who dismissed seventy-year-old Ronald Reagan, at the time the oldest man to assume the presidency, and the first to have been divorced, as a mental lightweight inattentive to the details of policy and management, underrated his many virtues, including the importance of his years in front of a camera. Politics is a performing art, all the more so in the age of television, and few politicians had Reagan's stage presence—or confidence. His ability to make voters again believe in American greatness won him two presidential elections, in 1980 and 1984. Just how revolutionary the "Reagan era" was remains a subject of intense debate among historians, but what cannot be denied is that Reagan's actions and beliefs set the tone for the decade's political and economic life.

REAGAN'S FIRST TERM

"Fellow conservatives," President Reagan said in a speech in 1981, "our moment has arrived." In his presidential inaugural address, he promised to help Americans "renew our faith and hope" in America as a "shining city on a hill" for the rest of the world to emulate.

President Reagan succeeded where Jimmy Carter failed for three main reasons. First, he focused on a few priorities like slowing the rate of inflation, lowering tax rates, reducing the scope of the federal government, increasing military spending, and conducting an anti-Soviet foreign policy. Second, he was a shrewd negotiator with congressional leaders and foreign heads of state. He also recognized early on that governing a representative democracy requires compromises. He thus combined the passion of a revolutionary with the pragmatism of a diplomat. Third, Reagan's infectious optimism, like that of Franklin Roosevelt before him, gave people a sense of common purpose and renewed confidence. "We have every right," he stressed, "to dream heroic dreams."

Reagan's first step as president was to freeze federal hiring. "Government," he declared, "is not the solution to our problems. Government *is* the problem." To drive home that theme, he ordered that the portrait of Harry Truman in the Cabinet Room be replaced with one of Calvin Coolidge, the most anti-government president of the twentieth century—and, like Reagan, a man who loved afternoon naps.

Public affection for Reagan spiked just two months into his presidency when John Hinckley Jr., an emotionally disturbed young man, fired six shots at the president as he was returning to his limousine after a speaking engagement at the Hilton Hotel in Washington, D.C. In his deranged mind, Hinckley thought by killing the president he would impress actress Jodie Foster, a woman he had never met but was obsessed with and had been stalking.

Hinckley's bullets wounded a police officer and a Secret Service agent, and critically wounded press secretary James Brady, who remained paralyzed the rest of his life. Another bullet ricocheted off the presidential limousine and punctured the president's lung. Still conscious as he was wheeled into a nearby hospital, Reagan asked the medical team preparing him for life-saving surgery, "Please tell me you're Republicans." His witty and gritty response to the assassination attempt created an outpouring of support that gave his presidency added momentum. The Democratic Speaker of the House, Tip O'Neill, told colleagues that Reagan "has become a hero. We can't argue with a man as popular as he is." (At his trial, John Hinckley was found not guilty by reason of insanity and confined to a psychiatric hospital).

Reagan inherited an economy in shambles. The annual rate of inflation had reached 13 percent, and unemployment hovered at 7.5 percent. At the same time, the Cold War was heating up again. The Soviet Union had placed missiles with nuclear weapons in the nations of Central and Eastern Europe under its control—which threatened the entire continent. Reagan refused to be intimidated and adopted a confrontational posture against the Soviet Union, which he summarized as "We win, you lose." He convinced Congress to support a huge increase in the military budget, deployed U.S. missiles in Europe, and sought to root out Communist insurgencies in Central America.

REAGANOMICS On August 1, 1981, President Reagan signed the Economic Recovery Tax Act (ERTA), which cut personal income taxes by 25 percent, lowered the maximum tax rate from 70 to 50 percent for 1982, and offered a broad array of tax concessions. The bill was the centerpiece of Reagan's "common sense" economic plan. While theorists called the philosophy behind the plan supply-side economics, journalists dubbed the president's proposals **Reaganomics**.

Simply put, Reaganomics grew out of the assumption that the stagflation of the 1970s had resulted from excessive corporate and personal income taxes, which weakened incentives for individuals and businesses to increase productivity, save money, and reinvest in economic expansion. The solution, according to Reagan, was to slash tax rates, especially on the wealthy, in the belief that they would spend their tax savings on business expansion and consumer goods (the "supply side" of the economy). Such spending, Reagan and others believed, would provide "trickle down" benefits to the masses. Reaganomics promised to produce enough new tax revenues from rising corporate profits and personal incomes to pay for the tax cuts. In the short term, however, ERTA did not work as planned. The federal budget deficit grew, and by November 1981, the economy was officially in recession.

MANAGING THE BUDGET   To offset the loss of government tax revenues, David Stockman, President Reagan's budget director, proposed sharp reductions in federal spending, including Social Security and Medicare, the two most expensive—and most popular—federal social welfare programs. Liberal Democrats howled, and Reagan responded that he was committed to maintaining the "safety net" of government services for the "truly needy." According to Stockman, Reagan was "too kind, gentle, and sentimental" to make the drastic cuts needed to balance the budget.

Rallying against Reaganomics In 1982, a throng of more than 5,000 senior citizens staged a demonstration in downtown Detroit against Reagan's decision to cut federal budgets for Social Security and other programs to aid the elderly.

In the end, the president and Congress agreed to cut the budget for food stamps (government subsidies to help poor people buy groceries) only 4 percent from what the Carter administration had planned to spend. The Reagan administration also continued to provide huge federal subsidies to corporations and agribusinesses—what critics called "welfare for the rich." In the end, Reagan never dismantled the major New Deal programs that he had savagely criticized. Conservative political columnist George Will explained Reagan's failure to make substantial cuts in federal spending by noting that "Americans are conservative. What they want to conserve is the New Deal."

Within a year, budget director David Stockman realized that the actual cuts in domestic spending had fallen far short of what the president had promised. Massive increases in military spending complicated the situation. In essence, Reagan gave the Defense Department a blank check, telling the secretary of defense to "spend what you need." Over the next five years, the administration would spend $1.2 trillion on military expenses, the highest amount ever. Something had to give.

In the summer of 1981, Stockman warned that "we're heading for a crash landing on the budget. We're facing potential deficit numbers so big that they could wreck the president's entire economic program." The fast-growing federal deficit, which had helped trigger the worst recession since the 1930s, was Reagan's greatest failure. During 1982, an estimated 10 million Americans, more than 10 percent of the workforce, were jobless. "The stench of failure hangs over Ronald Reagan's White House," declared the *New York Times*.

Stockman and other aides finally convinced the president that the government needed "revenue enhancements" (tax increases). With Reagan's support, Congress passed a tax bill in 1982 that would raise almost $100 billion, but the economic slump persisted. In the 1982 congressional midterm elections, Democrats picked up twenty-six seats in the House of Representatives.

Yet Reagan's determination to "stay the course" with his economic program slowly began to pay off as he had promised. By the summer of 1983, a robust economic recovery was underway, in part because of increased government spending and lower interest rates, and in part because of lower tax rates. Inflation subsided, as did unemployment. Reaganomics was not helping to balance the budget as promised, however. In fact, the federal deficits had grown larger—so much so that the president had run up an accumulated debt larger than that of all his predecessors combined.

REAGAN'S ANTI-LIBERALISM During Ronald Reagan's presidency, organized labor suffered severe setbacks. In 1981, he fired 11,359 members

Sandra Day O'Connor O'Connor, the first woman to serve on the Supreme Court, was confirmed in September 1981, at a hearing that was picketed by conservatives who decried her pro-abortion stance.

of the Professional Air Traffic Controllers Organization who had participated in an illegal strike intended to shut down air travel. (Air traffic controllers are deemed essential to public safety and therefore are prohibited from striking by the Taft-Hartley Act of 1947.) Reagan's actions broke the political power of the American Federation of Labor–Congress of Industrial Organizations (AFL-CIO), the national confederation of labor unions that traditionally supported Democratic candidates. Although record numbers of jobs were created during the 1980s, union membership steadily dropped. By 1987, unions represented only 17 percent of the nation's full-time workers, down from 24 percent in 1979.

Reagan also opposed the Equal Rights Amendment, abortion rights, and proposals by women's rights organizations to require comparable pay for jobs of comparable worth. In affirming his conservative credentials, he cut funds for civil rights enforcement and the Equal Employment Opportunity Commission, and he opposed renewal of the Voting Rights Act of 1965.

Reagan did name Sandra Day O'Connor, an Arizona judge, as the first woman Supreme Court justice in 1981, despite the Religious Right's objections that O'Connor supported abortion rights for women. O'Connor gained the support of both Democrats and Republicans, and she was confirmed by a vote of 99–0 in the U.S. Senate. She would serve on the Supreme Court for a quarter of a century.

THE ELECTION OF 1984 By 1983, prosperity had returned, the stock market was soaring, and Reagan's supply-side economic theory was at last working as advertised—except for the growing federal budget deficit, which had always been a sore subject to fiscal conservatives. Reporters began to speak of the "Reagan Revolution." In 1984, the slogan at the Republican National Convention was "America is back and standing tall."

The Democrats' presidential nominee, Walter Mondale, Jimmy Carter's vice president, was endorsed by the AFL-CIO, the National Organization for Women (NOW), and many prominent African Americans. He made history by choosing as his running mate Geraldine Ferraro, a New York congresswoman who was the first female vice presidential candidate.

A bit of frankness in Mondale's acceptance speech ended up hurting his campaign. "Mr. Reagan will raise taxes [to reduce budget deficits], and so will I," he told the convention. "He won't tell you. I just did." Reagan responded by vowing never to approve another tax increase (a promise he could not keep). Reagan also repeated a theme he had used against Carter: "It's morning again in America," and record numbers of Americans were finding jobs. In the end, Reagan took 59 percent of the popular vote and lost only Minnesota (Mondale's home state) and the District of Columbia. It was the worst defeat ever for a Democratic candidate.

REAGAN'S SECOND TERM

Spurred by his landslide reelection, Ronald Reagan called for "a Second American Revolution of hope and opportunity." Through much of 1985, he drummed up support for a tax-simplification plan. After vigorous debate, Congress passed a comprehensive Tax Reform Act in 1986. It cut the number of federal tax brackets from fourteen to two and reduced rates from the maximum of 50 percent to 15 and 28 percent—the lowest since Calvin Coolidge was president in the 1920s.

REAGAN'S HALF-HEARTED REVOLUTION Although Ronald Reagan had promised to "curb the size and influence of the federal establishment," the number of federal employees actually grew during his two terms as president. Neither Social Security nor Medicare, the two largest federal social programs, was overhauled, and the federal agencies that Reagan had threatened to abolish, such as the Department of Education, not only survived but saw their budgets grow.

The federal deficit almost tripled during Reagan's two terms. He blamed Congress for the problem, "since only Congress can spend money," but the legislators essentially approved the budgets Reagan submitted to them. As Dick Cheney, a future Republican vice president, quipped, "Reagan showed that deficits don't matter."

The cost of Social Security, the most expensive "entitlement" program, grew by 27 percent under Reagan, as some 6,000 people each day turned sixty-five years old. Moreover, he failed to fulfill his campaign promises to the Religious Right, such as reinstituting daily prayer in public schools and banning abortion. Reagan did follow through on his pledge to reshape the federal court system by appointing 368 mostly conservative judges, including Supreme Court justices Antonin Scalia and Anthony Kennedy.

Reagan also ended the prolonged period of stagflation and set in motion what economists called the "Great Expansion," an unprecedented twenty-year burst of productivity and prosperity. True, Reagan's presidency left the nation with a massive debt burden that would cause major problems, but the Great Communicator also renewed the nation's strength, self-confidence, and soaring sense of possibilities.

An Anti-Communist Foreign Policy

On a flight to Detroit, Michigan, to accept the Republican party's presidential nomination in the summer of 1980, Ronald Reagan was asked why he wanted to be president. He answered: "To end the Cold War." As president, Reagan systematically promoted what he called his "peace through strength" strategy. He would build up U.S. military strength to the point at which it would overwhelm the Soviet Union, both financially and militarily. At the same time, Reagan launched a widespread "war of ideas" against communism by charging that the Soviet Union was "the focus of evil in the modern world."

What came to be called the Reagan Doctrine pledged to combat Soviet adventurism throughout the world, even if it meant partnering with brutal dictatorships. Reagan believed that aggressive CIA-led efforts to stymie Soviet expansionism would eventually cause the unstable Soviet system to implode "on the ash heap of history."

A MASSIVE DEFENSE BUILDUP   Ronald Reagan's conduct of foreign policy reflected his belief that trouble in the world stemmed mainly from Moscow, the capital of what he called the "evil empire." Reagan believed that Richard Nixon and Gerald Ford (who followed Henry Kissinger's advice) had been too soft on the Soviets. Kissinger's emphasis on détente, Reagan said, had been a "one-way street" favoring the Soviets.

Reagan wanted to reduce the risk of nuclear war by convincing the Soviets that they could not win such a conflict. To do so, he and Secretary of Defense Caspar Weinberger embarked upon a major buildup of nuclear

Strategic Defense Initiative President Reagan addresses the nation on March 23, 1983, promoting the development of a space-age shield to intercept Soviet missiles.

and conventional weapons. During Reagan's two presidential terms, defense spending came to represent a fourth of all federal government expenditures. Reagan claimed that such military spending would bankrupt the Soviets by forcing them to spend much more on their own military budgets.

On March 23, 1983, two weeks after denouncing the Soviet Union as "the focus of evil in the modern world," Reagan escalated the nuclear arms race when he announced that he was authorizing the Defense Department to develop the controversial **Strategic Defense Initiative (SDI)**. The plan featured a complex antimissile defense system using satellites equipped with laser weapons to "intercept and destroy" Soviet missiles in flight before they could harm the United States. The program was controversial because it relied upon untested technology and violated a 1972 U.S.-Soviet treaty banning such anti-missile defensive systems. The media, many scientists, and even government officials insisted that such a "Star Wars" defense system could never be built (Secretary of State George Shultz called it "lunacy"). Nevertheless, Congress approved the first stage of funding, eventually allocating $30 billion to the program. Although SDI was never implemented, it did force the Soviets to launch an expensive research-and-development effort of their own, which helped bankrupt their economy. As a Soviet foreign minister later admitted, Reagan's commitment to SDI "made us realize we were in a very dangerous spot."

COMMUNIST INSURGENCIES IN CENTRAL AMERICA

President Reagan's foremost international concern was Central America, where he detected the most serious Communist threat. The tiny nation of El Salvador was caught up in a brutal struggle between Communist-supported revolutionaries and the right-wing military government, which received U.S. economic and military assistance. Critics argued that U.S. involvement ensured that the revolutionary forces would gain public support by capitalizing on "anti-Yankee" sentiment. Reagan's supporters countered that allowing a Communist victory in El Salvador would lead all of Central America into the Communist camp (a new "domino" theory). By 1984, however, the U.S.-backed government of President José Napoleón Duarte had brought some stability to El Salvador.

Even more troubling to Reagan was the situation in Nicaragua. The State Department claimed that the Cuban-sponsored Sandinista socialist government, which had seized power in 1979, was sending Soviet and Cuban weapons to leftist Salvadoran rebels. In response, the Reagan administration ordered the CIA to train, equip, and finance anti-Communist Nicaraguans, or Contras (short for *contrarevolucionarios*, or "counterrevolutionaries"), who staged attacks on Sandinista bases from sanctuaries in Honduras.

In supporting these "freedom fighters," Reagan sought not only to impede the traffic in arms to Salvadoran rebels but also to replace the Sandinistas with a democratic government friendly to the United States. Yet his anti-Communist interventionism fostered a prolonged civil war that killed tens of thousands of Nicaraguans on both sides. Critics of American involvement accused the Contras of being mostly right-wing fanatics who killed indiscriminately. They also feared that the United States might eventually commit its own combat forces, leading to a Vietnam-like intervention. Reagan warned that if the Communists prevailed in Central America, "our credibility would collapse, our alliances would crumble, and the safety of our homeland would be jeopardized."

STRIFE IN THE MIDDLE EAST   The Middle East remained a tinderbox of conflict during the 1980s. In September 1980, the Iraqi despot, Saddam Hussein, launched attacks on neighboring Iran. The brutal war involved the extensive use of chemical weapons and generated hundreds of thousands of casualties on both sides, but showed no sign of ending. In 1984, both Iran and Iraq began to attack oil tankers in the Persian Gulf, a major source of the world's oil. At the same time, the Soviet occupation forces had gotten bogged down in Afghanistan as badly as the Americans had in Vietnam.

Like the presidents before him, Ronald Reagan continued to consider Israel the strongest and most reliable U.S. ally in the volatile Middle East, while still seeking to encourage moderate Arab groups. But the forces of moderation were dealt a blow during the mid-1970s when Lebanon, long an enclave of peace, collapsed into an anarchy of warring groups. The most powerful of the rival factions was the Palestine Liberation Organization (PLO). Founded in 1964, the PLO sought the "liberation of Palestine" from Israeli control through armed struggle, with much of its violence aimed at Israeli civilians on Lebanon's southern border.

In 1982, Israeli forces pushed the PLO from southern Lebanon north to Beirut, where they began shelling PLO strongholds. The United States sent a special ambassador to negotiate a settlement. Israeli troops moved into Beirut and looked the other way when Christian militiamen slaughtered Muslim women and children in Palestinian refugee camps. French, Italian, and U.S. forces then moved into Lebanon as "peacekeepers," but in such small numbers that they became targets themselves. Islamists resentful of Western troops in their homeland constantly harassed them. American warships and planes responded by bombing Muslim positions in the highlands behind Beirut.

By 1983, Israel had driven the PLO from Beirut, but the city became increasingly unstable. In April, Islamist suicide bombers drove a truck laden with explosives into the U.S. embassy compound in Beirut, detonated it, and killed forty people, including seventeen Americans. On October 23, 1983, an Islamist suicide bomber attacked U.S. Marine headquarters at the Beirut airport; the explosion left 241 Americans and 58 French dead. In early 1984, Reagan announced that the marines remaining in Lebanon would be redeployed to warships offshore. The Israeli forces pulled back to southern Lebanon, while the Syrians remained in eastern Lebanon. Peaceful coexistence in the region proved to be an elusive dream.

U.S. INVASION OF GRENADA Luck, as it happened, presented Ronald Reagan the chance for an easy triumph closer to home that eclipsed news of the debacle in Lebanon. On the tiny Caribbean island of Grenada, whose population of 91,000 made it the smallest independent country in the Western Hemisphere, a leftist government had hired Cuban workers to build a new airfield and signed military agreements with Communist countries. In October 1983, a radical military council seized power and killed the prime minister. Appeals from neighboring countries convinced Reagan to send 1,900 U.S. Marines to invade Grenada, depose the new military government, and evacuate a small group of American students at the country's medical school. The United Nations General Assembly condemned the U.S. invasion, but it was popular among Grenadians, their neighbors, and in the United States. (The date of the invasion is now a national holiday in Grenada, called Thanksgiving Day.)

The decisive move served as notice to Latin American revolutionaries that Reagan might use military force elsewhere in the region.

THE IRAN-CONTRA AFFAIR During the fall of 1986, Democrats regained control of the Senate and picked up six seats in the House, increasing their already comfortable margin to 259–176. The election results meant that Reagan would face a Democrat-controlled Congress during the last two years of his presidency.

Worse for the administration were reports in late 1986 finding that the U.S. government had been secretly selling arms to U.S.-hating Iran (which Reagan had called an "outlaw state") in the hope of securing the release of American hostages held in Lebanon by extremist groups sympathetic to Iran. Such action contradicted Reagan's insistence that his administration would never negotiate with terrorists. The disclosures angered America's allies as well as many Americans who vividly remembered the 1979 Iranian hostage situation.

Over the next several months, revelations emerged about a complicated series of covert activities carried out by administration officials. At the center of what came to be called the **Iran-Contra affair** was U.S. Marine Corps lieutenant colonel Oliver North, a swashbuckling aide to the National Security Council who specialized in counterterrorism. Working from the basement of the White House, North had been secretly selling military supplies to Iran and using the proceeds to support the Contra rebels fighting in Nicaragua at a time when Congress had voted to ban such aid.

North's illegal activities, it turned out, had been approved by Reagan's national security adviser, Robert McFarlane; McFarlane's successor, Admiral John Poindexter; and CIA director William Casey. Both Secretary of State George Shultz and Secretary of Defense Caspar Weinberger criticized the arms sale to Iran, but their objections were ignored. On three occasions, Shultz had threatened to resign over the "pathetic" scheme. After information about the secret dealings surfaced in the press, North and others erased incriminating computer files and destroyed documents. McFarlane attempted suicide before being convicted of withholding information from Congress. Poindexter

Iran-Contra Hearings Admiral John Poindexter listens with apprehension to a question from the congressional investigation committee on July 21, 1987.

resigned, and North, described by the White House as a "loose cannon," was fired.

Facing a barrage of criticism, President Reagan appointed a three-member commission, led by former Republican senator John Tower, to investigate the scandal. Early in 1987, the Tower Commission issued a devastating report that placed much of the responsibility for the Iran-Contra affair on Reagan's loose management style. When asked if he had known of Colonel North's illegal actions, the president simply replied, "I don't remember." During the spring and summer of 1987, a joint House-Senate committee held hearings into the Iran-Contra affair. In his testimony, North claimed that he thought "he had received authority from the President."

The investigations led to six indictments in 1988. A jury found North guilty of three minor charges but innocent of nine more serious counts, apparently reflecting the jury's reasoning that he had acted as an agent of higher-ups. An

The Iran-Contra Cover-Up In Paul Szep's 1987 cartoon, political figures, including President Ronald Reagan, Robert McFarlane, Lieutenant Colonel Oliver North, and Iran's Ayatollah Khomeini attempt to deflect blame for the Iran-Contra Affair. *(By permission of © Paul Szep and Creators Syndicate, Inc.)*

appellate court later overturned his conviction. Of those involved, only John Poindexter received a jail sentence—six months for obstructing justice and lying to Congress.

A HISTORIC TREATY The most notable foreign policy achievement at the end of Reagan's second term was a surprising arms-reduction agreement with the Soviet government. Under Mikhail Gorbachev, who became the Soviet president in 1985, the Soviets renewed the policy of détente, encouraging a reduction of tensions with the United States. In large part, they did so to reduce their runaway military spending and focus on more-pressing problems, chiefly an inefficient economy and the waging of a losing war in Afghanistan.

THE REYKJAVIK SUMMIT In October 1986, Ronald Reagan and Mikhail Gorbachev met for the first time in Reykjavik, Iceland, to discuss ways to reduce the threat of nuclear war. During ten hours of intense negotiations, Reagan shocked Gorbachev and the Soviets by saying, "It would be fine with

Reykjavik Summit Pictured here with President Reagan at the Reykjavik Summit, Gorbachev took major strides to improve relations with the United States.

me if we eliminated all nuclear weapons." Equally shocking was Gorbachev's reply: "We can do that."

By the end of the meeting, however, the two sides remained far apart. Reagan famously walked out of the conference when Gorbachev demanded that the United States abandon the Strategic Defense Initiative (SDI, or "Star Wars").

THE INF TREATY The logjam in the disarmament negotiations suddenly broke in 1987, when Mikhail Gorbachev announced that he was willing to consider mutual reductions in nuclear weaponry. A member of the Soviet negotiating team acknowledged Ronald Reagan's role in the breakthrough. The U.S. president, he explained, "takes you by the arm, walks you to the cliff's edge, and invites you to step forward for the good of humanity."

After nine months of strenuous negotiations, Reagan and Gorbachev met amid much fanfare in Washington, D.C., on December 9, 1987, and signed the **Intermediate-Range Nuclear Forces (INF) Treaty**, an agreement to eliminate intermediate-range (300- to 3,000-mile) missiles. Reagan's steadfast show of strength against the Soviets and a new kind of Soviet leader in Mikhail Gorbachev combined to produce the most sweeping reduction in nuclear weaponry in history.

The INF treaty marked the first time that the two nations had agreed to destroy a whole class of weapons systems. Under the terms of the treaty, the United States would destroy 859 missiles, and the Soviets would eliminate 1,752. Still, the reductions represented only 4 percent of the total nuclear-missile count on both sides.

REAGAN'S GLOBAL LEGACY Ronald Reagan achieved the unthinkable by helping to end the Cold War. Although his massive defense buildup almost bankrupted the United States, it did force the Soviet Union to the bargaining table.

By negotiating the nuclear disarmament treaty and lighting the fuse of democratic freedom in Soviet-controlled East Germany, Hungary, Poland, and Czechoslovakia, Reagan set in motion events that would lead to the collapse of the Soviet Union.

In June 1987, Reagan visited the huge concrete-and-barbed-wire Berlin Wall separating East Berlin from West Berlin and, in a dramatic speech, called upon the Soviet Union to allow greater freedom within the countries under its control. "General Secretary Gorbachev, if you seek peace, if you seek prosperity for the Soviet Union and Eastern Europe, if you seek liberalization: Come here to this gate! Mr. Gorbachev, open this gate! Mr. Gorbachev, tear down this wall!" It was great theater and good politics.

THE CHANGING ECONOMIC AND SOCIAL LANDSCAPE

During the 1980s, profound economic and technological changes transformed American life. The economy went through a wrenching transformation in adapting to an increasingly interconnected global marketplace. The nations most devastated by the Second World War—France, Germany, the Soviet Union, Japan, and China—had by the 1980s developed formidable economies with higher levels of productivity than in the United States. More and more American manufacturing companies shifted their production overseas to take advantage of lower labor costs, accelerating the transition of the economy from its once-dominant industrial base to a more services-oriented economy. Driving all these changes was the impact of the computer revolution and the development of the internet.

THE COMPUTER REVOLUTION The idea of a programmable machine that would rapidly perform mental tasks had been around since the eighteenth century, but it took the Second World War to gather the intellectual and financial resources needed to create such a "computer." In 1946, a team of engineers at the University of Pennsylvania developed ENIAC (electronic numerical integrator and computer), the first all-purpose, all-electronic digital computer. It required 18,000 vacuum tubes to operate and an entire room to house it. The following year, researchers at Bell Telephone Laboratories invented the transistor, which replaced the bulky vacuum tubes and enabled much smaller, yet more-powerful, computers—as well as being the foundation for new devices such as hearing aids and transistor radios.

The next major breakthrough was the invention in 1971 of the **microprocessor**—virtually a tiny computer on a silicon chip. The microprocessor chip revolutionized computing by allowing for the storage of far more data in much smaller machines.

The microchip made possible the personal computer. In 1975, an engineer named Ed Roberts developed the Altair 8800, the prototype of the personal computer. Its potential excited a Harvard University sophomore named Bill Gates, who improved the software of the Altair 8800, dropped out of college, and formed a company called Microsoft to sell the new system.

During the 1980s, IBM (International Business Machines), using a microprocessor made by the Intel Corporation and an operating system provided by Microsoft, helped transform the personal computer into a mass consumer product. In 1963, a half-million computer chips were sold worldwide; by 1970, the number was 300 million.

Macintosh In 1984, Apple launched its personal computer, the Macintosh, with the tagline "For the rest of us," marketing it as an affordable and easy-to-use computer designed for the average user.

Computer chips transformed a variety of electronic products—televisions, calculators, wristwatches, clocks, ovens, phones, laptops, and automobiles—while facilitating efforts to land astronauts on the moon and launch satellites into space. The development of the internet, electronic mail (email), and cell-phone technology during the 1980s and 1990s allowed for instantaneous communication, thereby accelerating the globalization of the economy, dramatically increasing productivity in the workplace, and transforming the way people communicated with each other.

CAREFREE CONSUMERS AND THE STOCK MARKET PLUNGE During the 1980s, Ronald Reagan reduced tax rates so people would have more money to spend. Americans preferred Reagan's emphasis on prosperity to Carter's focus on propriety. Reagan, however, succeeded too well in shifting the public mood back to the "bigger is better" tradition of heedless consumerism. During the "age of Reagan," advertisements celebrated instant gratification. Many consumers went on self-indulgent spending sprees, and the more they bought, the more they wanted. As the stock market soared, the number of multimillionaires working on Wall Street and in the financial industry mushroomed as income inequality in the United States widened. The national economy during the 1980s shifted from manufacturing to service industries, where wages were lower (a process known as "deindustrialization"). Most new jobs created during the 1980s paid only the minimum wage.

Yet affluent Americans showed little concern about those struggling to make ends meet. The money fever was contagious. Compulsive spenders donned T-shirts proclaiming: "Born to Shop." By 1988, some 110 million Americans had an average of seven credit cards each. Money—lots of it—came to define the American dream. In the hit movie *Wall Street* (1987), the high-flying land developer and corporate raider Gordon Gekko, played by actor Michael Douglas, announced, "Greed . . . is good. Greed is right."

During the 1980s, many Americans began spending more than they earned. All categories of debt dramatically increased. Americans in the 1960s had saved, on average, 10 percent of their income; in 1987, the figure was less than 4 percent. The federal debt more than tripled, from $908 billion in 1980 to $2.9 trillion at the end of the 1989 fiscal year.

On October 19, 1987, the bill collector suddenly arrived at the nation's doorstep. On that "Black Monday," the stock market experienced a tidal wave of selling reminiscent of the 1929 crash, as investors worried that the United States would never address its massive budget deficits. The Dow Jones Industrial Average plummeted 22.6 percent, nearly doubling the 12.8 percent fall on October 28, 1929. Wall Street's selling frenzy sent stock prices plummeting in Tokyo, London, Paris, and Toronto.

In the aftermath of Black Monday, fears of an impending recession led business leaders and economists to attack President Reagan for allowing such huge budget deficits. He responded by agreeing to work with Congress to develop a deficit-reduction package. For the first time, Reagan indicated a willingness to increase taxes to help reduce the deficit. The eventual compromise plan, however, was so modest that it did little to restore investor confidence.

THE POOR The eighties were years of vivid contrast. Despite unprecedented prosperity, growing numbers of jobless Americans were without hope. Widespread homelessness (estimated at 400,000 people) became the most acute social issue. Several factors had led to a shortage of low-cost housing. The government had given up on building public housing, urban-renewal programs had demolished blighted areas but provided no housing for those who were displaced, and owners had abandoned unprofitable buildings in poor inner-city neighborhoods or converted them into expensive condominiums for high-income city dwellers, a process called gentrification.

In addition, the working poor during the 1980s saw their incomes decline at the same time that the Reagan administration was making deep cuts in federal social welfare programs. By 1983, over 15 percent of adults were living below the poverty line, even though half of them lived in households where at least one person worked. Still another factor affecting the homelessness epidemic was the unintended effects of new medications that allowed some patients to be discharged from mental institutions. Once released, many of them ended up on the sidewalks of America, homeless and without care, because promised mental-health services failed to materialize. Between 1982 and 1985, federal programs targeted to the poor were reduced by $57 billion.

Drug and alcohol abuse was rampant among the homeless, mostly unemployed single adults. In Los Angeles County, for example, there were 400,000 cocaine addicts and 200,000 other drug addicts in need of treatment by the late 1980s. An estimated 100,000 of them were homeless or poor. Nationwide, a quarter of the homeless (about 100,000 people) had spent time in mental institutions; some 40 percent had spent time in jail; a third were delusional.

THE AIDS EPIDEMIC Another group of severely marginalized people were those suffering from a new disease called AIDS (acquired immunodeficiency syndrome). At the beginning of the 1980s, public health officials had reported that gay men and intravenous drug users were especially at risk for developing AIDS. People contracted the human immunodeficiency virus (HIV), which causes AIDS, through contact with the blood or body fluids of an infected person. Those infected with the virus showed signs of extreme fatigue, developed a strange combination of infections, and soon died.

The Reagan administration showed little interest in AIDS in part because it was viewed as a "gay" disease. Reagan himself did not specifically mention AIDS in public until 1985, even though some 5,000 Americans had died of the disease. Patrick Buchanan, who served as Reagan's director of communications, said that gays had "declared war

ACT UP! Members of the influential AIDS activist group ACT UP! demonstrate for increased availability of life-saving medication.

on nature, and now nature is extracting an awful retribution." Buchanan and others convinced Reagan not to address the **HIV/AIDS** issue. In part because of federal government indifference, by 2001, 774,467 persons had contracted AIDS in the United States, and 448,060 of them had died. Nearly 1 million Americans were carrying the deadly virus, and it had become the leading cause of death among men aged twenty-five to forty-four.

Frustrated by the lack of concern shown by the Reagan administration, activists led by Larry Kramer, a playwright, novelist, and army veteran, founded the AIDS Coalition to Unleash Power (ACT UP) in 1987. It quickly became the most effective voice for fighting AIDS. Its members marched into the New York Stock Exchange and into the headquarters of pharmaceutical corporations and the offices of the Food and Drug Administration, all in an effort to accelerate research into the causes of AIDS in hopes of finding a cure.

The courage of Kramer and ACT UP helped transform medical practice. The number of newly reported AIDS cases has significantly declined from nearly 200,000 a year in 1988 to 35,000 in 2021. Dr. Anthony Fauci, the federal government's leading immunologist, credited Kramer for the successful effort to combat AIDS. "In American medicine," he said, "there are two eras. Before Larry and after Larry."

The Presidency of George H. W. Bush

In his farewell address in January 1989, Ronald Reagan said with a smile, "My friends, we did it. We . . . made a difference." Over his two terms, Reagan had become a transformational president. While restoring the stature of the presidency, helping to defuse the Cold War, and reviving the economy, he had accelerated the nation's shift toward conservatism and rejuvenated the Republican party after the Watergate scandal. He put the Democratic party on the defensive and forced conventional New Deal "liberalism" into a panicked retreat. For the next twenty years or so, Reagan's anti-government, anti-tax conservative agenda would dominate the national political landscape.

Reagan would prove a tough act to follow. His two-term vice president, George H. W. Bush, won the Republican presidential nomination in 1988 because he pledged to ensure an ethical government, be a more "hands-on" president than Reagan, and promote "a more compassionate conservatism." It was time to deal more seriously with the thorny problems of inner-city poverty, homelessness, and drug abuse.

A man of old-fashioned dignity who had committed much of his life to public service, Bush knew the value of conciliation, compromise, and common

George H. W. Bush His son, George W. Bush, would also serve as president, making them the second father-son presidential duo in history (the first was John Adams and John Quincy Adams).

sense. He viewed those on the other side of issues as opponents, not enemies. In short, he considered himself a doer, a problem solver, a man of action. The voters, he stressed in the White House, "did not send us here to bicker." It was now time, he said, to deal more seriously with the thorny problems of inner-city poverty, homelessness, and drug abuse.

Born into a prominent New England family, the son of a U.S. senator, George H. W. Bush had, at the age of eighteen, enlisted in the U.S. Navy at the start of the Second World War, becoming America's youngest combat pilot. After his distinguished military service, Bush graduated from Yale University and thereafter moved with his family to west Texas, where he became a wealthy oil executive before entering government service. He served first as a member of the U.S. House of Representatives and then as U.S. ambassador to the United Nations. He was elected chair of the Republican National Committee, became a diplomat in China, and was appointed director of the CIA before becoming vice president in 1981.

In all those roles, Bush had displayed intelligence, integrity, and courage, but he lacked Reagan's charm and eloquence. One Democrat described the wealthy Bush as having been born "with a silver foot in his mouth."

Bush was a centrist Republican who had never embraced right-wing conservatism. He promised to use the White House to fight bigotry, illiteracy,

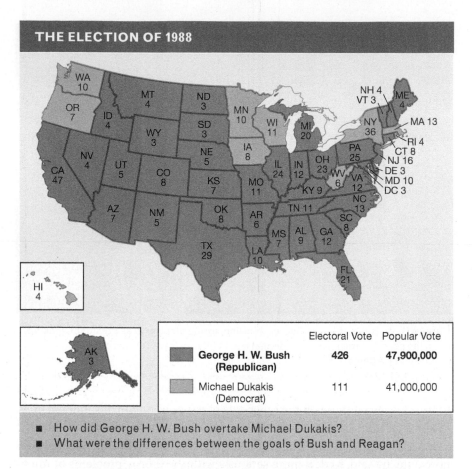

THE ELECTION OF 1988

	Electoral Vote	Popular Vote
George H. W. Bush (Republican)	426	47,900,000
Michael Dukakis (Democrat)	111	41,000,000

- How did George H. W. Bush overtake Michael Dukakis?
- What were the differences between the goals of Bush and Reagan?

and homelessness. "I want a kinder, gentler nation," Bush said in accepting the Republican nomination. Yet the most memorable line in his speech was a defiant statement ruling out any tax increases to deal with the massive budget deficits created during the Reagan years: "The Congress will push me to raise taxes, and I'll say no, and they'll push, and I'll say no, and they'll push again. And I'll say to them: Read my lips. *No new taxes.*"

In the end, Bush won decisively over the Democratic nominee, Massachusetts governor Michael Dukakis. Dukakis carried only ten states plus the District of Columbia, with clusters of support in the Northeast, Midwest, and Northwest. Bush carried the rest, with a margin of about 54 percent to 46 percent in the popular vote and 426 to 111 in the Electoral College, but the Democrats retained control of the House and Senate.

As the new president, George H. W. Bush felt the need to show that he was his own man, not a Reagan clone. To that end, he replaced Calvin Coolidge's portrait in the White House with one of Theodore Roosevelt, and he ordered all Reagan appointees to submit their resignations. Bush ended support for the Contras in Nicaragua and abandoned Reagan's unworkable "Star Wars" missile defense program.

Yet, for the most part, Bush sought to consolidate the initiatives that Reagan had put in place rather than launch his own array of programs and policies. "We don't need to remake society," he announced. As an example of his "compassionate" conservatism, Bush supported the Democratic-proposed Americans with Disabilities Act (ADA) in 1990, which strengthened the civil rights of those who are physically or mentally disabled in areas such as employment, public transportation, and housing. The ADA also required organizations to provide amenities such as mechanized doors, wheelchair ramps, and elevators to ensure that people with physical disabilities could more easily access facilities.

IMMIGRATION ACT OF 1990   On November 29, 1990, President Bush signed the bipartisan Immigration Act of 1990, which amended the Immigration and Nationality Act of 1965. It initially increased the total number of immigrants allowed each year to 700,000 between 1992 and 1994, and then the number would be capped at an annual 675,000 thereafter. Most of the visas would still be allocated to family members of U.S. citizens, but the bill added other preferences: people of "extraordinary ability" or "special skills," or with professional degrees in law, medicine, accounting, engineering, and other fields, all designed to attract the "best and the brightest" in the global labor market. In addition, the amendment introduced a "diversity lottery" system to assign visas to immigrants randomly, regardless of their country of origin. The act also lifted the ban on suspected gay and lesbian immigrants.

In signing the legislation, President Bush described it as the most comprehensive revision of immigration laws in decades and applauded its emphasis on ensuring greater diversity among immigrants being welcomed into the United States. He added that he was "also pleased to note that this Act facilitates immigration not just in numerical terms, but also in terms of basic entry rights of those beyond our borders." The new immigration act had a greater impact than its proponents imagined. During the 1990s, more immigrants entered the country than in any previous decade.

THE FEDERAL DEBT AND RECESSION   The biggest problem facing the Bush administration was the huge national debt, which stood at $2.9 trillion in 1989, nearly three times its 1980 level. President Bush's pledge not to increase taxes made it all the more difficult to reduce the annual budget deficits or trim the accumulating national debt. Likewise, Bush was not willing to make substantial spending cuts to defense or social welfare programs like

Social Security, Medicare, and food stamps. As a result, by 1990 the country faced "a fiscal mess."

During the summer of 1990, a frustrated Bush broke his promise and proposed several tax increases, including a spike in federal gasoline taxes. His reversal on raising taxes set off a revolt among conservative Republicans, from which the Bush presidency never recovered. Newt Gingrich, a Republican leader from Georgia in the House of Representatives, accused the president of "betrayal." A Republican-aligned New York newspaper expressed its views with a banner headline: "Read My Lips: I Lied."

Republicans in Congress were so angry at the president that they joined with Democrats in nixing Bush's budget proposal. A fuming Bush lashed out at Newt Gingrich: "You're killing us. You're killing us." With Congress and the White House unable to reach agreement on the budget, government agencies and offices, including national parks, shut down. People were furious, and their widespread anger forced Bush to admit defeat and sign a new resolution that reopened government offices. To do so, however, he had to agree to a new budget drafted by Democrats. It replaced the president's proposed gasoline tax with an increase in the top income tax rate, from 28 to 31 percent. Only a fourth of Republicans went along with the idea, but the Democrats marshaled enough votes for it to become law in October 1990.

The budget fiasco and tax increase created a lasting divide between congressional Republicans and President Bush. Even more worrisome was that the economy barely grew during the first three years of the Bush administration—the worst record since the end of the Second World War. By 1991, the economy was in a recession, the unemployment rate had spiked to 8 percent, and public disapproval of the president had risen accordingly.

THE DEMOCRACY MOVEMENT ABROAD   George H. W. Bush entered the White House with more foreign-policy experience than most presidents, and like Richard Nixon, he preferred to deal with international relations rather than domestic problems.

In the Soviet Union, amazing changes were under way. In December 1988, Soviet leader Mikhail Gorbachev shocked the world by renouncing his country's actions in fomenting the Cold War. New circumstances, he said, were causing the Soviets "to abandon traditional stereotypes and outdated views, and free ourselves from illusions." A new world was emerging that required "a different road to the future."

With the Soviet economy failing, Gorbachev responded with policies of *perestroika* ("economic restructuring") and *glasnost* ("openness"), a loosening of centralized economic planning and censorship of the press.

Gorbachev sought greater harmony and trade with the West. Early in 1989, Soviet troops left Afghanistan after nine years. Gorbachev then renounced the right of the Soviet Union to intervene in the internal affairs of other Communist countries. Soon thereafter, the old Communist regimes in Eastern Europe were toppled with surprisingly little bloodshed. Communist rule enforced by the Soviet Union ended first in Poland and Hungary, then in Czechoslovakia and Bulgaria. In Romania, the year of peaceful revolution ended in a bloodbath when the people joined the army in a bloody uprising against Nicolae Ceaușescu, the country's brutal dictator. He and his wife were captured, tried, and then executed on Christmas Day.

THE END OF THE BERLIN WALL The most spectacular event in the collapse of the Soviet empire came on November 9, 1989, when tens of thousands of East Germans gathered at the Berlin Wall and demanded that the border guards open the gates to West Berlin to allow them to flee. The guards reluctantly did so, and soon Germans on both sides—using hand tools and even their bare hands—tore down the Berlin Wall, the chief symbol of the Cold War. What Germans called the "peaceful revolution" had occurred with dramatic suddenness. With the borders to West Germany now fully open, the Communist government of East Germany collapsed. (On October 3, 1990, the five states of East Germany were reunited with West Germany.)

On December 3, 1989, Bush and Gorbachev met on a ship off the coast of Malta, an island in the Mediterranean. After Gorbachev declared that the Soviet Union no longer regarded "the United States as an adversary," Bush announced that "we stand at the threshold of a brand new era of U.S.-Soviet relations." With startling suddenness, the long Cold War was over.

A Hammer to the Soviet Empire A West German demonstrator pounds away at the Berlin Wall on November 11, 1989, while East Berlin border guards look on. Two days later, all the crossings between East and West Germany were opened.

The reform impulse that Gorbachev helped unleash in the Eastern-bloc countries sped out of control within the Soviet Union itself, however. Gorbachev had proven unusually adept at political restructuring, yielding the Communist monopoly of government but building a presidential system that gave him, if anything, increased powers. His skills, however, could not salvage an antiquated government-stifled economy that resisted change. In addition, as various Soviet states sought their independence, hardline Communist leaders questioned Gorbachev's leadership.

SOVIET COUP FAILS   Mikhail Gorbachev's popularity shrank in the Soviet Union as it grew abroad. Communist hard-liners saw in his reforms the unraveling of their bureaucratic and political empire. In August 1991, a group of "old guard" political and military leaders accosted Gorbachev at his vacation retreat in Crimea and demanded that he proclaim a state of emergency and transfer his powers to them. Gorbachev replied, "Go to hell," whereupon he was arrested. All political activity was suspended, and newspapers were shut down.

The coup, however, was poorly planned and clumsily implemented. The plotters neglected to close airports or cut off telephone and television communications, and they were opposed by key elements of the military and KGB (the Soviet secret police). The hard-liners also failed to arrest popular leaders such as Boris Yeltsin, the feisty president of the Russian Republic who energized nationwide resistance to the coup.

President Bush responded favorably to Yeltsin's request for support and persuaded other leaders to refuse to recognize the new Soviet government. On August 2, the coup collapsed, and the plotters fled. Several committed suicide, and a freed Gorbachev ordered the others arrested.

Gorbachev admitted that the coup "weakened my position as president" and set the Soviet Union hurtling into dissolution, with no clear sense of what would arise in its place. Four months later, on December 25, 1991, Gorbachev resigned and handed governing authority to Boris Yeltsin. That evening, the Soviet flag was lowered from the Kremlin and replaced with the Russian flag.

The Soviet Union was no more. Ronald Reagan's strategy of spending the Soviet Union into bankruptcy had triggered the astonishing disintegration of a superpower that had fascinated and frightened the world for seventy years. What had begun as a reactionary coup against Gorbachev turned into a powerful accelerant for the "Soviet Disunion," as one journalist termed it. Most of the fifteen Soviet republics proclaimed their independence from Russia, with the Baltic states of Latvia, Lithuania, and Estonia regaining the status of independent nations, with their own currencies, their own foreign policies, even their own armies. The Communist party was dismantled, prompting celebrating crowds to topple statues of Lenin and other Communist heroes. As 1989 ended, so too did the international Communist movement.

REDUCING THE NUCLEAR THREAT The collapse of the Soviet Union accelerated efforts to reduce their stockpiles of nuclear weapons. In late 1991, President Bush announced that the United States would destroy all its tactical nuclear weapons in Europe and Asia. Bush explained that the prospect of a Soviet invasion of Western Europe was "no longer a realistic threat" and that this transformation provided an unprecedented opportunity for reducing the threat of nuclear holocaust. President Gorbachev responded by announcing similar Soviet cutbacks. The sudden end of the Cold War led many to believe that the United States could greatly reduce the vast global military responsibilities it had developed over four decades of anti-communism.

U.S. INVASION OF PANAMA The end of the Cold War and the implosion of the Soviet Union did not spell the end of international tensions, however. Before the close of 1989, some 26,000 U.S. troops were engaged in combat in Panama.

In 1983, General Manuel Noriega had become the head of the Panamanian Defense Forces, which made him head of the government—in fact if not in title. He indulged himself with luxurious mansions and cocaine-fueled parties. He lusted after power and became a tyrant; he lusted after wealth and became an international criminal.

In 1988, federal grand juries in Florida indicted Noriega and fifteen others on charges of conspiring with Colombia's drug lords to ship cocaine through Panama to the United States. The next year, the Panamanian president tried to fire Noriega, but the National Assembly ousted the president and named Noriega "maximum leader."

In 1989, the National Assembly declared war on the United States. On December 16, Noriega's soldiers shot and killed an unarmed U.S. Marine in Panama City, wounded another, and arrested and roughed up a third American, a navy officer, and threatened his wife with sexual assault. "That was enough," President Bush said as he ordered an invasion (Operation Just Cause) "to protect American lives, restore the democratic process, preserve the integrity of the Panama Canal treaties and apprehend Manuel Noriega."

Early on December 20, U.S. troops struck at strategic targets in Panama City. Noriega surrendered within hours. Twenty-three U.S. servicemen were killed and more than 300 wounded; estimates of Panamanian casualties were as high as 4,000, including civilians. In April 1992, Noriega was convicted in the United States on eight counts of racketeering and drug distribution and sentenced to forty years in a federal prison.

THE GULF WAR In August 1990, Saddam Hussein, dictator of Iraq, focused U.S. attention back upon the Middle East when his huge army suddenly invaded Kuwait, its tiny but oil-rich neighbor. The invasion became the first major crisis of the post–Cold War era. Kuwait had increased its oil production, contrary to agreements with the Organization of the Petroleum Exporting Countries (OPEC). The resulting drop in global oil prices offended the Iraqi regime, which was deeply in debt and heavily dependent upon oil revenues.

Although most foreign leaders assumed that nothing could or should be done to protect Kuwait, President Bush condemned Iraq's "naked aggression" and declared that "this will not stand." If Saddam Hussein were not stopped, Bush feared, he might next invade Saudi Arabia. The president dispatched warplanes and troops to defend Kuwait and Saudi Arabia and then recruited other nations to support the U.S. effort. British forces soon joined in, as did Arab troops from Egypt, Morocco, Syria, Oman, the United Arab Emirates,

Operation Desert Storm Allied soldiers patrol the southern Iraqi city of Salman Pak on February 27,.1991. On the side of a building is a propaganda mural of dictator Saddam Hussein in military uniform.

Qatar, and other countries. Iraq refused to yield, and on January 12, 1991, Congress authorized the use of force to liberate Kuwait. The United Nations Security Council, including Russia and China, agreed that Iraq must withdraw from Kuwait.

Four days later, U.S. military units and those from thirty-three other nations, including ten Islamic countries, launched **Operation Desert Storm** against Iraq. During the next six weeks, Iraqi soldiers surrendered by the thousands, and on February 28, Bush called for a cease-fire. The Iraqis accepted. Although coalition forces occupied about a fifth of Iraq, Hussein's tyrannical regime remained intact. Bush believed that removing Hussein would have only brought more instability to an already unstable region.

What came to be called the Gulf War was thus a triumph without victory. Hussein had been defeated, but he remained in power. The war's consequences would be played out in the future, as Arabs humiliated by the American triumph began plotting revenge that would spiral into a new war of terrorism.

BUSH'S "NEW WORLD ORDER" For months after the first Gulf War in 1991, George H. W. Bush seemed unbeatable; his public approval rating soared to 91 percent. Yet the aftermath of Desert Storm was mixed, with Saddam Hussein's iron grip on Iraq still intact. The Soviet Union meanwhile stumbled on to its surprising end. As a result, the United States had become the world's only dominant military power.

Containment of the Soviet Union, the bedrock of U.S. foreign policy for more than four decades, had suddenly become irrelevant. For all its potential horrors, the Cold War brought stability because the two superpowers, the United States and the Soviet Union, had restrained themselves from an all-out war that may well have involved the use of nuclear weapons. Now the world would witness a growing number of unresolved political crises and unstable regimes, some of which had access to weapons of mass destruction—nuclear as well as chemical and biological weapons.

President Bush struggled to interpret the fluid new international scene. He spoke of a "new world order" but never defined it, admitting that he had trouble with "the vision thing." By the end of 1991, the euphoria of the Gulf War victory had worn off and a listless Bush faced a challenge in the Republican primary from the feisty conservative commentator and former White House aide Patrick Buchanan, who adopted the slogan "America First" and called on Bush to "bring home the boys."

The excitement over the allied victory in the Gulf War quickly gave way to anxiety over the depressed economy. In addressing the recession, Bush tried a clumsy balancing act, on the one hand acknowledging that "people are hurting" while on the other telling Americans that "this is a good time to buy a car." By 1991, the public approval rating of his economic policy had plummeted to 18 percent.

THE 1992 ELECTION   At the 1992 Republican National Convention, Patrick Buchanan, who had won about a third of the votes in the party's primaries, blasted Bush for breaking his pledge not to raise taxes and for becoming the "biggest spender in American history." Rush Limbaugh, the popular conservative Republican radio commentator, showed equal disdain for Bush, charging that he had "compromised his promises and beliefs on nearly every important principle he articulated." According to Limbaugh, Bush had "rolled over for the liberals," and the result was a failed presidency.

As the 1992 election unfolded, however, Bush's real problem proved to be his failure to improve the economy. In a reflection of the high unemployment rate, a popular bumper sticker expressed the public's frustration: "Saddam Hussein still has his job. What about you?"

In contrast to the divided Republicans, the Democrats at their 1992 convention presented an image of centrist or moderate forces in control. For several years, the Democratic Leadership Council, led by Arkansas governor William Jefferson Clinton, had been pushing the party from the liberal left to the center of the political spectrum. Clinton called for a "third way" positioned between conservatism and liberalism.

The 1992 campaign also featured a third-party candidate, Texan H. Ross Perot, a puckish billionaire who found a large audience for his criticism of Reaganomics as "voodoo economics" (a phrase originally used in the 1980 Republican primary by then-contender George H. W. Bush before he was named the vice-presidential candidate on the Reagan presidential ticket) and his warnings about the impending crisis posed by the huge federal debt. Perot appealed to those fed up with government "gridlock" created by the polarization of the two major parties. As the CEO of a high-tech company, Perot initially won support for a unique proposal: an electronic town hall that would enable voters to express their preferences for major policies through instantaneous digital polling.

Bill Clinton, however, attracted most of the media attention. Born in 1946 in Hope, Arkansas, he was a brilliant student who attended Georgetown University in Washington, D.C., won a Rhodes Scholarship to Oxford University, and earned a law degree from Yale University, where he met his future wife, Hillary Rodham. Clinton returned to Arkansas and won election as the state's attorney general. By 1979, at age thirty-two, he was the youngest governor in the country. He served three more terms as "boy governor" and emerged as a dynamic leader of the "**New Democrats**," who were committed to winning back the middle-class Whites ("Reagan Democrats") who had voted Republican during the 1980s.

A self-described moderate seeking the Democratic presidential nomination, Clinton promised to cut the defense budget, provide tax relief for the middle class, and create a massive economic aid package for the former republics of the Soviet Union to help them forge democratic societies. Witty, intelligent, and charismatic, with an in-depth knowledge of public policy, Clinton was a superb campaigner; he projected energy, youth, and optimism, reminding many political observers of John F. Kennedy, Clinton's boyhood hero.

But beneath Clinton's charisma and public-policy expertise lurked several flaws. Self-absorbed and self-indulgent, he, like Lyndon Johnson, yearned to be loved. Biographers explained that Clinton was "emotionally needy, indecisive and undisciplined." During his four terms as governor, his critics accused him of flip-flopping on major issues and pandering to special interest groups. There were also allegations that he had altered his ROTC service record to avoid serving in the Vietnam War. Even more enticing to the media were rumors that Clinton was a chronic adulterer. His evasive denials of both accusations could not dispel a lingering mistrust of his character.

After a series of bruising party primaries, Clinton won the Democratic presidential nomination in the summer of 1992, promising to restore the "hopes of the forgotten middle class." He chose Senator Albert "Al" Gore Jr. of Tennessee as his running mate. Gore described himself as a "raging moderate." Flushed with their convention victory and sporting a ten-point lead over President Bush in the polls, the Clinton-Gore team hammered Bush on economic issues to win over working-class voters. Clinton pledged that, if elected, he would cut the federal budget deficit in half in four years while cutting taxes paid by middle-class Americans.

Such promises helped Clinton win the election with 370 electoral votes and about 42 percent of the popular

Bill Clinton and Al Gore The Democratic candidates round out their campaign in Clinton's hometown of Little Rock, Arkansas, on November 3, 1992.

vote; Bush received 168 electoral votes and 39 percent of the popular vote; and Ross Perot garnered 19 percent of the popular vote, more than any other third-party candidate since Theodore Roosevelt in 1912.

As 1992 came to an end, Bill Clinton, the "New Democrat," prepared to lead the United States through the last decade of the twentieth century. "The urgent question of our time," he said, "is whether we can make change our friend and not our enemy." During his eight years as president, Clinton would embrace many unexpected changes while ushering America into the twenty-first century.

THE CLINTON PRESIDENCY (1993–2001)

Bill Clinton brought to the White House extraordinary gifts—and robust weaknesses. At forty-six years old, he was the third-youngest president in history. Like Ronald Reagan, Clinton charmed people, and his speeches inspired them. He embraced politics as a civic duty and painstakingly learned the details of major policies and programs.

Clinton's inexperience in international affairs and congressional maneuvering led to several missteps in his first year as president. Like George H. W. Bush before him, he reneged on several campaign promises. In a bruising battle with Congress, he was forced to abandon his proposed middle-class tax cut in order to keep another campaign promise to reduce the federal deficit. Then he dropped his promise to allow gays, lesbians, and bisexuals to serve openly in the armed forces after military commanders expressed strong opposition. He later announced an ambiguous policy called "don't ask, don't tell" (DADT), which allowed gays, lesbians, and bisexuals to serve in the military but only if they kept their sexual orientation secret (DADT did not mention transgender service members). "I got the worst of both worlds," Clinton later confessed. "I lost the fight, and the gay community was highly critical of me for the compromise."

THE ECONOMY   As a candidate, Bill Clinton had pledged to reduce the federal deficit without damaging the economy or hurting the nation's most vulnerable people. To this end, he proposed $241 billion in higher taxes for corporations and for the wealthiest individuals over a period of four years, and $255 billion in spending cuts over the same time frame. The hotly contested bill passed the Democratic-controlled Congress by the slimmest of margins: 218 to 216 in the House and 51 to 50 in the Senate, with Vice President Al Gore providing the tie-breaking vote.

Rally for the Violence Against Women Act A group of marchers at a rally in support of the Violence Against Women Act.

For virtually the first time since 1945, Congress had passed a major bill without a single Republican vote, a troubling indication of the nation's growing partisan divide. Bipartisanship in Congress was a dying tradition. Clinton's deficit-reduction effort worked as planned. It led to lower interest rates, which, along with low energy prices, helped spur economic growth.

An equally difficult battle for Clinton was gaining congressional approval of the **North American Free Trade Agreement (NAFTA)**, which the Bush administration had negotiated with Canada and Mexico. In 1994, Clinton urged Congress to approve NAFTA, which would make North America the largest free-trade zone in the world. Opponents favored tariffs to discourage the importation of cheaper foreign products, especially from Mexico. Yet Clinton prevailed with solid Republican support. A sizable minority of Democrats, mostly labor unionists and southerners, opposed NAFTA, fearing that textile mills would lose business (and millions of jobs) to "cheap labor" countries—as they did.

CONFRONTING RISING CRIME Democrats were eager to address the startling rise in urban crime, particularly violent crime, that had begun in the 1960s and continued, on and off, through the 1990s (in part because of the crack cocaine epidemic). Senator Joe Biden, a Delaware Democrat who chaired the Senate Judiciary Committee, took the lead in drafting the Violent Crime Control and Law Enforcement Act, which both parties supported and President Clinton signed in 1994.

The crime bill included a long list of controversial items depending on your ideological worldview. It funded new prisons and tens of thousands of community police officers and drug courts, banned assault weapons for ten years, and mandated life sentences for criminals convicted of a violent felony after two or more prior convictions, including drug crimes. The mandated life sentences were known as the "three-strikes" provision.

The bill also included The Violence Against Women Act, which provided more resources to stop domestic violence and rape. The law also encouraged states to create drug courts to divert drug offenders from prison into treatment, and also helped fund some addiction treatment.

HEALTH-CARE REFORM Clinton's major public-policy initiative was an ambitious plan to overhaul the nation's health-care system. "If I don't get health care," he declared, "I'll wish I didn't run for president." Public support for government-administered health insurance had increased as medical costs skyrocketed and some 37 million Americans, most of them poor or unemployed, went without coverage. The Clinton administration argued that providing medical insurance to everyone, regardless of income, would reduce the costs of health care, but critics in Congress questioned the savings—and the ability of the federal government to manage such a huge program efficiently.

Clinton's plan called for everyone to be enrolled in a qualified health insurance plan, either through their individual initiative or through their employer. Those too poor to afford coverage were to receive government subsidies to enable them to enroll. All large businesses (over 5,000 employees) would have to pay for most of the medical insurance expenses of their employees while small businesses would be required to form "health alliances" so that they, too, could provide subsidized health insurance to their workers.

By the summer of 1994, Clinton's bulky 1,364-page health-insurance plan, developed by a 500-person task force of "experts" headed by the First Lady, Hillary Rodham Clinton, rather than congressional leaders, was doomed, in part because the president opposed any changes to his wife's plan and in part because the report was impossibly complicated. Strenuously opposed by Republicans and health-care interest groups, especially the pharmaceutical and insurance industries, Clinton's prized health-care bill, officially called the Health Security Act, lost in Congress in 1994. As the president lamented, "We . . . took too long and ended up achieving nothing."

THE CONTRACT WITH AMERICA The health-care disaster and the growing federal budget deficit played a dramatic role in the 1994 midterm elections. In the most astonishing congressional victory of the twentieth century, the Republicans captured both houses of Congress for the first time since 1953. They also won thirty-two governorships, including those in the most populous states of California, New York, and Texas, where George W. Bush, son of the former president and a future president himself, won handily. "We got the living daylight beat out of us," Bill Clinton admitted.

A Georgia conservative named Newton (Newt) Leroy Gingrich orchestrated the Republican congressional victories. In early 1995, he became the first Republican Speaker of the House in forty-two years. Gingrich, a former history professor with a lust for controversy, an unruly ego, and an overweening ambition, was a superb tactician who had helped mobilize conservative voters associated with the Christian Coalition.

The Christian Coalition, organized by television evangelist Pat Robertson in 1989 to replace Jerry Falwell's Moral Majority (which had disbanded that year), was pro–school prayer, antiabortion, anti-feminist, and anti–LGBTQ (lesbian, gay, bisexual, transgender, queer) rights. In many respects, the Religious Right took control of the political and social landscape in the nineties.

In 1994, Gingrich and other Republican candidates rallied conservative voters by lambasting Bill Clinton as "the enemy of normal Americans." Gingrich was determined to end the congressional tradition of bipartisan compromise and replace it with all-out partisan warfare. He and his congressional colleagues promised to bring forward a **Contract with America**, an audacious pledge to dismantle the "corrupt liberal welfare state" created by Democrats.

The ten-point, anti-big-government "contract" promised a smaller federal

Newt Gingrich Joined by 160 of his fellow House Republicans, Speaker of the House Newt Gingrich promotes the Contract with America in April 1995.

government by reducing taxes and regulations, requiring term limits for members of Congress, slashing social welfare and racial affirmative-action programs, and passing a constitutional amendment requiring a balanced federal budget. As Texan Tom DeLay, a leading House Republican, explained, "You've got to understand, we are ideologues. We have an agenda. We have a philosophy."

Yet the much-trumpeted Contract with America quickly fizzled. The conservatives pushed too hard and too fast, realizing too late that their slim majority in Congress could not launch a revolution. Gingrich's combative tactics contributed to the disintegration of the Contract with America. He was too ambitious, too abrasive, too divisive. When Clinton refused to go along with Republican demands for a balanced-budget pledge, Gingrich twice shut down the federal government during the fall of 1995, sending 800,000 employees home and closing national parks, Social Security offices, and other agencies. The tactic backfired. By 1996, Republicans had abandoned their Contract with America.

THE SUPREME COURT AND RACE The conservative resurgence also revealed itself in Supreme Court rulings that undermined affirmative-action programs, which gave African American students special consideration in college admissions and financial-aid awards. Between 1970 and 1977, African American enrollment in colleges and universities doubled, even as White students and their parents complained about "reverse discrimination."

Two major 1996 rulings affected affirmative action in college admissions. In *Hopwood v. Texas*, a federal court ruled that race could not be used as a consideration for admission in higher education. Later that year, California voters passed Proposition 209 (also known as the California Civil Rights Initiative, or CCRI), which ruled out preferential treatment (affirmative action) in government hiring, government contracting, and public schools and colleges based on race, sex, ethnicity, or national origin.

Similar complaints were directed against affirmative-action programs that awarded government contracts to businesses owned by women and people of color. In 1995, the Court in *Adarand Constructors v. Peña* declared that affirmative-action programs had to be "narrowly tailored" to serve a "compelling national interest." The implication of such vague language was clear: the mostly conservative justices on the Court had come to share the growing public suspicion of the legitimacy of programs designed to benefit a particular race, gender, or ethnic group.

LEGISLATIVE BREAKTHROUGH After the surprising 1994 Republican takeover of Congress, Bill Clinton shrewdly resolved to reinforce his claim that he was a "centrist." He co-opted much of the energy of the conservative movement by announcing that "the era of big government is over" and by reforming the federal system of welfare payments to the poor.

Late in the summer of 1996, the Republican-controlled Congress passed a comprehensive welfare-reform measure, the **Personal Responsibility and Work Opportunity Act of 1996 (PRWOA)**. It illustrated Clinton's efforts to move the Democratic party away from the liberalism it had promoted since the 1930s.

The PRWOA abolished the Aid to Families with Dependent Children (AFDC) program, which had provided poor families almost $8,000 a year, and replaced it with the Temporary Assistance for Needy Families program, which limited the duration of welfare payments to two years in an effort to encourage unemployed people—including immigrants—to get self-supporting jobs.

President Clinton privately called the new measure "a decent welfare bill wrapped in a sack of s–t," but he signed it anyway to help ensure his reelection. Liberal Democrats bitterly criticized Clinton's "welfare reform" deal. Yet it was a statistical and political success. Both the number of welfare recipients and poverty rates declined during the late 1990s, leading the editors of the left-leaning *New Republic* to report that the PRWOA had "worked much as its designers had hoped." Its passage also enabled Clinton to reposition himself as a centrist.

IMMIGRATION REFORM Bill Clinton's efforts to move the Democratic party away from "excessive liberalism" included a new immigration bill that he signed in 1996. Called the Illegal Immigration Reform and Immigration Responsibility Act (IIRIRA), it addressed the dramatic increase in the number of undocumented immigrants in the United States. The new law broadened the scope of those immigrants eligible to be deported. It also gave immigration officers the authority to arrest and deport people without bringing them before a judge. Under IIRIRA, all noncitizens, including many immigrants who had been in the United States for years, even decades, were subject to deportation without a hearing. The IIRIRA also provided substantial increases in funding for the Border Patrol and enabled the federal government to construct barrier fencing along the border with Mexico. President Clinton maintained that the new legislation strengthened "the rule of law by cracking down on illegal

March against Immigration Reform In 1996, the Illegal Immigration Reform and Immigration Responsibility Act (IIRIRA) permitted the deportation of undocumented immigrants without trial. In protest, undocumented immigrants demanded a simpler process toward citizenship.

immigration at the border, in the workplace, and in the criminal justice system—without punishing those living in the United States legally."

THE 1996 CAMPAIGN The Republican takeover of Congress in 1994 had given the party hope that it could prevent President Clinton's reelection. After clinching the GOP presidential nomination in 1996, Senate majority leader Bob Dole of Kansas resigned his seat to devote his attention to the campaign. Clinton, however, maintained a large lead in the polls, in part because he now had successfully portrayed himself as a centrist.

Concern about Dole's age (seventy-three) and his gruff personality, as well as tensions between economic and social conservatives over volatile issues such as abortion and gun control, hampered Dole's efforts to generate widespread support, especially among independent voters. Dole portrayed himself as a pragmatist willing to "downsize government, [but] not devastate it." Clinton, however, framed the election as a stark choice between Dole's desire to build a bridge to the past and Clinton's promise to build a bridge to the future.

On November 5, 1996, Clinton won with an electoral vote victory of 379 to 159 and 49 percent of the popular vote. Dole received 41 percent of the popular vote. Third-party candidate Ross Perot got 8 percent.

THE "NEW ECONOMY" Bill Clinton's presidency benefited from a prolonged period of unprecedented prosperity. During the 1996 campaign, he took credit for having generated "ten million new jobs, over half of them high wage jobs." During his last three years in office (1998–2000), the federal government generated unheard-of budget *surpluses*. What came to be called the **new economy** featured high-flying electronics, computer, software, tele-communications (cell phones, cable TV, etc.), and e-commerce internet firms called "dot-com" companies.

These dynamic tech enterprises helped the U.S. economy set records in every area: low inflation, low unemployment, corporate profits, and personal fortunes. Alan Greenspan, the Federal Reserve Board chairman, suggested that "we have moved beyond history" into an economy that seemed only to grow. He would soon be proven wrong.

GLOBALIZATION Another feature of the new economy was **globalization**, the process by which people, goods, information, and cultural tastes circulated across national boundaries. People began talking about a "border-less economy" as high-tech companies like Microsoft, Apple, and Amazon developed a worldwide presence. The end of the Cold War and the disintegration of the Soviet Union accelerated economic globalization by opening many opportunities for U.S. companies in international trade. In addition, new globe-spanning communication technologies, the internet, and massive new container-carrying ships and cargo jets shortened time and distance, enabling multinational companies to conduct more business abroad. In 1994, more than a hundred nations sent representatives to the founding meeting of the World Trade Organization (WTO), whose primary purpose was to facilitate free trade worldwide.

Bill Clinton accelerated the process of globalization. "The global economy," he said, "is giving more of our own people, and billions around the world, the chance to work and live and raise their families with dignity." He especially welcomed the World Wide Web, which opened the internet to everyone, and, by doing so, greatly accelerated U.S. dominance of the international economy.

By 2000, more than a third of the production of U.S. multinational companies was occurring abroad, compared with only 9 percent in 1980. In 1970, there were 7,000 American multinational companies; by the year 2000, there were 63,000. Many multinational companies pursued controversial *outsourcing* strategies—moving their production facilities "offshore" to nations such as Mexico and China to take advantage of lower labor costs and fewer workplace and environmental regulations. At the same time, many European and Asian companies, especially automobile manufacturers, built large plants in the United States to reduce the shipping expenses required to get their products to American markets.

FOREIGN POLICY IN THE NINETIES

Unlike George H. W. Bush, Bill Clinton had little interest in global politics. Untrained and inexperienced in international relations, he sought to create opportunities around the world for U.S. business expansion. Yet, as international analyst Leslie Gelb cautioned Clinton, "A foreign economic policy is not a foreign policy, and it is not a national security strategy." Events soon forced Clinton to intervene to help foreign nations in crisis.

THE MIDDLE EAST During the 1990s, the Middle East remained a region fractured by ethnic and religious conflict and ruled by authoritarian regimes. President Clinton continued George H. W. Bush's policy of orchestrating patient negotiations between the Arabs and the Israelis. A new development was the inclusion of the Palestine Liberation Organization (PLO) in the discussions.

In 1993, secret talks between Israeli and Palestinian representatives in Oslo, Norway, resulted in a draft agreement that provided for the restoration of Palestinian self-rule in the occupied Gaza Strip and in Jericho, in the West Bank, in a "land for peace" exchange as outlined in United Nations Security Council resolutions. A formal signing occurred at the White House on September 13, 1993. With President Clinton presiding, Israeli prime minister Yitzhak Rabin and PLO leader Yasir Arafat exchanged handshakes, and their foreign ministers signed the agreement.

However, the Middle East peace process suffered a terrible blow in early November 1995, when Rabin was assassinated by an Israeli militant upset by efforts to negotiate with the Palestinians. Seven months later, conservative hard-liner Benjamin Netanyahu narrowly defeated U.S.-backed Shimon Peres in the Israeli national elections. Nevertheless, in October 1998, Clinton brought Yasir Arafat, Netanyahu, and King Hussein of Jordan together to reach an agreement. Under the Wye River Accords, Israel agreed to surrender land in return for security guarantees by the Palestinians.

THE BALKANS President Clinton also felt compelled to address turmoil in the eastern European nations recently freed from Soviet domination. In

1991, Yugoslavia had disintegrated into ethnic warfare as four of its six multi-ethnic republics declared their independence. Serb minorities, backed by the new Republic of Serbia, stirred up civil wars in neighboring Croatia and Bosnia. In Bosnia, the conflict involved genocidal efforts to eliminate Muslims. Clinton decided that the situation was "intolerable" because the massacres of thousands of Bosnian Muslims "tore at the very fabric" of human decency. He ordered food and medical supplies sent to Bosnia and dispatched warplanes to stop the massacres.

In 1995, U.S. negotiators finally persuaded the foreign ministers of Croatia, Bosnia, and Yugoslavia (by then a loose federation of the Republics of Serbia and Montenegro) to agree to a comprehensive peace plan. Bosnia would remain a single nation divided into two states: a Muslim-Croat federation controlling 51 percent of the territory, and a Bosnian-Serb republic controlling the rest. To enforce the agreement, 60,000 NATO peacekeeping troops were dispatched to Bosnia.

McRubble Pro-Milošević residents of Belgrade, Yugoslavia, destroy the storefront of a McDonald's fast-food restaurant in 1999 to protest NATO and the United States' air strikes on their homeland.

In 1998, the Balkan tinderbox flared up again, this time in the Yugoslav province of Kosovo, long considered sacred ground by Christian Serbs, although 90 percent of the 2 million Kosovars were in fact Albanian Muslims. Yugoslav president Slobodan Milošević began a program of "ethnic cleansing" whereby Yugoslav forces burned Albanian villages, murdered men, raped women, and displaced hundreds of thousands of Muslim Kosovars.

On March 24, 1999, NATO, relying heavily upon U.S. military support, launched air strikes against Yugoslavian military targets. After seventy-two days of bombardment, Milošević sued for peace on NATO's terms, in part because his Russian allies had abandoned him. An agreement was reached on June 3, 1999, and Clinton pledged extensive U.S. aid to help the Yugoslavs rebuild their war-torn economy.

The Scandal Machine

For a time, Bill Clinton's preoccupation with foreign crises helped deflect attention from several investigations into his personal conduct. During his first term, he was dogged by old charges about investments he and his wife had made in Whitewater, a planned resort community in Arkansas. The project turned out to be a fraud and a failure, and people accused the Clintons of conspiring with the developer. In 1994, Kenneth Starr, a former judge and a conservative Republican, was appointed to investigate the Whitewater case.

Starr found no evidence that the Clintons were directly involved in the Whitewater fraud, but in the course of another investigation, he happened upon evidence of a White House sex scandal. Between 1995 and 1997, President Clinton had a sixteen-month-long sexual affair with an unpaid twenty-two-year-old White House intern, Monica Lewinsky. Even more disturbing, he had pressed her to lie about their relationship, even under oath.

Clinton initially denied the charges, telling the nation in late January 1998, "I did *not* have sexual relations with that woman, Miss Lewinsky." Yet the scandal would not disappear. A former aide, David Gergen, warned that if the president was lying, "he has betrayed the public trust and is a scoundrel." A desperate Clinton went to extraordinary lengths to camouflage the truth, even drawing his secretary into his web of deceit.

For the next thirteen months, the media circus surrounding the "Monicagate" affair captured public attention like a daily soap opera. With the economy booming, however, Clinton's public approval ratings actually rose during

1998. In August, however, the bottom fell out of Clinton's denials when Monica Lewinsky provided a federal grand jury with a detailed account of her intimate relationship with the president.

Soon thereafter, knowing that he was about to be proven a liar, Clinton confessed to his wife and daughter before becoming the first president in history to testify before a grand jury. On August 17, the self-pitying, defiant Clinton admitted in a televised address to having had "inappropriate, intimate physical contact" with Lewinsky but insisted that he had done nothing illegal.

Public reaction was mixed. A majority expressed sympathy for Clinton throughout his ordeal because of his humiliation and because the Lewinsky affair was a private act of consensual sex. Others, however, were eager to see the president resign. Republicans were convinced they could impeach him— and they set about to do so.

THE CLINTON IMPEACHMENT On September 9, 1998, Special Prosecutor Kenneth Starr submitted to Congress documents that included a graphic account of the Lewinsky episode. The Starr Report claimed that there was "substantial and credible" evidence of presidential wrongdoing (perjury, obstructing justice, and abuse of power). On October 8, the Republican-dominated House of Representatives began a wide-ranging impeachment inquiry, which led Clinton to claim that he was the victim of a rogue prosecutor run amok. "When this thing is over," Clinton said, "there's only going to be one of us left standing. And it's going to be me."

On December 19, 1998, William Jefferson Clinton was impeached (accused of "high crimes and misdemeanors"). The House of Representatives charged Clinton with obstructing justice and lying under oath to a federal grand jury.

House Speaker Newt Gingrich initially led the impeachment effort, even though he himself was secretly engaged in a long-standing sexual affair with a congressional staff member. (Gingrich resigned as Speaker in November 1998 and left both the House and his wife, escaping with his new wife from elected office altogether.)

Journalists began calling Clinton's Senate trial the "soap opera" impeachment after Gingrich's successor as Speaker, Robert Livingston of Louisiana, suddenly resigned after admitting that he, too, had been involved in adulterous affairs.

The impeachment trial began on January 7, 1999. Five weeks later, on February 12, Clinton was acquitted, largely on a party-line vote. A majority of senators, mostly Democrats and a few Republicans (55–45), decided that Clinton had not committed the "high crimes and misdemeanors" required to remove a president from office.

Impeachment Witnesses testifying before the House Judiciary Committee as part of President Clinton's impeachment over "high crimes and misdemeanors" in December 1998.

After presiding over the trial, Chief Justice William Rehnquist congratulated the senators. He was "impressed" by their debate "on the entire question of impeachment as provided for under the Constitution." Most Americans agreed. As historian Steven Gillon observed, "The only thing most Americans disliked more than a devious middle-aged man lying about sex was moralizing, self-righteous hypocrites telling other people how to lead their lives." Years later, Kenneth Starr admitted that his four-year-long effort to impeach Clinton "had been a mistake."

ASSESSING THE CLINTON PRESIDENCY

For all his faults, Bill Clinton presided over an unprecedented period of peace and prosperity (115 consecutive months of economic growth and the lowest unemployment rate in thirty years), generated record federal budget surpluses, and passed a welfare-reform measure with support from both parties. Crime rates fell during his presidency, and he facilitated the rapid rise of the internet and the rapid expansion of globalization. At the same time, he revitalized the Democratic party by moving it from the left to the "vital center" of the political spectrum. Clinton also helped bring peace and stability to the Balkans.

At times, however, he displayed arrogant recklessness, and his effort to bring health insurance to the uninsured was a clumsy failure. Yet in 2000, his last year in office, his public approval rating was 65 percent, the highest end-of-term rating since Dwight D. Eisenhower. Bill Clinton's popularity was not enough, however, to ensure the election of his vice president, Al Gore, as his successor.

CHAPTER REVIEW

SUMMARY

- **The Carter Presidency**   Jimmy Carter had notable achievements, such as the 1978 *Camp David Accords*. Yet his administration suffered from legislative inexperience, a deepening economic recession, soaring inflation, and the *Iranian hostage crisis* (1979). His sermonizing about the need for Americans to lead simpler lives compounded the public's loss of faith in his presidency.

- **Ronald Reagan and the Rise of Conservatism**   The Republican insurgency won Reagan the election in 1980 and was dominated by the *Christian Right* characterized in part by a cultural backlash against the feminist movement. Sunbelt voters were socially conservative and favored lower taxes and a smaller, less intrusive federal government. California's property-tax-lowering referendum, Proposition 13, led to a nationwide tax revolt.

- **The Reagan Revolution**   Reagan introduced a "supply-side" economic philosophy, commonly called *Reaganomics*, that championed tax cuts for the rich, reduced government regulation, cuts to social welfare programs, and increased defense spending. In practice, however, Reagan was unable to cut domestic spending significantly, and the tax cuts failed to pay for themselves as promised. The result was a dramatic increase in the national debt. Reagan also did much to weaken unions and the feminist movement, and to shift the political landscape away from the New Deal liberalism that had dominated American politics since 1932.

- **The End of the Cold War**   Reagan's massive military buildup, including preliminary development of the *Strategic Defense Initiative (SDI)* in 1983, brought the Soviets to agreement in 1987 on the *Intermediate-Range Nuclear Forces (INF) Treaty*—the beginning of the end of the Cold War. But Reagan's foreign policy was badly tarnished in 1987 by the *Iran-Contra affair*.

- **The Changing Economic and Social Landscape: America in the 1980s**   The eighties brought not only unprecedented prosperity but also rising poverty and homelessness. The prevailing conservative mood condemned *HIV/AIDS* as a "gay" disease. The *microprocessor* ignited the computer revolution, which dramatically increased productivity and communications while generating new industries. Consumerism flourished all too well, resulting in massive public and private debt.

- **A New World Order: The Presidency of George H. W. Bush**   In the late 1980s, democratic political movements erupted. Gorbachev's steps to restructure the Soviet Union's economy (*perestroika*) and promote more open policies (*glasnost*) ultimately led to the collapse of the Soviet empire. Iraq, led by Saddam Hussein, invaded Kuwait in 1990. The United States led allied forces in *Operation Desert Storm* (1991); the Iraqis soon surrendered. Despite the success of the first Gulf War, the sluggish economy led to Bush's defeat by the *New Democrats* under Bill Clinton.

- **Divided Government: The Bill Clinton Presidency**   Two years into the Clinton presidency, Republican Speaker of the House Newt Gingrich crafted his *Contract with America* (1994) against the "corrupt liberal welfare state" and achieved a Republican landslide in the 1994 midterm elections. The *North American Free*

Trade Agreement (NAFTA) (1994) and the *Personal Responsibility and Work Opportunity Act of 1996 (PRWOA)* were bipartisan successes. The prosperous high-tech *new economy* helped Clinton balance the federal budget, but the controversial process of *globalization*, whereby huge U.S. corporations came to dominate the everyday consumer choices of people across the globe, generated unexpected consequences and backlashes against U.S. economic "imperialism." In the end, Bill Clinton's personal scandals tarnished his presidency, and in 1998 he was impeached, though ultimately acquitted by the Senate.

CHRONOLOGY

1971	Microprocessor developed
1975	First personal computer, the Altair 8800, produced
1978	Camp David Accords; Tax revolt in California leads to the passage of Proposition 13
1979	Jerry Falwell organizes the Moral Majority
November 1979	Iranian hostage crisis begins
1980	Ronald Reagan elected president
1981	Reagan enacts major tax cuts
1983	Strategic Defense Initiative (SDI) authorized
1987	Tower Commission reports on Iran-Contra affair; Reagan delivers Berlin Wall speech
1988	George H. W. Bush elected president
November 1989	Berlin Wall torn down
December 1989	U.S. troops invade Panama and capture Manuel Noriega
1990–1991	First Gulf War; Soviet Union dissolves
1992	Bill Clinton elected president
1991	Ethnic conflict explodes in Yugoslavia
1994	NAFTA goes into effect; Contract with America
1996	Congress passes welfare reform
1998	President Clinton impeached

KEY TERMS

Camp David Accords (1978) p. 1488
Iranian hostage crisis (1979) p. 1490
Christian Right p. 1495
Reaganomics p. 1499
Strategic Defense Initiative (SDI) (1983) p. 1505
Iran-Contra affair (1987) p. 1508
Intermediate-Range Nuclear Forces (INF) Treaty (1987) p. 1511
microprocessor p. 1512
HIV/AIDS p. 1516
perestroika p. 1520

glasnost p. 1520
Operation Desert Storm (1991) p. 1525
New Democrats p. 1527
North American Free Trade Agreement (NAFTA) (1994) p. 1529
Contract with America (1994) p. 1531
Personal Responsibility and Work Opportunity Act of 1996 (PRWOA) p. 1533
new economy p. 1535
globalization p. 1535

30 Twenty-First-Century America

2000–Present

Black Lives Matter Protest People gathered all over the world to protest the deaths of Black Americans George Floyd, Breonna Taylor, and Ahmaud Arbery, among others, to denounce racism and police brutality.

The United States entered the final decade of the twentieth century triumphant. American persistence in the Cold War had brought about the collapse of the Soviet Union and the birth of democracy and capitalism in Eastern Europe. During the 1990s, the U.S. economy became the world's marvel as remarkable gains in productivity boosted by new digital technologies led to the greatest prosperity in modern history.

Yet America's sense of physical security and material comfort was shattered in 2001 by terrorist assaults on New York City and Washington, D.C. The attacks killed thousands, deepened an ongoing recession, and raised profound questions about national security, personal safety, and civil liberties.

In leading the fight against Islamist terrorism, the United States became embroiled in long, costly, and controversial wars in Iraq and Afghanistan. Opposition to those wars would provide much of the momentum for Democrat Barack Obama's election in 2008 as the nation's first African American president.

Obama entered the White House when the United States and Europe were experiencing the Great Recession, a prolonged economic downturn that

focus questions

1. What were the major population trends (demographics) in the United States during the twenty-first century? How did they influence the nation's politics?

2. What was the impact of global terrorism during the presidency of George W. Bush? How effective was his "war on terror"?

3. What were the issues and developments during Bush's second term that helped lead to Barack Obama's historic victory in the 2008 presidential election?

4. What were President Obama's priorities at home and abroad? How effective were his efforts to pursue them?

5. What were the factors that led to Donald Trump's 2016 presidential election? How would you assess his presidency?

6. What were the impacts of the Black Lives Matter movement and the COVID-19 pandemic on American society and on the 2020 presidential election?

7. What steps did the Joe Biden administration take to confront the COVID-19 pandemic? How effective were they?

threatened the global banking system, caused widespread unemployment, and ignited social unrest and political tensions.

Eight years later, those tensions gave rise to an unconventional Republican presidential candidate, billionaire New York real estate developer Donald Trump. In 2016, he surprised pollsters by winning the Republican nomination and then narrowly defeating Democrat Hillary Clinton in the general election.

Trump's election exposed the deep divide in America between those whose worldview embraced economic nationalism ("America First!") and those eager to integrate international economies and cultures through intensifying the forces of globalization. Trump's presidency saw tremendous economic growth and the appointment of three new conservative Supreme Court justices, but his confrontational leadership style and his controversial policies promoting economic nationalism at the expense of globalization outraged his opponents and thrilled his supporters. Chief among the bitterly divisive policies were his efforts to build a massive wall along the border with Mexico, his indifference to tragic incidents involving White police officers killing unarmed African Americans, and his aggressive trade war with China. Ultimately, however, it was his inability to manage the COVID-19 pandemic that led to his narrow reelection defeat in November 2020. His clumsy efforts to overturn the election results and his role in fomenting the storming of the U.S. Capitol by his supporters as the Electoral College votes were being counted in January 2021 would lead to his second impeachment trial just after Joseph Biden was sworn in as the 46th president of the United States.

AMERICA'S CHANGING POPULATION

By 2020, America's population had surpassed 331 million, with more than 80 percent living in cities or suburbs. Overall, the slowing of immigration, especially from Mexico, and a declining national birth rate between 2010 and 2020 brought the second slowest population growth rate since the government began counting in 1790. Western and southern states such as Texas, Colorado, Montana, Oregon, Florida, and North Carolina continued to experience the fastest growth rates. In 1970, western and southern states combined to host just under half the national population; in 2020 those Sunbelt regions made up 62 percent of the population. One in five Americans lived in two states, California and Texas.

More importantly, the nation's racial and ethnic composition was rapidly changing. In 2005, Hispanics (the term used by the Census Bureau), surpassed African Americans as the nation's largest minority group. Yet Asian Americans

Mexican Immigrants Pictured here in Arizona, millions of undocumented Mexican immigrants traveled through border towns for the prospect of a new life and American citizenship.

were the fastest-growing racial or ethnic group in the United States. Between 2000 and 2020, the Asian population grew 81 percent, compared to a 70 percent growth among Hispanic Americans, a 61 percent growth among Native Hawaiian and Pacific Islanders, and a 20 percent growth among Black Americans. For the first time ever, the White population decreased in size, dropping 2.6 percent. Another fast-growing cohort was the 10 million people who described themselves as "multiracial" and who represented more than 3 percent of the population.

These dramatic changes in the nation's ethnic mix resulted from an immigration surge during the late twentieth and early twenty-first centuries. In 1996, U.S. immigration reached its highest level since before the First World War. By 2020, the United States had more foreign-born residents than ever—over 46 million, 11 million of whom were undocumented immigrants (formerly classified as *illegal aliens*). For the first time, most immigrants came not from Europe, but from Asia, Latin America, and Africa. Mexicans composed the largest share of Hispanics, followed by Puerto Ricans and Cubans. Most Americans born during and after the Second World War considered the surge in diversity a "cause for concern." They worried that Hispanics, now most frequently referred to as Latinos/Latinas, would never assimilate into mainstream culture but would remain a permanent underclass of people tied closely to their ancestral homelands.

Yet such concerns ignored the growing evidence that Latinos/Latinas were integrating well into society. They provided the nation with a surge of youthful energy and vitality—and demonstrated such traditional American attributes as self-reliance, rugged individualism, thrift, close family ties, strong religious beliefs, support for the military, and an ethic of hard work.

The nation's African American population also experienced significant changes in the early twenty-first century. In a reverse of the Great Migration of the 1920s and after, a steady stream of young Blacks moved out of Rust Belt states, like Michigan and Illinois, to the South. Atlanta replaced Chicago as the metro area with the largest population of African Americans. By 2010, some 57 percent of African Americans lived in the states of the former Confederacy, the highest percentage in fifty years.

A Chaotic Start to a New Century

Wild celebrations ushered in the year 2000, and Americans led the cheering at the start of a new millennium. The Cold War was over, the United States reigned as the world's only superpower, and its high-tech economy dominated global trade. During the early twenty-first century, for example, Google came to control 90 percent of search-engine use in Europe and America. YouTube became the largest video-streaming service in the world. Amazon garnered more than half of every dollar spent online. Facebook recruited billions of followers worldwide.

Not since the late nineteenth century had the U.S. economy witnessed such a concentration of wealth and power in a handful of companies. By the twenty-first century, the entrepreneurs behind these megatech companies began to exercise almost godlike powers in the nation's cultural and political life. Mark Zuckerberg, founder of Facebook, claimed that his social media company was replacing the church as the bedrock of community life.

During the early twenty-first century, international relations grew more unstable. Powerful new forces were emerging across the globe, the most dangerous of which were sophisticated global networks of Islamist terrorists eager to disrupt and destroy American values and institutions.

2000: A DISPUTED ELECTION   The presidential election of 2000 was one of the closest and most controversial in history. The two major-party candidates, Vice President Albert Gore Jr., the Democrat, and Texas Republican governor George W. Bush, son of the former president, differed in their views on the role of the federal government, tax cuts, environmental regulations, and the best way to preserve Social Security and Medicare.

Gore, a Tennessee native and Harvard graduate whose father had been a U.S. senator, favored an active federal government that would do more to protect the environment. Bush campaigned on a theme of "compassionate conservatism." He promised to restore "honor and dignity" to the White House after the Clinton scandal.

The vote count created high drama. As the results rolled in, television networks initially reported that Gore had narrowly won Florida and its decisive twenty-five electoral votes. Later in the evening, however, they reversed themselves, saying Bush had won Florida. By the early morning hours of the next day, the networks again reversed course and claimed that Florida was too close to call. The final tally showed Bush with a razor-thin lead, but Florida law required a recount. The results would remain in doubt for weeks.

The Recount In yet another recount of presidential votes on November 24, 2000, Judge Robert Rosenberg examines a ballot with a magnifying glass. That Florida's voting machines had limited accuracy introduced a great margin of doubt in a close election.

As a painstaking by-hand recount of paper ballots proceeded, the two sides sparred in court, each accusing the other of trying to steal the election. The drama lasted five weeks, until, on December 12, a divided U.S. Supreme Court ruled 5–4 that the recount be halted. Bush had been elected by 537 votes. Gore had amassed a 540,000-vote lead nationwide, but losing Florida meant he lost the Electoral College by 2 votes. Although Gore "strongly disagreed" with the Supreme Court's decision, he asked voters to rally around Bush and move forward. "Partisan rancor," he urged, "must be put aside."

The ferocious sparring between the two national parties was not put aside, however, in part because Bush chose as key advisers men with strong ideological convictions. One of them, Richard "Dick" Cheney, a former Wyoming congressman and influential member of three Republican administrations, quickly became the most powerful vice president in modern history. The secretive Cheney used his long experience with government bureaucracy to

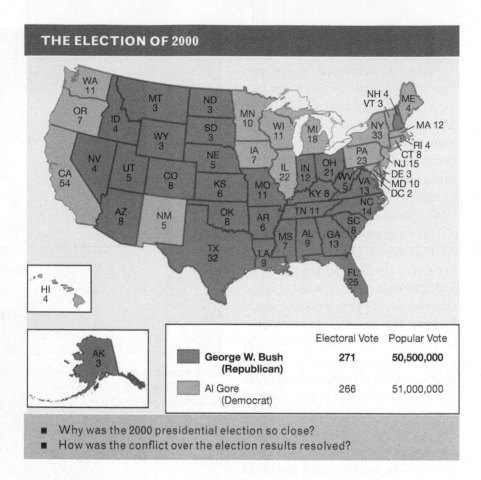

THE ELECTION OF 2000

	Electoral Vote	Popular Vote
George W. Bush (Republican)	271	50,500,000
Al Gore (Democrat)	266	51,000,000

■ Why was the 2000 presidential election so close?
■ How was the conflict over the election results resolved?

fill the administration with like-minded associates who helped him control the flow of information to the president.

A CHANGE OF DIRECTION   George W. Bush had promised to cut taxes for the wealthy, increase military spending, and eliminate "overly" strict environmental regulations. First, however, he had to deal with a sputtering economy, which in March 2001 languished in recession for the first time in more than a decade. Bush decided that cutting taxes was the best way to boost economic growth and generate jobs. On June 7, 2001, he signed the Economic Growth and Tax Relief Act, which slashed $1.35 trillion in taxes.

Instead of paying for themselves in renewed economic growth, however, the tax cuts led to a sharp drop in federal revenue, producing a fast-growing budget deficit. The wealthiest Americans benefited most from the lower tax rates. In addition, huge increases in the costs of Medicare and Medicaid resulting from the aging of the baby boom generation worsened the government deficit.

9/11—A NEW DAY OF INFAMY The inability of U.S. intelligence agencies to track the movements and intentions of militant extremists became tragically evident in the late summer of 2001. Early on the morning of September 11, 2001, Islamist terrorists hijacked four U.S. airliners filled with passengers. They commandeered one to New York City, where at 8:46 A.M. they slammed the fuel-laden jet into the upper floors of the North Tower of the World Trade Center in the heart of the nation's financial district. The twin Trade Center towers, each 110 stories tall and filled with Wall Street investment companies, had been viewed as iconic cathedrals of capitalism. Now they were being toppled.

Eighteen minutes later, a second hijacked jet crashed into the South Tower. The skyscrapers, filled with 50,000 workers, burned fiercely. Hundreds of trapped occupants, many of them on fire, saw no choice but to jump to their deaths. One couple held hands as they plummeted to the ground.

The mammoth steel structures quickly collapsed, destroying surrounding buildings and killing nearly 3,000 people, including more than 400 firefighters, police officers, and emergency responders. The southern end of Manhattan—"ground zero"—became a hellish scene of fires, twisted steel, broken concrete, suffocating smoke, wailing sirens, blood-covered streets, victims in agony, and thousands of panicked people.

While the catastrophic drama in New York City was unfolding, a third hijacked plane crashed into the Pentagon in Washington, D.C. A fourth airliner, most likely aimed toward the White House, missed its mark when passengers—who had heard reports of the earlier hijackings via cell phones—assaulted the knife-wielding hijackers to prevent the plane from being used as a weapon. During the cockpit struggle, the plane plummeted to the ground near Shanksville, Pennsylvania, killing everyone aboard.

September 11 Smoke pours out of the North Tower of the World Trade Center as the South Tower bursts into flames after being struck by a second hijacked airplane. Both buildings would collapse within an hour.

Within hours, the nineteen dead terrorists, fifteen of them from Saudi Arabia, were identified as members of al Qaeda (Arabic for "the Base"), a shadowy network of Islamist extremists led by a wealthy Saudi renegade, Osama bin Laden. Years before, bin Laden had declared *jihad* (holy war) on the United States, Israel, and the Saudi monarchy in his effort to create a single Islamist *caliphate* (global empire). Using remote training bases in Sudan and Afghanistan, bin Laden found a haven among the Taliban, a coalition of ultraconservative Islamists bent on waging war against the United States and its allies.

The governments of Islamic nations worldwide condemned the 9/11 attacks. But al Qaeda was not a nation; it was a new and dangerous type of organization—a virtual terrorist state, borderless yet global in its reach and populated by multinational Islamist zealots who hated America because of its support of Israel. As a Pakistani newspaper asserted, "September 11 was not a mindless terrorism for terrorism's sake. It was reaction and revenge, even retribution" for America's pro-Israeli policies.

THE "WAR ON TERROR" The 9/11 assault, like the Japanese attack on Pearl Harbor on December 7, 1941, transformed modern life. After an initial period of grief, confusion, and fear, many Americans were consumed by blinding anger and a desire for retaliation and revenge.

George W. Bush found his presidential voice and purpose as he skillfully forged a coalition of allied nations committed "to answer these attacks and rid the world of evil. . . . We will not waver, we will not tire, we will not falter, and we will not fail." In a speech to Congress and the world, he warned other nations: "either you are with us or you are with the terrorists." The **war on terror**, Bush stressed, would begin with al Qaeda–but would "not end until every terrorist group of global reach has been found, stopped, and defeated."

Congress readily authorized military force against anyone or any group that helped plan, aid, or commit the acts of violence against the United States. A wave of patriotic fervor swept the nation as Americans embraced Bush's war on terror.

Finding the al Qaeda terrorists required ousting the Taliban movement in Afghanistan, which gave shelter to al Qaeda. Bush demanded that the Taliban government surrender the terrorists or risk military attack. When the Taliban leadership refused, the United States, supported by some sixty allied nations, launched on October 7, 2001, an invasion of Afghanistan dubbed Operation Enduring Freedom. Bush pledged that U.S. forces would stay until they finished the job of ousting the Taliban and establishing a stable democratically elected government in Afghanistan. (The war is now in its twenty-first year, the longest conflict in American history.)

Afghanistan was a desperately poor country hobbled by a dysfunctional and corrupt government and inhabited by a largely rural population whose life expectancy was forty-seven years; the literacy rate was only 38 percent, in large part because the Taliban prohibited girls over 8 years old from attending school.

On December 9, the Taliban regime collapsed in the face of the U.S. military onslaught, and the American-led coalition was suddenly faced with rebuilding a government infrastructure. Yet rarely has a great power taken control of another nation with such a flawed understanding of the challenges it faced. As U.S. Army General Douglas Lute admitted, "We didn't have the foggiest notion of what we were undertaking." The United States proved unable to improve the Islamic nation's quality of life. As a result, the war in Afghanistan transitioned into a high-stakes manhunt for the elusive Osama bin Laden.

FIGHTING TERROR AT HOME While fighting continued in Afghanistan, officials in Washington worried that terrorists might attack the United States with biological, chemical, or even nuclear weapons. To address the threat, President Bush established the Office of Homeland Security and gave it sweeping authority to spy on Americans. Another new federal agency, the Transportation Security Administration (TSA), assumed responsibility for screening airline passengers for weapons and bombs.

At the same time, Bush convinced Congress to create the **USA Patriot Act**, which gave government agencies authority to eavesdrop on confidential conversations between prison inmates and their lawyers. It also permitted suspected terrorists to be tried in secret military courts and jailed in a military prison at the Guantánamo naval base in Cuba, where they could be held indefinitely and without access to attorneys. Civil liberties groups voiced concerns that the measures jeopardized constitutional rights and protections, but most Americans supported them.

Yet the public was unaware that Vice President Cheney, Secretary of Defense Donald Rumsfeld, and other so-called neoconservatives (neocons) in the departments of State and Defense had convinced Bush to authorize—illegally—the use of torture ("enhanced interrogation techniques") when interviewing captured terrorist suspects. Such tactics violated international law and compromised human rights. When asked about this approach, Cheney scoffed that America sometimes had to work "the dark side."

THE BUSH DOCTRINE In the fall of 2002, George Bush unveiled a new national security policy. The **Bush Doctrine** said that the growing menace posed by "shadowy networks" of terrorist groups and unstable rogue nations

War Fever President George W. Bush addresses members of the Special Forces in July 2002 as part of an appeal to Congress to increase defense spending after the September 11 attacks.

with **"weapons of mass destruction" (WMDs)** required the United States at times to use *preemptive* military action and to act unilaterally if necessary to eliminate the threat of nations like Iraq using WMDs. "If we wait for threats to fully materialize," or wait for allies to join America, Bush explained, "we will have waited too long. In the world we have entered, the only path to safety is the path of action. And this nation will act."

THE SECOND IRAQ WAR During 2002 and 2003, Iraq emerged as the focus of the Bush administration's policy of preemptive military action. Vice President Cheney, Secretary of Defense Rumsfeld, and Deputy Defense Secretary Paul Wolfowitz repeatedly urged the president to use U.S. power to reshape the Islamist world in America's image. This included sponsoring "regime change" in authoritarian nations lacking "political and economic freedom." The goal was to create a new democratic world order "friendly to our security, our prosperity, and our principles." These cabinet members convinced Bush that the dictatorial Iraqi regime of Saddam Hussein represented a "grave and gathering danger" because of its support of global terrorism and its supposed possession of biological and chemical weapons of mass destruction.

Yet neither Bush nor his hawkish advisors found any tangible evidence of such weapons. In addition, none of Bush's advisors understood the bewildering complexities of religion, culture, politics, and rivalries between traditionalists and modernists within Islamist nations. The administration placed too little faith in diplomacy and too much faith in intelligence agencies and military intervention.

On March 17, 2003, Bush issued Saddam Hussein an ultimatum: leave Iraq within forty-eight hours or face an invasion. Hussein refused. Two days later, on March 19, American and British forces attacked Iraq. None of the other major American allies, nor the United Nations, agreed to participate; thus the two-nation force that entered Iraq was referred to as the "coalition of the willing." The war was legitimate, Bush claimed, because Hussein "promotes international terror" and "seeks nuclear weapons."

The Second Iraq War began with a massive bombing campaign, followed by a fast-moving ground assault. On April 9, after three weeks of intense fighting, U.S. forces captured Baghdad, the capital of Iraq. Hussein's regime and his demoralized army collapsed a week later.

The U.S. management of the six-week war was ferociously efficient: fewer than 200 of the 300,000 allied troops were killed, compared to more than 2,000 Iraqis; civilian casualties numbered in the tens of thousands. Bush hurriedly staged a celebration onboard a U.S. aircraft carrier at which he announced victory under a massive banner proclaiming "mission accomplished."

But the president, as he later admitted, had spoken too soon; the initial military triumph carried with it the seeds of deception and disaster, as no weapons of mass destruction were found in Iraq. Bush said that the absence of WMD left him with a "sickening feeling," for he knew that his primary justification for the war had evaporated. As former presidential candidate and conservative commentator Pat Buchanan said, America had "invaded a country that did not attack us, and did not want war with us, to disarm it of weapons we have since discovered it did not have."

REBUILDING IRAQ It proved far easier to win the brief war against Iraq than to reconstruct the Islamist nation in America's image. As Secretary of State Colin Powell had warned Bush, conquering Iraq would make him "the proud owner of 25 million people. You will own all their hopes, aspirations, and problems. You'll own it all."

Unprepared U.S. officials faced the daunting task of installing a democratic government in a nation fractured by religious feuds and ethnic tensions made worse by the allied invasion. Large parts of the country quickly fell into civil war as sectarian tribalism replaced the dictatorship. Looting was widespread and chaos reigned.

Rather than reducing the number of Islamist terrorists, the U.S. intervention in Iraq served to increase them. Soon, Iraq became a quagmire for

Freedom for Whom? The American torture of Iraqi prisoners in Abu Ghraib prison only exacerbated the anger and humiliation that Iraqis experienced since the first Gulf War. In response to America's incessant promises of peace and autonomy, a Baghdad mural fires back: "That Freedom For B[u]sh."

American forces. Vengeful Islamist radicals streamed into Iraq to wage a campaign of terror, sabotage, and suicide bombings against American troops and bases.

Bush's bold reaction to the surge of terrorism—"Bring 'em on!"—revealed the limits of the American government's actual level of knowledge about the internal dynamics in Iraq. The newly elected pro-American Iraqi prime minister, Prime Minister Nouri al-Maliki, imposed an authoritarian, Shiite-dominated regime that discriminated against the Sunnis, Kurds, and other ethnic and religious minorities. Soon the civil war had grown beyond America's capacity to understand, control, afford, or end.

By the fall of 2003, Bush admitted that substantial numbers of American troops (around 150,000) would have to remain in Iraq much longer than anticipated, and many of them would end up serving multiple tours there. He also acknowledged that rebuilding Iraq would take years and cost almost a trillion dollars.

Americans grew dismayed as the number of casualties and the expense of the military occupation soared. The nation became more alienated when journalists revealed graphic pictures of U.S. soldiers abusing and torturing

Arab detainees in the Abu Ghraib prison near Baghdad. By 2004, a Republican journalist dismissed Bush's Middle East strategy as "shiftless, reactive, irrelevantly grandiose; our war aims undefined; our preparations insufficient; our civil defense neglected."

Regardless, Bush insisted that a democratic Iraq would bring stability to the Middle East and blunt the momentum of Islamist terrorism. Yet even though Saddam Hussein was captured in December 2003 and later hanged, Iraq seemed less secure than ever.

By the beginning of 2004, some 1,000 Americans had died, and more than 10,000 had been wounded, many of them having lost limbs in explosions. Many other veterans suffered from post–traumatic stress disorder (PTSD). The ethnic and religious tensions only worsened as Sunni jihadists allied with al Qaeda to undermine the Iraqi government and assault U.S. forces.

The U.S. effort in Iraq became the wrong war in the wrong place fought in the wrong way. It was hugely expensive. It also distracted attention from the revival of the Taliban and other terrorist groups in Afghanistan. Journalist Roger Cohen distilled perhaps the most important lesson from the wars in Iraq and Afghanistan when he said that the American ideal of democracy "can still resonate" with people around the world, but U.S. leaders "must embody it rather than impose it."

THE 2004 ELECTION Growing concern about Iraq complicated George W. Bush's campaign for a second presidential term in 2004. The Democratic nominee, Senator John Kerry of Massachusetts, condemned Bush for misleading the nation about weapons of mass destruction and his slipshod handling of the reconstruction of postwar Iraq. Kerry also highlighted the administration's record budget deficits. Bush countered that the efforts to create a democratic government in Iraq would enhance America's long-term security.

On Election Day, November 2, 2004, exit polls suggested a Kerry victory. As it turned out, the election hinged on the swing state of Ohio, where late returns tipped the balance toward Bush, even as rumors of electoral "irregularities" began to circulate. Nevertheless, Kerry conceded. "The outcome," he stressed, "should be decided by voters, not a protracted legal battle."

By winning Ohio, Bush captured 286 electoral votes to Kerry's 251. Yet in some respects, the election was not so close. Bush received 3.5 million more votes nationwide than Kerry, and Republicans increased their majorities in both houses of Congress. Bush pledged to bring democracy and stability to Iraq, trim the federal deficit, pass a major energy bill, create more jobs, and "privatize" Social Security funds by investing them in the stock market.

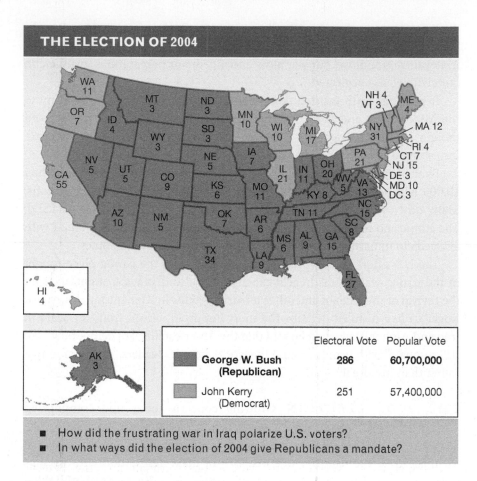

THE ELECTION OF 2004

		Electoral Vote	Popular Vote
	George W. Bush (Republican)	**286**	**60,700,000**
	John Kerry (Democrat)	251	57,400,000

■ How did the frustrating war in Iraq polarize U.S. voters?
■ In what ways did the election of 2004 give Republicans a mandate?

SECOND-TERM BLUES

George Bush's second term featured thorny political problems, a sluggish economy, and continuing turmoil in Iraq. In 2005, he pushed through Congress an energy bill and a Central American Free Trade Act (CAFTA). But his effort to privatize Social Security retirement accounts only provoked fear and distrust among retired Americans. At the same time, soaring budget deficits dismayed many fiscal conservatives.

HURRICANE KATRINA   In late August 2005, President Bush's eroding public support suffered another blow after killer-hurricane Katrina slammed into the Gulf coast, devastating large areas of Alabama, Mississippi, and Louisiana. Hardest hit was New Orleans, where floodwaters drowned the city.

Katrina left more than 1,500 dead, wiped out whole towns, and destroyed 160,000 homes and apartments. Hundreds of thousands were left homeless

The Aftermath of Katrina Two men paddle through high water with wooden planks in a New Orleans devastated by the storm.

and hopeless. In New Orleans, where local officials and the Federal Emergency Management Agency (FEMA) were caught unprepared, confusion and incompetence abounded as dead bodies floated in the flooded streets.

President Bush, who was vacationing when the hurricane hit, made no public statement for four days and initially appeared indifferent to the storm's toll. In the face of blistering criticism, he came out of seclusion and took responsibility for the balky federal response.

The backlash over the poor federal response to Katrina generated an overwhelming defeat for Republicans in the November 2006 congressional elections. The Democrats won control of the House of Representatives, the Senate, and a majority of governorships and state legislatures. The election also included a significant milestone: Californian Nancy Pelosi, leader of the Democrats in the House, became the highest-ranking woman in the history of the U.S. Congress upon her election as House Speaker in January 2007.

Nancy Pelosi The first female Speaker of the House (pictured here at a news conference on Capitol Hill), Pelosi's success coincided with the mounting public disapproval of the Republican party.

THE "SURGE" IN IRAQ George W. Bush received the blame for the costs and casualties of the unending war in Iraq, where violence increased throughout the fall of 2006. Bush eventually responded by creating the Iraq Study Group, a bipartisan task force that surprised the president by issuing a report recommending the withdrawal of combat forces by the spring of 2008.

Bush disagreed. On January 10, 2007, he announced that he was sending a "surge" of an additional 20,000 (eventually 30,000) troops to Iraq, bringing the total to almost 170,000. From a military perspective, the surge succeeded. By the fall of 2008, violence in Iraq had declined dramatically, and the Iraqi government had grown in stature and confidence.

The U.S. general who oversaw the increase in troops admitted, however, that the gains were "fragile and reversible." As the number of U.S. combat deaths in Iraq passed 4,000, Bush acknowledged that the conflict was "longer and harder and more costly than we anticipated." By 2008, more than 60 percent of Americans believed the Iraqi invasion had been a mistake.

ECONOMIC SHOCK: THE GREAT RECESSION After the intense but brief 2001 recession, America's high tech–driven economy had begun another period of prolonged expansion. Between 1997 and 2006, home prices rose an astounding 85 percent, leading to a frenzy of irresponsible mortgage lending. Homebuyers were often freed from making down payments or even demonstrating creditworthiness. At the same time, consumers binged on a debt-financed spending spree fed by the overuse of credit cards and home equity loans. Millions of people bought houses they could not afford, refinanced their mortgages, or tapped home equity for loans to make discretionary purchases. It was irrational and reckless to believe that home prices would continue to rise, but lenders, regulatory agencies, and a willing public rode that wave of false hope together.

In 2007, the easy-credit bubble burst, and home values and real estate sales plummeted. The loss of trillions of dollars in home values set off a seismic shock across the economy, as record numbers of homeowners defaulted on their mortgage payments. Foreclosures and bankruptcies soared as banks lost billions, first on the shaky mortgages, then on other categories of overleveraged debt: credit cards, car loans, student loans, and commercial mortgage-backed securities. Lax government oversight and President Bill Clinton's deregulation of the financial sector in 1999 contributed to the meltdown.

The economy fell into a recession in 2008, and some of the nation's most prestigious banks, investment firms, and insurance companies went belly up. The entire financial system teetered on the brink of collapse. The price of food and gasoline spiked, and unemployment soared. What had begun as a sharp decline in home prices became a global economic meltdown.

The speed and scale of the economic collapse were so startling that people imagined another Great Depression. On October 3, 2008, President Bush signed into law the Troubled Asset Relief Program (TARP). It authorized the Treasury Department to spend $700 billion to keep big banks and other large financial institutions and mortgage lenders afloat. These institutions were deemed "too big to fail," while small banks and homeowners went under. Yet

Rio Vista, California With an $816,000 deficit, this northern California city filed for bankruptcy and pulled the plug on its massive 750-home housing development in November 2008. Here, abandoned model homes stand eerily in a blank landscape of sidewalks and cul-de-sacs.

TARP, while shoring up the large financial institutions, did little to restore the public's confidence in the economy.

In early October 2008, stock markets around the world began to crash. It was the onset of what came to be called the **Great Recession** and it lasted from December 2007 to January 2009 and forced 9 million people out of work. Federal Reserve chairman Ben Bernanke called it "the worst financial crisis in modern history," prompting the Fed to inject trillions of dollars into the collapsing world economy.

The Great Recession was devastating. The economic recovery that began in June 2009 would be the weakest in more than fifty years. Between 2009 and 2013, economic growth averaged just 2.2 percent, barely half the 4.2 percent average of the seven previous recoveries.

The never-ending wars in Afghanistan and Iraq, coupled with a slumping economy, shattered public support for the Bush administration. During Bush's last year in office, his approval rating was 25 percent, just one point higher than Richard Nixon's during the Watergate investigations.

Bush's roller-coaster presidency ended in failure. By cutting taxes while increasing spending, his administration created the largest budget deficits in history. In the end, Bush's presidency weakened the Republican Party, strained the military, and eroded American prestige abroad.

A HISTORIC NEW PRESIDENCY Bush's mistakes excited Democrats about the possibility of regaining the White House in 2008. The early front-runner for their party's nomination was New York senator Hillary Rodham Clinton, the spouse of ex-president Bill Clinton. Like her husband, she displayed an impressive command of policy issues and mobilized a well-funded campaign team. Moreover, as the first woman with a serious chance of gaining the presidency, she had widespread support among voters eager for female leadership.

As the primaries played out, however, an overconfident Clinton lost the nomination to Barack Obama of Illinois, a little-known first-term senator. Young, handsome, and intelligent, a vibrant mixture of idealism and pragmatism, coolness and passion, Obama was an inspiring speaker who promised a "politics of hope," the "energy of change," and the revival of bipartisanship. In June 2008, he gained enough delegates to secure the nomination, and he named veteran senator Joseph Biden of Delaware as his running mate.

THE FIRST AFRICAN AMERICAN PRESIDENT Barack Obama was the first African American presidential nominee of either party. Born in Hawaii in 1961, he was the son of a White mother from Kansas and a Black father from Kenya, who left the household and returned to Africa when Barack was a toddler. Raised in Indonesia, where his mother was an anthropologist, and Hawaii, where his maternal grandparents lived, Obama attended Occidental College in Los Angeles and graduated from Columbia University in New York City before earning a law degree from Harvard.

The forty-seven-year-old senator presented himself as a leader who could inspire, unite, and forge collaborations across the partisan divide. He vowed to end the "forever" wars in Afghanistan and Iraq, stop the use of torture, reduce nuclear weapons, tighten regulation of the banking industry, secure the border with Mexico, provide a path to citizenship for undocumented immigrants, and offer medical coverage to millions of uninsured Americans.

Barack Obama The president-elect and his family wave to the crowd of supporters in Chicago's Grant Park.

Obama and his strategists mastered the use of social media to organize rock-concert-like campaign rallies. His vitality created a movement that reinvigorated political activism at a time when voter disgust with politics was widespread.

By contrast, his Republican opponent, seventy-two-year-old Arizona senator John McCain, was the oldest presidential candidate in history. A twenty-five-year veteran of Congress, McCain had developed a reputation as a GOP "maverick," willing to work with Democrats to achieve legislative goals. As his running mate, he chose little-known, former Alaska governor Sarah Palin, to serve as a bridge to female voters and the evangelical base of the Republican party. Initial enthusiasm over her candidacy dimmed quickly after a series of prominent interviews clearly revealed that she lacked the depth and experience to serve as a major national candidate.

On November 4, 2008, Obama made history by becoming the first person of color to be elected president. He won the popular vote by 53 percent to 46 percent, won the Electoral College 365 to 173, and penetrated the solidly Republican South by winning Florida, North Carolina, and Virginia. He also helped the Democrats win majorities in both houses of Congress. Voter turnout, especially among African Americans and young adults, was the highest since 1968.

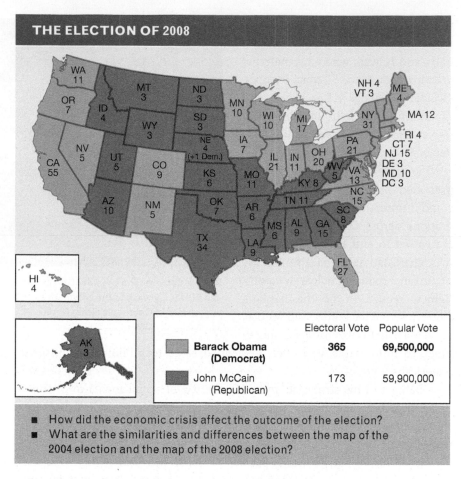

THE ELECTION OF 2008

		Electoral Vote	Popular Vote
	Barack Obama (Democrat)	**365**	**69,500,000**
	John McCain (Republican)	173	59,900,000

■ How did the economic crisis affect the outcome of the election?
■ What are the similarities and differences between the map of the 2004 election and the map of the 2008 election?

Obama considered his election a "defining moment." He urged Americans to "resist the temptation to fall back on the same partisanship and pettiness and immaturity that has poisoned our politics for so long." But his idealistic appeal had little chance of unifying the bitterly divided electorate.

THE OBAMA ADMINISTRATION

In his 2009 inaugural address, President Obama acknowledged that America was in a crisis. His administration had inherited two unpopular wars, rising unemployment, a staggering national debt, and the weakest economy in eighty years. He vowed to change the culture of "greed and irresponsibility" and pledged to create a foreign policy based on diplomacy rather than military intervention. He promised to bring home all U.S. troops from Iraq and to end the use of torture in the war against terrorism.

To do so, he proposed "a new politics for a new time"—without explaining what that meant or how he planned to implement it. In the end, despite several notable achievements, Obama would prove to be more inspirational than effective as the nation's chief executive.

ENDING THE GREAT RECESSION Barack Obama's most pressing challenge was to keep the Great Recession from becoming a prolonged depression. Unemployment had passed 8 percent and was still rising. The financial sector remained paralyzed, and public confidence in the economy had plummeted.

The Obama administration chose to bail out Wall Street. It continued the TARP program by providing massive funding for huge banks and financial corporations. Critics attacked the bailouts as deeply unfair to most Americans. Treasury Secretary Timothy Geithner later explained, "We had to do whatever we could to help people feel their money was safe in the [banking] system, even if it made us unpopular." Had they not saved the big banks, Obama and Geithner argued, the economy would have crashed.

Preserving the banking system did not create many jobs, however. To do so, in mid-February 2009, Congress passed, and Obama signed, an $832 billion economic-stimulus bill called the American Recovery and Reinvestment Act. It included cash distributions to states for construction projects to renew the nation's infrastructure (roads, bridges, levees, government buildings, and the electricity grid), money for renewable-energy systems, $212 billion in tax reductions for individuals and businesses, as well as funds for food stamps and unemployment benefits.

It was the largest government infusion of cash into the economy in history. The steps taken by the Obama administration saved the nation—and the world economy—from a financial meltdown. Another Great Depression was averted. Yet the Great Recession also created a convergence of forces with long-term political consequences. Stagnant wages, widening economic inequality, anger over immigration and immigrants, and a deepening distrust of political elites and government bureaucrats combined to create the populist revolt among growing numbers of working-class Republicans that would elevate Donald Trump to the presidency in 2016.

HEALTH-CARE REFORM From his first day in office, Barack Obama stressed that his foremost goal was to reform a health-care system that was "bankrupting families, bankrupting businesses, and bankrupting our government at the state and federal level." The United States was (and still is) the only developed nation without a national health-care program. Since 1970, the number of uninsured people had been steadily rising, as had health-care costs. In 2010, roughly 50 million Americans (16 percent of the population), most of them poor, young, or people of color, had no health insurance.

The president's goal in creating the **Affordable Care Act (ACA)**, which critics labeled "Obamacare," was to make health insurance more affordable and health care more accessible. The $940 billion law, proposed in 2009 and hotly debated for a year, centered on the "individual mandate," which required uninsured adults to buy a private insurance policy through state-run exchanges (websites where people could shop for insurance), or pay a tax penalty. Low-income Americans would receive federal subsidies to help pay for their coverage, and insurance companies could no longer deny coverage to people with preexisting illnesses. To fund the plan, companies that did not offer health insurance to their employees would have to pay higher taxes, and drug companies and manufacturers of medical devices would have to pay government fees. Everyone would pay higher Medicare payroll taxes.

Requiring people to buy health insurance was controversial. Critics questioned not only the individual mandate but the administration's projections that the program would eventually reduce federal expenditures. The ACA passed without a single Republican vote, and Obama signed it on March 23,

Go Obama Go! A Democrat holds up a sign in support of the Affordable Care Act, more commonly known as Obamacare, in a march in Washington, D.C., in 2010.

2010. Its complex provisions, to be implemented over a four-year period, would bring health insurance to 32 million people, half of whom would be covered by expanded Medicaid and the other half by the individual mandate. In the end, about half those numbers enrolled. In its scope and goals, the ACA was a breakthrough in the history of health and social welfare—as well as the expansion of the federal government.

REGULATING WALL STREET The near collapse of the nation's financial system beginning in 2008 had prompted calls for overhauling the financial regulatory system. On July 21, 2010, Obama signed the Wall Street Reform and Consumer Protection Act, also called the Dodd-Frank Bill after its two congressional sponsors, Democratic senator Chris Dodd of Connecticut and Democratic representative Barney Frank of Massachusetts. The 2,319-page law required government agencies to exercise greater oversight over complex new financial transactions and protected consumers from unfair practices in loans and credit cards by establishing the Consumer Financial Protection Bureau.

FOREIGN AFFAIRS

President Obama had more success in foreign affairs than in reviving the economy at home. What journalists came to call the Obama Doctrine was much like the Nixon Doctrine, stressing that the United States could not afford to police the world.

THE OBAMA DOCTRINE The loosely defined Obama Doctrine grew out of efforts to end the wars in Iraq and Afghanistan. In essence, the president wanted to replace confrontation and military intervention with cooperation and negotiation.

On February 27, 2009, President Obama announced that all 142,000 U.S. troops would be withdrawn from Iraq by the end of 2011, as the Iraqi government and the Bush administration had agreed in 2008. True to his word, the last U.S. combat troops left Iraq in December 2011. Their departure marked the end of a divisive war that had raged for nearly nine years, killed more than 110,000 Iraqis, and left the nation shattered and unstable. More than 4,500 Americans had been killed, 30,000 wounded (many grievously so), and the war had cost $2 trillion. Perhaps the greatest embarrassment was that the Iraqi government the United States left in power was inept and unfriendly to American interests.

The war was an expensive mistake. As it turned out, there were no weapons of mass destruction, despite what officials in the Bush administration

Home from Iraq U.S. troops returned from Iraq to little celebration or even notice.

had claimed, nor was there a direct link between the al Qaeda terrorists and Saddam Hussein. Al Qaeda, in fact, did not arrive in Iraq until after the invasion. American efforts at nation building had failed, and Obama and Bush's hopes that the United States could avoid fighting in the Middle East and that the Iraqis could sustain a stable government proved fruitless. Iraq's woeful government and constant sectarian strife required continued infusions of U.S. military assistance, daily bombing raids, and massive economic aid.

"SURGE" IN AFGHANISTAN At the same time that President Obama was drawing down U.S. military involvement in Iraq, he dispatched 21,000 additional troops to Afghanistan. While doing so, however, he narrowed the focus of the U.S. mission to one of suppressing terrorists rather than transforming the country into a stable capitalist democracy.

The "surge" worked as hoped. During the summer of 2011, Obama announced that the "tide of war was receding" and that the United States had largely achieved its goals, setting in motion a withdrawal of forces that lasted until 2014. "We will not try to make Afghanistan a perfect place," Obama said. "We will not police its streets or patrol its mountains indefinitely. That is the responsibility of the Afghan government."

Thereafter, however, the situation in Afghanistan deteriorated, and substantial U.S. forces remained in place for a decade. The Taliban increased the amount of territory they controlled, and the Afghan government continued to be ineffective, unstable, and often corrupt. In 2020, the *Washington Post* published 2,000 pages of top-secret government documents revealing that senior U.S. officials had failed to tell the truth about the war in Afghanistan throughout the lengthy campaign. They knowingly released upbeat yet false assessments, and they hid evidence showing that the war had become unwinnable. Since 2001, more than 775,000 U.S. troops were sent to Afghanistan. Of those, 2,300 were killed, and 20,589 were wounded in action. During that period, the U.S. government spent some $1 trillion on the war.

THE DEATH OF OSAMA BIN LADEN After the 9/11 attacks in the United States, Osama bin Laden eluded an intensive manhunt. In August 2010, however, U.S. intelligence analysts discovered his sanctuary outside Abbottabad, Pakistan. On May 1, 2011, President Obama authorized a daring night raid by a Navy SEAL team transported by helicopters from Afghanistan. After a brief firefight, the SEALs killed bin Laden. His death was a watershed moment but did not end Islamist terrorism.

THE "ARAB AWAKENING" In late 2010 and early 2011, a chaotic series of spontaneous uprisings erupted throughout much of the Arab world as long-oppressed peoples rose up against repressive regimes. Young idealists, inspired by the hope of democracy and

Arab Awakening Thousands of protesters converge in Cairo's Tahrir Square to call for an end to President Hosni Mubarak's rule.

connected by social media, transformed passionate street protests into political revolutions that forced corrupt tyrants from power. The essentially leaderless uprisings seemed to herald a new era in the Middle East.

Yet building new democratic governments proved harder than expected. The Middle East had no models of open societies to follow, and the essential elements of democratic governance had to be established from scratch. As a result, most of the grassroots revolutionary movements stalled by 2014. Egypt reverted to an even harsher authoritarian government, Libya lapsed into chaos, and Yemen exploded in civil war. The Arab uprisings sank into the desert sands. Only Tunisia sustained a fragile democracy.

THE CUBAN THAW   At the end of 2014, President Obama surprised the world by announcing that the United States and Cuba would restore normal relations after more than fifty years of hostility. As a first step, Obama relaxed restrictions on tourists visiting Cuba, many of them aboard large cruise ships. Six months later, the two nations reestablished embassies in each other's capital cities.

The powerful anti-Communist Cuban community in south Florida fiercely criticized Obama's decision, and congressional Republicans threatened to block the appointment of a U.S. ambassador to Cuba because of its Communist government. But Obama insisted that isolating Cuba had not worked. "Americans and Cubans alike are ready to move forward," he said. "I believe it's time for Congress to do the same."

POLARIZED POLITICS

Barack Obama had campaigned in 2008 on the promise of bringing dramatic change while reducing the partisan warfare between the two national parties. By the end of his first year, however, a Gallup poll found that he had become the most polarizing president in modern history. In part, the problem stemmed from Obama's detached style and distaste for political infighting. Like Jimmy Carter, he did not like to horse-trade his way to legislative approval. Republican senator John McCain quipped that Obama preferred "leading from behind." Even Democrats criticized his "aloofness."

Yet the standoff with Congress was not solely his fault. His Republican opponents had no interest in negotiating with him. In fact, the Senate minority leader, Mitch McConnell of Kentucky, hosted key Republican leaders on the night of Obama's inauguration. That evening they pledged to obstruct the new president's every initiative.

Political culture had become so divided that it resembled two separate nations. Each party had its own cable-news station and partisan commentators, its own newspapers, its own think tanks, and its own billionaire donors. Governing, Obama quickly discovered, was far more difficult than campaigning.

THE TEA PARTY No sooner was Barack Obama sworn in than grass-roots conservatives mobilized against the "tax-and-spend" liberalism he represented in their eyes. In January 2009, a New York stock trader named Graham Makohoniuk urged people to send tea bags to their congressional representatives to symbolize the Boston Tea Party of 1773, when colonists protested against the tax policies imposed by the British government.

Soon, the revolt became a national **Tea Party** movement, with chapters in all fifty states. The Tea Party was not so much a cohesive political organization as it was an attitude and an ideology, a collection of self-described "disaffected," "angry," and "very conservative" activists. They were mostly White, male, married, middle-class Republicans over forty-five years of age who had grown incensed by corporate bailouts, the "invasion" of immigrants, and the unprecedented federal government spending (by both Bush and Obama) to check the Great Recession. Democrats, including President Obama, initially dismissed the Tea Party as a fringe group, but the 2010 election results proved it had become a fast-brewing political force, using social media to help mobilize almost 25 percent of voters.

Democratic House and Senate candidates (as well as moderate Republicans), including many long-serving leaders, were defeated in droves when conservative Republicans, many of them aligned with the Tea Party, gained sixty-three seats to recapture control of the House of Representatives. They won a near majority in the Senate as well. It was the most lopsided midterm election since 1938.

OCCUPY WALL STREET The emergence of the Tea Party was mirrored on the left by the Occupy Wall Street (OWS) movement. In the fall of 2011, a call went out over the Internet to "Occupy Wall Street. Bring tent." Dozens, then hundreds, then thousands of people converged on Zuccotti Park in lower Manhattan to "occupy" Wall Street, protesting economic inequality and the "tyrannical" power of major banks and investment companies. Similar OWS encampments sprang up in hundreds of cities.

The protesters described themselves as the voice of the 99 percent who were being victimized by the 1 percent—the wealthiest and most politically connected elite who controlled 38 percent of the nation's wealth. Unlike the Tea Party, however, OWS did not have staying power. Within a year, its

Occupy Wall Street The Manhattan-born grassroots movement grew rapidly from rallies to massive marches in financial districts worldwide, like this demonstration in downtown Los Angeles.

energies and visibility had waned, in part because of mass arrests and in part because it was an intentionally "leaderless" movement more interested in saying what it was against than explaining what it was for.

Occupy Wall Street and the Tea Party were opposite expressions of an anti-establishment rage sweeping the country, fed by a conviction that political and business elites had colluded to bilk "the system" to serve their own greed. The radical left blamed corrupt corporate leaders while the radical right targeted minority groups and immigrants. Public faith in American institutions plunged to an all-time low.

BOLD DECISIONS

For all the political sniping, however, attitudes toward some hot-button cultural values were slowly changing. In December 2010, Congress repealed the "don't ask, don't tell" (DADT) military policy that, since 1993, had resulted in some 9,500 gays and lesbians being discharged from the armed forces. A year later, a report by army officers concluded that the repeal "had no overall negative impact on military readiness or its component dimensions, including cohesion, recruitment, retention, assaults, harassment, or morale."

THE DACA PROGRAM AND THE DREAM ACT In 2012, the Census Bureau reported that 39.5 million residents, some 13 percent of the total population, had been born outside the United States. In June 2012, President Obama sought Congressional approval of a program called the Development, Relief and Education for Alien Minors Act. The DREAM Act would have allowed 2.1 million undocumented immigrants (Dreamers) brought to the United States as children (before the age of sixteen) to remain and pursue formal citizenship. The policy had been debated in Congress since 2001 but

Refugees from Gangland Braving hundreds of miles on foot, Honduran and Salvadorian children are sent off by their parents for a better life in the United States, away from the drugs and violence of Central America. Here, border guards stop a group of child refugees in Granjeno, Texas.

had never been passed. Although it gained more legislative support in 2012, it was rejected by only five votes in the Senate. As a consequence, Obama on June 15 bypassed the Republican-controlled Congress and issued an executive order announcing that the administration would stop deporting undocumented immigrants under a new policy called the Deferred Action for Childhood Arrivals (DACA) program. Hundreds of thousands of immigrants applied for the new program.

DACA, however, had unexpected consequences. It prompted masses of Central Americans willing to endure enormous risks to migrate to America. Panicked parents in El Salvador, Guatemala, and Honduras, worried about widespread drug-related gang violence, sent their children through Mexico to the United States in hopes of connecting with relatives and being granted citizenship. At the same time, the Obama administration was deporting record numbers of undocumented immigrants. By the end of 2014, this "great expulsion" had deported more than 2 million, some of whom had been working in the nation for decades. Obama, called the Deporter in Chief by critics, claimed that he was only following the laws written by anti-immigration Republicans.

MARRIAGE EQUALITY In May 2012, President Obama became the first sitting president to support the right of gay and lesbian couples to marry.

While asserting that it was the "right" thing to do, Obama knew that endorsing **marriage equality** had powerful political implications. The LGBTQ community would come to play an energetic role in the 2012 presidential election, and the youth vote—the under-thirty electorate who most supported marriage equality—would be crucial. No sooner had Obama made his announcement than polls showed that voters were evenly split on the issue, with Democrats and independent voters providing the bulk of support.

THE SUPREME COURT The Supreme Court surprised observers in 2013 by overturning the Defense of Marriage Act (DOMA) of 1996, which had denied federal benefits to gay and lesbian couples who married. In *United States v. Windsor*, the Court voted 5–4 that the federal government could not withhold spousal benefits from couples of the same sex who had been legally married in states allowing single-sex unions. During 2014, federal courts repeatedly overturned state laws banning marriage between same-sex couples.

While the *Windsor* decision disappointed social conservatives, the Court's five conservative justices continued to restrict the powers of the federal government. In June 2013, in *Shelby County v. Holder*, the Court gutted key provisions of the 1965 Voting Rights Act (VRA), which had outlawed discrimination toward voters "on account of race or color." The majority opinion declared that in five of the six southern states originally covered by the VRA, Black voter turnout now exceeded White turnout. To the judges, this single statistic seemed to prove there was no evidence of continuing racial discrimination. Today's laws "must be justified by current needs," Chief Justice John Roberts wrote.

Soon after the Court's ruling, counties and states in the South pushed through new laws that had the effect of making voting more difficult for people of color, poor people, and immigrants (more such laws were passed by Republican-controlled state legislatures in 2021). Voting hours were reduced, and voters had to have a driver's license or other government-issued ID to vote. That there was little evidence of voter fraud led critics to charge that the new requirements were intended to suppress Democratic votes.

THE 2012 ELECTION The 2012 presidential election would be the most expensive ever, in part because the Supreme Court had ruled in *Citizens United v. Federal Elections Committee* (2010) that corporations could spend as much as they wanted in support of candidates.

Mitt Romney, a former governor of Massachusetts (2003–2007), emerged as the Republican nominee. Two factors hurt his candidacy. The first was his decision to cater to right-wing voters by opposing immigration reforms that might allow undocumented immigrants a pathway to citizenship. The second was a startling statement made to wealthy Republican donors. He was caught on tape saying that he "did not care" about the 47 percent of Americans who "will vote for the president no matter what" because they are "dependent upon government . . . believe that they are victims . . . [who] believe the government has a responsibility to care for them . . . these are people who pay no income tax."

The Obama campaign seized on the impolitic statement and demonized Romney as an uncaring wealthy elitist. On Election Day, Obama won with 66 million votes to Romney's 61 million, and 332 electoral votes to 206.

Nearly 60 percent of White voters chose Romney. But the nation's fastest-growing groups—Latinos, Asian Americans, and African Americans—voted overwhelmingly for Obama, as did college-educated women. David Frum, a Republican speechwriter and columnist, confessed that his party was becoming "increasingly isolated and estranged from modern America."

BLACK LIVES MATTER In 2013, three African American activists—Alicia Garza, Patrisse Cullors, and Opal Tometi—created a civil rights organization called **Black Lives Matter (BLM)** to address mounting evidence that African Americans were being treated unfairly by law enforcement officers and the judicial system. In 2012, 31 percent of people killed by police were

Black Lives Matter The founders of the movement stand with arms linked at a protest in Cleveland, Ohio. Left to right: Opal Tometi, Alicia Garza, and Patrisse Cullors.

African American (often unarmed young men), even though Blacks made up just 13 percent of the total population.

Garza, Cullors, Tometi, and others generated widespread support. Black Lives Matter, the organizers explained, "is an ideological and political intervention in a world where Black lives are systematically and intentionally targeted for demise. It is an affirmation of Black folks' humanity, our contributions to this society, and our resilience in the face of deadly oppression."

BLM gained added urgency on August 9, 2014, when Michael Brown, an unarmed Black teenager, was shot and killed by a White police officer in Ferguson, Missouri. Police left his lifeless body broiling in the summer heat for more than four hours. The failure of a grand jury to indict the police officer prompted civil unrest and protests around the country. The phrase "Black Lives Matter" became a rallying cry for people who had grown indignant with police brutality against people of color. "We have made enormous progress in race relations over the course of the past several decades," President Obama said. "But what is also true is that there are still problems, and communities of color aren't just making these problems up."

What happened in Ferguson initially seemed to mark a turning point. Protests spread nationwide, and blue-ribbon commissions were appointed to explore the causes of racist policing. As months passed, however, reforms were modest, and the pattern of police brutality against young Black men continued.

OBAMACARE ON THE DEFENSIVE   President Obama's proudest achievement, the Affordable Care Act (ACA), provided 20 million people, especially African Americans, Asians, and Latinos, with health insurance. Yet the program was so massive and complicated that the scheduled rollout took four years. In the fall of 2013, the federal online health insurance "exchange," where people without insurance could sign up, opened with great fanfare. Obama assured people that using the online system would be "real simple."

It was not. On October 1, millions tried to sign up; only six succeeded. The website was hobbled with technical glitches. It also became evident that Obama had misled the nation when he told voters that if they liked their current health-insurance plan, they could, under Obamacare, "keep that insurance. Period. End of story." As it turned out, many saw their policies canceled by insurers.

Eventually, the ACA website was fixed, and by August 2014, more than 9 million people, well above the original target number, had signed up for health insurance. "The Affordable Care Act is here to stay," Obama said. But public skepticism about the government's ability to manage the program continued. Over the next ten years, congressional Republicans would try seventy times to dismantle, defund, or change the ACA, but the essential programs remained intact, in part because data showed that the ACA had improved the overall health of the nation.

New Global Challenges in an Age of Insecurity

Rarely are presidents more popular than on their first day in office. To govern requires making decisions, and decisions in democratic nations inevitably produce disappointments, disagreements, and criticism—even among a president's supporters.

During his presidency, Barack Obama discovered the difficulties of leading the world's economic and military superpower in the post–Cold War era. He struggled to stabilize unstable nations—Iraq, Afghanistan, Libya, Ukraine, and Syria—that craved U.S. resources but resented American meddling.

Overall, Obama adopted a posture of restraint in world affairs. He was determined to "avoid stupid errors," wind down the wars in Iraq and Afghanistan, and reduce the use of U.S. military power abroad.

Yet he and others were naive to think that the United States could avoid the burdens of being the only superpower in a post–Cold War world of growing anarchy and violence. Democratic senator Diane Feinstein of California wondered in September 2014 if Obama had become "too cautious" about the use of force in world affairs.

AN IRANIAN NUCLEAR DEAL AND A SYRIAN CRISIS In 2013, the United States and diplomats from other nations held the first high-level talks with Iran since 1979, when Iranian militants took U.S. embassy employees in Tehran hostage. Two years later, Secretary of State John Kerry announced the signing of the Joint Comprehensive Plan of Action (JCPOA). Under its terms, Iran agreed to dismantle much of its nuclear program and open its facilities to more extensive international inspections in exchange for the removal of stringent economic sanctions imposed on Iran by the United States and five other nations.

At the same time that negotiations were occurring in Iran, a bloody civil war in Syria began to have major international repercussions after the Syrian government in August 2013 used chemical weapons to kill 1,400 of its own citizens, many of them children.

President Obama had repeatedly warned that such use of weapons of mass destruction was a "red line" that would trigger international military intervention of "enormous consequences." In late August, he hesitantly approved a military strike against Syria, but then reversed himself, triggering sharp criticism.

In the fall of 2013, Kerry defused the crisis by signing an agreement with Russia to dispose of Syria's chemical weapons. By the end of October, the chemical weapon stockpiles had supposedly been destroyed or dismantled, but the civil war raged on.

RUSSIA'S ANNEXATION OF CRIMEA For nearly twenty years, Vladimir Putin of Russia had viewed the disintegration of the Soviet Union as the "greatest geopolitical catastrophe of the century." On February 27, 2013, now-President Putin sent troops into Crimea, part of the former Soviet republic of Ukraine. A week later, the Crimean parliament voted to become part of the Russian Federation. Putin, claiming that Crimea had "always been an inseparable part of Russia," made the illegal annexation official by positioning Russian troops there, even though he denied their presence.

The speed and ruthlessness with which Putin seized control of Crimea ended hopes that Russia would become a cordial partner of the United States and its European allies. In response to the actions, the United States and the European Union refused to recognize the annexation of Crimea and announced economic sanctions against Russia while pledging financial assistance to Ukraine. By a vote of 100–11, the United Nations General Assembly also opposed the annexation. Yet Putin's popularity in Russia rose, leaving the United States to revert to the Cold War stance of containing Russia's expansionist ambitions.

ISLAMISTS ON THE MOVE In June 2014, events in the Middle East gave President Obama an opportunity to take decisive action. Sunni Jihadists, who had been fighting in Syria, invaded northern Iraq and announced the formation of ISIS, the Islamic State. Most alarming was their brutality—they quickly became infamous for circulating videos of their beheading of prisoners of war.

ISIS represented the culmination of decades of Arab Islamist rage against Europe and the United States. Within months, the terrorist organization undermined governments and security in Syria and Iraq. ISIS seized huge tracts of territory while enslaving, terrorizing, raping, or massacring thousands of men, women, and children.

In August 2014, after ISIS terrorists beheaded two captured Americans, Obama ordered systematic airstrikes, first in Iraq and later in Syria, as ISIS fighters assaulted Christians, Yazidis, and Kurds in the region. If George W. Bush had plunged the United States too deeply into Iraq, Obama seemed to have withdrawn U.S. support too quickly.

POLITICAL GRIDLOCK

During Barack Obama's two presidential terms, the efforts of congressional Republicans to reject all proposals from the White House meant that stalemate had become the controlling political principle.

Intense partisanship dominated the 2014 congressional elections, when Republicans gained control of the Senate for the first time since 2006. They also strengthened their hold on the House, added governorships, and tightened their control of state legislatures. The GOP had campaigned on the dual themes of the "failure" of President Obama and the "disaster" of Obamacare.

Political moderates became a dying breed. By late 2014, the percentage of voters who described themselves as liberals or conservatives had doubled since 1994. More than twice as many Democratic and Republican voters as in 1994 had a "very unfavorable" view of the other party. Congress included mostly Republicans on the Far-Right, Democrats on the Far-Left, and hardly anyone in the middle. "That alignment," said Gerald Seib of the *Wall Street Journal*, created a Congress "that does less, and does it less well, than any time in memory."

Voters hoping for a more energetic and engaged Obama after his reelection were disappointed. He seemed disheartened by the "gap between the magnitude of our challenges and the smallness of our politics" and blamed Republicans for stalemating his second term. But he was not blameless. As political scientist Ian Bremmer said, "George W. Bush was a leader who didn't like to think. Barack Obama is a thinker who doesn't like to lead."

RENEWED ENERGY Yet during the summer of 2015, in the sunset of his presidency, Obama regained his energy. He also benefited from two surprising Supreme Court rulings.

For years, Republicans had waged war on the Affordable Care Act. Unable to halt its implementation in Congress, critics turned to the courts. The claim raised in *King v. Burwell* (2015)—that individuals who purchase insurance on the federal government's health-care exchange are not entitled to the tax subsidies available to those purchasing on state exchanges—would have greatly weakened the ACA.

But in a surprising 6–3 decision, the Supreme Court saved the law. Chief Justice John Roberts explained in the majority opinion that some of the sloppy language in the original legislation should not be used to destroy the program. "Congress passed the Affordable Care Act to improve health insurance markets, not to destroy them," Roberts stressed. "If at all possible, we must interpret the Act in a way that is consistent with the former and avoids the latter."

Married with Pride A California couple poses in front of the United States Supreme Court building in Washington, D.C., while the justices hear arguments on the constitutional right for same-sex couples to wed. On June 26, 2015, in a landmark 5–4 decision, the Court ruled in favor of upholding marriage equality in all fifty states.

Just a day later, the Supreme Court announced a 5–4 decision in *Obergefell v. Hodges*, which banned states from preventing marriages between same-sex couples. The Court's affirmation of same-sex marriage reflected the recent change in public attitudes toward LGBTQ rights.

The momentum of the Court decisions bolstered Obama's efforts in foreign policy. In his 2009 inaugural address, he had vowed to international enemies that "we will extend a hand if you are willing to unclench your fist." That effort finally paid off with the normalizing of relations with Cuba but also when the United States and other major world powers (Russia, China, Germany, Britain, France, and the European Union) announced a draft treaty with Iran intended to thwart its efforts to develop a nuclear weapon. In exchange for ending the international trade embargo against Iran, the agreement called for the Iranians to dismantle much of their nuclear program and allow international inspectors to confirm that destruction. Obama warned congressional critics that any attempt to veto the treaty (called the Joint Comprehensive Plan of Action) would mean "a greater chance of war in the Middle East." In July 2015, the Iran nuclear deal was formalized.

THE TRUMP ADMINISTRATION

In 1780, future president John Adams proclaimed that "division of the republic into two great parties . . . is to be dreaded as the greatest political evil under our Constitution." His fears were well founded. During the twenty-first century, politics devolved into an "us versus them" zero-sum game, a death match energized by mutual contempt and savage attacks. A growing number of voters gave up on the two major parties and identified as independents, a group that soon claimed more people than either the Democrats or Republicans.

THE 2016 PRESIDENTIAL PRIMARIES

Ferocious political polarization shaped the 2016 presidential campaign. Surveys showed that voters were more intensely divided about the opposing political party than they were about race, class, gender, and age. The growing partisanship was evident in a single data point: in 1960, some 5 percent of Republicans and 4 percent of Democrats said they objected to their child marrying someone with the opposing party affiliation. A survey fifty years later found that 49 percent of Republicans objected to their child marrying a Democrat, and 33 percent of Democrats felt the same about their child marrying a Republican.

ANGRY WHITE MEN During the new century, many working-class (those receiving an hourly wage) and lower-middle-class White men (small farmers and shopkeepers, small business owners, policemen, firemen, servicemen, and craft workers—plumbers, electricians, carpenters, truck drivers) felt left behind by the economic recovery. The dramatic widening of the income gap was especially galling. In 1965, heads of companies were paid 20 times that of a typical worker. By 2011, CEOs earned 383 times more than the average worker, for whom the American Dream of endless upward social mobility had vanished.

Some had seen their factory jobs go offshore. Some struggled with stagnant wages. Their prospects were diminished, in part, because labor unions had lost membership and their influence with management. Many blamed an economic system that favored the wealthy, government-subsidized minorities ("welfare cheats"), low-wage immigrant laborers, and a political elite that favored minorities over the White majority. Dashed hopes had fostered despair that morphed into anger and rage fueled by the "grievance media," radio and television talk shows that fed upon and reinforced the anger felt by grassroots Americans.

As sociologist Michael Kimmel explained in his book, *Angry White Men* (2017), the surging popularity of gender and racial equality and immigrant rights had left many White men "feeling betrayed and bewildered," and represented a direct assault on them and their values. In response, White working-class voters mobilized to oppose policies and programs promoting diversity, from busing and affirmative action to bilingual education and gay rights. They fumed about companies and schools giving preference to what they perceived to be less qualified minorities to achieve greater diversity. And they fought liberals who, in their view, championed multiculturalism and the contribution of minorities while denigrating the achievements of White men.

By the twenty-first century, the shared anxieties and resentments of "these angry White males" had coalesced into a well-documented backlash against the multiculturalism evident during Obama's presidency. Non-college-educated Whites worried that their children's lives would be worse than their own, resented immigrants for "taking our jobs," begrudged African Americans for getting what they felt was too much government support, and became convinced that the nation's growing racial and ethnic diversity would push them even further to the margins of society.

TRUMP THE OUTSIDER The emergence of these "angry White men" proved crucial to the unprecedented presidential campaign of Donald Trump, a celebrity real estate developer and reality-television star who had never held elected office. Born in 1946 in Queens, a borough of New York City, he attended a military high school where he was known as a "ladies' man." He then enrolled at Fordham University for two years before transferring to the Wharton School of Business at the University of Pennsylvania, where he earned a degree in economics in 1968. After college, Trump parlayed a large loan from his wealthy father into a sprawling real estate development business called the Trump Organization.

Trump expanded his business empire into the casino gambling industry and later acquired numerous golf resorts around the world. All the while, he focused on building the Trump brand, despite numerous business failures and bankruptcies. Trump's visibility earned him a starring role in a popular NBC television reality series called *The Apprentice*, in which contestants competed for a job within the Trump Organization.

Trump had been a Republican until 2000 when he switched to the Democratic party because Republicans, he said, were "crazy" right-wingers. During Barack Obama's presidency, however, Trump switched back to the Republican party, convinced that the future belonged to "nonpoliticians" like himself. Yet he was a new type of Republican. He showed little interest in reducing government spending, balancing the federal budget, or reducing government entitlement programs—the centerpiece of "Reagan Republicanism." Instead, he focused on economic growth, job creation, and stopping free trade, immigration, and U.S. military interventions abroad.

MAKE AMERICA GREAT AGAIN Initially, Trump's candidacy wasn't taken seriously by many Washington "insiders." Bob Schieffer, the political journalist for *CBS News*, reported that he could not find "a single Republican" who thought Trump could win the nomination. Unlike the other sixteen Republican primary candidates in 2016, however, Trump (similar to Patrick Buchanan in the 1990s), had national name recognition and a unique personality suited to his raucous rallies. He nursed the grievances and anger in his large crowds, and made it clear and easy for supporters to see what he was thinking, while assuring listeners that he would get things done.

Trump fed upon and reinforced the anger felt by so many Americans who had been left out of the economic recovery. He was one of the few candidates to discuss the terrible problems confronting those buffeted by the opioid drug epidemic, declining manufacturing jobs, and the rising cost of health care. He depicted a weakening America besieged by Muslim terrorists and illegal immigrants ("bad dudes"), police killers, and self-serving liberal "elites" championing an unconstrained diversity at the expense of national security.

Republican Rally Donning his "Make America Great Again" cap, Donald Trump speaks at a rally in Orlando, Florida, six days before the 2016 presidential election.

Candidate Trump repeatedly promised to "Make America Great Again." His gospel combined populism with America-first nationalism. His campaign fed upon voter frustrations with conventional politics and conventional politicians. Trump positioned himself as an "outsider," promising to "drain the swamp" of corruption created by political insiders in Washington, D.C.

Trump's campaign also benefited from the surging influence of social media such as Twitter and Facebook. People could now discuss politics online in an unmediated way, reading and expressing themselves in the language of resentment not allowed on television or in newspapers. And candidate Trump relentlessly used Twitter, sending dozens of daily tweets to his growing number of followers.

To the surprise of pundits and the chagrin of party leaders, Trump won the 2016 Republican nomination and named Mike Pence, the conservative former governor of Indiana, as his running mate.

A CAMPAIGN LIKE NO OTHER   The 2016 contest between Donald Trump and Hillary Clinton was one of the most negative in political history, a campaign more memorable for its drama and insults than its issues or proposals. Trump dismissed "crooked Hillary" as a "nasty woman," calling her the "most corrupt person ever to seek the presidency," and lampooning her as a creature of the Washington and Wall Street elite who masqueraded as a friend of the people while raking in millions of ill-gotten dollars. If elected president, he promised, he would "put her in jail," leading his supporters to wear T-shirts shouting, "Lock Her Up."

For her part, Clinton portrayed Trump as unfit for the highest office in the land, labeling him a dangerous and unpredictable leader incapable of exercising the mature temperament demanded of the modern presidency. She hurt her cause when, amid a fit of frustration, she claimed that "you could put half of Trump's supporters into what I call the 'basket of deplorables.'"

The fall presidential campaign featured one startling surprise after another. On October 7, 2016, just two days before the second televised debate with Clinton, the *Washington Post* released a videotape from 2005 that showed a married Trump lewdly describing his unsolicited kissing and groping of women he had met during his frequent business trips. "You know I'm automatically attracted to beautiful women," he bragged. "I just start kissing them. It's like a magnet. Just kiss. I don't even wait [to be asked]. And when you're a star [like me], they let you do it. You can do anything [to them]." The taped comments ignited a media furor, yet Trump dismissed the controversy as simply "locker room banter" that he claimed all men engage in.

Hillary Clinton confronted her own scandals. For years, people had questioned how she and her husband, former president Bill Clinton, had channeled huge donations to the Clinton Foundation from foreign and domestic corporations and individuals. In March 2015, the *New York Times* reported that Clinton, as secretary of state between 2009 and 2013, had used her family's email server for her official communications rather than the State Department server. Her doing so violated departmental protocols, created a security risk that confidential (classified) diplomatic emails might be hacked and monitored by foreign agents, and prevented the State Department from archiving her 62,000 messages.

After an exhaustive investigation, the FBI director, James B. Comey, concluded that Clinton had been "extremely careless" in handling her email, but saw no point in prosecuting her. Clinton acknowledged that her decision to use a personal server was a "mistake" resulting from her desire for "personal convenience," but Republican critics used the issue to call into question Clinton's honesty and reliability. Donald Trump charged that Clinton's use of a personal email server was "worse than Watergate."

Then came more surprises. During the summer of 2016, agents of the Russian government "hacked" the email system of the Democratic National Committee and forwarded the data to WikiLeaks, which released tens of thousands of confidential messages intended to embarrass and distract the Clinton campaign. On October 28, 2016, just eleven days before the presidential election, FBI director James Comey informed Congress that "in connection with an unrelated case, the FBI has learned of the existence of emails that appear pertinent to the investigation" of Hillary Clinton's use of her personal email server.

This revelation was like a bomb hitting the Clinton campaign. It raised new questions about her presidential fitness and revealed that the ongoing investigation into her emails would not be concluded by Election Day. Clinton would later claim that Comey's revelation ("October surprise") cost her the election. Perhaps it did, but Clinton also struggled throughout the fall to articulate a unifying vision or fashion a compelling explanation for why she should be the next president.

Still, Clinton's narrow loss to Trump on November 8 surprised virtually everyone. Most observers believed that she had won the three televised debates, and all the major polls predicted a narrow Democratic victory. Yet Trump ended up with 309 electoral votes to her 228. True, Clinton won 3 million more votes than Trump out of the 136 million ballots cast, garnering the largest total ever by a losing candidate, but she lost by 78,000 votes the crucial swing states of Michigan, Ohio, Pennsylvania, and Wisconsin. Their

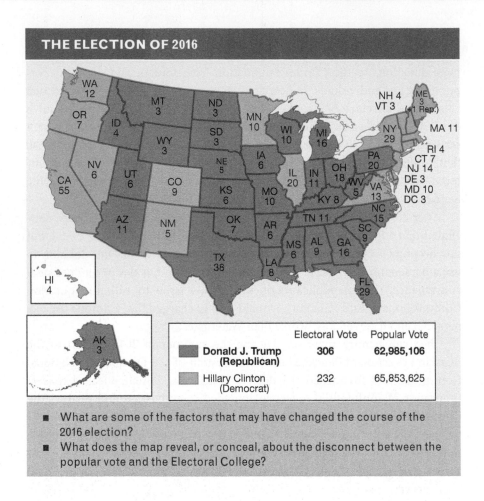

THE ELECTION OF 2016

	Electoral Vote	Popular Vote
Donald J. Trump (Republican)	306	62,985,106
Hillary Clinton (Democrat)	232	65,853,625

■ What are some of the factors that may have changed the course of the 2016 election?

■ What does the map reveal, or conceal, about the disconnect between the popular vote and the Electoral College?

46 electoral votes gave Trump the edge he needed. Clinton's totals fell far short of Obama's numbers in 2012.

Surveys revealed that voters by a 2–1 margin cared most about which candidate could bring change to Washington politics. Clinton struck many voters as offering more of the same. Her failure to win over White working- and lower-middle-class males in the Rust Belt states was her downfall, along with the fact that many minority voters did not go to the polls. While Trump positioned himself as the candidate of change, Clinton struggled as a lackluster defender of the status quo. At the close of her campaign, she could only offer a final promise, "I'm not *him*." Voters wanted more. Shannon Goodin, a twenty-four-year-old first-time voter in Michigan, explained that Trump won her vote by being a "big poster child for change." She added that traditional "politicians don't appeal to us. Clinton would go out of her way to appeal to minorities, immigrants, but she didn't really care for everyday Americans."

A POPULIST PRESIDENT

President-elect Trump could claim a long list of firsts: the first president never to have served in the military or held public office, the oldest president, and the president with the lowest popularity upon taking office as measured by opinion polls. Like Andrew Jackson, whom he claimed to emulate, Trump could appear wild and ruthless at times, and, like Richard Nixon, he could display open contempt for both the media ("fake news") and career government officials, many of whom he viewed as incompetent and unnecessary.

Trump, however, would preside over a deeply divided nation. While his supporters were thrilled with their victory, millions of stunned Americans viewed his victory on November 8 with unprecedented foreboding. The two

Women's March on Washington On January 21, 2017, the day after the Trump inauguration, demonstrators flooded the National Mall in support of women's rights and reproductive justice, health care, immigration reform, racial justice, LGBTQ rights, and other interconnected issues. The Washington demonstration was grounded in the nonviolent ideology of the civil rights movement and went down as the largest coordinated protest in U.S. history; combined with hundreds of counterpart marches worldwide, the event drew 5 million participants.

Democratic leaders of the California legislature released a joint statement that reflected the feelings of most Democrats: "Today, we woke up feeling like strangers in a foreign land."

Women concerned about Trump's election organized mass demonstrations in January 2017 on behalf of women's rights, immigrants and refugees, improved health care, reproductive rights, LGBTQ (lesbian, gay, bisexual, transgender, queer/questioning) rights, racial equality, freedom of religion, and workers' rights. Although a worldwide phenomenon, the Women's March was the largest one-day demonstration in U.S. history, encompassing demonstrations in some 400 American cities. The Women's March on Washington, D.C., which included a half million protesters, was designed to "send a bold message to our new administration on their first day in office, and to the world that women's rights are human rights." One of the speakers, feminist leader Gloria Steinem, directed her comments at President Trump: "Our Constitution does not begin with 'I, the President.' It begins with, 'We, the People.'"

At the same time, Trump's supporters relished a future of unconventional presidential action designed to end their alienation and bitterness. In his inaugural address, he assured the nation that his swearing-in ceremony would be "remembered as the day the people became the rulers of this nation again." He told his ecstatic working-class supporters that "you will never be ignored again," for he intended to uproot the political "establishment." An unapologetic hypernationalism would be the theme of his administration: "From this day forward, it is going to be only America first—America first."

A CHAOTIC FIRST HUNDRED DAYS   Chaos characterized Trump's presidency. He was a disrupter and divider by choice, eager to exploit and worsen the cultural and political polarization that had fragmented Americans for the past twenty years. No modern president had displayed so little understanding or so little interest in how government operates—its norms, procedures, and constraints. He even used Twitter to announce those he had fired and policies he had created.

President Trump forged a cabinet and group of senior advisers dominated by family members and wealthy loyalist bankers and businessmen, mostly older White men with little government experience. Some of his closest aides, such as Steve Bannon, his chief strategist, and senior policy adviser Stephen Miller, were leaders of "Alt-Right" (alternative right) organizations that promoted White supremacy, anti-immigrant nativism, and America-first trade policies.

As the months passed, the Trump administration experienced constant turnover. Despite the president's promise to "surround myself with only the best and most serious people," an unprecedented number of cabinet members, senior aides, advisers, and presidential attorneys came and went. More than 90 percent of cabinet officers and White House senior aides either resigned or were fired, including three presidential chiefs of staff.

Trump vigorously denied that his untested new administration was anything but perfect. "I turn on the TV, open the newspapers, and I see stories of chaos" at the White House, he grumbled. "Chaos! This administration is running like a fine-tuned machine."

Additional worries for the Trump administration came with the news that the FBI was investigating the possibility that Trump campaign staffers had secretly collaborated with Russia to torpedo Hillary Clinton's campaign. Trump vigorously denied that he or his campaign staff ever "colluded" with Russian officials. As journalist Timothy Noah explained, however, "the Trump administration in its infancy [was] creating enough blunders, scandals, and controversies to strain the resources" of the White House press corps.

AN ACTIVIST PRESIDENT   Amid all the personnel turnover, most Republicans were pleased overall with his efforts to reduce federal regulation and the size of the government and grow the economy. President Trump in his first year signed thirty-two executive orders removing federal protections for consumers, the environment, food safety, internet privacy, transgender Americans, and victims of sexual abuse. He froze most federal hiring, cut aid payments to foreign governments, and curbed federal efforts to constrict the coal industry. Trump's greatest success early in his presidency was the appointment of two conservative justices to the Supreme Court: Neil Gorsuch and Brett Kavanaugh, both federal court of appeals judges. In 2020, he would add a third conservative justice to the Court, Amy Coney Barrett. With the help of a Republican majority in the Senate, Trump also appointed some 220 conservative federal judges during his presidency.

VETOING EFFORTS TO SLOW CLIMATE CHANGE   On June 1, 2017, President Trump announced that the United States, which ranked as the world's second-highest emitter of greenhouse gases, would withdraw from the 2015 Paris Climate Agreement addressing climate change. He claimed that the accord, signed by 195 nations, penalized American businesses and workers, while other major countries simply ignored the terms and benchmarks of the agreement to reduce carbon emissions. Trump's withdrawal from the agreement represented his most sweeping assertion of an "America First" foreign policy. Thereafter, he systematically rolled back more than eighty federal environmental regulations, even as the changing climate triggered more widespread fires in western states and more powerful hurricanes.

BANNING MUSLIMS OR SECURING BORDERS?   One of Trump's most controversial executive orders was a temporary ban on immigrants and refugees from seven nations with large Muslim populations. The response that rose against the "Muslim ban" was immediate and widespread, with adherents of both the center and the left voicing their dismay at such a prejudicial policy. Thousands protested across the nation while lawyers for various organizations filed suits to stop the order from taking effect. The acting attorney general, Sally Yates, refused to enforce the new policy. Trump fired her. Even Dick Cheney, George Bush's hard-nosed former Republican vice president, declared that the proposed travel ban "went against everything we stand for." The pro-Trump editors of the *Wall Street Journal* also took issue with the order describing it as "so poorly explained and prepared for, that it has produced fear and confusion at airports, an immediate legal defeat, and political fury at home and abroad."

Within days, federal judges dismissed the travel ban as an unconstitutional assault on a particular religious group. In response, on March 6, 2017, President Trump issued a revised executive order, but it too was rejected by federal judges. In mid-2018, the Supreme Court by a 5–4 vote in *Trump v. Hawaii* approved a third version of the executive order banning immigrants from seven Muslim nations. This time the order was based on the president's claim that the countries were "terrorist risks." Speaking for the majority, Chief Justice John Roberts acknowledged that the court had "no view on the soundness of the policy," but insisted that the president had the authority to impose

Muslim Ban A crowd of protesters gather at the Los Angeles International Airport on January 29, 2017, speaking out against President Trump's executive order to ban immigrants from certain Muslim-majority countries from entering the United States.

such a ban. In her dissenting opinion, Justice Sonia Sotomayor, the daughter of Puerto Rican immigrants who was the first Latina to serve on the Supreme Court, argued that any "reasonable observer" would conclude that the travel ban was "motivated by anti-Muslim animus."

A similar culture-wars battle with the courts greeted Trump's reversal of Barack Obama's 2016 decision to allow transgender people to serve openly in the military. The United States "will not accept or allow" transgender people in the military "in any capacity," Trump tweeted in July 2017. He added that the military "cannot be burdened with the tremendous medical costs and disruption that transgender in the military would entail."

Lawsuits filed in several federal courts delayed implementation of the ban, which affected some 15,000 people. In issuing an injunction against the ban, U.S. District Court Judge Colleen Kollar-Kotelly found "absolutely no support for the claim that the ongoing service of transgender people would have any negative effects on the military."

ASSAULTING OBAMACARE Throughout the 2016 presidential campaign, Trump had lambasted Obamacare, promising to replace it "on day one" with a much better health-care program "at a tiny fraction of the cost, and it is going to be so easy." To that end, he and House Speaker Paul Ryan unveiled in early 2017 the American Health Care Act (AHCA). It would have removed many of the pillars of Obamacare, including phasing out Medicaid subsidies that had enabled millions to gain coverage for the first time.

Yet surveys showed that only 17 percent of voters liked the new bill. For that reason and others, Republican congressional leaders withdrew the AHCA without a formal vote. Trump remained committed to the destruction of Obamacare, but neither he nor the Republican congressional leadership offered a concrete alternative to Obamacare. Nonetheless, during his presidential term, some 4 million Americans lost their medical coverage.

BUILDING A WALL Trump's other showcase campaign promise proved equally difficult to implement. He pledged to build a "huge" anti-immigrant wall along the 2,000-mile-long Mexican border and that Mexico would pay for it. In late April 2017, the president acknowledged that he could not convince Congress or Mexico to finance the wall.

Rebuffed on Capitol Hill, Trump made the controversial decision to divert billions of dollars from the defense budget to build a small section of the much-trumpeted wall. Critics challenged the legality of such funding, but in July 2019, the Supreme Court approved the reallocation of $2.5 billion in Department of Defense anti-drug funding to construct the wall. Two months later, an additional $3.6 billion was diverted from military construction projects.

Trump had promised to erect 500 miles of new metal fencing by the end of his first term. By mid-2020, with more than $11 billion spent, only 110 miles of what he called his "impenetrable" barrier had been erected.

FORGING FOREIGN POLICIES

In foreign affairs, Donald Trump's America First policy led him to criticize NATO allies for not paying enough for their own defense needs and he pledged to bring more U.S. troops home from foreign bases. Yet his early actions were minimal, in part because he had so little preparation for global leadership. Other than hosting several foreign dignitaries, waving a big stick toward rogue nations such as North Korea and Iran, and twice launching cruise missiles at Syrian airbases in retaliation for chemical attacks on civilians by the Syrian government, the president's view of America's role in the world remained confused.

SYRIA In 2013, for example, when President Assad of Syria had first used chemical weapons against government opponents, killing a thousand people, citizen Trump had urged President Obama: "Do not attack Syria. There is no upside and tremendous downside." Similarly, during his presidential campaign, he had told Reuters news service that "we should not be focusing on Syria. You're going to end up in World War III over Syria if we listen to Hillary Clinton." As president, however, he adopted a strategy of meeting America's needs first, treating allies like secondary partners that needed constant reminders of the nature of the alliance, while engaging more openly with America's traditional enemies. His America First policy pleased his supporters, but it remained to be seen whether it truly benefited national interests.

On October 6, 2019, President Trump ordered the U.S. troops in Syria to leave, thereby liberating thousands of ISIS prisoners captured by U.S. forces. Three days later, Turkish soldiers invaded Syria to suppress the Kurdish minority who had been launching attacks across the border. Trump's collaboration with Turkey frustrated America's traditional NATO allies.

LAUNCHING A TRADE WAR In March 2018, President Trump abruptly announced punitive tariffs on imported steel and aluminum. This policy change caught his aides and fellow Republicans off guard, hurt American companies that had to buy imported steel and aluminum at higher prices. and infuriated America's most reliable global trading partners. Hardest hit was China, who predicted a retaliatory trade war. By 2020, American tariffs on imports were the highest they had been since 1993, and, as always, higher tariffs meant higher prices for consumers.

The trade war with China involved more than high tariffs. President Trump complained about American companies having unequal access to China's markets and China's long history of stealing the intellectual property of U.S. companies.

The president claimed that "trade wars are good, and easy to win," which stunned economists—and Republicans. The president's chief economic adviser resigned in protest. More than a hundred congressional Republicans urged the president to reconsider launching a trade war, claiming that no nation wins such vengeful efforts. In the end, while the trade war showed his willingness to stand up to China, it appears to have achieved much less than promised in the short run. The tariffs hurt U.S. manufacturers, disrupted supply chains, and raised the cost of producing factory goods.

IRAN Just weeks later, on May 8, 2018, President Trump again angered America's western European allies. He announced that the United States would

"Iran Deal" Withdrawal President Trump displays his signature on a document reinstituting sanctions against Iran after withdrawing the United States from the Joint Comprehensive Plan of Action in May 2018.

withdraw from the Joint Comprehensive Plan of Action (JCPOA) agreement with Iran limiting its ability to create nuclear weapons and reinstitute economic sanctions against the Islamist nation. It was Trump's most consequential foreign policy action. The withdrawal was enthusiastically welcomed in Israel and by its strong supporters. Yet worldwide it left many confused and unsettled about the destabilizing ramifications it could produce in the Middle East. Trump abandoned the JCPOA even though the United Nations had verified that Iran was abiding by their agreement not to develop nuclear weapons. Consequentially, America's withdrawal from the JCPOA also called into question the U.S. government's commitment to other treaties around the world. Britain, France, and Germany admonished Trump and vowed to continue honoring the deal with Iran.

NORTH KOREA Soon after, Trump again surprised the world when he announced that he and North Korean leader Kim Jong-un would hold a summit meeting to discuss the future of nuclear weapons in the Communist nation. On June 12, 2018, the two met in Singapore and announced that discussions would continue "to work toward complete denuclearization of the Korean Peninsula." Ten days later, President Trump claimed that North Korea had begun to dismantle its nuclear test sites, only to be contradicted by his secretary of defense, James Mattis, who said there was no evidence of North Korea taking any concrete steps to denuclearize. In the end, none of the early promise for successful negotiations came to fruition.

RUSSIA In July 2018, President Trump traveled to Helsinki, Finland, to meet with Vladimir Putin, the authoritarian Russian leader. There he did not address the U.S. government's displeasure with any of the issues pushing the two countries farther and farther apart. Topics to be discussed included the Russian annexation of Crimea and their shootdown of a Malaysian passenger jet over eastern Ukraine in 2014, and the hot-button issue of Russian interference in the 2016 U.S. election on behalf of Trump. At the postsummit press conference, with the whole world watching, President Trump did just the opposite and took Putin's side on most of the matters dividing the two nations. A reporter asked who he believed—Putin or America's intelligence agencies—about Russian interference in the 2016 U.S. election. Trump responded, "My people came to me, [Director of National Intelligence] Dan Coats came to me and some others saying they think it's Russia. I have President Putin, he just said it's not Russia," Trump said. "I will say this, I don't see any reason why it would be. . . . I have confidence in both parties."

2018 Russia–United States Summit Meeting President Donald Trump and First Lady Melania Trump met with Vladimir Putin of Russia in Helsinki, Finland to discuss the possibility of Russian interference in the 2016 U.S. election.

The president was widely criticized back home for his handling of the summit. Newt Gingrich, a strong Trump supporter, labeled the Russian summit "the most serious mistake of his presidency." The editors of the pro-Trump newspaper, *The Arizona Republic*, said the summit with Putin revealed that the U.S. president "hasn't got a clue what it means to be president."

AFGHANISTAN In Afghanistan, the Trump administration dispatched more troops and intensified the bombing campaign against the Taliban, but the military stalemate continued. In December 2017, Vice President Mike Pence made a brief visit to the war-torn Islamist nation. There, he reaffirmed America's commitment: "We're here to stay until freedom wins." Three years later, however, little had changed in what President Trump had called a "stupid" war that had cost America more than a trillion dollars and 2,500 lives. The Afghan War, by far America's longest conflict, had become a costly quagmire like the Vietnam War.

DEEPENING DIVISIONS

By the end of Trump's first 100 days in office, his presidency was struggling to lay claim to any major legislative victories, and as a result, he had the lowest public approval rating (37 percent) of any first-term president at that benchmark.

LEGAL ISSUES In May 2017, President Trump stunned the nation by firing James Comey, the FBI director, who was leading that agency's investigation into contacts between Trump campaign officials and Russian groups assisting them. White House aides initially claimed that Trump had acted on the advice of the deputy attorney general. The next day, however, President Trump contradicted them. He acknowledged firing Comey because he wanted the Russian investigation ended.

Only days later, the media reported that Comey had kept detailed summaries of his meetings with the president. One of the entries revealed that Trump on February 14 had urged Comey to drop an investigation into Michael Flynn, the director of national security, who had engaged in illegal contacts with Russian officials. Trump saw his position further eroded when Jeff Sessions, the attorney general, recused himself from the investigation because he, too, had been in contact with Russian officials during the 2016 campaign.

On May 18, 2017, Rod Rosenstein, the deputy attorney general, appointed a special counsel, Robert Mueller III, a decorated Vietnam War marine veteran, former FBI director, and longtime Republican. Mueller's assignment was to lead a criminal investigation into Russian involvement in the 2016 Trump campaign.

President Trump now faced the prospect of a prolonged criminal investigation that would impede his efforts to fulfill campaign promises.

TAX REFORM VICTORY President Trump had promised on the campaign trail to generate the greatest economic growth in U.S. history. To do so, he created the Tax Cuts and Jobs Act, which Congress passed without a single Democrat vote at the end of 2017. It was his first major legislative victory nearly one year into office. It cut the corporate tax rate from 35 percent to a permanent 21 percent, lowered income tax rates overall (not permanent), doubled the standard deduction, and eliminated many personal exemptions.

It was the first major reduction in federal taxes in more than thirty years, and it provided a well-timed stimulus to the economy. Within months, the tax cut boosted corporate profits and stimulated sustained economic growth while boosting employment. At the same time, Trump ordered federal agencies to roll back environmental regulations that he claimed were stifling economic growth. By the end of 2019, unemployment was at its lowest level for half a century, and wage levels had risen more than 4 percent over the 2018 average. With the stock market increasing dramatically and unemployment levels at record lows, many thought the country was headed in a good direction economically.

SHUTTING OFF IMMIGRATION   With the economy on the upswing, the Trump administration decided to deliver on another big campaign pledge, which was to close the U.S. border with Mexico and pass immigration reform. Initially, his administration shut down the asylum program offering refuge to victims of authoritarian regimes and deported more than 600,000 people. In the spring of 2018, the federal government announced a zero-tolerance policy regarding undocumented Mexican immigrants. The Department of Homeland Security and the U.S. Border Patrol took the controversial step of separating several thousand children from their detained parents. An internal Department of Homeland Security memo surfaced that admitted "harm to children is being deliberately used for its deterrent effect."

When videos surfaced of children being held in metal cages, having to sleep on concrete floors, and crying for their parents, nationwide protests erupted against the new policy; Evangelist Franklin Graham, an ardent Trump booster, called the new policy "disgraceful," and even First Lady Melania Trump issued an unusual statement deploring the situation. When large numbers of Republicans condemned the separation of undocumented immigrant parents and

Children in Migrant Detention Centers Due to the zero-tolerance immigration policy, undocumented Mexicans were held in migrant detention centers. While the adults faced prosecution, children were controversially separated from their parents and supervised by federal authorities.

children, President Trump reversed himself on June 20, 2018, signing an executive order that allowed families at the border to be detained together.

IMPEACHING PRESIDENT TRUMP

As the political divisions in the country deepened, President Trump continued to enjoy intense support among his "base"—those loyal voters who carried him into office. They were drawn to him for his directness, toughness, and their shared vision of what would make America great again. The president seemed determined to fend off all challenges by staying on the offensive, dismissing his critics and journalists as biased whiners.

THE MUELLER REPORT On March 22, 2019, after twenty-two months of investigation, special counsel Robert Mueller submitted to Attorney General William Barr his much-anticipated report. The "Report on the Investigation into Russian Interference in the 2016 Presidential Election," detailed the "systematic" Russian government-sponsored efforts to ensure a Trump victory in the 2016 presidential election. Mueller and his team of 19 attorneys and 40 FBI agents had interviewed more than 500 people and perused thousands of documents.

The Mueller report revealed that the Russian Internet Research Company weaponized social media, especially Facebook, to manipulate U.S. voters in 2016. Trump campaign officials had secretly welcomed Russian help, but the evidence was insufficient to warrant charges that Donald Trump the candidate "conspired or coordinated" with Russians.

As to President Trump's efforts to impede, misrepresent, and end the investigation, Mueller did not pursue the issue, citing a Justice Department opinion that prohibits a federal indictment of a sitting president. But the report specifically did not "exonerate" the president of culpability.

On March 24, Attorney General Barr sent Congress a letter giving his summarization of the report, claiming that it had cleared President Trump of *any* wrongdoing. Democrats widely criticized Barr's synopsis as a "whitewash." Mueller himself wrote Barr, stressing that the attorney general's letter "did not fully capture the context, nature, and substance of this office's work and conclusions" and that this caused "public confusion." For his part, President Trump claimed that Mueller's "witch hunt" had "totally" exonerated him.

FIRST IMPEACHMENT The failure of the Mueller report to provide evidence of illegal behavior by President Trump did not deter congressional Democrats from pursuing an array of investigations. In the fall of 2019, the

House of Representatives launched an investigation to determine if Trump should be impeached. A survey showed that more than half of voters thought he had tried to impede the Russian investigation.

The House Judiciary Committee hearings centered on one issue: did President Trump withhold Congress-approved military aid to Ukraine until its president, Volodymyr Zelensky, launched an investigation into Hunter Biden, the son of Joe Biden, the former vice president and the likely Democratic presidential candidate in 2020? The younger Biden had served on the board of a Ukrainian natural-gas company, and Trump hoped to find evidence about his relationships that would embarrass Joe Biden and undermine his candidacy.

After fiery debate, the House in December passed two articles of impeachment on a party-line vote, with all Democrats voting in favor:

> 1. Abuse of power by "pressuring Ukraine to investigate his political
> rivals ahead of the 2020 election while withholding a White House
> meeting and $400 million in U.S. security aid from Kyiv."
> 2. Obstruction of Congress by directing defiance of subpoenas issued
> by the House and ordering officials to refuse to testify.

Donald Trump was the third president to be impeached, following Andrew Johnson in 1868 and Bill Clinton in 1998. Yet most Democrats knew that the Republican-controlled Senate was unlikely to convict the president. Senate majority leader Mitch McConnell said, "there's no chance" Trump would be convicted. He and others argued that impeachment was the wrong way to address the charges against the president. Let the voters decide the issue in the 2020 election, they insisted.

On February 5, 2020, as McConnell predicted, the Senate found Trump not guilty by a vote of 48–52, with all forty-seven Senate Democrats voting guilty on both counts. Former Republican presidential nominee Mitt Romney was the only senator—and the first in U.S. history—to cross party lines by voting to convict.

In the aftermath of the impeachment vote, the polarization of the political system only widened. Voters were deeply divided along racial, generational, ideological, cultural, and rural/urban lines. On average, Republicans grew more conservative and Democrats grew more liberal, leaving the prospect of hard-fought and evenly balanced elections in which the two political tribes fight to the death. Republican senator Jeff Flake said "Tribalism is ruining us. It is tearing our country apart. It is no way for sane adults to act."

The toxic bitterness between the president and Democrats in Congress was on full display at President Trump's 2020 State of the Union address, which coincided with the impeachment vote. As the president arrived at the podium,

Donald Trump's First Impeachment A majority among members of the House of Representatives were so concerned with President Trump's perceived abuse of power regarding the U.S. policy with Ukraine and Hunter Biden that they filed charges against him (impeachment). The Republican-controlled Senate, however, acquitted Trump.

House speaker Pelosi extended her hand, but President Trump refused to shake it. Pelosi responded in kind when the president finished his speech by theatrically ripping in half her paper copy of his remarks.

SIDESWIPED BY A PANDEMIC

President Trump's impeachment victory was cut short by a report that a potentially global medical crisis was unfolding in China. On December 31, 2019, Chinese officials had notified the World Health Organization (WHO) about several unusual cases of pneumonia in Wuhan City, the cultural and economic hub of central China. Within a week, the number of cases had grown to sixty, and the tally was increasing exponentially, as was the number of people dying of the unknown illness.

On January 7, 2020, a Chinese laboratory isolated and identified the new coronavirus. It became known as COVID⊠19, and it quickly spread across the world. The virus, which could be transmitted through the air and by physical contact, was extremely contagious. It attacked the respiratory system, and there was no clear treatment for it, much less a cure. On March 11, 2020, the World Health Organization (WHO) announced that COVID-19 had become a pandemic (an epidemic that spreads beyond a single country or continent). By August 2021, more than 190 million people worldwide had contracted the disease and more than 4 million had died. In the United States, the virus infected more than 35 million people and killed more than 625,000.

Those infected with the virus displayed a variety of symptoms to varying degrees. Some had little discomfort; others developed fevers, chills, painful aches and coughs, and respiratory distress. The aggressive virus frequently transitioned into pneumonia, which was often deadly for the elderly and those with preexisting conditions such as diabetes, obesity, heart disease, and respiratory issues.

ORIGINS Medical researchers believed that the virus originated in animals, probably bats, before crossing into humans at an unsanitary "wet market" in Wuhan City, where vendors sold live animals for food. After the infection spread across Wuhan City, it did not take long to spread around the world. Soon, people were calling COVID-19 the "globalization virus."

IMPACT Over the centuries, pandemics have reshaped the course of world history. The black death caused by the bubonic plague in the mid-fourteenth century killed as many as two thirds of Europeans. The Spanish flu epidemic of 1918–1920 cost as many as 100 million lives worldwide.

The **COVID-19 pandemic** did not have the same physical impact as those epidemics because medical knowledge, technology, and communications are far superior today. Still, the 2019–2021 pandemic had a colossal effect on daily life throughout the world. As the head of the International Red Cross warned, "We run the risk of an unprecedented humanitarian crisis."

To slow the spread of infection, nations went into quarantine mode as early as February 2020. Governments urged or ordered people to stay at home. Spectator sports banned in-person attendance. Airlines and subways shut down. Businesses, schools, and colleges closed, and many white-collar employees were forced to work from home using computers—if they still had a job. But many "essential workers"—physicians and nurses, delivery drivers, garbage haulers, postal and construction workers, grocery-store employees, farm laborers—could not work from home and therefore were more susceptible to the viral infection.

THE PANDEMIC IN AMERICA

The first case of the virus in the United States emerged on January 19, 2020, when a thirty-five-year-old man in Washington State went to a clinic complaining of a stubborn cough, fever, and vomiting. He had recently returned from China. Tests confirmed that he had the COVID-19 virus.

Two previous presidents, George W. Bush and Barack Obama, had established detailed protocols and maintained a federal office to deal with epidemics, but the Trump administration had closed the office. Public health officials and infectious disease experts warned President Trump that the pandemic would soon sweep across America. The national security adviser, Robert O'Brien, stressed that the coronavirus represented the "biggest national security threat" of the Trump presidency.

Yet the president dismissed such dire predictions and persistently downplayed the pandemic. On January 23, he claimed, "We have it totally under control." The virus would soon disappear, he promised, as the weather turned warmer. That did not happen. Instead, the virus spread—triggering lockdowns nationwide.

On February 29, 2020, officials reported the first American death from the coronavirus. While public health officials urged people to self-quarantine and to cancel social events and large gatherings, the Trump administration continued to downplay the threat.

Scientists stressed that the key element in fighting any virus pandemic is diagnostic tests providing prompt results, yet the Trump administration failed to develop a national testing strategy, leaving the effort mostly in the hands of the states. While other nations were testing thousands of people for infection, the Centers for Disease Control (CDC), the federal government's primary agency for dealing with epidemics, had screened just 500 people by the end of February 2020. Dr. Anthony Fauci, the nation's leading infectious-disease specialist, called the national testing effort "a failure."

In the early months of the pandemic, President Trump viewed it primarily as a threat to the economy. His administration was slow to address an alarming shortage of basic supplies needed by medical workers to fight a pandemic— diagnostic test kits, face masks, ventilators, protective clothing, gloves, and intensive-care hospital beds. Rather than call for more testing capacity, President Trump said the United States should be testing *less*. He repeatedly blamed rising numbers of cases on increased testing. "If we didn't do testing, we'd have no cases," the president said, baffling public health professionals. The president also sent mixed signals about whether wearing masks was effective at limiting the spread of the virus.

SOCIAL DISRUPTIONS   For everyone, rich and poor, young and old, the pandemic upended everyday life. Apartments and homes became workplaces, classrooms, fitness centers, yoga studios, and child-care centers—and crossroads of tension. Many nonessential businesses closed down in March 2020, sending employees home in an effort to stem the spread of the virus. Some were able to continue working from home, but many were not, and unemployment soared. At the end of March, President Trump finally heeded the advice of medical advisors to order a national shutdown of all non-essential functions.

Life ground to a halt by early April 2020 as most Americans closeted themselves in their homes or apartments. The basic human need for social interaction was frustrated by the greater need for social distancing. Americans struggled with loneliness and boredom amid the "new normal" of self-isolation. Uncertainty and anxiety abounded, as no one knew how long the pandemic and the lockdown it triggered would last.

As the number of cases and deaths rose and the days and weeks passed in dull, drab isolation, people grew grumpy as their despair over an uncertain future deepened. "My god," wrote journalist Frank Bruni. "We're hurting like we seldom hurt. We're quarreling like we seldom quarrel. We're exceptional in our death count, in our [political] divisions. It's easy to feel hopeless. It's hard to press forward."

Unable to pay their rent or mortgage, millions of suddenly unemployed people faced eviction or foreclosure. In March 2020, the economy experienced

Covid-19 Testing Health-care professionals utilized coronavirus tests, like the nasal swab test pictured here, to determine if someone had contracted COVID-19.

a sharp, sudden downturn that some economists called a pandemic depression. The stock market plunged 30 percent, the fastest and deepest drop in history. Unemployment increased from 3.5 percent in February to 15 percent in April, the highest level since the Great Depression of the 1930s.

In response to the economic shock, Congress and President Trump passed the Cares Act at the end of March 2020. It distributed more than half a trillion dollars in direct aid to more than 150 million Americans. The infusion of cash helped some struggling households but was not sufficient to generate an economic recovery.

For a period in the spring of 2020, America made progress against the virus. The number of cases in hard-hit states like New York and New Jersey dropped, thanks largely to a statewide shutdown of nonessential businesses such as restaurants, movie theaters, and hair salons, and new requirements that everyone wear masks in public areas and practice "social distancing"— staying at least six feet apart.

VIRAL POLITICS   The pandemic deepened political divisions. Following President Trump's lead, Republicans were much less willing than Democrats to respect CDC guidelines for social distancing and wearing masks, insisting that it was their constitutional right to do whatever they wanted, wherever they pleased, even if doing so endangered others. As American behavior during the Second World War had demonstrated, however, the necessity of collective sacrifice in pursuit of the greater good during a national crisis should not be confused as an assault on individual liberty.

By late April 2020, against the advice of medical experts, the president demanded that businesses and schools reopen. On April 17, the president tweeted, "LIBERATE MICHIGAN" in support of armed protesters demanding an end to the state's lockdown. By early to mid-May, some states began to reopen to varying degrees, while the worst-hit states remained on more severe lockdowns until mid-June.

To address the slumping economy, Trump authorized Treasury secretary Steven Mnuchin to distribute a staggering $1.6 trillion in stimulus grants and loans to individuals, companies, and nonprofit organizations. The aid package calmed markets, prevented many businesses from collapsing, slowed layoffs, and stabilized household income.

Still, the number of Americans infected by the virus rose as various states chose to reopen an even larger range of businesses, bars, beaches, swimming pools, and parks during the summer. The United States soon had the highest number of cases—and deaths—in the world. With less than 5 percent of the world's population, the United States had 25 percent of the world's confirmed coronavirus cases.

Those killed by the virus were disproportionately old, poor, African American, Native American, and Latino. Because people were twenty times more likely to become infected indoors than outdoors, congested spaces—prisons, nursing homes, and meat processing plants—became "hot spot" incubators for the virus. Wherever the coronavirus emerged, area hospitals were overwhelmed. President Trump's approval ratings began to drop noticeably throughout the summer of 2020, as the number of cases and deaths steadily rose and the economy limped along.

During the fall of 2020 as the presidential election approached, the United States experienced a third wave of new cases coming off of Labor Day weekend and growing fatigue among the American people from wearing masks and social distancing. Americans still wrestled with an unknown future; many worried about how to pay bills, support their families, and sustain their mental and physical health. In late 2020, in tandem with the national elections, the pandemic spiked yet again, and the total infection count reached 9 million. The coronavirus seemed likely to leave the United States weakened and adrift, with hundreds of thousands of its citizens dead and no sign of a return to normalcy.

GEORGE FLOYD RACIAL JUSTICE PROTESTS Amid the pandemic, more highly publicized killings of African Americans by White police officers and White supremacists ignited a wave of **racial justice protests** nationwide. On May 25, 2020, George Floyd, a forty-six-year-old security guard suspected of passing counterfeit money, was killed when a White Minneapolis police officer handcuffed him, threw him down on the pavement, and dug his knee into the back of his neck for nine minutes, all the while ignoring his anguished gasps, "I can't breathe."

The gruesome ten-minute cell phone video of Floyd's killing outraged Americans—people of color and Whites—and triggered nationwide protests with a scale and momentum that had not been seen in decades. That, on average, an African American was killed by police every day in the United States fueled the call for meaningful reforms. For weeks, the nation witnessed spontaneous protests that coalesced into a grassroots movement demanding substantial changes in the criminal justice system. Valerie Rivera, whose son Eric was shot and killed by police in 2017, took comfort in the groundswell of protests in scores of cities. "We have been waiting for these days to come, for these people to scream into these streets."

George Floyd's killing also focused worldwide attention on America's persistent racial inequalities and discrimination. "It's either COVID-19 killing us, cops are killing us, or the economy is killing us," said Priscilla Borkor, a Black social worker participating in one of the demonstrations.

Before Floyd's murder, race relations were already frayed. Hate crimes in 2018 had reached a sixteen-year high. The Department of Homeland Security reported that White supremacist groups had become the deadliest terrorist threat in the United States. Two thirds of Americans surveyed believed that racism had increased during Donald Trump's presidency.

Floyd's death crystallized a renewed commitment to address the dehumanizing effects of systemic racism. Although the Minneapolis police officers involved in Floyd's death were arrested and charged with murder and manslaughter, righteous anger over the incident spilled into the streets with massive multiracial demonstrations involving 20 million people in more than 2,000 cities and towns in the United States and around the world. The primary officer involved in the killing was convicted of murder in April 2021.

The demonstrations against racism and police brutality represented the largest protest movement in U.S. history, as support for the Black Lives Matter movement skyrocketed. For the first time since BLM was founded in 2013, most Whites expressed support for the organization, and substantial numbers of Whites joined in the street protests. George Floyd's killing seemed to be the urgent catalyst for widespread reform. "There is literally a brewing civil war," said Alicia Garza, one of the founders of Black Lives Matter.

For months, the mass protests continued. Most of the demonstrations were peaceful, but some participants engaged in rioting, looting, and violence. Police stations were torched, police officers assaulted, shops gutted, and windows broken. Rather than trying to quell the unrest and unify the country, President Trump fanned the flames of racial unrest by praising right-wing protesters and by dismissing racial justice demonstrators as "bad people" eager to "demolish both justice and society." He called BLM a "symbol of hate." Some of President Trump's most militant supporters clashed frequently in the streets with BLM protesters. In an intentional echo of former president Richard Nixon, Trump pledged "I am your president of law and order." He warned on Twitter that looters would be shot and that he would unleash "vicious dogs" against demonstrators, prompting Twitter to take the unprecedented step of limiting his access to their media platform. President Trump also ordered riot police on horseback in Washington, D.C., to use tear gas and rubber bullets to disperse a group of peaceful demonstrators and journalists so that he could stage a photo of himself standing with a Bible in front of a vandalized church.

While President Trump's staunchest supporters approved of his handling of the racial justice protests, the backlash from the center and left was

Protests for Racial Justice Spurred by the video-recorded killing of George Floyd, protesters took to the street amid the COVID-19 pandemic to call for racial justice. Here, a protester is holding a sign that says, "racism is a pandemic."

substantial. Amid the turmoil, journalists reminded Americans of some stubborn facts: despite the civil rights revolution of the sixties, African American income remained only 60 percent of White income, further evidence of the racism that had plagued the nation since its founding.

THE 2020 GENERAL ELECTION

In 2020, voters faced a presidential campaign like no other. Twenty-nine Democrats initially sought the nomination, the largest number of candidates ever. In the end, the Democrats chose Joe Biden, a former U.S. senator from Delaware and Barack Obama's two-term vice president. Biden selected Senator Kamala Harris from California as his running mate. The daughter of immigrants from Jamaica and India, she was the first woman to serve as California's attorney general, and the first African American and Indian American to be nominated as vice president by one of the two major parties.

The 2020 campaign was less a contest between two candidates than it was a referendum on Donald Trump. Joe Biden stated forthrightly to a journalist that "The story is Trump." Issues of racial justice, social protest, unemployment, urban violence, natural disasters fueled by a changing climate, and the growing COVID-19 pandemic were pushed to the background.

The differences between Trump and Biden in style, tone, and vision were striking. Trump sought change through disruption and division, Biden was a healer and unifier whose campaign highlighted Trump's widely viewed mis-management of the pandemic and the need for reviving traditional values such as trust, compassion, and inclusion. Trump repeatedly used his Twitter account to charge that the Democrats were "rigging" the election against him and that he might not accept the election results should he lose. In September 2020, he declined to commit to a peaceful transfer of power should he lose the election.

The death of Supreme Court justice Ruth Bader Ginsberg just weeks before the election added an incendiary issue to the presidential campaign. Only the second woman to serve on the U.S. Supreme Court, and the first Jewish woman justice, Ginsberg had been a liberal stalwart on the Court for twenty-seven years. When President Trump and Senate Republicans rushed to appoint conservative Amy Coney Barrett as a successor for Ginsberg before the November election, Democrats cried foul, for these were the same Senate Republicans who had blocked Barack Obama's efforts to fill a vacancy on the Court before the 2016 election. At that time, they had argued that the *next* president (chosen by the voters in the upcoming election) should have that responsibility, contradicting their stance.

In early October, just a month before the election and only a day after President Trump insisted that "the end of the pandemic is in sight," he and Melania Trump, the First Lady, and their son Barron contracted the coronavirus, as did several White House aides and advisers, three Republican senators, Trump's campaign manager, and military leaders. Aides rushed the president to a hospital, where he stayed three nights and received supplemental oxygen and the latest drug treatments.

The blockbuster news of President Trump's illness hurt his efforts to win a second term. "It's hard to imagine that this doesn't end his hopes for reelection," said Rob Stutzman, a Republican campaign consultant. The news of his own infection also became the president's greatest political liability.

By late October, just days before the election, another surge in coronavirus cases threatened Trump's reelection hopes. October 23 witnessed the highest number of new cases in the United States since the pandemic started. By late November, the daily totals set all-time records, topping 200,000.

As the November 3 Election Day approached, most pollsters predicted Biden would win and the Democrats would likely take over control of the Senate. But it took far longer than usual to determine a new president. The vote count was slowed by the huge number of ballots mailed in by voters eager to reduce the possibility of them contracting the coronavirus infection: nearly half of this record number of voters, disproportionately Democrats, opted to mail their ballots rather than vote in person. After midnight on Election Day,

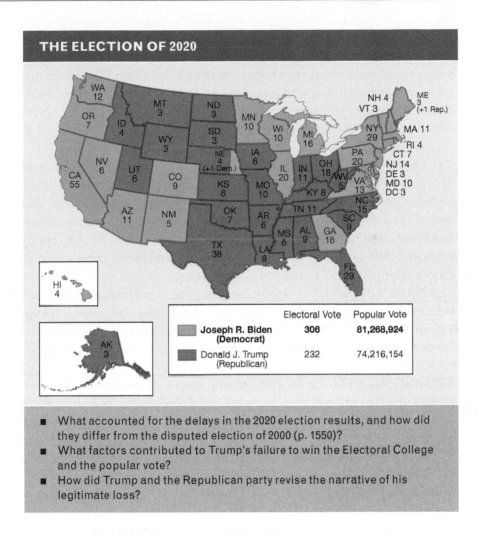

THE ELECTION OF 2020

	Electoral Vote	Popular Vote
Joseph R. Biden (Democrat)	306	81,268,924
Donald J. Trump (Republican)	232	74,216,154

- What accounted for the delays in the 2020 election results, and how did they differ from the disputed election of 2000 (p. 1550)?
- What factors contributed to Trump's failure to win the Electoral College and the popular vote?
- How did Trump and the Republican party revise the narrative of his legitimate loss?

President Trump claimed victory before key results were in, baselessly asserting that the election was "a fraud on the American public."

After more than a week of tedious vote counting and recounting, Joe Biden won by retaking three long-held Democratic states that Trump had won in 2016, Michigan, Pennsylvania, and Wisconsin, while flipping two traditionally Republican states, Arizona and Georgia. He beat President Trump 52 to 47 percent in the popular vote, with a winning margin of more than 7 million votes nationwide. The Electoral College final tally was 306 votes for Biden and 232 for Trump, the identical total that Donald Trump won by in 2016. More than 65 percent of U.S. voters cast a ballot, the highest percentage in more than a century.

The 2020 electoral pain continued for Republicans as they lost control of the Senate in January 2021 when Democratic candidates won both Georgia Senate runoff races, thanks to a huge turnout by Black voters. This meant that president-elect Joe Biden, who at age seventy-seven would be the oldest president ever, would be able to get major legislation through Congress and appoint cabinet members and federal judges of his choosing.

CHALLENGING BIDEN'S VICTORY Furious that he was one of only four presidents ever to lose reelection, Donald Trump spent the next six weeks in an unprecedented effort to intervene in the electoral process and reverse the outcome of an election. He charged, without evidence, that there had been widespread election fraud. For weeks after the election, his lawyers promoted the "Big Lie" by filing more than fifty lawsuits in various "swing" states challenging the legitimacy of the vote count.

William Barr, the U.S. attorney general and one of the president's strongest supporters, contradicted the president's claim that the election was stolen from Trump. Barr reported that Justice Department investigators had found no evidence of voting fraud widespread enough to have changed the election result.

STORMING THE CAPITOL Trump and most Republicans, however, refused to accept the legitimate verdict of the voters, and in the final weeks of his term the president urged his supporters to converge on Washington, D.C., to protest the election results.

On January 6, 2021, a joint session of Congress prepared to certify the election victory of Joe Biden. President Trump called his famously loyal vice president, Michael Pence, to pressure him as the presiding officer of the joint session to invalidate the results of the presidential election. The vice president, however, explained that he had no constitutional authority to overturn Biden's victory.

Just hours after his tense exchange with Vice President Pence, President Trump addressed thousands of ardent followers whom he had summoned to Washington, D.C. He again claimed without evidence that the election was stolen from him. He then encouraged his raucous supporters (who called themselves patriots) to go to the Capitol building and disrupt the process of Congress certifying the Electoral College vote for president-elect Joe Biden. "We will never give up. We will never concede," the president pledged, urging them to "show strength" and promising that "I'll be there with you. . . . If you don't fight like hell, you're not going to have a country anymore." As the president finished speaking, the crowd began chanting, "Storm the Capitol!" as they moved forward to stop the constitutional transfer of power to Joe Biden.

As the large crowd marched to the Capitol, it morphed into a mob of self-styled revolutionaries armed with bats, crowbars, shields, riot gear, spears, pipe bombs, stun guns, and chemical spray. Once they arrived, the world looked on in horror as hundreds of them swarmed past barricades, shattered windows, climbed walls, clashed with police, and forced their way inside the marble-floored Capitol Building while legislators were in the process of certifying the Biden presidency. Some of the rioters chanted, "Hang Mike Pence!"

As the vice president, his family, and panicked members of Congress and their staffs fled the unimaginable scene, rioters stampeded through hallways, ransacked offices, and vandalized the nation's most cherished legislative building, the very symbol of America's commitment to democracy. "Our president wants us here," a rioter shouted. "We take orders from our president." One of the rioters was shot and killed while storming the House chamber as the unprepared Capitol police gave way. Four others died, including a policeman; dozens of Capitol police were injured. (A few days later, another Capitol policeman committed suicide.) More than 500 of the rioters were arrested

Violence at the Capitol After Joe Biden's presidential election was certified, protesters who rejected the legitimate result marched to the Capitol. The armed insurrectionists were confronted by police, but ultimately they broke through and turned the scene into a riot, vandalizing the Capitol Building while injuring many and killing a police officer.

and charged with federal crimes. The horrifying scene of thousands of Trump loyalists storming the Capitol stood in stark contradiction to a nation committed to the rule of law.

The fallout from the shocking riot continued for weeks. Several cabinet members and senior White House aides resigned in protest of President Trump's role in instigating the violence on Capitol Hill. Twitter, Facebook, and YouTube executives shut down President Trump's social media accounts after his "repeated and severe" violations of its rules of conduct. At the same time, legislators and commentators called for Trump's impeachment or removal. The pro-Trump *Wall Street Journal* demanded that he resign.

Early in the morning of January 7, Congress overwhelmingly ratified the vote in the Electoral College to name Joe Biden the new president and Kamala Harris the new vice president. "While I may be the first woman in this office," Harris said, "I will not be the last, because every little girl watching tonight sees that this is a country of possibilities."

A SECOND IMPEACHMENT OF PRESIDENT TRUMP On January 13, Democrats in the House of Representatives, its chambers now protected by National Guard troops, introduced a single article of impeachment against President Trump for inciting the mob that assaulted the Capitol five days earlier. It was the first time that a president had been impeached twice, and this time ten Republicans voted with the Democrats compared to none at the first impeachment. Even Kevin McCarthy, the Republican minority leader in the House, declared that Trump "bears responsibility" for the attack on the Capitol buildings. Although McCarthy opposed impeachment, he acknowledged that President Trump should have "immediately denounced the mob when he saw what was unfolding."

The second impeachment of Donald Trump and the 2020 election results confirmed that Americans remained more polarized than ever. The Pew Research Center documented that partisan rage was growing "more intense, more personal" with each passing year. That President Trump refused to participate in the inauguration of President Joe Biden symbolized the toxic polarization of the political system.

AN UNCERTAIN FUTURE At his inauguration, President Joe Biden sought to salve the wounds from the toxic campaign. "We the People voted," he said. "Faith in our institutions held. The integrity of our elections remains intact. And so, now it is time to turn the page, as we've done throughout our history. To unite. To heal."

President Biden and Vice President Harris Joseph Biden and Kamala Harris were officially inaugurated as president and vice president on January 20, 2021.

The still bleeding wounds of civil unrest, however, would prove hard to heal. "We are not together," observed Eddie Glaude, an essayist writing in *Time* magazine. "Americans are disaffected, distrustful, and full of disdain" for the political system. As the world greeted a new president amid a still-raging pandemic, the nation's political and cultural civil war seemed more likely to worsen than improve.

BIDEN'S FIRST 100 DAYS

President Joe Biden had no time to waste. He confronted a runaway pandemic that had cost more than a half million American lives, a series of natural disasters exacerbated by climate change, a sputtering economy still bleeding millions of jobs, and the fallout from President Trump's foreign policies that had left America's global leadership in doubt in terms of longtime partners and enemies.

No sooner was Biden inaugurated than he began fulfilling his pledge to be a quite different leader than Donald Trump. His focus was on crafting policies, getting legislation passed, and producing results for a wide range of American families. The new president was far less visible than his predecessor. Rather than using Twitter as his primary means of communication, he made carefully crafted public addresses to convey his stances on critical issues. His efforts to dampen the political combat bore fruit early in his presidency, as he made efforts to reach out to Republican opponents both inside and outside of Washington. Republican senator John Thune acknowledged that Biden's "tone is moderate and he's an affable person, he's a likeable individual and a lot of us know him, have relationships with him, and it's probably harder to attack somebody who is relatable and likeable."

During Biden's first 100 days in office, he signed dozens of executive orders, most of them dealing with the coronavirus pandemic or reversing Trump's executive orders such as the ban on transgender people serving in the military. Other executive orders took steps to reduce greenhouse gas emissions, renew U.S. membership in the Paris Climate Agreement, revamp immigration policies, end Mexican border wall construction, and reverse Trump's travel ban targeting Muslims. Supporters worried that leaning too heavily on executive orders would not create lasting change. "I'm not making new law. I'm eliminating bad policy," the new president explained.

At the same time, however, Biden faced a challenging crisis on the Mexican border as a surge of desperate immigrants from across Mexico and Central America tried to enter the United States illegally in the aftermath of his election. A record number of unaccompanied children were being held in detention centers as immigration officials struggled to handle the crisis. In April 2021, Biden reversed Trump's ban on refugees from many key regions of the world and pledged to increase the number of refugees allowed to enter the United States.

As a result, the Biden administration faced growing criticism from both the right and left. Critics on the right complained that he was too welcoming to refugees, whereas critics on the left felt that his administration wasn't doing enough to process those desperate to enter America.

On March 11, 2021, Biden signed the American Relief Plan, a COVID-19 relief package, which narrowly gained congressional passage on party-line votes in the House and Senate, even though it was widely popular with those people still struggling with the pandemic's effects. It was the largest job creation and anti-poverty program since the New Deal. At the same time, administration agencies dramatically accelerated the distribution of coronavirus vaccines. At his first news conference, on March 25, Biden promised the delivery of "200 million [vaccine] shots in 100 days." He also proposed a whopping $2.3 trillion infrastructure rebuilding program intended to address deteriorating highways, bridges, railways, airports, and the electricity grid.

Following on the heels of a decision already made by the Trump Administration, on April 14, 2021, President Biden announced that the roughly 3,500 U.S. military personnel remaining in Afghanistan would begin withdrawing on May 1. "It's time to end America's longest war," Biden said. "It's time for American troops to come home."

By mid-April 2021, the economy was surging again thanks to the infusion of stimulus checks; the stock market continued to rise, and nearly half the nation had been vaccinated. Biden's favorable rating among voters was significantly higher than was Trump's after his first 100 days in office. The president showcased the end of his first 100 days by delivering a major speech to Congress. "America is on the move again," he asserted. "Turning peril into possibility. Crisis into opportunity. Setback into strength." Biden celebrated his administration's accomplishments, highlighting how Americans had received over 220 million COVID vaccinations in his first 100 days in office, an accomplishment he called "one of the greatest logistical achievements this country has ever seen."

Then President Biden showcased his two huge spending proposals: the American Jobs Plan and American Family Plan—a combined $4 trillion in spending aimed at everything from roads and bridges to prekindergarten and child-care and tuition-free community college that would usher in a government-led economic boom.

Biden concluded his address by invoking the rhetoric of his favorite former president: "In another era when our democracy was tested, Franklin Roosevelt reminded us: In America, we do our part," Biden said. "That's all I'm asking. That we all do our part." But Americans remained sorely divided on what doing their part should entail. Biden faced a huge challenge in his efforts to bring a sharply divided America together and to convince a stalemated Congress to endorse his proposals.

A determined President Biden secured a huge victory in August 2021 when a bipartisan majority in the Senate passed a $1 trillion bill to rebuild the nation's deteriorating infrastructure (roads, bridges, ports, and airports) and fund new climate resilience and internet initiatives.

Yet no sooner had the White House celebration of the infrastructure bill subsided when President Biden suffered an embarrassing foreign policy setback in Afghanistan. As the last American military units left the beleaguered Islamic nation, the Taliban quickly routed the U.S.-trained and -equipped Afghan army and security forces.

While President Biden was heavily criticized for the unexpected chaotic collapse of the Afghan government, most informed observers agreed that it would have made little difference if U.S. forces had stayed for another month or another decade. The longest war in American history was finally over.

CHAPTER REVIEW

SUMMARY

- **Changing Demographics**   From 1980 to 2020, the population of the United States grew by 40 percent, reaching 331 million. A wave of immigration from Latin America allowed Latinos/Latinas to surpass African Americans as the nation's largest minority. By 2018, the U.S. population included more foreign-born and first-generation residents than ever.

- **Global Terrorism**   The 9/11 attacks led President George W. Bush to declare a *war on terror* that commenced with the U.S. invasion of Afghanistan to capture Osama bin Laden and oust the Islamist Taliban government. In 2001, Congress approved the *USA Patriot Act*, which gave new powers to federal, state, and local agencies to deter and punish terrorist acts in the United States and around the world. The *Bush Doctrine* declared America's right to initiate preemptive military strikes against terrorists or rogue nations possessing *weapons of mass destruction (WMDs)*. In 2003, Bush invoked this doctrine against Saddam Hussein, the leader of Iraq. The ensuing Second Iraq War removed Hussein from power but turned up no WMDs.

- **A Historic Election**   The 2008 presidential primary campaigns featured Democratic senators Hillary Rodham Clinton, the first formidable female candidate, and Barack Obama, the first truly contending African American candidate, as well as Republican senator John McCain, the oldest candidate in history. Obama won his party's nomination and went on to take the election in large part due to public dismay about the *Great Recession* (2007–2009).

- **Obama's Priorities**   Obama's first priority was to shore up the failing economy, which he attempted through controversial Wall Street "bailouts" and a huge economic stimulus package. Yet the recovery remained slow and unequal, widening the economic divide and spawning the short-lived Occupy Wall Street movement. The *Affordable Care Act (ACA)* incited increasingly bitter opposition from the conservative *Tea Party*. Obama was more successful in winning public support to reduce American military deployment abroad, remove all combat troops from Iraq in 2011, and downsize their presence in Afghanistan. In addition, he endorsed *marriage equality* for LGBTQ couples, as did the U.S. Supreme Court in *Obergefell v. Hodges* (2015).

- **Make America Great Again**   The election of Donald Trump in 2016 in part reflected how divided American society had become over the previous four decades. His promise to "Make America Great Again" appealed to those voters who felt alienated as American society moved toward becoming part of an interconnected, global world. Efforts early in his administration to enact economic nationalism-based policies to limit immigration, protect jobs, and abandon various treaties with other nations were met with strong resistance from those who looked to intensify the forces of globalization. Eventually, the new president would be able to bring to fruition some campaign promises, namely, tax reform, rolling back environmental regulations, and the appointment of three new conservative U.S. Supreme Court justices.

- **The COVID-19 Pandemic and Racial Justice Protests** The global *COVID-19 pandemic* posed the greatest challenge to the Trump administration upon its arrival in the United States in early 2020. The president and his medical team downplayed the seriousness of the virus early on, but the highly infectious disease soon swept out of control, shuttering schools and businesses and killing tens of thousands of people. The Trump administration struggled to consistently develop an effective strategy for containing its spread. There were not enough testing kits or protective masks. By November 2020, some 9,000,000 cases had been reported with over 500,000 killed by the virus or health issues related to the virus.

  The country was further rocked in May of 2020, when George Floyd, an unarmed 46-year-old Black man, was killed in the custody of police in Minneapolis, Minnesota. The tragic incident provoked a storm of *racial justice protests* across the country and throughout the world. Millions of marchers demanded meaningful police reform, support for the Black Lives Matter movement skyrocketed, and many cried out for a national conversation to be held on the impact of systemic racism on people of color.

- **The First 100 Days of the Biden Administration** Newly inaugurated President Joe Biden faced enormous challenges as he began his presidential term. His victory remained contested in the eyes of Donald Trump and his supporters, he had the slimmest of margins in Congress to pass legislation, and the pandemic continued to race out of control. His top priorities were to jumpstart an economic recovery and get a substantial portion of the population vaccinated. On March 11, 2021, he signed the American Relief Plan, the largest job creation and anti-poverty program since the New Deal. As the national vaccination effort gained momentum, people were able to begin returning to some sense of normalcy after more than a year of enforced isolation.

CHRONOLOGY

2000	George W. Bush elected after controversial recount
September 11, 2001	Terrorists attack New York City and the Pentagon
October 2001	Operation Enduring Freedom begins in Afghanistan
March 2003	Iraq War begins
2007	Global financial markets collapse; Great Recession begins
2009	Barack Obama inaugurated as nation's first Black president
	American Recovery and Investment Act
2010	Congress passes the Affordable Care Act (Obamacare)
May 2011	Al Qaeda leader Osama bin Laden killed
2013	Black Lives Matter movement formed

2015	U.S. Supreme Court affirms marriage equality
2016	Donald Trump elected president
2017	Muslim travel ban
2018	Tax Cut and Jobs Act
2018	U.S.–North Korea Summit
2019	First impeachment of President Trump
2020	U.S.–Mexico border wall funds released
	COVID-19 pandemic sweeps the world
2021	Pro-Trump riot at U.S. Capitol
	Racial justice protests
	Second impeachment of Donald Trump
	COVID-19 vaccine distribution begins
	Joseph Biden inaugurated as the forty-sixth U.S. president

KEY TERMS

war on terror p. 1552

USA Patriot Act (2001) p. 1553

Bush Doctrine p. 1553

weapons of mass destruction (WMDs) p. 1554

Great Recession (2007–2009) p. 1562

Affordable Care Act (ACA) p. 1566

Tea Party p. 1571

marriage equality p. 1574

Black Lives Matter (BLM) p. 1575

COVID-19 pandemic p. 1601

racial justice protests p. 1605

⚀ INQUIZITIVE

Go to InQuizitive to see what you've learned—and learn what you've missed—with personalized feedback along the way.

GLOSSARY

abolitionism Movement that called for an immediate end to slavery throughout the United States.

affirmative action Programs designed to give preferential treatment to women and people of color as compensation for past injustices and to counterbalance systematic inequalities.

Affordable Care Act (ACA) (2010) Vast health-care-reform initiative championed by President Obama and widely criticized by Republicans that aimed to make health insurance more affordable and make health care accessible to everyone, regardless of income or prior medical conditions.

Agricultural Adjustment Act (1933) Legislation that paid farmers to produce less in order to raise crop prices for all; the AAA was later declared unconstitutional by the U.S. Supreme Court in the case of *United States v. Butler* (1936).

Albany Plan of Union (1754) A failed proposal by the seven northern colonies in anticipation of the French and Indian War, urging the unification of the colonies under one Crown-appointed president.

Alien and Sedition Acts of 1798 Four measures passed during the undeclared war with France that limited the freedoms of speech and press and restricted the liberty of immigrants.

alliance with France Critical diplomatic, military, and economic alliance between France and the newly independent United States, codified by the Treaty of Alliance (1778).

American Anti-Imperialist League Coalition of anti-imperialist groups united in 1899 to protest American territorial expansion, especially in the Philippine Islands; its membership included prominent politicians, industrialists, labor leaders, and social reformers.

American Colonization Society (ACS) Established in 1816, an organization whose mission was to return freed, formerly enslaved people to Africa.

American Federation of Labor Founded in 1886 as a national federation of trade unions made up of skilled workers.

American System Economic plan championed by Henry Clay of Kentucky that called for federal tariffs on imports, a strong national bank, and federally financed internal improvements—roads, bridges, canals—all intended to strengthen the national economy and end American economic dependence on Great Britain.

American Tobacco Company Business founded in 1890 by North Carolina's James Buchanan Duke, who combined the major tobacco manufacturers of the time, controlling 90 percent of the country's booming cigarette production.

Anaconda Plan Union's primary war strategy calling for a naval blockade of major Southern seaports and then dividing the Confederacy by gaining control of the Tennessee, Cumberland, and Mississippi Rivers.

anti-Federalists Opponents of the Constitution as an infringement on individual and states' rights, whose criticism led to the addition of a Bill of Rights to the document. Many anti-Federalists later joined Thomas Jefferson's Democratic-Republican party.

Appomattox Court House Virginia village where Confederate general Robert E. Lee surrendered to Union general Ulysses S. Grant on April 9, 1865.

Articles of Confederation The first form of government for the United States, ratified by the original thirteen states in 1781; weak in central authority, it was replaced by the U.S. Constitution drafted in 1787.

Atlanta Compromise (1895) Speech by Booker T. Washington that called for the Black community to strive for economic prosperity before demanding political and social equality.

Atlantic Charter (1941) Joint statement crafted by Franklin D. Roosevelt and British prime minister Winston Churchill that listed the war goals of the Allied Powers.

"Axis" alliance Military alliance formed in 1937 by the three major fascist powers: Germany, Italy, and Japan.

baby boom Markedly high birth rate in the years following World War II, leading to the biggest demographic "bubble" in U.S. history.

Bacon's Rebellion (1676) Unsuccessful revolt led by planter Nathaniel Bacon against Virginia governor William Berkeley's administration, which, Bacon charged, had failed to protect settlers from Indian raids.

Bank of the United States (1791) National bank responsible for holding and transferring federal government funds, making business loans, and issuing a national currency.

Bank War Political struggle in the early 1830s between President Jackson and financier Nicholas Biddle over the renewing of the Second Bank's charter.

Barbary pirates North Africans who waged war (1801–1805) on the United States after Jefferson refused to pay tribute (a bribe) to protect American ships.

Battle of Antietam (1862) Turning-point battle near Sharpsburg, Maryland, leaving almost 25,000 soldiers dead or wounded, in which Union forces halted a Confederate invasion of the North.

Battle of Gettysburg (1863) A monumental three-day battle in southern Pennsylvania, widely considered a turning point in the war, in which Union forces defeated Lee's Confederate army and forced it back into Virginia.

Battle of Midway A 1942 battle that proved to be the turning point in the Pacific front during World War II; it was the Japanese navy's first major defeat in 350 years.

Battle of New Orleans (1815) Final major battle in the War of 1812, in which the Americans under General Andrew Jackson unexpectedly and decisively countered the British attempt to seize the port of New Orleans, Louisiana.

Battle of Tippecanoe (1811) Battle in northern Indiana between U.S. troops and Native American warriors led by prophet Tenskwatawa, the half-brother of Tecumseh.

Battle of Trenton (1776) First decisive American victory that proved pivotal in reviving morale and demonstrating General Washington's abilities.

Battle of Vicksburg (1863) A protracted battle in northern Mississippi in which Union forces under Ulysses S. Grant besieged the last major Confederate fortress on the Mississippi River, forcing the inhabitants into starvation and then submission on July 4, 1863.

Battle of Yorktown (1781) Last major battle of the Revolutionary War; General Cornwallis, along with over 7,000 British troops, surrendered to George Washington at Yorktown, Virginia, on October 17, 1781.

Battles of Saratoga (1777) Decisive defeat of almost 6,000 British troops under General John Burgoyne in several battles near Saratoga, New York, in October 1777; the American victory helped convince France to enter the war on the side of the Patriots.

Bay of Pigs (1961) Failed CIA operation that deployed Cuban rebels to overthrow Fidel Castro's Communist regime.

Beats Group of bohemian writers, artists, and musicians who flouted convention in favor of liberated forms of self-expression.

Berlin airlift (1948–1949) Effort by the United States and Great Britain to fly massive amounts of food and supplies into West Berlin in response to the Soviet land blockade of the city.

Berlin Wall Twenty-seven-mile-long concrete wall constructed in 1961 by East German authorities to stop the flow of East Germans fleeing to West Berlin.

Bill of Rights (1791) First ten amendments to the U.S. Constitution, adopted in 1791 to guarantee individual rights and to help secure ratification of the Constitution by the states.

birth rate Proportion of births per 1,000 of the total population.

Black codes Laws passed in southern states to restrict the rights of formerly enslaved people.

Black Lives Matter (BLM) Sociopolitical movement in protest of police brutality toward Black people, with origins in Missouri and a growing global presence.

Black Power movement Militant form of civil rights protest focused on urban communities in the North that emerged as a response to impatience with the nonviolent tactics of Martin Luther King, Jr.

Bleeding Kansas (1856) A series of violent conflicts in the Kansas Territory between anti-slavery and pro-slavery factions over the status of slavery.

blitzkrieg (1940) The German "lightning war" strategy characterized by swift, well-organized attacks using infantry, tanks, and warplanes.

Bonus Expeditionary Force (1932) Protest march on Washington, D.C., by thousands of military veterans and their families, calling for immediate payment of their service bonus certificates; violence ensued when President Herbert Hoover ordered their tent villages cleared.

Boston Massacre (1770) Violent confrontation between British soldiers and a Boston mob on March 5, 1770, in which five colonists were killed.

Boston Tea Party (1773) Demonstration against the Tea Act of 1773 in which the Sons of Liberty, dressed as Indians, dumped hundreds of chests of British-owned tea into Boston Harbor.

bracero program (1942) System that permitted seasonal farmworkers from Mexico to work in the United States on yearlong contracts.

***Brown v. Board of Education* (1954)** Landmark Supreme Court case that struck down racial segregation in public schools and declared "separate but equal" unconstitutional.

burial mounds A funereal tradition, practiced in the Mississippi and Ohio Valleys by the Adena-Hopewell cultures, of erecting massive mounds of earth over graves, often shaped in the designs of serpents and other animals.

Bush Doctrine National security policy launched in 2002 by which the Bush administration claimed the right to launch preemptive military attacks against perceived enemies, particularly outlaw nations or terrorist organizations believed to possess WMD.

Cahokia The largest chiefdom of the Mississippian Indian culture located in present-day Illinois and the site of a sophisticated farming settlement that supported up to 15,000 inhabitants.

California Gold Rush (1849) A massive migration of gold hunters, mostly young men, who transformed the national economy after massive amounts of gold were discovered in northern California.

campaign of 1828 Bitter presidential contest between Democrat Andrew Jackson and National Republican John Quincy Adams (running for reelection), resulting in Jackson's victory.

Camp David Accords (1978) Peace agreement facilitated by President Carter between Prime Minister Menachem Begin of Israel and President Anwar el-Sadat of Egypt, the first Arab head of state to officially recognize the state of Israel.

Carnegie Steel Company Corporation under the leadership of Andrew Carnegie that came to dominate the American steel industry.

Central Intelligence Agency (CIA) Intelligence-gathering government agency founded in 1947; under President Eisenhower's orders, it secretly undermined elected governments deemed susceptible to communism.

Chicago Democratic National Convention Convention in 1968 where the social unrest over the Vietnam War and civil rights movement came to a violent head between student protesters and the Chicago police. Hubert H. Humphrey was ultimately nominated as the presidential candidate for the Democratic Party.

Chinese Exclusion Act (1882) Federal law that barred Chinese laborers from immigrating to America.

Christian Right Christian conservatives with a faith-based political agenda that includes prohibition of abortion and allowing prayer in public schools.

citizen-soldiers Part-time non-professional soldiers, mostly poor farmers or recent immigrants who had been indentured servants, who played an important role in the Revolutionary War.

Civil Rights Act of 1964 Legislation that outlawed discrimination in public accommodations and employment, passed at the urging of President Lyndon B. Johnson.

civil service reform An extended effort led by political reformers to end the patronage system; led to the Pendleton Act (1883), which called for government jobs to be awarded based on merit rather than party loyalty.

Clayton Anti-Trust Act (1914) Legislation that served to enhance the Sherman Anti-Trust Act (1890) by clarifying what constituted "monopolistic" activities and declaring that labor unions were not to be viewed as "monopolies in restraint of trade."

clipper ships Tall, slender ships favored over older merchant ships for their speed; ultimately gave way to steamships because clipper ships lacked cargo space.

Coercive Acts (1774) Four parliamentary measures that required the colonies to pay for the Boston Tea Party's damages: closed the port of Boston, imposed a military government, disallowed colonial trials of British soldiers, and forced the quartering of troops in private homes.

Columbian Exchange The transfer of biological and social elements, such as plants, animals, people, diseases, and cultural practices, among Europe, the Americas, and Africa in the wake of Christopher Columbus's voyages to the New World.

Committee of Correspondence Group organized by Samuel Adams to address American grievances, assert American rights, and form a network of rebellion.

Common Sense **(1776)** Popular pamphlet written by Thomas Paine attacking British principles of hereditary rule and monarchical government and advocating a declaration of American independence.

Compromise of 1850 A package of five bills presented to the Congress by Henry Clay intended to avoid secession or civil war by reducing tensions between North and South over the status of slavery.

Compromise of 1877 Secret deal forged by congressional leaders to resolve the disputed election of 1876; Republican Rutherford B. Hayes, who had lost the popular vote, was declared the winner in exchange for his pledge to remove federal troops from the South, marking the end of Reconstruction.

Comstock Lode A mine in eastern Nevada acquired by Canadian fur trapper Henry Comstock that between 1860 and 1880 yielded almost $1 billion worth of gold and silver.

Congressional Reconstruction Phase of Reconstruction directed by Radical Republicans through the passage of three laws: the Military Reconstruction Act, the Command of the Army Act, and the Tenure of Office Act.

conquistadores Term from the Spanish word for "conquerors," applied to Spanish and Portuguese soldiers who conquered lands held by indigenous peoples in central and southern America as well as the current states of Texas, New Mexico, Arizona, and California.

consumer culture A society in which mass production and consumption of nationally advertised products comes to dictate much of social life and status.

containment U.S. cold war strategy to exert political, economic, and, if necessary, military pressure on global Soviet expansion as a means of combating the spread of communism.

Continental Army Army authorized by Continental Congress, 1755–1784, to fight the British; commanded by George Washington.

contrabands Freedom seekers who sought refuge in Union military camps or who lived in areas of the Confederacy under Union control.

Contract with America (1994) List of conservative promises in response to the supposed liberalism of the Clinton administration; drafted by Speaker of the House Newt Gingrich and other congressional Republicans as a campaign tactic for the 1994 midterm elections.

corrupt bargain Scandal in which presidential candidate and Speaker of the House Henry Clay secured John Quincy Adams's victory over Andrew Jackson in the 1824 election, supposedly in exchange for naming Clay secretary of state.

cotton White fibers harvested from plants that made comfortable, easy-to-clean products, especially clothing; the most valuable cash crop driving the economy in nineteenth-century United States and Great Britain.

cotton gin Hand-operated machine invented by Eli Whitney that quickly removed seeds from cotton bolls, enabling the mass production of cotton in nineteenth-century America.

cotton kingdom Cotton-producing region, relying predominantly on slave labor, that spanned from North Carolina west to Louisiana and reached as far north as southern Illinois.

counterculture Unorganized youth rebellion against mainstream institutions, values, and behavior that more often focused on cultural radicalism rather than political activism.

COVID-19 pandemic Global pandemic resulting from the airborne and contagious coronavirus disease which took millions of lives, debilitated governments and institutions, and necessitated new cultural norms of distancing and face masking.

crop-lien system Credit system used by sharecroppers and share tenants who pledged a portion ("share") of their future crop to local merchants or landowners in exchange for farming supplies, food, and clothing.

Cuban missile crisis (1962) Thirteen-day U.S.-Soviet standoff sparked by the discovery of Soviet missile sites in Cuba; closest the world has come to nuclear war since 1945.

cult of domesticity Pervasive nineteenth-century ideology urging women to celebrate their role as manager of the household and nurturer of the children.

Dartmouth College v. Woodward (1819) Supreme Court ruling that enlarged the definition of *contract* to put corporations beyond the reach of the states that chartered them.

Daughters of Liberty Colonial women who protested the British government's tax policies by boycotting British products, such as clothing, and who wove their own fabric, or "homespun."

Dawes Severalty Act of 1887 Federal legislation that divided ancestral Native American lands among the heads of each Indian family in an attempt to "Americanize" Indians by forcing them to become farmers working individual plots of land.

death rate Proportion of deaths per 1,000 of the total population; also called *mortality rate*.

Declaration of Independence (1776) Formal statement, principally drafted by Thomas Jefferson and adopted by the Second Continental Congress on July 4, 1776, that officially announced the thirteen colonies' break with Great Britain.

Declaration of Rights and Sentiments (1848) Document based on the Declaration of Independence that called for gender equality, written primarily by Elizabeth Cady Stanton and signed by Seneca Falls Convention delegates.

détente Period of improving relations between the United States and Communist nations, particularly China and the Soviet Union, during the Nixon administration.

Deists Those who applied Enlightenment thought to religion, emphasizing reason, morality, and natural law rather than scriptural authority or an ever-present god intervening in the daily life of humans.

de Lôme letter (1898) Private correspondence written by the Spanish ambassador to the United States, Depuy de Lôme, that described President McKinley as "weak"; the letter was stolen by Cuban revolutionaries and published in the *New York Journal* in 1898, deepening American resentment of Spain and moving the two countries closer to war in Cuba.

Dien Bien Phu Cluster of Vietnamese villages and site of a major Vietnamese victory over the French in the First Indochina War.

Distribution Act (1836) Law requiring distribution of the federal budget surplus to the states, creating chaos among unregulated state banks dependent on such federal funds.

Dixiecrats Breakaway faction of White southern Democrats who defected from the national Democratic party in 1948 to protest the party's increased support for Black civil rights and to nominate their own segregationist candidates for elective office.

dollar diplomacy Practice advocated by President Theodore Roosevelt in which the U.S. government fostered American investments in less developed nations and then used U.S. military force to protect those investments.

Dred Scott v. Sandford (1857) U.S. Supreme Court ruling that enslaved people were not U.S. citizens and that Congress could not prohibit slavery in territories.

Dust Bowl Vast area of the Midwest where windstorms blew away millions of tons of topsoil from parched farmland after a long drought in the 1930s, causing great social distress and a massive migration of farm families.

Eastern Woodland peoples Various Native American societies, particularly the Algonquian, Iroquoian, and Muskogean regional groups, who once dominated the Atlantic seaboard from Maine to Louisiana.

Economic Opportunity Act of 1964 Key legislation in President Johnson's "War on Poverty" that created the Office of Economic Opportunity and programs like Head Start and the work-study financial-aid program for low-income college students.

election of 1800 Presidential election involving Thomas Jefferson and John Adams that resulted in the first Democratic-Republican victory after the Federalist administrations of George Washington and John Adams.

election of 1864 Abraham Lincoln's successful reelection campaign, capitalizing on Union military successes in Georgia, to defeat his Democratic opponent, former general George B. McClellan, who ran on a peace platform.

Emancipation Proclamation (1863) Military order issued by President Abraham Lincoln that freed enslaved people in areas still controlled by the Confederacy.

Embargo Act (1807) A law promoted by President Thomas Jefferson prohibiting American ships from leaving for foreign ports, in order to safeguard them from British and French attacks. This ban on American exports proved disastrous to the U.S. economy.

encomienda A land-grant system under which Spanish army officers (*conquistadores*) were awarded large parcels of land taken from Native Americans.

Enlightenment A revolution in thought begun in Europe in the seventeenth century that emphasized reason and science over the authority and myths of traditional religion.

Environmental Protection Agency (EPA) Federal environmental agency created by Nixon to appease the demands of congressional Democrats for a federal environmental watchdog agency.

Erie Canal (1825) Most important and profitable of the many barge canals built in the early nineteenth century, connecting the Great Lakes to the Hudson River and conveying so much cargo that it made New York City the nation's largest port.

ethnic cleansing Systematic removal of an ethnic group from a territory through violence or intimidation in order to create a homogeneous society; the term was popularized by the Yugoslav policy brutally targeting Albanian Muslims in Kosovo.

Exodusters African Americans who migrated west from the South in search of a haven from racism and poverty after the collapse of Radical Republican rule.

Fair Deal (1949) President Truman's proposals to build upon the New Deal with national health insurance, the repeal of the Taft-Hartley Act, new civil rights legislation, and other initiatives; most were rejected by the Republican-controlled Congress.

"falling-domino" theory The theory that if one country fell to communism, its neighboring countries would necessarily follow suit.

Farmers' Alliances Like the Granger movement, these organizations sought to address the issues of small farming communities; however, Alliances emphasized more political action and called for the creation of a third party to advocate their concerns.

fascism A radical form of totalitarian government that emerged in 1920s Italy and Germany in which a dictator uses propaganda and brute force to seize control of all aspects of national life.

Federal Deposit Insurance Corporation (FDIC) (1933) Independent government agency, established to prevent bank panics, that guarantees the safety of deposits in citizens' savings accounts.

Federal Reserve Act (1913) Legislation passed by Congress to create a new national banking system in order to regulate the nation's currency supply and ensure the stability and integrity of member banks that made up the Federal Reserve System across the nation.

Federal Trade Commission (1914) Independent agency created by the Wilson administration that replaced the Bureau of Corporations as an even more powerful tool to combat unfair trade practices and monopolies.

Federal-Aid Highway Act (1956) Largest federal project in U.S. history, which created a national network of interstate highways.

federalism Concept of dividing governmental authority between the national government and the states.

The Federalist Papers Collection of eighty-five essays, published widely in newspapers in 1787 and 1788, written by Alexander Hamilton, James Madison, and John Jay in support of adopting the proposed U.S. Constitution.

field hands Enslaved people who toiled in the cotton or cane fields in organized work gangs.

Fifteenth Amendment (1870) Amendment to the U.S. Constitution forbidding states to deny any male citizen the right to vote on grounds of "race, color or previous condition of servitude."

First New Deal (1933–1935) Franklin D. Roosevelt's ambitious first-term cluster of economic and social programs designed to combat the Great Depression.

First Red Scare (1919–1920) Outbreak of anti-Communist hysteria that included the arrest without warrants of thousands of suspected radicals, most of whom (especially Russian immigrants) were deported.

flappers Young women of the 1920s whose rebellion against prewar standards of femininity included wearing shorter dresses, bobbing their hair, dancing to jazz music, driving cars, smoking cigarettes, and indulging in illegal drinking and gambling.

Force Bill (1833) Legislation, sparked by the nullification crisis in South Carolina, that authorized the president's use of the army to compel states to comply with federal law.

Fourteen Points President Woodrow Wilson's proposed plan for the peace agreement after the Great War, which included the creation of a "league" of nations intended to keep the peace.

Fourteenth Amendment (1866) Amendment to the U.S. Constitution guaranteeing equal protection under the law to all U.S. citizens, including formerly enslaved people.

Freedmen's Bureau Federal Reconstruction agency established to protect the legal rights of formerly enslaved people and to assist with their education, jobs, health care, and land ownership.

Freedom Riders Activists who, beginning in 1961, traveled by bus through the South to test federal court rulings that banned segregation on buses and trains.

Free-Soil party A political coalition created in 1848 that opposed the expansion of slavery into the new western territories.

French and Indian War (Seven Years' War) (1756–1763) The last and most important of four colonial wars between England and France for control of North America east of the Mississippi River.

French Revolution Revolutionary movement beginning in 1789 that overthrew the monarchy and transformed France into an unstable republic before Napoléon Bonaparte assumed power in 1799.

frontier revivals Religious revival movement within the Second Great Awakening, which took place in frontier churches in western territories and states in the early nineteenth century.

Fugitive Slave Act (1850) A part of the Compromise of 1850 that authorized federal officials to help capture and then return freedom seekers to their owners without trials.

Ghost Dance movement A spiritual and political movement among Native Americans whose followers performed a ceremonial "ghost dance" intended to connect the living with the dead and make the Native Americans bulletproof in battles intended to restore their homelands.

Gibbons v. Ogden **(1824)** Supreme Court case that gave the federal government the power to regulate interstate commerce.

GI Bill of Rights (1944) Provided unemployment, education, and financial benefits for World War II veterans to ease their transition back to the civilian world.

Gilded Age (1860–1896) An era of dramatic industrial and urban growth characterized by widespread political corruption and loose government oversight of corporations.

glasnost Russian term for "openness"; applied to the loosening of censorship in the Soviet Union under Mikhail Gorbachev.

globalization An important and controversial transformation of the world economy led by the growing number of multinational companies and the internet, whereby an international marketplace for goods and services was created.

Glorious Revolution (1688) Successful coup, instigated by a group of English aristocrats, that overthrew King James II and instated William of Orange and Mary, his English wife, to the English throne.

Granger movement Began by offering social and educational activities for isolated farmers and their families and later started to promote "cooperatives" where farmers could join together to buy, store, and sell their crops to avoid the high fees charged by brokers and other middlemen.

Great Awakening Emotional religious revival movement that swept the thirteen colonies from the 1730s through the 1740s.

Great Depression (1929–1941) Worst economic downturn in American history; it was spurred by the stock market crash in the fall of 1929 and lasted until the Second World War.

Great Migration Mass exodus of African Americans from the rural South to the Northeast and Midwest during and after the Great War.

Great Recession (2007–2009) Massive, prolonged economic downturn sparked by the collapse of the housing market and the financial institutions holding unpaid mortgages; resulted in 9 million Americans losing their jobs.

Great Sioux War Conflict between Sioux and Cheyenne Indians and federal troops over lands in the Dakotas in the mid-1870s.

Great Society Term coined by President Lyndon B. Johnson in his 1965 State of the Union address, in which he proposed legislation to address problems of voting rights, poverty, diseases, education, immigration, and the environment.

greenbacks Paper money issued during the Civil War, which sparked currency debates after the war.

Harlem Renaissance The nation's first self-conscious Black literary and artistic movement; centered in New York City's Harlem district, which had a largely Black population in the wake of the Great Migration from the South.

Hartford Convention (1814) A series of secret meetings in December 1814 and January 1815 at which New England Federalists protested American involvement in the War of 1812 and discussed several constitutional amendments, including limiting each president to one term, designed to weaken the dominant Republican party.

Haymarket Riot (1886) Violent uprising in Haymarket Square, Chicago, where police clashed with labor demonstrators in the aftermath of a bombing.

headright A land-grant policy that promised fifty acres to any colonist who could afford passage to Virginia and fifty more for each accompanying servant. The headright policy was eventually expanded to include any colonists—and was also adopted in other colonies.

Hessians German mercenary soldiers who were paid by the British royal government to fight alongside the British army.

Hiroshima (1945) Japanese port city that was the first target of the newly developed atomic bomb on August 6, 1945. Most of the city was destroyed.

HIV/AIDS Human immunodeficiency virus (HIV) transmitted via the bodily fluids of infected persons to cause acquired immunodeficiency syndrome (AIDS), an often-fatal disease of the immune system when it appeared in the 1980s.

holding company Corporation established to own and manage other companies' stock rather than to produce goods and services itself.

Holocaust Systematic efforts by the Nazis to exterminate the Jews of Europe, resulting in the murder of over 6 million Jews and more than a million other "undesirables."

Homestead Act (1862) Legislation granting "home-steads" of 160 acres of government-owned land to settlers who agreed to work the land for at least five years.

Homestead Steel Strike (1892) Labor conflict at the Homestead steel mill near Pittsburgh, Pennsylvania, culminating in a battle between strikers and private security agents hired by the factory's management.

horses The animals that the Spanish introduced to the Americas, eventually transforming many Native American cultures.

House Committee on Un-American Activities (HUAC) Committee of the U.S. House of Representatives formed in 1938; originally tasked with investigating Nazi subversion during the Second World War and later focused on rooting out Communists in the government and the motion-picture industry.

Immigration Act of 1924 Federal legislation intended to favor northern and western European immigrants over those from southern and eastern Europe by restricting the number of immigrants from any one European country to 2 percent of the total number of immigrants per year, with an overall limit of slightly over 150,000 new arrivals per year.

Immigration and Nationality Services Act of 1965 Legislation that abolished discriminatory quotas based upon immigrants' national origin and treated all nationalities and races equally.

imperialism The use of diplomatic or military force to extend a nation's power and enhance its economic interests, often by acquiring territory or colonies and justifying such behavior with assumptions of racial superiority.

indentured servants Settlers who signed on for a temporary period of servitude to a master in exchange for passage to the New World.

Independent Treasury Act (1840) System created by Van Buren that moved federal funds from favored state banks to the U.S. Treasury, whose financial transactions could only be in gold or silver.

Indian Removal Act (1830) Law permitting the forced relocation of Indians to federal lands west of the Mississippi River in exchange for the land they occupied in the East and South.

Indian wars Bloody conflicts between U.S. soldiers and Native Americans that raged in the West from the early 1860s to the late 1870s, sparked by American settlers moving into ancestral Indian lands.

Industrial Revolution Major shift in the nineteenth century from handmade manufacturing to mass production in mills and factories using water-, coal-, and steam-powered machinery.

infectious diseases Also called contagious diseases, illnesses that can pass from one person to another by way of invasive biological organisms able to reproduce in the bodily tissues of their hosts. Europeans unwittingly brought many such diseases to the Americas, devastating the Native American peoples.

The Influence of Sea Power upon History, 1660–1783 Historical work in which Rear Admiral Alfred Thayer Mahan argued that a nation's greatness and prosperity come from the power of its navy; the book helped bolster imperialist sentiment in the United States in the late nineteenth century.

Intermediate-Range Nuclear Forces (INF) Treaty (1987) Agreement signed by U.S. president Ronald Reagan and Soviet premier Mikhail Gorbachev to eliminate the deployment of intermediate-range missiles with nuclear warheads.

internal improvements Construction of roads, canals, and other projects intended to facilitate the flow of goods and people.

Interstate Commerce Commission (ICC) (1887) An independent federal agency established in 1887 to oversee businesses engaged in interstate trade, especially railroads, but whose regulatory power was limited when tested in the courts.

Iran-Contra affair (1987) Reagan administration scandal over the secret, unlawful U.S. sale of arms to Iran in partial exchange for the release of hostages in Lebanon; the arms money in turn was used illegally to aid Nicaraguan right-wing insurgents, the Contras.

Iranian hostage crisis (1979) Storming of the U.S. embassy in Tehran by Iranian revolutionaries, who held fifty-two Americans hostage for 444 days, despite President Carter's appeals for their release and a botched rescue attempt.

iron curtain Term coined by Winston Churchill to describe the cold war divide between Western Europe and the Soviet Union's Eastern European satellite nations.

Iroquois League An alliance of the Iroquois Nations, originally formed sometime between 1450 and 1600, that used their combined strength to pressure Europeans to work with them in the fur trade and to wage war across what is today eastern North America.

J. Pierpont Morgan and Company An investment bank under the leadership of J. Pierpont Morgan that bought or merged unrelated American companies, often using capital acquired from European investors.

Jay's Treaty (1794) Controversial agreement between Britain and the United States, negotiated by Chief Justice John Jay, that settled disputes over trade, prewar debts owed to British merchants, British-occupied forts in American territory, and the seizure of American ships and cargo.

Jazz Age Term coined by writer F. Scott Fitzgerald to characterize the spirit of rebellion and spontaneity among young Americans in the 1920s, a spirit epitomized by the hugely popular jazz music of the era.

Jeffersonian Republicans Political party founded by Thomas Jefferson in opposition to the Federalist party led by Alexander Hamilton and John Adams; also known as the Democratic-Republican party.

Johnson's Restoration Plan A plan to require southern states to ratify the Thirteenth Amendment, disqualify wealthy ex-Confederates from voting, and appoint a Unionist governor.

joint-stock companies Businesses owned by investors, who purchase shares of stock and share the profits and losses.

Kansas-Nebraska Act (1854) Controversial legislation that created two new territories taken from Native Americans, Kansas and Nebraska, where resident males would decide whether slavery would be allowed (popular sovereignty).

King Philip's War (1675–1678) A war in New England resulting from the escalation of tensions between Native Americans and English settlers; the defeat of the Native Americans led to broadened freedoms for the settlers and their dispossessing the region's Native Americans of most of their land.

Knights of Labor A national labor organization with a broad reform platform; reached peak membership in the 1880s.

Know-Nothings Nativist, anti-Catholic third party organized in 1854 in reaction to large-scale German and Irish immigration.

Ku Klux Klan A secret terrorist organization founded in Pulaski, Tennessee, in 1866 targeting formerly enslaved people who voted and held political offices, as well as people the KKK labeled as carpetbaggers and scalawags.

laissez-faire An economic doctrine holding that businesses and individuals should be able to pursue their economic interests without government interference.

League of Nations Organization of nations formed in the aftermath of the Great War to mediate disputes and maintain international peace; despite President Wilson's intense lobbying for the League of Nations, Congress did not ratify the Versailles Treaty, and the United States failed to join.

Lend-Lease Act (1941) Legislation that allowed the president to lend or lease military equipment to any country whose own defense was deemed vital to the defense of the United States.

Lewis and Clark expedition (1804–1806) Led by Meriwether Lewis and William Clark, a mission to the Pacific coast commissioned for the purposes of scientific and geographical exploration.

Lincoln-Douglas debates (1858) In the Illinois race between Republican Abraham Lincoln and Democrat Stephen A. Douglas for a seat in the U.S. Senate, a series of seven dramatic debates focusing on the issue of slavery in the territories.

Louisiana Purchase (1803) President Thomas Jefferson's purchase of the Louisiana Territory from France for $15 million, doubling the size of U.S. territory.

Lowell system Model New England factory communities that provided employees, mostly young women, with meals, a boardinghouse, moral discipline, and educational opportunities.

Loyalists Colonists who remained loyal to Britain before and during the Revolutionary War.

Lusitania British ocean liner torpedoed and sunk by a German U-boat; the deaths of nearly 1,200 of its civilian passengers, including many Americans, caused international outrage.

maize (corn) The primary grain crop in Mesoamerica, yielding small kernels often ground into cornmeal. Easy to grow in a broad range of conditions, it enabled a global population explosion after being brought to Europe, Africa, and Asia.

manifest destiny The widespread belief that America was "destined" by God to expand westward across the continent into lands claimed by Native Americans as well as European nations.

Marbury v. Madison **(1803)** First Supreme Court decision to declare a federal law—the Judiciary Act of 1789—unconstitutional ("judicial review").

March on Washington (1963) Civil rights demonstration on the National Mall, where Martin Luther King, Jr. gave his famous "I Have a Dream" speech.

market economy Large-scale manufacturing and commercial agriculture that emerged in America during the first half of the nineteenth century, displacing much of the premarket subsistence and barter-based economy and producing boom-and-bust cycles while raising the American standard of living.

marriage equality Legal right for gay and lesbian couples to marry; the most divisive issue in the culture wars of the early 2010s as increasing numbers of court rulings affirmed this right across the United States.

Marshall Plan (1948) Secretary of State George C. Marshall's post–World War II program providing massive U.S. financial and technical assistance to war-torn European countries.

Massachusetts Bay Colony English colony founded by Puritans in 1630 as a haven for persecuted Congregationalists.

massive resistance White rallying cry for disrupting federal efforts to enforce racial integration in the South.

massive retaliation Strategy that used the threat of nuclear warfare as a means of combating the global spread of communism.

Mayflower Compact (1620) A formal agreement signed by the Separatist colonists aboard the *Mayflower* to abide by laws made by leaders of their choosing.

McCarthyism Anti-Communist hysteria led by Senator Joseph McCarthy's witch hunts attacking the loyalty of politicians, federal employees, and public figures, despite a lack of evidence.

McCormick reaper Mechanical reaper invented by Cyrus Hall McCormick in 1831 that dramatically increased the production of wheat.

McCulloch v. Maryland **(1819)** Supreme Court ruling that prohibited states from taxing the Bank of the United States.

Medicare and Medicaid Health-care programs designed to aid the elderly and disadvantaged, respectively, as part of President Johnson's Great Society initiative.

mercantilism Policy of England and other imperial powers of regulating colonial economies to benefit the mother country.

Mexica Empire The dominion established in the fourteenth century under the imperialistic Mexicas, or Aztecs, in the valley of Mexico.

Mexicas Otherwise known as Aztecs, a Mesoamerican people of northern Mexico who founded the vast Aztec Empire in the fourteenth century, later conquered by the Spanish under Hernán Cortés in 1521.

microprocessor An electronic circuit printed on a tiny silicon chip; a major technological breakthrough in 1971, it paved the way for the development of the personal computer.

Middle Passage The hellish and often deadly middle leg of the transatlantic "triangular trade" in which European ships carried manufactured goods to Africa, then transported enslaved Africans to the Americas and the Caribbean, and finally conveyed American agricultural products back to Europe.

Militia Act (1862) Congressional measure that permitted formerly enslaved people to serve as laborers or soldiers in the U.S. Army.

militias Part-time "citizen-soldiers" called out to protect their towns from foreign invasion and ravages during the American Revolution.

Mississippi Plan (1890) Series of state constitutional amendments that sought to disenfranchise Black voters and was quickly adopted by nine other southern states.

Missouri Compromise (1820) Legislative decision to admit Missouri as a slave state while prohibiting slavery in the area west of the Mississippi River and north of the parallel 36°30'.

moderate Republicanism Promise to curb federal government and restore state and local government authority, spearheaded by President Eisenhower.

modernism An early twentieth-century cultural movement that rejected traditional notions of reality and adopted radical new forms of artistic expression.

money question Late nineteenth-century national debate over the nature of U.S. currency; supporters of a fixed gold standard were generally moneylenders and thus preferred to keep the value of money high, while supporters of silver (and gold) coinage were debtors who owed money, so they wanted to keep the value of money low by increasing the currency supply (inflation).

monopoly Corporation so large that it effectively controls the entire market for its products or services.

Monroe Doctrine (1823) U.S. foreign policy that barred further colonization in the Western Hemisphere by European powers and pledged that there would be no American interference with any existing European colonies.

Montgomery bus boycott Boycott of bus system in Montgomery, Alabama, organized by civil rights activists after the arrest of Rosa Parks in 1955.

Mormon Church The Church of Jesus Christ of Latter-day Saints, founded by Joseph Smith, emphasizing universal salvation and a modest lifestyle; often persecuted for separateness and practice of polygamy.

Morrill Land-Grant College Act (1862) Federal statute that granted federal lands to states to help fund the creation of land-grant colleges and universities, which were founded to provide technical education in agriculture, mining, and industry.

muckrakers Writers who exposed corruption and abuses in politics, business, consumer safety, working conditions, and more, spurring public interest in progressive reforms.

Mugwumps Reformers who bolted the Republican party in 1884 to support Democrat Grover Cleveland for president over Republican James G. Blaine, whose secret dealings on behalf of railroad companies had brought charges of corruption.

Mulattoes Mixed-race people who constituted most of the South's free Black population.

Nat Turner's Rebellion (1831) Insurrection in rural Virginia led by Black overseer Nat Turner, who murdered slave owners and their families; in turn, federal troops indiscriminately killed hundreds of enslaved people in the process of putting down Turner and his rebels.

National Association for the Advancement of Colored People (NAACP) Organization founded in 1910 by Black activists and White progressives that promoted education as a means of combating social problems and focused on legal action to secure the civil rights supposedly guaranteed by the Fourteenth and Fifteenth Amendments.

National Banking Act (1863) The U.S. Congress created a national banking system to finance the enormous expense of the Civil War. It enabled loans to the government and established a single national currency, including the issuance of paper money ("greenbacks").

National Recovery Administration (NRA) (1933) Controversial federal agency that brought together business and labor leaders to create "codes of fair competition" and "fair-labor" policies, including a national minimum wage.

National Security Act (1947) Congressional legislation that created the Department of Defense, the National Security Council, and the Central Intelligence Agency.

National Trades' Union Organization formed in 1834 to organize all local trade unions into a stronger national association; dissolved amid the economic depression in the late 1830s.

nativism Reactionary conservative movement characterized by heightened nationalism, anti-immigrant sentiment, and laws setting stricter regulations on immigration.

nativists Native-born Americans who viewed immigrants as a threat to their job opportunities and way of life.

natural rights An individual's basic rights (life, liberty, and property) that should not be violated by any government or community.

Navigation Acts (1651–1775) Restrictions passed by Parliament to control colonial trade and bolster the mercantile system.

neutrality laws Series of laws passed by Congress aimed at avoiding a Second World War; these included the Neutrality Act of 1935, which banned the selling of weapons to warring nations.

New Democrats Centrist ("moderate") Democrats led by President Bill Clinton that emerged in the late 1980s and early 1990s to challenge the "liberal" direction of the party.

new economy Period of sustained economic prosperity during the 1990s marked by federal budget surpluses, the explosion of dot-com industries, low inflation, and low unemployment.

New Freedom Program championed in 1912 by the Woodrow Wilson campaign that aimed to restore competition in the economy by eliminating all trusts rather than simply regulating them.

New Frontier Proposed domestic program championed by the incoming Kennedy administration in 1961 that aimed to jump-start the economy and trigger social progress.

new immigrants Wave of newcomers from southern and eastern Europe, including many Jews, who became a majority among immigrants to America after 1890.

New Left Term coined by the Students for a Democratic Society to distinguish their efforts at grassroots democracy from those of the 1930s Old Left, which had embraced orthodox Marxism and admired the Soviet Union under Stalin.

New Mexico A region in the American Southwest, originally established by the Spanish, who settled there in the sixteenth century, founded Catholic missions, and exploited the region's indigenous peoples.

New Netherland Dutch colony conquered by the English in 1667, out of which four new colonies were created—New York, New Jersey, Pennsylvania, and Delaware.

Nineteenth Amendment (1920) Constitutional amendment that granted women the right to vote in national elections.

nonviolent civil disobedience The principled tactic that Martin Luther King Jr. advocated: peaceful lawbreaking as a means of ending segregation.

North American Free Trade Agreement (NAFTA) (1994) Agreement eliminating trade barriers that was signed in 1994 by the United States, Canada, and Mexico, making North America the largest free-trade zone in the world.

North and South Carolina English proprietary colonies, originally formed as the Carolina colonies, officially separated into the colonies of North and South Carolina in 1712, whose semitropical climate made them profitable centers of rice, timber, and tar production.

North Atlantic Treaty Organization (NATO) Defensive political and military alliance formed in 1949 by the United States, Canada, and ten Western European nations to deter Soviet expansion in Europe.

Northwest Ordinance (1787) Land policy for new western territories in the Ohio Valley that established the terms and conditions for self-government and statehood while also banning slavery from the region.

NSC-68 (1950) Top-secret policy paper approved by President Truman that outlined a militaristic approach to combating the spread of global communism.

nullification Right claimed by some states to veto a federal law deemed unconstitutional.

Old Southwest Region covering western Georgia, Alabama, Mississippi, Louisiana, Arkansas, and Texas, where low land prices and fertile soil attracted droves of settlers after the American Revolution.

Open Door policy (1899) Official U.S. assertion that Chinese trade would be open to all nations; Secretary of State John Hay unilaterally announced the policy in 1899 in hopes of protecting the Chinese market for U.S. exports.

open shop Business policy of not requiring union membership as a condition of employment; such a policy, where legal, has the effect of weakening unions and diminishing workers' rights.

Operation Desert Storm (1991) Assault by American-led multinational forces that quickly defeated Iraqi forces under Saddam Hussein in the First Gulf War, ending the Iraqi occupation of Kuwait.

Operation Overlord The Allies' assault on Hitler's "Atlantic Wall," a seemingly impregnable series of fortifications and minefields along the French coastline that German forces had created using captive Europeans for laborers.

Oregon Fever The lure of fertile land and economic opportunities in the Oregon Country that drew hundreds of thousands of settlers westward, beginning in the late 1830s.

Overland Trails Trail routes followed by wagon trains bearing settlers and trade goods from Missouri to the Oregon Country, California, and New Mexico, beginning in the 1840s.

Pacific Railway Act (1862) Congress provided funding for a transcontinental railroad from Nebraska west to California.

Panic of 1819 A financial panic that began a three-year economic crisis triggered by reduced demand in Europe for American cotton, declining land values, and reckless practices by local and state banks.

Panic of 1837 A financial calamity in the United States brought on by a dramatic slowdown in the British economy and falling cotton prices, failed crops, high inflation, and reckless state banks.

Panic of 1873 Financial collapse triggered by President Grant's efforts to withdraw greenbacks from circulation and transition the economy back to hard currency.

Panic of 1893 A major collapse in the national economy after several major railroad companies declared bankruptcy, leading to a severe depression and several violent clashes between workers and management.

Parliament Legislature of Great Britain, composed of the House of Commons, whose members are elected, and the House of Lords, whose members are either hereditary or appointed.

party boss A powerful political leader who controlled a "machine" of associates and operatives to promote both individual and party interests, often using informal tactics such as intimidation or the patronage system.

Patriots Colonists who rebelled against British authority before and during the Revolutionary War.

patronage An informal system (sometimes called the "spoils system") used by politicians to reward their supporters with government appointments or contracts.

Pearl Harbor (1941) Surprise Japanese attack on the U.S. fleet at Pearl Harbor on December 7, which prompted the immediate American entry into the war.

peculiar institution Phrase used by Whites in the antebellum South to refer to slavery without using the word *slavery*.

People's party (Populists) Political party formed in 1892 following the success of Farmers' Alliance candidates; Populists advocated a variety of reforms, including free coinage of silver, a progressive income tax, postal savings banks, regulation of railroads, and direct election of U.S. senators.

perestroika Russian term for economic restructuring; applied to Mikhail Gorbachev's series of political and economic reforms that included shifting a centrally planned Communist economy to a mixed economy allowing for capitalism.

Personal Responsibility and Work Opportunity Act of 1996 (PRWOA) Comprehensive welfare-reform measure aiming to decrease the size of the "welfare state" by limiting the amount of government unemployment aid to encourage its recipients to find jobs.

plain white folk Yeoman farmers who lived and worked on their own small farms, growing food and cash crops to trade for necessities.

plantation mistress Matriarch of a planter's household, responsible for supervising the domestic aspects of the estate.

planters Owners of large farms in the South that were worked by twenty or more enslaved people and supervised by overseers.

Pontiac's Rebellion (1763) A series of Native American attacks on British forts and settlements after France ceded to the British its territory east of the Mississippi River as part of the Treaty of Paris without consulting France's Native American allies.

popular sovereignty Legal concept by which the White male settlers in a U.S. territory would vote to decide whether to permit slavery.

Powhatan Confederacy An alliance of several powerful Algonquian societies under the leadership of Chief Powhatan, organized into thirty chiefdoms along much of the Atlantic coast in the late sixteenth and early seventeenth centuries.

Proclamation Act of 1763 Proclamation drawing a boundary along the Appalachian Mountains from Canada to Georgia in order to minimize occurrences of settler–Native American violence; colonists were forbidden to go west of the line.

professions Occupations requiring specialized knowledge of a particular field; the Industrial Revolution and its new organization of labor created an array of professions in the nineteenth century.

Progressive party Political party founded by Theodore Roosevelt to support his bid to regain the presidency in 1912 after his split from the Taft Republicans.

Prohibition (1920–1933) National ban on the manufacture and sale of alcohol, though the law was widely violated and proved too difficult to enforce effectively.

Protestant Reformation Sixteenth-century religious movement initiated by Martin Luther, a German monk whose public criticism of corruption in the Roman Catholic Church and whose teaching that Christians can communicate directly with God gained a wide following.

public schools Elementary and secondary schools funded by the state and free of tuition.

Pullman Strike (1894) A national strike by the American Railway Union, whose members shut down major railways in sympathy with striking workers in Pullman, Illinois; ended with intervention of federal troops.

Puritans English religious dissenters who sought to "purify" the Church of England of its Catholic practices.

race-based slavery Institution that uses racial characteristics and myths to justify enslaving a people by force.

racial justice protests Largest collection of multiracial and intergenerational protests across the United States in opposition to racism toward Black people, prompted by the documented murder of George Floyd, a Black man, by a Minneapolis police officer.

Radical Republicans Congressmen who identified with the abolitionist cause and sought swift emancipation of the enslaved, punishment of the Rebels, and tight controls over former Confederate states.

railroads Steam-powered vehicles that improved passenger transportation, quickened western settlement, and enabled commercial agriculture in the nineteenth century.

Reaganomics President Reagan's "supply-side" economic philosophy combining tax cuts with the goals of decreased government spending, reduced regulation of business, and a balanced budget.

Reconstruction Finance Corporation (RFC) (1932) Federal program established under President Hoover to loan money to banks and other corporations to help them avoid bankruptcy.

redeemers Postwar White Democratic leaders in the South who supposedly saved the region from political, economic, and social domination by Northerners and Blacks.

Red Power Activism by militant Native American groups to protest living conditions on Indian reservations through demonstrations, legal action, and at times, violence.

republican ideology Political belief in representative democracy in which citizens govern themselves by electing representatives, or legislators, to make key decisions on the citizens' behalf.

republican simplicity Deliberate attitude of humility and frugality, as opposed to monarchical pomp and ceremony, adopted by Thomas Jefferson in his presidency.

return to normalcy Campaign promise of Republican presidential candidate Warren G. Harding in 1920, meant to contrast with Woodrow Wilson's progressivism and internationalism.

***Roe v. Wade* (1973)** Landmark Supreme Court decision striking down state laws that banned abortions during the first trimester of pregnancy.

Roman Catholicism The Christian faith and religious practices of the Roman Catholic Church, which exerted great political, economic, and social influence on much of western Europe and, through the Spanish and Portuguese Empires, on the Americas.

Roosevelt Corollary (1904) President Theodore Roosevelt's revision (1904) of the Monroe Doctrine (1823) in which he argued that the United States could use military force in Central and South America to prevent European nations from intervening in the Western Hemisphere.

Rough Riders The First Volunteer Cavalry, led in the Spanish-American War by Theodore Roosevelt; victorious in their only engagement, the Battle of San Juan Hill.

Sacco and Vanzetti case (1921) Trial of two Italian immigrants that occurred at the height of Italian immigration and against the backdrop of numerous terror attacks by anarchists; despite a lack of clear evidence, the two defendants, both self-professed anarchists, were convicted of murder and were executed.

salutary neglect Informal British policy during the first half of the eighteenth century that allowed the American colonies freedom to pursue their economic and political interests in exchange for colonial obedience.

Sand Creek Massacre (1864) Colonel Chivington's unprovoked slaughter of the Cheyenne and Arapaho in Colorado, initially reported as a justified battle but soon exposed for the despicable massacre it was.

Scopes Trial (1925) Highly publicized trial of a high-school teacher in Tennessee for violating a state law that prohibited the teaching of evolution; the trial was seen as the climax of the fundamentalist war on Darwinism.

Second Bank of the United States Established in 1816 after the first national bank's charter expired; it stabilized the economy by creating a sound national currency; by making loans to farmers, small manufacturers, and entrepreneurs; and by regulating the ability of state banks to issue their own paper currency.

Second Great Awakening Religious revival movement that arose in reaction to the growth of secularism and rationalist religion; spurred the growth of the Baptist and Methodist denominations.

Second Industrial Revolution Beginning in the late nineteenth century, a wave of technological innovations, especially in iron and steel production, steam and electrical power, and telegraphic communications, all of which spurred industrial development and urban growth.

Second New Deal (1935–1938) Expansive cluster of legislation proposed by President Roosevelt that established new regulatory agencies, strengthened the rights of workers to organize unions, and laid the foundation of a federal social welfare system through the creation of Social Security.

Securities and Exchange Commission (SEC) (1934) Federal agency established to regulate the issuance and trading of stocks and bonds in an effort to avoid financial panics and stock market crashes.

Seneca Falls Convention (1848) Convention organized by feminists Lucretia Mott and Elizabeth Cady Stanton to promote women's rights and issue the pathbreaking Declaration of Rights and Sentiments.

separate but equal Underlying principle behind segregation that was legitimized by the Supreme Court ruling in *Plessy v. Ferguson* (1896).

separation of powers Strict division of the powers of government among three separate branches (executive, legislative, and judicial), which in turn check and balance each other.

Seventeenth Amendment (1913) Constitutional amendment that provided for the public election of senators rather than the traditional practice allowing state legislatures to name them.

sharecropping A farming system developed after the Civil War by which landless workers farmed land in exchange with the landowner for farm supplies and a share of the crop.

Shays's Rebellion (1786–1787) Storming of the Massachusetts federal arsenal in 1787 by Daniel Shays and 1,200 armed farmers seeking debt relief from the state legislature through issuance of paper currency and lower taxes.

Sherman's "March to the Sea" (1864) The Union army's devastating march through Georgia from Atlanta to Savannah led by General William T. Sherman, intended to demoralize civilians and destroy the resources the Confederate army needed to fight.

silent majority Term popularized by President Richard Nixon to describe the great majority of American voters who did not express their political opinions publicly; "the non-demonstrators."

Sixteenth Amendment (1913) Constitutional amendment that authorized the federal income tax.

slave codes Laws passed by each colony and later states governing the treatment of enslaved people that were designed to deter freedom seekers and rebellions and often included severe punishments for infractions.

social Darwinism The application of Charles Darwin's theory of evolutionary natural selection to human society; social Darwinists used the concept of "survival of the fittest" to justify class distinctions, explain poverty, and oppose government intervention in the economy.

social gospel Mostly Protestant movement that stressed the Christian obligation to address the mounting social problems caused by urbanization and industrialization.

Social Security Act (1935) Legislation enacted to provide federal assistance to retired workers through tax-funded pension payments and benefit payments to the unemployed and disabled.

Sons of Liberty First organized by Samuel Adams in the 1770s, groups of colonists dedicated to militant resistance against British control of the colonies.

Southern Christian Leadership Conference (SCLC) Civil rights organization formed by Dr. Martin Luther King, Jr. that championed nonviolent direct action as a means of ending segregation.

Spanish Armada A massive Spanish fleet of 130 warships that was defeated at Plymouth in 1588 by the English navy during the reign of Queen Elizabeth I.

spirituals Songs with religious messages sung by enslaved people to help ease the strain of field labor and to voice their suffering at the hands of their masters and overseers.

Square Deal Theodore Roosevelt's progressive agenda of the "Three Cs": control of corporations, conservation of natural resources, and consumer protection.

stagflation Term coined by economists during the Nixon presidency to describe the unprecedented situation of stagnant economic growth and consumer price inflation occurring at the same time.

Stamp Act (1765) Act of Parliament requiring that all printed materials in the American colonies use paper with an official tax stamp in order to pay for British military protection of the colonies.

Standard Oil Company Corporation under the leadership of John D. Rockefeller that attempted to dominate the entire oil industry through horizontal and vertical integration.

staple crops Profitable market crops, such as cotton, tobacco, and rice, that predominate in a region.

state constitutions Charters that define the relationship between the state government and local governments and individuals, while also protecting individual rights and freedoms.

steamboats Ships and boats powered by wood-fired steam engines that made two-way traffic possible in eastern river systems, creating a transcontinental market and an agricultural empire.

Stonewall Uprising (1969) Violent clashes between police and gay patrons of New York City's Stonewall Inn, seen as the starting point of the modern gay rights movement.

Stono Rebellion A 1739 slave uprising in South Carolina that was brutally quashed, leading to executions as well as a severe tightening of the slave codes.

Strategic Arms Limitation Treaty (SALT I) Agreement signed by President Nixon and Premier Leonid Brezhnev prohibiting the development of missile defense systems in the United States and Soviet Union and limiting the quantity of nuclear warheads for both.

Strategic Defense Initiative (SDI) (1983) Ronald Reagan's proposed space-based anti-missile defense system, dubbed "Star Wars" by the media, which aroused great controversy and escalated the arms race between the United States and the Soviet Union.

Student Nonviolent Coordinating Committee (SNCC) Interracial organization formed in 1960 with the goal of intensifying the effort to end racial segregation.

suburbia Communities formed from mass migration of middle-class Whites from urban centers.

Suez crisis (1956) British, French, and Israeli attack on Egypt after Nasser's seizure of the Suez Canal; President Eisenhower interceded to demand the withdrawal of the British, French, and Israeli forces from the Sinai Peninsula and the strategic canal.

Taft-Hartley Labor Act (1947) Congressional legislation that banned "unfair labor practices" by unions, required union leaders to sign anti-Communist "loyalty oaths," and prohibited federal employees from going on strike.

Tariff of 1816 Taxes on various imported items, to protect America's emerging iron and textile industries from British competition.

Tariff of Abominations (1828) Tax on imported goods, including British cloth and clothing, that strengthened New England textile companies but hurt southern consumers, who experienced a decrease in British demand for raw cotton grown in the South.

tariff reform (1887) Effort led by the Democratic party to reduce taxes on imported goods, which Republicans argued were needed to protect American industries from foreign competition.

Taylorism Labor system based on detailed study of work tasks, championed by Frederick Winslow Taylor, intended to maximize efficiency and profits for employers.

Tea Party Right-wing populist movement, largely made up of middle-class, White male conservatives, that emerged as a response to the expansion of the federal government under the Obama administration.

Teapot Dome Scandal (1923) Harding administration scandal in which Secretary of the Interior Albert B. Fall profited from secret leasing of government oil reserves in Wyoming to private oil companies.

Tecumseh's Indian Confederacy A group of Native American nations under leadership of Shawnees Tecumseh and Tenskwatawa; its mission of fighting off American expansion was thwarted at the Battle of Tippecanoe (1811), when the Confederacy fell apart.

telegraph system System of electronic communication invented by Samuel F. B. Morse that could transmit messages instantaneously across great distances.

Teller Amendment (1898) Addition to the congressional war resolution of April 20, 1898, which marked the U.S. entry into the war with Spain; the amendment declared that the United States' goal in entering the war was to ensure Cuba's independence, not to annex Cuba as a territory.

temperance A widespread reform movement led by militant Christians that focused on reducing the use of alcoholic beverages.

tenements Shabby, low-cost inner-city apartment buildings that housed the urban poor in cramped, unventilated apartments.

Tet offensive (1968) Surprise attack by Viet Cong guerrillas and North Vietnamese army on U.S. and South Vietnamese forces that shocked the American public and led to widespread sentiment against the war.

Texas Revolution (1835–1836) Conflict between Texas colonists and the Mexican government that resulted in the creation of the separate Republic of Texas in 1836.

Thirteenth Amendment (1865) Amendment to the U.S. Constitution that ended slavery and freed all enslaved people in the United States.

tobacco A "cash crop" grown in the Caribbean as well as the Virginia and Maryland colonies, made increasingly profitable by the rapidly growing popularity of smoking in Europe after the voyages of Columbus.

Tonkin Gulf Resolution (1964) Congressional action that granted the president unlimited authority to defend U.S. forces abroad after an allegedly unprovoked attack on American warships off the coast of North Vietnam.

Townshend Acts (1767) Parliamentary measures to extract more revenue from the colonies; the Revenue Act of 1767, which taxed tea, paper, and other colonial imports, was one of the most notorious of these policies.

Trail of Tears (1838–1839) The Cherokees' 800-mile journey from the southern Appalachians to Indian Territory.

transcendentalism Philosophy of New England writers and thinkers who advocated personal spirituality, self-reliance, social reform, and harmony with nature.

Transcontinental Treaty (1819) Treaty between Spain and the United States that clarified the boundaries of the Louisiana Purchase and arranged for the transfer of Florida to the United States in exchange for cash.

Treaty of Ghent (1814) Agreement between Great Britain and the United States that ended the War of 1812.

Treaty of Guadalupe Hidalgo (1848) Treaty between United States and Mexico that ended the Mexican-American War.

Treaty of Paris (1763) Settlement between Great Britain and France that ended the French and Indian War.

Treaty of Paris (1783) The treaty that ended the Revolutionary War, recognized American independence from Britain, created the border between Canada and the United States, set the western border at the Mississippi, and ceded Florida to Spain.

Treaty of Versailles Peace treaty that ended the Great War, forcing Germany to dismantle its military, pay immense war reparations, and give up its colonies around the world.

trench warfare A form of prolonged combat between the entrenched positions of opposing armies, often with little tactical movement.

triangular trade A network of trade in which exports from one region were sold to a second region; the second sent its exports to a third region that exported its own goods back to the first country or colony.

Triple Alliance (Central Powers) One of the two sides during the Great War, including Germany, Austria-Hungary, Bulgaria, and Turkey (the Ottoman Empire).

Triple Entente (Allied Powers) Nations fighting the Central Powers during the Great War, including France, Great Britain, and Russia; later joined by Italy and, after Russia quit the war in 1917, the United States.

Truman Doctrine (1947) President Truman's program of "containing" communism in Eastern Europe and providing economic and military aid to any nations at risk of Communist takeover.

trust Business arrangement that gives a person or corporation (the "trustee") the legal power to manage another person's money or another company without owning those entities outright.

Tuskegee Airmen U.S. Army Air Corps unit of African American pilots whose combat success spurred military and civilian leaders to desegregate the armed forces after the war.

two-party system Domination of national politics by two major political parties, such as the Whigs and Democrats during the 1830s and 1840s.

U-boat German military submarine used during the Great War to attack warships as well as merchant ships of enemy and neutral nations.

Underground Railroad A secret system of routes, safe houses, and abolitionists that helped freedom seekers reach freedom in the North.

Unitarians Members of the liberal New England Congregationalist offshoot, who profess the oneness of God and the goodness of rational worshippers, often well-educated and wealthy.

United Farm Workers (UFW) Organization formed in 1962 to represent the interests of Mexican American migrant workers.

Universalists Generally working-class members of a New England religious movement, who believed in a merciful God and universal salvation.

USA Patriot Act (2001) Wide-reaching congressional legislation, triggered by the war on terror, which gave government agencies the right to eavesdrop on confidential conversations between prison inmates and their lawyers and permitted suspected terrorists to be tried in secret military courts.

U.S. battleship *Maine* American warship that exploded in the Cuban port of Havana on February 15, 1898; though later discovered to be the result of an accident, the destruction of the *Maine* was initially attributed by war-hungry Americans to Spain, contributing to the onset of the Spanish-American War.

utopian communities Ideal communities that offered innovative social and economic relationships to those who were interested in achieving salvation—now.

Valley Forge (1777–1778) American military encampment near Philadelphia, where more than 3,500 soldiers deserted or died from cold and hunger in the winter.

Viet Cong Communist guerrillas in South Vietnam who launched attacks on the Diem government.

Vietnamization Nixon-era policy of equipping and training South Vietnamese forces to take over the burden of combat from U.S. troops.

Virginia Statute of Religious Freedom (1786) A Virginia law, drafted by Thomas Jefferson in 1777 and enacted in 1786, that guarantees freedom of, and from, religion.

virtual representation The idea that the American colonies, although they had no actual representative in Parliament, were "virtually" represented by all members of Parliament.

Voting Rights Act of 1965 Legislation ensuring that all Americans were able to vote; ended literacy tests and other means of restricting voting rights.

Wagner Act (1935) Legislation that guaranteed workers the right to organize unions, granted them direct bargaining power, and barred employers from interfering with union activities.

War of 1812 (1812–1815) Conflict fought in North America and at sea between Great Britain and the United States over American shipping rights and British-inspired Indian attacks on American settlements. Canadians and Native Americans also fought in the war on each side.

war on terror Global crusade to root out anti-Western and anti-American Islamist terrorist cells launched by President George W. Bush as a response to the 9/11 attacks.

War Powers Act (1973) Legislation requiring the president to inform Congress within forty-eight hours of the deployment of U.S. troops abroad and to withdraw them after sixty days unless Congress approves their continued deployment.

War Production Board Federal agency created by Roosevelt in 1942 that converted America's industrial output to war production.

war relocation camps Detention camps housing thousands of Japanese Americans from the West Coast who were forcibly interned from 1942 until the end of the Second World War.

Watergate (1972–1974) Scandal that exposed the criminality and corruption of the Nixon administration and ultimately led to President Nixon's resignation in 1974.

weapons of mass destruction (WMD) Lethal nuclear, radiological, chemical, or biological devices aimed at harming people, institutions, and a nation's sense of security.

Western Front Contested frontier between the Central and Allied Powers that ran along northern France and across Belgium.

Whig party Political party founded in 1834 in opposition to the Jacksonian Democrats; supported federal funding for internal improvements, a national bank, and high tariffs on imports.

Whiskey Rebellion (1794) Violent protest by western Pennsylvania farmers against the federal excise tax on corn whiskey, put down by a federal army.

Wilmington Insurrection (1898) Led by Alfred Waddell in Wilmington, North Carolina, White supremacists rampaged through the Black community, overthrew the local government, and forced over 2,000 African Americans into exile.

Wilmot Proviso (1846) Proposal by Congressman David Wilmot, a Pennsylvania Democrat, to prohibit slavery in any lands acquired in the Mexican-American War.

Women's Army Corps Women's branch of the U.S. Army; by the end of the Second World War, nearly 150,000 women had served in the WAC.

women's movement Wave of activism sparked by Betty Friedan's *The Feminine Mystique* (1963); it argued for equal rights for women and fought against the cult of domesticity that limited women's roles to the home as wife, mother, and homemaker.

women's suffrage Movement to give women the right to vote through a constitutional amendment, spearheaded by Susan B. Anthony and Elizabeth Cady Stanton's National Woman Suffrage Association.

women's work Traditional term referring to routine tasks in the house, garden, and fields performed by women; eventually expanded in the colonies to include medicine, shopkeeping, upholstering, and the operation of inns and taverns.

Works Progress Administration (1935) Government agency established to manage several federal job programs created under the New Deal; it became the largest employer in the nation.

Yalta Conference (1945) Meeting of the "Big Three" Allied leaders—Franklin D. Roosevelt, Winston Churchill, and Josef Stalin—to discuss how to divide control of postwar Germany and eastern Europe.

yellow journalism A type of news reporting, epitomized in the 1890s by the newspaper empires of William Randolph Hearst and Joseph Pulitzer, that intentionally manipulates public opinion through sensational headlines, illustrations, and articles about both real and invented events.

Zimmermann telegram Message sent by a German official to the Mexican government urging an invasion of the United States; the telegram was intercepted by British intelligence agents and angered Americans, many of whom called for war against Germany.

APPENDIX

THE DECLARATION OF INDEPENDENCE (1776)

When in the Course of human events, it becomes necessary for one people to dissolve the political bands which have connected them with another, and to assume among the powers of the earth, the separate and equal station to which the Laws of Nature and of Nature's God entitle them, a decent respect to the opinions of mankind requires that they should declare the causes which impel them to the separation.

We hold these truths to be self-evident, that all men are created equal, that they are endowed by their Creator with certain unalienable Rights, that among these are Life, Liberty and the pursuit of Happiness. —That to secure these rights, Governments are instituted among Men, deriving their just powers from the consent of the governed, —That whenever any Form of Government becomes destructive of these ends, it is the Right of the People to alter or to abolish it, and to institute new Government, laying its foundation on such principles and organizing its powers in such form, as to them shall seem most likely to effect their Safety and Happiness. Prudence, indeed, will dictate that Governments long established should not be changed for light and transient causes; and accordingly all experience hath shewn, that mankind are more disposed to suffer, while evils are sufferable, than to right themselves by abolishing the forms to which they are accustomed. But when a long train of abuses and usurpations, pursuing invariably the same Object evinces a design to reduce them under absolute Despotism, it is their right, it is their duty, to throw off such Government, and to provide new Guards for their future security.—Such has been the patient sufferance of these Colonies; and such is now the necessity which constrains them to alter their former Systems of Government. The history of the present King of Great Britain is a history of repeated injuries and usurpations, all having in direct object the establishment of an absolute Tyranny over these States. To prove this, let Facts be submitted to a candid world.

He has refused his Assent to Laws, the most wholesome and necessary for the public good.

He has forbidden his Governors to pass Laws of immediate and pressing importance, unless suspended in their operation till his Assent should be obtained; and when so suspended, he has utterly neglected to attend to them.

He has refused to pass other Laws for the accommodation of large districts of people, unless those people would relinquish the right of Representation in the Legislature, a right inestimable to them and formidable to tyrants only.

He has called together legislative bodies at places unusual, uncomfortable, and distant from the depository of their public Records, for the sole purpose of fatiguing them into compliance with his measures.

He has dissolved Representative Houses repeatedly, for opposing with manly firmness his invasions on the rights of the people.

He has refused for a long time, after such dissolutions, to cause others to be elected; whereby the Legislative powers, incapable of Annihilation, have returned to the People at large for their exercise; the State remaining in the mean time exposed to all the dangers of invasion from without, and convulsions within.

He has endeavoured to prevent the population of these States; for that purpose obstructing the Laws for Naturalization of Foreigners; refusing to pass others to encourage their migrations hither, and raising the conditions of new Appropriations of Lands.

He has obstructed the Administration of Justice, by refusing his Assent to Laws for establishing Judiciary powers.

He has made Judges dependent on his Will alone, for the tenure of their offices, and the amount and payment of their salaries.

He has erected a multitude of New Offices, and sent hither swarms of Officers to harrass our people, and eat out their substance.

He has kept among us, in times of peace, Standing Armies without the Consent of our legislatures.

He has affected to render the Military independent of and superior to the Civil power.

He has combined with others to subject us to a jurisdiction foreign to our constitution, and unacknowledged by our laws; giving his Assent to their Acts of pretended Legislation:

For quartering large bodies of armed troops among us:

For protecting them, by a mock Trial, from punishment for any Murders which they should commit on the Inhabitants of these States:

For cutting off our Trade with all parts of the world:

For imposing Taxes on us without our Consent:

For depriving us in many cases, of the benefits of Trial by Jury:

For transporting us beyond Seas to be tried for pretended offences

For abolishing the free System of English Laws in a neighbouring Province, establishing therein an Arbitrary government, and enlarging its Boundaries so as to render it at once an example and fit instrument for introducing the same absolute rule into these Colonies:

For taking away our Charters, abolishing our most valuable Laws, and altering fundamentally the Forms of our Governments:

For suspending our own Legislatures, and declaring themselves invested with power to legislate for us in all cases whatsoever.

He has abdicated Government here, by declaring us out of his Protection and waging War against us.

He has plundered our seas, ravaged our Coasts, burnt our towns, and destroyed the lives of our people.

He is at this time transporting large Armies of foreign Mercenaries to compleat the works of death, desolation and tyranny, already begun with circumstances of Cruelty & perfidy scarcely paralleled in the most barbarous ages, and totally unworthy the Head of a civilized nation.

He has constrained our fellow Citizens taken Captive on the high Seas to bear Arms against their Country, to become the executioners of their friends and Brethren, or to fall themselves by their Hands.

He has excited domestic insurrections amongst us, and has endeavoured to bring on the inhabitants of our frontiers, the merciless Indian Savages, whose known rule of warfare, is an undistinguished destruction of all ages, sexes and conditions.

In every stage of these Oppressions We have Petitioned for Redress in the most humble terms: Our repeated Petitions have been answered only by repeated injury. A Prince whose character is thus marked by every act which may define a Tyrant, is unfit to be the ruler of a free people.

Nor have We been wanting in attentions to our Brittish brethren. We have warned them from time to time of attempts by their legislature to extend an unwarrantable jurisdiction over us. We have reminded them of the circumstances of our emigration and settlement here. We have appealed to their native justice and magnanimity, and we have conjured them by the ties of our common kindred to disavow these usurpations, which, would inevitably interrupt our connections and correspondence. They too have been deaf to the voice of justice and of consanguinity. We must, therefore, acquiesce in the necessity, which denounces our Separation, and hold them, as we hold the rest of mankind, Enemies in War, in Peace Friends.

We, therefore, the Representatives of the united States of America, in General Congress, Assembled, appealing to the Supreme Judge of the world for the rectitude of our intentions, do, in the Name, and by Authority of the good People of these Colonies, solemnly publish and declare, That these United Colonies are, and of Right ought to be Free and Independent States; that they are Absolved from all Allegiance to the British Crown, and that all political connection between them and the State of Great Britain, is and ought to be totally dissolved; and that as Free and Independent States, they have full Power to levy War, conclude Peace, contract Alliances, establish Commerce, and to do all other Acts and Things which Independent States may of right do. And for the support of this Declaration, with a firm reliance on the protection of divine Providence, we mutually pledge to each other our Lives, our Fortunes and our sacred Honor.

Georgia
Button Gwinnett
Lyman Hall
George Walton

North Carolina
William Hooper
Joseph Hewes
John Penn

South Carolina
Edward Rutledge
Thomas Heyward, Jr.
Thomas Lynch, Jr.
Arthur Middleton

Massachusetts
John Hancock

Maryland
Samuel Chase
William Paca
Thomas Stone
Charles Carroll of
   Carrollton

Virginia
George Wythe
Richard Henry Lee
Thomas Jefferson
Benjamin Harrison
Thomas Nelson, Jr.
Francis Lightfoot Lee
Carter Braxton

Pennsylvania
Robert Morris
Benjamin Rush
Benjamin Franklin
John Morton
George Clymer
James Smith
George Taylor
James Wilson
George Ross

Delaware
Caesar Rodney
George Read
Thomas McKean

New York
William Floyd
Philip Livingston
Francis Lewis
Lewis Morris

New Jersey
Richard Stockton
John Witherspoon
Francis Hopkinson
John Hart
Abraham Clark

New Hampshire
Josiah Bartlett
William Whipple

Massachusetts
Samuel Adams
John Adams
Robert Treat Paine
Elbridge Gerry

Rhode Island
Stephen Hopkins
William Ellery

Connecticut
Roger Sherman
Samuel Huntington
William Williams
Oliver Wolcott

New Hampshire
Matthew Thornton

ARTICLES OF CONFEDERATION (1787)

TO ALL TO WHOM these Presents shall come, we the undersigned Delegates of the States affixed to our Names send greeting.

Whereas the Delegates of the United States of America in Congress assembled did on the fifteenth day of November in the Year of our Lord One Thousand Seven Hundred and Seventy-seven, and in the Second Year of the Independence of America agree to certain articles of Confederation and perpetual Union between the States of Newhampshire, Massachusetts-bay, Rhodeisland and Providence Plantations, Connecticut, New York, New Jersey, Pennsylvania, Delaware, Maryland, Virginia, North-Carolina, South-Carolina and Georgia in the Words following, viz.

Articles of Confederation and perpetual Union between the States of Newhampshire, Massachusetts-bay, Rhodeisland and Providence Plantations, Connecticut, New-York, New-Jersey, Pennsylvania, Delaware, Maryland, Virginia, North-Carolina, South-Carolina and Georgia.

ARTICLE I. The stile of this confederacy shall be "The United States of America."

ARTICLE II. Each State retains its sovereignty, freedom and independence, and every power, jurisdiction and right, which is not by this confederation expressly delegated to the United States, in Congress assembled.

ARTICLE III. The said States hereby severally enter into a firm league of friendship with each other, for their common defence, the security of their liberties, and their mutual and general welfare, binding themselves to assist each other, against all force offered to, or attacks made upon them, or any of them, on account of religion, sovereignty, trade or any other pretence whatever.

ARTICLE IV. The better to secure and perpetuate mutual friendship and intercourse among the people of the different States in this Union, the free inhabitants of each of these States, paupers, vagabonds and fugitives from justice excepted, shall be entitled to all privileges and immunities of free citizens in the several States; and the people of each State shall have free ingress and regress to and from any other State, and shall enjoy therein all the privileges of trade and commerce, subject to the same duties, impositions and restrictions as the inhabitants thereof respectively, provided that such restrictions shall not extend so far as to prevent the removal of property imported into any State, to any other State of which the owner is an inhabitant; provided also that no imposition, duties or restriction shall be laid by any State, on the property of the United States, or either of them.

If any person guilty of, or charged with treason, felony, or other high misdemeanor in any State, shall flee from justice, and be found in any of the United States, he shall upon demand of the Governor or Executive power, of the State from which he fled, be delivered up and removed to the State having jurisdiction of his offence.

Full faith and credit shall be given in each of these States to the records, acts and judicial proceedings of the courts and magistrates of every other State.

ARTICLE V. For the more convenient management of the general interests of the United States, delegates shall be annually appointed in such manner as the legislature of each State shall direct, to meet in Congress on the first Monday in November, in every year, with a power reserved to each State, to recall its delegates, or any of them, at any time within the year, and to send others in their stead, for the remainder of the year.

No State shall be represented in Congress by less than two, nor by more than seven members; and no person shall be capable of being a delegate for more than three years in any term of six years; nor shall any person, being a delegate, be capable of holding any office under the United States, for which he, or another for his benefit receives any salary, fees or emolument of any kind.

Each State shall maintain its own delegates in a meeting of the States, and while they act as members of the committee of the States.

In determining questions in the United States, in Congress assembled, each State shall have one vote.

Freedom of speech and debate in Congress shall not be impeached or questioned in any court, or place out of Congress, and the members of Congress shall be protected in their persons from arrests and imprisonments, during the time of their going to and from, and attendance on Congress, except for treason, felony, or breach of the peace.

ARTICLE VI. No State without the consent of the United States in Congress assembled, shall send any embassy to, or receive any embassy from, or enter into any conference, agreement, alliance or treaty with any king, prince or state; nor shall any person holding any office of profit or trust under the United States, or any of them, accept of any present, emolument, office or title of any kind whatever from any king, prince or foreign state; nor shall the

United States in Congress assembled, or any of them, grant any title of nobility.

No two or more States shall enter into any treaty, confederation or alliance whatever between them, without the consent of the United States in Congress assembled, specifying accurately the purposes for which the same is to be entered into, and how long it shall continue.

No State shall lay any imposts or duties, which may interfere with any stipulations in treaties, entered into by the United States in Congress assembled, with any king, prince or state, in pursuance of any treaties already proposed by Congress, to the courts of France and Spain.

No vessels of war shall be kept up in time of peace by any State, except such number only, as shall be deemed necessary by the United States in Congress assembled, for the defence of such State, or its trade; nor shall any body of forces be kept up by any State, in time of peace, except such number only, as in the judgment of the United States, in Congress assembled, shall be deemed requisite to garrison the forts necessary for the defence of such State; but every State shall always keep up a well regulated and disciplined militia, sufficiently armed and accoutred, and shall provide and constantly have ready for use, in public stores, a due number of field pieces and tents, and a proper quantity of arms, ammunition and camp equipage.

No State shall engage in any war without the consent of the United States in Congress assembled, unless such State be actually invaded by enemies, or shall have received certain advice of a resolution being formed by some nation of Indians to invade such State, and the danger is so imminent as not to admit of a delay, till the United States in Congress assembled can be consulted: nor shall any State grant commissions to any ships or vessels of war, nor letters of marque or reprisal, except it be after a declaration of war by the United States in Congress assembled, and then only against the kingdom or state and the subjects thereof, against which war has been so declared, and under such regulations as shall be established by the United States in Congress assembled, unless such State be infested by pirates, in which case vessels of war may be fitted out for that occasion, and kept so long as the danger shall continue, or until the United States in Congress assembled shall determine otherwise.

ARTICLE VII. When land-forces are raised by any State of the common defence, all officers of or under the rank of colonel, shall be appointed by the Legislature of each State respectively by whom such forces shall be raised, or in such manner as such State shall direct, and all vacancies shall be filled up by the State which first made the appointment.

ARTICLE VIII. All charges of war, and all other expenses that shall be incurred for the common defence or general welfare, and allowed by the United States in Congress assembled, shall be defrayed out of a common treasury, which shall be supplied by the several States, in proportion to the value of all land within each State, granted to or surveyed for any person, as such land and the buildings and improvements thereon shall be estimated according to such mode as the United States in Congress assembled, shall from time to time direct and appoint.

The taxes for paying that proportion shall be laid and levied by the authority and direction of the Legislatures of the several States within the time agreed upon by the United States in Congress assembled.

ARTICLE IX. The United States in Congress assembled, shall have the sole and exclusive right and power of determining on peace and war, except in the cases mentioned in the sixth article—of sending and receiving ambassadors— entering into treaties and alliances, provided that no treaty of commerce shall be made whereby the legislative power of the respective States shall be restrained from imposing such imposts and duties on foreigners, as their own people are subjected to, or from prohibiting the exportation or importation of and species of goods or commodities whatsoever—of establishing rules for deciding in all cases, what captures on land or water shall be legal, and in what manner prizes taken by land or naval forces in the service of the United States shall be divided or appropriated—of granting letters of marque and reprisal in times of peace—appointing courts for the trial of piracies and felonies committed on the high seas and establishing courts for receiving and determining finally appeals in all cases of captures, provided that no member of Congress shall be appointed a judge of any of the said courts.

The United States in Congress assembled shall also be the last resort on appeal in all disputes and differences now subsisting or that hereafter may arise between two or more States concerning boundary, jurisdiction or any other cause whatever; which authority shall always be exercised in the manner following. Whenever the legislative or executive authority or lawful agent of any State in controversy with another shall present a petition to Congress, stating the matter in question and praying for a hearing, notice thereof shall be given by order of Congress to the legislative or executive authority of the other State in controversy, and a day assigned for the appearance of the parties by their lawful agents, who shall then be directed to appoint by joint consent, commissioners or judges to constitute a court for hearing and determining the matter in question: but if they cannot agree, Congress shall name three persons out of each of the United States, and from the list of such persons each party shall alternately strike out one, the petitioners beginning, until the number shall be reduced to thirteen; and from that number not less than seven, nor more than nine names as Congress shall direct, shall in the presence of Congress be drawn out by lot, and the persons whose names shall be so drawn or any five of them, shall be commissioners or judges, to hear and finally determine the controversy, so always as a major part of the judges who shall hear the cause shall agree in the determination: and if either party shall neglect to attend at the day appointed, without reasons, which Congress shall judge sufficient, or being present shall refuse to strike, the Congress shall proceed to nominate three persons out of each State, and the Secretary of Congress shall strike in behalf of such party absent or refusing; and the judgment and sentence of the court to be appointed, in the manner before prescribed, shall be final and conclusive; and if any of the parties shall refuse to submit to the authority of such court, or to appear or defend their claim or cause, the court shall nevertheless proceed to pronounce sentence, or judgment, which shall in like manner be final and decisive, the judgment or sentence and other proceedings being in either case transmitted to Congress, and lodged among the acts of Congress for the security of the parties concerned: provided that every commissioner, before he sits in judgment, shall take an oath to be administered by one of the judges of the supreme or superior court of the State where the case shall be tried, "well and truly to hear and determine the matter in question, according to the best of his judgment, without favour, affection or hope of reward:" provided also that no State shall be deprived of territory for the benefit of the United States.

All controversies concerning the private right of soil claimed under different grants of two or more States, whose jurisdiction as they may respect such lands, and the states which passed such grants are adjusted, the said grants or either of them being at the same time claimed to have originated antecedent to such settlement of jurisdiction, shall on the petition of either party to the Congress of the United States, be finally determined as near as may be in the same manner as is before prescribed for deciding disputes respecting territorial jurisdiction between different States.

The United States in Congress assembled shall also have the sole and exclusive right and power of regulating the alloy and value of coin struck by their own authority, or by that of the respective States—fixing the standard of weights and measures throughout the United States—regulating the trade and managing all affairs with the Indians, not members of any of the States, provided that the legislative right of any State within its own limits be not infringed or violated—establishing and regulating post-offices from one State to another, throughout all of the United States, and exacting such postage on the papers passing thro' the same as may be requisite to defray the expenses of the said office—appointing all officers of the land forces, in the service of the United States, excepting regimental officers—appointing all the officers of the naval forces, and commissioning all officers whatever in the service of the United States—making rules for the government and regulation of the said land and naval forces, and directing their operations.

The United States in Congress assembled shall have authority to appoint a committee, to sit in the recess of Congress, to be denominated "a Committee of the States," and to consist of one delegate from each State; and to appoint such other committees and civil officers as may be necessary for managing the general affairs of the United States under their direction—to appoint one of their number to preside, provided that no person be allowed to serve in the office of president more than one year in any term of three years; to ascertain the necessary sums of money to be raised for the service of the United States, and to appropriate and apply the same for defraying the public expenses—to borrow money, or emit bills on the credit of the United States, transmitting every half year to the respective States an account of the sums of money so borrowed or emitted,—to build and equip a navy—to agree upon the number of land forces, and to make requisitions from each State for its quota, in proportion to the number of white inhabitants in such State; which requisition shall be binding, and thereupon the Legislature of each State shall appoint the regimental officers, raise the men and cloath, arm and equip them in a soldier like manner, at the expense of the United States; and the officers and men so cloathed, armed and equipped shall march to the place appointed, and within the time agreed on by the United States in Congress assembled: but if the United States in Congress assembled shall, on consideration of circumstances judge proper that any State should not raise men, or should raise a smaller number of men than the quota thereof, such extra number shall be raised, officered, cloathed, armed and equipped in the same manner as the quota of such State, unless the legislature of such State shall judge that such extra number cannot be safely spared out of the same, in which case they shall raise officer, cloath, arm and equip as many of such extra number as they judge can be safely spared. And the officers and men so cloathed, armed and equipped, shall march to the place appointed, and within the time agreed on by the United States in Congress assembled.

The United States in Congress assembled shall never engage in a war, nor grant letters of marque and reprisal in time of peace, nor enter into any treaties or alliances, nor coin money, nor regulate the value thereof, nor ascertain the sums and expenses necessary for the defence and welfare of the

United States, or any of them, nor emit bills, nor borrow money on the credit of the United States, nor appropriate money, nor agree upon the number of vessels to be built or purchased, or the number of land or sea forces to be raised, nor appoint a commander in chief of the army or navy, unless nine States assent to the same: nor shall a question on any other point, except for adjourning from day to day be determined, unless by the votes of a majority of the United States in Congress assembled.

The Congress of the United States shall have power to adjourn to any time within the year, and to any place within the United States, so that no period of adjournment be for a longer duration than the space of six months, and shall publish the journal of their proceedings monthly, except such parts thereof relating to treaties, alliances or military operations, as in their judgment require secresy; and the yeas and nays of the delegates of each State on any question shall be entered on the Journal, when it is desired by any delegate; and the delegates of a State, or any of them, at his or their request shall be furnished with a transcript of the said journal, except such parts as are above excepted, to lay before the Legislatures of the several States.

ARTICLE X. The committee of the States, or any nine of them, shall be authorized to execute, in the recess of Congress, such of the powers of Congress as the United States in Congress assembled, by the consent of nine States, shall from time to time think expedient to vest them with; provided that no power be delegated to the said committee, for the exercise of which, by the articles of confederation, the voice of nine States in the Congress of the United States assembled is requisite.

ARTICLE XI. Canada acceding to this confederation, and joining in the measures of the United States, shall be admitted into, and entitled to all the advantages of this Union: but no other colony shall be admitted into the same, unless such admission be agreed to by nine States.

ARTICLE XII. All bills of credit emitted, monies borrowed and debts contracted by, or under the authority of Congress, before the assembling of the United States, in pursuance of the present confederation, shall be deemed and considered as a charge against the United States, for payment and satisfaction whereof the said United States, and the public faith are hereby solemnly pledged.

ARTICLE XIII. Every State shall abide by the determinations of the United States in Congress assembled, on all questions which by this confederation are submitted to them. And the articles of this confederation shall be inviolably observed by every State, and the Union shall be perpetual; nor shall any alteration at any time hereafter be made in any of them; unless such alteration be agreed to in a Congress of the United States, and be afterwards confirmed by the Legislatures of every State.

And whereas it has pleased the Great Governor of the world to incline the hearts of the Legislatures we respectively represent in Congress, to approve of, and to authorize us to ratify the said articles of confederation and perpetual union. Know ye that we the undersigned delegates, by virtue of the power and authority to us given for that purpose, do by these presents, in the name and in behalf of our respective constituents, fully and entirely ratify and confirm each and every of the said articles of confederation and perpetual union, and all and singular the matters and things therein contained: and we do further solemnly plight and engage the faith of our respective constituents, that they shall abide by the determinations of the United States in Congress assembled, on all questions, which by the said confederation are submitted to them. And that the articles thereof shall be inviolably observed by the States we respectively represent, and that the Union shall be perpetual.

In witness thereof we have hereunto set our hands in Congress. Done at Philadelphia in the State of Pennsylvania the ninth day of July in the year of our Lord one thousand seven hundred and seventy-eight, and in the third year of the independence of America.

The Constitution of the United States (1787)

We the People of the United States, in Order to form a more perfect Union, establish Justice, insure domestic Tranquility, provide for the common defence, promote the general Welfare, and secure the Blessings of Liberty to ourselves and our Posterity, do ordain and establish this Constitution for the United States of America.

Article. I.

SECTION. 1. All legislative Powers herein granted shall be vested in a Congress of the United States, which shall consist of a Senate and House of Representatives.

SECTION. 2. The House of Representatives shall be composed of Members chosen every second Year by the People of the several States, and the Electors in each State shall have the Qualifications requisite for Electors of the most numerous Branch of the State Legislature.

No Person shall be a Representative who shall not have attained to the Age of twenty five Years, and been seven Years a Citizen of the United States, and who shall not, when elected, be an Inhabitant of that State in which he shall be chosen.

Representatives and direct Taxes shall be apportioned among the several States which may be included within this Union, according to their respective Numbers, which shall be determined by adding to the whole Number of free Persons, including those bound to Service for a Term of Years, and excluding Indians not taxed, three fifths of all other Persons. The actual Enumeration shall be made within three Years after the first Meeting of the Congress of the United States, and within every subsequent Term of ten Years, in such Manner as they shall by Law direct. The Number of Representatives shall not exceed one for every thirty Thousand, but each State shall have at Least one Representative; and until such enumeration shall be made, the State of New Hampshire shall be entitled to chuse three, Massachusetts eight, Rhode-Island and Providence Plantations one, Connecticut five, New-York six, New Jersey four, Pennsylvania eight, Delaware one, Maryland six, Virginia ten, North Carolina five, South Carolina five, and Georgia three.

When vacancies happen in the Representation from any State, the Executive Authority thereof shall issue Writs of Election to fill such Vacancies.

The House of Representatives shall chuse their Speaker and other Officers; and shall have the sole Power of Impeachment.

SECTION. 3. The Senate of the United States shall be composed of two Senators from each State, chosen by the Legislature thereof for six Years; and each Senator shall have one Vote.

Immediately after they shall be assembled in Consequence of the first Election, they shall be divided as equally as may be into three Classes. The Seats of the Senators of the first Class shall be vacated at the Expiration of the second Year, of the second Class at the Expiration of the fourth Year, and of the third Class at the Expiration of the sixth Year, so that one third may be chosen every second Year; and if Vacancies happen by Resignation, or otherwise, during the Recess of the Legislature of any State, the Executive thereof may make temporary Appointments until the next Meeting of the Legislature, which shall then fill such Vacancies.

No Person shall be a Senator who shall not have attained to the Age of thirty Years, and been nine Years a Citizen of the United States, and who shall not, when elected, be an Inhabitant of that State for which he shall be chosen.

The Vice President of the United States shall be President of the Senate, but shall have no Vote, unless they be equally divided.

The Senate shall chuse their other Officers, and also a President pro tempore, in the Absence of the Vice President, or when he shall exercise the Office of President of the United States.

The Senate shall have the sole Power to try all Impeachments. When sitting for that Purpose, they shall be on Oath or Affirmation. When the President of the United States is tried, the Chief Justice shall preside: And no Person shall be convicted without the Concurrence of two thirds of the Members present.

Judgment in Cases of Impeachment shall not extend further than to removal from Office, and disqualification to hold and enjoy any Office of honor, Trust or Profit under the United States: but the Party convicted shall nevertheless be liable and subject to Indictment, Trial, Judgment and Punishment, according to Law.

SECTION. 4. The Times, Places and Manner of holding Elections for Senators and Representatives, shall be prescribed in each State by the Legislature thereof; but the Congress may at any time by Law make or alter such Regulations, except as to the Places of chusing Senators.

The Congress shall assemble at least once in every Year, and such Meeting shall be on the first Monday in December, unless they shall by Law appoint a different Day.

SECTION. 5. Each House shall be the Judge of the Elections, Returns and Qualifications of its own Members, and a Majority of each shall constitute a Quorum to do Business; but a smaller Number may adjourn from day to day, and may be authorized to compel the Attendance of absent Members, in such Manner, and under such Penalties as each House may provide.

Each House may determine the Rules of its Proceedings, punish its Members for disorderly Behaviour, and, with the Concurrence of two thirds, expel a Member.

Each House shall keep a Journal of its Proceedings, and from time to time publish the same, excepting such Parts as may in their Judgment require Secrecy; and the Yeas and Nays of the Members of either House on any question shall, at the Desire of one fifth of those Present, be entered on the Journal.

Neither House, during the Session of Congress, shall, without the Consent of the other, adjourn for more than three days, nor to any other Place than that in which the two Houses shall be sitting.

SECTION. 6. The Senators and Representatives shall receive a Compensation for their Services, to be ascertained by Law, and paid out of the Treasury of the United States. They shall in all Cases, except Treason, Felony and Breach of the Peace, be privileged from Arrest during their Attendance at the Session of their respective Houses, and in going to and returning from the same; and for any Speech or Debate in either House, they shall not be questioned in any other Place.

No Senator or Representative shall, during the Time for which he was elected, be appointed to any civil Office under the Authority of the United States, which shall have been created, or the Emoluments whereof shall have been encreased during such time; and no Person holding any Office under the United States, shall be a Member of either House during his Continuance in Office.

SECTION. 7. All Bills for raising Revenue shall originate in the House of Representatives; but the Senate may propose or concur with Amendments as on other Bills.

Every Bill which shall have passed the House of Representatives and the Senate shall, before it become a Law, be presented to the President of the United States; If he approve he shall sign it, but if not he shall return it, with his Objections to that House in which it shall have originated, who shall enter the Objections at large on their Journal, and proceed to reconsider it. If after such Reconsideration two thirds of that House shall agree to pass the Bill, it shall be sent, together with the Objections, to the other House, by which it shall likewise be reconsidered, and if approved by two thirds of that House, it shall become a Law. But in all such Cases the Votes of both Houses shall be determined by yeas and Nays, and the Names of the Persons voting for and against the Bill shall be entered on the Journal of each House respectively. If any Bill shall not be returned by the President within ten Days (Sundays excepted) after it shall have been presented to him, the Same shall be a Law, in like Manner as if he had signed it, unless the Congress by their Adjournment prevent its Return, in which Case it shall not be a Law.

Every Order, Resolution, or Vote to which the Concurrence of the Senate and House of Representatives may be necessary (except on a question of Adjournment) shall be presented to the President of the United States; and before the Same shall take Effect, shall be approved by him, or being disapproved by him, shall be repassed by two thirds of the Senate and House of Representatives, according to the Rules and Limitations prescribed in the Case of a Bill.

SECTION. 8. The Congress shall have Power To lay and collect Taxes, Duties, Imposts and Excises, to pay the Debts and provide for the common Defence and general Welfare of the United States; but all Duties, Imposts and Excises shall be uniform throughout the United States;

To borrow Money on the credit of the United States;

To regulate Commerce with foreign Nations, and among the several States, and with the Indian Tribes;

To establish an uniform Rule of Naturalization, and uniform Laws on the subject of Bankruptcies throughout the United States;

To coin Money, regulate the Value thereof, and of foreign Coin, and fix the Standard of Weights and Measures;

To provide for the Punishment of counterfeiting the Securities and current Coin of the United States;

To establish Post Offices and post Roads;

To promote the Progress of Science and useful Arts, by securing for limited Times to Authors and Inventors the exclusive Right to their respective Writings and Discoveries;

To constitute Tribunals inferior to the supreme Court;

To define and punish Piracies and Felonies committed on the high Seas, and Offences against the Law of Nations;

To declare War, grant Letters of Marque and Reprisal, and make Rules concerning Captures on Land and Water;

To raise and support Armies, but no Appropriation of Money to that Use shall be for a longer Term than two Years;

To provide and maintain a Navy;

To make Rules for the Government and Regulation of the land and naval Forces;

To provide for calling forth the Militia to execute the Laws of the Union, suppress Insurrections and repel Invasions;

To provide for organizing, arming, and disciplining, the Militia, and for governing such Part of them as may be employed in the Service of the United States, reserving to the States respectively, the Appointment of the Officers, and the Authority of training the Militia according to the discipline prescribed by Congress;

To exercise exclusive Legislation in all Cases whatsoever, over such District (not exceeding ten Miles square) as may, by Cession of particular States, and the Acceptance of Congress, become the Seat of the Government of the United States, and to exercise like Authority over all Places purchased by the Consent of the Legislature of the State in which the Same shall be, for the Erection of Forts, Magazines, Arsenals, dock-Yards, and other needful Buildings;—And

To make all Laws which shall be necessary and proper for carrying into Execution the foregoing Powers, and all other Powers vested by this Constitution in the Government of the United States, or in any Department or Officer thereof.

SECTION. 9. The Migration or Importation of such Persons as any of the States now existing shall think proper to admit, shall not be prohibited by the Congress prior to the Year one thousand eight hundred and eight, but a Tax or duty may be imposed on such Importation, not exceeding ten dollars for each Person.

The Privilege of the Writ of Habeas Corpus shall not be suspended, unless when in Cases of Rebellion or Invasion the public Safety may require it.

No Bill of Attainder or ex post facto Law shall be passed.

No Capitation, or other direct, Tax shall be laid, unless in Proportion to the Census or enumeration herein before directed to be taken.

No Tax or Duty shall be laid on Articles exported from any State.

No Preference shall be given by any Regulation of Commerce or Revenue to the Ports of one State over those of another; nor shall Vessels bound to, or from, one State, be obliged to enter, clear, or pay Duties in another.

No Money shall be drawn from the Treasury, but in Consequence of Appropriations made by Law; and a regular Statement and Account of the Receipts and Expenditures of all public Money shall be published from time to time.

No Title of Nobility shall be granted by the United States: And no Person holding any Office of Profit or Trust under them, shall, without the Consent of the Congress, accept of any present, Emolument, Office, or Title, of any kind whatever, from any King, Prince, or foreign State.

SECTION. 10. No State shall enter into any Treaty, Alliance, or Confederation; grant Letters of Marque and Reprisal; coin Money; emit Bills of Credit; make any Thing but gold and silver Coin a Tender in Payment of Debts; pass any Bill of Attainder, ex post facto Law, or Law impairing the Obligation of Contracts, or grant any Title of Nobility.

No State shall, without the Consent of the Congress, lay any Imposts or Duties on Imports or Exports, except what may be absolutely necessary for executing it's inspection Laws: and the net Produce of all Duties and Imposts, laid by any State on Imports or Exports, shall be for the Use of the Treasury of the United States; and all such Laws shall be subject to the Revision and Controul of the Congress.

No State shall, without the Consent of Congress, lay any Duty of Tonnage, keep Troops, or Ships of War in time of Peace, enter into any Agreement or Compact with another State, or with a foreign Power, or engage in War, unless actually invaded, or in such imminent Danger as will not admit of delay.

ARTICLE. II.

SECTION. 1. The executive Power shall be vested in a President of the United States of America. He shall hold his Office during the Term of four Years, and, together with the Vice President, chosen for the same Term, be elected, as follows:

Each State shall appoint, in such Manner as the Legislature thereof may direct, a Number of Electors, equal to the whole Number of Senators and Representatives to which the State may be entitled in the Congress: but no Senator or Representative, or Person holding an Office of Trust or Profit under the United States, shall be appointed an Elector.

The Electors shall meet in their respective States, and vote by Ballot for two Persons, of whom one at least shall not be an Inhabitant of the same State with themselves. And they shall make a List of all the Persons voted for, and of the Number of Votes for each; which List they shall sign and certify, and transmit sealed to the Seat of the Government of the United States, directed to the President of the Senate. The President of the Senate shall, in the Presence of the Senate and House of Representatives, open all the Certificates, and the Votes shall then be counted. The Person having the greatest Number of Votes shall be the President, if such Number be a Majority of the whole Number of Electors appointed; and if there be more than one who have such Majority, and have an equal Number of Votes, then the House of Representatives shall immediately chuse by Ballot one of them for President; and if no Person have a Majority, then from the five highest on the List the said House shall in like Manner chuse the President. But in chusing the President, the Votes shall be taken by States, the Representation from each State having one Vote; A quorum for this purpose shall consist of a Member or Members from two thirds of the States, and a Majority of all the States shall be necessary to a Choice. In every Case, after the Choice of the President, the Person having the greatest Number of Votes of the Electors shall be the Vice President. But if there should remain two or more who have equal Votes, the Senate shall chuse from them by Ballot the Vice President.

The Congress may determine the Time of chusing the Electors, and the Day on which they shall give their Votes; which Day shall be the same throughout the United States.

No Person except a natural born Citizen, or a Citizen of the United States, at the time of the Adoption of this Constitution, shall be eligible to the Office of President; neither shall any Person be eligible to that Office who shall not have attained to the Age of thirty five Years, and been fourteen Years a Resident within the United States.

In Case of the Removal of the President from Office, or of his Death, Resignation, or Inability to discharge the Powers and Duties of the said Office, the Same shall devolve on the Vice President, and the Congress may by Law provide for the Case of Removal, Death, Resignation or Inability, both of the President and Vice President, declaring what Officer shall then act as President, and such Officer shall act accordingly, until the Disability be removed, or a President shall be elected.

The President shall, at stated Times, receive for his Services, a Compensation, which shall neither be increased nor diminished during the Period for which he shall have been elected, and he shall not receive within that Period any other Emolument from the United States, or any of them.

Before he enter on the Execution of his Office, he shall take the following Oath or Affirmation:—"I do solemnly swear (or affirm) that I will faithfully execute the Office of President of the United States, and will to the best of my Ability, preserve, protect and defend the Constitution of the United States."

SECTION. 2. The President shall be Commander in Chief of the Army and Navy of the United States, and of the Militia of the several States, when called into the actual Service of the United States; he may require the Opinion, in writing, of the principal Officer in each of the executive Departments, upon any Subject relating to the Duties of their respective Offices, and he shall have Power to grant Reprieves and Pardons for Offences against the United States, except in Cases of Impeachment.

He shall have Power, by and with the Advice and Consent of the Senate, to make Treaties, provided two thirds of the Senators present concur; and he shall nominate, and by and with the Advice and Consent of the Senate, shall appoint Ambassadors, other public Ministers and Consuls, Judges of the supreme Court, and all other Officers of the United States, whose Appointments are not herein otherwise provided for, and which shall be established by Law: but the Congress may by Law vest the Appointment of such inferior Officers, as they think proper, in the President alone, in the Courts of Law, or in the Heads of Departments.

The President shall have Power to fill up all Vacancies that may happen during the Recess of the Senate, by granting Commissions which shall expire at the End of their next Session.

SECTION. 3. He shall from time to time give to the Congress Information of the State of the Union, and recommend to their Consideration such Measures as he shall judge necessary and expedient; he may, on extraordinary Occasions, convene both Houses, or either of them, and in Case of Disagreement between them, with Respect to the Time of Adjournment, he may adjourn them to such Time as he shall think proper; he shall receive Ambassadors and other public Ministers; he shall take Care that the Laws be faithfully executed, and shall Commission all the Officers of the United States.

SECTION. 4. The President, Vice President and all civil Officers of the United States, shall be removed from Office on Impeachment for, and Conviction of, Treason, Bribery, or other high Crimes and Misdemeanors.

ARTICLE. III.

SECTION. 1. The judicial Power of the United States shall be vested in one supreme Court, and in such inferior Courts as the Congress may from time to time ordain and establish. The Judges, both of the supreme and inferior Courts, shall hold their Offices during good Behaviour, and shall, at stated Times, receive for their Services a Compensation, which shall not be diminished during their Continuance in Office.

SECTION. 2. The judicial Power shall extend to all Cases, in Law and Equity, arising under this Constitution, the Laws of the United States, and Treaties made, or which shall be made, under their Authority;—to all Cases affecting Ambassadors, other public Ministers and Consuls;—to all Cases of admiralty and maritime Jurisdiction;—to Controversies to which the United States shall be a Party;—to Controversies between two or more States;—between a State and Citizens of another State,—between Citizens of different States,—between Citizens of the same State claiming Lands under Grants of different States, and between a State, or the Citizens thereof, and foreign States, Citizens or Subjects.

In all Cases affecting Ambassadors, other public Ministers and Consuls, and those in which a State shall be Party, the supreme Court shall have original Jurisdiction. In all the other Cases before mentioned, the supreme Court shall have appellate Jurisdiction, both as to Law and Fact, with such Exceptions, and under such Regulations as the Congress shall make.

The Trial of all Crimes, except in Cases of Impeachment, shall be by Jury; and such Trial shall be held in the State where the said Crimes shall have been committed; but when not committed within any State, the Trial shall be at such Place or Places as the Congress may by Law have directed.

SECTION. 3. Treason against the United States, shall consist only in levying War against them, or in adhering to their Enemies, giving them Aid and Comfort. No Person shall be convicted of Treason unless on the Testimony of two Witnesses to the same overt Act, or on Confession in open Court.

The Congress shall have Power to declare the Punishment of Treason, but no Attainder of Treason shall work Corruption of Blood, or Forfeiture except during the Life of the Person attainted.

Article. IV.

SECTION. 1. Full Faith and Credit shall be given in each State to the public Acts, Records, and judicial Proceedings of every other State. And the Congress may by general Laws prescribe the Manner in which such Acts, Records and Proceedings shall be proved, and the Effect thereof.

SECTION. 2. The Citizens of each State shall be entitled to all Privileges and Immunities of Citizens in the several States.

A Person charged in any State with Treason, Felony, or other Crime, who shall flee from Justice, and be found in another State, shall on Demand of the executive Authority of the State from which he fled, be delivered up, to be removed to the State having Jurisdiction of the Crime.

No Person held to Service or Labour in one State, under the Laws thereof, escaping into another, shall, in Consequence of any Law or Regulation therein, be discharged from such Service or Labour, but shall be delivered up on Claim of the Party to whom such Service or Labour may be due.

SECTION. 3. New States may be admitted by the Congress into this Union; but no new State shall be formed or erected within the Jurisdiction of any other State; nor any State be formed by the Junction of two or more States, or Parts of States, without the Consent of the Legislatures of the States concerned as well as of the Congress.

The Congress shall have Power to dispose of and make all needful Rules and Regulations respecting the Territory or other Property belonging to the United States; and nothing in this Constitution shall be so construed as to Prejudice any Claims of the United States, or of any particular States.

SECTION. 4. The United States shall guarantee to every State in this Union a Republican Form of Government, and shall protect each of them against Invasion; and on Application of the Legislature, or of the Executive (when the Legislature cannot be convened), against domestic Violence.

ARTICLE. V.

The Congress, whenever two thirds of both Houses shall deem it necessary, shall propose Amendments to this Constitution, or, on the Application of the Legislatures of two thirds of the several States, shall call a Convention for proposing Amendments, which, in either Case, shall be valid to all Intents and Purposes, as Part of this Constitution, when ratified by the Legislatures of three fourths of the several States, or by Conventions in three fourths thereof, as the one or the other Mode of Ratification may be proposed by the Congress; Provided that no Amendment which may be made prior to the Year One thousand eight hundred and eight shall in any Manner affect the first and fourth Clauses in the Ninth Section of the first Article; and that no State, without its Consent, shall be deprived of its equal Suffrage in the Senate.

ARTICLE. VI.

All Debts contracted and Engagements entered into, before the Adoption of this Constitution, shall be as valid against the United States under this Constitution, as under the Confederation.

This Constitution, and the Laws of the United States which shall be made in Pursuance thereof; and all Treaties made, or which shall be made, under the Authority of the United States, shall be the supreme Law of the Land; and the Judges in every State shall be bound thereby, any Thing in the Constitution or Laws of any State to the Contrary notwithstanding.

The Senators and Representatives before mentioned, and the Members of the several State Legislatures, and all executive and judicial Officers, both of the United States and of the several States, shall be bound by Oath or Affirmation, to support this Constitution; but no religious Test shall ever be required as a Qualification to any Office or public Trust under the United States.

ARTICLE. VII.

The Ratification of the Conventions of nine States, shall be sufficient for the Establishment of this Constitution between the States so ratifying the Same.

The Word, "the," being interlined between the seventh and eighth Lines of the first Page, the Word "Thirty" being partly written on an Erazure in the fifteenth Line of the first Page, The Words "is tried" being interlined between the thirty second and thirty third Lines of the first Page and the Word "the" being interlined between the forty third and forty fourth Lines of the second Page.

Attest William Jackson Secretary

Done in Convention by the Unanimous Consent of the States present the Seventeenth Day of September in the Year of our Lord one thousand seven hundred and Eighty seven and of the Independance of the United States of America the Twelfth In witness whereof We have hereunto subscribed our Names,

G°. Washington
Presidt and deputy from Virginia

Delaware	Geo: Read Gunning Bedford jun John Dickinson Richard Bassett Jaco: Broom	New Hampshire	John Langdon Nicholas Gilman
		Massachusetts	Nathaniel Gorham Rufus King
Maryland	James McHenry Dan of St Thos. Jenifer Danl. Carrol	Connecticut	Wm. Saml. Johnson Roger Sherman
		New York	Alexander Hamilton
Virginia	John Blair James Madison Jr.		
North Carolina	Wm. Blount Richd. Dobbs Spaight Hu Williamson	New Jersey	Wil: Livingston David Brearley Wm. Paterson Jona: Dayton
South Carolina	J. Rutledge Charles Cotesworth Pinckney Charles Pinckney Pierce Butler	Pennsylvania	B Franklin Thomas Mifflin Robt. Morris Geo. Clymer Thos. FitzSimons Jared Ingersoll James Wilson Gouv Morris
Georgia	William Few Abr Baldwin		

Amendments to the Constitution

The Bill of Rights: A Transcription

THE PREAMBLE TO THE BILL OF RIGHTS
congress of the United States
begun and held at the City of New-York, on
Wednesday the fourth of March, one thousand seven hundred and eighty nine.

THE Conventions of a number of the States, having at the time of their adopting the Constitution, expressed a desire, in order to prevent misconstruction or abuse of its powers, that further declaratory and restrictive clauses should be added: And as extending the ground of public confidence in the Government, will best ensure the beneficent ends of its institution.

RESOLVED by the Senate and House of Representatives of the United States of America, in Congress assembled, two thirds of both Houses concurring, that the following Articles be proposed to the Legislatures of the several States, as amendments to the Constitution of the United States, all, or any of which Articles, when ratified by three fourths of the said Legislatures, to be valid to all intents and purposes, as part of the said Constitution; viz.

ARTICLES in addition to, and Amendment of the Constitution of the United States of America, proposed by Congress, and ratified by the Legislatures of the several States, pursuant to the fifth Article of the original Constitution.

Note: The first ten amendments to the Constitution were ratified December 15, 1791, and form what is known as the "Bill of Rights."

Amendment I

Congress shall make no law respecting an establishment of religion, or prohibiting the free exercise thereof; or abridging the freedom of speech, or of the press; or the right of the people peaceably to assemble, and to petition the Government for a redress of grievances.

Amendment II

A well regulated Militia, being necessary to the security of a free State, the right of the people to keep and bear Arms, shall not be infringed.

Amendment III

No Soldier shall, in time of peace be quartered in any house, without the consent of the Owner, nor in time of war, but in a manner to be prescribed by law.

Amendment IV

The right of the people to be secure in their persons, houses, papers, and effects, against unreasonable searches and seizures, shall not be violated, and no Warrants shall issue, but upon probable cause, supported by Oath or affirmation, and particularly describing the place to be searched, and the persons or things to be seized.

Amendment V

No person shall be held to answer for a capital, or otherwise infamous crime, unless on a presentment or indictment of a Grand Jury, except in cases arising in the land or naval forces, or in the Militia, when in actual service in time of War or public danger; nor shall any person be subject for the same offence to be twice put in jeopardy of life or limb; nor shall be compelled in any criminal case to be a witness against himself, nor be deprived of life, liberty, or property, without due process of law; nor shall private property be taken for public use, without just compensation.

Amendment VI

In all criminal prosecutions, the accused shall enjoy the right to a speedy and public trial, by an impartial jury of the State and district wherein the crime shall have been committed, which district shall have been previously ascertained by law, and to be informed of the nature and cause of the accusation; to be confronted with the witnesses against him; to have compulsory process for obtaining witnesses in his favor, and to have the Assistance of Counsel for his defence.

Amendment VII

In Suits at common law, where the value in controversy shall exceed twenty dollars, the right of trial by jury shall be preserved, and no fact tried by a jury, shall be otherwise re-examined in any Court of the United States, than according to the rules of the common law.

Amendment VIII

Excessive bail shall not be required, nor excessive fines imposed, nor cruel and unusual punishments inflicted.

Amendment IX

The enumeration in the Constitution, of certain rights, shall not be construed to deny or disparage others retained by the people.

Amendment X

The powers not delegated to the United States by the Constitution, nor prohibited by it to the States, are reserved to the States respectively, or to the people.

Amendment XI

Passed by Congress March 4, 1794. Ratified February 7, 1795.

Note: Article III, section 2, of the Constitution was modified by amendment 11.

The Judicial power of the United States shall not be construed to extend to any suit in law or equity, commenced or prosecuted against one of the United States by Citizens of another State, or by Citizens or Subjects of any Foreign State.

Amendment XII

Passed by Congress December 9, 1803. Ratified June 15, 1804.

Note: A portion of Article II, section 1 of the Constitution was superseded by the 12th amendment.

The Electors shall meet in their respective states and vote by ballot for President and Vice-President, one of whom, at least, shall not be an inhabitant of the same state with themselves; they shall name in their ballots the person voted for as President, and in distinct ballots the person voted for as Vice-President, and they shall make distinct lists of all persons voted for as President, and of all persons voted for as Vice-President, and of the number of votes for each, which lists they shall sign and certify, and transmit sealed to the seat of the government of the United States, directed to the President of the Senate; — the President of the Senate shall, in the presence of the Senate and House of Representatives, open all the certificates and the votes shall then be counted; — The person having the greatest number of votes for President, shall be the President, if such number be a majority of the whole number of Electors appointed; and if no person have such majority, then from the persons having the highest numbers not exceeding three on the list of those voted for as President, the House of Representatives shall choose immediately, by ballot, the President. But in choosing the President, the votes shall be taken by states, the representation from each state having one vote; a quorum for this purpose shall consist of a member or members from two-thirds of the states, and a majority of all the states shall be necessary to a choice. [And if the House of Representatives shall not choose a President whenever the right of choice shall devolve upon them, before the fourth day of March next following, then the Vice-President shall act as President, as in case of the death or other constitutional disability of the President. —]* The person having the greatest number of votes as Vice-President, shall be the Vice-President, if such number be a majority of the whole number of Electors appointed, and if no person have a majority, then from the two highest numbers on the list, the Senate shall choose the Vice-President; a quorum for the purpose shall consist of two-thirds of the whole number of Senators, and a majority of the whole number shall be necessary to a choice. But no person constitutionally ineligible to the office of President shall be eligible to that of Vice-President of the United States.

AMENDMENT XIII

Passed by Congress January 31, 1865. Ratified December 6, 1865.

Note: A portion of Article IV, section 2, of the Constitution was superseded by the 13th amendment.

SECTION 1. Neither slavery nor involuntary servitude, except as a punishment for crime whereof the party shall have been duly convicted, shall exist within the United States, or any place subject to their jurisdiction.

SECTION 2. Congress shall have power to enforce this article by appropriate legislation.

Superseded by section 3 of the 20th amendment.

AMENDMENT XIV

Passed by Congress June 13, 1866. Ratified July 9, 1868.

Note: Article I, section 2, of the Constitution was modified by section 2 of the 14th amendment.

SECTION 1. All persons born or naturalized in the United States, and subject to the jurisdiction thereof, are citizens of the United States and of the State wherein they reside. No State shall make or enforce any law which shall abridge the privileges or immunities of citizens of the United States; nor shall any State deprive any person of life, liberty, or property, without due process of law; nor deny to any person within its jurisdiction the equal protection of the laws.

SECTION 2. Representatives shall be apportioned among the several States according to their respective numbers, counting the whole number of persons in each State, excluding Indians not taxed. But when the right to vote at any election for the choice of electors for President and Vice-President of the United States, Representatives in Congress, the Executive and Judicial officers of a State, or the members of the Legislature thereof, is denied to any of the male inhabitants of such State, being twenty-one years of age,* and citizens of the United States, or in any way abridged, except for participation in rebellion, or other crime, the basis of representation therein shall be reduced in the proportion which the number of such male citizens shall bear to the whole number of male citizens twenty-one years of age in such State.

SECTION 3. No person shall be a Senator or Representative in Congress, or elector of President and Vice-President, or hold any office, civil or military, under the United States, or under any State, who, having previously taken an oath, as a member of Congress, or as an officer of the United States, or as a member of any State legislature, or as an executive or judicial officer of any State, to support the Constitution of the United States, shall have engaged in insurrection or rebellion against the same, or given aid or comfort to the enemies thereof. But Congress may by a vote of two-thirds of each House, remove such disability.

SECTION 4. The validity of the public debt of the United States, authorized by law, including debts incurred for payment of pensions and bounties for services in suppressing insurrection or rebellion, shall not be questioned.

---

*Changed by section 1 of the 26th amendment.

But neither the United States nor any State shall assume or pay any debt or obligation incurred in aid of insurrection or rebellion against the United States, or any claim for the loss or emancipation of any slave; but all such debts, obligations and claims shall be held illegal and void.

SECTION 5. The Congress shall have the power to enforce, by appropriate legislation, the provisions of this article.

AMENDMENT XV

Passed by Congress February 26, 1869. Ratified February 3, 1870.

SECTION 1. The right of citizens of the United States to vote shall not be denied or abridged by the United States or by any State on account of race, color, or previous condition of servitude—

SECTION 2.
The Congress shall have the power to enforce this article by appropriate legislation.

AMENDMENT XVI

Passed by Congress July 2, 1909. Ratified February 3, 1913.

Note: Article I, section 9, of the Constitution was modified by amendment 16.

The Congress shall have power to lay and collect taxes on incomes, from whatever source derived, without apportionment among the several States, and without regard to any census or enumeration.

AMENDMENT XVII

Passed by Congress May 13, 1912. Ratified April 8, 1913.

Note: Article I, section 3, of the Constitution was modified by the 17th amendment.

The Senate of the United States shall be composed of two Senators from each State, elected by the people thereof, for six years; and each Senator shall have one vote. The electors in each State shall have the qualifications requisite for electors of the most numerous branch of the State legislatures.

When vacancies happen in the representation of any State in the Senate, the executive authority of such State shall issue writs of election to fill such vacancies: *Provided*, That the legislature of any State may empower the executive thereof to make temporary appointments until the people fill the vacancies by election as the legislature may direct.

This amendment shall not be so construed as to affect the election or term of any Senator chosen before it becomes valid as part of the Constitution.

AMENDMENT XVIII

Passed by Congress December 18, 1917. Ratified January 16, 1919. Repealed by amendment 21.

SECTION 1. After one year from the ratification of this article the manufacture, sale, or transportation of intoxicating liquors within, the importation thereof into, or the exportation thereof from the United States and all territory subject to the jurisdiction thereof for beverage purposes is hereby prohibited.

SECTION 2. The Congress and the several States shall have concurrent power to enforce this article by appropriate legislation.

SECTION 3. This article shall be inoperative unless it shall have been ratified as an amendment to the Constitution by the legislatures of the several States, as provided in the Constitution, within seven years from the date of the submission hereof to the States by the Congress.

AMENDMENT XIX

Passed by Congress June 4, 1919. Ratified August 18, 1920.

The right of citizens of the United States to vote shall not be denied or abridged by the United States or by any State on account of sex.

Congress shall have power to enforce this article by appropriate legislation.

AMENDMENT XX

Passed by Congress March 2, 1932. Ratified January 23, 1933.

Note: Article I, section 4, of the Constitution was modified by section 2 of this amendment. In addition, a portion of the 12th amendment was superseded by section 3.

SECTION 1. The terms of the President and the Vice President shall end at noon on the 20th day of January, and the terms of Senators and Representatives at noon on the 3rd day of January, of the years in which such terms would have ended if this article had not been ratified; and the terms of their successors shall then begin.

SECTION 2. The Congress shall assemble at least once in every year, and such meeting shall begin at noon on the 3d day of January, unless they shall by law appoint a different day.

SECTION 3. If, at the time fixed for the beginning of the term of the President, the President elect shall have died, the Vice President elect shall become President. If a President shall not have been chosen before the time fixed for the beginning of his term, or if the President elect shall have failed to qualify, then the Vice President elect shall act as President until a President shall have qualified; and the Congress may by law provide for the case wherein neither a President elect nor a Vice President shall have qualified, declaring who shall then act as President, or the manner in which one who is to act shall be selected, and such person shall act accordingly until a President or Vice President shall have qualified.

SECTION 4. The Congress may by law provide for the case of the death of any of the persons from whom the House of Representatives may choose a President whenever the right of choice shall have devolved upon them, and for the case of the death of any of the persons from whom the Senate may choose a Vice President whenever the right of choice shall have devolved upon them.

SECTION 5. Sections 1 and 2 shall take effect on the 15th day of October following the ratification of this article.

SECTION 6. This article shall be inoperative unless it shall have been ratified as an amendment to the Constitution by the legislatures of three-fourths of the several States within seven years from the date of its submission.

AMENDMENT XXI

Passed by Congress February 20, 1933. Ratified December 5, 1933.

SECTION 1. The eighteenth article of amendment to the Constitution of the United States is hereby repealed.

SECTION 2. The transportation or importation into any State, Territory, or Possession of the United States for delivery or use therein of intoxicating liquors, in violation of the laws thereof, is hereby prohibited.

SECTION 3. This article shall be inoperative unless it shall have been ratified as an amendment to the Constitution by conventions in the several States, as provided in the Constitution, within seven years from the date of the submission hereof to the States by the Congress.

Amendment XXII

Passed by Congress March 21, 1947. Ratified February 27, 1951.

SECTION 1. No person shall be elected to the office of the President more than twice, and no person who has held the office of President, or acted as President, for more than two years of a term to which some other person was elected President shall be elected to the office of President more than once. But this Article shall not apply to any person holding the office of President when this Article was proposed by Congress, and shall not prevent any person who may be holding the office of President, or acting as President, during the term within which this Article becomes operative from holding the office of President or acting as President during the remainder of such term.

SECTION 2. This article shall be inoperative unless it shall have been ratified as an amendment to the Constitution by the legislatures of three-fourths of the several States within seven years from the date of its submission to the States by the Congress.

Amendment XXIII

Passed by Congress June 16, 1960. Ratified March 29, 1961.

SECTION 1. The District constituting the seat of Government of the United States shall appoint in such manner as Congress may direct:

A number of electors of President and Vice President equal to the whole number of Senators and Representatives in Congress to which the District would be entitled if it were a State, but in no event more than the least populous State; they shall be in addition to those appointed by the States, but they shall be considered, for the purposes of the election of President and Vice President, to be electors appointed by a State; and they shall meet in the

District and perform such duties as provided by the twelfth article of amendment.

SECTION 2.
The Congress shall have power to enforce this article by appropriate legislation.

AMENDMENT XXIV

Passed by Congress August 27, 1962. Ratified January 23, 1964.

SECTION 1. The right of citizens of the United States to vote in any primary or other election for President or Vice President, for electors for President or Vice President, or for Senator or Representative in Congress, shall not be denied or abridged by the United States or any State by reason of failure to pay poll tax or other tax.

SECTION 2. The Congress shall have power to enforce this article by appropriate legislation.

AMENDMENT XXV

Passed by Congress July 6, 1965. Ratified February 10, 1967.

Note: Article II, section 1, of the Constitution was affected by the 25th amendment.

SECTION 1. In case of the removal of the President from office or of his death or resignation, the Vice President shall become President.

SECTION 2. Whenever there is a vacancy in the office of the Vice President, the President shall nominate a Vice President who shall take office upon confirmation by a majority vote of both Houses of Congress.

SECTION 3.
Whenever the President transmits to the President pro tempore of the Senate and the Speaker of the House of Representatives his written declaration that he is unable to discharge the powers and duties of his office, and until he transmits to them a written declaration to the contrary, such powers and duties shall be discharged by the Vice President as Acting President.

SECTION 4. Whenever the Vice President and a majority of either the principal officers of the executive departments or of such other body as Congress may by law provide, transmit to the President pro tempore of the Senate and the Speaker of the House of Representatives their written declaration that the President is unable to discharge the powers and duties of his office, the Vice President shall immediately assume the powers and duties of the office as Acting President.

Thereafter, when the President transmits to the President pro tempore of the Senate and the Speaker of the House of Representatives his written declaration that no inability exists, he shall resume the powers and duties of his office unless the Vice President and a majority of either the principal officers of the executive department or of such other body as Congress may by law provide, transmit within four days to the President pro tempore of the Senate and the Speaker of the House of Representatives their written declaration that the President is unable to discharge the powers and duties of his office. Thereupon Congress shall decide the issue, assembling within forty-eight hours for that purpose if not in session. If the Congress, within twenty-one days after receipt of the latter written declaration, or, if Congress is not in session, within twenty-one days after Congress is required to assemble, determines by two-thirds vote of both Houses that the President is unable to discharge the powers and duties of his office, the Vice President shall continue to discharge the same as Acting President; otherwise, the President shall resume the powers and duties of his office.

Amendment XXVI

Passed by Congress March 23, 1971. Ratified July 1, 1971.

Note: Amendment 14, section 2, of the Constitution was modified by section 1 of the 26th amendment.

SECTION 1. The right of citizens of the United States, who are eighteen years of age or older, to vote shall not be denied or abridged by the United States or by any State on account of age.

SECTION 2. The Congress shall have power to enforce this article by appropriate legislation.

AMENDMENT XXVI

Originally proposed Sept. 25, 1789. Ratified May 7, 1992.

No law, varying the compensation for the services of the Senators and Representatives, shall take effect, until an election of representatives shall have intervened.

PRESIDENTIAL ELECTIONS

Year	Number of States	Candidates	Parties	Popular Vote	% of Popular Vote	Electoral Vote	% Voter Participation
1789	11	**GEORGE WASHINGTON**	No party designations			69	
		John Adams				34	
		Other candidates				35	
1792	15	**GEORGE WASHINGTON**	No party designations			132	
		John Adams				77	
		George Clinton				50	
		Other candidates				5	
1796	16	**JOHN ADAMS**	Federalist			71	
		Thomas Jefferson	Democratic-Republican			68	
		Thomas Pinckney	Federalist			59	
		Aaron Burr	Democratic-Republican			30	
		Other candidates				48	
1800	16	**THOMAS JEFFERSON**	Democratic-Republican			73	
		Aaron Burr	Democratic-Republican			73	
		John Adams	Federalist			65	
		Charles C. Pinckney	Federalist			64	
		John Jay	Federalist			1	
1804	17	**THOMAS JEFFERSON**	Democratic-Republican			162	
		Charles C. Pinckney	Federalist			14	

Year	Number of States	Candidates	Parties	Popular Vote	% of Popular Vote	Electoral Vote	% Voter Participation
1808	17	**JAMES MADISON**	Democratic-Republican			122	
		Charles C. Pinckney	Federalist			47	
		George Clinton	Democratic-Republican			6	
1812	18	**JAMES MADISON**	Democratic-Republican			128	
		DeWitt Clinton	Federalist			89	
1816	19	**JAMES MONROE**	Democratic-Republican			183	
		Rufus King	Federalist			34	
1820	24	**JAMES MONROE**	Democratic-Republican			231	
		John Quincy Adams	Independent			1	
1824	24	**JOHN QUINCY ADAMS**	Democratic-Republican	108,740	30.5	84	26.9
		Andrew Jackson	Democratic-Republican	153,544	43.1	99	
		Henry Clay	Democratic-Republican	47,136	13.2	37	
		William H. Crawford	Democratic-Republican	46,618	13.1	41	
1828	24	**ANDREW JACKSON**	Democratic	647,286	56.0	178	57.6
		John Quincy Adams	National-Republican	508,064	44.0	83	
1832	24	**ANDREW JACKSON**	Democratic	688,242	54.5	219	55.4
		Henry Clay	National-Republican	473,462	37.5	49	
		William Wirt	Anti-Masonic	101,051	8.0	7	
		John Floyd	Democratic			11	
1836	26	**MARTIN VAN BUREN**	Democratic	765,483	50.9	170	57.8
		William H. Harrison	Whig			73	
		Hugh L. White	Whig	739,795	49.1	26	
		Daniel Webster	Whig			14	
		W. P. Mangum	Whig			11	

Year	Number of States	Candidates	Parties	Popular Vote	% of Popular Vote	Electoral Vote	% Voter Participation
1840	26	WILLIAM H. HARRISON	Whig	1,274,624	53.1	234	80.2
		Martin Van Buren	Democratic	1,127,781	46.9	60	
1844	26	JAMES K. POLK	Democratic	1,338,464	49.6	170	78.9
		Henry Clay	Whig	1,300,097	48.1	105	
		James G. Birney	Liberty	62,300	2.3		
1848	30	ZACHARY TAYLOR	Whig	1,360,967	47.4	163	72.7
		Lewis Cass	Democratic	1,222,342	42.5	127	
		Martin Van Buren	Free Soil	291,263	10.1		
1852	31	FRANKLIN PIERCE	Democratic	1,601,117	50.9	254	69.6
		Winfield Scott	Whig	1,385,453	44.1	42	
		John P. Hale	Free Soil	155,825	5.0		
1856	31	JAMES BUCHANAN	Democratic	1,832,955	45.3	174	78.9
		John C. Frémont	Republican	1,339,932	33.1	114	
		Millard Fillmore	American	871,731	21.6	8	
1860	33	ABRAHAM LINCOLN	Republican	1,865,593	39.8	180	81.2
		Stephen A. Douglas	Democratic	1,382,713	29.5	12	
		John C. Breckinridge	Democratic	848,356	18.1	72	
		John Bell	Constitutional Union	592,906	12.6	39	
1864	36	ABRAHAM LINCOLN	Republican	2,206,938	55.0	212	73.8
		George B. McClellan	Democratic	1,803,787	45.0	21	

Year	Number of States	Candidates	Parties	Popular Vote	% of Popular Vote	Electoral Vote	% Voter Participation
1868	37	ULYSSES S. GRANT	Republican	3,013,421	52.7	214	78.1
		Horatio Seymour	Democratic	2,706,829	47.3	80	
1872	37	ULYSSES S. GRANT	Republican	3,596,745	55.6	286	71.3
		Horace Greeley	Democratic	2,843,446	43.9	66	
1876	38	Rutherford B. Hayes	Republican	4,036,572	48.0	185	81.8
		Samuel J. Tilden	Democratic	4,284,020	51.0	184	
1880	38	JAMES A. GARFIELD	Republican	4,453,295	48.5	214	79.4
		Winfield S. Hancock	Democratic	4,414,082	48.1	155	
		James B. Weaver	Greenback-Labor	308,578	3.4		
1884	38	GROVER CLEVELAND	Democratic	4,879,507	48.5	219	77.5
		James G. Blaine	Republican	4,850,293	48.2	182	
		Benjamin F. Butler	Greenback-Labor	175,370	1.8		
		John P. St. John	Prohibition	150,369	1.5		
1888	38	BENJAMIN HARRISON	Republican	5,477,129	47.9	233	79.3
		Grover Cleveland	Democratic	5,537,857	48.6	168	
		Clinton B. Fisk	Prohibition	249,506	2.2		
		Anson J. Streeter	Union Labor	146,935	1.3		
1892	44	GROVER CLEVELAND	Democratic	5,555,426	46.1	277	74.7
		Benjamin Harrison	Republican	5,182,690	43.0	145	
		James B. Weaver	People's	1,029,846	8.5	22	
		John Bidwell	Prohibition	264,133	2.2		
1896	45	WILLIAM MCKINLEY	Republican	7,102,246	51.1	271	79.3
		William J. Bryan	Democratic	6,492,559	47.7	176	

Year	Number of States	Candidates	Parties	Popular Vote	% of Popular Vote	Electoral Vote	% Voter Participation
1900	45	**WILLIAM McKINLEY**	Republican	7,218,491	51.7	292	73.2
		William J. Bryan	Democratic; Populist	6,356,734	45.5	155	
		John C. Wooley	Prohibition	208,914	1.5		
1904	45	**THEODORE ROOSEVELT**	Republican	7,628,461	57.4	336	65.2
		Alton B. Parker	Democratic	5,084,223	37.6	140	
		Eugene V. Debs	Socialist	402,283	3.0		
		Silas C. Swallow	Prohibition	258,536	1.9		
1908	46	**WILLIAM H. TAFT**	Republican	7,675,320	51.6	321	65.4
		William J. Bryan	Democratic	6,412,294	43.1	162	
		Eugene V. Debs	Socialist	420,793	2.8		
		Eugene W. Chafin	Prohibition	253,840	1.7		
1912	48	**WOODROW WILSON**	Democratic	6,296,547	41.9	435	58.8
		Theodore Roosevelt	Progressive	4,118,571	27.4	88	
		William H. Taft	Republican	3,486,720	23.2	8	
		Eugene V. Debs	Socialist	900,672	6.0		
		Eugene W. Chafin	Prohibition	206,275	1.4		
1916	48	**WOODROW WILSON**	Democratic	9,127,695	49.4	277	61.6
		Charles E. Hughes	Republican	8,533,507	46.2	254	
		A. L. Benson	Socialist	585,113	3.2		
		J. Frank Hanly	Prohibition	220,506	1.2		

Year	Number of States	Candidates	Parties	Popular Vote	% of Popular Vote	Electoral Vote	% of Voter Participation
1920	48	WARREN G. HARDING	Republican	16,143,407	60.4	404	49.2
		James M. Cox	Democratic	9,130,328	34.2	127	
		Eugene V. Debs	Socialist	919,799	3.4		
		P. P. Christensen	Farmer-Labor	265,411	1.0		
1924	48	CALVIN COOLIDGE	Republican	15,718,211	54.0	382	48.9
		John W. Davis	Democratic	8,385,283	28.8	136	
		Robert M. La Follette	Progressive	4,831,289	16.6	13	
1928	48	HERBERT C. HOOVER	Republican	21,391,993	58.2	444	56.9
		Alfred E. Smith	Democratic	15,016,169	40.9	87	
1932	48	FRANKLIN D. ROOSEVELT	Democratic	22,809,638	57.4	472	56.9
		Herbert C. Hoover	Republican	15,758,901	39.7	59	
		Norman Thomas	Socialist	881,951	2.2		
1936	48	FRANKLIN D. ROOSEVELT	Democratic	27,752,869	60.8	523	61.0
		Alfred M. Landon	Republican	16,674,665	36.5	8	
		William Lemke	Union	882,479	1.9		
1940	48	FRANKLIN D. ROOSEVELT	Democratic	27,307,819	54.8	449	62.5
		Wendell L. Willkie	Republican	22,321,018	44.8	82	
1944	48	FRANKLIN D. ROOSEVELT	Democratic	25,606,585	53.5	432	55.9
		Thomas E. Dewey	Republican	22,014,745	46.0	99	
1948	48	HARRY S. TRUMAN	Democratic	24,179,345	49.6	303	53.0
		Thomas E. Dewey	Republican	21,991,291	45.1	189	
		J. Strom Thurmond	States' Rights	1,176,125	2.4	39	
		Henry A. Wallace	Progressive	1,157,326	2.4		
1952	48	DWIGHT D. EISENHOWER	Republican	33,936,234	55.1	442	63.3
		Adlai E. Stevenson	Democratic	27,314,992	44.4	89	

Year	Number of States	Candidates	Parties	Popular Vote	% of Popular Vote	Electoral Vote	% Voter Participation
1956	48	**DWIGHT D. EISENHOWER**	Republican	35,590,472	57.6	457	60.6
		Adlai E. Stevenson	Democratic	26,022,752	42.1	73	
1960	50	**JOHN F. KENNEDY**	Democratic	34,226,731	49.7	303	62.8
		Richard M. Nixon	Republican	34,108,157	49.5	219	
1964	50	**LYNDON B. JOHNSON**	Democratic	43,129,566	61.1	486	61.9
		Barry M. Goldwater	Republican	27,178,188	38.5	52	
1968	50	**RICHARD M. NIXON**	Republican	31,785,480	43.4	301	60.9
		Hubert H. Humphrey	Democratic	31,275,166	42.7	191	
		George C. Wallace	American Independent	9,906,473	13.5	46	
1972	50	**RICHARD M. NIXON**	Republican	47,169,911	60.7	520	55.2
		George S. McGovern	Democratic	29,170,383	37.5	17	
		John G. Schmitz	American	1,099,482	1.4		
1976	50	**James E. CARTER**	Democratic	40,830,763	50.1	297	53.5
		Gerald R. Ford	Republican	39,147,793	48.0	240	
1980	50	**RONALD REAGAN**	Republican	43,901,812	50.7	489	52.6
		James E. Carter	Democratic	35,483,820	41.0	49	
		John B. Anderson	Independent	5,719,437	6.6		
		Ed Clark	Libertarian	921,188	1.1		
1984	50	**RONALD REAGAN**	Republican	54,451,521	58.8	525	53.1
		Walter F. Mondale	Democratic	37,565,334	40.6	13	

Year	Number of States	Candidates	Parties	Popular Vote	% of Popular Vote	Electoral Vote	% Voter Participation
1988	50	GEORGE H. W. BUSH	Republican	47,917,341	53.4	426	50.1
		Michael Dukakis	Democratic	41,013,030	45.6	111	
1992	50	WILLIAM J. CLINTON	Democratic	44,908,254	43.0	370	55.0
		George H. W. Bush	Republican	39,102,343	37.4	168	
		H. Ross Perot	Independent	19,741,065	18.9		
1996	50	WILLIAM J. CLINTON	Democratic	47,401,185	49.0	379	49.0
		Robert Dole	Republican	39,197,469	41.0	159	
		H. Ross Perot	Independent	8,085,295	8.0		
2000	50	GEORGE W. BUSH	Republican	50,455,156	47.9	271	50.4
		Al Gore	Democrat	50,997,335	48.4	266	
		Ralph Nader	Green	2,882,897	2.7		
2004	50	GEORGE W. BUSH	Republican	62,040,610	50.7	286	60.7
		John F. Kerry	Democrat	59,028,444	48.3	251	
2008	50	BARACK OBAMA	Democrat	69,456,897	52.9	365	63.0
		John McCain	Republican	59,934,814	45.7	173	
2012	50	BARACK OBAMA	Democrat	65,915,795	51.1	332	57.5
		Mitt Romney	Republican	60,933,504	47.2	206	
2016	50	DONALD J. TRUMP	Republican	62,979,636	46.1	304	60.2
		Hillary Rodham Clinton	Democrat	65,844,610	48.2	227	
2020	50	JOSEPH R. BIDEN	Democrat	81,268,924	51.31	302	66.8
		Donald J. Trump	Republican	74,216,154	46.86	232	

Candidates receiving less than 1 percent of the popular vote have been omitted. Thus the percentage of popular vote given for any election year may not total 100 percent. Before the passage of the Twelfth Amendment in 1804, the Electoral College voted for two presidential candidates; the runner-up became vice president.

ADMISSION OF STATES

Order of Admission	State	Date of Admission	Order of Admission	State	Date of Admission
1	Delaware	December 7, 1787	26	Michigan	January 26, 1837
2	Pennsylvania	December 12, 1787	27	Florida	March 3, 1845
3	New Jersey	December 18, 1787	28	Texas	December 29, 1845
4	Georgia	January 2, 1788	29	Iowa	December 28, 1846
5	Connecticut	January 9, 1788	30	Wisconsin	May 29, 1848
6	Massachusetts	February 7, 1788	31	California	September 9, 1850
7	Maryland	April 28, 1788	32	Minnesota	May 11, 1858
8	South Carolina	May 23, 1788	33	Oregon	February 14, 1859
9	New Hampshire	June 21, 1788	34	Kansas	January 29, 1861
10	Virginia	June 25, 1788	35	West Virginia	June 30, 1863
11	New York	July 26, 1788	36	Nevada	October 31, 1864
12	North Carolina	November 21, 1789	37	Nebraska	March 1, 1867
13	Rhode Island	May 29, 1790	38	Colorado	August 1, 1876
14	Vermont	March 4, 1791	39	North Dakota	November 2, 1889
15	Kentucky	June 1, 1792	40	South Dakota	November 2, 1889
16	Tennessee	June 1, 1796	41	Montana	November 8, 1889
17	Ohio	March 1, 1803	42	Washington	November 11, 1889
18	Louisiana	April 30, 1812	43	Idaho	July 3, 1890
19	Indiana	December 11, 1816	44	Wyoming	July 10, 1890
20	Mississippi	December 10, 1817	45	Utah	January 4, 1896
21	Illinois	December 3, 1818	46	Oklahoma	November 16, 1907
22	Alabama	December 14, 1819	47	New Mexico	January 6, 1912
23	Maine	March 15, 1820	48	Arizona	February 14, 1912
24	Missouri	August 10, 1821	49	Alaska	January 3, 1959
25	Arkansas	June 15, 1836	50	Hawaii	August 21, 1959

POPULATION OF THE UNITED STATES

Year	Number of States	Population	% Increase	Population per Square Mile
1790	13	3,929,214		4.5
1800	16	5,308,483	35.1	6.1
1810	17	7,239,881	36.4	4.3
1820	23	9,638,453	33.1	5.5
1830	24	12,866,020	33.5	7.4
1840	26	17,069,453	32.7	9.8
1850	31	23,191,876	35.9	7.9
1860	33	31,443,321	35.6	10.6
1870	37	39,818,449	26.6	13.4
1880	38	50,155,783	26.0	16.9
1890	44	62,947,714	25.5	21.1
1900	45	75,994,575	20.7	25.6
1910	46	91,972,266	21.0	31.0
1920	48	105,710,620	14.9	35.6
1930	48	122,775,046	16.1	41.2
1940	48	131,669,275	7.2	44.2
1950	48	150,697,361	14.5	50.7
1960	50	179,323,175	19.0	50.6
1970	50	203,235,298	13.3	57.5
1980	50	226,504,825	11.4	64.0
1985	50	237,839,000	5.0	67.2
1990	50	250,122,000	5.2	70.6
1995	50	263,411,707	5.3	74.4
2000	50	281,421,906	6.8	77.0
2005	50	296,410,404	5.3	77.9
2010	50	308,745,538	9.7	87.4
2015	50	321,931,311	4.3	91.1
2020	50	331,449,281	7.4	93.8

IMMIGRATION BY REGION AND SELECTED COUNTRY OF LAST RESIDENCE, FISCAL YEARS 1820–2020

Region and country of last residence	1820 to 1829	1830 to 1839	1840 to 1849	1850 to 1859	1860 to 1869	1870 to 1879	1880 to 1889	1890 to 1899
Total	128,502	538,381	1,427,337	2,814,554	2,081,261	2,742,137	5,248,568	3,694,294
Europe	99,272	422,771	1,369,259	2,619,680	1,877,726	2,251,878	4,638,677	3,576,411
Austria-Hungary	—	—	—	—	3,375	60,127	314,787	534,059
Austria	—	—	—	—	2,700	54,529	204,805	268,218
Hungary	—	—	—	—	483	5,598	109,982	203,350
Belgium	28	20	3,996	5,765	5,785	6,991	18,738	19,642
Bulgaria	—	—	—	—	—	—	—	52
*Former Czechoslovakia	—	—	—	—	—	—	—	—
Denmark	173	927	671	3,227	13,553	29,278	85,342	56,671
Finland	—	—	—	—	—	—	—	—
France	7,694	39,330	75,300	81,778	35,938	71,901	48,193	35,616
Germany	5,753	124,726	385,434	976,072	723,734	751,769	1,445,181	579,072
Greece	17	49	17	32	51	209	1,807	12,732
Ireland	51,617	170,672	656,145	1,029,486	427,419	422,264	674,061	405,710
Italy	430	2,225	1,476	8,643	9,853	46,296	267,660	603,761
Netherlands	1,105	1,377	7,624	11,122	8,387	14,267	52,715	29,349
Norway-Sweden	91	1,149	12,389	22,202	82,937	178,823	586,441	334,058
Norway	—	—	—	—	16,068	88,644	185,111	96,810
Sweden	—	—	—	—	24,224	90,179	401,330	237,248
Poland	19	366	105	1,087	1,886	11,016	42,910	107,793
Portugal	177	820	196	1,299	2,083	13,971	15,186	25,874
Romania	—	—	—	—	—	—	5,842	6,808
Russia	86	280	520	423	1,670	35,177	182,698	450,101
Spain	2,595	2,010	1,916	8,795	6,966	5,540	3,995	9,189
Switzerland	3,148	4,430	4,819	24,423	21,124	25,212	81,151	37,020
United Kingdom	26,336	74,350	218,572	445,322	532,956	578,447	810,900	328,759
*Former Yugoslavia	—	—	—	—	—	—	—	—
Other Europe	3	40	79	4	9	590	1,070	145

Asia	34	55	121	36,080	54,408	134,128	71,151	61,285
China	3	8	32	35,933	54,028	133,139	65,797	15,268
Hong Kong	—	—	—	—	—	166	—	102
India	9	38	33	42	50	—	247	102
Iran	—	—	—	—	—	—	—	—
*Israel	—	—	—	—	—	—	—	—
Japan	—	—	—	—	138	193	1,583	13,998
Jordan	—	—	—	—	—	—	—	—
*Korea	—	—	—	—	—	—	—	—
Philippines	—	—	—	—	—	—	—	—
Syria	—	—	—	—	—	—	—	—
Taiwan	—	—	—	—	—	—	—	—
Turkey	19	8	45	94	129	382	2,478	27,510
Vietnam	—	—	—	—	—	—	—	—
Other Asia	3	1	11	11	63	248	1,046	4,407
North America	9,655	31,905	50,516	84,145	130,292	345,010	524,826	37,350
Canada and Newfoundland	2,297	11,875	34,285	64,171	117,978	324,310	492,865	3,098
Mexico	3,835	7,187	3,069	3,446	1,957	5,133	2,405	734
Caribbean	3,061	11,792	11,803	12,447	8,751	14,285	27,323	31,480
Cuba	—	—	—	—	—	—	—	—
Dominican Republic	—	—	—	—	—	—	—	—
Haiti	—	—	—	—	—	—	—	—
Jamaica	—	—	—	—	—	—	—	—
Other Caribbean	3,061	11,792	11,803	12,447	8,751	14,285	27,323	31,480
Central America	57	94	297	512	70	173	279	649
Belize	—	—	—	—	—	—	—	—
Costa Rica	—	—	—	—	—	—	—	—
El Salvador	—	—	—	—	—	—	—	—
Guatemala	—	—	—	—	—	—	—	—
Honduras	—	—	—	—	—	—	—	—
Nicaragua	—	—	—	—	—	—	—	—
Panama	—	—	—	—	—	—	—	—
Other Central America	57	94	297	512	70	173	279	649

Region and country of last residence	1820 to 1829	1830 to 1839	1840 to 1849	1850 to 1859	1860 to 1869	1870 to 1879	1880 to 1889	1890 to 1899
South America	405	957	1,062	3,569	1,536	1,109	1,954	1,389
Argentina	—	—	—	—	—	—	—	—
Bolivia	—	—	—	—	—	—	—	—
Brazil	—	—	—	—	—	—	—	—
Chile	—	—	—	—	—	—	—	—
Colombia	—	—	—	—	—	—	—	—
Ecuador	—	—	—	—	—	—	—	—
Guyana	—	—	—	—	—	—	—	—
Paraguay	—	—	—	—	—	—	—	—
Peru	—	—	—	—	—	—	—	—
Suriname	—	—	—	—	—	—	—	—
Uruguay	—	—	—	—	—	—	—	—
Venezuela	—	—	—	—	—	—	—	—
Other South America	405	957	1,062	3,569	1,536	1,109	1,954	1,389
Other America	—	—	—	—	—	—	—	—
Africa	15	50	61	84	407	371	763	432
Egypt	—	—	—	—	4	29	145	51
Ethiopia	—	—	—	—	—	—	—	—
Liberia	1	8	5	7	43	52	21	9
Morocco	—	—	—	—	—	—	—	—
South Africa	—	—	—	—	35	48	23	9
Other Africa	14	42	56	77	325	242	574	363
Oceania	3	7	14	166	187	9,996	12,361	4,704
Australia	2	1	2	15	—	8,930	7,250	3,098
New Zealand	—	—	—	—	—	39	21	12
Other Oceania	1	6	12	151	187	1,027	5,090	1,594
Not Specified	19,523	83,593	7,366	74,399	18,241	754	790	14,112

Region and country of last residence	1900 to 1909	1910 to 1919	1920 to 1929	1930 to 1939	1940 to 1949	1950 to 1959	1960 to 1969	1980 to 1989
Total	8,202,388	6,347,380	4,295,510	699,375	856,608	2,499,268	3,213,749	6,244,379
Europe	7,572,569	4,985,411	2,560,340	444,399	472,524	1,404,973	1,133,443	668,866
Austria-Hungary	2,001,376	1,154,727	60,891	12,531	13,574	113,015	27,590	20,437
Austria	532,416	589,174	31,392	5,307	8,393	81,354	17,571	15,374
Hungary	685,567	565,553	29,499	7,224	5,181	31,661	10,019	5,063
Belgium	37,429	32,574	21,511	4,013	12,473	18,885	9,647	7,028
Bulgaria	34,651	27,180	2,824	1,062	449	97	598	1,124
*Former Czechoslovakia	—	—	101,182	17,757	8,475	1,624	2,758	5,678
Denmark	61,227	45,830	34,406	3,470	4,549	10,918	9,797	4,847
Finland	—	—	16,922	2,438	2,230	4,923	4,310	2,569
France	67,735	60,335	54,842	13,761	36,954	50,113	46,975	32,066
Germany	328,722	174,227	386,634	119,107	119,506	576,905	209,616	85,752
Greece	145,402	198,108	60,774	10,599	8,605	45,153	74,173	37,729
Ireland	344,940	166,445	202,854	28,195	15,701	47,189	37,788	22,210
Italy	1,930,475	1,229,916	528,133	85,053	50,509	184,576	200,111	55,562
Netherlands	42,463	46,065	29,397	7,791	13,877	46,703	37,918	11,234
Norway-Sweden	426,981	192,445	170,329	13,452	17,326	44,224	36,150	13,941
Norway	182,542	79,488	70,327	6,901	8,326	22,806	17,371	3,835
Sweden	244,439	112,957	100,002	6,551	9,000	21,418	18,779	10,106
Poland	—	—	223,316	25,555	7,577	6,465	55,742	63,483
Portugal	65,154	82,489	44,829	3,518	6,765	13,928	70,568	42,685
Romania	57,322	13,566	67,810	5,264	1,254	914	2,339	24,753
Russia	1,501,301	1,106,998	61,604	2,463	605	453	2,329	33,311
Spain	24,818	53,262	47,109	3,669	2,774	6,880	40,793	22,783
Switzerland	32,541	22,839	31,772	5,990	9,904	17,577	19,193	8,316
United Kingdom	469,518	371,878	341,552	61,813	131,794	195,709	220,213	53,644
*Former Yugoslavia	—	—	49,215	6,920	2,039	6,966	17,990	16,267
Other Europe	514	6,527	22,434	9,978	5,584	11,756	6,845	3,447

Region and country of last residence	1900 to 1909	1910 to 1919	1920 to 1929	1930 to 1939	1940 to 1949	1950 to 1959	1960 to 1969	1980 to 1989
Asia	299,836	269,736	126,740	19,231	34,532	135,844	358,605	2,391,356
China	19,884	20,916	30,648	5,874	16,072	8,836	14,060	170,897
Hong Kong	—	—	—	—	—	13,781	67,047	112,132
India	3,026	3,478	2,076	554	1,692	1,850	18,638	231,649
Iran	—	—	208	198	1,144	3,195	9,059	98,141
*Israel	—	—	—	—	98	21,376	30,911	43,669
Japan	139,712	77,125	42,057	2,683	1,557	40,651	40,956	44,150
Jordan	—	—	—	—	—	4,899	9,230	28,928
*Korea	—	—	—	—	83	4,845	27,048	322,708
Philippines	—	—	—	391	4,099	17,245	70,660	502,056
Syria	—	—	5,307	2,188	1,179	1,091	2,432	14,534
Taiwan	—	—	—	—	—	721	15,657	119,051
Turkey	127,999	160,717	40,450	1,327	754	2,980	9,464	19,208
Vietnam	—	—	—	—	—	290	2,949	200,632
Other Asia	9,215	7,500	5,994	6,016	7,854	14,084	40,494	483,601
North America	277,809	1,070,539	1,591,278	230,319	328,435	921,610	1,674,172	2,695,329
Canada and Newfoundland	123,067	708,715	949,286	162,703	160,911	353,169	433,128	156,313
Mexico	31,188	185,334	498,945	32,709	56,158	273,847	441,824	1,009,586
Caribbean	100,960	120,860	83,482	18,052	46,194	115,661	427,235	790,109
Cuba	—	—	12,769	10,641	25,976	73,221	202,030	132,552
Dominican Republic	—	—	—	1,026	4,802	10,219	83,552	221,552
Haiti	—	—	—	156	823	3,787	28,992	121,406
Jamaica	—	—	—	—	—	7,397	62,218	193,874
Other Caribbean	100,960	120,860	70,713	6,229	14,593	21,037	50,443	120,725
Central America	7,341	15,692	16,511	6,840	20,135	40,201	98,560	339,376
Belize	77	40	285	193	433	1,133	4,185	14,964
Costa Rica	—	—	—	431	1,965	4,044	17,975	25,017
El Salvador	—	—	—	597	4,885	5,094	14,405	137,418
Guatemala	—	—	—	423	1,303	4,197	14,357	58,847
Honduras	—	—	—	679	1,874	5,320	15,078	39,071
Nicaragua	—	—	—	405	4,393	7,812	10,383	31,102

Panama	7,264	—	—	1,452	5,282	12,601	22,177	32,957
Other Central America	—	15,652	16,226	2,660	—	—	—	—
South America	15,253	39,938	43,025	9,990	19,662	78,418	250,754	399,862
Argentina	—	—	—	1,067	3,108	16,346	49,384	23,442
Bolivia	—	—	—	50	893	2,759	6,205	9,798
Brazil	—	—	4,627	1,468	3,653	11,547	29,238	22,944
Chile	—	—	—	347	1,320	4,669	12,384	19,749
Colombia	—	—	—	1,027	3,454	15,567	68,371	105,494
Ecuador	—	—	—	244	2,207	8,574	34,107	48,015
Guyana	—	—	—	131	596	1,131	4,546	85,886
Paraguay	—	—	—	33	85	576	1,249	3,518
Peru	—	—	—	321	1,273	5,980	19,783	49,958
Suriname	—	—	—	25	130	299	612	1,357
Uruguay	—	—	—	112	754	1,026	4,089	7,235
Venezuela	—	—	—	1,155	2,182	9,927	20,758	22,405
Other South America	15,253	39,938	38,398	4,010	7	17	28	61
Other America	—	—	29	25	25,375	60,314	22,671	83
Africa	6,326	8,867	6,362	2,120	6,720	13,016	23,780	141,990
Egypt	—	—	1,063	781	1,613	1,996	5,581	26,744
Ethiopia	—	—	—	10	28	302	804	12,927
Liberia	—	—	—	35	37	289	841	6,420
Morocco	—	—	—	73	879	2,703	2,880	3,471
South Africa	—	—	5,299	312	1,022	2,278	4,360	15,505
Other Africa	6,326	8,867	9,860	909	3,141	5,448	9,314	76,923
Oceania	12,355	12,339	8,404	3,306	14,262	11,353	23,630	41,432
Australia	11,191	11,280	935	2,260	11,201	8,275	14,986	16,901
New Zealand	—	—	521	790	2,351	1,799	3,775	6,129
Other Oceania	1,164	1,059	930	256	710	1,279	4,869	18,402
Not Specified	33,493	488	—	—	135	12,472	119	305,406

Region and country of last residence	1990 to 1999	2000 to 2009	2010	2011	2012	2013	2014	2015
Total	9,775,398	10,299,430	1,042,625	1,062,040	1,031,631	779,929	653,416	730,259
Europe	1,348,612	1,349,609	95,429	90,712	86,956	80,333	71,325	78,074
Austria-Hungary	27,529	33,929	4,325	4,703	3,208	1232	1,114	1148
Austria	18,234	21,151	3,319	3,654	2,199	248	223	207
Hungary	9,295	12,778	1,006	1,049	1,009	984	891	941
Belgium	7,077	8,157	732	700	698	513	408	505
Bulgaria	16,948	40,003	2,465	2,549	2,322	2,646	2,226	2,336
*Former Czechoslovakia	8,970	18,691	1,510	1,374	1,316	232	303	371
Denmark	6,189	6,049	545	473	492	127	129	243
Finland	3,970	3,970	414	398	373	300	274	301
France	35,945	45,637	4,339	3,967	4,201	2,534	2,589	2,784
Germany	92,207	122,373	7,929	7,072	6,732	4,066	4,375	4,380
Greece	25,403	16,841	966	1,196	1,264	938	780	867
Ireland	65,384	15,642	1,610	1,533	1,694	1,295	1,413	1,375
Italy	75,992	28,329	2,956	2,670	2,946	2,355	2,313	2,760
Netherlands	13,345	17,351	1,520	1,258	1,294	786	665	778
Norway-Sweden	17,825	19,382	1,662	1,530	1,441	863	816	965
Norway	5,211	4,599	363	405	314	80	92	80
Sweden	12,614	14,783	1,299	1,125	1,127	783	724	885
Poland	172,249	117,921	7,391	6,634	6,024	8,697	8,304	7,886
Portugal	25,497	11,479	759	878	837	1,585	1,587	1,690
Romania	48,136	52,154	3,735	3,679	3,477	4,050	3,267	3,478
Russia	433,427	167,152	7,502	8,548	10,114	8,222	6,824	6,552
Spain	18,443	17,695	2,040	2,319	2,316	1,367	1,326	1,414
Switzerland	11,768	12,173	868	861	916	452	388	411
United Kingdom	156,182	171,979	14,781	13,443	13,938	9,459	8,906	10,095
*Former Yugoslavia	57,039	131,831	4,772	4,611	4,488	4,445	—	—
Other Europe	29,087	290,871	22,608	20,316	16,865	17,839	—	—

Asia	2,859,899	3,470,835	410,209	438,580	416,488	275,700	233,163	261,374
China	342,058	591,711	67,634	83,603	78,184	35,387	30,284	31,241
Hong Kong	116,894	57,583	3,263	3,149	2,642	2,093	1,801	1,716
India	352,528	590,464	66,185	66,331	63,320	49,897	37,854	42,213
Iran	76,899	76,755	9,078	9,015	8,955	11,623	9,620	10,344
*Israel	41,340	54,081	5,172	4,389	4,640	3,466	3,015	3,182
Japan	66,582	84,552	7,100	6,751	6,581	1,837	1,635	1,858
Jordan	42,755	53,550	9,327	8,211	7,014	2,816	2,427	2,461
*Korea	179,770	209,758	22,022	22,748	—	—	—	—
Philippines	534,338	545,463	56,399	55,251	55,441	43,489	34,591	40,815
Syria	22,906	30,807	7,424	7,983	6,674	2,196	1,832	2,004
Taiwan	132,647	92,657	6,785	6,206	5,295	5,255	4,326	4,420
Turkey	38,687	48,394	7,435	9,040	7,362	3,990	2,925	3,150
Vietnam	275,379	289,616	30,065	33,486	27,578	24,277	18,837	21,976
Other Asia	637,116	745,444	112,320	122,417	122,000	107,232	—	—
North America	5,137,743	4,441,529	426,981	423,277	409,664	271,807	222,547	247,492
Canada and Newfoundland	194,788	236,349	19,491	19,506	—	—	—	—
Mexico	2,757,418	1,704,166	138,717	142,823	145,326	99,385	94,889	105,958
Caribbean	1,004,687	1,053,357	139,389	133,012	126,615	121,349	—	—
Cuba	159,037	271,742	33,372	36,261	32,551	30,482	24,092	25,770
Dominican Republic	359,818	291,492	53,890	46,036	41,535	39,590	23,775	26,665
Haiti	177,446	203,827	22,336	21,802	22,446	23,480	13,676	14,053
Jamaica	177,143	172,523	19,439	19,298	20,300	16,442	13,547	16,566
Other Caribbean	181,243	113,773	10,352	9,615	9,783	9,384	—	—
Central America	610,189	591,130	43,597	43,249	39,837	44,056	—	—
Belize	12,600	9,682	997	933	875	966	773	851
Costa Rica	17,054	21,571	2,306	2,230	2,152	1,661	1,461	1,633
El Salvador	273,017	251,237	18,547	18,477	15,874	18,401	15,598	16,930
Guatemala	126,043	156,992	10,263	10,795	9,857	9,530	8,549	9,344
Honduras	72,880	63,513	6,381	6,053	6,773	5,462	4,433	5,039
Nicaragua	80,446	70,015	3,476	3,314	2,943	5,064	3,775	3,951
Panama	28,149	18,120	1,627	1,447	1,363	1,598	1,277	1,412
Other Central America	—							

Region and country of last residence	1990 to 1999	2000 to 2009	2010	2011	2012	2013	2014	2015
South America	570,624	856,508	85,783	84,687	77,748	76,167	60,665	67,927
Argentina	30,065	47,955	4,312	4,335	4,218	4,177	3,683	3,886
Bolivia	18,111	21,921	2,211	2,113	1,920	1,961	1,527	1,689
Brazil	50,744	115,404	12,057	11,643	11,248	9,565	8,625	10,516
Chile	18,200	19,792	1,940	1,854	1,628	1,649	1,435	1,486
Colombia	137,985	236,570	21,861	22,130	20,272	22,196	16,478	17,207
Ecuador	81,358	107,977	11,463	11,068	9,284	9,470	6,952	7,664
Guyana	74,407	70,373	6,441	6,288	5,282	6,295	4,327	5,162
Paraguay	6,082	4,623	449	501	454	331	256	338
Peru	110,117	137,614	14,063	13,836	12,414	11,782	9,572	10,701
Suriname	2,285	2,363	202	167	216	160	127	183
Uruguay	6,062	9,827	1,286	1,521	1,348	933	812	902
Venezuela	35,180	82,087	9,497	9,229	9,464	7,648	6,871	8,192
Other South America	28	2	1	2	—	1	—	—
Other America	37	19	4	—	—	1	—	—
Africa	346,416	759,734	98,246	97,429	103,685	71,872	62,175	71,492
Egypt	44,604	81,564	9,822	9,096	10,172	6,213	5,094	5,693
Ethiopia	40,097	87,207	13,853	13,985	15,400	8,323	7,002	8,312
Liberia	13,587	23,316	2,924	3,117	3,451	3,923	3,035	3,042
Morocco	15,768	40,844	4,847	4,249	3,534	3,768	3,538	3,805
South Africa	21,964	32,221	2,705	2,754	2,960	2,283	2,083	2,538
Other Africa	210,396	494,582	64,095	64,228	68,168	61,455	—	—
Oceania	56,800	65,793	5,946	5,825	5,573	3,849	3,399,	3,811
Australia	24,288	32,728	3,077	3,062	3,146	1,296	1,159	1,379
New Zealand	8,600	12,495	1,046	1,006	980	482	453	514
Other Oceania	23,912	20,570	1,823	1,757	1,447	1,505	—	—
Not Specified	25,928	211,930	5,814	6,217	9,265	10,127	—	—

— Represents zero or not available.

*Note that (a) Korea split into North Korea and South Korea in 1945; (b) Czechoslovakia separated into the Czech Republic and the Slovak Republic in 1993; (c) Former Yugoslavia, beginning in the 1990s, broke into the six nations of Serbia, Montenegro, Slovenia, Croatia, Macedonia, and Kosovo; (d) and due to the way United States immigration statistics are recognized and collected, immigrants from the Occupied Palestinian Territories are grouped together with immigrants from Israel.

Region and country of last residence[1]	2016	2017	2018	2019	2020
Total	1,183,505	1,127,167	1,096,611	1,031,765	
Europe	98,043	89,706	85,486	90,810	
Austria-Hungary[2,3]	2,620	2,886	3,154	2,247	
Austria[2,3]	1,621	1,962	2,289	1,201	
Hungary[2,3]	999	924	865	1,046	
Belgium	821	742	628	765	
Bulgaria[4]	2,560	2,070	1,717	1,697	
Czechoslovakia[5]	1,299	1,142	1,138	1,200	
Denmark	562	536	412	467	
Finland[6]	512	478	456	523	
France	5,473	4,973	4,537	5,009	
Germany[3]	5,895	5,369	5,022	5,276	
Greece	1,664	1,495	1,367	1,537	
Ireland[7]	1,895	1,685	1,477	1,912	
Italy	4,385	4,055	3,545	4,072	
Netherlands	1,550	1,285	1,154	1,348	
Norway-Sweden[8]	1,729	1,523	1,347	1,445	
Norway[8]	404	377	301	349	
Sweden[8]	1,325	1,146	1,046	1,096	
Poland[3]	5,287	4,592	4,161	4,561	
Portugal[9]	1,017	910	914	959	
Romania	3,322	2,722	2,397	2,532	
Russia[3,6,10]	9,280	8,841	8,883	10,006	
Spain	4,018	3,555	3,210	3,465	
Switzerland	1,090	837	732	730	
United Kingdom[11]	14,887	13,318	11,867	12,951	
Yugoslavia[12]	5,392	4,966	4,522	5,065	
Other Europe	22,785	21,726	22,846	23,043	
Asia	442,854	404,371	383,145	352,593	
China	77,658	66,479	61,848	60,029	
Hong Kong	2,982	2,893	2,480	2,377	
India	61,691	57,155	56,761	51,139	
Iran	9,596	9,311	5,334	4,463	
Israel	4,652	4,227	4,009	4,702	
Japan	5,709	5,176	4,760	4,897	
Jordan	7,345	8,219	15,417	7,442	
Korea[13]	21,329	18,559	17,253	18,120	
Philippines	50,609	46,542	44,776	43,478	
Syria[14]	3,800	3,010	1,877	1,708	

Region and country of last residence[1]	2016	2017	2018	2019	2020
Taiwan	5,062	4,787	5,093	5,770	
Turkey[14]	8,635	9,144	13,097	9,135	
Vietnam	40,412	37,541	33,236	38,944	
Other Asia	143,374	131,328	117,204	100,389	
America	502,639	489,676	489,291	452,941	
Canada and Newfoundland[15,16,17]	19,349	18,469	14,337	14,723	
Mexico[16,17]	172,726	168,980	160,132	153,502	
Caribbean	180,479	173,724	180,628	135,605	
Cuba	66,120	64,749	75,159	39,580	
Dominican Republic	60,613	58,384	57,286	49,815	
Haiti	23,185	21,501	21,091	16,991	
Jamaica[18]	22,833	21,517	19,986	21,337	
Other Caribbean[18]	7,728	7,573	7,106	7,882	
Central America	54,512	52,907	58,387	61,087	
Belize	878	754	637	817	
Costa Rica	2,295	2,259	2,241	2,466	
El Salvador	21,268	21,920	22,884	24,326	
Guatemala	12,548	12,792	15,172	13,111	
Honduras	12,996	11,147	13,492	15,543	
Nicaragua	3,397	3,014	2,967	3,689	
Panama[19]	1,130	1,021	994	1,135	
Other Central America	-	-	-	-	
South America	75,571	75,595	75,806	88,022	
Argentina	3,783	3,191	2,863	3,753	
Bolivia	1,481	1,399	1,398	1,425	
Brazil	13,528	14,832	15,286	19,607	
Chile	1,711	1,664	1,566	1,817	
Colombia	16,830	16,341	15,950	18,715	
Ecuador	10,779	10,826	11,775	11,189	
Guyana	4,909	4,683	4,573	4,837	
Paraguay	400	364	361	435	
Peru	10,519	9,767	9,488	9,873	
Suriname	130	111	161	149	
Uruguay	911	952	904	1,063	
Venezuela	10,590	11,465	11,481	15,159	
Other South America	-	-	-	-	
Other America	2	1	1	2	
Africa	110,754	116,667	112,745	110,048	

Region and country of last residence[1]	2016	2017	2018	2019	2020
Egypt	13,367	11,166	11,657	10,415	
Ethiopia	13,699	15,678	13,965	10,109	
Liberia	3,545	4,085	3,008	3,419	
Morocco	4,447	4,066	2,961	3,659	
South Africa	3,441	3,438	3,575	3,337	
Other Africa	72,255	78,234	77,579	79,109	
Oceania	6,489	5,986	5,422	6,209	
Australia[20]	4,173	3,818	3,394	3,823	
New Zealand[20]	939	900	831	979	
Other Oceania	1,377	1,268	1,197	1,407	
Not Specified[21]	22,726	20,761	20,522	19,164	

[1] Prior to 1906, refers to country of origin; from 1906 onward, refers to country of last residence. Because of changes in country boundaries, data for a particular country may not necessarily refer to the same geographic area over time.

[2] Austria and Hungary not reported separately for all years during 1860 to 1869, 1890 to 1899, and 1900 to 1909.

[3] Poland included in Austria, Germany, Hungary, and Russia from 1899 to 1919.

[4] Bulgaria included Serbia and Montenegro from 1899 to 1919.

[5] Includes Czechia, Czechoslovakia (former), and Slovakia.

[6] Finland included in Russia from 1899 to 1919.

[7] Northern Ireland included in Ireland prior to 1925.

[8] Norway and Sweden not reported separately until 1861.

[9] Cape Verde included in Portugal from 1892 to 1952.

[10] Refers to the Russian Empire from 1820 to 1920. Between 1920 and 1990, refers to the Soviet Union. From 1991 to 1999, refers to Russia, Armenia, Azerbaijan, Belarus, Georgia, Kazakhstan, Kyrgyzstan, Moldova, Tajikistan, Turkmenistan, Ukraine, and Uzbekistan. Beginning in 2000, refers to Russia only.

[11] United Kingdom refers to England, Scotland, Wales, and Northern Ireland since 1925.

[12] Includes Bosnia and Herzegovina, Croatia, Kosovo, Macedonia, Montenegro, Serbia, Serbia and Montenegro (former), and Slovenia.

[13] Includes North Korea and South Korea.

[14] Syria included in Turkey from 1886 to 1923.

[15] Includes British North America and Canadian provinces.

[16] Land arrivals not completely enumerated until 1908.

[17] No data available for Canada or Mexico from 1886 to 1893.

[18] Jamaica included in British West Indies from 1892 to 1952.

[19] Panama Canal Zone included in Panama from 1932 to 1972.

[20] New Zealand included in Australia from 1892 to 1924.

[21] Includes 32,897 persons returning in 1906 to their homes in the United States.

Note: Official recording of immigration to the United States began in 1820 after the passage of the Act of March 2, 1819. From 1820 to 1867, figures represent alien passenger arrivals at seaports; from 1868 to 1891 and 1895 to 1897, immigrant alien arrivals; from 1892 to 1894 and 1898 to 2014, immigrant aliens admitted for permanent residence; from 1892 to 1903, aliens entering by cabin class were not counted as immigrants. Land arrivals were not completely enumerated until 1908. For this table, Fiscal Year 1843 covers 9 months ending September 30, 1843; Fiscal Years 1832 and 1850 cover 15 months ending December 31 of the respective years; Fiscal Year 1868 covers 6 months ending June 30, 1868; and Fiscal Year 1976 covers 15 months ending September 30, 1976.

LEGAL IMMIGRATION TO THE UNITED STATES

	Number of Legal Immigrants
2016	1,183,505
2017	1,127,167
2018	1,096,611
2019	1,031,765
2020	TO BE RELEASED
Total	4,439,048

PRESIDENTS, VICE PRESIDENTS, AND SECRETARIES OF STATE

President	Vice President	Secretary of State
1. George Washington, Federalist 1789	John Adams, Federalist 1789	Thomas Jefferson 1789 Edmund Randolph 1794 Timothy Pickering 1795
2. John Adams, Federalist 1797	Thomas Jefferson, Dem.-Rep. 1797	Timothy Pickering 1797 John Marshall 1800
3. Thomas Jefferson, Dem.-Rep.1801	Aaron Burr, Dem.-Rep. 1801 George Clinton, Dem.-Rep. 1805	James Madison 1801
4. James Madison, Dem.-Rep. 1809	George Clinton, Dem.-Rep. 1809 Elbridge Gerry, Dem.-Rep. 1813	Robert Smith 1809 James Monroe 1811
5. James Monroe, Dem.-Rep. 1817	Daniel D. Tompkins, Dem.-Rep. 1817	John Q. Adams 1817
6. John Quincy Adams, Dem.-Rep. 1825	John C. Calhoun, Dem.-Rep. 1825	Henry Clay 1825
7. Andrew Jackson, Democratic 1829	John C. Calhoun, Democratic 1829 Martin Van Buren, Democratic 1833	Martin Van Buren 1829 Edward Livingston 1831 Louis McLane 1833 John Forsyth 1834
8. Martin Van Buren, Democratic 1837	Richard M. Johnson, Democratic 1837	John Forsyth 1837
9. William H. Harrison, Whig 1841	John Tyler, Whig 1841	Daniel Webster 1841

	President	Vice President	Secretary of State
10.	John Tyler, Whig and Democratic 1841	None	Daniel Webster 1841 Hugh S. Legaré 1843 Abel P. Upshur 1843 John C. Calhoun 1844
11.	James K. Polk, Democratic 1845	George M. Dallas, Democratic 1845	James Buchanan 1845
12.	Zachary Taylor, Whig 1849	Millard Fillmore, Whig 1848	John M. Clayton 1849
13.	Millard Fillmore, Whig 1850	None	Daniel Webster 1850 Edward Everett 1852
14.	Franklin Pierce, Democratic 1853	William R. King, Democratic 1853	William L. Marcy 1853
15.	James Buchanan, Democratic 1857	John C. Breckinridge, Democratic 1857	Lewis Cass 1857 Jeremiah S. Black 1860
16.	Abraham Lincoln, Republican 1861	Hannibal Hamlin, Republican 1861 Andrew Johnson, Unionist 1865	William H.Seward 1861
17.	Andrew Johnson, Unionist 1865	None	William H.Seward 1865
18.	Ulysses S. Grant, Republican 1869	Schuyler Colfax, Republican 1869 Henry Wilson, Republican 1873	Elihu B. Washburne 1869 Hamilton Fish 1869
19.	Rutherford B. Hayes, Republican 1877	William A. Wheeler, Republican 1877	William M. Evarts 1877

20.	James A. Garfield, Republican 1881	Chester A. Arthur, Republican 1881	James G. Blaine 1881
21.	Chester A. Arthur, Republican 1881	None	Frederick T. Frelinghuysen 1881
22.	Grover Cleveland, Democratic 1885	Thomas A. Hendricks, Democratic 1885	Thomas F. Bayard 1885
23.	Benjamin Harrison, Republican 1889	Levi P. Morton, Republican 1889	James G. Blaine 1889 John W. Foster 1892
24.	Grover Cleveland, Democratic 1893	Adlai E. Stevenson, Democratic 1893	Walter Q. Gresham 1893 Richard Olney 1895
25.	William McKinley, Republican 1897	Garret A. Hobart, Republican 1897 Theodore Roosevelt, Republican 1901	John Sherman 1897 William R. Day 1898 John Hay 1898
26.	Theodore Roosevelt, Republican 1901	Charles Fairbanks, Republican 1905	John Hay 1901 Elihu Root 1905 Robert Bacon 1909
27.	William H. Taft, Republican 1909	James S. Sherman, Republican 1909	Philander C. Knox 1909
28.	Woodrow Wilson, Democratic 1913	Thomas R. Marshall, Democratic 1913	William J. Bryan 1913 Robert Lansing 1915 Bainbridge Colby 1920
29.	Warren G. Harding, Republican 1921	Calvin Coolidge, Republican 1921	Charles E. Hughes 1921
30.	Calvin Coolidge, Republican 1923	Charles G. Dawes, Republican 1925	Charles E. Hughes 1923 Frank B. Kellogg 1925

President	Vice President	Secretary of State
31. Herbert Hoover, Republican 1929	Charles Curtis, Republican 1929	Henry L. Stimson 1929
32. Franklin D. Roosevelt, Democratic 1933	John Nance Garner, Democratic 1933 Henry A. Wallace, Democratic 1941 Harry S. Truman, Democratic 1945	Cordell Hull 1933 Edward R. Stettinius, Jr. 1944
33. Harry S. Truman, Democratic 1945	Alben W. Barkley, Democratic 1949	Edward R. Stettinius, Jr. 1945 James F. Byrnes 1945 George C. Marshall 1947 Dean G. Acheson 1949
34. Dwight D. Eisenhower, Republican 1953	Richard M. Nixon, Republican 1953	John F. Dulles 1953 Christian A. Herter 1959
35. John F. Kennedy, Democratic 1961	Lyndon B. Johnson, Democratic 1961	Dean Rusk 1961
36. Lyndon B. Johnson, Democratic 1963	Hubert H. Humphrey, Democratic 1965	Dean Rusk 1963
37. Richard M. Nixon, Republican 1969	Spiro T. Agnew, Republican 1969 Gerald R. Ford, Republican 1973	William P. Rogers 1969 Henry Kissinger 1973
38. Gerald R. Ford, Republican 1974	Nelson Rockefeller, Republican 1974	Henry Kissinger 1974
39. James E. Carter, Democratic 1977	Walter Mondale, Democratic 1977	Cyrus Vance 1977 Edmund Muskie 1980

40.	Ronald Reagan, Republican 1981	George H. W. Bush, Republican 1981	Alexander Haig 1981 George Schultz 1982

40.	Ronald Reagan, Republican 1981	George H. W. Bush, Republican 1981	Alexander Haig 1981 George Schultz 1982
41.	George H. W. Bush, Republican 1989	J. Danforth Quayle, Republican 1989	James A. Baker 1989 Lawrence Eagleburger 1992
42.	William J. Clinton, Democratic 1993	Albert Gore, Jr., Democratic 1993	Warren Christopher 1993 Madeleine Albright 1997
43.	George W. Bush, Republican 2001	Richard B. Cheney, Republican 2001	Colin L. Powell 2001 Condoleezza Rice 2005
44.	Barack Obama, Democratic 2009	Joseph R. Biden Jr., Democratic 2009	Hillary Rodham Clinton 2009 John Kerry 2013
45.	Donald J. Trump, Republican 2017	Michael R. Pence, Republican 2017	Rex W. Tillerson 2017 Michael R. Pompeo 2018
46.	Joseph R. Biden Jr., Democrat 2021	Kamala D. Harris, Democrat 2021	Antony J. Blinken

FURTHER READINGS

CHAPTER 15

The most comprehensive treatment of Reconstruction is Eric Foner's *Reconstruction: America's Unfinished Revolution, 1863–1877* (1988). See also Foner's *The Second Founding: How the Civil War and Reconstruction Remade the Constitution* (2020). Good brief histories include Michael W. Fitzgerald's *Splendid Failure: Postwar Reconstruction in the American South* (2007), Alan Guelzo's *Reconstruction: A Concise History* (2018), and Kate Masur's *Until Justice Be Done: America's First Civil Rights Movement* (2021). On Andrew Johnson, see Hans L. Trefousse's *Andrew Johnson: A Biography* (1989) and David D. Stewart's *Impeached: The Trial of Andrew Johnson and the Fight for Lincoln's Legacy* (2009). Robert S. Levine's *The Failed Promise* (2021) analyzes Reconstruction through the relationship between President Andrew Johnson and Frederick Douglass, the most prominent African American leader.

Scholars have been sympathetic to the aims and motives of the Radical Republicans. See, for instance, Herman Belz's *Reconstructing the Union: Theory and Policy during the Civil War* (1969) and Richard Nelson Current's *Those Terrible Carpetbaggers: A Reinterpretation* (1988). A fine biography of one of the leading Radicals is Bruce Levine's *Thaddeus Stevens* (2021). The ideology of the Radicals is explored in Michael Les Benedict's *A Compromise of Principle: Congressional Republicans and Reconstruction, 1863–1869* (1974). On the Black political leaders, see Phillip Dray's *Capitol Men: The Epic Story of Reconstruction through the Lives of the First Black Congressmen* (2008).

The intransigence of southern White attitudes is examined in Michael Perman's *Reunion without Compromise: The South and Reconstruction, 1865–1868* (1973) and Dan T. Carter's *When the War Was Over: The Failure of Self-Reconstruction in the South, 1865–1867* (1985). Allen W. Trelease's *White Terror: The Ku Klux Klan Conspiracy and Southern Reconstruction* (1971) covers the various organizations that practiced vigilante tactics. On the massacre of African Americans, see Charles Lane's *The Day Freedom Died: The Colfax Massacre, the Supreme Court, and the Betrayal of Reconstruction* (2008).

The difficulties former slaves had in adjusting to the new labor system are documented in James L. Roark's *Masters without Slaves: Southern Planters in the Civil War and Reconstruction* (1977). Books on southern politics during Reconstruction include Michael Perman's *The Road to Redemption: Southern Politics, 1869–1879* (1984), Terry L. Seip's *The South Returns to Congress: Men, Economic Measures, and Intersectional Relationships, 1868–1879* (1983), and Mark W. Summers's *Railroads, Reconstruction, and the Gospel of Prosperity: Aid under the Radical Republicans, 1865–1877* (1984).

Numerous works study the freed Blacks' experience in the South. Start with Leon F. Litwack's *Been in the Storm So Long: The Aftermath of Slavery* (1979). The Freedmen's Bureau is explored in William S. McFeely's *Yankee Stepfather: General O. O. Howard and the Freedmen* (1968). The situation of freed slave women is the focus of Jacqueline Jones's *Labor of Love, Labor of Sorrow: Black Women, Work and the Family, from Slavery to the Present* (1985). On the "scalawags," see James Alex Bagget's *The Scalawags: Southern Dissenters in the Civil War and Reconstruction* (2003). For a provocative interpretation of the lasting effects of the Civil War and Reconstruction, see Heather Cox Richardson's *How the South Won the Civil War: Oligarchy, Democracy, and the Continuing Fight for the Soul of America* (2020).

The politics of corruption outside the South is depicted in William S. McFeely's *Grant: A Biography* (1981). The best recent biography of the eighteenth president is Ron Chernow's *Grant* (2017). The political maneuvers of the election of 1876 and the resultant crisis and compromise are explained in Michael Holt's *By One Vote: The Disputed Presidential Election of 1876* (2008).

CHAPTER 16

For masterly syntheses of post–Civil War industrial development, see Walter Licht's *Industrializing America: The Nineteenth Century* (1995) and Maury Klein's *The Genesis of Industrial America, 1870–1920* (2007). On the growth of railroads, see Richard White's *Railroaded: The Transcontinentals and the Making of Modern America* (2011) and Albro Martin's *Railroad Triumphant: The Growth, Rejection, and Rebirth of a Vital American Force* (1992). For the role of Chinese immigrants in the construction of railroads, see Gordon H. Chang's *Ghosts of Gold Mountain: The Epic Story of the Chinese Who Built the*

Transcontinental Railroad (2019). An excellent biography of the colossal inventor Thomas Edison is Edmund Morris's *Edison* (2019).

On entrepreneurship in the iron and steel sector, see Thomas J. Misa's *A Nation of Steel: The Making of Modern America, 1865–1925* (1995). The best biographies of the leading business tycoons are Ron Chernow's *Titan: The Life of John D. Rockefeller, Sr.* (1998), David Nasaw's *Andrew Carnegie* (2006), and Jean Strouse's *Morgan: American Financier* (1999). Nathan Rosenberg's *Technology and American Economic Growth* (1972) documents the growth of invention during the period.

For an overview of the struggle of workers to organize unions, see Philip Bray's *There Is Power in a Union: The Epic Story of Labor in America* (2010). On the 1877 railroad strike, see David O. Stowell's *Streets, Railroad, and the Great Strike of 1877* (1999). For the role of women in the changing workplace, see Alice Kessler-Harris's *Out to Work: A History of Wage-Earning Women in the United States* (1982) and Susan E. Kennedy's *If All We Did Was to Weep at Home: A History of White Working-Class Women in America* (1979). On Mother Jones, see Elliott J. Gorn's *Mother Jones: The Most Dangerous Woman in America* (2001). To trace the rise of socialism among organized workers, see Nick Salvatore's *Eugene V. Debs: Citizen and Socialist* (2007) and Patrick Renshaw's *The Wobblies: The Story of the IWW* (1999). The key strikes are discussed in James Green's *Death in the Haymarket: A Story of Chicago, the First Labor Movement and the Bombing That Divided Gilded Age America* (2006), W. F. Burns's *The Pullman Boycott: A Complete History of the Railroad Strike* (2015), and Les Standiford's *Meet You in Hell: Andrew Carnegie, Henry K. Frick and the Bitter Partnership that Transformed America* (2005).

CHAPTER 17

On southern efforts to rationalize their defeat in the Civil War, see Edward H. Bonekemper's *The Myth of the Lost Cause: Why the South Fought the Civil War and the North Won* (2015). The classic study of the emergence of the New South remains C. Vann Woodward's *Origins of the New South, 1877–1913* (1951). A more recent treatment of southern society after the end of Reconstruction is Edward L. Ayers's *Southern Crossing: A History of the American South, 1877–1906* (1995). A thorough survey of industrialization in the South is James C. Cobb's *Industrialization and Southern Society, 1877–1984* (1984).

On race relations, see Howard N. Rabinowitz's *Race Relations in the Urban South, 1865–1890* (1978). Leon F. Litwack's *Trouble in Mind: Black*

Southerners in the Age of Jim Crow (1998) treats the rise of legal segregation, while Michael Perman's *Struggle for Mastery: Disfranchisement in the South, 1888–1908* (2001) surveys efforts to keep African Americans from voting. An award-winning study of White women and the race issue is Glenda Elizabeth Gilmore's *Gender and Jim Crow: Women and the Politics of White Supremacy in North Carolina, 1896–1920* (1996). On W. E. B. Du Bois, see David Levering Lewis's *W. E. B. Du Bois: Biography of a Race, 1868–1919* (1993). On Booker T. Washington, see Robert J. Norrell's *Up from History: The Life of Booker T. Washington* (2009).

For stimulating reinterpretations of the frontier and the development of the West, see William Cronon's *Nature's Metropolis: Chicago and the Great West* (1991), Patricia Nelson Limerick's *The Legacy of Conquest: The Unbroken Past of the American West* (1987), Richard White's *"It's Your Misfortune and None of My Own": A New History of the American West* (1991), and Walter Nugent's *Into the West: The Story of Its People* (1999). The most famous western outlaw, William Henry McCarty ("Billy the Kid"), is profiled in Ron Hansen's *The Kid* (2016). The cattle industry is the subject of Christopher Knowlton's *Cattle Kingdom: The Hidden History of the Cowboy West* (2017).

The role of African Americans in western settlement is the focus of William Loren Katz's *The Black West: A Documentary and Pictorial History of the African American Role in the Westward Expansion of the United States*, rev. ed. (2005), and Nell Irvin Painter's *Exodusters: Black Migration to Kansas after Reconstruction* (1977).

The role of women in the West is the focus of Winifred Gallagher's *New Women in the Old West* (2021), Cathy Luchetti and Carol Olwell's *Women of the West* (2017), and Glenda Riley's *Women and Nature: Saving the Wild West* (1999).

Excellent accounts of the conflicts between Native Americans and Whites are Peter Cozzens's *The Earth Is Weeping: The Epic Story of the Indian Wars* (2016) and Robert M. Utley's *The Indian Frontier of the American West, 1846–1890* (1984). For the Sand Creek massacre, see Ari Kellman's *A Misplaced Massacre: Struggling over the Memory of Sand Creek* (2013). On the Battle of the Little Bighorn, see Nathaniel Philbrick's *The Last Stand: Custer, Sitting Bull, and the Battle of the Little Bighorn* (2010). On Crazy Horse, see Thomas Powers's *The Killing of Crazy Horse* (2010). The massacre at Wounded Knee is the focus of David Treuer's *The Heartbeat of Wounded Knee: Native America from 1890 to the Present* (2019). On General Custer, see T. J. Stiles's *Custer's Trials: A Life on the Frontier of a New America* (2015) and Jerome A. Greene's *American Carnage: Wounded Knee, 1890* (2014).

For a presentation of the Native American side of the story, see Peter Nabokov's *Native American Testimony: A Chronicle of Indian-White Relations from Prophecy to the Present, 1492–2000*, rev. ed. (1999). On the demise of the buffalo herds, see Andrew C. Isenberg's *The Destruction of the Bison: An Environmental History, 1750–1920* (2000).

For comprehensive overviews of the Hispanic influence in U.S. history, see Felipe Fernández-Armesto's *Our America: A Hispanic History of the United States* (2014), Carrie Gibson's *El Norte: The Epic and Forgotten Story of Hispanic North America* (2020), and Paul Ortiz's *An African American and Latinx History of the United States* (2018).

CHAPTER 18

For a survey of urbanization, see David R. Goldfield's *Urban America: A History* (1989). Gunther Barth discusses the emergence of a new post–Civil War urban culture in *City People: The Rise of Modern City Culture in Nineteenth-Century America* (1980). John Bodnar offers a synthesis of the urban immigrant experience in *The Transplanted: A History of Immigrants in Urban America* (1985). See also Roger Daniels's *Guarding the Golden Door: American Immigration Policy and Immigrants since 1882* (2004). Walter Nugent's *Crossings: The Great Transatlantic Migrations, 1870–1914* (1992) provides a wealth of demographic information and insight. Efforts to stop Chinese immigration are detailed in Erika Lee's *At America's Gates: Chinese Immigration during the Exclusion Era* (2003) and *The Making of Asian America: A History* (2015).

On urban environments and sanitary reforms, see Martin V. Melosi's *The Sanitary City: Urban Infrastructure in America from Colonial Times to the Present* (2000), Joel A. Tarr's *The Search for the Ultimate Sink: Urban Pollution in Historical Perspective* (1996), and Suellen Hoy's *Chasing Dirt: The American Pursuit of Cleanliness* (1995).

For the growth of urban leisure and sports, see Roy Rosenzweig's *Eight Hours for What We Will: Workers and Leisure in an Industrial City, 1870–1920* (1983) and Steven A. Riess's *City Games: The Evolution of American Urban Society and the Rise of Sports* (1989). Saloon culture is examined in Madelon Powers's *Faces along the Bar: Lore and Order in the Workingman's Saloon, 1870–1920* (1998).

On the impact of Darwin's theory of evolution, see Barry Werth's *Banquet at Delmonico's: Great Minds, the Gilded Age, and the Triumph of Evolution in America* (2009). On the rise of realism in thought and the arts during the second half of the nineteenth century, see David E. Shi's *Facing Facts: Realism in American Thought and Culture, 1850–1920* (1995). The rise of pragmatism is featured in Louis Menand's *The Metaphysical Club: A Story of Ideas in America* (2001).

Helpful overviews of the Gilded Age are Alex Axelrod's *The Gilded Age, 1876–1912: Overture to the American Century* (2017), Sean Cashman's *America in the Gilded Age: From the Death of Lincoln to the Rise of Theodore Roosevelt* (1984), and Richard White's *The Republic for Which It Stands: The U.S. during Reconstruction and the Gilded Age* (2017).

For a stimulating overview of the political, social, and economic trends during the Gilded Age, see Jack Beatty's *Age of Betrayal: The Triumph of Money in America, 1865–1900* (2007). On the development of city rings and bosses, see Kenneth D. Ackerman's *Boss Tweed: The Rise and Fall of the Corrupt Pol Who Conceived the Soul of Modern New York* (2005). Excellent presidential biographies include Hans L. Trefousse's *Rutherford B. Hayes* (2002), Scott S. Greenberger's *The Unexpected President: The Life and Times of Chester A. Arthur* (2017), Henry F. Graff's *Grover Cleveland* (2002), and Robert W. Merry's *President McKinley: Architect of the American Century* (2003). On the political culture of the Gilded Age, see Charles Calhoun's *Minority Victory: Gilded Age Politics and the Front Porch Campaign of 1888* (2008).

Balanced accounts of Populism can be found in Charles Postel's *The Populist Vision* (2007) and Michael McGerr's *A Fierce Discontent: The Rise and Fall of the Progressive Movement, 1870–1920* (2005). The election of 1896 is the focus of R. Hal Williams's *Realigning America: McKinley, Bryan, and the Remarkable Election of 1896* (2010). On the role of religion in the agrarian protest movements, see Joe Creech's *Righteous Indignation: Religion and the Populist Revolution* (2006). The best biography of William Jennings Bryan is Michael Kazin's *A Godly Hero: The Life of William Jennings Bryan* (2006).

CHAPTER 19

Excellent surveys of the diplomacy of the era include Charles S. Campbell's *The Transformation of American Foreign Relations, 1865–1900* (1976) and Daniel Immerwahr's *How to Hide an Empire: A History of the Greater United States* (2019). For background on the events of the 1890s, see David Healy's *U.S. Expansionism: The Imperialist Urge in the 1890s* (1970). The dispute over American policy in Hawaii is covered in Thomas J. Osborne's *"Empire Can Wait": American Opposition to Hawaiian Annexation, 1893–1898* (1981).

Ivan Musicant's *Empire by Default: The Spanish-American War and the Dawn of the American Century* (1998) is the most comprehensive volume on the conflict. A colorful treatment of the powerful men promoting war is Evan Thomas's *The War Lovers: Roosevelt, Lodge, Mahan, and the Rush to*

Empire, 1898 (2010). On the war itself, see Clay Risen's *The Crowded Hour: Theodore Roosevelt, the Rough Riders, and the Dawn of a New Century* (2019). For the war's aftermath in the Philippines, see Stuart Creighton Miller's *"Benevolent Assimilation": The American Conquest of the Philippines, 1899–1903* (1982). On the Philippine-American War, see David J. Silbey's *A War of Frontier and Empire: The Philippine-American War, 1899–1902* (2007).

A good introduction to American interest in China is Michael H. Hunt's *The Making of a Special Relationship: The United States and China to 1914* (1983). John Taliaferro's *All the Great Prizes: The Life of John Hay* (2013) examines the role of this key secretary of state in forming policy.

For U.S. policy in the Caribbean and Central America, see Walter LaFeber's *Inevitable Revolutions: The United States in Central America*, 2nd ed. (1993). Ada Farrer examines the relationship between Cuba and the United States in *Cuba: An American History* (2021). David McCullough's *The Path between the Seas: The Creation of the Panama Canal, 1870–1914* (1977) presents an admiring account of how the United States secured the Panama Canal. A more sober assessment is Julie Greene's *The Canal Builders: Making America's Empire at the Panama Canal* (2009). For a detailed treatment of Theodore Roosevelt's diplomacy as president, see James Bradley's *The Imperial Cruise: A Secret History of Empire and War* (2009).

CHAPTER 20

Splendid analyses of progressivism can be found in John Whiteclay Chambers II's *The Tyranny of Change: America in the Progressive Era, 1890–1920*, rev. ed. (2000), Steven J. Diner's *A Very Different Age: Americans of the Progressive Era* (1997), Maureen A. Flanagan's *America Reformed: Progressives and Progressivisms, 1890–1920* (2006), Michael McGerr's *A Fierce Discontent: The Rise and Fall of the Progressive Movement in America* (2003), and David Traxel's *Crusader Nation: The United States in Peace and the Great War, 1898–1920* (2006). On Ida Tarbell and the muckrakers, see Steve Weinberg's *Taking on the Trust: The Epic Battle of Ida Tarbell and John D. Rockefeller* (2008).

The evolution of government policy toward business is examined in Martin J. Sklar's *The Corporate Reconstruction of American Capitalism, 1890–1916: The Market, the Law, and Politics* (1988). Mina Carson's *Settlement Folk: Social Thought and the American Settlement Movement, 1885–1930* (1990) examines the social problems in the cities. Robert Kanigel's *The One Best Way: Frederick Winslow Taylor and the Enigma of Efficiency* (1997) highlights the role of efficiency and expertise in the Progressive Era.

An excellent study of the role of women in progressivism's emphasis on social justice is Kathryn Kish Sklar's *Florence Kelley and the Nation's Work: The Rise of Women's Political Culture, 1830–1900* (1995). On the tragic fire at the Triangle Shirtwaist Company, see David Von Drehle's *Triangle: The Fire That Changed America* (2003). The best study of the settlement house movement is Jean Bethke Elshtain's *Jane Addams and the Dream of American Democracy: A Life* (2002).

On Theodore Roosevelt and the conservation movement, see Douglas Brinkley's *The Wilderness Warrior: Theodore Roosevelt and the Crusade for America* (2009). For insights into Republicans and Progressivism, see Michael Wolraich's *Unreasonable Men: Theodore Roosevelt and the Republican Rebels Who Created Progressive Politics* (2014). The immensely important election of 1912 is covered in James Chace's *1912: Wilson, Roosevelt, Taft, and Debs—The Election That Changed the Country* (2004). Excellent biographies include Kathleen Dalton's *Theodore Roosevelt: A Strenuous Life* (2002) and Patricia O'Toole's *The Moralist: Woodrow Wilson and the World He Made* (2019). On the tensions with Mexico during Wilson's presidency, see Jeff Guinn's *War on the Border: Villa, Pershing, the Texas Rangers, and an American Invasion* (2021).

The racial blind spot of Progressivism is in the focus of David W. Southern's *The Progressive Era and Race: Reform and Reaction, 1900–1917* (2006). On anti-Mexican prejudice and violence in Texas, see Monica Martinez's *The Injustice Never Leaves You: Anti-Mexican Violence in Texas* (2018).

CHAPTER 21

A lucid overview of international events in the early twentieth century is Robert H. Ferrell's *Woodrow Wilson and World War I, 1917–1921* (1985). For a vivid account of U.S. intervention in Mexico, see Frederick Katz's *The Life and Times of Pancho Villa* (1999). On Wilson's stance toward the European war, see Robert W. Tucker's *Woodrow Wilson and the Great War: Reconsidering America's Neutrality, 1914–1917* (2007). An excellent biography is John Milton Cooper, Jr.'s *Woodrow Wilson: A Biography* (2010).

For the European experience in the Great War, see Adam Hochschild's *To End All Wars: A Story of Loyalty and Rebellion, 1914–1918* (2011), Margaret MacMillan's *The War That Ended Peace: The Road to 1914* (2013), and William Philpott's *Attrition: Fighting the First World War* (2015). For the efforts to keep the United States out of the Great War, see Michael Kazin's *War against War: The American Fight for Peace, 1914–1918* (2017). Edward

M. Coffman's *The War to End All Wars: The American Military Experience in World War I* (1968) is a detailed presentation of America's military involvement. See also Peter Hart's *The Great War: A Combat History of World War I* (2015) and Gary Mead's *The Doughboys: America and the First World War* (2000).

For a survey of the impact of the war on the home front, see Meirion Harries and Susie Harries's *The Last Days of Innocence: America at War, 1917–1918* (1997). Maurine Weiner Greenwald's *Women, War, and Work: The Impact of World War I on Women Workers in the United States* (1980) discusses the role of women in the war effort. John Maxwell Hamilton's *Manipulating the Masses: Woodrow Wilson and the Birth of American Propaganda* (2020) reveals how Wilson manipulated the information about the war shared with the public. Richard Polenberg's *Fighting Faiths: The Abrams Case, the Supreme Court, and Free Speech* (1987) examines the prosecution of a case under the 1918 Sedition Act. See also Ernest Freeberg's *Democracy's Prisoner: Eugene V. Debs, the Great War, and the Right to Dissent* (2009).

How American diplomacy fared in the making of peace has received considerable attention. Thomas J. Knock connects domestic affairs and foreign relations in his explanation of Wilson's peacemaking in *To End All Wars: Woodrow Wilson and the Quest for a New World Order* (1992). See also John Milton Cooper, Jr.'s *Breaking the Heart of the World: Woodrow Wilson and the Fight for the League of Nations* (2002), Charles L. Mee's *1919 Versailles: The End of the War to End All Wars* (2014), G. J. Meyers's *The World Remade: America in World War I* (2018), and Adam Tooze's *The Deluge: The Great War, America, and the Remaking of the Global Order* (2014).

The problems of the immediate postwar years are chronicled by several historians. The best overview is Ann Hagedorn's *Savage Peace: Hope and Fear in America, 1919* (2007). On the Spanish flu, see John M. Barry's *The Great Influenza: The Epic Story of the Deadliest Plague in History* (2004). Labor tensions are examined in David E. Brody's *Labor in Crisis: The Steel Strike of 1919* (1965) and Francis Russell's *A City in Terror: Calvin Coolidge and the 1919 Boston Police Strike* (1975). On racial strife, see Jan Voogd's *Race Riots and Resistance: The Red Summer of 1919* (2008). The fear of Communists is analyzed in Robert K. Murray's *Red Scare: A Study in National Hysteria, 1919–1920* (1955).

On the ratification of the Nineteenth Amendment granting women the vote, see Elaine Weiss's *The Woman's Hour: The Great Fight to Win the Vote* (2018).

CHAPTER 22

The best introduction to the culture of the 1920s remains Roderick Nash's *The Nervous Generation: American Thought, 1917–1930* (1990). See also Lynn Dumenil's *The Modern Temper: American Culture and Society in the 1920s* (1995).

The impact of woman suffrage is treated in Kristi Anderson's *After Suffrage: Women in Partisan and Electoral Politics before the New Deal* (1996). The best study of the birth control movement is Ellen Chesler's *Woman of Valor: Margaret Sanger and the Birth Control Movement in America* (1992).

On the African American migration from the South, see James N. Gregory's *The Southern Diaspora: How the Great Migrations of Black and White Southerners Transformed America* (2005). See Charles Flint Kellogg's *NAACP: A History of the National Association for the Advancement of Colored People* (1967) for his analysis of the pioneering court cases against racial discrimination. Nathan Irvin Huggins's *Harlem Renaissance* (1971) assesses the cultural impact of the Great Migration on New York City.

On the radio craze, see Alfred Balk's *The Rise of Radio, from Marconi through the Golden Age: Charles Lindbergh's Daring and Immortal 1927 Transatlantic Crossing* (2005). For the automobile culture, see Richard Snow's *I Invented the Modern Age: The Rise of Henry Ford* (2014). On the emergence of airplanes, see Dan Hampton's *The Flight: Charles Lindbergh's Daring and Immortal 1927 Transatlantic Crossing* (2017), Mike Campbell's *Amelia Earhart: The Truth at Last; Propaganda versus Fact in the Disappearance of America's First Lady of Flight* (2016), and Keith O'Brien's *Fly Girls: How Five Daring Women Defied All Odds and Made Aviation History* (2018).

The emergence of jazz is documented in Burton W. Peretti's *The Creation of Jazz: Music, Race, and Culture in Urban America* (1992). Scientific breakthroughs are analyzed in Manjit Kumar's *Quantum: Einstein, Bohr, and the Great Debate about the Nature of Reality* (2010). The best overviews of cultural modernism in Europe are Ann L. Ardis's *Modernism and Cultural Conflict, 1880–1922* (2008) and Peter Gay's *Modernism: The Lure of Heresy from Baudelaire to Beckett and Beyond* (2009). Stanley Coben's *Rebellion against Victorianism: The Impetus for Cultural Change in 1920s America* (1991) surveys the appeal of modernism among writers, artists, and intellectuals.

On President Harding, see Charles L. Mee's *The Ohio Gang: The World of Warren G. Harding* (2014). See Nan Britton's account of her affair with Harding, *The President's Daughter* (2008). On President Coolidge, see Robert Sobel's *Coolidge: An American Enigma* (2012). On President Hoover, see Kenneth Whyte's *Hoover: An Extraordinary Life in Extraordinary Times* (2017).

John Higham's *Strangers in the Land: Patterns of American Nativism, 1860–1925*, 2nd ed. (2002), details the story of immigration restriction. The controversial Sacco and Vanzetti case is the focus of Moshik Temkin's *The Sacco-Vanzetti Affair: America on Trial* (2009). For analysis of the revival of Klan activity, see Linda Gordon's *The Second Coming of the KKK: The Ku Klux Klan of the 1920s and the American Political Tradition* (2017) and Thomas R. Pegram's *One Hundred Percent American: The Rebirth and Decline of the Ku Klux Klan in the 1920s* (2011). The best analysis of the Scopes trial is Edward J. Larson's *Summer for the Gods: The Scopes Trial and America's Continuing Debate over Science and Religion* (1997). On Prohibition, see Lisa McGirr's *The War on Alcohol: Prohibition and the Rise of the American State* (2015).

On the stock market crash in 1929, see Maury Klein's *Rainbow's End: The Crash of 1929* (2000). For an overview of the depressed global economy, see Charles R. Morris's *A Rabble of Dead Money: The Great Crash and the Global Depression* (2017). For the human impact of the Great Depression, see Murray Rothbard's *America's Great Depression* (2019). On the removal of the Bonus Army, see Paul Dickson and Thomas B. Allen's *The Bonus Army: An American Epic* (2004).

CHAPTER 23

Two excellent overviews of the New Deal are Ira Katznelson's *Fear Itself: The New Deal and the Origins of Our Time* (2013) and David M. Kennedy's *Freedom from Fear: The American People in Depression and War, 1929–1945* (1999). A lively biography of Franklin D. Roosevelt as political figure is Robert Dallek's *Franklin D. Roosevelt: A Political Life* (2018). A fine biography of the First Lady is David Michaelis's *Eleanor: A Life* (2020).

The busy first year of the New Deal is ably detailed in Anthony J. Badger's *FDR: The First Hundred Days* (2008). Perhaps the most successful of the early New Deal programs is the focus of Neil M. Maher's *Nature's New Deal: The Civilian Conservation Corps and the Roots of the American Environmental Movement* (2008). For the crucial role played by Frances Perkins in creating and managing New Deal programs, see Kirstin Downey's *The Woman behind the New Deal: The Life of Frances Perkins, FDR's Secretary of Labor and His Moral Conscience* (2009). On the political opponents of the New Deal, see Alan Brinkley's *Voices of Protest: Huey Long, Father Coughlin, and the Great Depression* (1982). Roosevelt's battle with the Supreme Court is detailed in Jeff Shesol's *Supreme Power: Franklin Roosevelt vs. The Supreme Court* (2010).

The effects of the New Deal on the economy are detailed in Elliot A. Rosen's *Roosevelt, the Great Depression, and the Economics of Recovery* (2005).

Critical assessments of Roosevelt and the New Deal are Burton Folsom's *New Deal or Raw Deal?: How FDR's Economic Legacy Has Damaged America* (2009) and Amity Schlaes's *The Forgotten Man: A New History of the Great Depression* (2008). James N. Gregory's *American Exodus: The Dust Bowl Migration and Okie Culture in California* (1989) describes the migratory movement. The dramatic Scottsboro court case is the focus of James Goodman's *Stories of Scottsboro* (1995). On the environmental and human causes of the Dust Bowl, see Donald Worster, *Dust Bowl: The Southern Plains in the 1930s* (1979). On cultural life during the 1930s, see Morris Dickstein's *Dancing in the Dark: A Cultural History of the Great Depression* (2009).

Robert Dallek's *Franklin D. Roosevelt and American Foreign Policy, 1932–1945* (1979) provides a judicious assessment of Roosevelt's foreign policy initiatives during the 1930s. On Roosevelt's war of words with isolationists, see Lynne Olsen's *Those Angry Days: Roosevelt, Lindbergh, and America's Fight over World War II, 1939–1942* (2013) and Nicholas Wapshott's *The Sphinx: Franklin Roosevelt, the Isolationists, and the Road to World War II* (2015). The British efforts to get America in the war is the focus of Henry Hemming's *Our Man in New York: The British Plot to Bring America into the Second World War* (2015). For the Japanese perspective on the outbreak of war, see Eri Hotta's *Japan 1941: Countdown to Infamy* (2014). On the surprise attack on Pearl Harbor, see Gordon W. Prange's *Pearl Harbor: The Verdict of History* (1986).

CHAPTER 24

For a sweeping survey of the Second World War, consult Anthony Roberts's *The Storm of War: A New History of the Second World War* (2011). The events leading up to the war in Europe are outlined in James Holland's *The Rise of Germany, 1939–1941* (2015). A detailed treatment of U.S. involvement is Rick Atkinson's multivolume Pulitzer prize–winning series, *An Army at Dawn: The War in North Africa, 1942–1943* (2007), *The Day of Battle: The War in Sicily and Italy, 1943–1944* (2008), and *The Guns at Last Light: The War in Western Europe, 1944–1945* (2013). Roosevelt's wartime leadership is analyzed in Eric Larrabee's *Commander in Chief: Franklin Delano Roosevelt, His Lieutenants, and Their War* (1987).

Books on specific European campaigns include Anthony Beevor's *D-Day: The Battle for Normandy* (2010), Jonathan Dimbleby's *The Battle of the Atlantic:*

How the Allies Won the War (2016), Jonathan Dimbleby's *Barbarossa: How Hitler Lost the War* (2021), and Peter Caddick-Adams's *Snow and Steel: The Battle of the Bulge* (2017). On the Allied commander, see Carlo D'Este's *Eisenhower: A Soldier's Life* (2002). Richard Overy assesses the controversial role of air power in *The Bombing War: Europe, 1939–1945* (2013).

For the war in the Far East, see John Costello's *The Pacific War, 1941–1945* (1981), Ronald H. Spector's *Eagle against the Sun: The American War with Japan* (1985), John W. Dower's award-winning *War without Mercy: Race and Power in the Pacific War* (1986), and Dan van der Vat's *The Pacific Campaign: The U.S.-Japanese Naval War, 1941–1945* (1991).

An excellent overview of the war's effects on the home front is Michael C. C. Adams's *The Best War Ever: America and World War II* (1994). On the transformation to the wartime economy, see Arthur Herman's *Freedom's Forge: How American Business Produced Victory in World War II* (2012) and Maury Klein's *A Call to Arms: Mobilizing America for World War II* (2013). Susan M. Hartmann's *The Home Front and Beyond: American Women in the 1940s* (1982) treats the new working environment for women. Kenneth D. Rose tells the story of problems on the home front in *Myth and the Greatest Generation: A Social History of Americans in World War II* (2008). Neil A. Wynn looks at the participation of Blacks in *The Afro-American and the Second World War* (1976). The story of the oppression of Japanese Americans is told in Greg Robinson's *A Tragedy for Democracy: Japanese Confinement in North America* (2009). The role of Japanese Americans in the U.S. armed forces is the focus of Daniel James Brown's *Facing the Mountain: A True Story of Japanese American Heroes* (2021).

On the development of the atomic bomb, see Jim Baggott's *The First War of Physics: The Secret History of the Atomic Bomb* (2010). The devastation caused by the atomic bomb is the focus of Paul Ham's *Hiroshima Nagasaki: The Real Story of the Atomic Bombings* (2015) and Susan Southard's *Nagasaki: Life after Nuclear War* (2015). For the controversy over America's policies toward the Holocaust, see Richard Breitman and Alan J. Lichtman's *FDR and the Jews* (2013).

A detailed introduction to U.S. diplomacy during the conflict can be found in Gaddis Smith's *American Diplomacy during the Second World War, 1941–1945* (1985). To understand the role that Roosevelt played in policy making, consult Warren F. Kimball's *The Juggler: Franklin Roosevelt as Wartime Statesman* (1991). The most important wartime summit meeting is assessed in S. M. Plokhy's *Yalta: The Price of Peace* (2010). The issues and events that led to the deployment of atomic weapons are addressed in Martin J. Sherwin's *A World Destroyed: The Atomic Bomb and the Grand Alliance*

(1975). See also Michael Dobbs's *Six Months in 1945: FDR, Stalin, Churchill, and Truman—From World War to Cold War* (2013).

CHAPTER 25

The Cold War remains a hotly debated topic. The traditional interpretation is best reflected in John Lewis Gaddis's *The Cold War: A New History* (2005). Both superpowers, Gaddis argues, were responsible for causing the Cold War, but the Soviet Union was more culpable. The revisionist perspective is represented by Gar Alperovitz's *Atomic Diplomacy: Hiroshima and Potsdam: The Use of the Atomic Bomb and the American Confrontation with Soviet Power*, 2nd ed. (1994). Also see H. W. Brands's *The Devil We Knew: Americans and the Cold War* (1993), Melvyn P. Leffler's *For the Soul of Mankind: The United States, the Soviet Union, and the Cold War* (2007), Ralph Levering's *The Cold War: A Post-Cold War History* (2016), and Odd Arne Westad's *The Cold War: A World History* (2017). On the architect of the containment strategy, see John L. Gaddis's *George F. Kennan: An American Life* (2011). For the Marshall Plan, see Benn Steil's *The Marshall Plan: Dawn of the Cold War* (2018).

Frank Constigliola assesses Franklin Roosevelt's role in the start of the Cold War in *Roosevelt's Lost Alliances: How Personal Politics Helped Start the Cold War* (2013). Arnold A. Offner indicts Truman for clumsy statesmanship in *Another Such Victory: President Truman and the Cold War, 1945–1953* (2002). For a positive assessment of Truman's leadership, see Robert Dallek's *The Lost Peace: Leadership in a Time of Horror and Hope, 1945–1953* (2010). On the Berlin blockade and airlift, see Giles Milton's *Checkmate in Berlin: The Cold War Showdown That Shaped the Modern World* (2021).

The domestic policies of Truman's Fair Deal are treated in William C. Berman's *The Politics of Civil Rights in the Truman Administration* (1970), Richard M. Dalfiume's *Desegregation of the U.S. Armed Forces: Fighting on Two Fronts, 1939–1953* (1969), and Maeva Marcus's *Truman and the Steel Seizure Case: The Limits of Presidential Power* (1977). The most comprehensive biography of Truman is David McCullough's *Truman* (1992).

For an introduction to the tensions in Asia, see Akira Iriye's *The Cold War in Asia: A Historical Introduction* (1974). For the Korean conflict, see Callum A. MacDonald's *Korea: The War before Vietnam* (1986) and Max Hastings's *The Korean War* (1987).

The anti-Communist crusade is surveyed in Larry Tye's *Demagogue: The Life and Long Shadow of Senator Joe McCarthy* (2020). For a well-documented account of how the Cold War was sustained by superpatriotism, intolerance, and suspicion, see Stephen J. Whitfield's *The Culture of the Cold War*, 2nd ed. (1996).

CHAPTER 26

Two excellent overviews of social and cultural trends in the postwar era are William H. Chafe's *The Unfinished Journey: America since World War II*, 6th ed. (2006), and William Hitchcock's *The Age of Eisenhower: American and the World in the 1950s* (2018). For insights into the cultural life of the 1950s, see David Halberstam's *The Fifties* (1993).

The baby boom generation and its impact are vividly described in Paul C. Light's *Baby Boomers* (1988). The emergence of the television industry is discussed in Erik Barnouw's *Tube of Plenty: The Evolution of American Television*, 2nd rev. ed. (1990).

On the process of suburban development, see Kenneth T. Jackson's *Crabgrass Frontier: The Suburbanization of the United States* (1985). Equally good is Tom Martinson's *American Dreamscape: The Pursuit of Happiness in Postwar Suburbia* (2000).

The middle-class ideal of family life in the 1950s is examined in Elaine Tyler May's *Homeward Bound: American Families in the Cold War Era*, rev. ed. (2008). Thorough accounts of women's issues are found in Wini Breines's *Young, White, and Miserable: Growing Up Female in the Fifties* (1992). For an overview of the resurgence of religion in the 1950s, see George M. Marsden's *Religion and American Culture: A Brief History*, 2nd ed. (2000). On the crusade to identify and fire homosexuals working for the federal government, see Eric Cervini's *The Deviant's War: The Homosexual vs. the United States of America* (2020).

The origins of rock and roll music are surveyed in Carl Belz's *The Story of Rock*, 2nd ed. (1972). The colorful Beats are brought to life in Steven Watson's *The Birth of the Beat Generation: Visionaries, Rebels, and Hipsters, 1944–1960* (1995) and Dennis McNally's *Desolate Angel: Jack Kerouac, the Beat Generation, and America* (2003).

Scholarship on the Eisenhower years is extensive. Balanced treatments include Jim Newton's *Eisenhower: The White House Years* (2012) and Jean Edward Smith's *Eisenhower: In War and Peace* (2012). For Eisenhower's foreign policies, see Evan Thomas's *Ike's Bluff: President Eisenhower's Secret Battle to Save the World* (2012).

The best overview of American foreign policy since 1945 is Stephen E. Ambrose and Douglas G. Brinkley's *Rise to Globalism: American Foreign*

Policy since 1938, 9th ed. (2011). For the buildup of U.S. involvement in Indochina, consult Fredrik Logevall's *Embers of War: The Fall of an Empire and the Making of America's Vietnam* (2012). The Cold War strategy of the Eisenhower administration is the focus of Chris Tudda's *The Truth Is Our Weapon: The Rhetorical Diplomacy of Dwight D. Eisenhower and John Foster Dulles* (2006). To learn about the CIA's secret activities in Iran, see Ervand Abrahamian's *The Coup: 1953, the CIA, and the Roots of Modern U.S.-Iranian Relations* (2013). On the Suez crisis, see Alex von Tunzelmann's *Blood and Sand: Suez, Hungary, and the Crisis that Shook the World* (2017).

The impact of the Supreme Court during the 1950s is the focus of Archibald Cox's *The Warren Court: Constitutional Decision as an Instrument of Reform* (1968). A masterly study of the important Warren Court decision on school desegregation is James T. Patterson's *Brown v. Board of Education: A Civil Rights Milestone and Its Troubled Legacy* (2001).

For the story of the early years of the civil rights movement, see Taylor Branch's *Parting the Waters: America in the King Years, 1954–1963* (1988), Robert Weisbrot's *Freedom Bound: A History of America's Civil Rights Movement* (1990), and David A. Nicholas's *A Matter of Justice: Eisenhower and the Beginning of the Civil Rights Revolution* (2007). On Rosa Parks, see Jeanne Theoharis's *The Rebellious Life of Mrs. Rosa Parks* (2013).

Chapter 27

A superb analysis of John Kennedy's life is Thomas C. Reeves's *A Question of Character: A Life of John F. Kennedy* (1991). The 1960 campaign is detailed in Gary A. Donaldson's *The First Modern Campaign: Kennedy, Nixon, and the Election of 1960* (2007). The best study of the Kennedy administration's domestic policies is Irving Bernstein's *Promises Kept: John F. Kennedy's New Frontier* (1991). See also Robert Dallek's *Camelot's Court: Inside the Kennedy White House* (2013), Fredrik Logevall's *JFK: Coming of Age in the American Century, 1917–1956* (2020), and Ira Stoll's *JFK, Conservative* (2013). On Kennedy's handling of civil rights, see Nick Bryant's *The Bystander: John F. Kennedy and the Struggle for Black Equality* (2006). On the space program, see Jeff Shesol's *Mercury Rising: John Glenn, John Kennedy, and the New Battleground of the Cold War* (2021). For details on the still swirling conspiracy theories about the assassination, see David W. Belin's *Final Disclosure: The Full Truth about the Assassination of President Kennedy* (1988).

On Barry Goldwater and the rise of modern conservatism, see Rick Perlstein's *Before the Storm: Barry Goldwater and the Unmaking of the*

American Consensus (2009). On LBJ, see the magisterial multivolume biography by Robert Caro titled *The Years of Lyndon Johnson* (1990–2013). Also helpful is Randall B. Woods's *Prisoners of Hope: Lyndon B. Johnson, the Great Society, and the Limits of Liberalism* (2016). On the Johnson administration, see Vaughn Davis Bornet's *The Presidency of Lyndon B. Johnson* (1984). For an insider's perspective, see Joseph A. Califano's *The Triumph and Tragedy of Lyndon Johnson* (2015). For the story of Johnson's White House, see Joshua Zeitz's *Building the Great Society: Inside Lyndon Johnson's White House* (2018). Also insightful is Randall B. Woods's *Prisoners of Hope: Lyndon B. Johnson, the Great Society, and the Limits of Liberalism* (2016).

Among the works that interpret Johnson's social policies during the 1960s, John E. Schwarz's *America's Hidden Success: A Reassessment of Twenty Years of Public Policy* (1983) offers a glowing endorsement of Democratic programs. For a contrasting perspective, see Charles Murray's *Losing Ground: American Social Policy, 1950–1980* (1994). Also see Martha J. Bailey and Sheldon Danzinger's *Legacies of the War on Poverty* (2015). The controversy spawned by the Kerner Commission report is the focus of Steven Gillom's *Separate and Unequal: The Kerner Commission and the Unraveling of American Liberalism* (2018).

On foreign policy, see *Kennedy's Quest for Victory: American Foreign Policy, 1961–1963* (1989), edited by Thomas G. Paterson, and Patrick J. Sloyan's *The Politics of Deception: JFK's Secret Decisions on Vietnam, Civil Rights, and Cuba* (2015). To learn more about Kennedy's problems in Cuba, see Mark J. White's *Missiles in Cuba: Kennedy, Khrushchev, Castro and the 1962 Crisis* (1997). See also Serhii Ploky's *Nuclear Folly: A History of the Cuban Missile Crisis* (2021).

American involvement in Vietnam has received voluminous treatment from all political perspectives. For excellent overviews, see Geoffrey C. Ward's *The Vietnam War: An Intimate History* (2017) and Mark Moyar's *Triumph Forsaken: The Vietnam War, 1954–1965* (2018). An analysis of policy making concerning the Vietnam War is David M. Barrett's *Uncertain Warriors: Lyndon Johnson and His Vietnam Advisors* (1993). On the legacy of the Vietnam War, see Arnold R. Isaacs's *Vietnam Shadows: The War, Its Ghosts, and Its Legacy* (1997).

Many scholars have dealt with various aspects of the civil rights movement and race relations in the 1960s. See especially Taylor Branch's *The King Years: Historic Moments in the Civil Rights Movement* (2013), David J. Garrow's *Bearing the Cross: Martin Luther King, Jr., and the Southern Christian Leadership Conference* (1986), Adam Fairclough's *To Redeem the Soul of*

America: The Southern Christian Leadership Conference and Martin Luther King, Jr. (1987), and Thomas Holt's *The Movement: The African American Struggle for Civil Rights* (2021).

CHAPTER 28

An engaging overview of the cultural trends of the 1960s is Maurice Isserman and Michael Kazin's *America Divided: The Civil War of the 1960s*, 3rd ed. (2007). The New Left is assessed in Irwin Unger's *The Movement: A History of the American New Left, 1959–1972* (1974). On the Students for a Democratic Society, see Kirkpatrick Sale's *SDS* (1973) and Allen J. Matusow's *The Unraveling of America: A History of Liberalism in the 1960s* (1984). Also useful are Todd Gitlin's *The Sixties: Years of Hope, Days of Rage*, rev. ed. (1993), and Bryan Burrough's *Days of Rage: America's Radical Underground, the FBI, and the Forgotten Age of Revolutionary Violence* (2015).

For insights into the Black Power movement, see Peniel E. Joseph's *Stokely: A Life* (2014) and Joshua Bloom and Waldo E. Martin, Jr.'s *Black against Empire: The History and Politics of the Black Panther Party* (2013).

Two influential assessments of the counterculture by sympathetic commentators are Theodore Roszak's *The Making of a Counter-Culture: Reflections on the Technocratic Society and Its Youthful Opposition* (1969) and Charles A. Reich's *The Greening of America: How the Youth Revolution Is Trying to Make America Livable* (1970). A good scholarly analysis that takes the hippies seriously is Timothy Miller's *The Hippies and American Values* (1991). A more recent assessment of the "culture wars" since the sixties is Andrew Hartman's *A War for the Soul of America: A History of the Culture Wars* (2015).

The best study of the women's liberation movement is Ruth Rosen's *The World Split Open: How the Modern Women's Movement Changed America*, rev. ed. (2006). On Betty Friedan, see Daniel Horowitz's *Betty Friedan and the Making of the Feminine Mystique* (2000). For the point of view of a militant feminist, see Vivian Gornick, *Essays in Feminism* (1978). On the gay liberation movement, see Jim Downs's *Stand by Me: The Forgotten History of Gay Liberation* (2016) and Sarah Schulman's *Let the Record Show: A Political History of Act Up New York, 1987–1993* (2021). The Stonewall riots are featured in Ann Bausum's *Stonewall: Breaking Out in the Fight for Gay Rights* (2016). See also Joanne Meyerowitz's *How Sex Changed: A History of Transexuality in the United States* (2004) and Vicki L. Eklors's *Queer America: A People's LGBT History of the United States* (2011).

The union organizing efforts of Cesar Chavez are detailed in Miriam Pawel's *The Crusades of Cesar Chavez: A Biography* (2014). The struggles of Native Americans for recognition and power are sympathetically described in Stan Steiner's *The New Indians* (1968).

The best overview of the 1970s and 1980s is James T. Patterson's *Restless Giant: The United States from Watergate to* Bush v. Gore (2005). On Nixon, see Melvin Small's thorough analysis in *The Presidency of Richard Nixon* (1999). A good slim biography is Elizabeth Drew's *Richard M. Nixon* (2007). A massive biography is Evan Thomas's *Being Nixon: A Man Divided* (2015). For excellent overviews of the Watergate scandal, see Michael Dobbs's *King Richard: Nixon and Watergate* (2021) and Stanley I. Kutler's *The Wars of Watergate: The Last Crisis of Richard Nixon* (1990). For the way the Republicans handled foreign affairs, consult Tad Szulc's *The Illusion of Peace: Foreign Policy in the Nixon Years* (1978). The Nixon White House tapes make for fascinating reading. See *The Nixon Tapes* (2014), edited by Douglas Brinkley and Luke Nichter. Rick Perlstein traces the effects of Nixon's career on the Republican party and the conservative movement in two compelling books: *Nixonland: The Rise of a President and the Fracturing of America* (2007) and *The Invisible Bridge: The Fall of Nixon and the Rise of Reagan* (2014).

The Communist takeover of Vietnam and the end of American involvement there are traced in Larry Berman's *No Peace, No Honor: Nixon, Kissinger, and Betrayal in Vietnam* (2001). William Shawcross's *Sideshow: Kissinger, Nixon and the Destruction of Cambodia*, rev. ed. (2002), deals with the broadening of the war. The most comprehensive treatment of the anti-war movement is Tom Wells's *The War Within: America's Battle over Vietnam* (1994).

A comprehensive treatment of the Ford administration is contained in John Robert Greene's *The Presidency of Gerald R. Ford* (1995). The best overview of the Carter administration is Burton I. Kaufman's *The Presidency of James Earl Carter, Jr.*, 2nd rev. ed. (2006). More sympathetic to the Carter administration are Kai Bird's *The Outlier: The Unfinished Presidency of Jimmy Carter* (2021) and John Dumbrell's *The Carter Presidency: A Re-evaluation*, 2nd ed. (1995). Gaddis Smith's *Morality, Reason, and Power: American Diplomacy in the Carter Years* (1986) details Carter's foreign policies. Background on how the Middle East came to dominate much of American policy is found in William B. Quandt's *Decade of Decisions: American Policy toward the Arab-Israeli Conflict, 1967–1976* (1977). For a biography of Carter, see Randall Balmer, *Redeemer: The Life of Jimmy Carter* (2014).

CHAPTER 29

The rise of modern political conservatism is well explained in Patrick Allitt's *The Conservatives: Ideas and Personalities throughout American History* (2009) and Michael Schaller's *Right Turn: American Life in the Reagan-Bush Era, 1980–1992* (2007).

On Reagan, see John Patrick Diggins's *Ronald Reagan: Fate, Freedom, and the Making of History* (2007), Richard Reeves's *President Reagan: The Triumph of Imagination* (2005), Sean Wilentz's *The Age of Reagan: A History, 1974–2008* (2008), and Thomas C. Reed's *The Reagan Enigma: 1964–1980* (2015). The best political analysis is Robert M. Collins's *Transforming America: Politics and Culture during the Reagan Years* (2007). On Reaganomics, see David A. Stockman's *The Triumph of Politics: Why the Reagan Revolution Failed* (1986).

For Reagan's foreign policy in Central America, see James Chace's *Endless War: How We Got Involved in Central America— and What Can Be Done* (1984) and Walter LaFeber's *Inevitable Revolutions: The United States in Central America*, 2nd ed. (1993). On Reagan's second term, see Jane Mayer and Doyle McManus's *Landslide: The Unmaking of the President, 1984–1988* (1988). For a masterly study of the Iran-Contra affair, see Theodore Draper's *A Very Thin Line: The Iran Contra Affairs* (1991).

The 41st president is the focus of Timothy Naftali's *George H. W. Bush* (2007). The best biography is Jon Meacham's *Destiny and Power: The American Odyssey of George Herbert Walker Bush* (2015). For a social history of the decade, see John Ehrman's *The Eighties: America in the Age of Reagan* (2005). On the Persian Gulf conflict, see Lester H. Brune's *America and the Iraqi Crisis, 1990–1992: Origins and Aftermath* (1993). For the end of the Cold War, see Jeffrey Engel's *When the World Seemed New: George H. W. Bush and the End of the Cold War* (2017).

CHAPTER 30

Analysis of the Clinton presidency can be found in Joe Klein's *The Natural: The Misunderstood Presidency of Bill Clinton* (2002). More recent biographies include John F. Harris's *The Survivor: Bill Clinton in the White House* (2006) and Patrick J. Maney's *Bill Clinton: New Gilded Age President* (2016). Clinton's impeachment is assessed in Richard A. Posner's *An Affair of State: The Investigation, Impeachment, and Trial of President Clinton* (1999).

On changing demographic trends, see Sam Roberts's *Who We Are Now: The Changing Face of America in the Twenty-First Century* (2004). For a textured account of the exploding Latino culture, see Roberto Suro's *Strangers among Us: How Latino Immigration Is Transforming America* (1998). On social and cultural life in the 1990s, see Haynes Johnson's *The Best of Times: America in the Clinton Years* (2001). Economic and technological changes are assessed in Daniel T. Rogers's *Age of Fracture* (2011). The onset and growth of the AIDS epidemic are traced in *And the Band Played On: Politics, People, and the AIDS Epidemic*, 20th anniversary ed. (2007), by Randy Shilts.

On the religious right, see George M. Marsden's *Understanding Fundamentalism and Evangelicalism*, new ed. (2006). On the invention of the computer and the internet, see Paul E. Ceruzzi's *A History of Modern Computing*, 2nd ed. (2003), Janet Abbate's *Inventing the Internet* (1999), and Michael Lewis, *The New New Thing: A Silicon Valley Story* (1999). The booming economy of the 1990s is well analyzed in Joseph E. Stiglitz's *The Roaring Nineties: A New History of the World's Most Prosperous Decade* (2003).

For further treatment of the end of the Cold War, see Michael R. Beschloss and Strobe Talbott's *At the Highest Levels: The Inside Story of the End of the Cold War* (1993) and Richard Crockatt's *The Fifty Years War: The United States and the Soviet Union in World Politics, 1941–1991* (1995).

On the transformation of American foreign policy, see James Mann's *Rise of the Vulcans: The History of Bush's War Cabinet* (2004), Claes G. Ryn's *America the Virtuous: The Crisis of Democracy and the Quest for Empire* (2003), and Stephen M. Walt's *Taming American Power: The Global Response to U.S. Primacy* (2005).

The disputed 2000 presidential election is the focus of Jeffrey Toobin's *Too Close to Call: The Thirty-Six-Day Battle to Decide the 2000 Election* (2001). On the Bush presidency, see *The Presidency of George W. Bush: A First Historical Assessment*, edited by Julian E. Zelizer (2010) and Jean Edward Smith's *Bush* (2017).

On the terrorist attacks of September 11, 2001, and their aftermath, see *The Age of Terror: America and the World after September 11*, edited by Strobe Talbott and Nayan Chanda (2001). For a devastating account of the Bush administration by a White House insider, see Scott McClellan's *What Happened: Inside the Bush White House and Washington's Culture of Deception* (2008).

On the historic 2008 election, see Michael Nelson's *The Elections of 2008* (2009). The best biography of Obama is Peter Baker's *Obama: The Call of History* (2017). A conservative critique is provided in Edward Klein's *The Amateur: Barack Obama in the White House* (2012). For insiders' accounts of the Obama administration, see David Axelrod's *Believer: My Forty Years in*

Politics (2015) and Ben Rhodes's *The World as It Is: A Memoir of the Obama White House* (2018). Barack Obama writes better than most presidents. See the former president's memoir, *A Promised Land* (2020), for his insights into modern politics and civil strife.

The Great Recession is explained in Adam Toozes's *Crashed: How a Decade of Financial Crises Changed the World* (2018). The recession's effects on modern politics are the focus of John B. Judis's *The Populist Explosion: How the Great Recession Transformed American and European Politics* (2016).

The Tea Party movement is assessed in Theda Skocpol and Vanessa Williamson's *The Tea Party and the Remaking of Republican Conservatism* (2012). The polarization of politics is the focus of Russell Muirhead's *The Promise of Party in a Polarized Age* (2015). The partisan gridlock in Congress is analyzed in Thomas E. Mann and Norman J. Ornstein's *The Broken Branch: How Congress Is Failing America and How to Get It Back on Track* (2012). The tension between the conservative majority on the U.S. Supreme Court and the Obama administration is examined in Jeffrey Toobin's *The Oath: The Obama White House and the Supreme Court* (2012). On the growing economic inequality in America, see Joseph Stiglitz's *The Price of Inequality: How Today's Divided Society Endangers Our Future* (2013).

The emergence of Islamist radicalism is explained in Michael Weiss and Hassan Hassan's *ISIS: Inside the Army of Terror* (2015) and Jessica Stern and J. M. Berger's *ISIS: The State of Terror* (2015). The conflicts in the Middle East are the focus of Dominic Tierney's *The Right Way to Lose a War: America in an Age of Unwinnable Conflicts* (2015).

The dramatic presidential election of 2016 is assessed in Larry Sabato and Kyle Kondik's *Trumped: The 2016 Election That Broke All the Rules* (2017) and Doug Wead's *Game of Thorns: The Inside Story of Hillary Clinton's Failed Campaign and Donald Trump's Winning Strategy* (2017). For the emergence of populism, see Salena Zito and Brad Todd's *The Great Revolt: Inside the Populist Coalition Reshaping American Politics* (2018).

On the two impeachments of President Trump, see Kevin Sullivan and Mary Jordan's *Trump on Trial: The Investigation, Impeachment, Acquittal and Aftermath* (2020) and Jeffrey Toobin's *True Crimes and Misdemeanors: The Investigation of Donald Trump* (2020). For how the Trump administration mismanaged the COVID pandemic, see Yasmeen Abutaleb and Damian Paletta's *Nightmare Scenario: Inside the Trump Administration's Response to the Pandemic That Changed History* (2021).

Assessments of the chaotic Trump White House include Michael Cohen's *Disloyal: The True Story of the Formal Personal Attorney to President Donald*

Trump (2020), James Comey's *A Higher Loyalty: Truth, Lies, and Leadership* (2018), Michael Wolff's *Landslide: The Final Days of the Trump Presidency* (2021), and Bob Woodward's *Fear: Trump in the White House* (2018). On the disputed 2020 presidential election, see Larry Sabato's *A Return to Normalcy? The 2020 Election That (Almost) Broke America* (2021). On America's longest war, see Carter Malkasian's *The American War in Afghanistan: A History* (2021) and Craig Whitlock's *The Afghanistan Papers: A Secret History of the War* (2021).

CREDITS

Chapter 15: p. 700: Sarin Images/GRANGER; p. 703: Library of Congress; p. 707: Sarin Images/ GRANGER; p. 709: Science History Images/Alamy Stock Photo; p. 711: Library of Congress; p. 712: Sarin Images/GRANGER; p. 714: Everett Collection/Shutterstock; p. 716: Library of Congress; p. 721: Science History Images/Alamy Stock Photo; p. 722: Library of Congress p. 724: GRANGER; p. 726 & p. 728: Library of Congress; p. 731: Sarin Images/GRANGER; p. 735: John Kraljevich/John Kraljevich Americana; p. 738: Library of Congress; p. 742 akg-images/Fototeca Gilardi; p. 749: Library of Congress.

Chapter 16: p. 755: Historia/Shutterstock; p. 756: David J. & Janice L. Frent/Corbis via Getty Images; p. 758: Sarin Images/GRANGER; p. 762: The Bookworm Collection/Alamy Stock Photo; p. 764: GRANGER; p. 765: Historia/Shutterstock; p. 770: Science History Images/Alamy Stock Photo; p. 772: National Archives; p. 776: GL Archive/Alamy Stock Photo; p. 777: from John J. McLaurin, Sketches in Crude-Oil, 1902, www.archive.org, public domain; p. 779 & p. 780: Library of Congress; p. 781: GRANGER; p. 783: Peter Newark American Pictures/Bridgeman Images; p. 785: © Museum of the City of New York, USA/Bridgeman Images; p. 787: Archives and Special Collections, Vassar College Libraries. Archives 08.07.05; p. 788: Retro AdArchives/Alamy Stock Photo; p. 790: Library of Congress; p. 793: Peter Newark American Pictures/Bridgeman Images; p. 795 & 797: Library of Congress; p. 801: Historia/Shutterstock; p. 804: Smith Archive/Alamy Stock Photo; p. 806: Library of Congress.

Chapter 17: p. 810: Bill Manns/Shutterstock; p. 812: Impress/Alamy Stock Photo; p. 815: Heritage Image Partnership Ltd./Alamy Stock Photo; p. 817: Library of Congress; p. 823 & p. 825: Corbis/Getty Images; p. 828: Everett Collection Historical/Alamy Stock Photo; p. 829 & p. 831: Library of Congress; p. 833: Library of Congress, Rare Book and Special Collections Division; p. 834: Library of Congress; p. 840 Julia Macias Brooks/Courtesy Wickenburg Chamber of Commerce; p. 843: Library of Congress; p. 847: National Archives; p. 848: Glasshouse Images/Alamy Stock Photo; p. 850: Eric J. Garcia; p. 852: Art Collection 3/Alamy Stock Photo; p. 857: World History Archive/Alamy Stock Photo.

Chapter 18: p. 866: Collection of Mr. and Mrs. Paul Mellon, Courtesy National Gallery of Art, Washington; p. 871: Bettmann/Getty Images; p. 874: Library of Congress; p. 875: GRANGER; p. 878: New York Public Library Digital Collection; p. 880: Bettmann/Corbis/Getty Images; p. 881: © Museum of the City of New York, USA/Bridgeman Images; p. 882: Chronicle/Alamy Stock Photo; p. 885: Hinman B. Hurlbut Collection. The Cleveland Museum of Art: p. 887, p. 892 & p. 895: Library of Congress; p. 897: GRANGER; p. 902: Library of Congress; p. 904: Jimlop collection/Alamy Stock Photo; p. 907 both: David J. & Janice L. Frent/Corbis via Getty Images; p. 908: Library of Congress.

Chapter 19: p. 914: Courtesy Frederic Remington Art Museum, Ogdensburg, New York; p. 917: Wikimedia Commons, The life and letters of John Fiske, 1874, Harvard University; p. 918: Sarin Images/GRANGER; p. 920: Library of Congress; p. 923: Everett Collection Historical/Alamy Stock Photo; p. 926: Library of Congress; p. 927: Betmann/Getty Images; p. 931: Sarin Images/GRANGER;

Congress; **p. 1223**: MGPhoto76/Alamy Stock Photo; **p. 1227**: Chronicle/Alamy Stock Photo; **p. 1228**: Glasshouse Images/Alamy Stock Photo; **p. 1231**: Herbert Gehr/The Life Picture Collection/ Getty Images; **p. 1232**: MPVHistory/Alamy Stock Photo; **p. 1240**: Science History Images/Alamy Stock Photo; **p. 1241**: Niday Picture Library/Alamy Stock Photo.

Chapter 25: **p. 1247**: Eugene Gordon/The New-York Historical Society/Getty Images; **p. 1249**: Allstar Picture Library Ltd./Alamy Stock Photo; **p. 1252**: Bettmann/Getty Images; **p. 1254** & **p. 1257**: Library of Congress; **p. 1260**: Shawshots/Alamy Stock Photo; **p. 1262**: Hulton-Deutsch Collection/Corbis via Getty Images; **p. 1263**: David Lichtneker/Alamy Stock Photo; **p. 1267**: National Archives; **p. 1269**: Bettmann/ Corbis/Getty Images; **p. 1272** & **p. 1274**: Bettmann/Getty Images; **p. 1275**: Loomis Dean/The LIFE Picture Collection via Getty Images; **p. 1277** & **p. 1280**: Everett Collection Historical/Alamy Stock Photo; **p. 1281**: World History Archive/Alamy Stock Photo; **p. 1282**: Walter Sanders/The LIFE Picture Collection via Getty Images; **p. 1285**: Bettmann/Corbis/Getty Images; **p. 1288**: Sarin Images/GRANGER; **p. 1292**: J. T. Vintage/Bridgeman Images.

Chapter 26: **p. 1298**: GraphicaArtis/Getty Images; **p. 1300**: National Archives; **p. 1304**: Heritage Image Partnership Ltd/Alamy Stock Photo; **p. 1307**: Photo by Kay Tobin © Manuscripts and Archives Division, The New York Public Library; **p. 1309**: John Dominis//Time Life Pictures/Getty Images; **p. 1310**: Heritage Image Partnership Ltd/Alamy Stock Photo; **p. 1313**: World of Triss/Alamy Stock Photo; **p. 1315**: Schomburg Center for Research in Black Culture, Manuscripts, Archives and Rare Books Division, The New York Public Library Digital Collections. 1956; **p. 1317 left**: Everett Collection Historical/Alamy Stock Photo; **p. 1317 right**: AF archive/Alamy Stock Photo; **p. 1319**: Three Lions/Getty Images; **p. 1321**: Everett Collection Historical/Alamy Stock Photo; **p. 1322**: Allan Grant/The LIFE Picture Collection/Getty Images; **p. 1324**: Album/Alamy Stock Photo; **p. 1326**: Elliott Erwitt/Magnum Photos; **p. 1327**: Bruce Davidson/Magnum Photos; **p. 1330 left**: IanDagnall Computing/Alamy Stock Photo; **p. 1330 right**: American Photo Archive/Alamy Stock Photo; **p. 1332**: Everett Collection Inc./Alamy Stock Photo; **p. 1336**: A 1956 Herblock Cartoon, © Herb Block Foundation; **p. 1339**: AFP/Getty Images; **p. 1343**: AP Photo; **p. 1347**: Associated Press; **p. 1348**: Sovfoto/Universal Images Group/Shutterstock.

Chapter 27: **p. 1352**: Library of Congress; **p. 1355**: Archive PL/Alamy Stock Photo; **p. 1358**: Bettmann/Getty Images; **p. 1361**: Sueddeutsche Zeitung Photo/Alamy Stock Photo; **p. 1363**: NASA; **p. 1364**: John F. Kennedy Library, National Archives; **p. 1369**: Carl Mydans/The LIFE Picture Collection/ Getty Images; **p. 1371**: GRANGER; **p. 1372**: Everett Collection Inc/Alamy Stock Photo; **p. 1376**: AP Photo; **p. 1379**: Mariano Garcia/Alamy Stock Photo; **p. 1382**: AP Photo/William J. Smith, File; **p. 1384**: ASSOCIATED PRESS; **p. 1386**: Library of Congress; **p. 1388**: National Archives; **p. 1390**: AP Photo; **p. 1392**: Everett Collection Historical/Alamy Stock Photo; **p. 1393 left**: David J. & Janice L. Frent/ Corbis via Getty Images; **p. 1393 right**: Heritage Auctions, HA.com; **p. 1397**: AP Photo/File; **p. 1401**: Tim Page/Corbis Historical/Getty Images; **p. 1402**: Bettmann/Getty images; **p. 1407**: Jack Kightlinger, Lyndon Baines Johnson Library and Museum.

Chapter 28: **p. 1416**: Bettmann/Getty Images; **p. 1419**: AP Photo/Robert W. Klein/File; **p. 1420**: Library of Congress; **p. 1422**: AP Photo; **p. 1425**: David Graves/Shutterstock; **p. 1426**: David Parker/Alamy Stock Photo; **p. 1429**: John Olson/The LIFE Picture Collection/Getty Images; **p. 1430**: Michael Ochs Archive/Getty Images; **p. 1433**: ZUMA Press, Inc./Alamy Stock Photo; **p. 1436**: Tribune Content Agency LLC/Alamy Stock Photo; 1439 **left**: Eugene Gordon/The New-York Historical Society/Getty Images; **p. 1439 right**: Bettmann/Getty Images; **p. 1440**: H. William Tetlow/Getty Images; **p. 1443**: Arthur Schatz/The LIFE Picture Collection/Shutterstock; **p. 1445**: Bettmann/Getty Images; **p. 1446**: Fred W. McDarrah/Getty Images; **p. 1448**: NASA; **p. 1453**: Lee Lockwood/The Life Images Collection/Getty Images; **p. 1455**: AP Photo; **p. 1459**: CPA Media Pte Ltd/Alamy Stock Photo; **p. 1463**: Bettmann/Corbis/Getty Images; **p. 1467**: CPA Media Pte Ltd/Alamy Stock Photo; **p. 1473** mccool/Alamy Stock Photo; **p. 1475**: The Color Archives/Alamy Stock Photo; 1477: Courtesy Gerald R. Ford Library.

Chapter 29: **p. 1482**: Wally McNamee/CORBIS via Getty Images; **p. 1485**: ZUMA Press, Inc./Alamy Stock Photo; **p. 1488**: World History Archive/Alamy Stock Photo; **p. 1491**: Library of Congress; **p. 1492**: Mohsen Shandiz/Sygma/Getty Images; **p. 1493**: GL Archive/Alamy Stock Photo; **p. 1495** & **p. 1500**: Bettmann/Getty Images; **p. 1502**: Library of Congress; **p. 1505**: National Archives; **p. 1508**: Bettmann/Getty Images; **p. 1509**: By permission of © Paul Szep and Creators Syndicate, Inc.; **p. 1510**: World History Archive/Alamy Stock Photo; **p. 1513**: Bridgeman Images; **p. 1515**: AP photo; 1517: World Politics Archive (WPA)/Alamy Stock Photo; **p. 1521**: Allstar Picture Library Ltd/Alamy Stock Photo; **p. 1524**: Mike Nelson/Getty Images; **p. 1527**: AP Photo/Susan Ragan; **p. 1529**: Frances Roberts/Alamy Stock Photo; **p. 1531** & **p. 1534**: Richard Ellis/Alamy Stock Photo; **p. 1537** & **p. 1540**: REUTERS/Alamy Stock Photo.

Chapter 30: **p. 1544**: Sheila Fitzgerald/Alamy Stock Photo; **p. 1547**: OMAR TORRES/AFP via Getty Images; **p. 1549**: Robert King/Getty Images; **p. 1551**: Tamara Beckwith/Shutterstock; 1554: Kevin Lamarque/REUTERS/Newscom; **p. 1556**: Ali Jasim/REUTERS/Newscom; **p. 1559**: Mario Tama/Getty Images; **p. 1560**: AP Photo/Pablo Martinez Monsivais; **p. 1561**: Justin Sullivan/Getty Images; **p. 1563**: AP Photo/Jae C. Hong; **p. 1566**: Jewel Samad/AFP via Getty Images; **p. 1568**: AP Photo/Erich Schlegel; **p. 1569**: Jeff J. Mitchell/Getty Images; **p. 1572**: AP Photo/Ringo H.W. Chiu; **p. 1573**: AP Photo/Eric Gay; **p. 1575**: Ben Baker/Redux; **p. 1580**: Mladen Antonov/AFP/Getty Images; **p. 1583**: The Photo Access/Alamy Stock Photo; **p. 1587**: Amy Sussman/REX/Shutterstock; **p. 1590**: Brian van der Brug/LA Times via Getty Images; **p. 1593**: Shutterstock; **p. 1595**: Planetpix/Alamy Live News; **p. 1597**: REUTERS/Alamy Stock Photo; **p. 1600**: AP Photo/Evan Vucci; **p. 1603**: National Guard/Alamy Stock Photo; **p. 1607**: Simone Hogan/Alamy Stock Photo; **p. 1611**: AP Photo/zz/STRF/STAR MAX/IPx; **p. 1613**: REUTERS/Alamy Stock Photo.

INDEX

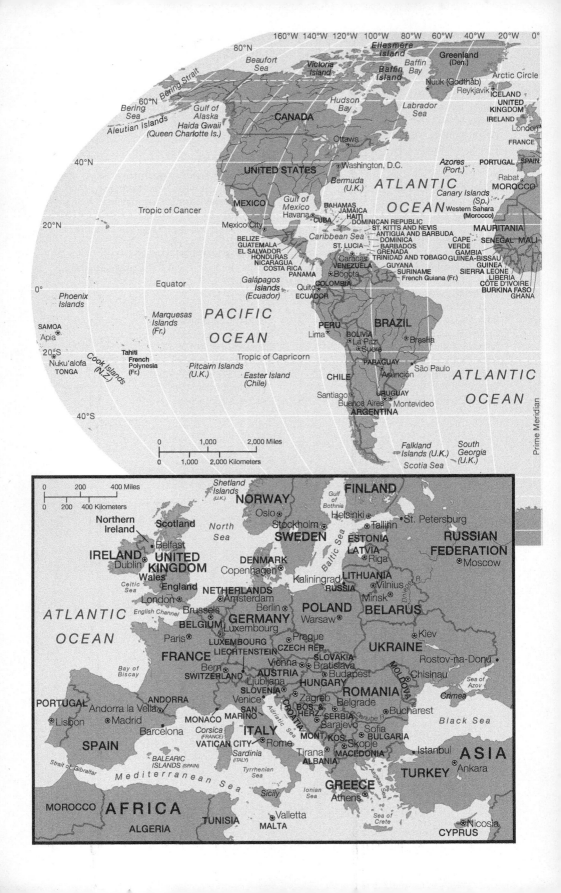

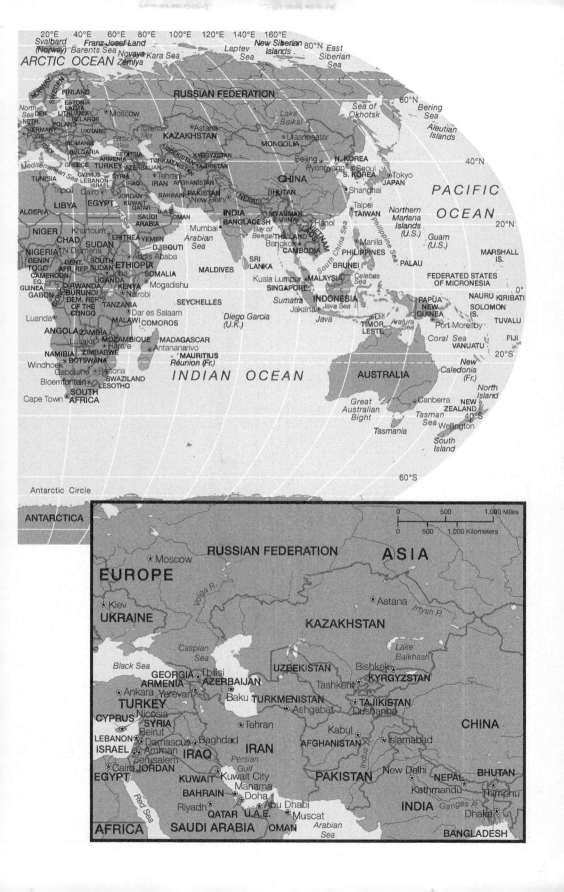